P9-BUH-353

Jimmy Swaggart Bible Commentary

Acts

- Genesis [639 PAGES 11-201]
- Exodus [639 PAGES 11-202]
- Leviticus [435 PAGES 11-203]
- Numbers
  Deuteronomy [493 PAGES 11-204]
- Joshua
  Judges
  Ruth [329 PAGES 11-205]
- I Samuel
  II Samuel [528 PAGES 11-206]
- I Kings
  II Kings [560 PAGES 11-207]
- I Chronicles
  II Chronicles [505 PAGES 11-226]
- Ezra
  Nehemiah
  Esther [288 PAGES 11-208]
- Job [320 PAGES 11-225]
- Psalms [688 PAGES 11-216]
- Proverbs [320 PAGES 11-227]
- Ecclesiastes
  Song Of Solomon [245 PAGES 11-228]
- Isaiah [688 PAGES 11-220]
- Jeremiah
  Lamentations [688 PAGES 11-070]
- Ezekiel [520 PAGES 11-223]
- Daniel [403 PAGES 11-224]
- Hosea
  Joel
  Amos [496 PAGES 11-229]
- Obadiah
  Jonah
  Micah
  Nahum
  Habakkuk
  Zephaniah [530 PAGES 11-230]
- Haggai
  Zechariah
  Malachi [448 PAGES 11-231]
- Matthew [625 PAGES 11-073]
- Mark [606 PAGES 11-074]
- Luke [626 PAGES 11-075]
- John [717 PAGES 11-076]
- Acts [832 PAGES 11-077]
- Romans [536 PAGES 11-078]
- I Corinthians [632 PAGES 11-079]
- II Corinthians [589 PAGES 11-080]
- Galatians [478 PAGES 11-081]
- Ephesians [550 PAGES 11-082]
- Philippians [476 PAGES 11-083]
- Colossians [374 PAGES 11-084]
- I Thessalonians
  II Thessalonians [498 PAGES 11-085]
- I Timothy
  II Timothy
  Titus
  Philemon [687 PAGES 11-086]
- Hebrews [831 PAGES 11-087]
- James
  I Peter
  II Peter [730 PAGES 11-088]
- I John
  II John
  III John
  Jude [377 PAGES 11-089]
- Revelation [602 PAGES 11-090]

JIMMY SWAGGART BIBLE COMMENTARY

For prices and information please call: 1-800-288-8350
Baton Rouge residents please call: (225) 768-7000
Website: www.jsm.org • E-mail: info@jsm.org

Jimmy Swaggart Bible Commentary

Acts

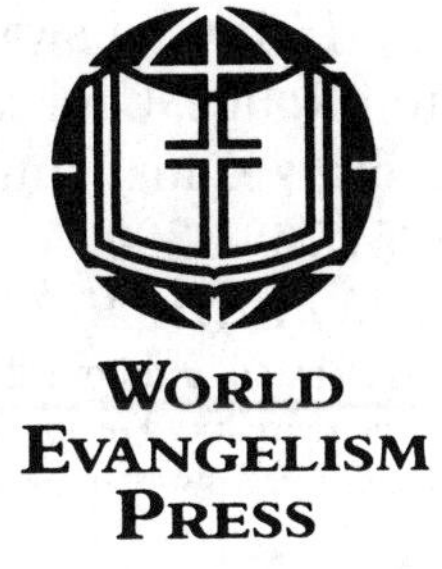

World Evangelism Press

ISBN 978-1-934655-08-5

P.O. Box 262550 • Baton Rouge, Louisiana 70826-2550
Website: www.jsm.org • E-mail: info@jsm.org
(225) 768-8300
15 16 17 18 19 20 21 22 23 24 / RRD / 15 14 13 12 11 10 9 8 7 6

TABLE OF CONTENTS

1. Introduction v

2. Acts 1

3. Index 797

INTRODUCTION

ABOUT LUKE

As most know, Luke, referred to as *"the beloved physician,"* is the instrument used by the Holy Spirit to give us the Book of Acts. As well, that would include the Gospel that bears his name.

Some have claimed that Luke was a Gentile. While that possibility exists, it is my personal opinion that he was a Jew. I say that because all of the other writers who were used by the Holy Spirit to write the Canon of Scripture were Jews. As well, and even more telling, the Psalmist said: *"He shows His Word unto Jacob, His Statutes and His Judgments unto Israel"* (Ps. 147:19). Some even think that he may have been the *"Lucius"* of Romans 16:21. If so, the possibility also exists that he was personally related to Paul.

It is believed that he spent at least 12 years with the Apostle Paul, thereby, being personally involved in this great Move of God that shook the world and has not stopped unto this hour.

It is almost of unanimous agreement that Luke completed the Book of Acts in the year A.D. 63. It seems that much of the work was done during Paul's the two years that Paul was imprisoned at Rome. This would have given Luke the time to accomplish this task which, no doubt, was derived from prepared notes and memoranda prepared several years before while on the journeys with Paul.

It is almost certain that the book could not have been completed earlier because the narrative comes down without a break, in one continuous flow, to the time of the imprisonment we have just mentioned.

It may be concluded that the book was finished before Paul's trial before Nero, his acquittal and his journey into Spain (if indeed he went to Spain), and his second trial and martyrdom. If the narrative continued through this time, surely Luke would have mentioned them.

There is really no knowledge of Luke's life after the close of the Acts of the Apostles, except the mention of him being still with Paul at the time of the writing of Paul's second Epistle to Timothy (II Tim. 4:11). So, we have no record of his death or how long he lived after *"The Acts of the Apostles"* was finished.

THE PATTERN AND EXAMPLE

The Book of Acts is meant to portray what the Church must be. The Holy Spirit and not man drew the blueprints, set the course, and described the method. Consequently, if the modern local Church (or any Church at any time for that matter) does not have the earmarks of the Book of Acts Church, then one must conclude that it is not of the Spirit, but rather of man and, therefore, worthless!

In this account we find powerful preaching and teaching of the Gospel. We find the sick being healed in the Name of Jesus and miracles being performed. We find the oppressed being set free and demons cast out. We find Believers being baptized with the Holy Spirit with the evidence of speaking with other tongues. We find the Gifts of the Spirit in operation. Consequently, this is the pattern that all Churches must follow.

HOLY SPIRIT DIRECTED GOVERNMENT

We do not find religious denominations in the Book of Acts, and one will look in vain for any type of religious hierarchy. Such does not exist!

We do find a fellowship of Churches with a common bond or purpose and with like doctrine.

We find the local Church with its collective leadership as the high spiritual authority. In other words, the government as laid down by the Holy Spirit is simple, but yet, extremely effective.

THE GOAL AND PURPOSE OF THE HOLY SPIRIT

As is obvious in this account, the establishment of the local Church is the purpose of the Spirit. However, even more particularly, the taking of the Gospel ever forward—even to the furtherest regions—becomes blatantly obvious in the Book of Acts as the Spirit ever drives onward in the hearts and lives of those whom He has called. In other words, world evangelism holds priority!

DOCTRINE?

Some have claimed that the Book of Acts is not meant to serve in a doctrinal capacity as it is mainly a portrayal of experience; however, that is error pure and simple.

The Book of Acts is, in fact, doctrine carried out in the actions, ways, and means of the principle players. I speak of Peter and Paul and a host of others! Consequently, to deny its doctrinal portrayal by example is to deny much of the purpose and intent of the Holy Spirit.

THE HOLY SPIRIT

Over 50 times the title or name *"Holy Spirit," "Spirit,"* or *"Spirit of God"* is used in this great book. Therefore, it vastly becomes obvious as to the identity of the principle player in this great story. It is the Holy Spirit carrying out the designs of the Head of the Church, the Lord Jesus Christ. He is paramount, predominant, probing, and powerful in everything that is done. There is no mistaking His identity and direction.

This tells us that He must be the same presently, that is, if we are to get anything done for God.

Sadly, this leaves out the far greater majority of congregations that call themselves *"Churches,"* especially considering that the Holy Spirit in these local groups (and they number in the tens of thousands) is little obvious, if at all. As such, most of what is done is man-instituted, man-directed, man-inspired, and, therefore, not of God. Considering that everything done on this Earth by God the Father and God the Son is done through the person, agency, office, and ministry of the Holy Spirit, His Leadership should be eagerly sought by the Church.

A PERSONAL EXPERIENCE

I was baptized with the Holy Spirit when I was 8 years old. The means which the Lord used to bring this about will be addressed at greater length elsewhere in this volume. However, the many souls we have seen brought to Christ and the many baptized with the Holy Spirit, along with numberless lives changed by the Power of God, must go in totality to the credit of the Holy Spirit. Someone has well said that the Holy Spirit works and operates in the individual's life according to the degree that Jesus is Lord in that life.

My grandmother was the first one in our family to be baptized with the Holy Spirit with the evidence of speaking with other tongues. It was to be a red-letter day! Even though I was only a child when this happened, the memory of it is fresh in my mind and ever shall be. I came to find that it was the Holy Spirit Who opened up the Word of God and, as well, wondrously glorified Christ.

Salvation is God's greatest Gift to the world. The Baptism with the Holy Spirit is His greatest Gift to the Church. As Salvation separates the believing sinner from the world, likewise, the Holy Spirit separates the Believer from dead, cold, and formal religion.

MY PERSONAL FEELINGS

In attempting to write a commentary on the entirety of the Word of God, it has been a project that has already taken some 20 years, and in one sense of the word, a lifetime. In writing this commentary, I have faced the prospect of certain books with great trepidation; the Acts of the Apostles is one of those books. And yet, I am so thankful to the Lord for giving me the opportunity and privilege of attempting this task. The spiritual growth I have personally enjoyed in doing this could not be measured by any dimension. This I do know: My love for the Word of God seems to grow with intensity as I go forward. Countless times as I have held the dictaphone in my hands, I have sensed the Presence of God—at times even to the point of tears—as the Holy Spirit would open up the Scriptures. If our efforts affect you in its study as it has affected me in its compilation, then I know you will be signally blessed. If in this volume we have lifted up Jesus (and this I believe the Holy Spirit has helped us do), then the effort is a success, irrespective of the thoughts of others.

AND FINALLY

I make no claims at being a scholar, but if I did make such claims, I would be quickly exposed! However, I do claim to be an avid student of the Word, even to the point of compulsion. At the same time, I have benefited from and freely used the scholarship of many others who have gone before me. As someone has said, *"Other men labored, and I have entered into their labors."* Therefore, if the research material in this volume proves to be of benefit to you, the only credit I deserve is the labor and efforts in ferreting it out.

I pray that you will study this volume and that it will be interesting enough that you will desire to do so. If it does prove to be a blessing, which we certainly pray it shall, it is the Lord Who has given the increase, and to Him we owe all praise.

Perhaps the cry of the Book of Acts can be summed up in the old song written by Charles Gabriel so long ago:

"There's a call comes ringing o're the restless wave,
"Send the light! Send the light!
"There are souls to rescue, there are souls to save,
"Send the light! Send the light!"

"Send the light! Send the blessed Gospel light!
"Let is shine from shore to shore,
"Send the light! That blessed Gospel light,
"Let it shine forevermore."

THE

BOOK OF ACTS

NOTES

(1) "THE FORMER TREATISE HAVE I MADE, O THEOPHILUS, OF ALL THAT JESUS BEGAN BOTH TO DO AND TEACH."

The exegesis is:

1. The Cross of Christ is the Story of the entire Bible.

2. One might also say that the Bible is the Story of the Cross of Christ.

3. The Cross of Christ is the Foundation of all Biblical Doctrine.

THE FORMER TREATISE

The phrase, *"The former treatise have I made,"* refers to the Gospel of Luke, which was probably finished a year or so before the writing of this account, which is called, *"The Acts of the Apostles."*

The word *"treatise"* has the following connotations:

- It refers to the inward thoughts expressed in speech.
- It refers to the reasoning powers of the mind.
- In this respect, it refers to the Word of God, *"The embodiment of and expression of all wisdom and prudence."* It can probably be expressed best with two Greek words:

1. *"Logos"*: has to do with a concept or idea.

2. *"Rhema"*: has to do with the expression of that idea in proper, intelligent, and grammatical form in words and sentences.

Therefore, as Luke used the word *"treatise,"* referring to his Gospel that bears his name and, as well, the *"Book of Acts,"* he was implying that both of these works are inspired by the Holy Spirit, which is absolutely correct (we will discuss inspiration in more detail momentarily).

The exclamation and name *"O Theophilus"* is the same person addressed by Luke in that Gospel.

It was a common Roman name and is mentioned only in these two places. The name means *"dear to God."*

Inasmuch as the title, *"Most Excellent,"* was given to him in Luke 1:3, such may have denoted some official position, or it may have been merely a courtesy title.

Some have suggested that it refers to Titus Flavius Clemens, the Emperor Vespasian's nephew, but there is no proof of that.

OF ALL THAT JESUS BEGAN BOTH TO DO AND TEACH

The phrase, *"Of all that Jesus began both to do and teach,"* presents an extremely weighty statement.

This one statement sets the stage for the entirety of this Book of Acts, which records the continuation of Jesus' Ministry through Believers and by the Power of the Holy Spirit (Mk. 16:15-20; Jn. 14:12).

The progression is according to the following:

- That which Jesus *"began both to do and teach"* is the Standard, the Principle, and the Foundation of the Gospel.

What did He do and teach?

He preached the Gospel, healed the sick, and cast out demons. As well, the Second Chapter of Acts records that Jesus is the One Who baptizes with the Holy Spirit, as was predicted by John the Baptist (Mat. 3:11).

He *"taught"* the Word of God, which referred to the Old Testament, and laid the Foundation for the New Covenant, the meaning of which would be given to the Apostle

Paul. Consequently, His Teaching took Israel, and the world for that matter, beyond the Law of Moses. Actually, He was the Fulfillment of that Law, which necessitated it being laid aside (Col. 2:8-23).

However, while the ritual or ceremonial Law was fulfilled in Christ and, therefore, set aside, the moral Law, which was also ensconced in the Law of Moses, was not set aside but, in a sense, brought over into the New Testament. The reason is simple: moral Law cannot change.

At the starting gate, the Holy Spirit through Luke presented Jesus as the Foundation, Principle, and Standard for all things.

THE PATTERN

- Consequently, the Book of Acts, even as described by Luke, is to serve as the pattern and description of all that Jesus did and taught. In other words, we must look at the Book of Acts as the criterion and model for our present Churches. To be more precise, if our local church is not like the Church presented in the Book of Acts, at least in some ways, that means that we are not continuing what Jesus began to both do and teach.
- The Holy Spirit is the same now as He was then, and, in fact, He laid down the criteria in the Book of Acts, which we are to emulate. Sadly and tragically, very few modern churches carry the earmarks of the Book of Acts; however, for the few that do, they touch the world. The reason is simple:

They are continuing what Jesus began both to do and teach. The word *"began"* in the Greek Text is *"archomai"* and means *"through the implication of precedence."*

Inasmuch as this is so very, very important, I think the following concerning Jesus is necessary:

JESUS AND THE BELIEVER TODAY

(The following pertaining to the Believer and Jesus is derived from the scholarship of Kenneth Wuest.)

God has so created man that he never enjoys a complete satisfaction and rest of heart until he finds it in a vital experience of companionship with his Creator. King Solomon had at his disposal all that wealth could give him. As well, he had a supernatural wisdom that has never been available to any other man. After thoroughly investigating its possibilities, he cried, *"Vanity of vanities, all is vanity."* That, put into modern English is, *"emptiness of emptiness, all is emptiness,"* or *"futility of futilities, all is futility."*

All that Earth can offer is futile when it comes to giving a person complete soul satisfaction.

In the next few paragraphs, we are told how the Word of God gives us information as to how a person can be brought into a right relationship with God through Jesus Christ and, as well, how to maintain and cultivate that relationship.

WHO JESUS IS!

If someone today claimed that he was a constant companion of Julius Caesar, enjoyed his fellowship day-by-day, and knew him very well, what would your reaction be? You would say, *"Julius Caesar is dead. No one can have intimate companionship of this man today."*

However, suppose for a moment that Julius Caesar were alive today and on some remote planet, and that there was some means of communication so that people on Earth could converse with him. If 10,000 people all claimed to have him for a constant companion, what would you say?

Your answer would be, *"Julius Caesar, although alive, can only have intelligent contact with one person at a time because he is a human being."*

This very thing that is impossible in the case of Julius Caesar, or any other man for that matter, is possible in the case of the Lord Jesus because He is not only Human but God, as well. Also, He is alive and there is a supernatural means whereby millions of people may be in constant touch with Him at the same time, 24 hours a day.

It is concerning this fellowship of the Believer with the Lord Jesus that we wish now to speak.

We will approach our subject from the angle of what the Believer must do to cultivate and maintain a day-by-day fellowship with this Jesus, Who lived on Earth in the First Century, Who died and was raised

NOTES

from the dead, and Who now resides in Heaven in His Glorified Body.

To be sure, He is localized in His Human Body as a Man, but as God, He is ever Omnipresent, and thus, as close to the Believer as any human companion on Earth could be, and actually must closer!

THE FIRST THING THE BELIEVER MUST DO

• This first thing is to not only know the Lord Jesus as Saviour but as one's Lord and one's constant Helper, Guide, and Friend. To begin correctly, one must study the account of Jesus' Life in the four Gospels. Here, we come to know what the Lord Jesus is like. The Holy Spirit will paint the Portrait of Jesus in the mind's eye of the Believer.

Erasmus, the great Greek scholar and humanist, a contemporary of Martin Luther, said in the preface of his Greek New Testament: *"These holy pages will summon up the living image of the Mind of Christ. They will give you Christ Himself, talking, healing, dying, rising, the whole Christ in a word; they will give Him to you in an intimacy so close that He would be less visible to you if He stood before your eyes."*

The strange thing concerning this statement by Erasmus is that he was an unsaved man. However, if he, even in his unsaved state, could see some of the Beauties of the Lord Jesus in the pages of the four Gospels, how much clearer is the portrait that the Holy Spirit can paint for the Believer as he meditates upon the Story of Jesus.

ALL THE SCRIPTURES

• In addition to the Believer's study of the four Gospels, he should become well acquainted with the other parts of the Scriptures also, for in these, the Lord Jesus will talk with him. Thus, in the study of the Bible, the Believer has a Spirit-drawn Portrait of the Lord Jesus before him and the Words of Jesus spoken to him.

• The Believer should maintain a day-by-day fellowship with Him in prayer, in realizing His Nearness, and in living in His Presence. This is the sweet mystical communion of the Believer, who is yielded to the Holy Spirit, with his Lord and Master.

NOTES

ALL

As well, the word *"all"* in the statement, *"All that Jesus began both to do and teach,"* means exactly what it says.

Now, in all of this, there is one thing that stands out above all, and that is that the Believer must have a proper understanding of the Cross of Christ, what Jesus came to this mortal coil to do, and what He did do. Until one understands the Cross relative to both Salvation and Sanctification, one cannot properly understand the Lord Jesus as one should. Most Christians have at least a working knowledge of the Cross of Christ respecting Salvation. *"Jesus died for me"* is perhaps the greatest statement that's ever been made; however, the problem is, with most Christians, it stops there. In other words, they don't have the slightest clue regarding the part the Cross of Christ plays in our Sanctification experience. We are speaking of how we live for God and how we grow in Grace and the Knowledge of the Lord. Until that is understood, one cannot have a proper understanding of Christ. In other words, one is teaching, preaching, and living a partial gospel. Considering the price that Jesus paid at Calvary's Cross, for us not to have all for which He paid such a price is the greatest tragedy for the Child of God.

THE CROSS OF CHRIST

The Story of the Bible is the Story of Jesus Christ and Him Crucified (I Cor. 1:23). That subject matter, the Foundation of the Word, runs like a golden thread all the way from Genesis 1:1 through Revelation 22:21. The very first Foundation principle of Redemption, or *"the primary Doctrine,"* one might say, is the Cross of Christ. It was formulated in the Mind of God from even before the foundation of the world.

Peter said, **"Forasmuch as you know that you were not redeemed with corruptible things, *as* silver and gold** *(presents the fact that the most precious commodities [silver and gold] could not redeem fallen man)*, **from your vain conversation** *(vain lifestyle)* ***received*** **by tradition from your fathers** *(speaks of original sin that is passed on from father to child at conception)***;**

"But with the Precious Blood of Christ *(presents the payment, which proclaims the poured out life of Christ on behalf of sinners)*, **as of a lamb without blemish, and without spot** *(speaks of the lambs offered as substitutes in the old Jewish economy; the death of Christ was not an execution or assassination, but rather a sacrifice; the offering of Himself presented a Perfect Sacrifice, for He was perfect in every respect [Ex. 12:5])*:

BEFORE THE FOUNDATION OF THE WORLD

"Who verily was foreordained before the foundation of the world *(refers to the fact that God, in His Omniscience, knew He would create man, man would fall, and man would be redeemed by Christ going to the Cross; this was all done before the universe was created; this means the Cross of Christ is the Foundation Doctrine of all Doctrine, referring to the fact that all Doctrine must be built upon that Foundation, or else it is specious)*, **but was manifest in these last times for you** *(refers to the invisible God Who, in the Person of the Son, was made visible to human eyesight when He assumed a human body and human limitations)*" **(I Pet. 1:18-20).**

So, we are told here that *"the Cross"* is the Foundation Doctrine of all Doctrine.

THE CROSS AND SANCTIFICATION

As we have previously stated, most Believers have at least a modicum of understanding of how the Cross concerns Salvation (Jn. 3:16); however, almost none of the church world has understanding of how the Cross concerns the Sanctification of the Saint.

When Jesus came to this world, He came for one purpose, with His Face even set like a flint toward that purpose, which was to die on Calvary. While His Virgin Birth was absolutely necessary, still, that within itself could not redeem mankind. His Miracles and Healings were absolutely astounding, such as the world had never seen before, but, still, had it stopped there, no one could have been saved. Again, His Perfect Life was totally necessary and was absolutely beyond reproach; and yet, had it ended there, not a single human being would have ever been saved.

NOTES

All of these things were absolutely necessary, but that which had to be was the Cross, that is, if man was to be redeemed. The Cross was the reason Jesus came. In fact, every single thing that the Believer receives from the Lord comes exclusively through Christ as the Source and the Cross as the Means. In other words, that's the reason we must ever make the Cross the Object of our Faith. The Believer never outgrows the Cross because it is not possible to outgrow the Cross. Paul called it, *"The Everlasting Covenant"* (Heb. 13:20).

ROMANS, CHAPTER 6

The Sixth Chapter of Romans is the great *"how to"* Chapter of the Bible as it refers to the Sanctification of the Saint. In this particular Chapter, the Holy Spirit through Paul tells the Believer how to live for God. If we don't understand the Sixth Chapter of Romans, it is impossible to live a sanctified life. It simply cannot be done.

The following will give in brief that which the Holy Spirit through the Apostle taught us as it regards this all-important truth:

SIN

In the first two Verses of Romans, Chapter 6, Paul tells us that the problem is *"sin,"* or better yet, *"the sin nature."* Unfortunately, the modern church has tried to ignore sin or has tried to chart a course where sin is not mentioned. That is tragic! Sin in the life of the Believer has to be dealt with; ignoring the issue does not solve the problem. There is only one way it can be addressed, which is by and through the Cross of Christ.

THE CROSS

In answer to the problem of sin, or the sin nature, Paul now takes the Believer straight to the Cross of Christ. Please understand, Paul is not speaking here of the unredeemed; he is speaking solely of Believers, and that means you and me. He said: **"Do you not know, that so many of us as were baptized into Jesus Christ** *(plainly says that this Baptism is into Christ, not water [I Cor. 1:17; 12:13])* **were baptized into His**

Death? *(When Christ died on the Cross, in the Mind of God, we died with Him; in other words, He became our Substitute; our identification with Him in His Death gives us all the benefits for which He died; the idea is, He did it all for us!)*

"Therefore we are buried with Him by baptism into death *(not only did we die with Him, but we were buried with Him as well, which means that all the sin and transgression of the past were buried; when they put Him in the Tomb, they put all of our sins into that Tomb also)***: that like as Christ was raised up from the dead by the Glory of the Father, even so we also should walk in newness of life** *(we died with Him, we were buried with Him, and His Resurrection was our Resurrection to a 'newness of life')***.**

"For if we have been planted together *(with Christ)* **in the likeness of His Death** *(Paul proclaims the Cross as the instrument through which all blessings come; consequently, the Cross must ever be the object of our Faith, which gives the Holy Spirit latitude to work within our lives)***, we shall be also *in the likeness* of *His* Resurrection,** *(i.e., 'Live this resurrection Life,' only as long as we understand the 'likeness of His Death,' which refers to the Cross as the Means by which all of this is done)***" (Rom. 6:3-5).**

Plainly, clearly, and unequivocally, these three Verses take us to the Cross, which is the scene of Victory; spiritually speaking, it is the only scene of Victory there is.

FAITH

Having taken us to the Cross, the Apostle then tells us, **"Likewise reckon** *(account)* **you also yourselves to be dead indeed unto** *(the)* **sin** *(the sin nature—while the sin nature is not dead, we are dead unto the sin nature by virtue of the Cross and our Faith in that Sacrifice, but only as long as our Faith continues in the Cross)***, but alive unto God** *(living the Resurrection Life)* **through Jesus Christ our Lord** *(refers to what He did at the Cross, which is the means of this Resurrection Life)***" (Rom. 6:11).**

Due to what Christ did at the Cross, we are to understand that this is the Means by which we can have total Victory and, in fact, the only Means. It all comes through Faith, but ever with the Cross as the Object of that Faith.

(2) "UNTIL THE DAY IN WHICH HE WAS TAKEN UP, AFTER THAT HE THROUGH THE HOLY SPIRIT HAD GIVEN COMMANDMENTS UNTO THE APOSTLES WHOM HE HAD CHOSEN."

The overview is:

1. The phrase, *"Until the day in which He was taken up,"* means that Christ did His Works until He ascended.

2. *"After that He through the Holy Spirit,"* refers to the fact that the Spirit of God is the Speaker and Actor in this Book.

3. This tells us that everything that Jesus does on this Earth is done through the Power, Agency, Office, and Ministry of the Holy Spirit. To ignore Him, as sadly, most of the church world does, is to shut the door on all that God does.

4. Regrettably, most preachers, and I think I exaggerate not, little seek the Face of the Lord respecting guidance and direction. In the case of most churches, they simply make their own plans, and consequently, little or nothing is done for the Lord!

5. *"Had given Commandments unto the Apostles whom He had chosen,"* refers to the time before His Ascension.

6. The *"Commandments"* here mentioned refer to all the instructions given to these various men in the four Gospels, and especially the last Word given before the Ascension.

7. Is He still giving *"Commandments"* presently to modern Apostles whom He has called?

8. If the word *"Commandments"* is to be used in the sense of the Canon of Scripture as it here speaks, in a word, *"No!"* Every evidence is that the Holy Spirit closed out the Canon of Scripture with the giving of the Book of Revelation to John on the Isle of Patmos. No more has been given and, in fact, no more will be given for the simple reason that such is not needed.

9. However, if one uses the word *"Commandments"* in the realm of instruction or leading, Jesus is definitely doing this, and whatever He does give, it will always

coincide with the Word of God. If not, then it was not the Lord Who gave it.

10. In that case, to be sure, whatever He does give is definitely *"A Word of God,"* but not *"The Word of God!"*

(3) "TO WHOM ALSO HE SHOWED HIMSELF ALIVE AFTER HIS PASSION BY MANY INFALLIBLE PROOFS, BEING SEEN OF THEM FORTY DAYS, AND SPEAKING OF THE THINGS PERTAINING TO THE KINGDOM OF GOD."

The exegesis is:

1. One never matures beyond the Cross of Christ!

2. The whole of the Christian life from beginning to end, day-by-day, moment by moment, is simply learning what it means to live by Grace through Faith alone in Christ alone.

3. The great Plan of Redemption cost God everything, but it costs us nothing.

INFALLIBLE PROOFS

The phrase, *"To whom also He showed Himself alive after His passion by many infallible proofs,"* concerns His Appearances after the Resurrection.

The words, *"He showed Himself alive,"* have reference to the fact of him proving to the Disciples and others that He was not a spirit but actually a flesh and bone Body (Jn. 20:27).

There is no evidence that His Glorified Body contained any blood. In fact, I think the evidence shows that it did not. Regarding the body, which is physical only, the life normally is in the blood; however, the Holy Spirit is the Life of the Glorified Body, although continuing to be physical. Still, due to the Spirit, it is an entirely different dimension.

It is argued that the word *"proofs"* does not need the associate superlative *"infallible"* inasmuch as a *"proof"* is already infallible; however, Hervey says, *"The manner in which Luke used this word is quite justified."* He went on to say that inasmuch as Luke was a physician, it was quite common for medical writers to use such terms. *"Infallible symptoms,"* etc., is a case in point.

It means to go far beyond the normal meaning of the word, in this case, *"proof."*

NOTES

With the word *"infallible"* attached, even as Luke did, it expresses the certainty of the conclusion based on those particular proofs. In other words, there was absolutely no way that anyone who experienced these *"proofs,"* regarding the Resurrection of Jesus, could successfully dispute these happenings. The *"proofs"* are ironclad.

FORTY DAYS

The phrase, *"Being seen of them forty days,"* tells us several things:

- All that was done at Calvary was ratified by the Resurrection. However, it must be understood, the Cross of Christ was not dependent on the Resurrection, but rather the Resurrection was dependent on the Cross.
- In other words, if Jesus had failed to atone for even one sin, due to the fact that the wages of sin is death, He could not have been raised from the dead. The very fact that He was raised proclaims the fact of the veracity of Calvary.
- Jesus did not make just one appearance after the Resurrection but, in fact, several, probably about 12 appearances.
- These appearances were not brief and momentary, but actually, very involved, even with Jesus performing further Miracles (Jn. 21:6).
- These appearances were spread out over 40 days, putting to silence any skepticism.
- The number *"40"* refers to a probationary period. Moses fasted 40 days and nights as well as Jesus, and Israel wandered a probationary time of 40 days in the wilderness because of unbelief.

So, this period of time spent by Jesus between the Resurrection and Ascension satisfied all doubts and put to rest all skepticism concerning His Resurrection.

SPEAKING

The phrase, *"And speaking of the things pertaining to the Kingdom of God,"* addressed many things.

Israel had been offered the Kingdom both by John the Baptist and by Christ; however, despite the fact that Christ fulfilled all Scriptural admonitions as it regarded His Person as the Messiah, still, Israel would not accept Him. Religious leaders didn't accept Him simply because they didn't really know the Lord, despite all their religious profession. In fact, they were far worse than those who made no profession of Faith whatsoever. It was so bad, as is obviously known, that they crucified Christ.

They intended it as murder and, in fact, God held them accountable for murder and, above all, the murder of the Son of God; still, it was the Cross of Christ that ushered in the Kingdom of God. It could not have come without the Cross.

At the Cross, the terrible sin debt was paid totally and completely, past, present, and future, at least for all who will believe (Jn. 3:16). So, while they thought they were getting rid of this *"problem,"* they were actually carrying out the Will of God whether they realized it or not, and, of course, they didn't. No! It was definitely not the Will of God that they commit this terrible crime, but it was the Will of God that Christ would die on the Cross. That is, in fact, the very reason He came to this Earth (Gen. 3:15; Isa., Chpt. 53).

THE KINGDOM OF GOD

However, irrespective of their murderous intent, the Cross of Calvary, ordained of God, was carried out in totality in that the price was completely paid that the fallen sons of Adam's lost race might go free.

The *"Kingdom of God"* was offered to Israel but refused! However, while that did delay the physical and material aspects of the Kingdom, it did not delay the Spiritual aspects of the Finished Work of Christ.

The *"Kingdom of God"* resides in the hearts and lives of all Believers. Jesus is the Head of this Kingdom and will come back soon to guarantee its totality.

Then the Earth will be *"filled with the knowledge of the Glory of the LORD, as the waters cover the Sea"* (Hab. 2:14).

Entrance into this Kingdom is by the New Birth only (Jn. 3:3).

(4) "AND, BEING ASSEMBLED TOGETHER WITH THEM, COMMANDED THEM THAT THEY SHOULD NOT DEPART FROM JERUSALEM, BUT WAIT FOR THE PROMISE OF THE FATHER, WHICH, SAID HE, YOU HAVE HEARD OF ME."

NOTES

The synopsis is:

1. What is the alternative to the Cross of Jesus Christ?

2. The only alternative is to fall back once again upon our own resources.

3. Such a direction guarantees failure in every capacity.

THE COMMAND

The phrase, *"And, being assembled together with them,"* speaks of the time He ascended back to the Father. This was probably the time the *"above five hundred"* were gathered (I Cor. 15:6).

"Commanded them that they should not depart from Jerusalem," pertains to the coming Day of Pentecost.

The word *"Commanded"* in the Greek Text is *"Paraggelia,"* and means *"to charge,"* as in a military command. In other words, it was not a suggestion!

What the Lord was actually saying to His Followers was that they were not to go testify of Him, try to hold services, or try to preach revivals. In fact, they were to do nothing for Him until they were first baptized with the Holy Spirit. As stated, this was not a suggestion; it was and is a command.

This means that without the Holy Spirit, very little if anything is going to be done for the Lord Jesus Christ. There may be much religious machinery in motion, with much racket taking place, but still, it's just noise and not truly a work for God. Before they were to do anything for the Lord, they were to be first baptized with the Holy Spirit, which would come on the Day of Pentecost.

IS THIS COMMAND IN FORCE PRESENTLY?

Yes, it is!

The Holy Spirit is needed just as much presently as it was 2,000 years ago. In fact, there has never been a time that He wasn't needed, and greatly so.

Unfortunately, most of the Pentecostal denominations in America and Canada are relying less and less on the Holy Spirit and more and more on men's ways, which spells disaster. Let us say it again, *"Without the Holy Spirit, nothing is going to be*

NOTES

done for the Lord."

Unfortunately, racket and activity are mistaken for the Holy Spirit.

WHY JERUSALEM?

Jerusalem was the city chosen by God where He would place His Name (II Chron. 6:6). Consequently, the Temple was built there, with the further Command that all sacrifices were to be offered at the Temple and no place else. As well, all the Feast Days were celebrated there.

The reason is that God dwelt in the Temple, in fact, between the Mercy Seat and the Cherubim, or at least was supposed to dwell there.

Inasmuch as the Holy Spirit has now been given due to what Jesus did at the Cross, the Believer does not have to go to Jerusalem or any other designated place respecting the Infilling of the Holy Spirit, or anything pertaining to God for that matter. Due to the Blood of Jesus Christ cleansing from all sin, the Holy Spirit can now reside in the hearts and lives of all Believers, which He does. Consequently, they can be *"saved"* or *"baptized with the Holy Spirit"* any place where Faith reaches out to the Lord. By His Death at Calvary, Jesus had removed the middle wall of partition that kept the Gentiles from having access and, as well, from entering the Holy of Holies, spiritually speaking, where God was supposed to reside. Now, due to Calvary, all of that has changed.

They did not go to Jerusalem to be filled with the Spirit, even though that most definitely happened. They went there to wait for the Holy Spirit to come, which He did some 10 days after the Ascension of Christ.

THE PROMISE OF THE FATHER

The phrase, *"But wait for the Promise of the Father,"* spoke of the Holy Spirit, which had been promised by the Father (Lk. 24:49; Joel, Chpt. 2).

The phrase, *"Which, said He, You have heard of Me,"* pertains to that which Christ had already said concerning the Spirit Baptism, which the Disciples and others had heard (Jn. 7:37-39; 14:12-17, 26; 15:26; 16:7-15).

Believers must understand that we are opposed by the spirit world of darkness attempting to steal, kill, and destroy (Jn. 10:10). Within our own ability, education, motivation, talent, will power, etc., such has no effect on the powers of darkness. This, among other things, is why the Holy Spirit is so much needed by every single Believer. The Holy Spirit gives the Believer Power and, as well, reveals to him that which the Lord desires to be done (Jn. 16:7-15; Acts 1:8).

Consequently, regarding any so-called work done for God, if it's not done by the Power of the Holy Spirit, it constitutes a work of man and not of God. Therefore, God cannot accept it. As we have stated, everything the Lord does on Earth, He does through the Person, Power, Agency, Office, and Ministry of the Holy Spirit.

As we have already said, this statement given by Christ concerning His Command is not a suggestion. It is a military term, which demands obedience. If we ignore it, we do so at our peril.

(5) "FOR JOHN TRULY BAPTIZED WITH WATER; BUT YOU SHALL BE BAPTIZED WITH THE HOLY SPIRIT NOT MANY DAYS HENCE."

The order is:

1. When Paul wrote the Book of Galatians, he was upset.

2. Interlopers (the Judaizers) had come in and were trying to get these Galatians to resort to Law, which would destroy the only hope that they had of a right relationship with God.

3. That right relationship with God is through the Cross of Jesus Christ, and only through the Cross of Jesus Christ.

BAPTIZED WITH WATER

The phrase, *"For John truly baptized with water,"* merely symbolized the very best baptism that Believers could receive before the Day of Pentecost. The reasons are obvious.

The Holy Spirit could not come into the heart and life of the Believer in the realm of baptism until Jesus died on Calvary, thereby, taking the sin of man away, which the blood of bulls and goats could never do (Jn. 1:29; 7:39; Heb. 10:4).

Before Calvary, the Holy Spirit definitely

helped Followers of the Lord and even anointed some of them for service; however, as Jesus said, He (the Holy Spirit) dwelt then with Believers, whereas now, He dwells in Believers (Jn. 14:17).

Before the sin debt was paid by Jesus at Calvary, those in Covenant were definitely Saved, even as we are Saved now, but their sins were only covered and not taken away. Consequently, the Holy Spirit could not occupy them as a temple as He does presently (I Cor. 3:16).

Since Calvary, the sin and sins of all Believers have been taken away with no charge against them at all, even by Satan; consequently, the Holy Spirit can now come into this cleansed temple and there abide forever (Jn. 14:16).

BAPTIZED WITH THE HOLY SPIRIT

The phrase, *"But you shall be baptized with the Holy Spirit not many days hence,"* spoke of the coming Day of Pentecost, although Jesus did not at that time use that term.

As well, the Holy Spirit could not be sent, at least in this capacity, until Jesus ascended back to Heaven, signifying a Finished Work. He said, *"It is expedient for you that I go away: for if I go not away, the Comforter (Helper) will not come unto you; but if I depart, I will send Him unto you"* (Jn. 16:7).

Of course, the Holy Spirit coming on the Day of Pentecost signified that Jesus did, in fact, ascend to the Father.

The word *"baptized"* means *"to dip under."* Actually, it means that the Believer can be immersed in the Holy Spirit and the Holy Spirit immersed in the Believer. As stated, this is now possible because of the Blood of Jesus Christ having washed, i.e., *"taken away all sin."*

Jesus here is meaning to contrast the difference in the Old Covenant and the New Covenant. Under the Old Covenant, *"Water Baptism"* was basically a ceremony or ritual and was introduced alone by John. In fact, it was referred to as *"John's baptism"* (Acts 19:3).

This baptism of John's was the result of the sinner's Repentance and not the cause. In fact, Jesus was baptized in water by John, even though He needed no Repentance but did so to *"fulfill all Righteousness"* (Mat. 3:15).

NOTES

WHY DID JOHN BAPTIZE IN WATER?

Considering that none of the Prophets of old did this before him, why did he do so?

John was the forerunner of Christ, actually raised up to introduce Jesus as the Messiah. That was his sole purpose. When he did that, the Lord took him home because his Ministry was finished.

"Water Baptism" was introduced by John because it was commanded by the Holy Spirit in order that Jesus be manifested as the Messiah to Israel (Jn. 1:25-31).

Water Baptism, which continues under the New Covenant, was and is symbolic of the Death, Burial, and Resurrection of Christ. Whenever the Believer is put under the water in baptism and then brought out, it is a sign also of his spiritual death and Spiritual Resurrection.

The Prophets of old did not do such because they were not introducing Christ.

That which John did was ceremonial, ritualistic, and symbolic; however, that which Jesus does (baptizing the Believer with the Holy Spirit) is not ceremony, ritual, or symbol.

- The Holy Spirit is a Person and not something impersonal, such as water.

As well, Jesus is the One Who does the baptizing with the Holy Spirit (Mat. 3:11).

- Whenever the believing sinner comes to Christ, it is the Holy Spirit Who baptizes that person into Christ, all made possible by the Cross (Rom. 6:3-5). At the Spirit Baptism, it is Jesus Who baptizes that person with the Spirit (Mat. 3:11).

- The Holy Spirit is to help us in every conceivable activity we perform for Christ and every Work He performs in us; however, this Baptism is potential in its nature. The mere Indwelling of the Spirit does not guarantee the full efficacy of His Work in us since that Indwelling is not automatic in its nature.

THE HOLY SPIRIT

The Spirit has been sent to the Believer's heart to make His Home there. That means that the Christian must make Him feel at home. He can do that by giving the Holy

Spirit absolute liberty of action in his heart, the home in which He lives.

This means that the Believer is to yield himself, all of himself, to the Spirit's Control and depend upon the Spirit for guidance, teaching, and strength. Then will the potential power resident in the Presence of the Spirit in the heart of the Believer be operative in one's life.

This union is to be of such magnitude that it is explained by the word *"baptized,"* which means, in essence, *"The Believer is immersed into the Holy Spirit, and the Holy Spirit is immersed into the Believer."*

For the Holy Spirit to function in our lives as He can function and desires to function, our Faith must ever be in the Cross of Christ (Rom. 8:2). In other words, the Cross of Christ must be the Object of our Faith, and the only Object of our Faith.

The entire Story of the Bible is the Story of *"Jesus Christ and Him Crucified."* While Jesus is the Source of all things we receive from God, it is the Cross that is the means by which all of these things are given to us. So, our Faith must ever be in the Finished Work of Christ. Then the Holy Spirit will work on our behalf, and do so constantly. Please understand that this is something we have to have, or we simply cannot live a victorious life.

While a Believer can be Saved and not place his Faith exclusively in Christ and the Cross, he can never walk in victory, but rather the opposite. Let us say it again:

The Desire of the Holy Spirit is to give us victory over the world, the flesh, and the devil, which helps us to grow in Grace and the Knowledge of the Lord. For Him to work within our lives as He desires to do so, our Faith must at all times be in the Cross of Christ. Then the Holy Spirit will work mightily within our hearts and within our lives (Rom. 8:1-11; I Cor. 1:17-18, 23; 2:2; Col. 2:10-15).

(6) "WHEN THEY THEREFORE WERE COME TOGETHER, THEY ASKED OF HIM, SAYING, LORD, WILL YOU AT THIS TIME RESTORE AGAIN THE KINGDOM TO ISRAEL?"

The form is:

1. It is so foolish to turn from the Cross of Christ.

2. It is foolish to exchange the free Grace of God for the bondage of one's own works. This is what abandoning the Cross means.

3. The Law did not come to make you good; the Law came to crush all your self hopes and to drive you out of yourself to Christ and the Cross.

NOTES

THEY ASK OF HIM

The phrase, *"When they therefore were come together, they asked of Him, saying,"* seemingly presents the last meeting before the Ascension. Every evidence is that these were the last Words Jesus would speak before He went to the Father. If our calculations are correct, and without enumerating them here, this was the twelfth Appearance of the Lord during this 40 days and nights from the Resurrection to the Ascension.

By now it should be obvious that, even though this was the same Jesus and, as well, with a human body, albeit glorified, still, there was a vast difference in Him. His Demeanor, Persona, Familiarity, and Presence were of a higher dimension. While He was still human, His Deity now shone forth exceedingly so!

THE RESTORATION OF THE KINGDOM

The question, *"Lord, will You at this time restore again the Kingdom to Israel?"* presents the thinking of the Disciples even now.

In all fairness to them, the Old Testament is full of promises and predictions respecting the Restoration of Israel. Almost every Prophet spoke of it extensively. Naturally, they had read these things, and that is what they believed was coming now.

Admittedly, there is almost nothing in the Old Testament concerning the Church. It was mentioned in a veiled reference but couched in terminology not immediately understandable. I speak of the predictions that the Gentiles would come to know the Lord (Isa. 11:10; 42:1, 6; 49:6, 22; 60:3; 66:19; Mal. 1:11). As is obvious, most of these predictions came from Isaiah, who was also the great Millennial Prophet. So, the conclusion drawn from these statements was probably in the context of the Gentiles recognizing Israel as the premier Nation and serving her, etc. At any rate, they did not link it with what we refer to as the New Testament Church.

Even when Jesus plainly spoke of building His Church, they seemed not to grasp His Meaning (Mat. 16:18).

In fact, was the New Testament Church intended by God all along, and if so, why is it not mentioned more readily in the Old Testament?

Of course, it is obvious that the Lord knew that such would be; however, there is no evidence that this was His original Intention.

In attempting to understand the great Plan of God, one must understand that while His Will is seldom carried out in this present world, His Plan always ultimately comes to a successful conclusion. In other words, any plan that God has made will be carried out without fail; however, as should be obvious, at times there are delays in that plan.

THE PLAN OF GOD

For instance, it was not the Plan of God that Adam and Eve fall in the garden, bringing about misery, suffering, and dying to the extent that it beggars description. It was His Plan that Adam and Eve live as they were created, which means to serve God faithfully and to bring little Sons and Daughters of God into the world.

However, even though Adam and Eve failed, the Plan of God has not failed but has only been delayed. In fact, it will be totally realized in the coming Kingdom Age and then forever!

As well, it was not God's Plan that Israel reject her Messiah and even kill Him. Due to Adam's fall, it was the Plan of God that the Second Member of the Godhead would become a Man and die on a Cross. Still, it was not predestined as to who would commit this vile act.

Due to Israel rejecting her Lord, the Church, which was not in the original Plan of God, or at least as it is now known, became a necessity. Paul mentioned this when He said, **"I say then, Have they stumbled that they should fall?** *(Never to rise again?)* **God forbid: but *rather* through their fall Salvation *is come* unto the Gentiles, for to provoke them to jealousy.**

NOTES

THE FALL

He then said, **"Now if the fall of them *be* the riches of the world** *(made it a necessity for the Lord to now place the emphasis on the Gentiles)*, **and the diminishing of them the riches of the Gentiles; how much more their fullness?** *(How much greater blessing will it be, when they are restored!)*" **(Rom. 11:11-12).**

So, the Church was not originally planned by God but due to Israel's fall, it became a necessity.

As stated, the original plan was a world of no sin or failure, populated by Sons and Daughters of God, which would have happened had Adam and Eve not fallen.

Their fall necessitated Israel being brought into existence in order that the Word of God and the Messiah, Who would save mankind, be given to the world.

Due to events, Israel became a part of the Plan of God but was not so originally.

As a result of her being a part of the Plan of God, Israel will ultimately be restored, which will take place at the Second Coming, and then she will fulfill her destiny.

THE CHURCH

Also, the Church was not originally in the Plan of God, but due to Israel's fall, it now is a part of that plan. Therefore, the future will come out according to the following manner:

The natural people on Earth, who will be alive at the Second Coming and will go over into the Kingdom Age, will ultimately fulfill that which God originally intended. In the Perfect Age to come, which follows the Kingdom Age and is outlined in Revelation, Chapters 21 and 22, men and women through procreation will bring little Sons and Daughters of God into the world. (After the Fall, Adam and Eve could only bring about sons and daughters in the image of Adam, which spoke of a fallen race [Gen. 5:3; Rev. 22:2]).

Israel will fulfill her destiny, as planned by God after the Fall, and will serve as a Holy Nation and Holy Priesthood under Christ to the entirety of this world. However, this will come about in the Kingdom Age, with no information given concerning their status in the coming Perfect Age.

Regarding the Church, it is made up of both Gentiles and Jews (only a few Jews). As well, it includes all Israelites of the Old Testament who were in Covenant, and those, such as they were, who lived from Adam to Abraham and died in the Faith. It will be as follows:

GOD, ALL IN ALL

All of this group, which is by far the largest, will have a part in the First Resurrection and, as such, will be given Glorified Bodies exactly as Christ had after His Resurrection. They will help Him rule His vast Creation forever and ever (I Cor. 15:51-57; Rev., Chpts. 21-22).

Paul said, *"Then comes the end (the end of all rebellion which will take place at the conclusion of the Kingdom Age, and immediately preceding the Perfect Age), when He (Christ) shall have delivered up the Kingdom to God, even the Father; when He (Christ) shall have put down all rule and all authority and power."*

He then said, *"And when all things shall be subdued unto Him (Jesus Christ), then shall the Son also Himself be subject unto Him (God the Father) Who put all things under Him (Jesus Christ), that God may be all in all"* (I Cor. 15:24, 28).

When God shall be *"All in All,"* then His Plan, although having been delayed, will finally be realized. At that time, all evil and unrighteousness will be no more, with the entirety of the world knowing nothing but the Righteousness of God.

Then the New Jerusalem is going to come down from God out of Heaven, with God literally changing His Headquarters from Heaven to Earth (Rev. 21:2-3).

John said, *"Behold, the Tabernacle of God is with men, and He will dwell with them, and they shall be His people, and God Himself shall be with them, and be their God"* (Rev. 21:3).

(7) "AND HE SAID UNTO THEM, IT IS NOT FOR YOU TO KNOW THE TIMES OR THE SEASONS, WHICH THE FATHER HAS PUT IN HIS OWN POWER."

NOTES

The exegesis is:

1. It is foolish, as stated, to exchange what is free for the relentless demands of the Law.
2. The Gospel of Grace says: God gives and gives! The Law says: you must do and do!
3. It is foolish to exchange the infinite Merit of Christ for my finite merit before God.

SEVERAL THINGS ARE SAID IN THIS VERSE

In essence, Jesus was telling His Disciples, and all His Followers for that matter, that the things which they asked were not important to know. It was the business of the Disciples and others to attend to the work at hand. In other words, *"Occupy till I come"* (Lk. 19:13).

While these things certainly are of great significance, the task at hand is of far greater import.

Verse 8 will proclaim that the entirety of the thrust of this meeting is that world Evangelism is priority with God and should be priority with the Disciples and all others, and for all time! This does not mean that other things pertaining to God are of no significance. In fact, anything that is of the Lord is of overwhelming import; however, that which is of priority here, and which continues to show such through the entirety of the Book of Acts, is the taking of the Gospel to the entirety of the world. If that is priority with God, it must be priority with the Church. If it is not, and sadly, it is not in most churches, then the church is not functioning in a manner intended by the Lord.

THE LAST INSTRUCTIONS

When we consider that these things said by Christ at this time were the last instructions before the Ascension, we should realize how significant they really are. Believers are told to do these things:

- Get baptized with the Holy Spirit, which is a work separate and apart from Salvation, as we shall see. Without the Holy Spirit, nothing will be done for God, no matter how much is attempted. This is an absolute essential! As we have already stated, it is not a suggestion, but rather a

"Command," even as Verse 4 tells us.

• The Holy Spirit is given to us for many and varied reasons, but one of the greatest reasons of all is to help us take the Gospel to the world.

• In effect, Jesus does say in this Verse that Israel is going to be restored, but not when!

• These *"times and seasons"* are in the Domain of the Father and will be brought about accordingly.

The word *"times"* in the Greek Text refers to *"an indefinite period of time,"* while the word *"seasons"* refers to *"a set time."*

So, it seems that some of these *"times"* concerning coming events could vary according to particulars.

TIMES AND SEASONS

Conversely, it seems that the word *"seasons"* implies the very opposite, in other words, *"a fixed time."* However, in these *"times and seasons,"* there is no indication that man has anything to do with the fixation of these events, but rather are in the Domain of God exclusively. Actually, the word *"power,"* as it is used here, in the Greek is *"exousia"* and means *"control."* In other words, the control is in His Hands.

From Matthew 24:36, we know that the Lord has a set day and hour concerning the fulfillment of futuristic events, such as the Rapture, Great Tribulation, Second Coming, etc.

Therefore, the word *"times"* refers to the conduct and action of the Church on Earth, which may vary and are not predetermined. However, whatever those *"times"* may be, such will not affect the *"seasons,"* which are already fixed in the Mind of God.

(8) "BUT YOU SHALL RECEIVE POWER, AFTER THAT THE HOLY SPIRIT IS COME UPON YOU: AND YOU SHALL BE WITNESSES UNTO ME BOTH IN JERUSALEM, AND IN ALL JUDAEA, AND IN SAMARIA, AND UNTO THE UTTERMOST PART OF THE EARTH."

The exegesis is:

1. Look at all the wonderful things that God has done for you in your Christian experience. Did those things come to you because of your effort?

NOTES

2. Do those things come to you because of your merit?

3. No, they came to you because of what Jesus did at the Cross and your Faith in Him and His Finished Work.

POWER

The phrase, *"But you shall receive Power,"* presents a different type of *"Power"* than the same word in Verse 7.

"Power," as Jesus used it here, in the Greek Text is *"Dunamis"* and means *"Miracle-working Power."* It means *"to make able or possible"* that which was not heretofore so!

As well, it is *"inherent Power,"* which is capable of reproducing itself like a dynamo (II Pet. 1:3).

In essence, this means that the Power Plant has moved inside the Believer, which is exactly what has happened. The Holy Spirit, Who is God, literally comes to abide in the Believer (Jn. 14:17).

Science has dreamed of finding the secret to perpetual motion, that is, if such exists. This means that the motion does not have to have an outside source of power, such as electricity, atomic energy, gasoline, etc. In other words, it runs on its own.

However, this Perpetual Power, which needs no outside source, has come into being in the Believer in the form of God the Holy Spirit. Before Pentecost, the Holy Spirit was with the Believer, which spoke of an outside Source. However, since Pentecost, that Source has taken up abode, literally speaking, in the Believer (I Cor. 3:16). Therefore, there is no way that Satan or demon spirits can get at this *"Source,"* that is, if the Believer truly follows the Lord.

In a sense, this means that the same Power Jesus had in His public Ministry, and Him alone we might quickly add, now is ensconced in the heart and life of every single Spirit-filled Believer. In other words, instead of Satan having to contend with one Jesus, in essence, he now has to contend with multiplied millions of Believers, who have been granted the privilege and Power that was previously incumbent on Jesus alone. This is the reason that Jesus told His Disciples hours before the Crucifixion, *"It is expedient for you that I go away: for if I go not away, the Comforter (Holy Spirit) will not come unto you; but if I depart, I will send Him unto you"* (Jn. 16:7).

FOR WHAT IS THIS POWER TO BE USED?

Jesus told us the answer to that question as well. *"He who believes on Me, the works that I do shall he do also; and greater works than these shall he do; because I go unto My Father"* (Jn. 14:12).

The Spirit-filled Believer is to preach the Gospel, pray for the sick and see them healed, perform Miracles, and cast out demons (Mk. 16:17-18).

However, this Miracle-working Power is not meant to be used for greedy purposes of our own, even as Jesus did not use His Power in that fashion. It is to be used in a twofold manner:

1. To *"destroy the works of the devil"* (I Jn. 3:8). In other words, that which Jesus began, even as Luke said in the first Verse of this Book, is to be continued.

2. This *"Power"* is to be used to ever take the Gospel to the entirety of the world.

The phrase, *"After that the Holy Spirit is come upon you,"* specifically states that this *"Power"* is inherent in the Holy Spirit and solely in His Domain.

As well, it tells us that only Spirit-filled Believers have this Power. This means that all Believers who do not have the Acts 2:4 experience do not have this *"Power,"* and accordingly, can be of precious little service to the Lord. Such Believers, although Born-Again, will effect little or nothing for the cause of Christ. There may be much religious activity and much religious machinery, and many people may be fooled because of all of the activity and motion; however, it is not possible for any true Work of God to be accomplished without the Power of the Holy Spirit resident in the Believer's life.

EQUIPPED FOR SERVICE

Regrettably, millions teach and believe that all of this comes immediately at Salvation, which repudiates any other experience after being Born-Again. In other words, they claim they are baptized with the Holy Spirit at Conversion, that is, if they give any

NOTES

credence to the Holy Spirit at all.

However, there is no Scriptural validity for such thinking. The truth is, the *"Born-Again"* experience does not equip one for service. That is done through the Baptism with the Holy Spirit, which must be received after Salvation. While the sinner can definitely receive Christ into his heart, it is not possible for him to be baptized with the Holy Spirit at the same moment he is saved. Jesus said, *"Even the Spirit of Truth; Whom the world cannot receive"* (Jn. 14:17).

While the believing sinner definitely can be baptized with the Holy Spirit moments after Salvation, even as many have down through the centuries (Acts 10:44-48), still, the temple must be washed and cleansed by the Blood of Jesus before the Entrance of the Holy Spirit.

WITNESSES UNTO ME

The phrase, *"And you shall be witnesses unto Me,"* does not refer to witnessing to souls about their Eternal Salvation, as important as that is!

The word for *"witnesses"* in the Greek Text is *"martus"* and means *"a martyr for Christ."* It actually refers to one giving his all in every capacity for Christ, even to the laying down of his life. Actually, that is exactly what is supposed to happen when one accepts Christ. One is to forfeit one's life in favor of Christ. Of course, when this happens, one truly finds one's life (Mat. 10:39).

If the reader is to notice, Jesus said, *"Unto Me,"* rather than, *"For Me!"* So, this word does not mean to witness for Jesus, as important as that is, but rather *"unto Jesus."*

The idea is that one cannot properly witness unto Jesus, regarding His Salvation and all that He is, without being baptized with the Holy Spirit. While the Believer can certainly learn the Rudiments of Christ without this experience, still, Christ will never be made completely real to him, nor will he be able to make Christ real to others. Please allow me to say it again:

This of which Jesus speaks, the Baptism with the Holy Spirit, is meant to equip one for service. If a Believer does not obey Christ in this regard, which means to be baptized with the Holy Spirit with the evidence of speaking with other Tongues, his service for the Lord will be inconsequential.

WAITING FOR THE PROMISE OF THE FATHER

Paul mentioned that there were about 500 people who saw Jesus at one time, with it probably being the time of the Ascension of Christ (I Cor. 15:6). If that is the case, then we know that about 380 of them, or at least some portion, did not obey Him relative to *"waiting for the Promise of the Father."*

About 120, or whatever number there was, did obey and were present on the Day of Pentecost and were baptized with the Holy Spirit exactly as Jesus said would happen. Now, quite possibly, some, or most, of the remaining number, ever how many that would be, did receive the Holy Spirit a little later, and no doubt did. We do know that ever how many were there on the Day of Pentecost, they shook the world for Jesus Christ; however, to those who did not obey regarding the Baptism with the Holy Spirit, one can be certain that their lives little counted for God, as far as His Work and Service were concerned. Make no mistake about it, it is the same presently!

And yet, there is an excellent possibility, and, no doubt, was correct, that many of these people who saw Jesus and heard Him give the Command to *"wait for the Promise of the Father,"* although not filled on the Day of Pentecost because they were not present, were filled later.

UNTO THE UTTERMOST PART OF THE EARTH

The phrase, *"Both in Jerusalem, and in all Judaea, and in Samaria, and unto the uttermost part of the Earth,"* proclaims the Work of God as being worldwide, as is here obvious.

While it certainly began in Jerusalem, it quickly spread to *"all Judaea,"* and then elsewhere, even to hated *"Samaria,"* and then all over the world.

While the reader may think little concerning this statement as given by Christ, actually, it is of tremendous import.

"Jerusalem" was the city God had chosen in order to place His Name. Consequently, it would be there, Jerusalem and Judaea, where the Holy Spirit would move first of all. However, then He mentioned *"Samaria."*

NOTES

Samaria was hated by the Jews; therefore, we know that with this simple statement, Jesus was striking down all racial prejudice and bias. Please allow me to make this statement:

Any church that does not have people of all races and colors worshipping together, as well as every strata of society, whether rich or poor, cannot honestly call itself a New Testament Church, at least if such ethnic groups reside in the area. If the Gospel is truly preached, there will be no racial prejudice and bias; there will be all types of people in such a Church.

As well, the worldwide thrust of the Gospel demanded by Jesus means that the Gospel of Jesus Christ is not a western gospel, eastern gospel, etc. Neither is it a white man's gospel or especially tailored for any other ethnic group.

All men are lost and need a Redeemer. Consequently, Jesus died for all. So, the Gospel is for all people everywhere!

(9) "AND WHEN HE HAD SPOKEN THESE THINGS, WHILE THEY BEHELD, HE WAS TAKEN UP; AND A CLOUD RECEIVED HIM OUT OF THEIR SIGHT."

The form is:

1. The phrase, *"And when He had spoken these things,"* refers to His last instructions to His Followers.

2. We understand that last words, at least in this context, are very important and that Jesus could have spoken of anything. Considering what He did say concerning the Holy Spirit, it should be evident to all as to how important this really is.

3. *"While they beheld, He was taken up,"* refers to Him ascending before their very eyes, which was something no human beings had ever witnessed in all of human history, with the exception of Elisha seeing the departure of Elijah. However, this was the Son of God, Who had completed the great Redemption Plan, and at great price. Therefore, it was unique within itself.

4. *"And a cloud received Him out of their sight,"* I think represents the Shekhinah Glory of God which enveloped Christ

as He ascended.

5. Even though the word *"cloud"* is here used, which speaks of an ordinary cloud that can be seen by anyone, from the manner in which the Text reads, we note several things:

a. This was *"a cloud"* and not just any cloud. The emphasis speaks of a certain cloud that was for this very purpose.

b. This cloud *"received Him,"* which could not be said of ordinary clouds, etc.

c. Because of the description given, I personally believe that this was the same *"cloud"* that led the Children of Israel out of Egypt, which hovered over the Tabernacle (Ex. 13:21; 40:34). The *"cloud"* in all cases, I think, was the Holy Spirit!

(10) "AND WHILE THEY LOOKED STEADFASTLY TOWARD HEAVEN AS HE WENT UP, BEHOLD, TWO MEN STOOD BY THEM IN WHITE APPAREL."

The order is:

1. The phrase, *"And while they looked steadfastly toward Heaven as He went up,"* refers to there being absolutely no doubt that He actually ascended. As stated, this very well could have been the time when approximately 500 people saw this Event of all Events.

2. These statements are important because of affirming His actual Ascension, which was testified to by eyewitnesses.

3. *"Behold, two men stood by them in white apparel,"* presents a necessity because the Law required two witnesses to establish a matter. So, two men appeared at the Transfiguration, two men (Angels) at the Resurrection, and two men (Angels) at the Ascension.

4. The *"white apparel"* here mentioned refers to the color white as actually more of a light than color itself. In other words, the garment was made translucent by the Presence of God emanating from the Angels. The garment did not cause this; the Angels themselves did (these two *"men"* were actually Angels).

(11) "WHICH ALSO SAID, YOU MEN OF GALILEE, WHY DO YOU STAND GAZING UP INTO HEAVEN? THIS SAME JESUS, WHICH IS TAKEN UP FROM YOU INTO HEAVEN, SHALL SO COME IN LIKE MANNER AS YOU HAVE SEEN HIM GO INTO HEAVEN."

NOTES

The structure is:

1. The question, *"Which also said, You men of Galilee, why do you stand gazing up into Heaven?"* does not mean that it was only men who were present, but rather that this was a common term used for both men and women in such circumstances.

2. As well, this statement by the Angels, although addressed to all, was probably more particularly addressed to the Eleven as it mentions Galilee, which was their home.

3. If, in fact, there were about 500 people present at this time, it is possible, but not likely, that everyone there was from Galilee. I find it difficult to think that Mary and Martha, along with Lazarus, whom Jesus had raised from the dead and who lived in Bethany, a suburb of Jerusalem, would not have been present at this occasion.

4. *"This same Jesus, which is taken up from you into Heaven,"* refers to the same Human Body with the nail prints in His Hands and Feet, etc.

5. *"Shall so come in like manner as you have seen Him go into Heaven,"* actually refers to the same place, which was the Mount of Olivet, and with clouds.

6. John said, *"Behold, He comes with clouds"* (Rev. 1:7). Daniel said, *"One like the Son of Man came with the clouds of Heaven"* (Dan. 7:13).

7. Inasmuch as these *"clouds"* were not ordinary clouds, but rather representative of redeemed men and Angels, likewise, the *"cloud"* that received Him out of their sight at the Ascension was representative of the Holy Spirit.

(12) "THEN RETURNED THEY UNTO JERUSALEM FROM THE MOUNT CALLED OLIVET, WHICH IS FROM JERUSALEM A SABBATH DAY'S JOURNEY."

The synopsis is:

1. The phrase, *"Then returned they unto Jerusalem from the Mount called Olivet,"* represents, as stated, the place of His Ascent and will also be the place of His Descent.

2. As men with natural eyes saw Jesus ascend, likewise will men with natural eyes see Him descend (Dan. 7:13-14; Zech. 14:1-5; Mat. 24:29-31; 25:31-46; II Thess. 1:7-10; Rev. 1:7; 19:11-21).

3. *"Which is from Jerusalem a Sabbath Day's journey,"* represented little over one-half mile.

4. Verses 12 through 14 represent these people, or at least some of them, obeying Jesus to go into Jerusalem and *"wait for the Promise of the Father."*

(13) "AND WHEN THEY WERE COME IN, THEY WENT UP INTO AN UPPER ROOM, WHERE ABODE BOTH PETER, AND JAMES, AND JOHN, AND ANDREW, PHILIP, AND THOMAS, BARTHOLOMEW, AND MATTHEW, JAMES THE SON OF ALPHAEUS, AND SIMON ZELOTES, AND JUDAS THE BROTHER OF JAMES."

The construction is:

1. The phrase, *"And when they were come in, they went up into an upper room,"* more than likely referred to the same room where they had eaten the Passover with Christ (Lk. 22:12). It is said by some that the house (which may have been the house of John Mark) containing this *"upper room"* was in back of the Temple and a very short distance from that edifice; however, that cannot be conclusively proven.

2. *"Where abode both Peter, and James, and John,"* presents as usual Peter being mentioned first (Mat. 10:2-5; Mk. 3:16-19; Lk. 6:14-16).

3. As is known, James and John were brothers, the sons of Zebedee.

4. *"And Andrew,"* speaks of Peter's brother.

5. *"Philip, and Thomas, Bartholomew,"* presents Philip and Bartholomew as brothers. *"Thomas"* is placed between Philip and Bartholomew, but it is not known why! (Bartholomew is the same as Nathaniel.)

6. *"And Matthew, James the son of Alphaeus, and Simon Zelotes, and Judas the brother of James,"* are, as well, thought possibly to have been brothers.

7. This Judas is also called Lebbaeus and Thaddaeus (Mat. 10:3; Mk. 3:18). As well, this was James the Less, to distinguish him from James the brother of John.

8. The word *"abode"* does not mean they lived there but that it was a large room used as a meeting place.

(14) "THESE ALL CONTINUED WITH ONE ACCORD IN PRAYER AND SUPPLICATION, WITH THE WOMEN, AND MARY THE MOTHER OF JESUS, AND WITH HIS BRETHREN."

NOTES

The synopsis is:

1. The Law was not given to make one good; the Law was given to crush all of our self hopes and to drive us out of ourselves to Christ.

2. It is foolish to return to the Law as a means to be accepted by God when the purpose of the Law was to crush the hopes of being accepted by God on one's own terms, and rather to drive one to Christ.

3. The Law takes, while Grace gives.

PRAYER AND SUPPLICATION

The phrase, *"These all continued with one accord in prayer and supplication,"* proclaims the manner in which these meetings were conducted. How long they stayed there each day, we are not told; however, this we do know, the word *"continued,"* as used here, means *"to persevere in a thing, or to adhere firmly."* Consequently, the greatest bulk of the time was taken up in prayer.

The word *"supplication"* means *"to request,"* so they were not only worshipping the Lord but asking Him to do certain things as well!

To be sure, there were many things they needed from the Lord. The threat to their own lives, especially at this time, was not the least of their concerns. As well, they still hardly knew what the future held, just that they were to wait there for the *"Promise of the Father."*

They really had no idea what this meant. These were uncharted waters, Scripturally speaking, other than the Second Chapter of Joel and a small portion of the Twenty-eighth Chapter of Isaiah.

While Peter and others instantly linked Joel with what had happened on the Day of Pentecost, it is doubtful if they were able to correlate any such thing before that momentous day.

While it is true that Jesus had spoken to them extensively about the Holy Spirit a few days before the Crucifixion, which would be far more understandable after the Day of Pentecost, once again, before the fact, their knowledge was very limited.

PRAYER

Nevertheless, they did the one thing that was important, and that was to *"pray."* It is tragic that at present, much of the modern church little knows anything about prayer. Considering that this is the greatest privilege that anyone could ever have—the ability to speak to Someone Who is All-powerful and All-knowing—is an opportunity unparalleled. Tragically, few take advantage of such.

If each one of you holding this book in your hands would set aside as little as 15 or even maybe 30 minutes a day solely for prayer, in a short while, you would find that every single thing would change, and I mean everything, and for the better. Prayer is basically twofold:

1. It is the only way that a proper relationship can be established with the Lord. It is a time of introspection where we speak to the Lord and He speaks to us. As always, He seeks our betterment in all things. In other words, He alone can make a better person out of you.

2. Prayer is also the opportunity for making our requests known to the Lord. He alone is able to meet any and every need. If the Believer really has Faith and understands at least a little about the Word of God, he will find that prayer and Faith in God's Word present the ticket to success in all things, at least all things that really count.

THE WOMEN

The phrase, *"With the women, and Mary the Mother of Jesus,"* concerns the women who followed Christ from Galilee (Mat. 27:55-56).

As well, it should be noticed that Mary, the Mother of Jesus, appears here not as an object of worship but as humbly joining in with the others in seeking the Lord.

The phrase, *"And with His Brethren,"* concerns His Half-brothers, one might say, who were, *"James, Joseph, Simon, and Jude"* (Mat. 13:55; Mk. 6:3).

Whether all four were present or not, we are not told; however, due to Jesus having appeared to James after the Resurrection, there is definitely a possibility that all four were there.

NOTES

In fact, this statement concerning Mary and His Brethren, as given by the Holy Spirit, brings deep and sweet relief to the Christian heart. At last, Mary and the Brothers of Jesus took their place publicly among the Disciples. Had they made this great decision at the beginning, how much happier they should have been!

It is humbling to religious self-esteem to learn that the Lords' daily, intimate, family life of perfect love and exquisite moral beauty failed to win His Brothers and Sisters to believe on Him, even though he was with them for many years in the home at Nazareth. This remained true even later when His Miracles and Teaching were obvious. Their unbelief makes more convincing the truth of the incurable corruption of the natural heart (Jer. 17:9). John recorded their attitude by saying, *"Neither did His brethren believe in Him"* (Jn. 7:5).

It is clear that Mary was willing to be the Mother of the King of Israel (Lk. 1:32-38), but unwilling, it seems, to be a Disciple of the despised Nazarene (Mk. 3:21, 31-35; Lk. 11:27-28).

Actually, the terrible sword of Luke 2:34-35 revealed the thoughts of many hearts and of her heart (Heb. 4:12).

The pain she felt when viewing the Crucifixion belonged to the realm of nature, but the double prediction of Luke, Chapter 2, belonged to the realm of judgment. She herself illustrated Luke 2:34.

The part of Christianity that is corrupt has composed a different history of her—and the natural heart prefers it—but the true Christian believes only what the infallible Spirit of God records.

(15) "AND IN THOSE DAYS PETER STOOD UP IN THE MIDST OF THE DISCIPLES, AND SAID, THE NUMBER OF NAMES TOGETHER WERE ABOUT AN HUNDRED AND TWENTY."

The structure is:

1. The phrase, *"And in those days Peter stood up in the midst of the Disciples, and said,"* represents Peter taking the lead, which has always been obvious, and continues to be so, despite the denial.

2. The words, *"those days,"* refer to the

following taking place sometime during the 10 days between the Ascension and the Day of Pentecost.

3. *"The number of names together were about an hundred and twenty,"* in essence, forms the beginning of the *"Church."*

(16) "MEN AND BRETHREN, THIS SCRIPTURE MUST NEEDS HAVE BEEN FULFILLED, WHICH THE HOLY SPIRIT BY THE MOUTH OF DAVID SPOKE BEFORE CONCERNING JUDAS, WHICH WAS GUIDE TO THEM WHO TOOK JESUS."

The construction is:

1. The Holy Spirit through Paul said that the Galatians, who were listening to the law-keepers, were being bewitched.

2. This means that false doctrine has a strange spell to it.

3. Without exception, such will always lead to despair.

FULFILLING OF THE WORD OF GOD

The phrase, *"Men and brethren, this Scripture must needs have been fulfilled,"* proclaims several things to us:

• As we have just stated, and as it is obvious, Peter had been selected by the Holy Spirit to serve in the capacity of leadership concerning the Twelve Apostles, as well as other segments of the Word of God; however, in no way does this place him in the position of *"Pope"* as Catholics claim. Actually, as we shall see, Jesus Christ is the *"Pope,"* and the only *"Pope."*

Functioning as the Head of the Church, and a very active Head at that, shortly, Christ would choose Paul to spearhead world Evangelism and the meaning of the New Covenant, which would be given to him. I can assure all concerned that had man been running the show, Paul, for reasons we will see later, would never have been chosen for this task.

• Considering how obvious it is, I think it should be noted that Peter, even before the soon-to-come Day of Pentecost, was functioning with a much greater straightforward authority. Of course, this would be greatly enhanced after the arrival of the Holy Spirit.

The only explanation for this is what Jesus did at Calvary. Without going into a long theological discussion, the wondrous price paid on that horrible day perfected a work in the spirit world, which immediately affected all Followers of the Lord in a positive sense. In effect, Satan now had no more claim on God's People as he did prior to Calvary.

NOTES

THE ATONEMENT

At that time, even though the terrible sin debt was covered by Atonement, the sins were not taken away and, therefore, were still against the Believer. As such, the Holy Spirit was greatly limited in what He could do in the lives of even the most devout followers of the Lord.

While it is true that the Holy Spirit came upon Bible Greats tremendously so in Old Testament Times, which occasioned them to do great things for the Lord, still, in their personal lives, due to the sin debt, there was just so much the Spirit could do.

However, when Jesus paid the price, the sin debt was completely removed (Jn. 1:29), which gave the Holy Spirit far greater access upon and within Believers. Of course, as stated, the Day of Pentecost, which would usher in the Advent of the Holy Spirit in a completely new dimension, would catapult Believers to a spiritual height and depth never before known.

SEARCHING THE SCRIPTURES

As is obvious, Peter and, no doubt, the others, even in these few short days since the Ascension, had begun to search the Scriptures relative to all these things. This shows two things:

1. They were soaking everything they did in prayer.

2. The Word of God became the criterion. Consequently, this must be the foundation of all Ministers of the Gospel as well!

The phrase, *"Which the Holy Spirit by the mouth of David spoke before concerning Judas,"* is derived from Psalms 69:25-28.

As well, we learn from this that the Holy Spirit is the true Author of the Scriptures, even though He used human instrumentation such as David, etc. So, the Word of God, even as Peter proclaimed, must be the criterion and Foundation of all that is done. The moment that is abrogated, that is the moment the person or even the Church denomination begins to go astray.

As well, Peter and others were able to discern what the Holy Spirit through David was saying in this particular Psalm.

"Which was guide to them who took Jesus," proclaims Judas fulfilling this Prophecy given about 1,000 years before, and says also that all of us are fulfilling Prophecy in one way or the other. We are either following the Lord and, therefore, reaping the benefits promised in the Scriptures, or doing otherwise with its negative results.

(17) "FOR HE WAS NUMBERED WITH US, AND HAD OBTAINED PART OF THIS MINISTRY."

The form is:

1. The phrase, *"For he was numbered with us,"* means he was one of the Apostles and chosen by the Lord.

2. *"And had obtained part of this Ministry,"* refers to Judas being treated as all the other Apostles. He was given Power to pray for the sick and to see them healed. He was also given instructions respecting the Word of God. In other words, he was just as much an Apostle of the Lord as Simon Peter and the others.

3. Actually, we will see that this man had been a Saved man but by transgression, fell.

(18) "NOW THIS MAN PURCHASED A FIELD WITH THE REWARD OF INIQUITY; AND FALLING HEADLONG, HE BURST ASUNDER IN THE MIDST, AND ALL HIS BOWELS GUSHED OUT."

The record is:

1. The phrase, *"Now this man purchased a field with the reward of iniquity,"* refers to the Pharisees taking the blood money from Judas, which he had been paid to betray Jesus, and buying his burying place (Mat. 27:6-8).

2. *"And falling headlong,"* pertains to the tree or gallows on which he hanged himself, committing suicide (Mat. 27:3-8).

3. Lightfoot, the historian, said that the devil took Judas up in the air and dashed his body on the ground after strangling him.

4. *"He burst asunder in the midst, and all his bowels gushed out,"* records, as is here obvious, the terrible result of his league with the devil.

5. Actually, it seems that Luke inserted this explanation in Verses 18 and 19, which are not a part of Peter's original discourse. He did this to explain more fully what had happened.

6. Peter's discourse picks back up at Verse 20.

(19) "AND IT WAS KNOWN UNTO ALL THE DWELLERS AT JERUSALEM; INSOMUCH AS THAT FIELD IS CALLED IN THEIR PROPER TONGUE, ACELDAMA, THAT IS TO SAY, THE FIELD OF BLOOD."

The overview is:

1. The phrase, *"And it was known unto all the dwellers at Jerusalem,"* actually means that *it "became known."*

2. *"Inasmuch as that field is called in their proper tongue, Aceldama, that is to say, The Field of Blood,"* was also known as the *"Potter's Field."* It was purchased with the 30 pieces of silver paid to Judas for his betrayal of Jesus. He did not himself purchase the field but caused it to be purchased by his actions.

3. When Judas brought the money back to the Chief Priests and Elders, he said, *"I have sinned in that I have betrayed the innocent blood."*

4. The Scripture says at that time, *"He cast down the pieces of silver in the Temple, and departed, and went and hanged himself"* (Mat. 27:4-5).

5. If, at that time, he had turned to Jesus instead, even as did Peter, he would have received the same forgiveness, Mercy, and Grace; however, this he did not do!

(20) "FOR IT IS WRITTEN IN THE BOOK OF PSALMS, LET HIS HABITATION BE DESOLATE, AND LET NO MAN DWELL THEREIN: AND HIS BISHOPRICK LET ANOTHER TAKE."

The structure is:

1. If you see Christ as an accuser, then that's not the Christ of the Bible.

2. The Word of God depicts Christ not as judge, tempter, or accuser, but rather Reconciler, the Mediator, the Comforter, and the Saviour.

3. In fact, Jesus Christ is *"The Throne of Grace."*

NOTES

THE BOOK OF PSALMS

The phrase, *"For it is written in the Book of Psalms,"* presents Luke now picking up Peter's narrative.

"Let his habitation be desolate, and let no man dwell therein," is derived from Psalm 69:25, and also says in Verse 28 of that Psalm that his name had been in the Book of Life and then blotted out because of his sin.

As well, there is indication that some of the other religious leaders of Israel fell into the same category simply because the pronoun *"them"* is used in Psalm 69:28.

BISHOP

"And his bishoprick let another take," refers to the office or position of a Bishop, which, in this case, referred to his Apostleship.

Actually, the words as used in the New Testament of *"Bishop, Overseer, Presbyter, Pastor, Elder, Shepherd, or Minister,"* all refer basically to the same thing, *"The Pastor of the Church or Minister of the Gospel in any capacity"* (Acts 20:17; Eph. 3:7; Col. 1:23, 25; I Tim. 1:1).

The ecclesiastical names for different offices in the Church, such as a *"Bishop"* over a group of Churches or an entire area, etc., only gradually came into being, which means that such is man-instituted and man-induced.

In other words, at times, the manner in which the title *"Bishop"* is presently used, and other such like titles, is not Scriptural. The wrong use of these titles came about as man gradually usurped the authority of Christ as the Head of the Church, thereby, instituting offices respecting Church denominations, etc., which have no Scriptural validity.

We must ever be conscious that whatever we do pertaining to the Work of God must have a strong Scriptural foundation. Otherwise, great harm will result.

THE HOLY SPIRIT

As the Book of Acts proclaims, and as we shall see, if anyone would have had the authority to promote their place and position above all others, the original Twelve, minus Judas, with Matthias taking his place, would surely have had that right. Considering that they were chosen personally by Jesus and that their names will forever be inscribed on the twelve foundations of the New Jerusalem (Rev. 21:14), one would surely think that they merited special attention in the Early Church. However, even though they are very important in the great Plan of God, still, we do not find the Holy Spirit showing them preeminence, at least respecting dictatorial authority, etc.

So, if the Holy Spirit did not do such with the original Twelve Apostles, and He did not, then, to be sure, it is unscriptural for others who occupy man-devised religious offices to conduct themselves in that manner. Actually, this has probably caused more hurt and harm to the Work of God down through the centuries, even unto this present time, than anything else. Men love to rule over other men, and religious men love to rule over other men most of all.

(21) "WHEREFORE OF THESE MEN WHICH HAVE COMPANIED WITH US ALL THE TIME THAT THE LORD JESUS WENT IN AND OUT AMONG US."

The synopsis is:

1. The phrase, *"Wherefore of these men which have companied with us all the time,"* tells us that there were a good number of others who traveled with Jesus along with the original Twelve.

2. *"That the Lord Jesus went in and out among us,"* presents the Resurrection Title of the Lord and will constantly appear in the Book of Acts.

3. In other words, Jesus Christ rose from the dead.

(22) "BEGINNING FROM THE BAPTISM OF JOHN, UNTO THAT SAME DAY THAT HE WAS TAKEN UP FROM US, MUST ONE BE ORDAINED TO BE A WITNESS WITH US OF HIS RESURRECTION."

The exegesis is:

1. The phrase, *"Beginning from the baptism of John, unto that same day that He was taken up from us,"* spans the entirety of the three and one-half years of the public Ministry of Jesus.

2. *"Must one be ordained to be a witness with us of His Resurrection,"* tells us several things:

NOTES

a. Whoever was chosen had to be one who had been there the entirety of the time, as all the other Apostles, and was a witness, therefore, of all that Jesus *"began both to do and teach."*

b. This person had to be a witness of the Resurrection of Christ, which meant that he had to have been in at least one of the groups to which Jesus appeared, if only the last one before the Ascension.

c. From these instructions, as given to Peter by the Holy Spirit, we know that the Apostle Paul could not have fit this description. He was not even a Follower of Christ at the time, much less a witness to the Resurrection. Consequently, this shoots down the theory held by some preachers that the Lord intended for Paul to take the place of Judas, etc.

d. We learn from this, as should be obvious, that the Resurrection of Christ from the dead is a Cardinal Doctrine of the Gospel.

3. The whole truth of Christ's Mission, the acceptance of His Sacrifice, the consequence of forgiveness of sins, and all man's hopes of Eternal Life turn upon it.

(23) "AND THEY APPOINTED TWO, JOSEPH CALLED BARSABAS, WHO WAS SURNAMED JUSTUS, AND MATTHIAS."

The record is:

1. The phrase, *"And they appointed two,"* seems to be the ones who fit the desired description more than all others.

2. The word *"appointed,"* in this case, means *"to present."* Consequently, they would present these two to the Lord for His Choice.

3. *"Joseph called Barsabas, who was surnamed Justus,"* is thought by some to be the same as Barnabas, who travelled some with the Apostle Paul (Acts 4:36).

4. If that, in fact, is true, Barnabas certainly did not allow his not being chosen to bother him at all. In fact, he was used mightily of God. However, it is not clear in Scripture if Joseph Barnabas is the same as Joseph Barsabas.

5. *"And Matthias,"* presents the one ultimately chosen.

6. Not much is known of him except it is said that he suffered martyrdom in Ethiopia as a result of preaching the Gospel.

7. It is thought that both Barsabas and Matthias were of the seventy who also were with Jesus (Lk. 10:1).

NOTES

(24) "AND THEY PRAYED, AND SAID, YOU, LORD, WHO KNOWS THE HEARTS OF ALL MEN, SHOW WHICH OF THESE TWO YOU HAVE CHOSEN."

The synopsis is:

1. The phrase, *"And they prayed,"* shows their utter dependence on the Lord.

2. They did not trust their judgment alone but took the matter before the Lord, believing Him for the correct choice.

3. As well, every Believer, irrespective as to whether they are Preachers or not, must seek the Lord about all things. How so much better things would be if all did this!

4. Too often, we make our plans and then ask God to bless them. We should let God make the plans, and then they are assured of Blessing.

5. *"You, Lord, Who knows the hearts of all men,"* tells us where alone the truth can be found. No man knows the heart of another. Actually, we do not even know our own hearts as we should (Jer. 17:9-10).

6. *"Show which of these two You have chosen,"* proclaims their desire for God's Choice.

7. The problem in the modern church and, in fact, always has been, is that God's Choice is seldom recognized in the church, with man's choice being preeminent most of the time.

8. It is sad that God's Choice in the Church is not only not recognized most of the time but is even bitterly opposed!

(25) "THAT HE MAY TAKE PART OF THIS MINISTRY AND APOSTLESHIP, FROM WHICH JUDAS BY TRANSGRESSION FELL, THAT HE MIGHT GO TO HIS OWN PLACE."

The record is:

1. Is Salvation by works? Even a good Christian can slide back into this dark way of thinking.

2. This kind of theology is a theology of doubt, despair, hopelessness, and one that breeds fear in the soul.

3. How do you see the Lord? Do you see Him as opposed to you or for you?

APOSTLESHIP

The phrase, *"That he may take part of*

NOTES

this Ministry and Apostleship," proves that Judas did have a part in the Ministry as one of the Twelve Apostles. In other words, he was legitimate, at least up until the time that he gave his will to Satan.

In all of human history, there was no greater honor than this of which Peter speaks. Only Twelve men out of all the billions who had lived or would ever live would be privileged to be selected personally by Christ at the Command of the Heavenly Father. And yet, Judas threw it away.

However, the honor and privilege of being able to hear the Gospel and to accept Christ, by anyone for that matter, is not far behind the privileged position of the Twelve Apostles. And yet, to those of us who have enjoyed this privilege and have accepted it, I wonder if we really know and understand how fortunate we are? How faithful are we to this great privilege within our lives? How much attention do we devote to this wonderful Life in Christ, which, in fact, will never end, versus the things of this world, which perish almost by the time they appear?

To be sure, the great cry of untold millions of Believers when they stand before Jesus will, no doubt, be that they took it all too lightly, with more attention given to insignificant things which mattered little.

JUDAS BY TRANSGRESSION FELL

The phrase, *"From which Judas by transgression fell,"* tells us plainly that Judas once knew the Lord, for how can one fall from something to which he has never attained?

Judas was not chosen a devil, as some claim, but was chosen as all the other Disciples. For a time he loved God, served Him, followed Jesus, and was granted the same Power and Authority as the other Apostles in preaching the Gospel, healing the sick, etc.

At some point in time, Satan began to work on him, even as he worked on Peter and others; however, Judas allowed himself to be taken further and was lost, i.e., *"fell!"*

Some preachers promote the idea that Judas was never saved in order to make it fit their unscriptural doctrine of Unconditional Eternal Security. In other words, this teaching says that if a person has ever once been truly Saved, he cannot lose his soul irrespective of what he might do. Consequently, people who have made no pretense at living for God in years are preached into Heaven at funerals. In fact, they have lived in deep sin, but because in years past, they made some type of so-called profession of Faith, they are still preached into Heaven, etc.

Some actually did give their hearts to God but, at a point in time, turned their backs on Him and ceased to believe in Christ and the Cross and, in fact, have not lived for Him or made any pretense at doing so for many years. They are still preached into Heaven, etc. This is a damnable doctrine that has caused untold millions to be eternally lost.

So, these false teachers have a choice. They can promote one of several things:

FALSE TEACHERS

- They can claim that the Heavenly Father told Jesus to choose Judas who was ungodly and actually was a hypocrite. This is what these teachers really believe.
- They can believe, as well, that Jesus gave an ungodly man, who, in effect, was serving Satan, the Power to preach the Gospel and to heal the sick, etc., which again is what they teach and believe.
- They can teach and believe that it was predestined that Judas would do this thing and, consequently, that he had no choice in the matter. However, to teach that means that no one has any say whatsoever in his eternal destiny, but that it has already been decided. To believe that ignores the very tenor of the Word of God, which is *"whosoever will"* (Rev. 22:17; Jn. 3:16).
- Or, they can believe that the Heavenly Father Personally selected Judas, even as He did all the other Apostles, and that Judas, of his own free will at a point in time, freely chose to discontinue serving the Lord, thereby, choosing his own way and *"by transgression fell!"* Whereas he had formerly been *"Saved,"* even as the other Apostles, at a point in time, he threw in his lot with Satan, meaning that he ceased to believe. This seems to have been at the Last Supper. At that moment, he was lost. There is every indication that Jesus attempted

several times to bring Judas to his senses, and I speak especially of the Last Supper, but to no avail! (Jn. 13:4-5, 21, 26-27).

TO HIS OWN PLACE

Even after he committed this foul deed, had he returned to Jesus, asking Mercy, pardon, and forgiveness, if truly sincere in his heart, Jesus would have extended him the same Mercy that He did Simon Peter. However, Judas did not do that, but instead, he hanged himself and, thereby, died eternally lost. That is the truth of the matter according to the Scriptures (Acts 1:25).

The phrase, *"That he might go to his own place,"* tells us several things:

• Neither Judas, nor anyone else for that matter, was predestined to go to either Heaven or Hell. Even though many factors are involved, still, the final determination is left up to the free moral agency of the individual.

• Every single person in the world, even as Judas, is preparing, in essence, *"his own place,"* whether that be Heaven or Hell. This is done either by acceptance or rejection of Jesus Christ, God's only Son.

• This statement speaks of eternal Hell and, thereby, proclaims its reality.

• Irrespective of who the person is, even if one of the Twelve Apostles, as Judas, all must answer alike. God plays no favorites. If we obey Him, we will reap Eternal Life; if not, eternal damnation!

(26) "AND THEY GAVE FORTH THEIR LOTS; AND THE LOT FELL UPON MATTHIAS; AND HE WAS NUMBERED WITH THE ELEVEN APOSTLES."

The structure is:

1. Why is it Christ Crucified?

2. It is because a Perfect Substitute was needed in order to reconcile you to God.

3. It is because a Perfect Substitute was needed in order that God's Justice be satisfied.

THEIR LOTS

The phrase, *"And they gave forth their lots,"* went back to the Urim and Thummim, of which the Disciples would have been familiar.

The *"Urim and Thummim,"* which means *"Lights"* and *"Perfection,"* were

NOTES

carried by the High Priest of Israel. These two items, of which no one is quite sure as to what they actually were, were contained in a pouch of sorts in the ephod, which was worn immediately under the breastplate worn by the High Priest. This pouch contained the 12 precious stones respecting the Twelve Tribes of Israel. This was one of the ways that God had made provision for giving guidance to His People (Deut. 33:8, 10), but particularly to the leaders of His People (Num. 27:21).

Almost everything, however, about this provision remains unexplained. It is not known as to exactly what these items were, with some thinking they may have been two flat objects, each with a *"yes"* side and each with a *"no"* side. However, that is mere speculation!

By the time of Jesus, such were no longer in use, probably because of the spiritual deterioration of the Priesthood, etc.

So, what Peter and the other Apostles did resembled that practice, which is probably what they were intending to do.

MATTHIAS

The phrase, *"And the lot fell upon Matthias,"* probably means that the names of the two men were placed on two stones, pieces of parchment, or pieces of wood, and then placed into an urn.

They then prayed, and someone put his hand in the urn and drew out one of the lots (Lev. 16:8-9; Josh. 14:2).

The name on the one drawn out was *"Matthias."* Consequently, they evidently felt they had the Mind of the Lord in this matter.

The phrase, *"And he was numbered with the Eleven Apostles,"* seems to indicate that he was God's Choice.

It should be noted that this is the closest thing to our modern *"voting"* found in the Book of Acts, or the entirety of the New Testament for that matter! To be sure, as should be obvious, the similarity is very distant.

Inasmuch as the practice of voting on preachers, etc., is not found in the New Testament, it would seem to me that such a practice presently is unscriptural. Such an

NOTES

effort as voting places the entire effort into the political more so than the spiritual.

Believers are to seek God about everything, but especially that which pertains to His Work.

All Preachers should definitely feel led of the Lord concerning where they are to minister, rather than most of the modern efforts of *"trying out"* for a church. The Lord little works in that manner.

If the Minister says he is definitely led of the Lord respecting a field of ministry, the people should hear him and then take it to the Lord in prayer. After that, it would certainly be proper for the people to discuss what they feel the Lord has said, but the deacons or Church leaders should probably make the final decision.

THE WILL OF GOD

I say this because the Eleven Apostles here took the initiative, as they should have, even though others of the 120 were, no doubt, very interested in this outcome and probably helped the Apostles to pray about the matter. Still, it was the Eleven who were ultimately responsible for the replacement of Judas.

We make a mistake if we think that Church or the Work of God in any capacity is a democracy. It is not! There is one Will and only one Will that is to be satisfied, and that is the Will of God. Whenever hundreds, or even thousands, of people are voting on something of this nature, it makes it increasingly difficult for the Will of God to be brought about.

As well, many times modern deacon boards function in an unscriptural manner, often through no fault of their own. Of course, when this happens, as it mostly does, it makes the situation increasingly more difficult to find the Mind of God.

Even though this particular subject is not meant to be addressed here and, in fact, will be addressed more extensively elsewhere in this Volume, I feel it imperative to make these few statements.

THE WORD OF GOD

The worst thing that a church can do is to do things because it seems to be the right way. Every effort made should be made on the basis of the Word of God. In other words, the Word of God must be the criterion, the Foundation, and the Standard. We should attempt to make everything line up with the Word, at least as far as possible. That is, I believe, the Intention of the Holy Spirit in the Book of Acts. He sets the pattern, and we are to follow.

Had the Churches outlined in the Book of Acts used the election process of each individual voting respecting these things, then I would say we should do accordingly. However, inasmuch as nothing like that was done then or is now done, we should try to see what actually is being done, ask the Lord to give us direction, and then attempt to follow what information we find, once again asking the Holy Spirit to lead, guide, and direct.

In this first Chapter of Acts, even that which sets the Standard, we find the Holy Spirit appearing four times, and with a specific direction each time:

1. In Verse 2, we find *"Commandments"* being given through the Holy Spirit concerning certain things which were to be done. In other words, they were not suggestions!

2. Verse 5 proclaims the *"Baptism"* with the Holy Spirit, which is an absolute necessity for each Believer.

3. In Verse 8, we find the Holy Spirit giving *"Power"* to those who had been *"baptized"* with the Spirit according to the *"Commandments"* of the Lord.

4. Verse 16 gives us *"teaching"* according to the Scripture and makes the Scripture the Foundation of all that is done.

So, we have *"Commandments," "Baptism," "Power,"* and *"Teaching,"* all through and by the Holy Spirit.

"I have left the land of bondage with its earthly treasures,
"I've journeyed to a place where there is love on every hand;
"I've exchanged a land of heartaches for a land of pleasure, "I'm camping, I'm camping in Canaan's happy land."
"Out of Egypt I have traveled, through the darkness dreary,

"Far over hills and valleys and across the desert sands;
"But I've landed safe at home where I shall not grow weary,
"I'm camping, I'm camping in Canaan's happy land."

"Yes, I've reached the land of promise with its scenes of glory,
"My journey ended in a place so lovely and so grand;
"I've been led by Jesus to this blessed land of story,
"I'm camping, I'm camping in Canaan's happy land."

CHAPTER 2

(1) "AND WHEN THE DAY OF PENTECOST WAS FULLY COME, THEY WERE ALL WITH ONE ACCORD IN ONE PLACE."

The synopsis is:

1. Fear is dispelled in no other way but by the Cross of Christ.
2. The infinite Son of God became Man, hung upon a Cross, and was made a curse so that you and I might not be cursed but be free from the curse.
3. How foolish then to walk in the labyrinth of works of self-righteousness.

THE DAY OF PENTECOST

The phrase, *"And when the Day of Pentecost was fully come,"* had to do with the Feast of Pentecost, which was one of the seven great Feasts ordained by God and practiced by Israel.

Actually, in the Greek, the word *"Pentecost"* means *"fifty"* or the fiftieth day from the waving of the sheaf of the Feast of First Fruits (Lev. 23:15-16). This was done at the beginning of the Passover, which was another feast.

Since the time elapsed from Passover or Feast of First Fruits was seven weeks, it was, as well, called at times, *"Feast of Weeks"* (Ex. 34:22; Deut. 16:10). It marked the completion of the wheat harvest, with the Passover conducted some seven weeks earlier at the time of the barley harvest.

NOTES

THE FEAST

The fruit harvest came during the time of the Feast of Tabernacles, which was in October.

The seven Feasts were:

1. Feast of Unleavened Bread
2. Feast of Passover
3. Feast of First Fruits

(These feasts covered a span of about eight days and took place in April. Representative males from each household in Israel were expected to attend, as with all other feasts.)

4. Feast of Pentecost

(This feast was conducted in the latter part of May.)

5. Feast of Trumpets
6. Feast (or Great Day) of Atonement
7. Feast of Tabernacles

(The last three, as stated, were conducted in October.)

As well, it was on the Day of Pentecost when the Law was given at Sinai, which took place 50 days after the first Passover in Egypt.

None of these feasts are incumbent upon Christians in that all were Types of Christ and, consequently, were fulfilled totally in Christ when He came.

- The Feast of Unleavened Bread pictured Jesus' Pure, Sinless, Human Body, which was without blemish.
- The Feast of Passover pictured the Death of Christ on the Cross.
- The Feast of First Fruits pictured the Resurrection of Christ.
- The Feast of Pentecost pictured Jesus as the Baptizer with the Holy Spirit.
- The Feast of Trumpets will be fulfilled at the Second Coming.
- The Great Day of Atonement will be fulfilled by the Jews accepting Christ, which they will do at the Second Coming.
- The Feast of Tabernacles will be fulfilled by Jesus reigning as King in the coming Kingdom Age.

As is obvious, the last three have not yet been fulfilled but will be shortly. As well, they could have been fulfilled at His First Advent but were not due to Israel's failure to accept Him as their Messiah. Consequently, this will not be rectified until the Second Coming, which will begin the Kingdom Age.

WITH ONE ACCORD

The phrase, *"They were all with one accord in one place,"* does not speak of the Upper Room where they had previously met at times, but inasmuch as it was the Day of Pentecost, it is certain they were in the Temple court where they had met regularly in the last few days for prayer (Lk. 24:53; Acts 2:46).

Considering what Jesus had told them about tarrying in Jerusalem until they had received the Promise of the Father, one has to understand that these individuals were expectant. They did not know what was to happen, in fact, had no idea, but they knew that something great and wonderful was going to take place because Jesus had said so. This means they were not uninterested, and they were not lukewarm, but rather eagerly awaiting what would happen.

We should understand the promise that Christ gave them is just as appropriate now as it was then. Every Believer who has not yet been baptized with the Holy Spirit should be greatly expectant of receiving. The Promise of the Father is for all.

(2) "AND SUDDENLY THERE CAME A SOUND FROM HEAVEN AS OF A RUSHING MIGHTY WIND, AND IT FILLED ALL THE HOUSE WHERE THEY WERE SITTING."

The diagram is:

1. The Cross is the Son of God bearing your sin, no matter what that sin has been.

2. That is the reality of the Cross, Christ as sin-bearer.

3. The Gospel of Jesus Christ is not based upon our feelings, but rather on Christ and what He did at Calvary's Cross and our Faith in that Finished Work.

THE RUSHING MIGHTY WIND

The phrase, *"And suddenly there came a sound from Heaven as of a rushing mighty wind,"* portrays the Coming of the Holy Spirit in a new dimension.

The word *"suddenly"* in the Greek Text is *"aphno"* and means *"unexpectedly."*

Actually, I think it is obvious that the Apostles, plus all who obeyed Christ and came into Jerusalem to wait for this great event, did not really know what to expect. At any rate, they surely did not expect what actually happened.

NOTES

What is meant by the words *"fully come,"* as given in Verse 1, is not completely known. The manner in which the Jews reckoned time then was different than our method presently. Then, the following day began at sundown. In other words, the *"Day of Pentecost,"* which was Sunday, actually began at sundown on Saturday according to our reckoning.

However, it is certain, I think, that the words *"fully come"* in Verse 1 referred to the next morning (Acts 2:15). As well, it is not for certain that there were 120 there at that particular time, with that number, no doubt, fluctuating each day. Of course, there certainly could have been 120 exactly, but whatever number, it was on the Day of Pentecost that they were all *"filled with the Holy Spirit."*

That which took place was cataclysmic, without warning, sudden, and, in effect, the second greatest happening in human history, with man's Redemption at Calvary being the greatest. This event would do more to change the world for good than anything else that has ever happened. The Holy Spirit, of course, is God. As Deity, He illuminates, empowers, and is sent for the express purpose of aiding and abetting the Child of God relative to the Father's Will. At that moment, the Church was visibly born and manifested.

THE MIGHTY WIND

The word *"wind"* in the Greek is *"pnoe"* and means *"respiration, breeze or breath."*

This well could have been and, no doubt, was the *"Breath of God,"* symbolized by Jesus *"breathing on the Apostles"* after the Resurrection and saying, *"Receive ye the Holy Spirit"* (Jn. 20:22).

Actually, the Hebrew word for *"breathed"* and used by John is *"naphach"* and means *"to breathe, or blow with force, exactly as God did to Adam when He breathed into his nostrils the breath of life"* (Gen. 2:7).

Inasmuch as the Holy Spirit is the Life of the Church, i.e., *"the Body of Christ,"* this was the *"Breath of God,"* i.e., *"the Holy Spirit."*

The word *"rushing"* in the Greek Text is *"phero"* and means *"to be driven, or to rush."* In other words, this was a powerful force that entered this place, and more particularly, these people.

The word *"mighty"* in the Greek actually speaks of *"violence."* One could perhaps even say *"violent"* to the powers of darkness but very gentle to the Believer.

IT FILLED ALL THE HOUSE

The phrase, *"And it filled all the house where they were sitting,"* does not indicate the Upper Room as many think, but rather, as stated, the Temple. Actually, Jesus had earlier said, speaking of the Temple, *"Is it not written, My House shall be called of all nations the House of Prayer?"* (Mk. 11:17).

So, other than the times Jesus was in the Temple, the Holy Spirit had not resided in this place at all, even since the Prophet Ezekiel had seen Him leave some 600 years before (Ezek. 11:22, 23). However, now there was a difference.

The Holy Spirit was coming back, not to occupy a building structure, but because of what Jesus did at Calvary. He came to occupy the hearts and lives of Born-Again Believers. It is a moment of unprecedented Power and Glory.

(3) "AND THERE APPEARED UNTO THEM CLOVEN TONGUES LIKE AS OF FIRE, AND IT SAT UPON EACH OF THEM."

The overview is:

1. The Gospel of Jesus Christ is not based upon one's feelings!

2. The Gospel is not something that is based upon one's changing moods.

3. The Gospel does not depend upon our whims or changing emotions.

CLOVEN TONGUES LIKE AS OF FIRE

The phrase, *"And there appeared unto them cloven tongues like as of fire,"* actually has a little different meaning than that which appears in the phrase *"cloven tongues."*

In this case, it does not mean a *"forked tongue,"* as many think, but rather that the fire was *"distributed"* out over the entirety of the number of people. In other words, a *"tongue"* of fire appeared over the heads of all who were present.

NOTES

Why this phenomenon of *"fire"*?

This was in fulfillment of the Prophecy of John the Baptist when he said concerning Jesus, *"He shall baptize you with the Holy Spirit, and with fire"* (Mat. 3:11).

SYMBOLISMS OF THE HOLY SPIRIT

- Wind: this speaks of Power (Acts 2:2).
- Fire: this speaks of Purity (Mat. 3:11-12).
- Water: this speaks of Life (Jn. 7:37-39).
- Oil: this speaks of Anointing and Healing (James 5:14-15).
- Dove: this speaks of Gentleness (Jn. 1:32-33).

As we go forward, we will find all these Attributes of the Holy Spirit, all for the purpose of performing a work in the heart and life of the Believer.

Even though the Believer is totally cleansed from all sin at the time of Conversion, still, discipleship is only beginning, with the Holy Spirit taking on this task in the life of the Believer, even as He functioned in the capacity of Regeneration in the Salvation experience. In other words, the Holy Spirit is involved in every single thing done by the Lord. In fact, and as is known, the Holy Spirit is God.

Inasmuch as the two attributes of *"Wind"* and *"Fire"* were initially present at this grand Advent, I think this tells us that *"Power"* and *"Purity"* are the two paramount Works performed by the Holy Spirit in the lives of Believers. While the *"Power"* is instant, the *"Purity"* is a process carried out over a period of time.

We shall see that the *"Anointing"* would be manifested shortly, enabling Peter to preach the inaugural Message of the Church on that grand and glorious day. This speaks of the *"Oil,"* although unseen.

We will find that some 3,000 would accept the Lord, which speaks of the symbol of *"Water,"* although unseen, as well, which symbolizes *"Life."*

Despite the great Manifestations here recorded, I think the *"gentleness"* of those who had been filled will be evident. This is symbolized by the *"Dove,"* even though unseen.

IT SAT UPON EACH OF THEM

The phrase, *"And it sat upon each of them,"* means upon all who were there, whether 120 or whatever number, and not just the Apostles.

So, this opened up a completely new vista in the Work of God and the way God deals with His People.

In Old Testament Times, the Holy Spirit, at least the majority of the time, only used specified individuals. However, with all receiving this experience, at least all who obeyed Christ in going there to wait, it portrays that the Lord now would use any and all, along with the Apostles, irrespective of whom these people may have been. It was a completely new manner and way of doing things.

So, the Holy Spirit showed no favoritism whatsoever, treating all alike, be they Apostles or not!

(4) "AND THEY WERE ALL FILLED WITH THE HOLY SPIRIT, AND BEGAN TO SPEAK WITH OTHER TONGUES, AS THE SPIRIT GAVE THEM UTTERANCE."

The exegesis is:

1. We are saved on account of Christ through Faith, not making Faith into some kind of works.

2. Law and Grace are the differences between the life of joy and freedom filled with Grace and the life marked by self-torture and introspection.

3. There is no hope looking in on yourself. Hope is in Christ, and Christ alone.

AND THEY WERE ALL FILLED WITH THE HOLY SPIRIT

The phrase, *"And they were all filled with the Holy Spirit,"* once again proclaims that all were filled and not just merely the Apostles, etc.

The word *"filled"* in the Greek is *"pletho"* and means *"to soak up as with a sponge"* or to *"imbue, influence, supply, accomplish, furnish."*

This was in direct fulfillment of what Jesus had said to the Disciples shortly before His Crucifixion, *"For He dwells with you, and shall be in you"* (Jn. 14:17).

NOTES

Consequently, this milestone—incidentally, one of the greatest in human history—is direct proof that Jesus *"took our sin away"* (Jn. 1:29).

This means He not only took away *"sins,"* which speaks of particular acts of sin, but, as well, *"sin,"* which means the fact of sin, in other words, *"original sin."*

The whole sin question at the Cross was dealt with in its entirety, with every debt paid and, consequently, the grip of sin broken in the believing sinner's heart and life. As a result, Satan has no more hold within or claim upon any Believer who has trusted Jesus. The sin question has been settled, and by Faith, God has attributed or imputed Righteousness to the believing sinner. So now, the sin is gone, and Righteousness has come.

As a result, the subject becomes a fit habitation or temple of the Holy Spirit (I Cor. 3:16).

OTHER TONGUES

The phrase, *"And began to speak with other Tongues,"* presents that predicted by Isaiah (Isa. 28:9-12) and by Christ (Mk. 16:17; Jn. 15:26; 16:13), and brought to pass in Acts 2:4-13, and continues in Acts 10:44-48; 19:1-7; and I Corinthians, Chapters 12 through 14, even unto this very hour!

As well, there is no evidence whatsoever in the Greek Text that their speaking in Tongues was mere gibberish as distinct from language, or even language coined at the moment by the Holy Spirit. Every evidence is, as we shall see, these were languages unknown to the speaker but known somewhere in the world.

Also, the narrative in no way hints at any use afterward of the Gift of Tongues for missionary purposes, or in other words, to preach the Gospel in the native language of particular people, etc. There is no evidence of such whatsoever in the following examples in Acts. Neither did the Fathers of the first three centuries speak of Tongues being used in connection with preaching to foreign nations, etc.

As well, when Peter began to preach a little later, as we shall see, he preached in the language to all the people.

NOTES

When comparing Acts, Chapters 2, 10, and 19, we can arrive at no other Scriptural conclusion but that speaking with Tongues is the initial physical evidence that one has been baptized with the Holy Spirit. As well, unless one does speak with other Tongues, one has not been baptized with the Spirit. No other evidence is offered or suggested.

To say it again in another way, every Believer (for only Believers can receive this experience) who is baptized with the Holy Spirit will speak with other Tongues as the Spirit of God gives the utterance. If that is not the case, as stated, they have not been baptized with the Holy Spirit. There are no exceptions!

WHY TONGUES?

As some would ask, *"What good are Tongues?"*

• God gave this initial physical evidence. As well, anything He does is wonderful, glorious, and grand. Therefore, to speak derogatorily of that which He has done shows great Spiritual and Scriptural ignorance.

• Everything God does is important, not just because He does such, but because it is important!

• Paul said, *"For he who speaks in an unknown tongue speaks not unto men, but unto God"* (I Cor. 14:2).

• As well, when one speaks with other Tongues, one is speaking of the *"wonderful Works of God"* (Acts 2:11).

• Paul said, *"He who speaks in an unknown tongue edifies himself"* (I Cor. 14:4). Every Believer needs such edification.

• To argue that one can speak to the Lord in the native tongue better than the *"Tongue"* as supplied by the Spirit is, at the same time, saying that God does not know what He is doing.

While one certainly can pray and worship in one's native tongue, with most actually being done this way, still, praying and worshipping in the *"Tongue"* supplied by the Holy Spirit, which is a common occurrence with Spirit-filled Believers (or certainly should be), presents a depth of praying, worship, and petition that is unknown in any other manner.

• Inasmuch as the Holy Spirit is the One Who gives this utterance, that means that it is holy; consequently, to speak disparagingly of such is to speak disparagingly of the Holy Spirit, which no one desires to do, at least if he is sane.

• Every evidence is, as we have stated, that speaking with other Tongues is the initial physical evidence that one has been baptized with the Holy Spirit, which, therefore, makes it extremely significant.

• Isaiah said and Paul quoted in respect to this subject (I Cor. 14:21), *"For with stammering lips and another tongue will He speak to this people.*

"To whom He said, this is the rest wherewith you may cause the weary to rest; and this is the refreshing: Yet they would not hear" (Isa. 28:11-12).

REST AND REFRESHING

We are plainly told here by the Holy Spirit through the Prophet that speaking with other Tongues provides a *"rest,"* which pertains to the emotions and even the subconscious of the individual.

We are, as well, told that it is a *"refreshing,"* which speaks of replenishment.

I firmly believe if every Spirit-filled Believer would take advantage of this great Gift from God, there would be much less emotional disturbances, depression, sicknesses, etc. I am not saying that speaking with other Tongues will eliminate all of these things, but I do believe it would eliminate some of them.

The Believer should trust the Lord to implement these necessary helps in his everyday life with every assurance that He shall. That we do not understand how it is done is really not the question. It is Faith in Him that what He has said regarding speaking with other Tongues and its contribution will be done exactly as He has said.

If one is going to demand total understanding about God before acceptance of Him, very little will be received. In fact, if one could understand all that God does, then one would be as intelligent as God. Were that the case, most would have little desire to serve the Lord, and rightly so.

The truth is, the Lord does not owe us

explanations, but He does guarantee that which He has promised.

THE SPIRIT GIVES THE UTTERANCE

The phrase, *"As the Spirit gave them utterance,"* simply means that they did not initiate this themselves but that it was initiated by the Holy Spirit.

Though speaking in Tongues is done through immediate inspiration by new recipients when one has thus received the Gift, it then becomes a part of one's mental make-up so that he can, if he desires to do so, exercise it without direct inspiration.

To be frank, this can be done, and often is, when one is in a backslidden condition (I Cor. 13:1-3). However, this in no way makes it right, and neither does it mean that the one doing the speaking is right with God.

As should be obvious, the Gifts of the Spirit regarding Prophecy, Tongues, and Interpretation of Tongues have to be regulated and judged as to whether they are of the Lord or a product of the flesh (I Cor. 14:29-33).

(5) "AND THERE WERE DWELLING AT JERUSALEM JEWS, DEVOUT MEN, OUT OF EVERY NATION UNDER HEAVEN."

The exposition is:

1. The phrase, *"And there were dwelling at Jerusalem Jews, devout men,"* had to do with individuals who feared God but were not necessarily true Believers, even as we shall see.

2. *"Out of every nation under Heaven,"* could pertain to two groups of people:

a. At all Feast Days, Jews came to Jerusalem from all over the Roman Empire. At this time, they *"dwelt"* at Jerusalem for a particular period before going back home.

b. It could pertain to Jews who had lived in other nations of the world, but for various reasons, had come back to Jerusalem to live permanently. It could mean that some of these people had come to Jerusalem either to retire or possibly because they were anticipating the Messiah. He was looked for at this particular time and, in fact, did come in the Person of Jesus Christ but was rejected by Israel!

NOTES

3. *"Every nation under Heaven,"* did not necessarily mean every single country on the face of the Earth, but was rather used as a figure of speech denoting many nations, etc.

(6) "NOW WHEN THIS WAS NOISED ABROAD, THE MULTITUDE CAME TOGETHER, AND WERE CONFOUNDED, BECAUSE THAT EVERY MAN HEARD THEM SPEAK IN HIS OWN LANGUAGE."

The structure is:

1. The phrase, *"Now when this was noised abroad,"* means that when the Holy Spirit came, and especially the manner in which He came, such was noted by more than just the 120, or however many there were. No doubt, others heard the sound of the mighty rushing wind and even saw the tongues of fire sitting on the heads of these people. As well, as we shall see, they were staggering around like drunken men.

2. Almost instantly, people began coming hither and yon, telling all they saw of this strange phenomenon.

3. *"The multitude came together,"* means that many, possibly even thousands, began to rush to this part of the Temple court where all of this was taking place. In other words, it drew a huge crowd in a matter of minutes.

4. *"And were confounded, because that every man heard them speak in his own language,"* proclaims each one, it seems, speaking a different tongue. As the next Verse proclaims, this confounded the onlookers, and for the reason given in the next Verse.

(7) "AND THEY WERE ALL AMAZED AND MARVELLED, SAYING ONE TO ANOTHER, BEHOLD, ARE NOT ALL THESE WHICH SPEAK GALILEANS?"

The exposition is:

1. The phrase, *"And they were all amazed and marvelled, saying one to another,"* mostly centered upon the speaking with other Tongues.

2. The question, *"Behold, are not all these which speak Galileans?"* presents the cause of the amazement.

3. The Galilean accent was peculiar and well known (Mk. 14:70; Lk. 22:59).

4. Where it certainly would have been possible for one or even several *"Galileans"*

NOTES

to have known one or more of the exotic dialects, it was inconceivable and even impossible, at least in the natural, for all of these different people to be able to speak accordingly in this manner.

(8) "AND NOW HEAR WE EVERY MAN IN OUR OWN TONGUE, WHEREIN WE WERE BORN?"

The structure is:

1. Many of these Jews who were now living in Jerusalem, or else, visiting the city during the Feast days were actually native of other lands.

2. As such, the tongue or dialect of that particular land was their primary language, even though they could also speak Aramaic and possibly even Greek.

3. In other words, they were bilingual or even trilingual.

(9) "PARTHIANS, AND MEDES, AND ELAMITES, AND THE DWELLERS IN MESOPOTAMIA, AND IN JUDAEA, AND CAPPADOCIA, IN PONTUS, AND ASIA,

(10) "PHRYGIA, AND PAMPHYLIA, IN EGYPT, AND IN THE PARTS OF LIBYA ABOUT CYRENE, AND STRANGERS OF ROME, JEWS AND PROSELYTES,

(11) "CRETES AND ARABIANS, WE DO HEAR THEM SPEAK IN OUR TONGUES THE WONDERFUL WORKS OF GOD."

The synopsis is:

1. As we have already alluded, what these people were speaking was not gibberish or babble, but rather languages known somewhere in the world, as is here obvious, but not known by the speaker. And yet, all who were doing the speaking were *"Galileans,"* who had little or no knowledge at all of these foreign languages.

2. When individuals are baptized with the Holy Spirit presently and begin to speak with other Tongues, it is the same now as then! That which is being spoken is a language and is understood somewhere in the world but, as stated, not by the speaker.

3. *"We do hear them speak in our tongues the wonderful Works of God,"* simply referred to praises offered to the Lord, as well as telling great things the Lord had done and was doing.

4. However, even though this was understood perfectly by those who happened to speak that tongue, it was not understood at all regarding the speaker.

(12) "AND THEY WERE ALL AMAZED, AND WERE IN DOUBT, SAYING ONE TO ANOTHER, WHAT DOES THIS MEAN?"

The construction is:

1. The phrase, *"And they were all amazed,"* presents that which is certainly natural.

2. Without having to ask anyone, they knew that these Galileans were little, if at all, acquainted with these particular languages, so they knew what was happening was something extraordinary, to say the least. As well, according to what Peter would say momentarily, it seems that they suspected that it had something to do with the Lord.

3. *"And were in doubt,"* should have been translated, *"And were perplexed."* In other words, there was no rational answer to their perplexity.

4. The question, *"Saying one to another, What does this mean?"* was asked more in wonder than the demand for an answer.

(13) "OTHERS MOCKING SAID, THESE MEN ARE FULL OF NEW WINE."

The composition is:

1. The Gospel of Jesus Christ is not based upon your moral condition; it is based on His moral Condition.

2. Christ died not only for the sins of the unredeemed, but He died for the failures of the Saints as well.

3. It is not my worth that saves me, but the worth of Christ that saves me.

THE MOCKERS

The phrase, *"Others mocking said,"* means *"to scoff at, whether by gesture or word."* It means they jeered at the Testimony of this given by the Holy Spirit.

"These men are full of new wine," was actually an accusation that they were drunk, consequently, acting accordingly.

So, in Verses 12 and13, we have a compendium of the responses tendered then toward what God was doing, which remains unto the present. Some wonder and some mock!

Also, it should be noted that these various responses came from those who claimed to know God.

NOTES

This which the Lord did produced *"amazement," "perplexity,"* and *"mockery!"* on the part of the onlookers, all according to the response of the individuals.

It would seem that the majority here were merely in *"amazement and perplexity,"* with those who were *"mocking"* in the minority. It seems to be reversed presently!

MY INTRODUCTION TO THE HOLY SPIRIT

If I remember the year correctly, my parents came to Christ in 1940. I was five years old.

Our little church was small, with possibly only four or five people in the church who were Spirit-filled, if that! As well, it was the Pastor's first church.

I do not honestly remember if he preached about the Holy Spirit very much or not at that time; however, I do know that my parents then knew absolutely nothing about the Holy Spirit. They were Saved and actually had a wonderful experience with the Lord. Their lives had totally and completely changed. Jesus Christ had come to live in our home, and to be sure, it was somewhat like Heaven on Earth.

I remember as a child hearing my parents fuss and quarrel, that is, before they were Saved. It would hurt me so much, even as it does any little child, simply because I loved both of them very much.

However, when Jesus came into their hearts, the fussing and quarreling instantly stopped. That I will never forget! I think I was the happiest one of all. Mom and Dad did not fuss anymore, there were no more quarrels, they were not shouting names at each other, etc.

If one wants to know the answer to the marriage problem, this is it! Jesus Christ and Jesus Christ alone is the Answer. That may seem somewhat trite as it easily rolls off the tongue, but it just happens to be true.

MODERN MARRIAGE SEMINARS

I am appalled presently at preachers who have left the Bible way, opting instead for the psychological way as the answer to these very important problems. I speak of the myriad of marriage seminars, which seem to be constant. With some few exceptions, these seminars constitute the psychological way, with a Scripture or two thrown in. They are a waste of time!

When a person truly gets Jesus in his heart, even as my mother and dad did so long ago, He is the Perfect Marriage Counselor. To be frank, there is no other!

THE DAY I FIRST HEARD

As stated, my parents were wondrously Saved but did not have the mighty baptism with the Holy Spirit. Actually, as stated, it was something they knew nothing about.

The year was 1943, and it must have been the month of June. It was summer vacation, and by piecing together what happened in the next two or three months, it would have necessitated what I'm about to say happening at the first part of that month.

It must have been about 7 or 8 a.m. We were always early risers, and in my memory, the day had already long since begun.

I remember coming from the back of the house into the living room. My mother and dad were standing near my piano, and they were discussing my grandmother.

Due to my grandfather and grandmother on my dad's side taking up a lot of time with me, I was very close to them. So, when my grandmother's name was mentioned, I sort of slowed my pace to hear what was being said.

What they were saying was somewhat negative, so I listened a little closer.

A few weeks earlier, my grandmother had gone to a small campmeeting up in north Louisiana. There she had been baptized with the mighty Holy Spirit with the evidence of speaking with other Tongues. However, even though my mother and dad had discussed this before now, and surely I had overheard some of their remarks, I have no recollection of anything at all concerning the Holy Spirit before that particular morning.

"Mamma has gone crazy over religion," I heard my dad say! When he said that, I stopped completely to be certain that I overheard whatever else was to be said. It was to be one of the greatest moments in my life.

THE DAY I WAS SAVED

I had been saved just a few weeks earlier, and of all places, my Conversion took place while I was standing in a line of kids waiting for the local movie house to open in our little town of Ferriday, Louisiana. It was a Saturday afternoon.

Of course, my mother and dad had witnessed to me a number of times since they had been saved about two or three years earlier. As well, we were in Church every time the church doors opened. However, as of yet, I had not accepted Christ, but I am certain that all the services I was in, plus my mother's Spiritual attention to me, had affected my awareness of the Lord, etc.

At any rate, without warning, the Lord spoke to my heart that Saturday afternoon, saying, *"Do not go into this place. Give me your heart, for you are a chosen vessel to be used in My Service!"*

It was not an audible voice, but it was so nearly an audible voice that I was shaken greatly. Being only eight years old, I had little understanding of the Lord, but at the same time, I knew instantly it was God. Of that, I had no doubt!

The Voice in my spirit spoke again, *"Do not go into this place. Give me your heart, for you are a chosen vessel to be used in My Service!"*

Even though I may not be remembering the statement verbatim, it was approximately what I have just related. I was shaken! I knew this was God!

By that time, the ticket window had opened, and the line was inching forward. I found myself standing in front of the ticket booth, which was almost immediately after the Lord had spoken the second time.

I had laid my quarter on the counter in order to secure the ticket.

Before the lady could reach for my quarter, the ticket spool jammed, with her stopping to effect its release. I will always believe that the Lord did this in order to move even more heavily upon my heart. Finally, the ticket spool unjammed, and the lady began to reach for my quarter; however, I grabbed it first. I remember her looking at me and saying, *"Jimmy, do you want to go or not!"*

NOTES

I mumbled something, grabbed my quarter, and ran. At that moment I was Saved. I can't explain it anymore than what I've just said, but I knew at that very instant that Jesus came into my heart.

WALKING DOWN THE STREET

I remember that Saturday afternoon walking down the street past the Piggly Wiggly Supermarket (a very small supermarket), Doris' Dress Shop, Ellis' Five and Dime, and then walking into Vogt's Drugstore on the corner. I remember getting an ice cream cone of all the flavors then sold in that little drugstore, which was three.

Vogt, Jr., piled the ice cream on the cone and gave me a dime change from my quarter.

I walked out of the store with the ice cream cone and stood on the sidewalk for a few moments facing the street.

At that moment, the most glorious feeling I had ever experienced came over me. It was as though 50 pounds had been lifted from my shoulders. I knew I was Saved! Of course, being a child, I did not have much understanding, but I knew something wonderful and glorious had happened.

I have thought about it many times that if I felt that wonderful at that time, even though I really had not known too much what sin actually was, what must a man or woman feel who has gone deep into sin and then been wondrously saved by Jesus Christ?

Not going to the movie that afternoon, or any other afternoons for that matter, I went home early. My mother, not expecting me home that early, asked what had happened. Somewhat nonchalantly, I told her, *"I got Saved!"*

She looked at me strangely and asked how such could happen.

I related to her what I have just related here, and I will never forget, she began to weep as she pulled me close to her. I did not quite understand her weeping, but I look back now and know that it was for joy.

I'm not exactly certain as to what month this was, but looking back and attempting to correlate events, it must have been sometime in the first part of April. As stated, the year was 1943.

Of those few weeks prior to the time of

the event of this illustration concerning the Holy Spirit, I have little recollection, but now, things were about to gloriously change.

IT CAME TO MY EARS AND HEART AS POSITIVE

After hearing my dad that early morning say, *"Mamma has gone crazy over religion,"* as stated, I stopped to hear more clearly.

Then I heard my dad say words to this effect, *"All she does is talk about the Lord, and she keeps telling us we need to be filled with the Holy Spirit."*

He then said, *"It has made a fanatic out of her, and on top of all things, she speaks in some type of weird language which no one can understand."*

Like I said, they were somewhat upset with her, but for some reason, what they said about her, and especially about the Holy Spirit, quickened my interest greatly. I did not know what she had done or what she had, but I wanted to find out.

I remember listening for a few moments and then darting out the front door and going straight to her house.

SHE TOLD ME!

As she let me in the house, she took me back into the kitchen where she was preparing herself some hot tea.

I immediately went up to her, saying, *"Nannie* (for that is what I called her), *Mamma and Daddy say that you have something that you received at a Church service a short time back, and it makes you talk funny!"*

I remember it like it was yesterday. She laughed and turned around. She said, *"Wait for a moment until I prepare this tea, and I'll tell you about it."*

With a cup of hot tea in her hand, she came and sat down in one of the chairs in the living room, and I sat on the floor, Indian fashion, with my legs under me, looking up at her. I was eagerly awaiting what she would say.

It was to prove to be one of the greatest moments of my life. I would never be the same again. From that moment, I have seen literally hundreds of thousands, and I exaggerate not, brought to a Saving Knowledge of Jesus Christ. I have seen hundreds of thousands of lives changed by the Power of God all over the world. Without the mighty baptism with the Holy Spirit, none of this, I know, would have ever happened.

She began to tell me how she had gotten hungry to be baptized with the Holy Spirit. I don't remember if she explained it from the Bible or not. I think she just gave her Testimony, and that was about it. However, please believe me, the Power of God so accompanied what she was saying that it was more than enough to greatly excite my interest.

HER EXPERIENCE

As she began to relate this grand experience step-by-step, she told me how she had sought the Lord that morning in that meeting for the Holy Spirit but had not received.

Lunchtime came. She told her friends she was not going to eat anything, but instead, would continue praying.

She and a number of ladies went out of the tabernacle and knelt under a little cope of trees very near that crude structure and began to seek God.

She then said, *"Jimmy, I felt it begin to come. It was like something which flowed all over me, and then I began to speak with other Tongues as the Spirit of God gave the utterance."*

When my grandmother said that, the Power of God came on her as she sat in that chair, and I remember her raising her right hand to Praise the Lord and then beginning to speak with Tongues.

As I have stated, I was sitting on the floor looking up at her, but when the Power of God came upon her, it came upon me at the same time.

Even though I had felt mightily the convicting Power of the Holy Spirit when I was saved a few weeks earlier, as I have related, I had never really felt the Power of God. This was my first time, and I would never be the same again.

I remember looking down at my arms, and chill bumps had broken out all over, with the roots of my hair literally tingling. I am not exaggerating; I am saying it just as it happened.

NOTES

NOTES

A GREAT HUNGER!

In a few moments she stopped praising the Lord and speaking in Tongues and began to talk to me.

I don't remember her exact words, but she was telling me that the Lord would fill me with the Holy Spirit as well! *"He'll give you the same thing I have,"* she said!

I don't remember my reaction at that moment, at least what I said to her, but I know that afternoon at about 1 or 2 p.m., I was back again, asking her to tell me the same story again, which she did. The same thing happened again. She began to speak with other Tongues, and I sensed the Power of God greatly.

For the next several weeks, I would go to my grandmother's house two to three times each day, asking her to tell me the same story again, which she would always do. She did not seem to tire or grow impatient. Every single time the Power of God would come into the room, and I would sense it greatly. Once anyone has sensed the Power of God relative to the Holy Spirit, one will never be the same again. Dead preachers preaching dead sermons to dead congregations will no longer suffice. They have tasted of the Honey in the Rock and experienced the Living Waters, and nothing else will satisfy anymore.

INSTANTLY I BEGAN TO SEEK

This one thing I know: What my grandmother had, I wanted. Consequently, I began to seek the Lord exactly as she told me, expecting to receive.

I don't remember exactly how long the intervening time was, but it could not have been over two or three weeks. Our Church began a revival.

The Evangelist was a lady from Houston, Texas. Looking back now and knowing how much the Lord was leading her, I remember her Messages. She preached on the Holy Spirit every single service.

It made my mother and dad rather agitated because, as stated, they were somewhat put off by my grandmother's *"fanaticism,"* as they called it.

The meeting lasted a week, with the Pastor announcing that it would go another week. Once again, this dear lady preached on the Holy Spirit just about every service, if not every single service. I remember my parents complaining, wishing she would preach on something else. They were very vocal about the matter. However, the Lord knew exactly what He was doing, for they too would soon become hungry for the Holy Spirit.

The meeting ended, but the Church continued having prayer meetings every morning. My mother and dad, along with my grandmother and others, were at each one of these prayer meetings. Though my parents had been a little agitated at the sister preaching every Message on the Holy Spirit, nevertheless, the Word of God had its effect. My mother and dad began to hunger for what my grandmother had received. It is virtually impossible for a person to attend prayer meetings for any length of time where the Spirit of God is moving and not get hungry for the Holy Spirit if he has not already received Him.

THE DAY MY MOTHER RECEIVED

I cannot imagine why I did not attend the prayer meeting that particular morning, but for some reason, I did not go, and it was the morning my mother received. As well, our Church had begun another revival, this time with a young man.

I remember being with Jerry Lee (Jerry Lee Lewis) and two other boys that morning. I do not recall exactly what we were doing, but I know we were not far from the church, perhaps only 100 yards or so. I do not remember, as well, why I was not in prayer meeting.

It must have been about 9 a.m. All of a sudden, we heard someone shout loud, and I mean loud! Of course, it would have had to be loud for us to hear it at that distance.

I instantly recognized it as my mother. I knew she was at the prayer meeting, but I did not know what had happened.

I remember all the other boys stopped what they were doing and said, *"Did you hear that?"* One of them said, and I don't remember which one, *"It came from the church!"*

NOTES

As stated, I knew it was my mother, but I did not know what had happened. I did know she was at a prayer meeting, and I was embarrassed. I did not want the other boys to know it was my mother shouting this loud.

I remember saying to them, *"Oh, I don't believe it was from the church; it's probably a car wreck!"*

One of the boys said, *"No, it is coming from the church; let us go over there and see what it is!"*

Once again, embarrassed, I tried to draw their attention from the church because I knew it was my mother, and I could not understand why in the world she would be shouting that loud, so loud, in fact, that it was plainly audible even where we were. Somehow or the other, I was able to divert their attention, and we did not go to the church. I always wished we had, for this is what happened:

ALL THE THINGS MY MOTHER SAID SHE WOULD NOT DO

It happens at times that people sometimes get in the flesh in their worshipping the Lord, and certain things will be done which would probably be better left undone.

For instance, there was a dear lady, a very godly lady I might quickly add, in the little church that was our home Church, who at times could get a little loud in her worship. This irritated my parents, and they had made some statements about it that were somewhat negative.

As well, our church, as stated, had begun another revival meeting, which very shortly had followed the one conducted by the dear lady from Houston. The Lord was really moving, and the prayer meetings had been started each morning to seek the Lord for even a greater Outpouring of His Spirit.

During the course of the meeting, the Evangelist had gotten happy one night and danced across the platform or some such thing, which had once again impacted my parents in a negative way. They had made some remarks about such not being necessary, etc.

As well, there was an elderly gentleman who was blind, who came to our church occasionally. He was a dear brother, but at times, his hygiene may not have been quite what it should have been. Again, my parents had made some statements about him that pretty well said they wished he would attend Church somewhere else. At any rate, all of this was about to be addressed that morning when my mother was baptized with the Holy Spirit.

WE'LL UNDERSTAND IT BETTER BY AND BY

As I have mentioned previously, that particular morning, I had not gone to the prayer meeting for some reason and was with two or three other boys doing whatever boys of that particular age group do. As stated, I heard my mother shout.

I was told later that the Evangelist that morning had picked up his accordion and had begun to sing the old Hymn, *"We'll Understand It Better By And By."* As he began to sing, the Power of God began to fall. My mother was the first one that it came upon, if one could use such an expression. Mickey Gilley's mother, my aunt, was the second one. And then, all the things my mother had said she would not do and had actually made fun of others for doing, she found herself doing.

As I have already stated, even though I, along with several other boys, were at least 100 yards away from the church, I heard her shout aloud. As well, they said that all of a sudden, she ran all the way around the church and then began to speak with other Tongues as the Spirit of God gave the utterance. To be sure, I did not miss any more prayer meetings after that.

When she finally came to herself, she was hugging the elderly brother, who I mentioned was blind, and shouting all around him.

Now, do not misunderstand! None of these things really have anything at all to do with being baptized with the Holy Spirit. The idea is that one had better be careful as to what one tells the Lord one will not do. Most of the time, the Lord is going to see to such that we do exactly that!

Actually, I never heard my mother shout that loud again in all the remainder of her

NOTES

life, but she did that morning when she was baptized with the Holy Spirit.

I want the Believer to understand that as revolutionary as is Salvation to the sinner, such will be to the Believer when one is baptized with the Holy Spirit.

AND THEN THE LORD FILLED ME

As I have mentioned, to be sure, I did not miss any more prayer meetings. I do not remember exactly how long it was from the time my mother was filled until my experience, but it could not have been over a few weeks.

As I have already related, I had been seeking the Lord so earnestly for the Holy Spirit. Even though I was only eight years old, there seemed to be a consuming desire in my heart to be filled. I did get discouraged as I saw others go through, with me seemingly not able to receive; however, the seeking was about to end, with that which I had sought being made so real to me.

Little did I realize that the Lord would use me in evangelistic work to see literally tens of thousands baptized with the Holy Spirit.

Once again it was in one of the morning prayer meetings. I can see myself even yet kneeling at the Altar, praising the Lord. All of a sudden, it happened!

I saw a Light, which seemed to be so pure and so real that it was almost as though it was liquid. It seemed to settle all over me, even down in my very being, and then I began to speak with other Tongues.

When I began to speak, it was like an uninterrupted flow that would not stop. Actually, it was days before I said very much in English, for I was speaking in Tongues almost constantly.

I remember, a few days later, my mother sent me to the post office to purchase a stamp. I walked up to the window, laid the money on the counter, and the clerk asked me what I wanted.

I opened my mouth to tell him what I desired and began to speak with other Tongues. I did not mean to do such, and it took me completely by surprise. I remember the clerk looking at me somewhat funny, asking what I had said because, of course, he could not understand.

I made another attempt and once again began to speak in Tongues. Again he looked at me quizzically and said, *"I do not know what you are saying."*

I then made a third attempt and once again began to speak in Tongues, and then, not knowing what to do, grabbed the money and ran.

When I arrived home a few minutes later, my mother asked me if I had gotten the stamp. Then I could speak English and told her, *"No!"*

I then explained to her what had happened, and I remember her laughing, but I do not remember how we ever got the stamp.

No, I do not understand why it is that I could not speak English in the post office and then was able to do so at home. That is beyond me, but it is exactly the way it happened.

CALLED TO THE MINISTRY

Through the entirety of that summer, I was in one and sometimes two prayer meetings every single day. These would be conducted at the home of my grandmother, my aunt, or the church.

During these times, occasionally I would begin to pray and literally go into a trance. I would awaken sometime later, thinking it had only been a few minutes when it had actually been several hours.

During that time, the Lord told me that I would be an Evangelist and that our Ministry would be worldwide.

Years later, while conducting a Crusade in Little Rock, Arkansas, the Pastor, who had been our Pastor those long years before, was in the Service that night. He told me something after the Service that I had not known.

He mentioned one of the prayer meetings where only about four or five people were present. He said that an utterance was given in Tongues, with the interpretation stating, *"There is one in your midst whose Ministry will touch the entirety of the world."*

He told me that night in Little Rock that he looked around at the small gathering, and even though the interpretation had been very clear and plain, he wondered in his heart how in the world such could be.

He went on to say that he did not feel that the Lord would ever use him in that fashion or my dad, who was present and, incidentally, by now had also been baptized with the Holy Spirit. As well, there were two or three ladies present. Then there was no one left but me as he looked at all who were there.

At that time, I was nine years old and as he looked at me, he really could not see how that such a thing could be.

However, he stood there that night with tears in his eyes and said, *"Brother Jimmy, I now know that utterance in Tongues and interpretation was from the Lord!"*

Over and over again, I continue to thank the Lord that this great Gospel brought to our family so long ago included the mighty experience of the baptism with the Holy Spirit. To be sure, without this which Jesus promised and did give, I would not have been able whatsoever to have seen the hundreds of thousands of souls brought to Christ that we have seen; however, there is one further thing I desire to say....

I BELIEVE THE BEST IS YET TO COME

I believe the Lord is about to move around this world, resulting in hundreds of thousands, if not millions, brought to a saving knowledge of Jesus Christ, with untold hundreds of thousands also baptized with the Holy Spirit with the evidence of speaking with other Tongues. I believe it will be the greatest Move of God in relationship to these things mentioned that the world or the Church has ever known. I also believe the Lord has told me that it will be the last great Move before the coming Great Tribulation.

It is October, 2013, as I dictate these notes. In 2010, the Lord began to speak to my heart about things which are shortly to come to pass.

When I come to the office each morning, I always spend a little time with the Lord in prayer. Leaving the office and going home each evening, I, as well, spend some time with the Lord. It was in one of those times. As stated, it was 2010.

In prayer, the Spirit of the Lord began to flow over me, and the Lord spoke the following to my heart:

"The Evil One tried to close the door to this Ministry in the 1990s; however, I kept it open about ten percent as to what it had once been."

The Lord then said, *"I am now going to open this door wide."*

I had no doubt in my mind that it was the Lord Who had spoken this to me. And then, the very next evening while in prayer, the Lord spoke again. He said:

"When I told you yesterday that I would open the door wide, you were thinking that I was speaking only of the television programming."

I did think that! The so-called Christian channels would not allow our programming on their networks. Then the Lord said to me:

"I was speaking of the placement of the programming, but I was also referring to everything for which you have asked Me in the last few years." He then said, *"I am going to open the door wide for these things to be brought to pass."* There were four things for which I had sought His Face and had done so earnestly and ardently:

1. The placement of our programming in order to reach this nation and the world. Little did I realize at that time that the Lord was about to have us begin a network of our own, airing our programming 24 hours a day, 7 days a week, but that's exactly what He did. At the time of this writing, we cover about two-thirds of the entirety of the United States with programming, as stated, 24 hours a day, 7 days a week. As well, we are in hundreds of millions of homes all over the world in other countries, actually reaching most of the nations of the world by satellite.

2. To do all of this, the finances would have to be increased, and increased dramatically. We had struggled for years, trying to stay on the air, because that's what the Lord told us to do. However, now He had said that financially, He was going to open the door wide.

3. Knowing this task was not yet finished, I had asked the Lord for years to give Frances and me longevity, health, and strength that we might finish this course. The Lord is doing exactly that.

4. And then, that which is the most important of all, I had asked Him for an

NOTES

Anointing of the Holy Spirit such as we had never had before. I had begun to seek the Lord for that all the way back to 1992. To reach a lost world, one must have the Anointing of the Holy Spirit, the convicting Power of the Holy Spirit, and the Authority of the Spirit. The Lord has told me that He is going to open that door wide for all of these things to be brought to pass. It has already begun!

THE DREAM GIVEN TO PHARAOH AND INTERPRETED BY JOSEPH

Dreams played an important part in the life of Joseph, Jacob's son, and the most beautiful Type of Christ found in the entirety of the Old Testament. There was not one single sin that was attributed to Joseph. That didn't mean that he did not sin, for all have sinned. The Holy Spirit chose not to list any infraction against Joseph, not only because he was a Type of Christ, but the most perfect Type of Christ found in Old Testament Times.

As a young boy about 17 years of age, Joseph had two Dreams, which pertained to his day and age, with the second one yet to come to pass.

His first Dream concerned a sheaf of grain, which represented Joseph, and there were other sheaves of grain, which made obeisance to his sheaf (Gen. 37:6-7).

That was fulfilled some years later when his brethren bowed to him while in Egypt purchasing grain.

He dreamed a second time, and *"the sun and the moon and the eleven stars made obeisance to him"* (Gen. 37:9).

This Dream pertains to the Second Coming of the Lord when all Thirteen Tribes of Israel will bow to Him, recognizing Him as their Messiah, their Saviour, and their Lord. As is obvious, it has not yet been fulfilled.

The next set of Dreams concerns those given to Pharaoh by the Lord and interpreted by Joseph.

The first Dream concerned seven fat and healthy cattle that came up out of the river, which was followed by seven other cattle that were lean fleshed and emaciated. The thin cattle consumed the fat cattle.

The second Dream was a little different. He dreamed of seven stalks of grain that were healthy and fat fleshed. He then saw seven lean stalks that consumed the seven fat stalks.

Once again, the first Dream was fulfilled during the time of Pharaoh. It concerned seven years of the greatest harvest of grain that Egypt had ever known, represented by the seven fat cattle. It was followed by seven years of famine such as that part of the world had never known, once again typified by the seven lean cattle.

The second part of the Dream, even as Joseph's second Dream, has not yet been fulfilled. It is my belief that the explanation is according to the following:

Taking the last part of the Dream first, the seven wasted stalks of grain represent the coming Great Tribulation, which will also last for seven years. It will be the worst the world has ever known.

Looking at the first part of the second Dream, which concerns seven healthy stalks of grain, I believe it represents seven years of the harvest of souls, one might say, the greatest that the world or the Church has ever seen. I believe the Lord has shown me that. It is that which is very shortly to come to pass.

The Lord told me that this Ministry (Jimmy Swaggart Ministries) would play a great part in this harvest. He also told me this would be the last worldwide harvest before the coming Great Tribulation.

THE VISION

On July 1, 1985, which was a Monday morning if I remember correctly, the Lord gave me a Vision of the coming world harvest.

As was my custom at that time, every morning I would drive my car to a particular place by the side of railroad tracks, which afforded privacy and solitude. I would study the Word for awhile and then walk down the tracks for a period of time seeking the Lord. This particular morning would prove to be something spectacular.

As I finished my study of the Word and proceeded to walk down the tracks, praying as I went, all of a sudden, things changed.

As the Lord began to give me this Vision, I saw fields of cotton stretched in every direction over the horizon. It was the most bumper crop of cotton that I had ever seen. Every stalk was heavily laden. In the distance I could see a couple of mechanical pickers trying to gather the harvest.

Then I looked to my left, and there was the most awful storm that was brewing. The sky was inky black with jagged forks of lightning cutting across the skies. I realized that if that storm reached this cotton crop before it was gathered, it would destroy it all.

After the Vision, I wondered why the Lord showed me fields of cotton when Preachers normally use wheat fields as a sign of the harvest. Then I remembered what Jesus said:

"Do not say there are yet four months, and then comes harvest? Behold, I say unto you, lift up your eyes, and look on the fields, they are white already to harvest" (Jn. 4:35).

Then the Lord began to speak to my heart. He said the following to me:

"Put the television programming in every city of the world that will accept it. I will hold back the storm for a period of time until the work can be accomplished."

He then said, *"I have called others for localities around the world, but I have called this Ministry alone* (Jimmy Swaggart Ministries) *for the entirety of the world."*

Then He said, *"Do not fail Me because there is no other to get it done."*

Considering the events that followed, I did everything within my power to carry out what the Lord had told me to do, but I was unable to accomplish the task.

And then in 2011, while in prayer one afternoon, the Lord renewed that Vision in my mind all over again. I saw everything that I had seen at the beginning, and then the Lord spoke this to my heart:

"The commission that I gave you in 1985 is still in force. Do what I told you to do and get it done quickly."

To say the least, for the Lord to tell me that, that the commission was still in force, was almost more than I could comprehend. However, that is the reason that we are striving as hard as we are to take *"The Message of the Cross"* to the entirety of the world.

NOTES

We have a mandate from the Lord to get it done. In fact, that's the reason that THE SONLIFE BROADCASTING NETWORK is the fastest growing network in the world today. It is the Lord Who is opening the doors. It is the Lord Who makes the way. Consequently, I believe that despite the condition of the modern church, the Lord is going to use modern technology to touch untold millions with the Gospel of Jesus Christ. Please understand, when the Spirit of God anoints the Preacher, which means the Message, thereby, is also anointed, there is no limit as to what can be done in just a short period of time. Still, the greatest export that the United States has is not Apple, Microsoft, etc., but is rather the Gospel of Jesus Christ. As long as the Gospel, the Message of the Cross, which is the Gospel, goes out over the world, I believe the Lord is going to see this nation through.

(14) "BUT PETER, STANDING UP WITH THE ELEVEN, LIFTED UP HIS VOICE, AND SAID UNTO THEM, YOU MEN OF JUDAEA, AND ALL YOU WHO DWELL AT JERUSALEM, BE THIS KNOWN UNTO YOU, AND HEARKEN TO MY WORDS:"

The form is:

1. The Gospel of Jesus Christ is not something that is based upon our changing moods.

2. The Gospel does not depend upon our whims or our changing emotions.

3. Faith has no virtue of its own. We are saved on account of Christ through Faith, not making Faith some type of work.

PETER

The phrase, *"But Peter, standing up with the eleven, lifted up his voice, and said unto them,"* presents, as is obvious, Peter taking the lead and above all, preaching the inaugural Message of the Church on the Day of Pentecost.

It is somewhat ironic that if Peter had belonged to one of several modern Pentecostal denominations, he would not have been allowed to do this thing. It would have been two years or some such period of time in which he would have been placed on probation; consequently, the Book of Acts would read entirely differently. However, it

NOTES

would be a difference not sanctioned by the Holy Spirit.

One must ever understand that the Grace of God is not probationary. Were that so, then it would hold little validity at all!

No! The moment Peter was forgiven of his denial, he was just as pure in the Sight of God as anyone could ever be. To be sure, the Blood of Jesus cleanses from all sin and does so immediately upon Faith being exercised (I Jn. 1:7, 9).

HEARKEN TO MY WORDS

The phrase, *"You men of Judaea, and all you who dwell at Jerusalem, be this known unto you, and hearken to my words,"* presents this spoken somewhere in one of the Temple courts. A great crowd had gathered, possibly even several thousands of people. They had been attracted, as stated, by the strange happenings, whether the speaking with Tongues or the tongues of fire on their heads, that is, if such were visible to at least some of these onlookers.

Some may well ask the question that if we presently believe in speaking in Tongues (which we do), then why do we not also teach the other two phenomena, *"The mighty rushing wind and the tongues of fire"*? It is very simple to answer that question.

When we read of the other incidents in the Book of Acts of individuals being baptized with the Holy Spirit, two other times, even other than this initial response, it mentions that they spoke with Tongues (Acts 2:4; 10:45, 46; 19:1-7). Even though it's not mentioned, the other two occasions strongly suggest that they spoke with Tongues, as well; however, on all the occasions, there is no mention whatsoever of the *"mighty rushing wind"* or the *"tongues of fire!"*

Why?

• The *"sound of the mighty rushing wind"* was the initial Coming of the Holy Spirit. He has remained here ever since. Were He to come and go, then the sound would, no doubt, be forthcoming. However, inasmuch as He does not come and go, it tells us that He came to stay and is still doing the Work now that He did on the Day of Pentecost and continued to do.

• Also, the *"tongues of fire"* sitting on each of them in the initial outpouring was in fulfillment of the Prophecy of John the Baptist when he said concerning Jesus, *"He shall baptize you with the Holy Spirit and with fire"* (Mat. 3:11).

Inasmuch as it did not happen again and that it was actually a fulfillment of that Prophecy, it is not something that should be expected presently respecting one being baptized with the Holy Spirit.

As well, the Scripture tells us that in the mouth or the word of two or three witnesses shall every word be established (Mat. 18:16).

THE WORD OF GOD IS THE CRITERION

However, the account does continue to mention speaking with other Tongues, and as such, we are to expect that all Believers, upon initially being baptized with the Holy Spirit, will without exception speak with other Tongues.

Acts 2:4 states that *"all"* were *"filled with the Holy Spirit, and* (all) *began to speak with other Tongues,"* not just some!

If there is anything that is incumbent upon the Believer, it is that the Word of God must serve as the criterion for all things. It does not really matter what a denomination teaches or thinks; it is what the Word of God says.

One day every Believer will stand at the Judgment Seat of Christ and will be judged according to the works we carried out for the Lord on Earth. The Word of God and the Word of God alone will serve as the criterion; consequently, we must base what we believe entirely upon the Word and nothing else. Therefore, if the church you are attending does not teach what the Word says, you should find a Church, at least if possible, that does. It should be as near as possible to the Word. If that fails, then you have the privilege of joining FAMILY WORSHIP CENTER MEDIA CHURCH.

So, when Peter began to speak, he would anchor what had happened to the Word of God. That should be done by all others as well.

(15) "FOR THESE ARE NOT DRUNKEN, AS YOU SUPPOSE, SEEING IT IS BUT THE THIRD HOUR OF THE DAY."

The pattern is:

1. The Gospel is not based upon our moral condition; it is based upon His Moral Condition.

2. Jesus died for the failures of the Saints as well as for the lost!

3. It is not my worth that saves me but the Worth of Christ that saves.

THE HOLY SPIRIT IS A PERSON

Evidently there was much comment taking place respecting the speaking with Tongues and emotionalism, which were obvious.

The people who had gathered that day in the Temple evidenced so much joy that onlookers thought they were drunk.

I wonder how many modern churches exhibit the same type of Manifestation. To be honest, most have never exhibited anything that even remotely resembles that which took place on that Day of Pentecost. The reason is simple: the Holy Spirit is not present in most modern congregations because He is not wanted.

No! This is not a plea for emotionalism for the sake of such! That's not the idea at all.

The idea is that genuine Bible Christianity, which will always be characterized by the Holy Spirit, will always produce something similar in the hearts and lives of those who follow Christ. The Holy Spirit is a Person; consequently, His Moving in our hearts and lives always causes some type of response. While that response may differ, it will nevertheless be a response. I speak of the clapping of hands, the lifting of hands, praises to the Lord, laughing, crying in the Spirit, and even as these evidently were doing, staggering because of the Moving of the Holy Spirit within and upon them.

If such happened, and it did as is here obvious, then it should happen now!

DRUNK?

The phrase, *"For these are not drunken, as you suppose,"* in effect, says they were drunk, but not in the normal manner.

The Holy Spirit produces many emotions in an individual, at least if He is allowed latitude. One of those emotions is great joy exactly as evidenced here. As such, it produces a sense of well-being and even euphoria that nothing in the world can match. Actually, this is one of the reasons that many professing Christians are troubled by stress, emotional disturbances, depression, etc. Most are not baptized with the Holy Spirit and even those who are little allow, at least for the most part, the Holy Spirit to have His Perfect Way.

NOTES

The truth is that this is the answer for stress, emotional disturbances, and anything else with which the human body and mind may be confronted. Regrettably, most Believers have little knowledge of that of which I speak.

The phrase, *"Seeing it is but the third hour of the day,"* speaks of nine o'clock in the morning.

Most Jews there, except the mockers, knew that not even most worldlings were inebriated at that early hour, much less these people, and especially considering the large number. So, that accusation was baseless, even at first glance.

(16) "BUT THIS IS THAT WHICH WAS SPOKEN BY THE PROPHET JOEL."

The pattern is:

1. If one is to notice, Peter did not say, *"This fulfills that spoken by the Prophet Joel,"* but rather, *"This is that,"* implying that it began on the Day of Pentecost and would continue even as it has done.

2. The phrase, *"Which was spoken by the Prophet Joel,"* is referring to Joel 2:28-29.

3. Inasmuch as *"Joel"* was the Prophet whom the Holy Spirit desired Peter to use as an example, he can thusly be called the Holy Spirit Prophet of the Old Testament.

4. As we have already stated, we find Peter basing everything that was done squarely on the Scriptures. Consequently, everything we do must be done accordingly.

(17) "AND IT SHALL COME TO PASS IN THE LAST DAYS, SAITH GOD, I WILL POUR OUT OF MY SPIRIT UPON ALL FLESH: AND YOUR SONS AND YOUR DAUGHTERS SHALL PROPHESY, AND YOUR YOUNG MEN SHALL SEE VISIONS, AND YOUR OLD MEN SHALL DREAM DREAMS."

The form is:

1. The good news of the Gospel declares that you must get rid of the idea that you can do anything to be accepted by God!

2. The Gospel is one hundred percent Christ and zero regarding ourselves, except for us having Faith.

3. Faith must have as its Object, and without fail, Christ and Him Crucified.

THE LAST DAYS

The phrase, *"And it shall come to pass in the last days, saith God,"* portrays these *"last days"* as beginning on the Day of Pentecost and continuing through the coming Great Tribulation; however, qualifications are needed:

We find in Joel's Prophecy that these *"last days"* are somewhat divided, even as Joel said:

"Be glad then, you children of Zion, and rejoice in the LORD your God: for He has given you the former rain moderately, and He will cause to come down for you the rain, the former rain, and the latter rain in the first month" (Joel 2:23).

The seasonal rainfall in Israel was divided into two particular times, the *"former rain"* beginning in mid or late October, with the *"latter rain"* beginning between April and early May. These seasonal rains generally lasted approximately two months each. Otherwise, rain was very sparse, virtually nonexistent.

As such, the Holy Spirit used these seasonal changes in Israel to describe that which He would do during this time known as the *"last days."*

One could say that the *"Former Rain"* was that of the Early Church, actually that which we are now describing. The Book of Acts gives this account. In fact, much of the civilized world of that day was touched with the Gospel of Jesus Christ primarily because of the mighty Power of the Holy Spirit.

After the last Apostles and those who knew them died, little by little the church began to apostatize. This began taking place strongly so in the Third Century.

THE CATHOLIC CHURCH

Out of this was gradually born that which is known as the Catholic church; however, one should readily understand that the Early Church was not the *"Catholic church,"* as Catholics claim, which is plainly obvious as we read the Scriptures. In other words, there is absolutely no resemblance whatsoever to the Book of Acts Church and the Catholic church, and many other types of churches for that matter.

NOTES

As the Catholic church gradually consolidated its power, it drifted farther and farther from the Word of God until the Dark Ages descended upon the Earth. However, in the Sixteenth Century the Reformation began, with the rejection of much Catholic doctrine and the establishment of Protestant Churches. All during this time, very few people were actually baptized with the Holy Spirit with the evidence of speaking with other Tongues. In truth, there were not very many people who were truly Born-Again during these times. Where the Word of God is not preached, these great things cannot come about, for *"Faith comes by hearing, and hearing by the Word of God"* (Rom. 10:17).

Out of the Reformation came the major Protestant denominations, such as the Baptist, Methodist, Lutheran, Presbyterian, etc.

Gradually the ardor of these began to cool, with the great Holiness Movement born in the 1800s. So, the first Move took the People of God back to the Bible, for this is what the Reformation spawned, and then the second Move took the Body of Christ to the way of Holiness.

However, little by little, the Holiness Movements, for the most part, degenerated into legalism; consequently, there was a hunger and thirst in the hearts and lives of people. They were searching for reality and not mere rules, which had degenerated into self-righteousness and Pharisaism.

Out of that was born the *"Latter Rain,"* actually, the great Pentecostal Movements. It was just about at the turn of the Twentieth Century that this happened.

THE PENTECOSTALS

Individuals began to be hungry for more of God and began to search the Scriptures referring to the Infilling of the Holy Spirit. Consequently, hungry hearts began to be filled, and Miracle of Miracles, Believers were once again being baptized with the Holy Spirit in tremendous numbers, and they spoke with Tongues as the Spirit of God gave the utterance, even as they did in the Early Church.

Of course, there was much opposition from the other churches to this which was called *"wildfire," "fanaticism," "emotionalism,"* etc.

It was said that only the poorest of the poor associated with such Doctrine, insinuating that many, if not most, were mentally unbalanced, that is, if they embraced the baptism with the Holy Spirit with the evidence of speaking with other Tongues. It was also suggested that it was no more than a fad, which would vanish away shortly.

However, this *"fad"* has girdled the globe until it is believed that over 500 million people have been baptized with the Holy Spirit according to Acts 2:4, spanning the time from the turn of the Twentieth Century to the present. As stated, it is the *"Latter Rain"* as prophesied by Joel.

Sadly and regrettably, many of the modern Pentecostal denominations seem to be now following in the footsteps of their predecessors. This is marked by a departure from the Word, and in many cases, even a repudiation of this that has made these denominations great, the baptism with the Holy Spirit. In truth, only about one-third of the people associated with major modern Pentecostal denominations, at least in America and Canada, even claim to be Spirit-filled. Consequently, these denominations cannot honestly even call themselves *"Pentecostal"* anymore!

HUNGER AND THIRST

And yet, at the same time, there is a hunger and a thirst for God that is being born in the hearts and lives of many all around the world. This hunger and thirst cries for a deeper walk with the Lord in that the Spirit of God will move even in greater ways today than ever before. To be sure, this that is happening is inspired by the Holy Spirit. It is in fulfillment of the Word of God.

According to that which Peter will yet quote from Joel, I personally believe this Moving of the Holy Spirit is going to be the greatest yet, even greater than in the Early Church, even extending into the coming Great Tribulation.

NOTES

THE POURED OUT SPIRIT

The phrase, *"I will pour out of My Spirit upon all flesh,"* means exactly what it says.

The word *"pour"* in both the Hebrew and Greek mean to *"pour out"* or *"gush out."* Consequently, this speaks of a mighty Move and Operation of the Holy Spirit, at least where He is allowed to have His Way, which, sadly, is not much or often.

The *"all flesh"* speaks of all people everywhere and, therefore, is not limited to some particular geographical location. As well, it is not limited respecting race, color, or creed.

So, the Gospel of Jesus Christ is not a *"white man's gospel,"* as some claim, but is in reality for all. All were lost, and Jesus died for all, and so all are included!

The phrase, *"And your sons and your daughters shall prophesy,"* as well, as is obvious, includes both genders. The Outpouring of the Holy Spirit shows no partiality, but according to Faith, comes into the hearts and lives of all alike, both men and women, and boys and girls.

This speaks of one having the *"Gift of Prophecy,"* one of the nine Gifts of the Spirit, and has little or nothing to do with foretelling, but rather pertains to *"forth telling."* Speaking of this Gift of the Spirit, Paul said, *"But he who prophesies speaks unto men to edification, and exhortation, and comfort"* (I Cor. 14:3).

All who stand in the Office of the Prophet, which is not that of which Joel spoke, and engage in *"foretelling"* also have the *"Gift of Prophecy"* (I Cor. 12:8-10), but all who have the *"Gift of Prophecy"* do not stand in the Office of the Prophet. In fact, precious few do!

Actually, individuals who presently stand in the Office of the Prophet also have several of the other Gifts of the Spirit, *"the Word of Wisdom," "the Word of Knowledge," "the Gift of Faith,"* and *"Discerning of spirits."* So, as would be obvious, the Office of the Prophet is powerful, actually second only to the Office of the Apostle.

A PERSONAL EXPERIENCE

The year was 1944. I was nine years old.

NOTES

The prayer meetings that I previously mentioned were continued even through the school year but on an abbreviated basis; however, with the advent of the summer vacation, we once again began having prayer meetings each day.

During that time, the Lord began to speak through me concerning the invention of the atomic bomb. No, that term was not used, only that a bomb was being developed that would be so powerful that it could destroy an entire city.

These Prophecies lasted for a period of some days, even several weeks. Of course, only a handful of people in the world at that particular time knew of such a project; however, even at that moment a handful of men were working on this proposed super weapon. Actually, in today's inflated dollars, taxpayers spent about 25 billion dollars on this project, which ended World War II.

Of course, it should be understood that a nine year old boy in 1944 could not have had any knowledge whatsoever of such a doomsday weapon. Consequently, that which was given was solely of the Holy Spirit.

In the month of August, 1945, this Prophecy was fulfilled, with Hiroshima and Nagasaki, Japan, both being totally destroyed by an atomic bomb. Over 100,000 people were killed outright either in Hiroshima or in the coming near future after the explosion. Over 75,000 died in Nagasaki. These two cities looked like a moonscape after these horrible explosions.

The question, of course, must be asked as to why the Lord would give such information to a nine year old child, especially that of such consequences.

WHY?

To be frank, that I cannot answer! This I do know, the Lord does things in His own Way. The Holy Spirit through Paul said, *"But God has chosen the foolish things of the world to confound the wise; and God has chosen the weak things of the world to confound the things which are mighty."*

He does that in order *"that no flesh should glory in His Presence"* (I Cor. 1:27, 29).

During that time, the Lord also spoke through me that I would be an Evangelist and that my Ministry would touch much of the world. Of course, at that time (before television), such looked impossible, but the Spirit of God, Who knows all things, knew what would transpire in the future. He is never wrong, as He cannot be wrong.

The phrase, *"And your young men shall see visions, and your old men shall dream dreams,"* I am told that in the Hebrew, it actually reads, *"Both your young men and old men shall see Visions, and baoth your young men and old men shall dream Dreams."*

This refers to both *"Visions"* and *"Dreams"* as being from the Lord and being a result of the Infilling of the Holy Spirit.

This doesn't mean that all dreams are from the Lord but that some definitely can be.

(18) "AND ON MY SERVANTS AND ON MY HANDMAIDENS I WILL POUR OUT IN THOSE DAYS OF MY SPIRIT; AND THEY SHALL PROPHESY."

The order is:

1. Paul said to the Galatians, *"Before your very eyes, Jesus was clearly placarded as crucified."*

2. Paul was not saying that Christ is crucified over and over.

3. Rather, he was saying, the eternal efficacy of the Cross of Christ is placarded before your very eyes every time the Gospel is preached.

SERVANTS AND HANDMAIDENS

The Phrase, *"And on My servants and on My handmaidens I will pour out in those days of My Spirit,"* is meant purposely to address two particular classes of people who had been given very little shift in the past.

The word *"servants"* in the Greek is *"doulos"* and means *"a slave."* This means that these people, whomever they were, would be treated by the Lord exactly as all others. No discrimination would be shown respecting them receiving the things of God and being baptized with the Holy Spirit.

To take it a step further, the word *"handmaidens"* in the Greek is *"doule"* and means *"a female slave."*

So, the Holy Spirit here purposely pointed out those in the very lowest stratum of society and placed them on an equal footing with all others. Consequently, irrespective of what man thought of these people, we have here what God says, which is all that matters in the eternal scheme of things.

This means that no racism, prejudice, bias, or favoritism is practiced or shown to any.

THE GOSPEL OF JESUS CHRIST

Consequently, if the Gospel is properly understood and preached, it will attract all different types of people, whether they be rich, poor, or whatever color groups they may be. It is unscriptural for any church to tailor its message and actions so as to exclude any people, irrespective of whom they may be. While it certainly may be true that there are churches where only one color group attends, nothing is wrong with that, providing the doors are open to all; however, if certain groups are not made to feel welcome, that is sorely displeasing to the Lord.

When Jesus died on Calvary, He died for the whole of the human family. He placed no one group or color above others; His Blood was shed for all! As well, He showed absolutely no discrimination in His Ministry in any capacity, be they rich, cultured, slaves, beggars, male, or female. All were treated accordingly. As someone has said, *"The ground is level at the foot of the Cross!"*

I find it very difficult to understand how some entire religious denominations can open their doors basically to whites only and still claim to be Scriptural!

It's not right for a person to think of himself as better than others. This is highly displeasing to the Lord. Worse yet, to treat someone, or anyone for that matter, in a lesser way, especially those who have been Saved by the Precious Blood of Jesus, is downright insulting to God and the price Jesus paid at Calvary. In other words, it is a very serious offense, which should be obvious.

As we shall see just a little later, the Lord addressed Himself very succinctly to Simon Peter who in his heart was engaging in discrimination. He told Peter, *"What God has cleansed, you are not to call common"* (Acts 10:15).

On top of that, and so there would be absolutely no misunderstanding, He told him these very words three times. The

NOTES

lesson should be well taken!

IN THOSE DAYS OF MY SPIRIT

The phrase, *"In those days of My Spirit,"* is beautiful indeed!

However, we must make it clear that these wonderful *"days of My Spirit,"* meaning that it is available to all, are made possible by what Jesus did at the Cross. The Cross of Christ atoned for all sin, past, present, and future, at least for all who will believe (Jn. 3:16).

As well, the Cross dealt with not only acts of sin but the very cause of sin itself, speaking of original sin. It dealt with every facet of sin and in every capacity, making it possible for the Holy Spirit to now do what was impossible for Him to do previously.

As we have already stated, everything the Lord does on this Earth has always been done by and through the Person, Office, and Ministry of the Holy Spirit (Gen. 1:1-2; Zech. 4:6; Jn. 1:1). Consequently, to the extent the Holy Spirit is hindered in the lives of individuals, to that extent they will suffer loss.

Much of the church world teaches that there is no such thing as an experience of being baptized with the Holy Spirit after Conversion. In other words, they teach that one gets everything at Conversion, which is a repudiation of this very Chapter.

Even many of these who would teach some type of experience after Conversion deny that speaking with other Tongues is the initial physical evidence. Some even go as far as to claim that speaking in other Tongues is of the devil, etc.

To be frank, the latter group is treading on very thin ice and actually coming very close to blaspheming the Holy Spirit (Mat. 12:24-32).

While others do not go that far, nevertheless, their repudiation of this baptism with the Holy Spirit as a definite Work of Grace, which follows Conversion either immediately or soon after, shuts them off respecting most anything that the Lord does. If God works exclusively through the Holy Spirit, and He definitely does, then they have closed off the only avenue that the Lord uses; consequently, all they do, at least for the most part, is man-originated, man-induced, and man-performed. As such, and as we have stated, even though there may be much religious machinery and activity, little if anything will actually be done for the Lord.

POTENTIAL IN NATURE

Regrettably, and again as we have stated, even those who have been baptized with the Holy Spirit do very little for the Lord at times; however, that's not the fault of the Spirit, but rather the individuals in question.

The Working of the Spirit in our lives is potential in nature. In other words, none of these great things are automatic but always come about as the person cooperates with the Holy Spirit. The potential is there, but regrettably, seldom utilized in the hearts and lives of many, if not most.

We believe the Bible teaches the following:

• Salvation by Faith in Christ and Faith alone (Jn. 3:16; Rom. 5:1; Eph. 2:9).

• Immediately following Salvation, the Believer, who is now a cleansed temple and made so by the Precious Blood of Christ, must seek to be baptized with the Holy Spirit. As stated, this experience did not, nor does it, happen automatically at Conversion. It is an experience separate and apart from Salvation, which gives one Power to do and carry out the Works of Christ (Acts 1:8). Actually, the Holy Spirit does many things for the Child of God. He leads us, guides us, empowers us, strengthens us, comforts us, enables us, aids us, and does so in many and varied ways.

It is certainly true that all Believers have the Holy Spirit simply because He has a part in everything done by the Heavenly Father and through the Authority of Jesus Christ, even as we have already said. However, the Work of the Holy Spirit in Regeneration, which takes place in the heart and life of every sinner upon Faith in Christ, is totally different than the baptism with the Spirit, which this Second Chapter of Acts portrays. In other words, being born of the Spirit is one thing while being baptized with the Spirit is something else altogether (Acts 1:4; 2:4; 8:14-15; 9:17; 10:44; 19:1-7).

• We believe the Bible teaches that all recipients of the Holy Spirit speak with other Tongues as the Spirit of God gives the utterance, and without exception. We teach that this is the initial physical evidence that one has been baptized with the Holy Spirit (Acts 2:4; 10:46; 19:6).

To not believe this and, thereby, fail to receive this that Jesus commanded (Acts 1:4) is to cut off oneself from much of that which the Lord does within a person and through a person.

CHURCHES WITHOUT THE HOLY SPIRIT

Consequently, in churches that repudiate the First and Second Chapters of Acts, either by unbelief or claiming it is not for us today, one finds almost nothing of the Works of Christ carried out in these churches.

There is little or no praying for the sick, no casting out of demons, little or no manifestation of worship, and no anointing of the Holy Spirit on the preacher, or anyone else for that matter! Consequently, there is very little conviction of sin, of Righteousness, and of judgment (Jn. 16:7-15). In truth, even though many people join these churches, there are actually very few true Conversions.

As a result, these types of churches are guided and ruled primarily by committees of one form or the other. As well, their gospel is little more than a social gospel, and if straight as far as it goes, it has little or no anointing of the Holy Spirit. As a result, just about anyone with problems is referred to counselors or psychologists.

Whenever the Holy Spirit is repudiated in any fashion, whether by denial or unbelief, the supernatural factor is taken away, with nothing left but that which is man-induced.

I realize that what we are saying is very serious. I also realize it characterizes most churches, even those that call themselves *"Pentecostal!"* Tragically and sadly, many of these in the latter group are following their old-line contemporaries.

If the Word of God is obeyed, with the Spirit of God given proper latitude, there will be earmarks of the Book of Acts Church. If it doesn't have the same earmarks, it is not a New Testament Church but something else altogether! As it was in the *"days of the Spirit"* then, it is in the *"days of the Spirit"*

NOTES

NOTES

now! So, they should be very similar.

(19) "AND I WILL SHOW WONDERS IN HEAVEN ABOVE, AND SIGNS IN THE EARTH BENEATH; BLOOD, AND FIRE, AND VAPOR OF SMOKE."

The form is:

1. The phrase, *"And I will show wonders in Heaven above,"* pertains to the Great Tribulation that will come upon this Earth immediately before the Second Coming.

2. *"And signs in the Earth beneath; blood, and fire, and vapor of smoke,"* is proclaimed in greater detail in Ezekiel 38:22; Revelation 8:5-8; 9:2-3, 17-18; 11:5-6; 16:3-6, 8; 18:8-9, 18; 19:3.

3. These *"signs"* will take place in both the *"Heaven above"* and *"Earth beneath."* It will be a time of such sorrow as the world has never known before.

4. Jesus said, *"For then shall be great tribulation, such as was not since the beginning of the world to this time, no, nor ever shall be"* (Mat. 24:21).

5. These things have to do with the *"Seven Seal Judgments"* (Rev., Chpts. 6-8), *"the Seven Trumpet Judgments"* (Rev., Chpts. 8-11), and *"the Seven Vial Judgments"* (Rev., Chpts. 15-16).

(20) "THE SUN SHALL BE TURNED INTO DARKNESS, AND THE MOON INTO BLOOD, BEFORE THAT GREAT AND NOTABLE DAY OF THE LORD COME."

The pattern is:

1. In brief, God's Way is *"Jesus Christ and Him Crucified."*

2. That's why Paul said, *"We preach Christ Crucified"* (I Cor. 1:23).

3. He said he realized that this was an offense to the Jews and foolishness to the Greeks (Gentiles), but he preached Christ and Him Crucified because that was God's Way and His only Way.

DARKNESS

The phrase, *"The sun shall be turned into darkness,"* does not mean that it will be extinguished. The word *"darkness"* means simply that the sun will be shaded, which could easily happen by disturbances on Earth that could fill the air with dust or particles, thereby, shading the sun, etc.

"And the moon into blood," seems to imply, according to Revelation 6:12, that this does not have a literal meaning, but rather will look blood-red because of atmospheric conditions. While it is certainly possible for the Lord to literally turn the moon to blood, or anything else for that matter, comparing Scripture to Scripture, the Bible does not seem to bear out the literalness of this statement (Mat. 24:29; Rev. 6:12).

THE DAY OF THE LORD

The phrase, *"Before that great and notable Day of the Lord come,"* speaks of the Second Coming (Mat. 24:29-31; 25:31-46; Rev. 19:11).

This completely shoots down the theory promoted by some that the Books of Daniel and Revelation have already been fulfilled. However, this that Peter quoted from Joel plainly tells us that these things will not happen until just before the Second Coming.

This teaching, incidentally, is promoted by many and is referred to by several names, such as *"Kingdom now"* or *"Kingdom teaching."* It basically claims, with some variations, that the entirety of the world is gradually getting better, with Christianity making great inroads, which will ultimately usher in the Kingdom Age. The basic means of attaining this end is the promotion of the political message. In other words, it is claimed that all of this will be brought about by high political offices, etc. Consequently, organizations, such as *"Christian Coalition,"* as well as others, are formed and funded for this very purpose.

It looks and sounds very good to the Christian public because all the right words are said. Actually it is far better in this country if suitable men and women can be elected to high political offices. While that within itself is not wrong, but rather right, it deceives many people.

However, these false apostles (for that is what they are) are at the same time repudiating world Evangelism according to the Bible, which is carried out by the preaching of the Gospel. As well, the Bible teaches the very opposite of what Kingdom Agers are promoting.

The situation is not improving, but rather

the very opposite, with the church ultimately apostatizing and perilous times ultimately coming upon this world, which will culminate with the greatest time of sorrow the world has ever known. It is called the Great Tribulation and on the horizon of events, it is right around the corner, so to speak (Mat. 24:21; Rev., Chpts. 6-19).

(21) "AND IT SHALL COME TO PASS, THAT WHOSOEVER SHALL CALL ON THE NAME OF THE LORD SHALL BE SAVED."

The record is:

1. Jesus Christ is the New Covenant (Jn. 1:1-3, 14, 29; Col. 2:10).

2. The Cross of Christ is the meaning of the New Covenant (I Cor. 1:17-18; 2:2).

3. The meaning of the New Covenant, which is the Cross of Christ, was given to the Apostle Paul, and he gave it to us in his 14 Epistles.

IT SHALL COME TO PASS

The phrase, *"And it shall come to pass,"* is used in the past tense because Peter was quoting Joel, who gave this Prophecy about 750 years before Christ.

At that particular time, it was not a simple thing to be saved. While individuals have always been saved in the same identical manner, which refers to trust in Christ, before Calvary, the process was much more involved. While it definitely did come by Faith exactly as it does presently, still, Faith was exhibited in the sacrifices, which within themselves could not save anyone but did point to the One Who could, the Lord Jesus Christ.

Consequently, even though there were some proselyte Gentiles brought in, considering the whole, they were few and far between.

So, Joel was saying, as Peter quoted him, that all of this would one day change exactly as it did when Jesus went to Calvary and was raised from the dead. Then the door opened to all and on the same basis, which constitutes the New Covenant.

CALLING ON THE NAME OF THE LORD

The phrase, *"That whosoever shall call on the Name of the Lord shall be saved,"* presents one of the most glorious statements ever made:

NOTES

- As stated, that which Jesus did at Calvary made it possible for the door to be opened to all!
- The word, *"Whosoever,"* means exactly what it says, that Gentiles are now placed on the same level as the Jews.
- All one has to do to be saved is to simply *"call upon the Name of the Lord,"* which presupposes Faith. No sacrifices are required simply because Jesus was and is the Sacrifice.
- As well, there is no limitation on the locality or geography. It doesn't matter where a person may be, he can call on the Lord at that time and in that place, and if he is sincere and really believes, he will be instantly saved (Jn. 3:16).
- Also, concerning this great Promise, Peter did not say as with the Holy Spirit, *"This fulfills that which was spoken by the Prophet Joel,"* but rather, *"This is that."* In other words, this glorious Salvation process, which is the single most important thing in the world, began the moment Jesus was crucified and rose from the dead. It is called the New Covenant and continues unto this very hour and will not stop (Lk. 22:20). As stated, Jesus Christ is the New Covenant.
- This will be true as long as there are sinners to repent. There is no doctrine in Scripture that says the door of Mercy will be closed to Jews or Gentiles at any time before their death (Heb. 9:27).
- This means that people will continue to be saved and baptized with the Holy Spirit in the coming Great Tribulation exactly as they were on the Day of Pentecost and even unto this very hour.
- This tells us also that ceremonies, churches, rituals, and other religious acts are unnecessary regarding the Salvation process. Actually, if anyone attempts to add these things to simple Faith, his Faith is instantly nullified. That is the sad reason that multiple tens of millions of people in churches are very lost although very religious. They have attempted to add something to the Finished Work of Christ, which cannot be done for the obvious reasons, which the Lord cannot allow. Either Jesus did it all, or else, He left certain things that need to be done respecting the Salvation process.

We know that He left nothing hanging, with every single thing done, which means that nothing needs to be added.

- In order to be saved, one must call solely on the Lord. The reason is obvious! He is the One Who suffered, bled, and died for our sins. In other words, He alone paid the price. As well, He is the One Who defeated death and did so by rising from the dead.
- The word *"Saved"* implies *"Deliverance,"* which is exactly the word used by Joel (Joel 2:32).

Consequently, for one to be delivered, there must be a *"Deliverer!"*

The action of the Deliverer, in this case Jesus, effects a release from the circumstances that caused the suffering, sin, and bondage in the first place. Thus, Salvation portrays movement—from distress to safety.

Both Testaments express conviction that it is God and God only Who can save His People. Thus, in the Bible, Salvation focuses on the relationships between God and human beings; however, it is Jesus alone Who has opened up the way to God (Jn. 14:6).

THREE ASPECTS OF SALVATION

The New Testament presents three different aspects of the Salvation that Jesus has purchased for us.

These may be thought of as the past, present, and future aspects of Salvation.

THE FIRST ASPECT OF SALVATION

Historically, Jesus died for us and thus accomplished our Salvation. Our initial belief in Jesus comes in conjunction with God's application of Redemption to us by means of Justification and Regeneration.

In other words, even though sinners, we are justified by placing our Faith exclusively in Christ, Who took the punishment that we should have taken.

When this happens, the Holy Spirit performs the Work of Regeneration within our hearts and lives. In other words, we are made *"a new creature in Christ Jesus"* (II Cor. 5:17).

Thus, in both the historic and subjective senses, it is proper for the New Testament to speak of our having been saved, in other words, *"past tense." "According to His Mercy He saved us,"* Paul writes (Titus 3:5), and he says to Timothy, *"God, Who has saved us and called us to a holy life"* (II Tim. 1:9).

NOTES

THE SECOND ASPECT OF SALVATION

While it is true that Jesus has saved us, it is also true that Jesus is presently saving us. Salvation has an impact on our present experience. Reconciled to God, we are being saved through Jesus' Life (Rom. 5:10), in other words, the Life that He gave up on the Cross.

This aspect of Salvation is taught in Romans, Chapter 6. Released from slavery to sin, we offer ourselves to God to serve Him in Righteousness (Rom. 6:5-14).

THE THIRD ASPECT OF SALVATION

It is true that we have been saved, we are saved, and we shall be saved, future tense.

The ultimate impact of the Salvation that Jesus won for us will be known only at the Trump of God. Then the last taint of sin will be removed, and we will be perfected at last and given a Glorified Body. The certitude of this future is beautifully expressed in Romans 8:18-39 and I Corinthians 15:12-58.

SALVATION FROM WHAT?

It is Salvation from sin!

Sin has a double hold on humanity. Due to the Fall, man is afflicted with the fact of sin, which is original sin, into which he was born. In other words, all are born in sin, therefore, lost, and within themselves have no way to be delivered or saved (Ps. 51:5).

However, I believe the Bible teaches that even though they are born in original sin, all babies and children below the age of accountability are protected, respecting their soul's Salvation, until they reach the age of accountability. I believe this is true because of their innocence. Also, the age of accountability varies with children (Mat. 18:3).

As well, man is afflicted not only with original sin but with acts of sin, which in the life of the unbeliever are constant and extremely destructive and debilitating.

However, Jesus dealt with sin at Calvary, and through Him Salvation entered the world (Jn. 3:17). Through Jesus we are

NOTES

saved from the coming wrath (Rom. 5:9), all made possible by the Cross of Christ. It should be obvious that our Lord paid a terrible price at Calvary's Cross in order that man might be redeemed. At the Cross Jesus dealt not only with original sin, but He dealt with all acts of sin as well. In other words, He atoned for all sin, past, present, and future, at least for all who will believe (Jn. 3:16).

If you take the Cross out of this mix, then you're left with *"another Jesus,"* which God can never accept (II Cor. 11:4).

Jesus came into the world to accomplish Salvation for us (I Tim. 1:15), and there is no other name under Heaven to which we can look for Deliverance (Acts 4:12). God's Power was exercised to the fullest on our behalf in the Death of Jesus for our sins and in the Resurrection of Jesus to guarantee what His Death had purchased (II Tim. 4:18; Heb. 7:25).

WHAT IS OUR PART IN SALVATION?

Paul's answer to the Philippian jailer expresses the consistent Testimony of Scripture: *"Believe in the Lord Jesus Christ, and you will be saved"* (Acts 16:31).

Salvation is a gracious Gift of God received through Faith (Eph. 2:5-8). The human responsibility now, as in Old Testament Times, is simply to rely completely on the Lord. Thus, Salvation today comes in the context of one's relationship with God and is never based on any human acts.

It was God Who acted and Who acts; the Law required man to act. This requirement demonstrated man's impotency. The Son of God requires nothing from man other than his confidence.

THE BASIC CONCEPT

Salvation is a basic concept in both Testaments. It clearly defines the human condition, as well as the relationship that must exist between God and human beings.

Salvation implies human helplessness in the face of life-threatening danger. Thus, Deliverance must come through the actions of another. Throughout Scripture, the Source of Salvation always is God. He alone can act to deliver His People from the dangers in this present world and from the spiritual, eternal danger. In each Testament, the one in danger may simply turn to the Lord, rely fully on Him, and trust Him to act.

Also, both the Old Testament and the New Testament present a basis for confidence in the Lord. The Covenant Promises that God made to Abraham and his descendants were based on the future Coming of Christ as Redeemer, and the Promises to New Testament Believers are based on the Finished Work of Christ Jesus, that is, His Death on Cavalry's Cross. To all Believers, Faith is an expression of a person's confidence in the Trustworthiness of God.

We can then be sure of our Salvation, for we can rely on God Who has acted for us and Whose Promise cannot be a lie.

Now, we must remember and, in fact, never forget that it is the Cross of Christ that has made Salvation possible, and only the Cross of Christ. Jesus Christ is the Source of all things that we receive from God, but the Cross is the Means and the only Means by which these wonderful things are given to us. Without the Cross there would be no Salvation, no baptism with the Holy Spirit, and no communion with the Lord, in fact, nothing. It is the Cross of Christ that has made everything possible.

Of course, when we speak of the Cross, we aren't speaking of the wooden beam on which Jesus died, but rather what He there did, what He there accomplished, and what He there won, which was all for us and none for Himself.

Understanding that the Cross of Christ is the Means and the only Means by which all of these wonderful things are given to us, then the Cross of Christ must be the Object of our Faith. That's why Paul said, *"We preach Christ Crucified"* (I Cor. 1:23).

That's why he also said to the Church at Corinth and to all of us, as well, *"I determined to know nothing among you save Christ and Him Crucified"* (I Cor. 2:2). That's why the great Apostle also stated:

"God forbid that I should glory (boast), *save in the Cross of our Lord Jesus Christ, by Whom the world is crucified unto me, and I unto the world"* (Gal. 6:14).

And then, *"Blotting out the handwriting*

of ordinances that was against us, which was contrary to us, and took it out of the way, nailing it to His Cross" (Col. 2:14).

It was at the Cross and the Cross alone where all sin was atoned, past, present, and future (Jn. 3:16). The Cross is where Satan, all fallen Angels, and demon spirits were totally and completely defeated. Concerning this, Paul also said:

"And having spoiled principalities and powers (fallen Angels), *He made a show of them openly, triumphing over them in it"* (Col. 2:15).

It is impossible for a Believer to walk in victory without understanding the Cross of Christ as it relates to Sanctification, in other words, how we live for God.

THE HOLY SPIRIT

Then we must understand, the Holy Spirit is God, and He works entirely within the parameters, so to speak, of the Finished Work of Christ, i.e., *"the Cross."* The Holy Spirit doesn't demand much of us, but He does demand one thing, and that is that our Faith be exclusively in Christ and what Christ did for us at the Cross (Rom. 8:1-11).

The Holy Spirit works exclusively by and through the Cross of Christ. In other words, it is the Cross, what Jesus there did, that makes it possible for the Holy Spirit to work within our hearts and lives, without Whom we simply cannot be what we ought to be. That's how important the Cross of Christ is and how important the Holy Spirit is.

(22) "YOU MEN OF ISRAEL, HEAR THESE WORDS; JESUS OF NAZARETH, A MAN APPROVED OF GOD AMONG YOU BY MIRACLES AND WONDERS AND SIGNS, WHICH GOD DID BY HIM IN THE MIDST OF YOU, AS YOU YOURSELVES ALSO KNOW."

The record is:

1. Unredeemed man is loath to accept the Cross.

2. The reason is the Cross tells man how Righteous God is and how unrighteous man is.

3. Simple man does not like to admit that he is so sinful, so wicked, and so vile that it would take such a price, the price of the Cross, in order to redeem him.

NOTES

ISRAEL

The phrase, *"You men of Israel, hear these words,"* now presents a Message that is straightforward and pulls no punches whatsoever!

Considering this Message, in effect, the inaugural Message of the Church, we should understand and comprehend what the Spirit was saying through the Apostle. This we do know, that which Peter said was Divinely orchestrated. Among other things, it resulted in the Salvation of *"about three thousand souls"* (Acts 2:41).

The Message was directed to Israel, as is obvious, and for the obvious reasons. Most who heard this Message that day were Jews. Therefore, the Holy Spirit would direct His Attention to these people simply because those were the ones who were listening.

The Holy Spirit always knows the need of the moment, and if the Preacher of the Gospel will seek the Face of the Lord, each Message, even as here, will be tailored for that particular audience, etc. However, this can only be brought about as the Preacher of the Gospel walks in close fellowship with the Lord.

When I preach, I earnestly seek the Lord that He give me the Message that He desires for that particular time simply because He knows all things.

JESUS OF NAZARETH

The phrase, *"Jesus of Nazareth, a Man approved of God among you,"* tells us several things:

• Jesus was the Theme of this Message and should be the Theme either directly or indirectly of every Message.

• As well, the Holy Spirit wanted Peter to strongly bear down on the Person of Christ, irrespective of the fact that the Jews hated Christ and, in fact, had murdered Him.

By this we see that the Holy Spirit gives people what they need and not exactly what they want.

• By Peter using the words, *"a Man,"* he was directing attention to the Incarnation of Christ, God becoming Man (Isa. 7:14).

To be frank, His Incarnation was at least one of the reasons the religious leaders

NOTES

would not accept Him. In their eyes He was a Peasant and, as such, could not be the Messiah. Of course, these were only their conclusions and not that which was given in the Word of God.

• Even though He was not approved by the religious leaders of Israel, He definitely was *"approved of God."*

So, one can have the approval of man or the Approval of God. One cannot have both!

Peter was saying that they disapproved that which was approved by God. Such was a very serious charge, and sadly, characterizes modern religion as well!

The Believer must not look to outward appearances or even circumstances, but rather find the Mind of God relative to that which He has approved. Most follow that approved by man, thinking it is God but, in reality, is not!

• As well, all of the things done by Jesus were done in the very midst of the people with nothing done in secret. As such, the religious leaders of Israel should have easily known and understood the Source of this Power, but regrettably, they accused Him of performing Miracles by the power of Satan (Mat. 12:24-32).

MIRACLES, WONDERS, AND SIGNS

The phrase, *"By Miracles and wonders and signs, which God did by Him in the midst of you,"* proclaims that which Peter knew firsthand because he was there.

If it is to be noticed, Jesus did not and, in fact, could not perform these Miracles of Himself as Man, for man has no such Power. It was God Who did these things through Him by the Power of the Holy Spirit (Lk. 4:18-19).

"As you yourselves also know," means that so many of these things were done that there was absolutely no excuse for them not to know.

As well, according to the Words of Christ, *"Miracles, Wonders, and Signs,"* should continue in the lives of Believers even unto this present hour (Mk. 16:17).

Actually, this is at least one of the great reasons the Holy Spirit is given to Believers. The Scriptures say, *"For this purpose the Son of God was manifested, that He might destroy the works of the devil"* (I Jn. 3:8).

Such are to continue in the lives and ministries of all Believers.

Tragically, much of the modern church world denies *"Miracles, Wonders, and Signs!"* Unbelief registers itself in many as, *"The days of Miracles are over," "Such passed away with the Apostles," "It is not for us today,"* etc. However, *"Let God be true, and every man a liar"* (Rom. 3:4).

So, not only did Peter make Jesus the main Theme of this Message, but he also proclaimed that which Jesus did and continued in the lives and Ministry of the Apostles and others. Correspondingly, in this inaugural Message of the Church, the Holy Spirit was saying that such must continue with us as well!

(23) "HIM, BEING DELIVERED BY THE DETERMINATE COUNSEL AND FOREKNOWLEDGE OF GOD, YOU HAVE TAKEN, AND BY WICKED HANDS HAVE CRUCIFIED AND SLAIN."

The record is:

1. It is not only true that unredeemed man thinks he can save himself, but redeemed man, who ought to know better, thinks he can sanctify himself.

2. That is, no doubt, the biggest problem in the church presently.

3. However, let the Redeemed understand that we can no more sanctify ourselves than the unredeemed can save themselves.

THE DETERMINATE COUNSEL AND FOREKNOWLEDGE OF GOD

The phrase, *"Him, being delivered by the determinate counsel and Foreknowledge of God,"* tells us certain things about the Plan of God and the manner in which it was carried out.

It was the Plan of God that Jesus would die on Calvary; however, it was not the Plan of God for the religious leaders of Israel to do this thing. That was of their own making and choice.

Even though they desired the Crucifixion of Christ, still, they could not have done such, which should be overly obvious, if not permitted by God.

Pilate mentioned the authority he thought he had over Jesus and was answered by the Lord, *"You could have no power at all against Me, except it were given you from above"* (Jn. 19:11).

The phrase, *"Determinate counsel,"* has to do with predestination. In other words, the sending of Jesus, His Death, and Resurrection were all predestined (I Pet. 1:20). However, this was brought about by the *"Foreknowledge of God."*

This means that God has the ability to look down through time and see what is going to happen in the future. It is called *"Omniscience"* or *"Foreknowledge."*

However, this does not mean that God has wound up His Creation like a person would wind up a clock and then sits back and watches it unwind on its own. In fact, God is very much involved in all aspects of the human family. However, in this involvement, He never violates the free moral agency of man. Being God, He can bring things to pass without violating this principle.

BY WICKED HANDS HAVE CRUCIFIED

From this we learn that predestination is based on the *"Foreknowledge of God,"* and as such, always holds sacred man's free will.

"You have taken, and by wicked hands have crucified and slain," presents a charge so serious that it absolutely defies description!

This one thing we do know: Peter was not pulling any punches in delivering this Message. He called it what it was and said what it did! Of course, as we shall see, the religious leaders of Israel who had committed this dastardly crime were not too happy about being reminded of such, especially in this fashion.

As well, the bravado of which Peter had boasted some 50 days earlier was now very much present; however, whereas it was then of himself, it was now by the Power of the Holy Spirit. Consequently, there is a vast, vast difference.

How many Preachers presently address sin as Peter did, and how many dare address the sinner in this fashion?

Actually, Peter's Message would have been rejected and disapproved for this very reason by most of the modern church; however, such is done only because the

NOTES

perpetrators do not want the Mind of God, desiring to preach their own message. Regrettably, such spiritual pabulum is swallowed down by most Christians.

However, when it is *"Thus saith the Lord,"* such becomes something else altogether.

Peter was there to say what the Lord wanted him to say, and that he would do, irrespective of the outcome.

Actually, the outcome of a Message sent from God is never the concern of the Messenger. His concern is delivering it as it should be delivered and in the right way. This Peter did!

(24) "WHOM GOD HAS RAISED UP, HAVING LOOSED THE PAINS OF DEATH: BECAUSE IT WAS NOT POSSIBLE THAT HE SHOULD BE HOLDEN OF IT."

The structure is:

1. The phrase, *"Whom God has raised up,"* concerns the Resurrection of Christ.
2. *"Having loosed the pains of death,"* simply means that death could not hold Him, even though it had held all others!
3. Death is the end result of sin and, consequently, holds sway over the human family, for all have sinned (Rom. 3:23; 6:23). This speaks of death in every form.
4. Physical death was ultimately brought about by the Fall, with man originally created to live forever. Spiritual death came immediately, which means separation from God.
5. So, before Jesus died on Calvary, thereby, settling the debt of sin, death overwhelmed every person, even beyond physical death. Consequently, all, even Believers, were taken captive by Satan at death. While he could not put them into the burning side of Hell, he could force them to stay in the place called Paradise, which was separated from Hell only by a gulf and located in the heart of the Earth (Mat. 12:40; Lk. 16:22-31).
6. However, Jesus liberated these souls during the three days and nights He was in the Earth, with them transported to Heaven and that compartment remaining empty from then until now (Mat. 27:52-53; Eph. 4:8-10).
7. When Jesus died, He did so by His own volition, with none taking His Life from Him, although attempting to do so; however, death could not hold Him simply

NOTES

because He had never sinned and, therefore, was due none of sin's wages. As such, He walked out victorious over sin, death, and Hell.

8. The word *"loosed"* carries the sense that death attempted to bind Him in its grip but could not hold Him, that grip being dissolved. Consequently, from that moment, death could not hold any Believer in its vice. Even though the Believer does ultimately physically die, still, the soul and the spirit go to be with Jesus, there to await the Resurrection morn when the soul and the spirit will be reunited with a Glorified Body, which will last forever.

9. *"Because it was not possible that He should be holden of it,"* had to do with the things I have just stated concerning Jesus never having sinned and, therefore, not subject to its wages, which are death. So, what death was attempting to do was impossible!

10. Because of its significance, we need to state again that death attempted to hold Him but simply did not have the power to do so.

(25) "FOR DAVID SPEAKS CONCERNING HIM, I FORESAW THE LORD ALWAYS BEFORE MY FACE, FOR HE IS ON MY RIGHT HAND, THAT I SHOULD NOT BE MOVED."

The record is:

1. God's Way is *"Jesus Christ and Him Crucified."*

2. Man can only be changed by the Power of God.

3. It is the Power of God alone that is greater than the power of Satan.

DAVID

The phrase, *"For David speaks concerning Him,"* is taken from Psalms 16:8-11.

How did Peter know that this Psalm referred to Christ and His Experience in the nether world?

The Spirit of the Lord told him.

However, these Passages, plus many others of similar import concerning the Psalms as they relate to Christ, tell us that in truth, the entirety of the Psalms speak of Christ, with the exception of those that address themselves to the Evil One. That is not understandable to most simply because of some of the terminology involved.

For instance, Psalm 51 is an excellent example but in truth, only one among many.

David said in this Psalm, *"Wash me thoroughly from mine iniquity, and cleanse me from my sin"* (Ps. 51:2). In fact, almost the entirety of this Psalm is in that vein.

Of course, we know that Jesus never sinned and, consequently, never had to ask the Father for forgiveness, etc. So, how can this Psalm, especially considering its terminology, portray Christ?

While this Psalm definitely pertains to David as he prayed this prayer of Repentance concerning his sin with Bath-sheba and against Uriah, still, it points to our Greater David in His Intercessory Role on our behalf.

Most Believers do not properly understand the Intercessory Role of Christ.

INTERCESSION

Everything Jesus did on this Earth was on our behalf in every respect.

For example, His Perfect Life was lived for us, and upon Faith in Him, becomes our Perfect Life. He was and is the Representative Man.

His Death on Cavalry was on our behalf, as was His Resurrection. In other words, we were in Him when He lived the Perfect Life, died on Calvary, and rose from the dead (Rom. 6:3-6).

As well, we are still in Him as He is seated by the Father in Heavenly Places (Eph. 2:6).

However, it does not end there as we continue to be in Him and Him in us in His Intercessory Role (Jn. 14:20; Heb. 7:25).

The Greek word for *"Intercession"* is *"Entugchano,"* and means *"to plead on behalf of someone"* and *"to give self wholly to."*

In essence, it means that as Jesus became one with us in our sin as He died on the Cross, likewise, He remains one with us after our Conversion, even when we fail. Consequently, He not only pleads for us to the Father in this intercessory role but, in fact, He pleads as us, which accounts for suchlike terminology in the Psalms.

Actually, when one reads Psalm 51, one is reading the intercessory prayer that stands for all Believers everywhere, and for all time. In other words, whenever a

NOTES

Saint does wrong, Jesus does not turn to the Father and plead the cause as we would think. He does plead it, but it's in a different way. It was done when David prayed that prayer outlined in Psalm 51. Not only was it David's prayer, but it was the prayer of our Lord in His Intercessory Role, all on our behalf. In other words, the Intercession really has already been done and will stand for the entirety of the ages to come.

Because of its significance, I will say it again:

He pleads for us when we sin, and He pleads as us! Again, read Psalm 51, and you can see the Intercessory Prayer of Christ that every one of us has had to fall back on time and time again. As somebody has well said, *"Were it not for the Intercessory Work of Christ on our behalf, we wouldn't last out a day, not even an hour."*

So, when you read the Psalms again, hopefully, you will read them in a different light. Even though they do point to people and events of particular times, we must understand that as secondary. Its principle predictions concern the Perfections, the Sufferings, and the succeeding Glories of the Messiah, i.e., the Lord Jesus Christ.

THE HIGH PRIEST OF HIS PEOPLE

With God having been dishonored by human unbelief and disobedience, it was necessary that a Man should be born Who would perfectly love, perfectly trust, perfectly serve Him, and Who would be the True Adam, Noah, Abraham, Israel, Moses, David, etc.

God's Moral Glory demanded that sin should be judged and that sinners should repent, confess, and forsake sin, and worship and obey Him. Being God, His Nature required perfection in these emotions of the heart and will.

Such perfection was impossible to fallen man, and it was equally out of his power to provide a sacrifice that could remove his guilt and restore his relationship with God.

The Psalms reveal Christ as satisfying all the Divine requirements in these relationships. Though Himself sinless, He declares Himself in these Psalms to be the sinner, at least in the intercessory role, and He expresses to God the abhorrence of sin accompanied by the Repentance and sorrow, which man ought to feel and express but will not and cannot.

Similarly, the faith, love, obedience, and worship that man fails to give, He perfectly renders.

Thus, as the High Priest of His People, He, the True Advocate, charges Himself with the guilt of their sin and declares them to be His Own. He confesses them and repents of them, declaring at the same time His own sinlessness, and atones for them. Thus, these Psalms, and especially Psalm 51 in which the Speaker declares His Sinfulness and His Sinlessness, become quite clear of comprehension when it is recognized Who the Speaker actually is.

HIS OTHER OFFICES

Messiah's other Offices and Ministries as Son of God and Son of Man, as King and Priest, as Servant of Jehovah, as Angel of Jehovah, as the Word of God, as the Burnt-Offering, the Meal-Offering, the Peace-Offering, the Sin-Offering, the Trespass-Offering, and as the Resurrection and the Life, are all sung of in the Psalms, together with the sufferings and glories appropriate to each office.

The Gospels record the fact that He prayed; the Psalms furnish the Words of the Prayer.

THE PSALTER

The Psalter (Psalmist) is an inexhaustible source of strength, guidance, consolation, and moral teaching to the People of God, and many valuable commentaries point out these treasures. It may, therefore, in this aspect be justly regarded as a diary kept by the Lord when on Earth in which are recorded His own experiences and the experiences proper to those in whom He dwells.

However, this Commentary studies the Psalter in relation to the Messiah, His Feelings, His Manner, and His Way.

Some of these Messianic experiences were entirely personal, others representative, others sympathetic, and others proper to Him as the True Israel, the True Man, and the True Church.

The interpretation of the Psalms, therefore, belongs to Him as Messiah, to Israel as His People, and to the nations as His Possession. Its application is to all who feel their need of a Saviour from sin and from its consequences.

THE SINLESS MESSIAH

Williams said, *"Only the sinless Messiah can sing the Psalms in their fullness. It deeply affects the heart to listen to Him as He sings; especially when, as the Representative and Sin-Bearer of His people, He declares their sins, sorrows, sufferings, and chastisements to be His Own.*

"The Psalms have an application to all who in any dispensation hunger and thirst after Righteousness and in consequence suffer persecution. The Messiah as Man here suffers with His people—for how could He suffer if He were not Man? And as God He delivers them—for how could He deliver if He were not God?

"Therefore, when you read the Psalms, you are reading Jesus."

I FORESAW THE LORD

Even though the words, *"I foresaw the Lord always before My Face,"* are the words of David and, as well, pertain to the burden of his heart, still, they are more perfectly of Christ. It speaks of Jesus keeping His Eyes, Heart, Thoughts, Direction, and Very Being continually on His Father. This is actually the crux of His Prayer in the Garden of Gethsemane when He said, *"Nevertheless not My will, but Yours, be done"* (Lk. 22:42).

Even though all the Psalms, I believe, pertain to Christ, with the exception of those which pertain to the Evil One, I personally think those written by David carry one to a closer vision of Jesus than others. The reason should be obvious!

David's life was a Type of Christ in His Redemptive Role as Solomon was a Type of Christ in His Kingdom Role. David was constantly at war in one way or the other during most of his reign, typifying the battles fought by Christ for the Redemption of the souls of men. On the other hand, Solomon's reign was characterized by peace, which portrays Christ in that coming Kingdom Day.

NOTES

DAVID

Inasmuch as Jesus is called, *"The Son of David,"* the characteristics of David in this capacity are portrayed on every hand.

For instance, as Saul attempted to kill David, the religious leaders of Israel followed suit concerning Christ. As David's life was marked by constant opposition and warfare, so was the Life of Christ on Earth.

As David was ultimately betrayed by Ahithophel, his closest adviser, likewise was Jesus betrayed by Judas.

David was not only a Type of Christ but, as well, a type of Israel.

When David sinned terribly regarding Bath-sheba and his murder of her husband Uriah, this pictured Israel as having murdered Christ in the most perfidious, diabolic way. As well, David's prayer of Repentance in Psalm 51 will be the cry of Israel in that coming day when Jesus reveals Himself to them at the Second Coming (Zech. 12:10-14; 13:1-6).

The phrase, *"For He is on My Right Hand, that I should not be moved,"* refers to power, for this is what the *"Right Hand"* implies!

In Jesus it is the same, as well, with every Believer. We must not be moved from the Direct and Perfect Will of God. As well, the Lord is at our right hand in order to sustain us.

(26) "THEREFORE DID MY HEART REJOICE, AND MY TONGUE WAS GLAD; MOREOVER ALSO MY FLESH SHALL REST IN HOPE."

The record is:

1. The phrase, *"Therefore did My Heart rejoice,"* concerns Christ rejoicing over His Father's Guarantee and Protection concerning His Descent into the death world. He rejoiced in the fact that God would bring Him out, which He did!

2. The phrase, *"And My Tongue was glad,"* refers to the things He said regarding His Resurrection (Mat. 16:21; 17:23; 20:17-19; Mk. 8:31).

3. What does our *"tongue"* say regarding the Promises of God?

4. Do we speak doubt and unbelief, or do we speak the gladness of the Word?

5. *"Moreover also My Flesh shall rest in*

NOTES

hope," refers to resting in the Promises of God, referring to the Resurrection.

6. The word *"rest"* is interesting, inasmuch as it means *"a place to lodge."* So, Jesus was lodging in the Promises of God. The *"flesh"* here speaks of passions the same as in Acts 2:17.

7. The Passions of Christ were always holy because they lodged in the Promises of God.

8. This of which Jesus speaks presents the only way that the Believer can have victory over the flesh. As Jesus rested in that which His Father said He would do, we rest in that which the Father has done! Of course, He did it through Jesus Christ, which is the very Subject of Peter's Message.

(27) "BECAUSE YOU WILL NOT LEAVE MY SOUL IN HELL, NEITHER WILL YOU SUFFER YOUR HOLY ONE TO SEE CORRUPTION."

The structure is:

1. While it was definitely *"Who"* He was that effected Salvation, it was more so *"What"* He did, which refers to the Cross, that effected Salvation.

2. Jesus has always been God but merely as God, as important as that was, it really did not save anyone.

3. It took the Cross for man to be saved.

YOU WILL NOT LEAVE MY SOUL IN HELL

The phrase, *"Because You will not leave My soul in Hell,"* speaks of the three days and nights that Jesus was in the heart of the Earth following His Death by Crucifixion (Mat. 12:40).

The entirety of that region in the heart of the Earth is called *"Hell,"* which also includes the burning part of Hell and Paradise, which is separated by a gulf (Lk. 16:19-31).

Even though the entirety of the place is a prison, one might say, still, there is indication that there are special prisons even within this particular prison (I Pet. 3:18-20).

There is no Biblical evidence whatsoever that Jesus ever went into the burning side of Hell. He did go into Paradise, called *"Abraham's Bosom"* (Eph. 4:8-10). There He rescued all the righteous souls from that place who were held captive by Satan, which included every single Believer from the time of Adam to the Death of Christ on the Cross.

Since the Death and Resurrection of Christ, the souls and spirits of all Believers now go instantly to be with Jesus in Heaven at death (II Cor. 5:8; Phil. 1:21-24; Heb. 12:23; Rev. 6:9-11).

All wicked souls continue to go to Hell (the burning side) where they will remain until the Second Resurrection of Damnation, where all, even including Satan, will be placed into the Lake of Fire, there to remain forever (Isa. 14:9; Rev. 20:11-15).

THE HOLY ONE WOULD NOT SEE CORRUPTION

The phrase, *"Neither will You suffer Your Holy One to see corruption,"* can be explained in two ways:

1. Having never sinned, the Body of Jesus was perfect. Consequently, there was no seed of sin in Him, which carries with it the penalty of sickness, disease, decay, rot, and eventual death.

As a result, His Body, although dead, could not corrupt and rot as all other dead bodies; therefore, the spices of embalming placed there by Joseph were unnecessary, etc. If there is no corruption, there is no odor, which the spices were meant to stifle.

2. God raised Him from the dead even as an eternal, immortal flesh and bone Body, which had never seen corruption and could not see corruption. It is the same Body that all Believers will have in the Resurrection, referred to as *"Glorified!"* So, not only did His Physical Body not decay, it was rather *"Glorified."*

Due to the fall in the Garden of Eden, the human body begins to age immediately at birth, which is caused by corruption due to original sin. This is actually what causes the aging process, which, as well, is aided by sickness, affliction, and disease. This corruption shows in the face of all as the body ages.

As He was kept from corruption, so will all Believers at the Resurrection. Paul said, *"In a moment, in the twinkling of an eye, at the last trump: for the Trumpet shall sound, and the dead shall be raised incorruptible, and we shall be changed."*

He then said, *"For this corruptible* (corruption) *must put on incorruption, and this mortal must put on immortality"* (I Cor. 15:52-53).

(28) "YOU HAVE MADE KNOWN TO ME THE WAYS OF LIFE; YOU SHALL MAKE ME FULL OF JOY WITH YOUR COUNTENANCE."

The exegesis is:

1. The phrase, *"You have made known to Me the ways of Life,"* presents Christ as the Pattern for all to follow and, as well, presents the Resurrection not only of Himself but all Believers.

2. These *"Ways of Life"* actually refer to Jesus as *"the Way, the Truth, and the Life"* (Jn. 14:6).

3. This, as well, speaks of the Incarnation, presenting Jesus as the Representative Man. In this, the Father showed Him every single thing that was to be done because as a Man, even though The Man Christ Jesus, He had to look to the Father totally for direction. As God, He was Omniscient and had to learn nothing; however, as Man, He had to learn everything and did so from the Father, Who made known to Him the *"Ways of Life."*

4. The phrase, *"You shall make Me full of joy with Your countenance,"* speaks of the privilege of looking full into the Face of God.

5. The Psalmist said, *"Cause Your Face to shine; and we shall be saved"* (Ps. 80:3).

6. The *"Face of God"* shining upon anyone refers to the Blessings of God.

7. The *"Ways of Life"* in the first phrase, as stated, also speak of the Confidence of Christ in view of His Death and Resurrection. His Incorruption and His Soul in Sheol believed for *"The Ways of Life,"* i.e., for Resurrection and for the certitude of Ascension, i.e., the joy of Jehovah's Countenance.

(29) "MEN AND BRETHREN, LET ME FREELY SPEAK UNTO YOU OF THE PATRIARCH DAVID, THAT HE IS BOTH DEAD AND BURIED, AND HIS SEPULCHRE IS WITH US UNTO THIS DAY."

The synopsis is:

1. The phrase, *"Men and Brethren, let me freely speak unto you of the Patriarch David,"* presents the only time David is referred to in Scripture as a *"Patriarch."* Heretofore, it was applied only to Abraham and the 12 sons of Jacob (Heb. 7:4, 8-9). It is a title of dignity, signifying the head of a house.

2. It is applied here to David because he is spoken of as head of the family from which Christ sprang.

3. As well, as Abraham and Jacob's sons were founders of the Nation of Israel, David was founder of the monarchy through whom the Messiah would come.

4. *"That he is both dead and buried, and his sepulchre is with us unto this day,"* is given here to dispel the erroneous notions held by the Pharisees and religious leaders of Israel concerning the Messiah.

5. This that Peter would give showed that Christ was a Descendant of David and, as such, the True King of Israel. As well, Peter was reminding them that the Genealogy of Jesus back to David was perfect. Through Joseph, His Foster Father, Jesus went back to David through Solomon, which guaranteed the Throne rights.

6. Through Mary, His Mother, Jesus went all the way back to David also through another son, Nathan. Consequently, the genealogy was impeccable through both lines.

7. Josephus spoke of David's tomb (calling it, as Peter here did, his sepulchre) as consisting of several chambers and related how one of these chambers was opened by the High Priest, Hyrcanus, who took from it 3,000 talents of gold to give to Antiochus Pius, who was at that time laying siege to Jerusalem.

8. He added that another chamber was opened later by King Herod, who abstracted a great quantity of gold and ornaments from it; but neither of them penetrated to the vaults where the bodies of David and Solomon were deposited because the entrance to them was so carefully concealed.

9. He further mentioned that Herod, having been terrified by the bursting out of flames that stopped his further progress, built a most costly marble monument at the entrance of the tomb.

(30) "THEREFORE BEING A PROPHET,

NOTES

AND KNOWING THAT GOD HAD SWORN WITH AN OATH TO HIM, THAT OF THE FRUIT OF HIS LOINS, ACCORDING TO THE FLESH, HE WOULD RAISE UP CHRIST TO SIT ON HIS THRONE."

The order is:

1. The phrase, *"Therefore being a Prophet,"* pertains not only to what God told him concerning the Messiah coming through his lineage but, as well, the many Prophecies contained in some of the Psalms he wrote (II Sam. 7:11-16; Ps. 5, 16, 22, etc.).

2. The phrase, *"And knowing that God had sworn with an oath to him,"* refers not only to II Samuel 7:28 but, as well, to Psalm 89 where the Lord said, *"I have made a Covenant with My chosen, I have sworn unto David My servant,*

"Your seed will I establish forever, and build up your throne to all generations. Selah" (Ps. 89:3-4).

The phrase, *"That of the fruit of his loins, according to the flesh, He would raise up Christ to sit on his throne,"* pertains to the Incarnation, God becoming Man through the lineage of David.

3. David did not beget a spirit being but a flesh being with a soul and spirit.

4. The same Body of Flesh that descended from him was crucified and raised from the dead and will sit forever on His Throne (Isa. 9:6-7; Lk. 1:32-33; Rev. 11:15).

5. Furthermore, this is further proof of the bodily, fleshy Resurrection of Jesus. He was not resurrected as a spirit, but rather as a Man, exactly as He had died, albeit a Glorified Man.

6. Consequently, this shot to pieces some of the erroneous concepts held by the religious leaders of Israel regarding the Messiah. Some taught He would be a Reincarnation of one of the Prophets of old, such as Jeremiah, Isaiah, etc. Others taught He would be an extremely charismatic individual, Who would suddenly appear, etc.

As well, most knew that He would be linked to David, hence, called, *"The Son of David;"* however, almost none understood that He would be God manifest in the flesh.

(31) "HE SEEING THIS BEFORE SPOKE OF THE RESURRECTION OF CHRIST, THAT HIS SOUL WAS NOT LEFT IN HELL, NEITHER HIS FLESH DID SEE CORRUPTION."

NOTES

The diagram is:

1. The phrase, *"He seeing this before spoke of the Resurrection of Christ,"* told the religious leaders of Israel that David plainly prophesied that Jesus would be raised from the dead (Ps. 16:8-11). Therefore, they should have known Who He was and could have done so had they taken the time to properly study the Word of God; however, they, as most today, came up with ridiculous conclusions, as all will who do not know the Word.

2. It is amazingly beautiful as to how the Holy Spirit through the Apostle carefully delineated all these things from Jesus from a Scriptural viewpoint. In doing so, He portrayed the utter simplicity of what was said and should have been easily understood; however, their black hearts and rebellious ways would not allow them to properly interpret the Word of God, which is the same with many presently.

3. The phrase, *"That His soul was not left in Hell, neither His flesh did see corruption,"* proclaims the fact of His Resurrection as the first phrase proclaimed the Promise. As well, He only went to the Paradise side of Hell and not the burning side.

4. So, Peter was saying that exactly as David prophesied, it happened!

(32) "THIS JESUS HAS GOD RAISED UP, WHEREOF WE ALL ARE WITNESSES."

The composition is:

1. The phrase, *"This Jesus has God raised up,"* speaks of the physical Jesus and not some spirit.

2. *"Whereof we all are witnesses,"* spoke not only of the Apostles and others who had been in the Company of Jesus but, as well, spoke to all Israel.

3. In other words, Peter was telling them that despite what they said, they knew that Jesus was raised from the dead.

(33) "THEREFORE BEING BY THE RIGHT HAND OF GOD EXALTED, AND HAVING RECEIVED OF THE FATHER THE PROMISE OF THE HOLY SPIRIT, HE HAS SHED FORTH THIS, WHICH YOU NOW SEE AND HEAR."

The form is:

1. Why is it so difficult for man to accept Christ and the Cross?

2. Millions accept Christ or pay lip service to Him, but they reject the Cross.

3. In doing so, they are left with *"another Jesus"* (II Cor. 11:4).

THE RIGHT HAND OF GOD EXALTED

The phrase, *"Therefore being by the Right Hand of God exalted,"* proclaims where Jesus was at that particular time. As well, this was a direct repudiation—and publicly given—of the contention of the religious leaders of Israel that Jesus' Body had been stolen by His Disciples and hidden away. It's interesting to understand how they could have done this with four Roman soldiers guarding the Tomb at all times. The truth is obvious:

Jesus is the Son of David in fulfillment of the Prophecies, therefore, the Messiah, and He died to redeem humanity and was raised from the dead. As well, He appeared to many after His Resurrection, even for a period of some 40 days, and then ascended, which was also witnessed. He now sits by the Right Hand of the Father exalted!

THE PROMISE OF THE HOLY SPIRIT

The phrase, *"And having received of the Father the Promise of the Holy Spirit,"* proclaims the fact that Jesus did get back to the Father, for the Holy Spirit, which had been promised by the Father, had now come, which was obvious for all to see and hear. Jesus had said that He would send the Holy Spirit back, and that is exactly what He did (Jn. 16:7).

WHICH YOU SEE AND HEAR

The phrase, *"He has shed forth this, which you now see and hear,"* would have been better translated, *"He has poured forth this,"* for the word *"shed"* has the same meaning as the word *"pour"* in Acts 2:17.

As well, the baptism with the Holy Spirit produced something that all could *"see and hear."*

All could obviously *"see"* the individuals who had just been baptized with the Spirit, respecting certain displays of emotionalism, which caused some to think they were drunk.

NOTES

As well, many, even hundreds or more, had heard them speak with other Tongues as the Spirit of God gave the utterance.

So, when modern skeptics demean the Pentecostal experience, claiming that all is received at Conversion, such thinking is obviously unscriptural.

To be factual, almost none who are saved in these circles ever claim to have been baptized with the Holy Spirit. Actually, they know little or nothing about the Holy Spirit, with their knowledge little improved after Conversion, simply because of unbelief.

The truth is that precious few of these people, whomever they may be, are truly Born-Again. Some are, but most aren't! Most of such *"conversions"* in those circles are merely a philosophical approach, which carries no true spiritual emphasis. These preachers do not believe in the Holy Spirit, at least in the Biblical way; consequently, precious few preach any type of Anointing of the Holy Spirit for the simple reason they do not even really believe in such a thing. As a result, the Spirit of God has very little opportunity to do much of anything in such an atmosphere.

This one thing is sure: in those circles, little is produced, if at all, that one can *"see and hear."*

(34) "FOR DAVID IS NOT ASCENDED INTO THE HEAVENS: BUT HE SAID HIMSELF, THE LORD SAID UNTO MY LORD, YOU SIT ON MY RIGHT HAND."

The composition is:

1. It is the Cross of Christ that made the baptism with the Holy Spirit possible.

2. The blood of bulls and goats could not take away sins, so individuals before the Cross could not be baptized with the Spirit (Heb. 10:4).

3. Where the Holy Spirit before the Cross was with the Saints, since the Cross, He is in the Saints. There is a vast difference in this.

A MISINTERPRETATION OF SCRIPTURE

The phrase, *"For David is not ascended into the Heavens,"* was stated by Peter to prove that these Prophecies were not given to David concerning himself, but rather the One to come, namely the Lord Jesus Christ. As he had already said concerning

David, *"That he is both dead and buried, and his sepulchre is with us unto this day"* (Acts 2:29).

Evidently, some of the religious leaders were attempting to claim that these Prophecies had nothing to do with Jesus, but rather pertained to David personally, which Peter here repudiated.

"But he said himself," refers to the Prophecy given by David concerning the coming Messiah, which the next phrase will prove (Ps. 110:1). *"The LORD said unto my Lord, You sit on My Right Hand,"* harks back to the very words Jesus had spoken in Mark 12:35-37. Peter was using this Passage pretty much as it was used by Jesus.

Jesus had asked this question of the people: How is it that the Scribes say that Christ (Messiah) is the Son of David? (Mk. 12:35).

The word or title, *"Christ,"* is the transliteration of the Greek word, *"Christos,"* which means, *"The Anointed One."* It also means *"Messiah."*

It has the idea of the future King of Israel Who will someday reign on the Throne of David.

When Jesus used the word, *"Son,"* as in, *"Son of David,"* he was speaking of a descendant.

LORD

As well, the word *"Lord"* is the translation of the Greek word *"Kurios,"* which itself means *"Master, one Who has power over another,"* and, in effect, is the translation of the august title of God in the Old Testament, namely Jehovah. It has implications of Deity, as should be obvious!

Both the Scribes and the people, at least for the most part, believed that the Jewish Messiah would come from the Royal Line of David. David was human, and so would the Messiah be human. Thus, He would be David's son.

Our Lord reminded His Hearers that David called the Messiah his Lord (Ps. 110:1). That is, he recognized Him as Deity, the Jehovah of the Old Testament.

Consequently, the difficulty our Lord put before His Listeners and, at the same time, tossed into the lap of the Pharisees, was how, since Messiah is Jehovah, Deity, He could also be human. At once the Incarnation was brought before them, God becoming Man, and through the lineage of David.

NOTES

However, the Jewish leaders, despite the incontestable proof, rejected the teaching of the Incarnation and Jesus' Claim to Deity.

It is well to notice our Lord's Testimony to the Divine Inspiration of David.

So Peter used the same argument as used previously by Jesus, which proclaimed Jesus as the Messiah and showed exactly how it was done, with God becoming Man through the lineage of David and, therefore, *"David's Son."*

As the religious leaders were speechless before Jesus, they continued to be speechless before Peter. They had no answer to the obvious Biblical proof!

(35) "UNTIL I MAKE YOUR FOES YOUR FOOTSTOOL."

The exposition is:

1. Man is what the Holy Spirit says he is.
2. He is ungodly with no righteousness whatsoever!
3. To this dilemma, the Cross of Christ alone holds the answer.

THE FOES

This Scripture tells us that even though the Plan of Redemption is complete, even with the Mighty Holy Spirit sent back in order to occupy the hearts and lives of Believers, still, all the *"foes"* of Righteousness, although defeated, have not yet been banished. However, the Feet of Christ on their heads is a foregone conclusion!

So, the Lord is presently seated by the Right Hand of the Father, with the Holy Spirit, the Third Person of the Trinity, on Earth, working through the Body of Christ to destroy the works of the devil (I Jn. 3:8).

About 3,000 years have come and gone since David prophesied these words and about 2,000 years since repeated by Peter. Consequently, we are closer than ever to this glorious moment being fulfilled.

According to Bible Prophecy, the Rapture of the Church could take place at any time. Regrettably and sadly, the church has already entered into the great apostasy predicted by Paul (II Thess. 2:3; I Tim. 4:1; II Tim. 2:1-5).

NOTES

The world after the Rapture will then be plunged into the Great Tribulation, predicted by Jesus in Matthew 24:21.

At the end of that dread time, Jesus Christ will come back to this Earth and will instantly overthrow the Antichrist and set up a Kingdom, ruling Personally from Jerusalem. Most of the *"foes"* will be then put away.

THAT WHICH IS COMING

However, at the conclusion of the one thousand year Reign, Satan will be loosed from the bottomless pit where he has been incarcerated for the past one thousand years, with the last battle between good and evil being fought at that time (Rev. 20:7-10).

Satan will then be locked away forever in the Lake of Fire, along with all demons and fallen Angels, as well as every unbeliever (Rev. 20:10-15).

At that time, there will be a *"New Heaven and a New Earth,"* actually referring to them passing from one condition to another rather than being destroyed. According to Peter, they will be cleansed by fire, which will rid all of God's Creation of all evil (II Pet. 3:10-13).

At that time, the New Jerusalem will come down from Heaven to Planet Earth, with God literally changing His Headquarters to this new address (Rev., Chpts. 21-22).

Paul wrote, *"Then comes the end, when He* (Jesus) *shall have delivered up the Kingdom to God, even the Father; when He* (Jesus) *shall have put down all rule and all authority and power."*

He then said, *"For He* (Jesus) *must reign, till He has put all enemies under His Feet"* (I Cor. 15:24-25).

As well, as an aside, it is well to notice the recognition by David of the two other Persons of the Trinity, the Father saying to the Son, *"You sit on My Right Hand, till I make Your enemies Your footstool."* Thus, when we consider that Jesus (Mk. 12:35-37) and Peter both ascribed Divine Inspiration to David, which is done by the Holy Spirit (II Pet. 1:20-21), we have the Trinity mentioned in an Old Testament setting in Mark 12:36, as well as by Peter.

(36) "THEREFORE LET ALL THE HOUSE OF ISRAEL KNOW ASSUREDLY, THAT GOD HAS MADE THAT SAME JESUS, WHOM YOU HAVE CRUCIFIED, BOTH LORD AND CHRIST."

The synopsis is:

1. The phrase, *"Therefore let all the house of Israel know assuredly,"* is leveled by Peter directly toward the religious leadership of Israel and is inspired by the Holy Spirit. In other words, the Holy Spirit wanted him to say that which he did say; consequently, we find a totally different type of preaching than most of the modern variety.

2. Thousands of preachers boast that they never say anything negative. Regrettably, they seldom preach the Gospel either!

3. This which the Holy Spirit demanded that Peter say is about as negative as anything could ever be; however, it was necessary, as should be obvious. When Peter was finished, the *"House of Israel"* would have absolutely no doubt as to what had been said and what it meant. It must also be said that this is the manner in which the Holy Spirit works.

4. The stakes are too high for people to leave not knowing exactly what the Holy Spirit has said!

5. *"That God has made that same Jesus, Whom you have crucified, both Lord and Christ,"* laid down the gauntlet exactly as it was.

6. The religious leadership of Israel rejected Jesus, but God, Whom they professed to serve, did not. Actually, He made the very one they crucified *"Both Lord and Christ."*

7. The title *"Lord"* means that Jesus was and is *"Jehovah,"* and the title *"Christ"* means that He was and is Israel's *"Messiah"* and the world's *"Redeemer."*

8. So, in effect, they killed the Lord in the Name of the Lord!

(37) "NOW WHEN THEY HEARD THIS, THEY WERE PRICKED IN THEIR HEART, AND SAID UNTO PETER AND TO THE REST OF THE APOSTLES, MEN AND BRETHREN, WHAT SHALL WE DO?"

The composition is:

1. The phrase, *"Now when they heard this, they were pricked in their heart,"* shows us what the Word of God does when preached under the Anointing of the Holy Spirit. These people were convicted mightily by the Holy Spirit! Consequently, we are

given here a description as to what happens when individuals are convicted of sin.

2. Actually, other than the Ministry of Jesus, this was the first time that the Holy Spirit could work exactly in this manner. It was a new day made possibly by what Jesus did at Calvary and the Resurrection.

3. Now the Holy Spirit was in Peter, giving him the Message to preach and anointing him to preach it.

4. That is why the preaching of the Gospel under the Anointing of the Spirit is the most powerful, persuasive factor on the face of the Earth. It alone brings souls to Christ; however, as we shall see, it also arouses tremendous opposition among most religious leaders, as well as the world.

5. This is the only type of preaching that gets results. If it is possible for a person, city, or nation to be saved, this is the only way it can be done.

6. *"And said unto Peter and to the rest of the Apostles,"* presents the convicting Power of the Holy Spirit taking a deadly toll among these thousands who stood there that day; consequently, they addressed Peter and the other Apostles. Their question would be just as pointed as his Message.

7. The question, *"Men and Brethren, what shall we do?"* proclaims these people ready to get right with God.

8. Inasmuch as this was the Day of Pentecost, untold thousands of Jews were in Jerusalem from all over the Roman Empire, as well as Israel itself. Consequently, of many of those who gave their hearts to the Lord that day, undoubtedly, some were from Gentile areas far off, even as Acts 2:7-11 proclaims. So, they would take the Gospel back to their places of domicile, wherever that may have been.

(38) "THEN PETER SAID UNTO THEM, REPENT, AND BE BAPTIZED EVERY ONE OF YOU IN THE NAME OF JESUS CHRIST FOR THE REMISSION OF SINS, AND YOU SHALL RECEIVE THE GIFT OF THE HOLY SPIRIT."

The record is:

1. If Christ and His Cross are not accepted fully, God will not accept the seeker.

2. Unredeemed man is loath to accept the Cross because the Cross tells man how Righteous God is and how unrighteous man is.

3. The fact that man is so sinful, wicked, and vile that it would take such a price, the price of the Cross, in order to redeem him strikes a nerve.

NOTES

PETER

The phrase, *"Then Peter said unto them, Repent,"* proclaims the answer not only of Peter but that of which the Holy Spirit had given him. In other words, the Holy Spirit through the Apostle demanded Repentance on the part of the people.

To repent is to make a decision that changes the total direction of one's life.

In Jesus' Ministry, He concentrated on the same theme (Mat. 4:17; Mk. 6:12). Later, when Jesus Himself had become the issue, the call to Repentance was a call to change one's mind about Him and to make a personal commitment to Him (Lk. 13:3, 5; Acts 3:19).

In this Age of Grace, it is God's Kindness in withholding merited judgment that gives human beings time to repent (Rom. 2:4).

Actually, God requires both Repentance and Faith on the part of the individual in order for one to be saved.

Paul said, *"Testifying both to the Jews, and also to the Greeks* (Gentiles), *Repentance toward God, and Faith toward our Lord Jesus Christ"* (Acts 20:21).

Repentance toward God is required because it is God Whom we have offended.

FAITH TOWARD JESUS CHRIST

As well, we must have *"Faith toward Jesus Christ"* because He is the One Who has paid the price for man's Salvation, making it possible for man to be saved.

Actually, one who truly repents has Faith, for it is Faith in God that is expressed when we carry out a decision to turn from our old ways and to commit ourselves to God's Ways, which characterizes Repentance.

It is regrettable when many in the modern Charismatic community deny Repentance as a New Testament Doctrine, claiming that it belongs entirely to the Old Covenant Doctrine. As should be obvious, such portrays a lack of knowledge concerning man's offense toward God, which does not change the Covenant whatsoever.

While it is true that Paul greatly expressed Faith in Jesus Christ as a requirement for Salvation while mentioning Repentance only sparingly, this was for a reason (Eph. 2:8).

Repentance has never been the issue, with it held out constantly in Old Testament Times and, as well, carried over into the New Covenant, which is fundamental; however, Faith in Christ was the great controversy then and actually still is.

Consequently, Paul, under the Guidance of the Holy Spirit, placed far more emphasis on Faith in Christ, as he should have done.

Actually, somewhere around the world, millions repent each day, but without Faith in Christ, which does them no good whatsoever.

Untold numbers repent concerning the imbibing of alcohol, but no change is effected. The same could be said for gambling, drugs, etc.

For Repentance to be effective it must not only be directed toward God but, as well, one must have Faith in Jesus Christ and what He did for us at the Cross. Without the latter, the former is not recognized by God and, in fact, cannot be, and is therefore useless.

At the same time, proper Faith toward Christ will also result in a proper Repentance toward God. Properly carried out, the two are inextricable.

BECAUSE YOUR SINS HAVE BEEN REMITTED

The phrase, *"And be baptized every one of you in the Name of Jesus Christ for the remission of sins,"* should have been translated, *"Because of remission of sins."*

The word *"for"* in the Greek is *"eis,"* and points to something that has already been done, in other words, past tense.

The way it is presently translated, it makes it sound as if Water Baptism within itself remits sins, which it does not!

Water Baptism takes place after Repentance and, consequently, after one's sins have been washed away by the Blood of Jesus.

Water Baptism is *"the answer of a good conscience toward God,"* and has nothing to do with one's Salvation (I Pet. 3:21).

NOTES

Regrettably, false doctrines have been vigorously promoted respecting this very Scripture, with its words twisted and, consequently, its meaning distorted.

THE CLAIM THAT WATER BAPTISM SAVES

Water Baptism does not save.

As Peter was the one speaking in Acts 2:38, let us quote that which he also said in the first Book that bears his name:

"Which sometime were disobedient, when once the longsuffering of God waited in the days of Noah, while the Ark was a preparing, wherein few, that is, eight souls were saved by water.

"The like figure whereunto even Baptism does also now save us (not the putting away of the filth of the flesh, but the answer of a good conscience toward God), *by the Resurrection of Jesus Christ"* (I Pet. 3:20-21).

The phrase, *"Eight souls were saved by water,"* in speaking of Noah's Ark, does not mean these people were saved from sin, but that they were saved from drowning by being in the Ark, which was carried forth by the water, as is obvious.

As well, Water Baptism does not save us, but the *"like figure whereunto even Baptism does also now save us."*

Is it the water that saves or the thing of which it is a figure?

It was not the water that saved the eight persons in Noah's Ark, but it was actually the Ark itself that saved them from drowning in the flood, which was borne up by the water.

So, baptism in water does not save the soul, but Faith in the Death, Burial, and Resurrection of Jesus Christ, that of which baptism is a figure, does save the soul (Rom. 6:4-5; I Cor. 15:1-4; Eph. 1:13-14; Col. 1:20-22).

A MERE FIGURE HAS NO SALVATION

A mere figure can have no power to save, but the reality of the figure can.

Peter, lest some should trust in Water Baptism to save the soul (as many have) made it very clear that baptism does not save one from the filth or moral depravity of the flesh. He showed Water Baptism to be only the answer of a good conscience toward God, one that has been made clean by Faith in Christ and what He did for us at the Cross.

It is clear here that at baptism, the conscience is already supposed to be good and clean, and baptism merely answers to it.

As the waters of the Flood could not have saved the eight persons in Noah's Ark had they not made use of the Ark, so the water of baptism does not save the soul of anyone, but does testify figuratively to the Salvation that has already come to the individual by Faith (Rom. 1:16; 3:24-25; 10:9-10)

WHAT WATER BAPTISM SYMBOLIZES

It symbolizes the Death, Burial, and Resurrection of Christ.

- Water Baptism also symbolizes the death of the old man, what we were before we came to Christ. In the Mind of God, when you accepted Christ as your Saviour, you were literally placed in Christ, in His Death (Rom. 6:3-5).
- When you were placed under the water, that, as well, was a symbolism of all your sins forever being buried. In other words, when Christ was put in the Tomb, all your sins were, in essence, put in that Tomb with Him. One might even say that you were buried with Him.
- When you were brought up out of the water, that was a symbolism of Christ being raised from the dead and you, in essence, being raised from the dead with Him that you might now walk in Newness of Life. This is the way that Paul put it:

"Do you not know, that so many of us as were baptized into Jesus Christ were baptized into His Death?" (This is not speaking of Water Baptism as many believe, but rather the Crucifixion, Burial, and Resurrection of Christ, and us being in Him when all of this took place).

"Therefore we are buried with Him by baptism into death," which refers to all of our sins being buried with Him as well.

Then it says, *"Like as Christ was raised up from the dead by the Glory of the Father, even so we also should walk in newness of life"* (Rom. 6:3-5).

- We died with Him....

NOTES

- We were buried with Him....
- His Resurrection was our Resurrection to a *"Newness of Life."*

BY GRACE ARE YOU SAVED THROUGH FAITH

Paul said, *"For by Grace are you saved through Faith; and that not of yourselves, it is the Gift of God:*

"Not of works, lest any man should boast" (Eph. 2:8-9).

The moment that one trusts in the water to save, or anything else for that matter other than Christ and what He did for us at the Cross, that is the moment one has entered into *"works,"* which nullifies Grace. This means that anytime we tie anything to Salvation, such as Water Baptism, the Lord's Supper, or joining a church, irrespective as to what it might be, we have then left Grace and have gone into works, which God can never accept.

As someone has said, *"Water Baptism is an outward sign of an inward work, already accomplished."*

THE WATER BAPTISM FORMULA

Trinitarians baptize according to Matthew 28:19, using the Words of the Lord Jesus Christ where He said that we should baptize, *"In the Name of the Father, and of the Son, and of the Holy Spirit."*

As well, there is a group of Pentecostals, good people I might quickly add, who sincerely love the Lord, who baptize in the Name of Jesus only, using a variety of formulas among themselves, etc.

Let us look for a moment at baptismal formulas.

THE ARGUMENTS

The Jesus Only people affirm that the Matthew 28:19 method is not once found in the Book of Acts and was unknown in the Early Church but was introduced centuries later by apostates in total disregard of apostolic practice.

Trinitarians are, therefore, admonished to conform to the Scriptural pattern and to follow the example of those who have the true *"Revelation"* of the Name. This is taken to mean that unless one is baptized in the Name of Jesus Christ only, he cannot be forgiven his sins, etc.

(Even though very brief, I think this is probably the sum total of the Jesus Only doctrine concerning the *"method"* of Water Baptism.)

NAMES

The Jesus Only people claim that the words, *"Father"* and *"Son,"* do not constitute names. We maintain they do!

We believe that Matthew 28:19 definitely confirms that *"Father"* is a Name, that *"Son"* is a Name, and that *"Holy Spirit"* is a Name simply because we are not generalizing just any father or just any son. We are talking about God the Father and God the Son. Most anyone in Christendom today would readily recognize and know of Whom is being spoken.

In Isaiah 9:6, the Bible says His Name shall be called, *"Wonderful, Counselor, the Mighty God, the Everlasting Father, the Prince of Peace."* Each one of these appellations would be labeled a title by Jesus Only interpreters, but Isaiah's Text calls each one a *"Name."*

This is also the one Verse in the entirety of God's Word where Jesus Christ is called the Father; and still, somehow these people are blinded to the fact that the Verse actually disproves their theory concerning titles and names simply because it gives the name of *"Father"* to Jesus.

Incidentally, the Holy Spirit referred to Jesus in this capacity as *"Father"* because Jesus is, in fact, the Father of Salvation.

Concerning this, Paul said, *"For Whom He* (God the Father) *did foreknow* (had foreknowledge as God does), *He also did predestinate to be conformed to the image of His Son, that He* (Jesus) *might be the Firstborn among many Brethren"* (Rom. 8:29).

The word *"firstborn"* in the Greek is *"prototokos"* and means in this case that Jesus is the Father of the great Salvation Plan, and is so by virtue of His going to the Cross and paying there the price for man's Redemption.

So, Jesus was referred to as *"Father"* by the Prophet Isaiah because He is the Father of all Redemption. It does not mean that Jesus Christ is God the Father. Jesus Christ is God, but He is not the Father, but rather the *"Only Begotten Son of the Father"* (Mat. 3:17).

Going back to Isaiah 9:6, according to that Prophet, isn't *"Wonderful"* a Name? Isn't *"Prince of Peace"* a Name? Isaiah used five different Names here, and yet, under Divine Inspiration, he specifically chose the singular when he said, *"And His Name shall be called...."* So what more needs to be said in answer to this strange insistence that if *"Father, Son, and Holy Spirit"* are Names (plural), then Matthew 28:19 should be read, *"In the Names of"*?

The writers, under Divine Inspiration, used the singular in Matthew instead of the plural. They did it for a Divine reason. The Trinity must be acknowledged.

THE BOOK OF ACTS AND THE BAPTISMAL FORMULA

There is not a single incident in the Book of Acts where any particular baptismal method is given. There is no record of the dialogue of the Baptizer while standing in the water with the Convert. You will look in vain for any Scripture which states, *"I baptize you in the Name of Jesus Christ"* (or any other variation of the Precious Name of our Lord). If one could produce such an explicit procedure, I would be thrilled to admit that we have a Scriptural right to baptize thus, but it cannot be produced because it does not exist.

THE WEAKNESS OF THIS POSITION

This immeasurably weakens the Jesus Only position. They have read into the record that which is not there. They have taken the words of Peter, assumed that they were the properly expressed formula, and placed them onto the lips of those who baptized in water—without a shred of Biblical evidence to support their action.

The Jesus Only proponents claim that Acts 2:38 is the baptismal formula. And yet, Acts 8:16 and Acts 19:5 simply state they were baptized in the Name of the Lord Jesus. If you will notice in these two latter Verses, the word, *"Christ,"* is omitted altogether.

If Peter, on the Day of Pentecost, received a baptism *"Revelation,"* which the Jesus

NOTES

Only proponents claim is, *"In the name of Jesus Christ,"* why, we may ask, is this later variation produced?

You see, there is no fixed wording to follow. There is no regular or prescribed usage of certain words. So the question has to be asked, *"Should we baptize in the Name of Jesus Christ, in Christ Jesus, in the Lord, in the Lord Jesus, or in the Lord Jesus Christ?"* Which would be correct? Was Peter right, was Philip right, or was Paul right?

Jesus Only exponents say they are sticklers (fanatics) for the exact Words of Scripture and that they use the identical words of the Apostles; yet their demands are not accompanied by quotations from God's Word.

Even in those Passages where their purported words are found, their full formula is lacking. One of their chief proponents some years ago stated that the following formula should be used: *"I baptize you in the Name of the Lord Jesus Christ, which is the Name of the Father, and of the Son, and of the Holy Spirit."* When this particular brother was asked to cite Chapter and Verse for this formula, he was speechless. Apparently it had not occurred to him that the formula he had conjured up had no Scriptural connotation whatsoever.

SO WHAT IS THE RIGHT BAPTISMAL FORMULA TO BE USED?

The question still must be asked, *"Which is the right way to baptize and what was the meaning of Peter's or Paul's words in the Book of Acts?"*

There is no way one can take the Passages in the Book of Acts to be intended as a baptismal formula. Therefore, the words in Acts should be regarded as a compendious description of the entire rite. In Acts 2:38, 8:16, 10:48, and 19:5, the details of the baptismal ceremony are not set forth. What is set forth is a condensed, brief, and abridged reference to the Sacred experience. The words described the sphere, the foundation, or the ground of baptism, rather than the prescribed words of the formula.

Every Trinitarian using the Matthew 28:19 formula refers to Water Baptism as *"Christian Baptism,"* and this is as it should be, for Christ is assuredly the central figure in Water Baptism.

Jesus Christ is the one Who died and rose again, not the Father and not the Holy Spirit. It is into His Death that we are symbolically buried, and in the likeness of His Resurrection, we are raised to walk in Newness of Life; therefore, belief in and confession of the Lord Jesus Christ is a central part of our baptismal ceremony.

THE REASONS WE ACCEPT THE MATTHEW 28:19 BAPTISMAL FORMULA

- Both the Minister and the Believer render obedience to the Master's own explicit Command whenever the words are used, *"In the Name of the Father, and of the Son, and of the Holy Spirit."*
- Matthew 28:19 fits the definition of a formula. It is an orderly statement of Faith and Doctrine. It is the prescribed works of a ceremony or rite. The Words of the Lord Himself are all contained in one concise declaration.

It is not necessary, as in the Jesus Only formula, to combine it with other Scriptures in order to get the complete Name. It is complete within itself.

- Matthew 28:19 incorporates an orderly statement of Faith. It summarizes the scattered and unsystematized thought and language of the entire New Testament concerning the Nature of the Godhead.

Actually, if one will carefully read the four Gospels, one will find that Jesus constantly reduced extremely complex subjects into short, abbreviated statements, which, in effect, explained those complex subjects so readily that they could be understood even by a child. Please check the following Passages: Matthew 19:4-9; 22:21, 29-32, 37-40; 29:19.

Jesus spoke the Words of Matthew 28:19 and did so that they may be used as the formula. This Passage is purposely designed to set forth the Doctrine of the Trinity in this initiatory Christian rite. The Master's own Baptism by John was a vivid precedent for associating the Trinity with baptism. Jesus was there in Person. God spoke from Heaven and the Holy Spirit descended like a Dove upon Him.

NOTES

THE COMMAND

• Matthew 28:19 is the only Command in the entire Bible given specifically to those performing the Rite of Water Baptism. If you will examine all of the Passages in Acts dealing with baptism, you will discover that the Commands there are to the Believers themselves and not to the Baptizer or the Minister.

Matthew 28:19 is a direct order given by Christ to those who administer the ordinance informing them to baptize *"In the Name of the Father, and of the Son, and of the Holy Spirit."*

• It is unthinkable that the Disciples disobeyed the express Command of their Lord. The only logical and Scriptural conclusion is that the Apostles and other leaders not only obeyed His Command to baptize, but also obeyed His Command to *"baptize in the Name of the Father, and of the Son, and of the Holy Spirit."*

• The Matthew 28:19 baptismal formula is abundantly confirmed by the earliest Christian writings, while the Jesus Only formula has no historical support at all.

Justin's first apology was written in A.D. 153 about 90 years after the death of Peter and Paul. It was about 60 years after the death of John the Apostle.

Justin was a contemporary of Polycarp, who was a disciple of John himself, and he stated that Matthew 28:19 was the correct formula.

There is another book called the, *"Teaching of the Twelve Apostles,"* and it is the oldest book outside the New Testament. It is also known as the *"Didache"* and is dated by most authorities between the years A.D. 70 and 100.

Although the author of the book is unknown, it is a compilation of the teachings of the Apostles, which he had apparently learned either by personal instruction, oral tradition, through their (the Apostles') own writings, or other New Testament writings then in circulation.

MORE PROOF

While it does not possess the inspiration of the Scriptures, the *"Didache"* is an authentic record of primitive Christianity. It includes as instructions for baptizing in water that we ought to baptize *"In the Name of the Father, and of the Son, and of the Holy Spirit,"* and also that we ought to baptize in living or running water.

There again, the Matthew 28:19 formula is used. Lest we forget, I would remind you that there is not a single recorded incident in the Bible, or any other genuine First Century book, where any other formula was ever used in the first 100 years of the Christian era.

It should go without saying that if the Apostles and others baptized in a different manner, surely something would have been said about such in all the material that was produced in that particular time. Nothing was said because such was not done.

• Matthew 28:19 can be used as the formula and the baptism still be in the Name of Jesus Christ because the Son is Jesus Christ. Jesus Christ is the Sphere, the Foundation, and the Ground for Trinitarian baptism.

Belief in and confession of Christ is the very heart of our baptism. Consequently, the words spoken by most Ministers of the Gospel, baptizing according to Matthew 28:19, follow this pattern: *"On the confession of your Faith in the Lord Jesus Christ, I baptize you in the Name of the Father, and of the Son, and of the Holy Spirit."*

THE GIFT OF THE HOLY SPIRIT

The phrase, *"And you shall receive the Gift of the Holy Spirit,"* tells us two things:

1. A person has to be Saved, in other words, have his sins remitted by Faith in Christ, before he can be baptized with the Holy Spirit.

2. As closely attached as this Promise is to the Salvation experience, we learn that it is absolutely imperative that after Conversion, the Believer go on immediately and be baptized with the Holy Spirit. In other words, after Salvation, whether moments after or shortly after, the Believer should ask the Lord for the Holy Spirit baptism which, as should be obvious, is totally different than Water Baptism.

Also, as Salvation is a Gift, the Holy Spirit likewise falls into the same pattern. As the sinner cannot merit Salvation, neither can

NOTES

the Believer merit the Infilling of the Holy Spirit. All is given by the Grace of God, and all must be received in the same manner.

• The Believer must understand, when we come to Christ, we are literally baptized into His Death, His Burial, and His Resurrection (Rom. 6:3-5). This baptism has absolutely nothing to do with Water Baptism. In fact, the Holy Spirit through the Apostle and others uses the word *"baptism"* either literally or figuratively. Many people confuse the word *"baptism"* in Romans, Chapter 6, with Water Baptism. The Apostle was not speaking there, as stated, of Water Baptism, but rather, as also stated, the baptism into Christ, which takes place at Conversion. Please notice the following Scripture:

"I indeed baptize you with water unto Repentance: but He Who comes after me is mightier than I, Whose shoes I am not worthy to bear: He shall baptize you with the Holy Spirit, and with fire" (Mat. 3:11).

The Prophet John the Baptist used the word *"baptized"* in this Eleventh Verse at first literally, and then, when he spoke of the Holy Spirit, he used the word *"baptized"* figuratively.

In fact, the Believer is to be subjected to three baptisms. Let me explain:

1. The baptism into Christ, which takes place when we are converted (Rom. 6:1-5; Col. 2:10-15).

2. Baptism into Water (Mat. 28:19).

3. The baptism with the Holy Spirit (Acts 2:4).

(39) "FOR THE PROMISE IS UNTO YOU, AND TO YOUR CHILDREN, AND TO ALL WHO ARE AFAR OFF, EVEN AS MANY AS THE LORD OUR GOD SHALL CALL."

The record is:

1. The answer to victorious, overcoming, Biblical living is the Cross of Christ.

2. In fact, the Cross of Christ is the solution to every problem.

3. It was there that Christ paid the price for everything that we might need.

THE PROMISE

The phrase, *"For the Promise is unto you,"* was directed toward the many Jews standing in the Temple listening to Peter that day, as well as all Believers at that time.

He was telling them that what was happening was not just for the Apostles or the other Believers who had been filled but, as well, was extended to those listening, and all others for that matter.

So, this shoots down the idea promoted by some that this was for the Apostles only. A mere preliminary investigation of the Outpouring of the Holy Spirit will debunk this error.

The word *"Promise"* as here used signifies a *"pledge"* on the Part of God.

As well, as should be obvious, the entire tenor of that which Peter said portrays Salvation and the Gift of the Holy Spirit as two different experiences altogether. Assuredly, this totally abrogates the erroneous contention made by many in the modern church that all people upon Salvation automatically are baptized with the Spirit, and consequently, there is no experience thereafter. Verses 38 and 39 completely repudiate such thinking.

At the same time, as Jesus used the word, *"Promise,"* concerning the Infilling of the Holy Spirit (Acts 1:4), it holds the connotation of much more than meets the eye.

The Lord would not *"promise"* something unless it was of infinite value. It would be pointless otherwise. Accordingly, there is absolutely nothing more valuable or significant to the Believer than the baptism with the Holy Spirit. As Salvation is such to the world, the baptism with the Holy Spirit is such to the Believer.

If one fully recognizes the significance of this, understanding that everything the Lord does in the heart and life of the Believer is done through the Person and Agency of the Holy Spirit, then one begins to realize how very important this is.

TO ALL WHO ARE AFAR OFF

The tragedy is that even most Believers who are Spirit-filled little take advantage of what the Spirit can actually do within their hearts and lives. Perhaps all of us fall into this category, at least to a certain extent! My prayer is that the Lord will help us to understand the significance of this, and to take full advantage of all that He can do and what He can help us to be.

"And to your children," means that this great Outpouring of the Holy Spirit did not stop with the initial outpouring, but continues on.

"And to all who are afar off," speaks of geography, meaning that this was not given just for Jerusalem but, in fact, for the entirety of the world, and for all Believers for all time.

"Even as many as the Lord our God shall call," does not place a limit on this call as some teach and believe.

Jesus said, *"Come unto Me, all you who labor and are heavy laden, and I will give you rest"* (Mat. 11:28).

The word *"all"* tells us the extent of this *"call."* It covers all of humanity for all time! The *"Promise"* is to *"Whosoever will"* and will never change (Jn. 7:37-39; Rev. 22:17).

(40) "AND WITH MANY OTHER WORDS DID HE TESTIFY AND EXHORT, SAYING, SAVE YOURSELVES FROM THIS UNTOWARD GENERATION."

The diagram is:

1. Peter's Message was much longer than the compendium of which we are given here.

2. When he said, *"Save yourselves from this untoward generation,"* little did he realize how prophetic that was.

3. In A.D. 70, which would be about 37 years into the future, this entire city of Jerusalem would be completely destroyed by the Romans, with over one million Jews killed in this carnage.

MANY WORDS

The phrase, *"And with many other words did he testify and exhort,"* tells us that the part of his Message recorded in this Second Chapter of Acts is only part of that which he said. Actually, I suspect that the account of most of the Messages we are given in the Word of God is only a part of what was originally said; however, we do have that which the Holy Spirit wanted us to have, and that is all that is necessary.

"Saying, Save yourselves from this untoward generation," although simply put, is one of the weightiest statements that these people would ever hear.

NOTES

Of course, it was a call to Repentance, as is obvious; however, for these who were listening that day, this statement pointed to something that was about to happen, which would be the most terrible thing that Israel had ever experienced up to this present time.

"This untoward generation," of which Peter spoke, is, as is obvious, the generation that crucified Christ. Consequently, their sin was more than heavy; it was absolutely devastating. In fact, no generation that has ever lived in human history would compare with this generation, as far as rebellion against God is concerned.

THE DESTRUCTION OF JERUSALEM

About 37 years later, the Roman general Titus, commanding the Roman Tenth Legion, laid siege to Jerusalem and when it was all over, the city was completely destroyed, with over one million Jews dying in that carnage. The Roman commanders crucified Jews by the literal tens of thousands. Actually, had one stood on a nearby hill overlooking the city, the sight would have been gruesome beyond comprehension.

Josephus, the Jewish historian, said that so many were crucified that there were simply no more places to put crosses. In other words, every available foot of ground in the city and surrounding the city was used for this gruesome task.

Hundreds of thousands of Jews were sold as slaves for trifling prices, so much so, in fact, that the price per slave in all markets dropped drastically.

Remarkably enough, not one Christian lost his life in this carnage. They all remembered the Words of Jesus when He said, *"And when you shall see Jerusalem compassed with armies, then know that the desolation thereof is nigh."*

He then said, *"Then let them which are in Judaea flee to the mountains; and let them which are in the midst of it depart out; and let not them who are in the countries enter thereinto"* (Lk. 21:20-21).

In respect to this terrible time, it is said that Titus himself groaned and threw up his hands in horror and called God to witness that he was not responsible.

No fewer than 600,000 who were thrown out the gates were counted by the Romans. As stated, over one million died at that time, plus multitudes of others not counted who perished in other ways.

So, Peter's Message was of far greater import than anyone could ever know. Likewise, it is little different at present:

SAVE YOURSELF

The call to come to God is the most serious call that anyone could ever entertain. In essence, it is little different, if at all, than that said by Peter some 2,000 year ago, *"Save yourself from this untoward generation."*

Regrettably, as stated many times, a great segment of the modern church claims that this generation is the best one of all, with the next one to be even better; however, that is not what the Bible says. It says the opposite (II Tim. 2:1-5).

In truth, this is the generation of apostasy. Sadly, it will not get better, but rather continue to degenerate. I realize that most do not desire to hear such statements, but they happen to be true.

Whether believed or not, the world is heading toward Armageddon, but before that, the Antichrist is going to make his debut. He will be Satan's trump card, in other words, his last effort so to speak. The Rapture of the Church is getting closer by the moment, and yet, most of the church has little knowledge whatsoever of the Doctrine called the *"Rapture."* Scores who do know of this Bible Doctrine do not believe it, claiming other things. Nevertheless, despite the unbelief, the Trump of God is soon to sound. We had better believe that (I Thess. 4:16-17).

However, at the same time that the apostasy is deepening, a great Move of God, I believe, at least as it regards people being saved and Believers being baptized with the Holy Spirit, is going to touch this world, even as it was during the time of the Early Church. However, because of modern technology, it can cover the entirety of the world.

THE FORMER RAIN AND THE LATTER RAIN

The Jews and Israel were about to be destroyed while, at the same time, the Lord was pouring out His Spirit in an unprecedented way. The same identical thing is going to happen now, except this judgment will touch the entirety of the world along with the Jews. So, the parallels in the *"Former Rain"* are very similar to the *"Latter Rain."* They must not be overlooked or dismissed lightly.

Matthew, Chapter 24, deals with these very days in which we live now, which speaks of the coming Great Tribulation and Israel's coming sorrow.

Luke, Chapter 21, says almost the same words, but yet, certain things are given that let us know that Jesus was now speaking of the carnage that was soon to come on Israel a short time later, even in A.D. 70. Even though all given by Jesus, whether in Matthew or Luke, pertains basically to the Jews and, as stated, deal with two periods of time, still, as the Church was impacted then, it will be impacted now.

Then Israel was the apostate church and was ultimately destroyed. The true Church, which we refer to as the *"Early Church,"* was not destroyed, but only because they heeded the warning to flee from the area.

At present, the apostate church is in the realm of Christianity. To be sure, it will continue to apostatize more and more, eventually aiding and abetting the Antichrist when he makes his bid for power.

However, the true Church, which parallels the Early Church, is, in effect, told to *"flee"* as well! It will do so by virtue of the Rapture (Resurrection).

Therefore, Peter's words are as appropriate now as then!

(41) "THEN THEY WHO GLADLY RECEIVED HIS WORD WERE BAPTIZED: AND THE SAME DAY THERE WERE ADDED UNTO THEM ABOUT THREE THOUSAND SOULS."

The pattern is:

1. The phrase, *"Then they who gladly received his word were baptized,"* simply means that they believed what Peter said and gave their hearts to God, repenting of their sins. Nothing is said as to whether some or any of these people were baptized with the Holy Spirit; however, they were

NOTES

baptized in water.

2. Exactly when this was done, the Scripture does not say. As well, we have no information either of where it was done.

There is no river or lake in the immediate vicinity of Jerusalem. Also, the Brook Kidron was all but dry at that time of the year, which was probably the last days of May.

3. It is possible that they could have used the Pool of Siloam, but as would be obvious, it would take quite some time to baptize approximately 3,000 people; however, it was done, ever how long it took and wherever it took place.

4. *"And the same day there were added unto them about three thousand souls,"* proclaims the response to Peter's Message on this glorious day.

5. It should be noted that the Law of Moses was given on this same day about 1,600 years before (Ex., Chpts. 20-21). However, when the total of all the Law was finally given, being completed some 40 days later, with Moses being gone that long, the people made an idol and began to worship it as God. Because of this idolatry, the Scripture says, *"There fell of the people that day about three thousand men"* (Ex. 32:28). However, on the Day of Pentecost when the Holy Spirit came, *"About three thousand souls"* were saved!

6. Under Law, 3,000 were lost; under Grace, 3,000 were saved!

7. The words, *"Added unto them,"* refer to the approximate 120, now making a total of 3,120.

8. As is obvious, the Church, even on its first day, was growing rapidly.

9. As well, one should quickly add that the Church cannot even be said to have begun until the Day of Pentecost, which signaled the Advent of the Holy Spirit. We are safe in saying this because of the Command given by Jesus in Acts 1:4. They were to go and *"wait for the Promise of the Father."*

10. So, if the Church did not even really begin until the Advent of the Holy Spirit, how can the Church continue without the Holy Spirit?

11. Of course, it cannot! Therefore, if the Holy Spirit is not pertinent and prevalent in the midst of God's People and recognized as such, it may be a gathering of people, but it cannot be called *"Church!"*

(42) "AND THEY CONTINUED STEADFASTLY IN THE APOSTLES' DOCTRINE AND FELLOWSHIP, AND IN BREAKING OF BREAD, AND IN PRAYERS."

The structure is:

1. The sin nature, which is a result of the Fall, means that the nature of the individual is bent totally and completely toward sin.

2. While the Lord does not remove the sin nature at Conversion, He does tell us how to have victory to where it no longer bothers us.

3. That Way is the Cross of Christ! We are to maintain Faith in Christ and what He did for us at the Cross.

THE APOSTLES' DOCTRINE

The phrase, *"And they continued steadfastly in the Apostles' Doctrine,"* constitutes what?

If *"they continued steadfastly in the Apostles' Doctrine,"* should we not do the same?

The Apostles' Doctrine is found in Acts 2:38:

• Repentance: If we believe that Peter was inspired by the Holy Spirit in this Message preached and, therefore, what he was saying was not out of his own mind and that this was the *"Church"* under the New Covenant, then we must understand and conclude that the Message of Repentance should be the foundation of our Message presently. While many other things should be preached, even as we will see elsewhere in the Book of Acts, still, the undergirding must be the Message of Repentance.

As we've already stated, Repentance is a Message needed by both the world and the Church. Actually, the Believer should live a repentant life. No, that does not mean constant sinning and, thereby, constant Repentance.

One can describe a repentant life by the Believer as one that remains broken and contrite before the Lord. Actually, this was the foundation of Jesus' Sermon on the Mount, *"Blessed are the poor in spirit: for theirs is the Kingdom of Heaven"* (Mat. 5:3). This spirit is that which characterized

Christ (Mat. 11:28-29). Jesus was *"meek and lowly in heart,"* and so must we be!

Going back to the original meaning of Repentance, which means to *"turn around,"* sins cannot be remitted unless there is Repentance (I Jn. 1:9). It is impossible to confess sins away, educate them away, or anoint with oil and cause them to go away, and neither must they be ignored. The only method given by the Holy Spirit is *"Repentance."*

It must be remembered, to five of the seven Churches of Asia (Rev., Chpts. 2-3), Repentance was demanded by our Lord.

WATER BAPTISM

As we've already stated, Water Baptism is an extremely important part of the Christian experience, even though it contains no Salvation within itself. Inasmuch as it symbolizes the Death, Burial, and Resurrection of Christ and speaks of the fulfillment of all Righteousness (Mat. 3:15), its significance becomes very obvious. Therefore, it is the same for Believers, at least in a spiritual sense.

However, allowing for the great spiritual symbolism and its significance, Water Baptism stresses (possibly more than anything else) the person's commitment and allegiance to Christ and, therefore, severance from the world's system as well. It is an outward portrayal of an inward act already performed and is meant to label the Believer as a Follower of Christ.

THE BAPTISM WITH THE HOLY SPIRIT

After Salvation, whether immediately, as with the house of Cornelius, or shortly thereafter, as with the Samaritans (Acts, Chapt. 8), it is absolutely imperative, and I think stressed exceedingly so by the Word of God, that one must go on and receive *"the Gift of the Holy Spirit."*

As should be obvious, Satan has attempted to subvert *"the Apostles' Doctrine"* in every way possible. Many in the modern Charismatic church, and others, as well, deny that Repentance is a New Testament Doctrine, claiming it had validity only under the Old Covenant.

NOTES

As well, others go to the opposite end of the spectrum respecting Water Baptism, claiming that the ceremony itself contains Salvation, even with babies being baptized, etc. That is gross error as well! There is no such thing as baptismal regeneration.

Much of the modern church world denies the Baptism with the Holy Spirit with the evidence of speaking with other Tongues or any part of His Manifestation or Operation.

So, these churches, of whatever stripe they may be, are not continuing in the Apostles' Doctrine and, consequently, are of no service to the Kingdom of God.

Not only did they continue in this Doctrine, but they did so *"steadfastly,"* which means *"to persevere, be constantly diligent, and to attend assiduously all the exercises."*

It means that one must not veer whatsoever from that laid down by the Holy Spirit.

FELLOWSHIP

The phrase, *"And fellowship, and in breaking of bread,"* actually has to do with the bond of union of the Christian Family and Household of Faith.

The *"breaking of bread"* had to do with the celebration of the Lord's Supper, which was probably a much more informal setting than presently. It was an occasion of joy as they partook of the bread, symbolizing His Broken Body, and the cup, which symbolized His shed Blood.

As well, as should be overly obvious, the Apostles' Doctrine, although containing the rudiments of Verse 38, as we have mentioned, is actually portrayed in the clearest of terms as being anchored in Jesus Christ. He alone is the One Glorified by the Holy Spirit. It is through His Name and Faith in His Name that gives us Salvation. As well, His Name symbolizes what He has done for the human family.

"Jesus Christ," or more perfectly, *"The Lord Jesus Christ,"* proclaims Him as *"Jehovah, Saviour, Anointed."*

Only God could redeem man, and He did this by becoming Man and, therefore, our Representative Man.

As such, He became the *"Saviour"* of all who will believe. He did this by dying on the Cross of Calvary, thereby, satisfying the claims of Heavenly Justice and breaking the grip of sin that Satan had on the human family.

CHRIST THE ANOINTED ONE

As Christ the *"Anointed One,"* He not only spoiled Satan's goods and his house but, as well, rose from the dead by the Power of the Holy Spirit upon and within Him. So, Jesus is All in All. He alone saves!

Even though Repentance is required when one sins and, consequently, is an absolute necessity, still, that within itself does not save anyone. We are to repent because we have offended God, but it is Faith in Christ and what He did for us at the Cross that actually saves.

As well, as we have stated, Water Baptism contains no Salvation, but the One it represents, the Lord Jesus Christ, does save, and absolutely so.

Also, it is impossible for anyone to be baptized with the Holy Spirit unless he first has had every sin washed away by the Precious Blood of Jesus Christ. As well, only the Blood of Jesus can accomplish such a task.

Also, He is the One Who actually does the baptizing with the Spirit (Mat. 3:11).

RELIGION

The biggest mistake the church makes, and that which Satan grandly promotes, is the divorcing of these important rudiments and requirements, such as Repentance, Water Baptism, etc., from the Person of Christ. If that is done, and it is done in much, if not most, of that which calls itself *"Christian,"* then these requirements and ordinances simply degenerate into a religion, actually of no more consequence than the Muslim's prayers carried out five times a day, etc.

Even though the Lord's Supper, spoken of here as the *"breaking of bread,"* is very sacred, special, and holy, still, the modern manner in which it is taken probably causes its meaning to be lost.

The Lord's Supper is the symbol of the New Covenant, representing a great price that was paid by our Lord. It is a portrayal of the greatest Victory ever won for the human family and was done so by Christ.

NOTES

"And in prayers," simply meant it was a praying Church.

It is not possible for any Believer to have any type of quality relationship with the Lord without having a strong prayer life at the same time. There simply is no other method. Of course, the study of the Word of God goes hand-in-hand with *"prayer."*

And yet, the far greater majority of Christians, in fact, almost all, and that includes preachers, have little prayer life at all! Consequently, there is precious little true knowledge of Jesus Christ or His Word.

(43) "AND FEAR CAME UPON EVERY SOUL: AND MANY WONDERS AND SIGNS WERE DONE BY THE APOSTLES."

The overview is:

1. The phrase, *"And fear came upon every soul,"* simply spoke of the Moving and Operation of the Holy Spirit. God was in their midst and working mightily; therefore, in seeing the things before their very eyes that He was doing, a feeling and sense of awe, wonder, and fear filled their hearts, as it will do any under these circumstances.

2. The type of *"fear"* here mentioned is a healthy fear because one realizes two things:

a. God is in our midst.

b. He is doing great things.

3. There is little fear of God in most circles presently because little, if anything, is being done by the Holy Spirit. When He begins to move, even as here, *"fear"* will be the result, and rightly so.

4. *"And many wonders and signs were done by the Apostles,"* presents that which normally happens whenever the Lord is working in the midst of His People. The true Moving and Operation of the Holy Spirit will always result in many things, as the Book of Acts proclaims; however, if He is there and allowed to have His Way, sooner or later, there will be *"Signs and Wonders."* This speaks of Miracles, Healings, and even Manifestations of the Holy Spirit, which may affect a person in respect to his emotions, such as laughing, weeping, shaking, unable to stand, etc.

5. As well, the Working of the Holy Spirit was not only in the Apostles but even others,

such as Philip who performed Miracles and cast out demons, etc. (Acts 8:5-8).

6. Actually, Jesus did not place a limitation on the Moving and Operation of the Holy Spirit (for He is the Author of these things), regarding the ones through whom He works, but rather said, *"These signs shall follow them who believe,"* referring to any Believer (Mk. 16:17).

(44) "AND ALL WHO BELIEVED WERE TOGETHER, AND HAD ALL THINGS COMMON."

The composition is:

1. The phrase, *"And all who believed were together,"* has a much greater meaning than meets the eye.

2. Even though they were together in Doctrine and fellowship, which spoke of a common bond of unity in Jesus, their togetherness was accelerated by other sources as well.

3. Every Jew who came to Christ in Jerusalem at that time (and most, if not all, were Jews at the beginning) were instantly excommunicated from the synagogue. This meant they were barred from any and all functions in the synagogue and not even allowed to attend. If they had children in school (the synagogues were the schools), they had to be removed.

4. As well, if they were living in an apartment or flat that was not their own, they were instantly evicted and not allowed to secure another place unless they could find one owned by a Publican, etc. As well, they were also terminated from their employment.

5. It was total banishment, which affected every part and parcel of their lives. Consequently, many of these people were left completely destitute. As such, they had to be taken in by others who were not affected as adversely.

6. So, when it says, *"And all who believed were together,"* it meant exactly that.

7. *"And had all things common,"* spoke of those who were not placed in such a position as sharing with those who were. In effect, they said, *"What is mine is yours!"*

8. Some have read these Scriptures, thinking that the Apostles were advocating socialism or communism; however, there was nothing political in this, but rather a necessity due to the times in which they lived. It was not socialistic!

9. It meant something then to accept Christ! Those who did not only lost things of monetary value but, as well, were removed from their families, at least those families who did not accept Christ, with their names not even allowed to be mentioned anymore. In other words, they were to be thought of as dead.

10. If one wants to know the earmarks of religion, such attitudes, more or less, always characterize religion. They seek to destroy those who leave their ranks for any reason.

(45) "AND SOLD THEIR POSSESSIONS AND GOODS, AND PARTED THEM TO ALL MEN, AS EVERY MAN HAD NEED."

The exegesis is:

1. The phrase, *"And sold their possessions and goods,"* simply means they sold things that they did not absolutely need in order that they may be able to help those who were in great need.

2. *"And parted them to all men, as every man had need,"* proclaimed a Christlike community because of the great persecution at hand.

3. Regrettably, this situation did not ameliorate soon! The religious leaders of Jerusalem continued their persecution and hatred. Inasmuch as they controlled almost everything in the city, be it religious, economic, or governmental, they held, as should be obvious, great sway. Hating Christ as they did, they likewise hated His Followers, even as Jesus had predicted (Jn. 15:18-21).

4. As well, inasmuch as people were being saved constantly in Jerusalem, this problem would continue for many years. Actually, the great dissertation given by the Apostle Paul regarding giving in II Corinthians, Chapters 8 and 9, concerned helping the Saints in Jerusalem. This was about 26 or 27 years after the initial Day of Pentecost when the Spirit first fell.

(46) "AND THEY, CONTINUING DAILY WITH ONE ACCORD IN THE TEMPLE, AND BREAKING BREAD FROM HOUSE TO HOUSE, DID EAT THEIR MEAT WITH GLADNESS AND SINGLENESS OF HEART."

The synopsis is:

1. If the Believer doesn't understand the Cross as it regards Sanctification, he simply cannot walk after the Spirit, no matter how hard he may try.

2. He will rather walk after the flesh, despite the fact that he is trying not to do so.

3. The flesh refers to the ability, personal strength, motivation, education, talent, etc., of a human being.

WITH ONE ACCORD

The phrase, *"And they, continuing daily with one accord in the Temple,"* must have presented an awesome sight. Thousands by now had come to Christ, and they were meeting daily in the Temple preaching, worshipping, praying for the sick, and glorifying God. I wonder what the thoughts of the religious leaders were respecting this, which they thought they had stopped with the Crucifixion of Christ.

Instead of the Influence of Christ being stopped, it had, in fact, multiplied thousands of times over, and it was just getting started!

It should be understood that the Believers then did not consider themselves at all to be separate from Judaism. They felt that this was Judaism rather perfected, which, in a sense, it was! So, in no way did they consider themselves to be antagonistic to the Law of Moses, etc.

Consequently, they would meet in the Temple each day; however, about eight years later, the Lord would send Peter to the house of Cornelius, a Gentile if you will, with the Gospel presented for the first time to these people. Also, the Lord would give the particulars of the New Covenant to Paul, which probably began about 10 years after the Day of Pentecost's Outpouring.

With the Gospel ultimately going to the Gentiles and the persecution from the religious leaders of Israel increasing constantly, it soon came to the place that Followers of Christ were forced to separate themselves from the synagogue and the Temple as well. Of course, when Gentiles were ultimately brought in, as they were by the thousands very shortly, wherever they were, they had no link whatsoever with Judaism, etc.

NOTES

However, at that time, which was very shortly after the Outpouring on the Day of Pentecost, the Followers of Christ thought of the Temple as being as much theirs as anyone's.

HOUSE TO HOUSE

The phrase, *"And breaking bread from house to house,"* indicates that when they did not meet in the Temple, even as this would become increasingly difficult, they met in different houses all across the city. No doubt, this incorporated quite a few houses, especially among those who owned their homes. In effect, this would become their church.

In fact, many, if not most, Church services during the time of the Book of Acts were conducted in people's homes. This spoke of Gentiles, as well, as the Church expanded to much of the civilized world of that day.

However, this was of necessity. Rome would not tolerate the construction of church buildings as we think of such today; consequently, the people had to meet in homes, caves, or any such place that was suitable. Of course, *"Church"* is not a building, but rather the abiding of the Holy Spirit in the hearts and lives of Believers.

There are, no doubt, hundreds of thousands of beautiful church edifices which the Lord recognizes not at all as *"Church."* At the same time, He wondrously recognizes other gatherings as *"Church"* because they are meeting in His Name and do their very best to abide by the Word of God. Whether they are in a building or under a tree really does not matter. Such, in the Mind of God, is *"Church!"*

CELL GROUPS

From these *"house churches,"* the modern method of cell groups has sprung up. I speak of a central church, wherever it may be, having groups to meet in particular houses during the week, with the basic objective being the bringing in of new people, hopefully to Christ, in an informal setting.

While I do not question the motive, I personally feel, at least in many cases, that this type of method is unscriptural. While it is certainly proper to have Church in a *"house,"* which basically made up the Early Church, still, doing such purposely, even in an organized manner, I think will not achieve the spiritual results desired, even though it may achieve some type of numerical results. The reasons are these:

• I think if it had been possible for the Early Church to have had church buildings of some sort, they would have assembled there instead of their houses. However, as stated, a house can be, and should be, a perfect place to have Church, but not in the sense of the modern cell groups.

• Irrespective of the excellent motives and good intentions, and even considering proper training being given to those who are in charge of each cell group, still, it is not possible to make spiritual leaders out of people whom God has not called for such. That is what this method attempts to do.

While there are certainly exceptions, for the most part, even though proper lessons may be prepared by others, still, it cannot be properly delivered by most laypeople. Most of them have not been Called by the Holy Spirit for this task, and consequently, they little have His Help, at least as it should be.

Nearly all of the people I have encountered over the years who faithfully attended these groups have said, almost without exception, that there was almost no spiritual depth to anything that was done. While there certainly may be fellowship, that is about as far as it goes.

METHODS OF THE WORLD

Actually, one of the major problems in the modern church is people who have been brought into its confines but have really never been Born-Again. Many offer a mental acquiescence to whatever is being given but have really experienced little or no convicting Power of the Holy Spirit. As such, most in this category are not actually saved.

Regrettably, the church more and more is getting away from the teaching and preaching of the Word of God under the Anointing of the Holy Spirit by people called for that task (Eph. 4:11-12). This then affects the hearts and lives of the listeners, be they Believers or unbelievers. As the Holy Spirit through the Word touches their souls, they are convicted of *"sin, Righteousness, and judgment."* Consequently, an extremely favorable Work is accomplished in their hearts and lives.

However, the modern church has succumbed to methods that, in effect, are not Scriptural, such as the modern so-called cell ministry and especially the so-called Seeker Sensitive groups.

The phrase, *"Did eat their meat with gladness and singleness of heart,"* means that despite the persecution they were enduring concerning their excommunication from the synagogue, with all its attendant problems, still, such did not take their joy because their joy was untouchable.

(47) "PRAISING GOD, AND HAVING FAVOR WITH ALL THE PEOPLE. AND THE LORD ADDED TO THE CHURCH DAILY SUCH AS SHOULD BE SAVED."

The exegesis is:

1. The phrase, *"Praising God, and having favor with all the people,"* means that Jerusalem as a whole was favorably impressed by what they saw respecting these Followers of Christ.

2. As well, their *"praising God"* was a far cry from the cold, liturgical, formal methods of the Pharisees and religious leaders of Israel. This thing was real! There was an obvious change in people's lives, which produced a joy unspeakable and full of Glory. So, what the people saw, they wanted!

3. *"And the Lord added to the Church daily such as should be saved,"* proclaims the results of the Working and Manifestation of the Holy Spirit in the hearts and lives of those who had come to Jesus. In essence, people were getting saved right and left. It was a tremendous beginning for the Church.

4. However, it should be noticed that in the final alternative, it was the Holy Spirit Who attracted the people, convicting them of *"sin, Righteousness, and judgment."* While He used the people respecting the change in their lives and their exuberant joy, still, it was the *"Lord"* Who gave the increase.

NOTES

"There is a song in my heart today,
"Something I never had;
"Jesus has taken my sins away,
"O say, but I'm glad!"

"O say, but I'm glad, I'm glad,
"O say, but I'm glad!
"Jesus has come and my cup's overrun,
"O say, but I'm glad!"

CHAPTER 3

(1) "NOW PETER AND JOHN WENT UP TOGETHER INTO THE TEMPLE AT THE HOUR OF PRAYER, BEING THE NINTH HOUR."

The diagram is:

1. The phrase, *"Now Peter and John went up together,"* proclaims the friendship of these two Apostles.

2. This is not something that had come about recently but, no doubt, began with their partnership in the fishing business, which they had pursued before being Called by Christ.

3. Now we find these two spearheading the Work of God at the outset of the Early Church.

4. *"Into the Temple at the hour of prayer, being the ninth hour,"* pertains to 3:00 in the afternoon.

5. The Jews had three particular times of prayer each day. Those times were 9 a.m., 12 p.m., and 3 p.m.

6. It is believed that Abraham instituted the first time, Isaac the second, and Jacob the last.

7. As well, this particular hour was the time of the evening sacrifice. The Priest at that time offered the sacrifice and burnt the Incense, hence, the Psalm of David, *"Let my prayer be set forth before You as incense; and the lifting up of my hands as the evening Sacrifice"* (Ps. 141:2).

8. As we stated in the previous Chapter, none of the people who had come to Christ at that time, including the Apostles, looked at themselves any differently than any other Jews. Theirs, at least in their minds, was a completed Judaism, which, in fact, it actually was!

NOTES

(2) "AND A CERTAIN MAN LAME FROM HIS MOTHER'S WOMB WAS CARRIED, WHOM THEY LAID DAILY AT THE GATE OF THE TEMPLE WHICH IS CALLED BEAUTIFUL, TO ASK ALMS OF THEM WHO ENTERED INTO THE TEMPLE."

The overview is:

1. The phrase, *"And a certain man lame from his mother's womb was carried, whom they laid daily,"* seemed to be a daily occurrence that had taken place in one way or the other since this man was a child.

2. Little did he realize that this would be the greatest day of his life, and little did the ones who carried him realize that this would be their last day at this task.

3. *"At the gate of the Temple which is called Beautiful,"* presents this gate, according to Josephus, as made of beautiful and costly Corinthian brass. It was said to be about 62 feet wide and 31 feet high.

4. *"To ask alms of them who entered into the Temple,"* presented an occasion of barely eking out an existence; however, on this day, this man was to receive something that would change his life forever.

(3) "WHO SEEING PETER AND JOHN ABOUT TO GO INTO THE TEMPLE ASKED AN ALMS."

The exegesis is:

1. The phrase, *"Who seeing Peter and John,"* at first glance, presented just two more people going through the gate. But yet, these two at that particular time were probably closer to God than anyone on the face of the Earth.

2. *"About to go into the Temple, asked an alms,"* seems at first to have asked without really looking at them.

3. As well, Peter and John were, no doubt, strangers to him!

(4) "AND PETER, FASTENING HIS EYES UPON HIM WITH JOHN, SAID, LOOK ON US."

The exegesis is:

1. The phrase, *"And Peter, fastening his eyes upon him with John,"* indicates that they were moved upon by the Holy Spirit to do this thing.

2. *"Said, Look on us,"* has to do with the

Power of God about to be administered.

3. Peter wanted him to hear what he was about to say!

(5) "AND HE GAVE HEED UNTO THEM, EXPECTING TO RECEIVE SOMETHING OF THEM."

The record is:

1. The phrase, *"And he gave heed unto them,"* proclaims their request as commanding, and yet, of expectancy. This was something he had never encountered before and would prove to be the greatest moment of his life.

2. *"Expecting to receive something of them,"* points to expectation and possibly even Faith, but never dreaming what he actually would receive.

3. Most people only see their problems and their needs and, consequently, do not go beyond that. While these things are certainly important, the Holy Spirit is always attempting to take us beyond, much beyond, these particulars. In essence, I am saying that God not only meets our need but, as well, He gives us so much more beyond what we could even ask or think. It was the case with this crippled beggar, and it is the case with all who come in contact with the Power of God.

4. As well, how blessed at this time Jerusalem was to have men of the likes of Peter and John, as well as all of the Apostles and others who had recently accepted Christ. This is the strength (the true strength) of a city, a nation, and a people. Regrettably, such is seldom known or even understood, and most of the time is opposed!

(6) "THEN PETER SAID, SILVER AND GOLD HAVE I NONE; BUT SUCH AS I HAVE GIVE I TO YOU: IN THE NAME OF JESUS CHRIST OF NAZARETH RISE UP AND WALK."

The form is:

1. If the Believer doesn't understand the Cross as it regards Sanctification, he simply cannot walk after the Spirit.

2. No matter how hard he tries, he will rather walk after the flesh, despite the fact that he is trying not to do so.

3. We *"walk after the Spirit,"* not by doing something, but rather by trusting in something that's already done. I speak of the Cross!

NOTES

SILVER AND GOLD

The phrase, *"Then Peter said, Silver and gold have I none,"* was spoken in regard to what the man was expecting.

I wonder how this statement as given by Peter concerning silver and gold relates to the modern greed message.

Yes! The Lord does bless His People, and abundantly so. He blesses in monetary and material things, as well as all else; however, whenever these things become priority and actually the thrust of our message, then it becomes unscriptural and is heresy.

Many in the modern church measure their Faith by the amount of silver and gold they possess; however, it is the very opposite here!

It is not that silver and gold have no significance, for they do, but actually, very little in comparison to the Power of God manifested in one's life.

CAN ONE HAVE BOTH?

Quite possibly one can; however, it really should not even be the question.

Jesus plainly said, *"But seek ye first the Kingdom of God, and His Righteousness; and all these things shall be added unto you"* (Mat. 6:33).

Righteousness must be the quest and not material riches!

"But such as I have give I to you," pertains to the greatest thing anyone could ever have.

Peter had the Power of God within his heart and life. With that, all things are possible.

The phrase, *"In the Name of Jesus Christ of Nazareth rise up and walk,"* proclaims that Peter remembered what Jesus had said, *"In My Name"* (Mk. 16:17).

This is actually the power of attorney given to all Believers who truly follow the Word of God. As well, this glorious privilege pertains not only to those such as Peter and John but, as well, to all Preachers of the Gospel, and to any Believer in any capacity for that matter. Jesus said, *"These signs shall follow them* (and that means any and all) *who believe"* (Mk. 16:17).

As well, Peter would use the definitive Name of Christ by saying, *"Jesus Christ of*

Nazareth," so as not to mistake the One of Whom he spoke.

In other words, this One from Nazareth, hated by the religious leaders, was the very One Who made it possible for all of these things to happen.

It is not the name of Muhammad, Confucius, Joseph Smith, or any other fake luminary for that matter, it is *"Jesus Christ of Nazareth."*

(7) "AND HE TOOK HIM BY THE RIGHT HAND, AND LIFTED HIM UP: AND IMMEDIATELY HIS FEET AND ANKLE BONES RECEIVED STRENGTH."

The exegesis is:

1. The phrase, *"And He took him by the right hand, and lifted him up,"* presents Faith in action; however, let us quickly add that this was not presumption but Faith in God. Many attempt to do these things but with little or no direction by the Holy Spirit. Such is always presumption, and such always fails! To be led by the Spirit, as Peter and John evidently were, always brings guaranteed success.

2. *"And immediately his feet and ankle bones received strength,"* refers to *"instantly,"* for that is what the word *"immediately,"* as it is here used, actually means.

3. As such, and considering that it was Divine intervention that brought this about, this certainly could be labeled as a *"Miracle!"*

(8) "AND HE LEAPING UP STOOD, AND WALKED, AND ENTERED WITH THEM INTO THE TEMPLE, WALKING, AND LEAPING, AND PRAISING GOD."

The pattern is:

1. Most of the modern church understands not at all the manner of the sin nature.

2. I would suspect that most Christians have never even heard a message on the sin nature.

3. That is tragic, considering that the Holy Spirit through Paul gave us such a voluminous amount of instruction.

WALKING AND LEAPING AND PRAISING GOD

The phrase, *"And he leaping up stood, and walked,"* presents him now doing what he could not do before.

NOTES

"And entered with them into the Temple, walking, and leaping, and praising God," presents a sight that must have been a wonder to behold!

Whether he was recognized immediately, we do not know; however, he was so happy at what happened to him that he could not contain himself. To be sure, such is understandable and would to God that it would happen to all!

Previously, he had not even been able to walk, having to be carried by others wherever he went (Acts 3:2), but now he was completely whole.

Is Faith in God always the sole ingredient in Healings and Miracles of this nature, or anything else we receive from God for that matter?

No!

While Faith is certainly a vast significance without which we cannot receive from God, still, it is not the only ingredient in this mix.

Much teaching has been done in the last few years claiming that if one has enough Faith, one can receive whatever one desires. In this manner, Faith becomes the only ingredient, which completely nullifies all other particulars. Surely there were other beggars in Jerusalem who were crippled, blind, or with other types of malformities! Was it not the Will of God that they be healed as well?

LACK OF FAITH?

I have to assume that it is the Will of God for all to be healed. We learn this from the Ministry of Christ. He healed all who came to Him, irrespective of who they were or what they were. He never turned one away because Grace cannot turn one away. So, from that we deduce that it is always God's Will to heal the sick.

However, even though such is God's Will, all types of other things must be factored in as well! Beyond that, we cannot say, inasmuch as no mortal can lay claim to Omniscience; however, I think it unwise and even unscriptural to label every case as a *"lack of Faith"* if healing does not come, or even other things. While a lack of faith is definitely the cause in many situations, it is not the cause all the time.

In fact, this man who experienced this great Healing actually did not evidence much faith, if any, on his part. It was all resident in Peter and John.

The only way he could have failed to receive Healing was simply to rebel against them. Tragically, many do that very thing, believe it or not!

For His own reasons, the Lord wanted to give Healing to this man specifically and, thereby, caused the Holy Spirit to move upon Peter and John to minister to him. There would be many other Miracles in Jerusalem in the coming days, as well, but I think if all were investigated properly, one would find that prayer for the sick was not altogether indiscriminate. Always, the Apostles were led by the Holy Spirit in all they did!

While it is always God's Will for good things to happen to people, sometimes, due to the actions of the people, whatever they might be, it is not His Wisdom. There is a vast difference in the Will of God and the Wisdom of God.

(9) "AND ALL THE PEOPLE SAW HIM WALKING AND PRAISING GOD."

The overview is:

1. There was no doubt about this man's Healing, as there is no doubt about anything truly done by the Lord.

2. The evidence was irrefutable, and the results were obvious to all.

3. The man was hilariously happy and conducted himself accordingly, and one can certainly understand why!

(10) "AND THEY KNEW THAT IT WAS HE WHICH SAT FOR ALMS AT THE BEAUTIFUL GATE OF THE TEMPLE: AND THEY WERE FILLED WITH WONDER AND AMAZEMENT AT THAT WHICH HAD HAPPENED UNTO HIM."

The synopsis is:

1. When Paul spoke of Faith, without exception, he was speaking of what Jesus did at the Cross.

2. In essence, he described it as, *"The Faith"* (Gal. 2:20).

3. This means that the Object of Faith must always be the Cross of Christ, and we are speaking here not of the wooden beam on which Jesus died, but rather what He there accomplished at the Cross.

NOTES

A HEART CRY!

The phrase, *"And they knew that it was He which sat for alms at the Beautiful Gate of the Temple,"* just might give us a clue as to why the Holy Spirit singled out this man for this great Miracle. He would not be retiring at all respecting his exhibition to all as to what the Lord had done for him. As well, it seems that he was constantly praising God!

I think it is obvious that the Holy Spirit desired this. He wanted this to be a Testimony, and He wanted it to be obvious to all and for none to have any doubt about what had been done. Quite possibly, some or even most would not have been as bold as this man. What better way to get the attention of the people!

Also, I believe that everything that God does for a person is at least generated in part by a heart cry from that individual. Others may not know about it, but God does! As such, He will bring things to pass which will place the person in a position in order for him to receive that for which he has asked.

WONDER AND AMAZEMENT

We are given no history at all regarding this man before his great Miracle. However, I greatly suspect that if the truth were known, one would find that he had called out to the Lord, no doubt, many times respecting his physical and social plight. I am almost positive that such was the case; consequently, the Holy Spirit, at a certain time, was given instructions by the Father, based on the Authority of the Son, to bring about this Miracle through Peter and John.

The phrase, *"And they were filled with wonder and amazement at that which had happened unto him,"* proclaims that which is absolutely indisputable.

Some of them had probably seen the man sitting at the gate that morning before his Healing, and others had probably seen him there many times. So, there was no way this Miracle could be denied. It was open and obvious to all!

I believe that the Lord is presently on the verge of performing a Work that is going to

NOTES

be so grand and glorious that the world and the Church are going to be filled with *"wonder and amazement."* I feel that and sense that in my spirit as never before. God is able to make the entirety of the world take notice in *"wonder and amazement,"* and actually, He desires to do now what He did then. As it was God's Time then, I believe it is God's Time now!

(11) "AND AS THE LAME MAN WHICH WAS HEALED HELD PETER AND JOHN, ALL THE PEOPLE RAN TOGETHER UNTO THEM IN THE PORCH THAT IS CALLED SOLOMON'S, GREATLY WONDERING."

The exposition is:

1. The phrase, *"And as the lame man which was healed held Peter and John,"* means that he stood very close to them, even with the idea that he did not want them to depart out of his sight. It is almost as if he feared if they left, the malady would return.

2. It is somewhat like Mary Magdalene, who had been delivered by Jesus of some seven demons, desiring to stay close even to His Corpse after His Death at Calvary. Of course, she was to receive far, far more; the Crucified One was risen!

3. Before now, this man had no life except that of begging and depending on others to carry him wherever he went. Now he was a whole man, and all because of the Power of God resident within these two men. No wonder he desired to *"hold Peter and John."*

4. *"All the people ran together unto them in the porch that is called Solomon's,"* is said to have been about 800 feet long and built on the east side of the outer court.

5. As should be obvious, there would be room enough there for many people, even thousands to see and hear.

6. The words *"greatly wondering"* speak of a very strong emotion of awe and astonishment. They knew it had been a Miracle and that God through these two men had done this great thing. As well, they knew that it had been done in the *"Name of Jesus Christ of Nazareth."*

(12) "AND WHEN PETER SAW IT, HE ANSWERED UNTO THE PEOPLE, YOU MEN OF ISRAEL, WHY DO YOU MARVEL AT THIS? OR WHY DO YOU LOOK SO EARNESTLY ON US, AS THOUGH BY OUR OWN POWER OR HOLINESS WE HAVE MADE THIS MAN TO WALK?"

The structure is:

1. The phrase, *"And when Peter saw it, he answered unto the people,"* proclaims another Message about to be delivered, which would result in even a greater number being Saved, even *"about five thousand men"* besides the women and children (Acts 4:4). As well, this Message would pull no punches, even as the last, and would strike conviction in the hearts of the people, which was exactly what the Holy Spirit intended to do.

2. The question, *"You men of Israel, why do you marvel at this?"* is meant to point to Jesus, which it graphically did, and reminded the people that Jesus had performed an astounding number of Miracles, but still, the religious leaders would not believe.

3. The idea is that this which Jesus *"began both to do and teach"* (Acts 1:1) is continuing right on, and even in greater measure. Then, Jesus was only one Person, but now, multiple thousands, and even many more, will exhibit the same type of Power.

4. The question, *"Or why do you look so earnestly on us, as though by our own power or holiness we have made this man to walk?"* presents the very opposite of what too many presently do and say.

5. Peter instantly portrayed Jesus as the Power behind this Miracle, with the idea that no dead man could perform this type of Miracle, or any Miracle for that matter.

6. The problem with too many in the modern church is that they try to do things of their *"own power."* It is tied to their self-righteousness, which they think is *"holiness,"* but is no such thing!

7. While it was *"Power,"* true enough, which had brought about this great Miracle, still, it was the Power of the Holy Spirit resident within these two men, who acted on the Authority of the Lord Jesus Christ, with all being triggered by the use of the Name of Jesus.

8. So, we have men here who were given authority to use the Name of Jesus and were

NOTES

empowered by the Holy Spirit, Who was instructed to act in accordance with the proper use of that Name. In fact, there is no power like the Power of the Name of Jesus!

(13) "THE GOD OF ABRAHAM, AND OF ISAAC, AND OF JACOB, THE GOD OF OUR FATHERS, HAS GLORIFIED HIS SON JESUS; WHOM YOU DELIVERED UP, AND DENIED HIM IN THE PRESENCE OF PILATE, WHEN HE WAS DETERMINED TO LET HIM GO."

The form is:

1. Most Believers have little or no knowledge at all as it regards the sin nature.

2. And yet, it is one of the most important subjects in the entirety of the New Testament.

3. However, to understand the sin nature, one also has to understand the Cross of Christ relative to Sanctification (Rom., Chpt. 6).

THE GOD OF ABRAHAM, ISAAC, AND JACOB

The phrase, *"The God of Abraham, and of Isaac, and of Jacob, the God of our fathers, has glorified His Son Jesus,"* presents Peter connecting the present Miracle with all that God had done for their fathers in days gone by.

If one is to notice, he does not seem conscious of any break or transition, or of any change of posture or position. Only a new incident, long since promised by the Prophets, has been added.

Chrysostom said, *"He thrusts himself upon the Fathers of old, lest he should appear to be introducing a new doctrine."*

In effect, he told them that this Miracle was not something new but actually a continuance of that given in Old Testament Times. Consequently, in his statement concerning the Fathers, he told us that the Old Testament is the New Testament concealed, while the New Testament is the Old Testament revealed.

The Glorification of Jesus Christ took place at the Resurrection. This meant that the Mission for which Jesus had come, and had even been given a body to carry out in detail, had now been finished. Consequently, God would glorify this very Body, which had been offered in Sacrifice, thereby, purchasing the Redemption of lost humanity because of what He did. The Holy Spirit in baptismal measure was promised and given, as the Day of Pentecost proclaimed.

THE GUILT OF ISRAEL

The phrase, *"Whom you delivered up,"* pertains to the action of Judas in delivering Jesus into the hands of the Chief Priests (Jn. 19:11), who delivered Him to Pilate to be crucified.

"And denied Him in the presence of Pilate, when he was determined to let Him go," seems here to absolve Pilate of at least some, if not most, of the blame in the Death of Jesus, placing it squarely on the shoulders of the religious leaders of Israel.

This does not mean that Pilate did not share at all in the guilt, simply because he had the power had he only used it to set Jesus free; however, he allowed himself to be bullied and threatened, thereby, carrying out the blood thirst of these reprobates. But still, the major part of the guilt belonged to Israel, as is here portrayed.

This one thing is sure: Upon hearing Peter, the people had absolutely no doubt as to what he was saying, clearly understanding exactly what it meant. Inasmuch as Peter was preaching under the Anointing of the Holy Spirit and, as well, and more perfectly, was inspired, we now get an idea as to exactly how the Holy Spirit operates respecting His Dealings with sinful men.

Also, the Holy Spirit through the Apostle did not limit this guilt to the religious leaders only but included, as well, almost all of the people of Israel. It was a very serious indictment!

(14) "BUT YOU DENIED THE HOLY ONE AND THE JUST, AND DESIRED A MURDERER TO BE GRANTED UNTO YOU."

The pattern is:

1. The only way that sin can be properly addressed is by and through the Cross.

2. That's why Paul said that the emphasis must always be on the Cross and never on anything else (I Cor. 1:17).

3. It is by and through what Jesus did at the Cross that effects the Salvation of the sinner and the Sanctification of the Saint.

NOTES

THE DENIAL OF JESUS CHRIST

The phrase, *"But you denied the Holy One and the Just,"* proclaims the terrible sin of Israel. As well, it proclaims the terrible sin of most of humanity for all time!

The Muslim world denies Jesus as the *"Holy One,"* i.e., *"The Messiah, The Son of God,"* although they would probably refer to Him as *"Just."* However, it is impossible for Him to be *"Just"* if He is not Who He says He is. A person cannot be *"Just"* and a liar and deceiver at the same time, which Jesus would have had to have been, if He is not what He said He is, the Son of God.

As well, this issue faces not only the Muslims, but actually the entirety of the world for all time.

Was Jesus, as many claim, merely *"a Good Man"* and a Miracle Worker, but not actually the Son of God?

Once again we are faced with the problem that it is impossible for Christ to have been a *"Good Man"* if He is at the same time a liar and a deceiver!

Jesus plainly said that He is God and the Fulfillment of the Promises (Isa. 7:14; Mat. 16:16; Jn. 14:8-11; 15:26; 16:14-15, 28; 17:1-3; 20:28; Rev. 1:12-18; 19:11-16).

WHO JESUS IS!

Therefore, if Jesus Christ is not the Son of God, i.e., *"The Holy One,"* then neither is He a Good Man, but rather the worst impostor and deceiver who has ever lived! By sheer definition, it is an absolute necessity that He be one or the other.

So, anyone who denies Him as the Son of God is at the same time calling Him a liar, deceiver, impostor, and actually the brigand of the ages!

Of course, most would not dare say such a thing; however, it is not possible to reach any other conclusion. One either *"denies"* Him altogether or *"accepts"* Him altogether!

The phrase, *"And desired a murderer to be granted unto you,"* speaks of Barabbas (Mat. 27:15-26).

Why would Israel deny Christ?

Why would anyone deny Christ?

Of all the major religions of the world, Islam, Buddhism, Shintoism, Mormonism, etc., not a single one of their founders claimed to be God. The reasons are obvious!

If they had made such claims, such would have been treated as a joke, and for all the obvious reasons.

However, Jesus did claim to be God, in effect, making claims no one else had ever made.

JESUS CHRIST HAD THE CREDENTIALS

Even though great anger was registered toward Jesus by the religious leaders of Israel because of these claims, even though rejected, they were not disputed. I speak of the Miracles He performed, which were so numerous, so powerful, and so absolutely wondrous, even to the raising of the dead, that they simply could not be disputed. Not able to deny their veracity, they simply accused Him of doing such by the powers of Satan (Mat. 12:24-32).

As well, He cited the Scriptures (the Old Testament, which was then the Bible), saying, *"And they are they which testify of Me"* (Jn. 5:36-42).

In other words, Jesus Christ had the credentials that He claimed, which no other human being in history ever had.

So, the only reason that the majority of mankind denies Him is because of deception and rank unbelief. The proof as to Who He was and is remains incontestable.

With the proliferation of Bibles around the world and the Testimonies of unnumbered millions who have had their lives gloriously and miraculously changed by this One we call *"Jesus Christ, the Saviour of mankind,"* there remains no excuse for any not to know.

No one has ever denied Christ for noble, right, honest, truthful, or proper reasons. They have always denied Him from the most impure and wicked motives. Such was so regarding the religious leaders of Israel, and such has remained the same ever since. Most of humanity would rather have a *"murderer"* than the Prince of Life.

Why?

It is because they are far more like the *"murderer"* than they are the Christ of

Glory! That is a serious charge, but true nevertheless.

(15) "AND KILLED THE PRINCE OF LIFE, WHOM GOD HAS RAISED FROM THE DEAD; WHEREOF WE ARE WITNESSES."

The synopsis is:

1. There's only one way that the Believer can live a victorious Christian life.
2. That way is the Way of the Cross!
3. It simply means that our Faith must be maintained in Christ and what He did for us at the Cross. Then the Holy Spirit will grandly help us.

THEY KILLED THE PRINCE OF LIFE

The phrase, *"And killed the Prince of Life,"* refers to Jesus, as is obvious.

The word *"Prince"* in the Greek is *"archegos"* and means *"leader or author; one who stands at the head or the beginning of a list or rank."*

Jesus is called *"The Prince of Life."*

This means that Christ doesn't merely have life but, in reality, is the Source of Life; however, while He is the Source of Life, the means by which this Life is given to Believers is through the Cross. In fact, everything that Jesus did while on this Earth, especially that which He did at the Cross, was all for you and me. None of it was for Angels or the Godhead, but rather all for sinners.

An analogy is drawn in Verses 14 and 15, which must not be overlooked.

If Jesus is denied, and that means respecting His rightful Place and Position as the Son of God and the Lord of Glory, the position of the one who denies such does not remain static. Denial of Christ always brings acute degeneration and, barring Repentance, will eventually conclude in killing the Lord of Glory.

While, of course, that is not now possible in a literal sense as with the Jews of old, still, it definitely is true respecting the motives and actions of the one who denies.

As well, this denial of which Peter spoke does not come from the world, but rather the church. While the world definitely denies Christ, still, it little seeks to kill Him, as was evident in the efforts of Pilate. It is the religious sector that carries the denial to the depth of murder. Also, such is not new.

NOTES

SELF-RIGHTEOUSNESS

It began with Cain killing Abel. It was self-righteousness versus God's Imputed Righteousness. It was self-will versus God's Will. It is man's wicked substitute for Salvation versus God's True Prince of Salvation, the Lord Jesus Christ.

Self-righteousness always attempts to kill God's Imputed Righteousness.

The word *"denied"* means to *"reject, disavow, contradict, abnegate, and refuse."*

What do we exactly mean regarding self-righteousness opposing God's Imputed Righteousness?

It speaks of man's efforts to save himself by his own machinations, i.e., *"good works in one form or the other."* This is the driving force behind all the religions in the world. It is the driving force behind man in general. Almost all who do not know the Lord think of themselves in the plus column because of certain things they have done or certain things they have not done. The Pharisees of St. Luke is a perfect case in point.

To fine tune the subject and to point out that which seems so right to the religious mind, but yet is so wrong, please allow me to be specific.

Only a tiny percentage of those who call themselves *"Believers"* actually accept in totality God's Imputed Righteousness. Imputed Righteousness is that which God freely or instantly gives to one who has exhibited simple Faith in Christ, which means to accept that which Christ has done for humanity, which refers to the Cross. That means the sinner can be unclean one moment and clean the next, and be that without any type of merit or works but simply, as stated, by exhibiting Faith in Christ.

LAW AND GRACE

Many in the Church will accept that respecting the sinner who initially comes to Christ, but will not accept it at all respecting Believers. However, we must remind all concerned that when Jesus died on the Cross, He did so not only for sinners but, as well, for Saints.

In other words, much of the church

NOTES

demands some type of penance or punishment for Believers who fail, which is anathema to the Finished Work of Christ.

In truth, if any Believer agrees to submit to any type of penance, etc., at that moment the individual nullifies the Grace of God. Paul said, *"Christ is become of no effect unto you, whosoever of you are justified by the Law* (or seek to be justified by penance or works)*; you are fallen from Grace"* (Gal. 5:4).

Consequently, the very thing that much of the church seeks to impose actually falls out to the very opposite effect. It is impossible for one to trust in performance and promise at the same time; in self-righteousness and imputed Righteousness at the same time; and law and Grace at the same time.

It would be bad enough if those who promote self-righteousness in one form or the other simply refused God's Imputed Righteousness and let it go at that; however, such is never the case. The very nature of self-righteousness, as the Jews of old, must of necessity kill God's Imputed Righteousness, *"The Prince of Life."*

This is the battle that has raged from the very beginning and rages unto this very hour. This is the dividing line of the Church. To be frank, it is that which Paul combated more then anything else, i.e., the Law/Grace issue! Make no mistake about it, it is just as much the issue now as it was then.

The phrase, *"Whom God has raised from the dead,"* presents the crowning Glory of Salvation. The Resurrection ratified what was done at Calvary. Along with Jesus, the old man of the believing sinner also died at Calvary; consequently, the price was paid for man's Redemption, with the sin debt forever settled and the grip of sin forever broken.

However, if everything had stopped there, man's Salvation, although completely purchased, would still be incomplete. Jesus Christ had to be raised from the dead in order that the Newness of Life would now replace that which was dead even as it lived (Rom. 6:4; I Tim. 5:6). However, it must be remembered that the Cross was not dependent on the Resurrection, but rather the Resurrection was dependent on the Cross. In other words, if Jesus did what He set out to do at the Cross, which was to atone for all sin, past, present, and future, at least for all who will believe, He would then come from the dead. In fact, due to the fact that *"the wages of sin is death,"* had He failed to atone for one sin, even the smallest sin, He could not have been raised from the dead. The fact of Him being raised from the dead tells us that He most definitely did atone for all sin.

The phrase, *"Whereof we are witnesses,"* simply means, and yet is so profound, that they had personally seen the Resurrected Christ. There is no greater witness than an eyewitness.

As well, to all who witnessed His Resurrection, that He had actually been raised from the dead and was not a mere apparition or spirit, was proven beyond doubt. They ate with Him, walked with Him, and even touched and handled Him (I Jn. 1:1).

(16) "AND HIS NAME THROUGH FAITH IN HIS NAME HAS MADE THIS MAN STRONG, WHOM YOU SEE AND KNOW: YEA, THE FAITH WHICH IS BY HIM HAS GIVEN HIM THIS PERFECT SOUNDNESS IN THE PRESENCE OF YOU ALL."

The structure is:

1. The Object of one's Faith must always be Christ and the Cross (I Cor. 2:2).

2. The Story of the entirety of the Bible is *"Jesus Christ and Him Crucified"* (Gal. 6:14).

3. The Cross of Christ is the Means and the only Means by which all of these wonderful things are given to us (Col. 2:10-15).

FAITH IN HIS NAME

The phrase, *"And His Name through Faith in His Name has made this man strong,"* presents the key to all things!

His Name and Faith in His Name will make a life strong, a marriage strong, a home strong, and even the entirety of the nation strong!

This means that all the self-help programs in the world, irrespective of how cleverly they may be presented, can effect nothing positive for anyone, at least respecting any lasting results. However, simple Faith in the Name of Jesus, which refers to all He has done for humanity, will bring about miraculous results. Actually, this and this alone is the answer! No other alleged panacea will suffice, and no other panacea is needed.

THE MEANING IN THE NAME

"Name" is a significant concept in both Testaments.

In Biblical cultures a name did more than identify; it communicated something of the essence, character, or the reputation of the person or thing named.

NAMES LINKED WITH REVELATION ABOUT GOD

The Messiah would be called Immanuel (*"With us is God"*). Mary and Joseph were told to name her infant, *"Jesus"* (meaning *"Deliverer or Saviour"*), *"because He will save His people from their sins"* (Mat. 1:21; Lk. 1:31).

It is the linkage of the name with the identity and essential character of the person named that helps us to understand several misunderstood phrases in Scripture.

THE THIRD OF THE TEN COMMANDMENTS

The Third of the Ten Commandments is as follows: *"You shall not misuse the Name of the LORD your God"* (Ex. 20:7; Deut. 5:11).

The reference is not to cursing or profanity as we would think of such, but to any use of the Name of God that treats Him as anything but what He is—the Sovereign Source of all things and the Redeemer of His People.

In addition, Christians who bear the Name of Christ should not misuse the Name by behavior that is unbecoming to it.

TO PRAY IN THE NAME OF JESUS

Jesus told the Apostles that after He left, they were to pray to the Father in His Name (Jn. 14:13-14; 15:16; 16:23-24, 26). He was not merely referring to an expression tacked on to the end of a prayer. To pray *"In Jesus' Name"* means:

- To identify the content and motivation of prayer with all that Jesus is.
- To pray with full confidence in Him as He has revealed Himself. Jesus promised that prayer in His Name would be answered. Of course, He was speaking of those who have the proper relationship with Him and, therefore, will ask all things subject to His Will.

Without going into detail regarding the Will of God, suffice to say that some things are the Will of God for all Believers in any and all circumstances, while other things might be His Will to some and not for others. We must always remember that we want His Will and not ours.

IN THE OLD TESTAMENT

If one is to notice, the Lord addressed Himself in Old Testament Times by various names. He did this to express Himself in a certain capacity.

For instance, in Genesis 22:14, when addressing Abraham, He referred to Himself as *"Jehovah-jireh,"* which means *"The Lord will see or provide."*

Sometime later in addressing Moses, He referred to Himself as *"Jehovah-nissi,"* which means *"The Lord our Banner"* (Ex. 17:15). This refers to the fact that we fight under His Banner.

In Exodus 15:26, the Lord referred to Himself as *"Jehovah-ropheka,"* which means *"The Lord our Healer."*

IN THE NEW TESTAMENT

To which we have already alluded, the Name of Jesus, as given to the Son of God (Lk. 1:31), means *"Deliverer-Saviour."* Therefore, His Name expresses His Mission and Purpose. (Jesus is the Greek derivative of the Hebrew Joshua.)

So, having Faith in His Name refers to having Faith in that which He did and can do. He alone is the Deliverer of humanity from sin, which, as well, delivers from poverty, sickness, self-will, self-righteousness, religion, etc. His Name signifies Who He is and What He is!

It is not that His *"Name"* is some type of magic talisman, which some seem to think, but rather an expression of His Purpose and Ability.

NOTES

NOTES

As well, the Name of *"Jesus"* summarizes all the Names used by God in the Old Testament. In other words, all were brought to bear in that one Name.

THE SPIRIT WORLD

The Name of Jesus strikes terror to all demon spirits, fallen Angels, and Satan himself. Paul said, *"Wherefore God also has highly exalted Him, and given Him a Name which is above every name:*

"That at the Name of Jesus every knee should bow, of things in Heaven, and things in earth, and things under the earth;

"And that every tongue should confess that Jesus Christ is Lord, to the Glory of God the Father" (Phil. 2:9-11).

The reason that these spirit beings have to bow the knee to Jesus even at the mention of His Name is because He has defeated every power of darkness, every fallen Angel, every demon spirit, and even Satan himself.

They were not merely defeated, but the Scripture says, *"And having spoiled principalities and powers, He made a show of them openly, triumphing over them in it"* (Col. 2:15).

This means that Jesus exposed Satan to public infamy and shame, respecting the spirit world of darkness.

The allusion is to the custom of conquerors making a public demonstration of conquered enemies.

Satan and his human agents made a public shame out of Christ by crucifying Him. By that they thought they would triumph over Him, putting an end to His New Covenant, but the Cross turned out to be their public defeat and shame (I Jn. 3:8).

As well, Jesus entered the house of the strong man Satan, and because He was Infinitely Stronger, actually All-powerful, spoiled Satan's goods and spoiled his house (Mat. 12:29).

Man's true problem, whether he knows it or not, comes from the spirit world of darkness. Demon spirits under their master Satan seek to influence and even possess human beings. They steal, kill, and destroy (Jn. 10:10).

All the world can do is address the evil handiwork of Satan, which is actually the result; however, Jesus went to the source of the problem, dealing with it in the spiritual realm, thereby, breaking Satan's hold on this world. Of course, he is still active, but that time of activity is about over (Rev. 20:1-3).

THE PRIVILEGE OF THE BELIEVER TO USE THAT NAME

All Believers have the privilege of the use of the Name Jesus (Mk. 16:17-18); however, it cannot be used relative to other people but only against the spirit world of darkness. Inasmuch as this is the seat, as stated, of the problems of man, this is where its use is greatly needed.

Consequently, for the church to deny, ignore, or fail to use His Name in that capacity, whether attempting to solve these problems by political means or any other way, is tantamount to blasphemy, or gross spiritual ignorance to say the least. As we study the Book of Acts, we will see how the Name is used, and we will see not at all any political foray on the part of the Apostles, etc.

The example laid down for all Believers should be followed meticulously, always remembering that it was the Holy Spirit Who gave these examples.

The phrase, *"Whom you see and know,"* means simply that many who were present that day knew this man, and consequently, knew that he had been a cripple, and now they saw him perfectly sound and whole. There was no denying the Miracle!

FAITH

The phrase, *"Yes, the Faith which is by Him has given him this perfect soundness in the presence of you all,"* refers to the Object of Faith, Who is Jesus.

Even though the Believer is to use Faith respecting any and all things asked of the Lord, in actuality, those things, be they Healing, finances, Salvation for lost loved ones, etc., are not to be the object of faith, but rather the results of Faith. Jesus Christ alone and what He did at the Cross is to be the Object of all Faith. The writer of Hebrews said, *"Looking unto Jesus the Author and Finisher of our Faith"* (Heb. 12:2).

Peter was unequivocally portraying Jesus as the One responsible for this man's

NOTES

Miracle; consequently, he drew attention away from himself, as he should have!

As well, that which the Lord does is always *"given freely"* and produces a *"perfect soundness."* Nothing else can do such.

(17) "AND NOW, BRETHREN, I BELIEVE THAT THROUGH IGNORANCE YOU DID IT, AS DID ALSO YOUR RULERS."

The order is:

1. When it comes to victory over the sin nature, it seems from the Sacred Text that the Lord gave to Paul first the meaning of the sin nature.
2. After showing him how that man was saved, *"Justification by Faith,"* He then showed him the meaning of the sin nature (Rom., Chpt. 6).
3. Romans, Chapter 7, proclaims Paul trying to address this thing in the wrong way and failing constantly (Rom. 7:15).

IGNORANCE

The phrase, *"And now, brethren, I believe that through ignorance you did it,"* places the people of Israel as culpable for the murder of Jesus Christ, as well as their rulers.

Millions hide behind so-called leadership, thinking to absolve themselves of responsibility; however, such is not the case!

In fact, how guilty were the people of Israel, considering that they had little or no personal part in this dastardly deed, at least as far as the act itself was concerned?

We know at least that the far greater majority was culpable because the judgment which followed in A.D. 70 touched not only the rulers but over one million of the people, as well, who died, with almost the entirety of the balance of the population negatively affected in some way. When one considers that not a single Believer lost his life in this carnage, even more light is thrown upon the subject.

The judgment that ultimately came probably had more to do with their failure to repent even than the actual act of murdering the Lord of Glory. I think this is obvious, especially considering the tone of the Messages brought by the Apostle.

In essence, the Holy Spirit here responded to the prayer offered by Jesus while on the Cross, *"Father, forgive them for they know not what they do"* (Lk. 23:34). Guilty as they were of this terrible sin of having put the King's Son to death, the King remitted this terrible sin and sent a Message of Mercy, that is, if they would heed the Message and repent.

This tells us something wonderful!

THE MERCY OF GOD

There could be no more terrible sin than the murder of Jesus Christ. Of all the perfidious things done in human history, this crime reached the lowest of the low and the deepest of the deep. It is one thing to sin against man, but it is even worse to sin against God. However, to sin against God, Who has taken upon Himself the form of man, even for the very purpose of redeeming man, is the sin of all sins. And yet, Jesus had said, *"And whosoever speaks a word against the Son of Man, it shall be forgiven him"* (Mat. 12:32).

Of course, we are speaking of sins which can be forgiven, not that of blaspheming the Holy Spirit, for which there is no forgiveness (Mat. 12:32).

The phrase, *"As did also your rulers,"* places all, in essence, on the same footing.

As we shall see, even after this dastardly deed, actually the most horrible in the history of mankind, the Lord in His Mercy and Grace will offer pardon and Salvation to all who will believe.

In this, actually the beginning of the great Dispensation of Grace, never will one find the Grace of God exhibited more than at this time. To offer pardon to the murderers of His only Son is beyond the ability of humankind to comprehend.

WILLFUL IGNORANCE

One can somewhat understand the *"ignorance"* of the people as a whole, but as for the rulers, how is it that they were *"ignorant"* as well?

Their *"ignorance"* did not in any way excuse them, as it in no way excuses anyone else. In other words, ignorant or not, this terrible sin was laid to their charge, with Repentance being the only way it could be expunged. So, ignorance is no excuse!

However, one must understand that their

"ignorance" was a *"willful ignorance,"* as it is more or less with all.

WHAT IS WILLFUL IGNORANCE?

The problem in spiritual ignorance is a misunderstanding that comes from a wrong perception of that which is known. Jesus' Listeners heard what He told them, but they could not understand its meaning for them (Mk. 9:32; Lk. 9:45).

Ignorance lies at the core of pagan worship (Acts 13:27) and explains the failure of all the lost to realize that it is God's Kindness only, designed to lead them to Repentance, that delays God's Judgment (Rom. 2:1-4).

It is one thing for pagans to be in ignorance, but something else altogether for those who have heard the Word to remain in ignorance. As well, the people of Israel, and especially the rulers (religious leaders), had had the opportunity to hear, see, grasp, and understand the Gospel more so than any other people who have ever lived. One must conclude that due to the Ministry of Christ, the level of spiritual intelligence had never been higher. Isaiah had prophesied nearly 800 years before, *"The people who walked in darkness have seen a great light: they who dwell in the land of the shadow of death, upon them has the light shined"* (Isa. 9:2). So, the sin of Israel, and especially her rulers, was a sin against *"Revealed Light,"* and that *"Light"* was *"Christ!"*

Willful ignorance pertains to those who can readily know because this *"Light"* has been given unto them, but they purposely choose to remain in ignorance. It is a willful choice on their part.

So, such is an ignorance that is totally unlike the pagan who has never had the opportunity, or at least very little opportunity, to hear the Gospel and, therefore, to know Christ.

It is somewhat like the adage that points to a person who tells a particular lie so long that he comes to believe that what he says is true.

Even though they were ignorant, there was no excuse for their ignorance, which, within itself, constitutes the understatement of all time.

NOTES

Why does a person, even as these rulers of Israel of so long ago, desire to remain in ignorance after hearing the Word?

Of course, only God would know the motives and reasonings of each individual heart; however, the basic problem is *"unbelief."* They simply will not allow themselves to believe, even though the proof is obvious before their eyes. They actually will purposely turn away. This tells us two things:

1. TOTAL DEPRAVITY

The total depravity of the human heart is a result of the Fall. Man is not just somewhat lost, but totally lost! He is not somewhat a sinner, but altogether a sinner! He is not only devoid of Spiritual Light, but devoid of all Spiritual Light! Within himself, man cannot initiate any type of favorable response toward God. Therefore, the Holy Spirit must act upon the Word that is delivered to the sinner, who is spiritually dead, in order for him to have the capacity to accept the Lord.

However, even then, the far greater majority choose to do exactly what the rulers of Israel did so long ago—reject Jesus Christ.

This very scenario, even this that is so obvious before our very eyes concerning the Message of Peter to Israel, proves beyond the shadow of a doubt the free moral agency of man. The Lord presents, and even deals strongly with the individual, but in no way tampers with one's free moral agency. The choice is always that of the person.

2. SINCERITY

Sincerity is not enough! One can be sincerely wrong, as most are.

Billions will one day stand before God at the Great White Throne Judgment and declare their innocence, or lack of guilt as a result of ignorance. They will claim that they sincerely thought such and such was right; therefore, due to this, they will demand pardon by reason of ignorance. However, the Word of God tells us, *"And the times of this ignorance God winked at; but now commands all men every where to repent"* (Acts 17:30).

The word *"winked"* in the Greek is *"hupereido"* and means *"to overlook in the realm of not punishing."* It has nothing to do with the fact of sin and that these people before Christ were sinners and died lost.

The idea is that these pagans had absolutely no Light whatsoever respecting God and, therefore, will suffer less punishment in Hell than those who have had the Light. This is what Jesus meant when He said, *"And that servant, which knew his Lord's will, and prepared not himself, neither did according to His will, shall be beaten with many stripes* (punished severely in Hell, which will last forever).

"But he who knew not, and did commit things worthy of stripes, shall be beaten with few stripes. For unto whomsoever much is given, of him shall be much required: and to whom men have committed much, of him they will ask the more" (Lk. 12:47-48).

In these remarks in Luke, Jesus plainly tells us that ignorance is not Salvation. If ignorance constituted Salvation, then we should close all churches, burn all Bibles, and discontinue the presentation of all Gospel, thereby, insuring the Salvation of all. Of course, such is opposed to all sensible and rational thinking.

An individual may swallow poison in ignorance, but that in no way absolves him of its deadly results.

So, the *"ignorance"* of which Peter spoke in no way absolved these people of blame in any capacity.

(18) "BUT THOSE THINGS, WHICH GOD BEFORE HAD SHOWN BY THE MOUTH OF ALL HIS PROPHETS, THAT CHRIST SHOULD SUFFER, HE HAS SO FULFILLED."

The record is:

1. The phrase, *"But those things, which God before had shown by the mouth of all His Prophets,"* proclaims to us the Inspiration of the Scriptures.

2. The Words, the Statements, and the Doctrines were God's Words, God's Statements, and God's Doctrines.

3. Inasmuch as Israel was the recipient of the very Word of God, they should have known Who and What Jesus was and is. This tells us that the criterion for all spiritual things is the Word of God. When men stand before God, they will not answer according to what their denomination said, or anyone else for that matter, but according to what the Word of God says.

4. Consequently, every Believer must avail himself of the knowledge of the Word of God because he will be judged on that basis.

5. *"That Christ should suffer,"* proclaims Peter now preaching the very Doctrine of the Suffering Messiah, against which Doctrine he had protested (Mat. 16:22).

6. Christ came into the world to *"suffer,"* i.e., to die on Calvary, thereby, paying the price for humanity's sin.

7. *"He has so fulfilled,"* proclaims that such was predestined, but not who would commit this dastardly deed of crucifying Him.

8. The Eighteenth Verse tells us that in some way, every single Prophet listed in the Old Testament spoke of Jesus and what He would do and its necessity.

(19) "REPENT YOU THEREFORE, AND BE CONVERTED, THAT YOUR SINS MAY BE BLOTTED OUT, WHEN THE TIMES OF REFRESHING SHALL COME FROM THE PRESENCE OF THE LORD."

The order is:

1. One never matures beyond the Cross!

2. The whole of the Christian life from beginning to end is simply learning what it means to live by Grace through Faith alone in Christ alone.

3. The Gospel of Jesus Christ is a Gospel of Grace.

REPENTANCE

The phrase, *"Repent you therefore, and be converted,"* was addressed directly to those to whom Peter was speaking, including their rulers, but, as well, speaks to all, and for all time!

The pronoun *"you"* is emphatic, pointing to these particular people, which strongly convicted them of their terrible sin.

The very word *"convert"* in the Greek is *"epistrepho"* and means *"to turn about,"* in this case, toward God.

"That your sins may be blotted out," speaks of Justification by Faith, even though that term at that time would not have been understood.

The Greek word for *"blotted out"* is *"exaleipho"* and means *"to remove completely, to obliterate."*

It not only refers to the account being

NOTES

stricken from the record (Rev. 20:12), but in the Mind of God, it actually never happened.

What a Promise!

This means that all sin, even the horrible sin of these people personally rejecting Christ, and even the most horrible sin of the rulers actually crucifying Christ, could be blotted out through Repentance as if it was never committed. There is no way that one could even begin to imagine or comprehend the magnitude of such Mercy and Grace.

It may not be too difficult for many to understand how God could forgive a so-called good person, but to forgive the very ones who murdered His only Son is beyond the pale of human comprehension. So, if God would forgive that terrible sin, and He definitely did for all who responded to Peter's Message, then no one should ever question God forgiving his sin.

REFRESHING

The phrase, *"When the times of refreshing shall come from the Presence of the Lord,"* should have been translated, *"In order that, the times of refreshing shall come from the Presence of the Lord."*

In other words, upon Repentance, the terrible guilt with its heavy weight is lifted, thus, not having to carry such anymore.

The Greek word for *"refreshing"* is *"anapsuxis"* and means *"to recover one's breath."*

This actually speaks of the terrible load and weight of sin carried by all unbelievers, and as would be obvious, some loads and weights are greater than others. In fact, the Holy Spirit through the Apostle is affirming the fact that due to her murder of Christ, the weight being borne by Israel was the heaviest of all!

This tells us somewhat the cause of all stress, emotional disturbances, and even to a degree, of mental imbalance. All of this contributes heavily toward breakdowns of every description and even sickness and disease.

Only conversion, which is brought about by Repentance, can assuage this terrible condition, which tells us that all the self-help programs and efforts instituted by man to alleviate these problems are less than worthless. This can only come from the *"Presence of the Lord,"* which completely debunks the modern psychological way presently grabbed at by many, if not most, so-called Christian leaders!

(20) "AND HE SHALL SEND JESUS CHRIST, WHICH BEFORE WAS PREACHED UNTO YOU."

The diagram is:

1. The phrase, *"And He shall send Jesus Christ,"* pertains to the Second Coming (Rev., Chpt. 19).

2. *"Which before was preached unto you,"* refers to the approximate three years of the public Ministry of Christ to Israel.

3. In other words, Israel thought they had done away with Christ by crucifying Him, but Peter here said that Jesus is coming back, and Israel will have to face Him, and face Him they will.

(21) "WHOM THE HEAVEN MUST RECEIVE UNTIL THE TIMES OF RESTITUTION OF ALL THINGS, WHICH GOD HAS SPOKEN BY THE MOUTH OF ALL HIS HOLY PROPHETS SINCE THE WORLD BEGAN."

The overview is:

1. Salvation cost God's Son everything, but it cost us nothing.

2. When we turn to the Book of Galatians and, in fact, all of Paul's writings, we see this great Gospel of Grace outlined before our very eyes.

3. To forget the Grace of God in Christ is foolish indeed!

THE RESTITUTION OF ALL THINGS

The phrase, *"Whom the Heaven must receive until the times of restitution of all things,"* refers, in effect, to the Dispensation of the Church Age, which is presently almost over. In fact, if the calendars are correct, as of 2013, the Church is 1,980 years old. The Church Age will be followed by the Kingdom Age when and where the Lord Jesus Christ ultimately will bring all things into perfection.

Concerning this, Paul said, **"Then *comes* the end** *(does not refer to the time immediately following the Rapture or even the Second Coming, but rather to when all Satanic rule and authority have been put*

NOTES

down, which will take place at the conclusion of the Kingdom Age [Rev., Chpt. 20]), **when He** *(Jesus)* **shall have delivered up the Kingdom to God, even the Father; when He shall have put down all rule and all authority and power.** *(He will have put down all of Satan's rule, etc.; the means of which were made possible by the Cross and the Resurrection.)* **For He** *(Jesus)* **must reign** *(refers to the 1,000 year reign of Christ on Earth after He returns)*, **till He has put all enemies under His Feet** *(the subjugation of all evil powers, which will take place at the conclusion of the Kingdom Age [Rev., Chpt. 20])*.

DEATH

"The last enemy *that* shall be destroyed *(abolished)* ***is*** **death** *(Death is the result of sin [Rom. 6:23], and the Cross addressed all sin. After the Resurrection, when all Saints are given glorified bodies, it will be impossible to sin. Even during the Millennial Reign, sin will still be in the world, but not in the Glorified Saints. Sin will be forever eradicated when Satan and all his fallen angels and demons spirits, plus all people who follow him, are cast into the Lake of Fire, where they will remain forever [Rev., Chpt. 20]. Death will then be no more.)*

"For He has put all things under His feet. *(God the Father has put all things under the Feet of Jesus.)* **But when He said all things are put under *Him*, *it is* manifest that He is excepted, which did put all things under Him.** *(This has reference to the fact that 'all things' do not include God the Father being made subject to Jesus. God is excepted, as should be obvious.)*" **(I Cor. 15:24-27).**

The phrase, *"Which God has spoken by the mouth of all His Holy Prophets since the world began,"* proclaims Peter once again basing everything squarely on the Scriptures.

In other words, there is no reason, nor was there any reason, for Israel not to know all of these things. As well, even at the very beginning of the Fall, God foretold the Restoration of all things by the Seed (Jesus) of the woman (Mary) (Gen. 3:15).

Enoch predicted the Second Coming of Christ, which Prophecy was given about 5,500 years ago (Jude, Vs. 14). In fact, most Prophets predicted the final and complete Restoration of all things, which most definitely will take place.

So, there was no excuse for Israel then as there is no excuse for man now. The Word of God is available to all. It proclaims exactly what is coming so that no one need be in ignorance.

SPIRITUAL POVERTY

Observing Israel during the time of Christ, and even at this particular time, it is easy to observe how far these people had fallen from the original Intentions of God. The lame man at the gate, plus untold thousands of others like him in Israel, was a sign of their spiritual poverty.

As well, being ruled by Rome was another penalty for their fallen condition.

When God brought them out of Egypt about 1,500 years before, the Scripture says, *"He brought them forth also with silver and gold: and there was not one feeble person among their tribes"* (Ps. 105:37). Furthermore, the Lord told Moses, *"If you will diligently hearken to the Voice of the Lord your God, and will do that which is right in His Sight … I will put none of these diseases upon you, which I have brought upon the Egyptians: For I am the Lord Who heals you"* (Ex. 15:26).

Concerning nations, it is said, *"And the Lord shall make you the head, and not the tail; and you shall be above only, and you shall not be beneath; if that you hearken unto the Commandments of the Lord your God, which I command you this day, to observe and to do them"* (Deut. 28:13).

Also, He said, *"The Lord shall cause your enemies who rise up against you to be smitten before your face: they shall come out against you one way, and flee before you seven ways"* (Deut. 28:7).

Consequently, it is easy to observe what God intended for these people. There was to be no poverty and no sickness among them, no enemies able to hinder them, and they were to be the mightiest Nation on the face of the Earth.

So, due to their turning away from God,

they now found themselves sick and in bondage to another nation, with many, if not most, of their people poverty stricken. We should take a lesson from this.

If God promised all of that under the Old Covenant, and He certainly did, then He surely will do as much, and even much more, under the New Covenant, which is based on better Promises (Heb. 7:22; 8:6).

THE BLESSINGS OF THE CROSS

How so much we live beneath that which God intends for us. How so much He would bless if we would only line up with His Ways and follow after the Spirit (Rom. 8:6).

What are His Ways? The answer to that is simple: It is the Cross of Christ. That's the reason that Paul said:

"Christ sent me not to baptize, but to preach the Gospel: not with wisdom of words, lest the Cross of Christ should be made of none effect" (I Cor. 1:17).

Paul was not denigrating Water Baptism. He was merely stating that the Cross of Christ must always be preeminent. We must not allow any other great Doctrine of the Bible to take the place of the Cross. It is there where all sin was atoned and all Victory was won by our Saviour over every power of darkness. In fact, without the Cross, no one could be saved, and without the Cross, no Believer could live a victorious life. No one ever matures beyond the Cross. In fact, if one goes beyond the Cross, without fail, one loses one's way.

According to the Word of God, I believe that God intends for all of His Children to be prosperous, healthy, and spiritually strong. That does not mean that there will never be a problem, but it does mean that the Lord will deliver us out of whatever problems do come our way and continue to bless us at all times.

Of course, the condition now of keeping His Word is basically the same as it was under the Old Covenant, with one exception.

The Law of Moses functioned on the premise of performance, to which no one could measure up; however, the great Covenant of Grace is based on Promise, which is centered in Christ and what Christ did for us at the Cross. In effect, it cannot fail

NOTES

because it is all in Jesus. We *"rest"* in that (Mat. 11:28-30).

Jesus has already kept all the Laws, Commandments, and Precepts, and He did it all on our behalf as our Representative Man. As we live by Him, of Him, for Him, and in Him, this great life victory is awarded to us by Faith as well (Rom. 6:11).

(22) "FOR MOSES TRULY SAID UNTO THE FATHERS, A PROPHET SHALL THE LORD YOUR GOD RAISE UP UNTO YOU OF YOUR BRETHREN, LIKE UNTO ME; HIM SHALL YOU HEAR IN ALL THINGS WHATSOEVER HE SHALL SAY UNTO YOU."

The exegesis is:

1. The phrase, *"For Moses truly said unto the Fathers,"* refers to Deuteronomy 18:15-19.

2. Once again, Peter linked everything he was saying, plus the Person of Jesus, to the Scriptures.

3. *"A Prophet shall the Lord your God raise up unto you of your brethren, like unto me,"* presents another Promise given by God concerning the Messiah as it was given to Moses.

4. Referring to this Passage, the Jews would ask John, *"Are you that Prophet?"* (Jn. 1:21).

5. As well, after the Miracle of the loaves and fish, some that day said of Jesus, *"This is of a truth that Prophet Who should come into the world"* (Jn. 6:14; 7:40).

6. In fact, the people were right respecting the fulfillment of that Prophecy, but yet, most would not go so far as to say that Jesus is the Messiah.

7. *"Him shall you hear in all things whatsoever He shall say unto you,"* could not be clearer.

8. They were to recognize Who He was, and they were to hearken unto what He said, but tragically, precious few actually did so.

9. There were many reasons they did not, but the primary reason was that He was not saying what they desired to hear.

10. The religious leaders of Israel desired that He place Himself under their authority and, thereby, do according to their dictates. Of course, that was not the case and in no way could be the case. Therefore, they

opposed Him, even as most so-called religious leaders do presently! There are a few exceptions, but not many.

11. The travesty of their rebellion knows no equal in human history. The evidence as to Who and What He was, was so overwhelming as to be above question. But yet, their rebellious hearts would not accept Him, and as the Holy Spirit through Peter said, *"They killed the Prince of Life, Whom God has raised from the dead"* (Acts 3:15).

(23) "AND IT SHALL COME TO PASS, THAT EVERY SOUL, WHICH WILL NOT HEAR THAT PROPHET, SHALL BE DESTROYED FROM AMONG THE PEOPLE."

The exposition is:

1. The phrase, *"And it shall come to pass, that every soul,"* now extends the Person of Christ not only to the Jews but to the entirety of the world for all time.

2. Even though Jesus almost totally confined His Ministry to the Jews, which is what He should have done, nevertheless, He came for the entirety of the world, and for all time. While He was the Jewish Messiah, He was the world's Saviour.

3. *"Which will not hear that Prophet, shall be destroyed from among the people,"* means to be eternally lost!

4. The Greek word for *"destroyed,"* as used here, is *"exolothreuo"* and means *"to utterly destroy,"* and refers to the destruction of one who refuses to hearken to the Voice of God through Christ.

5. However, the word does not mean extinction of existence, but rather the extinction of all Salvation. In other words, if men refuse to accept Christ, there remains nothing for them but spiritual destruction.

(24) "YES, AND ALL THE PROPHETS FROM SAMUEL AND THOSE WHO FOLLOW AFTER, AS MANY AS HAVE SPOKEN, HAVE LIKEWISE FORETOLD OF THESE DAYS."

The structure is:

1. The phrase, *"Yes, and all the Prophets from Samuel,"* proclaims this Prophet as being the first one to be labeled as such, even though others were spoken of as Prophets before him, such as Abraham and Moses. Though a Prophet, Abraham was looked at more as a Patriarch, even as Moses was looked at mostly as the Law-Giver.

NOTES

2. As well, many believe that Samuel actually served as the last judge of Israel, at least until Saul became king; however, the weight of his Prophetic Office eclipsed that of his judgeship.

3. *"And those who follow after, as many as have spoken, have likewise foretold of these days,"* speaks of all the Prophets, at least in one way or the other, pointing to the coming Redeemer, Who would be the Lord Jesus Christ.

4. So, as we can see, Peter was weaving a Scriptural position that could not be refuted by the religious leaders of Israel.

(25) "YOU ARE THE CHILDREN OF THE PROPHETS, AND OF THE COVENANT WHICH GOD MADE WITH OUR FATHERS, SAYING UNTO ABRAHAM, AND IN YOUR SEED SHALL ALL THE KINDREDS OF THE EARTH BE BLESSED."

The construction is:

1. What is the alternative to the Cross of Jesus Christ?

2. The only alternative is to fall back once again upon our own resources.

3. Of course, when one does fall back on his own resources, failure is the inevitable result.

THE PROPHETS

The phrase, *"You are the children of the Prophets,"* means simply that they should have known what the Prophets had said.

That they knew very little of what the Word of God actually said about the Messiah is overly obvious. However, their ignorance, as stated, was a self-willed ignorance in that they put everything else ahead of the Word of God or twisted the Word to suit their own desires. To be frank, millions are in the same situation presently.

There are not many in America or Canada, or many other countries in the world for that matter, who cannot know exactly what the Word of God says about any and all things. Of course, the unsaved have no interest, and even if they attempted to read the Word, they would have precious little understanding of its contents. However, many unsaved and attempting to read the Bible have become convicted and, thereby, given their hearts and lives to Jesus Christ, but in view of the whole, that number is small.

Sadly, most Believers little study the Word of God, either out of apathy, or they somehow think that ignorance of the Word absolves them of responsibility.

It does not!

Just as this generation that crucified Christ was not absolved of responsibility, neither are all those who have followed in their train.

THE COVENANT

The phrase, *"And of the Covenant which God made with our Fathers,"* actually refers to the Abrahamic Covenant (Gen. 12:1-3).

"Saying unto Abraham, And in your Seed shall all the kindreds of the earth be blessed," speaks of Jesus Christ as that *"Seed."* Consequently, Jesus is referred to as, *"The Son of David, the Son of Abraham"* (Mat. 1:1). Truly, Jesus Christ has brought the greatest *"Blessing"* of all to this Earth, in effect, blessing all people everywhere.

I thank God that my *"kindred"* (family) had the privilege of hearing about Jesus, which, if I remember correctly, was in 1940. This would be a red-letter day in our lives, especially in mine, even though I was only a child. I was only five years old when my parents were saved, but in effect, our whole world changed. Without a doubt, it was our greatest day, the day that Jesus Christ was introduced to us.

In order to bring the Redeemer into the world, thereby, fulfilling that which God had promised in the Garden of Eden (Gen. 3:15), it was necessary to do certain things.

God would have to become Man (Isa. 7:14), thereby, becoming the Last Adam and taking the place of the first Adam who fell. In order to do this, a human lineage, beginning, as is obvious, with Adam, had to go in an unbroken line toward the *"Seed of the woman,"* spoken of by the Lord.

To do this, God chose Abraham out of Ur of the Chaldees, where he had formerly been an idol-worshipper; however, he heeded the Voice of the Lord, thereby, in effect, accepting Christ Jesus as his Saviour. The Lord made a Covenant with him, of which Peter here spoke. That Covenant was at least one of the grandest in human history, promising a Redeemer for all of mankind.

NOTES

The Miracle Child Isaac was born to him and Sarah; and to Isaac, Esau and Jacob.

FAITH

Jacob was chosen by God to serve in the lineage of the coming Redeemer, even though he was not the firstborn. Faith has always superseded Law and did so in that case. Esau had no faith in the coming Redeemer, while Jacob had great Faith. From his loins came the Patriarchs, who would head up the Thirteen Tribes of Israel, thereby, forming a Nation of people who would give the world the Word of God and the Messiah, Who would be the Lord Jesus Christ. Before Jacob died, he prophesied that of those Tribes, the Tribe of Judah was thus chosen to be the favored one (Gen. 49:10), who would give the world the Promised *"Seed."* The Lord then told David that it would be through his family that this Promised *"Seed"* would come. David was a member of the Tribe of Judah (II Sam., Chpt. 7). In due time, the *"Seed"* was born, Who was Jesus Christ, born, we might quickly add, of the Virgin Mary, and Who has blessed the entirety of the world for time and eternity.

(26) "UNTO YOU FIRST GOD, HAVING RAISED UP HIS SON JESUS, SENT HIM TO BLESS YOU, IN TURNING AWAY EVERY ONE OF YOU FROM HIS INIQUITIES."

The synopsis is:

1. The phrase, *"Unto you first God,"* refers to the offer of Salvation being made first to the Jews (Lk. 24:47; Rom. 1:16; 2:10). However, they did not accept Him, even crucifying Him.

2. *"Having raised up His Son Jesus,"* refers to the Resurrection. Therefore, they did not rid themselves in any way of the Person of Christ.

3. *"Sent Him to bless you,"* refers to God being the Blesser and the Bearer of the Blessing, the Lord Jesus Christ. The object of the Blessing was to be Israel, *"You first!"* Regrettably, they were *"murderers."*

4. *"In turning away every one of you from his iniquities,"* proclaims the

"Blessing" of which Peter spoke.

5. Even though there are many wonderful side effects to the Gospel, such as prosperity, healing, Blessings of every nature, etc., nevertheless, the main thrust of the Gospel always has been, is now, and will ever be the saving of man from sin. The nature of this Blessing is a definite separation from everything sinful.

6. The Apostolic Gospel was based upon the Bible, as is here obvious. Its authority was decisive and infallible. Upon this basis was placed a personal Testimony.

7. Man's moral ruin as a sinner and the certitude of the Wrath of God upon sin and sinners were enforced. The note dominating all was the Person and Work of The Lord Jesus Christ, Who paid the price for all of us at Calvary's Cross. Belief in Him and what He has done for us secured Eternal Life and necessitated a definite break with sin and sinning. This can only come about by one placing one's Faith exclusively in Christ and what Christ has done for us at the Cross, and maintaining it exclusively in Christ and the Cross.

8. As in I Corinthians 15:1-8, so here the facts and Doctrines of the Gospel were based upon the infallible Word of God. It decided everything. From it, there was no appeal. Then, human Testimony was added to assure man's doubting heart.

9. However, the Testimony of the Bible came first and was decisive. Regrettably, a school of modern thought reverses this so as to place man above the Bible; however, all such thinking leads to ruin, while adhering to the Word of God leads to unparalleled Blessings.

One particular preacher, a member of one of the largest Pentecostal denominations in the world, foolishly stated that modern man is facing problems of which solutions are not found in the Bible and, therefore, modern man, he went on to state, needs the help of humanistic psychology.

How foolish can we be!

Peter said: *"Grace and Peace be multiplied unto you through the knowledge of God, and of Jesus our Lord.*

"According as His Divine Power has given unto us all things that pertain unto life and godliness, through the knowledge of Him Who has called us to Glory and Virtue:

"Whereby are given unto us exceeding great and Precious Promises: that by these you might be partakers of the Divine Nature, having escaped the corruption that is in the world through lust" (II Pet. 1:2-4).

So, one can take the word of Peter, which was given to him by the Holy Spirit, or the word of that foolish preacher. As for me and my house, we will take the Word of God.

"When pangs of death seized on my soul,
"Unto the Lord I cried,
"Till Jesus came and made me whole,
"I would not be denied."

"As Jacob in the days of old,
"I wrestled with the Lord,
"And instant, with a courage bold,
"I stood upon His Word."

"Old Satan said my Lord was gone,
"And would not hear my prayer,
"But, praise the Lord! the work is done,
"And Christ the Lord is here."

CHAPTER 4

(1) "AND AS THEY SPOKE UNTO THE PEOPLE, THE PRIESTS, AND THE CAPTAIN OF THE TEMPLE, AND THE SADDUCEES, CAME UPON THEM."

The composition is:

1. The phrase, *"And as they spoke unto the people,"* pertains, as is obvious, to the Word of God going forth to the hungry hearts of those who were there that day, even thousands.

2. It is Satan's business to stop the Gospel, and the far greater majority of the time, he uses the so-called church to do so. Let the Preacher understand that if he preaches the Truth and has the Holy Spirit working through him mightily, he is the very one Satan is going to attack and will pull no punches in doing so. As stated, it will come from the religious sector almost

all of the time.

3. *"The Priests, and the captain of the Temple, and the Sadducees, came upon them,"* probably represents both Pharisees and Sadducees, for in all likelihood, some, if not the majority, of these *"Priests"* were Pharisees.

4. Even though some *"Priests"* accepted Christ, even as we shall see, most were strident enemies of Christ from the very beginning.

5. It is thought that the *"captain of the Temple"* was the son of the High Priest Ananias. He had under him the Levitical Guard, whose duty it was to keep order in the Temple courts at all times.

6. The *"Sadducees"* pretty well controlled the High Priesthood, and actually most of the Priestly duties of the Temple, at least as far as overseership was concerned.

7. Satan used the Pharisees to oppose Christ in Atonement and the Sadducees to oppose Him in Resurrection; both were his instruments.

8. The one was self-righteous and sought Eternal Life through personal moral merit; the others were self-thinkers, denied the fact of Resurrection, and hence, became prominent as opposing the Gospel.

9. The section from Acts 4:1 to Acts 5:16 may be termed the *"Great"* section. It records *"Great Conversions"* (Acts 4:4; 5:14); *"Great Opposition"* (Acts 4:6; 5:17); *"Great Boldness"* (Acts 4:13); *"Great Faith"* (Acts 4:24); *"Great Bible Intelligence"* (Acts 4:25); *"Great Expectation"* (Acts 5:30); *"Great Unity"* (Acts 4:32); *"Great Power"* (Acts 5:33); *"Great Grace"* (Acts 4:33); *"Great Sacrifice"* (Acts 4:34); *"Great Fear"* (Acts 5:5, 11); *"Great Miracles"* (Acts 4:16); and, *"Great Love"* (Acts 4:34) (Williams).

(2) "BEING GRIEVED THAT THEY TAUGHT THE PEOPLE, AND PREACHED THROUGH JESUS THE RESURRECTION FROM THE DEAD."

The exegesis is:

1. The phrase, *"Being grieved that they taught the people,"* proclaims their consternation. In the Greek the word *"grieved"* means *"worried."*

2. They were greatly upset because of the success of the Gospel, and because the Name of Jesus was being used freely and seeing tremendous results, as with the Miracle performed on the lame man. They may have thought that they had rid themselves of this Jesus, but they now found that the whole thing had multiplied manyfold and seemed to be unending.

3. The phrase, *"And preached through Jesus the Resurrection from the dead,"* concerns the area of their greatest difficulty.

4. The Sadducees denied that there was any such thing as a Resurrection (Lk. 20:27). So, what Peter and John were preaching impacted their doctrines in a strong way, especially considering that these men were preaching under a heavy Anointing of the Holy Spirit. Consequently, their arguments were irrefutable, even as the Holy Spirit was convicting people of their sins, which greatly validated their Doctrine and lifted up Jesus.

5. However, the Temple must not be misunderstood as being similar to the modern church, for it was not! It was for Jews, and even Gentiles, that is, if the Gentiles were in the place reserved for them, which was the Court of the Gentiles.

6. Concerning the preaching of a Resurrection, even though the Sadducees would have been greatly opposed, still, in all likelihood, they normally would have probably said nothing, inasmuch as the Pharisees strongly believed in a Resurrection.

However, the Apostles were not only preaching the Resurrection but strongly linking it to Jesus. The Sadducees probably thought that with that being the case, the Pharisees would not object to their strong-arm methods.

(3) "AND THEY LAID HANDS ON THEM, AND PUT THEM IN HOLD UNTO THE NEXT DAY: FOR IT WAS NOW EVENTIDE."

The synopsis is:

1. The phrase, *"And they laid hands on them,"* refers to the methods just mentioned.

2. It is said that the harsh persecution of the Apostles at Jerusalem at this time when the Sadducees were in power is in exact accordance with the statement of Josephus that the Sadducees were more severe and cruel in their administration of so-called

NOTES

justice than any other Jews. Their tenet of no life to come, hence, no Resurrection, made them look to severe punishments in this life.

3. *"And put them in hold unto the next day,"* was probably a small prison in the confines of the Temple.

4. *"For it was now eventide,"* referred to night drawing on; however, despite the persecution, this day would record a tremendous number of people being brought to Christ and, therefore, receiving the great Gift of Salvation.

(4) "HOWBEIT MANY OF THEM WHICH HEARD THE WORD BELIEVED; AND THE NUMBER OF THE MEN WAS ABOUT FIVE THOUSAND."

The construction is:

1. The only way that sin can be properly addressed is by and through the Cross.

2. That's why Paul said that the emphasis must always be on the Cross. It is by and through what Jesus did at the Cross that effects the Salvation of the sinner and the Sanctification of the Saint.

THE WORD

The phrase, *"Howbeit many of them which heard the Word believed,"* has reference to the fact that they believed on Christ, thereby, accepting Him as the Messiah of Israel and the Saviour of men.

The Greek word for *"believed"* is *"pisteuo"* and means *"to have Faith in, upon, or with respect to, a person or thing,"* in this case, the Lord Jesus Christ.

So, this was not a mere mental affirmation but a decision made after all the facts had been assimilated and observed. In other words, these publicly accepted Christ in the confines of the Temple, even though they knew it would mean tremendous opposition on the part of the powers that be, as is now obvious.

There is no such thing as a silent Believer. Such is impossible, at least for any length of time. Ultimately, when it comes to Christ, the Believer must make a bold announcement to all concerning his Faith and allow the Lord to take care of the results. This does not mean that all have to shout such from the housetops; however, it does mean that, in most cases, ultimately a confession of Faith before others must be made. It seems these people did exactly that!

This method of preaching the Gospel was instigated by the Holy Spirit even in the preparation of the coming Messiah, as carried out by John the Baptist. He came preaching!

PREACHING

Christ conducted Himself in the same manner, and we find here the Holy Spirit continuing the process. Consequently, this is the main means in which the Gospel is given to all of mankind. To be sure, the Lord has not changed from that day until this. He still calls men and women to preach the Gospel and anoints them with the Holy Spirit. To seek any other method only constitutes Spiritual and Scriptural ignorance of the highest order.

However, let it be known that the hotter the Church, the hotter the preaching!

As well, let it be known that the colder the church, the colder the preaching until it little exists, if at all! The moment the church begins to stress other things is the moment the Holy Spirit ceases to function. He will only work according to His Prescribed manner, and rightly so! He is God; therefore, He knows all things.

And yet, it is not uncommon at all to hear religious men belittle the preaching of the Gospel. These people constitute such as vulgar, crude, and outdated. Of course, whenever these things are said, the insult is toward the Holy Spirit!

It is sad when one realizes that much of this sarcasm comes from those who refer to themselves as Pentecostal but obviously are not, as should be obvious!

The Holy Spirit anoints the preaching of the Word, at least if the Word is truly being preached, and the Preacher in question has truly sought the Lord. There is nothing more powerful than the preaching of the Gospel under the Anointing of the Holy Spirit. That alone can truly bring great numbers to Christ!

PEOPLE BEING SAVED

The phrase, *"And the number of the men*

NOTES

was about five thousand," seems to speak only of men, and for whatever reason, does not count the women and children who came to Christ that day.

Some have claimed that this number includes the 3,000 of Acts 2:41; however, such does not seem to be the case.

In Acts 2:41, it says, *"And the same day there were added unto them about three thousand souls,"* so that tells us that this number was saved on that particular day, while the latter number pertained to an entirely different situation altogether.

At that time, there could have been well over 10,000 people who had already given their hearts and lives to Christ since the Day of Pentecost. The Message was spreading fast!

(5) "AND IT CAME TO PASS ON THE MORROW, THAT THEIR RULERS, AND ELDERS, AND SCRIBES."

The synopsis is:

1. Believers are able to *"walk after the Spirit,"* not by doing something, but rather by trusting in something that's already done.
2. That trust pertains to Christ and what He did for us at the Cross.
3. The Object of Faith for the Believer must always be *"Jesus Christ and Him Crucified."*

INSTITUTIONALIZED RELIGION

The phrase, *"And it came to pass on the morrow,"* refers to the following day, as is obvious, and would be a day of confrontation.

As outlined in this Chapter, that which was to happen is that which confronts every true Preacher of the Gospel in one form or the other, sooner or later! By far, the greatest hindrance to the Cause of Christ is not the world system or the vices that are paramount in that system, but rather that which purports to be of God and, thereby, a part of the Work of God. If such could be labeled, it could be referred to as *"Institutionalized Religion."* However, the type of institutionalization of which I speak has little to do with denominations, etc., and neither has it anything to do with organization. For that of which I speak is just as rampant in so-called independent churches as in the denominational variety.

NOTES

I speak of that which is controlled by man and not by the Holy Spirit.

The very word *"institution"* actually refers to *"organization."* That within itself is not wrong. The greatest organization in the world is found in the Kingdom of God; however, it is His organization and not man's. As well, His organization (institution) is not that of the world and actually has no resemblance to the systems of the world. For one to follow God's organization, one must be totally and completely led by the Holy Spirit. I might quickly add, God's Kingdom is not a democracy; therefore, it is not subject to popular vote or conventional wisdom. Inasmuch as it takes a close walk with God to function in such a government, the field is sparsely populated.

MAN'S ORGANIZATION

On the other hand, institution and organization derived by man in the realm of the Work of God constitute the far greater majority of that which calls itself *"Christian"* or *"Church."* To be sure, even by its very nature, this *"organization"* originated by man, which means it has deviated from the Word of God, will greatly oppose that which is ordained by God and, thereby, led by the Holy Spirit. It began with Cain and Abel and has continued unchecked unto this very hour.

As previously stated, if a man or woman sets out to follow the Lord in the realm of Ministry and determines to continue in that vein, the confrontation with man's religious government is going to come sooner or later.

Sadly, most give in, going the way of man, which meets with man's approval; consequently, their ministry thereafter is compromised, with the Holy Spirit not allowed to take them to the height of His Plan for their lives.

At this moment, tens of thousands of pastors are saying, respecting their particular denominations, *"I do not approve of what is being done, but it has no effect on me."* However, it does have an effect!

If we support something that is wrong, even to the slightest degree, we automatically become a part of the wrong, with such leaven ultimately corrupting the whole. There is no way that one can stay in an unscriptural position and remain static. If it is unscriptural, the very law of such demands a constant regression, which may be slow, but is prevalent nevertheless.

A PERSONAL EXPERIENCE

Just a few days ago, an Evangelist, whom I have known for many years, came by Family Worship Center on a Sunday night. The Lord moved especially so that evening, with an obvious Outpouring of the Holy Spirit, which affected everyone in the congregation, including the Evangelist and his wife.

After the service and during a short time of fellowship, he mentioned something about coming to our church and ministering, etc.

"My Brother," I said, *"If you did that, the denomination with which you are associated would excommunicate you immediately, and in a very derogatory way."*

"You can't be serious," he said! *"Do they not see and know how the Power of God is present in this place?"*

I went on to relate to him that the Moving and Operation of the Holy Spirit has nothing to do with that of which I speak. In other words, even as the *"rulers, Elders, and Scribes"* of Peter's day, who had no regard whatsoever that the lame man at the gate called Beautiful had been healed, likewise, this is not the criterion in its modern counterpart.

The criterion for the true Preacher of the Gospel is the Leading and Operation of the Holy Spirit. The criterion for institutionalized religion is control. That is what it all boils down to—control. Therefore, it is not possible, at least in most cases, to listen to the Voice of the Holy Spirit and the voice of man at the same time, even as this Chapter will prove.

So, what should that Evangelist do, whom I have just mentioned?

He can take the position that most take, that it little affects him and, therefore, he will say nothing; or, he can pass the rulings of this particular denomination under the judgment of the Word of God, which must be done sooner or later. If he honestly does that, he will bid these people a quiet farewell.

NOTES

Of course, most preachers take the position that if such is done, *"Where will I preach?"*

In that case, the Lord will have to provide, as He desired to be doing all along but was little allowed. Regrettably, most preachers make their decision according to money and welfare, which spells to them security; consequently, they are now totally controlled, whether they realize it or not, by the powers that be.

THE WORD OF GOD

At this moment, many Catholic priests and nuns know and realize that their system is ungodly, unscriptural, and corrupt; however, they ask themselves the question as to what they will do if the church no longer supports them. Where will they go? What type of ministry, if any, will they have?

Of course, all such thinking, whether Catholic or Protestant, shows a lack of trust respecting God and His Word. The truth is, most preachers in the world are not looking to God for their upkeep, support, leading, or direction, but rather their man-devised and man-operated religious denominations. As such, the Holy Spirit has little or no part!

It is impossible to have both!

The phrase, *"That their rulers, and Elders, and Scribes,"* speaks of the assembly of the Sanhedrin, or the Grand Council of the Jews.

(6) "AND ANNAS THE HIGH PRIEST, AND CAIAPHAS, AND JOHN, AND ALEXANDER, AND AS MANY AS WERE OF THE KINDRED OF THE HIGH PRIEST, WERE GATHERED TOGETHER AT JERUSALEM."

The structure is:

1. The phrase, *"And Annas the High Priest,"* actually meant that he was an associate High Priest with Caiaphas (Lk. 3:2; Jn. 18:13, 19, 24). He had been High Priest for 11 years, bore the title all his life, and had the honor of seeing five sons fill the office after him. As well, he was the father-in-law to Caiaphas.

Actually, the succession of the High Priests at this time was so irregular, and their tenure of the office so uncertain due to

NOTES

Roman control, that in the later years of the Jewish Commonwealth, the office was filled at the caprice of the civil rulers, who appointed and deposed them at their pleasure.

2. Consequently, the Aaronic Priesthood, at least regarding the High Priests as originally designed by the Holy Spirit and given to Moses, had long since gone by the boards, so to speak. It was now far more a political office than spiritual.

3. The words, *"And Caiaphas,"* presents the one who actually occupied the Office of High Priest at this time and through whom the real power, Annas, actually worked!

4. Caiaphas served as the trial judge of Jesus (Mat. 26:2-3, 57, 63-65; Jn. 18:24-28), Peter, and others, as is here obvious.

5. Two years after the Crucifixion, both he and Pilate were deposed by Vitellius, then governor of Syria, and afterward, the Roman Emperor.

6. It is said that Caiaphas, who was probably guiltier of the murder of Christ than any other man except Judas, committed suicide.

7. The words, *"And John,"* leave no hint as to who exactly he was; however, some think he could have been Johanan Ben Zakkai, a famous rabbi of that time.

8. The words, *"And Alexander,"* could possibly refer to Alexander Lysimachus, who was a very rich man, and who also was a friend of King Agrippa.

9. The phrase, *"And as many as were of the kindred of the High Priest,"* speaks of the certain families from which the High Priests were taken. They would naturally be the near relations of the High Priest; consequently, there is a possibility that some or all of the five sons of Annas were also present.

10. *"Were gathered together at Jerusalem,"* implies that some of them may not have lived in the city normally but found themselves here at this particular time.

(7) "AND WHEN THEY HAD SET THEM IN THE MIDST, THEY ASKED, BY WHAT POWER, OR BY WHAT NAME, HAVE YOU DONE THIS?"

The record is:

1. The phrase, *"And when they had set them in the midst,"* proclaims Peter and John being brought from jail and made to stand before the Sanhedrin. Considering that there were 71 members of the Sanhedrin, counting the High Priest, and that others were present, as well, the total number could have been significant, possibly over 100. This portrays how serious they considered what had happened on the Day of Pentecost and following. They thought they were rid of Jesus when they crucified Him, but now they were faced with the scores of witnesses and Testimonies who claimed that He was raised from the dead and that they saw Him with their own eyes. As well, His Disciples, who had been somewhat retiring before the Crucifixion, now seemed to exhibit the same Powers that Jesus had! So, the situation was multiplying, and fast!

2. The question, *"They asked, By what power, or by what name, have you done this?"* pertained to that of which they already knew the answer.

3. As well, the pronoun, *"You,"* is emphatic and was said with contempt.

4. Once again, the sectarian spirit, which evidenced itself in these men all during the Ministry of Jesus, continues presently on the same path. They were the elite of Israel; consequently, these unlearned Apostles were nothing, at least in their eyes, and would be treated accordingly. Such is religion!

5. Self-righteousness and elitism characterize many, if not most, religious denominations. However, such is never of God and always opposes God.

6. The words, *"By what name?"* actually mean, *"By what authority?"*

(8) "THEN PETER, FILLED WITH THE HOLY SPIRIT, SAID UNTO THEM, YOU RULERS OF THE PEOPLE, AND ELDERS OF ISRAEL."

The form is:

1. The Object of one's Faith must always be *"Jesus Christ and Him Crucified"* (I Cor. 1:17-18, 21, 23; 2:2, 5).

2. The modern church talks about Faith constantly, but the type of faith it talks about is not really the type of Faith that Paul talked about.

3. When Paul spoke of Faith, without exception, he was speaking of what Jesus did at the Cross, which, in essence, is described

as *"the Faith"* (Gal. 2:20).

THE HOLY SPIRIT

The phrase, *"Then Peter, filled with the Holy Spirit, said unto them,"* proclaims the strength of these men, and actually that of the entirety of the Early Church. Over 50 times in the Book of Acts, the Holy Spirit is mentioned in one way or the other. He is either addressing the situation, or else, He is portrayed in the pivotal role.

As this was the secret of the strength of these, and the Early Church in general, it is the secret presently. Without the Holy Spirit, irrespective of all the other accouterments one may have, nothing is going to be done for the Lord. With the Holy Spirit, all types of things can be done, even as we are here seeing proclaimed.

About one-half of the churches presently in Christendom do not even believe in the Baptism with the Holy Spirit according to Acts 2:4. While they agree that it was valid then, they claim it is no longer valid, and for any number of reasons. They say it passed away with the Apostles or ceased after the Book of Revelation was concluded, thereby, finishing the Canon of Scripture.

Others twist and pervert Scripture, attempting to make it mean something that is illogical as one compares Scripture with Scripture. Irrespective, in these circles, the Holy Spirit is vigorously opposed, even though such would be denied.

CONTROLLED BY THE HOLY SPIRIT

In these churches, nothing is done for the Lord, irrespective of all the religious machinery. Even though my statements are blunt, I believe them to be true. As far as the Lord is concerned, this is not church. If the Holy Spirit is not present and, in fact, is not even desired, by no stretch of the imagination can these gatherings or organizations even be called *"Church,"* that is, if His Word is to be the criterion. Without the Holy Spirit it is simply not possible to have Church, properly understand the Word of God, or do anything for the Lord for that matter!

We must not forget that the Lord especially forbade the beginning of the Church until the Holy Spirit was present. That's the reason He *"Commanded"* His Followers to go to Jerusalem and wait for the Promise of the Father (Acts, Chpt. 1).

The word *"filled"* in the Greek is *"pletho"* and means *"to imbue, influence, or supply."* So it would probably have been better translated *"controlled by the Holy Spirit."*

All Believers who are baptized with the Holy Spirit have all the Holy Spirit and not a part. The Holy Spirit is a Person and not a mere substance or emanation. As such, when He comes in, He does so totally.

Therefore, no Believer can partially have the Holy Spirit as if one would have a container half filled with water or some such type of substance.

Therefore, the problem is control rather than filling. The Holy Spirit desires to control us but can only do so as we earnestly give Him permission and, as well, provide a suitable temple for Him, which can only be done by the means of the Cross (I Cor. 3:16).

For God the Holy Spirit to dwell in the heart and life of a mere mortal is absolutely wonderful to behold, as should be obvious. This was made possible only by the Death and Resurrection of Christ, which then made it possible for the Holy Spirit to literally indwell the Believer.

So, Peter here was being totally controlled by the Holy Spirit, Who empowered him to speak boldly and empowered him formerly to be an instrument in bringing about the Healing of the lame man at the gate called Beautiful. This, and only this, is the manner in which things are done for the Lord. All else is man-conceived and man-instituted and, as a result, serves no purpose for God, but rather the very opposite; however, with the Holy Spirit leading and guiding, plus empowering, miraculous things are done for God!

A WARNING BY THE HOLY SPIRIT

The phrase, *"You rulers of the people, and Elders of Israel,"* was used by Peter in this manner for purpose.

The Holy Spirit, through him, was pointing out the responsibility they held as the spiritual guides of the people, even as Peter addressed them with respect. Whether they

NOTES

NOTES

realized it at that time or not, no rulers on Earth had ever been so privileged and, at the same time, so culpable.

They were privileged in that which the Prophets had spoken concerning the coming of the Redeemer, which had taken place in their time. No rulers could be more privileged or blessed; however, they did not know the time of their visitation. Consequently, they killed the Lord of Glory, bringing upon themselves the most horrifying judgment ever experienced by any people. It resulted in the destruction of their Nation and their sinking into spiritual darkness, where they have remained for nearly 2,000 years.

And yet, the Holy Spirit would continue to try to reach them through Peter and later through Paul, but sadly, to no avail!

It is not known at this time as to the disposition of Joseph of Arimathaea or of Nicodemus, concerning their continuing to be members of the Sanhedrin. After coming out publicly for Jesus at His Death, no doubt, they had by now resigned as there is no mention of them in the Book of Acts as having continued in this position.

(9) "IF WE THIS DAY BE EXAMINED OF THE GOOD DEED DONE TO THE IMPOTENT MAN, BY WHAT MEANS HE IS MADE WHOLE."

The form is:

1. The phrase, *"If we this day be examined of the good deed done to the impotent man,"* proclaims Peter, in effect, asking as to how or why a good deed such as this would be questioned! It would seem that the rulers would be thrilled beyond words; however, it was not really the deed in question but how it was done, and more particularly, by Whom it was done!

2. *"By what means he is made whole,"* presents the cause of the attitude and action of the ruling body of Israel.

3. Such is religion! It has little or no regard at all for souls being saved, the sick being healed, bondages being broken, and lives being changed, unless such is done under its authority, which it seldom, if ever, is. In the first place, it will not admit that such can be done outside of its authority and, therefore, will not recognize the authority of anyone else, even that of God. In fact, such religious leaders do not even believe in the Power of God. Religion is to them a business.

4. In effect, these rulers would rather have seen people die eternally lost, or this man remain crippled the rest of his life, living (if one could call it that) as a beggar, rather than be healed in the Name of Jesus. That seems incredible, but it is true!

5. Such has not changed unto this hour. Even though most of the laity in Pentecostal churches would have little knowledge of what I speak, still, it is true that most of their leaders presently, at least in America and Canada, would rather see people die eternally lost, even as those rulers of Israel of so long ago, than to come to Christ under someone who is not of their choosing. I realize that sounds harsh, and most would not even believe what I am saying; however, it is true! And yet, I pray so much that it will change.

While these leaders would deny this, even as the rulers of Israel, their actions prove differently.

6. These men would seek to stop Peter and John, which had they been successful, would have stopped the Healing of anyone else, or any other work for God for that matter! Therefore, one can truly conclude that they cared not at all about the lost, sick, and suffering, but only that their so-called authority had been abrogated. The spirit of their modern counterparts is identical!

As here, there is no evil like religious evil!

A PERSONAL EXPERIENCE

Let me give you an idea of this of which I speak.

Right at the beginning of the Soviet Union coming out from communism, the Lord opened the door for us to air television programming over the largest television channel in the world, TV-1 out of Moscow. It covered all 15 Soviet Republics, with some 7,000 repeater stations.

We had to translate the program into Russian, and the Lord ultimately gave us an excellent translator. We saw a tremendous work for God accomplished in the former Soviet Union.

However, before the Lord gave us the

translator that we used, we heard of another brother who was Russian and could speak both Russian and English.

My associate, Jim Woolsey, called him and asked if he would be interested in doing the translation work. He instantly stated that he would very much like to do such, but then he added that he belonged to a certain denomination and would have to get their permission.

Jim called the leader, whomever he was. I did not know him, had never heard of him, and had had no dealings with him whatsoever.

At any rate, when Jim mentioned the programming and that he would be translating for me, the man went into a tirade and said that under no circumstances would he be allowed to do the translation work.

Jim told him that these people would be hearing the Gospel for the first time, and without the Gospel, they would die and go to Hell. The man's answer was startling!

Even though he was a pastor of a so-called church, he answered Jim by saying, *"I would rather see them go to Hell than to hear the Gospel preached by Jimmy Swaggart."*

That's what I mean! There is no evil like the evil of religion. That's the type of evil that nailed Christ to a Cross.

(10) "BE IT KNOWN UNTO YOU ALL, AND TO ALL THE PEOPLE OF ISRAEL, THAT BY THE NAME OF JESUS CHRIST OF NAZARETH, WHOM YOU CRUCIFIED, WHOM GOD RAISED FROM THE DEAD, EVEN BY HIM DOES THIS MAN STAND HERE BEFORE YOU WHOLE."

The pattern is:

1. There's only one way the Believer can live a victorious Christian life.

2. That way is by the means of the Cross of Christ.

3. The Believer is to place his Faith exclusively in Christ and what Christ has done for us at the Cross, and maintain it thusly (I Cor. 1:17-18; 2:2; Col. 2:10-15).

STRONG PREACHING

The phrase, *"Be it known unto you all, and to all the people of Israel,"* specifies that this Message concerning Jesus Christ was to be given both to the rulers and the people of Israel. As we have already stated, the portent of this Message was so very significant, even beyond its normal impact of the Salvation of eternal souls. Of course, nothing is more important than that; however, there was an added impetus here in that the very Nation of Israel was hanging in the balance, respecting their response. Not only would the decision of the rulers impact themselves but, in fact, would impact all future generations of Jews, even up to the Second Coming of our Lord, which has not yet happened.

A Jewish friend mentioned to me once that they (this present generation), etc., were not responsible for what someone did nearly 2,000 years ago, respecting a Man Whom none of them had ever seen, or millions who had lived and died in the intervening time.

While that is true, certain things are brought into focus here:

What we do, especially in the spiritual sense, greatly affects others, even coming generations, etc. For instance, as the Spirit of God deals with a young man about Salvation, if he accepts the Lord, his children—that is, if he does have children at a later time—will be greatly affected in a positive sense (and even all after them). However, if Jesus is rejected, the reverse is true!

At the Crucifixion of Christ, the Jews had said, *"His Blood be on us, and on our children"* (Mat. 27:25).

So, the decision they made that day did exactly what they said. It adversely affected their children and their children's children, even to a degree that is beyond comprehension.

BY THE NAME OF JESUS CHRIST OF NAZARETH

The unbeliever, as I have stated the fact, may claim that such is unfair, even as my Jewish friend; however, the entirety of the warp and woof of life is inextricably bound up in this very fashion. The mother contracts AIDS, and her baby is born with AIDS. While it could be argued that such is not fair simply because the baby was not culpable of any sin or wrongdoing, which is certainly true, irrespective, the baby has AIDS, etc.

NOTES

NOTES

Even though my Jewish friend was right respecting him being far removed from this day of darkness of so long ago, still, he had no more love for Jesus Christ than his forefathers and frankly admitted such to me. Neither do most other Jews! Consequently, the curse called upon them so long ago continues to operate.

However, any Jew at any time, as well as any Gentile, can say *"Yes"* to Jesus Christ and as far as they or their children are concerned, the situation graphically and drastically changes, and for the good I might quickly add!

The phrase, *"That by the Name of Jesus Christ of Nazareth,"* proclaims Peter speaking of Jesus in the same fashion as he did in his Message on the Day of Pentecost. He wanted all and sundry to know which Jesus it was of Whom he spoke.

A HOLY BOLDNESS

However, I personally believe that Peter's boldness and constant portrayal of Jesus, even in the face of the most strident enemies of our Lord, were, in a sense, a response to his denial of Christ on the Day of the Crucifixion. It seems as if the Holy Spirit gave him a holy boldness to proclaim this Name, in other words, turning what had been Peter's weakness (cowardness) into his great strength.

It is somewhat like a broken bone being properly set. When it heals, it is stronger at the place of the break than any other part of the appendage. The Lord will take that which had been our gross weakness and turn it into that which is now our great strength, and actually, that is His very Business.

Moses is a case in point in that he had been a firebrand in his own personal actions at the beginning of his obedience to the Lord. In anger, he killed a man (Ex. 2:11-14). However, at a point in time, the Scripture says, *"Now the man Moses was very meek, above all the men which were upon the face of the Earth"* (Num. 12:3).

Whereas Peter had once failed regarding the owning of Jesus, even in the presence of a young girl, he now proudly owned that Name before the highest tribunal of Israel. Of course, it was the Spirit of God Who gave him this boldness, even as the first part of Acts 4:8 declares.

PULLING NO PUNCHES

The phrase, *"Whom you crucified,"* places the emphasis on the word *"you,"* thereby, pointedly and directly fastening the terrible sin of crucifying their Messiah squarely on their shoulders.

What must have been their thoughts when he said this, considering that he was anointed heavily by the Holy Spirit to utter these words; consequently, his declaration was driven to the very depths of the black hearts of these reprobates.

These men had been accustomed to making judgments and handing down decisions, with their authority never questioned at all. However, it is easy to observe that Peter and John held the authority at this time, with the persons of these two men looming heavily over these rulers. In effect, they were the instruments as the Spirit of God did with the Apostles exactly what Jesus had previously said, *"And you shall be brought before Governors and Kings for My sake, for a testimony against them and the Gentiles.*

"But when they deliver you up, take no thought how or what you shall speak: for it shall be given you in that same hour what you shall speak.

"For it is not you that speaks, but the Spirit of your Father which speaks in you" (Mat. 10:18-20).

THE RESURRECTION

The phrase, *"Whom God raised from the dead,"* says several things:

- The Sadducees, who mostly made up this ruling clique, did not believe in a Resurrection. Irrespective, Peter, in no uncertain terms, hit that error head on, declaring the Glory of the Resurrection by the fact that Jesus Christ had been raised from the dead. Such would guarantee a future Resurrection!
- By crucifying Jesus, they thought they were ridding themselves of Him when, in reality, it did no such thing, even increasing His Person, His Influence, and His Power, to an extent even beyond comprehension.

• As well, and pointedly so, the Holy Spirit was using these words to convict these rulers of their terrible sin with an invitation to come to Repentance. Tragically, at least as far as the rulers were concerned, it was ignored.

• The phrase, *"Even by Him does this man stand here before you whole,"* proclaims the Apostle passing from the Name to Him Whose Name it was. Consequently, this put an entirely different complexion on the matter.

• The only Power that could bring about such a thing had to be that which came from Deity. So, that meant that Israel had crucified not just a Man, but their Messiah, actually, the Lord of Glory. The implications were absolutely awful, the significance of which was not lost at all upon these rulers.

(11) "THIS IS THE STONE WHICH WAS SET AT NOUGHT OF YOU BUILDERS, WHICH IS BECOME THE HEAD OF THE CORNER."

The exegesis is:

1. The phrase, *"This is the Stone,"* is derived from Psalm 118:22-23.

2. The phrase, *"Which was set at nought of you builders,"* places the responsibility squarely on their heads. In other words, they were attempting to build without Christ, as the entirety of the world seeks to do.

3. Men, even from the very beginning, have attempted to rebuild the Garden of Eden without the Tree of Life, i.e., *"Jesus Christ."* Such cannot be and, in fact, is impossible!

4. Actually, this points to each and every human being who rejects Jesus Christ, attempting to build their lives without the Cornerstone. It is a house built on sand and is easily destroyed (Mat. 7:26).

5. The phrase, *"Which is become the Head of the corner,"* proclaims the fact that even though Israel rejected Him, in no way did that stop the Plan of God from being carried out; however, it did destroy Israel, as such rebellion will ultimately destroy all.

6. Rejecting Jesus Christ in no way negates the Kingdom of God, but such rejection definitely does destroy the rejecter. Jesus said, *"And whosoever shall fall on this Stone shall be broken* (to be made contrite, thereby, accepting Jesus): *But on Whomsoever it shall fall, it will grind him to powder"* (Mat. 21:44).

NOTES

7. The idea is not a lack of Mercy on the part of Christ, but rather the proclamation that all attempts to destroy this Cornerstone, substituting another to take His Place, will never meet with success. As well, the direction taken by the rebellious ones will ultimately always fall out to their destruction.

(12) "NEITHER IS THERE SALVATION IN ANY OTHER: FOR THERE IS NONE OTHER NAME UNDER HEAVEN GIVEN AMONG MEN, WHEREBY WE MUST BE SAVED."

The diagram is:

1. The phrase, *"Neither is there Salvation in any other,"* proclaims unequivocally that Jesus alone holds the key to Salvation and, in fact, is Salvation.

2. *"Salvation"* covers far more than the initial Conversion experience. It actually includes every phase and facet of one's life and living, including Sanctification, and especially including Sanctification. It extends to all that the Cross afforded, even the Glorified Body, which Saints of God presently do not have but most definitely will have in the coming Resurrection of Life.

3. So, we make a mistake when we limit Salvation to merely the Born-Again experience, as important, of course, as that actually is. This means that it refers to freedom not only from sin, which, of course, is the greatest victory of all, but also freedom from poverty, ignorance, superstition, etc., all made possible by the Cross of Christ.

4. If we do not experience all that Salvation affords, and regrettably, most Christians don't, considering the price that Jesus paid, we are seriously shortchanging ourselves. *"Salvation,"* therefore, cannot be limited to the initial stage of Redemption.

5. The phrase, *"For there is none other name under Heaven given among men, whereby we must be saved,"* says it all!

6. The very Name *"Jesus"* means *"Salvation, Deliverance."* As well, He alone came down from Heaven and was born of the Virgin Mary in order that He would be born without sin. He walked a perfect life before

man and God and then died on Calvary, literally becoming the Sin-Offering. This settled the sin debt forever and broke the grip of sin on the human family, thereby, defeating Satan and all of his cohorts, at least for all who will believe (Jn. 3:16).

7. As well, He was raised from the dead, and some 40 days later, ascended to the Father; consequently, it is understandable as to how He is the only One Who can save and deliver.

8. Therefore, if anything is added to His Finished Work, it negates that Finished Work, constituting a falling from Grace (Gal. 5:4).

9. Whenever the Catholic church demands allegiance to the church and its so-called sacraments, claiming that such ensures Salvation, Jesus has been relegated to a minor position, whether they agree or not. As such, every individual who thinks that their faithfulness to the Catholic church, or any church for that matter, saves them, actually falls out to the very opposite. In other words, they have substituted a human organization for Jesus, which means they cannot be saved in this fashion. Such can be said for any and all Protestant churches as well! The same goes for *"good works," "Water Baptism"* and even the *"Lord's Supper."*

10. Dependence on anything other than Christ and the Cross solely is a forfeiture of Salvation, which, sadly, includes most of the world, and for all time.

11. To be blunt, it is Jesus alone or Hell!

(13) "NOW WHEN THEY SAW THE BOLDNESS OF PETER AND JOHN, AND PERCEIVED THAT THEY WERE UNLEARNED AND IGNORANT MEN, THEY MARVELED; AND THEY TOOK KNOWLEDGE OF THEM, THAT THEY HAD BEEN WITH JESUS."

The synopsis is:

1. When the Cross is removed from Christianity, nothing is left but a vapid philosophy.

2. One of the reasons the Cross of Christ is an offense is because it tells us what man is and what God is.

3. Man doesn't like the Cross because he is loath to admit that it took something so drastic to save his soul.

NOTES

THE BOLDNESS OF PETER AND JOHN

The phrase, *"Now when they saw the boldness of Peter and John,"* proclaims not only the freedom to speak but, as well, pertains to that which was spoken and the Power with which it was spoken. Actually, the Sanhedrin had never encountered anything quite like this. They did not realize, and neither would they have believed, that this *"boldness"* was the result of the Holy Spirit abiding in the Apostles.

"And perceived that they were unlearned and ignorant men," simply means that they had not studied in the rabbinical schools. In fact, they were not *"unlearned and ignorant,"* but rather the very opposite!

Their education had come from Christ and was now buttressed by the Holy Spirit. As well, they had great knowledge of the Scriptures, far beyond the Sanhedrin, which Peter graphically portrayed.

The actual truth is, the Sanhedrin was *"unlearned and ignorant."* It is the same presently!

Irrespective of how much education individuals may have, if they do not know Christ and the Word of God, they are *"ignorant and unlearned"* about the things that really matter.

Of course, while the world recognizes its own, irrespective of what direction it takes, it will never recognize that which is of God, always referring to it as *"ignorant and unlearned."*

However, a person can be extremely educated in many and various things concerning science and the arts and still not know how to live. Therefore, all of their other learning has helped them very little, at least in this capacity. Only the Bible can show men the way to live simply because it introduces man to the Author and Giver of Life, The Lord Jesus Christ.

THEY HAD BEEN WITH JESUS

The phrase, *"They marveled; and they took knowledge of them, that they had been with Jesus,"* pretty well says it all!

He who knows Jesus knows Life. As well, he who knows Jesus then becomes a recipient of the Holy Spirit, Who is God, and actually takes up abode within one's heart and life. Such provides the ultimate Grace and Help!

It was certainly known by some members of the Sanhedrin that Peter and John had been Disciples of Jesus. As well, they knew, no doubt, that these men had been raised in the fishing business, and while honorable, still, this provided no training whatsoever in this great subject of Salvation that was being addressed. Consequently, the only answer to their *"boldness,"* their *"learning and education,"* which was here obvious to all, was their association with Jesus.

Therefore, once again, Jesus was brought before them as the Messiah, One Who is capable of changing men, as is here glaringly obvious. So, this Power not only heals the sick but saves men, and even gives them a degree of intelligence they have not previously known, especially about the things of life and the things which really matter. All of it is tied to *"Jesus,"* the life, the Baptism with the Holy Spirit, the Healing, the Power to change, etc.

(14) "AND BEHOLDING THE MAN WHICH WAS HEALED STANDING WITH THEM, THEY COULD SAY NOTHING AGAINST IT."

The overview is:

1. Why is it Christ Crucified?

2. It is because a Perfect Substitute was needed in order to reconcile you to God.

3. It is because a Perfect Substitute was needed in order that God's Justice be satisfied.

THE MAN WHO WAS HEALED

The phrase, *"And beholding the man which was healed standing with them,"* presents a picture that must have been beautiful to behold.

Hours before, he had sat at a gate begging, even as he had done for many years, and had to be carried by others wherever he went. And now, he was standing before the highest tribunal in the land, the subject of conversation, and above all, no longer a beggar or a cripple. Only Jesus could do such a thing! As well, that is how quickly, grandly, gloriously, and miraculously He can change things.

To be sure, as Jesus did such for this man of long ago, He has done such for untold millions ever since, which reaches unto this very hour. There is nothing else that can remotely compete or compare with this of which I speak. And yet, most desire to remain crippled and begging. What an awful deception!

On the other side, this former cripple was risking excommunication and even death as he boldly identified himself with the Apostles, voluntarily taking his stand with them in court. However, I do not think that was a problem to him whatsoever!

The Lord Who had just healed him could protect him. However, if He chose not to do so, that would not be a problem either.

The phrase, *"They could say nothing against it,"* proclaims the proof, which was obvious to all!

Why would they desire to say anything at all against such a notable Miracle!

When men come face-to-face with the Gospel, even as these here did, they are never left in a neutral position. If one is not for Jesus, one is against Jesus! If one is not against Jesus, one is for Jesus! There is no middle ground.

How could anyone rationalize or justify being *"against"* something this wonderful?

CONTROL

Why did these rulers in Israel hate Jesus so much? Why did they hate His Followers or even those who had been healed by the Lord?

I suppose, as I have stated in a previous Chapter, the real problem is *"control."* Religious men who are not following the Word of God love to rule over other men. When such rule is not accepted because it is unscriptural, the anger of these individuals knows no bounds. As the Sanhedrin of old, they will do almost anything to protect their authority although it is not authority given by God or taken from the Bible.

Everything we do must line up with the Word of God. If we fail the Lord in any way or turn aside from His Word, we must repent of such action and then come back to the Way of the Lord, which is the Word of the Lord. If we are going to make up rules that have no basis or foundation in the Word of God, then we are guilty of writing our own Bible, which, as with Israel of old, will sooner or later bring destruction.

Many modern denominations desperately need to repent respecting positions that have no scriptural foundation. If they will not, sooner or later, the *"leaven"* of false doctrine and false direction will ultimately corrupt the whole. This is exactly what is happening presently and will continue unabated unless there is a change, which does not presently seem to be in the offing. However, my prayer is that it will change, but if not, they will find themselves more and more opposing that which is of God until, ultimately, they are in the other camp entirely. To be frank, they are very close to that position now.

In effect, Peter boldly told these clergy (Acts 4:5-6) that they needed to be saved, and he shut them up to Salvation in the one Person Whom they had set at naught (Acts 4:11) and crucified (Acts 4:10), but Whom God had raised from the dead and appointed the Head of the corner. Thus, he contrasted their treatment of the Messiah and God's Treatment of Him.

This is the very thing of which I speak. We had best treat that which belongs to God exactly as He treats that which belongs to Him. With the Power and Anointing of the Holy Spirit resting upon an individual, all others must recognize such for what it is, for to not do so is to deny the Holy Spirit, which is a very dangerous position to take!

(15) "BUT WHEN THEY HAD COMMANDED THEM TO GO ASIDE OUT OF THE COUNCIL, THEY CONFERRED AMONG THEMSELVES."

The focus is:

1. The phrase, *"But when they had commanded them to go aside out of the Council,"* proclaims the fact that God had left this council a long time ago.

2. *"They conferred among themselves,"* portrays an evil that is common in meetings of this nature.

3. Men in committees or groups of this nature will do things in an evil sense that they would not dare do alone. They somehow seem to think that agreement among themselves justifies the action they take.

NOTES

4. As well, it must be quickly added that men in these circumstances seldom consult the Bible. They consult mostly their constitution and by-laws, which should be Scriptural but oftentimes are not.

(16) "SAYING, WHAT SHALL WE DO TO THESE MEN? FOR THAT INDEED A NOTABLE MIRACLE HAS BEEN DONE BY THEM IS MANIFEST TO ALL THEM WHO DWELL IN JERUSALEM; AND WE CANNOT DENY IT."

The structure is:

1. The question, *"Saying, What shall we do to these men?"* poses another question. Why would they want to do anything negative to these men? What had they done that was harmful to anyone and especially the Work of God?

2. The answer is simple: They had done nothing to hurt anyone, but rather the very opposite. As well, not only did they not hurt the Work of God, but they were actually carrying out the Work of God exactly as the Holy Spirit desired that it be done.

3. If one is to notice (which is very obvious), Rome, which represented the system of the world and controlled Israel, offered no reproof or opposition whatsoever. It was religion that opposed Peter and John (actually Christ within them), which is pretty much always the case.

4. The phrase *"For that indeed a notable miracle has been done by them is manifest to all them who dwell in Jerusalem,"* implies that the news of this man's Miraculous Healing had spread far and wide, even in the last few hours. Even these reprobates, if you will, recognized this that was done as a *"Miracle!"* As well, Peter had avowed that it was done in the Name of Jesus. So, how did they rationalize all of this in their minds?

5. If indeed it was a Miracle, and it definitely was, and if it had been done in the Name of Jesus, and it definitely had, did this not tell them Who Jesus actually was?

6. I suspect that at this time, the weight of their awful sin was beginning to tell. In their heart of hearts, they had to know Who Jesus actually was. This is so much the case that Caiaphas, as we have stated, committed suicide about two years later.

7. To remedy the situation, they would

have to repent (and do so publicly), which they obviously felt they could not do. How so much their pride destroyed them, and how so much the destruction could have been avoided had they only repented.

8. The phrase, *"And we cannot deny it,"* presents that which is exactly right!

9. They could not deny it, but at the same time, they would not accept it.

10. This is what made their sin so awful! The proof concerning Jesus was so abundant as to be undeniable, even as this Text states, for to admit to the Miracle was to admit to the veracity of Jesus Christ.

(17) "BUT THAT IT SPREAD NO FURTHER AMONG THE PEOPLE, LET US STRAITLY THREATEN THEM, THAT THEY SPEAK HENCEFORTH TO NO MAN IN THIS NAME."

The composition is:

1. The phrase, *"But that it spread no further among the people,"* seems to present their great fear. Actually, this is the fear of most of institutionalized religion. Religion must control the people, doing all within its power to keep them from thinking. This is at least one of the reasons that the Catholic church fought mightily for centuries to keep the Bible out of the hands of the people. They did not want the people to think for themselves.

2. It is also one of the reasons institutionalized religion would stop most radio and television ministries, that is, if they had the power to do so. Of course, they would place their seal of approval upon someone who touted the party line. However, for the Evangelist who gets his instructions from Heaven, if the truth be known, they would not sanction that, irrespective of the Moving and Operation of the Holy Spirit.

3. The phrase, *"Let us straitly threaten them, that they speak henceforth to no man in this Name,"* automatically places the situation into a posture that cannot be obeyed. The Name spoken of is Christ, as is obvious. As well, the term *"Name,"* as expressive of the Person, continually occurs in this Book.

(18) "AND THEY CALLED THEM, AND COMMANDED THEM NOT TO SPEAK AT ALL NOR TEACH IN THE NAME OF JESUS."

NOTES

The form is:

1. The devil's chief purpose is to stop the propagation of the Gospel, which, of course, is centered up in Jesus Christ, and he will do anything he can to carry forth this effort. As we have repeatedly stated, Satan will use religion more than anything else, even as here, to fulfill this task.

2. Satan does not mind at all some preachers being on radio and television, or any other capacity one may name. Many of them preach a compromised message, which may gain the plaudits of the crowd and the acceptance of many in the world, but will see no results for the Lord; or else, they preach without any Anointing of the Holy Spirit, which falls out to the same end results. If the truth be known, Satan actually helps those who preach false doctrine, or what Paul referred to as another Jesus, another Spirit, and another Gospel (II Cor. 11:4).

3. However, for those such as Peter and John, who truly have a mandate from the Lord and are heavily anointed to deliver the Message, which will always be *"in the mighty Name of Jesus,"* Satan will fight with every ounce of strength that Hell possesses to stop the Message. He would cause Paul to be locked up in prison for years, seeking to stop his voice.

However, the Lord allows Satan only so much latitude and uses whatever is done, as with Paul, to bring the individual even closer to Him. So, in the long run, Satan always loses out, even as the account of our Text proclaims.

(19) "BUT PETER AND JOHN ANSWERED AND SAID UNTO THEM, WHETHER IT BE RIGHT IN THE SIGHT OF GOD TO HEARKEN UNTO YOU MORE THAN UNTO GOD, JUDGE YE."

The order is:

1. Fear is dispelled in no other way but by the Cross of Christ.

2. The Infinite Son of God became Man, hung upon a Cross, and was made a Curse so that you and I might not be cursed but be free from the curse.

3. How foolish then to walk in the maze of works of self-righteousness.

NOTES

THE ANSWER OF PETER AND JOHN

The phrase, *"But Peter and John answered and said unto them,"* proclaims that which the Sanhedrin was not too much desiring to hear.

"Whether it be right in the Sight of God to hearken unto you more than unto God, judge ye," once again puts the ball back in their court and poses a question, the answer to which will expose them.

In effect, Peter and John were saying that these men were not of God, were not doing the Work of God, and consequently, did not have the Mind of God, irrespective of their claims. Actually, they were in juxtaposition to God.

Inasmuch as these were the spiritual guides of the people, there are many who feel, even now, that such must be obeyed, etc.

The only reason people would think such a thing is because they do not know the Word of God.

The Jewish Sanhedrin did not have a Scriptural foundation. In other words, it was a man-devised organization with no counterpart in the Word of God.

In the Old Testament, and that which was ordained of God, there were Patriarchs, Judges, Prophets, and kings. There was no Sanhedrin, at least that was ordained by the Holy Spirit. Consequently, John the Baptist and Jesus were given instructions by the Holy Spirit to completely ignore this group as if they did not exist, at least as far as carrying out the Work of God was concerned. It is identical at this present time and, actually, has always been.

BIBLICAL GOVERNMENT

While God definitely does have a Biblical Government respecting His Work, which is outlined in the Book of Acts, much of that which passes presently for church government has no Scriptural foundation. Even though I will not at this time go into this subject, saving it for a later time, still, we must quickly say that religious denominations have no Scriptural validity, and neither do many of the offices in these denominations, such as superintendent, general superintendent, overseer, bishop, etc.

In the strict sense of the word, the forming of a religious denomination carries with it no connotation of wrongdoing. Ideally, it should be an instrument or a tool to help further the Kingdom of God. If it is looked at in that sense, especially by those who occupy its positions, no harm is done, with the possibility of good being carried out.

However, the moment it is looked at, addressed, and treated as something spiritual, which it is not, it then becomes sin, and grossly so! This leads to religious hierarchy, which, as well, has no counterpart in the Word of God, but rather the very opposite.

When this stage is reached, the people occupying these positions begin to think of themselves in the light of spiritual authority and demand obedience, etc., exactly as the Sanhedrin of old! Incidentally, they were not called or appointed by the Lord, at least in these offices, for they are not Scriptural. The true Preacher of the Gospel sooner or later has to say to them, *"Whether it be right in the Sight of God to hearken unto you more than unto God, judge ye."*

The answer is obvious!

(20) "FOR WE CANNOT BUT SPEAK THE THINGS WHICH WE HAVE SEEN AND HEARD."

The order is:

1. How foolish it is to walk in the labyrinth of self-righteousness.

2. The Gospel is Christ Crucified for sinners.

3. Calvary is the Son of God bearing your sin, no matter what that sin has been.

SPEAKING

Williams says that there are two groups of Christians: those who *"cannot speak"* and those who *"cannot but speak."* The little word *"but"* distinguishes between these groups. The one group is so inflamed with love for Christ that they cannot *"but"* speak; the other is so wanting in love for Him that they cannot speak.

These men had *"seen and heard"* something, as all who truly follow Christ. What they had *"seen and heard"* was not to be filtered through committees, denominational boards, or in this case, the Sanhedrin. Of course, as is obvious, this did not set too well with the Sanhedrin!

The true Preacher of the Gospel must ever understand the following:

While all of us, at least those who truly love the Lord, are very appreciative of our brothers and sisters in Christ and definitely do seek their prayers, counsel, and advice, still, whatever is truly given to us by the Lord must never be subject to the approval of others.

At the same time, no man is infallible and, therefore, is subject to mistakes. So, any advice or counsel given respecting that which is claimed should be weighed heavily in the light of the Scripture.

However, after doing that, if it is determined that what is being *"seen and heard"* is Scriptural, and Scriptural, as well, in its application, the true Preacher of the Gospel will forge ahead irrespective of the cost or consequences.

SUBMISSION

I place no confidence in, and neither do I have respect for, those who claim that God has called them to do a certain thing and then submit it to some type of religious board for approval or rejection, and then abide by that decision. Either the Holy Spirit is leading the individual, or man is. Both cannot serve in this capacity!

It is certainly not wrong and is actually proper at times to submit such for counsel and advice to those who are spiritual. This counsel all of us sorely need, but never in the capacity of others having the final say.

If God has truly called someone to do a certain thing, it will be obviously sensible and Scriptural. If it is not, others have the duty to point out such erroneous direction (I Cor. 14:29). If it is Scriptural, one must forge ahead, irrespective of the cost.

A PERSONAL EXPERIENCE

Back in 1968, after much prayer and consecration on my part, the Lord instructed me to begin a daily radio program, Monday through Friday. He instructed me what to do and told me how to carry it out. It was His Will that we basically cover the nation, which we did, airing over some 600 stations daily, with many of these stations airing twice or even three times a day.

NOTES

The Lord used it in a spectacular way to touch untold numbers of hearts and lives for the Cause of Christ. Many were Saved and baptized with the Holy Spirit as a result of the teaching the Lord instructed us to do. There was no way that anyone could look at the Fruit of this effort and not know that it was ordained by the Lord, at least if they desired to be honest.

Not long after the initiation of the program, I received a letter from an official in the Assemblies of God, of which I was then a part. This was a man I had not met, having only heard his name.

He wanted to know what I was doing on radio, and who had given me the authority to do this, or words to that effect. The tone of his letter was that it had not been passed upon by the Assemblies of God leadership, and therefore, we must cease and desist.

In effect, he was saying that they would recognize only those whom they chose, appointed, etc.

I was somewhat flabbergasted when I received the letter. It was true that I had not asked permission to do this because to have done so would have been wrong. This which God had told me to do was never to be held up for someone else's approval; consequently, it never entered my mind to do such a thing.

WE HAVE TO DO WHAT THE LORD WANTS US TO DO

I wrote back a kind letter telling him that the Lord had called me to do this, and I was doing my very best to carry out that Call. The Word was my Authority, and the Holy Spirit was the One Who anointed me to carry out this task. As well, the Fruit of this Ministry to which the Lord had called me was obvious for all to see.

Once again, the objection was not that I was preaching erroneous doctrine, conducting myself in an unethical way, or doing anything unscriptural. The objection was that they had not chosen me for this task, and they could not accept anyone whom they had not chosen.

I think it is easy to see that the Lord and His Will had little place in their thinking,

NOTES

with them actually setting themselves up as God and demanding obedience. This is the major problem with most denominations.

Regarding my position, I was basically in the same situation as Peter and John, and millions of others down through the centuries for that matter, who *"could not but speak the things which we had seen and heard."*

Incidentally, this same man who wrote me later became a friend, at least in a distant way. He told others after he had retired from the particular office he had been holding in that denomination that he did such terrible things while in office that he was not even sure if he was really Saved or not. He said, I am told, *"It was like a spirit that was upon me, which did not leave until I no longer held that position."*

The reason for this situation was, at least in part, because he was occupying an office that was not Scriptural, but which he claimed to be Scriptural. As such, he assumed Spiritual Authority, which the Bible did not give him, or anyone in those particular types of positions. As a result, if the truth be known, he was very close to losing his soul as all are, I believe, who function accordingly. Thank God, he did come to his spiritual senses!

(21) "SO WHEN THEY HAD FURTHER THREATENED THEM, THEY LET THEM GO, FINDING NOTHING HOW THEY MIGHT PUNISH THEM, BECAUSE OF THE PEOPLE: FOR ALL MEN GLORIFIED GOD FOR THAT WHICH WAS DONE."

The synopsis is:

1. The Gospel is not based upon your moral condition; it is based upon His Moral Condition.

2. Jesus Christ died for the failures of the Saints as well as dying for the sins of the sinners.

3. It is not my worth but the Worth of Christ that saves.

A SAD STATE OF AFFAIRS

The phrase, *"So when they had further threatened them, they let them go, finding nothing how they might punish them,"* presents a sad state of affairs.

Why did they desire to punish them, even though they found no way to do so?

In fact, does any Christian or so-called religious leader have the right to punish another Believer?

No!

James answered that very succinctly. He said, *"Who are you who judges another?"* In other words, who do you think you are, thinking you are qualified to judge and punish another Believer? (James 4:12).

Why should we want to do so? Didn't Jesus suffer all the punishment that needed to be suffered when He died upon Calvary? For us to take it upon ourselves to punish someone else, in effect, states that what Jesus suffered was not enough, and we have to add other to it. This is a gross insult to the Lord that, to be sure, He does not take lightly.

The truth is, no Believer has the right to punish another Believer. Such is always left up to God, with no man ever given that latitude (Rom. 12:19). Of course, I am speaking of Church government and not civil government, which does have that right (Rom. 13:1-7).

That means it is not proper to impose penance, punishment, or anything of that nature on a fellow Believer. If the individual is unscriptural and will not repent, that is, if something wrong is being done, the most that Believers are allowed to do is to disfellowship that person.

Even then, we have no right to take any further steps, at least in that direction, with the person going his own way. By all means, we should continue to pray for the individual but never do anything attempting to hurt him (II Thess. 3:15).

Such actions always carry with it a dictatorial, un-Christlike attitude, which is more ungodly than the one they are attempting to punish.

BECAUSE OF THE PEOPLE

The phrase, *"Because of the people,"* presents the only thing seemingly that stopped them. In other words, if they had not been fearful of an uprising, they would have probably stoned Peter and John to death.

Actually, this is what this entire situation was all about. They saw themselves losing control of the people, with control always being paramount with religion.

To those who truly follow the Lord, such control is never sought or even desired. While Preachers of the Gospel are responsible for proper instruction and naturally warn of hirelings, still, the Holy Spirit is the One Who alone exercises control; however, He will only do such when it is freely given.

The phrase, *"For all men glorified God for that which was done,"* proclaims, as stated, the news of this man's Healing being spread all across the city.

As well, the type of response it brought from the people was that which glorified God, which is what should have happened.

Of course, these *"rulers"* had no desire to glorify God, but were rather interested in maintaining their control in the occupation of their positions.

Religion is a sick business, and the reader is here getting a good introduction into that which purported to be of God (the Sanhedrin) but, in reality, was of Satan.

(22) "FOR THE MAN WAS ABOVE FORTY YEARS OLD, ON WHOM THIS MIRACLE OF HEALING WAS SHOWN."

The synopsis is:

1. Any direction other than the Cross always, and without fail, leads to self-righteousness.

2. The only way any Believer can successfully live for the Lord is by placing his or her Faith exclusively in Christ and what Christ did for us at the Cross.

3. With that being done, the Holy Spirit, Who works entirely within the parameters of the Finished Work of Christ, will work grandly on our behalf (Rom. 8:1-11).

THE MIRACLE OF HEALING

The phrase, *"For the man was above forty years old,"* carries with it the meaning that this was not a child that someone could coax, and neither was it someone with senility. This man was responsible and, therefore, could be believed.

The phrase, *"On whom this Miracle of Healing was shown,"* proclaims that which was true.

I personally feel it is very displeasing to the Lord for great Healings or Miracles to be claimed when there is no proof of such or no obvious positive results.

God does not need fake glory, and neither does He desire such!

It was obvious to all that this man had been gloriously and wondrously healed by the Power of God. Hundreds or even thousands knew him, or at least knew of him, as he was placed each day at the gate called Beautiful or elsewhere, seeking to beg alms, etc. All knew that his condition of being crippled was not fake or put-on.

As well, when he was healed instantly and began to walk, leap, and praise God, whether one liked it or not, it was obvious as to the reality of what had happened to him.

It is very easy to announce someone as *"healed!"* As well, it is certainly proper to do so if, in fact, one is healed, or God has told one to say such.

However, that not being the case, it would be best to wait and see so as not to bring reproach to the Cause of Christ.

Due to false teaching, the climate of Healing at this particular time (2013) has become so unscriptural that in many circles, to *"wait and see"* is tantamount to a lack of faith. So, whether healed or not, many, if not most, are encouraged to claim their Healing immediately, etc.

No! Such discretion is not a lack of faith, but rather a desire to please God and not tell something untrue. While a good confession is definitely important, we must make certain that it is Scriptural. A so-called good confession can quickly degenerate into a lie, which is wrong no matter how it is sliced.

To casually announce mass Healings or to quickly announce someone is healed without the proper evidence, I think can be greatly displeasing to the Lord! The very Characteristic of Christ, which is overly obvious, is honesty. Therefore, dishonesty, even with the best of intentions, cannot please the Lord. As well, neither is it faith but only presumption!

It is a wonderful thing and brings great glory to God when people are truly healed; however, to claim such when it really has not happened brings Him no glory at all, but rather reproach.

Could it be possible that the reason for such false announcements is because preachers too often desire personal glory? The answer is known only to the Lord, for only God can see a person's heart; however, I am afraid that such may be the case too often!

(23) "AND BEING LET GO, THEY WENT TO THEIR OWN COMPANY, AND REPORTED ALL THAT THE CHIEF PRIESTS AND ELDERS HAD SAID UNTO THEM."

The form is:

1. The phrase, *"And being let go, they went to their own company,"* refers to other Apostles, as well as Believers of the original group on the Day of Pentecost.

2. However, that *"company"* was now growing at a tremendous rate and would continue to do so.

3. The phrase, *"And reported all that the Chief Priests and Elders had said unto them,"* presents the first account of opposition against the Early Church. It was not long in coming!

(24) "AND WHEN THEY HEARD THAT, THEY LIFTED UP THEIR VOICE TO GOD WITH ONE ACCORD, AND SAID, LORD, YOU ARE GOD, WHICH HAS MADE HEAVEN, AND EARTH, AND THE SEA, AND ALL THAT IN THEM IS."

The composition is:

1. The phrase, *"And when they heard that, they lifted up their voice to God with one accord, and said,"* proclaims several things:

a. I think it is clear from this account that all the people were praying at the same time but that the gist of their prayer was according to that which is given unto us.

b. They took the entire situation to the Lord in prayer, which set a precedent for us and all others.

c. We will see in this prayer, as it is inspired by the Holy Spirit, the entire disposition of the Sovereignty of God, as well as a petition for His Guidance and Protection.

2. The phrase, *"Lord, You are God, which has made Heaven, and Earth, and the sea, and all that in them is,"* proclaims His unlimited Power over all that He has made. The Church in danger finds support and solace in the thought of God's absolute Sovereignty.

3. God is recognized as the Creator and, as well, the Maintainer. As such, nothing can happen to the Child of God but that the Lord causes or allows such. Make no mistake about it, Satan does not have free course or latitude except that granted by God (Job, Chpt. 1).

4. Of course, God does not cause sin or failure of any nature; however, He does allow such, with the Believer having to bear the responsibility. As well, He does allow Satan some latitude respecting persecution, hindrance, etc.

5. While Satan, of course, means such for our harm and even destruction, the Lord intends for such to push us closer to Him, thereby, gaining Spiritual strength, trust, and obedience.

(25) "WHO BY THE MOUTH OF YOUR SERVANT DAVID HAS SAID, WHY DID THE HEATHEN RAGE, AND THE PEOPLE IMAGINE VAIN THINGS?"

The form is:

1. Grace is the only means and manner in which the Believer can function in perpetual victory.

2. The Bible does not teach sinless perfection.

3. It does teach that sin is not to have dominion over us (Rom. 6:14).

THE PSALMS

The phrase, *"Who by the mouth of Your Servant David has said,"* refers to Psalm 2.

Some Bibles have a superscription before each Psalm, giving the name of the writer. (The Author of all the Psalms, as well as the entirety of the Word of God, irrespective of the writer, is the Holy Spirit.)

About 73 of the Psalms are ascribed to David when, in actuality, he probably wrote others as well. Two were ascribed to Solomon, 12 to Asaph, who was the music director under David, one to Heman, one to Ethan, and 10 to the sons of Korah, with one ascribed to Moses. That leaves 50 Psalms with the writer not named. Actually, Psalm 2, which is the subject of this statement by Peter, has no superscription giving the name of the writer.

Nevertheless, we know from what they said that David was the writer. Actually, he probably wrote a goodly number of the 50 where the writers were not named.

NOTES

Irrespective, all the Psalms are the Word of God.

So, if there were no superscription, how did they know that David was the writer?

They knew it in one of two ways:

1. The Holy Spirit told them.

2. Many of the Jewish scholars at that time had knowledge of some of the particulars of which we speak, with the information being handed down through the centuries, which was probably the case concerning who wrote Psalm 2.

THE RAGING OF THE HEATHEN

The question, *"Why did the heathen rage, and the people imagine vain things?"* is used by those praying, and I must quickly add, led by the Holy Spirit to do so, as an example of what these religious leaders were doing concerning Jesus.

These Verses state that the Messiah is the Person of whom Psalm 2 speaks, and thus, a flood of light is thrown upon the entire Book of Psalms.

In other words, as we have previously stated, the entirety of the Psalms, other than those addressed to Satan, speaks of Christ, even those that are not looked at as Messianic Psalms. Incidentally, Psalm 2 is referred to as a Messianic Psalm.

As the Holy Spirit is using it through Peter, the idea is that the spirit of the world as well as the spirit of religion are greatly opposed to Christ.

The Greek word for *"heathen"* is *"ethnos"* and refers to those who are *"pagan."* In the strict interpretation of the word, this refers to those who are driven by sensual pleasures and, thereby, ruled by unholy passions; however, in the spiritual sense, it refers to those outside the Gospel of Jesus Christ, such as the Hindus, Muslims, Buddhists, etc.

So, as should be obvious, those in these religions, or else, no religion at all but yet antagonistic toward Christ, oppose Him in a manner totally unlike their opposition to anything else. The opposition against Christ is vocal and often violent, even taking the form of bodily harm at times to some Believers.

This stems from the *"vanity"* of people in these religions. The idea that ethics, good works, etc., merit no salvation at all is offensive to them. As well, and even more importantly, the idea that one must accept Jesus Christ alone as the Son of God and as one's Saviour is even more offensive. So, they *"rage"* against Him and *"imagine vain things."*

NOTES

(26) "THE KINGS OF THE EARTH STOOD UP, AND THE RULERS WERE GATHERED TOGETHER AGAINST THE LORD, AND AGAINST HIS CHRIST."

The composition is:

1. The phrase, *"The Kings of the Earth stood up,"* pertains not only to Herod and others, even as they would say in this prayer, but has a more sweeping meaning that we will address momentarily.

2. *"And the Rulers were gathered together against the Lord,"* speaks of Pilate and others similar, as they would say, but, as well, has a larger meaning.

3. If one is to notice, the title *"Lord"* is used in this instance of God the Father.

4. *"And against His Christ,"* speaks of Jesus and means that if one opposes Jesus, one opposes the Father and, as well, the Holy Spirit, whether realized or not.

5. This Psalm refers to all opposition against Christ, even from the time of His First Advent, as is here obvious. However, in its strictest interpretation, it refers to the coming Great Tribulation when the Antichrist will lead many leaders of the Earth and even most of the people against Christ. Its climax is the Battle of Armageddon when the Antichrist will lead many armies against Israel, making one final attempt to destroy these ancient people (Ezek., Chpts 38-39). He will think that if he can destroy Israel, even as Satan used Hitler and scores of others down through the centuries, the Promises and Prophecies of the Lord will fall to the ground, especially considering that so many of these predictions are centered up in Israel and her Restoration. Of course, he will fail and will actually be stopped by the Coming of the Lord (Rev., Chpt. 19).

6. The phrase, *"Against His Anointed,"* as it is used in Psalm 2:2, and as Peter used it in Acts, 4:27, refers to Christ, Who is the True Israel exactly as He is the True Church.

7. This should give us an idea as to how sweeping many of these Passages are respecting their interpretation. Since it is the Word of God, it has the capacity to cover a broad area, as it generally does.

(27) "FOR OF A TRUTH AGAINST YOUR HOLY CHILD JESUS, WHOM YOU HAVE ANOINTED, BOTH HEROD, AND PONTIUS PILATE, WITH THE GENTILES, AND THE PEOPLE OF ISRAEL, WERE GATHERED TOGETHER."

The diagram is:

1. The modern church understands some things about the Cross referring to Salvation but virtually nothing concerning Sanctification.

2. The only way a Believer can live a victorious life is by understanding the Cross as it refers to Sanctification.

3. Faith in Christ and the Cross is all that is required.

JESUS, THE FULFILLMENT OF THE PROPHECIES

The phrase, *"For of a truth against Your Holy Child Jesus, Whom You have anointed,"* proclaims Jesus as the Fulfillment of all the Prophecies, the Son of God, the Incarnate One, and the Saviour of men.

The title *"Christ"* in the Greek actually means *"Anointed"* and refers to *"One consecrated to an office or service."* In fact, men can anoint other men in the secular sense for secular purposes, even as is done constantly. However, when it pertains to God, it always speaks of His Purposes and Services.

As it referred to the coming Jewish Messiah and the Saviour of all men, the Holy Spirit first used the word *"Anoint"* or *"Anointed"* through the lips of Hannah as she consecrated her little son Samuel to the service of the Lord (I Sam. 2:10). From this point on, others took up the Theme of God's Anointed One—the Messiah (I Sam. 2:35; Ps. 2:2; 45:7; Isa. 61:1; Dan. 9:25-26; Jn. 1:41; 4:25).

Of course, the *"Anointing"* speaks of the Holy Spirit, Who actually carries out the task of equipping one for service, etc. (Lk. 4:18-19).

The phrase, *"Both Herod, and Pontius Pilate, with the Gentiles, and the people of Israel, were gathered together,"* points to these who *"gathered together against the Lord and against His Christ."* In other words, they were *"gathered together"* for the express purpose of crucifying Christ.

While it was true that Herod or Pilate seemed to have little stomach for this extreme, still, neither one used his office to stop this greatest crime of all the ages. I remind all and sundry, it was the church of that day who crucified Christ.

NOTES

OPPOSITION

The opposition is very pronounced and actually had its beginning with Satan in the Garden of Eden; however, when the Person of Christ appeared in the Incarnation, the opposition intensified because He was the True Object of the animosity. He was Righteousness while they were unrighteousness! He was Light while they were darkness! He was Salvation while they were sin!

As well, the Holy Spirit through those praying (Acts 3:12-15) refers not only to those leaders but, as well, to the *"people in general."*

This refers to the fact that great numbers of people in Israel were opposed to Christ as well as their rulers. How large was this number, only God knows; however, for the Holy Spirit to mention it several times tells us that it must have been substantial. This is proven somewhat in the last year of Jesus' Public Ministry.

The first approximate two years saw Jesus ministering constantly in synagogues all over Galilee, etc. However, the last year of His Public Ministry saw Him very little in the synagogues. The reason is that the synagogue leaders did not want Him, or even if they did, they bowed to the demands of the hierarchy in Jerusalem, as many presently continue to do in similar situations. There is very little record, if any, that any of the leaders of the synagogues in the various cities and towns in Israel stood up publicly for Jesus, at least during the last year.

Consequently, the Holy Spirit holds all of these people somewhat responsible in the murder of the Lord, even though they had no direct part in this travesty. Such should be a lesson to all others as well!

One cannot be neutral regarding Jesus Christ, and neither can he be a silent witness. Sooner or later, he must stand up for Jesus and publicly confess Christ. To not do so places one altogether in the other camp.

(28) "FOR TO DO WHATSOEVER YOUR HAND AND YOUR COUNSEL DETERMINED BEFORE TO BE DONE."

The overview is:

1. The phrase, *"For to do whatsoever Your Hand and Your Counsel determined,"* speaks of predestination concerning Christ, His Death on Calvary's Cross, and then His Resurrection from the dead. However, it does not mean that it was predestined that these people named, or any others for that matter, were to commit this foul deed! That was done strictly by their choice.

2. *"Before to be done,"* refers to eternity past when such was predetermined.

3. This speaks of the time—even before the foundation of the world—when God through foreknowledge knew that He would create man and that man would fall. It was then predetermined that man would be redeemed by God becoming Man and, thereby, serving as a Sacrifice on the Cross of Calvary in order that man might be saved (I Pet. 1:18-20).

(29) "AND NOW, LORD, BEHOLD THEIR THREATENINGS: AND GRANT UNTO YOUR SERVANTS, THAT WITH ALL BOLDNESS THEY MAY SPEAK YOUR WORD."

The exegesis is:

1. The phrase, *"And now, Lord, behold their threatenings,"* proclaims those praying turning over these rulers and others to the Lord in order that He might handle the situation.

2. In effect, their threatenings were against the Lord and only against Peter, John, and other Followers of the Lord as they exhibited the Lord in their lives and Ministries.

3. They were commanding that Peter and John, and all others for that matter, cease and desist respecting the use of the Name of Jesus or anything whatsoever about Jesus. The implication was of serious consequences if such were not heeded; however, it was something that could not be heeded.

NOTES

Therefore, the Lord would have to take steps to protect His People.

The word *"behold"* in the Greek is *"epeidon"* and means, at least in this instance, *"To behold unfavorably for the purpose of frustrating or even punishing."*

4. This tells us that Christians are not to take up their own defense, but rather turn it over to the Lord. If we take it up, the Lord does not!

5. The phrase, *"And grant unto Your Servants, that with all boldness they may speak Your Word,"* proclaims the very opposite of that demanded by the religious leaders of Israel.

6. They were telling them to cease and desist respecting Jesus, while the Apostles and others here prayed that the Lord would grant even greater *"boldness that they may speak Your Word."*

7. Consequently, it is Evangelism full speed ahead, irrespective of the threats. In other words, the Disciples were preparing for an even greater thrust!

(30) "BY STRETCHING FORTH YOUR HAND TO HEAL; AND THAT SIGNS AND WONDERS MAY BE DONE BY THE NAME OF YOUR HOLY CHILD JESUS."

The exposition is:

1. The phrase, *"By stretching forth Your Hand to heal,"* proclaims the request for more Miracles, such as the healing of the lame man at the gate called Beautiful.

2. As is here obvious, it is the Lord Who does the healing, but at the same time, He had promised that *"these signs shall follow them that believe"* (Mk. 16:17).

3. The phrase, *"And that signs and wonders may be done by the Name of Your Holy Child Jesus,"* speaks of the Power of God but done in the *"Name of Jesus."*

4. If one is to notice, the Apostles did not necessarily pray for protection from persecution or even deliverance from possible death, but for courage to keep on preaching and for a continuance of the Divine endorsement of their Testimony.

5. Should *"Healings"* and *"signs and wonders"* be resident in the modern Church?

6. Most definitely they should. Jesus said, *"These signs shall follow them that believe,"* and He placed no time limitation

NOTES

on that Promise.

7. The reason most preachers do not have such in their ministries, or laypersons for that matter, is simply because *"they do not believe!"*

8. If one is to notice, the Baptism with the Holy Spirit, as given in Acts 2:4, carries with it certain things. Those things are great Faith in God, leading and direction given by the Holy Spirit, signs, wonders, and Miracles, as well as great Anointing to preach the Gospel, which results in many people being saved.

9. When the Baptism with the Holy Spirit is not accepted according to Acts 2:4, all of the things just mentioned are lacking in the ministries and lives of those who take such positions. With the Holy Spirit, the Church enjoys and experiences all of these things mentioned in the Book of Acts. Without the Holy Spirit, none of these things are present because the supernatural has been removed; consequently, all that is left is that which pertains to man and not God. Everything the Lord does on Earth is done through the Power and Office of the Holy Spirit in the Name of Jesus. If that is denied, even as it is in many churches, the door is closed!

(31) "AND WHEN THEY HAD PRAYED, THE PLACE WAS SHAKEN WHERE THEY WERE ASSEMBLED TOGETHER; AND THEY WERE ALL FILLED WITH THE HOLY SPIRIT, AND THEY SPOKE THE WORD OF GOD WITH BOLDNESS."

The structure is:

1. There is only one place to address sin, and that is at the Cross.

2. The Cross is where all sin was atoned, past, present, and future, at least for all who will believe (Jn. 3:16).

3. In fact, God can meet with sinful man only at the Cross.

THE PRAYER LIVES OF THE APOSTLES

The phrase, *"And when they had prayed,"* proclaims the foundation of the Early Church. Prayer was a constant privilege in which they engaged frequently, and which was the great pillar of their success.

Regrettably, the modern church is little a praying church. It has been attacked by false doctrines and by sheer unbelief to the extent that prayer, at least in many circles, is engaged only as a matter of a last resort. Concerning problems and difficulties, the great thrust of the modern church is toward psychologists and psychological counseling. Sometimes it is claimed to be Biblical counseling, and some certainly is; however, for the most part, even though it is referred to as such, it is the psychological way.

This has pulled generations of Christians away from God and the Bible, resorting to man-instituted solutions that, in reality, are no solutions at all. If man could solve behavioral problems, which psychology purports to do, then Jesus wasted His Time coming down here and, above all, having to suffer a horrible death. Of course, we know Jesus did not waste His Time. He carried out the great Plan of Redemption simply because the plight of man was so serious that this was the only way it could have been handled.

Others just simply do not believe. In other words, they do not believe that God answers prayer, even though many would deny that charge. However, a lack of prayer on their part pretty well gives away their doubt and unbelief.

Another segment of the modern church, especially of the Charismatic variety, actually does not even believe in prayer, but rather confession. In other words, for a Believer to resort to prayer means that something is wrong, at least according to these false teachers. In their way of thinking, nothing can be wrong with a *"new creation"* man, etc. So, they set about to confess into existence that which is needed or desired, which really has no Scriptural foundation whatsoever.

WHY SHOULD CHRISTIANS PRAY?

If Jesus had a strong prayer life, and He did, then it should seem incumbent upon us to follow suit as He is our example.

As all Believers know, Jesus was Perfect. He is the Son of God. As well, even in the Incarnation, He was filled with the Spirit beyond measure, in other words, to a degree that no other human being has ever known (Jn. 3:34).

As well, the Heavenly Father was His own unique Father in a way that no other person can boast. All Believers are in the Family of God by adoption, whereas Jesus, although Incarnate in His Earthly Sojourn, was the Son of God by eternal generation.

And yet, Jesus felt the need of constant prayer (Mat. 14:23; 26:36; Mk. 6:46; 14:32; Lk. 6:12; 9:28; Jn. 17:9). Considering Who He was, where does that leave us?

He set the example for us, and He did it for a purpose and a reason. If a prayer life was a necessity for Him, surely we must understand what a necessity it is for us as well!

A HABITUAL PRAYER LIFE IS FOR THREE PURPOSES

Of course, some have attempted to make a law out of prayer, which, if done, cancels out the worth of prayer and avails nothing.

By that I mean that if we have the idea that God blesses us solely because we put in so much prayer time, it then becomes a law, which, in essence, is attempting to earn something from God, etc. Such is doomed to failure before it even begins.

The actual source of victory for the Child of God is the Cross of Christ. In fact, the Cross of Christ must be the Object of our Faith in every capacity and for all time. Once we understand the Cross as it regards our everyday living for God, understanding that the Holy Spirit works exclusively within the parameters, so to speak, of the Finished Work of Christ, then our prayer life will take on a brand new perspective. In other words, we will not pray thinking that so much prayer gives so many Blessings, etc. It doesn't! However, once the Believer properly understands the Cross of Christ not only for Salvation but for Sanctification, as well, then, as stated, our prayer life will be totally different, which we hope to bring out in these Passages. Let's say it this way:

• Jesus Christ is the Source of all things we receive from God (Jn. 1:1-3, 14, 29; 14:6, 20; Col. 2:10-15).

• The Cross of Christ is the Means and the only Means by which we receive all of these good things from God (Rom. 6:1-14; I Cor. 1:17-18, 23; 2:2).

NOTES

• With Jesus as our Source and the Cross as our Means, then the Cross of Christ must ever be the Object of our Faith (Gal. 6:14; Col. 2:10-15).

• With Jesus as the Source, the Cross as the Means, and the Cross of Christ ever the Object of our Faith, the Holy Spirit, Who works exclusively within the parameters of the Finished Work of Christ, will then grandly help us, without which, we cannot hope to succeed (Rom. 8:1-11; Eph. 2:13-18).

THE FIRST PURPOSE IS FOR COMMUNION WITH OUR HEAVENLY FATHER

Communion speaks of relationship. In other words, it is impossible to establish a relationship with your Heavenly Father without communion. Without prayer, communion cannot be established. As well, relationship is the foundation of the Christian experience. To do such, there must be prayer and the study of the Word of God. The two go hand in hand, without which, communion cannot be engaged or relationship established.

Respecting communion, when the Believer begins to pray, he should do exactly as the Psalmist said so long ago, *"Enter into His Gates with thanksgiving, and into His Courts with praise: be thankful unto Him, and bless His Name"* (Ps. 100:4).

Of course, the Psalmist was speaking of one's entrance into the Temple of old; however, the same principle holds true respecting our entering into the Presence of God by prayer at this present time.

As the Believer begins to pray, he should always begin by praising the Lord, acknowledging His many Blessings, and simply thanking Him for all the things He has done, is doing, and shall do. This shows gratitude on the part of the Believer.

Oftentimes the Believer will not even get beyond this stage as the Holy Spirit begins to fill his heart, taking him into a place of communion, which is based strictly upon praise and thanksgiving.

THE HOLY SPIRIT

As well, after beginning to pray, the Believer should ask the Lord for the Holy

Spirit to lead him into the area of prayer needed the most. Actually, one of the great Works of the Holy Spirit in the life of the Believer is making Intercession for us, which actually speaks of helping us to pray (Rom. 8:26-27).

Unless one prays in the Spirit, one is actually not going to make much headway with the Lord. In doing such, the Holy Spirit may lead us to pray in Tongues some, but more than likely, most of our supplication will be in English or our native language, whatever that may be.

As stated, the Believer should earnestly seek the help of the Holy Spirit when he prays, which should be often, even daily.

I have heard many Christians go to prayer and immediately begin to petition the Lord for certain things without even bothering to thank Him for what He has already done. As well, I have heard them making petitions before the Lord as if they were reading a grocery list without the Spirit of God helping them to pray. In truth, that is really not prayer. At best, it is just some type of prayerful exercise, which will really avail little or nothing.

There is no greater privilege for the Child of God than the privilege of prayer. The ability to go before One Who is supreme and, consequently, able to do anything that needs to be done is a privilege indeed! Therefore, we should avail ourselves of the opportunity to engage in this privilege in the highest manner, especially considering how important this is.

THE SECOND PURPOSE OF PRAYER IS CONSECRATION

In prayer, we have the privilege of talking to the Lord and of Him talking to us.

Many times in prayer, even as I have already stated, we may never even get beyond the praise stage, and sometimes we will just keep quiet before the Lord and allow Him to speak to our hearts.

In prayer, the Lord always deals with us about particular things. Actually, it is virtually impossible for any Believer to have a prayer life while at the same time practicing sin. One of the first things the Holy Spirit is going to do is to convict of sin, that is, if sin is actually in the life of the Believer. It is His Business to get it out, and to be sure, He will do just that if we allow Him proper latitude.

NOTES

The Lord desires the Believer to walk so closely to Him that the Believer can always hear the still, small voice as it whispers. In turn, He gives us leading, guidance, and direction, which speaks of consecration. He points out things in our lives that are displeasing to Him, as well as leading us in the direction He desires that we go.

Consequently, I am positive that one can see how absolutely significant this is! Prayer is to help us move into God's Ways rather than our ways or the ways of man, which are always unproductive. God has a way, and not only does He have a way, but He has a special way tailored just for you, the individual Believer. In other words, He wants you to know and understand the very special, unique plan that He has outlined for you and is especially for your benefit. There is no other way this can come about except through prayer and the study of the Word of God.

Therefore, prayer is really the only method of consecration afforded by the Heavenly Father. To be sure, it is for our benefit and not His!

THE THIRD PURPOSE OF PRAYER IS PETITION

Regrettably, many Believers think that prayer consists of petition totally. As we have attempted to prove, it is only a part of prayer, but a very important part, as should be obvious.

Over and over again, we are told in the Word of God to petition our Lord for what we want and need (Mat. 21:22; Mk. 11:22-24; Jn. 14:14; 15:7).

Of course, every Believer must pray according to the Will of God because that is the only way the Holy Spirit will help us pray (Rom. 8:26-27).

The question is asked as to how we can know what the Will of God actually is.

The stock answer is, *"The Will of God is the Word of God."* Of course, that is correct, but as we have stated, God has an overall plan, and then He has a plan tailor-made just for you. Consequently, what may be His Will for others just might not be His Will for you. While there are many things I believe that are standard, meaning the Will of God for all, such as Spiritual growth, prosperity, and Healing, still, how these things are brought about can vary with Believers.

Therefore, as we have already stated, when we have the proper communion with the Lord, which will ensure the proper consecration, then we will know what is the Mind of the Spirit and the Will of God personally for us. Communion and consecration ensure this, which makes these twin privileges a necessity.

If we have proper communion with the Lord, which ensures relationship, we will not ask for things that are not the Will of God for our lives. We will know that Will. If at times we do not know exactly what His Will is concerning a certain thing, we will simply tell Him that above all, we desire His Will and will actually settle for nothing else (Lk. 22:42).

In this context, the Lord has promised that He will give us what we want and need!

MY PERSONAL PRAYER LIFE

When I was but a child, my grandmother taught me the value of prayer and, in effect, how to pray. She taught me how to have Faith in God, believing His Word. One might say that she was my Bible School and my teacher, all under the Guidance of the Holy Spirit.

I can see her face even now as it literally would be wreathed in glory, with her eyes having a far-away look and her telling me, *"Jimmy, God is a big God, so ask big!"* I have never forgotten that, with it helping me to touch a great part of this world for the Cause of Christ.

So, I was raised with that type of aura as it regards prayer, which helped chart the course of my life. Without it, I doubt very seriously if I would have made it.

In late October, 1991, at an extremely serious crisis time of this Ministry, which was my fault I might quickly add, the Lord spoke to my heart and told me to have two prayer meetings a day, which we did for over 10 years, and which I personally continue to this day.

NOTES

When the Lord first told me to do this, the only instruction that He gave was, *"Do not seek Me so much for what I can do, but rather for Who I am."* He wasn't telling me that I wasn't to ask Him for that which we needed, but that I must make relationship priority. No other instructions were given.

At that time, I had no idea whatsoever that the Lord was going to give me a Revelation of the Cross of Christ that would revolutionize my life and Ministry and millions of others as well.

Those prayer meetings lasted for over 10 years, and actually, as stated, I still personally keep the same schedule morning and night.

At a particular time, I grew somewhat discouraged, not quite knowing that for which I was seeking the Face of the Lord. As I've just stated, the Lord only stated, *"Seek Me mostly for Who I am."*

I began to ask the Lord why it was taking so long. Little did I know and realize many things that lay ahead. Then one night in a prayer meeting, the Lord answered that particular prayer, and did so by using one of the strangest Texts in the Bible.

That night He said to me, *"You have asked Me why it is taking so long. Here is My Answer to you."*

"For precept must be upon precept, precept upon precept; line upon line, line upon line; here a little, and there a little" (Isa. 28:10).

I knew beyond the shadow of a doubt that it was the Lord speaking to me, but yet, this was a strange answer.

It took me years to fully understand what He was telling me that night.

The idea is that everything must be measured by the Word of God. No other *"measurement"* will be accepted. In reality, what He was telling me, which I then did not know, was that He would give me the great Word of the Cross and until that was done, *"Precept would not be upon precept"* and *"line would not be upon line."* That took about seven years, and to be frank, continues unto this hour, and I think will ever continue. It's impossible to exhaust the potential of the Finished Work of Christ.

That's the reason that Paul referred to it as *"the Everlasting Covenant"* (Heb. 13:20).

THE CROSS

Then in 1997, the Lord began to open up to me the great Message of the Cross. It was nothing new but actually that which He had long since given to the Apostle Paul, which Paul gave to us in his 14 Epistles. The Lord gave me this great word in three stages:

1. He first showed me what the sin nature was. I learned that this was the first thing the Lord showed the Apostle Paul after the great Apostle had come to Christ (Rom. 6:1-23; 7:1-25).

2. Secondly, He showed me the solution to the sin nature, which is the Cross of Christ. Actually, He gave me this simple Revelation in three sentences:

a. The answer you seek is found in the Cross.

b. The solution you seek is found in the Cross.

c. The answer you seek is found only in the Cross.

Once again, He took me to the great Sixth Chapter of Romans to show me this, as well as the First Chapter of I Corinthians. Then, as I learned the Cross, I found that the entirety of the Story of the Bible was *"Jesus Christ and Him Crucified"* (I Cor. 1:23; Gal. 6:14).

THE HOLY SPIRIT

3. Thirdly, the Lord showed me how the Holy Spirit works in all of this.

When the Lord told me, *"The answer for which you seek is found only in the Cross,"* the word *"only"* somewhat confused me. Where did the Holy Spirit come in regarding all of this?

I had always strongly preached the Holy Spirit through my Ministry. In fact, by the Grace of God, through our Ministry I had seen tens of thousands (and I exaggerate not) baptized with the Holy Spirit with the evidence of speaking with other Tongues. But yet, the Lord said that *"the answer for which you seek is found only in the Cross."* So again I asked, *"Where does the Holy Spirit come in regarding all of this?"*

For several weeks I earnestly sought the Lord about the matter, and then at a particular time, the Lord answered that prayer in a phenomenal way.

NOTES

To address this, I have to go all the way back to 1988. It was a time so dark in this Ministry that I did not know if I would make it or not. In fact, if I had not had a strong prayer life, I know that I would not have made it.

That particular morning while seeking the Lord, I experienced an attack by the powers of darkness that was greater than anything I had ever previously encountered. As he does, Satan began to tell me, *"You have disgraced yourself, your family, your Church, the work that God has called you to do, and you are nothing but an embarrassment. You ought to draw out what money you have in the bank,"* which was about $800, *"and just disappear."*

As that was rolling through my mind, and with a power that I had never experienced before, which was a power of destruction, I began to plead with the Lord for help. I said to Him, *"Lord, You promised that You would not put on us anything any harder than we could bear, but with every temptation, You would make a way of escape."* I then went on to say, *"I think You are allowing the Evil One too much latitude. No human being can stand this. Please help me."*

Instantly it happened!

One moment, it was like 500 pounds were crushing me down, and the next moment, it was like I was floating on clouds as the Spirit of God washed all over me. Then the Lord spoke to my heart and said to me:

"I am going to show you things about the Holy Spirit that you do not now know."

Instantly, I began to wonder what He was talking about. I knew that the Holy Spirit is God, and I also knew that there were all kinds of things about the Holy Spirit that I did not know. And yet, I knew that somehow the Lord was talking about the problem at hand.

As time rolled by, I thought about that moment again and again. Still, there was nothing that happened that I could put my finger on that let me know the Lord was answering the prayer regarding that which He would show me respecting the Holy Spirit.

Then it happened! It was 1997, some nine years after He had first spoken to my heart concerning this all important subject.

The great Revelation of the Cross had just begun. The Ministry at that time had two radio stations. I was endeavoring to teach on the Cross what the Lord at that time had been so gracious to open up to me. On that particular morning as we went through the program, something happened that had never taken place in my life before or since.

The program had almost ended, lacking only a few minutes until we would close. All of a sudden, without premeditation and without even knowing what I was talking about, I made the following statement:

"The Holy Spirit works entirely within the parameters of the Cross of Christ and will not work outside of those parameters."

When I said it, it shocked me. I didn't even know what I had said. I had never heard such a statement! I had never read anything like that in a book. I had not known anything of that nature. As stated, I had never done anything like that before or since.

As I sat there lost in my thoughts for a few moments, knowing that what I said was right but not understanding it, all of a sudden, Loren Larson, who was on the program with me, asked, *"Can you give me Scripture for that?"*

How could I when I had never heard the statement before in my life?

THE LORD KEPT HIS PROMISE

I looked down at my Bible, and Romans 8:2 literally leaped up at me. The Holy Spirit through Paul said:

"The Law of the Spirit of Life in Christ Jesus has made me free from the Law of Sin and Death" (Rom. 8:2).

There it was in black and white.

I read the Text and then the program ended.

I got up from the table and turned to my right to walk out of the little room when the Spirit of God came all over me. The Lord then spoke to my heart, saying:

"Do you remember back in 1988 when I told you that I would show you things about the Holy Spirit which you did not then know?"

NOTES

Of course, I remembered and quietly answered in the affirmative as the tears rolled down my face.

The Lord then said, *"I have just kept My Word to you. I have shown you something about the Holy Spirit you did not then know. I have shown you how that He works within hearts and lives."*

At the moment, I did not fully realize how important it was what I had just been given. Of course, this great Truth was given to the Apostle Paul nearly 2,000 years ago.

However, as to how the Holy Spirit works in the hearts and lives of Believers, helping us to live this life we ought to live, I do not think this great Truth has been known by many since the days of the Early Church. As should be obvious, it is a phenomenal Truth. It is actually one of the great Truths of the New Covenant made possible by the Cross.

Yes, while the answer is found only in the Cross, still, it is the Holy Spirit Who makes these great Truths of Christ, Who is the New Covenant, relevant and mighty within our hearts and lives (Rom. 8:1-11).

YOU, THE BELIEVER

If you will take to heart the following statements, irrespective as to who you might be and irrespective of the past—whatever that has been—and you will do that which I will state, I guarantee that you will know Blessings unexcelled. So, whatever you do, take advantage of what we are going to say.

At this moment, if you as a Believer will vow to set aside each day a period of time (even 15 minutes) for the study of the Word and some 15 minutes for prayer, you will see your world change for the better one thousand times over.

Now, you may say, *"Brother Swaggart, that sounds good, but I am so busy that I simply don't have the time to set aside 30 minutes, etc."* If that is the case, then you are busier than you ought to be. It doesn't matter how busy you are, and it doesn't matter what you have to do to faithfully hold to that which I have stated; if you will do it, let me say it again, your world will change, and for the better.

NOTES

SATAN WILL TRY TO STOP YOU

Once you make up your mind to do this that I have stated, you will find that Satan will throw everything as a roadblock in front of you to hinder you, and I mean everything. He knows your world will change if you will faithfully adhere to that which I have said, so he will try to stop you.

However, you must not allow that to happen. In other words, I don't care how tired you are, I don't care how your mind wanders when you try to pray, and I don't care how many things come up that you think you must attend to immediately, if you will persevere and let nothing stop you, you are on your way to victory.

PRAYER IS NOT EASY

You will find that the study of the Word of God is much easier than prayer. I will give you a little clue: The way you study the Word is that you begin with THE EXPOSITOR'S STUDY BIBLE. It will help you to understand the Word as nothing else that you have ever read or studied. Start with the Book of Genesis and go straight through, reading and studying about 15 minutes a day, or longer if you so desire. You will find the Lord at times speaking to you through the Word as you slowly draw closer to the Lord.

When you begin to pray each day, begin praying by thanking the Lord for what He has done for you. The Scripture says, *"Enter into His Gates with thanksgiving, and into His Courts with praise: be thankful unto Him, and bless His Name"* (Ps. 100:4).

Many times, you will find that the entire 15 minutes or longer will be spent just in praising Him and thanking Him for His Goodness to you. That's the way it ought to be, and then at other times, the Holy Spirit will anoint you to petition the Lord for the things that you need. It doesn't matter if they are financial, physical, social, or above all, spiritual, tell the Lord what you need.

Now don't get discouraged and quit. Sometimes the Lord answers prayer very quickly, and sometimes it's a period of time, even years before a prayer is answered. However, this one thing is certain: If you will persevere and not give up and quit, the answer most definitely will come. It will come at God's Time and in God's Way, but it will come.

Incidentally, as your prayer life strengthens, you will learn to pray according to His Will. In other words, you'll come to the place that you don't want anything except that which He wants you to have, and your praying will be in that capacity.

THE HOLY SPIRIT

As well, we must understand that everything done on this Earth for the Lord and by the Lord is done through the Person, Agency, Office, and Ministry of the Holy Spirit and by the Authority of the Lord Jesus Christ, and actually in His Name. With Him, anything can be done; without Him, nothing can be done!

Now it's up to you! You belong to the Lord. He has paid a tremendous price for your soul, and He loves you more than words could ever begin to express. He wants to bless you! He wants to help you! However, it must be done His Way. In other words, for the Lord to be to us what He desires to be, there must be a relationship with Him. That relationship can only be brought about by prayer and the study of the Word. Please understand that the Cross of Christ is the Means and the only Means by which all of these wonderful things are given to us. In other words, Jesus paid the price at the Cross for everything we need. He defeated every power of darkness at the Cross, and there He atoned for every sin, so the Cross of Christ must ever be the Object of our Faith. With that being done, the Holy Spirit, Who works exclusively within the parameters of the Finished Work of Christ, will then work mightily on our behalf.

(32) "AND THE MULTITUDE OF THEM WHO BELIEVED WERE OF ONE HEART AND OF ONE SOUL: NEITHER SAID ANY OF THEM THAT OUGHT OF THE THINGS WHICH HE POSSESSED WAS HIS OWN; BUT THEY HAD ALL THINGS COMMON."

The exegesis is:

1. The phrase, *"And the multitude of them who believed were of one heart and*

NOTES

of one soul," speaks of the unity that can only be brought about by the Holy Spirit. Man's efforts and attempts to establish unity simply cannot be done. Only the Holy Spirit can do such, and the proper atmosphere has to be provided in order even for Him to bring these things to pass.

2. It is very obvious in the Text that despite the threatened persecution, which, incidentally, was very real, these people had no fear because they knew beyond the shadow of a doubt that God was with them. As stated, they *"were of one heart and of one soul."*

3. This meant *"one"* in Faith, in purpose, in direction, and in leading according to the Holy Spirit.

4. The phrase, *"Neither said any of them that ought of the things which he possessed was his own; but they had all things common,"* tells us several things:

a. A oneness with Jesus, generated by the Holy Spirit, produced a oneness among themselves, as it is meant to be.

b. As we have already stated, thousands of these people were being excommunicated from the synagogue due to their acceptance of Christ, and as a consequence, many of them lost their jobs, were evicted from their homes and, in effect, were left destitute. However, others, who were better off financially, sold things they did not need to help meet this expense, which it did.

5. Also, when they did this, it was freely given, with no obligation on the part of the recipient, which is the way it ought to be with true Christianity.

6. Due to what was happening, Satan did not succeed in what he was trying to do (the choking of them to death financially), with the Holy Spirit giving them guidance as to how the problem could be solved, and was solved easily.

(33) "AND WITH GREAT POWER GAVE THE APOSTLES WITNESS OF THE RESURRECTION OF THE LORD JESUS: AND GREAT GRACE WAS UPON THEM ALL."

The synopsis is:

1. The phrase, *"And with great Power gave the Apostles witness of the Resurrection of the Lord Jesus,"* proclaims the Holy Spirit greatly anointing the Apostles to attest to the Resurrection of Christ, and that they were personal witnesses of this, the greatest event in the annals of human history.

2. If it is to be noticed, the Apostles said almost nothing about the Cross of Christ at this particular time. The reason is that this great Truth concerning the Cross, which is actually the meaning of the New Covenant, had not yet been given. This Truth would be given several years later to the Apostle Paul, who would give it to us in his 14 Epistles.

Of course, the Holy Spirit wanted the Resurrection preached strongly and solidly simply because the Nation of Israel, and by that I speak of its religious leaders, was claiming that Jesus had not been raised from the dead, but His Body had been stolen, etc. So, the Holy Spirit wanted the Resurrection preached then in no uncertain terms, which it was.

Of course, He wants the Resurrection preached now, as well, but it is the Cross of Christ, which we now learn from the Apostle Paul, that is the Foundation of the Faith (I Cor. 1:17-18, 23; 2:2; Gal. 6:14; Col. 2:10-15).

3. The demands of the Priests that the Apostles keep quiet about the Resurrection of Christ were not heeded at all. How could they keep quiet about such a thing? To be sure, they were not supposed to keep quiet about this great Miracle—the Miracle of the ages (I Cor. 15:1-23).

4. *"And great Grace was upon them all,"* is a portrayal of the beginning of the great Dispensation of Grace, which actually began on the Day of Pentecost.

5. The Church would not know the full ingredients of Grace or understand its import fully until the Lord gave the particulars, as stated, to the Apostle Paul. At this time, he was not a Believer and was actually a hater of Christ. As well, he was doing everything within his power, as we shall see, to destroy the Early Church, but how wonderful is our God!

6. *"Grace"* speaks of the Favor of God, and *"great Grace"* speaks of great favor. One might say that Grace is simply the Goodness of God given to undeserving people.

7. As well, I think one can say without fear of contradiction that the *"great Grace"*

was a result of the mighty Filling and Operation of the Holy Spirit within their hearts and lives.

8. In the very face of the threatenings of the religious leadership of Israel, the Lord was pouring out His Grace on His People in an unprecedented way. To be frank, nothing could be more wonderful or greater!

(34) "NEITHER WAS THERE ANY AMONG THEM WHO LACKED: FOR AS MANY AS WERE POSSESSORS OF LANDS OR HOUSES SOLD THEM, AND BROUGHT THE PRICES OF THE THINGS THAT WERE SOLD."

The record is:

1. The phrase, *"Neither was there any among them who lacked,"* refers to those who had been excommunicated from the synagogue, as we have just stated. As the Holy Spirit began to move, not only was the spiritual problem handled but the financial problem as well!

2. *"For as many as were possessors of lands or houses sold them, and brought the prices of the things that were sold,"* refers to extra possessions, etc. There is no hint here that anyone impoverished himself, but rather the very opposite.

3. Without a doubt, the Holy Spirit began to move upon individuals respecting these extra possessions and directed them as to what they should do. They would follow His Leading and then bring the money to the Apostles in order that it be properly distributed among those who were in need.

4. As well, even though none was aware of such at this particular time, in about 27 years, Rome would completely destroy Jerusalem, and most of Israel for that matter. Consequently, when that time came, houses and lands had little value, with most everything being destroyed or confiscated.

(35) "AND LAID THEM DOWN AT THE APOSTLES' FEET: AND DISTRIBUTION WAS MADE UNTO EVERY MAN ACCORDING AS HE HAD NEED."

The order is:

1. The phrase, *"And laid them down at the Apostles' feet,"* spoke of them as the leaders and, thereby, entrusted with this largesse.

2. *"And distribution was made unto every man according as he had need,"* speaks of an orderly account with proper distribution.

NOTES

3. Once again, the Lord met the need by encouraging people to give to His Cause and His Work.

(36) "AND JOSEPH, WHO BY THE APOSTLES WAS SURNAMED BARNABAS, (WHICH IS, BEING INTERPRETED, THE SON OF CONSOLATION,) A LEVITE, AND OF THE COUNTRY OF CYPRUS."

The order is:

1. The phrase, *"And Joseph, who by the Apostles was surnamed Barnabas,"* is actually, *"Joseph Barnabas."* Some think that this is the same man as Joseph Barsabas in Acts 1:23. Whether that is correct or not, no one knows!

2. Barnabas became a Prophet and an Apostle (Acts 13:1; 14:14).

3. He is the one who brought the newly converted Paul (Saul) to the Apostles in Jerusalem (Acts 9:25-27). As well, he became a co-worker with Paul (Acts 11:30; 12:25; 13:1-15).

4. Some say the phrase, *"Which is, being interpreted, The son of consolation,"* should have been translated, *"Son of Exhortation,"* for the Hebrew favors the latter.

5. At any rate, the name fit Barnabas in every capacity.

6. He seemed to be a man who had unlimited patience and seldom gave up on people. He was used greatly by the Holy Spirit to help spearhead the Work of God in the Early Church, and above all, respecting the spread of the Gospel to the world of that day.

7. He was, without a doubt, one of the most important men in the Early Church and was used mightily by the Holy Spirit.

8. *"A Levite, and of the country of Cyprus,"* simply meant that he was a Jew who was born in Cyprus and lived there for a considerable period of time, as likely his father had done before him.

9. Being of the Tribe of Levi and, consequently, a *"Levite"* meant that he was of the priestly class, although not a Priest.

(37) "HAVING LAND, SOLD IT, AND BROUGHT THE MONEY, AND LAID IT AT THE APOSTLES' FEET."

The pattern is:

1. As we have stated, the Cross was little discussed by the Early Church until the time of the Apostle Paul.

2. It was little discussed because the meaning of the New Covenant, which is the meaning of the Cross, was not yet given. It would be given to the Apostle Paul.

3. As well, due to the fact that the leaders of Israel were claiming that Jesus did not rise from the dead but that His Body had been stolen, the Holy Spirit wanted the great Doctrine of the Resurrection to be preached constantly, which it was at those times, and rightly so.

THE SON OF CONSOLATION

The phrase, *"Having land, sold it,"* probably referred to property in Cyprus, but which is not certain.

The phrase, *"And brought the money, and laid it at the Apostles' feet,"* singles him out specifically, which the Holy Spirit desired to do. In other words, what Barnabas did, no doubt, inspired many others to do the same thing.

Going back to the phrase, *"The Son of consolation,"* it is thought that Luke, in writing this account, desired more specifically to indicate the man's character rather than anything else. At any rate, it was an apt description.

Also, when Barnabas sold the land, which evidently brought a large sum of money, and then gave it to the Apostles for proper distribution, it seems that possibly this may have represented a very large gift, which caused many people to speak kindly of Barnabas.

If, in fact, that is the case, it seems that Ananias and Sapphira, who we will study in the next Chapter, concocted a scheme that, in effect, was a lie, which they thought would bring them great accolades as well. It was to bring the very opposite as we shall see!

Luke said of Barnabas that he was *"a good man, full of the Holy Spirit and of Faith"* (Acts 11:24).

When the converted Saul arrived in Jerusalem only to discover that the Christians thought him a spy, it was Barnabas who introduced him to the *"pillar"* Apostles and convinced them of his Conversion and sincerity (Acts 9:27; Gal. 1:18).

NOTES

It was Barnabas who represented the Apostles at Antioch when, for the first time, Gentiles had been evangelized in significant numbers, and where fellow Cypriots had been prominent (Acts 11:19).

He saw the movement as a Work of God and as a fitting sphere for the forgotten Saul, whom he brought to share his labors.

BARNABAS

However, Barnabas was not the man to withstand Peter to his face when he succumbed to Judaizing pressure. Even Barnabas temporarily broke fellowship with the Gentiles at that time, which caused problems and brought the rebuke of Paul (Gal. 2:13).

However, in the total scope of things, Barnabas was committed to full acceptance of Gentiles on Faith in Christ (Acts 13:46). The journey with Paul (Acts, Chpts. 13-14), beginning in his own Cyprus, resulted in a chain of predominantly Gentile Churches far into Asia Minor and a surging Jewish opposition.

As well, back at Antioch, the Circumcision question became so acute that he and Paul were appointed to bring the matter before the Jerusalem Council. Their policy was triumphantly vindicated (Acts 15:1-29).

Somewhat later, Barnabas insisted on including Mark, who was actually his cousin, in a missionary journey. Paul refused because Mark had not proven faithful regarding a previous expedition. This occasioned a separation between Barnabas and Paul, which I think was not the Will of God (Acts 15:36-40).

However, even though this close partnership was broken, it seems that the friendship was not. Whenever Paul mentioned Barnabas, his words implied sympathy and respect (Gal. 2:13).

In principles and practice, they were identical, and we shall never know how much Paul owed to Barnabas, but we do know it was much.

This much we do know: God used this man in a mighty way and had there not been a

NOTES

Barnabas, there just might not have been a Paul.

"I heard an old, old story,
"How a Saviour came from Glory,
"How He gave His Life on Calvary,
"To save a wretch like me;
"I heard about His groaning,
"Of His precious Blood's atoning,
"Then I repented of my sins,
"And won the victory."

"I heard about His healing,
"Of His cleansing Power revealing,
"How He made the lame to walk again,
"And caused the blind to see,
"And then I cried 'dear Jesus,
"Come and heal my broken spirit,'
"And somehow Jesus came and brought
"To me the victory."

"I heard about a mansion
"He has built for me in Glory,
"And I heard about the streets of gold
"Beyond the crystal sea;
"About the Angels singing,
"And the old Redemption Story,
"And some sweet day I'll sing up there
"The song of victory."

CHAPTER 5

(1) "BUT A CERTAIN MAN NAMED ANANIAS, WITH SAPPHIRA HIS WIFE, SOLD A POSSESSION."

The exegesis is:

1. God's Way, for whatever problem, is *"Jesus Christ and Him Crucified."*

2. Man can only be changed by the Power of God, and that Power is registered in the Holy Spirit (Rom. 8:1-11).

3. This Power is made available to Believers on the basis of Faith placed in Christ and the Cross exclusively (I Cor. 1:17-18, 23; 2:2).

ANANIAS AND SAPPHIRA

The story of this man and his wife was placed here in graphic detail by the Holy Spirit as a warning.

The One and Self-same Holy Spirit, Who was the Spirit of Life to the impotent man of the Third Chapter, was a Spirit of Death to Ananias and Sapphira. If electricity is obeyed, it is a beneficent force; if disobeyed, a deadly force.

The Presence of God in the camp meant death to the carnal nature, for God is intolerant of evil, hence, the terrible judgments of the wilderness and of the Acts of the Apostles.

When the Holy Spirit withdrew from the *"camp"* because of disobedience, both in the days of Moses and Peter, these judgments ceased, and their cessation proved His Departure.

When the mighty Spirit of God works, His Operation is sure to manifest the evil and opposition of the carnal nature. His Power manifested itself outside the Church in Grace to the helpless, diseased, and sinful, and inside the Church in judgment upon falsehood and evil.

He will have Holiness in His House; and it is a fearful thing to sin against God. Like Ananias and Sapphira, many today in that which professes to be His Church effect a devotion that is false.

In graphic, glaring detail, this is the very reason that many people seek a church where the Spirit of God is *not* moving. In such a false religious atmosphere, they can continue in their sin without ever fearing Conviction, which definitely comes about when one is in a Spirit-led service.

THE SPIRIT OF GOD

While these individuals would strongly deny this, claiming other reasons, that of which we have spoken is the real cause. This group actually outnumbers by far the true Servants of God. People love their sin, and religious people most of all. They seek to continue their wrongful direction while at the same time appeasing their conscience by associating with some church that will cause them no spiritual discomfort whatsoever. There are many churches that fit that category.

This one thing is certain: Where the

Spirit of God is present and prevalent, He will never fail to carry out His Office Work to convict of sin, of righteousness, and of judgment, as well as comfort, strengthen, help, and anoint those who truly desire to follow the Lord in all His Fullness. However, if the Holy Spirit is not eagerly sought, with latitude, leading, and guidance given totally to Him, He simply will not remain. He cannot bless that which is not Scriptural, and neither can He bless sin. He will definitely help the individual who is truly crying out to God to become Scriptural, and will greatly bless and help the one who confesses and forsakes sin.

As we stated at the conclusion of the last Chapter, what Barnabas did respecting the sale of property and the giving of money must have been the catalyst that initiated the response of this couple. In fact, that is not out of the ordinary at all concerning spiritual things.

When God truly moves and people truly follow Him, even as Barnabas, Satan immediately places into the hearts of his dupes to do something similar, but with an entirely different motivation in mind. Thus was *"Ananias and Sapphira!"*

We learn from Verses 3 and 8 that it was land that was sold.

(2) "AND KEPT BACK PART OF THE PRICE, HIS WIFE ALSO BEING PRIVY TO IT, AND BROUGHT A CERTAIN PART, AND LAID IT AT THE APOSTLES' FEET."

The record is:

1. The phrase, *"And kept back part of the price, his wife also being privy to it,"* instantly proclaims the conception of this great sin and its deception in carrying it out. In other words, this was a carefully crafted scenario, which was authored by Satan but carried out by his dupes.

The phrase, *"And brought a certain part, and laid it at the Apostles' feet,"* carries forth in the word *"brought"* a detailed plan with a very wide application. In other words, it was done a certain way with a certain purpose in mind. That purpose was to carry out deception, having the people laud them, with them looking very high and spiritual, etc. In other words, it was done with fanfare, wide publication, and great ado.

NOTES

However, the Holy Spirit stresses the fact that while they desired to have the entirety of the Church with all its thousands think very highly of them, more than all they wanted the Apostles to regard them accordingly, hence, *"laying the money at the Apostles' feet."*

2. From this scenario and as carefully outlined by the Holy Spirit, we are given an idea as to the Spiritual Authority of those whom God has called, such as the Apostles. In this Calling is authority; however, it is not authority over other people, but rather to be exercised in the spirit world, such as authority over Satan, demon spirits, etc. To be sure, it was not Peter who struck these people dead, but rather the Lord. However, it is impossible to deal with God's called without at the same time dealing with God.

3. Turning this scenario in the opposite direction, I wonder how many times this scene is repeated but with altogether different results. In other words, the preacher is not close enough to God to properly discern, and because it is money in question, the modern Ananias and Sapphira are roundly praised and even given prominent positions in the church, which were the intentions of the original duo.

However, if the Holy Spirit is as prominent in our efforts presently as He was in the Early Church, and desires to be in ours I might quickly add, Satan's schemes make little headway.

(3) "BUT PETER SAID, ANANIAS, WHY HAS SATAN FILLED YOUR HEART TO LIE TO THE HOLY SPIRIT, AND TO KEEP BACK PART OF THE PRICE OF THE LAND?"

The form is:

1. The question, *"But Peter said, Ananias, why has Satan filled your heart to lie to the Holy Spirit?"* presents here two Gifts of the Spirit in operation: *"Discerning of Spirits"* and *"a Word of Knowledge."* As I have stated, this is why some people do not desire to attend a Church where the Spirit of the Lord is prominent. They want to keep lying to the Holy Spirit, so they find a church that is such in name only, which characterizes most sad to say, and where they will not be confronted. To be sure, the Spirit of God

will always confront the individual but, of course, only seldom to this degree.

2. The conclusion of the question, *"And to keep back part of the price of the land?"* details their insidious plan.

3. Coupling the Name *"God"* in the Fourth Verse with the Name *"Holy Spirit"* in this Verse affirms the Personality and Godhead of the Holy Spirit.

(4) "WHILE IT REMAINED, WAS IT NOT YOUR OWN? AND AFTER IT WAS SOLD, WAS IT NOT IN YOUR OWN POWER? WHY HAVE YOU CONCEIVED THIS THING IN YOUR HEART? YOU HAVE NOT LIED UNTO MEN, BUT UNTO GOD."

The pattern is:

1. Why is it so difficult for man to accept Christ and the Cross?

2. Millions accept Christ, but they reject the Cross.

3. In doing so, they are left with *"another Jesus,"* which means it's a Jesus not of the Bible (II Cor. 11:4).

SUBTERFUGE

The question, *"While it remained, was it not your own?"* tells us, as is obvious, that they had sold the land for a particular sum of money, heralding it far and wide that they were going to give it all to the Work of God. Evidently, they made a big thing of this.

However, neither the people nor the Apostles had any knowledge as to what the original sale price was and really did not care.

Ananias and Sapphira then concocted a story between themselves that the sale price was so much when actually, it was much more, making it seem as if they were doing a great thing in giving all the money. To be sure, if they lied to the Apostles, the people, and the Holy Spirit, which they did, one can be certain that they went to all lengths to impress people regarding the supposed generosity of their hearts. Evidently they had gone to great lengths to make people believe they were in great need themselves but had unselfishly ignored this, giving all they had to the Lord. Naturally, this was supposed to elicit praise and, above all, to make them look good in the eyes of the Apostles. However, they reckoned without the Holy Spirit, Who knows all things.

NOTES

WHY?

The question, *"And after it was sold, was it not in your own power?"* means simply that God did not require them to sell the land or to give all the money received to the Work of the Lord. In fact, the Lord would have been pleased with whatever part they did actually give had they only been honest. It was not the amount in question, but rather the deception!

The question, *"Why have you conceived this thing in your heart?"* proclaims to us where sin originates. It comes from within, and if it is dealt with, it must be dealt with from within.

This is the reason that all of the self-help efforts generated by men, irrespective of their nature, are all to no avail! Man can only address himself to the externals, such as environment, participation, association, etc. None of that works, even as it cannot work, simply because it really does not address the problem but only the symptoms.

Man's problem is a spiritual problem and has to be dealt with spiritually. This is what makes psychology (psychoanalysis) so wrong! It can only address the externals, even though it attempts to probe into the minds of people, etc. However, even if it could affect the mind in a positive way, which it actually cannot, this still would not solve the problem. Even though man is definitely affected by his physical body and certainly his mind, still, the real problem lies in the soul and spirit of man, which can only be addressed by the Lord.

THE NEW BIRTH

The New Birth is a Spiritual Birth and has nothing to do with one's physical body or mind, even though it will greatly affect them in a positive sense. In addressing this very thing, Paul spoke to Believers (people who were already Saved), *"That you present your bodies a living sacrifice, holy, acceptable unto God, which is your reasonable service."*

Regarding the mind, he then said, *"And be not conformed to this world: But be you transformed by the renewing of your mind, that you may prove what is that good, and acceptable, and perfect, Will of God"* (Rom. 12:1-2).

The point is that all the religious ceremonies in the world, which can only affect the body, cannot truly help anyone. As well, all of man's efforts to develop mind power will not truly affect the real problem, which is in the spirit of man. Once again, when men address themselves to these particulars, they are only addressing themselves to symptoms.

Still, even though God totally changes a person by changing his heart, which deals with the real seat of the problem, this does not mean that the individual will never again do wrong. Even though the Believer should not sin and is commanded not to sin, due to the sin nature remaining in the Believer, sin is always possible, which, if committed, will affect the Believer in a very negative way (Rom. 6:16).

The phrase, *"You have not lied unto men, but unto God,"* actually portrays the object of all sin. Satan directs it against God because sin is meant to do just that—be an affront to God. All sin is a form of rebellion against God, which is the very intention of Satan in the first place.

The act committed by Ananias and Sapphira was one of deliberate hypocrisy—an attempt to deceive God Himself, as if such could be done!

Acts 4:31 says, *"They were all filled with the Holy Spirit."* This Verse says, *"Why has Satan filled your heart?"*

There is an excellent possibility that Ananias and Sapphira were at the prayer meeting of the previous Chapter and were filled with the Holy Spirit with all the others. This we do know: If they were there, they were filled because the word *"all"* is used (Acts 4:31). Actually, every evidence is that they did fall into that category.

Let us look at the two sins of passion and pride, with all sins falling into one category or the other.

NOTES

SINS OF PASSION

The sins of passion fall under the category of *"lusts of the flesh,"* and result in *"works of the flesh,"* such as *"adultery, fornication, uncleanness, lasciviousness, idolatry, witchcraft, hatred, variance, etc."* (Gal. 5:19-21).

These sins are wicked, as should be obvious; however, they fall into an entirely different category than sins of pride. While they are wicked and awful, still, it is much easier to bring one to Repentance of this nature than those who are engaged in sins of pride. Jesus addressed Himself to this very thing:

He said, *"That the Publicans and the harlots go into the Kingdom of God before you"* (Mat. 21:31).

No! Jesus was not condoning stealing, graft, or immorality, but was rather pointing out the fact that it was much easier to bring these to Repentance than those who were guilty of the sin of pride, as the Pharisees.

SINS OF PRIDE

Sins of pride are much more subtle. They come from the spirit of man and are rather a direct frontal assault against God, which cleverly subverts the Truth, even as Satan did in the Garden of Eden. Actually, this is the great sin of religion. It substitutes another way to victory or even to Salvation other than the Bible.

I think I can say without fear of contradiction that the sin of pride (religious pride) always carries with it deceit, a form of hypocrisy, deception, subterfuge, and self-righteousness while all the time being very religious.

In fact, the sin of pride is the cause of all false doctrine in the church and all false ways of Salvation.

This is what the Lord through Isaiah was saying when He gave the Word, *"But to this man will I look, even to him that is poor and of a contrite spirit, and trembles at My Word"* (Isa. 66:2).

The broken and contrite spirit is the very opposite of pride.

This is what made the sin of Ananias and Sapphira so bad. It was a sin of pride, which caused them to selfishly desire preeminence in the Church and favor with the Apostles in a deceitful, lying, and ungodly way. They were not only trying to buy their way in, even as multiple millions have done, but they were lying about it as well. Also, it was not just a lie that came quickly, but rather one that was schemed and planned, and if allowed to continue, would ultimately have greatly corrupted the Church.

CORRUPTION IN THE MODERN CHURCH

Actually, if one wants to look at this scenario involving Ananias and Sapphira, one finds the reason for most of the corruption in the modern church.

Of course, some may ask the question as to why God does not strike people dead now as then. There are two answers to that:

1. In fact, He is doing so at certain times. While it may not be as dramatic or as obvious as that of our Text, and it may be labeled by doctors as a heart attack, etc., if the truth be known, it is the Lord Who executes judgment because of this same sin being committed.

2. As we have already alluded, such judgment basically only happens where the Holy Spirit is totally in control as during the first days of the Early Church. If there is very little True Gospel preached, the Holy Spirit is little present, if at all, and for the obvious reasons. Consequently, He takes little hand, if any at all, whether of judgment or Blessing.

To be frank, when true Holy Spirit Revival comes, it will always work in both directions. People are greatly blessed as they repent and come back to the Lord, and others are judged because of their refusal to repent, and some are judged very severely.

(5) "AND ANANIAS HEARING THESE WORDS FELL DOWN, AND GAVE UP THE GHOST: AND GREAT FEAR CAME ON ALL THEM WHO HEARD THESE THINGS."

The composition is:

1. Unredeemed man is loath to accept the Cross because the Cross tells man how Righteous God is and how unrighteous man is.

2. Redeemed man is loath to accept the Cross because the Cross says that man within himself, although redeemed, cannot live the life he ought to live.

3. It is the Cross alone that can cause the Believer to walk in victory.

NOTES

JUDGMENT

The phrase, *"And Ananias hearing these words fell down, and gave up the ghost,"* means that he was stricken dead on the spot.

Ananias, with the approval of his wife, laid their deceitful money at the Apostles' feet, and judgment swiftly laid their deceitful selves there.

"And great fear came on all them who heard these things," presents that which the Holy Spirit demands, and which is lacking, for the most part, in the modern church. In other words, there is very little fear of God! Were there proper fear in the modern church as it ought to be, there would be much more fear of God in the world, but there is almost none.

The type of *"fear"* spoken of here is not the type of fear a slave would have for a harsh taskmaster. It is actually a healthy fear, even a very healthy fear, without which man cannot properly function.

This type of *"fear"* simply knows and understands that God is Loving, Kind, Longsuffering, and Merciful. However, at the same time, He hates sin, even though He does love the sinner.

In accordance, He has said some very merciful and beautiful things to the sinner while at the same time saying very harsh things about sin. Healthy fear knows that God says what He means and means what He says. Without that type of respect, which incorporates awe, God's correct Government breaks down.

FEAR

Men at times lose respect for other men simply because of wrongdoing or failure. However, man has never had a reason to lose respect for God, inasmuch as He has never failed in anything but has always been faithful in His Government and, as a matter of fact, always will be. So, the loss of such fear or respect never has its roots in God but always in the prideful and deceitful hearts of men. When this happens, men crucify Christ exactly as the Pharisees and religious leaders of old.

With the death of Ananias and Sapphira, and especially the manner in which they

NOTES

died, the Holy Spirit was serving notice on Israel, *"Repent or else!"*

It stands to reason and is almost certain that the religious leaders heard of the deaths of these two people, and that they had died as a direct result of the Judgment of God. However, the Seventh Chapter will show us that they little hearkened but went even deeper into their rebellion by murdering Stephen.

Even after that, the very man who held the clothes of them who stoned Stephen would come to Christ, and Paul was, no doubt, the instrument chosen by God to deliver the final Message, but again, to no avail (Acts, Chpt. 22-23).

About 10 years after Paul's final Message to Israel, they were completely destroyed by the Romans, even ceasing to be a Nation.

The Former Rain came as prophesied by Joel and constituted the Early Church, which was followed by judgment, even as we have said. To be sure, the Latter Rain outpouring, also prophesied by Joel, which began at about the turn of the century, will be followed by judgment as well (Joel, Chpt. 2). It is called the Great Tribulation and will affect Israel exactly as before but with one distinction. In this coming judgment, Jesus Christ will return, and Israel will at long last accept Him and thus be brought back to God (Rev., Chpt. 19; Zech., Chpt. 14).

(6) "AND THE YOUNG MEN AROSE, WOUND HIM UP, AND CARRIED HIM OUT, AND BURIED HIM."

The synopsis is:

1. The phrase, *"And the young men arose, wound him up,"* seems to imply that the process then used consisted of the body being wrapped in linen (or some such type of cloth), with pleasant smelling spices wrapped with it. Whether spices were used here or not, we are not told, but probably not.

2. As well, there was no embalming used then as now, at least in Israel.

3. *"And carried him out, and buried him,"* does not refer to being interred in a grave, but rather placed in a tomb, or else, prepared him for such without the process being completed, which is probably the case.

4. It is conceivable that they would have prepared his body as stated, which was the custom in that day, but it is doubtful that they would have done much else, especially considering that at this stage, his wife was not even aware of what had happened.

5. They would not have done anything illegal, especially considering the anger that the authorities were already registering against them.

6. Consequently, the religious leaders of Israel would have thrown the Body of Jesus into the potter's field, even though He was the Son of God, had Joseph of Arimathaea not given Him his special Tomb. However, the leaders of the Early Church took special care of the bodies of these two people, even though they had been wicked and evil. What a contrast! Such is the difference in those who truly know the Lord and those who truly do not!

(7) "AND IT WAS ABOUT THE SPACE OF THREE HOURS AFTER, WHEN HIS WIFE, NOT KNOWING WHAT WAS DONE, CAME IN."

The pattern is:

1. The time stated in the phrase, *"And it was about the space of three hours after,"* represents a hallmark in the Early Church. As we have already alluded, every time the Holy Spirit moves greatly, it will always result in great Blessing. However, at the same time, everything must be brought under the judgment of the Word of God, and that the Holy Spirit will do.

2. Considering the severity of what happened to Ananias and Sapphira, very few with a carnal heart and mind would label it as a great Move of God, but it was! It is identical to the time when Uzzah put his hand against the Ark to steady it as it was being brought into Jerusalem, and the Lord struck him dead (II Sam. 6:1-7).

3. If the skeptic who claims that the Lord was overly severe in these cases (and countless others of similar comport) knew the background of all these situations, there would not be wonder at what the Lord did, but that He had not done such much sooner. If one knew the background, one would see that the Lord had been overly Gracious and Merciful with these people for a long, long period of time (as He is with all) before the

final step was taken of major judgment. The Scripture plainly tells us that the Lord *"is longsuffering to us-ward, not willing that any should perish, but that all should come to Repentance"* (II Pet. 3:9).

4. So, when measures such as these are taken, it is only after Mercy and Grace have been spurned over and over again.

5. *"When his wife, not knowing what was done, came in,"* presents this woman as not suspecting at all what had happened, and what was about to happen.

(8) "AND PETER ANSWERED UNTO HER, TELL ME WHETHER YOU SOLD THE LAND FOR SO MUCH? AND SHE SAID, YES, FOR SO MUCH."

The construction is:

1. The phrase, *"And Peter answered unto her,"* seems to speak to the fact that these two people were somewhat known in the Early Church, and were not merely strangers among the thousands who had gotten Saved since the Outpouring of the Holy Spirit very shortly before.

2. Ever how many days it had been, it seems that Ananias and Sapphira had begun almost at the outset to promote themselves by claiming great things from God in order to make themselves look big before the Apostles, and all others for that matter.

3. The question, *"Tell me whether you sold the land for so much?"* could have easily been her moment of Mercy had she answered correctly. If she had done so, she would have been forgiven instantly and not suffered the same fate as her husband.

4. *"And she said, Yes, for so much,"* seems to indicate that she was ready to receive the praises of men, never dreaming what was about to happen.

(9) "THEN PETER SAID UNTO HER, HOW IS IT THAT YOU HAVE AGREED TOGETHER TO TEMPT THE SPIRIT OF THE LORD? BEHOLD, THE FEET OF THEM WHICH HAVE BURIED YOUR HUSBAND ARE AT THE DOOR, AND SHALL CARRY YOU OUT."

The composition is:

1. The question, *"Then Peter said unto her, How is it that you have agreed together to tempt the Spirit of the Lord?"* presents an extremely serious scenario.

NOTES

2. The Spirit of the Lord is generally extremely gentle, even as He is typified by the dove (Jn. 1:32); however, He can, as well, speak by fire, which is judgment (Lev. 10:1-2).

3. Some have erroneously concluded that God looks at sin differently under the New Covenant than He did the Old; however, as should be obvious, such is blatantly untrue. In fact, God cannot change His Mind or Attitude toward sin simply because His Nature does not change and, in fact, cannot change. He is a Merciful God, Whose Mercy actually surpasses anything that can be comprehended by mere mortals; however, as we have stated, Mercy repeatedly refused is judgment ultimately come.

4. Peter's statement concerning the tempting of the Holy Spirit seems to imply that the Spirit of God dealt with them greatly, but to no avail. They pushed aside His Warnings, Pleadings, and Admonitions, determined to go their own way, which, if it had succeeded, would have greatly hurt the Work of God, which Satan knew.

5. So, Satan's plan (Acts 5:3) is shown to us in glaring detail and the checks of the Holy Spirit. Actually, I think this is little different, if any at all, than that which happened to Judas, at least this spiritual confrontation.

6. The phrase, *"Behold, the feet of them which have buried your husband are at the door, and shall carry you out,"* seems to imply that the Lord had already told Peter what her reaction would be, and that these same young men who had attended her husband were waiting in order to do the same with her.

7. This scheme, which Satan had promoted, did not bring them in as planned, but rather took them out. By all means, this should be a somber warning to all.

(10) "THEN FELL SHE DOWN STRAIGHTWAY AT HIS FEET, AND YIELDED UP THE GHOST: AND THE YOUNG MEN CAME IN, AND FOUND HER DEAD, AND, CARRYING HER FORTH, BURIED HER BY HER HUSBAND."

The synopsis is:

1. The phrase, *"Then fell she down straightway at his feet, and yielded up the ghost,"* presents the Judgment of God

striking her exactly as it had stricken her husband.

2. *"And the young men came in, and found her dead, and, carrying her forth, buried her by her husband,"* presents them together in judgment as they had been together in deception.

3. As I have already stated several times, because of the severity of what we are here shown, please allow me to say it again:

4. I greatly suspect that this has happened countless times in the past, and continues unto this present hour, as God exacts judgment against those who would seek to hinder His Work and make a mockery of the Holy Spirit. It may seldom be thought of as the Judgment of God, with it simply being labeled something else. However, if the truth be known, I have to believe that such has happened repeatedly, especially during times of great Movings of the Holy Spirit.

5. This we do know: Satan never ceases his efforts in this capacity, even as with Ananias and Sapphira. As well, the Holy Spirit does not change simply because He cannot change. Therefore, from that premise, we know that such is ongoing and always has been.

(11) "AND GREAT FEAR CAME UPON ALL THE CHURCH, AND UPON AS MANY AS HEARD THESE THINGS."

The construction is:

1. Inasmuch as the Holy Spirit made the same statement again as He had made in Verse 5, we come to realize that God is to be feared as well as to be praised.

2. Once again, it lends credence to the thought that the Holy Spirit desires that we understand that God says what He means and means what He says!

(12) "AND BY THE HANDS OF THE APOSTLES WERE MANY SIGNS AND WONDERS WROUGHT AMONG THE PEOPLE; AND THEY WERE ALL WITH ONE ACCORD IN SOLOMON'S PORCH."

The exposition is:

1. The price of the Cross was what it took to redeem mankind.

2. If the Cross is removed from Christianity, which by and large it has been presently, you have nothing left but a vapid philosophy.

NOTES

3. Please understand that without the Cross of Christ, there is no Salvation and no Sanctification.

SIGNS AND WONDERS

The phrase, *"And by the hands of the Apostles were many signs and wonders wrought among the people,"* tells us two things:

1. There is a good possibility that the judgment rendered on Ananias and Sapphira came to the ears of the religious leaders of Israel, which doubtless gave a temporary check to the persecutions, but as we shall see, not for long.

2. When the Word of the Lord is minutely followed, great things are always done by the Lord, even such as these *"signs and wonders."* This speaks of great Healings, as we shall see, and of demon spirits being cast out. What had brought death to the two now brought life to countless numbers.

However, it should be clearly understood that it was not Peter who struck these people dead, but the Lord. As well, it was not the Apostles who were healing the sick, etc., but it was the Spirit of the Lord. Peter and the Apostles were the instruments in both cases, but the action was that of the Spirit.

This I do believe: as the Former Rain of the Holy Spirit, even as prophesied by Joel, was accompanied by *"signs and wonders,"* the *"Latter Rain,"* also prophesied by Joel, will experience the same (Joel 2:23-32).

In fact, there have been mighty demonstrations of the Power of God in this very capacity since the turn of the Twentieth Century; however, I personally believe that the closer we get to the end, the greater these manifestations are going to be. In other words, I personally believe the world is about to experience an Outpouring of the Holy Spirit as it has never known before, which will be accompanied by all of these things that we see in the Book of Acts and possibly, even in greater measure. Actually, this is what the Church is supposed to be like.

ONE ACCORD

"And they were all with one accord in Solomon's porch," portrays a roofed

colonnade bearing Solomon's name, which ran along the eastern wall in the Court of the Gentiles of Herod's Temple. It had double columns.

This was the scene of Christ's Teaching at the Feast of the Dedication (Jn. 10:22-23).

This Passage implies that the Apostles went to this place each day, or at least often, along with thousands of others gathering, as well. There were tremendous numbers saved and Healings of every description being carried out among the people.

The Scripture again emphasizes the fact that *"they were all with one accord."* Inasmuch as this is said several times (Acts 2:4, 42, 46; 4:24, 32; 5:12), the Holy Spirit is informing Believers of how significant this really is.

When the Holy Spirit has His Way, and things are being done according to what Jesus, the Head of the Church, wants done, there will be an *"accord."* It is impossible for it to be otherwise!

In watching the Move of God that is presently taking place at Family Worship Center, I am noticing the same thing among our people. There is a *"oneness"* and an *"accord"* that I think we have never had before. It is not something that we have striven to obtain, which I think can hardly be done accordingly anyway, but it is rather a Work of the Spirit.

A man-devised *"accord"* is of no consequence because it is of the flesh. However, that which is generated by the Holy Spirit is always right because it is an *"accord"* that comes from the inside out instead of from the outside in, which is backward, and which the flesh attempts to do.

(13) "AND OF THE REST DOES NO MAN JOIN HIMSELF TO THEM: BUT THE PEOPLE MAGNIFIED THEM."

The structure is:

1. The phrase, *"And of the rest does no man join himself to them,"* has reference to the fact that inasmuch as great Miracles were being performed at the hands of the Apostles, people held them in awe. In other words, the effect of the Miracles was that the Jews looked with awe and reverence upon the Apostles, with none joining them out of mere curiosity. The situation with Ananias and Sapphira had become well known, with all now treating the Apostles with great respect.

2. The phrase, *"But the people magnified them,"* refers to the fact that the people knew that the Apostles were of the Lord and that the Lord was greatly using them, as the evidence was plainly obvious.

(14) "AND BELIEVERS WERE THE MORE ADDED TO THE LORD, MULTITUDES BOTH OF MEN AND WOMEN."

The exposition is:

1. The phrase, *"And Believers were the more added to the Lord,"* simply means *"those who believed"* or *"they came to believe."*

2. They became Believers because they saw the Miracles and Healings and, as well, heard the Word.

3. *"Multitudes both of men and women,"* signifies a great number and that the Spirit of God was dealing with both men and women, as should be obvious!

4. Most of this was taking place at the Temple, more specifically, at Solomon's Porch.

(15) "INSOMUCH THAT THEY BROUGHT FORTH THE SICK INTO THE STREETS, AND LAID THEM ON BEDS AND COUCHES, THAT AT THE LEAST THE SHADOW OF PETER PASSING BY MIGHT OVERSHADOW SOME OF THEM."

The exegesis is:

1. All Believers must understand that we can no more sanctify ourselves than the unredeemed can save themselves.

2. The Lord's Solution to this problem is the Cross of Christ, and only the Cross of Christ.

3. The Cross of Christ is not one of several solutions but, in fact, is the only solution.

MIRACLES

The phrase, *"Insomuch that they brought forth the sick into the streets, and laid them on beds and couches,"* evidently refers to two or three different streets on which Peter and the Apostles came to the Temple each day. It seems that the crowds may have been so large that they could not all get into the Temple Court, which, incidentally, would hold thousands. The people would try to anticipate which street Peter would walk down as he and others would come to the Temple, with the sick being placed along the sides.

Inasmuch as they were bringing them from all over Israel, that must have been quite a sight! This is what happens when the Holy Spirit has total and complete control in the hearts and lives of Believers. Several things always will happen, with possibly some things happening more than others, but nevertheless, all will be obvious. These are the earmarks of the Holy Spirit. These things are:

EARMARKS

• People are saved. Actually, there were thousands brought to Christ beginning on the Day of Pentecost and following.

• Believers are baptized with the Holy Spirit. Acts 4:31 says, *"And when they had prayed, the place was shaken where they were assembled together; and they were all filled with the Holy Spirit, and they spoke the Word of God with boldness."*

We know this, as well, because as Philip went to Samaria preaching the Gospel, many were saved and healed; however, none were baptized with the Holy Spirit, at least at that time.

However, almost immediately, Peter and John came from Jerusalem and, *"Who, when they were come down, prayed for them, that they might receive the Holy Spirit"* (Acts 8:15).

This shows, I think, the absolute insistence that Believers be baptized with the Holy Spirit as soon as possible after Salvation. As well, the evidence is clear that all spoke with Tongues when they were filled (Acts 2:4; 10:46; 19:1-7).

• There were signs, wonders, Healings, and Miracles.

• Demon spirits were cast out of people.

Those are the earmarks of the Presence of the Holy Spirit. If He is present in the full capacity He desires and is given latitude, these things will happen exactly as they happened then.

The foolish idea as propagated by some that all of this ceased after the Apostles died, etc., is not substantiated whatsoever in Scripture. What the Lord did then, He will more or less do now, that is, if people will believe Him and allow Him to have His Way (Mk. 16:15-18).

NOTES

THE SHADOW OF PETER

"That at the least the shadow of Peter passing by might overshadow some of them," implies that when this happened, Healing resulted.

There is no place in this account that indicates that Peter, or anyone else for that matter, suggested that this would happen. It just seemed to happen of its own accord, with people instantly noticing the results. As well, there is no record that it ever happened again after this episode.

In other words, as Peter, accompanied by other Apostles, would start out to the Temple each day (or whenever), he and others, no doubt, prayed for many, but there seems to have been such a great number that it would have been impossible for him to have physically prayed for everyone. Consequently, as he passed by, the Power of God was so prevalent and present that people simply were healed as his shadow touched them. To be sure, there was no healing virtue in his shadow, and neither is that the point the Holy Spirit desires to make. The Healings came about as a result of Faith in God and in His Servant being used, but which all can enjoy if they will only believe (Mk. 16:17).

Also, this was the beginning of the Early Church, and it is obvious that the Lord would do great things, which He did, in order to establish the Church.

As to how long this continued, the Scripture is silent. We do not read of it happening anymore, at least regarding the shadow; however, the Healings and Miracles continued, but not as prolific.

As well, the way the word *"shadow"* is here used, it does not necessarily refer to a *"shadow"* as we think of such, but it also referred to those who were merely close, somewhat as if one would be in the shade or shadow of another person. For them to be healed, it was not necessary that the sun be shining, etc.

As we have already stated, the Healing Power was not in these things but was resident in the Holy Spirit, Who filled Peter's heart and life.

(16) "THERE CAME ALSO A MULTITUDE OUT OF THE CITIES ROUND ABOUT UNTO JERUSALEM, BRINGING SICK FOLKS, AND THEM WHICH WERE VEXED WITH UNCLEAN SPIRITS: AND THEY WERE HEALED EVERY ONE."

The exegesis is:

1. The phrase, *"There came also a multitude out of the cities round about unto Jerusalem, bringing sick folks,"* proclaims the extent that this Move of God had reached.

2. The news was going out all over Israel as to what was happening in Jerusalem. As a result, the sick, no doubt with every type of disease that one could imagine, were being brought into the city. This must have created quite a stir. As we have already stated, when one considers that the streets nearby the Temple were lined with sick people, there is even a possibility that Peter, knowing that he could not personally pray for all of these people, took to just simply walking down the streets between the rows of ill, sick, and suffering, and the moment he passed by, each was healed. One can well imagine the joy and praises to the Lord that filled the air as every type of sickness and disease was healed.

3. The phrase, *"And them which were vexed with unclean spirits,"* tells us two things:

a. Much of the sickness was probably caused by unclean spirits, and these went out, etc.

b. Some of the people were, no doubt, demon possessed and were delivered, which is somewhat different than demon spirits causing sickness, etc.

4. The phrase, *"And they were healed every one,"* simply means there were no failures.

5. This meant that the Power of God was so great that Faith was high, and even for those who had little Faith, they were healed as well. It was somewhat like a tidal wave sweeping everything before it.

6. When the Spirit of God functions as He desires and is given the latitude He must have, I think this will be the case every time. *"All will be healed!"*

NOTES

(17) "THEN THE HIGH PRIEST ROSE UP, AND ALL THEY WHO WERE WITH HIM, WHICH IS THE SECT OF THE SADDUCEES, AND WERE FILLED WITH INDIGNATION."

The exegesis is:

1. In a sense, the Cross of Christ is Christianity.

2. When we speak of the Cross, we aren't speaking of the wooden beam on which Jesus died, but rather what He there did.

3. At the Cross, our Lord atoned for all sin, past, present, and future, at least for all who will believe, and, as well, defeated Satan, every fallen Angel, and every demon spirit (Col. 2:14-15).

OPPOSITION

The phrase, *"Then the High Priest rose up,"* either speaks of Annas or Caiaphas, but it is not clear.

As we shall see, two powers and their instruments are seen here in opposition—the Holy Spirit, with the Apostles and Angels as His Instruments, and the evil spirit, with the Priests and Sadducees as his instruments. Wherever the Holy Spirit manifests His Power, there Satan manifests his.

"And all they who were with him, which is the sect of the Sadducees," presents the party that pretty much controlled the Office of the High Priest in Israel.

The Sadducees denied the Resurrection of the body and did not believe in Angels or spirits (Mat. 22:23; Acts 23:8).

It is thought that after the return from Babylonian captivity, the High Priest drew to himself all powers, civil and religious. During that time, as far as the Persian authorities were concerned, he was as the king of the Jews.

SADDUCEES

By the time of Jesus, they had allied themselves with the Herodians, who were subservient to Rome.

At first, the Sadducees regarded the struggle between our Lord and the Pharisees as a matter with which they had no concern. They did not intervene until the Lord claimed to be the Messiah, and the people became more and more excited because of

NOTES

it. They felt that this would likely draw the attention of the Roman authorities; therefore, they intervened.

The Sadducees felt that should Tiberius learn that among the Jews there was widespread belief in the coming of a Jewish King Who was to rule the world, and that One had appeared Who claimed to be this Messiah, then very soon would the independence enjoyed by the Jews be taken from them.

If that happened, they reasoned, the influence of the Sadducees would be lost as well.

An oligarchy (a government in which a small group exercises control for corrupt and selfish purposes) is proverbially sensitive to anything that threatens its stability. A priesthood is unmeasured in its vindictiveness, and the Sadducees were a priestly oligarchy. Hence, it is not so strange that only the Death of Jesus would satisfy them.

PHARISEES

After the Resurrection, it seems that the Pharisees became a little less hostile to the Followers of Christ, but the Sadducees maintained their attitude of suspicion and hatred, as is here obvious.

Although a Pharisee, it was as an agent of the Sadducean High Priest that Paul persecuted the Believers. Ultimately, the Sadducees gained complete ascendancy in the Sanhedrin, and later, under the leadership of Annas, they put James, the brother of our Lord, to death.

In looking at the Ministry of Jesus, one finds that He did not denounce the Sadducees nearly as much as He did the Pharisees.

Inasmuch as His Position, both doctrinal and practical, was much nearer that of the Pharisees, it was necessary that He should clearly mark Himself off from them. There was not the same danger of His Position being confused with that of the Sadducees.

The Sadducees had influence with the rich, while Jesus drew His adherents chiefly from the poor, from whom also the Pharisees drew.

As well, the Gospels mainly recount our Lord's Ministry in Galilee, whereas the Sadducees were chiefly to be found in Jerusalem and its neighborhood. As well, there may have been severe denunciations of the Sadducees by Jesus that have not come down to us, and most probably were.

Also, the Sadducees felt that Jesus was weakening the influence of the Pharisees, whom they hated. Not until self-interest compelled them to do so did they join with the Pharisees in opposition to Christ.

If one is to notice, Luke referred to the Sadducees as a *"sect."* The word itself has no evil meaning. It simply refers to a doctrinal view or belief at variance with the recognized and accepted tenets of a system, church, or party.

HERETIC

The word *"heretic"* is used once in Scripture (Titus 3:10), and means one who holds a heresy; a dissenter, a nonconformist. It only takes on an evil meaning when sound doctrine is rejected, and fallacy is accepted and taught in preference to truth. If the doctrine is unsound and one dissents from the main body that holds to fallacy, then he is a heretic in a good sense.

The word *"heretic"* signifies a sect or party, whether good or bad, which is distinguished in some way from all others.

For instance, Catholics conclude all who are not members of the Catholic church as *"heretics."* So, one being labeled as a *"heretic"* does not necessarily mean that such a person is wrong. He might be, but not necessarily so!

One might say, and be Scripturally correct, that all who place their faith in other than the Cross of Christ could be labeled as *"heretics"* (Gal. 1:8-9).

THE GOSPEL

Paul actually describes the Gospel in his statement to the Church at Corinth. He said:

"For Christ sent me not to baptize *(presents to us a Cardinal Truth)*, **but to preach the Gospel** *(the manner in which one may be saved from sin)*: **not with wisdom of words** *(intellectualism is not the Gospel)*, **lest the Cross of Christ should be made of none effect.** *(This tells us in no uncertain terms that the Cross of Christ must always be the emphasis of the Message)*" **(I Cor. 1:17).**

As well, we are told here what the Gospel

NOTES

of Jesus Christ actually is. Anything other than the Cross of Christ is heresy.

The phrase, *"And were filled with indignation,"* refers here to *"envy"* or *"jealousy."*

The Priests were envious of the influence by which the Apostles were winning over the people, so they lodged all the Apostles in the prison in which common criminals were confined.

(18) "AND LAID THEIR HANDS ON THE APOSTLES, AND PUT THEM IN THE COMMON PRISON."

The exegesis is:

1. The phrase, *"And laid their hands on the Apostles,"* referred to all Twelve, with the Greek indicating that they did this publicly.

2. They made the arrest of the Twelve with the whole crowd looking on. Apparently the Priests and Sadducees had become desperate. Thousands of people were coming to Christ, with the Apostles and their use of the Name of Jesus, Who they claimed had been raised from the dead, fastly becoming overly prominent among all the people.

3. Hundreds, if not thousands, were coming from all over Israel, and the streets near the Temple were littered with the sick, who were being instantly healed by the Power of God. Because of this, it was a situation that was absolutely glorious as far as the Work of God was concerned, but yet, extremely negative respecting organized religion.

4. If it is to be remembered, they were afraid to arrest Jesus publicly because of the possible adverse reaction of the crowds. When they finally did arrest Him, it was at night when the crowds were absent.

5. However, now the situation had become so desperate, or so they thought, that they dared to risk the disapproval of the crowds by publicly arresting the Apostles. As well, they probably desired to show their authority.

6. *"And put them in the common prison,"* was to become an altogether too common occurrence, especially with Paul after he came to Christ.

7. However, this must quickly be said, *"When they touched the Apostles, they were touching the Lord."* Sadly, down through the many centuries, untold thousands have followed the sordid example of the Sadducees; however, if all the truth could be known, one can be absolutely certain that judgment has always followed.

(19) "BUT THE ANGEL OF THE LORD BY NIGHT OPENED THE PRISON DOORS, AND BROUGHT THEM FORTH, AND SAID."

The diagram is:

1. The phrase, *"But the Angel of the Lord by night opened the prison doors,"* should have been translated, *"An Angel."* Inasmuch as the Greek does not have the definite article, it refers to one of the many Angels who serve as ministering spirits to Believers and are sent to serve those who are and *"shall be heirs of Salvation"* (Heb. 1:14).

2. This Angel was a Messenger sent from the Lord with the Power to open the doors of the prison, which he proceeded to do.

3. From the description given in Verse 23, it seems that possibly the Lord caused a deep sleep to come upon the guards, so they were totally unaware of the opening of the gates and the departure of the Twelve.

4. *"And brought them forth, and said,"* must have been quite an experience when all of a sudden, an Angel was standing before the Apostles in the prison cell.

5. This is another of the *"many signs and wonders"* (Acts 5:12).

(20) "GO, STAND AND SPEAK IN THE TEMPLE TO THE PEOPLE ALL THE WORDS OF THIS LIFE."

The diagram is:

1. The phrase, *"Go, stand and speak in the Temple to the people,"* presents instructions directly opposite of that which the religious leaders had given.

2. The instructions were to be carried out to the letter, which they were, and, as well, were to serve as a warning to the Sadducees. However, when unbelief completely saturates people, as it did the Sadducees, it is very difficult to break out of this bondage. To be frank, religion is the worst bondage of all. It is so bad simply because people think they are right in what they are doing. They are spiritually blind and as such, cannot really *"see"* anything.

3. For the few who are pulled out of this

darkness, only the Holy Spirit can do such. However, even then, even as portrayed here, most never come out.

4. *"All the Words of this life,"* could be translated, *"All the Words of this Resurrection Life."* These were *"Words"* announcing Eternal Life to dying men.

5. In essence, the Angel gave them instructions to bear down even heavier on the Doctrine of the Resurrection, irrespective of what the Sadducees thought, who, incidentally, did not believe in such.

(21) "AND WHEN THEY HEARD THAT, THEY ENTERED INTO THE TEMPLE EARLY IN THE MORNING, AND TAUGHT. BUT THE HIGH PRIEST CAME, AND THEY WHO WERE WITH HIM, AND CALLED THE COUNCIL TOGETHER, AND ALL THE SENATE OF THE CHILDREN OF ISRAEL, AND SENT TO THE PRISON TO HAVE THEM BROUGHT."

The overview is:

1. The solution to victorious, overcoming, Biblical living is the Cross of Christ.

2. In fact, the Cross of Christ is the solution, and the only solution, to every spiritual problem.

3. The price He there paid included every need.

OBEDIENCE

The phrase, *"And when they heard that, they entered into the Temple early in the morning, and taught,"* proclaims that it was the night before that they were released by the Angel.

It is very doubtful that they got any sleep that night at all, especially considering that they went to the Temple at daybreak.

It is certain that at least some of the people present that morning knew that the Apostles had been arrested the day before, and must have wondered as to how they were now able to be here and teach.

There is some indication in Verse 26 that Peter and the others told the people what happened concerning the Angel delivering them. This must have been a great encouragement to the Believers, which made it obvious that God was with the Apostles, especially considering what had just happened. It was a further confirmation that their Message was true, and God was standing behind both them and His Word, which they were proclaiming with boldness.

NOTES

"But the High Priest came, and they who were with him, and called the Council together, and all the senate of the children of Israel," speaks of the Jewish Sanhedrin. Actually, the words *"council"* and *"senate"* all refer to the same thing, the Sanhedrin.

THE SANHEDRIN

The Sanhedrin claimed that it was constituted by Moses and reorganized by Ezra immediately after the return from exile. However, there is no Biblical or historical evidence to show that prior to the Greek period, there existed an organized, aristocratic, governing tribunal among the Jews.

Consequently, as we have previously stated, there was no Scriptural authority for such a group. Pharisees and Sadducees alike made up its members.

The acting High Priest was as such always head and president. Caiaphas was president at the trial of our Lord, while at Paul's trial, Ananias was president.

During the time of Christ and immediately after, the Sanhedrin enjoyed a very high measure of independence. It exercised not only civil jurisdiction, according to Jewish Law, but also in some degree, criminal jurisdiction. It had administrative authority and could order arrests by its own officers of so-called justice.

As well, it was empowered to judge cases that did not involve capital punishment, which later required the confirmation of the Roman Procurator.

For one offense, the Sanhedrin, on their own authority, could put to death even a Roman citizen, namely in the case of a Gentile passing the fence that divided the Inner Court of the Temple from that of the Gentiles (Acts 21:28).

The only case known of capital punishment in the New Testament in connection with the Sanhedrin is that of our Lord. The stoning of Stephen (Acts 7:54) was probably the illegal act of an enraged multitude.

"And sent to the prison to have them brought," referred to the Apostles. They were in for quite a surprise!

(22) "BUT WHEN THE OFFICERS CAME, AND FOUND THEM NOT IN THE PRISON, THEY RETURNED, AND TOLD."

The exegesis is:

1. The phrase, *"But when the officers came,"* presents a situation that should have been enough to have turned these men toward God. In effect, they were privileged to be a part of this Miracle.

However, a religious mind-set that is built on unbelief and doubt, but yet, supported by self-righteousness, can little see what God is really doing. In truth, the Lord does things constantly that, if recognized, would be enough to lead anyone to Christ; however, unbelief, which characterizes the human family, stops people from seeing what is really happening.

2. The Lord had done enough in Jerusalem, not only in the miraculous Ministry of Christ, but even in the last few days, to cause the entirety of Israel, and especially the religious leadership, to turn to the Lord. However, it seemed to have little effect on these leaders.

3. *"And found them not in the prison, they returned, and told,"* presents a scenario that is absolutely unbelievable, but yet, totally true!

(23) "SAYING, THE PRISON TRULY FOUND WE SHUT WITH ALL SAFETY, AND THE KEEPERS STANDING WITHOUT BEFORE THE DOORS: BUT WHEN WE HAD OPENED, WE FOUND NO MAN WITHIN."

The synopsis is:

1. The phrase, *"Saying, The prison truly found we shut with all safety,"* presents the fact that nothing seemed unusual and that the locks had not been tampered with, or anything else for that matter.

2. *"And the keepers standing without before the doors,"* presents the fact that the guards had no idea as to what had happened. As we have stated, the Angel, no doubt, put them to sleep for a short period of time, during which he released the Apostles. How this was done, we are not told! However, inasmuch as this was an Angel sent from the Lord, there were many things he could have done to effect their release.

3. *"But when we had opened, we found no man within,"* must have presented a situation of great surprise.

NOTES

4. What must these jailers have thought when they opened the doors for the officers, expecting to see the Twelve Apostles, but found nothing? The implication seems to be that all were in one cell, which had, as almost all cells, only one door. There was no way they could effect a release themselves, especially considering the keepers at the door who would have barred any entrance or exit.

5. So, a Miracle is the only explanation!

(24) "NOW WHEN THE HIGH PRIEST AND THE CAPTAIN OF THE TEMPLE AND THE CHIEF PRIESTS HEARD THESE THINGS, THEY DOUBTED OF THEM WHEREUNTO THIS WOULD GROW."

The exegesis is:

1. The phrase, *"Now when the High Priest and the Captain of the Temple and the Chief Priests heard these things,"* proclaims the entirety of this situation growing by the day, even by the hour.

2. Sadly, these men were supposed to be the spiritual guides of the people, which they were. However, despite being so very religious and even holding high religious offices, in fact, they did not know God. These offices were merely cushy appointments, which furnished them high salaries and gave them authority over the people. It was merely a business, actually, the religion business!

3. The scenario that unfolds before us in these Chapters pretty well portrays the present spiritual climate also. The ones who truly know the Lord are very seldom, if ever, accepted by the powers that be, and most of the time, even strongly opposed, even as here.

4. The phrase, *"They doubted of them whereunto this would grow,"* tells us two things:

a. The word *"doubted"* in the Greek is *"diaporeo"* and means *"to be thoroughly nonplussed, perplexed."* They simply could not explain that which had happened, for, in effect, there was no explanation other than the Lord. However, this they would not admit!

b. They were wondering what was going

to happen next. They saw themselves losing control of the people; consequently, all the measures taken were designed to salvage their position.

Had they simply done what this called for, which was to repent, they would have saved themselves and their Nation, but this they would not do!

(25) "THEN CAME ONE AND TOLD THEM, SAYING, BEHOLD, THE MEN WHOM YOU PUT IN PRISON ARE STANDING IN THE TEMPLE, AND TEACHING THE PEOPLE."

The overview is:

1. The phrase, *"Then came one and told them,"* presents a message that now adds considerably to their present perplexity.

2. *"Saying, Behold, the men whom you put in prison are standing in the Temple, and teaching the people,"* proclaims several things:

a. The Apostles were doing exactly what the Angel had told them to do and making no effort to hide themselves.

b. The sentence structure seems to imply that the Apostles were calm, registering absolutely no fear whatsoever. The idea is that they need not worry considering the protection they were being afforded.

It is my belief that the Angel who appeared to them and effected their release was still present, but yet, invisible. Actually, Angels only do what they are sent by the Lord to do. Still, I think they are in constant attendance respecting the Saints of the Lord (Ps. 91:11-12; Heb. 1:14; 12:22).

c. The modern church should, as well, expect the Lord to be as involved presently even as He was then. If Jesus Christ is properly glorified, which the Holy Spirit will always do if He is allowed to have His Way, Healings and Miracles, as well as signs and wonders, will often be the case. The trouble is modern Christianity, at least in too many circles, has been so watered down and compromised that philosophy is about all that is left.

3. It is pretty well the case that those who deny the Baptism with the Holy Spirit with the evidence of speaking with other Tongues are bereft of the Lord working in any capacity. It is *"a form of godliness, which denies the Power thereof."* Paul said, *"From such turn away"* (II Tim. 3:5).

NOTES

(26) "THEN WENT THE CAPTAIN WITH THE OFFICERS, AND BROUGHT THEM WITHOUT VIOLENCE: FOR THEY FEARED THE PEOPLE, LEST THEY SHOULD HAVE BEEN STONED."

The structure is:

1. The phrase, *"Then went the Captain with the Officers, and brought them without violence,"* means they did not bind them but simply asked that they follow.

2. *"For they feared the people, lest they should have been stoned,"* proclaims their fear of the people, but they did not fear Him Who manifested His Power in opening their prison, for their hearts and consciences were hardened with hatred against Jesus and His Followers.

3. In fact, they need not have feared the Apostles or their followers simply because Followers of the Lord do not resort to *"stoning,"* etc. However, there were, no doubt, many who were hearing Peter and the others, but who had not yet accepted the Lord. To be sure, these, and there probably were many, could very well have resorted to such!

4. Consequently, the Lord held the passions of the persecutors in check by using others who very well could have also resorted to such measures.

(27) "AND WHEN THEY HAD BROUGHT THEM, THEY SET THEM BEFORE THE COUNCIL: AND THE HIGH PRIEST ASKED THEM."

The composition is:

1. The phrase, *"And when they had brought them, they set them before the Council,"* implies the full Sanhedrin of 71 members, plus onlookers who were, no doubt, present as well.

2. *"And the High Priest asked them,"* presents the second time that Peter and John had appeared here, but it was the first time for all of the Apostles.

(28) "SAYING, DID NOT WE STRAITLY COMMAND YOU THAT YOU SHOULD NOT TEACH IN THIS NAME? AND, BEHOLD, YOU HAVE FILLED JERUSALEM WITH YOUR DOCTRINE, AND INTEND TO BRING THIS MAN'S BLOOD UPON US."

The exegesis is:

1. In Old Testament Times, Israel constituted God's People, and as such, their ethics were to assume a character and time worthy of Him.

2. Mackintosh said, *"It was no longer a question as to what they were, either in themselves or in comparison with others; but of what God was in comparison with all."*

DEMANDING COMPLIANCE

The question, *"Saying, Did not we straitly command you that you should not teach in this Name?"* says to us the following:

• As the rulers of Israel, they were demanding obedience, and according to the climate in much of the modern church, they demand the same thing. However, as we have stated, this is one of Satan's chief weapons respecting the hindrance of the Gospel. He uses those in man-made positions of religion, who have a pseudo-authority and demand compliance.

Satan's methods change little!

It must always be remembered, that which is not Scriptural must be ignored. The sadness is, many Believers, even preachers, little know or understand what the Word of God actually says and, therefore, find it very easy to allow someone else to do their thinking for them.

• If one is to notice, these religious leaders never referred to Jesus by His Name. It was *"this Name," "this Man,"* etc.

In some of the writings, He is even referred to as *"the Hung!"* Of course, this speaks of Him being crucified on a Cross, which carried with it the curse of God. However, what they failed to realize was that Jesus was actually made a curse, which is different than being cursed, but not for His sins, for He had none, but rather for our sins. In other words, He suffered the curse that I should have suffered, and all of humanity for that matter!

• The Apostles taught *"in His Name"* and healed *"in His Name."* In effect, they did everything in *"His Name."*

He gave them, and all Believers for that matter, the authority to use His *"Name,"* which, with proper Faith, will bring forth the intended results (Jn. 16:23-24).

NOTES

The phrase, *"And, behold, you have filled Jerusalem with your doctrine,"* proclaims the success of their preaching and teaching.

The word *"doctrine"* simply means *"teaching."*

WHAT WAS THEIR DOCTRINE OR TEACHING?

At this stage, the New Covenant had not yet been given. Actually, it would be approximately 20 years before Paul would write I Thessalonians, which is believed to be the first of his Epistles, with the others following over a period of some 10 to 12 years. Consequently, the Doctrine presently of the Apostles was very simple.

They taught and preached that Jesus was the Jewish Messiah and that He was God manifest in the flesh. They taught that He died on Calvary for the sins of man, and simple Faith in His Name ensured Salvation. This is evident from the thousands who *"believed"* (Acts 4:4).

They also taught, and strongly so, that Jesus had been resurrected from the dead and had ascended to the Father. They taught that Believers could be baptized with the Holy Spirit exactly as they had been (Acts 10:46-47).

They also taught that they, as well as any and all Believers, could use the Name of Jesus in order to pray for the sick, etc. (Acts 3:16).

Inasmuch as the New Covenant was not yet given, they would have continued to teach the people, at least at this time, that they should continue to follow the Law of Moses, etc.

THE NEW COVENANT?

However, when the New Covenant was given to the Apostle Paul, these things of the Law gradually fell off as being no more applicable because Jesus had fulfilled them in totality.

In other words, the Law was no longer incumbent upon Believers for the simple reason that it had been satisfied in every respect by Christ. He was the Law-keeper, in fact, the only one, and as the Representative Man, Faith in Him makes all Believers Law-keepers as well.

"And intend to bring this man's blood upon us," seems they now sought to avoid their own imprecation, where they had prayed that His Blood might be on them and on their children (Mat. 27:25).

In effect, their guilty consciences winced at every word that spoke of Jesus Christ, and especially of Him as now resurrected from the dead.

(29) "THEN PETER AND THE OTHER APOSTLES ANSWERED AND SAID, WE OUGHT TO OBEY GOD RATHER THAN MEN."

The record is:

1. The phrase, *"Then Peter and the other Apostles answered and said,"* represents their answer being instant and, as well, unequivocally clear. To be blunt, the religious leaders did not at all like what they heard.

2. *"We ought to obey God rather than men,"* although short, is without a doubt one of the most important statements in history.

In this brave reply, there was neither pride nor self-will. There was faithfulness, subjection to Truth, and intelligence in the Scriptures.

3. Concerning this, Hervey said, *"The rule is a golden one for all men, all circumstances, and all time. Peter does not deny having received the prohibition, but pleads the superior force of the Command of God, as set forth in the following Verses."*

4. When it comes down to basics, every person on the face of the Earth has to face this very question of whether they will obey God or men. More particularly, preachers will face this glaringly so, even as the Apostles.

5. The tragedy is that the far greater majority obey men instead of God. It is my personal belief that the slightest compromise starts one on a downward path, with the Holy Spirit little able to function, at least to any degree, in such a life or Ministry. There is no way that one can please God and men at the same time.

(30) "THE GOD OF OUR FATHERS RAISED UP JESUS, WHOM YOU KILLED AND HUNG ON A TREE."

The form is:

NOTES

1. The phrase, *"The God of our fathers raised up Jesus,"* says two things:

a. Peter linked Jesus with the Patriarchs and Prophets of old and, as well, with God. Therefore, he made it very clear that Jesus was the fulfillment of the Prophecies, actually, the very One to Whom the Prophets pointed.

b. He proclaimed that God raised Jesus from the dead, hence, the Resurrection, which must have been grating on the nerves of these unbelievers.

2. The phrase, *"Whom you killed and hung on a tree,"* places the responsibility of the murder of Christ squarely on the shoulders of the Sanhedrin.

3. The words, *"You killed,"* actually carry the connotations in the Greek that as far as God was concerned, they killed Him with their own hands, even though He actually laid down His own Life.

(31) "HIM HAS GOD EXALTED WITH HIS RIGHT HAND TO BE A PRINCE AND A SAVIOUR, FOR TO GIVE REPENTANCE TO ISRAEL, AND FORGIVENESS OF SINS."

The exposition is:

1. The Cross.
2. Our Faith.
3. The Holy Spirit.

THE EXALTATION OF CHRIST

The phrase, *"Him has God exalted with His Right Hand,"* refers to the fact that the Power of God not only raised Jesus from the dead but, as well, has seated Him at His own right Hand in the heavenlies (Rom. 8:34; Eph. 1:20).

"To be a Prince and a Saviour" proclaims the One Whom they concluded to be but a Peasant to be none other than the *"Prince of Glory."* He is the Titular Leader of the Church, even as He was the Titular Leader of Israel, but rejected.

As well, He is the *"Saviour,"* i.e., *"Deliverer."* Also, He is the only Saviour, as there is no other and, in fact, there will never be a need for another, for Jesus paid it all!

These titles, *"Prince and Saviour,"* express Royalty and Atonement.

The phrase, *"For to give repentance to Israel, and forgiveness of sins,"* tells us that not only is the Lord Jesus the Medium of Forgiveness and Life, but He is the dispenser of both.

He gives, not sells, Repentance and forgiveness. Forgiveness of sins means release from the eternal punishment of sins, and Repentance expresses and involves a moral revulsion against sin and a determined breach with it. Repentance is a Divine Gift as forgiveness is a Divine Gift.

REPENTANCE, AS *"TO TURN"*

The term *"to turn"* or *"return"* is most generally employed to express the Scriptural idea of genuine Repentance. It was used extensively by the Prophets and makes prominent the idea of a radical change in one's attitude toward sin and God.

It implies a conscious, moral separation and a personal decision to forsake sin and to enter into fellowship with God. It is employed extensively with reference to man's turning away from sin to Righteousness (Deut. 4:30; Neh. 1:9; Ps. 7:12; Jer. 3:14).

The term *"repentance"* is employed to indicate the thorough spiritual change that God alone can effect (Ps. 85:4).

REPENT, *"AS IN REMORSE"*

The feeling indicated by the word, as it is used at times in the New Testament, may issue in genuine Repentance, or it may degenerate into mere remorse (Mat. 21:29-32; 27:3).

Judas repented only in the sense of regret and remorse, and not in the sense of the abandonment of sin.

This type of Repentance God will not accept simply because it is not true Repentance.

True New Testament Repentance has the same meaning as in the Old Testament, which means an abandonment of sin, which quickly becomes obvious.

REPENT, *"TO CHANGE THE MIND"*

The Greek word *"metanoeo"* signifies *"to have another mind."* It means that one changes the opinion or purpose with regard to sin. It is equivalent to the Old Testament word *"turn."* Thus, it is employed by John the Baptist, Jesus, and the Apostles (Mat. 3:2; Mk. 1:15; Acts 2:38).

NOTES

REPENT, *"TO TURN OVER," "UPON,"* OR *"UNTO"*

The Greek word expressing this is *"epistrepho"* and refers to the distinct change wrought in Repentance. It is employed quite frequently in Acts to express the positive side of a change involved in New Testament Repentance or to indicate the return to God, of which the turning from sin is the negative aspect.

The word is used to express the spiritual transition from sin to God (Acts 9:35; I Thess. 1:9); to strengthen the idea of Faith (Acts 11:21); and to complete and emphasize the change required by New Testament Repentance (Acts 26:20).

The Latin version, as propagated by the Catholic church, has rendered Repentance as *"an exercise in penitence."* However, *"penitence"* signifies pain, grief, and distress rather than a change of thought and purpose.

Thus, the word has been corrupted, at least by Catholicism, by the error of presenting grief over sin rather than abandonment of sin as the primary idea of New Testament Repentance.

Dissecting the Greek word *"epistrepho"* makes it easy to make the transition from the error of *"penitence"* to *"penance."* Consequently, the Romanists represent Jesus and the Apostles as urging people to do *"penance,"* which carries with it the idea of *"paying for one's sin," "atoning for one's sin by some particular act or the giving of money,"* etc.

However, the exhortations of the ancient Prophets, of Jesus, and of the Apostles show that the change of mind is the dominant idea of the words employed, while the accompanying grief and consequent Reformation enter into one's experience from the very nature of the case.

There definitely will be grief and pain in the Repentance process, but nowhere does the Bible teach *"penance,"* which is strictly an invention of the Catholic church.

THE SPIRITUAL ELEMENTS OF REPENTANCE

Repentance is that change of a sinner's mind, which leads him to turn from his

NOTES

evil ways and life. The change wrought in Repentance is so deep and radical as to affect the whole spiritual nature and to involve the entire personality.

The intellect must function, the emotions must be aroused, and the will must act.

Repentance is profound, personal, and all-pervasive. Man must apprehend sin as unutterably heinous, the Divine Law as perfect and inexorable, and himself as coming short or falling below the requirements of a Holy God (Job 42:5-6; Ps. 51:3; Rom. 3:20).

However, at the same time, there may be a knowledge of sin without turning from it, which is an awful thing that dishonors God and ruins man. This change of view may lead only to a dread of punishment and not to the hatred and abandonment of sin (Ex. 9:27; Num. 22:34; Josh. 7:20; I Sam. 15:24; Mat. 27:4).

However, these things fall short of true Bible Repentance.

There must be a consciousness of sin, its effect on man, and its relation to God before there can be a hearty turning away from unrighteousness. The feeling naturally accompanying Repentance implies a conviction of personal sin and sinfulness, which is brought about by the Holy Spirit, and results in an earnest appeal to God to forgive according to His Mercy (Ps. 51:1-2, 10-14).

THE BIBLE CALL TO REPENTANCE

That men are called upon to repent, there can be no doubt, and that God is represented as taking the initiative in Repentance is equally clear.

The solution of the problem belongs to the spiritual sphere; consequently, this deals with sin in the heart and life of the individual, which is where it originates. There can be no external substitute for the internal change. Sackcloth for the body and remorse for the soul are not to be confused with a determined abandonment of sin and return to God.

Not material sacrifice but a spiritual change is the inexorable demand of God in both the Old and New Testaments simply because the problem of man, which is sin, does not change, and the solution, which is Bible Repentance and Faith in Christ and what He did for us at the Cross, does not change either (Ps. 51:17; Isa. 1:11; Jer. 6:20; Hos. 6:6).

REPENTANCE AND SALVATION

Repentance is only a condition of Salvation and not its meritorious ground. The motives for Repentance are chiefly found in the Goodness of God, in Divine love, in the pleading desire to have sinners Saved, in the inevitable consequences of sin, in the universal demands of the Gospel, and in the hope of Spiritual Life and membership in the Kingdom of Heaven (Ezek. 33:11; Mk. 1:15; Lk. 13:1-5; Jn. 3:16; Acts 17:30; Rom. 2:4; I Tim. 2:4).

Someone has said that the first four Beatitudes (Mat. 5:3-6) form a heavenly ladder by which penitent souls pass from the dominion of Satan into the Kingdom of God:

- A consciousness of spiritual poverty dethroning pride.
- A sense of personal unworthiness producing grief.
- A willingness to surrender to God in genuine humility.
- A strong spiritual desire developing into hunger and thirst after Righteousness.

These things definitely enter into the experience of one who wholly abandons sin and heartily turns to Him Who grants Repentance unto life.

Forgiveness of sins accompanies Repentance, with the two going hand in hand.

WHAT IS FORGIVENESS?

Christ taught that forgiveness is a duty. No limit can be set to the extent of forgiveness (Lk. 17:4), and it must be granted without reserve.

Jesus will not admit that there is any wrong so gross or so often repeated that it is beyond forgiveness. To Him, an unforgiving spirit is one of the most heinous of sins.

This is the offense that God literally will not forgive—the offense of unforgiveness (Mat. 18:34-35).

In fact, Jesus was so strong respecting the grace of forgiveness that in popular language, *"a Christian spirit"* is synonymous with a forgiving disposition. His Answer to Peter that one should forgive not merely *"seven times"* a day, but *"seventy times seven"* (Mat. 18:21-22), not only shows that He thought of no limit to one's forgiveness, but that the principle could not be reduced to a definite formula.

This is demanded on the part of Believers simply because the understanding and realization of what Jesus has done for us in forgiving our many sins can only be portrayed in our forgiving others. If one will not forgive, then it just might be that one has not been forgiven himself—in other words, he is not even saved.

ARE THERE CONDITIONS ATTACHED TO FORGIVENESS?

If forgiveness is to be total and complete, it must be a part of a mutual relationship. The other part is the Repentance of the offender.

While one should forgive, irrespective of the lack of Repentance on the part of the offender, still, such cannot truly be completed until there is Repentance, as should be obvious.

Actually, God does not forgive without Repentance, and in that sense of the word, forgiveness without Repentance on the part of the offending party is not required either.

The effect of forgiveness is to restore to its former state the relationship that was broken by sin. Such a Restoration requires the cooperation of both parties. There must be both a granting and an acceptance of the forgiveness.

Sincere, deep-felt sorrow for the wrong, which works Repentance (II Cor. 7:10), is the condition of the mind that ensures the acceptance of the forgiveness. Hence, Jesus commands forgiveness when the offender turns again, saying, *"I repent"* (Lk. 17:3-4).

It was this state of mind that led the Father joyfully to welcome the prodigal before he even gave utterance to his newly-formed purpose (Lk. 15:21).

However, even as we have mentioned, it is not to be supposed that failure to repent upon the part of the offender releases the offended from all obligation to extend forgiveness. As we have stated, even without the Repentance of the one who has wronged him, he can have a forgiving state of mind, which is an absolute necessity in the heart of the offended one, lest a root of bitterness spring up. This Jesus requires, as is implied by, *"If ye forgive not everyone his brother from your hearts"* (Mat. 18:35).

Such is also implied by the past tense in the Lord's Prayer: *"As we also have forgiven our debtors"* (Mat. 6:12).

It is this forgiving spirit that conditions God's Forgiveness of our sins (Mat. 6:14-15; Mk. 11:25).

However, forgiveness extended toward one who has not repented is altogether for the benefit of the one who has been offended. Even though forgiveness in the heart of the offended one should be prevalent, that doesn't mean that fellowship can be restored. In fact, it would be impossible to restore fellowship with one who has not repented.

If it is to be remembered, Joseph did not run and jump into the arms of his brothers when he saw them, even though they did not recognize him. He tested these men to see if they were the same as before, or if they had changed. Thankfully, they had changed; therefore, there came an hour whenever he revealed himself to them, but only when he determined in his mind that they had repented of their terrible sin and lifestyle of some years back.

Of all acts, is not forgiveness the most Divine for a man?

TAKING FORGIVENESS THE EXTRA MILE

The offended is to go even farther and is to seek to bring the wrongdoer to Repentance. This is the purpose of the rebuking commanded in Luke 17:3. More explicitly, Jesus said, If your brother sin against you, go, show him his faults between you and him alone (Mat. 18:15-17).

He is to carry his pursuit to the point of making every reasonable effort to win the wrongdoer, and only when he has exhausted every effort may he abandon it. The object is the gaining of his brother. Only when this is evidently unattainable is all effort to cease.

NOTES

GOD'S CONDITIONS FOR FORGIVENESS

That there is a close analogy between human and Divine forgiveness is clearly implied (Mat. 5:23-24; 6:12; Mk. 11:25; Lk. 6:37; Col. 1:14; 3:13).

God's Forgiveness is conditional upon man's forgiveness of the wrongs done him, not because God forgives grudgingly, but because forgiveness alone indicates that disposition of mind that will humbly accept the Divine pardon.

Repentance, as we have stated, is a necessary ingredient of the fully developed forgiveness. Actually, there is no essential difference between the human and the Divine pardon, though the latter is necessarily more complete, as would be obvious. However, if there is a difference, it is not true forgiveness.

It results in the complete removal of all estrangement and alienation between God and man. It restores completely the relationship that existed prior to the sin. The total removal of the sin as a result of the Divine forgiveness is variously expressed in the Scriptures: *"You have cast all my sins behind Your back"* (Isa. 38:17); *"You will cast all their sins into the depths of the sea"* (Micah 7:19); *"I will forgive their iniquity, and their sin will I remember no more"* (Jer. 31:34).

Ideally, this same result is attained in human forgiveness, but actually, the memory of the sin remains with both parties as a barrier between them. Even when there is a complete Restoration of amity, the former state of alienation cannot entirely be removed from memory because we are humans.

When God forgives, however, He restores man to the condition of former favor. Release from punishment is involved, though Divine forgiveness is more than this.

In most cases, the consequences, which, in some instances, are spoken of as punishment, are not removed, but they lose all penal character and become disciplinary.

The forgiveness does not remove from the human mind the consciousness of sin and the guilt which that involved, but it does remove the mistrust that was the ground of the alienation.

NOTES

Mistrust is changed into trust, and this produces peace of mind (Ps. 32:5-7; Rom. 5:1). As well, there is a consciousness of the Divine love and Mercy (Ps. 103). Also, and certainly not the least significant, forgiveness removes the fear of punishment (II Sam. 12:13).

PAUL AND FORGIVENESS

Paul rarely used the term *"forgiveness,"* preferring the word *"Justification"* in its place. They seem to be according to his understanding practically synonymous.

He seemed to prefer the latter, and rightly so, because it was better fitted to express the idea of secure, present, and permanent acceptance in the sight of God. It connoted both a complete and a permanent state of Grace.

In popular thought, forgiveness is not so comprehensive, but in the Biblical sense, it means no less than this. It removes all the guilt and cause of alienation from the past. It assures a state of Grace for the present and promises Divine Mercy and aid for the future. Its fullness cannot adequately be conveyed by any one term or formula.

THE NECESSITY OF AN ATONEMENT

Though forgiveness on God's part is an act of pure Grace prompted by His Love and Mercy, and though He forgives freely all those who comply with the condition of Repentance and abandonment of sin, yet this does not dispense with the necessity of an Atonement.

The Parable of the Prodigal Son was spoken to teach the freedom of God's Forgiveness, Acceptance of returning sinners, and the duty of men to assume the same attitude toward them. This much it teaches, but it fails to set forth entirely God's Attitude toward sin.

With reference to the sinner, God is Love and Mercy, but with reference to sin, He is Righteous, and this element of God's Nature is no less essential to Him than His Love, and must be considered in any effort to set forth completely the Doctrine of God's Forgiveness of sinners.

The Atonement of Christ and the many

NOTES

Atonements of the Law were manifestations of this phase of God's Nature.

The idea of an Atonement is fundamental in the teachings of the New Testament (Rom. 5:10; II Cor. 5:18-21; Col. 1:21).

It is very clearly implied in such terms as Reconciliation and propitiation, and is no less present in pardon, remission, and forgiveness. The Doctrine of the Atonement is not developed by Jesus, but it is strongly hinted at and is unmistakably implied in the language of Matthew 20:28; 26:28; Mark 10:45; Luke 24:46-47.

The statement of John, *"Behold the Lamb of God, that takes away the sin of the world!"* clearly implies it (Jn. 1:29).

In the writings of the Apostles, it is repeatedly and clearly affirmed that our forgiveness and reconciliation to God are based upon the Death of Christ. That is the Atonement of which we speak (Acts 4:12; Rom. 3:24; 5:11; II Cor. 5:19; Gal. 3:13).

As well, that which was so perfectly accomplished by the Offering of Christ was also presented symbolically by the sacrifices required by the Law, although imperfectly. The Law was *"a shadow of good things to come"* (Heb. 10:1).

THE EFFECT OF SIN

The unvarying effect of sin is to produce an estrangement between the injurer and the wronged. The Nature of God is such, and the relationship between Him and man is of such a character that sin brings about an alienation between them. It is this presupposition of an estrangement between them that renders the Atonement necessary before forgiveness can be extended to man. This estrangement must be removed and the alienation be transformed into a Reconciliation. In what then does the alienation consist?

SIN PRODUCES A CHANGED ATTITUDE

The sin of man produces a changed attitude toward each other on the part of both God and man. God holds no personal grudge against man because of his sin. The New Testament language is very carefully chosen to avoid any statement that would seem to convey such a conception. Yet, God's Holy Righteousness is such that He cannot be indifferent to sin. His Wrath must rest upon the disobedient, that is, if He is to remain absolutely Holy and Righteous (Jn. 3:36; Rom. 1:18).

In fact, God's hatred of sin is not merely impersonal. It is not enough to say He hates the sin. Man's unrighteousness has not merely alienated him from God, but God also from him.

The word *"enemies"* of Romans 5:10 is passive and means *"the object of God's enmity."* It was because of this fact that *"God set forth Christ to be a propitiation to show His Righteousness because of the passing over of sins done aforetime"* (Rom. 3:25-26).

BEFORE CALVARY?

God's passing over the sins of pre-Christian times without inflicting punishment had placed in jeopardy His Righteousness and had exposed Him to the implication that He could tolerate sin. God could not be true to Himself while He tolerated such an imputation, and so, instead of visiting punishment upon all who sin—which would have been one way of showing His Righteousness—He sent forth Christ to death (*"In His Blood"*). In this way, He placed Himself beyond the imputation of unrighteousness while it enabled Him to show Mercy to sinners.

This in no way means that due to their ignorance, the people who lived before Christ were not responsible for their sins. They most definitely were! This does not speak of the fact of sin, of which all were guilty, and for which they would die lost.

However, it does say that God did not hold sin to account as He now does, except when the situation became intolerable, with Sodom and Gomorrah serving as an example.

The effect of sin upon man was to estrange him from God and to lead him farther and farther away from his Maker. Each successive sin produced a greater barrier between the two. The Atonement was designed to remove the cause of this estrangement and restore the former relationship between God and man.

THE PURPOSE OF FORGIVENESS

This too, it has been observed, is the purpose of forgiveness so that the Atonement finds its completion in forgiveness. It should be noted that the Reconciliation originates with God and not with man (Rom. 3:25; II Cor. 5:19).

God woos man before the latter seeks God. The effect of the Atonement on man is to reconcile him and attract him to God.

It shows him God's Love for man and the forgiveness in that it removes sin completely, takes away the estranging factor between them, and so wins man back to God! *"We love, because He first loved us."*

At the same time, the Atonement is such a complete expression of both the love and the Righteousness of God that, while on the one hand, it exhibits His yearning for man, on the other, it shows that he is not tolerant toward sin.

In the Atonement of Christ, therefore, is the meeting place and the reconcilement of God's Holy horror of sin and the free bestowal by Grace of forgiveness upon penitent Believers.

(32) "AND WE ARE HIS WITNESSES OF THESE THINGS; AND SO IS ALSO THE HOLY SPIRIT, WHOM GOD HAS GIVEN TO THEM WHO BELIEVE HIM."

The form is:

1. The only way sin can be properly addressed was and is by and through the Cross.

2. That's why Paul said that the emphasis must always be on the Cross and never on anything else, as important as these other things sometimes are (I Cor. 1:17).

3. It is by and through what Jesus did at the Cross that effects the Salvation of the sinner and the Sanctification of the Saint.

WITNESSES

The phrase, *"And we are His Witnesses of these things,"* in effect, says that the things being said were not mere philosophy, but rather eyewitness accounts. In other words, they knew Who Jesus was simply because they had experienced Who He was. They were witnesses to the fact that God had raised Jesus from the dead. Of course, it was very obvious to all as to who had murdered Him. Peter and all the other Apostles were standing before the very ones who had done this horrible thing.

They also knew that Jesus was Israel's Messiah and the world's Saviour. So, they knew that of which they spoke!

THE HOLY SPIRIT

The phrase, *"And so is also the Holy Spirit, Whom God has given to them who obey Him,"* tells us several things:

• The Infilling of the Holy Spirit is an absolute necessity for all Believers. I trust we have satisfactorily brought this out, even several times; however, due to the great significance of what is being said here, I think it would be impossible to overstate the case. Without the Holy Spirit to help the Believer, absolutely nothing is going to be done for the Lord.

• Obedience to God is the requirement for one to be baptized with the Holy Spirit.

What did Peter mean by obedience to God in this respect?

The Lord had told His Followers just before the Ascension that they were to go into Jerusalem and wait for the Promise of the Father, i.e., the Holy Spirit. They were to obey in doing this, and the ones who did were given the great Gift on the Day of Pentecost.

Even though Jerusalem was required then respecting the Day of Pentecost, after that event, Jerusalem was no longer required, at least respecting this particular location. From then on, Believers were baptized with the Holy Spirit wherever they happened to be, which continues thusly unto this moment (Acts 2:39).

The point is, by this act, and as Peter here declared, they needed to understand the significance of being baptized with the Holy Spirit, which was shown by their obedience. Then they obeyed (at least those who did) simply because Jesus said so. To be frank, at that time they would have had no knowledge whatsoever as to the vast significance of this Gift. Of course, since that momentous day, which is overly obvious in the Ministry and conduct of the Early Church, it is now very obvious as to why Jesus commanded this.

The idea is, He commanded it then (Acts 1:4), and to be sure, that command holds true unto this very hour.

After coming to Christ, the Believer must immediately set about to receive this gracious Gift of the Holy Spirit. It is that important!

THE COMMAND

Failure to obey this command as given by Christ regarding the Baptism with the Holy Spirit (Acts 1:4), which is just as apropos now as it was then, is a great failure indeed!

In fact, the beginning of the Church was dependent upon being baptized with the Holy Spirit. That's how important it was and is. In other words, without the Holy Spirit, while there may be much religious machinery, there is not going to be anything done for the Lord Jesus Christ. So, as previously stated, failure to obey this command is failure indeed!

Regrettably, many at the present time, who once knew of the Holy Spirit, are now denying Him. Many are saying, *"It was for the Early Church but not for the present Church," "All of this passed away with the Apostles,"* or *"When one is Born-Again, one is automatically baptized with the Holy Spirit at the same time!"*

Of course, none of this is true, which an honest investigation of the Word of God will bear out.

So, a lack of obedience in this is a direct affront to Christ and, as well, cuts off the Believer from his Power Source, which is the Holy Spirit.

Let us say it again: Believers being baptized with the Holy Spirit is so important that the great institution called *"the Church"* could not even begin, much less accomplish something, without this Baptism. It is the same presently!

(33) "WHEN THEY HEARD THAT, THEY WERE CUT TO THE HEART, AND TOOK COUNSEL TO KILL THEM."

The pattern is:

1. To *"walk after the Spirit"* is simply to place one's Faith exclusively in Christ and what Christ did at the Cross (Rom. 8:1-2).

2. The Object of one's Faith must always be *"Jesus Christ and Him Crucified"* (I Cor. 1:17-18, 21, 23; 2:2, 5).

NOTES

HEARING THE GOSPEL

The phrase, *"When they heard that,"* pertains to a Message that was somewhat negative, at least as it addressed them, i.e., the religious leaders of Israel. But yet, Peter, as well as the others, said exactly what the Spirit of God wanted them to say.

Considering all who claim to be preachers, it is not very easy for the Lord to have most proclaim that which He desires to have proclaimed. Many who call themselves preachers are such in name only, never having really been Called by the Lord in the first place.

As well, there are many who have definitely been Called by the Lord, but have compromised their messages to such an extent that what they deliver is not from the Lord but out of their own minds or the minds of other men.

Few and rare are those who truly seek the Lord, seek to know His Mind, and are then willing to deliver what He gives!

CUT TO THE HEART

The phrase, *"They were cut to the heart,"* simply means that the Word of God cut into them like a knife, even down into their very hearts.

The Greek word is *"diaprio"* and means *"to cut through or to saw asunder."* It is the same word used again in Acts 7:54.

It is not the same word as *"katanusso,"* which means *"to be pricked to the quick"* or *"to agitate violently,"* as in Acts 2:37. There it brought remorse and Repentance, whereas here it filled them with hate and anger.

The Word of God, when preached under a mighty Anointing of the Holy Spirit, will seldom leave one as found. Most of the time, it produces a powerful reaction, whether to Repentance or to anger. This is because of two factors:

1. It is the Word of God and, consequently, totally unlike the various religions and philosophies of the world, which are solely of man. As such, it has a powerful effect.

2. When accompanied by the Holy Spirit, as is obvious with the Apostles, it presents a

NOTES

force and Power totally unlike anything else in the world, which goes far beneath the surface, even down into the very being of a person. In other words, it goes down into the heart and soul. As such, I think one can say that it is always accompanied by conviction (Jn. 16:8-11).

Conviction is meant to draw the person to their need and the Solution to that need, Who is Christ. If the person refuses to yield, most of the time, it turns to anger, exactly as here recorded concerning the religious leaders.

MURDEROUS HEARTS

The phrase, *"And took counsel to kill them,"* is the reaction that normally comes from the world of religion.

Inasmuch as we live in a land that does not allow such action, modern individuals take the next best step, which is to stop the Message, to which they will go to any length.

Please allow me to say again that this is Satan's greatest weapon. He uses the Church (apostate church) to stop the Messenger and the Message and will justify himself in using any tactics to do so. What I am about to say is not said with gladness of heart, but yet, I feel it must be said.

Most of that which calls itself *"church"* is actually doing all within its power to hinder the true Message of Jesus Christ. This is true whether it is *"institutionalized religion"* or all other varieties. Even though they are making great religious show, which, incidentally, deceives many people, still, they are hindering the true Message. They function primarily exactly as the religious leadership that killed Christ. It is ironic, but they killed the Lord in the Name of the Lord! Their modern counterparts do exactly the same!

They may use any variety of excuses or alleged reasons for their actions, but the true intent is exactly as the religious leaders who opposed the Early Church. As stated, they must stop the Message and the Messenger. As murder was in their hearts of so long ago, murder is in the hearts of those presently so occupied!

(34) "THEN STOOD THERE UP ONE IN THE COUNCIL, A PHARISEE NAMED GAMALIEL, A DOCTOR OF THE LAW, HAD IN REPUTATION AMONG ALL THE PEOPLE, AND COMMANDED TO PUT THE APOSTLES FORTH A LITTLE SPACE."

The pattern is:

1. There's only one way that the Believer can live a victorious, overcoming Christian life.

2. That way is the Cross of Christ!

GAMALIEL

The phrase, *"Then stood there up one in the Council, a Pharisee named Gamaliel,"* constitutes one of the most celebrated and honored Jewish rabbins.

Gamaliel was the thirty-fifth receiver of the traditions and of the Law given at Mount Sinai. He was the grandson of Hillel, one of the great theologians of Israel, and succeeded as president of the Sanhedrin on the death of his father, Rabbi Simeon, who was the son of Hillel.

As it is known, Paul studied under Gamaliel (Acts 22:3). He died about 18 years before Titus destroyed Jerusalem. In fact, his son Simeon died in the siege of the city in A.D. 70.

There are some who claim that Gamaliel favored the Apostles and that he ultimately became a Christian. However, all the evidence is to the contrary.

The high place accorded him in Jewish tradition, and the fact that the title of rabbin, higher even than rabbi or master, was first bestowed upon him testifies that he remained a Pharisee to the end.

His speech was rather indicative of one who knew the deeper truth in the Old Testament of the universal Governance of God, and who recognized that the presence of His Power was the deciding factor in all human enterprise. As well, his social enactments were permeated by the same broad-minded spirit. Thus, his legislation on behalf of the poor in Jerusalem was formulated so as to include Gentiles as well as Jews; however, as stated, there is no proof that he ever accepted Christ.

A DOCTOR OF THE LAW

The phrase, *"A Doctor of the Law, had in reputation among all the people,"* presents

NOTES

another instance to where the people think one thing because of outward circumstances or observances when, in reality, the situation is something else altogether.

While Gamaliel did do a good thing here, as the Lord evidently impressed him to do, still, in the final sense, his heart was not right with God. In a sense, he seems to have been attempting to play both sides of the fence.

It is a case, as it so often is, of one having an excellent *"reputation"* with the people, but whose *"character"* is not right with God. As we have previously stated, *"reputation"* is what people think you are while *"character"* is what God knows you are. Only God can develop character!

"And commanded to put the Apostles forth a little space," was for the purpose, as is obvious, for a short meeting to be held in order that his word of wisdom might be given to the other members of the Sanhedrin.

(35) "AND SAID UNTO THEM, YOU MEN OF ISRAEL, TAKE HEED TO YOURSELVES WHAT YOU INTEND TO DO AS TOUCHING THESE MEN."

The form is:

1. The phrase, *"And said unto them, You men of Israel,"* proclaims a voice to which the Sanhedrin would bow.

2. As we have already stated, Gamaliel was probably the most respected man in Israel at this time. As well, being a Pharisee, he would have been opposed to some of the violence of the Sadducees, who felt they had to put down all opposition with sternness and even force.

3. *"Take heed to yourselves what you intend to do as touching these men,"* presents a stand that is taken for one of several reasons:

a. In his wisdom, Gamaliel knew that brutal action taken against certain things has the very opposite effect intended. Actually, this is what happened!

b. There is a possibility that he had been previously touched by the Ministry of Christ, although he is not mentioned at all according to that particular time, even though the Crucifixion was only about two months earlier. If he had been present that awful night, quite possibly his position toward the Apostles was an effort at Atonement.

c. The Spirit of God definitely could have dealt with him and, no doubt, did at that particular time.

d. Even though the words of Gamaliel were heeded at present, the Sanhedrin would not restrain their anger for long. Their bloodlust would not stop until they opposed the Followers of Christ to the limit of their power, which, at the same time, succeeded in destroying themselves instead.

(36) "FOR BEFORE THESE DAYS ROSE UP THEUDAS, BOASTING HIMSELF TO BE SOMEBODY; TO WHOM A NUMBER OF MEN, ABOUT FOUR HUNDRED, JOINED THEMSELVES: WHO WAS SLAIN; AND ALL, AS MANY AS OBEYED HIM, WERE SCATTERED, AND BROUGHT TO NOUGHT."

The order is:

1. The phrase, *"For before these days rose up Theudas, boasting himself to be somebody,"* evidently concerned a particular insurrection led by this man, which had recently taken place.

2. It seems this man had claimed to be led by the Lord, etc., with Gamaliel showing that the claim had no relationship to reality.

3. *"To whom a number of men, about four hundred, joined themselves: who was slain; and all, as many as obeyed him, were scattered, and brought to nought,"* referred to these people as becoming dupes of this self-pronounced Messiah, or some such!

(37) "AFTER THIS MAN ROSE UP JUDAS OF GALILEE IN THE DAYS OF THE TAXING, AND DREW AWAY MUCH PEOPLE AFTER HIM: HE ALSO PERISHED; AND ALL, EVEN AS MANY AS OBEYED HIM, WERE DISPERSED."

The pattern is:

1. The phrase, *"After this man rose up Judas of Galilee in the days of the taxing, and drew away much people after him,"* as well, seems to proclaim another who claimed to have the Blessings of the Lord, etc.

2. *"He also perished; and all, even as many as obeyed him, were dispersed,"* proclaims these as coming to the same end as those under Theudas.

3. Gamaliel gave two examples to prove

NOTES

his point, which seems to have been well taken at the time.

4. Also, these are but examples of the untold thousands of false prophets who have lured gullible individuals into believing their lie, consequently, going to destruction.

5. Some would think that proper education would forgo such directions; however, deception does not bow to education.

(38) "AND NOW I SAY UNTO YOU, REFRAIN FROM THESE MEN, AND LET THEM ALONE: FOR IF THIS COUNSEL OR THIS WORK BE OF MEN, IT WILL COME TO NOUGHT."

The composition is:

1. The phrase, *"And now I say unto you, Refrain from these men, and let them alone,"* constitutes advice given with this idea in mind:

The Roman authorities were ever mindful of anything that tended to usurp authority over their rule. Of course, the reason these other groups mentioned by Gamaliel were so quickly destroyed is because they ran afoul of Roman power. In effect, Gamaliel was saying, *"Let them alone; Rome will handle the problem."*

2. *"For if this counsel or this work be of men, it will come to nought,"* is given on that pretext.

3. Some have misunderstood Gamaliel and, thereby, believed that if something succeeds, it must be of God. However, that is untrue!

4. Many false religions succeed. They do so because they appeal to existing prejudices, because their founders are extremely intelligent and possess great learning, or they have access to great sums of money or to certain individuals who have great influence, which seems to legitimize their false efforts.

5. Christianity has none of these things. It was hated, reviled, despised, and looked down upon. In fact, concerning Christianity, one of the Jewish leaders in Rome said to the Apostle Paul, *"But we desire to hear of you what you think: for as concerning this sect, we know that everywhere it is spoken against"* (Acts 28:22).

6. All of this simply means that if the Lord had not been the Sponsor of Bible Christianity, it would never have succeeded.

7. The Cross of Christ is the basic reason for the animosity against the true Way of the Lord. The reason?

8. It strikes down everything that is not totally of the Lord, dealing with every aspect of our lives personally, and, as well, the entirety of our belief system.

(39) "BUT IF IT BE OF GOD, YOU CANNOT OVERTHROW IT; LEST HAPLY YOU BE FOUND EVEN TO FIGHT AGAINST GOD."

The synopsis is:

1. Every victory won through the Cross gives glory to God.

2. Every so-called victory otherwise gives glory to man.

3. God can only accept that which glorifies Christ.

IF IT BE OF GOD ...

The phrase, *"But if it be of God, you cannot overthrow it,"* presents the first of two great truths given by Gamaliel.

Did he suspect that this thing that had taken Jerusalem by storm, bringing about tremendous Miracles and Healings, as well as thousands accepting Christ, just might be of God?

I think his statement proclaims that these thoughts were definitely in his mind. This great truth has held even from the very beginning.

Sometime ago, I stood on the top of Masada in Israel, the renowned place where a great number of Jews committed suicide rather than kneel to the Romans. It overlooks the Dead Sea and is a place of tremendous interest, as should be obvious.

As one stands on the top looking down at the sides, the earthworks built by the Romans, even at great expense, are still visible. Actually, the signs of their encampment are also visible on the desert floor.

However, mighty Rome, which ruled the world of that day, is now gone, with Israel once again a state and tremendously strong considering her size. In the natural, such would not be possible; however, Israel has survived, even as the Church has survived, simply because it is of God. I might quickly add, even though Israel has been out of Covenant with the Lord for over 2,000 years, still, she will be restored at the Second Coming.

THE BLOOD OF THE MARTYRS IS THE SEED OF THE CHURCH

In fact, mighty empires have come and gone, with some of them having made every effort to destroy Christianity, but without success! Actually, as someone has said, *"The blood of the martyrs is the seed of the Church."*

This very day, as the Twelve Apostles stood before the vaunted Sanhedrin, little did any of the members of this august body understand that in about 27 years from this time, Israel would literally cease to be a Nation, with the Church, the true Body of Christ, stronger than ever.

Let it ever be known, that which is *"of God"* is *"from God"* and cannot be overthrown. To fight that which is of God is to fight God! As someone has said, *"Many hammers beat upon the anvil. The hammers break, the anvil remains."*

A PERSONAL EXPERIENCE

If the reader will permit me to bring up our own Ministry, it will serve as an excellent example of that of which I speak. While I take full responsibility for any actions on my part, I am not responsible for the unscriptural actions of others. As well, I might quickly add that such was only an excuse and not the reason.

The reason that so much opposition came against us was and is because this Ministry is of God. I say that strongly because it is so and because its fruit is found all over the world in the form of lives changed, souls saved, bondages broken, and Christ made real in the hearts and lives of untold numbers of people. We give the Lord all the praise and the glory!

However, the truth is, powerful religious denominations did all within their power to destroy this Ministry, even going so far as to say, *"We will get him off of television and will use any tactic at our disposal to do so."*

Why?

As I have already stated elsewhere in this

NOTES

Volume, the reason had nothing to do with doctrine or honesty. Actually, there was nothing they could point to legitimately that was unscriptural.

There is only one conclusion! That which is truly of God will not oppose that which is of God. It only does so because it is not of God.

That is why the Pharisees became so angry when Jesus addressed them, saying, *"You are of your father the devil, and the lusts of your father you will do"* (Jn. 8:44).

THE BLESSINGS OF THE LORD

Never mind that virtually all of the church world has done its very best to overthrow this Ministry, but by the Grace of God, we are still here and continuing to tell the grandest Story ever told, the Story of Jesus Christ. At this writing (November, 2013), we are covering nearly two-thirds of America with programming 24 hours a day, seven days a week. Also, the SONLIFE BROADCASTING NETWORK is airing in several hundreds of millions of homes all over the world, translated into several languages. All of that is because this Ministry is of God.

Our prayer is that those who attempted to steal, kill, and destroy would come to the knowledge of the truth and, thereby, realize that if something is of God, it cannot be overthrown. It might be delayed, and it might be hindered, but it will not be stopped.

FIGHTING AGAINST GOD

The phrase, *"Lest haply you be found even to fight against God,"* presents the very worst position in which anyone can find himself. It is a battle that one cannot win, irrespective of the resources at one's disposal.

Actually, this is exactly what Israel did! They were fighting against God, and it was a battle they could not hope to win. It did not matter their seeming strength and the seeming weakness of the Apostles. It was not possible for Israel to win or for the Apostles to lose!

As well, it should be quickly understood that God was not with Israel at this time, even though they were His Chosen People after a fashion. In fact, they had given the world the Prophets, the Bible, and had

NOTES

actually served as the womb of the Messiah, even though they disowned Him. However, they were unscriptural, and grossly so, in their thinking, their actions, and their direction. Consequently, there was nothing God could do but to oppose them, as He opposes all things that are unscriptural. Never misunderstand, the Word of God is the criterion!

It does not matter how rich or powerful that a person or a group may be, and neither does it matter how much they profess to be of God. If they are not Scriptural, God is unalterably opposed to the person or a group.

Jesus plainly said concerning these very situations, *"The Kingdom of God shall be taken from you, and given to a nation bringing forth the fruits thereof"* (Mat. 21:43).

(40) "AND TO HIM THEY AGREED: AND WHEN THEY HAD CALLED THE APOSTLES, AND BEATEN THEM, THEY COMMANDED THAT THEY SHOULD NOT SPEAK IN THE NAME OF JESUS, AND LET THEM GO."

The construction is:

1. The phrase, *"And to him they agreed,"* presents them heeding this sound advice, at least about not killing them. It should be quickly said that they wanted to kill them because they were murderers at heart (Jn. 8:44).

2. *"And when they had called the Apostles, and beaten them,"* presents a cruel and brutal punishment, which was cowardly and unjust.

3. However, hatred of Christ drives men to their lowest depths of moral degradation.

4. As well, it should be said of Gamaliel, neutrality in relation to the Gospel is hostility to Christ, as Jesus Himself said (Lk. 11:23).

5. Deuteronomy 25:3 fixed the mode of a Jewish flogging and limited the number of blows to 40. It seems the flogging was administered by a rod.

6. It seems not to have been quite as horrible as the Roman scourging, which often left individuals permanently maimed or even killed, which is what Jesus experienced at the hands of His captors.

7. But yet, the Jewish beatings were bad enough so that some even think if Paul had experienced one more such flogging, it would have killed him, or at least made it impossible for him to walk the rest of his life (II Cor. 11:23-25).

8. *"They commanded that they should not speak in the Name of Jesus, and let them go,"* presents the second command not to preach in this Name (Acts 4:17-18, 21).

9. However, they had already informed the Sanhedrin as to what they would do respecting these commands. Their answer was clear and concise, *"We ought to obey God rather than men"* (Acts 5:29).

(41) "AND THEY DEPARTED FROM THE PRESENCE OF THE COUNCIL, REJOICING THAT THEY WERE COUNTED WORTHY TO SUFFER SHAME FOR HIS NAME."

The structure is:

1. The phrase, *"And they departed from the presence of the Council,"* proclaims the fact that the Lord had long since departed.

2. These were supposed to be the godliest men in Israel when, in reality, they were the most wicked. But yet, at least for the most part, they had excellent reputations over Israel.

3. So, the Believer must know the Word of God and be led by the Spirit accordingly so that he may know that which is of God and which is not. The Apostles knew, along with thousands of others in the area, but most of Israel did not know!

4. *"Rejoicing that they were counted worthy to suffer shame for His Name,"* presents the first sharp stroke of persecution. It was bitter and painful to the flesh, but yet, caused rejoicing in the spirit. Shame is glory if suffered for the Name (Williams).

(42) "AND DAILY IN THE TEMPLE, AND IN EVERY HOUSE, THEY CEASED NOT TO TEACH AND PREACH JESUS CHRIST."

The exposition is:

1. The phrase, *"And daily in the Temple,"* presents them boldly and properly disregarding their illegal judges as they kept on preaching that Jesus was the promised Messiah.

2. How long they continued this before Stephen appeared before the Sanhedrin, we are not told. Irrespective, thousands were coming to Christ.

3. *"And in every house, they ceased not to teach and preach Jesus Christ,"* tells us

that the churches were in houses for the most part, if not altogether.

4. As should be obvious, there was no way they could secure a building of any size, especially at this time.

5. The Jews would have considered such as rival worship to the synagogues. As well, Rome would never have countenanced such bold proclamation. So, they conducted services at countless houses all over Jerusalem, etc.

6. Actually, this continued to be the manner of worship, with some minor exceptions, throughout the entirety of the Book of Acts and the Early Church.

7. If one is to notice, the very theme of their Message was *"Jesus Christ."*

8. The spirit and conduct of the Apostles here recorded is a precious example to their successors.

9. To glory in the Cross, to count shame endured for Christ's Sake the highest honor, and to be unwearied and undaunted in teaching and preaching Jesus Christ through good report and through evil report is the true character and work of every bishop of souls.

"He pardoned my transgressions,
"He sanctified my soul,
"He honors my confessions,
"Since by His Blood I'm whole.
"It is truly wonderful what the Lord has done!
"It is truly wonderful! It is truly wonderful!
"It is truly wonderful what the Lord has done!
"Glory to His Name."

CHAPTER 6

(1) "AND IN THOSE DAYS, WHEN THE NUMBER OF THE DISCIPLES WAS MULTIPLIED, THERE AROSE A MURMURING OF THE GRECIANS AGAINST THE HEBREWS, BECAUSE THEIR WIDOWS WERE NEGLECTED IN THE DAILY MINISTRATION."

The exegesis is:

NOTES

1. Faith is talked about presently more than any other time in history.

2. However, is it the kind of Faith that Paul talked about?

3. *"Jesus Christ and Him Crucified,"* was the Faith that Paul constantly discussed (Gal. 2:20).

BELIEVERS MULTIPLIED

The phrase, *"And in those days, when the number of the Disciples was multiplied,"* implies several things:

- The Church at this time was growing by the proverbial leaps and bounds. In other words, thousands had been saved, with a constant and continuous stream of new Converts continuing even unto this moment.
- In this growth, problems arose, which is par for the course in such situations.
- We are shown in this Chapter how the Holy Spirit through the Apostles handled the problems, which should be a lesson to us as well!
- We are also given direction respecting ministry and regarding priority.

"There arose a murmuring of the Grecians against the Hebrews," does not pertain to Gentiles (referring to the Grecians) as some think, but rather to Jews who spoke Greek as a result of having once lived in various countries where Greek was spoken. The other Jews referred to here as *"Hebrews"* spoke Aramaic (Acts 21:40; II Cor. 11:22; Phil. 3:5).

THE WIDOWS

"Because their widows were neglected in the daily ministration," speaks of relief in the form of food and money given to *"widows"* in the Church in Jerusalem, who had no way to provide for themselves.

There were no social programs provided by the government in those days for people in need, and, as well, great persecution was being leveled against all the Followers of Christ at this time, which exacerbated the problem.

This practice in the Church of caring for *"widows"* who had no support was continued in all places, it seems, throughout the account of the Early Church. However, guidelines were later laid down by Paul.

He insinuated that younger widows were not to be included in this as they would likely remarry (I Tim. 5:11-14), and those with families were to be cared for by their relatives (I Tim. 5:3-8).

So, this practice that actually began under the Law of Moses (Ex. 22:22; Deut. 10:18; 24:19-21; 26:12-13), and was addressed, as well, in Acts, Chapter 6, as we are here discussing, was continued by the Church, but only for those who met certain qualifications. It seems these *"widows,"* who were supported by the Church, were to serve the Body in whatever way they could in order to earn their keep.

(2) "THEN THE TWELVE CALLED THE MULTITUDE OF THE DISCIPLES UNTO THEM, AND SAID, IT IS NOT REASON THAT WE SHOULD LEAVE THE WORD OF GOD, AND SERVE TABLES."

The overview is:

1. The Grace of God is simply the Goodness of God extended to undeserving Believers.

2. Grace is made possible by our Faith.

3. However, it must be Faith in Christ and the Cross for Grace to be realized.

THE TWELVE APOSTLES

The phrase, *"Then the Twelve called the multitude of the Disciples unto them, and said,"* constitutes probably the very first business meeting in the Early Church.

Due to these particular problems, the Twelve Apostles found themselves bogged down in administration, as well as attempting to settle squabbles, etc., which were demanding all of their time. Even though these things were important, this is not what God called them to do. Consequently, the main thrust of the Gospel was being neglected because of details resulting from growing pains.

The word *"Disciples,"* as it is used here, simply refers to *"a pupil or learner."*

The Greek word for *"Disciple"* is *"Mathetes."* It is used in several different ways in the Gospels.

THE WORD *"DISCIPLE"*

It designates the Twelve whom Jesus chose to be with Him. The Twelve are unique in that Jesus chose them and trained them to both teach and serve (Mk. 3:14). Responding to Jesus' Call, the Twelve made a Disciples' total commitment. They surrendered everything to live in obedience to Jesus (Lk. 14:26).

The New Testament also describes a much wider circle beyond the Twelve who were also called Disciples, even as mentioned here in Verse 2.

These were adherents to the movement associated with Jesus. At times, the word *"Disciple"* may seem to carry the sense of *"Believer"* (Jn. 8:31; 13:35; 15:8). However, it would be a mistake to think that all those who were called Disciples in the Gospels were persons who had made a firm commitment to Jesus.

In fact, many were only initially attracted to Jesus. When they found His teachings difficult, as after His discourse on the Bread of Life, Many of His Disciples turned back and no longer followed Him (Jn. 6:66).

After the Resurrection, Jesus charged His Followers to go and make Disciples of all Nations (Mat. 28:19). The mission was not to win adherents merely for a movement. Instead, Jesus said to His Disciples that they were to teach those who believe to obey everything He had commanded them (Mat. 28:20).

(It seems, however, that the manner in which the word *"Disciple"* is used in the Book of Acts always and without exception refers to Believers in Christ.)

DISCIPLESHIP AT PRESENT

In the Book of Acts, the word *"Disciple"* continues to be used but seems to be synonymous with *"Believer."*

However, Luke even recorded the point at which the believing community began its break with the language of both Jewish and Greek culture, from which the word *"Disciple"* sprang. He told of the time at Antioch when *"the Disciples were first called Christians"* (Acts 11:26).

Although it is dangerous to build on silence, it does seem significant, however, that the term *"Disciple"* is simply not used in the Epistles. This may be because

NOTES

it carried too many associations at a time when a new process was demanded within the Church to equip God's People for growth and ministry.

THE GOAL OF DISCIPLING

Jesus defined the goal of discipling when He said, *"The Disciple is not above his master: but everyone who is perfect (mature) shall be as his master"* (Lk. 6:40). Consequently, likeness, not simply knowledge, was the goal of Jewish Discipleship, and likeness to Jesus Himself is the goal God has for you and me (Rom. 8:29; I Jn. 3:2).

Although complete likeness to Jesus awaits our Resurrection, even now, God is actively at work within Believers. We *"are being transformed into His* (Jesus') *Likeness with ever-increasing glory"* (II Cor. 3:18).

A number of New Testament Passages give insight into the processes that are involved in individual and community growth toward Christlikeness (Eph. 4:11-16).

CHRIST'S BODY

The New Testament has several images that replace the image of Disciples gathered around a rabbi, as it was commonly understood in the Israel of Jesus' Day.

The Epistles speak of the Christian community as family, teaching us that we must build intimate relationships with our brothers and sisters.

There is the image of Christ's Body, a living organism, and this teaches us to look to each other for ministries that will facilitate our transformation. There is the image of a Holy Temple, indicating that we are to serve God and others.

The Epistles, especially in contexts that emphasize the family and the body, present new interpersonal processes that, in effect, supplant those by which the Disciples of Judaism were trained.

We can learn much from a study of Jesus' Relationship with the Twelve. However, just as the word *"Disciple"* was discarded when new terminology was needed to express new Truths, so we should study the Epistles for nurture principles by which modern men and women of Faith and commitment can be developed.

NOTES

PREACHERS

The phrase, *"It is not reason that we should leave the Word of God, and serve tables,"* refers to the voluminous administrative duties that accompanied great growth of the Early Church in Jerusalem, etc.

The word *"serve"* in this Verse, and the word *"ministration"* in Verse 1, as well as the word *"Deacon,"* all spring from the Greek word *"diakonos."*

The Minister of the Gospel is here given a great lesson respecting the Call of God and the carrying out of that Call.

The Preacher of the Gospel is not to purposely involve himself in any type of business activity that divides his attention and takes his time away from that which God has first called him to do. The business of the Preacher is to be *"the Word of God"* and its presentation.

However, it is certainly true at times that Preachers are forced to take secular jobs for particular reasons, exactly as Paul supported himself (Acts 18:3).

As well, Preachers of the Gospel, at least those who are truly Called of God, will not spend great amounts of their time on golf courses or any other such entertainment or pursuits. While those things are not wrong if done in moderation, they can quickly become wrong if such causes the Word of God to be neglected.

Nothing must draw the Preacher's mind, attention, or total diligence from the Word of God and its presentation. As we shall see, such demands a heavy prayer life also.

(3) "WHEREFORE, BRETHREN, YOU LOOK OUT AMONG YOU SEVEN MEN OF HONEST REPORT, FULL OF THE HOLY SPIRIT AND WISDOM, WHOM WE MAY APPOINT OVER THIS BUSINESS."

The form is:

1. There is no way that Righteousness can come by the law, by rules, by regulations, by merit, or by works.

2. If Righteousness can come by these various means, then *"Christ is dead in vain."*

3. Righteousness can only come as the Believer places his Faith exclusively in Christ and what Christ did for us at the Cross (I Cor. 1:17; 2:2).

NOTES

THE FIRST DEACONS?

The words, *"Wherefore, brethren,"* linked to the word *"Multitude"* in Verse 2, means this was quite a number of people, possibly several hundreds, or maybe even thousands.

"You look out among you seven men of honest report, full of the Holy Spirit and Wisdom," is thought by some to represent the first Deacons, even though they are not called that in this Chapter. Accordingly, it might not be wise to attempt to force this situation into the mold of Deacons but allow it to serve in principle only. It is the task of the Believer to see what the Holy Spirit is doing and learn the lesson thereof without forcing the issue.

For instance, the Church in Jerusalem at this time had between 10,000 and 20,000 people who had recently come to the Lord. Naturally, problems would arise in a Church this size, even as it did; consequently, the steps taken to correct the problems, which were, no doubt, designed by the Holy Spirit, are obvious.

As well, seven men were to be chosen to attend this business; the number was probably given to Peter by the Holy Spirit. Consequently, if this is the criterion for *"Deacons,"* then the number *"seven"* must be maintained as well; however, that would be impossible in many Churches.

Regarding Pentecostal and Charismatic churches presently, the *average* size is 50 people. That means that quite a few of them have an attendance of only 15, 20, etc. In churches that size, it would be impossible, at least in some of them, to find seven people, even including women, who would fit the qualifications laid down, *"Full of the Holy Spirit and Wisdom."*

As we shall see, of the seven men chosen, at least two of them, Stephen and Philip, were Preachers of the Gospel. The others may well have been, as well, even though no more information is given concerning them.

So, as stated, the principle of what was done here might well serve respecting the office of Deacons, but otherwise, it would be improper, I think, to use these particulars as a pattern designed by the Holy Spirit for that particular office. While we must never make too little of what the Holy Spirit says and does, likewise, at the same time, we must not make more than He intends.

The phrase, *"Whom we may appoint over this business,"* means to *"designate, ordain, or set."*

The Holy Spirit told the *"Twelve"* what to do, the number of men to choose, and how they were to be chosen.

Exactly how this was done, we are not told! However, it is almost certain that these men were not elected by popular ballot, especially considering the tremendous number of people in the Early Church. To attempt to do such, even as some of our modern churches, would have been chaotic, with hundreds of different men proposed, etc.

The idea seems to be that the task was left up to this *"multitude of Disciples,"* ever how many those were, with them making the selection.

It is a mistake to think of the government of the Church as a democracy. Pure and simple, it is not!

In simplistic form, the Biblical pattern is that God speaks to the Pastor of the Church, which in no way negates the fact that the Lord can and does speak to other people in the local Church, whether of leadership or laity. In other words, Jesus Christ is the Head of the Church, the Chief *"Shepherd and Bishop of our souls"* (I Pet. 2:25). The Pastor or Pastors of the local Church serve as undershepherds.

Concerning the *"business end"* of the Church, however these men or women are chosen for these positions, the final decision must always be made by the Pastor, as proven by the word *"appoint."*

There is very little Scriptural evidence, if any, concerning the modern method of electing church leaders or attending to church business by popular ballot. However, that does not mean that it is necessarily wrong for such a method to be used, providing the people will earnestly seek the Lord regarding His Decision. Actually, the Will of God in all things is what the local Church must strive for and seek to obtain. To do otherwise is to invite disaster.

NOTES

CHURCH GOVERNMENT

Church government is extremely important, even as government in any function is important. The word *"government"* in its simplest form means *"the act or process of authoritative direction or control."*

Inasmuch as we are speaking of the Church, the Body of Christ, the Bible must serve as the pattern and more particularly, the Book of Acts and the Epistles.

Satan's greatest effort to hinder the Work of God could very well be his efforts in bringing civil government over into the Church, of which he is mostly successful. In other words, the Church adopts the ways of the world, which is totally unscriptural, and leaven will ultimately corrupt the whole.

If one desires to make up his own rules, which many seem to do, perhaps the following material will not be to your liking; however, if you desire what the Bible says, perhaps some light may be offered. Then I must ask, *"If the Bible is not the pattern or standard, then what is?"*

THE BOOK OF ACTS AND THE EPISTLES

The Holy Spirit is the Author of the Word of God, even though He used human instrumentation; consequently, inasmuch as its Author is God, this means that it is inspired and error free. Paul said, *"All Scripture is given by Inspiration of God, and is profitable for Doctrine, for reproof, for correction, for instruction in Righteousness"* (II Tim. 3:16). Thus, it is to serve as the pattern, guide, and direction for all things.

In that light, we have the Book of Acts and the Epistles, given to us by the Holy Spirit, which are meant to serve as our pattern respecting the Church and its functions. Understanding that the things done in these accounts are not the efforts of men, but rather the directions of the Holy Spirit, we then know and understand that these are to serve as our guidelines. As stated, if one does not use the Book of Acts and the Epistles as the standard and pattern for the Church, then what is to be used? So, the reader is down to two choices. You can choose the Word of God or choose that which is instigated by man.

As for me and my house, we will take the Word of God.

Some preacher, actually, one who called himself Pentecostal, made the foolish statement sometime back that due to education and modern technology, we have gone beyond the Book of Acts; therefore, he went on to say that this Book should not serve as a pattern.

Such foolishness shows Spiritual and Scriptural ignorance to the highest degree, one might quickly add. If the Book of Acts was the mere efforts of men, that would be one thing; however, if that which is done respecting the Church is the Work and Leading of the Holy Spirit, then that is something else altogether. For any person to think he knows more than the Holy Spirit is ludicrous indeed!

THE CHURCH

We must understand that the Church, and I speak of the true Body of Christ, is a group of *"Called-out Believers,"* who, because of their Faith in Christ, have now become a part of the Body of Christ. The one qualification is to be *"Born-Again"* (Jn. 3:3).

While Water Baptism is the outward sign of that inward work already accomplished by Faith in Christ, still, it adds nothing to one's Salvation, which has come about solely by Faith (Eph. 2:8-9).

So, the idea that one has to become a Catholic, Baptist, Pentecostal, etc., to be saved is error! The many and varied church organizations around the world possibly are of some blessing and help to the furtherance of the Cause of Christ. However, regarding association and participation, they have absolutely nothing to do with one's Salvation. In other words, the Church, at least within itself, contains no Salvation. It is all in Jesus.

The idea that one is Saved because he belongs to a certain Church constitutes Scriptural ignorance. Where one attends Church is very important simply because of what is taught behind the pulpit. However, the act of belonging to or associating with a particular church organization and thinking it adds to one's Salvation, as stated, is error pure and simple.

WHAT TYPE OF CHURCH SHOULD ONE ATTEND?

If one's Spiritual Life is to be considered, the reason for one to attend a particular church should be and, in fact, must be in one of two categories:

1. That which is taught and preached behind the pulpit.
2. The Moving and Operation of the Holy Spirit in the Church.

Those are the only two things that matter. What type of social programs the Church may have is of little consequence. The fact that it is the same type of Church that one's family has always attended has no bearing either. Again, the name on the door is of little consequence. It is always to be judged according to the Word of God preached behind the pulpit and the Moving and Operation of the Holy Spirit in the services.

WHAT DOCTRINE IS SCRIPTURAL?

Of course, what is preached and taught behind the pulpit constitutes its doctrine, whatever that may be.

Naturally, the doctrine must be Biblical. And yet, almost all preachers claim to preach correct doctrine that is squarely based on the Word of God. So, it should be obvious that two individuals cannot be right if they have divergent conclusions.

According to the Word of God, the Doctrine should be as follows:

• Salvation by Faith in the shed Blood of Jesus, and Salvation by Faith in the shed Blood of Jesus Christ alone! (Eph. 2:8-9).

• The Baptism with the Holy Spirit with the evidence of *"speaking with other Tongues as the Spirit of God gives the utterance,"* which should be received shortly after being Born-Again. It is a separate and distinct experience with God that is separate and apart from Salvation. It does not make one more Saved but is meant to give one Power to do the Work of the Lord (Acts 2:4; 10:44-48; 19:1-7).

• Water Baptism *"in the Name of the Father, and of the Son, and of the Holy Spirit"* (Mat. 28:19).

• Divine Healing (Mk. 16:17-18).

• The Gifts of the Spirit in operation in the local Body (I Cor. 12:8-10).

• A victorious, overcoming Christian life, which can only be had by the Believer placing his or her Faith exclusively in Christ and what Christ has done for us at the Cross, and maintaining it exclusively in Christ and the Cross (Rom. 6:1-14; Lk. 9:23; Rom. 8:1-11).

• The Rapture of the Church, which could take place at any time (I Thess. 4:16-17).

• The Second Coming of the Lord with the Saints to rule and reign on this Earth (Rev., Chpt. 19).

Of course, there are many other particulars that enter into the Doctrine as here expressed; however, the guidelines we have given are Scriptural, and that should ever be the basis and foundation of our beliefs.

As well, there are so many divergent thoughts and opinions concerning Bible Doctrine, and common sense tells one that all cannot be correct. Considering how greatly significant all of this actually is, and especially considering that it pertains to our soul's Salvation, Jesus told us to also check the Fruit (Mat. 7:15-23).

CHURCH DENOMINATIONS

There is no such thing as a Church denomination in the Book of Acts or the Epistles. There is rather a fellowship of Churches, which I think the Holy Spirit actually intends.

The word *"Denomination"* actually means *"a designation or general name for a category, uniting in a single legal and administrative body, incorporating a number of local congregations."*

Within itself, there is nothing inherently wrong or unscriptural about forming a religious denomination or belonging to such. Ideally, such should be a tool to help promote the Cause of Christ, constituted by people of like Faith.

If it remains in that mode, no harm is done and, in fact, it can be a cause of great good.

However, the moment that its officers or adherents begin to apply unscriptural

NOTES

practices, such then becomes unscriptural and detrimental to the Cause of Christ. Regrettably, most religious denominations, even if they begin correctly, which some, no doubt, have, ultimately begin to think of their particular organization as something other than what it actually is. In other words, they attach spiritual elitism to their particular group and, as stated, add unscriptural practices, which we will momentarily discuss.

SCRIPTURAL OFFICES IN THE CHURCH

The only offices in the Church that are truly Spiritual and are Scriptural are those listed by the Apostle Paul, *"And He gave some, Apostles; and some, Prophets; and some, Evangelists; and some, Pastors and Teachers."*

He then said, *"For the perfecting of the Saints, for the Work of the Ministry, for the edifying of the Body of Christ"* (Eph. 4:11-12).

Anything other than these designations is man-originated and, therefore, man-instituted. In other words, that devised by man carries no Spiritual Authority.

That means that denominational offices, such as *"bishop* (the erroneous manner in which it came to be used), *superintendent, general superintendent, president, overseer, moderator,"* etc., are, in fact, not Scriptural offices.

However, once again, it is not wrong or unscriptural to have or hold these designations as long as one understands that they are merely administrative and hold no Scriptural Authority.

Of course, one holding one of these particular offices, who, most of the time, is elected by popular ballot, may at the same time have a definite Scriptural Calling, such as *"Apostle, Prophet, Evangelist, Pastor and Teacher."* However, the point must be made that these elected, man-devised offices add nothing whatsoever to the Scriptural Authority already ensconced in these Callings by the Lord.

The major problem occurs when men attach Spiritual Authority to these man-devised designations and then attempt to force others to subscribe to such pseudo-authority.

NOTES

When we go beyond the Word of God, we sin! It is that plain and simple!

RELIGIOUS HIERARCHY

A hierarchy is *"a ruling body of clergy organized into orders or ranks each subordinate to the one above it."*

Despite many religious denominations having such, which is characterized most of all by the Catholic church but is prominent in Protestant circles, as well, one will look in vain for any type of hierarchy in the Early Church. It simply does not exist. As well, it does not exist because it is improper, ungodly, and unscriptural.

The idea of a hierarchy is that God speaks to a committee, with them filtering such down to the subordinates and then to the masses; or else, they devise their own direction with God little consulted, if at all, which is generally the case. The Holy Spirit Personally leading individuals, which is the Bible way, is frowned on greatly by the hierarchy. The hierarchy demands total allegiance in that preachers are told where to go, what to do, how long to stay, and at times, what to preach! Regrettably, most religious denominations drift into the unscriptural direction of *"hierarchy,"* which more or less demands control. This pretty well stops the Holy Spirit from dealing with individual preachers, or anyone for that matter. If the Preacher in such an environment claims that God has given him directions to do some particular thing, such will not be looked at too favorably by the hierarchy.

THE EARLY CHURCH

If the Holy Spirit had desired for such to be, there would have been no better time than the Early Church. The Twelve Apostles who had walked shoulder-to-shoulder with Jesus for some three and one-half years would have been ideal candidates; however, they took no such position simply because such was not the Will of God.

Yes, there were leaders, as is obvious. However, these were men selected by the Holy Spirit.

For instance, even though Peter was initially the leader in the Early Church,

James, the Lord's half-brother, ultimately came to be the Pastor of the Church in Jerusalem.

As well, to spearhead world Evangelism, the Lord chose Paul, who did not accept Christ until approximately two years after the Day of Pentecost's Outpouring.

To be sure, had there been a religious hierarchy at that time, it is very doubtful that Paul would have written any Books of the New Testament, much less the meaning of the New Covenant, which is the Cross, given to him by the Lord. A religious hierarchy would have closed the door to such action immediately. The idea that God would give something of this nature to someone else other than them would not be tolerated.

So, from this, I hope that one can see how absolutely ungodly and unscriptural that such is. And yet, as stated, religious hierarchies are far more prominent in modern church circles than most realize.

DENOMINATIONALISM

Someone has defined *"denominationalism"* as somewhat akin to racism, which is an excellent comparison.

Racism, as most know, claims that if one is of a different color group or social standing, etc., he or she, consequently, is inferior.

Likewise, *"denominationalism"* is that which takes the *"denomination"* to the extreme. In other words, its adherents come to believe that one must belong to their particular denomination if one is to be saved. While some will not go that far, they do claim spiritual inferiority for all who are not members of their particular Church, etc.

When this happens, as it does very often, the truth is, such individuals nullify their own Salvation. Paul plainly said that if one attempts to add something to the Finished Work of Christ, *"Christ is become of no effect unto you, whosoever of you are justified by the Law* (claiming a particular Church saves, etc.); *you are fallen from Grace"* (Gal. 5:4).

Denominationalism adds to the Finished Work of Christ, in effect, claiming that what Jesus did at Calvary was necessary but not totally sufficient for one's Salvation. To complete the process, they say, other things must be done, such as *"Water Baptism," "membership in their church,"* etc.

NOTES

I suspect that more church members than one would realize are closer to *"denominationalism"* than many would think.

For instance, there are many Baptists who think that one has to be a Baptist in order to be saved. Actually, there are many Pentecostals in the same vein. Of course, it is obvious that Catholics believe this and say so openly! In other words, to be saved, one has to be a member of the Catholic church and faithful to its sacraments, etc.

As we have already stated, denominationalism has the direct opposite effect from that claimed by its adherents.

When a denomination begins to claim Spiritual Authority, that's when denominationalism sets in.

LOCAL CHURCH AUTHORITY

When one looks at the Book of Acts, one finds that the local Church constituted the highest Spiritual Authority.

This means that there was no such thing as a *"headquarters"* that decided policy for local Churches. To be sure, as stated, if the Holy Spirit had desired such, the Early Church would have been the time to have done such a thing.

In fact, what city in the world could compare with Jerusalem as a *"headquarters"*? While some doctrine was decided there according to Acts, Chapter 15, still, Jerusalem never did serve as a headquarters for the Move of God, even though it all began there on the Day of Pentecost. In fact, the Holy Spirit shifted the thrust from Jerusalem to Antioch as time went on (Acts 13:1-2).

As well, when Jesus addressed His Messages to the seven Churches of Asia, if one is to notice, He did not address the Message to *"headquarters"* at Jerusalem or Antioch, or any other place for that matter, other than the seven Churches in question, which He addressed each personally (Rev., Chpts. 2-3). If He had desired the recognition of some overall *"headquarters,"* once again, this would have been the perfect time to have done so. However, as stated, the Lord addressed His Message to each Church, and even to the Pastor of each Church. This tells us that there is no such thing as an outside authority respecting the local Church, other than the Lord Himself as the Chief Shepherd and Bishop.

In fact, in the New Testament, there is no warrant for ecclesiastical grades in the Ministry of the Churches by which there may be created an ascending series of rulers who shall govern the Churches that are merged into one vast ecclesiastical organization called *"the Church."* Such does not exist!

So, also, we are in position to see that there is no warrant for an ascending series of courts that may review any *"case"* that originates in a local Church. On the contrary, we may see that to each local Church has been committed by Christ the management of its own affairs, and that He had endowed every such Church with competency to perform every function that any ecclesiastical body has a right to perform.

Also, as the Churches are not to be dominated by any external ecclesiastical authority, so they are not to be interfered with in their Church life by civil government.

A FELLOWSHIP OF CHURCHES

While each local Church, according to the New Testament, is independent of every other in the sense that no other has jurisdiction over it, yet cooperative relations were entered into by New Testament Churches. Examples and indications of that may be found in Romans 15:1, 26-27; II Corinthians, Chapters 8 and 9; Galatians 2:10; and III John, Verse 8.

If a fellowship of Churches is that which the Holy Spirit has designed in the Book of Acts and the New Testament as a whole, it should stand to reason that such has continued to be His Will.

Fellowship consists of like doctrine, similar mission, and overall efforts. However, as stated, we do not find that any outside authority ever usurped the position of the local Church.

If this fundamental place and position is abrogated, the Headship of Christ, Who, incidentally, is a very active Head, will be impugned and maligned with man taking His Place. If such happens and, in fact, it happens constantly, the Spirit of God pulls back because man has usurped authority over the Lord. Such always characterizes the destruction of the Church, for the Holy Spirit will be subordinate to no one but Christ, and, as well, the Word of God must always govern all that is done (Eph. 1:22-23; Col. 1:18).

NOTES

CHURCH DISCIPLINE

Church discipline must always be handled by the local Church. In Matthew 18:17, our Lord, by anticipation, lodged final action in the sphere of the local Church. When the local Church, with no interference by outside ecclesiastical authorities, has taken action, the matter is ended. There is no direction given in Scripture to take it to a higher court. In fact, we are given a perfect example in the Word of God.

In I Corinthians, Chapter 5, there was a man brought to Paul's attention who was guilty of an infamous offense against purity (incest).

In that Chapter, Paul told the Church what they should do, but final action was left up to them.

If the individual, who seemed to be a Church leader, insisted on continuing on this sinful path, therefore, refusing to repent, he was to be disfellowshiped.

However, in II Corinthians, Chapter 2, a reference, which seems to be to this very case, shows that the Church acted upon Paul's advice and that proper action was taken.

The evidence is that the man truly repented, with Paul then counseling Restoration of this excluded member now right with God.

It is ironic! In I Corinthians, Chapter 5, the man was on trial. In II Corinthians, Chapter 2, the Church was now on trial. They were to restore him, which it seems they did.

Some claim that the individual in II Corinthians, Chapter 2, is not the same man as in I Corinthians, Chapter 5. That certainly may be true; however, in no way does it change the principle of the situation respecting discipline, irrespective as to who it was.

REPENTANCE

With wrongdoing, irrespective as to

who the offender may be, Repentance is demanded, which speaks of making things right with God and a forsaking of the particular sin or sins in question. That is all that is required in the Word of God. If anything else is added, such as *"penance,"* it constitutes an abrogation of the Grace of God and, in fact, nullifies the Gift of Grace.

After Repentance, Restoration is to be immediate with no penalties attached. In fact, the very principle of forgiveness sets aside the penalty.

Whatever the situation, the local Church must make the decision and do so to the best of their ability according to the Word of God.

Some cases may certainly require further wisdom, which will surely be granted by the Holy Spirit if needed (James 1:5).

For example, if a man is serving in the capacity of leadership respecting boys and is found to have molested one or more, even though he certainly may repent, and with all encouragement from the local Body, still, it would not be wise for him to be put back in the same position immediately, and maybe never. In fact, he should not even desire that particular position at the time inasmuch as his problem can cause hurt to others.

Believing that the Lord can do all things and knowing that He can set the captive free, such will become evident if the Lord has really performed the work of Deliverance sorely needed. That being the case, the brother can once again be used in any position.

RULES?

The idea is that it is unscriptural to lay down a set of rules that apply to any and all and for all situations. Each situation should be looked at by the leaders in the local Church respecting its merit or the lack thereof. Understanding that, each situation should be judged accordingly.

However, in all matters of discipline, the Love and Grace of God should be paramount in all decisions. The Word of God should be adhered to strictly concerning Repentance and Restoration. Last of all, even as Jesus said, *"Therefore all things whatsoever you would that men should do to you, you should do the same to them: For this is the Law and the Prophets"* (Mat. 7:12).

NOTES

As well, as the spirit of this Text proclaims, when it is necessary to pass judgment on others, do so as if you were judging yourself.

Respecting discipline, if Repentance is truly and Biblically engaged, forgiveness by all others is demanded.

The one sin that God will not forgive, other than blaspheming the Holy Spirit, is unforgiveness (Mat. 6:14-15).

(4) "BUT WE WILL GIVE OURSELVES CONTINUALLY TO PRAYER, AND TO THE MINISTRY OF THE WORD."

The overview is:

1. It is possible to frustrate the Grace of God, which means to hinder it coming to us, or even to stop it altogether (Gal. 2:21).

2. There is no way that Righteousness can come by law, rules, or regulations.

3. If Righteousness can come by these various means, then *"Christ is dead in vain."*

PROBLEMS!

It seems that the first contention in the Early Church was about the maintenance of widows, and it seemed that the answer of the Holy Spirit to this dilemma was seven men who were filled with the Holy Spirit and had the Wisdom of God.

Both Hebrews and Hellenists were Jews, as we have stated, but the Hebrews normally regarded the Hellenists as their inferiors.

This contention and its settlement show several things:

• How easily disputes may arise even among people who are filled with the Holy Spirit.

• How quickly they may be composed if grace and intelligence be used.

• How effective moderation and readiness to yield are in such misunderstandings, for all the seven men had Greek names, and they were undoubtedly appointed by the *"Hebrews"* who were in the majority.

• How free the Apostles were from the lust of power, for they handed the matter to the congregation for settlement. The selection of these officers rested with the people and their appointment with the Apostles.

In Verse 4, we are given direction by the Holy Spirit concerning the Will of God for

NOTES

those whom God has called for Ministry.

PRAYER

The phrase, *"But we will give ourselves continually to prayer,"* tells us that inasmuch as *"prayer"* is mentioned first, it is more important than preaching. The reason is obvious:

Without a proper prayer life, it is literally impossible for the Preacher of the Gospel to properly preach the Word or to have the Anointing of the Holy Spirit. Prayer is an absolute requirement and a requirement absolutely!

When I was a child, my grandmother taught me the value of prayer. I can see her face even unto this day. It would literally shine with anticipation when she would say to me, *"Jimmy, God is a big God so ask big."* That simple word of advice has helped me to touch this world for Christ. Any Believer who is too busy to pray is too busy.

Every morning before going to the studio for the telecast, I spend some time with the Lord, actually, about 20 minutes. Every afternoon after leaving the office and going home, I once again spend about 20 minutes with the Lord. I have many things to pray about, and the Lord has many things to say to me.

Let me say it again, *"If the preacher doesn't have a proper prayer life, he can forget about Ministry that will help or bless anyone."* That goes for laymen as well. If you want the Blessings of God, develop a prayer life, and your world will change a hundred times over for the better.

THE MINISTRY OF THE WORD

Even though we have alluded to the following elsewhere in these Volumes, due to the great significance of prayer, please allow me to address this very important subject again.

The phrase, *"And to the Ministry of the Word,"* proclaims the twin of prayer, which, without prayer, is of little consequence. In other words, for one to have a proper prayer life that brings outstanding results, one must know the Word of God. The two go hand in hand.

Of course, Peter was speaking here of preaching the Word, but one has to know the Word before one can successfully preach the Word.

Also, every layman should know the Word of God. In fact, every Believer should read the Bible completely through every year, beginning with Genesis, etc. If it's only 15 or 20 minutes a day that you can spend respecting the study of the Word of God, this you should do. As stated, start at the first of the Bible and go straight through. The Bible is a Story, the Story of man's Redemption, which is *"Jesus Christ and Him Crucified."*

However, at the outset, every single Believer must understand that while Jesus Christ is the Source of all things we receive from God, the Cross of Christ is the Means and the only Means by which all of these wonderful things are given to us. Consequently, one's Faith should ever be locked into Christ and the Cross.

Please understand, the entirety of the Story of the Bible is *"Jesus Christ and Him Crucified."* So, when your Faith is anchored in Christ and the Cross, then your Faith is anchored in the Word (Jn. 1:1-3, 14, 29; 14:6).

When one's Faith is properly anchored in Christ and the Cross, then prayer takes on a brand new meaning, and one will really then begin to understand the Word of God.

The Greek word for *"Ministry"* is *"Diakonia tou logou"* and means *"the Deaconship of the Word."*

As well, the actual Greek translation of the phrase, *"But we will give ourselves continually,"* says, *"but we will continue steadfastly."* In other words, this was not a momentary thing, but rather a lifestyle.

(5) "AND THE SAYING PLEASED THE WHOLE MULTITUDE: AND THEY CHOSE STEPHEN, A MAN FULL OF FAITH AND OF THE HOLY SPIRIT, AND PHILIP, AND PROCHORUS, AND NICANOR, AND TIMON, AND PARMENAS, AND NICOLAS A PROSELYTE OF ANTIOCH."

The diagram is:

1. We aren't holy because of what we *"do,"* but we are holy because of what He has already *"done."*
2. Consequently, our Faith must rest in the Finished Work of Christ, and that alone!

NOTES

THE WILL OF GOD

The phrase, *"And the saying pleased the whole multitude,"* proclaims wisdom the people could not fault. It was wisdom from above, consequently, given by the Lord.

If people truly want to do right, there is a solution for every problem. The evidence is that the Apostles earnestly sought the Lord respecting this difficulty, which could have caused division had it not been attended properly. The Lord gave them the answer, as He will do all who sincerely look to Him.

DEACONS

The phrase, *"And they chose Stephen, a man full of Faith and of the Holy Spirit, and Philip, and Prochorus, and Nicanor, and Timon, and Parmenas, and Nicolas a proselyte of Antioch,"* presents the seven men.

As we have stated, they all have Greek names, but some say that it does not necessarily mean they were Hellenists, for some Jews, it is said, had Greek or Latin names.

It is said of Stephen that he was *"a man full of Faith and of the Holy Spirit,"* which is the highest honor that could be paid any person. The next Chapter will relate his martyrdom, actually, the first one of the Early Church, or at least of which we are aware.

Nicolas was said to be a proselyte of Antioch.

There were two things required for the admission of a proselyte into the Jewish religion. They were circumcision and the offering of sacrifice. In the case of women, only the offering of sacrifice was required. For that reason, there were more women Converts than men.

The proselyte was received in the following manner: He was first asked his reason for wishing to embrace Judaism. He was told that Israel was in a state of affliction. If he replied that he was aware of the fact and felt himself unworthy to share these afflictions, he was admitted.

Then he received instruction in some of the *"light"* and *"heavy"* Commandments, the rules concerning gleaning and tithes, and the penalties attached to the breach of the Commandments.

If he was willing to submit to all of this, he was circumcised, and after his recovery, he was to offer the sacrifice without delay.

At this stage, a new name was given him. He was either named *"Abraham the son of Abraham,"* or the Scriptures were opened at hazard, and the first name that was read was given to him. Thenceforth, he had to put behind him all his past; even his marriage ties and those of kinship no longer held good.

Although he was now considered to be a new man, on the whole, he was looked down on as inferior to a born Jew.

So, all this that *"Nicolas"* did in order to become a Jewish proselyte would be laid aside as he was, no doubt, now excommunicated from the synagogue due to being a follower of Christ.

As previously stated, only Stephen and Philip are mentioned after this, with the others mentioned only here.

(6) "WHOM THEY SET BEFORE THE APOSTLES: AND WHEN THEY HAD PRAYED, THEY LAID THEIR HANDS ON THEM."

The form is:

1. The phrase, *"Whom they set before the Apostles,"* concerns the seven men chosen by the people now presented for acceptance or confirmation, etc.

2. *"And when they had prayed, they laid their hands on them,"* does not refer to the laying on of hands to impart the Holy Spirit or some such gift. In this case, the laying on of hands was to designate them for this particular work of the Ministry for which they had been called.

3. The *"laying on of hands"* is not something new, but rather has been practiced down through the ages, whether for blessing or to set individuals apart for a special work (Gen. 48:14; Deut. 34:9; Mat. 19:15; Mk. 6:5; 16:17-18; Lk. 4:40; 13:13; Acts 5:12; 6:6; 8:17-19; 9:17; 11:30; 13:3; 14:3; 19:6, 11; 28:8; Heb. 6:2).

4. The *"laying on of hands"* has no special power within itself and is not meant to convey such; however, it is meant, in a sense, to be the Hand of the Lord extended through Believers in order to bless or ordain. Inasmuch as it is meant to symbolically portray the Hand of the Lord extended, any

Believer can serve in that capacity (Mk. 16:17-18).

(7) "AND THE WORD OF GOD INCREASED; AND THE NUMBER OF THE DISCIPLES MULTIPLIED IN JERUSALEM GREATLY; AND A GREAT COMPANY OF THE PRIESTS WERE OBEDIENT TO THE FAITH."

The pattern is:

1. The moment the believing sinner evidences Faith in Christ, in the Mind of God, that person becomes one with our Substitute, Who is Jesus Christ.

2. Consequently, all of what He did at the Cross becomes ours.

THE WORD OF GOD INCREASED

The phrase, *"And the Word of God increased,"* means that more and more men were preaching the Gospel of Jesus Christ.

As we have already stated, that which they preached was the Old Testament Prophecies concerning the Lord Jesus Christ. As well, they preached His Crucifixion, Resurrection, and Ascension. They also preached strongly concerning the Baptism with the Holy Spirit and how He was intended for every Believer, as is evidenced in Acts 8:14-17.

"And the number of the Disciples multiplied in Jerusalem greatly," proclaims that which happens when the Word of God is faithfully preached. The Word increases and the Conversions multiply.

"And a great company of the Priests were obedient to the Faith," presents one of the greatest Testimonies to date of the Power of God. That many of these men were Saved who, in fact, had formerly been bitter enemies of Christ shows exactly how powerful this Move of God actually was.

It stands to reason that the *"Priests"* who came to Christ, especially at this time, would face terrible persecution by the Sanhedrin. However, no price is too high to pay, no sacrifice too great to make, no journey too long to undertake, and no way too hard to travel, even to the giving up of one's life in order to find, have, and hold the Lord Jesus Christ.

To know Him is to know life! To not know Him forfeits all life.

NOTES

A PERSONAL EXPERIENCE

As an example, some years ago, I had the occasion to preach a Service in San Jose, Costa Rica.

Actually, I had gone with my associates to visit a school that our Ministry had just built. While there, we conducted a short Service for the teachers, etc.

Even though I was preaching through an interpreter, the Spirit of God fell mightily over that small group that morning. I found out that either two or three of the teachers were former Catholic nuns, who had been brought to Christ as a result of hearing us preach the Gospel over television.

The Spirit of God moved upon them mightily that morning, which I am certain they very much needed. After the Service, they related to me how they were cut off from their families once they accepted Christ. After being sheltered in the Catholic church for all of those years, they were now turned out with no place to go and not knowing what they would do. However, two things came into vogue:

1. They had now found Jesus and actually knew what it meant to be truly Born-Again. As such, they had found a life in Christ that they had never known existed. Consequently, whatever price they had to pay was, in fact, nothing, considering what they had won in Christ.

2. Once they accepted Christ, they came under His Provision, and the Lord made a way for them, as He makes a way for all who take upon themselves His wonderful Name.

THE CAUSE OF CHRIST

But yet, being human, they hurt and suffered, realizing their loved ones had now turned their backs upon them, in effect, disowning them.

It should be mentioned that hundreds of thousands, if not millions, down through the centuries have given up their lives for the Cause of Christ.

In other words, they suffered death for their Testimony. Others have been maltreated in a terrible manner. The point is that if Christianity is a fake and Christ just another poor deluded Preacher, it is hardly likely that this tremendous number of people would have laid down their lives for such. To be sure, no religion in the world has ever even remotely garnered such allegiance.

These *"Priests"* left everything because, for the first time in their lives, they had found reality. They were not engaging a mere philosophy, but rather a Person, and even more than that, the Lord Jesus Christ, God manifest in the flesh, the Saviour of men. That is why millions have given up everything in order to serve Him.

(8) "AND STEPHEN, FULL OF FAITH AND POWER, DID GREAT WONDERS AND MIRACLES AMONG THE PEOPLE."

The record is:

1. The phrase, *"And Stephen, full of faith and power,"* speaks of a great knowledge of the Word of God, for Faith comes by hearing and hearing by the Word of God. It will be very obvious in the next Chapter just how knowledgeable in the Word this man was as he stood before the Sanhedrin.

As well, the *"Power"* speaks of the Holy Spirit and the control He had over Stephen.

"Did great wonders and miracles among the people," speaks of Healings and other things that are obviously beyond the ability of a mere human. In other words, these things were divinely done!

Actually, the Lord's use of Stephen, even as many others in the Acts account, portrays to us in glaring detail that this special Power was not limited only to the Twelve Apostles. This Power is available to anyone, with the only criterion being that one is baptized with the Holy Spirit and truly believes (Mk. 16:15-18).

We know from Verse 5 that Faith and Power accompany the Holy Spirit and without the Holy Spirit, there is no faith and power, at least to speak of. As well, I am speaking of the Baptism with the Holy Spirit with the evidence of speaking with other Tongues (Acts 1:8; 2:4).

(9) "THEN THERE AROSE CERTAIN OF THE SYNAGOGUE, WHICH IS CALLED THE SYNAGOGUE OF THE LIBERTINES, AND CYRENIANS, AND ALEXANDRIANS, AND OF THEM OF CILICIA AND OF ASIA, DISPUTING WITH STEPHEN."

NOTES

The pattern is:

1. The phrase, *"Then there arose certain of the synagogue, which is called the synagogue of the Libertines,"* speaks of Jews who had been taken as slaves to Rome or elsewhere in the Roman Empire but now had been set free, consequently, coming back to Jerusalem. They had a synagogue in Jerusalem, and maybe even several, which were especially for these particular people. Actually, there is said to have been 480 synagogues in Jerusalem at the time of Christ.

2. The phrase, *"And Cyrenians, and Alexandrians, and of them of Cilicia and of Asia,"* pertains to each one of these groups of Jews who had a synagogue in Jerusalem.

3. For instance, the population of Cyrene was about one-fourth Jews, with the population of Alexandria consisting of about 100,000 Jews, nearly one-half of the population of the city.

4. At the time of the Feasts, these Jews would come from these cities, plus others not named, with each group, it seems, having a synagogue in Jerusalem. As well, when many of them moved back to Jerusalem, whether to retire or for whatever purpose, they attended the synagogue that they had always considered to be theirs.

5. Cyrene was the chief city of North Africa, with Alexandria one of the chief cities of Egypt.

6. Cilicia was located in what is now known as Turkey. As well, there is a possibility that Saul of Tarsus could have been among those of Cilicia, as Tarsus was in that region.

7. Asia was also in the area now known as Turkey. It was also the area of the seven Churches addressed by Jesus in Revelation, Chapters 2 and 3.

8. The phrase, *"Disputing with Stephen,"* is especially interesting. It is thought by some that Paul, then known as Saul, was the leading disputer against Stephen.

9. Having been a student of the great Gamaliel, Paul was thought to have been at this time one of the greatest scholars of the Mosaic Law.

(10) "AND THEY WERE NOT ABLE TO RESIST THE WISDOM AND THE SPIRIT

NOTES

BY WHICH HE SPOKE."

The order is:

1. If, in fact, it was Paul who led the dispute against Stephen, this exchange would have been immensely interesting to behold. Paul, given up to be one of the leading Hebrew scholars of his time, and actually being groomed to take the place of the vaunted Gamaliel, would have thought of himself as able to batter the arguments of Stephen into the ground. After all, Stephen had no formal training, at least that is known, and would have been given no credence at all at that time by Paul, or anyone else for that matter, respecting Jewish scholars and teachers.

2. The word *"disputing"* means *"to argue, to debate, to fully investigate."*

3. The investigation was Jesus Christ and Who He was relative to the Word of God. To be sure, Paul was an able scholar, even as his writings portray; however, the difference was Jesus Christ and the Holy Spirit. In other words, Stephen was *"Born-Again"* and full of the Holy Spirit, while Paul was not Saved but merely religious. Consequently, Paul had no help at all from the Holy Spirit, while Stephen was helped greatly.

4. In front of the crowd, it seems, Stephen capably and powerfully portrayed Jesus Christ from the Scriptures and then countered every thrust made by Paul, which would have embarrassed Paul greatly, especially considering who he was and the contempt that he had for Stephen.

5. Of course, to lose an argument of this nature in front of all of these people, and to lose it to one of little note or none altogether, would have been a great blow to Paul's pride; consequently, all of these individuals would have grown very angry at Stephen.

6. Once again, I emphasize the fact that there is no concrete proof that Paul was actually the one disputing Stephen, but that it is possible that he could have done so. If so, this would have been approximately two years before his Conversion on the road to Damascus.

7. As well, I wish to maintain the position that one cannot properly know and understand the Word of God without one being baptized with the Holy Spirit (Acts 2:4); however, that in no way means that Spirit-filled Believers are Bible scholars, etc. In fact, sadly, many know very little about the Word of God; however, that is not the fault of the Spirit, but rather their fault.

8. When one receives the Baptism with the Holy Spirit, it is always total and complete respecting the Believer. As should be obvious, it is not possible to receive the Holy Spirit partly, etc. However, being baptized with the Holy Spirit within itself is only a beginning of what He can do in the life of the Believer if given the opportunity. In other words, that which He can do in the life of the individual is potential in nature. The potential is there but may or may not be realized according to the consecration and dedication of the person.

9. Stephen is an excellent example. The Scripture plainly says that he was full of Faith and Power, i.e., the Holy Spirit. It seems that he allowed the Holy Spirit to have total control within his life, which gave him an insight into the Scriptures over and beyond what one would normally have. However, this does not mean that all Spirit-filled Believers at that time had the same wisdom and Power as Stephen. They could have, and some few possibly did. However, there were, no doubt, many even at that time who little allowed, even as today, the Holy Spirit to have the control He desired in order that He might do and be what was necessary. As stated, His abiding in a person is potential in nature, with very little coming automatically.

(11) "THEN THEY SUBORNED MEN, WHICH SAID, WE HAVE HEARD HIM SPEAK BLASPHEMOUS WORDS AGAINST MOSES, AND AGAINST GOD."

The account is:

1. The phrase, *"Then they suborned men,"* speaks of the anger registered in the hearts of those who had been bested by Stephen in the disputation.

2. The word *"suborned"* means *"to do something by stealth, and to be in collusion."* In other words, they planned and formed a scheme together that held no validity or truth. Incidentally, the scholars say that if, in fact, Paul was the leading antagonist respecting the disputation, he

NOTES

was not a party to this scheme that cost Stephen his life.

3. The phrase, *"Which said, We have heard him speak blasphemous words against Moses, and against God,"* concerns their concocted scheme.

4. It must be remembered that at this time, the whole Jewish people were in a state of ill-suppressed frenzy and most sensitive jealousy for the honor of the Mosaic institutions—feelings that broke out in constant revolts against the Roman power. The accusation against the Apostles, and especially Stephen, of speaking blasphemies against Moses was, therefore, the most likely one they could have pitched upon to stir up ill will against them.

5. In truth, neither Stephen nor any of the Apostles had ever spoken anything *"against Moses, and against God."*

6. The word *"blasphemous"* in the Greek is *"blasphemos"* and means *"to say that which is scurrilous or calumnious against God or man."*

7. Exactly what Stephen said, we are not told. However, it is positive that he lifted up Jesus as the Messiah and the fulfillment of all the Prophecies. He, no doubt, exclaimed His Resurrection and Ascension. As well, as stated, he probably tied all of this to the Prophecies, which they were not able to successfully counter. Therefore, if they could not refute His Message, they would silence the Messenger.

8. Please forgive my repetition, but the spirit that characterized these individuals, which resulted in Stephen's death, is very much alive and well in the apostate church at the present time. What we will see in the death of Stephen is a perfect example of what I say. One cannot be on God's side and fight God at the same time! One cannot be obeying God and at the same time silencing one who is Called of God.

9. The truth is, as is obvious, even though these Jews talked about God constantly and were extremely religious, still, they did not really know God at all and were tools of Satan. In fact, the way these Jews conducted themselves at this particular time is very similar to the way the Muslims do presently. Actually, all of this, the Jews of 2,000 years ago and the Muslims at present, are perfect examples of religion.

(12) "AND THEY STIRRED UP THE PEOPLE, AND THE ELDERS, AND THE SCRIBES, AND CAME UPON HIM, AND CAUGHT HIM, AND BROUGHT HIM TO THE COUNCIL."

The structure is:

1. The phrase, *"And they stirred up the people, and the Elders, and the Scribes,"* refers to the lies they told and kept telling respecting Stephen.

2. As Jezebel employed false witnesses to accuse Naboth of speaking against God and against the government, so false witnesses were suborned to accuse Stephen of blaspheming God, Moses, and the Temple.

3. The phrase, *"And came upon him, and caught him, and brought him to the Council,"* refers to them getting permission from the Sanhedrin to arrest Stephen, which they did.

4. The *"Council"* was the Sanhedrin, before which he would be tried.

(13) "AND SET UP FALSE WITNESSES, WHICH SAID, THIS MAN CEASES NOT TO SPEAK BLASPHEMOUS WORDS AGAINST THIS HOLY PLACE, AND THE LAW."

The Word is:

1. The phrase, *"And set up false witnesses,"* proclaims the similarity of Stephen's trial with that of our Lord.

2. Hervey said, *"The same set purpose to silence a true-speaking tongue by death; the same base employment of false witnesses; the same wresting of good words into criminal acts; and the same meekness and patience unto death in the Righteous Martyrs."*

3. He then said, *"Blessed servant to tread so closely in thy Lord's Steps!"*

4. The phrase, *"Which said, This man ceases not to speak blasphemous words against this Holy Place, and the Law,"* is pretty much sum-med up in four accusations against Stephen. They are as follows:

a. They claimed he blasphemed Moses by making Christ greater than Moses. Of course, Christ was greater than Moses!

b. They claimed he blasphemed God by exalting Christ greater than the Temple and the Law. As well, Jesus was greater than these things.

c. They claimed he blasphemed the Temple by saying that Christ would destroy it. That is not really what Stephen said. He, no doubt, quoted the Words of Christ, Who said, concerning the Temple, that *"not one stone would be left upon another"* (Dan. 9:26; Mat. 24:1-3; Lk. 21:20-24).

d. They claimed he blasphemed the Law by saying that Christ had abolished the Law and made a New Covenant. In fact, Jesus had made a New Covenant, which was introduced at the Last Supper. However, the details of that Covenant had not yet been given and, in fact, would not be given for some time yet, when it was ultimately given to the Apostle Paul.

5. The truth is that the New Covenant definitely would replace the Old Covenant, which Stephen, no doubt, pointed out in the Law of Moses, which foretold of this coming day (Deut. 18:15).

6. While the detractors of Stephen would have possibly admitted all of these things, they would not admit that Jesus was the One Who fulfilled these Prophecies. They had murdered Him, and they now had to attempt to justify themselves in this horrible action by continuing to oppose Him. To be sure, it would fall out to their hurt, and great hurt at that.

7. If, in fact, Paul was the one who disputed with Stephen, it is ironic that this wonderful New Covenant mentioned by Stephen (if he did allude to such) would ultimately be given by the Lord to this very man Paul. At that moment, there was no way that anyone could have even remotely imagined that such a thing would happen. The greatest hater of Christ would be stricken down on the road to Damascus, even in the very midst of this hate, and as a result, would become possibly the greatest lover of Christ the world has ever known.

8. What a mighty God we serve!

(14) "FOR WE HAVE HEARD HIM SAY, THAT THIS JESUS OF NAZARETH SHALL DESTROY THIS PLACE, AND SHALL CHANGE THE CUSTOMS WHICH MOSES DELIVERED US."

The account is:

NOTES

1. The phrase, *"For we have heard him say,"* represents a distortion of what Stephen had probably said. They probably based their accusation upon some semblance of truth but totally distorted its meaning, as is obvious.

2. *"That this Jesus of Nazareth,"* is proclaimed in such a way as to be most contemptuous.

3. *"Shall destroy this place,"* probably referred to the Words said by Jesus, as stated, in the Olivet discourse.

4. His exact Words were, *"See ye not all these things? verily I say unto you, There shall not be left here one stone upon another, that shall not be thrown down"* (Mat. 24:2).

5. He did not say that He or His Followers would do such a thing but merely predicted what would happen, which, in fact, did happen when Titus destroyed the Temple in A.D. 70.

6. *"And shall change the customs which Moses delivered us,"* once again represents a play on words.

7. In fact, He would change the customs, which He had the right to do as God manifest in the flesh, and above all, He fulfilled what the *"customs"* represented.

8. In no way did He destroy or denigrate these *"customs,"* but rather fulfilled them, which is the very reason He came.

9. In fact, He was the very One Who gave these *"customs"* to Moses in the first place! Of course, they would not in any way admit to that! Stephen's undoubted Testimony that Jesus of Nazareth was God would be regarded by these men as blasphemy against God.

(15) "AND ALL THAT SAT IN THE COUNCIL, LOOKING STEDFASTLY ON HIM, SAW HIS FACE AS IT HAD BEEN THE FACE OF AN ANGEL."

The account is:

1. The phrase, *"And all that sat in the Council, looking stedfastly on him,"* represents them hearing this false testimony and then turning to Stephen to receive his answer to these charges.

2. The word *"stedfastly"* means *"to gaze intently"* for purpose and reason.

3. In other words, they saw something on his face that they probably had never

seen before in their lives. As a result, they stared in wide-eyed astonishment!

4. The phrase, *"Saw his face as it had been the face of an Angel,"* pertains to the Lord permitting His Glory to shine upon the face of Stephen so as to convince the people that what Stephen had said was the Truth. Just about everything in the Early Church was miraculous. It had to be, considering the opposition that Satan brought against this fledgling effort. If the Lord had not been with the Apostles and those in the Early Church, it simply could not have survived.

5. As we see here, this very Sanhedrin who had condemned Christ to death was still being dealt with by the Holy Spirit in miraculous ways in order to bring them to Repentance, but to no avail.

6. They had witnessed the miraculous Deliverance of the Apostles from the prison cell, which they could not deny. Now they observed Stephen's face as it shone with the Glory of God, which they could not deny either. In the face of incontrovertible proof, they continued to blaspheme and to rebel. Actually, they were doing the very thing (blaspheming) of which they accused Stephen, but which he did not do. While trying to destroy the Work of God, they were destroying themselves; however, they were so numb with hate and rebellion against God that they simply could not see.

7. A willful rejection of Truth always brings judicial judgment. No people on Earth had been offered more Light than these. Consequently, no people on Earth rejected such Light as these! As a result, no people on Earth have suffered such judgment as these—but judgment brought upon themselves, even after repeated warnings, as here!

"From Bethlehem's manger came forth a Stranger,
"Humble and lowly, I'd be like Him,
"Oh! Precious Saviour, with kindly favor,
"A Friend to all, I'd be like Him."

"The soldiers bound Him, with thorns they crowned Him,
"Enduring all that, I'd be like Him,
"They did deride Him and crucified Him,
"Submissive I'd be more like Him."

"To be like Jesus, to be like Jesus,
"I only ask to just be like Him,
"In life that's lowly, in heart that's holy,
"Oh how I long to be just like Him."

NOTES

CHAPTER 7

(1) "THEN SAID THE HIGH PRIEST, ARE THESE THINGS SO?"

The form is:

1. The Doctrine of the Cross of Christ is the very first Doctrine devised by the Holy Spirit.

2. It was devised before the world was even created (I Pet. 1:18-20).

3. Every Bible Doctrine is built squarely on the Cross (I Cor. 2:2).

THE JUDGMENT OF GOD

Stephen stood before the Sanhedrin, and once again the Lord would seek to turn them around. Of course, this group of men had no idea that their time was running short, with the most horrible judgment they had ever known soon to break upon them unless they repented.

Many Believers, and the world in general for that matter, have a wrong conception concerning the Judgment of God.

Inasmuch as this is the Dispensation of Grace, they have the idea that the Judgment of God is not pronounced during this time, or else, if it is, it is to a much lesser degree than in Old Testament Times. However, they have it directly backwards.

As we have previously stated, Paul would later say, speaking of Old Testament Times, *"And the times of this ignorance God winked at; but now commands all men every where to repent"* (Acts 17:30).

Inasmuch as the world had very little Light in Old Testament Times, God little called to account particular acts or degrees of sin. This did not mean that they were declared innocent or not guilty because of this ignorance, for they were sinners and died lost. It simply meant that the terrible wickedness that then prevailed was not called to account at that time unless the situation became intolerable. As a matter of fact, that is what happened concerning the flood and with Sodom and Gomorrah, as well as many other incidents that could be named.

THE WRATH OF GOD

Actually, that is why Jonah was told by the Lord to go to Nineveh and cry out against it. Their wickedness had become so great that if they had not repented at the preaching of Jonah, every indication is that the Lord would have destroyed them exactly as He did Sodom and Gomorrah. As it was, they had only 40 days to repent (Jonah 3:4).

To be sure, there is no way that a rival army could have besieged Nineveh in that length of time, and, in fact, there was no army in the world at that time capable of doing such. Therefore, had they not repented, the Lord would have taken them out with an earthquake, by plague, or even by calling fire down from Heaven exactly as He did the twin cities at the time of Abraham.

No! The truth is that inasmuch as this is the Day of Grace with great Light being given to the world due to the Advent of the Holy Spirit in the world, the Judgment of God is much more pronounced during this time than it was in Old Testament Times. Actually, Paul said concerning the Day of Grace, *"For the Wrath of God is revealed from Heaven against all ungodliness and unrighteousness of men, who hold the truth in unrighteousness"* (Rom. 1:18).

Concerning the Gospel Light, Jesus said, *"For unto whomsoever much is given, of him shall be much required"* (Lk. 12:48).

In truth, the Judgment of God against sin and sinners is more pronounced today and more active than ever before. As we have stated, due to the Advent of the Holy Spirit, much Gospel Light has been shed abroad in the world. As a result, sinning against that Light, which Old Testament Times were not able to do, brings the Wrath of God in a far more pronounced manner.

NOTES

In truth, the climactic conditions, such as tornadoes, storms, floods, earthquakes, etc., are all tied to the rejection of the Light. The same can be said for the economic and the social situations, which are all tied to the spirituality, or lack thereof, in a person, family, city, nation, continent, or even the entirety of the world.

Even in a more pronounced way, all of these things are basically tied to the spiritual temperature of the Church, i.e., the Body of Christ. The world is one thing, but God's People are something else altogether. Their spiritual conduct, be it negative or positive, decides to a great degree all that happens respecting these things I have just mentioned.

In other words, America has the president she has because of the spiritual condition of the church. If that improves, everything else improves as well. If it deteriorates, and I speak again concerning the Church, all else deteriorates as well!

Also, we should mention that sins of passion, as wicked as they are and as destructive as they are, are not really that which destroys the church. As we have already stated, it is the sin of pride in the church that destroys its effectiveness. It speaks of a wrong direction, a disbelief of the Word of God, the presentation of a false salvation, i.e. a departure from the Faith, etc. That is the real danger in the church and always has been.

So, the High Priest desired to know if these charges were true that were leveled against Stephen.

(2) "AND HE SAID, MEN, BRETHREN, AND FATHERS, HEARKEN; THE GOD OF GLORY APPEARED UNTO OUR FATHER ABRAHAM, WHEN HE WAS IN MESOPOTAMIA, BEFORE HE DWELT IN CHARRAN."

The record is:

1. Unfortunately, the greater part of the modern church now claims that psychology holds the solution to man's behavioral problems.

2. They simply do not believe that the Cross of Christ holds the answers (Heb. 4:1-11).

3. One cannot hold to humanistic

psychology and the Cross of Christ at the same time. Either one cancels out the other.

THE RELIGIOUS HIERARCHY OF ISRAEL

The phrase, *"And he said,"* even though coming from the mouth of Stephen, nevertheless was coming directly from God. In other words, his Message to these rulers of Israel was as if the Lord Himself was standing there delivering these words. Actually, it is the same with all who are truly God-called.

To speak to the issues, God uses those whom He has chosen. Consequently, they had better be heeded! As well, the Psalmist said, *"Touch not Mine Anointed, and do My Prophets no harm"* (Ps. 105:15).

The phrase, *"Men, brethren, and fathers,"* addresses (and is meant to address) the religious hierarchy of Israel.

These men were *"brethren"* of Stephen only in the sense that they were all Jews. They were *not "brethren"* according to service for the Lord.

The one word *"hearken"* speaks volumes! God was speaking through Stephen and, as such, must be heeded.

This offer of Salvation was made through the Hellenist Stephen and not through the chief Apostle Peter, and the offer was made at Jerusalem, which was the city of the Great King (the Lord Jesus Christ) and the ecclesiastical center of the Nation.

In a sense, Peter had declared (Acts 3:19-21) that if they repented, the King would return immediately, introduce *"the times of refreshing,"* and restore all things.

However, Israel rejected this Testimony, and as a consequence, the Holy Spirit, through the mouth of Stephen, pronounced judgment upon them.

THE LAST ADAM

The phrase, *"The God of Glory appeared unto our father Abraham,"* does not tell us exactly how this was done. It may have been a visible appearance, or the Lord may have used someone else to deliver the Message.

In fact, Shem, the son of Noah, was still alive at that particular time. It could very well be that the Lord used him to testify to Abraham.

NOTES

However, it does not really matter exactly how it was done, but that it was done.

In order for the Redeemer to come and for the Prophecy to be fulfilled, as given by the Lord in Genesis 3:15, it was necessary that God would literally become flesh, i.e., *"Man."* In effect, He was to be the Last Adam Who would succeed, whereas, the first Adam failed.

Due to the fact that the whole of humanity was in the loins of Adam, with him serving as the federal head of the human race, when he failed, all of humanity was thrust into the same condition. It is what is referred to as *"original sin."* Adam and Eve having the ability to bring offspring into the world and being the first parents, in essence, spoke and acted for the entirety of the human family for all time. So, in order that man be redeemed, another Adam would have to come upon the scene, which was done in the Person of Jesus Christ (Rom. 5:12, 17-18; I Cor. 15:22, 45-50).

In order that this be done (the coming of the Last Adam, Jesus Christ), certain things had to be done.

The Lord would have to raise up a particular people, who were not then in the world, and to whom He could give His Word and bring about the fulfillment of this Great Promise in Genesis 3:15.

ABRAHAM

After the Flood, the Lord spoke to Noah, saying to him, *"Blessed be the LORD God of Shem,"* who was one of Noah's sons. This meant that of the three sons of Noah—the other two being Ham and Japheth—through Shem's lineage would come the Messiah (Gen. 9:25-27).

To carry forth this Promise, the Lord called Abraham, who was of the lineage of Shem. From his loins would come the Jewish people, who would be different than any people on the face of the Earth. Concerning them and their uniqueness, the Lord would later say, *"Lo, the people shall dwell alone, and shall not be reckoned among the Nations"* (Num. 23:9). In fact, they would be a Nation, but not like other nations. They were to be a Holy People set apart for a special purpose.

To them the Lord would give His Word, which we refer to as the Bible, and, as well, they would serve as the womb of the Messiah.

Another Prophecy was given, saying, *"There shall come a Star out of Jacob, and a Sceptre shall rise out of Israel, and shall smite the corners of Moab, and destroy all the children of Sheth"* (Num. 24:17).

So, from Abraham's loins would come these people called Israelites, through whom the Messiah would come (Gen. 12:1-3).

Why did God specifically choose Abraham?

In fact, Abraham was an idolater when God spoke to him (Josh. 24:2). So, it was not because of any Righteousness on the part of Abraham that caused him to be selected. Actually, there were two reasons God chose him specifically:

1. As we have stated, whoever He called had to be of the lineage of Shem. Abraham was of that lineage.

2. God looked at his heart and despite the fact that he was an idol-worshiper at that time, knew that he hungered for something more than these dead idols. In fact, every evidence is that the Lord makes all choices of this nature on the basis of the heart condition, which only God can tell. The Lord said through Samuel, *"For the Lord sees not as man sees; for man looks on the outward appearance, but the Lord looks on the heart"* (I Sam. 16:7).

IRAQ

The phrase, *"When he was in Mesopotamia, before he dwelt in Charran,"* speaks of the country between the Tigris and Euphrates Rivers, actually modern Iraq. The exact place in that land was Ur of the Chaldees (Gen. 15:7).

It is said that this ancient city was dedicated to the worship of the moon god. It lay about 150 miles south of Babylon.

The city for the times was very developed. And yet, a part of its worship was the sacrifice of human beings.

Whenever particular kings died, at least with some of them, their most trusted aides were sacrificed and buried with them.

No wonder that when God would select a man of Ur through whom He would begin a new Revelation of hope to the world, He said, *"You must get out of your country, and from your kindred, and from your father's house, unto a land that I will show you"* (Gen. 12:1).

"Charran" was the *"Haran"* of Genesis 11:31. It was about 600 miles north of Ur.

From the Text, we know that the Lord spoke to Abraham while he was still living in Mesopotamia (Ur of the Chaldees), with him at the time relocating in Haran. However, as we shall see, it was not until his father, Terah, died that Abraham set out on the pilgrimage to the land of Canaan. He was 75 years old at that time and had probably lived in Haran after leaving Ur for about two or three years.

Incidentally, this place called *"Haran"* was where Isaac and Jacob got their wives and where most of Jacob's sons were born.

(3) "AND SAID UNTO HIM, GET OUT OF YOUR COUNTRY, AND FROM YOUR KINDRED, AND COME INTO THE LAND WHICH I SHALL SHOW YOU."

The form is:

1. The Cross was ever God's Answer to man's dilemma.

2. This was given at the very dawn of time immediately after the fall of Adam and Eve (Gen. 3:15).

SEPARATION BUT NOT ISOLATION

The phrase, *"And said unto him, Get out of your country,"* pertained to a land of idol-worship, as we have already stated.

In Stephen's review of the national history, he began with Abraham and recalled the Glory of the Grace that chose that idolater. It was the Glory of that Grace that gave meaning to the magnificent appellation, *"The God of Glory."* It was not an outward physical glory, but the Glory of absolutely free Grace, for Abraham was *"a Syrian ready to perish"* (Deut. 26:5).

Prior to the Flood, the Earth was filled with violence; subsequent to the Flood, it was filled with idolatry. Electing Grace chose one of these idolaters, Abraham, as we have already stated. Then Law was given to make Abraham's sons conscious that they were sinners and needed a Saviour.

The Prophets followed in patient Grace, and finally, the Son was sent. He was crucified, but in Grace, He sent the Holy Spirit.

Through Peter, He pleaded with Israel for Repentance, and upon their refusal, He reviewed their history by the mouth of Stephen and so judged them.

He manifested His Power and Glory in the tongues of fire on the heads of those who were baptized with the Holy Spirit on the Day of Pentecost, and in connection with Stephen, His Power and Glory in Heaven as it was displayed on Stephen's face.

Thus, Heaven and Earth united in testifying that Jesus of Nazareth was the God of Glory Who appeared to Abraham.

The phrase, *"And from your kindred,"* in effect, says they were idol-worshipers.

It has been argued that Abraham was wrong in taking Lot, his nephew, with him in that it was disobedient to the Command. However, Lot's father, Haran, had died, and it seems as if Abraham had taken the responsibility of raising the boy (Gen. 11:27-28; 12:5).

Flaws in Lot's character first appeared when he selfishly chose the well-watered Jordan Valley (Gen. 13:8-13). This brought him into the midst of the wicked men of Sodom, and he had to be rescued from the results of his folly, first by Abraham (Gen. 14:11-16), and then by the two Angels (Gen., Chpt. 19).

In the latter incident, he revealed both his weakness and his inclination to compromise.

Through his drunkenness, his two daughters obtained children by him, and these became the ancestors of the Moabites and the Ammonites, who were bitter enemies of Israel (Gen. 19:30-38; Deut. 2:9, 19, Ps. 83:8).

The Lord illustrated His Teaching on the subject of His Return from the story of Lot and his wife (Lk. 17:28-32), thus, setting His Seal upon its historicity. Peter, as well, asserted the Righteousness of Lot (II Pet. 2:7).

Even though Lot's situation did not seem to be positive at all, one finds it difficult to condemn Abraham for taking his nephew with him to Canaan, even though Isaac was not born to Abraham and Sarah until the separation from the nephew was complete (Gen. 21:1-3).

NOTES

The phrase, *"And come into the land which I shall show you,"* refers to the land of Canaan.

Consequently, in order that the Messiah could be brought into the world, the Lord had to have not only a particular people for this task but, as well, a particular land. There the Lord would get His People ready for the greatest event in the annals of human history, the giving of the Last Adam to mankind, i.e., all of humanity.

(4) "THEN CAME HE OUT OF THE LAND OF THE CHALDEANS, AND DWELT IN CHARRAN: AND FROM THENCE, WHEN HIS FATHER WAS DEAD, HE REMOVED HIM INTO THIS LAND, WHEREIN YOU NOW DWELL."

The diagram is:

1. The phrase, *"Then came he out of the land of the Chaldeans,"* was at the behest of God. In other words, everything Abraham did in this respect was according to Revelation and direction.

Incidentally, it is this area (the land of the Chaldeans) that is believed to have been the location of the original Garden of Eden. Some even think that ancient Babylon was actually built on its original site.

However, this much is known: due to the fact that the Scripture mentions the two rivers, Tigris and Euphrates, as flowing into the Garden, it is certain that this area is the cradle of civilization (Gen. 2:10-14).

Consequently, this throws away the idea that civilization began in Africa, as some evolutionists claim!

2. *"And dwelt in Charran,"* represents, as we have stated, approximately two or three years.

3. *"And from thence, when his father was dead, he removed him into this land, wherein you now dwell,"* indicates that the Lord was guiding and instructing in totality.

4. The Text indicates that the Lord allowed him to remain in this area until his father died and then hastened him on to the land of Canaan. As well, this could mean that Abraham's father formed the hindrance to Abraham's complete obedience.

NOTES

5. Abraham was 75 years old when he left Haran (Gen. 12:4).

(5) "AND HE GAVE HIM NO INHERITANCE IN IT, NO, NOT SO MUCH AS TO SET HIS FOOT ON: YET HE PROMISED THAT HE WOULD GIVE IT TO HIM FOR A POSSESSION, AND TO HIS SEED AFTER HIM, WHEN AS YET HE HAD NO CHILD."

The overview is:

1. Jesus Christ is the New Covenant (Jn. 1:1-3).

2. The meaning of the New Covenant is the Cross of Christ (I Cor. 1:17).

3. That meaning was given to the Apostle Paul (Gal. 1:12).

A POSSESSION

The phrase, *"And He gave him no inheritance in it, no, not so much as to set his foot on,"* means that Abraham personally never really owned any of the land of Canaan except the *"cave of Machpelah,"* which was used for a burial place for him and Sarah (Gen., Chpt. 23). Isaac and Rebekah were also buried there, as well as Jacob (Gen. 25:9; 49:30-31; 50:13). Leah was also buried there!

The idea was that Abraham owned no land in Canaan on which he could abide or have pasture for sheep. He was a pilgrim, going from place to place most of the time.

"Yet He promised that He would give it to him for a possession, and to his seed after him," is taken from Genesis, Chapter 15. Consequently, this land (Israel) has been the source of more contention and for a longer period of time than any other spot on Earth, and continues even unto this very hour.

Actually, Abraham's seed did not inherit the land until some 430 years after the Call was given to Abraham. However, from the time of Moses to the time of Christ, a period of approximately 1,600 years, the land of Israel was occupied by the Jews. There was a period of 70 years that interrupted this time because of the Babylonians, but even then, Jews remained in the land.

In A.D. 70, Titus, the Roman general, destroyed Jerusalem and Israel as a Nation. Even though Jews continued in the land, for the most part, they were scattered all over the world. In 1948, they once again became a Nation.

MY COVENANT

However, all of this is contested mightily by the Arabs, who claim that Abraham's rightful seed was Ishmael instead of Isaac. Of course, they derive this from the Koran, which was written about 600 years after Christ (Gen. 16:15). However, the Bible says, *"And you shall call his name Isaac: and I will establish My Covenant with him for an Everlasting Covenant, and with his seed after him"* (Gen. 17:19).

So, the Arabs, and more specifically, the Palestinians, claim Israel is theirs, which causes the problems of the present time.

Not counting the Bible or the Koran, Israel has the preponderance of evidence on its side, as is obvious from history. As we have stated, they have occupied the land, more or less, for a period of about 3,600 years. The Arabs can only claim some occupation for about the last 100 years, and even that was alongside the Jews. Therefore, historically or Biblically, the Arabs have no legitimate claim.

Of course, the real purpose of this contention, as it is engineered by Satan, is to hinder the fulfillment of the Prophecies concerning Israel, or even that they would fall to the ground.

Irrespective, Satan will lose, with Israel ultimately being restored at the Second Coming (Rev., Chpt. 19).

The phrase, *"When as yet he had no child,"* simply means that for all of this to be done, Abraham and Sarah had to have an heir, which they ultimately did have, who was Isaac.

(6) "AND GOD SPOKE ON THIS WISE, THAT HIS SEED SHOULD SOJOURN IN A STRANGE LAND; AND THAT THEY SHOULD BRING THEM INTO BONDAGE, AND ENTREAT THEM EVIL FOUR HUNDRED YEARS."

The overview is:

1. The phrase, *"And God spoke on this wise,"* concerns the Prophecy given to Abraham by the Lord respecting the future of his seed, i.e., the people who would later

be called *"Israel,"* who were offspring of the sons of Jacob (renamed Israel by God), who were the offspring of Isaac, who were the offspring of Abraham (Gen., Chpt. 15).

2. *"That his seed should sojourn in a strange land,"* had to do with their sojourn in Canaan before it became theirs, as well as Philistia and Egypt.

3. *"And that they should bring them into bondage, and entreat them evil four hundred years,"* pertains to the period of time they were in these countries before Canaan actually became theirs.

4. The whole length of the Dispensation of Promise, from Abraham to Moses, was 430 years (Ex. 12:40; Gal. 3:14-17).

5. Ishmael being cast out and Isaac being confirmed as the seed through whom the Messiah would come presents the beginning of the 400 years of Genesis 15:13 and Acts 7:6. The beginning of the time took place some five years after the birth of Isaac.

6. Concerning the 430 years mentioned, this deals with the departure of Abraham from Haran at the age of 75 years. This was some 25 years before Isaac was born and 30 years before Isaac was confirmed and Ishmael cast out.

(7) "AND THE NATION TO WHOM THEY SHALL BE IN BONDAGE WILL I JUDGE, SAID GOD: AND AFTER THAT SHALL THEY COME FORTH, AND SERVE ME IN THIS PLACE."

The exegesis is:

1. The phrase, *"And the nation to whom they shall be in bondage will I judge, said God,"* speaks of Egypt (Ex. 1:1-14:31), but yet, tells us something else as well:

a. As we have stated, from the time that Abraham left Haran to the time that God delivered Israel from Egyptian bondage was 430 years.

The first 215 years of that time was spent by the Patriarchs—Abraham, Isaac, and Jacob—in Canaan and Philistia (which was actually a part of Canaan), but without actually possessing any of it.

b. The last 215 years were spent in Egypt, beginning with Jacob and the 70 souls who comprised his family going into that land. However, he went in according to the Will of God (Gen. 46:1-4, 27). During that 215 years, they grew into a mighty Nation of millions, even though slaves. In the beginning, Joseph was viceroy of Egypt and their stay was pleasant. However, after Joseph died and another Pharaoh gained the throne (who did not recognize Joseph or his people), he made slaves of them.

c. God judged Egypt because they placed His People in bondage.

In those days, God directed everything according to His People Israel as He now directs everything according to His People, the Body of Christ, i.e., *"the Church!"* All will be judged who adversely affect His Children, be they one person or an entire nation.

d. The Lord said to Abraham and continues to say to every Believer, even up to this very moment, *"And I will bless those who bless you, and curse him who curses you: and in you shall all families of the Earth be blessed"* (Gen. 12:3).

Even though the Lord was speaking of the Messiah, Who would be of Abraham's seed, still, it is the true Body of Christ who proclaims Christ to the world, thereby, entering into the same Blessing as Israel of old.

2. The phrase, *"And after that shall they come forth, and serve Me in this place,"* speaks of the 400 years of Genesis 15:13, or the 430 years of Exodus 12:40 and Galatians 3:14-17.

3. As stated, the number of years depends upon whether one begins the count with Abraham coming out of Haran (430 years), or the 400 years that began with Isaac being weaned when he was five years old.

4. The Children of Israel were given the Promised Land, which Stephen referred to as *"this place."*

(8) "AND HE GAVE HIM THE COVENANT OF CIRCUMCISION: AND SO ABRAHAM BEGAT ISAAC, AND CIRCUMCISED HIM THE EIGHTH DAY; AND ISAAC BEGAT JACOB; AND JACOB BEGAT THE TWELVE PATRIARCHS."

The exposition is:

1. The Child of God has a choice; it is either law or Grace.

2. If law is chosen, then Grace falls by the wayside. If Grace is chosen, then law is laid aside.

3. However, to have the full embodiment of Grace, one must accept the Cross of Christ (I Cor. 2:2).

THE COVENANT OF CIRCUMCISION

The phrase, *"And He gave him the Covenant of Circumcision,"* refers to the Abrahamic Covenant of Genesis 12:1-3 and 17:9-27 and not the Mosaic Covenant, which continued circumcision but did not originate it.

Circumcision in Old Testament Times was a symbol in the flesh of separation from the world and its heathenistic practices unto God. In other words, Israel was a chosen people, a royal Priesthood.

If for some reason the adult male Israelite had not been circumcised, this act was to be performed forthwith.

Even though circumcision was practiced by other people in other nations, it did not at all have the same meaning as with Israel. It symbolized God's Covenant with Israel.

Thus, from its inception, infant circumcision was the distinctive Israelite custom. It was not derived from Egyptian or other practice, and it contrasted sharply with the puberty rites of other nations. The latter pointed to social acknowledgment of adult status, the former to a status before God and an avenue of Divine Grace.

Thus, those who became members of the Covenant were expected to show it outwardly by obedience to God's Law, which was expressed to Abram in the most general form, *"Walk before Me, and be blameless"* (Gen. 17:1). Consequently, the relationship between circumcision and obedience remains a Biblical constant (Jer. 4:4; Acts 15:5; Rom. 2:25-29; Gal. 5:3).

Therefore, circumcision, as it pertained to Israel, embodied and applied Covenant Promises and summoned one to a life of Covenant obedience.

Regrettably, Israel came to think of the Rite of Circumcision as Salvation within itself, even as they did the sacrifices, etc. As a result, it lost its meaning as a pledge between God and man.

In the New Testament, which is the New Covenant, circumcision plays no part as an actual rite, except in spirit (Col. 2:13).

NOTES

To Christians, who, in the words of the Apostle Paul, seek to enforce this Old Testament sign, he likened such to a heathenish gashing of the body (Phil. 3:3).

Many modern Christians have come to treat Water Baptism or the Lord's Supper exactly as Israel of old did circumcision. They attempt to make Salvation out of the ordinance, etc. Such is the wrong idea altogether! These things are to serve as the symbols they actually are, of a spiritual work carried out within our hearts and lives by Faith in Christ and what He did for us at the Cross, and Faith alone!

The phrase, *"And so Abraham begat Isaac, and circumcised him the eighth day,"* simply means that Abraham obeyed the Command of the Lord and that the Covenant extended to his son.

"And Isaac begat Jacob," proclaims that Jacob was also circumcised and, therefore, a part of the Covenant.

"And Jacob begat the Twelve Patriarchs," speaks of his sons, who headed up the Twelve Tribes of Israel, through which the Word of God would be given to the world, and through which also the Messiah would come.

As well, all who were born to these *"Twelve Patriarchs,"* ultimately numbering millions as the lineage continued down through the centuries, were also to enter into this Covenant.

These special people, who originated with Abraham, were separated unto God, as we have stated, for a specific purpose and reason, that being the bringing of the Messiah into the world. As well, they were given the Word of God, also, which was a part of the Covenant, and which made them the greatest people on the face of the Earth, at least when they were truly following the Lord.

America has been given by God the responsibility of Israel. In other words, we are to watch over and protect this tiny Nation for the simple reason that despite the fact of them being far, far from God, the Lord will ultimately bring them back. As stated, it will be at the time of the Second Coming. If our nation fails in this direction, the results will not be pleasant. The Lord meant what He said and said what He meant, *"And I will bless them who bless you, and curse him who curses you: and in you shall all families of the Earth be blessed"* (Gen. 12:3).

(9) "AND THE PATRIARCHS, MOVED WITH ENVY, SOLD JOSEPH INTO EGYPT: BUT GOD WAS WITH HIM."

The structure is:

1. The phrase, *"And the Patriarchs, moved with envy, sold Joseph into Egypt,"* proclaims to us several things:

• Joseph's brothers were jealous of him in that he was chosen by his father Jacob to inherit the birthright (I Chron. 5:1-2).

Normally, the birthright went to the firstborn and carried with it a double portion of the inheritance relative to a single portion given to the others.

By right, the birthright should have gone to Reuben, the firstborn; however, because of sin on his part, the Lord instructed Jacob to give it to Joseph.

Furthermore, even though the birthright was given to Joseph, the lineage that belonged to Christ was not included. That went to Judah! Judah was the fourth son of Leah, and his name means *"praise!"*

As stated, Reuben forfeited these rites by an act of infamy, while Simeon and Levi, who came next in order, were passed over because of their cruel and treacherous conduct at Shechem. The next in line was Judah, who was assigned the honors and responsibilities of the Lineage of Christ (Gen. 49:10), while Joseph received the other Blessings of the birthright.

• Joseph was a Type of Christ and one of the godliest men found in the history of the Word of God. It is peculiar that the Lord would give the birthright to Joseph but not, as well, give him the Genealogy of Christ, which normally went with the birthright, at least regarding the heirs of Abraham. Instead, it was given to Judah, who had something less than a pristine character (Gen., Chpt. 38).

The only answer is that God had other plans for the sons of Joseph, *"Manasseh and Ephraim."* As well, He wanted the Genealogy of Christ to be in the lineage of

NOTES

David, who would be born about 700 years later in the Tribe of Judah.

This example of the Patriarchs shows how the Israelites pretty well ill-used their greatest benefactors and resisted the leaders sent to them by God.

The phrase, *"But God was with him,"* tells us that irrespective of the plans of Joseph's brothers, who functioned in wickedness, at least at this time, God ultimately would prevail. Men rule, but God overrules!

If God is with someone, it does not matter what the present circumstances may be, the impossible odds stacked against them, or that no one gives them any chance at all; ultimately, they will prevail!

(10) "AND DELIVERED HIM OUT OF ALL HIS AFFLICTIONS, AND GAVE HIM FAVOUR AND WISDOM IN THE SIGHT OF PHARAOH KING OF EGYPT; AND HE MADE HIM GOVERNOR OVER EGYPT AND ALL HIS HOUSE."

The construction is:

1. The phrase, *"And delivered him out of all his afflictions,"* does not say that there were no afflictions, for, in fact, there were many, but the Lord delivered Joseph out of every snare set for him by Satan. Actually, the Scripture says, *"Many are the afflictions of the righteous: but the LORD delivers him out of them all"* (Ps. 34:19).

2. *"And gave him favour and wisdom in the sight of Pharaoh king of Egypt,"* proclaims much more than meets the eye.

3. It is believed that the Pharaoh who ruled Egypt at this time was named *"Apepi,"* who, according to the monuments, had only recently become king over all, having reigned with his father and grandfather for a time.

4. He was probably one of the Hyksos kings of the Fifteenth Dynasty, who were also called *"shepherd kings."*

5. Evidently, they had overrun Egypt at this time, which means that at the time of Joseph, a non-Egyptian sat on the throne, who would show more favor to Joseph than possibly an Egyptian Pharaoh.

6. The Hyksos were herdsmen or shepherds, at least this was the principle occupation of their country, while the Egyptians were a farming and industrial

NOTES

nation with nomadic people, such as shepherds, a far lower class in their eyes. So, the Lord would have this man on the throne when it was time for Joseph to be made viceroy of that great land. As well, the *"wisdom"* Joseph had was given to him by God.

7. At this time, it seems the only people on the face of the Earth who were truly serving God were Jacob and his son, Joseph, with possibly Benjamin, Joseph's younger brother, being a part of this tiny mix.

8. The phrase, *"And he made him governor over Egypt and all his house,"* portrays a wise ruler for a change!

9. One day Joseph was a faceless prisoner in the dungeons of Egypt, and the next day, he was the viceroy of that nation, the greatest on the face of the Earth.

(11) "NOW THERE CAME A DROUGHT OVER ALL THE LAND OF EGYPT AND CANAAN, AND GREAT AFFLICTION: AND OUR FATHERS FOUND NO SUSTENANCE."

The synopsis is:

1. The phrase, *"Now there came a drought over all the land of Egypt and Canaan,"* refers to the seven-year famine but does not say that the seven years of plenty, which preceded this time, extended any further than Egypt (Gen. 41:29).

2. In fact, it seems that Canaan did not experience the plenty but did suffer the famine, which caused them to go into Egypt to purchase food and, ultimately, to come in contact with Joseph.

3. The phrase, *"And great affliction: and our fathers found no sustenance,"* refers, as is obvious, to the inevitable.

4. All of this seems as if it was orchestrated purposely by the Lord, and, no doubt, it was, in order that His Plan be carried out respecting the Nation of Israel, which now only numbered about 70 people.

(12) "BUT WHEN JACOB HEARD THAT THERE WAS CORN IN EGYPT, HE SENT OUT OUR FATHERS FIRST."

The composition is:

1. All of this was in the Divine Plan but was known not at all at this time by Jacob.

2. As far as he knew, his son Joseph was dead, with this famine just another hardship added to all the others; consequently, he would send his sons into Egypt to buy food, which was the Plan of God.

3. Little did Jacob realize what was about to unfold!

(13) "AND AT THE SECOND TIME JOSEPH WAS MADE KNOWN TO HIS BRETHREN; AND JOSEPH'S KINDRED WAS MADE KNOWN UNTO PHARAOH."

The pattern is:

1. The phrase, *"And at the second time Joseph was made known to his brethren,"* refers to their second trip to Egypt, with Joseph testing them. The account of this moment, when Joseph finally revealed himself to his brothers, is found in Genesis 45:1-28.

2. *"And Joseph's kindred was made known unto Pharaoh,"* simply means they were introduced to Pharaoh, with Joseph seeking permission for his family to come into Egypt where they could be looked after by him, which was the Plan of God.

3. Pharaoh readily gave permission, knowing that the prosperity of Egypt was tied up in this Hebrew called *"Joseph,"* and above all, his touch with God.

4. How much this Pharaoh knew that he was involved in a Divine Plan that would ultimately touch the entirety of the world is not known; however, it is known that he showed extra favor to Joseph, which spoke very favorably of him.

(14) "THEN SENT JOSEPH, AND CALLED HIS FATHER JACOB TO HIM, AND ALL HIS KINDRED, THREESCORE AND FIFTEEN SOULS."

The pattern is:

1. The phrase, *"Then sent Joseph, and called his father Jacob to him,"* had to be one of the most striking moments in all of history.

2. As stated, during all of that time, Jacob had thought that Joseph was dead.

3. When the sons of Jacob returned from their second trip to Egypt after Joseph had revealed to them exactly who he was, they had to tell their father of this black sin they had committed approximately 20 years before.

4. When they told Jacob, saying, *"Joseph is yet alive, and he is governor over all the*

land of Egypt," the Scripture says, *"And Jacob's heart fainted, for he believed them not"* (Gen. 45:26).

5. However, they finally convinced him, with the Lord telling him that it was satisfactory for him to go into this land (Gen. 46:1-4).

6. The phrase, *"And all his kindred, threescore and fifteen souls,"* is different than the account given in Genesis 46:27 and Deuteronomy 10:22, where it says there were 70 souls who went into Egypt.

7. Stephen was quoting the Septuagint of Genesis 46:20, where the five sons of Manasseh and Ephraim are listed, which made 75 souls.

8. These five great-grandsons of Jacob were included, and necessarily so, simply because they were Israelites and, therefore, should have been counted. (The Septuagint includes these from Genesis 46:20, which are not mentioned in the regular Biblical account.)

(15) "SO JACOB WENT DOWN INTO EGYPT, AND DIED, HE, AND OUR FATHERS."

The order is:

1. Jacob lived 17 years in Egypt before he died (Gen. 47:28).

2. All his sons, including Joseph, died there, as well, with Joseph giving instructions that when the Children of Israel went back to the Promised Land, this time to take it as a possession, *"You shall carry up my bones from here"* (Gen. 50:25).

3. While his life and ministry were in Egypt, his heart was in Canaan.

4. Joseph lived in Egypt 93 years, for he was 17 years old when sold by his brothers. He was 110 years old when he died.

5. He lived about 56 years longer after his father Jacob died. It would be about 145 years before the Children of Israel would be delivered from Egypt; however, when they were delivered, they would do exactly what Joseph had requested; his bones would go with them (Ex. 13:19).

(16) "AND WERE CARRIED OVER INTO SYCHEM, AND LAID IN THE SEPULCHRE THAT ABRAHAM BOUGHT FOR A SUM OF MONEY OF THE SONS OF EMMOR THE FATHER OF SYCHEM."

NOTES

The form is:

1. The phrase, *"And were carried over into Sychem,"* referred to *"Shechem"* (Gen. 23:6-20; 33:19; 47:30; 49:29; 50:5; Ex. 13:19; Josh. 24:32).

2. *"And laid in the Sepulchre that Abraham bought for a sum of money of the sons of Emmor the father of Sychem,"* pertained to three couples who were buried there:

a. Abraham and Sarah

b. Isaac and Rebekah

c. Jacob and Leah (Rachel was buried close to Beth-lehem, Gen. 35:19.)

3. Joseph's bones were *"buried in Shechem in a parcel of ground which Jacob bought of the sons of Hamor the father of Shechem for an hundred pieces of silver"* (Josh. 24:32).

4. According to a tradition still surviving in the days of St. Jerome, the other Patriarchs (the brothers of Joseph) were buried there as well.

5. However, Josephus affirmed that all but Joseph were buried at Hebron, and that their beautiful marble monuments were to be seen at Hebron in his day.

6. Furthermore, it seems from the Text that Shechem was in Stephen's mind, which would have included the brothers of Joseph as well.

7. There also seems to be a discrepancy in that Stephen said that Abraham bought the piece of ground, while Joshua said it was purchased by Jacob (Josh. 24:32).

8. However, it is thought that quite possibly Abraham really did buy a field from Ephron in Sychem when he was there (Gen. 12:6). This was where Abraham built his first Altar, a site that he could very well have purchased. Due to the long span of time between Abraham and Jacob, Jacob possibly paid more money for the same place in order to satisfy any arguments that may have presently existed.

9. This much is certain: Stephen, as is plainly obvious, had a thorough knowledge of Bible history and would not have made a mistake.

10. What we have stated concerning both Abraham and Jacob, and the purchase of this site, is probably the way it went down.

(17) "BUT WHEN THE TIME OF THE

NOTES

PROMISE DREW NEAR, WHICH GOD HAD SWORN TO ABRAHAM, THE PEOPLE GREW AND MULTIPLIED IN EGYPT."

The form is:

1. The Cross of Christ is not merely a New Testament Doctrine.

2. The Cross goes all the way back to Genesis 3:15.

3. It includes every sacrifice offered up by Israel in Old Testament Times, which actually began with Adam and Eve.

THE PROMISE

The phrase, *"But when the time of the Promise drew near,"* contains a very important Truth respecting the *"time."*

God's Timing is just as important as His Promise. To be frank, it is quite possible, and even probable, that more people miss the Lord respecting His timing than anything else. By that I mean this:

When the Lord promises something, He almost always has a time factor built in; however, He very seldom tells us the exact length of that particular time. As a result, many Believers lose heart and give up. In other words, they allow the devil to tell them that God did not give them a Promise to start with, He has changed His Mind, the Promise cannot be fulfilled due to some particular failure on their part, etc. Satan will tell any lie that he can get a person to believe.

Consequently, most of the time, the waiting is the most difficult part of all, especially considering that we do not know exactly when the time of the Promise is to come about. However, God's Timing is important in several ways:

• For the Lord to bring certain things about, other things must be done that have absolutely no bearing at all upon the person in question, but yet, figure into that which the Lord will do. So, we have to trust that the Lord has a purpose behind His delay, and that He is working out certain things even at that very moment, exactly as He was doing with Israel of old.

This time of waiting is not meant to be without profit. Actually, it can be the most profitable time of all as the Lord deals with us about certain things that need to be addressed. The Scripture does not say for ought, *"But they that wait upon the LORD shall renew their strength; they shall mount up with wings as eagles; they shall run, and not be weary; and they shall walk, and not faint"* (Isa. 40:31).

• All of this is designed by the Lord for our profit and good. Waiting teaches us trust. It also strengthens our Faith. Peter said, *"That the trial of your Faith, being much more precious than of gold that perisheth, though it be tried with fire, might be found unto Praise and Honour and Glory at the appearing of Jesus Christ"* (I Pet. 1:7).

THE OATH

The phrase, *"Which God had sworn to Abraham,"* pertained to the Oath made by the Lord to the Patriarch.

Whenever the Lord gave this Promise to Abraham, to bind the Promise, *"He could swear by no greater* (therefore), *He swore by Himself, saying, Surely blessing I will bless you, and multiplying I will multiply you"* (Heb. 6:13-14; Gen. 22:17).

What the Lord bound Himself to perform was His Promises to His Covenant People.

In essence, the Guarantor and Fulfillment of all these Promises was Jesus Christ in Whom they found the answer *"Amen!"* (Isa. 65:16; II Cor. 1:19-20). In His First Advent, Jesus Christ fulfilled God's ancient Oaths to the Patriarchs (Lk. 1:68-73; 2:6-14).

The phrase, *"The people grew and multiplied in Egypt,"* spoke of the time from Jacob to the time they were delivered. As stated, they multiplied from just 70 people (75 counting the five sons of the two sons of Joseph), to a number of approximately 2,500,000 at the time of the Exodus.

(18) "TILL ANOTHER KING AROSE WHICH KNEW NOT JOSEPH."

The record is:

1. The phrase, *"Till another king arose,"* refers to the king of Assyria, who had conquered the land (Ex. 1:8-22; Ps. 105:25; Isa. 52:4).

2. *"Which knew not Joseph,"* simply means that this new Assyrian king had no regard for Egypt's past respecting Joseph and, consequently, had no regard for Joseph's people, the Israelites.

3. This also means that before this new king arose, the sons of Jacob were treated very well and allowed to prosper greatly! However, things would now change, which God allowed!

4. In fact, if it had not changed, the Children of Israel would not have wanted or desired to leave Egypt. Otherwise, being treated as slaves, they couldn't wait to leave.

(19) "THE SAME DEALT SUBTILLY WITH OUR KINDRED, AND EVIL ENTREATED OUR FATHERS, SO THAT THEY CAST OUT THEIR YOUNG CHILDREN, TO THE END THEY MIGHT NOT LIVE."

The record is:

1. The phrase, *"The same dealt subtilly with our kindred, and evil entreated our fathers,"* proclaims such being allowed by the Lord for purpose and reason!

2. Even though the harsh treatment by the Egyptians was very difficult to bear, the Lord had a purpose in all of this.

3. Up until the coming of this Assyrian king, it seems that Israel had prospered greatly in Egypt, both numerically and economically. If they had been allowed to remain in this posture, it is very doubtful that many of them would have desired to leave and go to this land called *"Canaan,"* which none of them had really ever seen.

4. Therefore, the Lord would allow measures to be taken that were very grievous to the flesh but invigorating to the spirit. In other words, due to this harsh treatment, they were now very willing to leave Egypt.

5. The phrase, *"So that they cast out their young children, to the end they might not live,"* speaks of the demand ordered by Pharaoh that all the boy babies of the Israelites were to be killed when they were born. As is obvious, the persecution was severe!

6. It is regrettable that many Believers will not obey God or seek to do His Will unless stringent measures are applied. This certainly does not include all Believers, but I think it definitely includes the majority. Most of the time, people obey God only if it is profitable to their self-interest. This simply means that most really are not attempting to do the Will of God, but

NOTES

rather the carrying out of their own will. So, the Lord allowed certain things to happen in order that Israel would desire to do His Will!

7. Remember this: Everything that happens to a Believer is either *"caused"* by the Lord or *"allowed"* by the Lord. There are no accidents with Believers, only opportunities.

(20) "IN WHICH TIME MOSES WAS BORN, AND WAS EXCEEDING FAIR, AND NOURISHED UP IN HIS FATHER'S HOUSE THREE MONTHS."

The account is:

1. The phrase, *"In which time Moses was born,"* presents, as well, another step in the Plan of God for Israel's Deliverance.

2. *"And was exceeding fair,"* describes the appearance of the child.

3. Josephus described Pharaoh's daughter as captivated by the beauty of the child, and as speaking of him to Pharaoh as of Divine beauty. In other words, the Lord caused this baby to literally radiate in order that it would catch the attention of Pharaoh's daughter.

4. *"And nourished up in his father's house three months,"* pertained to the time he was hidden by his parents in order that he not be killed as was demanded by Pharaoh of all newly-born Hebrew baby boys.

(21) "AND WHEN HE WAS CAST OUT, PHARAOH'S DAUGHTER TOOK HIM UP, AND NOURISHED HIM FOR HER OWN SON."

The diagram is:

1. The phrase, *"And when he was cast out,"* speaks of the time when he could not be hidden any longer, and, no doubt, led by the Lord, his mother made a tiny *"ark"* and *"put the child therein; and she laid it in the flags by the river's brink"* (Ex. 2:3).

2. *"Pharaoh's daughter took him up, and nourished him for her own son,"* presents this that was orchestrated totally by the Lord.

3. Moses was the seventh from Abraham, the line being: Abraham, Isaac, Jacob, Levi, Kohath, Amram, and Moses.

(22) "AND MOSES WAS LEARNED IN ALL THE WISDOM OF THE EGYPTIANS, AND WAS MIGHTY IN WORDS AND IN DEEDS."

The overview is:

1. The phrase, *"And Moses was learned in all the wisdom of the Egyptians,"* pertained to that which consisted of the mysteries of the Egyptian religion, arithmetic, geometry, poetry, music, medicine, and hieroglyphics.

2. Actually, at this time, the Egyptians were the most educated and instructed people on Earth.

3. Josephus said that Thermuthis spoke of Joseph as *"of a noble understanding"* and said that he was *"brought up with much care and diligence."*

4. The phrase, *"And was mighty in words and in deeds,"* is said to pertain to the fact that Moses ultimately became a general in the Egyptian Army and defeated the Ethiopians who had invaded Egypt. This was according to Josephus.

5. In essence, Stephen said that Moses was divinely beautiful (Acts 7:20); intellectually, he was highly cultured (Acts 7:22); and potentially, he was mighty in speech and action. Thus, he rebutted the charge of having spoken against Moses (Acts 6:11).

6. As well, Stephen had spoken of Joseph and the ill-treatment of him by the Patriarchs.

7. His argument was that both Joseph and Moses were Types of the Messiah, for just as God exalted Joseph, whom they had sold, and extolled Moses, whom they had thrust aside, and made them to be saviors to Israel, so God had exalted Jesus to be a Prince, like Joseph, and a Saviour, like Moses. As well, He was willing to deliver Israel from a greater bondage by giving them Repentance and Remission of sins, but they had treated Him as they had treated Joseph and Moses.

8. This seems to be what the Holy Spirit was saying to the Sanhedrin through Stephen.

(23) "AND WHEN HE WAS FULL FORTY YEARS OLD, IT CAME INTO HIS HEART TO VISIT HIS BRETHREN THE CHILDREN OF ISRAEL."

The overview is:

1. The phrase, *"And when he was full forty years old,"* pertains to the years Moses spent in Pharaoh's court. As well, he spent 40 years in Midian (the backside of the desert), and 40 years with the Children of Israel in the wilderness (Ex. 2:11; Deut. 2:7; 8:2; 31:2).

NOTES

2. *"It came into his heart to visit his brethren the Children of Israel,"* proclaims something placed there by the Holy Spirit. Before now, it seems that he had not been too occupied with the plight of *"his brethren."*

3. As well, it is believed that Moses was being groomed to be the Pharaoh of Egypt. However, whatever the direction, the Holy Spirit now began to move upon him in earnest respecting that which God had planned for him to do.

4. We do know that at about this time, he made a decision for the Lord because the writer of Hebrews said, *"By Faith Moses, when he was come to years, refused to be called the son of Pharaoh's daughter"* (Heb. 11:24).

(24) "AND SEEING ONE OF THEM SUFFER WRONG, HE DEFENDED HIM, AND AVENGED HIM THAT WAS OPPRESSED, AND SMOTE THE EGYPTIAN."

The exposition is:

1. The phrase, *"And seeing one of them suffer wrong, he defended him,"* tells us several things:

a. As stated, the Holy Spirit had already begun to move upon him concerning the Plan of God.

b. He now saw the wrong his people were suffering, whereas it seems that previously, he took little notice.

c. He now set out to do something about their plight; however, his efforts were in the flesh, and they did no good.

2. The phrase, *"And avenged him that was oppressed, and smote the Egyptian,"* is a perfect example of right motives but doing it in the wrong way.

3. The Call of God is only a part of the Mission. One must, as well, learn the Ways of the Spirit. However, as Moses, much of the Work of God is attempted in the flesh and brings forth the same results as it did with Moses—nothing! At least, nothing good!

(25) "FOR HE SUPPOSED HIS BRETHREN WOULD HAVE UNDERSTOOD HOW THAT GOD BY HIS HAND WOULD DELIVER THEM: BUT THEY

UNDERSTOOD NOT."

The exegesis is:

1. The phrase, *"For he supposed his brethren would have understood how that God by his hand would deliver them,"* proclaims a totally erroneous perception.

2. What had happened with Moses relative to the Lord speaking to him at this time is not known. However, the sentence structure tells us that the Lord had definitely dealt with Moses. Nevertheless, the people were not ready and neither was Moses!

3. *"But they understood not,"* probably pertained to their present feelings about him.

4. It is most probable that they really did not know Moses. They knew of him, but they really did not know him.

5. It is certain that the Israelites knew who he was, but what they knew did not at all endear him to their hearts. They were working as slaves while he was living in the lap of luxury and seemingly, before now, doing very little to lessen their plight. So, at present, they did not know his motives or understand his present activity. If he had mentioned anything about his proposed Mission regarding their Deliverance, they would have placed little credence in his statements.

(26) "AND THE NEXT DAY HE SHOWED HIMSELF UNTO THEM AS THEY STROVE, AND WOULD HAVE SET THEM AT ONE AGAIN, SAYING, SIRS, YOU ARE BRETHREN; WHY DO YOU WRONG ONE TO ANOTHER?"

The synopsis is:

1. The phrase, *"And the next day he showed himself unto them as they strove, and would have set them at one again,"* proclaims him attempting to take charge, for which they had little confidence or desire.

2. The question, *"Saying, Sirs, you are brethren; why do you wrong one to another?"* would bring forth an answer that he had not anticipated!

(27) "BUT HE WHO DID HIS NEIGHBOUR WRONG THRUST HIM AWAY, SAYING, WHO MADE YOU A RULER AND A JUDGE OVER US?"

The account is:

1. The phrase, *"But he who did his neighbour wrong thrust him away,"* plainly proclaims the man rejecting the leadership of Moses.

2. The question, *"Saying, Who made you a ruler and a judge over us?"* seems to indicate that Moses had said enough during the recent past, concerning the Call of God on his life, that a goodly number of people knew his intentions. However, they did not buy into his proposal, and neither did they have any respect, at least at this time, for his Call.

(28) "WILL YOU KILL ME, AS YOU DID THE EGYPTIAN YESTERDAY?"

The pattern is:

1. Evidently, Moses did not realize that his killing of the Egyptian was known; however, he had been seen!

2. Apparently, He had already renounced the adoption by Pharaoh's daughter and was now throwing in his lot with his people and, as a result, had no standing left in Egyptian circles. So, his situation suddenly became perilous!

(29) "THEN FLED MOSES AT THIS SAYING, AND WAS A STRANGER IN THE LAND OF MADIAN, WHERE HE BEGAT TWO SONS."

The form is:

1. The phrase, *"Then fled Moses at this saying,"* presents a situation that is not exactly conducive to the beginning of a Ministry. In other words, he began his Ministry by committing manslaughter!

2. *"And was a stranger in the land of Madian,"* proclaims him making good his escape. Whether Pharaoh simply did not try too hard to apprehend him or whether the Lord worked on his behalf is not exactly known. It might have been a combination of the two!

3. The land of Midian included the eastern coast of the Red Sea to the borders of Moab, taking in all of the Arabian Peninsula.

4. The area was named after Midian (Madian), the fourth son of Abraham and Keturah (Gen. 25:1-7).

5. The phrase, *"Where he begat two sons,"* proclaims in Exodus 2:22 and 18:3-4 that their names were Gershom and Eliezer.

(30) "AND WHEN FORTY YEARS WERE EXPIRED, THERE APPEARED TO

NOTES

HIM IN THE WILDERNESS OF MOUNT SINAI AN ANGEL OF THE LORD IN A FLAME OF FIRE IN A BUSH."

The pattern is:

1. The phrase, *"And when forty years were expired,"* proclaims that it took a very short time to get Moses out of Egypt but 40 years to get Egypt out of Moses. The flesh dies hard!

2. The phrase, *"There appeared to him in the wilderness of Mount Sinai an Angel of the Lord in a flame of fire in a bush,"* proclaims that this was actually God Himself appearing to Moses (Ex. 3:2; 4:17).

3. In the Bible, the designation of *"Angel"* can pertain to men, an Angel as we think of such, and even to God, as here!

4. The anguish of Israel continued under the taskmaster's lash, and the weakening of Israel's strength by the destruction of the male children went on, with what more or less rigor we know not. However, there in Midian, Moses was left by providence to mellow and mature that the haughty, impetuous prince, *"instructed in all the wisdom of the Egyptians,"* might be transformed into the wise, masterful leader, statesman, Law-giver, poet, and Prophet.

5. God usually prepares His Great Ones in the countryside or about some of the quiet places of Earth, farthest away from the busy haunts of men and nearest to the *"Sacred Place of the Most High."*

6. As David keeping his father's flocks, Elijah on the mountain slopes of Gilead, the Baptist in the wilderness of Judaea, and Jesus in the shop of a Galilean carpenter, so Moses was a shepherd in the Bedouin country in the *"waste, howling wilderness."*

(31) "WHEN MOSES SAW IT, HE WONDERED AT THE SIGHT: AND AS HE DREW NEAR TO BEHOLD IT, THE VOICE OF THE LORD CAME UNTO HIM."

The form is:

1. The phrase, *"When Moses saw it, he wondered at the sight,"* finds this man, more than likely, having long since given up the idea of delivering Israel. He probably had resigned himself to living out the rest of his days as a shepherd. I am certain that he contemplated many times the Call of God upon his life, but with no visible means or way to bring it to pass, he probably had resigned himself to the fact that the questions would never be answered.

NOTES

2. The phrase, *"And as he drew near to behold it, the Voice of the Lord came unto him,"* seems to have been the first time the Lord had spoken to him since the initial Call.

3. At about this time, the plight of the Children of Israel had become so serious that they were crying to God for help (Ex. 2:23-25). They had to be made willing to follow His appointed Man, and His appointed Man had to be made willing to follow God.

4. The former would have to endure the fire of persecution while the latter had to give up all hope of the flesh. Neither task came easily or quickly!

(32) "SAYING, I AM THE GOD OF YOUR FATHERS, THE GOD OF ABRAHAM, AND THE GOD OF ISAAC, AND THE GOD OF JACOB. THEN MOSES TREMBLED, AND DOES NOT BEHOLD."

The synopsis is:

1. The phrase, *"Saying, I am the God of your fathers, the God of Abraham, and the God of Isaac, and the God of Jacob,"* in essence, says that He was the same One Who had spoken to them.

2. All of this was for purpose and reason, actually, the single most important thing on the face of the Earth. God's Dealings with these men pertained to the Redemption of all of mankind.

3. Furthermore, that God would link Himself to poor, frail, fallen man is beyond the scope or comprehension of mere mortals. There was one ingredient that these men had to have. That ingredient was Faith. They believed what God told them, which, in essence, presents the greatest thing that a person can do. Many failures are tolerated if Faith is in evidence.

4. The phrase, *"Then Moses trembled, and does not behold,"* proclaims a great fear and Moses turning his face away, *"For he was afraid to look upon God"* (Ex. 3:6).

(33) "THEN SAID THE LORD TO HIM, PUT OFF YOUR SHOES FROM YOUR FEET: FOR THE PLACE WHERE YOU STAND IS HOLY GROUND."

The construction is:

NOTES

1. The phrase, *"Then said the Lord to him,"* begins a scenario that would only end some 40 years later.

2. Some have said that Moses receiving his Commission was the most appalling Commission ever given to a mere man (Ex. 3:10).

3. The phrase, *"Put off your shoes from your feet: for the place where you stand is Holy Ground,"* tells us several things:

a. Wherever God is, the place of consequence is Holy.

b. The demand for him to remove his shoes was, in effect, the sign that Moses had now become the slave of the Lord, for slaves did not wear shoes.

c. As well, the removal of the shoes signified that he gave up all pretense at ownership of anything, be it land, family, place, or position, for slaves own nothing!

4. However, to be able to stand on *"Holy Ground"* is the greatest privilege that anyone could ever have, by far eclipsing anything that Satan or the world would have to offer. Nothing, absolutely nothing, can compare with that.

(34) "I HAVE SEEN, I HAVE SEEN THE AFFLICTION OF MY PEOPLE WHICH IS IN EGYPT, AND I HAVE HEARD THEIR GROANING, AND AM COME DOWN TO DELIVER THEM. AND NOW COME, I WILL SEND YOU INTO EGYPT."

The structure is:

1. The phrase, *"I have seen, I have seen the affliction of My People which is in Egypt,"* tells us, as should be obvious, that God sees all, but especially that He does see the *"affliction"* of His People.

2. This should be a comfort to every Believer simply because God is able to do whatever is needed to bring about a successful conclusion. However, far too often, Believers attempt to make men see their *"afflictions,"* who, most of the time, cannot or will not do anything about the situation. For help, one must look to the Lord, and the Lord exclusively!

3. The phrase, *"And I have heard their groaning,"* pertains to sighing and of prayer. In other words, the Lord heard their prayers and cries for Deliverance.

4. So, He *"sees"* and He *"hears."*

5. The Lord is the only One Who can do anything about our plight. So, why do we as God's People resort to the foolishness of humanistic psychology or other man-devised efforts? It is bad enough for the world to look toward this broken cistern, but it is abominable for God's People to follow suit. However, the problem is found in the leadership. This is why it was said of Jesus, *"But when He saw the multitudes, He was moved with compassion on them, because they fainted, and were scattered abroad, as sheep having no shepherd"* (Mat. 9:36).

6. The phrase, *"And am come down to deliver them,"* proclaims that which He is able to do, and which He will do for all who will believe Him.

7. So, the Lord *"sees,"* He *"hears,"* and He *"delivers!"*

8. The phrase, *"And now come, I will send you into Egypt,"* presents, as stated, the most appalling task ever assigned to any man.

9. He was to deliver his kinsmen, over two million, from a dreadful slavery at the hand of the most powerful nation on Earth. Let not those who halt and stumble over the little difficulties of most ordinary lives think hardly of the faltering of Moses' Faith before such a task (Ex. 3:11-13; 4:1, 10-13).

10. Most men or women seldom have the Faith needed at the moment of the Commission. However, God increases the Faith proportionately as proper steps are taken.

11. As Exodus, Chapter 3, proclaims, Moses was very reluctant to proceed. Consequently, his retirement was just as obnoxious to God as had been his haste some 40 years before. Both were of the flesh, and both, therefore, a hindrance to the Spirit. However, Moses would ultimately obey!

(35) "THIS MOSES WHOM THEY REFUSED, SAYING, WHO MADE YOU A RULER AND A JUDGE? THE SAME DID GOD SEND TO BE A RULER AND A DELIVERER BY THE HAND OF THE ANGEL WHICH APPEARED TO HIM IN THE BUSH."

The exegesis is:

1. The question, *"This Moses whom they refused, saying, Who made you a ruler and a judge?"* is meant by Stephen to show that the Jesus Whom they had rejected and

crucified was their only present and Eternal Saviour.

2. *"The same did God send to be a ruler and a deliverer by the hand of the Angel which appeared to him in the bush,"* presents historical narrative of which the Sanhedrin was overly familiar; however, it cannot be that they did not catch or understand the implications! The Holy Spirit helped Stephen to so cleverly display this great Truth in front of them that they surely saw the great similarity, but there was a glaring difference!

3. Their fathers had taken the taskmaster's whip to such an extent that they were now willing to listen to God's Man.

4. Even though the Roman heel was on the head of Israel during the time of Stephen, it seemingly was not enough affliction to bend these prideful and arrogant rejecters of Christ. Therefore, they killed Him, even as ancient Israel first rejected Moses.

5. However, as some 40 years later, Israel was now ready to bend, likewise, at the Second Coming of our Heavenly Moses, Israel at that coming day will bend as well!

6. The parallel is overly obvious!

(36) "HE BROUGHT THEM OUT, AFTER THAT HE HAD SHOWN WONDERS AND SIGNS IN THE LAND OF EGYPT, AND IN THE RED SEA, AND IN THE WILDERNESS FORTY YEARS."

The overview is:

1. There is no salvation outside of the Cross of Christ.

2. There is no victory over sin by the Believer outside of the Cross of Christ (I Cor. 1:17).

SIGNS AND WONDERS IN THE LAND OF EGYPT

The phrase, *"He brought them out,"* as is obvious, speaks of Egypt; however, it is meant to convey the Deliverance effected regarding every believing sinner when God brings them out of sin and darkness unto the Gospel of His Dear Son and our Saviour, the Lord Jesus Christ. He brings us out of something and then places us into something. We are brought out of darkness and placed into Light. We are brought out of sin and placed into Salvation. We are brought out of slavery and placed into the freedom of God's Grace.

"After that He had shown wonders and signs in the land of Egypt," means that He manifested His great Power to Egypt so that there was no excuse for the Egyptians not knowing Who He was. He amply proved the falseness of the many gods they worshiped and with His display of Power, left them with no excuse.

Actually, it is the same presently! The proof of the veracity of the Bible as the Word of God and the Saving Grace of Jesus Christ is so amply provided that, as Paul said, *"They are without excuse"* (Rom. 1:20).

So, the destruction of Egypt was Egypt's own fault! Israel belonged to God, and He had the right to demand their release. When the Egyptians would not let them go, God had the right to do exactly as He did and should have done.

The phrase, *"And in the Red Sea,"* speaks of the greatest Miracle up to that time that had ever been performed.

The Believer needs to understand that the sinner's lost condition is so severe that only what Jesus did on Calvary can change the situation. That is why Jesus referred to it as being *"Born-Again!"*

DELIVERANCE

The Deliverance from Egypt is a perfect example. At that time, there was no earthly power that could have effected the release of the Children of Israel. Likewise, there is no earthly power that can effect a release from sin.

As well, Pharaoh is a type of Satan, who would not yield to the demands of Moses, as Satan will not yield to the demands of any mortal. Only the Power of God could break the will of Pharaoh, as only the Power of God has defeated Satan.

Also, as glorious as the *"signs and wonders"* were, they did not deliver Israel, with that being effected only by the shed Blood of the Lamb. That alone continues to hold true for the Salvation of sinners.

Also, the *"Red Sea"* stood as a barrier to freedom, even as the chains of sin stand as a barrier to the sinner. Only God, as should be obvious, could open a path through that sea, as only God can break the chains and shackles of sin, which He does upon Faith in Christ.

The phrase, *"And in the wilderness forty years,"* presents the Divine Protection of God this length of time, even though it was the Will of God that they be in this place only about two years, if that! Even in unbelief, the Miracles did not stop and neither did the *"signs and wonders,"* showing that God ever abides Faithful, even though His People do not at times.

(37) "THIS IS THAT MOSES, WHICH SAID UNTO THE CHILDREN OF ISRAEL, A PROPHET SHALL THE LORD YOUR GOD RAISE UP UNTO YOU OF YOUR BRETHREN, LIKE UNTO ME; HIM SHALL YOU HEAR."

The overview is:

1. Jesus Christ is the Source of all good things from God.
2. The Cross of Christ is the Means and the only Means by which all of these things are given to us.
3. With that being the case, the Object of our Faith must always be Christ and the Cross.

MOSES

The phrase, *"This is that Moses, which said unto the Children of Israel,"* and that which follows, presents Stephen as one of the first to conceive of the fact that Christianity, which it was not even then called, represented a new order of things and, as such, would inevitably supersede the old order. Thus, his teachings forecast that great controversy of the first Christian century, the controversy between Judaism and Christianity. It reached its culmination-point in the Council at Jerusalem, resulting in the independence of the Christian Church from the fetters of Judaistic legalism (Acts, Chpt. 15).

In accordance with the accusation against him, Stephen's defense was twofold: personal defense and defense of his teaching.

HIS PERSONAL DEFENSE

The charge of blasphemy against God and contempt of the Law are implicitly repudiated by the tenor of the whole speech.

NOTES

For instance, he recognized the Old Testament institutions as Divinely decreed, and his reference to the Divine sanction of the Law and its condemnation of those who had not kept it, at the close of his speech, show clearly his reverence, not only for the past history of the Jewish people but, as well, for its Sacred Writings and all its religious institutions.

It makes evident, beyond doubt, how ungrounded the accusation of blasphemy against him was. Not to impiety or frivolity in Stephen, but to some other cause, must be due, therefore, the difference between him and his opponents. What it was, Stephen himself showed unmistakably in the second part of his defense.

HIS DEFENSE OF HIS TEACHING

The fundamental differences between Stephen and his opponents, as is evident from the whole tone, drift, and purpose of his Message, lay in that he judged Old Testament history from the prophetic point of view, to which Jesus had also allied Himself, while his opponents represented the legalistic point of view that was so characteristic of the Jewish thought of that day.

In other words, he claimed (and rightly so) that all of the Old Testament rituals were prophetic in that they pointed to One Who was to come, namely Jesus Christ.

Regrettably, the Israel of Stephen's day no longer looked at this history as prophetic, but rather attempted to devise Salvation out of the rituals and ceremonies, which, of course, were gross error.

As a foundation for his teaching, he pointed out the disobedience on the part of their fathers and that, therefore, not he, but they, were disobedient to the Divine Revelation. Thus, in a masterful way, Stephen converted the charge of his being anti-Moses into a counter-charge of disobedience to the Divine Revelation, of which his hearers stood guilty in the present as their fathers had in the past.

In this sense, the Message as given by Stephen was a grand apology for the Christian Cause, which he represented, inasmuch as it showed clearly that the new way of following Christ was only the

Divinely-ordered development of the old and not in opposition to it.

The phrase, *"A Prophet shall the Lord your God raise up unto you of your brethren, like unto me; Him shall you hear,"* points directly to Jesus as the fulfillment of that Prophecy given by Moses so long before and who Stephen declared (Deut. 18:15).

(38) "THIS IS HE, WHO WAS IN THE CHURCH IN THE WILDERNESS WITH THE ANGEL WHICH SPOKE TO HIM IN THE MOUNT SINAI, AND WITH OUR FATHERS: WHO RECEIVED THE LIVELY ORACLES TO GIVE UNTO US."

The account is:

1. The modern Christian has a choice.
2. It is either law or Grace.

THE RELATIONSHIP BETWEEN THE CHURCH AND ISRAEL

The phrase, *"This is he, who was in the Church in the wilderness,"* refers to Moses, along with all the Israelites who were *"called out"* of Egypt. They represented God under the Mosaic Covenant until the Messiah should come (Mat. 11:11; Lk. 16:16; Gal. 3:19).

As Israel was *"called out"* of Egypt, likewise, the Body of Christ is *"called out"* of the world system. Soon it will be taken out of the world altogether (I Thess. 4:16-17).

Even though Israel and the Church have differences and similarities to which we will briefly allude, still, it must always be understood that the Church has its roots in Judaism of necessity.

As such, the entirety of the Bible must be looked at as one grand plan devised by the Lord in order to redeem humanity. In fact, the entirety of the Bible proclaims one personality, and that One is Jesus. He alone is the Subject, and for obvious reasons, even though there are many side issues.

As we have already stated, the main problem with Israel at the time of Christ was their misinterpretation of the Old Testament. It was prophetic in scope, which they would not recognize, except in a limited way and according to their own terms. Of course, the Prophecies pointed toward Jesus; consequently, in refusing to recognize the obvious, they attempted to make

NOTES

Salvation out of the rituals and ceremonies, which John the Baptist, as well as Jesus, so roundly condemned.

As someone has said, *"The Old Testament is the New Testament concealed, while the New Testament is the Old Testament revealed."* In other words, if one does not properly understand the Old Testament, one will have an erroneous concept of the New.

THE DIFFERENCES BETWEEN ISRAEL AND THE CHURCH

The New Testament portrait of the *"Called-out ones"* as a real spiritual entity, a Living Body of which the risen Jesus is Head, has led many to emphasize differences between the Church and Israel.

The Church, they say, began at Pentecost with the Spirit's Coming (Acts 2:1-4; I Cor. 12:13). The Church thus functions as a supernational entity while Israel functioned as a Nation.

The Church, they say, has a unique destiny as Christ's Bride while Israel has a unique destiny as Jehovah's Wife.

THE SIMILARITIES BETWEEN THE CHURCH AND ISRAEL

Others have stressed the similarities between the Church and Israel. They insist that there are not two communities of Faith, but one.

Israel and the Church were both intended to function as Faith-communities. Each looks to Abraham as father (Rom. 4:9-17; Gal. 3:6-9). Each enjoys Covenant relationship with God, and the New Covenant governing Christian experience is actually the same New Covenant promised to Israel (Jer. 31:31-34).

COVENANT

Actually, both differences and similarities do exist. The Church is not the same as Israel, and Old Testament Passages relating to Israel should not be spiritualized or forced out of context in an attempt to apply them to the Church.

However, at the same time, emphasizing the differences at the expense of many vital similarities is wrong.

We should understand Israel in the

context of which the Lord raised up these ancient people. Their purpose was to give the world the Word of God and to serve as the Womb of the Messiah. This they did.

They were also to evangelize the world, and under those whom they rejected, such as Paul and the other Apostles, they did succeed in carrying this out.

Their rejection of Christ has brought upon them untold sufferings and hardships, which has made them a spectacle to the world for nearly 2,000 years. However, at the same time, even though their rejection of Christ has delayed the Plan of God terribly so, for these people, ultimately, that Plan will be realized at the Second Coming of the Lord. God keeps His Covenants! Consequently, the Church, despite Israel's rebellion, must not forget the contribution they made and, as well, the Promise by God of a future Restoration.

At the same time, the Church has a Covenant as well. *"The New Covenant,"* was actually intended for the entirety of mankind, the Jew included, and to which the Old pointed. However, the rejection of this Covenant by the Jewish people in no way negates the Covenant, but only their part in its Promises.

One day soon (at the Second Coming) that will be rectified, and then the Church, the Body of Christ, will work, worship, and rule alongside a restored Israel (Isa. 11:11; 14:1-2; 43:5-6; Jer. 3:17-18; Chpts. 30-31, 33; Ezek. 28:25-26; 34:11-31; 36:6-38; Chpts. 37-39; Hos. 1:10-11; 3:4-5; Joel, Chpt. 3; Amos 9:9-15; Mic. 2:12-13; 4:1-8; 5:3-15; Zech. 2:8-13; 8:1-8; 10:6-12; 12:1-14:21; etc.).

THE LIVELY ORACLES

The phrase, *"With the Angel which spoke to him in the Mount Sinai,"* actually refers to God Himself, Who gave Moses the Law.

As should be obvious, the title or designation *"Angel"* can refer to either man, an Angel as we think of such, or God. The designation is used interchangeably and must be understood according to the associated Texts.

The phrase, *"And with our fathers,"* refers to the fact that the Elders of Israel were to help Moses, but rather did the opposite!

NOTES

The phrase, *"Who received the lively oracles to give unto us,"* in this instance refers to the Law of Moses.

The Greek word for *"lively Oracles"* is *"liege zonta"* and means *"living Doctrines that produce Life upon obedience to them."*

It is not referring to Salvation, at least as it is used here, but rather to the Blessing and prosperity of these Doctrines inasmuch as they were the Word of God.

In fact, in being given the Law of God, it gave Israel an unparalleled advantage over other nations. Whereas there were many and varied laws all over the world of that day, all were by man and, therefore, woefully inefficient.

These given by God addressed every single aspect of life in every capacity, whether toward one's fellowman or toward God. As such, Israel was guaranteed Blessing and prosperity, at least if they would walk according to this which God gave.

(39) "TO WHOM OUR FATHERS WOULD NOT OBEY, BUT THRUST HIM FROM THEM, AND IN THEIR HEARTS TURNED BACK AGAIN INTO EGYPT."

The overview is:

1. The phrase, *"To whom our fathers would not obey,"* marks the history of Israel, which ultimately led to their destruction. They disobeyed, even though God had bestowed such signal marks of favor upon them.

2. The phrase, *"But thrust him from them,"* refers not only to the initial response of Israel, but pretty much their history as well! In fact, had not God intervened at least several times, they would have killed Moses.

3. *"And in their hearts turned back again into Egypt,"* puts the finger right square on the problem. Their *"hearts"* were still in Egypt just like the hearts of many Believers presently are still in the world.

(40) "SAYING UNTO AARON, MAKE US GODS TO GO BEFORE US: FOR AS FOR THIS MOSES, WHICH BROUGHT US OUT OF THE LAND OF EGYPT, WE DO NOT KNOW WHAT IS BECOME OF HIM."

The exegesis is:

1. The phrase, *"Saying unto Aaron,"*

regrettably, proclaims these rebels receiving a sympathetic ear.

2. *"Make us gods to go before us,"* proclaims the sin that ultimately banished the Ten Tribes beyond Damascus and the Two Tribes beyond Babylon. In each case, it originated at the very start of their history.

3. Thus, Stephen laid bare the full measure of their guilt. Nothing now remained but their final banishment, which would come very shortly!

4. They had rejected all three Persons of the Trinity by despising the Law, rejecting the Prophets, and crucifying the Messiah. Man was judged and his nature revealed in the conduct of Israel, for Israel not only sinned, but being under the special care and love of God, sinned against that care and that love. They killed Christ in His humility and now rejected Him in His Glory.

5. The account of this failure unto Aaron is found in Exodus, Chapter 32.

6. The phrase, *"For as for this Moses, which brought us out of the land of Egypt, we do not know what is become of him,"* proclaims to us several things:

a. Without proper leadership, the end result almost always will be exactly as Israel of old, demanding a golden calf, etc. Regrettably, there is not much spiritual leadership in the modern church.

b. Idolatry was rampant then, and, regrettably, idolatry is rampant now (I Jn. 5:21).

c. As Israel's heart little left Egypt, likewise, the church's heart little leaves the world.

d. They were asking what had become of Moses, not dreaming or caring that they were about to be the recipients of the greatest instrument of Light in the world, the Law of God.

e. It is tragic, while God is preparing great things for us, even greater than one could begin to imagine, is it possible that we, at the same time, are preparing to worship idols?

(41) "AND THEY MADE A CALF IN THOSE DAYS, AND OFFERED SACRIFICE UNTO THE IDOL, AND REJOICED IN THE WORKS OF THEIR OWN HANDS."

The form is:

NOTES

1. The phrase, *"And they made a calf in those days,"* was the result of two things:

a. They wanted a God they could see.

b. The Egyptians worshiped living bulls at Memphis and Heliopolis as incarnations of the gods *"Ptah and Ra."* In fact, *"calf worship"* was almost, if not quite, universal among all the ancient Semite peoples.

2. In Canaan, the bull was the symbol of Baal and the cow of Astarte. Israel was supposed to have left *"calf"* worship in Egypt, but they would readily find it again in the Promised Land, which was a constant source of temptation.

3. *"And offered sacrifice unto the idol,"* probably represented a lamb but, in times to come, would include human sacrifice.

4. The phrase, *"And rejoiced in the works of their own hands,"* presents the problem of man from the very beginning. It is *"our own hands"* versus *"God's own Hands."*

5. Due to the Advent of the Holy Spirit nearly 2,000 years ago, and as a result of what Jesus did at Calvary and the Resurrection, *"Light"* has entered the world at an unprecedented rate; consequently, man is not quite so open presently in his worship of *"idols."* However, the principle is the same!

6. Today's idols are sports, money, power, entertainment, etc., all the work of men's hands.

7. In the Church, it is little different. Men make idols of religion, particular doctrines, education, psychology, money, power, etc., all devised by the hands of men and not God!

(42) "THEN GOD TURNED, AND GAVE THEM UP TO WORSHIP THE HOST OF HEAVEN; AS IT IS WRITTEN IN THE BOOK OF THE PROPHETS, O YOU HOUSE OF ISRAEL, HAVE YOU OFFERED TO ME SLAIN BEASTS AND SACRIFICES BY THE SPACE OF FORTY YEARS IN THE WILDERNESS?"

The pattern is:

1. The phrase, *"Then God turned, and gave them up to worship the host of Heaven,"* refers to the sun, moon, and stars.

2. Actually, the worship of the golden calf was star worship. It was the solar bull, the constellation Taurus, in which the sun was at the time of the spring equinox that was thus represented.

3. The question, *"As it is written in the Book of the Prophets, O you House of Israel, have you offered to Me slain beasts and sacrifices by the space of forty years in the wilderness?"* is asked in this manner for a purpose. While Israel did offer up sacrifices, they were not always to God. Actually, the words *"to Me"* are emphatic. His objection was that the sacrifices were not always to Him.

If God is not served alone and with the whole heart, He is not served at all. He regards no offering but the offerer himself. Moses said that Israel sacrificed to devils and not to God during part of this time (Deut. 32:17). Ezekiel declared that they went after their idols (Ezek. 20:16).

(43) "YES, YOU TOOK UP THE TABERNACLE OF MOLOCH, AND THE STAR OF YOUR GOD REMPHAN, FIGURES WHICH YOU MADE TO WORSHIP THEM: AND I WILL CARRY YOU AWAY BEYOND BABYLON."

The form is:

1. The phrase, *"Yes, you took up the tabernacle of Moloch,"* refers to the name of the main Ammonite deity to whom children were offered by fire (Lev. 18:21; 20:2; Deut. 18:10; II Ki. 16:3; 21:6; 23:10; Jer. 19:5; 32:35).

2. This was supposed to be the sun god. It was a hideous figure, with its outstretched arms heated red hot, and little children were tied to these arms and offered in sacrifice. They died a horrible death. To prevent the parents from hearing their cries, priests, dressed in black robes, would beat drums loudly.

3. The phrase, *"And the star of your god Remphan, figures which you made to worship them,"* refers to the Planet Saturn, called *"Chiun"* in Amos 5:26, which was the star god of Babylon. In those days, idolaters carried small images of their gods on their persons and even placed them in their houses. Sadly, Israelites began to emulate their heathen neighbors, such as the Moabites and Ammonites, etc., by doing the same thing.

4. If they wanted idols, that's exactly what they would get, as the Lord predicted by the Prophet Amos. They would be carried into captivity beyond *"Damascus"*

NOTES

and *"Babylon."*

5. And so they were!

6. The phrase, *"And I will carry you away beyond Babylon,"* presents Stephen quoting from Amos 5:25-27. However, he used the name *"Babylon"* while Amos used the name *"Damascus."* Nevertheless, there is no conflict!

7. The Ten Tribes were carried away by the Assyrians beyond Damascus as predicted by Amos, and the Two Tribes by the Chaldeans beyond Babylon as foretold by Moses, hence, the words, *"The Book of the Prophets,"* i.e., the Prophetic Books, i.e., the Bible.

8. Stephen did not say: *"As it is written in the Book of the Prophet Amos."*

(44) "OUR FATHERS HAD THE TABERNACLE OF WITNESS IN THE WILDERNESS, AS HE HAD APPOINTED, SPEAKING UNTO MOSES, THAT HE SHOULD MAKE IT ACCORDING TO THE FASHION THAT HE HAD SEEN."

The exegesis is:

1. The phrase, *"Our fathers had the tabernacle of witness in the wilderness, as He had appointed,"* simply means that God gave them the *"Tabernacle,"* plus the sacred vessels, in order that His People may have a way to worship Him. However, it was *"worship"* that was totally different from any other type of worship devoted to idols in the entirety of the world.

2. The latter represents worship one way only because idols are dead figures and cannot respond.

3. With God, when He is truly worshiped, He responds with His Presence filling the heart of the worshiper, which establishes communion and relationship. As such, the human heart is fulfilled, which nothing else can do.

4. So, with that being the case, why would Israel desire to worship idol gods, which were dead figures, rather than Jehovah, Who was real and alive?

5. Why will the modern church resort to the foolish drivel of man, such as humanistic psychology, etc., in the place of the Lord of Glory?

6. Perhaps the explanation is in many directions; however, the pull downward,

NOTES

spiritually speaking, is ever present. To be sure, Satan makes his way attractive and popular. As such, multitudes opt for the present glitter even as Israel of old!

7. Satan is very subtle! He seldom attacks head on. His error is quite content to ride into the Church on the back of Truth. As such, and because there is Truth, the *"lie"* is believable!

8. The phrase, *"Speaking unto Moses, that he should make it according to the fashion that he had seen,"* presents the design exclusively by the Lord, which is the only thing God can accept.

Men attempt to reach God in all types of ways, all by the devices of their own hands, even as the idols of old. That is even the problem in the modern church.

Men add to the Bible or take from the Bible, never content to leave it as is, but always feeling they must change the *"fashion"* in some manner.

9. God can be worshiped with tremendous results, but only on His Terms. As well, Salvation is available and freely given, but only on God's Terms, which man constantly attempts to change.

10. Man never seems to learn that as it pertains to God, it must always be *"according to the fashion,"* i.e., God's Word.

(45) "WHICH ALSO OUR FATHERS WHO CAME AFTER BROUGHT IN WITH JESUS (JOSHUA) INTO THE POSSESSION OF THE GENTILES, WHOM GOD DROVE OUT BEFORE THE FACE OF OUR FATHERS, UNTO THE DAYS OF DAVID."

The pattern is:

1. The phrase, *"Which also our fathers who came after brought in with Jesus into the possession of the Gentiles,"* should have been translated, *"Joshua,"* for that is who is meant. (Jesus is the Greek translation of the Hebrew Joshua. Jesus, the Son of God, was actually called *"Joshua,"* both meaning *"Saviour."*)

2. This *"possession of the Gentiles"* referred to the land of Canaan.

3. *"Whom God drove out before the face of our fathers, unto the days of David,"* refers to a time span of approximately 500 years.

4. After Joshua died, there was a terrible spiritual deterioration, albeit with some few spiritual highlights along the way. Due to this deterioration, it took much longer than it should have for victories to be brought about and milestones to be reached. I wonder how similar that is to our own lives!

5. When David became king of Israel—only after long years and much difficulties—Israel finally began to accomplish that intended by the Lord. Under David, at least for the most part, that which the Lord had promised to Abraham and to Moses was finally realized. By the Power of God, Israel became one of, if not the most, powerful nations in the world of its day. Every enemy was defeated, with tremendous spiritual victories won. Spiritually, Israel rose to its highest power under David, through whom the Son of David would ultimately come!

(46) "WHO FOUND FAVOR BEFORE GOD, AND DESIRED TO FIND A TABERNACLE FOR THE GOD OF JACOB."

The structure is:

1. The phrase, *"Who found favor before God,"* proclaims the greatest thing that could ever be said about any human being. The reason was simple: David had a heart after God and, actually, a heart after God's own Heart (I Sam. 13:14).

2. *"And desired to find a Tabernacle for the God of Jacob,"* speaks of the Ark of the Covenant being brought into Jerusalem after being untended for approximately 70 years (II Sam. 6:12; Ps. 132:6).

(47) "BUT SOLOMON BUILT HIM AN HOUSE."

The record is:

1. The plans for the Temple were given to David by the Lord, even down to the most minute detail, plus total instructions for the order of service and worship, but Solomon was the one who built the structure.

2. David was a Type of Christ, actually, more so than any other; however, he represented Christ as the Warrior Champion, Who would defeat all enemies, even as He did at Calvary and the Resurrection. For this cause was Christ manifested, that He might destroy the works of the devil (I Jn. 3:8).

3. Solomon was a Type of Christ, as well, but of the Victorious Christ with all enemies defeated, even as the reign of Solomon portrayed. The former represented the

kingdom realized while the latter represented the kingdom at peace.

4. The general outline of the structure (Temple) was based on that of the Tabernacle; however, the dimensions were in the main twice those of the Tabernacle, although there were exceptions to this rule.

5. It was built according to the directions of the Lord on Mount Moriah in Jerusalem. The Holy of Holies is supposed to have stood over the rock where Abraham was to offer Isaac but was stopped by the Lord at the last moment.

6. It took seven and one-half years to build this structure, and all of this time, *"There was neither hammer nor axe nor any tool of iron heard in the house, while it was in building"* (I Ki. 5:17-18; 6:7). The stones were cut, hewn, and polished at the places where they were taken.

7. The manner in which it was built would have cost approximately one trillion dollars in 2000 currency. Consequently, it was the most expensive building ever constructed.

8. It was destroyed by Nebuchadnezzar about 400 years after its construction. He carried off the treasures of the Temple and palace.

9. It was destroyed because Israel no longer desired to serve the Lord Who had dwelt between the Mercy Seat and the Cherubim in the Holy of Holies. The Prophet Ezekiel actually saw the Lord depart from this sacred edifice (Ezek. 11:22-25). Inasmuch as the Lord was no longer there, the building no longer served any purpose and, consequently, was destroyed.

10. When Judah served the Lord, there was no enemy on Earth who could defeat her; however, without the Lord, she was easy prey for the Babylonian dictator.

(48) "HOWBEIT THE MOST HIGH DWELLS NOT IN TEMPLES MADE WITH HANDS; AS SAYS THE PROPHET."

The record is:

1. If we ignore the Cross of Christ, we have just destroyed Christianity.

2. Everything we receive from the Lord comes by the means of the Cross.

3. In other words, it is the Cross of Christ that makes everything possible.

NOTES

THE MOST HIGH

The phrase, *"Howbeit the Most High dwells not in Temples made with hands,"* speaks of the prayer as offered by Solomon at the dedication of the Temple (I Ki. 8:27).

By quoting this as originally given by Solomon, Stephen justified himself from the charge of having spoken blasphemous words against the Temple. The idea is this:

The reason the Sanhedrin became so angry, even to the point of killing Stephen, which they did, is because they had made a god out of the Temple, the sacrifices, etc. They had long since lost all sight as to what these things represented and that their purpose was to point to One Who was to come, the Messiah, i.e., *"the Lord Jesus Christ."*

Such is the same presently with many religious denominations. The leaders and others have gradually turned the denomination into a god; consequently, if anyone makes a corrective statement about that particular denomination, it arouses intense anger, and for the same reason that it did with the Sanhedrin of old.

As we have previously said, a religious denomination ideally is to be a tool to help carry out the Work of God, pretty much the same as any helpful tool.

For someone to speak in a corrective sense about a mere tool, etc., would not arouse any animosity or anger. However, if the people in charge of the *"tool"* thought the thing was God, then the response would be one of anger, wrath, etc. The illustration may be crude, but I think it proves my point.

WILLFUL BLINDNESS AND IDOLATRY

Stephen made no defense but, on the contrary, accused his judges of hypocrisy. He declared that their devotion to the Law and to the Temple was hypocritical, for they continually resisted Him Who gave the Law and Whose House was the Temple.

To boast of the Temple and eject its Indweller was willful blindness and idolatry, and he charged them with being, at heart, idolaters from the very beginning of their national history, although professing obedience to the Law.

(The modern counterparts are idolaters, as well, having made a god [idol] out of their religious denominations, etc.)

Stephen pointed out that they had sold Joseph and thrust Moses from them, and that, as to the Temple, they were not entitled to pride themselves respecting it, for they had always resisted the Holy Spirit Who occupied it. As well, they had killed those whom He sent, with their wickedness culminating in their being now the betrayers and murderers of the Messiah Himself.

In his review of the national history, he began with Abraham and recalled the Glory of the Grace that chose that idolater. It was the Glory of that Grace that gave meaning to the magnificent appellation *"the God of Glory."*

It was not an outward physical glory but the Glory of absolutely free Grace, for Abraham was a Syrian ready to perish (Deut. 26:5).

The phrase, *"As says the Prophet,"* should have been in the next Verse, for it speaks and pertains to Isaiah.

(49) "HEAVEN IS MY THRONE, AND EARTH IS MY FOOTSTOOL: WHAT HOUSE WILL YOU BUILD ME? SAYS THE LORD: OR WHAT IS THE PLACE OF MY REST?"

The pattern is:

1. The *"Message of the Cross"* is, I believe, what the Holy Spirit is presently saying to the Churches (Rev. 3:13).

2. If that is the case, and I firmly believe it is, this means that this Message is the single most important Message in the world today.

HEAVEN AND EARTH

The phrase, *"Heaven is My Throne, and Earth is My Footstool,"* is taken, as is the balance of this Scripture and the next, from Isaiah 66:1-2.

The idea, as given by Isaiah and quoted by Stephen, is that God cannot be locked up in a building, a religious denomination, in philosophy, or in anything else. When one speaks of God, He must be spoken of in a manner totally unlike anything else or anyone else who is addressed.

While it was true that God dwelt between the Mercy Seat and the Cherubim in the Holy of Holies in the Temple, still, He was not confined to that place. That is at least one of the reasons Jesus said, *"But I say unto you, That in this place is One greater than the Temple,"* speaking of Himself (Mat. 12:6).

NOTES

The question, *"What House will you build Me? says the Lord,"* actually refers to the fact that it simply was not possible for anyone to build a house, as such, for the Lord. If Heaven is His Throne, and Earth is His Footstool, even as He says, how in the world did Israel think they could limit the Lord to the Temple?

The Temple was to be a stopgap measure, which enabled God's People to worship Him, and which pointed to the True Temple Who was coming.

The Lord even spelled it out in this Prophecy given by Isaiah as to the Character and Nature of the One Who was coming. The following is the description:

"But to this man will I look, even to him who is poor and of a contrite spirit, and trembles at My Word" (Isa. 66:2).

THE MESSIAH

In other words, the Scripture just quoted is the description of the Messiah, which fit Jesus totally, and which the religious leaders of Israel should have known!

The question, *"Or what is the place of My rest?"* pertains to the progressive Plan of God. The idea is this:

Israel had come to the place that they believed the Temple was all in all, in other words, the chief end of the Work and Ways of God. They did not see it as it truly was, only a step toward an ultimate goal.

The Greek word for *"rest"* is *"katapausis"* and means *"a putting down; to depose one from power."*

It refers to a complete putting down of enemies where one can rest secure from any danger of further uprising as referred to in Matthew 22:44 and Acts 2:35.

God's Rest from all Redemptive Work and of using force to put down rebellion will come at the end of the Millennium when Christ has put down all enemies and God becomes All in All (I Cor. 15:24-28; Eph. 1:10; Rev. 21:3-7; 22:3).

One of Satan's strategies is to get Believers, especially leaders, to veer away from the Word of God. If he can get them to add to the Word or take from the Word, to the extent this is done, to that extent will be harm.

Israel had made a god out of the Temple and all of its ceremonies, even as many modern Believers have made gods out of their particular churches or religious denominations, particular ordinances or doctrines, etc.

(50) "HAS NOT MY HAND MADE ALL THESE THINGS?"

The record is:

1. The idea of this question, as it is asked by the Lord, is that He has made the heavens and the Earth and all that is therein, so why would He want to confine Himself totally to one small building on Earth? The thing made must, of necessity, be less than the one who made it!

2. It is the same idea as some people thinking that the Lord is confined to their church alone, etc.

(51) "YOU STIFFNECKED AND UNCIRCUMCISED IN HEART AND EARS, YOU DO ALWAYS RESIST THE HOLY SPIRIT: AS YOUR FATHERS DID, SO DO YOU."

The pattern is:

1. To ignore the Cross is to ignore the Gospel (I Cor. 1:17).

2. Much of the modern church understands the Cross, at least somewhat, as it refers to Salvation, but not at all to Sanctification.

3. And yet, ninety-nine percent of Paul's writings are given over to this very subject, the Sanctification of the Saint.

UNCIRCUMCISED IN HEART

The phrase, *"You stiffnecked and uncircumcised in heart and ears,"* presented a blow to them, which went to the very heart of the matter.

In applying this expression to his hearers, Stephen was using the identical language of Moses when he conveyed God's rebuke to them.

Considering that they professed to be standing on Moses' side against Stephen, this must have made his words doubly cutting to them.

NOTES

The phrase, *"Uncircumcised in heart,"* only occurs here in the New Testament but is found, at least in the same spirit, in the Old Testament (Lev. 26:41; Deut. 10:16; Jer. 9:26; Ezek. 44:7, etc.). However, Paul basically said the same thing but in slightly different words (Rom. 2:28-29; Phil. 3:2-3; Col. 2:11, etc.).

The word as Stephen uttered it, in its application to his Jewish audience, contained a whole volume of rebuke.

They prided themselves on their circumcision. They trusted in it as a sure ground of favor in the Sight of God, but all the while, they were on a level with the heathen, whom they despised, and were to be reckoned among the uncircumcised, whom they loathed. The reason was simple: they were without the true Circumcision, that of the heart.

RESISTING THE HOLY SPIRIT

The phrase, *"You do always resist the Holy Spirit: as your fathers did, so do you,"* proclaims that which is very, very serious!

The Greek word for *"resist"* is *"antipipto"* and means to *"fall against or pull against like a backsliding heifer that will not be led"* (Hos. 4:16; 11:7).

As Stephen mentioned the *"fathers,"* he, as should be obvious, was not doing so in a positive way. In effect, he was stating that the Jews presently living were rebellious children of rebellious parents and, in fact, had been that way for many generations. Rebellion against God and His Ways is the worst sin of all. If such people have been given the Light of the Gospel, their rebellion becomes even worse.

When the Holy Spirit deals with human hearts and lives, this is a very special thing, as should be obvious. If His Pleadings are resisted, the individual does not remain static, but rather goes deeper into darkness. Anytime the Word of God is resisted, it produces the hardened heart; in fact, the more it is resisted, the more the heart becomes hardened.

All of this is in opposition to the Holy Spirit, whether the individual realizes it or not.

As an example: When we preach the

Cross through our television network, through the printed page, or however, if the Message is resisted, what they really are doing is resisting the Holy Spirit. This is true even though the people may think they are opposing me as an Evangelist, or Donnie, Gabriel, or any one of our Ministers. As such, it becomes very, very serious!

THE MESSENGER

Unfortunately, if the person doesn't like the Messenger, oftentimes, he will resist the Message. To do so, however, is to resist God! Man does not have the privilege of being able to choose the Messenger. That is the exclusive Domain of God!

Anything and everything that is truly of God is always carried out, superintended, overseen, and brought to fruition through and by the Person, Agency, Office, and Ministry of the Holy Spirit. So, if it is truly of God, the person is dealing with the Holy Spirit and, consequently, must never allow that truth to escape his consciousness.

When some of the Pharisees accused Jesus of casting out demons by the power of Satan, they were, in effect, subscribing the Moving and Operation of the Holy Spirit to Satan. Every evidence is that they blasphemed the Holy Spirit at that time, for which there is no forgiveness (Mat. 12:24-32).

As well, Believers should understand that while we must be very careful to measure everything according to the Word of God in order that false doctrine not be accepted, still, at the same time, we must be very careful that we do not speak in a negative sense of that which is truly of the Lord. Such is serious indeed!

Irrespective as to how weak a particular position may be, if it is of God, it ultimately will come out on top. Conversely, irrespective as to how strong a position may be, if it is not of God, ultimately, it will fail.

(52) "WHICH OF THE PROPHETS HAVE NOT YOUR FATHERS PERSECUTED? AND THEY HAVE KILLED THEM WHICH SHOWED BEFORE OF THE COMING OF THE JUST ONE; OF WHOM YOU HAVE BEEN NOW THE BETRAYERS AND MURDERERS."

The composition is:

NOTES

1. The question, *"Which of the Prophets have not your fathers persecuted?"* is very similar to that stated by Christ (Mat. 5:12; 23:30-31, 34-37; Lk. 13:33-34).

2. Some have surmised that Stephen may have been one of the 70. However, even though this is possible, there is no proof of such.

3. The phrase, *"And they have killed them which showed before of the coming of the Just One,"* proclaims the fact that the leadership of Israel down through the many years, with some few exceptions, had been just as much opposed to the Prophets who proclaimed the Coming of Jesus as these here who killed Him when He, in fact, did come. The pattern of unbelief began almost at the outset of Israel as a people and culminated in its truest form with the murder of Christ.

4. Always, the biggest hindrance to the Work of God on Earth carried out by the Holy Spirit, as stated, has always come from the religious side. Satan subverts that which is supposed to be of God, and is actually thought of by the world as of God, but, in reality, is doing the work of the Evil One.

5. *"Of Whom you have been now the betrayers and murderers,"* is about as strong as anything that could be said.

6. We know that Stephen was inspired by the Holy Spirit to say these words; therefore, this makes us know that those who claim to preach a positive gospel only, in fact, at least at times, are not preaching the gospel. For there to be a positive Gospel, there must, at the same time, be a negative Gospel!

7. Was this negative what Stephen was saying about the religious leadership of Israel?

8. Yes! In fact, it would hardly have been possible for it to have been more negative, but yet, this is exactly what the Holy Spirit wanted said.

9. As I have said elsewhere in these Volumes, when it comes to sinners who make little or no claim on God, the approach as used by the Holy Spirit, whether using Prophets or even Jesus Himself, has always been one of kindness, compassion, and love. However, to the professors of religion, even as here, that given by the Holy Spirit is much, if not

most, of the time very, very harsh!

(53) "WHO HAVE RECEIVED THE LAW BY THE DISPOSITION OF ANGELS, AND HAVE NOT KEPT IT."

The synopsis is:

1. The phrase, *"Who have received the Law by the disposition of Angels,"* speaks of the myriads of Angels who were present and were used in giving the Law of Moses to Israel. This is especially mentioned in Psalm 68:17, *"The chariots of God are twenty thousand, even thousands of Angels: the Lord is among them, as in Sinai, in the Holy Place."*

2. If we are to take this Verse literally, it means that 20,000,000 Angels were present when the Lord gave the Law at Sinai.

3. The phrase, *"And have not kept it,"* contradicts their claims!

(54) "WHEN THEY HEARD THESE THINGS, THEY WERE CUT TO THE HEART, AND THEY GNASHED ON HIM WITH THEIR TEETH."

The structure is:

1. The phrase, *"When they heard these things, they were cut to the heart,"* refers to the depth to which the Holy Spirit took Stephen's words, i.e., *"Word of the Lord."*

2. They were told bluntly and plainly that they had murdered the Lord of Glory and instead of abiding by the Law of Moses, they had instead broken it on every hand.

3. The manner in which the Word was given to them left them no room for rebuttal. In other words, there was nothing they could say!

4. The phrase, *"And they gnashed on him with their teeth,"* proclaims their answer to Stephen and the Holy Spirit.

5. They had only one choice, and that was Repentance. This they refused, so they would stop the Message by destroying the Messenger.

6. This is anger at a white-hot pitch!

(55) "BUT HE, BEING FULL OF THE HOLY SPIRIT, LOOKED UP STEDFASTLY INTO HEAVEN, AND SAW THE GLORY OF GOD, AND JESUS STANDING ON THE RIGHT HAND OF GOD."

The exegesis is:

1. The phrase, *"But he, being full of the Holy Spirit,"* proclaims this as being the second time as said of him (Acts 6:5).

NOTES

2. *"Looked up steadfastly into Heaven,"* means that Stephen saw something in Heaven that immediately seized his attention. Actually, he saw *"into Heaven,"* even as the Text proclaims, meaning he saw the very Throne of God itself.

3. The question must be asked, *"Did Stephen have a Vision, or did he see these things literally?"*

4. I think it really does not matter. Whether in Vision or not, it definitely was literal.

5. *"And saw the Glory of God,"* speaks of the splendor and magnificence of the Throne of God, but more so of God Who glorifies the Throne.

6. *"And Jesus standing on the Right Hand of God,"* is the opposite of the manner in which Jesus is usually presented respecting this position.

7. Sitting at the Right Hand of God is the usual attitude ascribed to the Lord in token of His Victorious Rest and waiting for the Day of Judgment. Here He is seen standing, as rising to welcome His faithful Martyr, and to place on his head the Crown of Life (Rev. 2:10).

8. In Verse 55, we have a clear portrayal of the Trinity. Stephen saw God the Father and Jesus standing at His Right Hand. The Third Person, the Holy Spirit, was filling Stephen, which enabled him to see the other Two.

(56) "AND SAID, BEHOLD, I SEE THE HEAVENS OPENED, AND THE SON OF MAN STANDING ON THE RIGHT HAND OF GOD."

The overview is:

1. The phrase, *"And said, Behold, I see the heavens opened,"* proclaims Jesus in His Glory as God just as the heavens had opened to see Jesus in His Humiliation on Earth as Man (Jn. 1:51).

2. *"And the Son of Man standing on the Right Hand of God,"* proclaims the rightful place of Christ as a result of His Exaltation, which was brought about solely by the Cross (Heb. 1:3-4).

3. Jesus used the title *"Son of Man"* of Himself some 84 times in the four Gospels. Actually, this is the 85th occurrence of this

title used 88 times in the New Testament. This is the only time that He is so styled after His Ascension except in Revelation 1:13 and 14:14.

4. The title speaks of His Incarnation, God becoming Man in order to serve as the Sacrifice in man's Redemption, and will have this human body forever, albeit glorified.

(57) "THEN THEY CRIED OUT WITH A LOUD VOICE, AND STOPPED THEIR EARS, AND RAN UPON HIM WITH ONE ACCORD."

The exegesis is:

1. The phrase, *"Then they cried out with a loud voice,"* presents their opposition to Stephen. Had they cried out in Repentance, the future of Israel could have been drastically changed for the good. However, their response was the same as it had been to Jesus.

2. *"And stopped their ears,"* means, as is obvious, that they no longer desired to hear anything that Stephen desired to say.

3. In other words, they *"stopped their ears"* to the Holy Spirit. In doing so, they sealed their doom!

4. The phrase, *"And ran upon him with one accord,"* pertains to the *"witness"* of Acts 6:13.

5. However, the Lord would hold them all guilty, both the false witnesses and the Sanhedrin.

6. Even though all possibly did not throw stones, all were in *"one accord"* that the stones be thrown, etc.

(58) "AND CAST HIM OUT OF THE CITY, AND STONED HIM: AND THE WITNESSES LAID DOWN THEIR CLOTHES AT A YOUNG MAN'S FEET, WHOSE NAME WAS SAUL."

The synopsis is:

1. The phrase, *"And cast him out of the city, and stoned him,"* presents pretty much the action of a mob.

2. *"And the witnesses laid down their clothes at a young man's feet,"* pertains, as stated, to that of Acts 6:13.

3. They took off their outer garments so as to be free to hurl the stones at their victim with greater force.

4. *"Whose name was Saul,"* presents the first mention of this man who would probably have a greater positive impact on Christianity than any other human being who has ever lived.

5. The Holy Spirit introduced Saul (Paul) in this posture for a reason.

6. Such would portray the Grace of God. Who that stood there and saw him keeping the clothes of the witnesses would have imagined that he would become the foremost Apostle of the Faith that he sought to destroy from the face of the Earth? But yet, that is exactly what happened!

7. Incidentally, the words *"young man,"* in the Greek is *"neanias"* and refers to one from 20 to 40 years of age. Paul was probably about 30 or 31 at this time.

(59) "AND THEY STONED STEPHEN, CALLING UPON GOD, AND SAYING, LORD JESUS, RECEIVE MY SPIRIT."

The order is:

1. The phrase, *"And they stoned Stephen, calling upon God,"* presents a monstrous offense on the part of his murderers.

2. When people do not know God and, in fact, are only immersed in religion, but yet, profess greatly and loudly to know Him, they will do anything to protect their position. They will even kill, exactly as here, in the Name of the Lord and feel justified in doing so. That is the very reason, among other things, that religion is a ghastly business!

3. One of the sure signs of religion and the absence of the Lord is when its adherents seek to protect what they consider to be theirs, and will go to any length to do so. Those who truly follow the Lord allow Him to defend their rights, place, position, etc.

4. As well, it would have been better translated to have inserted the title *"the Lord Jesus"* rather than *"God."*

5. The phrase, *"And saying, Lord Jesus, receive my spirit,"* presents Stephen rendering Divine worship to Jesus Christ in the most sublime form in the most solemn moment of his life.

6. Also, this statement by Stephen portrays to us that the spirit of man at death does not remain in the body but instantly goes to be with the Lord Jesus if the person is a Believer, and to Hell itself if an unbeliever (Mat. 10:28; Lk. 12:5; 16:19-31; II Cor. 5:8; Phil. 1:21-24; Heb. 12:23; James 2:26;

NOTES

I Pet. 1:3-4; Rev. 6:9-11).

(60) "AND HE KNEELED DOWN, AND CRIED WITH A LOUD VOICE, LORD, LAY NOT THIS SIN TO THEIR CHARGE. AND WHEN HE HAD SAID THIS, HE FELL ASLEEP."

The exegesis is:

1. When Jesus died on the Cross, He atoned for all sin, past, present, and future, at least for all who will believe.

2. This means that original sin was settled that day, and settled forever.

3. Now, the Holy Spirit has unlimited access to the Believer.

THE PRAYER OF STEPHEN

The phrase, *"And he kneeled down, and cried with a loud voice, Lord, lay not this sin to their charge,"* presents him dying on his knees and without malice toward his murderers.

One should note the comparison in his death and that of his Lord.

Jesus spoke with a *"loud voice"* at the very end, also, and said, *"Into Your Hands I commend My Spirit,"* with Stephen saying, *"Lord Jesus, receive my spirit"* (Lk. 23:46).

As well, Jesus prayed for His murderers while dying, as did Stephen (Lk. 23:34).

Stephen was stoned outside the city, as Jesus was crucified outside the city (Jn. 19:20).

"And when he had said this, he fell asleep," portrays the body falling asleep, with his soul and spirit instantly going to be with Jesus.

The body only sleeps at death and knows nothing in the grave. The spirit remains fully conscious after leaving the body, whether it goes to Hell or to Heaven (Isa. 14:9; Lk. 16:19-31; Rev. 20:11-15).

The experience of Stephen portrays that Heaven now is opened, and the Veil being rent, the Great High Priest is seen as the Son of Man in the Glory. All is open to the Believer—the Glory and He Who entered into it with His own Blood on behalf of His People.

He stands in Heaven, their Great High Priest, and bears their names upon His Breast. As King, He is seated; as Priest, He stands—though as to the perfection of His Atonement, He sat down.

NOTES

JESUS

Israel did not know until the High Priest came out on the Great Day of Atonement that his work was accepted for the Nation, but his reappearance assured them. So will it be by and by.

When they see Him coming out of the Heavens with His Pierced Hands and Feet, Israel will learn that His Atoning Work availed for their Justification.

That pertains to Israel; however, for Believers since the Day of Pentecost, it is otherwise, for the Holy Spirit has come out from the Glory to reveal the Perfection of Him Who is in the Glory, and to assure their hearts of the fact of the acceptance of His Atonement and the Power and sufficiency of His Mediation.

It is remarkable that prior to Revelation, Chapter 1, the only two men who saw the Man in the Glory were both Hellenists and not of the Twelve—Stephen and Paul.

SON OF MAN

Going back to the title *"Son of Man,"* Ezekiel was addressed accordingly; but the title *"the Son of Man"* belongs exclusively to the Messiah. It reveals Him as the representative Man, the long-promised and predicted Man, and the Seed of the Woman.

It is believed by many that the impression made by Stephen's death was even greater than that made by his life. Though it marks the beginning of the first great persecution of Christians, the death of the first Christian martyr resulted in the greatest acquisition Christianity has possibly ever made, the Conversion of Saul of Tarsus.

The Vision of the Risen and Exalted Jesus vouchsafed to the dying Stephen presented Christianity to Saul of Tarsus in a new light, tending to remove what had been its greatest stumblingblock to him in the Crucified One.

This Revelation coupled with the splendid personality of Stephen, the Testimony of his righteous life, the noble bravery of his sublime death, and above all, his dying prayer, fell upon the honest soul of Saul with an irresistible force and inevitably brought

NOTES

on the Damascus event.

Judged by his teaching, Stephen may be called the forerunner of Paul. He was one of the first to conceive of the fact that Christianity represented a new order of things and as such, would inevitably supersede the old order. Thus, his teachings forecast that great controversy of the first Christian century, the controversy between Judaism and Christianity, which reached its culmination point in the Council of Jerusalem, resulting in the independence of the Christian Church from the fetters of Judaistic legalism (Acts, Chpt. 15).

"Through the gates of Glory,
"Down the streets of gold,
"Marched a hero of the Lord,
"Into Heaven's fold.
"When he met the Master,
"At that Great White Throne,
"I believe Jesus smiled and said,
"'Stephen welcome home.'"

CHAPTER 8

(1) "AND SAUL WAS CONSENTING UNTO HIS DEATH. AND AT T HAT TIME THERE WAS A GREAT PERSECUTION AGAINST THE CHURCH WHICH WAS AT JERUSALEM; AND THEY WERE ALL SCATTERED ABROAD THROUGHOUT THE REGIONS OF JUDAEA AND SAMARIA, EXCEPT THE APOSTLES."

The exegesis is:

1. Jesus came to this world for one purpose, and that was to go to the Cross.

2. While everything else was of great significance, as should be obvious, still, the goal was always the Cross.

3. If man was to be redeemed, the Lord would have to do such by becoming man and giving Himself as a Sacrifice, which He did.

PAUL

The phrase, *"And Saul* (Paul) *was consenting unto his death,"* means that he was expressing hearty approval.

Paul was to mention this sad episode many times thereafter, and always with a great sadness and sorrow, which would be obvious (Acts 22:20; I Cor. 15:9; I Tim. 1:13).

Even though Paul was used of God as possibly no other man has ever been used, at least respecting the Church, still, we have very little knowledge of his background except a hint here and there.

For instance, it is said that he was *"a man little of stature, thin-haired upon the head, crooked in the legs, of good state of body, with eyebrows joining, and nose somewhat hooked, full of Grace: for sometimes he appeared like a man, and sometimes he had the face of an Angel."*

Paul says he was *"born at Tarsus in Cilicia"* (Acts 21:39; 22:3), and three times in this Book of Acts he is associated with this city (Acts 9:11, 30; 11:25).

Tarsus had a considerable reputation for culture, and, as a Hellenistic city in Cilicia—one of the early fields of Paul's missionary activity (Gal. 1:21)—it would provide the environment for his use of the common Greek speech and perhaps also for some acquaintance with the kind of thinking exposed in the streets and marketplace by Stoics, Cynics, and other propagandists.

He was given the name of Saul at birth, even though he never used any other name than Paul in his letters, primarily because they were addressed to Churches with many Gentiles. (Paul is the Greek derivative of the Hebrew Saul.)

He was of the Tribe of Benjamin (Rom. 11:1; Phil. 3:5).

A HELLENISTIC JEW

As well, it seems conclusive that Paul was a Hellenistic Jew, which simply means that he was influenced, as many other Jews of that day and time, by Greek thought and customs, although holding strongly to the Jewish Faith. It is generally assumed that Paul came from a family of some wealth and position but was disinherited when he came to Christ. As well, he was a Roman citizen, which was not easy for one to come by in those days if he were actually not a Roman. This gave him certain privileges that other people of the Roman Empire did not have.

He was trained in the Jewish religion

(for that is what it had become, just a mere religion) at the feet of Gamaliel in Jerusalem (Acts 5:34; 22:3).

Other than that, we know very little about him before his Conversion to Christ on the road to Damascus. I feel that there is a reason for this paucity of information.

Before coming to Christ, Paul's life was of no consequence, just as the lives of all are inconsequential before Christ. The moment a person accepts Jesus, that moment is actually the beginning of one's life. So it was with Paul!

Paul's Conversion is a never-ending Testimony to the Grace of God, of which we will say more in the Commentary on Chapter 9.

PERSECUTION

The phrase, *"And at that time there was a great persecution against the Church which was at Jerusalem,"* proclaims several things:

• The Church at Jerusalem was the first Christian Church, even though the name *"Christian"* was not even then in use. So, that means that the boast of others is unfounded.

• *"Great persecution"* generally follows a great Move of God. Satan is never pleased, as should be obvious, with many, even thousands, being taken from his kingdom of darkness into the Kingdom of God's dear Son, the Lord Jesus Christ.

• Jesus had commanded them to go everywhere preaching the Glad Tidings; however, it seems they were not too quick to carry out this Command but tended to remain in a great group at Jerusalem. Consequently, the *"persecution,"* although engineered by Satan, was allowed by God. Satan meant it for destruction, but the Lord allowed it in order that His People be scattered for the purpose of taking the Gospel to other places.

Also, it seems that Paul (Saul) was at least one of, if not the leader in this persecution.

The phrase, *"And they were all scattered abroad throughout the regions of Judaea and Samaria, except the Apostles,"* proclaims in the next Verses the results of this *"scattering."*

NOTES

The *"Apostles"* did not leave, at least at this time, and it seems it was according to the directions of the Holy Spirit.

This was perhaps done because of the need of anchoring the new Church in Jerusalem—new but tremendously large.

As well, this portrays the fact that the Lord would use others, such as Philip, even as He was using the Apostles. We learn from these Passages that all the activity was not contained solely within the circle of the Apostles, which informs us of the potency of the Holy Spirit in a yielded vessel, irrespective as to whom the vessel may be.

(2) "AND DEVOUT MEN CARRIED STEPHEN TO HIS BURIAL, AND MADE GREAT LAMENTATION OVER HIM."

The synopsis is:

1. The phrase, *"And devout men carried Stephen to his burial,"* proclaims the high esteem with which they held this man. He was the first martyr of the Church but definitely not its last! Following him, untold thousands would lay down their lives for the Cause of Christ in the Roman arenas, the Catholic inquisitions, etc. More than any other religion or faith in the world, Christianity has suffered this type of opposition. It does so because true Bible Christianity alone, which, in effect, is Christ, is the Way to God.

2. *"And made great lamentation over him,"* proclaims what was thought of him by the members of the Early Church.

3. It did not matter to them that he had been condemned by the Sanhedrin. They would publicly and audibly register their appreciation and love for Stephen, which, at the same time, repudiated the Sanhedrin.

4. Why would the Lord have allowed this death, especially considering that it seems that Stephen was in the very prime of his manhood?

5. Stephen's death would plant a seed that would play a great part in bringing forth Paul as its fruit. Consequently, in his death, even as Christ, many would live!

6. What a difference between his death and that of Ananias and Sapphira!

7. How many in the Body of Christ down through the centuries have died as Stephen, and how many as the duo of Acts, Chapter 5?

NOTES

(3) "AS FOR SAUL, HE MADE HAVOCK OF THE CHURCH, ENTERING INTO EVERY HOUSE, AND HALING MEN AND WOMEN COMMITTED THEM TO PRISON."

The structure is:

1. There has always been great persecution against Bible Christianity.

2. The reason is because it's the only way to God.

3. If the truth be known, as far as the powers that be, there would probably be more of those in America who would uphold Islam over Christianity. That's a strong statement, but I believe it to be true.

THE PERSECUTION OF THE CHURCH

The phrase, *"As for Saul, he made havock of the Church,"* means, *"To treat shamefully or with injury; to ravage; signifying the act of ferocious animals seeking prey."*

"Entering into every house," refers to those houses that he knew contained Followers of Christ.

"And haling men and women committed them to prison," means he spared no age or gender but forced them all before magistrates.

The Romans held the power of life and death. The Sanhedrin, the ruling body of Israel, could not sentence anyone to death except by special permission from the Romans (Acts 26:10). However, they could engage in murder, which was the case with Stephen.

During the period covered by the Acts, there was not much purely Gentile persecution. At that time, the persecution suffered by the Christian Church was chiefly Jewish.

There were, however, great dangers and risks encountered by the Apostles and by all who proclaimed the Gospel. Thus, at Philippi, Paul and Silas were most cruelly persecuted (Acts 16:19-40), and even before that time, Paul and Barnabas had suffered much at Iconium and at Lystra (Acts 14:5-19).

However, on the whole, the Roman authorities were not actively hostile during the greater part of Paul's lifetime. Actually, the purpose of Paul's trial being recorded at length in the Acts, Chapter 26 was to establish the fact that the preaching of the Gospel, at least at that time, was not forbidden by the laws of the Roman Empire.

THE ROMAN PERSECUTION BEGINS

The legal decisions that were favorable to the Christian Faith (Acts 18:14-16) were soon overturned on the occasion of the great fire in Rome, which occurred in July, A.D. 64.

The public feeling of resentment broke out against Nero to such a degree that he made the Christians the scapegoats, which he thought he needed. This was to avoid the stigma, just or unjust, of himself being guilty of setting the city on fire.

With the exception of such instances as those of Nero and Domitian, there is the surprising fact to notice that it was not the worst emperors, but the best (respecting administrative ability), who became the most violent persecutors of Christians.

One reason probably was that the ability of those emperors led them to see that Bible Christianity is really a divisive factor in any kingdom in which civil government and pagan religion are indissolubly bound up together.

The more that such a ruler was intent on preserving the unity of the empire, the more he would persecute the Christian Faith. Hence, among the rulers who were persecutors, there are the names Antonius Pius, Marcus Aurelius, who was referred to as the Philosopher-Emperor, and Septimius Severus.

CAUSES OF PERSECUTION

Persecution was no accident that chanced to happen, but rather an inevitable conclusion. It was the necessary consequence of the principles embodied in the heathen Roman government when these came into contact and into conflict with the essential principles of the Christian Faith.

The reasons for the persecution of the Christian Church by the Roman Empire were:

- Political
- On account of the claim that the Christian Faith makes, which it cannot help making, to the exclusive allegiance of the

heart and of the life.

Loyalty to Christ that the martyrs displayed was believed by the authorities of state to be incompatible with the duties of a Roman citizen. Patriotism demanded that every citizen should unite in the worship of the emperor, but Christians refused to take part in this worship on any terms, and so they continually lived under the shadow of a great hatred, which always slumbered, but might break out at any time.

The claim that the Christian Faith made to the absolute and exclusive loyalty of all who obeyed Christ was such that it admitted no compromise with heathenism. To receive Christ into the pantheon as another divinity as one of several was not the Christian Faith.

To every loyal Follower of Christ, compromise with other faiths was an impossibility. An accommodated Christianity would itself have been false to the only True God and Jesus Christ Whom He had sent, and would never have conquered the world.

To the heathen, there were many lords and many gods, but to the Christians, there was but one God the Father and one Lord Jesus Christ, the Saviour of the world (I Cor. 8:5-6).

Consequently, the essential absoluteness of the Christian Faith was its strength, but this was also the cause of it being hated.

THE THIRD RACE

This strange title, *"the third race,"* was probably invented by the heathen but was willingly accepted by the Christians without demur. It showed with what a bitter spirit the heathen regarded the Faith of Christ.

"The first race" was indifferently called the Roman.

"The second race" was anyone who was not Roman, i.e., *"barbarians,"* of which, Jews were accounted as such.

"The third race" was those who were Followers of Christ. The cry in the circus of Carthage was, *"How long must we endure this third race?"*

THE ROMAN CATHOLIC INQUISITION

Regrettably and sadly, the church slowly began to apostatize in the Second Century, and by the Third Century, was well on its way toward total apostasy.

NOTES

This took place after the Apostles passed on and those who knew them.

Actually, the persecution of the Christian Church by the empire of Rome came to an end in March, A.D. 313, when Constantine issued the document known as the *"Edict of Milan,"* which assured to each individual freedom of religious beliefs. This document marks an era of the utmost importance in the history of the world. Official Roman persecution had done its worst and had failed; it was ended now, but another persecution would take its place.

As the church began to apostatize into what ultimately became known as the Catholic church, then the same tyranny was practiced by its leadership upon those who would not join its ranks.

In effect, Constantine had brought the church and the state together, which ultimately brought the world into the Dark Ages. In totality, this scourge of the amalgamation of the church and state did not totally come to an end until the writing of the Constitution of the United States, which guaranteed religious freedom for all. That was in the late 1700s.

THE CATHOLIC CHURCH

As a result of attempting to make the church and the state one and, consequently, an empire on Earth, the Catholic church began to call itself the *"Holy Roman Catholic Church."* In fact, it was not holy or Roman, and neither was it universal, which the word *"Catholic"* actually means. As well, at least in the Eyes of God, it was no longer a church, that is, if the correct meaning of the word *"Church,"* which actually means *"Called out ones,"* is to be maintained. The Catholic church does not *"call out"* anyone from the world system but actually makes that system a part of the church, which once again obscures the very meaning of the word *"Church."*

In the doing of these things, great persecution was leveled against those who would not swear allegiance to the Pope, even as early Christians would not swear allegiance to Caesar.

NOTES

During the times of the Early Church, Rome demanded that Christians proclaim *"Caesar is Lord."* For those who would not do such, which numbered tens of thousands, the floors of the Roman arenas were wet with their blood.

Likewise, the Roman church continued to demand that Followers of the Lord proclaim allegiance to the Pope as the Vicar of Christ on Earth. For those who would not do such, and they numbered hundreds of thousands, they were tortured and slaughtered by every vile means that Hell could devise.

Today, the Roman church does not have the power it once had, or else, the inquisitions that stained entire nations with blood would once again be put into practice. They do not lack the will, only the power!

THE RESULTS OF PERSECUTION

Persecution raised up true witnesses for the Christian Faith. Men, women, and even children were among the martyrs, whom no cruelties, however refined and protracted, could terrify into denial of their Lord.

However, those who had adopted the Christian Faith in an external and formal manner only generally went back from their profession. The true Christian, as even the Roman proconsul Pliny testified, could not be made to do this.

The same stroke that crushed the straw separated the pure grain that the Lord had chosen.

Persecution showed that the Christian Faith is immortal even in this world. Of Christ's Kingdom, there shall be no end. *"Hammer away you hostile bands, your hammers break. God's Altar stands."*

Why was it necessary that the Church should have so terrible and prolonged experience of suffering?

It was in order to convince the world that though the kings of the Earth gather themselves against the Lord and against His Christ, yet all that they can do is vain. God is in the midst of His People; He shall help her, and that right early.

THE CHRISTIAN CHURCH

The Christian Church, as if suspended between Heaven and Earth, had no need of other help than that of the unseen but Divine Hand, which at every moment held it up and kept it from falling. Never was the Church freer, never stronger, never more flourishing, and never more extensive in its growth than in the days of persecution, especially the days of the Early Church.

What became of that great persecuting power, the Roman Empire?

It fell before the barbarians. Rome is fallen in its ruins, and its idols are utterly abolished. Its generals are peanut vendors, and its Caesars are organ grinders.

The Barbarians who overwhelmed the empire have become, at least in some way, the nominally Christian nations of modern Europe, and their descendants have carried the Christian Faith to America, Australia, Africa, and all over the world.

Likewise, the Reformation, which proclaimed the Bible as its Foundation and freedom to worship God according to the dictates of conscience, gradually overthrew the shackles of the Roman Catholic church until presently, its strength is but a shadow of what it once was.

CHRIST

Persecution made Christ very near and very precious to those who suffered. Many of the martyrs bore witness, even when in the midst of the most cruel torments, that they felt no pain but that Christ was with them.

Instances to this effect could be multiplied. Persecution made them feel how true Christ's Words were that even as He was not of the world, so they also were not of it. If they had been of the world, the world would love its own, but because Christ had chosen them out of the world, therefore, the world hated them. They were not greater than their Lord.

If men had persecuted Jesus, they would also persecute His True Disciples, but though they were persecuted, they were of good cheer; Christ had overcome the world. He was with them and He enabled them to be faithful unto death. He had promised them the Crown of Life.

Browning's beautiful lines describe what was a common experience of the martyrs, of how Christ *"in them"* and *"with them"* quenched the power of fire and made them more than conquerors:

"I was some time in being burned,
"But at the close a Hand came through
"The fire above my head, and drew
"My soul to Christ, Whom now I see.
"Sergius, a brother, writes for me
"This Testimony on the wall–
"For Me, I have forgot it all."

(4) "THEREFORE THEY WHO WERE SCATTERED ABROAD WENT EVERY WHERE PREACHING THE WORD."

The exegesis is:

1. If the *"Message of the Cross"* is unknown or ignored, the end result always is bondage.
2. The only answer for sin is the Cross of Christ.
3. If anything is trusted other than Christ and the Cross, in the Eyes of God, such is rebellion, therefore, sin.

PREACHING

The phrase, *"Therefore they who were scattered abroad,"* refers back to Verse 1 and, as stated, was a result of the persecution.

"Went every where preaching the Word," proclaims the criterion for Evangelism.

The word *"Preaching"* occurs seven times in this Chapter (Acts 8:4-5, 12, 25, 35, 40).

Satan dreads the preaching of the Gospel by the Anointing of the Holy Spirit but has no controversy with either ritualism or philanthropy; for it pleases God through the foolishness of preaching to save them who believe.

The Gospel is His Power unto Salvation, and the Preachers are not sinless Angels but pardoned rebels. Such is the simplicity of the Divine Plan for recovering humanity from the dominion of sin and Satan.

THE CALLED PREACHER

The Preacher of the Gospel is that one who has had an inner Call from the Holy Spirit and has been duly set apart as a Minister of Righteousness.

His task is that of addressing the popular mind and heart on Spiritual Truth as that Truth is set forth in the Sacred Scriptures. All of this is done for the spiritual profit of the hearer as its end.

The gravity and importance of this Calling, as set forth in the sacred Scriptures and amply illustrated in the history of the Church, surpasses those of any other calling among men. Luther said, *"The devil does not mind the Written Word so much, but he is put to flight whenever it is preached aloud."*

The work of the Preacher is always to be related to the Word of God, whether the Old Testament or the New Testament. He is a man with a Message and the preacher who has no message of the particular kind indicated in the Scriptures is in no true sense a preacher.

It has been well expressed that *"every living Preacher must receive his communication directly from God, and the constant purpose of his life must be to receive it uncorrupted and to deliver it without addition or subtraction."*

When he presents the Message of his Divinely-appointed ambassadorship in its integrity, he speaks with that peculiar kind of *"authority,"* which has been pronounced *"the first and indispensable requisite"* in giving a Message from God.

The true Preacher preaches from a Divine impulsion. He says with Paul, *"Necessity is laid upon me; yes, woe is unto me, if I preach not the Gospel!"* (Jer. 20:9; I Cor. 9:16).

He says with Peter, *"Whether it is right in the Sight of God to hearken unto you rather than unto God, judge ye.*

"For we cannot but speak the things which we saw and heard" (Acts 4:19-20).

THE MESSAGE IS GREATER

The Message of the Preacher is greater than the man because it is from God. It largely makes the man who preaches it in its fullness and power. Whatever are his own gifts or whatever the alleged recognition conferred by the laying on of hands, without the sense of the Message, he is not chosen of God to proclaim His Word.

Destitute of that, he does not have the

sustaining impulse of his vocation to enlist his entire personality in his work and give him mastery over the minds and hearts of men.

NOTES

THE OLDEST AGENCY

No agency of the Word of God is older than preaching. It is as old as the Bible itself (II Pet. 2:5). It is the manner chosen by God to communicate to man His Word, His Will, and His Way.

God has ordained that the agency for the spread of the Gospel is the preaching of that Gospel. No other means or way is provided.

CHRIST AS THE PREACHER

The mission of our Lord Jesus Christ, at least in part, was essentially one of proclaiming good tidings concerning the Kingdom of God (Mat. 4:17). He at once, on His entrance upon His Ministry, gave to preaching a spiritual depth and practical range that it never had before.

At that time preaching had manifestly become a fixed part of the synagogue worship and was made one of the chief instruments in the spread of the Gospel. In fact, our Lord constantly taught in the synagogues (Mat. 4:23; Mk. 1:21; Jn. 6:59). He thus read, interpreted, and applied the Law and the Prophets (Mk. 1:39; Lk. 4:16).

Christ's Testimony about Himself was that He came *"to bear witness to the Truth."* The spoken Word became His great Power in His Life and Ministry. Throughout His Life, Jesus was, above all things, a Preacher of the Truth of His Kingdom.

Telling men what He was in Himself, what He was in His Relation to man and his Salvation, and what He was to God the Father formed a large part of His Public Work.

PREACHED THE WORD

The first note of preaching is that it be the Word of God (II Tim. 4:2). Out of the Bible must the life of every generation of Christians be fed.

To Holy Scripture, therefore, ought the pulpit to abide faithful, for out of its treasures, the Preacher fulfills his double office of edifying Believers and subjugating the world to Christ. There must always be an organic connection between the Word in the Text and the Sermon.

The work of preaching is the fulfillment of a Divinely-instituted ambassadorship (II Cor. 5:20). The Gospel is put into the hands of men for a distinct purpose and is to be administered in accordance with the Plan of its Author, the Lord Jesus Christ.

The Preacher is in a very distinct sense a Trustee. *"But even as we have been approved of God to be entrusted with the Gospel, so we speak; not as pleasing men, but God Who proved our hearts"* (I Thess. 2:4).

Those who have accepted the responsibility imposed upon them by this Divine Commission, and a Divine Commission it is, are enjoined to exercise their office so as to warrant the approbation of Him Who has appointed them to a specific work.

The homiletic practice of taking the theme of every Message from a Passage of Holy Writ has been an almost invariable rule in the history of the Church. It is the business of the Preacher to present the Truth embodied in the Text in its integrity.

In the exercise of his Divinely-appointed ambassadorship, he is to administer God's Word revealed to Christian Faith, not human opinions or speculations.

(5) "THEN PHILIP WENT DOWN TO THE CITY OF SAMARIA, AND PREACHED CHRIST UNTO THEM."

The synopsis is:

1. Any direction taken other than the Cross of Christ always and without fail leads to spiritual adultery (Rom. 7:1-4).
2. Spiritual adultery is trusting in something other than Christ and the Cross.
3. As should be obvious, this greatly hinders the Holy Spirit from helping us.

THE SAMARITANS

The phrase, *"Then Philip went down to the city of Samaria,"* pertains to the Philip listed in Acts 6:5.

In using the phrase, *"City of Samaria,"* Luke was not meaning to refer to a city by that name, but rather *"a city of Samaria,"* which, although nameless, was probably Sychem.

This was the place of the heart of the Samaritan religion, and Mount Gerizim was the place of their temple. Actually, the Lord had already won many Converts there (Jn. 4:1-43).

During the Time of Christ and the Early Church, the Jews, at least for the most part, hated the Samaritans, and, as well, this hatred went back about 500 years.

Many of the Samaritans were half-breeds (part Jew and part Gentile), but the animosity was deeper than that.

Upon the return of the captive Jews from Babylon, the Samaritans asked permission to share in building the Temple under Zerubbabel. They claimed, and perhaps with good conscience, to serve God and to sacrifice to Him as the Jews did (Ezra 4:1); however, they were refused this request and, consequently, set themselves to frustrate the work in which they were not permitted to share (Ezra 4:4; Neh. 4:7).

Due to this, they instituted a rival religion, claiming the Pentateuch as the Word of God but denying the Psalms and the Prophets. As a result, the animosity only intensified.

Nevertheless, Jesus ministered to these people, even with great success, and now we see this great Move of God that took place under the Ministry of Philip.

PREACHING CHRIST

The phrase, *"And preached Christ unto them,"* refers to him proclaiming Jesus as the Messiah, God manifest in the flesh, and that He died on Calvary for the sins of man and rose from the dead. He preached Jesus as the Saviour and the Deliverer from sin!

The preaching of Christ must be the central core of our Message. To preach Christ is to preach Salvation, the Baptism with the Holy Spirit, the Cross, and the victorious, overcoming Christian life. As well, He is our Healer!

The problem with much modern preaching is that Christ is no longer held up as all of these things, but rather as a *"Good Man," "A Good Teacher,"* etc.

While He was truly all of these things, still, that within itself cannot redeem anyone. It is, as Paul said, *"Christ and Him Crucified,"* which is the Foundation of the Gospel.

NOTES

As a result of not holding Jesus up as the Saviour of man through what He did at Calvary, Christianity is reduced to a mere philosophy, and in that capacity, is no better than the religions of the world, etc. Jesus must be held up as the Son of God but, as well, as the One Who died on Calvary for our sins, thereby, taking the penalty upon Himself, which satisfied the claims of Heavenly Justice. Also, He rose from the dead, which ratified what He did on Calvary, and ascended to the Father, where He has remained, making Intercession for the Saints (Heb. 7:25).

(6) "AND THE PEOPLE WITH ONE ACCORD GAVE HEED UNTO THOSE THINGS WHICH PHILIP SPOKE, HEARING AND SEEING THE MIRACLES WHICH HE DID."

The record is:

1. The phrase, *"And the people with one accord gave heed unto those things which Philip spoke,"* proclaims a great acceptance of the Gospel.

2. *"Hearing and seeing the Miracles which he did,"* was that which verified the Message that he preached. These were, no doubt, *"Miracles"* of Healing, etc.

3. Actually, prayer for the sick and seeing them healed by the Power of God is meant to be a staple of true Christianity. The preaching of the Word and the *"Miracles"* should go hand in hand.

4. In this capacity, no religion on the face of the Earth can even remotely compare with that of our Risen Lord. However, sadly, much of Christianity has so watered down the Gospel, even openly denying the Miracle-working Power of God, that there is very little left, with the exception of a hollow shell. The primary reason for all of this is the denial of the Holy Spirit in the Office Work of His many Activities (Acts 1:8; 2:4).

(7) "FOR UNCLEAN SPIRITS, CRYING WITH LOUD VOICE, CAME OUT OF MANY WHO WERE POSSESSED WITH THEM: AND MANY TAKEN WITH PALSIES, AND WHO WERE LAME, WERE HEALED."

The order is:

1. The phrase, *"For unclean spirits, crying with loud voice, came out of many who were possessed with them,"* presents

NOTES

another aspect of the true Gospel Preacher using the Mighty Name of Jesus to cast out demons.

2. Jesus said, *"These signs shall follow them that believe; In My Name shall they cast out demons; they shall speak with new tongues;*

3. *"They shall take up serpents* (put away demon spirits)*; and if they drink any deadly thing, it shall not hurt them; they shall lay hands on the sick, and they shall recover"* (Mk. 16:17-18).

4. If one knew all the truth of the matter, one would find that demon spirits are the greatest cause of all types of aberrant activities and many sicknesses, etc. Regrettably, even though much of the modern church admits to the reality of demon spirits, they deny the Power of God, which alone can set the captive free (Lk. 4:18). For the most part, these types of needs and behavior problems are referred to psychologists. As such, they receive no help whatsoever and are actually harmed simply because they are kept from the Truth, which alone will set them free—the Power of God. Demon possession and oppression are just as real presently as they were in the time of Christ and the Early Church. As well, the only solution now is that which was the solution then, *"Jesus Christ and Him Crucified"* (I Cor. 1:23).

5. The phrase, *"And many taken with palsies,"* refers to a type of paralysis.

6. The phrase, *"And who were lame, were healed,"* probably has something to do with the *"palsies."* At any rate, there was a great Moving of the Holy Spirit in Samaria, which occasioned many coming to Christ, as well as *"signs and wonders"* being performed and carried out in the Name of Jesus.

(8) "AND THERE WAS GREAT JOY IN THAT CITY."

The synopsis is:

1. The *"joy"* was twofold, the Glad Tidings of the Gospel and the many Healings and Deliverances that were brought about.

2. In truth, if the Gospel is truthfully proclaimed, it will always result in people being saved, baptized with the Holy Spirit, healed, and delivered. If it is anything less, it is not the Gospel of Jesus Christ, which means that the far greater majority of that which claims to be the Gospel presently is, in fact, *"another gospel"* (II Cor. 11:4).

3. Down through the centuries, untold numbers of individuals, houses, and even entire cities, as here, have experienced the *"great joy"* that comes about as a result of the Gospel of Jesus Christ. It alone can bring about the fulfillment of the human heart. It alone can satisfy the spiritual craving in the soul of every man. It alone can set the captive free.

4. Anything that claims to be *"Salvation"* and does not produce *"great joy"* is, in fact, false!

(9) "BUT THERE WAS A CERTAIN MAN, CALLED SIMON, WHICH BEFORETIME IN THE SAME CITY USED SORCERY, AND BEWITCHED THE PEOPLE OF SAMARIA, GIVING OUT THAT HIMSELF WAS SOME GREAT ONE."

The form is:

1. The phrase, *"But there was a certain man, called Simon,"* presents a man around whom many legends grew, but of which there is no concrete proof.

2. However, it does seem to be correct that whatever the truth of the matter concerning this man, he was empowered by Satan and was able to do certain things accordingly.

3. To list some of the legends would require more time and space than should be given to a lie because whatever he claimed, it was all a fabrication.

4. The phrase, *"Which beforetime in the same city used sorcery,"* pertained to the practice of the rites of the art of the Magi. Consequently, many believe he was called *"Simon Magus,"* even though this last name is not recorded in the Bible.

5. To practice sorcery refers to seeking relief by magical means, which abounded in olden times, and is still prevalent today in many places.

6. Irrespective of whether it is called *"astrology, witchcraft, magic, sorcery, enchantments, etc.,"* it all pertains to trickery and fakery, or if it is something real, it is performed by demon spirits. The Bible forbids any traffic in this world of spiritual darkness, be it horoscopes, astrological

charts, etc.

7. The Believer is to be led by the Holy Spirit exclusively, Who will always lead one according to the Word of God (Jn. 16:13-15).

8. The phrase, *"And bewitched the people of Samaria,"* means they were amazed at the things he did.

9. *"Giving out that himself was some great one,"* proclaims this man called *"Simon"* claiming that he was the one who actually gave the Law to Moses. He claimed to be the Messiah and even the Holy Spirit. In other words, whatever he could get people to believe, that's what he claimed! The truth is, demon spirits used him and helped him to *"bewitch the people of Samaria."* However, now, possibly for the first time, the people of Samaria would hear the True Gospel of Jesus Christ.

The things of Satan always draw attention to the person, while that which is truly of God draws attention to Christ.

(10) "TO WHOM THEY ALL GAVE HEED, FROM THE LEAST TO THE GREATEST, SAYING, THIS MAN IS THE GREAT POWER OF GOD."

The account is:

1. The phrase, *"To whom they all gave heed, from the least to the greatest,"* proclaims that all were duped by his sorceries.

2. The phrase, *"Saying, This man is the great Power of God,"* means they attributed his magic and stunts as being done by the Power of God.

3. In fact, much of the world thinks that if something is supernatural, it automatically is of God! If one is to notice, many of the modern psychics who advertise over television and elsewhere claim to be of God. In fact, some of them are actually demon possessed, in this case, a familiar spirit. They can reveal certain things supernaturally and make the dupes think that there is help from this source.

4. Irrespective, it is all of Satan and designed ultimately to *"steal, kill, and destroy"* (Jn. 10:10).

5. The Believer must always understand that no matter how much something may be proclaimed as of God, and may even look like it is of God, if, in fact, it does not coincide perfectly with the Word of God, it is not to be accepted.

NOTES

6. For instance, the Catholics promote particular places, such as Lourdes in France, as a place where people can be healed, etc. In fact, every once in awhile someone is actually healed. In view of that, many are led to believe that it is of God; however, it is not of God because it is not according to the Word of God. There is nothing in the Word of God that proclaims Mary being used to heal people or bring about healing in any shape or form. So, irrespective of the claims, that and all others pertaining to Catholicism are not of God.

7. Of course, that necessitates an explanation as to how anyone is healed at this place, or others similar, if it is not of God.

8. The answer is simple: Satan can easily remove a disease that he put on a person in the first place; consequently, people are made to believe that what they receive is from God, which then deceives many others as well. Actually, deception is one of Satan's greatest weapons.

(11) "AND TO HIM THEY HAD REGARD, BECAUSE THAT OF LONG TIME HE HAD BEWITCHED THEM WITH SORCERIES."

The pattern is:

1. The phrase, *"And to him they had regard,"* means they had regard for someone who was of Satan and, therefore, of no benefit whatsoever, but rather was doing them great harm. Regrettably, many in the world, even in the church, have *"regard"* for that which is not of God, but rather of Satan, and of necessity, is packaged very deftly!

2. *"Because that of long time he had bewitched them with sorceries,"* can be said, as well, that almost the entirety of the world, and for all time, is *"bewitched."*

3. The word *"bewitched"* actually means that due to the power behind the sorcery, which, of course, is demon power, those who seek to such are, thereby, deprived of the ability to think or order their thoughts correctly. In other words, there is a touch of insanity involved!

4. That means that anyone who involves himself to any degree in horoscopes, psychics, Ouija boards, or any type of sorcery

NOTES

will suffer *"bewitchment"* the same as the Samaritans.

(12) "BUT WHEN THEY BELIEVED PHILIP PREACHING THE THINGS CONCERNING THE KINGDOM OF GOD, AND THE NAME OF JESUS CHRIST, THEY WERE BAPTIZED, BOTH MEN AND WOMEN."

The composition is:

1. The phrase, *"But when they believed Philip preaching the things concerning the Kingdom of God,"* means they now encountered a Power that was greater than the powers of darkness.

2. If the so-called preacher of the gospel does not preach a gospel that is stronger and more powerful than any other religion or witchcraft in the world, he is not really preaching the Gospel of Jesus Christ. Consequently, this means that preachers who refer people to psychologists are not truly preaching the Gospel of Christ. Were they doing so, that Gospel would set the captive free!

3. If preachers refer individuals to some type of 12-step program, this means, as well, that they are not truly preaching the Gospel of Jesus Christ. If so, Christ would set them free, which all the man-devised programs in the world can never do.

4. The phrase, *"And the Name of Jesus Christ,"* proclaimed that which, in reality, says everything. In other words, it is in *"the Name of Jesus Christ"* that the Gospel is preached, Salvation is obtained, people are baptized with the Holy Spirit, sick bodies are healed, etc.

5. He is the One Who has paid the price for all that we have, and consequently, it is in His Name that all of these things are done. To be sure, the Name of Jesus is far superior to that of Satan and anything he may possess.

6. The *"Name of Jesus"* represents His *"Authority"* and *"Power"* (Mat. 7:22; Mk. 9:39; Acts 4:7).

7. For something to be done *"in the Name of Jesus"* means *"as representing Him"* and, therefore, having His Authority.

8. To pray or ask as His Representatives on Earth, in His Mission and Stead, and in His Spirit and with His Aim, implies union with Christ and abiding in Him (Jn. 14:20).

9. *"They were baptized, both men and women,"* signifies that they had already come to the knowledge of Salvation through Christ and Faith in what He had done.

10. Water Baptism contributes nothing toward one's Salvation, but it definitely is an outward sign to the world that one has given one's heart and life to Jesus Christ, which it is meant to imply.

(13) "THEN SIMON HIMSELF BELIEVED ALSO: AND WHEN HE WAS BAPTIZED, HE CONTINUED WITH PHILIP, AND WONDERED, BEHOLDING THE MIRACLES AND SIGNS WHICH WERE DONE."

The synopsis is:

1. The phrase, *"Then Simon himself believed also,"* uses the same word as used in Verse 12. Consequently, every evidence is that Simon truly gave his heart and life to the Lord Jesus Christ, at least at that time! The word *"believed,"* as stated, is used here exactly as it was in the previous Verse and signifies Salvation, which is the requirement for that Gift of God (Jn. 3:16; Rom. 10:9-13).

2. *"And when he was baptized,"* plainly informs us that Philip saw enough evidence of Repentance and Faith in Christ that he baptized Simon exactly as he did the others, which he would not have done had it been a ploy as some claim!

3. As should be obvious, this completely shoots down the erroneous doctrine of Unconditional Eternal Security. It is quite possible for one to come to Faith but then to *"draw back unto perdition"* (Heb. 10:38-39).

4. The phrase, *"He continued with Philip, and wondered, beholding the Miracles and signs which were done,"* means that he watched very closely what Philip was doing, and his trained eye told him that no trickery was involved but that this was real—something, incidentally, he had never had!

(14) "NOW WHEN THE APOSTLES WHICH WERE AT JERUSALEM HEARD THAT SAMARIA HAD RECEIVED THE WORD OF GOD, THEY SENT UNTO THEM PETER AND JOHN."

The construction is:

1. The Cross of Christ is the Foundation Doctrine of all Doctrine.

2. The Cross was formulated in the Mind of God from before the foundation of the world (I Pet. 1:18-20).

3. This means that every Bible Doctrine is built squarely on the Cross.

4. If not, such a doctrine is specious.

THE HOLY SPIRIT

The phrase, *"Now when the Apostles which were at Jerusalem heard that Samaria had received the Word of God,"* proclaims a greater story than at first meets the eye.

Even though a great Move of God had taken place in Samaria, with many being saved, healed, and delivered, still, none had been baptized with the Holy Spirit.

Why?

The only answer is that Philip simply did not preach this great Doctrine, and for what reason, we do not know.

It is quite obvious that the Holy Spirit was working through him mightily to preach the Gospel and to perform Miracles, but nothing was said, it seems, about these individuals going on to receive the great Second Work of Grace, the mighty Baptism with the Holy Spirit (Acts 2:4).

Perhaps Philip felt he was not sufficiently informed in the Scriptures to preach this great Doctrine at this time. One must remember that at this early date, none of the New Testament had yet been written. As well, this was only a few weeks, or several months at the very most, after the Day of Pentecost.

A DEFINITE AND DISTINCT WORK OF GRACE

Irrespective as to what the reason was, when the news of this great harvest reached the ears of the Apostles in Jerusalem, they evidently inquired as to all the things that had happened. At some point, they must have asked as to how many had been baptized with the Holy Spirit, with Philip answering, *"None!"*

This tells us, even graphically so, that the Baptism with the Holy Spirit is a definite and distinct Work of Grace separate and apart from Salvation, and is actually received after Salvation.

So, if it is true, as many now proclaim, that when one is saved, one automatically receives the Holy Spirit, as well, then what the Apostles did in the sending of Peter and John made absolutely no sense.

No! The truth is that the Baptism with the Holy Spirit is an experience separate from Salvation. While the Holy Spirit is certainly involved in all that the Believer receives from the Lord, still, there is a great difference in being *"born of the Spirit"* than being *"baptized with the Spirit."*

As well, this shows us how much significance the Apostles placed in Believers being baptized with the Holy Spirit. The urgency and necessity is overly obvious! Consequently, the same emphasis should be had by modern Preachers as well.

The phrase, *"They sent unto them Peter and John,"* tells us that Peter was not the Pope of the Apostles, as claimed by the Catholic church, but actually their servant and agent. This fact destroys the claim of the papacy.

Of course, Catholics, as well as many Protestants, little regard the Bible, but rather their own tradition, which actually is made-up stories, etc.

(15) "WHO, WHEN THEY WERE COME DOWN, PRAYED FOR THEM, THAT THEY MIGHT RECEIVE THE HOLY SPIRIT."

The exposition is:

1. While the Lord may chastise His People, He never sends judgment because such judgment was tendered at Calvary.

2. Wisdom theology and legalistic theology discount the Cross of Christ. Both deprive it of its significance.

3. Paul's Doctrine of Justification is to be understood on the basis of the Cross. In fact, Justification and Sanctification are not possible outside of the Cross.

RECEIVING THE HOLY SPIRIT

The phrase, *"Who, when they were come down,"* refers to Peter and John. As well, it does not speak of geography, for Samaria was north and, therefore, up from Jerusalem. It did speak of topography, which means altitude-wise. Jerusalem was of higher altitude than Samaria, which then necessitated the

NOTES

Apostles *"going down."*

"Prayed for them that they might receive the Holy Spirit," proclaims the purpose for which Peter and John came.

Several things are here intimated. They are:

• This account tells us that the Baptism with the Holy Spirit is not an automatic process, as taught by some. It is certainly true that every person who is Saved is born of the Spirit, but that is certainly different from being baptized with the Spirit. Among other things, we learn here that one should pray to be baptized with the Spirit, which is done, of course, after one has been saved (Lk. 11:13; Acts 1:14; 9:17-18; 19:1-7; 1 Cor. 12:30; 14:1).

• It is evident in this account that the *"Holy Spirit"* referred to here is not Salvation, but rather an experience separate, different, and apart from Salvation, although Salvation must first be received before one can be baptized with the Spirit (Jn. 14:17).

• The account also tells us that the Baptism with the Holy Spirit is for all Believers, no matter who they might be.

THE PROMISE

Peter said on the Day of Pentecost, *"For the Promise* (of the Baptism with the Holy Spirit) *is unto you* (directed toward the many Jews standing in the Temple listening to Peter that day), *and to your children* (means that this great outpouring did not stop with the initial outpouring, but continues on), *and to all who are afar off* (meaning that it's not only for those in Jerusalem, but also the entirety of the world), *even as many as the Lord our God shall call (*that *'Call'* is *'whosoever will' [Jn. 7:37-39; Rev. 22:17])"* (Acts 2:39).

• We are also here told that it is Biblical to have special services delegated for Believers to be baptized with the Spirit (Acts 9:17-18; 19:1-7; I Tim. 4:14; II Tim. 1:6; Heb. 6:1-2).

If I remember correctly, the year was 1973. In prayer at one particular time, the Lord spoke to my heart and told me that I should set aside at least one service in every Crusade conducted here in the United States for Believers to be baptized with the Spirit. This we did, and we saw literally tens of thousands baptized with the Holy Spirit with, I might quickly add, the evidence of speaking with other Tongues as the Spirit of God gave the utterance (Acts 2:4).

The Lord also spoke to me and told me that if we would believe Him, we would see as many as 1,000 baptized in a single Service.

That was fulfilled at Madison Square Garden in New York City. Well over 1,000 were baptized with the Holy Spirit the last Sunday afternoon of the Crusade.

(16) "(FOR AS YET HE WAS FALLEN UPON NONE OF THEM: ONLY THEY WERE BAPTIZED IN THE NAME OF THE LORD JESUS.)"

The diagram is:

1. The phrase, *"For as yet He was fallen upon none of them,"* means, as it states, that even though many had been Saved, none in this place had been baptized with the Holy Spirit as of yet. However, that was soon to change!

2. *"Only they were baptized in the Name of the Lord Jesus,"* is meant to emphasize that the Water Baptism here inferred was not the same as the Baptism with the Holy Spirit.

3. As an aside, regarding Water Baptism in the Name of the Lord Jesus mentioned here and in Acts 2:38, as well as Acts 10:48 and 19:5, we are not to suppose that any other formula was used than that prescribed by our Lord (Mat. 28:19). However, as Water Baptism was and is preceded by a confession of Faith in the Lord Jesus, it is, therefore, a true description to speak of Water Baptism as being in the Name of Jesus Christ, which it is!

(17) "THEN LAID THEY THEIR HANDS ON THEM, AND THEY RECEIVED THE HOLY SPIRIT."

The overview is:

1. Paul presented Christ Crucified as the decisive Act of God in Salvation.

2. While the world attempts to manufacture another god, the church attempts to manufacture another sacrifice.

3. Religion is a man-made system used in place of a God-given Salvation.

NOTES

THE LAYING ON OF HANDS

The phrase, *"Then laid they their hands on them,"* once again proclaims this Doctrine.

As we have previously stated, the act of *"laying on of hands,"* in a sense, is to be the Hands of Jesus extended. Such serves as recognition respecting ordination or appointment, Healing Power, and as portrayed here, for Believers to be baptized with the Holy Spirit (Mk. 3:3; 14:3; 16:18; Acts 6:6; I Tim. 4:14; II Tim. 1:6).

"And they received the Holy Spirit," proclaims the greatest Gift any Believer can receive, even as Salvation is the greatest Gift that a sinner can receive.

A PERSONAL EXPERIENCE

The year was 1970, if I remember correctly. I had just gone on radio a little over one year before with our daily 15-minute program, Monday through Friday. The Lord was blessing; however, as I began to seek His Face early that particular morning, even before daylight, the Lord spoke some things to my heart that were to literally change our Ministry.

He told me that He was going to pour out His Spirit all over the world and that multiple thousands, even millions, would be baptized with the Holy Spirit.

He also told me that I was to set aside at least one Service in every Crusade here in the United States to be devoted exclusively to proclaiming the Baptism with the Holy Spirit for those who had been seeking this experience.

I remember very vividly the mighty Moving of the Holy Spirit that early morning hour. As well, I remember how inadequate I felt respecting this awesome task. I felt I did not know enough about the Holy Spirit to properly present Him as He should be presented. Actually, I *"argued"* with the Lord that I was really inadequate for the task, which I was correct.

What was His Answer to me? It was that I must obey the instructions He had delivered because this was His Message and His Mission, and I was nothing more than the instrument chosen to bring about His Results, at least as He dealt with my own life.

OUR FIRST HOLY SPIRIT SERVICE

How well I remember that meeting in Canton, Ohio. I announced that the Sunday afternoon Service would be a *"Holy Spirit"* Service. I was unprepared, however, for that which actually took place.

Over the years, I had prayed for many people and had seen many receive the Holy Spirit Baptism. In praying for these many individuals down through the years, I had pretty much always done even as I had seen it done, which was to pray for each individual until he received, etc., which could take several hours.

This particular Holy Spirit Service was conducted in a high school gymnasium, while all the other Services of this meeting had been conducted in a church. I was quite unprepared for what was to happen.

First of all, the building was nearly full, and secondly, after I preached on receiving the Holy Spirit and the absolute necessity of such, I then called people forward who desired to receive. I was somewhat shocked at the large number who responded, actually, several hundreds of people.

That Sunday afternoon, I attempted to deal with each one of the people as I had always done, but this method very quickly proved to be inadequate, especially considering the large number.

Of course, others were helping me pray, but at the same time, we really did not see many results. In other words, only a very few actually were baptized with the Holy Spirit despite the hunger in their hearts, which was obvious.

A DISAPPOINTMENT!

As I went back that evening to the motel room, I was greatly discouraged. I had tried my best to obey the Lord but seemingly without any success. To be frank, I did not know what to do respecting this dilemma. It was obvious that many people were hungry for the Holy Spirit, but it was also obvious that my present methods were, as stated, woefully inadequate. I wept before the Lord that evening as I reviewed these facts and asked where I had erred. No immediate answer was forthcoming.

Our next scheduled meeting was a Full Gospel businessmen's breakfast in Toledo, Ohio. It was a Saturday morning, if I remember correctly.

I arose sometime before daylight to prepare for the Service, which would convene at 10 a.m. Once again, I strongly felt that I should minister on the Holy Spirit and give the people an opportunity to receive. But yet, I felt that a repeat performance of the last Holy Spirit meeting would serve little purpose.

However, it was that morning that the Lord revealed to me the basic method I have followed ever since. It is this that I want to pass on to you, hopefully, that will assist you in receiving the mighty Baptism with the Spirit, that is, if you have not already been filled. Also, it will help Preachers and others pray for others to be filled and, in fact, to see many instantly go through to their own experience.

If so, perhaps the following instructions can help you to assist others in receiving this great experience from the Lord.

In praying about the situation, I looked in my briefcase and there were several tapes in there. I pulled them out and looked at each one. One was by Brother Kenneth Hagin. Even though Brother Hagin and I differed as it regarded some points of Doctrine, still, he had an insight into the Holy Spirit that precious few Preachers had, if any.

The Lord directed me to listen to that tape, which I did, several times. Step-by-step the brother outlined how to pray for people, even hundreds at a time, to be filled with the Spirit. I knew in my heart that what he was saying was right.

As the Lord clearly revealed to me this of which I was to do, I was so sure in my heart of what He had told me that I could hardly wait for the Service to begin.

THAT WHICH THE LORD DID

I remember preaching that morning and then calling people forward to be baptized with the Holy Spirit, with scores responding. They lined up, with the line seemingly stretching all the way across the building.

I began to do what the Lord had shown me that I was to do, which I had derived from the Message preached sometime back by Brother Hagin.

As I immediately began to do what the Lord had instructed me to do, the far greater majority, if not all, of those who came that day were gloriously and wondrously baptized with the Holy Spirit. I suppose there were 50 to 100 people instantly filled that morning. Neither they nor I would ever be the same again!

I remember an elderly Nazarene grandmother who had started attending our Meetings whenever we were in Ohio. She had become very hungry for the Holy Spirit. Actually, she would come forward every time we gave the invitation, but as of yet, she had not been filled.

However, that morning she was in that prayer line, and the Power of God hit her as I have seen it happen to many people, with her instantly falling to the floor and coming up almost immediately speaking with other Tongues as the Spirit of God gave the utterance. When she left that day, her countenance was wreathed in the Glory of God. No one had to tell her that she had received, for she knew that Pentecost had come to her.

NOT AN OPTIONAL EXPERIENCE

The Holy Spirit is not a denomination, a movement, or a church. It is a life-transforming experience that is meant to be received by every person who has turned his or her life over to the Lord Jesus Christ, accepting Jesus' Sacrifice for their sins.

The great Truth that this is not an optional experience but something intended for every Christian came to me while I was preaching a Message on the Holy Spirit in one of the Crusades. Although I do not recall the thrust of the Message I preached that night, I remember the sudden awareness that I must proclaim to everyone that the Baptism with the Holy Spirit is not a voluntary or elective move on the part of the Christian—it is an obligation within God's Plan for His Children.

THE COMMAND

Are those Christians who neglect or refuse to be baptized with the Holy Spirit

NOTES

going to lose their Salvation as a result?

No! That is not what I am saying; however, if Light is given and then rejected, there is the possibility that what Light is left will also be taken away. This much is certain:

The Baptism with the Holy Spirit is the one help that the Lord has given the Believer to enable us to be what we ought to be in Christ. If the Holy Spirit is refused, there is no other option to take His Place; consequently, in that case, the Believer can go no further in the Lord.

Jesus, in Acts 1:4, commanded His Disciples to remain in Jerusalem until they should receive the Promise of the Father, which was the Baptism with the Holy Spirit.

The specific word used is *"Commanded."* That is strong language. There is no suggestion of optional decision here, and we are quoting directly from the Word of God.

This was the Revelation that came to me suddenly the day I was preaching on the Holy Spirit. The Baptism with the Spirit is a must and is imperative, a circumstance and condition commanded by our Lord and Saviour Jesus Christ.

SUBSEQUENT TO SALVATION

I am well aware that it is commonly taught among many denominations that every individual *"receives"* the Holy Spirit at the moment of Conversion.

Theologically and Scripturally, this is correct, at least as far as it goes. It is impossible for anyone to receive anything from God unless the Holy Spirit is a Co-Participant in that which is done.

However, as we have stated, there is a very real and definite difference between being *"born of the Spirit"* and being *"baptized with the Spirit."* A person is not baptized with the Spirit at the moment he is Saved. He may be baptized moments later but not at the same time. The Baptism with the Holy Spirit is an experience completely separate from Salvation; it can only come after Salvation, and it must be consciously sought by the Believer (Lk. 11:13).

SPEAKING WITH OTHER TONGUES!

It is our belief that according to the Word of God, every recipient of the Spirit speaks with other Tongues at the time of receiving the Holy Spirit. There are no exceptions.

NOTES

Acts 2:4 says: *"And began to speak with other Tongues, as the Spirit gave them utterance."*

Acts, Chapter 10, says that Cornelius and his household spoke with Tongues and prophesied.

In Acts, Chapter 19, we see where the Apostles of John (when the Apostle Paul prayed for them to receive the Holy Spirit) spoke with Tongues and prophesied as they were filled.

As well, whenever the people in Samaria, as recorded in Acts, Chapter 8, were filled with the Spirit, it doesn't plainly state that they spoke with Tongues. However, the Scripture does say the following:

Simon the sorcerer, when he saw Peter and John praying for people to be filled with the Spirit and saw them filled, *"Thought that the Gift of God may be purchased with money"* (Acts 8:20).

Peter answered him, stating, *"You have neither part nor lot in this matter"* (Acts 8:21).

The word *"matter"* in the Greek, as it is used here, is *"Logos,"* and means *"a word or speech"*; Peter was referring to these Believers speaking with other Tongues.

As well, the Ninth Chapter of Acts records the Apostle Paul being baptized with the Spirit when Ananias prayed for him. No information is given; it just simply said in the words of Ananias, *"The Lord, even Jesus ... Has sent me, that you might receive your sight, and be filled with the Holy Spirit"* (Acts 9:17).

But yet, Paul himself stated, *"I thank my God, I speak with Tongues more than you all"* (I Cor. 14:18).

So, the Word of God is replete with the Scriptural proof that every recipient of the Holy Spirit speaks with other Tongues at the moment they are filled, and should continue on thereafter with their prayer language as the Lord helps them.

ONLY ONE REQUIREMENT

Many individuals and many denominations have conjured up and formalized any

NOTES

number of requirements that must be met before the saved person can aspire to the Baptism. In all honesty, there is one, and only one, requirement within God's set of rules, so to speak, and that is that the individual must be Born-Again.

Read Acts 8:14-17 and Acts 19:2. Both incidents clearly describe the condition of the Believers who had not yet received the Baptism with the Holy Spirit. They had not gone through any rituals or met any lists of preconditions. They were merely saved Believers.

Knowing this, the Apostles prayed for them for the reception of the Holy Spirit and they received! Clearly, this is confirmation in God's Word that Salvation is the only prior condition that must be met before the person may become a candidate for the Baptism (Jn. 14:17; Acts 2:1-4).

Satan is very well aware that the Holy Spirit is the source of the effective Christian's Power. Of all the things in the world that Satan does not want, more Spirit-filled Christians would, no doubt, lead the list. Consequently, he will put any stumbling-block in the path of the Christian, and do anything within his power to convince a wavering Christian that the Holy Spirit Baptism is not for him, etc.

SATAN'S LIES

He will tell you that you are unworthy, or he will try to get you to work out some solutions in some areas in which you are not yet victorious. He will point out your remaining faults. He will ask, *"What about your temper?"* or he will mention envy.

He will ask, *"What about the battle to overcome cigarettes (or alcohol or whatever)?"* Problem after problem will be brought to mind as failing after failing becomes grist for his mill.

However, the truth of the matter is that nowhere in God's Word are we cautioned to do certain things before we go before God and ask for the Infilling of the Holy Spirit. All these false preconditions are manufactured by Satan, not God.

Shocking as it may seem to some Christians, I have seen many Believers baptized with the Holy Spirit while they still smoked cigarettes, had bad tempers, or while they still worked to fight down improper sexual drives. Isn't it logical that once they experience the Baptism, then they have the Holy Spirit to help them to overcome these impulses by the Revelation of God's Word?

Recognizing our earthly weaknesses, how like God it is to send us the Comforter and the Strengthener while we are still imperfect, rather than to demand that we do all of these things on our own, which cannot be done anyway!

OUR PARACLETE

This, of course, is why Satan does everything at his command to prevent our seeking and receiving God's Help. I am sure Satan is capable of understanding Greek, and he surely knows that the Name of the Holy Spirit in the original Greek is *"Paraclete." "Paraclete"* is translated as *"One called alongside to help."*

What a beautiful way of expressing the role of the Holy Spirit! None of us is capable of being perfect, even with the help of the Holy Spirit, but how much greater our consecration when we have that wonderful help given to us by our loving Heavenly Father.

This is why it behooves the father of lies to set up a list of obstacles to prevent our seeking God's Help in our lives. The more things we have to do before we seek God's Help, the more time Satan has to work his devilment in our lives and in the lives of those we might have influenced.

THE HOLY SPIRIT BAPTISM CAN BE RECEIVED INSTANTLY

Another myth connected with the Baptism with the Holy Spirit is that we must *"tarry"* for some indeterminate time before we can expect to actually be filled. This is patently untrue.

No doubt, the basis for this is that the Disciples were commanded to wait in Jerusalem before departing to spread the Gospel. In effect, they were told that they should not go try to witness for the Lord, or do anything for the Lord for that matter, until they were first baptized with the Holy

Spirit. In fact, the Church could not even begin until the Holy Spirit came, which He did in a brand new dimension. The Cross of Christ, having washed and cleansed all sin—at least for all who will believe—now made it possible for the Holy Spirit to come into the hearts and lives of all Believers, and to remain there permanently, which could not be done before the Cross.

In effect, these Followers of Christ were not waiting to be filled; they were waiting for the Holy Spirit to come in a new dimension, which He did on the Day of Pentecost. After that particular day, people were to be filled immediately upon requesting this great and glorious Gift.

Unfortunately, these Commands, as given by Christ in the First Chapter of Acts, have been twisted to mean that a waiting period is part and parcel of the Holy Spirit Baptism. This simply is not true.

For instance, in the Eighth Chapter of Acts, the incident is recounted where Peter and John came from Jerusalem and prayed for the Believers in Samaria. These were saved Christians who had not yet been baptized with the Holy Spirit.

What happened?

They were immediately filled when Peter and John prayed for them and laid on hands.

Incidentally, others were filled, such as Cornelius and his household, without the laying on of hands.

TARRYING

Now, please do not misunderstand. It is wonderful to tarry before God. Quite frankly, I do not think a day goes by when I do not tarry before the Lord, awaiting direction as to what He would have me do with one or more situations. I truly believe this is a major component of the Spiritual Strength within my life.

However, the fact remains, tarrying as a precondition to receiving the Spirit is not discernable as a viable Scriptural Doctrine. All those mentioned in each of the Scriptures we have given received the Holy Spirit immediately. This should certainly indicate that we do not have to spend a tarrying time as we ask the Lord to baptize us with the Spirit.

NOTES

THE HOLY SPIRIT BAPTISM IS A GIFT

The idea that one can earn something from the Lord is not easily rooted out of the Believer. There is something in man, even the godliest, which desires to contribute something in the form of works for the things we obtain from the Lord. Perhaps it is tied up with the doctrine of *"doing penance."*

In truth though, God does not run a Redemption center where we come to pick up trinkets once we have saved enough *"brownie points,"* etc.

Acts 2:38 clearly describes an occasion when Peter pointed out that the assembled would receive the *"Gift"* of the Holy Spirit. A gift is something entirely different from wages. We earn wages, but we receive gifts without expending labor for them.

Every Christian knows that Salvation is a Gift, that is, if he is truly Saved, a Gift, in fact, which is unmerited and freely given to the undeserving through the generosity and Grace of God.

Yet, knowing this, some try to make the Baptism with the Holy Spirit (also defined Scripturally as a Gift) something to be earned. This is not consistent or reasonable within theology or Scripture.

The only major difference between the Gift of Salvation and the Gift of the Holy Spirit is that Salvation is God's Gift to the world, while the Holy Spirit is God's Gift to His Children. What do I mean as I say this time after time to congregations all over the world?

I simply mean this: Anyone, no matter the depth of his sins, may receive Salvation freely and without prerequisites. However, God's Gift of the Holy Spirit is reserved for His own Children—those who have come out of the world system through accepting Salvation. Only then do they become eligible to receive the Holy Spirit (Jn. 14:17).

Beyond this though, there are no prior conditions that must be met before one can aspire to receiving the Holy Spirit. As Paul said in Ephesians 2:8-9, "...it is the Gift of God. Not *of works, lest any man should boast."* Paul was speaking specifically of Salvation when he said this, but the conclusions are the same. The Baptism with the Holy Spirit is a Gift of God, and as such, it may be received instantly and without preconditions other than Salvation.

HINDRANCES TO RECEIVING: UNBELIEF

This perhaps is the greatest hindrance of all preventing the Christian from being baptized with the Holy Spirit.

The person who comes forward to receive the Holy Spirit can go away unfilled if he is harboring unbelief in his heart regarding the Holy Spirit. Personal reservations as to the validity of this experience will almost surely prevent the seeker from receiving. If one is not certain that something is real, one is not going to pursue and realize the end result.

Satan, of course, uses this doubt to prevent many from receiving the Holy Spirit. This is an important truth for every Christian to face. Satan always sends doubts, but it is up to the individual Christian to reject them and stand on Scripture, claiming that which God has promised.

The Christian must lay aside all unbelieving notions received from unbelieving preachers or others and allow the Word of God to serve as the sole criterion. We must never forget that it is not what man says, but it is what the Word of God declares. To be sure, the Word of God is replete with the guarantee of the Promise of the Holy Spirit (Acts 1:4; 2:1-4; 8:14-17; 9:17; 10:45-46; 19:1-7).

However, it must be remembered that most unbelieving preachers will usually not come out with a frontal assault against the Baptism with the Holy Spirit, but rather will cloud the issue with such unscriptural terminology as, *"This was valid in the Early Church, but it all stopped with the death of the last Apostle"*; *"These things were given until the Canon of Scripture was completed by John in the writing of the Book of Revelation, but when that was done, all of these things were laid aside"*; or *"It was for them then, but it is not for us now!"*

So, the Believer is going to have to come to the conclusion that he is not going to be swayed by people, but rather by the Word of God.

NOTES

HINDRANCES TO RECEIVING: YIELDING

Unfortunately, the second interfering factor presents a whole new set of problems. I speak of the matter of *"yielding one's heart, life, and spirit to the Holy Spirit when one has come to receive."*

Yielding is easily said but not easily explained simply because it is different for each person. All of us are wound up with our all-too-human need for individuality. We are taught from childhood to *"stand on our own two feet,"* to *"make our own way,"* and *"not to be beholden to others."* This may be good advice within the worldly realm and will, in most cases, stand us in good stead when dealing with most other people.

However, this human tendency becomes so ingrained in us that we find it difficult when confronted with the necessity of yielding our will to that of God.

The Lord does not want us independent of Him. In fact, such cannot be, that is, if we are to have a relationship with Him. He is the Loving Father Who wants us to turn to Him with our every need. We are, therefore, torn by conflicting forces. On one hand, our lifelong training says, *"Keep control of your life."* The other side, however, says, *"Give in and throw yourself on the Mercy of God."*

At the moment the Believer begins to ask the Lord to baptize him with the Spirit, if Faith is evident, there will be a strange pressure of sorts building up within the Believer, which demands expression. So, what are we to do?

Many times we push it down and literally force ourselves to go in the opposite direction of yielding, and that is where many Believers stop. They go away unfilled simply because they refuse to yield.

Let us say it in a simpler way:

When any individual comes to be filled with the Spirit and hands are laid on him, at the moment the Preacher tells him to yield his mind and his tongue to the Lord, that person will hear, sense, or feel words that are not English or any other language learned at his mother's knee. That's the Holy Spirit giving the utterance. He will not force one to speak but will only give the utterance.

NOTES

The individual has to do the speaking, and that's what we mean by yielding. Go ahead and speak these words that you hear down in your spirit, which, as I've stated, are not English or any other learned language. To be sure, it is a language known somewhere in the world but not by the Believer. All that you sense and feel is the Holy Spirit giving the utterance.

He will not speak for you, and neither will He force you to speak. He will give you the utterance, but you have to do the speaking yourself.

The moment you sense and feel these words coming up in your spirit, go ahead and start speaking them out and watch the river flow in your heart and life, so to speak, which is the Baptism with the Holy Spirit.

A PERSONAL EXAMPLE

I could probably give many, but I think the following will suffice:

At a particular Service where I had preached on the Holy Spirit, I invited those who wanted to be filled to come forward. Many did!

When the Service was almost over and hundreds of people were happy because the Lord had filled them with His Spirit, a dear lady approached me and was rather discouraged because she had not been filled. She wanted me to pray for her again to be filled with the Spirit.

"Sister," I asked, *"Why didn't you come forward with the others at the general call for this purpose?"*

"Oh, I did," she said.

"And you heard the instructions I gave to the group?"

"Oh, yes!"

"Did you feel a stirring inside you, a welling-up of unknown phrases or sounds crying to be brought forth?"

"Oh yes, I did, Brother Swaggart," she said. *"In fact, it took every ounce of my strength to keep from just blurting it all out."*

Naturally, God's Purposes are brought forth with difficulty when our carnal self marshals up our free will to thwart the impulses put there by God.

I placed my hand on this dear, confused soul and explained to her that she must stop fighting God's Leadings, but rather yield to Him.

As I laid hands on her, immediately she burst forth in Tongues, gloriously receiving the Gift of the Holy Spirit.

I sense the Spirit of God even as I dictate these words. Please understand, that which I have said of the dear lady is not meant to be negative, because all of us have done the same thing at one time or the other regarding our failing to yield as we should to the Moving and Operation of the Holy Spirit.

God will not force anyone to do anything. He wants our cooperation. He has designed us in that manner in the receiving of His Gifts. To be sure, He demands nothing of us in the realm of merit, etc., but He does demand that we yield to that which He desires to do.

HINDRANCES TO RECEIVING: PRIDE

I am not certain if pride is the biggest hindering factor of all, but I greatly suspect that it is.

All of us are very conscious as to what others think of us. We do not want to make a fool of ourselves, and rightly so! Consequently, we hold back, ever mindful of our actions, etc.

To be sure, the Lord is always a perfect Gentleman and will never do anything that will embarrass anyone. So, we do not have to worry ourselves about what He will do.

At the same time, it certainly may happen that the Believer may become so overjoyed and happy once the Lord gives him this great Gift that he just might praise the Lord louder than heretofore, or any number of things, but what is wrong with that?

The pride factor is a very big factor, but one must understand that the ways of the world are definitely not the Ways of God. To be sure, His Ways are the Ways we should seek, irrespective of what the world may think.

IT TAKES FAITH

This ingredient is a must respecting the Child of God. One must simply believe the Lord. And yet, the Faith of which I now speak is different from the *"belief"* or *"unbelief"* to which we have just referred. The type of unbelief of which we have just spoken has to do with the Word of God; however, there are millions who believe that the Baptism with the Holy Spirit is Biblical and, therefore, something that God gives presently. Nevertheless, even though they believe this, they have doubts that God will fill them. He may fill others, but they see all kinds of reasons He would not give this wonderful Gift to them.

This is another chief ploy of Satan. As we have already stated, the only requirement for being baptized with the Holy Spirit is for one to be Saved. If that is the case, despite all the other frailties and flaws that one may have, the Lord will baptize the honest seeker with the Holy Spirit. He has said He will, and He shall!

The Christian must believe that about God and about himself.

Please believe me, you are not a special case. In fact, God has no special cases. He is no respecter of persons; what He has done for others, He will do for you! Just simply have Faith that He will do it, and He certainly will!

THE HOLY SPIRIT WILL NOT SPEAK FOR YOU

What do we mean by that statement?

Even though we have briefly addressed this, it is so important that I ask you to please allow us to shed a little more light on the subject.

Many Believers who are asking the Lord to baptize them with the Holy Spirit erroneously believe that there is some type of coercion or possession involved in speaking in Tongues. In other words, they believe the Lord will force them to speak in Tongues, or else, they will do so because they are unable to help themselves. This simply is not the case.

A Spirit-filled Christian retains full control of all his faculties at all times. God's Holy Spirit, even as we have said, is the ultimate example of priority, courtesy, and restraint. The Holy Spirit does not impose; He suggests. No Leading of the Spirit will ever cause any Christian to do anything improper.

NOTES

By the same token, the Holy Spirit will never force anyone to speak in Tongues. This is always under the control of the individual, but this is where the problem arises.

Some object, saying, *"But if it is up to me to speak in Tongues after that the Lord has given the utterance, then it will be me speaking in Tongues and not the Lord."*

Yes, this is true. However, it is you whom the Lord desires to fill.

So, what am I saying?

Whenever the Believer asks the Lord to baptize him or her with the Holy Spirit, in response to that request (that is, if the Believer is sincere and properly yields), the Lord will set about to answer that prayer.

THE WORK OF THE SPIRIT

He will then give the utterance, which will take place deep inside the individual; however, that is as far as He will go. He will not force the person to speak in Tongues; he must do that himself.

In other words, the Believer must begin to speak the words or phrases that he hears or senses deep down inside his very being, which is the Holy Spirit giving the utterance. This is where the cooperation comes in.

"The Lord gives the utterance, and the Believer does the speaking." As we have stated, untold numbers have not been filled, or else, they were dramatically delayed in being filled simply because of this situation.

Acts 2:4 says, *"And they were all filled with the Holy Spirit, and began to speak with other Tongues."*

Notice that the Passage does not say, *"They were all filled with the Holy Spirit, and the Holy Spirit started to speak through them."* It is quite clear. They were filled—and they spoke with Tongues.

The important, almost crucial, point to remember is that the Spirit, as we have stated, gives the utterance (plants within the Believer the words or phrases, which are not in the Believer's normal language), but the Believer does the speaking! There is no place in the Bible where a single word expresses the thought that the Holy Spirit either speaks in Tongues himself or forces anyone to do so.

THIS MAY BE THE SINGLE GREATEST HINDRANCE

Acts 10:46 says, *"For they heard them speak with tongues."* Notice, they heard them, the people, speak in tongues; not the Holy Spirit. Again, in Acts 19:6, *"And they spoke with tongues and prophesied."*

I believe this may well be the greatest single hindrance to the Christians receiving the Holy Spirit. They have somehow come to believe God will speak in Tongues through them (like some kind of spiritual radio, etc.), He will take control of their tongues and force them to speak, etc.

However, the Lord does not suddenly overwhelm us with His Power and *"take over"* our normal functions. I believe there are thousands, perhaps millions, of Christians who are ready, willing, and able to receive the Holy Spirit. However, they are frustrated in their quest because they do not realize that they are the ones who must open their mouths and express the utterance formed inside them by the Holy Spirit.

RELAX IN HIM

Have you been asking the Lord to baptize you with the Holy Spirit?

How many times in doing this have you sensed the Presence of God?

You want to be baptized with the Holy Spirit. You have sensed God moving in your life. His Presence has flooded and overflowed you. Deep down inside there were stirrings of words you did not recognize as English or any other language you have ever heard.

However, did you take the positive step of Faith of opening your mouth and *"speaking out"* those sounds?

You probably did not. Why not?

Maybe you were frightened, but more likely, you waited for some miraculous *"expulsion"* of these words without your help. Unfortunately, this is not going to happen.

The next time this happens, even immediately after you read these words, you can receive the Holy Spirit. Actually, I sense the Presence of the Lord even as I dictate these words and know that He will honor His Word and give you that which you so desperately want and need. You can receive your Baptism right now!

NOTES

The moment you sense the Presence of God, at the same time, if you will notice carefully, you will sense the Holy Spirit giving you utterance deep down inside your heart and being. That is it! That is the Holy Spirit!

Now, go ahead and speak out what is bubbling up inside you! God has given you, yes, I said *"You,"* the Promise. The Lord Jesus is the Baptizer. He wants you to have this experience. He is not trying to hold it from you. You desperately need it, and He desires to give it to you. The only thing remaining is for you to step out in Faith and receive, and I believe that you will, even at this very moment.

YOU WILL SPEAK IN TONGUES

We have already stated that Tongues are a positive sign and an integral component of the Holy Spirit Baptism, but a few more words should be said in this regard.

The duration, *"quality,"* and expertise of your particular Gift of Tongues can vary dramatically from that of others or from what you thought it should be. Some preachers and teachers even go so far as to teach that one must speak for some specific period before one can be assured that one has been filled. This is not so!

Sometime ago, a dear brother in the Lord came to me in an ecstatic mood. When I asked him as to the reason for his joy, he told me that the Lord had baptized him with the Holy Spirit. Of course, that is certainly something to be happy about, and greatly so!

However, in the course of the conversation, he mentioned that his *"Tongue"* consisted of just one single word.

As I heard him say this, I was somewhat disturbed. I had never heard of such happening quite like this. I have spent the major part of my life in this great Pentecostal way, but I had never heard of someone receiving the Holy Spirit with just one word of Tongues (tongue).

I frowned and decided to caution him that perhaps he had not truly been baptized with the Holy Spirit.

However, before I could say anything, I felt a forewarning fill my heart. The Lord very quietly said to me, *"I am the One Who baptizes with the Holy Spirit, and I am the One Who decides how the Baptism will come. Just join him in praising Me for it."*

I choked back the reservations that I had and began to thank the Lord for what He had given my brother.

Sometime later, we met again. He smiled and said, *"Brother Swaggart, I grew tired of repeating just one word. Today, the Tongues flow forth like a river from my heart."*

IDEAS THAT ARE NOT SCRIPTURAL

What would have happened if I had blurted out what I intended to say? I might have thrown a stumblingblock in his path that would have disastrously impeded his walk with God. Thank God, the Lord prompted me otherwise, and I had enough spirituality to listen and hear what He was telling me.

All too often, our preconceived (and often predigested and secondhand) ideas are not Scriptural. Of course, we enjoy hearing people flowing forth with beautiful, rolling renditions in Tongues. We enjoy so much hearing those who can speak out Tongues for some extended periods, which seems to be edifying to our hearts, etc. However, there is nothing in Scripture that states that this is the way it must be all the time.

At the time of receiving the Holy Spirit, the Tongues given may be long and flowing, or they may consist of nothing more than a few stuttering syllables, or even as I have just said, just one word. However, this is no reflection on the validity of the experience, nor is it a mandate for the good Christians present to pass judgment on the validity of the experience. Almost without exception, those who do start out haltingly receive much greater facility as time goes by.

QUALITY DIFFERS

For those who have recently received the Baptism and who are *"disappointed"* in the *"quality"* of your particular Tongue, I would say this, *"Do not be disappointed or question the validity of the experience."*

NOTES

Any preconceived notions on exactly what Tongues *"should"* be can get you into trouble. Let me give an example:

Many years ago, one of my dear friends was saved from a life of gross sin and iniquity. God performed a Miracle of Redemption within his heart and life.

A few months later, he received the Baptism with the Holy Spirit. When he received the Tongues he was to speak, it was unlike anything I had ever heard before in my whole Christian experience. Although it may sound strange, more than anything else in the world, it sounded like a burst of machine gun fire. That is about as close as I can come to what it actually sounded like.

In my heart of hearts, I harbored secret doubts as to whether this was truly *"speaking in Tongues."* Was it a sham? Had he, in his desire for the Baptism, manufactured a strange tongue with which to comfort himself?

I was concerned enough about the matter that I went before the Lord with it. Should I counsel with him and explore this matter further?

Immediately, some questions popped into my mind, *"Is he faithful?"* and *"Is his life now clean?"* The answer was that his life was exemplary and there was no hint that he was not a godly, committed Christian before the Lord.

After this, I felt the assurance from the Lord that he had, indeed, been baptized with the Holy Spirit, and it was nothing I should concern myself with further. In my mind, I let the matter drop.

WHAT THE LORD SHOWED ME

I thought no more about it for almost 20 years, and then an incident brought it to mind rather dramatically.

I was at home on this particular evening during one of those rare times between Crusades when Frances and I actually enjoyed a few days off. I was watching the evening news, or at least half doing so, while reading something at the same time. If I remember correctly, Walter Cronkite was speaking. Half immersed in my reading, I was only vaguely aware of his stating that they would transfer the scene to the United

Nations where the newest member nation from Africa was being invested into that organization.

I only subconsciously noted the scene as the new representative came before the television cameras. He was wearing flowing robes typical of his country, etc. As soon as he opened his mouth to speak, I sat bolt upright. My flesh tingles with the Holy Spirit even as I recall the incident. The words that came forth from his mouth were exactly the same as my friend's prayer language that I had heard so skeptically on that long-past day. The detached outburst of *"speech"* caused me to freeze in rapt attention as the paper fell from my hand. Tears began to roll down my cheeks as the Spirit of God so vividly brought the whole incident back to me, which had happened so many years before.

HOW GOOD GOD IS

The Lord again gently spoke to me:

"Do you recall when you asked Me whether your friend's Gift was real? Here now, after a period of time, is your confirmation of the legitimacy of his Tongues."

How good God is and how different His time frame from the impatient, harried pace we set for ourselves here on Earth.

There are all kinds of Tongues. If all the languages of the Earth were to be cataloged and transcribed, I suppose the libraries of the world would be greatly enlarged.

It is up to the Lord as to what kind of Tongue we will receive at the time of being baptized with the Spirit. We make mistakes when we preconceive just what this Tongue should be like.

Whatever God gives you in this capacity, it will be His Will, and to be sure, it will be glorious! Just give Him the praise and the glory for what He has done.

WHY TONGUES?

Without going into a long dissertation, at least at this time, my answer to that question is, *"Why not Tongues?"*

It is given by God, and if that, in fact, is true, and it definitely is, surely we must understand that everything He does is good.

The criterion is not what men think, but

NOTES

what the Word of God says, and the Word of God says, *"And they were all filled with the Holy Spirit, and began to speak with other Tongues, as the Spirit gave them utterance"* (Acts 2:4).

As well, this was not merely praises in their own language.

• The following Verses speak of Jews who were present at that time in the Temple in Jerusalem who, in fact, had come in from all over the Roman Empire in order to keep the Feast of Pentecost. Incidentally, it was not in the Upper Room where this happened, but rather in the Temple.

All of these many Jews spoke all types of languages, as well as their own native tongue. So there would be no confusion, the Holy Spirit had Luke to list all the many areas of the Roman world, with its various languages and dialects that were spoken by the Jews, who observed this initial Outpouring of the Holy Spirit on the Day of Pentecost (Acts 2:5-13).

Their statement was, *"We do hear them speak in our tongues the wonderful Works of God"* (Acts 2:11).

I surely think that speaking about the *"wonderful Works of God"* should be very beneficial.

As it was then, so it is now: some were *"amazed,"* others *"doubted,"* and others *"mocked"* (Acts 2:12-13).

Irrespective, whatever these onlookers did, it had no bearing whatsoever on this number who received the Holy Spirit that day.

• So, Tongues are not merely incoherent babble or gibberish, but rather a language known somewhere in the world, but not by the speaker.

• As well, and even as Isaiah prophesied, *"For with stammering lips and another tongue will he speak to this people."*

He then said, *"This is the rest wherewith you may cause the weary to rest; and this is the refreshing"* (Isa. 28:11-12).

So, the Word of God tells us that speaking in Tongues as the Spirit gives the utterance produces a *"rest"* for the Believer concerning the stress and vicissitudes of life.

• As well, it is a *"refreshing,"* which is the same thing as a battery being recharged.

In these Passages, the Holy Spirit through the Prophet told us the value of Tongues even some 800 years before it was given on the Day of Pentecost. We would do ourselves well if we carefully heeded His Advice and Counsel.

Far too many Believers are resorting to the things of this world, attempting to bring about a *"rest"* and *"refreshing"* they so desperately need. Such is foolish and, as well, without merit, especially considering that God's Way is available to all.

Let the Holy Spirit flow through you. The Believer should even speak in Tongues subconsciously some of the time, for this is God's Method of refreshing your spirit and your soul.

THE REASON FOR YOUR SALVATION

When Jesus died on the Cross, He made it possible for all sin to be taken away from the believing sinner (Jn. 1:29). As a result, there is no sin account of any nature against any Believer. All sins as committed acts have been washed clean by the Blood of Jesus Christ, and the very fact of original sin has been taken away as well!

Consequently, it then became possible for the Believer to be perfectly clean and, therefore, a fit residence of God's Spirit (I Cor. 3:16).

Actually, Paul said in Ephesians 2:22 that the very reason for Salvation is that we can become a *"habitation of God through the Spirit!"*

Many Believers do not realize it, but this is the basic reason God has saved your soul—so that He may inhabit Himself within your life.

He once occupied a Tabernacle and Temple. However, He now desires to take up residence within you, the Believer, His Child.

Of course, God is Omnipresent, meaning that He is everywhere. Nevertheless, He still desires to take up abode within our lives, at least respecting the function that we so desperately need. Please allow me to say this:

As Salvation was completely revolutionary to the believing sinner, likewise, the Baptism with the Spirit will be as revolutionary to the Christian.

NOTES

"And it shall come to pass in the last days, says God, I will pour out of My Spirit upon all flesh ... For the Promise is unto you, and to your children, and to all who are afar off, even as many as the Lord our God shall call" (Acts 2:17, 39).

"Amen."

(18) "AND WHEN SIMON SAW THAT THROUGH LAYING ON OF THE APOSTLES' HANDS THE HOLY SPIRIT WAS GIVEN, HE OFFERED THEM MONEY."

The structure is:

1. The phrase, *"And when Simon saw that through laying on of the Apostles' hands the Holy Spirit was given,"* says much to us by what it does not say!
2. What did Simon see?
3. If the Apostles had merely laid hands on these people with nothing happening, such would have aroused no interest in Simon whatsoever. However, when we add Acts 2:4, 10:46, and 19:6, we know they began to speak with other Tongues. This is what Simon saw and heard.
4. The phrase, *"He offered them money,"* is where the term *"Simony"* originated. It refers to the purchase of offices in the church, which originated with the action of Simon as here recorded. However, of course, the things of God cannot be purchased with money, which is overly obvious!

(19) "SAYING, GIVE ME ALSO THIS POWER, THAT ON WHOMSOEVER I LAY HANDS, HE MAY RECEIVE THE HOLY SPIRIT."

The form is:

1. A true experience with God is a personal relationship with God.
2. This can only come through an acceptance of Jesus Christ and what He did for us at the Cross.
3. Christ left the starry crown of Heaven for the thorny crown of Earth in the activity of the love that seeks the lost till it is found.

THIS POWER

The phrase, *"Saying, Give me also this power,"* will garner the same for others as they look to men even as it did for Simon—namely nothing!

Much of the modern similarities are not so crass as the request of Simon, still, this problem continues to rear its ugly head. Even though it may be cloaked under spirituality, the idea is the same. Men look to other men to receive Gifts of God, and many men leave the impression that they can bestow such gifts.

All types of seminars are conducted, with people and preachers attending, because they have been led to believe that some preacher could lay hands on them and impart some Spiritual Gift. Others claim they can transfer the Anointing of the Holy Spirit by the laying on of hands.

Not any of this is Scriptural because no man can impart a Spiritual Gift or the Anointing of the Holy Spirit to others, this being the sole domain of Jesus and the Holy Spirit. While the laying on of hands is certainly valid, no mortal has the prerogative to bestow or transfer such to others. To be frank, those who propose they can do such are woefully lacking in these gifts and the anointing themselves.

Peter and John were not imparting the Holy Spirit to these people. That sole Authority is held by Jesus Christ alone (Mat. 3:11). They, in effect, as all others of similar effort, were simply His Hands extended.

Likewise, neither Paul nor others bestowed of themselves a *"Gift"* on Timothy when hands were laid on him. The Holy Spirit through Prophecy as given by someone had informed the Church that such would be done regarding Timothy and that they were to lay hands on him, which, in effect, recognized such (I Tim. 4:14).

AS THE LORD WILLS

Referring to Timothy, what the Gift was, we are not told. However, this one thing we do know: Even though the Lord uses human instrumentation constantly, it is not the person who heals, baptizes with the Holy Spirit, or imparts Gifts. The Lord does these things through the Person, Agency, Office, and Ministry of the Holy Spirit, Who allows, at times, human instrumentation to be involved. The Scripture plainly says regarding these Gifts, *"But all these* (Gifts) *work that one and the selfsame Spirit, dividing to every man severally as He will"* (I Cor. 12:11).

NOTES

It could not be clearer; it is as *"He"* (the Spirit) wills and not what man wills.

THE LAYING ON OF HANDS

The phrase, *"That on whomsoever I lay hands, he may receive the Holy Spirit,"* presents something that cannot be bought with money, etc.

However, from then until now, millions have been baptized with the Holy Spirit as hands were laid on them, even though it does not necessarily have to follow in that fashion.

On the Day of Pentecost, no one laid hands on those who were filled; however, Ananias did lay hands on Paul when he received the Holy Spirit (Acts 9:12-18).

In Acts, Chapter 10, no one laid hands on those who were in the house of Cornelius while Peter was preaching. The Scripture just says, *"The Holy Spirit fell on all them which heard the Word"* (Acts 10:44). Conversely, in Acts 19:1-6, Paul did lay hands on the Believers in Ephesus who were baptized with the Holy Spirit.

So, it should be very clear that even though the Lord definitely does use the *"laying on of hands,"* the Holy Spirit is not confined to this for people to be healed, delivered, baptized with the Holy Spirit, etc.

(20) "BUT PETER SAID UNTO HIM, YOUR MONEY PERISH WITH YOU, BECAUSE YOU HAVE THOUGHT THAT THE GIFT OF GOD MAY BE PURCHASED WITH MONEY."

The account is:

1. The only place where God can meet with sinful man is at the Cross.
2. The only thing standing between man and the wrath of God is the Cross.
3. The Life of Christ given on the Cross, and given as our Substitute, provides the only Remission of sin.

MONEY

The phrase, *"But Peter said unto him, Your money perish with you,"* proclaims mainly that the things of God cannot be purchased with money. Actually, the Prophet Isaiah said, *"Ho, every one who thirsts, come to the waters, and he who has no money; come, buy, and eat; yea, come, buy*

NOTES

wine and milk without money and without price" (Isa. 55:1). But yet, sad to say, much of the modern church world revolves around money instead of the Spirit of God.

Actually, this scenario, as offered in this Chapter, is meant to portray the very fact of what should govern the Work of God. I speak of money or the Spirit of God. Regrettably, except for a few times in history, money has played the dominant role, with the Holy Spirit little sought or heeded.

For instance, thousands of pastors remain in particular denominations, even though they know and realize that it has become grossly unscriptural, simply because they fear that if they leave, their economic picture could change. Even though it is an indirect manner, money instead of the Spirit of God fuels their decision.

THE GIFT OF GOD

Thousands of preachers are afraid to preach what they know the Truth to be for fear they will upset certain people in their church who give large sums of money. Consequently, they have become hirelings.

In truth, almost the entirety of that which I refer to as the *"greed gospel"* presents money as the criterion. In other words, a person's faith is judged by the model and make of car he drives, the amount of money he has or claims to have, etc.

So, in essence, much of the modern church is for sale and, in fact, always has been, with some few exceptions. Miracles are for sale! Prosperity is for sale! That is, if people will give so much money, they will in turn reap a certain amount of economic reward. While God certainly does bless His People, and abundantly so, still, the idea that we give to get is entirely contrary to the Word of God.

Consequently, let it be known that everything that purports to be the Work of God and engages in such monetary traffic, which is exactly what Peter said will surely happen, *"Your money perish with you."*

The phrase, *"Because you have thought that the Gift of God could be purchased with money,"* tells us two things of which we have already spoken:

1. These are *"Gifts of God"* and not gifts of the church, gifts of preachers, etc.

2. The very moment that money or any type of works are introduced, the door is automatically shut to receiving anything simply because if it is a *"gift,"* it cannot be wages, etc.

(21) "YOU HAVE NEITHER PART NOR LOT IN THIS MATTER: FOR YOUR HEART IS NOT RIGHT IN THE SIGHT OF GOD."

LOGOS

1. The phrase, *"You have neither part nor lot in this matter,"* presents something of great interest.

2. The word *"matter"* in the Greek as it is here used is *"logos"* and means *"a word, or speech, or discourse."* Consequently, Peter was referring to these Believers speaking with other Tongues.

3. He was saying that this Gift of God, the Baptism with the Holy Spirit, which is always accompanied by speaking with other Tongues, cannot be purchased, earned, or merited.

4. The speaking with other Tongues by the recipients of the Holy Spirit when hands were laid upon them is what aroused the curiosity and desire of Simon.

So, in effect, Peter said, *"You have neither part nor lot in this speaking with other Tongues as the Spirit of God gives the utterance."*

5. *"For your heart is not right in the Sight of God,"* proclaims the reason for this man's attitude and the reason for all such activity in any and all Believers, should such happen.

6. What constitutes the heart not being right with God, at least as it refers to Believers?

7. It can be summed up in this fashion: Anything and everything that is not exactly according to the Word of God and the leading and the administration of the Holy Spirit, of necessity, must be of man. Consequently, it is not of God and, therefore, pertains to self-will, which means the heart is not right.

(22) "REPENT THEREFORE OF THIS YOUR WICKEDNESS, AND PRAY GOD, IF PERHAPS THE THOUGHT OF YOUR HEART MAY BE FORGIVEN YOU."

The exegesis is:

1. God has no respect for any proposed way of Salvation other than *"Jesus Christ and Him Crucified."*

2. It is Christ and Him Crucified, or it is hellfire.

3. The Cross is the symbol of our union with Christ (II Cor. 5:14).

REPENT

The phrase, *"Repent therefore of this your wickedness,"* proclaims just how bad this sin was, but yet, that hope was offered.

"And pray God, if perhaps the thought of your heart may be forgiven you," in a sense, tells us that God alone could remedy this situation.

It was not so much the terrible sin committed but the reason for its commission.

WHAT IS WICKEDNESS?

Wickedness, like all forms and thoughts of wrong kept warm in the mind, seems to be a thing of growth; it begins with a thought, then a deed, then a character, and finally a destiny.

Men actually increase in wickedness until they have lost all desire for that which is good in the Sight of God. The Holy Spirit explained this to Isaiah in this fashion. He said, *"Woe unto them that call evil good, and good evil; that put darkness for light, and light for darkness"* (Isa. 5:20).

Jesus pointed out the origin of wickedness, and all wrong for that matter: He said, *"For from within, out of the heart of men, proceed evil thoughts ... Wickedness, deceit, lasciviousness ... All these evil things proceed from within, and defile the man"* (Mk. 7:21-23).

SIN!

Transgression of known law is sin, but so is wrong attitude, wrong desires, wrong set of the will, or self. Thus, sin is unbelief (Heb. 3:12-19). It is the centering of the self upon something or someone less than God Himself (Gen. 3:6; Rom. 1:28; 8:7).

Sin is any attitude of indifference, unbelief, or disobedience to the Will of God revealed in conscience, law, or Gospel—whether this attitude expresses itself in thought, word, deed, or settled disposition and conduct.

NOTES

According to the Bible, sin has direct effect upon the imminent laws of Creation and also brings on men the retributive action of God.

THE EFFECTS OF SIN

Under Spiritual Law, sin involves the whole self in perverting man from his highest possibilities, darkening the mind, inflaming the passions, hardening the will against God and, in fact, everything that is good (Rom. 1:21-32; Gal. 5:19).

Under the law of heredity, sin transmits evil tendency and guilt to the sinner's offspring. It is called *"original sin"* (Ps. 51:5-6; Eph. 2:3).

Thus, the first sin involved the entirety of the race and included all who were yet to be born. Sin tends to always be self-propagating, intensively and extensively.

Consequently, sin brings upon the sinner the direct punishment of God (Ps. 51:11; Rom. 1:28; 6:23).

ORIGINAL SIN

In Genesis 3:1-6, we have the account of how sin began, at least in the human family. There is a voluntary disobedience of an explicit Command of God, their Creator and Friend—the disobedience not being in any sense a necessity of their nature or state.

It was suggested to our first parents, by Satan using the faculties of the serpent, that the prohibition was not clearly understood, that the threatened punishment was not certain, and that a privilege was arbitrarily and selfishly denied them by God. Consequently, the appeal was made to an appetite innocent in itself.

The imagination of the woman was stirred by the prospect of promised enjoyment and power; desire was aroused; and then the deed followed as choice.

All of this is amazingly true to actual experience of temptation and sin. There are elements of the story especially worthy of notice.

A MORAL TEST

In a sense, it was a moral test and, of

necessity, truly a spiritual test. The test was whether they would believe God and trust Him or not do so! The prohibition tested whether they would make God the center and goal of their lives, or whether they would center their lives about their own purposes—the inevitable spiritual test we all face sooner or later.

Note too that the sin was first inner; the Fall was first in imagination, affection, thought, and then in deed. The sin must be seen against the facts that they knew God and His explicit Command, and against the fact that God's Love did not leave them but sought them even after the sinful deed.

The test, therefore, was necessary alike to the nature of man and the purpose of God—to wit, man's self-realization in right relation to God.

The narrative, moreover, is presented not only as spiritually true, but as actual fact, as the historical beginning of sin regarding the human family, and is so held in the rest of the Bible (Jn. 8:44; Rom. 5:12; I Cor. 15:21-22).

THE ONLY ANSWER TO SIN IS REPENTANCE

This simply means that one must recognize his sin, actually seeing himself as God sees him. As well, one must realize that within himself and by his own strength, there is no answer for sin. The answer is found solely in Christ and more perfectly, what Jesus did for us at Calvary.

The individual must confess the sin to God (I Jn. 1:9), be truly sorry for the sin, realize that it is actually against God, and be willing to turn aside from that erroneous direction.

Biblical Repentance is not so much actual words said or stated as it is a state and attitude of the heart. If that is as it should be, God never fails to accept the Repentance of any individual, irrespective as to how bad the sin may have been. The door of Mercy and Grace is open to all and without qualification, except that it must be on God's Terms and not man's.

The phrase, *"And pray God, if perhaps the thought of your heart may be forgiven you,"* portrays to us the seriousness of this matter as it pertained to Simon. This man was no longer dealing with mere mortals, but rather the Holy Spirit using the Apostle to look down deep into the very heart.

NOTES

SIN AND ITS FORGIVENESS

Sin and its forgiveness, the recovery of the forgiven sinner, and the Sanctification of the new humanity in Christ Jesus is thus the supreme Work of Redemption. Inasmuch as God is Holy and governs the world in Holiness; inasmuch as He has impressed His Law upon His Creation and upon the nature of man; and inasmuch as He must be true to Himself in His Holiness as well as in His Love of man, forgiveness must not be regarded as a simple matter of overlooking the past, as it is sometimes represented.

THE PRICE PAID IN ORDER THAT MEN COULD BE FORGIVEN

Overcoming of sin required nothing less than Atonement by the Gift of the Son of God, Himself a Human Sacrifice. It is not accomplished until through the Spirit, man becomes a New Creation, with a right attitude of Faith, love, and obedience to God.

(23) "FOR I PERCEIVE THAT YOU ARE IN THE GALL OF BITTERNESS, AND IN THE BOND OF INIQUITY."

The exegesis is:

1. If the Believer doesn't understand the Cross relative to Sanctification, he is a target for Satan (I Cor. 1:17).

2. The greatest hindrance to Faith in Christ and the Cross is works (Eph. 2:8-9).

3. No person can even begin to comprehend the truth as to Who Christ really is until he first understands what Christ really did, which refers to the Cross.

THE GALL OF BITTERNESS

The words, *"For I perceive,"* refer to the Holy Spirit informing Peter as to the exact cause and not mere symptoms.

"That you are in the gall of bitterness," is taken from Deuteronomy 29:18.

The *"bitterness"* in the Greek Text is *"pikria"* and means *"a condition of extreme wickedness."*

"And in the bond of iniquity," actually refers to Simon being bound by the greed for

money, power, and control over other men.

This *"iniquity"* had created within him a *"gall,"* or rather *"the receptacle of bile."*

Of course, the question must again be asked if the man had been truly Saved to begin with.

Yes, he was!

As men at times misunderstand the Grace of God, they also misunderstand the free moral agency of man.

The Grace of God and its acceptance instantly makes one clean and holy, and without works or merit.

Likewise and conversely, as quickly as the Work of Grace can be carried out, as quickly can one revert back to sin and iniquity, that is, if one so desires.

As the first is instant upon simple Faith in Christ, likewise can the second be instant. It is the choice of the heart that decides the issue. Once again, it is according to free moral agency.

No! This does not mean that a Believer reverts back to an unsaved state every time he sins. In fact, he does not! However, if the course of sin is purposely chosen with the repeated checks of the Holy Spirit ignored, at some state, the person is looked at by God as lost. In other words, the Lord does not save us in sin, but rather from sin. He is Merciful and Gracious and will always forgive, cleanse, and wash if the individual is sincere in his Repentance. As well, there is no limitation to the number of times that God will forgive (I Jn. 1:9). However, the Believer must understand that he cannot practice sin and at the same time expect continued Salvation (I Jn. 3:9).

Sin carries with it a terrible debilitating factor. In other words, it carries with it a bondage, which can happen very quickly, even as Peter here addressed respecting Simon.

Years ago, I heard a great Preacher state, *"Every attack by Satan, irrespective as to what course it takes, is for but one purpose, and that is to destroy our Faith, or at least seriously weaken it."* When an individual ceases to place his or her Faith exclusively in Christ and the Cross, sin always *"constantly attacks that position, losing such Faith, and a person will then be lost."*

NOTES

As we asked the question as to whether Simon had actually been Saved to begin with, we now must ask the question, *"With that being the case, has he now reverted back to a lost condition?"*

Every indication is that he had not, at least at this stage!

A BIBLICAL EXAMPLE

For instance, Jesus had portrayed to His Disciples that He must *"be killed, and raised again the third day."*

The Scripture continues, *"Then Peter took Him, and began to rebuke Him, saying, Be it far from You, Lord: this shall not be unto You.*

"But He turned, and said unto Peter, Get behind Me, Satan: you are an offence unto Me: for you savor not the things that be of God, but those that be of men" (Mat. 16:21-23).

Even though Peter had committed a grave sin at this time and had actually become a tool of Satan, still, he was not in a lost condition at that time. Ultimately he was brought to the right path.

Some may argue that Peter's sin was not nearly as bad as that of Simon; however, I beg to disagree! I think it was just as bad, if not worse.

Peter was questioning the Cross, which, in a sense, is the greatest sin of all. And yet, the Lord always looks at the heart in such circumstances. Actually, this is of far greater significance than the act of sin committed itself. In other words, the state of the heart determines the gravity of the offense.

(24) "THEN ANSWERED SIMON, AND SAID, PRAY TO THE LORD FOR ME, THAT NONE OF THESE THINGS WHICH YOU HAVE SPOKEN COME UPON ME."

The synopsis is:

1. The phrase, *"Then answered Simon, and said, Pray to the Lord for me,"* suggests a right attitude on the part of Simon.

2. *"That none of these things which you have spoken come upon me,"* had reference to him potentially perishing, that is, if he remained on that particular course.

3. The root meaning of the Greek Text in Verse 23 does not necessarily mean that Simon had sunk down to the level of *"the*

gall of bitterness, and the bond of iniquity," but that he was in grave danger of doing so. As well, it seems that his *"bitterness"* in part was caused by the people no longer looking to him as some great one, but now looking to the Lord, and even His Servants, Peter, John, and Philip.

4. Many stories have sprung up respecting Simon in later years; however, we are given nothing Biblical regarding this man after his request for prayer. Whether he continued to follow the Lord, getting victory over these things, or fell back into the old bondage is not known.

(25) "AND THEY, WHEN THEY HAD TESTIFIED AND PREACHED THE WORD OF THE LORD, RETURNED TO JERUSALEM, AND PREACHED THE GOSPEL IN MANY VILLAGES OF THE SAMARITANS."

The account is:

1. The phrase, *"And they, when they had testified and preached the Word of the Lord, returned to Jerusalem,"* speaks of Peter and John and implies a great preaching Mission with, no doubt, excellent results, which could have lasted many weeks.

2. *"And preached the Gospel in many villages of the Samaritans,"* refers to doing these things on the way back to Jerusalem from the meeting in which Philip was involved, etc.

3. There is even a possibility that one of these villages now visited by Peter and John was one that John had wanted to destroy some months before (Lk. 9:54).

4. At any rate, a mighty Move of God took place in Samaria exactly as it had in Jerusalem. Many were ushered into the Kingdom of God, with many signs and wonders performed, as well as many being baptized with the Holy Spirit.

(26) "AND THE ANGEL OF THE LORD SPOKE UNTO PHILIP, SAYING, ARISE, AND GO TOWARD THE SOUTH UNTO THE WAY THAT GOES DOWN FROM JERUSALEM UNTO GAZA, WHICH IS DESERT."

The order is:

1. The phrase, *"And the Angel of the Lord spoke unto Philip,"* proclaims another mission entirely for Philip, rather than going back to Jerusalem with Peter and John. Incidentally, the Text should have been translated *"an Angel of Jehovah,"* rather than *"the Angel of Jehovah,"* for *"the Angel of Jehovah"* is the Lord Jesus.

NOTES

In the Book of Acts, we see the Ministry of Angels according to the following:

a. We find that the Apostles were delivered from jail by an Angel of the Lord (Acts 5:19).

b. In this account, an Angel directed Philip to where he should go (Acts 8:26).

c. It was an Angel who told Cornelius how he could find a Preacher who would tell him how to be saved (Acts 10:3, 7, 22; 11:13-18; 15:5-11).

d. An Angel delivered Peter from jail (Acts 12:7-11, 15)

e. An Angel executed Herod (Acts 12:23).

f. An Angel comforted Paul (Acts 27:23).

2. The phrase, *"Saying, Arise, and go toward the south unto the way that goes down from Jerusalem unto Gaza, which is desert,"* probably referred to Old Testament Gaza, which was destroyed in 93 B.C. In 57 B.C., a new Gaza was built near the Mediterranean Sea.

3. So, the Angel was probably speaking of the road that led to old Gaza, and more perfectly, where it branched off from the road to the new Gaza. The old Gaza had been the last settlement before the wilderness desert leading toward Egypt. Consequently, the directions given by the Angel were probably far more specific than meets the eye at first glance.

(27) "AND HE AROSE AND WENT: AND, BEHOLD, A MAN OF ETHIOPIA, AN EUNUCH OF GREAT AUTHORITY UNDER CANDACE QUEEN OF THE ETHIOPIANS, WHO HAD THE CHARGE OF ALL HER TREASURE, AND HAD COME TO JERUSALEM FOR TO WORSHIP."

The synopsis is:

1. Christ cannot put the seal of His Approval upon nature's strength, its wisdom, or its glory.

2. We can only know God through Christ, and we can only know Christ through the Cross.

3. The Cross is the only means by which God can commune with man, and the

Cross is the only means by which man can commune with God.

A MAN OF ETHIOPIA

The phrase, *"And he arose and went,"* speaks of a distance of approximately 100 miles. He probably began his journey from Sychem. His obedience was immediate, even though he had no idea why the Lord wanted him there, etc.

To be frank, most of the time when the Lord tells us to do something, He gives very little information. This is done for purpose.

First of all, the Lord desires obedience on the part of His Children. Secondly, He wants us to learn trust. He gives us the first step, and we are to trust Him to make known the second step, etc., as the time arrives.

"And, behold, a man of Ethiopia, an eunuch of great authority under Candace queen of the Ethiopians," evidently presents a Gentile who was a proselyte to the Covenant of Israel. However, it is possible that he was Jewish, but most expositors think not.

The name *"Candace"* was not so much a name as it was a title then used by all Ethiopian queens.

About 1,000 years earlier, the queen of Sheba visited Solomon, and it is said that she became a proselyte to the God of Israel. It is also believed that the queen of Sheba was Ethiopian.

She is supposed to have established the worship of God in her realm on her return home. Tradition also says that she had a son by Solomon named Menelik, who succeeded her in the kingdom, and that her people have preserved the Jewish religion from that time until now.

THE QUEEN OF SHEBA

In fact, sometime in the 1980s, the State of Israel airlifted quite a number of Ethiopian Jews out of that particular country and took them to Israel. Actually, on one of our trips to Africa, we had the occasion to land at that particular airfield. There is no terminal there, only a grassy strip, which sufficed for our needs and that of Israel shortly before.

It seems that Israel would not have accepted these Ethiopians respecting the airlift to Israel if they had not been certain of their Jewish ancestry. So, in view of that, there is probably some validity to the tradition that the queen of Sheba and Solomon had a child.

(And yet, there are many in Israel who still contest the validity of the so-called Ethiopian Jews.)

Inasmuch as in those days, some kings had a number of wives, with Solomon actually having 700 wives and princesses, as well as 300 concubines, the possibility definitely exists that the queen of Sheba could have been included in this number (I Ki. 11:3).

Having said that, every evidence is that the worship of the God of Israel was prominent in Ethiopia, with this man to whom Philip was sent possibly having served God for most of his life.

The phrase, *"Who had the charge of all her treasure,"* simply refers to his status as the treasurer of that African country.

WORSHIP

The phrase, *"And had come to Jerusalem for to worship,"* could refer to the Feast of Tabernacles, which was held in October.

Eusebius says he was the very first Gentile to convert to Christ, with the beginning of the Early Church made up entirely of Jews.

It is said that Irenaeus reported that this man, the treasurer of Ethiopia, preached the Gospel to the Ethiopians and that Candace, the queen of that country, was baptized by him.

If that is true, one can well understand the Commission given by the Holy Spirit to Philip. As well, it is ironic and beautiful that the Lord would use Philip, who was not an Apostle, to win the very first Gentile Convert to the Lord, that is, if he was Gentile. What a mighty God we serve!

As well, how glad I am that in 1939, two dear ladies came to our little backwater town of Ferriday, Louisiana, in order to bring the Gospel. They were commissioned for that very purpose because that was where the Lord told them to go. Those two women were Lester Sumrall's mother and sister. There my parents heard the Gospel for the very first time in their lives. A short time

NOTES

later, my whole family came to God, with me being saved at eight years of age in 1943.

How so grateful I am that the Lord would commission someone to bring the Light to our darkness. I shall ever be thankful, and, as well, that is why I have a consuming burden to take the Gospel to others. All must have the same opportunity to hear and know exactly as I did.

(28) "WAS RETURNING, AND SITTING IN HIS CHARIOT READ ISAIAH THE PROPHET."

The structure is:

1. The two words, *"was returning,"* will spell for this man the greatest moment of his life. He had been to Jerusalem to worship, and now he would find out what all the sacrifices and Feast Days of the Covenant of Israel actually meant. He would meet the One to Whom all of this pointed!

2. *"And sitting in his chariot read Isaiah the Prophet,"* more than likely spoke of a translation into Greek. Actually, the entirety of the Old Testament had been translated from Hebrew to Greek at Alexandria, Egypt, about 250 years before Christ. It was called the *"Septuagint."*

(29) "THEN THE SPIRIT SAID UNTO PHILIP, GO NEAR, AND JOIN YOUR SELF TO THIS CHARIOT."

The account is:

1. The phrase, *"Then the Spirit said unto Philip,"* presents the state in which the Spirit of God desires that we be. As He spoke to Philip, He desires to speak to us all. However, for this type of relationship, the Believer must live a very consecrated life. Regrettably, even though the Holy Spirit abides in the hearts and lives of many millions, there are only a few that He can truly lead and guide. Most live far beneath their spiritual privileges and, therefore, miss out on so very much of what the Lord actually seeks to do.

An Angel told Philip to take this journey, but it was the Holy Spirit Himself Who told Philip to preach to the traveler.

2. These facts show the importance and solemnity of preaching: an Angel may be charged with directions as to a journey, but the Holy Spirit Himself immediately acts in the presentation of the Gospel.

3. *"Go near, and join yourself to this chariot,"* presents another step in an amazing series of events.

4. First of all, Philip had to be in a certain place exactly at a certain time in order to intercept this chariot. As well, Philip had no idea for what he was looking when he arrived at the destination, but then the Spirit spoke respecting this particular chariot.

5. Once again, allow me to say, *"What a mighty God we serve!"*

(30) "AND PHILIP RAN THITHER TO HIM, AND HEARD HIM READ THE PROPHET ISAIAH, AND SAID, DO YOU UNDERSTAND WHAT YOU ARE READING?"

The form is:

1. The phrase, *"And Philip ran thither to him,"* presents very little information.

2. However, it seems from Verse 28 that the chariot for the moment was not moving. Perhaps the driver had stopped to water and rest the horses, etc. So Philip immediately went to him.

3. The phrase, *"And heard him read the Prophet Isaiah,"* means that he was reading aloud. Consequently, Philip's appearance on the scene would not have seemed like an intrusion.

4. The question, *"And said, Do you understand what you are reading?"* was perhaps asked because the Holy Spirit told him to ask such a question, or it was obvious from the man's reading that he was having difficulty understanding what was being said.

(31) "AND HE SAID, HOW CAN I, EXCEPT SOME MAN SHOULD GUIDE ME? AND HE DESIRED PHILIP THAT HE WOULD COME UP AND SIT WITH HIM."

The account is:

1. The question, *"And he said, How can I, except some man should guide me?"* presents the perfect opening.

2. I think it is very obvious as to how important it is for the right person to explain the Scriptures. Tragically, very few have the privilege of being helped by someone such as Philip.

3. *"And he desired Philip that he would come up and sit with him,"* is exactly what

the Holy Spirit wanted and had orchestrated all along.

4. There was no way this man could know or understand, at least at this stage, all that the Lord had done to bring this about.

5. As well, for every person who is brought to Christ, if all the facts were known, all of us would marvel at all the things carried out by the Holy Spirit in order that we might have an opportunity to hear and receive the Gospel.

(32) "THE PLACE OF THE SCRIPTURE WHICH HE READ WAS THIS, HE WAS LED AS A SHEEP TO THE SLAUGHTER; AND LIKE A LAMB DUMB BEFORE HIS SHEARER, SO HE OPENED NOT HIS MOUTH."

The exegesis is:

1. The phrase, *"The place of the Scripture which he read was this,"* presents, as well, an orchestration carried out by the Holy Spirit.

2. Not only did the Lord bring Philip to this spot at exactly the right time, but, as well, He had this Ethiopian reading the very part of Isaiah that would be conducive to his Salvation. Incidentally, the *"place"* where he was reading was Isaiah 53:7-8.

3. *"He was led as a sheep to the slaughter,"* referred to Jesus being led to Calvary and making no protest, exactly as would a lamb.

4. *"And like a lamb dumb before his shearer, so opened He not His Mouth,"* refers to the Power He had that could have been used to call down legions of Angels had He so desired, but instead did nothing!

5. I have often wondered what the Jewish Sanhedrin thought concerning the Power of Christ. There is no doubt that they knew of His Great Power, even to the raising of the dead. As well, all the Miracles He performed were done in such a way as to lay to rest all skepticism. In other words, there was no doubt as to their being genuine.

6. Did they not realize the Power He actually had?

7. Did they not realize that they could do these things to Him only with His Permission?

8. Did that not say something to them?

9. Deception is a devilish thing. It blinds people to the truth to such an extent that their thinking is not rational. His defending Himself not at all should have said something to them! However, it seems their hatred was of such magnitude that they could see or think of nothing else!

NOTES

(33) "IN HIS HUMILIATION HIS JUDGMENT WAS TAKEN AWAY: AND WHO SHALL DECLARE HIS GENERATION? FOR HIS LIFE IS TAKEN FROM THE EARTH."

The overview is:

1. The Power of the Cross must be entered into before we can steadily walk with God.

2. Walking after the Spirit is simply looking totally and completely to Christ and what He has done for us at the Cross (Rom. 8:2).

3. The Holy Spirit works exclusively within the parameters of the Finished Work of Christ (I Cor. 1:18).

HUMILIATION

The phrase, *"In His Humiliation His Judgment was taken away,"* means that all justice was suspended, referring to the trial and execution of Jesus.

It was the custom among the Jews that at several points during a trial, they would try to find someone who could say something in favor of the accused. Even after the person was condemned, even being taken to execution, efforts were made to find someone to appear on behalf of the individual. In the case of Christ, no such effort was made!

"And who shall declare His Generation?" means that the Jewish Sanhedrin had engineered the execution of Christ in such a way of humiliation (by Crucifixion) so as to blot out all memory of Him. In other words, His Family would be so ashamed of Him, respecting the manner of His Death, considering that He died under the Curse of God, that He would be quickly forgotten (Deut. 21:22-23).

It was the frustration of this hope of Jesus being forgotten in consequence of His Death that so troubled the Sanhedrin.

THE LIFE OF CHRIST

The truth was and is, His Name was

NOTES

heralded and lifted up more so than any human being who has ever lived, and continues on a worldwide basis to this very hour. More has been written about Jesus Christ, a thousand times over, than all the fake luminaries of the world put together. His Followers, in one way or the other, number over 2 billion at this present time (2013).

By contrast, the Sanhedrin, who condemned Him to death in the most ignominious way, has been held up to ridicule and contempt as no other governing force in history.

"For His Life is taken from the Earth," presents that which was done purposely. However, despite their evil intentions, it carried out the Plan of God to the letter, which was necessary for the Redemption of humanity.

His Perfect *"Life"* was taken but only because it was freely given. He became the Sin-Offering, thereby, paying the price for the terrible sin debt that hung like a sword of Damocles over the heads of all! His Life was taken in order that it may be given to us in place of our death (Jn. 3:16).

(34) "AND THE EUNUCH ANSWERED PHILIP, AND SAID, I PRAY THEE, OF WHOM SPEAKS THE PROPHET THIS? OF HIMSELF, OR OF SOME OTHER MAN?"

The form is:

1. The phrase, *"And the Eunuch answered Philip, and said,"* presents, as will become obvious, a heart hungry for God. As we have stated, little does he realize that this man standing before him has been sent by the Lord from a great distance for the express purpose of presenting Jesus to him.

2. Incidentally, the primary meaning of the word *"eunuch"* is *"court officer."*

3. In Hebrew, a secondary meaning is found, namely, a *"castrate,"* which speaks of the man being surgically impaired to where he could not father children, etc. However, the word does not necessarily have to include the second meaning.

4. Actually, every evidence is that Daniel and his companions were not *"castrates,"* for they were *"without blemish,"* the Scripture says (Dan. 1:4).

5. In Matthew 19:12, Jesus mentioned three types of eunuchs:

a. The first are born that way, in other words, born impotent, and among other things, are unable to father children.

b. The second group would probably include surgical castration in order to care for apartments of queens, princesses, etc.

c. The third group makes themselves so for the sake of the Work of God, but not by castration. It is said that Origen, misinterpreting in a literal sense the third group, mutilated himself. That being the case, such would not be pleasing to God.

6. The question, *"I pray thee, of whom speaks the Prophet this? Of himself, or of some other man?"* presents exactly the correct question, which Philip would answer very succinctly.

7. Evidently, the Ethiopian treasurer had been meditating on this part of Isaiah, with the Holy Spirit purposely drawing his attention to these Scriptures. In other words, He created an intense longing in this man's heart to know the answer as to whom Isaiah was speaking. Consequently, we are given an excellent illustration in this account of the manner and working of the Holy Spirit as He deals with people.

8. At the same time the Lord prepared Philip, He, as well, was preparing the heart of this man. That is the reason that if we follow the Spirit, we will be led to those who are sincerely hungry for God, with the results being positive.

However, many times the Holy Spirit is ignored, with our own little soul-winning programs inserted, which oftentimes indoctrinates but seldom converts.

(35) "THEN PHILIP OPENED HIS MOUTH, AND BEGAN AT THE SAME SCRIPTURE, AND PREACHED UNTO HIM JESUS."

The pattern is:

1. The phrase, *"Then Philip opened his mouth,"* represents the very purpose and reason for which the Holy Spirit had brought all of this together.

2. *"And began at the same Scripture,"* refers to Isaiah 53:7-8, but did not stop there. It seems that he may have referred to other Passages in Isaiah concerning Jesus as well!

3. In those days, the Bible was not printed in a book, at least as we think of such. Each writing, whether by a Prophet or Apostle, was printed on either papyrus or vellum.

Papyrus was the pith of the papyrus plant cut in strips by the Egyptians and pressed into a writing material. It could then be made into a long scroll.

Vellum was actually the skins of animals, which were somewhat more durable than the papyrus. It too was rolled into scrolls.

4. So, the Ethiopian had a scroll of the Writings of the Prophet Isaiah.

5. *"And preached unto him Jesus,"* refers to Jesus being the One of Whom Isaiah spoke, which was explained to the Ethiopian.

6. In fact, the entirety of the Bible pertains to Jesus. So, if the Preacher truly preaches the Bible, he will preach Jesus! Every evidence is that this man accepted Christ as his Saviour.

7. It is amazing what can be done when Faith is present. The Sanhedrin could not see Jesus, and neither can most of the world, simply because they refuse to believe that He is the Son of God and, therefore, the Saviour of man. Consequently, the Word has little or no effect on them, at least for good!

(36) "AND AS THEY WENT ON THEIR WAY, THEY CAME UNTO A CERTAIN WATER: AND THE EUNUCH SAID, SEE, HERE IS WATER; WHAT DOES HINDER ME TO BE BAPTIZED?"

The composition is:

1. The phrase, *"And as they went on their way,"* obviously means that after Philip joined the Ethiopian in the chariot, the journey was continued. Actually, Ethiopia was well over 600 miles from where they presently were. Of course, Philip would have journeyed with the man only a few miles toward that destination.

2. *"They came unto a certain water,"* proclaims the fact that Philip had explained to him that Water Baptism was the outward sign that Jesus had been accepted in the heart. It presented an open confession, the explanation of which obviously registered strongly upon the man.

3. *"And the eunuch said, See, here is water,"* seems to portray the fact that a deep stream or pond was sighted at about the time Philip was explaining what Water Baptism actually was.

NOTES

4. The question, *"What does hinder me to be baptized?"* presents him, as is obvious, desiring to be baptized immediately. He had accepted Christ in his heart and now strongly desired that he partake of this beautiful symbolism.

(37) "AND PHILIP SAID, IF YOU BELIEVE WITH ALL YOUR HEART, YOU MAY. AND HE ANSWERED AND SAID, I BELIEVE THAT JESUS CHRIST IS THE SON OF GOD."

The overview is:

1. The only way that one can have victory over the *"Law of Sin and Death"* is by and through the *"Law of the Spirit of Life in Christ Jesus."*

2. The Cross was not dependent on the Resurrection, but rather the Resurrection was dependent on the Cross (I Cor. 2:2).

I BELIEVE

The phrase, *"And Philip said, If you believe with all your heart, you may,"* presents the only Scriptural requirement for Salvation.

"And he answered and said, I believe that Jesus Christ is the Son of God," is all that was necessary, and it shows that Philip had explained the Gospel program to this man very well!

These short Passages give us much information respecting the Gospel Message. First of all, it completely shoots down the idea that one must belong to a certain church, or any church at all for that matter.

Secondly, it proclaims that at the moment of Faith, one is Saved. In other words, the Water Baptism, even though very important, did not add anything to the man's Salvation. That came about strictly by Faith in Christ.

As well, this shows us that Salvation and the Baptism with the Holy Spirit are two different things altogether. While every evidence is that this man was wondrously saved, there is no mention whatsoever that he was baptized with the Holy Spirit with the evidence of speaking with other Tongues at this particular time. He definitely may have been, but the Bible is silent regarding that question.

NOTES

So, as important as the Baptism with the Holy Spirit is, as I feel we have adequately portrayed time and time again, still, we must ever emphasize that being born of the Spirit is the absolute requirement for Salvation. This is exactly what happened with this Ethiopian and all others who come to Christ.

SALVATION

Conversely, being baptized with the Spirit is something else altogether, and pertains not at all to Salvation but to one's work and service for the Lord, among other things.

From the simple statement made by the Ethiopian, we learn that Philip had told him that the One of Whom Isaiah spoke was, in fact, the Jewish Messiah and, as well, the Son of God.

Philip explained to him how Jesus died on Calvary in order to pay for the sins of man and then rose from the dead.

It is obvious that Philip told him these things, for he would have had to have done so to have properly explained Isaiah 53:7-8.

What does it mean to truly believe?

Actually, Faith and believing are basically the same.

Faith or believing is the attitude whereby a man abandons all reliance on his own efforts to obtain Salvation, be they deeds of piety, of ethical goodness, or anything else. It is the attitude of complete trust in Christ and of reliance on Him alone according to the price He paid on Calvary's Cross for our Redemption.

FAITH IS MORE THAN MERE FACTS

While Faith or believing is certainly concerned with facts, there is more to it than that. James tells us that the demons believe and tremble, but this *"faith"* does not profit them (James 2:19). They knew the facts, but that did not save them.

Demons have another agenda, and even though they definitely believe and know some facts about God, there are other things that they do not believe. Satan and demon spirits are so deceived that even though they believe that Jesus is the Son of God, and that He died on Calvary and rose from the dead, that is as far as their faith or facts go. They do not believe Him for Salvation, but rather believe that they ultimately will win in this conflict between good and evil. So, believing certain facts does not save one.

The man who really believes God will, of course, act on that belief. In other words, a genuine belief that what God has revealed is true will issue in a true Faith, which will always be acted on.

TO BELIEVE INTO

The word *"believe,"* at least as it pertains to Faith in Christ, literally means *"to believe into."*

It denotes a Faith which, so to speak, takes a man out of himself and puts him into Christ, hence, the phrase *"in Christ"* being constantly used regarding Believers (Rom. 8:1).

It denotes not simply a belief that carries an intellectual assent, even as many do have but are not saved, but one wherein the Believer cleaves to his Saviour with all his heart. The man who believes in this sense abides in Christ and Christ in him (Jn. 15:4).

So, Faith, as it pertains to Christ and Salvation, is not merely accepting certain things that are true, but rather trusting a Person, and that Person is Christ.

THE GOSPEL STORY

The Book of Acts, which we are now studying, proclaims the story of vigorous Missionary advancement. Thus, it is not surprising that the characteristic expression of *"believing in Christ"* is the term used, for it indicates the act of decision. This is exactly what happened to the Ethiopian. His Faith, or *"believing in Christ,"* brought with it a decision, as such Faith or believing always does. As we have stated, if it is truly Faith, it will truly act.

(38) "AND HE COMMANDED THE CHARIOT TO STAND STILL: AND THEY WENT DOWN BOTH INTO THE WATER, BOTH PHILIP AND THE EUNUCH; AND HE BAPTIZED HIM."

The account is:

1. The phrase, *"And he commanded the chariot to stand still,"* obviously portrays that the Ethiopian had a driver, who was now commanded to stop.

2. *"And they went down both into the water,"* tells us two things:

a. The water was deep enough that the correct manner of baptizing could be carried out.

b. This tells us that Water Baptism is by immersion and not by mere sprinkling as taught by some.

Actually, the *"sprinkling"* in no way portrays the portrait that Water Baptism paints. One must be immersed for the correct symbolism to apply.

3. Water Baptism typifies the Death (going into the water), Burial (being put under the water), and Resurrection of Christ (being brought up out of the water).

4. As well, Water Baptism is symbolic of the Believer's Conversion to Christ. He goes into the water, which typifies his death to the world and the old man. He is placed under the water, which typifies the burial of the old man (when living in an unconverted state). He is then brought out of the water, which typifies one as a New Creation in Christ, i.e., a New Man (Rom. 6:3-5).

5. *"Both Philip and the eunuch; and he baptized him,"* proclaims the acceptance of Christ as Lord by this man and the washing away of his sins, which were now signified by Water Baptism.

(39) "AND WHEN THEY WERE COME UP OUT OF THE WATER, THE SPIRIT OF THE LORD CAUGHT AWAY PHILIP, THAT THE EUNUCH SAW HIM NO MORE: AND HE WENT ON HIS WAY REJOICING."

The way is:

1. The phrase, *"And when they were come up out of the water, the Spirit of the Lord caught away Philip,"* means exactly what it says.

2. The Greek word for *"caught away"* is *"harpazo"* and means *"to seize, catch away, pluck, pull or take away by force."*

3. The implication is and, no doubt, was that Philip was transported bodily through the air in a few moments' time to a city called Azotus, about 25 miles distance.

4. To try to explain it away as Philip being in some type of trance does not remain true to the Text.

5. *"That the eunuch saw him no more,"* simply means that when Philip pulled him up out of the water, all of a sudden, he (Philip) disappeared. In other words, he vanished right in front of the Ethiopian's eyes.

NOTES

6. *"And he went on his way rejoicing,"* proclaims the *"joys of sins forgiven, and the bliss the blood washed know."* He was now Saved and, therefore, one with Christ. That is enough to make anyone happy.

7. The story this man had to tell upon arriving home in Ethiopia would have been a wonder to hear and behold.

8. As we have already stated, tradition says he immediately began to preach the Gospel upon his arrival, with many being saved and even the queen giving her heart to the Lord.

(40) "BUT PHILIP WAS FOUND AT AZOTUS: AND PASSING THROUGH HE PREACHED IN ALL THE CITIES, TILL HE CAME TO CAESAREA."

The diagram is:

1. The phrase, *"But Philip was found at Azotus,"* actually means that after his sudden transportation by the Holy Spirit, he found he was at *"Azotus."*

2. *"And passing through he preached in all the cities,"* no doubt, recorded the Salvation of many souls.

3. *"Till he came to Caesarea,"* presents a city about 60 miles north of Azotus (old Ashdod). This route borders the Mediterranean.

4. The Scripture tells us that he made his home in Caesarea (Acts 21:8). In that Passage, he is called *"Philip the Evangelist,"* and it is said that he *"had four daughters, virgins, which did prophesy"* (Acts 21:9).

5. Several things are learned in this account of the Lord working with Philip, which are overlooked at times. Some are as follows:

a. Philip saw God move as few men in history, and yet, he was not an Apostle, but rather an Evangelist. In fact, the great Moving and Operation of the Holy Spirit is not limited to any one group of people, but is rather available to all Believers, whether they are Preachers or not (Mk. 16:17).

b. It is possible that this Ethiopian was Jewish, due to the Queen of Sheba and Solomon about 1,000 years before; however, it is also possible that he was a Gentile. If so, which is likely, he was the very first Gentile Convert under the New Covenant, and not Cornelius as some believe.

c. As well, being an African, there is every likelihood that he was black.

6. If that is true, it should give our black brothers and sisters occasion for rejoicing that the very first Gentile Convert was of black origin.

7. Incidentally, his Conversion probably took place only several months after the Day of Pentecost. As well, it seems that all Converts up to now in the Early Church, which numbered into the thousands, were Jewish.

"Here among the shadows living in a lonely land,
"With strangers we're a band of pilgrims on the move,
"Through dangers burdened down with sorrows,
"Shunned on every hand,
"But we are looking for a city built above."

"Here in disappointment often we so sadly roam,
"And earthly friends no longer speak one word of love:
"But truly we have found contentment,
"Jesus promised us a home,
"So we are looking for a city built above."

"In this land of dangers, we are going here and there,
"We're simply trusting in the Blessed Saviour's Love,
"And Mercy though we may be strangers,
"Living in this world of care,
"We're always looking for a city built above."

CHAPTER 9

(1) "AND SAUL, YET BREATHING OUT THREATENINGS AND SLAUGHTER AGAINST THE DISCIPLES OF THE LORD, WENT UNTO THE HIGH PRIEST."

NOTES

The overview is:

1. The Cross of Christ is the dividing line in every Believer's life from his former state.
2. Everything we receive from God comes from Christ as the Source and the Cross as the Means.
3. The Cross is the channel through which Grace is given, and the Cross is the Means by which it is received by sinful man.

SAUL

The phrase, *"And Saul, yet breathing out threatenings and slaughter against the Disciples of the Lord,"* presents Paul as the leader, as is obvious, of the persecution against the Early Church. The action of this man is indicative of one who is under conviction by the Holy Spirit.

When one is introduced to the Lord in whatever capacity, even as Saul (Paul), most of the time, one either yields to Christ immediately or becomes more antagonistic. The Holy Spirit deals with the person, and immediately the war begins.

There is no way that Paul could have witnessed the death of Stephen as he did and not be accordingly moved (Acts 7:57-60). So, his response to the Holy Spirit was an intensified effort of *"threatenings and slaughter."*

The word *"slaughter"* in the Greek Text actually means *"murder."* Consequently, it is believed that Paul's rampage against the early Believers was of far greater severity than at first thought. There is no evidence that he personally committed murder, but in the Eyes of God, he was guilty of this hideous crime. He was the one who arrested the Believers and brought them before magistrates, testifying against them in order to bring about their execution.

GRACE

How many died in this fashion is not known, but the evidence seems to be that the number was considerable. In other words, there were a lot of empty places at a lot of tables due to being imprisoned or executed, and all by the hands of Paul.

Yet, Grace in its sovereignty elected him as a chosen vessel and sent him out to preach the Gospel of the Glory. Such Grace united

NOTES

him to a glorified Christ in the eternal glories of the highest heavens; consequently, he proclaimed the very One Whom he had persecuted, Jesus, and preached that He was the Son of God.

And yet, Grace, even with all of its sovereignty, does not force one to the acceptance of Christ. It only guarantees the acceptance by the Lord of such a person as the person comes of his own free will. Then Grace blots out the past! It is called *"Justification by Faith,"* which Paul proclaimed as the Foundation of the Gospel.

The phrase, *"Went unto the High Priest,"* does not tell us exactly when this was. If it was A.D. 35, which it probably was, Caiaphas was High Priest. Once again we see here the evil of religion.

Paul was a Pharisee and Caiaphas was a Sadducee, or whoever ruled then as High Priest. Normally they hated each other, but they would now join hands against a common foe, the Followers of Christ, exactly as they had in the execution of Christ.

(2) "AND DESIRED OF HIM LETTERS TO DAMASCUS TO THE SYNAGOGUES, THAT IF HE FOUND ANY OF THIS WAY, WHETHER THEY WERE MEN OR WOMEN, HE MIGHT BRING THEM BOUND UNTO JERUSALEM."

The exegesis is:

1. Any Christian who thinks he has outgrown the Cross has just invited disaster for himself.

2. Faith in the Cross claims the supremacy of the Saviour and the helplessness of the Believer.

3. Faith in the Cross tells us how good God is and how evil man is.

LETTERS

The phrase, *"And desired of him letters to Damascus to the synagogues,"* proclaims the persecution led by Paul as branching out to other cities.

Actually, the persecution had become so severe in Jerusalem that many, if not most, of the Believers *"were all scattered abroad throughout the regions of Judaea and Samaria, except the Apostles"* (Acts 8:1).

Evidently, Paul had been led to believe that there were quite a number of Believers in Damascus; therefore, he would begin there.

The *"letters"* were from the Sanhedrin giving Paul the authority to do this, and binding the rulers of various synagogues to comply in ferreting out Followers of Christ.

As we have previously stated, the Church at this time was exclusively Jewish, with them continuing to worship in synagogues, for the most part, as they had always done. In a short time, all of this would change as all Jewish doors were closed to them.

It is believed that there were approximately 30 or 40 synagogues in Damascus and not less than 40,000 resident Jews. Consequently, there were bound to be Followers of Christ there, as Verses 10 and 13 proclaim.

THE WAY OF CHRIST

The phrase, *"That if he found any of this Way,"* portrays the first description or name of the Early Church (Jn. 14:6; Acts 18:25-26; 19:9, 23; 22:4; 24:14, 22).

This term refers to a peculiar Doctrine and, in this case, that of Christ. It was the *"Way of Christ,"* referring to Him being the Messiah and the Son of God.

It is said that its application to Christians apparently lasted only so long as Christianity was considered to be a modification or peculiar form of Judaism, which it was not!

"Whether they were men or women, he might bring them bound unto Jerusalem," refers to them appearing before the Sanhedrin. Their trials were the very opposite of what we would now know. In other words, they were guilty until proven innocent.

Incidentally, Damascus was one of the oldest cities in the world. It was the capital of Syria and was once famous for its orchards and gardens, being irrigated by the clear Abana River and the adjacent Pharpar (II Ki. 5:12).

Evidently, Paul had plans for all the cities in which he thought Followers of Christ might be. However, a traumatic thing was about to happen to him, which would change his life dramatically, and would have the greatest impact on the Gospel of anything that would ever happen.

(3) "AND AS HE JOURNEYED, HE CAME NEAR DAMASCUS: AND SUDDENLY

THERE SHINED ROUND ABOUT HIM A LIGHT FROM HEAVEN."

The diagram is:

1. The phrase, *"And as he journeyed,"* does not tell us exactly how, whether by foot or horse. It is unlikely that he would have had a chariot as the Ethiopian of the previous Chapter.

2. *"He came near Damascus,"* evidently refers to the near entrance to the city. Damascus is approximately 175 miles from Jerusalem.

3. Nearing the city, Paul and those with him were, no doubt, tired after the long journey and anxious to get to their destination. However, he was about to encounter the very One Whom he had branded as an impostor and blasphemer.

4. *"And suddenly there shined round about him a light from Heaven,"* proclaims the Appearance of Christ in His Glory. It was of such magnificence that it would blind this man for some three days. Evidently he saw the Lord before this brilliant Light blinded him, for he referred to such in I Corinthians 15:8. Consequently, this Jesus Whom he had ridiculed was now found to be anything but the peasant Paul had previously thought.

5. As well, this *"Light"* was from Heaven, the abode of God.

(4) "AND HE FELL TO THE EARTH, AND HEARD A VOICE SAYING UNTO HIM, SAUL, SAUL, WHY DO YOU PERSECUTE ME?"

The overview is:

1. Faith in the Cross admits the Sacrifice as God's Solution and that man has no solution whatsoever.

2. Faith in the Cross creates humility—faith in ourselves or other things creates self-righteousness.

A PERSONAL EXPERIENCE

The phrase, *"And he fell to the earth,"* seems to imply that the Power of God was so strong that he simply could not stand, even though it seemingly did not affect in a similar manner the others who were with him.

The Lord saved me when I was eight years old and baptized me with the Holy Spirit a few weeks after my initial Conversion experience. After I was baptized with the Holy Spirit, several of us would assemble at the home of my grandmother or my aunt for prayer meetings. This was done two or three times a day. It was during the summer months when I wasn't in school.

The following probably happened several times, but one time stands out to me very vividly:

As we went to prayer at that particular meeting, and I forget whether it was morning or afternoon, after a few minutes of praying, the Spirit of the Lord came upon me greatly. For about two hours, I literally went into a trance. If I remember correctly, this was during the time that the Lord was speaking to my heart about being an Evangelist. Being only eight years of age, my knowledge was extremely limited in these areas, as would be obvious; however, I knew that the Lord had called me to this particular aspect of Ministry. In other words, I knew that I would be an Evangelist even from that early age.

Looking back, I know that all of this was done by the Lord that I might learn to look to Him exclusively for all things.

THE VOICE

The question, *"And heard a voice saying unto him, Saul, Saul, why do you persecute Me?"* proclaims to all that if one touches those who belong to God, one has touched God!

The same Voice that had said, *"Abraham, Abraham," "Samuel, Samuel," "Martha, Martha,"* and *"Simon, Simon,"* now said, *"Saul, Saul."*

So, Saul made a terrible discovery that overwhelmed his mind and heart and broke him, respecting what he was. He found that zealous as he was for the Law, he was fighting against God and destroying His People.

How awful it must be to claim to be of God and working for the Lord but, in fact, actually fighting against God!

I think it could be said without any fear of exaggeration or contradiction that, if the truth were known, most preachers would fall into this category. Instead of living for God and working for Him as they think, they are actually tools of Satan, even as Saul!

Deception is a terrible thing, actually Satan's greatest weapon. He is so powerful with this force of darkness that he is deceived himself. Consequently, he easily deceives others!

(5) "AND HE SAID, WHO ARE YOU, LORD? AND THE LORD SAID, I AM JESUS WHOM YOU PERSECUTE: IT IS HARD FOR YOU TO KICK AGAINST THE PRICKS."

The exegesis is:

1. Let all understand: God has no other way, no other path, and no other solution—only the Cross.

2. God's Answer to failing, sinning, dying, lost, wrecked, and destroyed humanity is the Cross of Christ and nothing else.

WHO ARE YOU, LORD?

The question, *"And he said, Who are You, Lord?"* is used by Paul in the realm of Deity and not merely as respect, as some have claimed. In other words, Paul now knew beyond a shadow of a doubt that he was addressing God.

"And the Lord said, I am Jesus Whom you persecute," presents the very Name being used that Paul hated.

The Lord could have identified Himself in many and varied ways. He could have used the Name Jehovah, which would have been greatly acceptable to the Jewish mind; however, instead, He used the Name that Paul and the Sanhedrin were attempting to blot out. Consequently, there was absolutely no mistake as to Who appeared to Paul.

Jesus used the word *"persecute"* again, proclaiming the severity of this action and how it was noted in Heaven. Emphatically, He stated that it was He, Jesus, Who was being persecuted. There must not be any mistake about that!

The lesson must not be lost on us. As we have already stated, to oppose that which belongs to God is to oppose God. Ultimately, it is a battle that no one has ever won, nor can they win!

KICKING AGAINST THE GOADS

The phrase, *"It is hard for you to kick against the pricks,"* has reference to sharp goads that were placed immediately behind the oxen and were attached to the plow. Consequently, when the oxen kicked, for

NOTES

whatever reason, their feet and legs would hit these sharp goads, which had a strong tendency to cure them of such action.

The implication, as used here by Jesus, seems to have two references and applied not only to Paul, but to all others as well! The two references are:

1. AGAINST GOD

As stated, to set oneself against God is an unwinnable situation. The mightiest nations in the world have been brought to a sorry end because of this one thing. They attempted to stop God, and they did so by opposing those who belonged to Him, whether Israel or His Church.

So, if entire nations, which includes the mightiest empires that have ever existed, could not and, in fact, cannot win this conflict, surely individuals must know and realize that the same fate awaits them as well.

Fighting God, in whatever capacity, is a mistake that no sane human being wants to make. In fact, the entire tides of history ebb and flow upon this very principle. Mighty nations and empires have come and gone, and if the truth be known, their fall was always predicated on their opposition to God and His Son, the Lord Jesus Christ, but directed at God's People.

Where today is mighty Egypt, once the greatest of all lands? She has been reduced to the state of a shabby sexton of ancient tombs.

Where is mighty Rome, which ruled the world for over 1,000 years? Today her mighty Caesars are organ grinders and her generals are peanut vendors.

Where is mighty Spain whose ships once sailed the great oceans, filling her coffers with gold from the New World? Today, she sits like a drowsy beggar watching the hands of a broken clock.

Where is the mighty Soviet Union, which conquered with its communistic enslavement hundreds of millions of souls? Today, broken and bleeding, she is no more, a victim of her own corruption!

With all of these, and scores unnamed, the reason is, they *"kicked against the pricks,"* exactly as Jesus said of Paul.

2. STEPHEN

I think this statement as made by Christ

NOTES

harks back to the death of Stephen. I know that Paul could not forget this moment and tried to drown the memory by even more persecution.

I personally feel that the words Stephen said while dying, *"Lord Jesus, receive my spirit,"* and then, *"Lord lay not this sin to their charge,"* were words that would not leave Paul's mind and spirit. Consequently, when Jesus appeared to him, it took only a moment to recognize Him as the One to Whom Stephen had prayed.

(6) "AND HE TREMBLING AND ASTONISHED SAID, LORD, WHAT WILL YOU HAVE ME TO DO? AND THE LORD SAID UNTO HIM, ARISE, AND GO INTO THE CITY, AND IT SHALL BE TOLD YOU WHAT YOU MUST DO."

The exposition is:

1. Every true Move of God will always be accompanied by a Call to the Cross, which results in strong preaching that convicts of sin and calls people to holiness.

2. Religious men have always wanted revival without Repentance, and above all, revival without the Cross, but such is not to be.

TERRIFIED

The phrase, *"And he trembling and astonished said,"* gives us his reaction, over which he had little control.

The Greek word for *"trembling"* is *"tremo"* and means *"to be terrified."*

The Greek word for *"astonished"* is *"thambeo"* and means *"to be stupefied or astounded."*

Surely, Paul had heard any number of things about Jesus respecting His Miracles and His Teaching and Preaching. As well, he had, no doubt, heard of the answers given by Jesus to the most perplexing questions, even those designed to snare Him, but with no success whatsoever. But yet, he had reasoned in his mind that Jesus, despite all these things, was but a peasant and an impostor. So now, he saw Him as He truly was, and in a moment's time was changed.

However, he was terrified, realizing what he had done and faced with such Glory and Magnificence, his blasphemy was now called to account, but now he would learn that Jesus did not come to destroy but to save.

LORD, WHAT WILL YOU HAVE ME TO DO?

The great question, *"Lord, what will You have me to do?"* constitutes Paul's Salvation. In other words, he was saved at that moment.

Also, the appellative *"Lord,"* as now used by Paul, as we have stated, was not a mere term of respect as some have claimed, but rather of Deity. Paul now knew, in a moment's time, that Jesus is the Jewish Messiah, is the Fulfillment of all the Prophecies, was God manifest in the flesh, and, in fact, is God!

As well, he was meaning that Jesus was now the *"Lord"* of his life. Hence, when later giving the Plan of Salvation, he would say, *"That if you shall confess with your mouth the Lord Jesus, and shall believe in your heart that God has raised Him from the dead, you shall be saved"* (Rom. 10:9).

The most brilliant scripturian could have argued with Paul before now concerning the veracity of Jesus Christ and would have made no headway. In fact, as we have stated, there is every reason to believe that Paul may have been one of those debating Stephen as recorded in Acts 6:10, but despite the fact that Stephen bested him, still, Paul was not at all convinced. However, when Paul saw Jesus, what could not have been done any other way was accomplished immediately.

Churches are filled with people who have seen a doctrine, a religious denomination, social activity, or a host of other things, but sadly, most have not seen Jesus; consequently, they are not saved!

Jesus is Salvation, not the church! Jesus is the Deliverer, not psychologists! Jesus is the Baptizer with the Holy Spirit, not some denomination or preacher!

The trouble with much of the Christian world is that it has embraced the philosophy of Christianity without making Jesus Lord! Without Christ, Christianity is little better, if at all, than the religions of the world. Men must see Jesus!

WHAT YOU MUST DO

The phrase, *"And the Lord said unto him,*

Arise, and go into the city, and it shall be told you what you must do," pertains to the Plan of God for Paul, which, in effect, would change the world.

"What he must do," was to first be prayed for that he might receive his sight and then be baptized with the Holy Spirit. As well, he must be a witness to both Israel and the Gentiles. He would be given the great Covenant of Grace, which, in effect, is the Cross of Christ, making him the Moses, one might say, of the New Covenant. As no other man, the Holy Spirit would use him to establish the Church and to take the Gospel Message to the ends of the Earth, for that was the result of what he did.

So, there is no way that one can even begin to grasp the significance of this Conversion on the road to Damascus. And yet, the blood of Stephen was the seed that helped bring forth this fruit.

IN THE FACE OF JESUS CHRIST

Going back to Stephen, it is my opinion that the words and death of this man (and possibly others) surely left a deeper mark than I think we rightly realize. Before Paul's Conversion, he majored in the nuances of the Law. However, due to the fact that neither the Law nor any of the ceremonies and rituals could save, in effect, Paul only had a philosophy—the warped and twisted philosophy of Judaism, which had been made that way by men adding to and subtracting from the Word of God. However, what he saw in Stephen, and, in fact, could not help but see, spoke to him of something far deeper than mere philosophy. It is impossible but that this pointed to something he did not have. In other words, despite all his religion, Paul was lost! As we have stated, he responded to these feelings by increased persecution of the Saints. It all boiled down to a hostility toward Christ, with the struggle against this Way constantly in the subconscious mind. It was like a volcano ready to burst!

To sum it all up, Paul saw Jesus in this blinding appearance and immediately surrendered to Him. As well, this surrender was not only instantaneous but complete. As he would later say, he saw *"the Light of the Knowledge of the Glory of God in the Face of Jesus Christ"* (II Cor. 4:6). Consequently, the god of this world could blind him no longer. He had seen Jesus, and all else had lost charm for Paul.

NOTES

As blindly as he had fought Him, he would now follow Him!

(7) "AND THE MEN WHICH JOURNEYED WITH HIM STOOD SPEECHLESS, HEARING A VOICE, BUT SEEING NO MAN."

The structure is:

1. The phrase, *"And the men which journeyed with him stood speechless,"* means they were very much aware that something had happened, but they did not know exactly what.

2. *"Hearing a voice, but seeing no man,"* means they heard a Voice speaking but could not tell what it was saying and, as well, did not share in the Vision of Jesus (Acts 22:9). Also, they saw the *"Light from Heaven"* but not the Glory of that Light (Acts 22:9-11).

3. However, this much is certain, whatever they did see, it left them speechless from terror, even struck dumb!

(8) "AND SAUL AROSE FROM THE EARTH; AND WHEN HIS EYES WERE OPENED, HE SAW NO MAN: BUT THEY LED HIM BY THE HAND, AND BROUGHT HIM INTO DAMASCUS."

The construction is:

1. The phrase, *"And Saul arose from the earth,"* proclaims him, at the Vision of Jesus, having fallen to the earth. I think it is obvious that the Power of God was so strong that he simply could not stand.

2. *"And when his eyes were opened, he saw no man,"* means that he opened his eyes, but he had no sight! However, while in the trance, he definitely saw the Lord.

3. *"But they led him by the hand, and brought him into Damascus,"* proclaims that which must have been quite a sight.

4. Paul had been the champion of the persecutors, but now, he was led like a blind man, which he temporarily was.

5. He was coming to Damascus in order to lead Followers of Christ to prison or even to death. Instead, he was being led himself!

6. The very first thing that the Lord did to Paul was to humble him, which, in

effect, was the very opposite of what he had previously been. There is infinite pathos in the picture of the blind Paul led by the hand into Damascus. All the pride of power was gone, as well as all the lust for vengeance. His hatred for Christ had been changed instantly to that of utter awe.

7. It must have entered his mind as he was led into Damascus as to why the Lord had not stricken him dead, especially considering the terrible things he had done against Christ and His Followers! However, he was to learn that which the Law could never teach him—that God is Love and that He takes no delight in the death of the wicked, but rather great delight in their Salvation (Lk. 15:7-10).

(9) "AND HE WAS THREE DAYS WITHOUT SIGHT, AND NEITHER DID EAT NOR DRINK."

The synopsis is:

1. The phrase, *"And he was three days without sight,"* speaks only of the physical sense. In fact, for the very first time, he was now able to *"see!"*

2. *"And neither did eat nor drink,"* presents him fasting these three days and nights, and for the obvious reasons. It seems to have been a voluntary self-abasement.

3. His sin in persecuting the Followers of Christ and their Divine Head, as well, coupled with his guilt in assisting at the death of God's Saints and in rejecting the Testimony to Christ's Resurrection, had been very great. Even though the fasting did not earn him anything, still, these three days of blindness and of fasting were, therefore, a fitting act of thankfulness for the Grace of forgiveness that had been so freely and fully given to him (I Tim. 1:12-16).

(10) "AND THERE WAS A CERTAIN DISCIPLE AT DAMASCUS, NAMED ANANIAS, AND TO HIM SAID THE LORD IN A VISION, ANANIAS. AND HE SAID, BEHOLD, I AM HERE, LORD."

The composition is:

1. Every problem in the life of the Christian is because of an improper knowledge of the Cross.

2. Everything in the Old Testament streams forward to the Cross, while everything in the New Testament streams backward to the Cross.

NOTES

ANANIAS

The phrase, *"And there was a certain Disciple at Damascus, named Ananias,"* proclaims a dear brother who was about to be used by the Lord in such a way that his name would be spoken of favorably forever. How privileged he was to be used of the Lord in this fashion! How so wonderful was his consecration that the Lord could speak to him accordingly.

I suspect that if the truth be known, there are very few who claim Christ who can actually be used by Him. For many Christians, living for Jesus is a one hour a week experience, if that! An addition is made to that hour only if there is a great need, etc. How so wonderful, and yet, how so rare is that person, such as Ananias, who can hear at any time and will obey.

The phrase, *"And to him said the Lord in a vision, Ananias,"* means that he actually saw the Lord, but in Vision form.

The borderline between Vision and Dream or trance is difficult, if not impossible, to determine. This is reflected in the Biblical vocabulary of *"Vision."*

The Hebrew word for Vision is *"hazon"* and comes from a root used to describe the beholding of a Vision by anyone while in an ecstatic state (Isa. 1:1; Ezek. 12:27).

Another Hebrew word is *"mar'a"* and means *"a Vision as a means of Revelation"* (Num. 12:6; I Sam. 3:15).

The New Testament uses two Greek words in this connection: *"Horama"* (Acts 9:10, 12; 10:3, 17, 19) and *"optasia"* (Lk. 1:22; Acts 26:19; II Cor. 12:1). They signify *"appearance"* or *"Vision."*

VISIONS

The circumstances in which the revelatory Visions came to those of the Bible are varied. They came in men's waking hours (Dan. 10:7; Acts 9:7)—by day (Acts 10:3) or by night (Gen. 46:2). However, the Visions seemed to have had a close connection with the dream-state (Num. 12:6; Job 4:13).

Actually, the outstanding examples of Visions in the Old Testament are Ezekiel and Daniel.

In the New Testament, Luke manifests the greatest interest in Visions. He reported the Visions of Zechariah (Lk. 1:22), Ananias (Acts 9:10), Cornelius (10:3), Peter (10:10), and Paul (18:9); although Paul treated Visions with much reserve (II Cor. 12:1).

The supreme set of Visions in the New Testament is that in the Book of Revelation, as given to John the Beloved.

Biblical Visions concerned both immediate situations (Gen. 15:1; Acts 12:7) and the *"far-off Divine events"* of the Kingdom of God, as the writings of Isaiah, Daniel, and John testify.

"And he said, Behold, I am here, Lord," proclaims an extensive familiarity with the Lord by Ananias, which I think is far beyond the normal.

The simplicity of Ananias' words and of the Lord's replies is most touching and reveals the nature of the relationship between them, for He spoke to Ananias as a man speaks to his friend. He did not say, *"Ananias, Ananias,"* just as in John 20:16, He did not say, *"Mary, Mary."* Intimacy and fellowship appear in the simple *"Ananias."*

How much the heart wants to know more about this wonderful man!

(11) "AND THE LORD SAID UNTO HIM, ARISE, AND GO INTO THE STREET WHICH IS CALLED STRAIGHT, AND ENQUIRE IN THE HOUSE OF JUDAS FOR ONE CALLED SAUL, OF TARSUS: FOR, BEHOLD, HE PRAYS."

The pattern is:

1. The phrase, *"And the Lord said unto him, Arise, and go into the street which is called Straight,"* proclaims a street, even after nearly 2,000 years, that still exists. It then ran from the east to the west gate. In Oriental cities, such would be the bazaar or marketplace. It is said that at one time, there were three lanes divided by Corinthian columns.

2. *"And enquire in the house of Judas for one called Saul, of Tarsus,"* expresses the name of the man who was the most notorious scourge of the Followers of Christ in the world at that time, which must have come as a shock to Ananias.

3. No further information is given respecting *"Judas,"* who was chosen by the Lord to lodge Paul. That Paul was taken there and that this man had a house on the street called Straight is the entirety of the information given. The Scripture is silent as to the reason this place was chosen, or was it where Paul had intended to go originally?

4. *"For, behold, he prays,"* is said by some to refer to the actual time of his Conversion; however, I think the entirety of the account proves otherwise. People are saved not so much by praying, but more so by believing. Every indication is that Paul did exactly this when he said to the Lord at His Appearance, *"Lord, what will You have me to do?"* (Acts 9:6).

5. When Ananias first met Paul, he addressed him immediately as *"Brother Saul."* As well, he was then baptized with the Holy Spirit, which always follows the Conversion experience (Acts 9:17). Paul was already a saved man, hence, his fasting and praying respecting what he was to do.

6. Actually, Paul was not given any more information by Jesus except, *"Arise, and go into the city, and it shall be told you what you must do"* (Acts 9:6). So, after arriving at the house of Judas, Paul was waiting on the Lord concerning the next step. The next Verse tells us what that step was.

(12) "AND HAS SEEN IN A VISION A MAN NAMED ANANIAS COMING IN, AND PUTTING HIS HAND ON HIM, THAT HE MIGHT RECEIVE HIS SIGHT."

The pattern is:

1. The phrase, *"And has seen in a vision a man named Ananias coming in,"* proclaims the second Vision that Paul had in a very short period of time.

2. How long into these three days and nights of fasting and praying before the Vision came concerning Ananias, we are not told. At any rate, he now knew the Lord was going to send someone to pray for him concerning certain things.

3. *"And putting his hand on him, that he might receive his sight,"* was probably said in this way because, up to the time of the Vision, Paul may not have known if his sight would return or not!

(13) "THEN ANANIAS ANSWERED, LORD, I HAVE HEARD BY MANY OF THIS

MAN, HOW MUCH EVIL HE HAS DONE TO YOUR SAINTS AT JERUSALEM."

The order is:

1. The phrase, *"Then Ananias answered, Lord, I have heard by many of this man,"* presents the fierceness of the name of Paul (Saul) portraying itself in the dread that Ananias had and the protest that he made to the Lord concerning him.

2. As well, the statement of Ananias to the Lord shows how the news of Paul's Commission had preceded him and caused terror among the Disciples at Damascus. Little did Ananias suspect that this dreaded enemy would be the channel of God's richest Blessings to His Church throughout all ages until the Coming of Christ.

3. How empty our fears often are! How ignorant are we where our chief good lies hidden! However, God knows. Let us trust Him.

4. *"How much evil he has done to Your Saints at Jerusalem,"* presents exactly what Paul had been doing. But yet, the Lord would so change this man until he would become the greatest blessing to the Saints of possibly anyone in history. In fact, I personally believe that the Apostle Paul was the greatest example for Christianity ever produced by Christ.

(14) "AND HERE HE HAS AUTHORITY FROM THE CHIEF PRIESTS TO BIND ALL WHO CALL ON YOUR NAME."

The form is:

1. The phrase, *"And here he has authority from the Chief Priests,"* presents that which was true. But yet, a higher Authority, much higher, had overridden the intentions of these evil men. Men rule, but God overrules!

2. *"To bind all who call on Your Name,"* refers to the Name of Jesus. That Name is the most beloved Name on the face of the Earth, while, at the same time, being the most hated!

3. So, Paul's evil intentions had preceded him; however, the Lord would invade those intentions, completely changing them.

(15) "BUT THE LORD SAID UNTO HIM, GO YOUR WAY: FOR HE IS A CHOSEN VESSEL UNTO ME, TO BEAR MY NAME BEFORE THE GENTILES, AND KINGS, AND THE CHILDREN OF ISRAEL."

NOTES

The record is:

1. The Cross was not, and is not, a place of defeat, but rather Victory upon Victory upon Victory and continued Victory.

2. The Cross is to ever be placed as the Foundation of all we are, all we have, and all that we receive in Christ.

A CHOSEN VESSEL

The phrase, *"But the Lord said unto him, Go your way,"* presents an urgency that demands instant obedience by Ananias.

"For he is a chosen vessel unto Me," gives us a little insight into the Mind of God.

The Greek word for *"chosen"* is *"ekloge"* and means *"divine selection."* It can be, as well, translated *"election."*

As the word *"chosen"* or *"election"* is here used, it speaks simply of God choosing someone, in this case Paul, for a particular task. That task is given unto us in the balance of this Fifteenth Verse.

In no way was the will of Paul subverted, coerced, or forced. Of course, through foreknowledge, the Lord knew what Paul's reaction would be, as He knows what the reaction of all will be.

He knew that upon revealing Himself to Paul, he would willingly give himself to the Lord Jesus Christ for the task that lay ahead. On this basis, he was chosen, elected, and even predestined.

WHAT IS ELECTION?

Election is a choice originating with God respecting certain plans and certain people. In other words, they are elected by God to do something or to be something, or both! However, God's Election of certain people for certain things never violates their free moral agency. Even though men are called and elected for certain things, they must make their Calling and Election sure by accepting what God wants, as stated in II Peter 1:10.

The idea that some people are elected by God to be eternally Saved and others to be eternally lost, with nothing the person can do about these situations, is patently false. Actually, such teaching runs counter to the entirety of the tenor of the Word of God (Jn. 3:16).

ELECTION IS A CHOICE PREDICATED ON GRACE (ROM. 11:5)

It is an act of undeserved favor freely shown toward members of a fallen race to which God owed nothing but wrath (Rom. 1:18). Not only does God choose and elect all sinners to be saved, that is, if they will meet God's Terms (Rom. 4:5; 5:6-8; Eph. 2:1-9), He chooses to save them in a way that exalts His Grace by magnifying their sinfulness.

He shuts up His Elect, both Jew and Gentile, in a state of disobedience and unbelief, so that they display their true character as sinners, which all have glaringly done. Consequently, they stand out in history, confessed as unbelievers, before He shows them His Mercy (Rom. 9:30; 10:20; 11:30-32).

ELECTION IS A SOVEREIGN CHOICE BY GOD

It must of necessity be sovereign, or else, it would not be a choice. It is prompted by God's own good pleasure alone (Eph. 1:5, 9), and not by any works of man, accomplished or foreseen (Rom. 9:11), or any human efforts to win God's Favor (Rom. 9:15-18).

Such efforts would be vain in any case, for however high sinners aspire and however fast they run, they still, in reality, only continue to sin (Rom. 8:7).

God in His Sovereign Grace has elected to treat all sinners alike, which, in effect, elects them to be lost; however, His Plan of Salvation, which is elected, as well, has also elected that as all are sinners, all can be saved (Rev. 22:17).

THE CROSS OF CHRIST

In the process of *"election,"* if the Cross of Christ is not properly understood, election cannot be properly understood, either.

In the erroneous teaching on *"election,"* there are some who contend that when Jesus died on the Cross, He died only for those who were to be saved, in other words, only those who were predestined to be saved. That is patently false!

The Scripture plainly says, **"For God so loved the world** *(presents the God kind of love)*, **that He gave His only Begotten Son** *(gave Him up to the Cross, for that's what it took to redeem humanity)*, **that whosoever believes in Him should not perish, but have Everlasting Life.**

"For God sent not His Son into the world to condemn the world *(means that the object of Christ's Mission was to save, but the issue to those who reject Him must be, and can only be, condemnation)*; **but that the world through Him might be saved** *(Jesus Christ is the only Salvation for the world; there is no other! As well, He is Salvation only through the Cross; consequently, the Cross must ever be the object of our Faith)*.

"He who believes on Him is not condemned *(not condemned to be eternally lost in the Lake of Fire forever and forever [Rev. 20:11-15])*: **but he who believes not is condemned already, because he has not believed in the Name of the only Begotten Son of God** *(all of this refers to Christ and what He did at the Cross in order to redeem humanity; Salvation is never by works, but rather by Grace through Faith, with the Cross ever the object of that Faith)*" **(Jn. 3:16-18).**

As is overly obvious in these Passages, Jesus died for the entirety of the world, i.e., the entirety of mankind, not only for those who would be saved.

THE POTENTIAL OF THE CROSS

When Jesus died on the Cross, He atoned for all sin, past, present, and future, at least for all who will believe (Jn. 3:16). In fact, had He not atoned for all sin, then He could not have risen from the dead. The Scripture also says, **"For the wages of sin *is* death** *(speaks of spiritual death, which is separation from God)*; **but the Gift of God *is* Eternal Life through Jesus Christ our Lord" (Rom. 6:23).**

This means that if Jesus had failed to atone for even one sin, He could not have risen from the dead. So, the fact that He rose from the dead tells us that all sin was atoned. This means that all those who died in the Faith before the Cross were Saved, even though the blood of bulls and goats

NOTES

could not take away sins. Their Salvation rested on what the animal sacrifices represented, namely, Christ and what He would do at the Cross.

So, at any time in history, if individuals placed their Faith in Christ and what He would do at the Cross all on our behalf (of which the animal sacrifices were a symbol), that person would be saved. It also means that every individual in the world presently, no matter who they might be, where they might be, or how sinful and wicked they have been in the past, can be saved if they will look to Christ and believe Him, which means to trust Him. That's what we mean by the potential of the Cross. It carries the potential to save all, not just a few, that is, if all will simply believe.

ELECTION IS A CHOICE OF INDIVIDUAL SINNERS TO BE SAVED IN AND THROUGH CHRIST

Election is *"in Christ,"* the Incarnate Son, Whose Historical Appearing and Mediation were themselves included in God's Eternal Plan (Acts 2:23; I Pet. 1:20).

Election in Christ means:

- The goal of election is that God's Chosen should bear Christ's Image and share His Glory (Rom. 8:29; II Thess. 2:14). They are chosen for holiness (which means Christlikeness in all their conduct) in this life (Eph. 1:4), and glorification (which means Christlikeness in all their being) (II Cor. 3:18; Phil. 3:21) in the life to come.
- The Elect are to be redeemed from the guilt and stain of sin by Christ through His Atoning Death and the Gift of His Spirit (Eph. 5:25-27; II Thess. 2:13; I Pet. 1:2).

As Jesus said, the Father has given Him those who would make their choice to come to Him, and He has undertaken the necessary steps to bring us all to Eternal Glory (Jn. 6:37-45; 10:14-16, 27-30; 17:2, 6, 9, 24).

- The means whereby the Blessings of election are brought to the Elect in union with Christ—His Union with them representatively as the Last Adam and vitally as the Life-Giver—indwelling them by His Spirit, and their union with Him by Faith, presents the proclamation of Salvation.

NOTES

ELECTION SHOWS THAT SALVATION IS ALL OF GOD AND NONE OF MAN

Election shows the Believer that his Salvation, first to last, is all of God, a fruit of sovereign discriminating Mercy. The Redemption that he finds in Christ alone and receives by Faith alone has its source, not in any personal qualification, but in Grace alone—the Grace of election, all made possible totally by the Cross of Christ.

Every Spiritual Blessing flows to him from God's Electing Decree (Eph. 1:3).

The knowledge of his election, therefore, should teach him to glory in God, and God only (I Cor. 1:31), and to give Him the praise that is His due (Rom. 11:36).

The ultimate end of election is that God should be praised (Eph. 1:6, 12, 14), and the thought of election should drive ransomed sinners to incessant praises and thanksgivings to the Lord, even as it did Paul (Rom. 11:33; Eph. 1:3; I Thess. 5:18; II Thess. 2:13).

Consequently, what God has revealed about election is to Paul a theme, not for argument, but for worship.

ELECTION ASSURES THE BELIEVER OF HIS SECURITY IN CHRIST

As the Believer has been elected by God to be holy and to praise His Name, likewise must the Believer elect to be these particular things and to remain in Christ. When this is done, as it should be done constantly by all Believers, it removes all grounds for fear and despondency. As the Election of God is continuous, likewise must the election of the Believer be continuous as well! Thus, nothing can affect our justified status (Rom. 8:33), that is, as long as we maintain our Faith in Christ and what He did for us at the Cross. In that case, nothing can cut us off from God's Love in Christ (Rom. 8:35-39). Accordingly, one will never be safer than one is, for one is already as safe as one can be. However, if one is to notice in these Passages in Romans 8:35-39, God protects the Believer from all outside sources and situations, whatever they may be, but He does not protect the Believer from himself. In other words, the Believer's free moral agency, which means freedom to choose, is never abrogated by God.

Concerning the term *"chosen vessel,"* it is very special to me. When the Lord saved me at eight years of age, His very Words to me were, *"You are a chosen vessel to be used in My Service."* Actually, He said these words to me twice!

In relationship to that, I was not the one who made the choice, at least, for His Service; it was made by God alone! However, it was up to me to choose whether I would obey Him or not. Thank God, I did obey the Heavenly Vision, even as Paul also said (Acts 26:19).

And yet, I am persuaded that the term *"chosen vessel"* will seldom draw the approval of the church. As with Paul, there is almost universal opposition. It is as if Satan makes such a special target. However, even as in the life of Paul, that which hurts the most is the opposition from those who claim the Name of Christ.

OPPOSITION

One would think that the Early Church in Jerusalem would have put its strength behind Paul, referring to the great Covenant of Grace and world Evangelism, but regrettably, little help was received from that source.

Paul had the seal of Divine Blessing on his work among the Gentiles but seemingly, very little blessing of the Jerusalem Church.

However, Paul did have the Leading, Guidance, Anointing, and Power of the Holy Spirit, which are absolute necessities.

F. F. Bruce said, *"Paul always respected Jerusalem, but it seems that Jerusalem little respected Paul!"*

So, the term *"chosen vessel"* carries with it great Blessing but, at the same time, will always garner great opposition and misunderstanding. Let not the one so designated think that anything else will be the case, other than a lonely vigil. Nevertheless, the task, by the Grace of God, will be accomplished.

The phrase, *"To bear My Name before the Gentiles, and kings, and the Children of Israel,"* proclaims what Paul was chosen to do.

NOTES

If one is to notice, the *"Gentiles"* were placed first because ministry to those who were non-Jewish was Paul's principal Calling. He actually referred to himself as an Apostle to the Gentiles (Acts 22:21; 26:17-18; Rom. 15:16; Gal. 2:7-9). In fact, it was always the Plan of God for the entire world to hear and know the Gospel of Redemption. While Israel definitely was elected or chosen to be a particular people, the purpose and reason for that choice was not that they be saved exclusively, as they later came to believe, but that they might be the vehicle or instrument through which Salvation could come to the entirety of the world (Jn. 3:16). The Word of God would be given to them, and, as well, they would be the people through whom the Messiah, the Saviour of mankind, would come.

However, as stated, Israel became sectarian, finally coming to the place where they believed even being born a Jew assured one of Salvation. That fact, as well, shut out all Gentiles, which actually pertained to the entirety of the world.

THE EARLY CHURCH AND GENTILES

Inasmuch as the Early Church was made up entirely of Jews, at least at the beginning, it was very difficult to get them to break with tradition, thereby, taking the Gospel to the very ones for whom Jesus came and died. Even though Philip quite possibly was the first one to preach the Gospel to a Gentile (the Ethiopian), that is, if he actually was a Gentile, it was Peter who officially performed this task, which we will study in Acts, Chapter 10. However, it was done only at the Command of the Lord, and with some reluctance. Even then, Peter was called on the carpet by the Jerusalem Church, and had it been anyone but Peter, every evidence is that he would have been sanctioned severely.

THE OLD TESTAMENT AND GENTILES

Going back to the Old Testament, the Gentiles were far less sharply differentiated from the Israelites than in New Testament Times. Under Old Testament regulations, Gentiles were simply non-Israelites, which meant they were not from the stock of

Abraham. However, they were not to be hated or despised for that reason. They were to be treated almost on a plane of equality, except certain Tribes in Canaan with regard to whom there were special regulations of non-intercourse.

Actually, the Gentile stranger enjoyed the hospitality of the Israelite who was commanded to love him (Deut. 10:19) and to sympathize with him, *"For you know the heart of the stranger, seeing you were strangers in the land of Egypt"* (Ex. 23:9). In fact, the Kenites were treated almost as brethren, as well as the children of Rechab (Judg. 1:16; 5:24; Jer., Chpt. 35).

Uriah the Hittite was a trusted warrior of David (II Sam., Chpt. 11), and Ittai the Gittite was captain of David's guard (II Sam. 18:2). Araunah the Jebusite was a respected resident of Jerusalem. They were all Gentiles.

The Gentiles had the right of asylum in the cities of refuge, the cities of which were all Types of Christ, the same as Israelites (Num. 35:15). As well, a Gentile servant was not to be defrauded of his wages (Deut. 24:15).

Gentiles could inherit in Israel even as late as the Exile (Ezek. 47:22-23).

Prayers and sacrifices were to be offered for Gentile rulers (Ezra 6:10; Jer. 29:7).

ISRAEL AND THE GENTILES

However, as we approach the Christian era, the attitude of the Jews toward the Gentiles changed until we find in New Testament Times the most extreme aversion, scorn, and hatred. They were regarded as unclean, with whom it was unlawful to have any friendly intercourse. They were enemies of God and His People, to whom the knowledge of God was denied unless they became Jewish proselytes, and even then, they could not, as in ancient times, be admitted to full fellowship.

Jews were forbidden to counsel them, and if they asked about Divine things, they were to be cursed. All children born of mixed marriages were considered to be illegitimate. Actually, this is what caused the Jews to be so hated by Greeks and Romans, as we have abundant evidence in the writings of Cicero Seneca and Tacitus.

NOTES

Something of this is reflected in John 18:28 and in Acts 10:28 and 11:3.

This hatred came about because of a departure from the Word of God. Little by little, the Jews had made an idol out of the Law of Moses, as well as the Temple, the Feast Days, the sacrifices, etc. Inasmuch as they had done this, and inasmuch as they were the only ones in the world who had the Temple and the Law of God, etc., they excluded all others, causing them to look down on the Gentiles as dogs.

THE EARLY CHURCH

All of this had a tremendous influence even on the Apostles and the entirety of the Early Church, at least in its beginning stages. Actually, without Paul, unless the Lord had raised up someone else of like caliber, it is doubtful that the Early Church could have gotten beyond its Jewish beginnings.

The words *"and kings"* were filled in totality respecting Paul.

Even though the name Nero does not occur in the New Testament, still, he was the Caesar to whom Paul appealed (Acts 25:11) and at whose tribunal Paul was tried after his first imprisonment.

Even though one cannot be certain, it is quite likely that Nero heard Paul's case in person, for the emperor showed much interest in provincial cases.

So, Paul witnessed to Nero either directly or indirectly, plus other kings and leaders of nations as well!

His witnessing to the *"Children of Israel,"* while extremely pronounced, at least at the beginning, soon saw that door closed because of continued rebellion on the part of the Jews. So, *"Gentiles"* were placed first by the Holy Spirit because that door would remain open, with Paul actually given a special Commission respecting that part of the Gospel.

The word *"bear"* in the Greek Text is *"bastazo"* and means *"to take up with the hands; raise as a flag; carry as a banner; support, exalt, and hold upright."* In other words, the *"Name"* of Jesus would be the Supreme Foundation of Paul's Message, around which everything centered.

(16) "FOR I WILL SHOW HIM HOW

GREAT THINGS HE MUST SUFFER FOR MY NAME'S SAKE."

The account is:

1. Concerning this Passage, we learn many things.

We learn that true Faith will always be greatly opposed by Satan. As someone has once said, *"Faith must be tested, and great Faith must be tested greatly."*

2. One should read the Sixteenth Verse very carefully because it disavows much of what passes for Gospel presently!

3. Immediately after Paul's Conversion, the Holy Spirit began to outline to him the extreme difficulties he would face in bearing this Name of Jesus. It would ultimately cost him his life and is the very opposite, at least for the most part, of much modern gospel.

4. Too much of the time at present, people are told to come to Christ, and they will very soon be financially rich. Some in this *"other gospel"* even claim that if Paul had had the Faith they possess, he would not have had to undergo the tremendous difficulties that he faced, such as stonings, imprisonment, shipwrecks, etc.

5. Of course, such drivel, and drivel it is, is not really worthy of a response. In truth, these people, whomever they may be, have no faith at all! True Faith will always be opposed greatly by Satan, and for the obvious reasons.

(17) "AND ANANIAS WENT HIS WAY, AND ENTERED INTO THE HOUSE; AND PUTTING HIS HANDS ON HIM SAID, BROTHER SAUL, THE LORD, EVEN JESUS, THAT APPEARED UNTO YOU IN THE WAY AS YOU CAME, HAS SENT ME, THAT YOU MIGHT RECEIVE YOUR SIGHT, AND BE FILLED WITH THE HOLY SPIRIT."

The way is:

1. The theology of the Cross reminds us that it is the Cross, the Crucified Christ, that lies at the heart of the Gospel.

2. The Resurrection is a Chapter in the Book on the theology of the Cross.

ANANIAS

The phrase, *"And Ananias went his way, and entered into the house,"* proclaims, as is obvious, this man obeying the Command

NOTES

of the Lord.

"And putting his hands on him said, Brother Saul," tells us two things:

1. Ananias was instructed by the Lord to lay his hands on Paul in order that his eyes would be healed, and that he would be *"filled with the Holy Spirit."* As we have already stated, the laying on of hands is a means used by the Holy Spirit to recognize a Calling, to impart healing or the Holy Spirit, etc.

2. Ananias addressed Paul as *"Brother Saul"* (Paul), not out of mere respect, but because Paul was already Saved and had been so for the last three days and nights.

Jesus Himself said, *"For whosoever shall do the will of My Father which is in Heaven, the same is My brother, and sister, and mother"* (Mat. 12:50).

At the appearance of Christ near Damascus, Paul had asked, *"Lord, what will You have me to do?"* (Acts 22:10) signifying that he had recognized Jesus for Who He was and yielded his heart and life to Him, which constituted Salvation (Jn. 3:16).

THE LORD HAS SENT ME

The phrase, *"The Lord, even Jesus, that appeared unto you in the way as you came, has sent me,"* presents the second appearance of Christ, probably about two days after His Appearance to Paul, or possibly on the third day.

To be sure, especially considering his recent Vision, Paul would not have doubted Ananias whatsoever.

The phrase, *"That you might receive your sight, and be filled with the Holy Spirit,"* presents the first instance, at least that is recorded, of the Holy Spirit being imparted through an ordinary Believer. One can compare Acts 8:14-23; 10:1-7; I Tim. 4:14; and, II Tim. 1:6.

It seems as if Paul received his sight and was baptized with the Holy Spirit almost simultaneously.

Even though this Passage does not give us any specifics whatsoever as to what happened at this time, one makes a mistake if he claims this is an instance of one being baptized with the Holy Spirit without speaking in Tongues. There is nothing here that suggests such a thing, with the statement being made only that Paul was filled.

However, Paul did say in his dissertation of I Corinthians, Chapter 14, regarding the proper use of Tongues, *"I thank my God, I speak with Tongues more than you all"* (I Cor. 14:18).

LINGUISTIC?

No! Paul was not speaking of his ability to converse in several languages, such as Hebrew and Greek. Such thinking does extreme violence to the Text of I Corinthians, Chapter 14. A casual reading of this Chapter portrays Paul dealing with the issue of the Gift of Tongues and how it is to be used, etc., along with Interpretation of Tongues and Prophecy. Actually, three great Truths are given to us in this Seventeenth Verse:

1. The absolute necessity of a Believer being baptized with the Holy Spirit is very obvious in this scenario. In fact, any and all things that come to the Believer must, of necessity, come through the Office and Person of the Holy Spirit. So, we see in this Passage just how significant this really is, which is borne out in all other Passages respecting Believers being filled with the Spirit (Acts 1:4; 8:14-15; 10:44-48; 19:1-7).

2. We learn from this scenario that the Infilling of the Holy Spirit is not instantaneous with Conversion as many teach, but is always subsequent to Salvation, even though it may take place only moments after (Acts 10:44-48).

Actually, it is not possible for a sinner to receive the Holy Spirit (Jn. 14:17). In fact, the temple must be cleansed and washed by the Blood of Jesus, with the individual made clean by the act of Sanctification, as he is legally declared clean by the act of Justification. All of this is a Work of the Spirit but is not the Baptism with the Holy Spirit. Then the Believer, after being cleansed by the Blood, is a fit candidate for the Holy Spirit.

3. As well, even though Luke does not give us any information here, still, we know from I Corinthians 14:18 that speaking in other Tongues as the Spirit of God gives the utterance is the initial, physical evidence that one has been baptized with the Holy Spirit. Otherwise, how would one know?

NOTES

(18) "AND IMMEDIATELY THERE FELL FROM HIS EYES AS IT HAD BEEN SCALES: AND HE RECEIVED SIGHT FORTHWITH, AND AROSE, AND WAS BAPTIZED."

The pattern is:

1. The phrase, *"And immediately there fell from his eyes as it had been scales,"* seems to represent some type of film over his eyes, which now came off.

2. There is a possibility that the Lord caused this substance to form over Paul's eyes when He appeared to him in order that the dazzling brilliance not blind him permanently. While those with Paul also saw the Light (Acts 22:9), they did not see, as we have stated, the full *"Glory of that Light,"* as Paul did (Acts 22:11). Consequently, it would not have been nearly as bright to them as it was to him.

3. *"And he received sight forthwith, and arose, and was baptized,"* refers to being baptized in water, which evidently was done after he was baptized with the Holy Spirit.

Water Baptism was probably carried out in one of the rivers that runs through Damascus.

4. Even though the Scripture is clear to delineate that Paul was baptized in water, it gives us no information at all concerning the Twelve Apostles. Quite possibly they were baptized by Christ Himself.

(19) "AND WHEN HE HAD RECEIVED MEAT, HE WAS STRENGTHENED. THEN WAS SAUL CERTAIN DAYS WITH THE DISCIPLES WHICH WERE AT DAMASCUS."

The account is:

1. The phrase, *"And when he had received meat, he was strengthened,"* refers to him ending his three-day fast.

2. The phrase, *"Then was Saul certain days with the Disciples which were at Damascus,"* probably means that Ananias introduced him to these Followers of Christ. It is ironic that Paul now joins the very people whom he had previously intended to place in prison, or even send some to their deaths.

3. Without a doubt, Paul's Conversion had to be one of, if not the most, miraculous

NOTES

experiences ever recorded. There is actually no way one can properly define the drama attached to this that only God could do.

(20) "AND STRAIGHTWAY HE PREACHED CHRIST IN THE SYNAGOGUES, THAT HE IS THE SON OF GOD."

The way is:

1. The phrase, *"And straightway he preached Christ,"* should have been translated, *"And straightway he preached Jesus."* The word *"straightway"* means that he did so immediately!

2. Some have claimed that Paul went into the desert in Arabia immediately after Ananias prayed for him, with Verse 20 referring to his return from that area; however, the Text does not seem to lean at all in that direction.

3. Even though the word *"straightway"* could refer to the time immediately following the desert experience, as some claim, every indication is that it refers to Paul immediately beginning to preach after his Salvation experience.

4. *"In the synagogues,"* pertains to the very synagogues to which the letters of the High Priest were addressed, empowering Paul to arrest either man or woman who called upon the Name of Jesus, and bring them as prisoners to Jerusalem to be tried before the Sanhedrin.

5. *"That He is the Son of God,"* proclaims the first time in Acts that Jesus is referred to by this title.

6. The Holy Spirit anointed Paul to preach immediately. Even though he had studied Scripture for years, due to not truly being Saved, he had a skewed understanding of the Word of God. He now found the Scriptures brought into proper focus.

7. I have every confidence that the Holy Spirit opened up the Old Testament to Paul, as it referred to Christ, in such a graphic way that it now became clear as crystal.

(21) "BUT ALL WHO HEARD HIM WERE AMAZED, AND SAID; IS NOT THIS HE WHO DESTROYED THEM WHICH CALLED ON THIS NAME IN JERUSALEM, AND CAME HERE FOR THAT INTENT, THAT HE MIGHT BRING THEM BOUND UNTO THE CHIEF PRIESTS?"

The exegesis is:

1. The phrase, *"But all who heard him were amazed,"* proclaims such done for several reasons:

a. They were utterly amazed that this one who had purposed to rid the synagogues of all the Followers of Christ was now doing the very thing that he had so strongly opposed.

b. They were *"amazed,"* as well, as to the validity and power of his argument concerning Jesus. It was obvious that he knew his subject!

2. The reader must understand that at this stage, the Followers of Christ did not consider themselves at all as being outside the periphery of Judaism. They considered themselves good Jews who followed the Law of Moses. The only basic difference, at least in their thinking, was that they accepted Jesus as the Messiah of Israel and the Son of God. Of course, this was an untenable position in that if one truly followed Christ, one would have to understand that He fulfilled all the Law, with it no longer being applicable as far as its rituals and ceremonies were concerned. Why was the Type needed when the Antitype was now available?

3. Why should one continue to observe the Sabbath when the One to Whom the Sabbath pointed and was meant to symbolize had now come?

4. A little later, the Holy Spirit would graphically outline the New Covenant to Paul, which was meant to be followed and, in fact, was meant to take the place of the Old. However, as stated, old habits die hard!

5. The question, *"And said; Is not this he who destroyed them which called on this Name in Jerusalem, and came here for that intent, that he might bring them bound unto the Chief Priests?"* means simply that the people had been expecting him, but not what he was now saying.

6. The appellative *"Chief Priests"* is given in the plural and marks how the High Priesthood at this period was passed from one to another. Caiaphas, Annas, Jonathan, and Theophilus would all be included eventually under the term.

(22) "BUT SAUL INCREASED THE MORE IN STRENGTH, AND CONFOUNDED THE JEWS WHICH DWELT

AT DAMASCUS, PROVING THAT THIS IS VERY CHRIST."

The synopsis is:

1. The phrase, *"But Saul increased the more in strength,"* refers to his greater understanding of the Word of God as the days wore on. Now that he was baptized with the Holy Spirit, the Scripture, as we have stated, opened up to him like a flower.

2. *"And confounded the Jews which dwelt at Damascus,"* means that Paul overwhelmed them with his knowledge of the Word of God concerning Christ.

3. Now he found himself in the exact place in which Stephen had been used by the Lord, with the possibility definitely existing that Paul was the very one who was bested by this Follower of Christ (Acts 6:9-15).

4. *"Proving that this is very Christ,"* presents the idea that when comparing the Life and Works of Christ with the Prophets, it was clear that He was the Messiah.

5. Regrettably, these people of Damascus little searched the Scriptures, if at all, to see if Paul was correct; consequently, there is no record in the Book of Acts of a church being built in Damascus.

6. The title *"Christ"* actually means *"Anointed,"* and was used of Christ in the Old Testament Prophecies. In fact, it was Hannah, the mother of Samuel, who used this title for the first time (I Sam. 2:10). After that, the Holy Spirit began to give this term to others concerning the theme of God's Anointed One—the Messiah (Ps. 2:2; 45:7; Isa. 61:1; Dan. 9:25-26; Jn. 1:41; 4:25).

(23) "AND AFTER THAT MANY DAYS WERE FULFILLED, THE JEWS TOOK COUNSEL TO KILL HIM."

The exegesis is:

1. The theology of the Cross insists upon the Cross being given priority over all other events in the history of Salvation.

2. Wherever the Church takes the Cross of Christ seriously, it can expect to encounter hostility.

PAUL

The phrase, *"And after that many days were fulfilled,"* speaks of a span of time of about three years when he came again to Damascus after being in Arabia that long (II Cor. 11:32; Gal. 1:18).

NOTES

Luke gives no account of this personal phase of Paul's career, but he allows room for it between Acts 9:22 and 23. It is Paul who tells of his retirement to Arabia (Gal. 1:17) to prove his independence of the Apostles in Jerusalem.

He did not go to them for instruction or for ecclesiastical authority. He did not adopt the merely traditional view of Jesus as the Messiah. He knew, of course, the contention well enough, for he had answered it often enough.

However, now his old arguments were gone, and he must work his way around to the other side and be able to put forth his new Gospel with clearness and force.

He was done with calling Jesus anathema (I Cor. 12:3). Henceforth, to him, Jesus was Lord.

We know nothing of Paul's life in Arabia for this approximate three years, nor do we know in what part of Arabia he was. Some even contend that he may have gone to Mt. Sinai and thought out Grace in the atmosphere of Law, but there is no evidence of that.

However, one thing is clear: Paul grew in apprehension of the things of Christ during these years, as indeed he grew to the very end; however, he never pulled away from the first clear Vision of Jesus. He claimed that God had revealed His Son to him that he might preach to the Gentiles (Gal. 1:16). He claimed that from the first and to the last.

A DEVELOPED FAITH

It is impossible to escape the conclusion that the significance and value of the Cross became clear to him almost simultaneously with the certainty of the Resurrection and of the Messiahship of Jesus. This narrow Jew had surrendered to Christ Who died for the sins of the world.

The universal Gospel had taken hold of his mind and heart, and it would work out its logical consequences in Paul. The time in Arabia seems to be when he received from the Lord the New Covenant. When he reappeared in Damascus, he had *"developed Faith"* and energy that bore instant fruit.

NOTES

He was now the slave of Christ.

For him, henceforth, to live was Christ. He was crucified with Christ. He was in Christ. The union of Paul with Christ was the real key to his life. It was far more than a Doctrine about Christ. It was real fellowship with Christ.

Thus it was that the man who probably never saw Christ in the flesh understood Him best.

Now Paul did not merely proclaim Christ as before, he *"proved Christ."*

As well, he did it with such marvelous skill that the Jews were first confounded and then enraged to the point of murder. Their former hero was now their foe.

The phrase, *"The Jews took counsel to kill him,"* portrays the method of operation of all religion. They are not content to oppose the Message only, but they feel they must destroy the Messenger as well!

(24) "BUT THEIR LAYING AWAIT WAS KNOWN OF SAUL. AND THEY WATCHED THE GATES DAY AND NIGHT TO KILL HIM."

The account is:

1. The phrase, *"But their laying await was known of Saul,"* presents Believers informing him of the proposed action of these Jewish zealots. He *"proved"* the Gospel of Jesus Christ with such marvelous skill that the Jews were first confounded and then enraged to the point of murder.

2. *"And they watched the gates day and night to kill him,"* of which he was informed, as well; therefore, he would escape by a different route.

(25) "THEN THE DISCIPLES TOOK HIM BY NIGHT, AND LET HIM DOWN BY THE WALL IN A BASKET."

The form is:

1. This episode not only proclaims his escape but, as well, proclaims the beginning of the active Ministry of the man who was called to be a chosen vessel to Gentiles, kings, and Jews.

2. In II Corinthians 11:32-33 and Galatians 1:17, Paul gave the account himself of his escape.

(26) "AND WHEN SAUL WAS COME TO JERUSALEM, HE ASSAYED TO JOIN HIMSELF TO THE DISCIPLES: BUT THEY WERE ALL AFRAID OF HIM, AND BELIEVED NOT THAT HE WAS A DISCIPLE."

The synopsis is:

1. The phrase, *"And when Saul was come to Jerusalem,"* presents his first visit there after his Conversion. It was after his three-year sojourn in Arabia as well!

2. *"He assayed to join himself to the Disciples: but they were all afraid of him,"* means that while they had heard that he had come to Christ, they simply did not believe such, thinking it was another ploy to trap them.

3. *"And believed not that he was a Disciple,"* probably stems from the fact that they thought if he had truly given his heart to Christ, surely he would have come to Jerusalem before now.

4. In fact, he had not avoided Jerusalem because he despised flesh and blood, but because he had no need of Light from the Apostles since *"the divine Revelation so completely absorbed his interest and attention."*

Paul probably knew that he would be an object of suspicion to the Disciples in Jerusalem. This was inevitable in view of the past. It was best to go, but he did not wish to ask any favors of the Apostles. Indeed, it seems he went in particular *"to visit Peter* (Cephas)*"* (Gal. 1:18).

(27) "BUT BARNABAS TOOK HIM, AND BROUGHT HIM TO THE APOSTLES, AND DECLARED UNTO THEM HOW HE HAD SEEN THE LORD IN THE WAY, AND THAT HE HAD SPOKEN TO HIM, AND HOW HE HAD PREACHED BOLDLY AT DAMASCUS IN THE NAME OF JESUS."

The form is:

1. The phrase, *"But Barnabas took him,"* presents the same one mentioned in Acts 4:36.

Barnabas, as we shall see, played a great part in Paul's life and Ministry and, accordingly, was greatly used of the Lord in this capacity. As we have said elsewhere, if there had not been a Barnabas, there just may not have been a Paul.

2. *"And brought him to the Apostles,"* actually refers to Peter and James only (Gal. 1:18-19).

NOTES

James was considered an Apostle, even though he did not refer to himself as one, because of Jesus' special Appearance to him after the Resurrection (I Cor. 15:7).

3. *"And declared unto them how he had seen the Lord in the way, and that He had spoken to him,"* proclaims Barnabas giving Paul's Testimony to Peter and James and, no doubt, the Elders in the Church at Jerusalem. By him relating this to them, it showed that he believed what Paul had said, which gave it authenticity. (The other Apostles seem to have been away.)

4. *"And how he had preached boldly at Damascus in the Name of Jesus,"* seems to mean that Barnabas had heard this report and now testified as to its veracity.

(28) "AND HE WAS WITH THEM COMING IN AND GOING OUT AT JERUSALEM."

The pattern is:

1. The phrase, *"And he was with them,"* refers to the approximate 15 days he spent there, most of it with Simon Peter (Gal. 1:18).

2. It is certain that Peter and Paul knew each other but, of course, as opponents. Paul came now with the olive branch to his old enemy.

3. *"Coming in and going out at Jerusalem,"* concerns the Church there. In other words, because of Barnabas, he was accepted!

(29) "AND HE SPOKE BOLDLY IN THE NAME OF THE LORD JESUS, AND DISPUTED AGAINST THE GRECIANS: BUT THEY WENT ABOUT TO KILL HIM."

The account is:

1. The phrase, *"And he spoke boldly in the Name of the Lord Jesus,"* means that he pulled no punches when it came to declaring Jesus Christ as Israel's Messiah and the world's Saviour. He did this, as is obvious, in the very center, or core, of Jesus hate. He trimmed his Message not at all and if anything, if possible, made it even stronger.

2. *"And disputed against the Grecians,"* in essence, means that he now took Stephen's place, for Stephen was a Hellenist, or as it is described here, a Grecian Jew. He was probably preaching in the very synagogues in which he had heard Stephen and maybe had even debated him. As we have stated, it's even possible that he may have been the chief spokesman against Jesus and Stephen.

3. Now he showed his dauntless spirit and perhaps his deep compunction at the part he had taken in Stephen's death by thus encountering the bitter and unrelenting enmity of these Grecian Jews.

4. *"But they went about to kill him,"* presents the same spirit against him as he had presented against Stephen some three years earlier.

5. It was a repetition of Damascus, but Paul did not wish to run again so soon.

6. He protested to the Lord Jesus, Who spoke in a Vision to him, and recalled the fate of Stephen, even though Luke does not mention this account here, but Paul did recall the incident in Acts 22:17-21.

7. At this time, the Lord told him, *"Depart: for I will send you far hence unto the Gentiles"* (Acts 22:21).

(30) "WHICH WHEN THE BRETHREN KNEW, THEY BROUGHT HIM DOWN TO CAESAREA, AND SENT HIM FORTH TO TARSUS."

The exegesis is:

1. The Cross of Christ brings home the full seriousness of sin.

2. The Cross declares the powerlessness of fallen humanity to achieve Salvation of themselves.

3. The Cross of Christ exposes human delusions of self-righteousness.

THE BRETHREN

The phrase, *"Which when the brethren knew,"* refers to what the Lord had told him to do respecting the Gentiles.

The idea of this Verse seems to be that the brethren in Jerusalem knew that Paul was now in great danger, and they did not quite know what to do. Now that the Lord had told him to depart, they had a clear signal and proceeded to help him flee the city. In fact, the situation was about to explode, which, if it had happened at that time, would have caused even greater difficulties for the Jerusalem Church.

The phrase, *"They brought him down to Caesarea,"* was actually up, as far as direction was concerned, because it lay north of Jerusalem. However, respecting the topography, Caesarea was *"down"* exactly as here given.

This was not Caesarea Philippi, which was actually about 50 miles south of Damascus, but rather the Caesarea on the Mediterranean Sea.

The purpose for taking him there was probably twofold:

1. This was one of the great ports of Israel, with shipping going in all directions.

2. There was a Roman garrison there, which would have given pause to the Jews respecting the killing of Paul.

TARSUS

The phrase, *"And sent him forth to Tarsus,"* speaks of his home. As a result, we hear no more of Paul until Acts 11:25. Some think that this period of obscurity covered a period of approximately five years, which speaks of about eight years after his Conversion.

Even though the Scripture does not plainly say, some think that during this time, Paul ministered in the regions of Syria and Cilicia (Acts 11:19; Gal. 1:21).

Some feel that at this time, he ministered not only to the Jews in these regions but unto the Gentiles as well. They reason accordingly because when he appeared at Antioch with Barnabas (Acts 11:25-30), he seemed to take hold like an old hand at the business. It is quite probable, therefore, that this obscure Ministry of several years may have had more results than we know.

As far as is known, there were no Followers of Christ in Tarsus, unless some of the Believers driven from Jerusalem by Paul himself some years earlier went that far, even as they did go to Antioch (Acts 11:19). So, who would have welcomed him home?

One can but wonder whether Paul was kindly received at home by his father and mother. They had looked upon him, no doubt, with pride as the possible successor of the great teacher Gamaliel, but now he was a Follower of the despised Nazarene and a Preacher of the humiliating Cross.

Is it possible that his own exhortations to the fathers not to provoke their children to wrath (Eph. 6:4) may imply that his own father had cast him out at this time?

NOTES

In fact, if one analyzes the situation carefully, we find Paul at this time almost like a square peg in a round hole. It is doubtful, at least now, that his parents were sympathetic toward him. As well, the Church in Jerusalem did not really know what to do with him and may have felt that he was more of a liability than an asset. Due to the fact that he drew opposition like a lightning rod, it seems he was not too welcome.

As well, he had the seal of the Divine Blessing on his work among the Gentiles, in which the Apostles and Elders of the Church at Jerusalem shared little enthusiasm. Consequently, there was a pang of disappointment over the attitude of the Jerusalem Church toward his work. Only such a feeling of disappointment can explain the tone of his references respecting his relations to the Apostles (Gal. 1:11-24).

There is no bitterness in this tone but, as we have stated, puzzled surprise.

Actually, a narrow Pharisaic element in the Church at Jerusalem was active and sought to shape the policy of the Church in its attitude toward the Gentiles. This is clear, as we shall see, in the treatment of Peter when he returned to Jerusalem after the experience at Caesarea with Cornelius (Acts 11:1-18).

It seems, as we shall see, that the Church at Jerusalem accepted what had happened with Peter, but with the notion that this was an exceptional case of the Lord's doing, and did not quite allow it to serve as the Lord intended, the taking of the Gospel to the Gentile world.

(31) "THEN HAD THE CHURCHES REST THROUGHOUT ALL JUDAEA AND GALILEE AND SAMARIA, AND WERE EDIFIED; AND WALKING IN THE FEAR OF THE LORD, AND IN THE COMFORT OF THE HOLY SPIRIT, WERE MULTIPLIED."

The synopsis is:

1. The phrase, *"Then had the Churches rest throughout all Judaea and Galilee and Samaria,"* speaks of *"rest"* from persecution.

It is thought that the attention of the Jews to the progress of the Faith of Jesus Christ was diverted at this time, and their active hostility stayed by the still greater danger to the Jew's religion that arose from the Roman Emperor Caligula's intention of placing a statue to himself as a god in the Temple and, in fact, in the Holy of Holies. Thus did God's gracious Providence intervene to give rest to his harassed Saints and to build up His Church in numbers, in holiness, and in heavenly comfort.

The phrase, *"And were edified,"* pertains to a special time.

The word *"edified"* in the Greek Text is *"oikodomeo"* and means *"to be a house-builder, i.e., to construct."* Without interruption, the Lord now builds His House.

2. *"And walking in the fear of the Lord,"* presents a healthy type of *"fear."* The Greek word is *"phobos"* and means *"a reverential fear of God, as a controlling motive of the life, in matters spiritual and moral, not a mere fear of His Power and righteous retribution, but a wholesome dread of displeasing Him, of fear which banishes the terror that shrinks from His Presence, and which influences the disposition and attitude of one whose circumstances are guided by trust in God, through the indwelling Spirit of God."*

3. As well, this reverential fear of God will inspire a constant carefulness in dealing with others in His Fear.

The phrase, *"And in the comfort of the Holy Spirit,"* actually goes to the second Beatitude, *"Blessed are they that mourn: for they shall be comforted"* (Mat. 5:4).

4. The idea is that we do not deserve the Blessings of God, and very well realize our continued shortcomings. We *"mourn"* over that and thus experience the *"comfort"* of the Holy Spirit.

5. The Holy Spirit will not comfort self-righteousness or spiritual pride. He will only comfort those who rightly see themselves, and most importantly, rightly see Jesus.

6. The phrase, *"Were multiplied,"* refers to *"edification"* and a proper *"walking before the Lord,"* which brings new additions to the Body of Christ.

(32) "AND IT CAME TO PASS, AS PETER PASSED THROUGHOUT ALL QUARTERS, HE CAME DOWN ALSO TO THE SAINTS WHICH DWELT AT LYDDA."

The construction is:

1. The phrase, *"And it came to pass, as Peter passed throughout all quarters,"* now shifts the attention to this Apostle, and for a reason.

NOTES

2. Not only did the Holy Spirit desire that we know that the mighty Power of God that rested within Peter at the beginning also was prevalent now, but, as well, He would use Peter to open the door to the Gentiles by sending him to the house of Cornelius, as we will see in Acts, Chapter 10.

3. If Paul had been the first one to take the Gospel to the Gentiles, it would have probably been discounted, with little credence or weight attached to its significance. However, inasmuch as the Lord used Peter for this task, the Church accepted it, but it seems, as stated, it was with some reluctance.

4. However, the way would now be paved for the Ministry of the Apostle Paul among the Gentiles, which was the Intention of the Holy Spirit.

5. Evidently, Peter was traveling from area to area, checking on the Saints in all quarters.

6. *"He came down also to the Saints which dwelt at Lydda,"* refers to a town about 30 miles west of Jerusalem and 10 miles east of Joppa.

(33) "AND THERE HE FOUND A CERTAIN MAN NAMED AENEAS, WHICH HAD KEPT HIS BED EIGHT YEARS, AND WAS SICK OF THE PALSY."

The account is:

1. The phrase, *"And there he found a certain man named Aeneas,"* presents the first of three people who will figure prominently in this account, the other two being Dorcas and Cornelius.

2. These represent the helpless, dead, and ignorant world into which the Messiah proposed, through His Chief Apostle, to introduce health, life, and salvation.

3. The impotency of science, benevolence, and observance stands forth upon the record. Science could not heal Aeneas, benevolence could not give life to Dorcas, and religious observance failed to secure Salvation for Cornelius. Science, benevolence, and observance are excellent in themselves, but they cannot give Healing, Life, and Light to the soul. However, Christ can give these, and He only can; and personal contact with

Him secures them (Williams).

4. *"Which had kept his bed eight years, and was sick of the palsy,"* portrays, as is obvious, his helplessness.

5. As we have stated, such represents the impotency of man to heal himself or to be healed by the systems of this world. But yet, men and even the Church continue to try to do what only God can do. As someone has said, *"Let God be God!"*

6. In a sense, the number *"eight,"* representing the years this man had spent bed-ridden, points to Resurrection. Jesus was raised from the dead on the first day of the week but, actually, the eighth day as it pertains to the full Sabbath week.

7. It also points to the coming Perfect Age when the Lord will transfer His Headquarters from Heaven to Earth, as is outlined in Revelation, Chapters 21 and 22. At that time, the world will have seen about 7,000 years of time as regards man. Hence, the New Eternal Age begins on the eighth day or millennia.

(34) "AND PETER SAID UNTO HIM, AENEAS, JESUS CHRIST MAKES YOU WHOLE: ARISE, AND MAKE YOUR BED. AND HE AROSE IMMEDIATELY."

The structure is:

1. The phrase, *"And Peter said unto him, Aeneas, Jesus Christ makes you whole,"* refers to Peter staunchly giving Christ the credit for these Miracles.

2. It is certainly not strange that he would do that, but it is the emphasis of which I speak, and is worthy of note. It, no doubt, harks back to Peter's denial and proclaims the lesson learned by him so graphically that it is portrayed in almost everything he said and did. In other words, Peter was depending solely upon Christ.

3. The phrase, *"Arise, and make your bed,"* indicates that Peter had gone to the man's house to pray for him, no doubt, by request, and now, after prayer, he was to get up and make up his bed as a token of his miraculous cure.

4. *"And he arose immediately,"* records him doing that which he had not been able to do for eight years.

5. He did it immediately, which caused, as the next Verse proclaims, many to turn to the Lord.

NOTES

(35) "AND ALL WHO DWELT AT LYDDA AND SARON SAW HIM, AND TURNED TO THE LORD."

The diagram is:

1. The phrase, *"And all who dwelt at Lydda and Saron saw him,"* means that his Healing was very obvious to all because they had previously known him.

2. Due to the notoriety, there is some thought that this was a man of means, whether of public position or wealth, which occasioned so many people knowing him and being influenced by this of which the Lord had done.

3. The phrase, *"And turned to the Lord,"* is that which is intended by the Holy Spirit.

4. This is why the Holy Spirit led the Apostles to pray early on, *"And grant unto Your servants, that with all boldness they may speak Your Word.*

"By stretching forth Your Hand to heal; and that signs and wonders may be done by the Name of Your Holy Child Jesus" (Acts 4:29-30).

5. However, if unbelief is the case, as it was with the Jewish leaders respecting Jesus, all the signs and wonders in the world will have little effect.

6. The word *"all,"* as it is given in the original Greek, does not necessarily mean every single person in these areas, but rather to those who *"saw him,"* which, no doubt, numbered many.

(36) "NOW THERE WAS AT JOPPA A CERTAIN DISCIPLE NAMED TABITHA, WHICH BY INTERPRETATION IS CALLED DORCAS: THIS WOMAN WAS FULL OF GOOD WORKS AND ALMSDEEDS WHICH SHE DID."

The overview is:

1. The phrase, *"Now there was at Joppa,"* refers to a town about 10 miles east of Lydda and located on the Mediterranean Sea.

2. Incidentally, this was the place where Jonah caught a vessel, thinking to go to Spain because he did not want to preach in the Gentile city of Nineveh. Ironically enough, the Lord selected the same place to speak to Peter, as we shall see, concerning the taking of the Gospel to the Gentile house of Cornelius.

NOTES

3. The phrase, *"A certain Disciple named Tabitha, which by interpretation is called Dorcas,"* simply means that it was Tabitha in Syriac and Dorcas in the Greek. Both names mean *"a gazelle."*

Incidentally, every time the word *"Disciple"* is used in the Book of Acts, it always refers to Followers of Christ, meaning that they are Saved people.

The beauty and grace of the gazelle made it an appropriate name for a woman. Some have thought, with probability, that she was a Deaconess of the Church in that city.

4. The phrase, *"This woman was full of good works and almsdeeds which she did,"* proclaims that she was a lady of fine reputation and love for God. As well, she showed or portrayed that love by helping others, which is the highest form of expression.

(37) "AND IT CAME TO PASS IN THOSE DAYS, THAT SHE WAS SICK, AND DIED: WHOM WHEN THEY HAD WASHED, THEY LAID HER IN AN UPPER CHAMBER."

The overview is:

1. The phrase, *"And it came to pass in those days,"* refers to the days when Peter was in Lydda.

2. *"That she was sick, and died,"* seems to refer to the fact that such was totally unexpected.

3. *"Whom when they had washed, they laid her in an upper chamber,"* means they laid her out, it seems, for viewing, which seems to have taken place the day she died.

(38) "AND FORASMUCH AS LYDDA WAS NIGH TO JOPPA, AND THE DISCIPLES HAD HEARD THAT PETER WAS THERE, THEY SENT UNTO HIM TWO MEN, DESIRING HIM THAT HE WOULD NOT DELAY TO COME TO THEM."

The exposition is:

1. The phrase, *"And forasmuch as Lydda was nigh to Joppa,"* pertained to, as stated, an approximate eight miles distance.

2. *"And the Disciples had heard that Peter was there,"* tells us there was a Church in Joppa.

3. There is no indication in the Text as to exactly what they desired Peter to do. There is some slight movement toward the idea that they expected a Miracle, and yet, more movement toward the idea that they did not, but simply needed the comfort and strength that Peter could provide.

4. *"They sent unto him two men, desiring him that he would not delay to come to them,"* portrays the thought that someone, or several among them, was believing God for a Miracle. But yet, Verse 40 seems to say otherwise!

(39) "THEN PETER AROSE AND WENT WITH THEM. WHEN HE WAS COME, THEY BROUGHT HIM INTO THE UPPER CHAMBER: AND ALL THE WIDOWS STOOD BY HIM WEEPING, AND SHOWING THE COATS AND GARMENTS WHICH DORCAS MADE, WHILE SHE WAS WITH THEM."

The exegesis is:

1. The phrase, *"Then Peter arose and went with them,"* indicates that he was led by the Lord to do so.

2. *"When he was come, they brought him into the upper chamber,"* refers to where Dorcas was laid out. It had probably taken about a day for these men to come to Lydda and return with Peter.

3. *"And all the widows stood by him weeping, and showing the coats and garments which Dorcas made, while she was with them,"* seems to indicate that Dorcas was a widow as well.

4. These *"widows"* were cared for by the Church but, at the same time, were responsible for carrying forth certain duties. Quite possibly, Dorcas was their leader.

(40) "BUT PETER PUT THEM ALL FORTH, AND KNEELED DOWN, AND PRAYED; AND TURNING HIM TO THE BODY SAID, TABITHA, ARISE. AND SHE OPENED HER EYES: AND WHEN SHE SAW PETER, SHE SAT UP."

The exposition is:

1. The phrase, *"But Peter put them all forth,"* is said somewhat strongly; however, we should not make too much of this act on Peter's part, inasmuch as it seems he desired privacy more than anything else.

2. *"And kneeled down, and prayed,"* gives us no indication as to what he said.

3. *"And turning him to the body said, Tabitha, arise,"* is actually the same as that said by Jesus when He raised the daughter of

Jairus from the dead (Mk. 5:41).

The actual language used by Jesus and Peter, as well, was Aramaic, which said, *"Talitha cumi."* The only difference is that Peter preceded this command by prayer, while Jesus did not!

4. *"And she opened her eyes: and when she saw Peter, she sat up,"* presents the first person being raised from the dead in the Early Church.

Since the Death, Resurrection, and Ascension of Jesus, upon the death of the body, righteous souls no longer go to Paradise, but rather immediately to be with Christ in Heaven. This was made possible by what Jesus did at Calvary and the Resurrection, satisfying the terrible sin debt held over the heads of men, even the Righteous. Due to Calvary, that sin debt is gone, making it possible for Believers to actually be inhabited by the Holy Spirit, and for the soul and the spirit of the sainted dead to instantly go to Heaven.

5. So, Tabitha (Dorcas) was with Jesus when she was summoned back. The Lord gave her leave to go, her soul and spirit once again taking up residence in her body, which was dead, but now came alive.

The death of the body actually occurs when the soul and the spirit leave that mortal house. If Saved, the person instantly goes to be with Christ, and if not, the person goes to Hell (Lk. 16:19-31).

(41) "AND HE GAVE HER HIS HAND, AND LIFTED HER UP, AND WHEN HE HAD CALLED THE SAINTS AND WIDOWS, PRESENTED HER ALIVE."

The structure is:

1. The phrase, *"And he gave her his hand, and lifted her up,"* does not present something done because she was too weak to sit up on her own, but rather as a common courtesy.

2. *"And when he had called the Saints and widows, presented her alive,"* had to be the scene at that time of rejoicing and praise to the Lord such as few houses have ever seen in history.

3. What a story that Tabitha must have had! Actually, she is one of the few in human history who has actually died and then come back to tell the story.

NOTES

(42) "AND IT WAS KNOWN THROUGHOUT ALL JOPPA; AND MANY BELIEVED IN THE LORD."

The structure is:

1. The phrase, *"And it was known throughout all Joppa,"* presents this tremendous Miracle as having the same impact as the healing of Aeneas had at Lydda.

2. *"And many believed in the Lord,"* constitutes exactly that, as we have already stated, which the Spirit desired.

3. John tells us that the very purpose of the record that he wrote of the Miracles of Christ is *"that you may believe that Jesus is the Christ, the Son of God; and that believing you might have Life through His Name"* (Jn. 20:31).

The Miracles performed by Jesus, Peter, and Paul, as well as others in the Early Church, had the desired effect because they were genuine, obvious, and open for all to see.

Too much of that which is labeled *"Miracles"* has little effect, if any at all, on the unsaved because most, sad to say, are not genuine and, therefore, not obvious. Far too often, things are labeled as *"Miracles,"* with the person declared healed, etc., when investigation a little later shows the very opposite. As well, a lot of things are spoken of as Miracles when, in reality, there is no way to ascertain if something has really been wrong with the person to begin with.

Then, far too often, those who are obviously sick, and seriously so, leave as they came—unhealed!

4. In no way are these statements meant to demean or criticize that which is truly of God; however, sadly, I do believe that too often such is merely a *"racket!"*

Nevertheless, the fake, unproven, and outright religious scams in no way negate the true Miracle-working Power of God. The Lord does perform Miracles today and, in fact, always has. He is a Prayer-answering God, and for that very reason, He does not desire fake glory.

5. These people under Peter's Ministry turned to the Lord because the Miracles they saw were obvious, evident, and genuine, which, in effect, needed no explanation.

While some may have argued that Tabitha really was not dead but only unconscious,

NOTES

too much proof presented itself otherwise and was known by too many for such skepticism to prevail.

(43) "AND IT CAME TO PASS, THAT HE TARRIED MANY DAYS IN JOPPA WITH ONE SIMON A TANNER."

The synopsis is:

1. The phrase, *"And it came to pass, that he tarried many days in Joppa,"* probably referred to several months. During this time, Peter, no doubt, ministered all over the city and in outlying areas.

2. *"With one Simon a tanner,"* speaks of a man whose trade was considered to be unclean by some Jews. However, we must not infer that Peter was already indifferent to ceremonial uncleanness because the very next Chapter will tell us that was not so.

3. Inasmuch as this ruling by the Pharisees concerning *"tanners"* was actually a gloss of their own making and not actually of the Law of Moses, it was probably ignored by Peter, as it should have been!

4. About eight years had passed now since Pentecost, during which time, the Gospel had been preached only to the Jews (Mat. 10:6; Jn. 1:11; Rom. 1:16). In fact, as we have said, the Church was founded by Jews and for Jews.

5. However, the time had now arrived when God demanded that the Gospel be taken to the Gentiles, for whom Jesus also died. Actually, the Conversion of Paul was a powerful step in that direction, with Peter opening the door by his presentation of the Gospel to Cornelius.

6. Beginning now, a gradual change would take place, with Gentiles coming to Christ, and with the Church little by little becoming mainly Gentiles because of rejection by most of the Jews.

There would be a powerful struggle with the Law/Grace issue, but little by little the Gospel was purged of all mixture with the Law of Moses, which was demanded by the Holy Spirit, with Paul leading the way.

7. The Will of God for humanity has never been accepted readily or easily, with most of the time, the greatest opponents being those who should have been its chief proponents. However, Satan does his work best from the inside. Nevertheless, the Ways of the Lord ultimately gain the victory as the Holy Spirit selects those who are determined to do God's Will at whatever price.

Thus was Paul, and thus should we be as well! Consequently, the bulk of the Book of Acts, which portrays the Early Church, is devoted to the Ministry of Paul because of this one factor. He determined to do the Will of God at whatever cost!

"I've believed the true report,
"Hallelujah to the Lamb!
"I have passed the outer court,
"Oh glory be to God!
"I am all on Jesus' Side,
"On the Altar sanctified,
"To the world and sin I've died,
"Hallelujah to the Lamb!"

"I'm a king and priest to God,
"Hallelujah to the Lamb!
"By the cleansing of the Blood,
"Oh glory be to God!
"By the Spirit's Power and Light,
"I am living day and night,
"In the holiest place so bright,
"Hallelujah to the Lamb!"

"I have passed the outer Veil,
"Hallelujah to the Lamb!
"Which did once God's Light conceal,
"Oh glory be to God!
"But the Blood has brought me in
"To God's Holiness so clean
"Where there's death to self and sin,
"Hallelujah to the Lamb!"

"I'm within the holiest pale,
"Hallelujah to the Lamb!
"I have passed the inner Veil,
"Oh glory be to God!
"I am sanctified to God,
"By the Power of the Blood,
"Now the Lord is my Abode,
"Hallelujah to the Lamb!"

CHAPTER 10

(1) "THERE WAS A CERTAIN MAN IN CAESAREA CALLED CORNELIUS, A

CENTURION OF THE BAND CALLED THE ITALIAN BAND."

The way is:

1. The Cross of Christ is not merely the basis of human Salvation.
2. It is also the basis of God's Self-Revelation.
3. The Cross of Christ is where the Knowledge of God alone can be found.

CORNELIUS

The phrase, *"There was a certain man in Caesarea called Cornelius,"* presents the beginning of one of the great turning points of history.

Satan had done his work well in locking up the Word of God among the Jews. Their self-righteous sectarianism had taken them down such erroneous paths that by the time of Christ, they had perverted the Word of God and, as a result, would murder their Messiah. As well, as we have previously stated, they hated Gentiles. Consequently, they stopped the Word from going to others and would not receive it or accept it themselves.

Despite that, the Lord was quickly breaking these bonds and setting the stage for the propagation of the Word to the entirety of the world. Of course, it began with Christ, but it actually had its launching with the Advent of the Holy Spirit on the Day of Pentecost, made possible by the Death, Resurrection, and Ascension of Christ. By now, some eight years after Pentecost, tens of thousands of Jews were Followers of Christ, with the Gospel now ready to be launched to the Gentile world. It would begin in the city of *"Caesarea."*

Caesarea was about 30 miles north of Joppa and situated, as well, on the Mediterranean coast. It was built by Herod the Great on the site of Stato's tower, and the name Caesarea Sebaste was given it in honor of Augustus.

With his usual magnificence, Herod lavished adornments on the city. He erected sumptuous palaces and public buildings, a theater, and an amphitheater with prospect to the sea.

THE GOSPEL

In the summer of 1996, Frances and I, along with the entirety of our family, plus approximately 100 other people, had the opportunity to be in this area.

There are many things of interest about this place, but one of the most interesting is the extensive system built to transport fresh water, which, in effect, was a pipeline made of bricks and standing about 12 or 15 feet high.

The grade on this structure, which ran for miles, was tabulated perfectly so that the water would run into the city as a result of gravity. This was a marvelous structure considering the technology of nearly 2,000 years ago. Much of this *"pipeline"* is still standing.

Into this city, as we shall see, Peter brought the Gospel to the house of Cornelius, which, for all practical purposes, was the first presentation to the Gentiles. Here dwelt Philip the Evangelist also (Acts 8:40; 21:8).

Thrice Paul passed through this city (Acts 9:30; 18:22; 21:8); as well, he was sent there under guard from Jerusalem to escape the Jews (Acts 23:23), and there was imprisoned about two years before his final departure for Rome.

The name *"Cornelius"* is Roman and belonged to distinguished families in the imperial city, such as the Scipio and Sulla. Thus, he was probably an Italian of Roman blood.

Julian the Apostate reckons him as one of the few persons of distinction who became a Christian.

He was evidently a man of importance in Caesarea and well-known to the Jews.

He was a man, as we shall see, who yearned for a better Faith than the myriad of gods and religions embraced by Rome.

He embraced Jehovah of the Jews, read the Scriptures, and practiced, more or less, the Jewish rites.

Moreover, he seems to have made his house a sort of Church, for his kinsfolk and friends were in sympathy with him, and among the soldiers who closely attended him were some devout ones.

THE TENTH CHAPTER OF ACTS

Other than the Tenth Chapter of Acts,

NOTES

nothing further is known of Cornelius, though one tradition asserts that he founded the Church in Caesarea, and another legend states that he became the Bishop (Pastor) of the Church of Scamandros.

Actually, he was not a proselyte totally to the Jewish Faith, but rather was labeled as a *"God-fearer."* These were Gentiles who somewhat embraced Judaism, but without joining the Church, so to speak!

So, under Divine direction, the first Gentile, not at all belonging to the old theocracy, became a Spirit-filled Christian by entering through the front door of Christianity without first going through the narrow gate of Judaism.

Consequently, this incident settled forever the great, fundamental question as to the relations of Jews and Gentiles in the Church. The experience of Cornelius plainly portrays to all that one did not have to first become a proselyte before one could be Saved. In other words, Salvation was by Faith alone in Christ and not with the addition of rituals and ceremonies.

Of course, this incident of Cornelius was only the first step in a long development and, as well, was overlooked by many in the Early Church, but the principle was forever settled, at least for those who truly wanted to do things God's Way.

CHRISTIANITY

By this tremendous experience, it was settled that Christianity was to be freed from the swaddling bands of Judaism, which Satan tried his best to bring about, and with some help from the infant Church, we might quickly add. In other words, the Christian Church was not to be an appendix to the synagogue.

The noble character of Cornelius was justly fitted to abate, as far as possible, the prejudices of the Jewish Christians against what must have seemed to them a dangerous, if not awful, innovation.

The phrase, *"A Centurion of the band called the Italian band,"* could refer to two particular numbers of men. Normally, a *"band"* was about 500; however, when spoken of auxiliary provincial troops, it meant a regiment of about 1,000 men. It probably refers to the higher sense here, inasmuch as according to Josephus also, most of the soldiers were Syrians.

NOTES

Referring to the name *"Italian,"* such designated a particular unit, of which, in the whole empire, there were approximately 32 *"bands"* or cohorts bearing the same name. In Acts 27:1, the cohort there is called the *"Augustan band."*

These were names of distinction, especially the name *"Italian."* Such generally provided security for the Roman governor or procurator. Consequently, *"Cornelius"* was one of the commanders in this group and had charge of 100 men.

(2) "A DEVOUT MAN, AND ONE WHO FEARED GOD WITH ALL HIS HOUSE, WHICH GAVE MUCH ALMS TO THE PEOPLE, AND PRAYED TO GOD ALWAYS."

The exegesis is:

1. In the description given concerning Cornelius, we will find some wonderful things said about this man, things which certainly are commendable; however, we will also find, as commendable as they may be, that they do not save the soul. Regrettably, much of the Christian world falls into the same category. Let us look at what the Holy Spirit says about Cornelius:

a. *"A devout man"*: The word *"devout"* speaks of one who is reverent and consecrated, in this case, to God. However, as commendable as this was, it did not save him.

b. *"And one who feared God with all his house"*: As we have stated, Cornelius was a *"God-fearer,"* which, in Jewish terminology, referred to one who had not become an outright proselyte to Judaism, but who was in sympathy with its teachings and followed them somewhat. As well, Cornelius not only did this, but the entirety of his family did likewise!

c. *"Which gave much alms to the people"*: this signifies that he was a wealthy man and, as well, was generous in his efforts to help those who were less fortunate.

d. *"And prayed to God always"*: even though such prayers did not save this man, still, as we shall see, the Lord heard and saw all that he was doing, and in a very positive sense.

(3) "HE SAW IN A VISION EVIDENTLY

NOTES

ABOUT THE NINTH HOUR OF THE DAY AN ANGEL OF GOD COMING IN TO HIM, AND SAYING UNTO HIM, CORNELIUS."

The Testimony is:

1. God's Way of Salvation fills the heart with love.

2. Man's way of salvation inflames it with hatred.

THE VISION

"He saw in a Vision evidently about the ninth hour of the day": this was about 3 p.m. when the Vision of the Angel occurred. The Lord was about to answer his prayers, but in a way that would be far beyond his comprehension.

The phrase, *"An Angel of God coming in to him, and saying unto him, Cornelius,"* proclaims this great Plan of God about to unfold, which will, in essence, touch the entirety of the world.

However, the main point that one should notice in this scenario, at least up to now, is that all of these wonderful things that Cornelius did, plus things which we have not yet addressed, such as *"fasting,"* etc., are extremely commendable, but they did not save Cornelius. In fact, he was an unsaved man as is brought out clearly in Acts 11:14. Of course, he would be Saved very shortly, as we shall see.

THINGS WHICH CORNELIUS DID

Several things must be graphically noted here and are very important, as should be obvious! They are:

• Doing good things, even as here, does not save anyone. And yet, the far greater majority of mankind believes that it does.

In fact, if the truth be known, most people think they are Saved because they do certain things, such as belong to a Church, get involved in its functions, give money, etc. However, the Scripture plainly says, *"For by Grace are you Saved through Faith; and that not of yourselves: it is the Gift of God:*

"Not of works, lest any man should boast" (Eph. 2:8-9).

• However, Cornelius was a step ahead of many people who are depending on works simply because that is all he knew to do. He was not trying to do these things to please Christ for the simple reason that he did not know Christ, having possibly only heard of Him.

Whether Cornelius had been stationed at Caesarea a long while or had recently been transferred there is not known. It had been about eight years since the Death and Resurrection of Christ, and much can happen during that period of time.

So, Cornelius was doing all he knew to do respecting God and was very sincere in his efforts. However, ignorance is not Salvation, and neither is sincerity, although very important.

• Being involved in spiritual things, even to the degree of having Visions, does not save one. Salvation is not religious ceremonies or rituals, or even great spiritual experiences, other than accepting Christ.

In fact, many, one could probably say, have seen apparitions in the spirit world, such as Mary the Mother of Jesus, but none of this affords any Salvation whatsoever!

However, the Vision that Cornelius had was from God, therefore, genuine, and was of extreme benefit respecting instructions as to what he was to do.

Even though none of these things saved Cornelius, as they save no one, still, the Lord, as is plainly obvious, was very mindful of all this man had done and was doing, and saw the hunger of his heart. To be frank, the Lord judges all by the motives and direction of their hearts.

(4) "AND WHEN HE LOOKED ON HIM, HE WAS AFRAID, AND SAID, WHAT IS IT, LORD? AND HE SAID UNTO HIM, YOUR PRAYERS AND YOUR ALMS ARE COME UP FOR A MEMORIAL BEFORE GOD."

The record is:

1. God's Righteousness can only come by the Cross.

2. Self-righteousness is by dependence on works.

WHAT IS IT, LORD?

The phrase, *"And when he looked on him, he was afraid, and said,"* pretty well describes the reaction of most upon a glimpse into the supernatural and, more specifically, the appearance of a Heavenly Being.

NOTES

The question, *"What is it, Lord?"* tells us several things:

• From the manner in which the Angel appeared, it was evidently obvious that he had a Message for Cornelius, hence, the question.

• The appellative or title *"Lord,"* in the manner in which it was used by Cornelius, does not refer to Deity, but rather refers to respect or honor.

• Little did this man realize what was happening, but his question would open up something so absolutely important that it would defy description. That for which Jesus died, the Redemption of man, was about to spread over the entirety of the Earth. In fact, it would change the entirety of mankind in one way or the other. It was the presentation of the Gospel to the Gentiles.

This which would begin this day, in fact, actually had its beginning in the Garden of Eden, for God had obligated Himself to save all of mankind, at least those who will believe.

More specifically, it harks back to the Prophecy of Noah, *"God shall enlarge Japheth, and he shall dwell in the tents of Shem"* (Gen. 9:27).

The entirety of all of the families of the Earth sprang originally from Adam and Eve but, more specifically, from the three sons of Noah: Japheth, Shem, and Ham.

The simple reason is that other than Noah, these were the only men left alive on the Earth at that time. So, of necessity, all spring from these three.

JAPHETH AND SHEM

All Gentiles who ultimately populated Europe, the Far East, and North America sprang from Japheth.

All Jews and Arabs who occupy the Middle East sprang from Shem.

All those who populate Africa and Central and South America sprang from Ham. Respecting the descendants of Japheth and Ham, there is a great deal of intermingling, but very little with the descendants of Shem.

Noah prophesied in Genesis 9:26 and said, *"Blessed be the LORD God of Shem,"* which spoke of the Jews in particular, who would be used of God to give the world the Word of God and, as well, the greatest Gift of all, the Messiah and Saviour of all mankind, the Lord Jesus Christ. In effect, Noah was thanking the Lord that He would use Shem in this fashion.

However, he also prophesied, *"God shall enlarge Japheth, and he shall dwell in the tents of Shem,"* meaning that Shem, i.e., the Jews, would forfeit their Blessing by murdering their Messiah. Consequently, the Blessing would be taken from them and given to the descendants of Japheth, the Gentiles, who, figuratively speaking, would then dwell in this tent of Blessing, which rightly belonged to Shem.

Consequently, Cornelius, at least as it refers to this Prophecy, was the very first descendant of Japheth who would have this Blessing, which would ultimately spread to the entirety of the world.

So, when Cornelius asked the question, *"What is it, Lord?"* the answer would be staggering, to say the least!

PRAYERS AND ALMS

The phrase, *"And he said unto him, Your prayers and your alms are come up for a memorial before God,"* presents to us a most glorious Truth.

If a sinner will truly cry out to God, even as did Cornelius, the Lord will do whatever has to be done in order that Salvation be brought to that person. It will be done even if he has to send an Angel, as here, or even appear Himself, if necessary. A seeking heart will always find God (Isa. 1:18; 55:1; Mat. 11:28-30; Jn. 7:37-39; Rev. 22:17).

As well, as is here obvious, good things done toward the Lord by the unsaved, although not purchasing Salvation, etc., nevertheless, are noted favorably by God. Naturally, all of this would depend on many things, such as the motivation, purpose, etc., of the sinner.

If one thinks that such good works atones for sin, then such activity cannot be favorably accepted by the Lord. However, as we have already stated, if the sinner is truly, honestly, and sincerely attempting to reach the Lord by such means (or anything else of that nature), even though it is unacceptable to God relating to Salvation, still, God favorably judges the seeking heart and will answer accordingly.

A perfect example is many Catholics who, although unsaved, are sincerely reaching out to God. They will find the Lord responding favorably to them as He will to all in such situations. However, that does not mean that the Lord saves them in Catholicism, which is error, but that He will see to it that the Truth is presented to them, even as it was to Cornelius, and has been to millions of others.

After finding the Truth, which is graciously delivered to them by the Holy Spirit because of the sincerity of their hearts, they then must forsake error.

ISLAM

I have just finished reading the story of a dear lady who was born into the religion of Islam and faithfully served that structure for many years. However, her heart became hungrier and hungrier for God, despite her deepening consecration to Islam, and the hunger and thirst remained with no satisfaction forthcoming.

She had been born with a physical disability that crippled her, and extensively so. Consequently, she sought *"Allah"* incessantly for healing, but to no avail.

Out of desperation and because the Koran had briefly mentioned Jesus and His Power to heal, she began to pray to the Lord instead of Allah.

This went on for several weeks, and then it happened!

The Lord appeared to her one night, and this is what she said:

THE HEALING OF THE MUSLIM GIRL

"What happened next is something that I find hard to put into words. I know the whole room filled with Light. At first I thought it was from my reading lamp beside the bed. Then I saw that its light looked dim. Perhaps it was dawn? But it was too early for that. The Light was growing, growing in brightness, until it surpassed the day. I covered myself with my shawl. I was so frightened.

"I came out from my shawl to look. But the doors and windows were fast shut, with curtains and shutters drawn. I then became aware of figures in long robes, standing in the midst of the Light, a short distance from my bed. There were twelve figures in a row and the figure in the middle, the thirteenth, was larger and brighter than the others.

"'Oh God,' I cried and the perspiration broke out on my forehead. I bowed my head and I prayed, 'Oh God, who are these people, and how have they come here when all the windows and doors are shut?'

"Suddenly a Force said, 'Get up. This is the path you have been seeking. I am Jesus, Son of Mary, to Whom you have been praying, and now I am standing in front of you. You get up and come to Me.'

"I started to weep. 'Oh Jesus, I'm crippled. I can't get up.'

"He said, 'Stand up and come to Me. I am Jesus.'

"When I hesitated, He said it a second time. Then as I still doubted, He said for the third time, 'Stand up.'

THE HEALING

"And I, Gulshan Fatima, who had been crippled on my bed for nineteen years, felt new strength flowing into my wasted limbs. I put my foot on the ground and stood up. Then I ran a few paces and fell at the feet of the Vision. I was bathing in the purest Light, and it was burning as bright as the Sun and Moon together. The Light shone into my heart and into my mind, and many things became clear to me at that moment.

"Jesus put His Hand on the top of my head, and I saw a hole in His Hand from which a ray of Light struck down upon my garments, so that the green dress looked white.

"He said: 'I am Jesus. I am Immanuel. I am the Way, the Truth, and the Life. I am alive and am soon coming. See, from today you are My witness. What you have seen now with your eyes you must take to My people. My people are your people, and you must remain faithful to take that to My people.'"

Her Healing was instantaneous, with her able to walk, which she had not done in many years. As well, she was to soon learn that when He said, *"My People,"* He was not talking about Muslims, but instead

NOTES

Followers of Christ.

Almost immediately, she left the religion of Islam, even with her family threatening to kill her. She had found Jesus, and consequently, the error had to be forsaken.

However, the point I am attempting to make is that this girl earnestly sought the Lord, even though her thinking toward Him was skewed due to her false religion. Still, the Lord looked past that, even as He does with all, and saw her heart was true and sincere. He consequently appeared to her, giving her not only healing for her sick body, which, in itself, was a Miracle, but, as well, Salvation for her soul.

(5) "AND NOW SEND MEN TO JOPPA, AND CALL FOR ONE SIMON, WHOSE SURNAME IS PETER."

The overview is:

1. The phrase, *"And now send men to Joppa,"* proclaims the Angel telling Cornelius what to do in order to hear the Gospel but not presenting the Gospel himself. That privilege is given to man and not Angels. Actually, the Angel did not give any further explanation or any additional teaching. He merely told him where this help could be found.

2. The only time in the Bible we are told that Angels, or rather an Angel, preaches the Gospel is found in Revelation 14:6-7. This will be during the last three and one-half years of the Great Tribulation period. As well, there is every evidence that this is a literal Angel, who will literally fly through the heavens at that time, preaching and proclaiming the *"everlasting Gospel."*

This, no doubt, will be allowed at this time because of the severity of the situation, inasmuch as greater judgments are about to come upon the Earth; therefore, God will use this miraculous method of an Angel preaching the Gospel in order to get the attention of men.

3. The phrase, *"And call for one Simon, whose surname is Peter,"* presents to the Apostle not only the tremendous privilege of winning souls to Christ but, above all, opening the door to the entirety of the world that Gentiles could now come to the Lord by simple Faith without all the rituals and ceremonies of Judaism, etc. That Peter was chosen to open this door presents an honor and privilege unexcelled!

4. As we have already stated, Peter was probably the only one who the Lord, at that time, could have used for such a thing, at least who the Church would accept. Even then, as we shall see, Peter had to explain to the Elders in Jerusalem exactly what he had done and why it was done, which should not have been necessary.

5. Even though the other Apostles would recognize that which had been done as from the Lord, still, they would remain somewhat tepid respecting Paul's great Covenant of Grace that he had received from the Lord, which excluded all of the Mosaic rituals and ceremonies.

(6) "HE LODGES WITH ONE SIMON A TANNER, WHOSE HOUSE IS BY THE SEA SIDE: HE SHALL TELL YOU WHAT YOU OUGHT TO DO."

The account is:

1. The phrase, *"He lodges with one Simon a tanner, whose house is by the sea side,"* presents, as should be obvious, the Lord knowing at all times exactly where His People are.

2. So, the directions given by the Angel began the fulfillment of the Promise made by the Lord to Abraham nearly 2,000 years earlier, *"And in you shall all families of the Earth be blessed"* (Gen. 12:3).

3. Thank God that in this wonderful Promise made to the Patriarch now nearly 4,000 years ago, my family was included in all of the myriad of families who have had the opportunity to know about Jesus Christ.

"More about Jesus would I know,
"More of His Grace to others show;
"More of His Saving Fullness see,
"More of His Love Who died for me."

4. The phrase, *"He shall tell you what you ought to do,"* makes it clear to Cornelius that all his *"doing"* had no saving power.

5. Notwithstanding his moral worthfulness and religious culture and earnestness, Cornelius was an unsaved sinner and was told by the Angel that he must listen to words whereby he should be Saved (Acts 11:14). Therefore, prior to hearing and believing the Gospel, despite all the good things he had done, he was unsaved.

(7) "AND WHEN THE ANGEL WHICH SPOKE UNTO CORNELIUS WAS DEPARTED, HE CALLED TWO OF HIS HOUSEHOLD SERVANTS, AND A DEVOUT SOLDIER OF THEM THAT WAITED ON HIM CONTINUALLY."

The way is:

1. The phrase, *"And when the Angel which spoke unto Cornelius was departed,"* signals the beginning of this scenario that would shape the world.

2. One must wonder at this stage exactly how Cornelius felt. The hunger and thirst of his heart was about to be satisfied. As well, and to be sure, only a few people in history ever had the privilege of being visited by an Angel. Even though at this stage he had absolutely no idea as to what was in store for him, still, due to this visitation, I am confident that he knew it would be wonderful. And so it would be!

3. The phrase, *"He called two of his household servants, and a devout soldier of them that waited on him continually,"* concerns the three who went to fetch Peter, according to the demand of Cornelius, at the direction of the Angel. It was about 35 miles from Caesarea to Joppa and probably took two days to make the trip.

(8) "AND WHEN HE HAD DECLARED ALL THESE THINGS UNTO THEM, HE SENT THEM TO JOPPA."

The pattern is:

1. The phrase, *"And when he had declared all these things unto them,"* no doubt, referred to the visitation by the Angel and what the Angel had said.

2. Inasmuch as Verse 2 says concerning Cornelius, *"A devout man, and one who feared God with all his house,"* more than likely, these two servants and the soldier were God-fearers also! This basically meant that they recognized Jehovah as being God and that He was one. Actually, Israel was the only Nation in the world that was monotheistic, in reference to all other nations that worshipped many gods, which, in fact, were no gods at all! Jesus had said about the Samaritans, which applied, as well, to all other nations other than Israel, *"Ye worship ye know not what: we know what we worship: for Salvation is of the Jews"* (Jn. 4:22).

NOTES

3. *"He sent them to Joppa,"* no doubt, meant that the journey commenced then.

I know these three men made this trip with eager anticipation, especially considering that their master Cornelius had actually been visited by an Angel, and this trip was according to the directions of that Heavenly Being. What must have been their conversation as they walked these miles (that is, if they did not ride horses, which does not seem to be the case)?

4. Even though mighty Rome took no notice whatsoever of this trip, and if informed would have paid no heed, still, one can be certain that all of Heaven was monitoring each footstep.

5. Regrettably, it is doubtful that a single person in the Church of that day would have paid any heed as well. To be sure, Peter only went because he was commanded by the Lord to do so.

6. Without a doubt, I think it is obvious that Paul would have been an eager participant because of his Commission. However, as we have already stated, Peter is probably the only man who could take the Gospel to these Gentiles and have it accepted by the Church! If that was true of the Apostles of the Early Church, and it was, how much should all of us be very careful that we do not allow prejudice, bias, or self-will to chart the course instead of the Holy Spirit!

Did not the Holy Spirit inform the church as to what He was about to do?

I think they were so prejudiced that they would not have heard, irrespective as to what would have been done, other than what actually happened.

(9) "ON THE MORROW, AS THEY WENT ON THEIR JOURNEY, AND DREW NEAR UNTO THE CITY, PETER WENT UP UPON THE HOUSETOP TO PRAY ABOUT THE SIXTH HOUR."

The form is:

1. Calvary is the greatest display of the Wisdom of God (I Cor., Chpt. 2).

2. All Victory is found exclusively in the Cross of Christ.

PRAYER

The phrase, *"On the morrow, as they went on their journey, and drew near*

NOTES

unto the city," probably means that they left Caesarea very shortly after being given instructions by Cornelius the day before. They probably travelled up into the night, got a few hours sleep, and began very early the next morning, even before daylight. This would have been necessary, or something similar, if they were to reach Joppa a little after noon, as they did.

"Peter went up upon the housetop to pray about the sixth hour," refers to noon.

This tells us that Peter was a man of prayer, which should be obvious, but is not so obvious concerning most preachers presently. If one is to notice, both Cornelius and Peter were praying when the Lord spoke to them.

Actually, in both the Acts and Epistles, we see the Apostolic Church giving effect to Christ's Teaching on prayer. It was in a praying atmosphere that the Church was born (Acts 1:14; 2:1); and throughout its early history, prayer continued to be its vital breath and native air (Acts 2:42; 3:1; 6:4-6).

The Epistles abound in references to prayer. Those of Paul in particular contain frequent allusions to his own personal practice in the matter (Rom. 1:9; Eph. 1:16; Phil. 1:9; I Thess. 1:2), and many exhortations to all Believers to cultivate the praying habit (Rom. 12:12; Eph. 6:18; Phil. 4:6; I Thess. 5:17).

PRAYER AND THE HOLY SPIRIT

The new and characteristic thing about prayer, at least since the giving of the New Covenant, is its connection with the Holy Spirit. Actually, the Holy Spirit has raised prayer to its highest power by securing for it a Divine cooperation (Rom. 8:15-26; Gal. 4:6). Thus, prayer in its full New Testament meaning is prayer addressed to God as Father, in the Name of Christ as Mediator, and through the enabling Grace of the indwelling Spirit.

PRAYER IS THE HIGHEST EXERCISE

Prayer is the highest exercise of man's spiritual nature. It is natural to the soul, even in perfect accord with God.

It is not only the expression of need, the supply of which is sought of God, but by the example of Christ, it is the highest expression of trust, submission, and union with God. It is to be used both in solitude and in society; it is personal and intercessory.

PRAYER IN THE NAME OF JESUS

Prayer may be accompanied by the plea of Christ's Name and for Christ's Sake. These are the laws that should direct it; that is to say, it should be based upon the Merit and the Intercession of Christ. It should be addressed to God under the limitations of the Kingdom of the Lord and His Purposes for good, both for the interest of the supplicant and others, under the conditions of the interest of the whole Kingdom.

PRAYER AND THE CROSS OF CHRIST

The Cross of Christ opened up everything. It made it possible for the Believer to come directly to the Throne of Grace, once again, all made possible by the Cross. In fact, although all Believers can pray and should pray, still, unless one understands the Cross of Christ as it regards our Sanctification—how we live for God, how we order our behavior, and how we have victory over the world, the flesh, and the devil—such a Believer will not have the prayer life that he or she should have. The Holy Spirit is limited in His Help to us according to our understanding of the Cross of Christ as it regards our Sanctification (Rom. 6:1-5; 8:1-11; I Cor. 1:17-18, 23; 2:2; Gal. 6:14; Col. 2:10-15).

The only real understanding that a Believer can have about God and how we talk to Him and listen to Him in prayer is by and through the Cross of Christ. Regrettably, virtually every Believer is grossly limited in their understanding regarding the Cross of Christ. They understand the Cross somewhat as it regards Salvation but none at all as it regards Sanctification. And yet, over ninety-nine percent of the entirety of the Bible is given over to telling us how to live for God, which, of course, involves one's Sanctification. Please note the following very carefully.

- Jesus Christ is the Source of all things we receive from God (Jn. 1:1-3; 14:6).
- The Cross of Christ is the Means by

which we receive all of these good things (I Cor. 1:17-18, 23; 2:2).

• The Cross of Christ must ever be the Object of our Faith. This is critical (Col. 2:10-15).

• With that being done, the Holy Spirit, Who works exclusively within the parameters of the Finished Work of Christ, will work mightily on our behalf (Rom. 8:1-11).

(10) "AND HE BECAME VERY HUNGRY, AND WOULD HAVE EATEN: BUT WHILE THEY MADE READY, HE FELL INTO A TRANCE."

The structure is:

1. The phrase, *"And he became very hungry, and would have eaten,"* proclaims that he was about to quit praying and have lunch when something happened that would change him, change the entirety of the Church, and, in fact, change the entirety of mankind.

2. *"But while they made ready, he fell into a trance,"* refers to one being unconscious to all surroundings, with the exception of the subject of the Vision.

(11) "AND SAW HEAVEN OPENED, AND A CERTAIN VESSEL DESCENDING UPON HIM, AS IT HAD BEEN A GREAT SHEET KNIT AT THE FOUR CORNERS, AND LET DOWN TO THE EARTH."

The composition is:

1. The phrase, *"And saw Heaven opened,"* carries with it a powerful meaning.

2. Before Jesus, Heaven had been closed. The reasons were obvious. The blood of bulls and goats could not take away sins but only cover them. Consequently, when Saints died before Jesus, their souls and spirits went down into Paradise where, in a sense, they were held captive by Satan, but not in the burning side of Hell (Lk. 16:19-31; Eph. 4:8-10).

3. However, upon the Death, Resurrection, and Ascension of Christ, which effectively took sin away, the heavens then opened, with the Holy Spirit being sent in a new dimension and capacity (Acts 2:1-4). Heaven has remained open from then until now, and will continue to be open, all because of what Jesus did.

4. *"And a certain vessel descending unto him, as it had been a great sheet knit at the four corners, and let down to the Earth,"* in a sense, corresponded to the Ark of Noah.

NOTES

It, like the Ark, provided Salvation for all nations, not just for one Nation, and without any moral distinction.

5. Some animals were more beautiful and more useful than others, and many were ceremonially unclean, but the representatives of all were found in these two great vessels.

6. So will it be in the earthly Kingdom. All the nations, including Israel, will be shepherded in one fold. This was a hard lesson for Peter to learn, and the entirety of the Twelve for that matter, as well as the entirety of the Jewish Early Church. However, Christ is *"Lord of all"* (Acts 10:36), and the Gospel is for *"whosoever"* (Acts 10:43).

7. Peter had proclaimed on the Day of Pentecost the election of the Gentiles to Salvation in Acts 2:21 and 39, but he was so dull and prejudiced that this Vision had to be given to him to make him realize the fact.

(12) "WHEREIN WERE ALL MANNER OF FOURFOOTED BEASTS OF THE EARTH, AND WILD BEASTS, AND CREEPING THINGS, AND FOWLS OF THE AIR."

The composition is:

1. The phrase, *"Wherein were all manner of fourfooted beasts of the Earth,"* proclaims the Gospel now available to *"all manner"* of people, irrespective of whom they may be or where they may be. Such was illustrated by this Vision of all manner of animals.

2. *"And wild beasts, and creeping things, and fowls of the air,"* seemed to pertain, at least concerning these mentioned, only to animals and fowls labeled unclean. Not only were they not to be eaten, but they were not to be offered in sacrifice either. The list is found in Leviticus, Chapter 11.

3. Now that Jesus has gone to the Cross, this opens the door for *"whosoever will."*

(13) "AND THERE CAME A VOICE TO HIM, RISE, PETER; KILL, AND EAT."

The composition is:

1. There is no victory outside of the Cross of Christ.

2. Any other direction is labeled by the Lord as *"spiritual adultery"* (Rom. 7:1-4).

THE VOICE

The phrase, *"And there came a Voice to*

him," proclaims the Lord speaking to Peter, and Peter readily recognizing the Voice as coming from the Lord.

The phrase, *"Rise, Peter; kill, and eat,"* literally says in the Greek Text, *"Sacrifice and eat."*

The Lord intended for the Gentiles to be represented by these unclean animals. By His telling Peter to *"sacrifice and eat,"* in effect, He was saying that the Sacrifice of Christ at Calvary was intended for all, both Jews and Gentiles. Consequently, not only could the Jews *"eat My Flesh, and drink My Blood,"* but so could the Gentiles (Jn. 6:54).

The eating of the Flesh and drinking of the Blood was not meant to be taken literally, but was meant to express Jesus being offered at Calvary, which represented the Flesh and the spilling of His Life's Blood. Those who have Faith in what He did reap its benefits, which is the same as *"eating and drinking,"* etc.

These dietary and sacrificial Laws given to Moses by God were meant only for Israel. There was a reason for that!

Israel was raised up from the loins of Abraham for the great purpose of bringing the Messiah, the Saviour of mankind, into the world. He, as the Second Man and Last Adam, would do what the first Adam failed to do. Therefore, for Him to be born into this world as a man, certain things were required of the people who would serve that purpose, namely Israel.

THE LAW OF MOSES

Even though the Law of Moses was given for many purposes, part of its regimen was for the express purpose of the coming Messiah; consequently, in preparation for this, Israel was to conduct herself in a certain way and according to certain principles. It was laid out in the Law of Moses to the minute degree.

Some may claim that Israel miserably failed in this, and that would be true for most; however, there was always a Remnant in Israel who followed the Lord as closely as was humanly possible. Through this Remnant, which included the House of David, Jesus came as the Son of David.

Now that Jesus had come and had performed the task for which He came, the Law of Moses—respecting the Temple, sacrifices, Feast Days, Sabbaths, etc.—was no longer needed. The One to Whom they had pointed and meant to symbolize had now come. Consequently, they would be laid aside, along with all of these dietary laws, etc.

The Law of Moses, respecting the *"moral code,"* was not set aside, with the Ten Commandments, minus the Fourth Commandment concerning the Sabbath, carried over into the New Covenant. The reasons are obvious! Moral Laws do not and, in fact, cannot change.

Regrettably, Israel little by little attempted to make Salvation out of the Law, thus adding many more laws. I suppose in their thinking, if a little was good, more was much better. Consequently, they lost most knowledge as to why the Law had been given in the first place and to Whom it constantly pointed. So, Peter had been prejudiced into wrong thinking, as had most all of Israel, and would now be shocked at the Command of the Lord.

(14) "BUT PETER SAID, NOT SO, LORD; FOR I HAVE NEVER EATEN ANY THING THAT IS COMMON OR UNCLEAN."

The pattern is:

1. It is ever the Cross! The Cross! The Cross!

2. While the Believer can be Saved without properly understanding the Cross of Christ relative to Sanctification, still, such a Believer, no matter how hard he tries, cannot live a victorious, overcoming life.

SIMON PETER

The phrase, *"But Peter said, Not so, Lord,"* presents Peter actually disobeying the Lord, and why?

There were no literal animals in front of Peter, only the Vision; however, the symbolism that the Vision was meant to portray was very, very real, as the Lord intended for it to be.

As we have already stated, Leviticus, Chapter 11, plainly says that these animals were not to be eaten, and now the Lord said the very opposite.

Does the Lord contradict Himself? Does He change His Mind?

The answer is *"no"* to both questions. So, how do we explain what looks to be an obvious contradiction?

As we have stated, this particular part of the Law of Moses, as given by God, contained no moral content. It was meant to serve a particular purpose at that time, and above all, to serve as symbolism. Due to the significance of this, and even at the risk of being overly repetitive, please allow me to deal with this again.

SYMBOLISM

When Jesus ultimately came, the symbolism was of no more use, as should be obvious, and was meant to be laid aside. In other words, it fulfilled its role, and when that was done, it was of no more purpose. Such applied to these dietary laws, Feast Days, Sabbaths, and sacrifices, plus all the Sacred Vessels of the Temple, such as the Brazen Altar, Brazen Laver, etc.

Because Jesus has come, that which pointed to Him is of no further purpose, as should be obvious. Consequently, Believers do not now offer up lambs for sacrifices. However, in not doing so, we are not violating the Word of God, even though the Law of Moses plainly commanded that such be done. We do not do such now because since Jesus has come, which all of this was meant to symbolically portray, such is no longer needed. Actually, it would be a gross insult to Him for such to be continued.

So, when the Lord told Peter to do this thing, He was not contradicting Himself or changing His Mind.

It is painfully obvious that despite the fact that Jesus had come and satisfied all the demands of the Law, the Church of that day was still trying to hold on to the Law and continue its practice.

Why?

COMMON OR UNCLEAN

The greatest reason is that Israel had lost sight of what the Law actually was and Who it actually represented. As we have already stated, the spiritual leadership of Israel had attempted to make Salvation out of the Law, which God never intended whatsoever. Consequently, this spirit that pervaded the whole of Israel at that time had taken its toll even upon the Apostles of our Lord, hence, Peter's foolish answer to the Lord.

NOTES

The phrase, *"For I have never eaten any thing that is common or unclean,"* refers to that which was defiled and forbidden by the Law (Lev., Chpt. 11; Deut., Chpt. 14; Mk. 7:2).

However, there is a note of self-righteousness in Peter's answer, whether he intended that or not!

Israel never could quite understand a simple Truth, which many in the modern church have trouble believing as well!

Walking as perfectly before God as one knew or knows how to do, whether under the Old Covenant or the New, does not earn or merit one anything from God. In other words, such brings about no Righteousness whatsoever, even though the doing of such is very important.

GRACE

However, failing to obey the Law under the Old Covenant, or failing to live above sin under the New, will make one unrighteous very quickly. So, the church has attempted to address itself to these things in many and varied ways, most of the time wrong!

While it is true that Grace is greater than sin, still, Grace does not give one the license to sin, but rather the liberty to live a Holy life. Once again, living a Holy life, as the Grace of God enables one to do, is exactly what the Holy Spirit is attempting to bring about. However, having done that, one still does not merit or earn any Righteousness (Eph. 2:8-9). Righteousness is awarded freely to the sinner and done so instantly as the sinner has Faith in Christ. That is the only way it can be obtained and, in fact, it has always been that way.

However, as we have stated, even though one cannot earn Righteousness, irrespective as to what he or she may do, one can become unrighteous very quickly. Sin and failure automatically make one unrighteous, irrespective of who he may be, whether Moses, David, Peter, or Paul. It is the same for all Believers! (Rom. 6:23).

IMPUTED RIGHTEOUSNESS

Consequently, *"imputed Righteousness"*

NOTES

is freely given to any and all who have simple Faith in Christ. It is the kind of Righteousness given by God and the only kind, thereby, recognized by God. It is a lesson that Peter would learn this day (Rom. 4:3).

It was hard for him to understand that Gentiles, who had no knowledge of God and were committing every kind of sin that one could think, could at the same time be justified instantly, especially considering their record! Considering that he had never eaten anything common or unclean, nor had he committed many sins that Gentiles had committed, and yet, the Gentile could receive from God just as readily as the Jew, was a bitter pill for Peter to swallow. In fact, that's why Paul had such a difficult time introducing the great Gospel of Grace.

However, that is exactly what the Lord was telling Peter, and all others as well! Yes, he wanted the Jews to do certain things, and for purpose and reason; however, those things did not merit the Jew anything with God, and this is where the problem began.

Inasmuch as they had the Law, the sacrifices, the Temple, the Sabbaths, the Circumcision, and the rites and ceremonies, the Jews came to believe that these things merited them something with God, but it did not, which was very difficult for them to accept.

(15) "AND THE VOICE SPOKE UNTO HIM AGAIN THE SECOND TIME, WHAT GOD HAS CLEANSED, DO NOT CALL COMMON."

The composition is:

1. The Cross of Christ is the answer and the only answer!

2. And yet, sadly and regrettably, most Believers are taught absolutely nothing about the Cross of Christ relative to Sanctification.

THE SECOND TIME

The phrase, *"And the Voice spoke unto him again the second time,"* proclaims a correction tendered toward Peter by the Lord.

Peter had used the appellative *"Lord"* in responding to the Vision, which means, in essence, that Jesus is the Lord of one's life and is to be explicitly obeyed. However, Peter was contradicting himself in that he refused to obey.

To be frank, the title *"Lord,"* as it refers to Jesus, is used very loosely in today's spiritual climate. However, the far greater majority of those who call themselves Christians little seek to obey the Lord. Actually, most Believers obey only as long as it is in their personal interest to do so. Rare is the Believer who will obey, irrespective of the personal cost.

WHAT GOD HAS CLEANSED

The phrase, *"What God has cleansed, do not call common,"* struck at the very heart of present Jewish beliefs.

In other words, they believed that only a Jew could truly be called *"clean."* Of course, their judgment in the situation revolved around them supposedly keeping the Law, etc. However, the Lord did not recognize any of this and, in fact, never had.

In the first place, the Law could not cleanse from sin and was never meant to do so. As well, man certainly cannot cleanse himself of this dread malady, as should be painfully obvious. Therefore, only God can do such, and He does it not through works or merit, etc., but rather through the shed Blood of His Son, the Lord Jesus Christ.

The Gospel really was not that difficult to understand, nor had it ever been; however, Israel had made it very difficult by inserting the Mosaic Law into that for which it was never intended. On top of that, the Pharisees made up about 600 more laws to add to what was already given, which was a travesty of unprecedented proportions; consequently, several things are said here in the Lord's reply:

THE ANSWER AS GIVEN BY THE LORD

- As we have stated, only God can cleanse from sin. And yet, I am afraid that many modern denominations, even those who should know better, are guilty of attempting to add something to the Finished Work of Christ. When that is done, we sin and we sin greatly, in effect, calling God a liar!
- Faith expressed in the precious shed Blood of Jesus Christ is to be recognized by any and all. When we put our Faith in the Blood, we reap its wonderful benefits, for

NOTES

the Blood does cleanse from all sin. To refer to something as *"common"* or *"unclean"* that God has cleansed is grievous in the sight of the Lord.

• The Words of Jesus used here to Peter are very emphatic and, in effect, say, *"Peter, you must never treat anything as unclean that God has cleansed, or even think of such in that capacity."*

• This was the Lord's Way of telling Peter, and all others for that matter, that the Gospel must go to the Gentiles for whom Christ died, and that they can be Saved without all the rudiments of the Law simply by trusting in Christ.

• As well, the statement in reverse says that Israel must come the same identical way as the Gentiles must come, by and through the precious Blood of Jesus Christ.

In other words, the middle wall of partition, which separated the Court of the Gentiles from that of the Jews at the Temple, must be torn down, spiritually speaking, that all may come and, in fact, must come the same way!

• Also, to refuse to recognize Mercy, Grace, and forgiveness on the part of God, as it regards someone who has sinned and fully repented, is, in effect, calling unclean what God has cleansed. It constitutes a grievous sin in the Eyes of God.

(16) "THIS WAS DONE THREE TIMES: AND THE VESSEL WAS RECEIVED UP AGAIN INTO HEAVEN."

The exegesis is:

1. The Cross of Christ is God's Solution to man's dilemma.

2. This means there is no forgiveness and cleansing from sin outside of the Cross.

THREE TIMES

The phrase, *"This was done three times,"* refers to the Lord telling Peter three times to *"kill and eat,"* and then implies that Peter refused three times. As well, the Lord said three times, *"What God has cleansed, do not call common."*

Let us deal with the patience of the Lord in dealing with His Apostle, and all others as well!

In reading this, we may tend to think harshly of Peter; however, have we done any better? Are we doing any better at present?

In fact, obedience does not come very easily, even with the most consecrated Believers. That is because of prejudice, bias, and preconceived notions, or, as we have stated, it does not serve our self-interest. So, the Lord has to deal with us over and over again concerning specifics. Even then, many do not obey!

However, I think that one of the most important lessons in this scenario is that which the Holy Spirit intends for us to learn respecting how easy it is to believe error. As well, even as here, most error produces self-righteousness.

Peter placed great stock in his faithfulness in obeying Leviticus, Chapter 11.

• It was certainly right for him to have done so up to the time Jesus came; however, upon His Coming, all of these symbolisms and types were no longer pertinent, applicable, or necessary, as indeed they could not be! Peter was more acquainted with this than possibly anyone else in the world.

MORAL

Did Peter not understand that there was nothing moral in this particular symbolism of dietary laws, at least as it applied to human beings?

As well, looking at the situation presently, there is nothing immoral about a lady wearing rings, jewelry, or any such thing; however, some Believers have fastly held to such thinking that it is not proper to wear jewelry, etc. Once again, as with Peter, self-righteousness generally follows in the train of such erroneous thinking.

Jesus said, *"Woe unto you, Scribes and Pharisees, hypocrites! for you pay tithe of mint and anise and cumin, and have omitted the weightier matters of the Law, judgment, Mercy, and Faith: these ought you to have done, and not to leave the other undone"* (Mat. 23:23).

Jesus is here telling us that some things are more important than others. He is not denigrating tithing and plainly says that it should continue; however, what He did oppose was the emphasis placed on that, while things far more important were totally ignored.

NOTES

The Pharisees would minutely select their one plant out of 10 in the paying of their tithes, or whatever it was, and then ignore things that were of great moral content.

It makes it ever worse still when Peter was strongly desiring to continue something that no longer had Scriptural validity and, at the same time, allowed Gentiles to go to Hell without any opportunity of ever hearing the Gospel.

What type of thinking is it when we gloat that we have not eaten a ham sandwich and, at the same time, let a person go to Hell? However, this is what Peter was doing, and I must quickly ask the question, *"What are we doing?"*

As a case in point, the Lord put us on television in 1989 in what was then referred to as the Soviet Union. At first, we were only on a single station in the country of Latvia, which was a republic of the Soviet Union. However, very shortly the Lord opened up the largest television network, then called TV-1, in that vast communistic empire. It reached all 15 Soviet Republics and had formerly been used as the propaganda channel for communism.

Over the next three years, the Lord did a mighty Work through the telecast in seeing untold thousands brought to a saving knowledge of Jesus Christ. For that, we give Him all the praise and all the glory.

OBEY OR DISOBEY

However, it was a gargantuan struggle each month to pay for the airtime for that particular program. Somehow the Lord made a way, but it brought us to the edge of bankruptcy.

Despite our appeals, and despite the tremendous numbers of people being Saved, of which there was abundant proof I might add, virtually all Christians refused to help us at all simply because their denominational heads had told them not to do so. Consequently, they would obey an unscriptural rule that had no rhyme or reason, but would not obey the command to take the Gospel to lost and hurting humanity.

Of course, their answer would be that they would gladly support others, but not us. However, to say or do such a thing is, at the same time, to insult God Who does the choosing and calling respecting His Work. As well, even as the Lord told Peter, they were calling common what God had cleansed.

Thank the Lord that Peter ultimately obeyed, but these of which I speak did not obey at all!

Where does that leave them?

I can only answer that by asking another question.

"Where would it have left Peter if he had not finally obeyed and had continued to rebel?"

Once again, and as we have already stated, God is very patient with us, and how thankful we are that He is. As patient as He has been with me, I want Him to be as patient with others. However, the Lord will not tolerate gross disobedience forever.

The phrase, *"And the vessel was received up again into Heaven,"* portrays the Vision ending with Peter seemingly not yet obeying. However, in his defense, as we shall see, he really did not understand what the Lord was saying. Nevertheless, do we have to understand in order to obey?

(17) "NOW WHILE PETER DOUBTED IN HIMSELF WHAT THIS VISION WHICH HE HAD SEEN SHOULD MEAN, BEHOLD, THE MEN WHICH WERE SENT FROM CORNELIUS HAD MADE INQUIRY FOR SIMON'S HOUSE, AND STOOD BEFORE THE GATE."

The overview is:

1. The phrase, *"Now while Peter doubted in himself what this Vision which he had seen should mean,"* proclaims that at this stage, Peter did not actually know what the Lord was telling him.

2. The word *"doubted"* in the Greek Text is *"diaporeo"* and means *"to be thoroughly nonplussed,"* in other words, *"perplexed."*

3. Peter did not have the slightest idea that the Lord was going to use him to take the Gospel to the Gentiles and, in fact, that he would be the first one to do so! However, the true meaning of the Vision would not be long in coming.

The phrase, *"Behold, the men which were sent from Cornelius had made inquiry for Simon's house, and stood before the gate,"* proclaims events unfolding very fast. Peter would soon know what the Vision meant and understand perfectly what the Lord was telling him.

(18) "AND CALLED, AND ASKED WHETHER SIMON, WHICH WAS SURNAMED PETER, WERE LODGED THERE."

The construction is:

1. The words, *"And called,"* even though speaking then of the three men from the house of Cornelius, as well, speaks of the multiple millions all over the world who truly hunger for the Lord but really do not know how to find Him. They are calling!

2. They are calling from Europe, Asia, and Africa, and even in North, Central, and South America. As well, they are calling from the Far East, the Middle East, and the islands of the sea. In fact, they are calling from all over the world. As these three were looking for Simon Peter, so many others are looking for someone to tell them the grand and glorious Story, in other words, the Greatest Story ever told!

3. The phrase, *"And asked whether Simon, which was surnamed Peter, were lodged there,"* emphatically specifies, as should be obvious, that only Peter would do!

This is the man the Angel had told Cornelius to find, and he would give them the Words of Life.

I emphasize this because the Lord has not changed His Methods from then until now. He does not call denominations, committees, or boards, but rather a man or a woman. This is where religious denominations run aground.

Religious hierarchies gradually come into being as the Headship of Christ is traded for that of man. Then the hierarchy does the telling instead of the Lord, with the consequences being that nothing is accomplished for Christ. God calls a man or a woman, and He expects them to obey. However, that man or woman will ultimately find that, most of the time, the greatest hindrances will not come from the world system, but rather from the church itself! That is sad but true.

(19) "WHILE PETER THOUGHT ON THE VISION, THE SPIRIT SAID UNTO HIM, BEHOLD, THREE MEN SEEK YOU."

NOTES

The composition is:

1. Remove the Cross from Christianity, and there is nothing left but a vapid philosophy.

2. The entirety of every Bible Doctrine is built around and thereon the Cross of Christ. Otherwise, it is specious.

THE VISION

The phrase, *"While Peter thought on the Vision,"* has reference to the fact that Peter did not really know what the Lord had portrayed unto him. As is obvious, the Lord telling him three times to do something that he had never done in his life, and actually looked at as sin, was unnerving to say the least. However, the Spirit of God would now institute the second step, which would bring Peter closer to understanding what was being said and done.

As we see, it was much easier for the Lord to deal with Cornelius and for him to take directions than it was for His choice Apostle.

This is the basic reason that millions of fundamentalists were not baptized with the Holy Spirit, at least when the Spirit began to fall all over the world some decades ago. While tens of thousands of Lutherans, Presbyterians, Methodists, and Catholics were receiving, not as many Baptists and Holiness were included in that number.

Why?

For the most part, the others knew they were spiritually bankrupt, while most Baptists and Holiness made great profession of believing the entirety of the Bible, hence, referred to as fundamentalists, etc. Consequently, the idea that the Baptism with the Holy Spirit with the evidence of speaking with other Tongues was real, which they had opposed all along, offended their spiritual pride. As a result, and in comparison to the overall numbers, not as many of these received.

Spiritual pride is a diabolical thing! It is something every Believer must address constantly. That is the reason the Lord said through Isaiah, *"But to this man will I look, even to him that is poor and of a contrite spirit, and trembles at My Word"* (Isa. 66:2).

The phrase, *"The Spirit said unto him,"* reflects the Third Person of the Godhead,

NOTES

Who was extremely active in Peter's life, as He should be in all!

This is part of what Jesus spoke when He said, *"He* (the Holy Spirit) *will guide you into all Truth."*

He then said, *"He shall glorify Me: for He shall receive of Mine, and shall show it unto you"* (Jn. 16:13-14).

If the Believer will follow close enough to the Lord and seek to please Him constantly, he will be very surprised at how often the Spirit of God will speak unto him, giving leading, guidance, and direction.

The phrase, *"Behold, three men seek you,"* presents that which He whispered to Peter's heart, and actually pertains to that which He had commanded Cornelius to do respecting the sending of men to Peter.

Actually, it was the Holy Spirit Who had performed and carried out all of these directions. He sent the Angel to Cornelius, even as He gave Peter a Vision.

He now spoke to Peter and gave him explicit instructions.

This is the manner and way that the Spirit works, and as He worked then, He seeks to work now. However, if one will notice, Cornelius was engaged in prayer when this happened, as we have stated, as well as Peter. Of course, it does not happen in this manner every time, but still, it should be overly obvious as to how significant that prayer really is.

PRAYER

If I attempted to put on paper all the times the Holy Spirit has spoken to me about certain things, I know beyond a doubt that the experiences and illustrations would fill up the remainder of this book.

(20) "ARISE THEREFORE, AND GET YOU DOWN, AND GO WITH THEM, DOUBTING NOTHING: FOR I HAVE SENT THEM."

The synopsis is:

1. The phrase, *"Arise therefore, and get you down,"* pertains to Peter being on the housetop, which, in those days, was flat.

2. Actually, the top of houses was designed to be used by the inhabitants. In many, if not most houses, a set of stairs went down into the house, plus another set outside the house. During many months, and especially those not of the rainy season, the top was used as a sitting parlor of sorts, and for sleeping, in order that the cool breezes might be enjoyed, etc.

3. The phrase, *"And go with them, doubting nothing,"* has the following meaning:

The Greek word for *"doubting"* is *"diakrino"* and means *"do not waver or hesitate to obey,"* in fact, do not hesitate at all!

4. *"For I have sent them,"* proclaims all of this, even as we have stated, being carried out by the Holy Spirit.

5. If the individual or church refuses to deal with the Holy Spirit, or misinterprets or misunderstands His Manner of working, even as most do, they are then left with nothing but human devices.

6. Tragically, most of the major religious denominations have denied the Working and Operation of the Holy Spirit simply because of not rightly dividing the Word of Truth and are, therefore, bereft of anything that is of God.

7. Sadly, many, if not most, of the so-called Pentecostal denominations have forsaken the Holy Spirit. Unless there is revival, their fate will be even worse than their denominational friends.

8. The Believer must understand that the Book of Acts, which is the story of the Early Church and the Working and Operation of the Holy Spirit in that Church, is meant to serve as the pattern for all Churches from then until now. Consequently, if our lives and churches are not patterned after this example that the Holy Spirit intends, we may call ourselves *"Believers"* and refer to our gatherings as *"church,"* but the truth is, God refers to such as *"unbelievers"* and unto such churches as *"church"* in name only!

(21) "THEN PETER WENT DOWN TO THE MEN WHICH WERE SENT UNTO HIM FROM CORNELIUS; AND SAID, BEHOLD, I AM HE WHOM YOU SEEK: WHAT IS THE CAUSE WHEREFORE YOU ARE COME?"

The account is:

1. The phrase, *"Then Peter went down to the men which were sent unto him from Cornelius,"* simply refers to the fact that he probably came down the outside stairs from

NOTES

the top of the house.

2. The phrase, *"And said, Behold, I am he whom you seek,"* proclaims Peter introducing himself, even as the Angel had told Cornelius that such would be. In other words, Peter was at Joppa exactly as it had been said by the Angel.

3. The question, *"What is the cause wherefore you are come?"* presents Peter obeying the Holy Spirit in courteously meeting these men, but if one is to notice, the Spirit did not tell Peter what they wanted or the reason for their coming. He just told Peter to go with them, *"doubting nothing."*

4. However, they would now state their reason for coming, which would begin to throw Light on the Vision that Peter had just experienced.

(22) "AND THEY SAID, CORNELIUS THE CENTURION, A JUST MAN, AND ONE WHO FEARS GOD, AND OF GOOD REPORT AMONG ALL THE NATION OF THE JEWS, WAS WARNED FROM GOD BY AN HOLY ANGEL TO SEND FOR YOU INTO HIS HOUSE, AND TO HEAR WORDS OF YOU."

CORNELIUS THE CENTURION

The phrase, *"And they said, Cornelius the centurion,"* portrays to Peter immediately that this man was a Gentile.

Whether or not the meaning of the Vision just given to Peter began to be revealed at this moment is not clear; however, whether then or a little later, this much is clear, Peter would get the message.

The phrase, *"A just man, and one who fears God, and of good report among all the Nation of the Jews,"* reveals to Peter a number of things.

The word *"just,"* as here used, refers to one being right or righteous; however, it is speaking of that which relates to man, and not Righteousness or Justification as given by God.

The fact that he *"feared God"* means that he had turned his back totally and completely on all the paganistic gods and had adopted totally the God of Israel, i.e., *"Jehovah."* As such, he had a *"good report among the Jews,"* but yet, the man was not Saved. Even though we have dealt with this earlier in this Chapter, due to its great significance, please allow me to investigate a little further.

Most of the world believes there is a God. Their interpretation of Him is mostly jaded or 180 degrees from reality, but still, they have some type of belief in some type of god. They may refer to Him as a *"higher power"* or *"the force,"* but still, they have some type of mystical belief in that regard.

GOD

Millions foolishly believe that in some way the human being is god, hence, the continued effort to bring out the *"Deity"* in us, as they would say. As is obvious, some are much closer to the Truth than others.

Nevertheless, irrespective of how God or Salvation is defined, most operate on the premise that all of it is judged by certain good deeds they perform, or certain bad things they have not done. Most think of their lives as having two columns, with the good in one column and the bad in the other. When they come to the end of their lives, if the good outweighs the bad, they are Saved, or so they think, or else, they will receive some type of reward of some nature, etc.

Looking at the assortment of humanity with its varied beliefs, the very highest that man can attain within himself is that which was attained by Cornelius. He was *"a just man,"* one *"that fears God,"* and had a *"good report."* However, as noble as all of that was and as helpful as it was to him, it still did not afford Salvation, for there is no Salvation in man or anything he does.

Salvation is strictly from the Lord and is given exclusively upon His Terms.

But yet, millions in churches presently live their lives somewhat akin to Cornelius. They are church members; they occasionally give a little money to what proposes to be the Work of God; and they try to adhere to some type of ethical and moral rule. However, the truth is, despite all of that, if, in fact, that is their claim to Salvation, as Cornelius, they are not Saved.

The Word of God is the criterion for all things. It alone sets the Standard. It alone is the Standard. It plainly tells us that one must accept Christ as one's Saviour, thereby, availing oneself of what He has done in order that man could be redeemed. As well, one must lay aside any faith or confidence in his good works, whatever those works may be, and trust solely in Christ. Otherwise, a person cannot be Saved (Jn. 3:16; Rom. 10:9-13; Eph. 2:8-9).

THE REVELATION OF GOD TO CORNELIUS

The phrase, *"Was warned from God by an Holy Angel to send for you into his house,"* presents an interesting statement.

The word *"warned"* in the Greek Text is *"chrematizo"* and means *"to be strongly admonished."* In effect, it is saying that despite all the good things one could say about Cornelius, all of these good things could not save him.

"And to hear words of You," proclaims that which Cornelius must hear in order to be Saved. Peter had been chosen to deliver those *"words,"* and now it was up to Cornelius to *"hear them."*

Sadly, the *"words"* so desperately needed in order for people to be Saved are missing in most churches. In these churches, the preacher preaches no truth at all, or else, a mixture of Truth and error. And then, some do preach the Truth but without the Anointing of the Holy Spirit, which destroys the effectiveness of the Truth. Jesus said, *"The Spirit of the Lord is upon Me, because He has anointed Me to preach the Gospel to the poor* (poor in spirit)*"* (Lk. 4:18).

The Truth, simply because it is the Truth, is not automatically anointed by the Holy Spirit. The Anointing comes as a result of the Preacher of the Gospel consecrating himself to the Lord and having a strong prayer life and study of the Word.

No! Those things do not earn one anything with God, but they do make it possible for the Holy Spirit to work within our lives.

(23) "THEN CALLED HE THEM IN, AND LODGED THEM. AND ON THE MORROW PETER WENT AWAY WITH THEM, AND CERTAIN BRETHREN FROM JOPPA ACCOMPANIED HIM."

The synopsis is:

1. The phrase, *"Then called he them in, and lodged them,"* tells me that Peter now knew what the Vision meant, or at least had a good idea. The word carries with it that he showed them hospitality, which was very unusual concerning a Jew responding to Gentiles. This broke down the wall of partition between him and them.

2. It sounds somewhat ridiculous, does it not, to speak of Peter showing hospitality to these people when such should be par for the course respecting Followers of Christ. However, this is but one example of what religion will do to a person. It always creates an elitism, which is an abomination in the Eyes of God, especially considering that all people, even the best of Christians, are woefully lacking in the Righteousness of God.

3. Considering that, before we malign Peter, we must take a look at ourselves. Is there any elitism in our lives? Do we have a superior or a holier than thou attitude?

4. *"And on the morrow Peter went away with them,"* proclaims his obedience to what the Lord had told him to do, *"Go with them, doubting nothing"* (Acts 10:20).

5. *"And certain brethren from Joppa accompanied him,"* tells us there was a Church in Joppa, and that six brethren (Jews) accompanied him (Acts 11:1-18; 15:7).

6. Peter took these brethren with him for several reasons, but the primary reason of all was that he would have ample witnesses of all that was done. As we have already stated, this was one of the most important days in history. In effect, it would have a bearing on the entirety of the world, and for all time. The Gospel was about to be given unto the Gentiles with no strings attached, no necessity of having to become a Jewish proselyte, etc., but by simple Faith in Christ. It is truly *"Good News,"* which is exactly what the Gospel means!

(24) "AND THE MORROW AFTER THEY ENTERED INTO CAESAREA. AND CORNELIUS WAITED FOR THEM, AND HAD CALLED TOGETHER HIS KINSMEN AND NEAR FRIENDS."

The exegesis is:

1. The phrase, *"And the morrow after they entered into Caesarea,"* evidently means they had spent the night at Apollonia, which was about halfway on the coast road.

2. The phrase, *"And Cornelius waited for them,"* proclaims the fact that he had absolutely no doubt that Peter would come. After all, the Angel sent directly by the Lord had given him instructions as to what to do, so he was fully confident.

3. *"And had called together his kinsmen and near friends,"* tells us that he estimated the probable time they would arrive and had everyone waiting.

4. No doubt, he had related to all of these people how the Angel of the Lord had appeared unto him, telling him to send for the Apostle. Consequently, considering the circumstances, they would have been very excited, as would be obvious. Actually, the excitement must have sparkled like electricity, considering that very few people in all the time of human history had been blessed by the visitation of an Angel. For these *"kinsmen and near friends"* to be a part of this was phenomenal, to say the least, which they evidently recognized and understood.

(25) "AND AS PETER WAS COMING IN, CORNELIUS MET HIM, AND FELL DOWN AT HIS FEET, AND WORSHIPPED HIM."

The account is:

1. The phrase, *"And as Peter was coming in, Cornelius met him,"* insinuates that this meeting took place outside the house, probably at the gate. Most houses in those days, especially ones of note, were surrounded by a fence, etc.

2. As well, Cornelius undoubtedly had someone standing outside the gate watching for their arrival, and at the first sign, immediately brought the news, with the centurion rushing out to meet them.

3. *"And fell down at his feet, and worshipped him,"* does not necessarily mean that Cornelius was worshipping Peter, but was merely worshipping, inasmuch as the pronoun *"him"* was added by the translators. However, the word *"worshipped"* as here used, in the Greek Text is *"proskuneo"* and means *"to kiss, like a dog licking his master's hand, or to fawn or crouch, or to prostrate oneself in homage."* However, the possibility does exist that Cornelius was actually worshipping Peter.

(26) "BUT PETER TOOK HIM UP, SAYING, STAND UP; I MYSELF ALSO AM A MAN."

NOTES

The diagram is:

1. The Cross of Christ is the Means and the only Means by which all of these wonderful things are given to us.

2. When we say the Cross, we aren't speaking of the wooden beam on which Jesus died, but what He there did.

PETER THE ROCK

Cornelius had been brought up as a pagan and was accustomed from boyhood to seeing Divine honors rendered to particular men. Considering this and what he had experienced regarding the visitation of the Angel, one can understand his actions.

However, Peter was quick to correct him, firmly but gently.

Consequently, this lays to rest the Catholic claim of Peter being the first Pope, with homage being paid to such as it presently is!

The character of Peter is transparent and easily analyzed, and it is doubtless true that no other *"in Scriptural history is drawn for us more clearly or strongly."*

He had been styled the prince of the Apostles and, indeed, seems to have been their leader on every occasion. He is always named first in every list of accounts and was their common spokesman.

He was hopeful, bold, confident, courageous, frank, impulsive, energetic, vigorous, strong, loving, and faithful to his Master, notwithstanding his defection prior to the Crucifixion.

It is true that he was liable to change and inconsistency, and because of his peculiar temperament, he sometimes appeared forward and rash. Yet, as another says, *"His virtues and faults had their common root in his enthusiastic disposition,"* and the latter were at length overruled by Divine Grace into the most beautiful humility and meekness, as evinced in his two Epistles.

LEADERSHIP

The leadership, to which we have referred, however, should not lead to the supposition that he possessed any supremacy over the other Apostles, for there is no proof. Such supremacy was never conferred upon him by his Master. It was never claimed by himself and was never conceded by his associates (Mat. 23:8-12; Acts 15:13-14; II Cor. 12:11; Gal. 2:11).

It is true that when Christ referred to the meaning of His Name (Mat. 16:18), He said, *"Upon this Rock I will build My Church,"* but He did not intend to teach that His Church would be built upon Peter, but upon Himself as confessed by Peter in Matthew 16:16.

Peter was careful to affirm this in the first of his two Epistles (I Pet. 2:4-9). Moreover, when Christ said, *"I will give unto you the Keys of the Kingdom of Heaven"* (Mat. 16:19), He invested him with no power not possessed in common with his brethren, since they also after would receive the same Commission (Mat. 18:18; Jn. 20:23).

In one sense of the word, Peter was privileged to use this key regarding the opening of the door of the Gospel to Israel on the Day of Pentecost (Acts 2:38-42) and to the Gentiles in the house of Cornelius, which we are now studying. However, in another sense, all Believers have the privilege of using this *"key"* in telling the grand Story of Jesus Christ to others.

"Saying, Stand up; I myself also am a man," simply refers to the fact that as a man, he was not to be worshipped, for such belongs only to God.

As well, as is very obvious, Peter did not want any praise for being used of God. Neither did he want anyone to give any human personality preeminence in the Church.

III John, Verse 9, warns us against those who love to have the preeminence. Christ is the Head of the Church. God resurrected Him from the dead that *"in all things He might have the preeminence"* (Col. 1:18).

(27) "AND AS HE TALKED WITH HIM, HE WENT IN, AND FOUND MANY WHO WERE COME TOGETHER."

The overview is:

1. The phrase, *"And as he talked with him,"* portrays Peter putting himself on the same level as Cornelius, which, as well, portrayed the beautiful equality tendered by Bible Christianity.

2. *"He went in, and found many who were come together,"* seems to imply that Cornelius had not told him of the crowd waiting, or at least that it involved quite a number of people.

3. As well, the implication is that when Peter and the others were brought in by Cornelius, these *"many people"* waiting were awestruck when they saw him.

4. Again, allow us to emphasize that one can well understand their feelings and thinking, especially considering that this man, for all practical purposes, had been sent by an Angel.

5. As a result, it is my thinking that none of them rushed forward to greet Peter, but rather stood in awe and silence, which is understandable.

(28) "AND HE SAID UNTO THEM, YOU KNOW HOW THAT IT IS AN UNLAWFUL THING FOR A MAN THAT IS A JEW TO KEEP COMPANY, OR COME UNTO ONE OF ANOTHER NATION; BUT GOD HAS SHOWN ME THAT I SHOULD NOT CALL ANY MAN COMMON OR UNCLEAN."

The composition is:

1. The phrase, *"And he said unto them,"* now presents Peter's first words.

Ironically enough, that which he would say intimates that he was being corrected as well as Cornelius. Of course, what Cornelius would learn was the all-important aspect of Salvation, of which nothing could be greater. And yet, as it regards this episode, that which would be learned by Peter was no small thing either. Without reservation, as we shall see, Peter would plainly reveal all his wrong and God's Correction.

2. *"You know how that it is an unlawful thing for a man that is a Jew to keep company, or come unto one of another nation,"* proclaims him relating something that was quite well known by all Gentiles who had resided in Israel for any length of time.

3. *"But God has shown me that I should not call any man common or unclean,"* tells us that Peter now understood completely what the Vision was all about concerning the sheet let down from Heaven.

4. It was notorious among the Romans that the Jews kept themselves aloof from other people, hence, the accusation against them of being haters of the human race.

5. Tacitus says of them that they hated

all people, except their own countrymen, as their enemies and refused to eat or intermarry with them (Hervey).

6. Peter being in the House of Cornelius did not mean that he was arbitrarily turning his back on Jewish ways and customs, but that God had dealt with him strongly about looking down on other people. While it was more so in the spiritual sense, still, it socially applied as well!

7. This strikes hard at racism, prejudice, and bias. As well, it strikes hard at class consciousness. In true Bible Christianity, all are looked at as equal. In fact, in the Early Church, every indication is that wealthy land or business owners sat side by side with slaves. Actually, tradition says that Onesimus, the runaway slave from the house of Philemon, after coming to Christ, went back to Philemon and ultimately became Pastor of the Church at Ephesus.

(29) "THEREFORE CAME I UNTO YOU WITHOUT GAINSAYING, AS SOON AS I WAS SENT FOR: I ASK THEREFORE FOR WHAT INTENT YOU HAVE SENT FOR ME?"

The structure is:

1. The phrase, *"Therefore came I unto you without gainsaying, as soon as I was sent for,"* means that in no way did he question those sent by Cornelius, as referring to the validity or veracity of their request. In other words, he obeyed the Holy Spirit, as stated, to *"go with them, doubting nothing: for I have sent them"* (Acts 10:20).

2. Referring to obedience, this is always what the Lord intends and demands of His Children.

3. There are many who claim that God has told them to do many things when, in reality, it was not the Lord, but rather something out of their own minds. However, Peter knew beyond the shadow of a doubt that this was the Spirit of the Lord speaking to him and not a figment of his imagination. Consequently, he obeyed immediately, as it was intended that he do.

4. The question, *"I ask therefore for what intent you have sent for me?"* actually pertains to that which he already knew. It had been related to him by those sent by Cornelius.

NOTES

5. However, he was proper in asking this question as it gave Cornelius the opportunity to personally and officially state what the Lord had said unto him. This had to be a beautiful moment as he related his experience.

As well, as we have stated, it would have an effect over the entirety of the world, and for all time. Now the Prophecy of Joel (2:28), *"It shall come to pass afterward, that I will pour out My Spirit upon all flesh* (Jews and Gentiles)," was about to come to pass! What a time and moment in history this presented!

(30) "AND CORNELIUS SAID, FOUR DAYS AGO I WAS FASTING UNTIL THIS HOUR; AND AT THE NINTH HOUR I PRAYED IN MY HOUSE, AND, BEHOLD, A MAN STOOD BEFORE ME IN BRIGHT CLOTHING."

The exegesis is:

1. The phrase, *"And Cornelius said, Four days ago I was fasting until this hour; and at the ninth hour I prayed in my house,"* referred to 3 p.m. It had evidently taken two days for those sent to come to Joppa and about two days in returning.

2. The phrase, *"And, behold, a man stood before me in bright clothing,"* tells us two things:

a. Angels are Spirit Beings (Heb. 1:14) and, as such, do not have physical bodies. Nevertheless, many of them have the appearance of a man, even as Cornelius here used the word.

b. Even though many Angels have the appearance of men, still, the *"bright clothing"* speaks of the Glory of God about them, which sets them apart.

3. Actually, the word *"bright,"* as used here, refers to something being *"radiant and magnificent."* It is not so much that the garment itself is radiant but that the person of the Angel is radiant, consequently, shining through the clothing.

4. This signifies one who has been in the Presence of God.

(31) "AND SAID, CORNELIUS, YOUR PRAYER IS HEARD, AND YOUR ALMS ARE HAD IN REMEMBRANCE IN THE SIGHT OF GOD."

The synopsis is:

NOTES

1. The phrase, *"And said, Cornelius, your prayer is heard,"* speaks of one particular prayer, even though Cornelius undoubtedly prayed about many things.

2. That particular prayer was a desire by Cornelius to draw closer to God. As I have previously said, for the heart that truly reaches out to God, it in some way must be instigated by the Holy Spirit. I have to believe that God will find a way to get the Gospel to that person, irrespective of what it may take. Every evidence points to such a conclusion.

3. As we have stated, even though Cornelius was very sincere, very generous, and very religious, still, he was not Saved, which, within itself, and despite all the works of religion, points to an unsatisfied hunger.

4. The phrase *"And your alms are had in remembrance in the sight of God,"* points to a conclusion.

5. It does not mean that God forgets things, but that such *"remembrance,"* as here stated, refers to God doing something about the situation.

One must ever understand that God remembers both the bad and the good. In His Time, He rewards both accordingly!

As well, nothing escapes His attention, be it small or large! For every single thing done, all must know and understand that irrespective as to who does it or what is done, all *"are in the sight of God."* That should be a sobering thought!

(32) "SEND THEREFORE TO JOPPA, AND CALL HITHER SIMON, WHOSE SURNAME IS PETER; HE IS LODGED IN THE HOUSE OF ONE SIMON A TANNER BY THE SEA SIDE: WHO, WHEN HE COMES, SHALL SPEAK UNTO YOU."

The synopsis is:

1. The major sin of the modern church is that it has left the Cross of Christ.

2. The modern church has replaced the Cross with humanistic psychology. What a sorry trade!

THE ANGEL THAT SPOKE TO CORNELIUS

The phrase, *"Send therefore to Joppa, and call hither Simon, whose surname is Peter,"* presents the second time this has been related, and actually will be related a third time in Acts, Chapter 11. This tells us how significant all of this is in the Mind of the Holy Spirit.

The biggest mistake made by man, and even Christian man, is that too much importance is attached too often to the wrong thing. In the Mind of God, this thing that was now occurring was the single most important thing on Earth. It would have eternal consequences for good, which literally beggars description. And yet, the world had no knowledge at all as to what was happening, nor could they.

However, even more important, the Church, even though godly, had no knowledge whatsoever of what was taking place, except that which was given to Peter.

The Believer must constantly seek the Lord in order that he always have the Mind of the Lord. The worst thing is for God to be doing something grand and glorious, and the Church have no idea what is taking place. Even worse still, oftentimes, the church opposes that which God is doing. This happens when men get control of the church and, little by little, force out Christ as the Head. They therefore forfeit the Holy Spirit. Then it becomes a man-devised institution with no supernatural power. Consequently, nothing is done for God, with the church at that stage becoming the greatest enemy to the Cause of Christ.

HE WILL TELL YOU WHAT YOU OUGHT TO DO

The Early Church, of course, was on fire for God at this particular time; however, even then, Peter had to explain fully. When the Apostles and those who knew them ultimately died, little by little the Church went into apostasy, which really began in the Second Century. By the Third Century, it was well on its way to total apostasy. Ultimately, it became what is now the Catholic church.

The phrase, *"He is lodged in the house of one Simon a tanner by the sea side,"* proclaims, as is obvious, that God knows where all are and at all times.

"Who, when he comes, shall speak unto you," referred to the way of Salvation made

clear by Peter as it was given to the house of Cornelius.

I wonder how many places there are in the world presently, how many cities, how many homes, and how many individual persons are waiting for the Preacher to come.

Peter was probably about the only one who could be sent at that time, who would fully obey the Lord, and whose decision would be accepted by the Church.

Is it possible at this present time that the Lord has no one He can send?

Is it possible that many who actually do go in one form or the other do not preach the Truth; or, if they do preach the Truth, how many truly are anointed by the Holy Spirit to do so?

(33) "IMMEDIATELY THEREFORE I SENT TO YOU; AND YOU HAVE WELL DONE THAT YOU ARE COME. NOW THEREFORE ARE WE ALL HERE PRESENT BEFORE GOD, TO HEAR ALL THINGS THAT ARE COMMANDED YOU OF GOD."

The pattern is:

1. The phrase, *"Immediately therefore I sent to you,"* implies that such was done within the hour.

2. The phrase, *"And you have well done that you are come,"* actually means, even though it seems to be phrased another way, that they were so very pleased that Peter had come and that he came as soon as possible.

3. *"Now therefore are we all here present before God, to hear all things that are commanded you of God,"* tells us two things:

a. They were eager to hear what the Lord had for them.

b. They knew that Peter would speak only what God gave him to speak.

(34) "THEN PETER OPENED HIS MOUTH, AND SAID, OF A TRUTH I PERCEIVE THAT GOD IS NO RESPECTER OF PERSONS."

The account is:

1. The phrase, *"Then Peter opened his mouth, and said,"* proclaims, as simple as it was, a profound truth. The Gospel had now broken the bounds of Judaism despite the efforts of man to do otherwise; consequently, millions the world over would now come to Christ.

2. *"Of a truth I perceive that God is no respecter of persons,"* is not meant to be implied by Peter that this Truth was new, for it was not. The Old Testament recognized this Truth (II Sam. 14:14), but up to this time, Peter had applied it to Jews only and not Gentiles.

3. Now more than ever, Peter knew the meaning of the Vision he was given some two days before.

(35) "BUT IN EVERY NATION HE WHO FEARS HIM, AND WORKS RIGHTEOUSNESS, IS ACCEPTED WITH HIM."

The way is:

1. The phrase, *"But in every nation,"* means that whatever God accepts in a Jew, He also accepts in a Gentile.

If the things done were good in themselves, they were equally good whoever did them. God is no respecter of persons; therefore, He does not accept or reject one or another because of who he is but because of what he does (Eph. 6:8).

2. The rule is *"Glory, honor, and peace, to every man who works good, to the Jew first, and also to the Gentile:*

"For there is no respect of persons with God" (Rom. 2:10-11).

As well, the Holy Spirit through Peter said, *"In every nation,"* not *"In every religion,"* as corruptors of Truth assert.

3. The phrase, *"He who fears Him, and works righteousness, is accepted with Him,"* proclaims that all are judged on the same basis.

As well, Peter would explain momentarily what it means to *"work Righteousness,"* which can be accepted by God.

Actually, Cornelius was a perfect example of one who *"feared God"* and *"worked Righteousness."*

4. The phrase does not mean that one can earn Salvation irrespective of what he does. It does mean that Cornelius diligently sought the Lord, which God always honors. He was walking in all the Light he knew, even though that Light was woefully insufficient. To that kind, God always gives more.

In just a few moments, Cornelius would find the *"Righteousness"* that only God can give, and which comes without price.

(36) "THE WORD WHICH GOD SENT UNTO THE CHILDREN OF ISRAEL,

NOTES

PREACHING PEACE BY JESUS CHRIST: HE IS LORD OF ALL."

The form is:

1. Unless the Cross of Christ is understood, then the Lord cannot be properly understood.

2. Everything that God has for the Believer is opened up by the Cross.

THE WORD

The phrase, *"The Word which God sent unto the Children of Israel, preaching peace by Jesus Christ,"* refers to peace with God, which can only come by Jesus Christ.

Paul would later write, but which Peter already knew, *"But now in Christ Jesus you who sometimes were far off are made near by the Blood of Christ."*

Paul then said, *"For He is our Peace, Who has made both one, and has broken down the middle wall of partition between us"* (Eph. 2:13-14).

This simply meant that Jews and Gentiles are one in Christ (Rom. 1:16; 10:9-13; I Cor. 12:13; Gal. 3:28; Col. 3:11).

Sadly, *"The Word which God sent unto the Children of Israel,"* was rejected by Israel. They would not have the Message or the Messenger.

HE IS LORD OF ALL

The *"peace"* of which Peter here speaks, in the Greek Text is *"eirene"* and means *"to set at one again."*

Due to the Fall, man has no peace with God, which means there is a perpetual war between God and unregenerate man. However, upon coming to Christ, the enmity that is between God and man is removed, which sets things right again because *"peace with God"* is made.

This can be done only through Christ!

The phrase, *"He is Lord of all,"* tells us much about the Kingdom of God and how it operates.

Of the Triune Godhead, Jesus Christ is the One Who paid the price for man's Redemption by dying on the Cross. He alone satisfied the claims of Heavenly Justice, taking the curse of the Law upon Himself, which rightly should have come upon all of mankind. As well, He rose from the dead, thereby, defeating death, Hell, and the grave.

He ascended to the Father where He abides still, but immediately upon His arrival, He sent back the Holy Spirit, Who He had promised (Jn., Chpt. 16).

Inasmuch as Jesus is the One Who has done all of this, it is only through Faith in Him that one can be Saved (Jn. 3:16; Jn., Chpt. 10). Through Him alone we have access to the Father (Jn., Chpt. 16). He, as well, is the Baptizer with the Holy Spirit (Mat. 3:11), and it is through Faith in His Name that the sick are healed, demons expelled, etc. (Mk. 16:15-18; Acts 3:16). Jesus is also the Head of the Church (Eph. 1:19-23).

JESUS IS GOD

It is forgotten how great a change in the center of gravity in the conception of Christ's Person and Work was necessarily involved in the facts of Christ's Death, Resurrection, and Exaltation to the Right Hand of Power.

His Life is not ignored—far from it. Its influence breathes in every page of Paul's Epistles, as well as that of Peter and John.

However, the weakness, the limitations, the self-suppression—what Paul in Philippians 2:7 calls the *"emptying"*—of that earthly Life have now been left behind; the rejected and Crucified One has now been vindicated, exalted, and has entered into His Glory.

PETER'S FIRST ADDRESS AT PENTECOST

This is the burden of Peter's first address at Pentecost: *"God has made Him both Lord and Christ, this Jesus Whom you crucified"* (Acts 2:36).

Could anything look quite the same after that? The change is seen in the growing substitution of the Name *"Christ"* for *"Jesus"* and in the habitual speaking of Jesus as *"Lord."*

THE SIGNIFICANCE OF CHRIST'S PERSON

With belief in the Lordship of Jesus went necessarily an enlarged conception of the significance of His Person. The elements were all there in what the Disciples had

NOTES

seen and known of Jesus while on Earth (Jn. 1:14; I Jn. 1:1-3). However, His exaltation, not only through that Light upon His claims while on Earth—confirmed, interpreted, and completed them—but, likewise, showed the ultimate ground of these claims in the full Divine dignity of His Person.

He Who was raised to the Throne of Divine dominion; Who was worshipped with honors due to God only; Who was joined with the Father and with the Holy Spirit as, coordinately, the Source of Grace and Blessing must in the fullest sense be Divine.

NO SUCH THING AS AN HONORARY GODHEAD!

In that Jesus is Divine is the substance of everything taught about Him in the Epistles: His Preexistence (the Lord's own Words had suggested this in Jn. 8:58; 17:5), His share in Divine Attributes (eternity and eternal), in Divine Works (Creation, etc., I Cor. 8:6; Col. 1:16-17; Heb. 1:2; Rev. 1:8; 3:14), in Divine Worship (Phil. 2:9-11; Rev. 5:11-12), and in Divine Names and Titles (Heb. 1:8).

It is an extension of the same conception when Jesus is represented as the end of Creation—the *"Head"* in Whom all things are finally to be summed up (Eph. 1:10; Heb. 2:6-9). These high views of the Person of Christ in the Epistles are everywhere assumed to be that possessed by Christ.

JESUS AND HIS DEATH

Jesus had furnished His Disciples with the means of understanding His Death as a necessity of His Messianic Vocation, endured for the Salvation of the world; but it was the Resurrection and Exaltation that shed Light on the utmost meaning of this also.

Jesus died, but it was for sins. He was a Propitiation for the sin of the world (Rom. 3:25; I Jn. 2:2; 4:10). He was *"made sin"* for us, actually being made a Sin-Offering (II Cor. 5:21).

The strain of Isaiah, Chapter 53, runs through the New Testament teaching on this theme (I Pet. 1:19; 2:22-25). Jesus' own Word *"ransom"* is reproduced by Paul (I Tim. 2:6).

The song of the Redeemed is, therefore, *"You did purchase unto God with Your Blood men of every Tribe"* (Rev. 5:9).

NOTES

In view of this, is it wonderful that in the Apostolic Writings—not in Paul only, but also in Peter and John—the Cross should assume the decisive importance it does? Paul only works out more fully in relation to the Law and the sinner's Justification a Truth shared by all. He himself declares it, *"Justification by Faith,"* to be the common Doctrine of the Churches (I Cor. 15:3-4).

JESUS AND THE SECOND COMING

Jesus taught His Disciples to look for His Coming again, and connected with the Coming the Perfection of His Kingdom. Such is plain to every honest student of the Gospels.

As well, the Apostolic Church retained this feature of the Teaching of Jesus. In accordance with the Promise in Acts 1:11, it looked for the Glorious Reappearing of its Lord. The Epistles are full of this Hope. Even John gives it prominence (I Jn. 2:28; 3:2).

In looking for the Coming as something immediately at hand, the early Believers went even beyond what had been revealed, and Paul had to rebuke harmful tendencies in this direction (II Thess., Chpt. 2).

According to Paul's writings in II Thessalonians, Chapter 2, certain things had to come to pass before the return of Jesus to this Earth.

In I Thessalonians 4:16-17, Paul spoke of the Rapture of the Church, which must take place before the Second Coming of the Lord, with cataclysmic happenings taking place immediately after that event, as described in II Thessalonians, Chapter 2, as well as Revelation, Chapters 6 through 19.

This we do know: if Prophecy is already being fulfilled regarding the coming Great Tribulation and the advent of the man of sin, which will immediately precede the Second Coming, how much closer must the Rapture of the Church be!

Admitting that there are many diverse thoughts and interpretations concerning end-time events, still, the Second Advent of our Lord remains the great fixed event of the future, the event that overshadows all others. This tells us that ultimately

NOTES

Righteousness shall triumph, and the Kingdom of God shall come.

THE PERSON AND MINISTRY OF THE HOLY SPIRIT

Even though Jesus is the Head of the Church, and all things are done in His Name, still, it is through the Person, Agency, Office, and Ministry of the Holy Spirit in which all these things are carried out. This is overly prominent in the Book of Acts, which is to be the pattern for what the Church should be and how the Church should be!

In all of this, the Holy Spirit never thrusts forward Himself, but rather glorifies Christ at all times (Jn. 16:7-15).

In other words, *"No man can say that Jesus is the Lord, but by the Holy Spirit"* (I Cor. 12:3).

This means that those outside of Jesus, i.e., who are not Saved, and who cannot really tell Who Jesus actually is, do not really understand the Incarnation or His Supreme Role in Redemption.

Only one who is Saved, thereby, having access to the Holy Spirit, can understand these things (I Cor. 2:14).

(37) "THAT WORD, I SAY, YOU KNOW, WHICH WAS PUBLISHED THROUGHOUT ALL JUDAEA, AND BEGAN FROM GALILEE, AFTER THE BAPTISM WHICH JOHN PREACHED."

The construction is:

1. Due to the paucity of preaching on the subject, the Cross of Christ is all but extinct in modern churches.

2. Not understanding the Cross simply means that Believers do not understand their Salvation.

THAT WORD, I SAY, YOU KNOW

The phrase, *"That Word, I say, you know,"* refers to the Life and Ministry of Jesus, as well as His Death, Resurrection, and Ascension. Accordingly, He is *"Lord of all,"* referring to both Jews and Gentiles.

In effect, Peter was saying that what Jesus did and Who Jesus is was not merely pertaining to a *"Jewish religion"* but, in fact, was for the entirety of the world. So, he immediately lifted Cornelius and those present that day, as well as all others for that matter, into a world's sphere of Salvation, removing it from a local setting. It is clear that the Holy Spirit was pushing Peter in this direction, and for the obvious purpose and reasons.

Most religions are localized in the sense that they are predominant in certain parts of the world. For instance, Buddhism and Shintoism are pretty well ensconced in the Far East. Islam is based in the Middle East, with tentacles elsewhere.

Some have attempted to localize or socialize Christianity, claiming it is a *"white man's religion,"* which has mostly come from Islam. As well, others have claimed that Christianity is a *"Western Gospel."*

While it is certainly true that far more people in the West have accepted Bible Christianity, which has resulted in the greatest freedoms and prosperity ever known in the history of man, still, Christianity has its roots in Judaism and its beginnings in Israel. Consequently, as far as locality is concerned, its origin is in the Middle East.

THE FIRST CENTURY

The First Century saw the spread of Christianity to both Europe and Asia, but with greater success in Europe.

By the Third Century, it had begun to apostatize, which greatly weakened what Bible Christianity truly is. However, the Reformation, which began in the Sixteenth Century, began to open the door to the greatest Move of God the world had ever known, at least after the days of the Early Church. This broke the hold of paganistic Catholicism, with the Bible once again becoming the Standard and Criterion, instead of the Church.

Not counting Catholicism, which is really not Christian, there are approximately one billion people on the Earth presently who recognize Christ in some fashion, but with only a small percentage of that number being truly Saved.

If one adds Catholicism, the number is approximately two billion, which means that Christianity in one form or the other is ensconced throughout the entirety of the world.

GALILEE

"Which was published throughout all Judaea, and began from Galilee, after the baptism which John preached," speaks of the Introduction of Jesus by John the Baptist and the Ministry of Christ.

Consequently, the greatest Move of God ever known began in Galilee. Some 800 years previously, Isaiah had prophesied, *"Beyond Jordan, in Galilee of the nations.*

"The people who walked in darkness have seen a great Light: they who dwell in the land of the shadow of death, upon them has the Light shined" (Isa. 9:1-2). God manifest in the Flesh began to walk among men, not only bringing Words of Life such as Israel had never previously heard but, as well, healing the sick, casting out demons, and performing Miracles by the thousands.

John's baptism was the *"baptism of Repentance,"* which had to be preached before the Advent of the Ministry of the Son of God. And so it was!

(38) "HOW GOD ANOINTED JESUS OF NAZARETH WITH THE HOLY SPIRIT AND WITH POWER: WHO WENT ABOUT DOING GOOD, AND HEALING ALL WHO WERE OPPRESSED OF THE DEVIL; FOR GOD WAS WITH HIM."

The direction is:

1. The primary reason that Jesus came to this world was to die on Calvary.
2. Calvary was absolutely essential, that is, if man was to be redeemed!

THE ANOINTING

The phrase, *"How God anointed Jesus of Nazareth with the Holy Spirit,"* speaks of Jesus as a Man needing the Anointing of the Holy Spirit in order that these Works might be done.

As God, no Anointing was needed in any capacity. However, when God became Man, it was absolutely imperative that He have the Holy Spirit, Who would Anoint Him to carry out His Mighty Works.

The word *"anointed,"* as used here, in the Greek Text is *"chrio"* and means *"to designate or consecrate to an office or ministry."* It also means *"to smear or rub with oil,"* which speaks of the great help given by the Holy Spirit to carry out the functions of a particular office or ministry, in this case, preaching the Gospel, healing the sick, performing Miracles, and casting out demons.

On the Day of Pentecost, due to what Jesus did at Calvary and the Resurrection, the Holy Spirit came in a completely new dimension, in fact, taking up abode in Believers just as He had done with Jesus. As a result, Believers are to continue to preach the Gospel exactly as Jesus, and to heal the sick and cast out demons exactly as Jesus! It is the same Holy Spirit in both cases and, consequently, the same Anointing.

However, there is a difference in that *"God gives not the Spirit by measure unto Him,"* whereas no Believer can say such (Jn. 3:34).

Nevertheless, the Holy Spirit is so Powerful, being God Himself, that astounding Miracles can be performed by all Believers if they consecrate totally to God's Ways (Mk. 16:16-18).

SPIRIT-FILLED BELIEVERS

The *"Anointing,"* which is so graphically described here, is known and understood only by Spirit-filled Believers. Even then, the Holy Spirit must be allowed to have His total Way within one's life in order that the *"Anointing"* may be present and prevalent. To be frank, the Anointing of the Holy Spirit, which alone can bring about souls Saved and lives changed, as well as Healings and Miracles, is rare. Such is not the fault of the Spirit but of the individuals!

Also, those who do not believe, preach, or proclaim the Baptism with the Holy Spirit according to Acts 2:4, little understand the Anointing or even believe that it exists. Consequently, almost all things done in that capacity, as religious as they may be, constitute works of man only and are of no benefit to God or man. Only that which is done through the Person, Leading, Agency, Office, and Ministry of the Holy Spirit is truly of God.

The phrase, *"And with Power,"* does not refer to something in addition to, but rather a result of the Holy Spirit.

The Greek word for *"Power"* is *"Dunamis"* and means *"ability, abundance, and*

NOTES

might." It also carries the idea of a reproducing dynamo, meaning that the Source of this Power is in the Holy Spirit, Who was in Jesus. It is the same for all Believers!

The *"Anointing with Power"* is the great need of the modern church!

As we spoke of such without measure concerning Jesus, Isaiah tells us what that means. It speaks of the Sevenfold Spirit of the Lord resting upon Jesus:

1. The Spirit of the Lord
2. Of Wisdom
3. Of Understanding
4. Of Counsel
5. Of Might
6. Of Knowledge
7. Of the Fear of the Lord (Isa. 61:1-2).

This corresponds with that which John saw, *"Seven lamps of fire burning before the Throne, which are the Seven Spirits of God"* (Rev. 4:5).

No, this does not mean that there are seven Holy Spirits, but that *"seven"* denotes totality, completeness, absoluteness, infinity, all-in-all, the beginning and the end, and perfection.

DOING GOOD

The phrase, *"Who went about doing good,"* means that everything He did was good, with nothing being bad. So, why did they crucify Him?

His *"Good"* made their hypocritical bad very obvious. His Light revealed the darkness of the Pharisees and religious leaders of Israel. Consequently, they had a choice:

• They could repent, thereby, giving their hearts and lives to Him, which He would gladly have accepted and changed.

• They could stop Him, which they opted to do, but whether they realized it or not, could only do so with His Permission.

OPPRESSED OF THE DEVIL

The phrase, *"And healing all who were oppressed of the devil,"* enlightens us greatly as to the Mission of Christ.

The word *"oppressed"* in the Greek Text is *"katadunasteuo"* and means *"to overpower or control someone by force."*

Consequently, from this, we learn that Satan is the instigator of diseases, which agrees with Job 2:7 and Luke 13:16. A good example of its force is Exodus 1:13; 6:7.

Oppression does not have anything to do with sin being in the life of the Believer, although that may be the case. It refers to Satan, through his demon spirits, overcoming a person in various ways, whether with sickness, poverty, depression, etc.

Inasmuch as the root cause of these things is spiritual, they do not respond to psychology, any type of man-devised therapy, etc. They respond only to the Power of God.

Sadly, millions of Christians suffer oppression by Satan, even as uncounted numbers in Israel suffered the same fate.

The latitude held and taken by Satan, at least in most cases, is because of a lack of faith on the part of the Believer, or else, faith misplaced. Our Faith without fail must ever be on Christ and what He did for us at the Cross. It was at the Cross that every demon spirit was defeated, every fallen Angel defeated, and Satan himself defeated (Col. 2:10-15). The Cross of Christ alone is the answer and, in fact, the only answer for the sin problem. So, if Satan is oppressing you with the powers of darkness, which can cause many types of sicknesses, emotional disturbances, and nervous disorders, in other words, making life miserable, the only answer is the Cross of Christ. Unfortunately, the modern church has opted for humanistic psychology rather than the Cross. As a result, the situation grows worse by the day, for there is no help whatsoever in humanistic psychology.

The truth is, every single Believer has been troubled by spiritual oppression at one time or the other. There is a vast difference in *"oppression"* and *"possession."* No Child of God can be possessed by demon spirits, but the Child of God can most definitely be oppressed by demon spirits. As we have stated, the answer for this, and the only answer, is the Cross of Christ.

FOR GOD WAS WITH HIM

The phrase, *"For God was with Him,"* presents a given, for the Holy Spirit will not anoint error or sin.

In other words, for the person who is

truly anointed to preach the Gospel, etc., and such *"Anointing"* being obvious resulting in *"much Fruit,"* this automatically says to all that this Preacher is not functioning in error, nor does he (or she) have unconfessed sin within his or her life. There is no higher sanction than the Holy Spirit. Unfortunately, the Holy Spirit is little the criterion in most church circles, but rather silly rules made up by men.

Conversely, many claim the Holy Spirit and His Anointing but without any evidence, or else, much evidence is claimed but with no substance.

The Church must recognize those who are Called of God! If not, they will soon find themselves totally controlled by man, even as the Jewish Sanhedrin of old!

(39) "AND WE ARE WITNESSES OF ALL THINGS WHICH HE DID BOTH IN THE LAND OF THE JEWS, AND IN JERUSALEM; WHOM THEY KILLED AND HANGED ON A TREE."

The pattern is:

1. The phrase, *"And we are witnesses of all things which He did both in the land of the Jews, and in Jerusalem,"* speaks of the Twelve Apostles chosen for that very purpose, among other things. They saw and observed all that He did!

2. Not only were the Twelve *"witnesses"* of all that Jesus did, but the entirety of Israel after a fashion were witnesses as well!

3. It is certain that Cornelius knew of Jesus, although he may not personally have heard Him speak, etc. What Jesus was doing and the possibility of Him being the Messiah were on the lips of all. He was the topic of most every conversation, so, in a sense, Cornelius was a witness also in that he was alive at that time and in the same general area of Jesus.

4. The phrase, *"Whom they killed and hanged on a tree,"* refers to the *"Sanhedrin,"* the religious leaders of Israel.

The word *"slew"* simply means, as is obvious, that they killed Him. They called it an execution because He, they claimed, had committed high crimes against God. However, God called it *"murder!"* (Acts 3:14-15).

The word *"hanged"* refers to being *"crucified."* The person is *"hung"* on the Cross and suspended there by nails or ropes, hence, *"hanged."*

The word *"tree"* stands for *"wood"* and is used to refer to any object made of wood, which spoke of the *"Cross."*

Peter seems to be using this word here rather than the ordinary word for *"crucify"* in order to emphasize the shamefulness of Christ's Death. It refers to Deuteronomy 21:23 and the curse there taken by Jesus.

The Romans sometimes crucified on an X-shaped Cross, but the fact that the inscription was placed over Jesus' Head shows that the usual *"T"* form of the Cross was used.

In essence, Peter was saying that this One Who did nothing but good and *"healed all who were oppressed of the devil"* was rewarded for this greatest good ever—having come to the world by being murdered in the most humiliating way possible—by being hanged on a Cross! Such is God and such is man!

(40) "HIM GOD RAISED UP THE THIRD DAY, AND SHOWED HIM OPENLY."

The form is:

1. *"Jesus Christ and Him Crucified,"* was the Message Paul preached.

2. It must be the Message that we preach as well!

THE RESURRECTION OF CHRIST

The phrase, *"Him God raised up the third day,"* is meant to announce several things:

- Peter was affirming the Resurrection of Christ, which is obvious. As well, Cornelius would accept Peter's statement without question. The reason was that the Angel had appeared unto Cornelius and had specified that he should send for Peter. So, he knew beyond the shadow of a doubt that Peter would not lie.
- As well, the Resurrection of Jesus was not some mere spiritual apparition, but rather the flesh and bone Body of Jesus that had been raised.
- The religious leadership of Israel was denying the Resurrection of Christ, claiming that His Disciples had stolen away His Body, and making it appear that He had been resurrected! Undoubtedly, Cornelius had heard these stories, etc.
- Furthermore, it was God Who raised

Jesus from the dead. So, if that, in fact, was true, which, of course, it was, this meant that Jesus was exactly Who He said He was, *"God manifest in the flesh"* (I Tim. 3:16).

Of course, if the religious leadership of Israel admitted that Jesus had indeed been resurrected, of which the proof was undeniable, then they would have to admit that He was not an impostor, etc. Therefore, irrespective as to how foolish were their stories, and in the face of a mountain of proper evidence, they must maintain that He was an impostor, or else, admit that they had murdered the Son of God.

THE DENIAL OF TRUTH

As we have alluded, denial of Truth is one of Satan's favorite tactics. Of course, he is always very subtle in this denial, most of the time causing the unspiritual heart to accept what he says.

Using our own Ministry as an example, that which the religious leaders did to Jesus, many of them continue to do. They are not concerned about how many people are Saved, baptized with the Holy Spirit, or delivered by the Power of God. As well, it doesn't matter to them about the Mighty Anointing of the Holy Spirit, which, within itself, is proof positive. They will not and, in fact, cannot admit that it is of God because in so doing, they would admit their wrong. Therefore, they continue to maintain their charade. However, that poses a distinct problem, as should be overly obvious.

To deny that which is of God is to deny God! There is no way that one taking such a tact can spiritually survive.

Sadly and regrettably, I have watched most of the Pentecostal denominations in America spiritually deteriorate until there is not much left.

PROCLAIMING CHRIST OPENLY

The phrase, *"And showed Him openly,"* means that Jesus revealed Himself after the Resurrection to quite a number of people. Paul speaks of such in I Corinthians 15:4-8. Of course, the four Gospels portray these Appearances.

However, the Lord only revealed Himself to Believers and not at all to unbelievers.

NOTES

In fact, before His Death and Resurrection, He revealed Himself as Messiah to a strange assortment of people, but not at all to the religious leaders of Israel.

For instance, He revealed Himself as the Messiah to a fallen woman (Jn. 4:25-26), and, as well, to a beggar (Jn. 9:35-38). Of course, such was revealed to His close Followers.

The point is that He did not reveal Himself whatsoever to unbelievers in any capacity, irrespective of their religious status, and neither does He reveal Himself to such presently.

Everything God does is open, aboveboard, obvious, and straightforward. The Resurrection of Christ was not something hidden, something mystical, or something merely spiritual.

(41) "NOT TO ALL THE PEOPLE, BUT UNTO WITNESSES CHOSEN BEFORE OF GOD, EVEN TO US, WHO DID EAT AND DRINK WITH HIM AFTER HE ROSE FROM THE DEAD."

The account is:

1. The phrase, *"Not to all the people,"* bears out what I have just said.

To be sure, He could easily have revealed Himself after the Resurrection in any way that one could think. He could have done so accompanied by multiple thousands of Angels, telling Jerusalem that He was risen from the dead, and then accompany His claim with a great spectacle. However, He did not do that because it would have been terribly wrong.

2. The phrase, *"But unto witnesses chosen before of God,"* refers to those who had Faith in Him and believed.

The word *"witnesses"* in the Greek Text is *"martus"* and means *"one who is a martyr."*

This speaks of one who is willing to lay down his life for what he believes, in other words, to become a *"martyr"* if necessary.

In truth, the Believer's life is to be so totally given over to the Lord that, in effect, he is already a *"martyr,"* hence, Paul calling himself *"a prisoner of Jesus Christ"* (Phile., Vs. 1).

3. The phrase, *"Even to us, who did eat and drink with Him after He rose from the dead,"* proclaims that Jesus was not a spirit

or mere apparition, but rather real, physical, and alive. As such, He ate food, drank water and grape juice, etc.

4. The idea of all of this is not only to portray the veracity of the Resurrection of Christ to Cornelius but, as well, to proclaim the fact that he (Peter) was an eyewitness of all these things. In addition, that which he witnessed, even as here stated, was irrefutable.

5. We also learn something about how God works. Millions around the world flippantly say that if the Lord would appear to them, etc., they would believe. However, Jesus Himself refuted that claim when He told of Abraham addressing the rich man who went to Hell, and had asked that one be sent back from the dead in order to convince his brothers, etc. Jesus responded by saying, *"If they hear not Moses and the Prophets, neither will they be persuaded, though one rose from the dead"* (Lk. 16:31). The Lord does not perform stunts or resort to circus acts in order to convince jaded sarcasm, but rather responds to Faith, and Faith only!

(42) "AND HE COMMANDED US TO PREACH UNTO THE PEOPLE, AND TO TESTIFY THAT IT IS HE WHICH WAS ORDAINED OF GOD TO BE THE JUDGE OF THE QUICK (LIVING) AND DEAD."

The direction is:

1. The Early Church was founded on the Message of the Cross.

2. Now the Holy Spirit is bringing this Message full circle. In other words, as the Church came in, it will go out.

PREACHING THE GOSPEL

The phrase, *"And He commanded us to preach unto the people,"* presents God's Way of spreading the Gospel.

Paul said, *"For after that in the Wisdom of God the world by wisdom knew not God, it pleased God by the foolishness of preaching to save them who believe"* (I Cor. 1:21).

Paul's statement actually refers to the fact that men cannot understand God or be Saved through the intellectual route. To be frank, were that the case, precious few people would be Saved.

However, the Lord deals with man on the simple basis of Faith, which anyone can have—rich, poor, educated, uneducated, great or small, etc.

NOTES

JESUS CHRIST IS THE JUDGE

The phrase, *"And to testify that it is He which was ordained of God to be the Judge of the quick* (living) *and dead,"* tells us several extremely important things:

- Jesus Christ is the One *"ordained"* by God to serve as Judge of the living and the dead. Consequently, when men stand before God, they will not be judged by Buddha, Confucius, Muhammad, Joseph Smith, or any other fake luminary, but rather by Jesus Christ.

Even though the world pays precious little heed to this statement, it is something they had better heed because as certain as is that which is certain, all will stand before Jesus Christ.

- Jesus is now the Saviour, but then He will be the *"Judge."*

So, whatever decision man makes, he still must deal with Jesus Christ. He deals with Him as Saviour, or he will deal with Him as Judge. This is an appointment that will be kept.

- All will face this appointment, both the *"quick* (living) *and dead."* This speaks of the unnumbered millions who have lived and died, even with death itself unable to abrogate this coming appointment.

This actually pertains to the *"Great White Throne Judgment"* as outlined in Revelation 20:11-15.

Even though Peter only briefly alludes to this tremendously important subject of judgment, what he did say is absolutely riveting. It deserves a little more treatment.

THE LAST JUDGMENT

In Christian Theology, the Last Judgment (Rev. 20:11-15) is an act in which God interposes directly into human history, brings the course of this world to a final close, determines the eternal fate of human beings, and places them in surroundings spiritually adapted to their final condition.

WHEN THIS JUDGMENT WILL BE

The Great White Throne Judgment will take place after the Millennium and the revolt of Satan, for immediately after these events (Rev. 20:1-10), John saw a Great White Throne occupied by God from Whose Face the Earth and Heaven fled away. This is, no doubt, the same Throne seen throughout the Book of Revelation; however, here is the only place that a description of the Throne is given.

God, the Occupant of the Throne, is described previously, but the Throne itself is not.

It will be at this Throne that all unbelievers, for all time, will stand. This speaks of everyone who has ever lived in all of history, but will not include Believers, whomever they may have been, and whenever they may have lived. Believers allowed their sins to be judged at Calvary, and as a result, such sins can never be held against them anymore.

WHO WILL BE THE JUDGES?

As we have already stated, God has ordained that His Son, the Lord Jesus Christ, will be the Judge.

However, God the Father will serve as the Foundational Principal of all judgment meted out by His Son (Acts 17:30-31; Rom. 2:12-16; Heb. 12:23-24; Rev. 6:10).

In actuality, God the Father will decree, and the Son will execute (Jn. 5:22-27; Rom. 1:32-2:5).

THE BASIS OF JUDGMENT

A man who passes through this judgment (and all unredeemed will and for all time) will have no excuse or criticism of the sentence passed, regardless of what the decision will be, for, in a sense, he will be his own judge.

The actual manifestation of his failure to live up to his conscience, the Law or the Gospel, the fact that his sins and misdeeds are like mountains before him in his conscience and in his character, and the absence of his name in the Book of Life will automatically condemn him.

The *"Books"* mentioned in Revelation 20:12 refer to two things. They are:

1. These Books contain a record of every single thing done by every individual for all time. The only thing that can be erased from these Books is our sins, which takes place upon our Repentance before the Lord.

2. These Books will also contain the Word of God, which is to judge man in the Day of Judgment. In other words, it will be the Law in proverbial black and white.

NOTES

THE LENGTH OF THE JUDGMENT

The judgment passed upon each individual at this particular time will be eternal. All will be cast into the Lake of Fire, for no Believers will appear at the Great White Throne Judgment.

The same terms that are used in describing the eternity of God are used in describing the eternity of Hell, so if one is eternal, the other one must be as well (Isa. 66:22-24; Mat. 5:22, 29-30; 10:28; 13:42, 50; 18:9; Heb. 6:2; 10:26-31; Rev. 14:9-11; 19:20; 20:10-15; 21:8).

(43) "TO HIM GIVE ALL THE PROPHETS WITNESS, THAT THROUGH HIS NAME WHOSOEVER BELIEVES IN HIM SHALL RECEIVE REMISSION OF SINS."

The construction is:

1. The only means of Salvation is Faith in Christ and what He did for us at the Cross.

2. Without the Cross there could be no Salvation.

THE WITNESS

The phrase, *"To Him give all the Prophets witness,"* simply means that He fulfilled all these Prophecies, which He could not have done had He not been the Messiah.

In effect, the entirety of the Old Testament pointed to Jesus. He was the True Tabernacle and the True Temple just as He was the True Israel. As well, He is the True Man and the True Church. Everything is in Him, of Him, by Him, and through Him.

He was the subject of the very first Prophecy (Gen. 3:15), and is the Fulfillment of the last Prophecy (Rev. 22:20-21), for He will be the One Who comes in Power and Glory!

The religious leaders of Israel gave Him no *"witness"* at all, but the Prophets did! That is what makes the sins of these religious leaders so diabolical! From the Prophets, they knew Who He was and was to be, and had they bothered to investigate, they would have seen that He met all criteria.

He was Virgin-born as prophesied by

Isaiah (Isa. 7:14). He was the Son of David as prophesied by the *"sweet singer of Israel"* (II Sam., Chpt. 7). He was the Suffering Messiah as prophesied in Isaiah, Chapter 53. As well, He will be the One Who will fulfill the Prophecy of Malachi, *"But unto you that fear My Name shall the Sun of Righteousness arise with Healing in His Wings"* (Mal. 4:2).

THROUGH HIS NAME

The phrase, *"That through His Name,"* tells us that the entirety of the Gift of God, as it pertains to Salvation, Eternal Life, the Baptism with the Holy Spirit, Divine Healing, Deliverance, and all forgiveness of sins, are wrapped up in Jesus Christ and what He did at Calvary. Consequently, all are done in *"His Name!"*

As well, this tells us that the coming judgment, of which Peter had just spoken, need not trouble any Believer, for all sins to them have been washed clean by the Blood of Jesus Christ and Faith in His Name.

"Whosoever believes in Him shall receive remission of sins," proclaims, without a doubt, the greatest statement ever made by man!

The Greek word for *"remission"* is *"aphesis"* and means *"freedom, deliverance, forgiveness."*

A CORRECT CONCEPTION

The correct conception of sin is necessary if we are to grasp at all the Biblical idea of how man is to be delivered.

Life for man and for society is to be found in the right relation to God (Jn. 17:3), and cannot be found outside that right relation. Sin is:

- A break with God.
- Rejection of His loving Purpose for the creature.
- Wrong relation to one's fellowman.
- Opposition to the Law of God given to His Creation.
- Perversion of man's own powers and laws of development, involving moral and spiritual death. At best, it is a thoughtless content with a low moral level of self-indulgence, which has implicit at the heart of its self-deification opposition toward God and man as one's brother. In other words, sin is:

- Directed against God.
- Is a glorification of self.

ONLY GOD CAN REMOVE SIN

The Biblical idea is that God Himself must take away the guilt and become the first Mover in bringing man back into harmony with Himself, hence, the idea of Atonement, Justification, and Redemption, all made possible by the Cross, and the Cross alone!

Consequently, the Bible portrays the idea of a burden laid on the conscience so that only by pardon can a man get peace and the right to forget (Rom. 5:1). Indeed, the whole conception of Salvation, whether as changed status before God, or as a complete inner change in the sinner at the beginning or in the continuance of his new life, is conceived through this conception of the actual nature and tendency of sin.

SALVATION ORIGINATES IN THE LOVE OF GOD

The whole process of saving the sinner, originating in the Love of God (Jn. 3:16), centers in Christ. His Life, particularly His Death, produces Atonement and Reconciliation of God's Wrath against the sinner and of the sinner's fear of God (Rom. 5:1-11); brings the new knowledge of God to minds darkened by sin (Jn. 1:18); imposes on the will the new motives that cause Repentance, Faith, and love (Gal. 2:19-20; Rom. 5:11); supplies continuous stimuli for the new life to turn from sin (Rom. 8:12); and gives Power and Guidance through the Spirit (Rom. 8:5, 26).

Indeed, it is Christ living, dying, and risen to live forevermore, Who supplies the Spirit that by Regeneration makes possible the new life in its beginning, continuance, and consummation (Mat. 3:11; Acts 2:33; Rom. 6:4-14).

It is, therefore, *"in Christ,"* that is, through being united with Him, with our Faith and trust placed in Christ and the Cross alone, that sin is overcome in the individual (Rom. 8:2; II Cor. 5:17; Eph. 2:10; Col. 3:4); and from union with Him results the union and fellowship of Believers in the

NOTES

NOTES

Kingdom (I Cor. 10:17; I Jn. 1:3).

THE NECESSITY OF CONVERSION

In the reception and experience of Salvation by the individual, the nature of sin makes necessary the experience of Conversion, involving Repentance and Faith.

For those who truly understand Salvation, as it is given by Christ, it is a conscious change of the whole self, from a self-centered life to a Christ-centered life. Such involves a change in material judgments, standards, affections, and attitude; all of which are very clear in all Biblical Words describing this subjective change. I speak of conviction, Repentance, Conversion, and Faith.

Conviction means new Light on our own life in view of God's Judgment, while Repentance means acceptance of this Judgment so that we have a *"new mind"* on the matter, with concern and grief.

Conversion means a turning away from sin, which is Repentance, but also a turning to God. Faith means reliance, trust, and love.

This is exactly the change of attitude of the total self, which is a reversal of what sin makes a man. No doubt, the degree of emotional upheaval depends on the individual's past aberration and on the standards, socially mediated, of what is considered proper Conversion.

However, irrespective of what the social mores may dictate or what the standards of the world may be, the Biblical view considers Conversion as a conscious crisis, which means that one breaks with sin. For that reason, the Bible presents Repentance and Conversion as duty, making appeal to the whole self.

Even though the Law and the Gospel are recognized as instruments in Conversion, still, the real cause is God Himself (Jn. 1:13), and the real Object to Whom man turns is Christ Jesus (I Pet. 1:8; Rom. 3:22).

REMISSION OF SINS

The Remission of sins, as should be obvious, is not a simple thing. God could not decree such by fiat, as He has done many things. For instance, He said, *"Let there be light: and there was light"* (Gen. 1:3), but He could not say, *"Let there be Redemption, and there was Redemption,"* and be true to His Nature.

For Remission of sins to be effected, God would have to become Man and do what the first man Adam did not do.

He would have to be virgin-born in order to escape original sin and would have to live a perfect life, which Jesus did. Then this perfect Body, unstained by sin, could be offered up as a Sin-Offering, which would satisfy the claims of Heavenly Justice, which it did! That's why the Cross is so very, very important!

Jesus would then have to be raised from the dead in order to ratify that which was done by His Death. Inasmuch as He had no sin within Himself, Satan had no claim on Him, and neither did death or Hell. Consequently, He overcame death and Hell and rose from the dead.

FAITH IN HIM

To receive Remission of sins, the only requirement is to *"believe"* (Jn. 3:16; Rom. 10:9-10, 13).

That means to believe that one is a sinner, in other words, I am what God says I am. As well, one must believe that one cannot save oneself or, for that matter, do anything within one's own ability to effect Salvation of any kind or nature.

The sinner must believe that Jesus is the Son of God, died for man's sins, and rose from the dead. He must have Faith in what Jesus did, throwing himself totally and completely on the Mercy and Grace of God.

In other words, Jesus took the penalty the sinner should have taken but did not stop there. To those who believe, He takes all the sin and guilt away and, on top of that, gives Eternal Life.

In all of this, the Cross is the central focus; however, when we speak of the Cross, we aren't speaking of the wooden beam on which Jesus died, but rather what our Lord accomplished at Calvary's Cross. There He atoned for all sin, past, present, and future, at least for all who will believe (Jn. 3:16). This means that Satan has no more legal right to hold man in bondage. It was sin that gave him that legal right but with all sin atoned, Satan has no more legal ground on which to stand. So, if men die and go to Hell, it will simply be because they do not believe in that which Jesus did.

If Christians live in spiritual bondage to some sin or the other, it is because they too will not trust what Christ did at the Cross. In other words, for the Believer to have total victory, the Believer must place his or her Faith exclusively in Christ and what Christ did at the Cross, and it must be maintained in Christ and the Cross, even on a daily basis (Lk. 9:23; Rom. 6:1-14; 8:1-11; I Cor. 1:17-18, 23; 2:2; Gal. 6:14; Col. 2:10-15).

(44) "WHILE PETER YET SPOKE THESE WORDS, THE HOLY SPIRIT FELL ON ALL THEM WHICH HEARD THE WORD."

The exegesis is:

1. The Cross of Christ is literally the Foundation of every Bible Doctrine.

2. Unfortunately, humanistic psychology has taken the place of the Cross of Christ in modern church circles.

THESE WORDS

The phrase, *"While Peter yet spoke these words,"* signals one of the greatest moments in human history.

"Words" in the Greek Text is *"Rhema"* and means *"something spoken or commanded."* However, it is not just anything spoken or commanded, but rather is the Word of the Lord directed to a particular situation or person. I think that comes under the heading of *"command"* and, therefore, does not do violence to the Text.

The Word of the Lord, inasmuch as it is the Word of the Lord, is alive within itself, but is designed to be energized by the Holy Spirit, as it here was. However, it goes much further than that!

Knowing what is needed, the Spirit of God not only energizes the *"Word"* but more particularly, energizes it toward the person(s) or situation in question. In this case, it was Cornelius and his household.

But yet, that does not mean that what Peter said that day was intended only for Cornelius. In fact, it was intended for the entirety of mankind and for all time. However, knowing the hunger of the heart, the Holy Spirit energized it specifically at that moment for Cornelius and his household as if the Lord had done all of this specifically for him, which, in a sense, he had.

That explains you as a Believer reading the Word of God, or else, hearing it preached, with, all of a sudden, the Holy Spirit energizing some part of it directly to you, which instantly meets a need within your life, whatever it may be. I think one could say and be grammatically correct, at least regarding the Greek, that it is a *"Rhema Word"* especially for you, even as it was for Cornelius and his household.

WHOSOEVER

The word *"whosoever"* in the Forty-third Verse is emphatic and is intended so by the Holy Spirit. This states that Jew or Gentile can believe with the same results.

It also tells us that both male and female are on the same level, irrespective of one's sinful past and how bad it has been. If they *"believe,"* all sins will be remitted.

As the song says, *"Whosoever meaneth me!"*

The phrase, *"The Holy Spirit fell on all them which heard the Word,"* presents a spectacular moment, to say the least.

The Holy Spirit waited until Peter made this great statement concerning the Deity and Supremacy of Christ and, in effect, that He died for all, and that Faith in Him would wash the sinner clean. At that moment, He burst like an explosion in that room. Several things are here said and done, of which we should take note:

The Forty-third Verse proclaims the Salvation Message being delivered first of all, and with Cornelius and his household receiving it. What they said or did at this time, we are not told, but possibly, little or nothing concerning outward expression. Faith must begin in the heart, and accordingly, a person can be Saved by simply believing without saying a word. Of course, whether moments later or shortly, the person will confess Jesus Christ publicly (Rom. 10:9-10).

My own personal experience was pretty much in the same manner. I was Saved without really saying a word except in my heart. However, the moment I said *"yes"* in my heart, I was Saved, and to be sure, I knew it beyond the shadow of a doubt and confessed it publicly very shortly.

THE HOLY SPIRIT

The Holy Spirit fell on them, which could not have been so if they had not already been made clean by the Precious Blood of Christ. He can only come into Saved hearts and, therefore, cleansed vessels (Jn. 14:17).

So, they accepted Christ in their hearts as Peter ministered, and immediately the Holy Spirit fell.

He did not fall on some of them, but rather *"all of them,"* which means that all that day in the house of Cornelius had given their hearts to Christ and were now candidates for the Holy Spirit, which they received as well.

The Salvation they received upon believing the Word is totally different than the Infilling of the Holy Spirit, which took place moments afterward. They are two different experiences altogether and may be received at two different times or immediately after Salvation as here!

However, as we have stated, for the Holy Spirit to come into the heart and life of a person, that person must first have been Saved by the Blood of Jesus, which makes one clean and is called *"Sanctification."* Then the Heavenly Father declares the person *"not guilty,"* which can only come after Sanctification and is referred to as *"Justification"* (I Cor. 6:9-11). In other words, one must be *"made clean"* before one can be *"declared clean."*

Of course, those things that we have just mentioned pertain to Salvation and are carried out by the Lord in their entirety. They are received strictly by Faith, and received instantly. This makes one *fit "for an habitation of God through the Spirit"* (Eph. 2:22).

THE WORD

The *"Word"* they heard pertained exclusively to Salvation and how there was no discrimination. If Peter had mentioned anything previously about them being baptized with the Holy Spirit, the Scripture does not say. Actually, he probably did not.

NOTES

Their great need was Salvation, which He readily delivered unto them through the Word of God. However, irrespective that it seemingly had not been preached, the Holy Spirit fell on them anyway, and they were all filled.

This entire episode tells us that it is impossible to put God in a box, demanding that He do certain things in a certain way all the time. For instance:

- Every indication is that these people were Saved by simply believing in their hearts what Peter was saying, and not saying anything at the moment.
- The Holy Spirit fell on them, seemingly without them having any information respecting this Gift of God.
- They were baptized in water after being Saved and baptized with the Holy Spirit, when normally Water Baptism follows Salvation, with the Baptism in the Holy Spirit coming afterward. However, as we see here, the time element for Water Baptism is not that important simply because the ordinance within itself contains no saving grace. The idea is that one be baptized in water as soon as possible, whether after Salvation or after being baptized with the Holy Spirit.
- All of these Gentiles spoke with other Tongues exactly as did all the Jews on the Day of Pentecost.
- The Holy Spirit fell at a certain time while Peter was preaching, with the people instantly being filled with the Spirit.

One would not say that the Holy Spirit interrupted Peter because it was the Holy Spirit Who was anointing Peter to say these things, and even telling him what to say. So, the Holy Spirit does not and, in fact, cannot interrupt Himself.

FOLLOWING THE HOLY SPIRIT

The idea is that no set protocol was followed, but this Move of the Holy Spirit did not bother Peter at all simply because he was flowing with the Spirit. Therefore, what was done was in perfect order, as the Holy Spirit will always be in perfect order. It is people who get out of order, not the Spirit.

I suppose the question should be asked as to how most preachers would fare with the Holy Spirit this prevalent in their respective services.

Some few would be right at home, with most, I fear, totally nonplussed, consequently, having no idea of what to do. Of course, sadly, the Holy Spirit is little present in the services of such preachers, etc., and the truth is, absolutely nothing is done in the hearts and lives of those who are present. Such is a futility and a waste as it regards time, etc. And yet, this constitutes by far most churches in America, and for that matter, around the world.

Countless times I have seen the Holy Spirit basically do similar things in our Services, even as the Tenth Chapter of Acts portrays.

A Spirit-instigated and Spirit-led service is the single most wonderful thing that could ever begin to happen. Lives are changed! Believers are baptized with the Holy Spirit! Sick bodies are healed, and people are delivered!

If that is not the case, and it is not in most religious circles, very little, if anything, is done for the Lord. It is only where the Holy Spirit has total access to the Preacher and the people that one can see mighty things done for God. That is Church!

(45) "AND THEY OF THE CIRCUMCISION WHICH BELIEVED WERE ASTONISHED, AS MANY AS CAME WITH PETER, BECAUSE THAT ON THE GENTILES ALSO WAS POURED OUT THE GIFT OF THE HOLY SPIRIT."

The synopsis is:

1. Every Believer has what he has, whatever that is, all because of the Cross of Christ.

2. If the Cross of Christ is ignored, as it is in most modern churches, then absolutely nothing is done for the Lord.

THE GENTILES AND THE HOLY SPIRIT

The phrase, *"And they of the circumcision which believed were astonished, as many as came with Peter,"* refers to the six Jews who accompanied him from Joppa.

Why were they astonished?

The phrase, *"Because that on the Gentiles also was poured out the Gift of the Holy Spirit,"* proclaims the reason for their astonishment.

NOTES

The question in Galatians 3:2 is here answered. Cornelius did not receive the Holy Spirit on the principle of works, but on the opposing principle of Faith.

Notwithstanding all the teaching they had received from the Lord and from the Holy Spirit through the Scriptures, it seems that these Jews from Joppa were amazed that the Holy Spirit should indwell Gentiles.

Had Cornelius and his friends refused to believe on the Lord Jesus Christ, and declared that they preferred to trust for Salvation to their own praying and almsgiving, they would have received neither their Remission of sins nor the Gift of the Holy Spirit.

The action of the Holy Spirit following upon belief in Christ, contrasted with the religious activities recorded in Verses 2, 4, 22, and 30, confirms the fundamental Doctrine that entrance into the Kingdom of God is not through works of Righteousness but through Faith in Jesus Christ (Titus 3:5, 7).

FALLEN FROM THE TRUTH

The thing that astonished the Jews so much at this time was actually twofold in concept:

1. As stated, these were Gentiles, who no Jew thought could receive anything from God, but they had received because of simple Faith in Christ Jesus, which is the very Foundation of all that one is in Christ.

However, the Jews had fallen so far from the Truth that it affected even the godly ones, as these actually were, and for the obvious reasons.

2. As well, not only were these people Gentiles, but they had not laboriously attempted to keep the Law of Moses with all of its Feast Days, Sabbaths, and sacrifices.

In fact, the great controversy began here this day, but not with those present. It seems that, even though they were astonished, the Jews readily accepted, and gladly so, what the Lord had done.

However, as time went on, the Law/Grace controversy threatened the entirety of the fabric of the Church. Many who truly believed in Christ also insisted that Followers of Christ must also keep the Law of Moses. They claimed that Jesus was the

NOTES

Completeness and Fulfillment of the Law, and consequently, the Law must remain in force along with Christ.

PAUL

Paul fought this with all his strength, as we shall later see. He insisted that Salvation is by Faith alone, with nothing that needed to be added and, in fact, nothing could be added. A lesser man than Paul probably would not have been able to stem the tide, but God gave him the strength to stand firm, insisting on Justification by Faith alone, with nothing added, even the great Law of Moses.

It is amazing, but if the detractors of Grace had only looked closely at this experience with Peter and Cornelius, understanding that the Holy Spirit orchestrated everything, there should not have been any problem respecting this issue. Everything was freely given to Cornelius and his household strictly on the merit of Faith, with nothing else added. What other proof was needed?

As well, it is the *"Gift of the Holy Spirit,"* which means it is something that cannot be earned or merited.

(46) "FOR THEY HEARD THEM SPEAK WITH TONGUES, AND MAGNIFY GOD. THEN ANSWERED PETER."

The overview is:

1. What is the flesh?

2. It is that which is indicative to any human being. It speaks of our talents, ability, education, motivation, etc.

3. While these things are necessary, the simple fact is, we cannot live for God by that means.

SPEAKING WITH TONGUES

The phrase, *"For they heard them speak with Tongues,"* presents exactly that, as stated, which took place on the Day of Pentecost.

The Greek tense indicates continuous action for both the speaking in Tongues and the magnifying or praising, extolling, exalting, and glorifying God.

The speaking with other Tongues as the Spirit of God gave the utterance was that which convinced Peter's associates that these Gentiles were truly Spirit-filled. Had that not been the case (the speaking with other Tongues), they would not have known they had been filled with the Spirit.

Has it changed from then unto now?

No! It is the same now as then and, in fact, always has been since Pentecost. One knows he has been baptized with the Holy Spirit, exactly as given here, when he speaks with other Tongues as the Spirit of God gives the utterance. Such is the initial physical evidence that one has been filled (Acts 2:4).

While there certainly are many other evidences, the speaking with Tongues is the only physical evidence given by the Lord that is instant, immediate, and totally of the Lord.

So, to repudiate such is to repudiate God and His Ways, which is foolish to engage.

The phrase, *"And magnify God,"* means they would stop speaking in Tongues momentarily and then continue to praise God in their natural language, magnifying His Name. Actually, this is obvious and happens constantly with Spirit-filled Believers.

One thing is certain: This was a happy time for this houseful of Gentiles, as well as for Peter and his associates. To be sure, anything that the Lord does, and He surely did this, is beautiful, wonderful, glorious, and edifying beyond compare. As we have stated, this is Church!

At this moment, Cornelius and all with him probably had little idea that this was the first time Gentiles had ever been Saved in this manner and baptized with the Holy Spirit. The evidence seems to be that Jewish Christians were still offering up sacrifices in the Temple, which the Lord now showed was pointless, considering the manner in which Cornelius and his people were Saved and Spirit-filled.

The Jewish Believers should have known that Jesus fulfilled all of these types and symbols, making them null and void; however, old habits die hard. Unless we too speedily criticize them, I wonder if we are not also hung up ourselves on things that are not too pleasing to the Holy Spirit!

At any rate, the Temple would be totally destroyed in A.D. 70, which would make it impossible for the Jews to continue the rituals and ceremonies. Also, Churches before then were being established all over the Roman Empire, with most of the Converts being Gentiles and having little knowledge of the Mosaic Law, except that which interlopers brought in. As we have said, this was a constant difficulty for the Apostle Paul.

"Then answered Peter," presents the Apostle about to take another step, which proclaimed to all that Cornelius and his household were accepted into the Family of God without any reservations, despite the fact that they had not taken upon themselves the various rituals and ceremonies of Judaism.

(47) "CAN ANY MAN FORBID WATER, THAT THESE SHOULD NOT BE BAPTIZED, WHICH HAVE RECEIVED THE HOLY SPIRIT AS WELL AS WE?"

The overview is:

1. All Salvation is made possible by the Cross.

2. Sanctification, as well, is made possible by the Cross, and only by the Cross.

WATER BAPTISM

The question, *"Can any man forbid water, that these should not be baptized?"* was the step Peter would now take, signifying that all had been accepted.

Water Baptism is still the outward symbol that one has made Christ one's Saviour. To be sure, it adds nothing to one's Salvation, as should be overly obvious in this experience with Cornelius. However, it does serve a beautiful function in symbolizing the Death, Burial, and Resurrection of Christ. As well, it typifies the death of the old man and the new life of the new man in Christ Jesus, which takes place with all Believers. However, all must understand and realize that Water Baptism, as beautiful as it is and as significant as is its symbolism, it actually adds nothing to one's Salvation. In other words, one is not partially Saved until Water Baptism and then fully Saved after Water Baptism. Such foolishness is not taught in the Word of God, despite the fact that millions erroneously believe that way.

When Jesus died on Calvary and rose from the dead, all the terrible sin debt for all of humanity and for all time was totally and completely paid. Actually, it was paid to such an extent that no one, be he man, devil, or Angel, will ever be able to stand and say that the price was insufficient.

NOTES

THE CROSS

As well, the only requirement given in the Word of God for a person to take unto himself the tremendous benefits purchased by Christ at Calvary is Faith, but it must be Faith in Christ and the Cross. The Holy Spirit through Paul plainly said, *"For by Grace are you Saved through Faith; and that not of yourselves: it is the Gift of God: Not of works, lest any man should boast"* (Eph. 2:8-9).

Consequently, for anyone, be he preacher or otherwise, to claim that something must be added to the Finished Work of Christ in order for someone to be Saved, such as Water Baptism, the Lord's Supper, speaking in Tongues, joining the Church, etc., it can be labeled only as sin, and above that, a monstrous sin. It is an insult to Christ of the highest order and, in effect, is saying that He did not complete the task of Redemption and that it needs something added. I would hope the reader can understand the cause and reason for my strong statements. I think there is very little that is worse than that particular sin! Tragically, such sin is committed by the far greater majority of the modern church and, in fact, has always been a terrible problem.

Men are not satisfied with what God has done but strongly desire to add something to His Work or to delete from His Work. Actually, that was the cause of man's fall in the Garden of Eden. As well, it is the cause of almost all problems, and if one knew the total truth, the complete and total cause of every failure and affliction of the human family.

THE GREAT QUESTION

The conclusion of the question, *"Which have received the Holy Spirit as well as we?"* as asked by Peter, presents a beautiful conclusion that we should consider very seriously.

Understanding that this was a unique

situation, actually, the entrance of Gentiles into the Kingdom of God, still, we find that Peter judged their Salvation by the fact that they had been baptized with the Holy Spirit and spoke with other Tongues.

Peter knew, of course, that the Holy Spirit could not come into a polluted temple, such as characterizes all unsaved people, but can only come into the hearts and lives of those who have been thoroughly cleansed by the Precious shed Blood of Jesus Christ, and Faith in that Atonement.

Inasmuch as the Holy Spirit had definitely come into these people, which was proven by their speaking in Tongues, Peter judged the evidence to be undeniable.

The question I ask is this:

"How many churches in Christendom presently, irrespective of where they may be in the world, would judge accordingly?"

The truth is that a great percentage of churches, if not the majority, not only would not accept one who speaks with other Tongues, but would summarily dismiss him from their congregation, which is the very opposite of what Peter did! That should tell us something.

Many may presently argue that such was done then during the time of the Early Church but is not appropriate for now, inasmuch as it all passed away with the death of the Apostles, etc. Of course, such thinking is not only unscriptural, but flies in the face of a mountain of evidence otherwise.

These were accepted because they had received the Holy Spirit, said Peter, *"As well as we."* In other words, it was the same thing they had received on the Day of Pentecost.

With that being so, as to the millions who have presently been baptized with the Holy Spirit exactly as they were in the Early Church, the question needs to be asked as to why such is not valid presently, as many claim.

Of course, as should be obvious, these experiences are valid because they are totally Scriptural!

(48) "AND HE COMMANDED THEM TO BE BAPTIZED IN THE NAME OF THE LORD. THEN PRAYED THEY HIM TO TARRY CERTAIN DAYS."

NOTES

The diagram is:

1. The phrase, *"And He commanded them to be baptized in the Name of the Lord,"* simply meant, *"By the Authority of the Lord."*

2. As we have previously stated, when one is *"baptized in the Name of the Father, and of the Son, and of the Holy Spirit,"* at the same time, he is baptized in the Name of the Lord, as should be obvious (Mat. 28:19).

3. The word *"commanded"* is a strong word, which means that it will not tolerate any opposing view or allow that which is commanded to be deterred or to veer in another direction.

As well, the *"command"* given by Peter was not so much directed toward the method of Baptism, but rather the fact or the act of Baptism itself.

In other words, it is somewhat akin to a person about to join a Church and the Pastor addressing the congregation, asking if anyone has any reason this person should not be accepted. Then, at times, he will say, *"Speak now or forever hold your peace!"*

Peter, as the leader at this particular time, felt in his heart that he was following that which the Spirit of God wanted and desired, as he certainly was, and he would not be deterred, as he should not have been deterred. What God had accepted, and He definitely had accepted Cornelius and those with him, man should certainly accept as well! However, too oftentimes, what God accepts, men reject, and then at times, what men accept, God rejects!

4. The phrase, *"Then prayed they him to tarry certain days,"* presents that which is certainly understandable.

These people had just received the greatest Gift that anyone could ever receive, and I speak of Salvation by the Blood of Jesus and the Baptism with the Holy Spirit. Consequently, there was a joy in their hearts that words could not even begin to describe. In effect, the entirety of their world had changed and would remain changed forever.

5. As a result, they wanted Peter and those with him to remain there for some time, actually, as long as they would, it seems, to, no doubt, teach them more about the Word of God, and especially about Jesus.

Thus concludes the Tenth Chapter of Acts, which is a pivot point in the history of humanity. In fact, every single person who has ever come to Christ since then has been able to do so because the Lord opened up the entirety of the world to the great and glorious Gospel of Jesus Christ. He began with a Roman soldier, along with his family and friends. It was truly a red-letter day and will forever remain so.

As someone has said:

"God works in mysterious ways, His Wonders to perform,

"He plants His Feet upon the seas and rides upon the storms."

CHAPTER 11

(1) "AND THE APOSTLES AND BRETHREN WHO WERE IN JUDAEA HEARD THAT THE GENTILES HAD ALSO RECEIVED THE WORD OF GOD."

The overview is:

1. The phrase, *"And the Apostles and brethren who were in Judaea,"* refers to the Twelve other than Peter. It would have also included James, the Lord's Brother, even though he did not refer to himself as an Apostle.

The *"brethren"* pertained to the Elders in the Church in Jerusalem. All were Jews!

2. *"Heard that the Gentiles had also received the Word of God,"* proclaims the news of Cornelius and his friends and relatives receiving the Gospel. This was before Peter returned to Jerusalem. This type of news travels fast.

3. They learned that Peter was the one who took the Message to them, and they learned that it was eagerly received. However, this which seems so simple and open to us presently was a major hurdle at that particular time.

4. As we have repeatedly stated, the Jews normally had absolutely nothing to do with Gentiles, even looking down upon them with contempt and disdain.

5. While it was true that Cornelius had an excellent name respecting the Jews in Caesarea, still, for the most part, this in no way made him acceptable to strict Jews of that time. As we have already stated, the Followers of Christ, even some eight years after Pentecost, still considered themselves as people of the Law. I speak of the Law of Moses. To them, which would have included most, if not all, of the Elders and Apostles in Jerusalem, following Christ simply meant an extension of the Law, or rather a more completed Law. They in no way considered or understood, at least at this time, that the Law was completely fulfilled in Christ. As a result, to continue keeping the Sabbath and the Feast Days—plus a host of other rituals and ceremonies—was now pointless. However, they in no way understood such at this time. Of course, I am sure the reader understands that I am not speaking of the Jewish Sanhedrin, but rather the Apostles, Elders, and all Jewish Believers then in the Early Church.

6. When it says that *"the Gentiles had also received the Word of God"* at that time, the Apostles and brethren would not have agreed that such was the case, that is, if the Law of Moses was ignored, etc. It was a lesson they did not easily learn and as we have stated, had it not been for the later Ministry of Paul, it is doubtless that the struggling Church could have climbed this hurdle.

(2) "AND WHEN PETER WAS COME UP TO JERUSALEM, THEY WHO WERE OF THE CIRCUMCISION CONTENDED WITH HIM."

The exegesis is:

1. There is only one freedom from spiritual bondage, and that is the Cross of Christ (Gal. 5:1).

2. This means that every Believer who isn't looking to Christ and the Cross is someway in bondage. It cannot be otherwise (Gal. 5:1).

PETER

The phrase, *"And when Peter was come up to Jerusalem,"* presents a time of extreme significance.

I have every confidence that he was earnestly desirous of sharing the good news with the Church as to what had transpired regarding the Angel appearing to Cornelius, the Vision the Lord had given him, and his subsequent visit at the Command of the Holy Spirit to the home of Cornelius.

Whether he expected the opposition that he encountered is anyone's guess. However, in this encounter, we find how easy it is to be very sincere but, at the same time, be pulling against the Word and ways of God. Consequently, it is very serious, as should be obvious.

The phrase, *"They who were of the Circumcision contended with him,"* has reference to the following:

In fact, all were of the *"Circumcision"* because all were Jews, or else, proselytes; however, there were some who were much more contentious for the Law of Moses than others. It is these to whom the Text points.

The word *"contended"* in the Greek Text is *"diakrino"* and means *"to separate thoroughly, to discriminate."* It means, at least at the outset, that they were not accepting Peter's explanation, feeling he had made himself unclean by associating with Gentiles.

This is a perfect example of people taking a truth and turning it upside down. Even though these were Followers of Christ and had accepted Him as Israel's Messiah and their Saviour, still, despite all the things Jesus said concerning these very things, they were still bound by religion to such an extent that it was difficult for them to see the Grace of God.

RELIGION

As the Pharisees were more interested in their petty rules (which they had actually devised out of their own minds) than Jesus setting captives free, likewise, these Followers of Christ had a Pharisaic spirit, following in the same train. That is the reason that religion is the very worst bondage of all, even worse than alcohol, drugs, etc.

Actually, religion has sent more people to Hell than all the vices in the world put together. If Satan had had his way in that which he was very much attempting to do, Christianity would have been destroyed by this very thing, even as it was being born.

Following Christ was not an extension of the Law of Moses and, in fact, was not meant to be. The Law of Moses was another era altogether, which had served its purpose and now was to be replaced by the Grace of God.

That does not mean that the Law of Moses was wrong, for it was not. It was given by God and, consequently, was perfect. However, when it fulfilled its mission, which it did, it was to be set aside. I speak of the ritualistic and ceremonial parts of the Law and not the moral Law, which cannot change. Consequently, all of the Ten Commandments, with the exception of the Fourth concerning the Sabbath, were carried over into the New Covenant. For instance, stealing was wrong 5,000 years ago, was wrong when the Law was given about 1,500 years before Christ, and it is wrong now. These things that are of moral content never change. So, that part of the Law was brought over into the New Covenant and made a part of this great Covenant of Grace, bought and sustained by Jesus Christ.

CIRCUMCISION

The word *"Circumcision"* is here used regarding these people because that name, more than anything else, describes these contenders with Simon Peter.

Circumcision as a rule or Law was originally given to Abraham as a Covenant sign between him and God and, actually, the entirety of his seed, which would pertain to the Children of Israel (Gen., Chpt. 17). It was included, as well, in the Law of Moses (Lev. 12:1-3).

The Covenant of Circumcision was meant to portray separation, in other words, God's People, Israel, were separated from the rest of the world unto Jehovah. It spoke of them as a holy people, a people dedicated to God's Cause and Purpose, in other words, *"His People!"* Refusal to engage in this rite, in essence, said that the person or family did not belong to the Lord. Consequently, they were not to take this lightly.

THE SYMBOL

However, this rite was only a symbol of separation from the world unto God, which, to be effective, spiritually speaking, the heart must be circumcised as well!

Unfortunately, Israel gradually came to

NOTES

NOTES

link the Rite of Circumcision with Salvation, even as they did all the other rituals and ceremonies. So, whenever Luke used the term *"they who were of the Circumcision,"* he was speaking of Jews who had truly accepted Jesus as Saviour and the Messiah of Israel, but who, as well, believed that one must continue to keep the Mosaic Law, of which Circumcision was the major symbol. As is obvious, they were still hung up on rituals and ceremonies, which, within themselves, could not save anyone, make anyone holy, or actually affect anything within one's heart and life. As we have repeatedly stated, inasmuch as these things had been mere symbols, albeit important, they were now of no more purpose, considering that the One they symbolized, the Lord Jesus, had now come.

(3) "SAYING, YOU WENT IN TO MEN UNCIRCUMCISED, AND DID EAT WITH THEM."

The composition is:

Several things are here said:

- It is easily observed how these particular Jews linked Salvation almost exclusively with these rituals and ceremonies, giving Faith little credence, if any at all.
- Even though there is nothing mentioned about Peter and the others eating with Cornelius and his friends, it is obvious this did happen.

Going back some eight years to the Ministry of Christ, the Pharisees were very angry at Him because He ate with certain Jews who they called sinners, etc. His Answer to them was revealing, *"They that be whole need not a physician, but they that are sick"* (Mat. 9:12).

There is nothing in the Law of Moses which forbids eating with Gentiles! Actually, it insinuates the opposite.

Moses said, *"Circumcise therefore the foreskin of your heart, and be no more stiffnecked. He does execute the judgment of the fatherless and widow, and loves the stranger* (Gentiles)*, in giving him food and raiment."*

He then said, *"Love ye therefore the stranger* (Gentiles)*: for you were strangers in the land of Egypt"* (Deut. 10:16-19).

If it is to be noticed, there is a total absence in this setting of anything like Papal domination on the part of Peter, which debunks the claims of Catholicism of Peter being the first Pope, etc.

(4) "BUT PETER REHEARSED THE MATTER FROM THE BEGINNING, AND EXPOUNDED IT BY ORDER UNTO THEM, SAYING."

The structure is:

1. The phrase, *"But Peter rehearsed the matter from the beginning,"* proclaims the Apostle being very patient, and for cause.

2. Only a few days before, Peter had been of the same frame of mind. Therefore, he could empathize and carefully explain his position.

3. *"And expounded it by order unto them, saying,"* portrays him taking the entire episode step-by-step.

4. One cannot help but notice that the Holy Spirit had Luke to give a description of this entire episode two times. This was done for purpose, emphasizing the significance of what the Lord had done, and that all must be very careful to take heed.

(5) "I WAS IN THE CITY OF JOPPA PRAYING: AND IN A TRANCE I SAW A VISION, A CERTAIN VESSEL DESCEND, AS IT HAD BEEN A GREAT SHEET, LET DOWN FROM HEAVEN BY FOUR CORNERS; AND IT CAME EVEN TO ME."

The exegesis is:

1. In the phrase, *"I was in the city of Joppa praying,"* Peter proclaimed the spirituality of this moment. In other words, this was not something that happened out of his own mind, but it came about as he was seeking the Lord.

2. As well, and what makes it even more graphic, is that he was not seeking the Lord about taking the Gospel to Gentiles, but something else entirely. So, what took place was all of the Lord and none of Him.

3. *"And in a trance I saw a Vision,"* proclaims very readily the manner in which this thing was done and, as we have said, that it was all of the Lord and not due to desire on Peter's part, etc.

4. *"A certain vessel descend, as it had been a great sheet, let down from Heaven by four corners; and it came even to me,"* proclaims what he saw and that he knew

NOTES

it was meant for him. The Lord intended for him to see and understand the Message given explicitly for him, which would be made clear very shortly.

(6) "UPON THE WHICH WHEN I HAD FASTENED MY EYES, I CONSIDERED, AND SAW FOURFOOTED BEASTS OF THE EARTH, AND WILD BEASTS, AND CREEPING THINGS, AND FOWLS OF THE AIR."

The synopsis is:

1. The phrase, *"Upon the which when I had fastened my eyes,"* refers to what was done being meant for his eyes and that he must see it plainly, which he did!

2. The phrase, *"I considered,"* means that he inspected it closely, as he was meant to do.

3. The phrase, *"And saw fourfooted beasts of the Earth, and wild beasts, and creeping things, and fowls of the air,"* refers to animals, reptiles, and birds, all of which were unclean, meaning not fit for sacrifice or table food. As well, some of these creatures were dangerous, as would be obvious!

(7) "AND I HEARD A VOICE SAYING UNTO ME, ARISE, PETER; KILL AND EAT."

The pattern is:

1. The phrase, *"And I heard a Voice saying unto me,"* speaks of that which he knew to be the Voice of the Lord. As well, the tone was authoritative, actually, a Command. In other words, Peter had no choice in the matter, that is, if he was to obey God.

2. *"Arise, Peter; kill and eat,"* presents, as stated, an imperative Command. It was the same thing as a general speaking to a private. Those instructions are guaranteed to be followed immediately and to the letter.

So, none of this was a suggestion! It was a Command intended to be obeyed.

(8) "BUT I SAID, NOT SO, LORD: FOR NOTHING COMMON OR UNCLEAN HAS AT ANY TIME ENTERED INTO MY MOUTH."

The account is:

1. The phrase, *"But I said, Not so, Lord,"* proclaims the Apostle flatly refusing to obey. As the Lord's Command had been imperative, Peter's reply was very similar.

2. *"For nothing common or unclean has at any time entered into my mouth,"* proclaims his adherence to the Law of Moses.

3. Inasmuch as Peter knew beyond the shadow of a doubt that this was the Lord speaking to him, he should not have been so rash to answer as quickly as he did, which, as we shall see, was roundly rebuked.

4. He did not know exactly what the Lord was saying to him and as a result, should have approached it in another way.

5. And yet, under the same circumstances, I wonder if any of us would have done any better, or even as well.

(9) "BUT THE VOICE ANSWERED ME AGAIN FROM HEAVEN, WHAT GOD HAS CLEANSED, THAT CALL NOT YOU COMMON."

The way is:

1. The phrase, *"But the Voice answered me again from Heaven,"* proclaims a Message now being given by the Lord, which had far greater consequences than Peter at that moment even dared think or realize.

2. *"What God has cleansed, that call not you common,"* was not only an answer to Peter but, at the same time, presented the Message the Lord wanted given. He was speaking of Gentiles who would trust Him as Saviour, would have their sins washed clean by His precious shed Blood, and would accordingly be judged by God as *"clean."* However, at that time, Peter did not understand that, but would very shortly.

3. The Lord had chosen to use the symbolism of the unclean animals to portray the Message He wanted given. It would, in effect, address itself to the entirety of the Law. As we have stated, Peter would understand very shortly.

4. And yet, despite this plain example given by the Lord, which should have been understandable by anyone, and especially the Elders of the Church, this battle between Law and Grace would be fought for years. Paul would stand his ground, and because of that, the Gospel prevailed, but not without price!

(10) "AND THIS WAS DONE THREE TIMES: AND ALL WERE DRAWN UP AGAIN INTO HEAVEN."

The form is:

1. The phrase, *"And this was done three*

NOTES

times," proclaims such for purpose and reason:

a. The three times portrayed the significance of the Vision.

b. It proclaimed that this was not just something out of Peter's mind but had been given three times in order to impress upon Peter its reality.

c. *"Three times"* symbolized the holiness of that which the Vision symbolized, the Salvation of Gentiles without going through Judaism. Before the Throne of God, the living creatures *"rest not day and night, saying, Holy, Holy, Holy, Lord God Almighty, which was, and is, and is to come"* (Rev. 4:8).

d. As well, the three times signified the fulfillment of the Command, *"That in the mouth of two or three witnesses every word may be established"* (Mat. 18:16).

2. The phrase, *"And all were drawn up again into Heaven,"* signified that all of this was totally of God and none of man and was, therefore, to be obeyed without question, hence, the Spirit saying to Peter, *"Arise therefore, and get you down, and go with them, doubting nothing"* (Acts 10:20).

3. The great problem with the church is that of adding to or subtracting from that which has been solely devised in Heaven.

4. As well, the words *"drawn up"* imply that it was slowly drawn up, signifying that even though the Vision was now completed, the instructions it gave were to serve as a standard.

(11) "AND, BEHOLD, IMMEDIATELY THERE WERE THREE MEN ALREADY COME UNTO THE HOUSE WHERE I WAS, SENT FROM CAESAREA UNTO ME."

The construction is:

1. The phrase, *"And, behold, immediately there were three men already come unto the house where I was,"* speaks of the action of the Holy Spirit in hurriedly bringing this to pass and, consequently, meaning for Peter to obey immediately and implicitly.

2. *"Sent from Caesarea unto me,"* is bound up in the word *"sent."*

3. In the Greek Text, the word is *"apostello"* and means *"to send out on a mission."* In other words, they were sent by God but through the intermediaries of the Angel and Cornelius. If Peter was to obey God, he had absolutely no choice but to go with them, for this was the very purpose and reason for which they had been *"sent."*

(12) "AND THE SPIRIT BADE ME GO WITH THEM, NOTHING DOUBTING. MOREOVER THESE SIX BRETHREN ACCOMPANIED ME, AND WE ENTERED INTO THE MAN'S HOUSE."

The direction is:

1. Jesus Christ is the New Covenant (Jn. 1:1-3, 14, 29).

2. The Cross of Christ is the meaning of the New Covenant (I Cor. 1:17-18; 2:2).

THE HOLY SPIRIT

The phrase, *"And the Spirit bade me go with them, nothing doubting,"* lends, if possible, even more emphasis.

Peter was not to have doubts within his mind, not to be hesitant, and not to make the journey in fear, but rather the very opposite. He was not to question anything and take no ulterior position toward them because they were Gentiles.

This meant he was not to follow them at a distance but was to join with them, actually walking with them as brethren, which meant as equals.

Always the answer of the Lord had to be paramount in Peter's mind, *"What God has cleansed, that call not you common"* (Acts 10:15).

"Moreover these six brethren accompanied me," portrays him taking these men, as we have stated, in order to be witnesses as to everything that transpired, which they were.

The phrase, *"And we entered into the man's house,"* speaks of Cornelius.

However, Peter told nothing of the man, regarding his favor with the Jews, his efforts to reach the Lord, etc. The brethren at Jerusalem either already knew that, or else, it made no difference anyway, which the latter is probably the case.

As far as all good Jews were concerned, every Gentile, irrespective of their good works or whatever, was a stranger to the commonwealth of Israel, a foreigner separated from the Covenants of Promise, and in their eyes, outside of Christ and without hope unless he became a Jew.

NOTES

In the eyes of all good Jews, Cornelius, and all Gentiles for that matter, were like lepers under the Law, who were condemned to live outside the camp of God's People.

However, the leper could be cleansed, but if so, the Priest would have to take sacrificial blood and put it on the leper in such a way that it symbolized complete covering. Then, over the blood, the Priest placed oil as a symbol or Type of the Holy Spirit (Lev. 14:14-18).

In actuality, the same identical thing was happening with Gentiles, which should have been obvious to the Elders of the Church in Jerusalem.

Jesus Christ, our Great High Priest, had cleansed these Gentiles upon proper Faith. This meant that the Blood He shed at Calvary, which was typified by the sacrificial blood applied by the Priests of old, was now applied by Faith, with the work being carried out by the Holy Spirit. He now has come in a new dimension due to what Jesus did at Calvary and the Resurrection, which was symbolized in the past by the Priests applying the oil. As He did with Cornelius and his household, so does He with all!

In view of what the Lord had said to Peter, he was not retiring at all about entering into the house of this Gentile, which would have been unthinkable before.

To have not done so would have been far greater than mere disobedience but, in fact, would have made a mockery out of what Jesus had done at Calvary and the Resurrection. His Death and Resurrection were for the entirety of the world, in other words, all of mankind, and not just for Jews.

As well, these people were not to be looked at or classified as second-class Believers, etc.

(13) "AND HE SHOWED US HOW HE HAD SEEN AN ANGEL IN HIS HOUSE, WHICH STOOD AND SAID UNTO HIM, SEND MEN TO JOPPA, AND CALL FOR SIMON, WHOSE SURNAME IS PETER."

The direction is:

1. The phrase, *"And he showed us how he had seen an Angel in his house,"* presents a powerful witness, especially considering that a Vision had been given to Peter to substantiate what had been told by the Angel to Cornelius.

People can claim they see a lot of things, which, in reality, have not happened. However, there was no doubting this visitation by the Angel, especially considering, as stated, what the Lord had shown to Peter. Each verified the other!

2. *"Which stood and said unto him, Send men to Joppa, and call for Simon, whose surname is Peter,"* once again, proclaims Peter emphasizing the word *"send,"* inasmuch as it represented a Mission for the Lord.

As well, Peter was plainly stating that the Lord had specifically sent for him; consequently, he had no alternative or choice but to go, that is, if he was to obey the Lord.

3. As well, the implications are strongly given that if Peter had not obeyed, the results to him spiritually, and in every way for that matter, would have been catastrophic. He knew there would be opposition to his action, as there was. Nevertheless, that must not be taken into consideration. In fact, it must not be given any credence at all.

4. In truth, only a precious few will truly listen to the Lord, doing what He explicitly commands. In the first place, there are only a few who can truly hear the Lord, and then again, most preachers give their allegiance to denominational leaders and not God.

5. While there are certainly a few godly men in positions of spiritual leadership around the world, which demands that these men (or women) be given the respect due their Calling, still, the allegiance must always be given first and foremost to the Lord Jesus Christ.

6. It is not the idea of a lone ranger riding his horse into the sunset and kicking dust in the faces of all others. This is actually the very opposite of what we are saying. Rather, it is one who is truly broken and humble but will hear the Lord and obey Him first and foremost, irrespective of the price.

(14) "WHO SHALL TELL YOU WORDS, WHEREBY YOU AND ALL YOUR HOUSE SHALL BE SAVED."

The diagram is:

1. The phrase, *"Who shall tell you words,"* proclaims the absolute necessity of the Word of God being given to sinners if

they are to be saved. These are the *"words"* here to be spoken, *"the Word of God."*

2. Once again, *"words"* in the Greek is *"rhema"* and implies *"a matter or topic,"* in this case, the Word of God specifically directed to Cornelius and his household, but for all others as well.

3. That is the reason the preaching of the Gospel is so very, very important. Without such, people simply cannot be saved.

4. The Holy Spirit acts upon the Word in whatever capacity it is given, thereby, energizing it to the soul of the sinner. The person is then brought to the place of recognizing his lost condition and his need, the Lord Jesus Christ.

5. This *"word"* can be given in the form of that which we think of as preaching or teaching, songs that are truly anointed by the Lord, literature, or even the Testimony of an individual to another. Irrespective as to how it is given, if it is the Word of God, the Holy Spirit then can work. In fact, this is the only manner that He has chosen to bring sinners to Christ (I Cor. 1:18-25).

6. The phrase, *"Whereby you and all your house shall be saved,"* plainly tells us that before this, Cornelius was not Saved, despite all his good works.

7. As well, it tells us by the use of the words, *"All your house,"* that this great Message was not for Cornelius only but for all his friends and relatives. It was, in fact, for all of humanity because, in a sense, *"all your house"* includes the entirety of the Gentile world for all time!

(15) "AND AS I BEGAN TO SPEAK, THE HOLY SPIRIT FELL ON THEM, AS ON US AT THE BEGINNING."

The diagram is:

1. The phrase, *"And as I began to speak,"* tells us several things that happened at this time:

a. All evidence points to the fact that Peter did not speak very long before the Holy Spirit fell.

b. These people instantly accepted Christ in their hearts whenever Peter said, *"To Him* (Jesus) *give all the Prophets witness, that through His Name whosoever believes in Him shall receive remission of sins"* (Acts 10:43).

NOTES

When they heard that word, they instantly believed in their hearts and, at that moment, were saved, even without saying a particular word at that time.

c. The Holy Spirit fell on them, with them receiving this great Gift of God, which was impossible to happen if they first had not been cleansed by the precious Blood of Jesus Christ. He can only come into a cleansed and purified heart, which can only be done by the Blood of Jesus.

They were saved first, as stated, even as Peter spoke, and then immediately thereafter baptized with the Holy Spirit.

2. They spoke with Tongues exactly as the Believers had done on the Day of Pentecost.

3. The phrase, *"The Holy Spirit fell on them, as on us at the beginning,"* speaks of Cornelius and his household receiving the same identical thing and in the same manner that Believers had received on the Day of Pentecost. They were baptized with the Holy Spirit.

4. The word *"fell"* in the Greek Text is *"epipipto"* and means *"to embrace with affection, or seize strongly."*

5. The idea is not so much as to how the Holy Spirit came, but the manner in which He came. He embraced and seized them powerfully, which left absolutely no doubt in their minds as to what had happened. This resulted in their speaking with other Tongues and magnifying God (Acts 10:46).

(16) "THEN REMEMBERED I THE WORD OF THE LORD, HOW THAT HE SAID, JOHN INDEED BAPTIZED WITH WATER; BUT YOU SHALL BE BAPTIZED WITH THE HOLY SPIRIT."

The exegesis is:

1. The phrase, *"Then remembered I the word of the Lord,"* pertains to something that Peter had not mentioned in the actual happening.

2. In other words, he knew that what was happening respecting these Gentiles being saved and baptized with the Holy Spirit was according to the Word of the Lord.

3. *"How that He said, John indeed baptized with water; but you shall be baptized with the Holy Spirit,"* is derived from Acts 1:5. They are the words of Jesus in fulfillment of what John prophesied concerning

Jesus, which is found in Matthew 3:11.

4. Horton said, *"There are some writers who teach that nothing can be called a 'Baptism' in the Holy Spirit except what happened on the Day of Pentecost, and they deny that what happened on that day was ever repeated.*

"These writers may admit that Believers can be filled or even refilled with the Holy Spirit, but they reject the idea of a personal Pentecost, a Baptism in the Holy Spirit for today. However, Peter does use the word 'Baptize' here. Thus, he clearly saw that this outpouring was also a Baptism in the Spirit. This Baptism in the Holy Spirit was for all, and is still for all Believers, no matter what their background, race, national origin, or other affiliation."

5. Oh, the lengths that men, especially religious men, will go to in order to deny that which God is doing!

(17) "FORASMUCH THEN AS GOD GAVE THEM THE LIKE GIFT AS HE DID UNTO US, WHO BELIEVED ON THE LORD JESUS CHRIST; WHAT WAS I, THAT I COULD WITHSTAND GOD?"

The synopsis is:

1. It is the Cross of Christ that made all of this possible.

2. Before the Cross, the Holy Spirit could come into a few hearts and lives, such as Prophets, etc., and help them carry out a work they were called to do. However, when that work was finished, the Holy Spirit would then depart.

3. Now, since the Cross, He comes into the heart and life of the Believer instantly at Conversion to remain there forever (Jn. 14:16).

NOTES

THE SAME GIFT

The phrase, *"Forasmuch then as God gave them the like Gift as He did unto us,"* tells us several things, and they must be heeded:

• The word *"like"* in the Greek means *"equal"* or *"identical."*

So, that which the Gentiles received was identical, even as the Holy Spirit here proclaims, as that which was given on the Day of Pentecost. To deny that is to deny the Word of God.

• The Holy Spirit is a *"Gift,"* which, in the Greek Text, is *"dorea"* and refers to *"a gratuity."* However, it also refers to the Greek word *"doron,"* which means *"a gift or offering made possible by a sacrifice."*

• In other words, even though it is a *"Gift"* to the Believer and, in fact, cannot be earned, still, that in no way means that it did not come with great price. In fact, the price or Sacrifice was so great that man was unable to pay. Consequently, Jesus paid it in our stead, making it possible for Believers to then receive the *"Gift"* of the Holy Spirit.

The *"Gift"* received by the Gentiles was identical to the *"Gift"* received by the Jews. This is given a second time in a little different form in order that there be no mistake concerning what the Gentiles had received.

BELIEVING ON THE LORD JESUS CHRIST

The phrase, *"Who believed on the Lord Jesus Christ,"* constituted the only requirement.

Consequently, this meant that simple Faith alone in Christ was sufficient for Salvation and to receive the Gift of the Holy Spirit.

In this episode we learn as much from what Peter did not say as from what he did say. This means that all the rudiments of the Law are now out and not necessary at all respecting one's Salvation and Infilling of the Holy Spirit.

Peter knew this to be emphatically true because of what had happened. He knew these Gentiles had not kept the Law of Moses and had not really made any attempt to do so, that is, if it is correct that they were not proselytes, which they did not seem to be.

Had they been full-fledged proselytes, Peter would not have thought it a stigma associating with them, and neither would he have been called before the Elders of the Church in Jerusalem. Full-fledged proselytes, though looked at as a little lower by most Jews, were still recognized as a part of the commonwealth and Covenants of Israel.

Peter knew the only thing these Gentiles had exhibited was Faith in Jesus Christ, hence, the statement as here used.

WITHSTANDING GOD

The question, *"What was I, that I could*

withstand God?" has simple reference to the fact that had Peter disobeyed in any way, he would have been withstanding God, which is a position no one wants to occupy.

At the same time, he was telling the Elders of the Church in Jerusalem that if they did not accept what he was saying, they would be *"withstanding God"* themselves, which, no doubt, came across loud and clear.

In fact, anything that is not according to the Word of God is a withstanding of God and always invites serious consequences.

The word *"withstand"* means *"to prevent"* and in the case of God, means that such is impossible.

(18) "WHEN THEY HEARD THESE THINGS, THEY HELD THEIR PEACE, AND GLORIFIED GOD, SAYING, THEN HAS GOD ALSO TO THE GENTILES GRANTED REPENTANCE UNTO LIFE."

The exegesis is:

1. The phrase, *"When they heard these things,"* tells us they believed Peter and accepted what he did. They understood that not to do so would have put them opposite of God, which is an untenable position.

2. *"They held their peace, and glorified God,"* means they not only stifled their own thoughts of opposition but, as well, glorified God for what had been done.

3. The phrase, *"Saying, Then has God also to the Gentiles granted Repentance unto Life,"* proclaims in no uncertain terms that they were given such *"Life"* strictly on Faith, which included none of the rituals and ceremonies of Judaism.

4. This also confirms the thought that Cornelius was not a proselyte.

5. However, despite this incontrovertible proof of what God was doing regarding Gentiles, the Church was still very slow to reach out to the Gentiles, even as the next Verse proclaims. Not only were they slow in this regard, but strong factions arose in the Jerusalem Church, attempting to mesh the Law with Grace, which was, without a doubt, the greatest hindrance to the Gospel, and that which Paul had to contest greatly.

(19) "NOW THEY WHICH WERE SCATTERED ABROAD UPON THE PERSECUTION THAT AROSE ABOUT STEPHEN TRAVELLED AS FAR AS PHENICE, AND CYPRUS, AND ANTIOCH, PREACHING THE WORD TO NONE BUT UNTO THE JEWS ONLY."

NOTES

The way is:

1. The phrase, *"Now they which were scattered abroad upon the persecution that arose about Stephen,"* concerns that which happened in Acts, Chapter 8, which was about six or seven years before.

2. *"Travelled as far as Phenice, and Cyprus, and Antioch,"* pertains to three areas of great importance.

3. *"Phenice"* is the country between Galilee and Syria, presently known as Lebanon. It was along the coastline of the Mediterranean Sea and included the two main cities of Tyre and Sidon.

4. *"Cyprus"* is an island in the Mediterranean Sea, which still goes by the same name.

5. *"Antioch"* was a city of Syria built by Antiochus Seleucus near the river Orontes. At that time, it was one of the most celebrated cities of the East, claimed by Josephus to be the third city in importance of the whole Roman Empire, with Rome and Alexandria being the first two.

6. *"Preaching the Word to none but unto the Jews only,"* pertained basically to proclaiming Jesus as the Messiah of Israel and the Saviour of the world, and that He had died for man and had risen from the dead.

7. These who participated in this effort of Evangelism had done all of this, at least for the most part, before Peter's experience. However, since Peter and Cornelius, word had begun to get out about this tremendous change, even as the next Verse proclaims.

(20) "AND SOME OF THEM WERE MEN OF CYPRUS AND CYRENE, WHICH, WHEN THEY WERE COME TO ANTIOCH, SPOKE UNTO THE GRECIANS, PREACHING THE LORD JESUS."

The exegesis is:

1. It is true that the Cross of Christ was little preached before Paul.

2. The reason was that the Apostles or others at that time did not know anything about the Cross.

3. They mostly preached Jesus as the Messiah of Israel and His Resurrection from the dead.

NOTES

PREACHING THE LORD JESUS

The phrase, *"And some of them were men of Cyprus and Cyrene,"* gives us little evidence as to who exactly these men were but does imply that they were late comers to Antioch.

The phrase, *"Which, when they were come to Antioch, spoke unto the Grecians, preaching the Lord Jesus,"* pertains to Gentiles, and not Hellenists as some claim.

Such is supported by the strongest authority of the oldest Manuscripts.

Moreover, there was nothing novel in the Conversion and admission into the Church of Hellenistic Jews, as some claim there was, which, in fact, had been going on from the very beginning. Actually, as previously stated, Stephen, plus all the other men chosen, were Hellenistic Jews (Acts, Chpt. 6), and some think they were the first Deacons. So, it is obvious that these were Greeks, i.e., Gentiles.

As well, the phrase, *"Preaching the Lord Jesus,"* seems to indicate that these Jews who preached to them were not demanding that they also keep the Law of Moses, etc.

So, there is some evidence that the great experience of Peter in taking the Gospel to the house of Cornelius was beginning to be heard by others, with them responding accordingly.

Antioch is here mentioned in the sense of the importance that it would become. In a sense, the Holy Spirit would transfer His Sphere of influence from the mother Church in Jerusalem to Antioch.

ANTIOCH

Inasmuch as Jerusalem continued to be somewhat bogged down in the Law/Grace issue, and because of other problems, as well, Antioch would become much more suited for world Evangelism of that day. Of course, the Gospel was for all, but inasmuch as the Jews would basically deny Jesus, at least as a whole, the greater thrust would go to the Gentiles, for which Antioch would be much better suited.

Actually, about 16 Antiochs were built by Seleucus in honor of his father, but this Antioch was by far the most populated and powerful. Josephus records that the Seleucids encouraged Jews to immigrate there in large numbers and gave them full Roman citizenship rights.

Antioch fell to Pompey in 64 B.C., and he made it a free city. It became the capital of the Roman Province of Syria and, as stated, became the third largest city of the empire. The Seleucids and Romans erected magnificent temples and other buildings in the city.

It was a city renowned for its culture, being commended in this respect by no less a person than Cicero.

Close by the city were the renowned groves of Daphne and a sanctuary dedicated to Apollo, where orgiastic rites were celebrated in the name of religion. Despite the bad moral tone, at the beginning of the Christian era, life in Antioch was rich and varied. Incidentally, Antioch was about 500,000 in population.

Apart from Jerusalem itself, no other city was so intimately connected with the beginnings of Christianity.

THE EARLY CHURCH IN ANTIOCH

Nicholas, one of the seven *"Deacons"* of Acts 6:5, was of Antioch and had been a Gentile Convert (proselyte) to Judaism. During the persecution that followed the death of Stephen, some of the Disciples went as far north as Antioch (Acts 11:19) and preached to the Jews. Later arrivals also took Christianity, even as we see here, to the Greek populace, and when numerous Conversions occurred, the Jerusalem Church sent Barnabas to Antioch.

When he had assessed the situation, he went to Tarsus, as we shall see, and brought Saul (Paul) back with him, and both of them taught in Antioch for a year. Actually, the name *"Christian"* originated there, which we will soon see.

It was Antioch to which some Jews later came and proclaimed the necessity of circumcision for Gentiles as a prerequisite to becoming Christians, resulting in the first Council being conducted at Jerusalem (Acts 15:1-2).

Paul began all three of his great missionary journeys at Antioch. Consequently, its

NOTES

evangelistic zeal afforded this city great status in the subsequent history of the Church.

Archaeological excavations at the site, now in modern Turkey, have unearthed over 20 ruined Churches dating from the Fourth Century A.D.

Antioch was about 500 miles north of Jerusalem and about 80 miles southeast of Tarsus.

(21) "AND THE HAND OF THE LORD WAS WITH THEM: AND A GREAT NUMBER BELIEVED, AND TURNED UNTO THE LORD."

The pattern is:

1. The phrase, *"And the Hand of the Lord was with them,"* signifies that God was very pleased with the Gospel being preached to these Gentiles. Consequently, He confirmed His Word through them with signs and wonders (Acts 4:30; 13:11).

2. As well, one would have to assume that they also had been baptized with the Holy Spirit with the evidence of speaking with other Tongues exactly as had been those of the house of Cornelius.

3. *"And a great number believed, and turned unto the Lord,"* simply means that these Gentiles gave their hearts and lives to the Lord Jesus Christ. The evidence is that there were far more Gentiles coming to Christ in Antioch than Jews.

(22) "THEN TIDINGS OF THESE THINGS CAME UNTO THE EARS OF THE CHURCH WHICH WAS IN JERUSALEM: AND THEY SENT FORTH BARNABAS, THAT HE SHOULD GO AS FAR AS ANTIOCH."

The form is:

1. Jesus Christ is the New Covenant.

2. This means that He does not merely have the New Covenant but, in fact, is the New Covenant.

3. This means that everything we receive from God the Father comes to us through and by Jesus Christ and what He did for us at the Cross.

GOOD NEWS

The phrase, *"Then tidings of these things came unto the ears of the Church which was in Jerusalem,"* speaks of *"good news"* or *"good tidings."* As is obvious, this was after the great experience of Peter with Cornelius, with the Church in Jerusalem not surprised at what was now being told them concerning Gentiles at Antioch.

The phrase, *"And they sent forth Barnabas,"* proclaims to us several things:

• Up to this time, Jerusalem, as the mother Church, was attempting to fulfill the role of leadership, even as it should have. This was where the Holy Spirit first fell and where most, if not all, of the Apostles were headquartered. Considering the thousands who had been won to Christ, it, as well, was a large Church.

They were very wise and, no doubt, had the Mind of the Lord respecting their sending Barnabas. He was a man of great wisdom and, as well, seemed to have a greater grasp of what God was doing, respecting the Gentiles and world Evangelism, even than possibly some of the Apostles.

Also, he would be used mightily respecting the Apostle Paul, which Jerusalem did not have in mind, but the Lord definitely did.

• Even though Jerusalem would continue to exert great influence over the Work of God as a whole, even as the first Council proclaimed (recorded in Acts, Chapter 15), from here on out, the thrust—especially regarding Evangelism—would basically come from Antioch.

THE HOLY SPIRIT

The phrase, *"That he should go as far as Antioch,"* proclaims several things but, most of all, that they considered Antioch to be a place of great importance, which it was.

Some writers have assumed that sending Barnabas meant the Church in Jerusalem wanted to maintain control over this new development. However, there is actually no evidence of this. It seemed to be more love and concern than anything else.

The same loving Spirit Who sent Peter and John to Samaria to help the people there seems to be the same One Who moved the Apostles in this incident also.

There is no record that Barnabas had to report back to Jerusalem, nor, it seems, did he have to seek their advice about further steps in Ministry, etc.

Actually, the government of the Early

NOTES

Church, which was definitely instituted by the Holy Spirit, seemed to exert no central control in any capacity. Men were free to hear from the Lord and follow what they felt He had said, which is the way it should have been. While there may have been discussions sometimes before and sometimes after, even as it should have been, this seemed to have been as far as it went.

In fact, if one carefully studies the Work of the Holy Spirit concerning Church government throughout the Book of Acts and the Epistles, one will look in vain for a central control, which seems to be so prevalent now, and which is so unscriptural. The emphasis is that each Church served as its own authority, which seems to be what the Holy Spirit intended. While they took advice from others, even as Acts, Chapter 15, proclaims, authority, it seems, was never usurped over local Churches by Jerusalem, or anywhere else for that matter.

To do so more or less abrogates the Authority of the Holy Spirit and the Headship of Christ.

(23) "WHO, WHEN HE CAME, AND HAD SEEN THE GRACE OF GOD, WAS GLAD, AND EXHORTED THEM ALL, THAT WITH PURPOSE OF HEART THEY WOULD CLEAVE UNTO THE LORD."

The way is:

1. The phrase, *"Who, when he came, and had seen the Grace of God, was glad,"* presents a strange but beautiful statement.

Seeing the *"Grace of God"* has reference to the fact that Barnabas saw the changed lives of these Gentiles, who had, no doubt, been brought from the worship of idols, along with gross immorality. But now, the Grace of God through the Lord Jesus Christ and Faith in His Name had effected miraculous changes in them, which were obvious to all.

2. It gladdened the heart of Barnabas, not only because of their wondrously changed lives but, as well, that it was the Gospel of Grace at work. In other words, it could not be denied!

3. The phrase, *"And exhorted them all, that with purpose of heart they would cleave unto the Lord,"* proclaims to us the necessity of such, and should warn us of the great danger of falling away from the Faith under the pressure of temptation.

4. The Grace of God with its enabling Power had brought them out of the terrible debauchery of sin; however, in no way did it give them a license to continue in this lifestyle, but rather liberty to live a Holy Life. In other words, they were to *"cleave unto the Lord,"* which in the Greek Text is *"proskollao"* and means *"to adhere, to glue to."*

5. The word *"purpose"* in the Greek is *"prothesis"* and means *"a setting forth, or something that is exposed before God."*

6. The Believer is to set his heart toward Christ, determine to live for Him, and do so by literally (in a spiritual sense) being glued to Him.

(24) "FOR HE WAS A GOOD MAN, AND FULL OF THE HOLY SPIRIT, AND OF FAITH: AND MUCH PEOPLE WERE ADDED UNTO THE LORD."

The order is:

1. The Cross alone holds the solution for mankind.

2. Anything else in which Believers put their trust is labeled by the Lord as *"spiritual adultery"* (Rom. 7:1-4).

FULL OF THE HOLY SPIRIT AND FAITH

The phrase, *"For he was a good man,"* is so pleasing to read as it was written by Luke, which means this is what the Holy Spirit wanted him to say about Barnabas. In truth, few men are given the accolades, such as given here by the Holy Spirit, as given to this man. It is quite one thing to have men say such things, but to have the Holy Spirit say such things, as said here, is something else altogether.

In the mentioning of this man's *"goodness,"* the Holy Spirit through Luke probably meant that he was entirely free from Pharisaic judgment (Lk. 18:11).

"And full of the Holy Spirit and of Faith," proclaims Barnabas being described in the same manner as Stephen (Acts 6:5).

"And much people were added unto the Lord," probably refers to the fact that along with the great number who had believed before the coming of Barnabas, many more were added because of his life and Ministry,

which was full of the Holy Spirit and Faith!

THE HOLY SPIRIT IN THE OLD TESTAMENT

The word for *"Spirit"* in the Old Testament is *"Ruach"* and is never translated *"Ghost."*

In the New Testament, the Greek word is *"Pneuma"* and is the equivalent to the Hebrew *"Ruach"* and, accordingly, should not have been translated *"Ghost."*

If one is to notice, when the singular word *"Spirit"* is used, as in *"The Spirit said unto him"* (Acts 10:19), the word *"Ghost"* is never used. Consequently, it should have always been carried over by the King James translators in the title *"Holy Spirit."*

The actual meanings of the word *"Ruach,"* as it is used in the Old Testament, is according to the following:

Wind: an invisible, mysterious, and powerful force (Gen. 8:1; Ex. 10:13, 19; Num. 11:31; I Ki. 18:45; etc.).

• Breath: This is the same mysterious force seen as the life and vitality of man. It can be disturbed or activated in a particular direction (Gen. 41:8; Num. 5:14, 30; Judg. 8:3; I Ki. 21:5; I Chron. 5:26; etc.).

• Divine Power: This is when men seem to be carried out of themselves—not just a surge of vitality but a supernatural force taking possession. This was particularly true of early leaders (Judg. 3:10; 6:34; 11:29; 13:25; I Sam. 11:6).

At the heart of the word *"Ruach"* is the experience of a mysterious, awesome Power—the mighty invisible force of the Wind, the mystery of vitality, the only Power that transforms—all *"Ruach,"* all manifestations of Divine Energy.

THE HOLY SPIRIT IN THE NEW TESTAMENT

In the New Testament, the Greek word *"Pneuma"* is used, with the same meaning as the Hebrew *"Ruach,"* but with a slightly different turn.

It is important to realize that for the first Christians, the Spirit was thought of in terms of Divine Power clearly manifest by its effects on the life of the recipient. The impact of the Spirit did not leave the individual or onlooker in much doubt that a significant change had taken place in him, and was done so by Divine Agency. Paul refers his readers back to their initial experience of the Infilling of the Holy Spirit again and again. For some, it had been an overwhelming experience of God's Love (Rom. 5:5); for others, of joy (I Thess. 1:6); for others, of illumination (II Cor. 3:14-17), of liberation (Rom. 8:2; II Cor. 3:17), or of moral transformation (I Cor. 6:9-11), and of various Spiritual Gifts (I Cor. 1:4-7; Gal. 3:5).

Actually, all of these attributes are indicative more or less in each individual Spirit-filled Believer. Even though the Spirit is invisible, His Presence is readily detectable (Jn. 3:8).

Life for the Believer is, therefore, qualitatively different from what it was prior to Faith. Our daily living becomes our means of responding to the Spirit's claim, enabled by the Spirit's Power (Rom. 8:4-6, 14; Gal. 5:16, 18, 25; 6:8). Actually, this was the decisive difference between Christianity and Judaism. The Spirit was *"upon"* those before Christ was Glorified but *"in"* Believers afterward, which constitutes a far greater dimension.

NO FINAL FULFILLMENT OF HIS WORK

At the same time, because the Spirit is only a beginning of final Salvation in this life, there can be no final fulfillment of His Work in the Believer so long as this life lasts.

The man of the Spirit is no longer dependent on this world and its standards for his meaning and satisfaction; however, he is still a man of human appetites and frailty and part of human society. Consequently, to have the Spirit is to experience tension and conflict between the old life and the new, between flesh and Spirit (Rom. 7:14-25; 8:10, 12; Gal. 5:16, I Heb. 10.29).

Strangely enough, Paul declared that the Spirit in Grace comes to its full expression only in and through weakness (Rom. 8:26; II Cor. 12:1-10).

THE CROSS OF CHRIST

The only way that the Holy Spirit can work in our lives as He so desires, and is meant to do, is that our Faith be properly placed. By that, I mean that our Faith must be in Christ and what Christ did for us at the Cross (Lk. 9:23-24; Rom. 6:1-14; 8:1-11; I Cor. 1:17-18, 23; 2:2; Col. 2:10-15).

It is the Cross of Christ that has given and does give the legal means for the Holy Spirit to do all that He does. That's the reason that Paul said, *"For the Law of the Spirit of Life in Christ Jesus has made me free from the Law of Sin and Death"* (Rom. 8:2).

When the believing sinner comes to Christ, the Holy Spirit instantly comes into the heart and life of such a Believer, there to abide permanently. It is the Cross of Christ that makes all of this possible. We must never forget that while Jesus is the Source, it is the Cross that provides the Means of all that we receive from God. If the Believer looks to anything except Christ and the Cross, that is tantamount to spiritual adultery, which should be overly obvious, and greatly hinders the Holy Spirit (Rom. 7:1-4). The key to all victory is in the Holy Spirit, but the key to the Holy Spirit working within our hearts and lives as He must do is by and through the Cross. The Cross of Christ makes everything possible. If we don't understand that, then we are going to go somewhat wrong, which will cause us untold difficulties and problems.

Incidentally, in closing this segment, the Holy Spirit is not a *"Ghost,"* which means *"the disembodied soul of a dead person believed to be an inhabitant of the unseen world."*

The Holy Spirit is God and should be referred to accordingly.

(25) "THEN DEPARTED BARNABAS TO TARSUS, FOR TO SEEK SAUL."

The order is:

1. The Cross is not merely the basis of human Salvation, but it is also the basis of God's Self-revelation, in which the Knowledge of God alone can be found.

2. The Cross brings home the full seriousness of sin, declares the powerlessness of fallen humanity to achieve Salvation, and exposes human delusions of self-righteousness.

WESTERN CIVILIZATION

This short Verse of Scripture (Vs. 25) is without a doubt one of the single most important Verses in the entirety of the Word of God. Its significance, which is understood not at all by the world and even very little by the church, is of such proportion that it literally boggles the mind.

In the early 1990s, an extremely wealthy individual in the southwest donated several millions of dollars to Yale University in order to establish a *"Chair"* on the study of *"Western Civilization."*

After some three years had passed with nothing being done, the money was returned with the explanation, *"We simply do not know how to address such a subject, therefore, we are returning your money,"* or words to that effect.

However, to those who truly know their Bibles, we know that western civilization had its roots in the Missionary Work of the Apostle Paul, who brought the Gospel of Jesus Christ to Western Europe, with it ultimately going to England, then to America, etc. In other words, the Gospel of Jesus Christ is the spark and foundation of what we refer to as western civilization. It alone is the cause of the greatest freedoms, prosperity, and above all, Salvation afforded in this present world. Paul, as no other man, brought that *"Light"* to the darkness. Consequently, this event of Barnabas going to Tarsus to seek Paul presents a pivotal point in history all out of proportion to the short statement made here. In effect, it was the Macedonian Call, *"Come over and help us."*

PAUL

First of all, we know that the Lord moved upon Barnabas to find Paul and bring him to Antioch. The Lord was now ready to launch the Ministry of this man who some have said, *"Is the greatest example for Christianity ever produced by Christ."* Whether that is true or not, only the Lord knows. However, this much is certain: few men, if any, have made the impact on civilization as the Apostle Paul has.

As well, I think the contribution made to the Cause of Christ by Barnabas is of far greater magnitude than anyone would dare believe. The manner in which this man was used by the Holy Spirit is astounding to say the least! His spirit, attitude, and demeanor are so Christlike as to be one of the greatest

NOTES

examples, I think, in Bible history.

It is believed that Barnabas finding Paul took place in the spring of the year A.D. 43, or about 10 years after the Crucifixion.

If Barnabas went by ship from Antioch to Tarsus, it would have taken about 12 hours, or by land, a journey of about 80 miles.

The word *"seek"* in the Greek Text implies that Paul was not easily found. In other words, Barnabas had to search for Paul.

Almost immediately after Paul's Conversion, which was approximately eight years before, he had spent three years in Arabia, where and when he had most likely been given the meaning of the Great New Covenant of Grace.

THE MINISTRY OF PAUL

After that, it seems that he came back and ministered again in Damascus, where the Jews attempted to kill him. He escaped and went to Jerusalem, where he ministered for a period of time, probably not longer than several months (Acts 9:23-30). After he left Jerusalem, he went to Caesarea and then back to Tarsus.

So, there was probably a timespan of approximately four years when it is not known exactly what Paul did. Some suggest that during this time, he evangelized Gentiles *"in the regions of Syria and Cilicia,"* of which there seems to be some small Scriptural evidence (Gal. 1:21). It is only the time frame that is in question.

However, considering that the Lord had given Paul the meaning of the New Covenant, it is highly unlikely that a man of his temperament would just simply sit down and do nothing for this period of time. So, it is very likely that he was ministering, possibly even having planted some Churches, when Barnabas came to get him.

(26) "AND WHEN HE HAD FOUND HIM, HE BROUGHT HIM UNTO ANTIOCH. AND IT CAME TO PASS, THAT A WHOLE YEAR THEY ASSEMBLED THEMSELVES WITH THE CHURCH, AND TAUGHT MUCH PEOPLE. AND THE DISCIPLES WERE CALLED CHRISTIANS FIRST IN ANTIOCH."

The direction is:

1. Wherever the Church takes the Cross of Christ seriously, it can expect to encounter hostility (Gal. 5:11).

2. The Theology of the Cross insists upon the Cross being given priority over all other events in the history of Salvation (Gal. 6:14).

FINDING PAUL

The phrase, *"And when he had found him, he brought him unto Antioch,"* seems to indicate, as stated, that he had difficulty finding him. This seems to say that he was not staying at his home with his parents, which would have been easily found, suggesting that he had been disinherited due to becoming a Follower of Christ.

At any rate, when he was found by Barnabas, whatever he was told seemed to coincide with what Paul believed was the Will of God, with both of them returning to Antioch.

The phrase, *"And it came to pass, that a whole year they assembled themselves with the Church, and taught much people,"* could well signal the beginning teaching of the New Covenant as it had been given to Paul. However, if, in fact, he did plant Churches in the regions of Syria and Cilicia, it would have been first introduced there.

How large the Church was in Antioch is not known; however, the Scripture does say that *"a great number believed, and turned unto the Lord,"* which could have been several hundreds or even several thousands (Acts 11:21).

It has been suggested that because of Paul's training in schools of Greek philosophy (if, in fact, he was trained in these schools), his eloquence and logic were needed among the polished scholars of Antioch, capital of Syria and third city of importance in all the Roman Empire.

However, I think that such was little used, if at all, due to Paul later saying at Corinth, *"When I came to you, came not with excellency of speech or of wisdom, declaring unto you the Testimony of God.*

"For I determined not to know any thing among you, save Jesus Christ, and Him Crucified" (I Cor. 2:1-2).

"And the Disciples were called Christians first in Antioch," proclaims the greatest

honor that could ever be bestowed upon any person.

The name *"Christian"* in the Greek Text means *"Follower of Christ."*

Heretofore, they had been called among themselves *"disciples, and brethren, and Saints,"* and by the Jews, people of *"the Way"* (Acts 9:2).

However, now, from the outside world, they received the name of *"Christians"* as Followers of Christ, and they accepted it (Acts 26:28; I Pet. 4:16).

Some have suggested that the name was first given by outsiders in derision, but there is no evidence of this. Actually, it seems the name was coined by those who were not followers of Christ simply because those who were Followers were continually speaking of Christ, etc.

With that being the case, how wonderful that Believers spoke so much of Christ that they were named accordingly by others.

WHAT BEING A CHRISTIAN ACTUALLY MEANS

This was not altogether unusual inasmuch as followers of particular teachers, or even soldiers serving under a particular general, were usually known by the name of the teacher, general, etc. These Believers were Followers of Christ, so it was perfectly natural for the name *"Christian"* to be applied.

This one thing is sure: The Believers in Antioch were very open about their consecration to Christ and, as a result, very vocal. To be frank, how could it be otherwise?

It is said that Ignatius used the name *"Christian"* frequently in his Epistles. He was Bishop (Pastor) of the Church at Antioch probably about 30 to 40 years after this particular time, and was also a friend of Polycarp, the disciple of John the Beloved. It is also said that Polycarp's dying words were, *"I am a Christian."*

The name of *"Christian"* at that time was tied distinctly to Christ, which is obvious. However, such is not so much the case presently.

Tens of millions presently embrace a form of *"Christianity"* without really knowing Christ as Lord and Saviour. Consequently, for these people, they are exactly as Paul said, *"Having a form of godliness, but denying the Power thereof."* He then said, *"From such turn away"* (II Tim. 3:5).

NOTES

In this case, Christianity has been reduced to a mere philosophy, which makes it little better than all other philosophies. The Power in Christianity and the Power of Christianity is Christ and Christ alone. That is why Paul also said, *"I am crucified with Christ: nevertheless I live; yet not I, but Christ lives in me: and the life which I now live in the flesh I live by the Faith of the Son of God, Who loved me, and gave Himself for me"* (Gal. 2:20).

(27) "AND IN THESE DAYS CAME PROPHETS FROM JERUSALEM UNTO ANTIOCH."

The pattern is:

1. The phrase, *"And in these days,"* probably refers to near the conclusion of the year spent by Paul and Barnabas in Antioch at this time.

2. *"Came Prophets from Jerusalem unto Antioch,"* presents the Church in Antioch as having become one of some repute, as should be obvious. Actually, as we shall see throughout the Book of Acts, it seems that quite a few visitors came from Jerusalem, and possibly elsewhere, to Antioch. As we have stated, the Church there was quickly becoming the launching point of missions' endeavors all over the Roman Empire.

3. The *"Prophets"* spoken of here basically followed the same trend as Old Testament Prophets. In other words, they stood in the Office of the Prophet. This means they both *"foretold"* (futuristic events) and *"forthtold"* (edification, exhortation, and comfort) (I Cor. 14:3).

4. However, it must be understood that people who have the Gift of Prophecy (I Cor. 12:10; 13:3-5) are not necessarily Prophets. Actually, very few are! So, the two must be distinguished.

(28) "AND THERE STOOD UP ONE OF THEM NAMED AGABUS, AND SIGNIFIED BY THE SPIRIT THAT THERE SHOULD BE GREAT DROUGHT THROUGHOUT ALL THE WORLD: WHICH CAME TO PASS IN THE DAYS OF CLAUDIUS CAESAR."

NOTES

The composition is:

1. The phrase, *"And there stood up one of them named Agabus,"* proclaims Agabus giving forth a prophetic utterance, as he did, as well, in Acts 21:10.

2. *"And signified by the Spirit that there should be great drought throughout all the world,"* tells us several things:

a. It was the Holy Spirit Who gave the Word to Agabus, who gave it to the Church.

b. The drought took place about one year later (A.D. 44).

c. The indication seems to be that there were several droughts, which ultimately touched much of the Roman Empire. In those days, *"all the world"* was thought of as that which consisted of the Roman Empire.

3. The first drought, which began about one year later, as stated, and lasted for about four years, seemed to fall upon Judaea exclusively, at least as far as it appears from Josephus, and was very severe there.

4. Ishmael was High Priest at the time, and Helena, queen of Adiabene, fetched large supplies of corn from Egypt and figs from Cyprus to Jerusalem to supply the wants of the people.

5. *"Which came to pass in the days of Claudius Caesar,"* seems to indicate several famines. We know that several other famines did take place during his reign, which lasted from A.D. 41 to 54.

(29) "THEN THE DISCIPLES, EVERY MAN ACCORDING TO HIS ABILITY, DETERMINED TO SEND RELIEF UNTO THE BRETHREN WHICH DWELT IN JUDAEA."

The overview is:

1. The phrase, *"Then the Disciples, every man according to his ability,"* tells us that they did not give beyond their means, and neither did they give because of an emotional appeal. Each one determined what he could give based on the way the Lord had prospered him and given him financial ability. Notice that there was no thought of giving in order to gain prosperity.

2. *"Determined to send relief unto the brethren which dwelt in Judaea,"* proclaims such done for a special reason, especially considering that Antioch, at least at some point, would suffer from a coming drought as well!

3. The Believers in Judaea, and especially Jerusalem, had suffered much even before such a drought. Thousands of them had been excommunicated from the synagogues simply because they were Followers of Christ. This meant they lost their places of employment, plus their homes, unless they were fortunate enough to personally own them. As one could well imagine, this created a terrible hardship, which lasted throughout the entirety of the time of the Book of Acts, resulting in quite a few offerings being sent to Jerusalem.

4. Of course, the Holy Spirit knew that a coming drought would add extra hardship to the Believers in Judaea; therefore, He gave notice of such some months in advance. Consequently, Believers in Antioch and, no doubt, elsewhere, were able to build up a fund in order to help when this time came.

5. Barnabas, being very knowledgeable of this situation in Jerusalem, was probably the instigator in helping to raise these funds because he had given heavily some years earlier to the crisis there (Acts 4:36-37).

(30) "WHICH ALSO THEY DID, AND SENT IT TO THE ELDERS BY THE HANDS OF BARNABAS AND SAUL."

The diagram is:

1. The Resurrection is a chapter in a book on the Theology of the Cross (Gal. 2:2).

2. The Theology of the Cross reminds us that it is the Cross, the Crucified Christ, that lies at the heart of the Gospel (Col. 2:10-15).

JERUSALEM

The phrase, *"Which also they did,"* seems to mean they did such in short order.

"And sent it to the Elders by the hands of Barnabas and Saul," seems to be a visit to Jerusalem with little time spent there, consequently, causing Paul to not mention it in Galatians, Chapter 2. The Church at that time in Jerusalem was under great persecution, with James, the son of Zebedee, John's brother, being killed, and Peter escaping only by a Miracle. All of this is recorded in the next Chapter.

Consequently, most of the Apostles were probably not even present in Jerusalem at this time, with Paul and Barnabas discussing very little Church business, if any, only handing over the collection to the Elders (Acts 12:25).

The *"Elders"* were actually the Pastors of the Church in Jerusalem. It must be understood that there could have been as many as 50,000 Believers in Jerusalem at this time. As well, it seems the Twelve Apostles were coming and going constantly, and even though serving as leaders, did not consider themselves as Pastors of the Church in Jerusalem. In other words, their field was the entirety of the world of that day and not merely Jerusalem.

In fact, James, the Lord's Brother, seemed to serve as the Senior Elder or Pastor of the Jerusalem Church, with many other Pastors (Elders) serving under him (Acts 15:13-21).

In fact, the titles of Pastor, Shepherd, Elder, Bishop, and Presbyter all refer to the same office—that of Pastor.

It was only later, when the Church began to apostatize, that men loving preeminence placed a different meaning on the title *"Bishop,"* claiming that such a person would be in charge of an entire area comprising many Churches.

BISHOP

Actually, there is no trace in the New Testament of government by a single Bishop. The position of James at Jerusalem (even as we have just stated) was quite exceptional and was the result of his personal relationship to Christ; but influence is a different thing from office.

Among the apostolic fathers, Ignatius is the only one who insists on monarchical episcopacy, and even he never stated that this was of Divine institution—an argument that would have been decisive if it had been available for him to use.

Jerome, commenting on Titus 1:5, remarked that the supremacy of a single Bishop—which came to be in the Catholic church and has been copied quite extensively in Protestant churches, as well—arose *"by custom rather than by the Lord's actual appointment,"* as a means of preventing schisms in the Church.

In other words, by this time, the church was little being led by the Spirit and, therefore, needed, it thought, a *"Bishop"* to issue forth demands of allegiance. Hence, Church government was gradually taken from the hands of Christ as the Head of the Church, with men taking this position, claiming Divine institution, which was the ruin of the Church. In this one area alone is probably Satan's greatest effort to undermine the Moving and Operation of the Holy Spirit. Such erroneous direction sooner or later always concludes in a Papal hierarchy of sorts, and despite the claims otherwise, has absolutely no Scriptural foundation for support.

NOTES

THE LOCAL CHURCH

The Book of Acts and the Epistles, as given by the Holy Spirit, position the local Church as the highest Spiritual Authority. Most all of the Churches at this time were of like Faith and practice and, therefore, experienced fellowship among themselves, as is here obvious. Still, no local Church then answered to any central authority, not even to Jerusalem. Although the leadership of each local Church sought and received counsel at times elsewhere, they never abrogated its Spiritual Authority to an outside central Church government. Jesus always served as the Head, with the Holy Spirit here leading, guiding, and giving direction, as is overly obvious in the Book of Acts.

Inasmuch as this was given by the Holy Spirit and was meant to serve as our pattern, every Believer, Church, and Preacher should strive to emulate that pattern. To do otherwise is to lay aside the revealed Will of God, which, of necessity, will ultimately bring spiritual ruin.

"My Heavenly home is bright and fair,
"I feel like traveling on,
"Nor pain, nor death can enter there,
"I feel like traveling on."

"Its glittering towers the sun outshine,
"I feel like traveling on,
"That Heavenly mansion shall be mine,
"I feel like traveling on."

"Let others seek a home below,

"I feel like traveling on,
"Which flames devour, or waves over-flow,
"I feel like traveling on."

"The Lord has been so good to me,
"I feel like traveling on,
"Until that blessed home I see,
"I feel like traveling on."

CHAPTER 12

(1) "NOW ABOUT THAT TIME HEROD THE KING STRETCHED FORTH HIS HANDS TO VEX CERTAIN OF THE CHURCH."

The composition is:

1. The Message of the Cross is the Gospel of Jesus Christ (I Cor. 1:17).
2. The Message of the Cross is what the Holy Spirit is presently saying to the Churches (Rev. 3:22).

HEROD

The phrase, *"Now about that time,"* pertains to the time that Paul and Barnabas went to Jerusalem, taking the offering that had been received for those in need. The Holy Spirit seems to desire to portray the state of the Church, regarding persecution at this time.

"Herod the king" speaks of Herod Agrippa, the son of Aristobulus, grandson of Herod the Great, who murdered the babes of Beth-lehem, and nephew of Herod Antipas, who killed John the Baptist, and brother to Herodias.

There were actually six Herods who reigned in one form or the other in the area referred to as Israel. They are all mentioned in the Gospels and the Book of Acts, with the exception of the first. They are as follows:

HEROD THE GREAT

Even though his father, Herod Antipater, ruled as governor before his son, *"Herod the Great,"* he is not mentioned in the Word of God.

The reign of Herod the Great was very eventful; however, he is remembered

NOTES

basically for two major happenings:

1. The reconstruction of the Jerusalem Temple, which was begun early in 19 B.C.; and,
2. The slaughter of the infants of Beth-lehem (Mat., Chpt. 2).

HEROD THE ETHNARCH

He is mentioned in Matthew 2:22. Even though he reigned in Judaea *"in place of his father Herod,"* he was not given the title of king.

He is said to have had the worst reputation of all the sons of Herod. He continued his father's building policy, but his repressive rule became intolerable.

A deputation of the Judaean and Samaritan aristocracy went to Rome to warn Augustus that unless he was removed, there would be a full-scale revolt. Consequently, Herod the Ethnarch was accordingly deposed and banished, with Judaea at that time becoming a Roman province, administered by prefects appointed by the emperor.

HEROD THE TETRARCH

He is mentioned in Luke 3:19. He also bore the distinctive name of Antipas.

He is conspicuous chiefly for his part in the imprisonment and execution of John the Baptist (Mk. 6:14-28), and for his brief encounter with Jesus when the latter was sent to him by Pilate for judgment (Lk. 23:7).

Jesus is recorded as having once described him as *"that fox"* (Lk. 13:32).

It is said that he was the ablest of Herod's sons, and like his father, was a great builder; the city of Tiberias on the lake of Galilee was built by him in A.D. 22 and named in honor of the emperor Tiberius. The city remains even unto the present.

Some years later, the Nabataean king Aretas declared war against Herod, with Herod being heavily defeated. Josephus said that many people regarded his defeat as Divine retribution for him killing John the Baptist.

HEROD THE KING

This is the Herod spoken of in Acts 12:1. He was known as Agrippa and was the nephew of Herod the Tetrarch.

NOTES

He was brought up in Rome in close association with the imperial family.

In A.D. 23, he became so heavily in debt that he had to leave Rome. For a time, he received shelter at Tiberias from his uncle, Herod the Tetrarch, thanks to his sister Herodias, whom his uncle had recently married.

However, this situation soon came to a head with him quarreling with his uncle, and in A.D. 36, he returned to Rome. There he offended the emperor Tiberius and was imprisoned, but on Tiberius' death the following year, he was released by the new emperor, Caligula, from whom he received the title of king.

He courted the goodwill of his Jewish subjects, who, for the most part, approved of him.

His attack on the Apostles, as recorded in Acts 12:2, was popular with the Jewish hierarchy, for the obvious evil reasons.

His sudden death at the age of 54 in A.D. 44 is recorded by Luke in Acts 12:20-23.

HEROD AGRIPPA

He was born in A.D. 27. He was adjudged too young to be made successor to his father's kingdom. Later, however, he received the title of king from Claudius.

He changed the name of his capital from Caesarea Philippi to Neronias as a compliment to the later emperor, Nero.

From A.D. 48 to 66, he had the prerogative of appointing the Jewish High Priests.

It is said that he did his best to prevent the outbreak of the Jewish war against Rome in A.D. 66, which resulted in the destruction of Jerusalem and Judaea as a whole in A.D. 70.

He is best known to New Testament readers from his encounter with Paul, as recorded in Acts 25:13-26:32.

VEX CERTAIN OF THE CHURCH

The phrase, *"Stretched forth his hands to vex certain of the Church,"* means this was probably done to ingratiate himself with the Jewish leadership. Undoubtedly, he had heard how some years earlier, the Sanhedrin had threatened the Apostles that they should not teach or preach anymore in the Name of Jesus, but how they kept on preaching in that Name, winning many Converts.

He probably was closer to the Jewish leadership than any other of the Herods. He had interposed his influence with the Emperor Caligula to prevent his statue (of Caligula) from being placed in the Holy of Holies in the Temple. Consequently, the Jewish leadership (incidentally, the same leadership that crucified Christ) looked upon him with favor.

Therefore, to please them further, he would *"vex certain of the Church."* More than likely, meetings were conducted between him and the leadership of Israel, with them encouraging his action in this regard. So, the apostate church would join with the world to stop the Move of God! Regrettably, it oftentimes continues in the same vein presently!

(2) "AND HE KILLED JAMES THE BROTHER OF JOHN WITH THE SWORD."

The structure is:

1. The Message of the Cross will be the last Move of God before the coming Great Tribulation (Mat. 24:32-33).

2. This Move of God will last for several years and is presently in the preparatory stages (Jn. 4:25-28).

THE MURDER OF JAMES, THE BROTHER OF JOHN

James and John were sons of Zebedee and among the first chosen by the Lord to be Apostles. Actually, it seems that Andrew and John were the very first two chosen (Jn. 1:35-39).

As well, it should be noted that no successor for James was ever chosen. In fact, none of these Eleven were ever followed by others in office, in other words, no apostolic succession, as taught by some.

Why was James selected by Herod to be killed?

James being singled out by death portrays to us the fact that he had been very zealous for the Lord. It doesn't appear that they gave him a trial of any sort, but rather that he was murdered by the henchmen of Herod.

In the eyes of all Jews, being killed by a sword was very disgraceful; consequently, all the Jews who hated Christ were very pleased that James had died in this manner.

Incidentally, as most know, Peter, James, and John were actually the inner circle of Jesus' Twelve Disciples.

The death of James probably took place about A.D. 44, meaning that he had about 11 years of Ministry after the Ascension of Christ. He was probably in his late thirties when he was killed.

There are many questions that arise out of this situation, of which we would hope to address at least some.

QUESTIONS

Why did the Lord allow James to be killed while at the same time delivering Peter?

In some present theology, many would claim that James did not have proper Faith and Peter did, etc.

To these people, and they are numerous, every single thing that happens to a Believer, be it good or bad, is always hinged to Faith and a proper confession. While Faith and a proper confession are definitely important, still, such thinking in no way lines up with Scripture. Carried out to its conclusion, Faith becomes an idol, with God subject to Faith instead of Faith subject to God. God will not allow His Word to be used against Himself.

In other words, a Believer cannot take a Promise of God, such as, *"What things soever you desire, when you pray, believe that you receive them, and you shall have them"* (Mk. 11:24), and many other such Scriptures, and use them against the Will of God. To say it in another way, a Believer cannot take this Promise, and many others similar, and become the president of the United States, etc.

If it is the Will of God, he can, but otherwise, he cannot! As should be obvious, all of these great Promises, of necessity, are subject to the Will of God.

So, James was not killed because he did not have proper Faith. Actually, such thinking is silly!

Some have ventured that the Apostles were not taking the Gospel to other parts of the world as quickly as they should have, staying too much in Jerusalem. Consequently, the Lord would have this happen to James in order that they be forced to go to other places because of the persecution.

NOTES

TRUSTING GOD

While there may be some small validity in such thinking, it should be obvious that the Lord could easily have handled that situation in other ways without taking such drastic action. The answer is according to the following:

First of all, God owes us no explanation for all the things He does. Accordingly, there are many things that happen (even such as what happened to James) with no explanation given. Actually, concerning James, and all other things for that matter, if the Holy Spirit had wanted us to know, He would have told us.

The Believer is to trust God, knowing that He loves us supremely, and that everything He does is always for our good and for the good of the Church as a whole. Even though we do not have answers—which sometimes we don't—we are to trust Him. In truth, proper trust does not demand an explanation for everything for the simple reason that it does trust, and that is enough.

As well, as someone has well said, proper Faith does not have any questions.

JOB

Millions, and I think I exaggerate not, have been plunged into gloom and despondency, unscripturally I might quickly add, simply because someone made them believe that adverse situations came upon them for the sole reason of them not having proper faith. Pure and simple, that is a lie!

On the other side of that coin, a lack of faith, as well as hidden sin, disobedience, self-will, etc., can definitely be the cause of some problems; however, that is not true all of the time.

For instance, some preachers have attempted to claim that Job's great afflictions came upon him simply because there was *"fear"* in his heart (Job 3:25). However, even an elementary perusal of Job's situation completely debunks such foolishness.

Job's experience had absolutely nothing to do with fear or Faith, and neither did it have anything to do with any type of hidden sin, disobedience, etc. Actually, the Lord said of the man, *"There is none like him in the Earth, a perfect and an upright man, one who fears God, and hates evil"* (Job 1:8). In truth, and according to what the Lord said, Job was closer to God than any human being on the face of the Earth when these terrible catastrophes came to him. No, it was not because of fear! The reason for Job's difficulties include the following:

• Satan accused Job before the Lord of certain things that were untrue (Job 1:9-10). In this test brought upon Job, the Lord would prove Satan wrong, thereby, establishing a foundation of service to the Lord built solely upon love.

• The Lord allowed this to happen in order that men would not be so judgmental, showing that bad things do happen to good people at times, and through no fault of their own. Yes, the Lord could stop all such things, but rather at times, uses them to draw the person even closer to God.

• This that the Lord allowed to come upon Job proved that God is Sovereign over all. In other words, Satan cannot do anything but that he first receive permission from the Lord. Even then, if permission is granted, it must be defined thoroughly. In this we learn that God is not a glorified Santa Claus, and neither is Jesus Christ a glorified bellhop. As well, the Holy Spirit is not in the Believer in order to tell the Father all the things the Believer wants, but rather the very opposite. Jesus said of the Spirit, *"He shall glorify Me* (not the Believer): *for He shall receive of Mine* (My Will), *and shall show it unto you"* (Jn. 16:14).

WHY?

We do not know why the Lord allowed Herod to kill James. He could easily have stopped such, had He so desired. However, there is one thing we do know:

God does all things well and always for our good. So, as hurtful as this was for the moment, overall, it was best. Paul would later write, *"And be not conformed to this world* (the ways of the world): *but be transformed by the renewing of your mind, that you may prove what is that good, and acceptable, and perfect, Will of God"* (Rom. 12:2).

In other words, it was the *"good, and acceptable, and perfect, Will of God,"* for James to be taken at this time and Peter delivered.

NOTES

Eusebius related an anecdote of the martyrdom of James, extracted from the lost work of Clement of Alexandria.

He claimed to have received this account by tradition from his predecessors, to the effect that the informer who accused James was so struck with the constancy of James in confessing Christ before the magistrate that he came forward and confessed himself a Christian as well.

It is said that the two were then led off to execution together, and on the way, the informer asked James' forgiveness.

After a moment's hesitation, it is said, James said to him, *"Peace be unto you,"* and kissed him. They were then both beheaded.

As Clement lived during the Second Century, consequently, not long removed from the time of James, there is a possibility of some truth in this account.

(3) "AND BECAUSE HE SAW IT PLEASED THE JEWS, HE PROCEEDED FURTHER TO TAKE PETER ALSO. THEN WERE THE DAYS OF UNLEAVENED BREAD."

The exegesis is:

1. The Cross of Christ is the Gospel (I Cor. 1:17).

2. Jesus Christ is the New Covenant, while the Cross of Christ is the meaning of that Covenant (Rom. 6:1-14).

PLEASING THE JEWS

The phrase, *"And because he saw it pleased the Jews,"* proclaims this which is indicative of too many politicians. They want to please certain groups so will set aside that which they know to be right. This man killed James and, thereby, reasoned that inasmuch as this was pleasing to the Sanhedrin, he would proceed accordingly with Peter.

Even though this phrase at the beginning of Verse 3 is very simple, it is the cause of many people being lost, as well as many Believers not coming up to what God truly has for them.

Preachers are prone to do things that oppose the Word of God because it pleases denominational heads. I speak of action and conduct toward others also in Christ.

The Believer has but one responsibility, and that is to please God. All else must take second place or no place at all!

The phrase, *"He proceeded further to take Peter also,"* proclaims him being used by Satan. However, his murdering James and the attempt to do the same with Peter is altogether different than anything he had ever done in all his life.

While murder, of course, is abominable in any and all cases, as is all sin, to adversely touch God's People is to touch God Himself. This is a position in which no man, be he king or otherwise, wants to find himself. The Twenty-third Verse of this Chapter bears this out, and graphically so!

THE PASSOVER

"Then were the days of Unleavened Bread," speaks of the time of the Passover; therefore, it was April.

There were three feasts at this time, which lasted a total of seven days (Ex. 12:15-18).

The Passover was eaten on the first day, which was also the first day of Unleavened Bread. This would have been a Wednesday, the day on which Jesus died, and not Friday, as many think.

On the first day (Sunday) after the Sabbath (Saturday), the Priest waved a sheaf of barley before the Lord, signifying the firstfruits of the barley harvest (Lev. 23:9-11). All of this typified our Lord.

He died on Calvary on the Day of the Passover (Wednesday), being put on the Cross at 9 a.m., the time of the morning sacrifice, and died at 3 p.m., the time of the evening sacrifice. He was the True Passover, to Whom some 1,600 years of previous Passovers (beginning in Egypt) had pointed.

The Feast of Unleavened Bread pointed strictly to His Perfect Life and Perfect Body, which He offered up in Perfect Sacrifice to God in order that men may be saved. He was the True Unleavened Bread.

When He was raised from the dead on the first day after the Sabbath, He became the Firstfruits to Whom all the previous firstfruits had pointed. In fact, *"firstfruits"* spoke of Resurrection.

NOTES

THE KINGDOM OF HEAVEN

The Jews were continuing all of these feasts, completely oblivious to the fact that the One to Whom they had pointed, namely Jesus, had already come, which, in effect, made all of this null and void. Tragically, they would not accept Him Who was the True Passover and, therefore, destroyed themselves.

With the First Advent of Christ, Israel's major task was completed. However, their second task of being the Priestly Nation of the world under Christ would have then begun had they accepted the *"Kingdom of Heaven"* as offered by Jesus. Regrettably, they rejected Him.

They will yet fulfill this role (Ezek., Chpts. 40-48), which will take place at the Second Coming (Rev., Chpt. 19). In the meantime, which has lasted already for nearly 2,000 years, seeing they have rejected Christ, there is no purpose for them. Consequently, Jerusalem and the Temple were completely destroyed in A.D. 70, making it impossible to continue the sacrifices, the Feast Days, etc., and with their Nation being lost as well.

Their being restored as a Nation in 1948 was the beginning of the fulfillment of the Prophecies respecting their Restoration, which will come, as we have stated, at the Second Coming (Zech., Chpts. 13-14).

(4) "AND WHEN HE HAD APPREHENDED HIM, HE PUT HIM IN PRISON, AND DELIVERED HIM TO FOUR QUATERNIONS OF SOLDIERS TO KEEP HIM; INTENDING AFTER EASTER TO BRING HIM FORTH TO THE PEOPLE."

The pattern is:

1. There is no victory outside of the Cross of Christ.

2. This means that every Believer must make the Cross of Christ—and we speak of what Jesus there did—the Object of his Faith.

PRISON

The phrase, *"And when he had apprehended him, he put him in prison,"* represents the third time Peter had been arrested (Acts 4:3; 5:18-19).

"And delivered him to four quaternions of soldiers to keep him," represented 16

soldiers, four to the watch, relieving the previous watch probably every six hours. He was chained to two soldiers and guarded by two others.

Quite possibly, members of the Sanhedrin had told Herod of them imprisoning the Twelve Apostles some years earlier and how, in some manner, they escaped, despite the guards (Acts 5:17-20). Consequently, Herod desired to make certain that such did not happen again, hence, the guards and chains.

The phrase, *"Intending after Easter to bring him forth to the people,"* presents an extremely unfortunate translation. It should have been translated *"Passover"* instead of *"Easter,"* for that is what it was.

EASTER, A PAGAN FESTIVAL

The name *"Easter"* was derived from one of the Babylonian goddesses, referred to as the *"Queen of Heaven"* and named *"Ishtar."* In fact, the name *"Ishtar"* is the same as the name *"Astarte,"* referred to as *"Ashtaroth"* in the Old Testament. Regrettably, Israel at times worshipped this heathenistic god, which the Lord referred to as an abomination (I Sam. 7:3; I Ki. 11:5, 33; II Ki. 23:13; Jer. 7:18; 44:18).

Easter, Lent, Lady Day, and Christmas were all borrowed from, and had their origination in, the Babylonian mysteries. None of these things have any relationship to Bible Christianity.

No, it is not wrong to use these names presently, inasmuch as we understand that they have no bearing on Christianity and merely serve as a designation.

In fact, the names of the days of the week were derived from the same source and once had to do with the worship of heavenly bodies, etc. However, as we presently use them, they are not sinful or wrong, inasmuch as they, as well, merely represent a particular designation.

After the seven days of Passover season, Herod was intending to bring Peter before the people and make a spectacle of his condemnation. In other words, it seems he intended to kill him publicly in order to further ingratiate himself with the religious leaders of Israel, and to show his power to the people. However, as we shall see, the situation was not to turn out as he had planned. Men rule, but God overrules!

NOTES

(5) "PETER THEREFORE WAS KEPT IN PRISON: BUT PRAYER WAS MADE WITHOUT CEASING OF THE CHURCH UNTO GOD FOR HIM."

The exegesis is:

1. If one doesn't understand the Cross of Christ relative to Sanctification, one simply does not know how to live for God.

2. God's Way is Jesus Christ and Him Crucified.

3. He has no other way because no other way is needed (I Cor. 1:17).

PETER

The phrase, *"Peter therefore was kept in prison,"* seems to present an untenable situation.

Considering that Herod had just killed James, and considering that he was fully intent upon doing the same with Simon Peter, there was no way, as should be obvious, that the situation could be altered, at least in the natural. However, nothing is impossible with God, and as circumstances will prove, the Church of that day believed that God could do anything and, consequently, resorted to that which it had always done—seek God in prayer.

PRAYER

The phrase, *"But prayer was made without ceasing of the Church unto God for him,"* presents the greatest weapon at the disposal of the Church, a weapon so strong, in fact, that there is absolutely nothing that cannot be done, providing, of course, it is the Will of God.

How many churches presently believe that God can do anything?

How many Believers believe it enough that they will go to the Lord in prayer simply because they believe God answers prayer?

While there are certainly some few Believers who believe accordingly, and some few Churches that fall into that category, as well, the far greater majority, sadly and regrettably, do not.

As I have already said several times in this particular Volume, the Book of Acts is the pattern laid down by the Holy Spirit and is intended for all Churches and for all time. Consequently, if the flavor of our church at present is not very similar to the Book of Acts Churches, in actuality, it is not really Church.

Sometime ago, there was a particular problem at one of the largest churches in the nation. Frances and I called the pastor and his wife, with whom we were not personally acquainted, but were simply desiring to do what we could to show understanding, love, etc.

The man and his wife were very gracious and at one particular point in my conversation with him, I diplomatically mentioned that before decisions were made, he should gather around him a group of people who really knew how to pray and get the Mind of the Lord on the situation.

After I made that statement, there was a silence on the other end of the line, and then he said, *"Would you please repeat that?"*

I made the statement again and about halfway through, I realized that he didn't have the slightest idea what I was talking about. He was polite, but he had no knowledge of prayer, of seeking God, or of asking the Lord for His Leading, etc.

TRUTH

Not meaning to be unkind, but yet, with truth demanded, this was not really a church, despite the thousands attending there. It was a religious social center of sorts, which comprises the majority of *"churches."*

Sadly, almost none of the people who attended the church that I have just mentioned truly knew the Lord. To be frank with you, I really do not believe the pastor was Saved either. I realize that most who read these words would think that such a statement is judgmental. However, it is not meant to be.

The point is there was absolutely no Biblical evidence that the Lord was present to any degree. Many think that all churches, although different, still are comprised of Believers. Nothing could be further from the truth!

If the Bible is not our pattern, then what is?

NOTES

We are told in the Epistles what the Doctrine of Redemption is. The Book of Acts portrays Redemption in action. If what we have does not match up, then we are not interpreting the Epistles correctly.

(6) "AND WHEN HEROD WOULD HAVE BROUGHT HIM FORTH, THE SAME NIGHT PETER WAS SLEEPING BETWEEN TWO SOLDIERS, BOUND WITH TWO CHAINS: AND THE KEEPERS BEFORE THE DOOR KEPT THE PRISON."

The synopsis is:

1. The phrase, *"And when Herod would have brought him forth,"* tells us several things.

Herod had probably let out the word all over Jerusalem that immediately upon the Passover ending, he was going to put on a great spectacle. Inasmuch as there were possibly as many as one million people in Jerusalem at this Passover time, he, in essence, urged all to stay over and witness the show.

2. It seems that Herod did intend to conduct a trial this time, whereas no trial at all was afforded James. However, the trial, if it had come off, would have been a mockery exactly as it was with Jesus.

3. The phrase, *"The same night Peter was sleeping between two soldiers, bound with two chains,"* presents a sight (Peter sleeping) that was not at all common for someone who expected to be killed the next day.

4. The truth is, I do not think Peter expected to die at this time. I am positive that he remembered what Jesus had told him after the Resurrection. Jesus had said, *"Verily, verily, I say unto you, When you were young, you girded yourself, and walked where you would: But when you shall be old, you shall stretch forth your hands, and another shall gird you, and carry you where you would not."*

John then said, *"This spoke He, signifying by what death he* (Peter) *should glorify God"* (Jn. 21:18-19).

5. Inasmuch as Peter was probably only in his early forties at this time, he could not be classified as *"old,"* such as Jesus had said he would be when he died; therefore, he did not at all at this time expect that his time had come.

NOTES

However, irrespective of that, I personally feel that Peter would have faced death in the same manner regardless! In fact, many, if not most, of the early Believers were so full of Christ that they did not fear death. Like Peter, they faced it without signs of worry or dismay, with multiple thousands of them being torn by wild beasts in the Roman arenas, etc.

6. *"And the keepers before the door kept the prison,"* portrays, as stated, two soldiers chained to Peter, with two standing at the door. Consequently, they felt that Peter was secure and was beyond the possibility of any type of rescue. However, they reasoned without the Lord!

(7) "AND, BEHOLD, THE ANGEL OF THE LORD CAME UPON HIM, AND A LIGHT SHINED IN THE PRISON: AND HE SMOTE PETER ON THE SIDE, AND RAISED HIM UP, SAYING, ARISE UP QUICKLY. AND HIS CHAINS FELL OFF FROM HIS HANDS."

The direction is:

1. The phrase, *"And, behold, the Angel of the Lord came upon him,"* should have been translated, *"An Angel of the Lord."*

The words, *"Came upon,"* contain the idea not only of presence but, as well, assigned for a particular task, in this case, the deliverance of Peter.

Did Peter expect an Angel?

2. Of course, we have no idea what Peter expected; however, I doubt that he knew what to expect. I do firmly believe, as stated, that he believed some type of deliverance would be effected due to what Jesus had said of him some 11 years before. That it would be this dramatic, however, there is no indication.

3. And yet, this is the man who had seen Jesus perform literally hundreds, if not thousands, of the most astounding Miracles the world has ever known, even to the raising of the dead. As well, he had seen some of the greatest Miracles ever himself, even rivaling those performed by the Master, even to the raising of the dead. So, this was a man who expected Miracles. Consequently, I do not think, even as glorious as this was, that it was a great surprise to him. I feel that the only question Peter had was if it was a Vision or reality.

4. *"And a Light shined in the prison,"* does not indicate if it was emanating from the Angel, which it probably was, or separate from the Angel! At any rate, there was no doubt that the Angel was not only *"of the Lord,"* but, as well, *"from the Lord."*

Even as I dictate these notes, I sense strongly the Presence of the Lord. What a mighty God we serve! And yet, I believe that which Peter experienced that night, and which, in fact, was somewhat common during the times of the Early Church, is once again going to reappear, even as it did then.

5. Of course, God has always done great things for those who believe Him, even through the entirety of man's existence. However, I feel what we are about to see is going to supersede anything that has ever happened, and, in fact, we are even now in the preparatory stages.

6. *"And he smote Peter on the side, and raised him up, saying, Arise up quickly,"* simply means that the Angel awakened him.

7. *"And his chains fell off from his hands,"* refers to the Angel unlocking them by the Power of God.

(8) "AND THE ANGEL SAID UNTO HIM, GIRD YOURSELF, AND BIND ON YOUR SANDALS. AND SO HE DID. AND HE SAID UNTO HIM, CAST YOUR GARMENT ABOUT YOU, AND FOLLOW ME."

The structure is:

1. The phrase, *"And the Angel said unto him, Gird yourself, and bind on your sandals. And so he did."* presents Peter somewhat in a daze, as would be obvious. From his later conversation, it seems that he somewhat thought he was having a Vision.

2. *"And he said unto him, Cast your garment about you, and follow me,"* speaks of the outer garment, with Peter now being fully dressed.

3. As is obvious, he had to be told what to do respecting each thing, which probably would be similar with anyone else.

(9) "AND HE WENT OUT, AND FOLLOWED HIM; AND WIST NOT THAT IT WAS TRUE WHICH WAS DONE BY THE ANGEL; BUT THOUGHT HE SAW A VISION."

The plan is:

1. The phrase, *"And he went out, and followed him,"* presents Peter doing something which, at the moment, he was not certain was real. He knew the Angel seemed real enough, and his being loosed from the guards seemed real; however, he probably wondered if he would awaken at any moment.

2. The phrase, *"And wist not that it was true which was done by the Angel; but thought he saw a Vision,"* simply means that he had difficulty believing and understanding that this was literal. Even for someone like Peter, our situations are so prone to the natural that it is very difficult to properly make the transition to the supernatural.

(10) "WHEN THEY WERE PAST THE FIRST AND THE SECOND WARD, THEY CAME UNTO THE IRON GATE THAT LEADS UNTO THE CITY; WHICH OPENED TO THEM OF HIS OWN ACCORD: AND THEY WENT OUT, AND PASSED ON THROUGH ONE STREET; AND FORTHWITH THE ANGEL DEPARTED FROM HIM."

The exegesis is:

1. The phrase, *"When they were past the first and the second ward,"* probably means that Herod had placed Peter in the inner prison. So, it probably meant that he passed one door with guards and then a second door with guards. It is obvious here that every precaution of which one could think had been taken, guaranteeing that fellow Disciples could not rescue him, or anyone else for that matter, at least other than God.

2. It is obvious that in some manner, the Angel shielded Peter and himself in such a way that they were invisible to these guards.

3. *"They came unto the iron gate that leads unto the city,"* pertained to the gate of the prison. So, it seems that Peter and the Angel had to pass through two doors and one gate, which were all locked tight.

4. *"Which opened to them of his own accord,"* means it opened automatically.

5. *"And they went out, and passed on through one street; and forthwith the Angel departed from him,"* signals Peter's total deliverance, which was so miraculous that it actually defies description. Now that there were no more obstacles to overcome, the Angel departed.

NOTES

6. Surely, the reader can grasp the workings of the supernatural on this occasion to such a degree that it leaves one all but speechless! To be sure, things of this nature do not happen often; however, as we have stated, I believe that is about to change.

(11) "AND WHEN PETER WAS COME TO HIMSELF, HE SAID, NOW I KNOW OF A SURETY, THAT THE LORD HAS SENT HIS ANGEL, AND HAS DELIVERED ME OUT OF THE HAND OF HEROD, AND FROM ALL THE EXPECTATION OF THE PEOPLE OF THE JEWS."

The order is:

1. The phrase, *"And when Peter was come to himself,"* means that he finally knew and understood that what had happened to him had not merely been a Vision or a Dream, but he had been truly delivered by an Angel.

2. The phrase, *"He said, Now I know of a surety, that the Lord has sent His Angel,"* does not, as some claim, portray a lack of Faith on the part of Peter.

3. As we have stated, the supernatural is not a simple thing even with the godliest of Believers. The question is not one of reality, for, in truth, the supernatural is far more real even than the natural simply because it is eternal. The difficulty is exactly as it was with Peter, knowing at times if it is a Dream or a Vision or something actually happening.

4. *"And has delivered me out of the hand of Herod,"* proclaims Peter giving God all the glory and portraying His Omnipotence, which is here obvious. In other words, this deliverance affecting Peter, at the same time, refers to Judgment upon Herod.

5. A display of God's Power and Mercy is an awesome thing, even as recorded here. However, there are always two sides to that coin. Judgment, of necessity, always accompanies God's Power manifested in Mercy, Grace, and long-suffering. In other words, the same Power that heals can also kill. The same Power that saves can also destroy. The same Power that delivers can also imprison.

6. *"And from all the expectation of the*

NOTES

people of the Jews," means that multiple thousands in Jerusalem at that time were looking forward to seeing the show. Of course, there were also thousands in the city who were sympathetic toward the Apostles.

7. The people had become very polarized, as all such situations ultimately develop.

Those who had thrown in their lot with the Sanhedrin, of which there were many, eagerly awaited the coming spectacle, which was probably scheduled to happen the very next day.

Some think that Peter was delivered between 3 and 6 a.m.

(12) "AND WHEN HE HAD CONSIDERED THE THING, HE CAME TO THE HOUSE OF MARY THE MOTHER OF JOHN, WHOSE SURNAME WAS MARK; WHERE MANY WERE GATHERED TOGETHER PRAYING."

The pattern is:

1. The Believer needs the Work of the Cross just as much as the unredeemed need the Work of the Cross.

2. One of the greatest tricks of Satan is the pretense of leading Believers into higher enlightenment outside of the Cross.

THE SPIRIT WORLD OF DARKNESS

The phrase, *"And when he had considered the thing,"* refers to his momentary reflections regarding what had just happened. In a way, it seemed to be surreal, but yet, he now knew, in fact, it was very real.

Actually, the spirit world is all around us, and as far as Christians are concerned, it is in us, as well, due to being born of the Spirit with many baptized in the Spirit also.

The spirit world is extremely real, even more so than the so-called natural world, and something with which every human being deals constantly, even though not understood by most.

It is divided into the spirit world of darkness and the spirit world of Light. That of darkness is comprised of demon spirits and fallen Angels, all headed up by Lucifer, the Prince of Darkness. As well, the far greater majority of the human family is in league with the Evil One.

Sometime in the past, Lucifer, who was originally created by God as holy, pure, beautiful, and mighty, rebelled against his Creator, with about one-third of the Angels rebelling with him (Isa. 14:12-15; Rev. 12:4). From that time, Satan has attempted to destroy man, the most prized Creation of God. That revolution, which began before the Earth was ever created but extended to man at the time of the Creation, has raged from then until now unchecked (Ezek. 28:11-19). This revolution against God has resulted in this Earth being soaked with blood enumerable times, with sorrow unparalleled and sickness, pain, war, guilt, sin, and death being the result.

HOW DOES SATAN THINK HE CAN SUCCEED?

In fact, Satan does think he can succeed in this conflict. His greatest weapon against the human family is deception. With that, he has caused most of the population of humanity for all time to be eternally lost. In other words, they were deceived into believing a lie.

He is so good at his effort because he is deceived himself. In other words, he actually thinks he can overthrow God, even though God is Almighty.

Yes, he can read the Bible and knows it far better than most Believers, but the truth is, he does not believe the Bible. Consequently, his billions of dupes fall into the same category; they simply do not believe the Word of God. Tragically, it seems that many Christians, if not most, fall into the same category.

According to the Word of God, he has two more great efforts in his plan to destroy the Kingdom of God and to take over the world totally and completely.

Of his many efforts in the past, which are actually unending, the next great spectacle will be the Great Tribulation, lasting for some seven years. Jesus said, *"For then shall be Great Tribulation, such as was not since the beginning of the world to this time, no, nor ever shall be."*

He even said, *"And except those days should be shortened, there should no flesh be saved: but for the elect's sake* (the sake of Israel) *those days shall be shortened"* (Mat. 24:21-22).

Satan's effort at that time to take over the world will be multifaceted. Even though he is now the god of this present world and, in fact, has been ever since the Fall, still, he has repeatedly lost ground due to what the Lord has done regarding the Redemption of the fallen race by the means of the Cross.

THE CROSS

The Word of God came into the world as God gave it to Prophets as well as the Apostles. Then, with the First Advent of Jesus, Satan was dealt a severe blow, in fact, a fatal blow, when Jesus died on Calvary and was raised from the dead. That broke his terrible grip of sin on the human family and, as well, totally and completely cleanses all sinners from sin who believe on Christ and what He did for us at the Cross (Jn. 3:16; Rom. 10:9-13).

The Cross of Christ made possible all types of wonderful things. It made it possible for Jesus to be raised from the dead. It made it possible for any believing sinner to take of the Water of Life freely.

Then, with the Ascension, which was all because of the Cross, the Holy Spirit was sent back in a different dimension than had ever been known previously, which has resulted in the Light of the Gospel being spread all over the world.

In the coming Great Tribulation, Satan will attempt to destroy Israel totally and completely. Of course, this is a task he has worked at from the time of Abraham. He knows that great Promises of God are wrapped up in these ancient people, even though they are now in a terrible state of rebellion. He knows that if he can destroy them, even as he attempted to do in the Holocaust, as well as countless other times, the great Plan of God will come unraveled. In other words, great segments of the Word of God concerning Israel's coming Restoration will fall to the ground (Jer., Chpts. 30-31; Ezek., Chpts. 37-48; Zech., Chpts. 12-14, etc.)

So, in destroying Israel, that is, if he can do so, he will, in effect, destroy God because if God's Word is broken, everything falls down. As we have said, Satan is deceived and actually thinks he can carry forth such a task.

NOTES

THE GREAT TRIBULATION

However, his efforts to destroy these ancient people, although looking for a time as if it will succeed, will be thwarted by the greatest event in human history, at least as far as the world is concerned. We speak of the Second Coming of the Lord (Rev., Chpt. 19). Then, the Evil One, along with all his demon spirits and fallen Angels, will be locked away in the *"bottomless pit"* (Rev. 20:1-3).

For 1,000 years, with Jesus reigning personally from Jerusalem, He will govern this Earth with no hindrance whatsoever from Satan. It will be a time of bliss, prosperity, Salvation, and Restoration such as the world has never known.

ONE FINAL ATTEMPT

The Word says, *"And when the thousand years are expired, Satan will be loosed out of his prison"* (Rev. 20:7).

Of course, all of his demon spirits and fallen Angels will be loosed, as well, making one final attempt to steal, kill and destroy (Jn. 10:10), but will be cut short.

Actually, we are not given much information regarding this situation, for the reason that it will be short-lived (Rev. 20:7-10).

At that time, Satan and his henchmen will be *"cast into the Lake of Fire and Brimstone ... And shall be tormented day and night for ever and ever"* (Rev. 20:10).

THE SPIRIT WORLD OF LIGHT

This great Kingdom, called the *"Kingdom of God"* or the *"Kingdom of Heaven,"* is headed up by the Triune Godhead, *"God the Father," "God the Son,"* and *"God the Holy Spirit."* All of the angelic host, minus the fallen Angels, are a part of this Kingdom, as well as every single Born-Again Believer (Jn. 3:3).

As the kingdom of darkness under Satan is constantly active, as well, the Kingdom of Light is active. In fact, the Cross of Christ opened up this Kingdom of Light as nothing that has ever previously been done or ever will be done. Satan and all of his minions of darkness were totally and completely defeated at the Cross. The Holy Spirit through Paul tells us this, and I quote

NOTES

directly from THE EXPOSITOR'S STUDY BIBLE, notes and all.

"And you, being dead in your sins and the uncircumcision of your flesh *(speaks of spiritual death [i.e., 'separation from God'], which sin does!)*, **has He quickened** *(made alive)* **together with Him** *(refers to being made spiritually alive, which is done through being 'born-again')* **having forgiven you all trespasses** *(the Cross made it possible for all manner of sins to be forgiven and taken away)*;

"Blotting out the handwriting of Ordinances that was against us *(pertains to the Law of Moses, which was God's standard of Righteousness that man could not reach)*, **which was contrary to us** *(Law is against us, simply because we are unable to keep its precepts, no matter how hard we try)*, **and took it out of the way** *(refers to the penalty of the Law being satisfied in Jesus, and thereby being removed)*, **nailing it to His Cross** *(the Law with its decrees was abolished in Christ's death, as if Crucified with Him)*;

"And having spoiled principalities and powers *(Satan and all of his henchmen were defeated at the Cross by Christ atoning for all sin; sin was the legal right Satan had to hold man in captivity; with all sin atoned, he has no more legal right to hold anyone in bondage)*, **He** *(Christ)* **made a show of them openly** *(what Jesus did at the Cross was in the face of the whole universe)*, **triumphing over them in it** *(The triumph is complete and it was all done for us, meaning we can walk in power and perpetual victory due to the Cross)*" **(Col. 2:13-15).**

Now, due to the Cross, the Holy Spirit abides in the hearts of all Believers, which has blessed this world in a manner that is absolutely inconceivable, but which is understood not at all by the world and, regrettably, very little by the church.

In this Kingdom of Light, Angels are, as well, at work, even as we have studied the great deliverance of Peter from prison. Things of this nature happen, no doubt, untold times, but are seldom made visible, as it was with Peter. Actually, the Scripture tells us, *"Be not forgetful to entertain strangers: for thereby some have entertained Angels unawares"* (Heb. 13:2). The Bible records over 100 appearances of Angels to men, and as we have stated, no doubt, enumerable times although unseen.

As well, the Holy Spirit is constantly leading and giving direction, at least for those who look to Him (Jn. 16:7-15).

MARY

The phrase, *"He came to the house of Mary the mother of John, whose surname was Mark,"* presents one of the six Mary's in Scripture. She was the aunt of Barnabas.

The John Mark mentioned here is the one who wrote the Gospel that bears his name.

He seems to have been a Convert of Peter (I Pet. 5:13), and later worked with Paul (Col. 4:10-11; II Tim. 4:11; Phile., Vs. 24).

Some think this may have been the house that contained the Upper Room, which would have been quite large considering that over 100 people may have gathered there at times (Acts 1:13-15).

The phrase, *"Where many were gathered together praying,"* proclaims they were praying for Peter around the clock. Some scholars think that Peter was rescued by the Angel, as stated, between 3 and 6 a.m., which meant, if correct, they were praying day and night.

Their only hope was God, as is overly obvious, as God is our only hope in any situation. So, it is very foolish for Believers to resort to men.

(13) "AND AS PETER KNOCKED AT THE DOOR OF THE GATE, A DAMSEL CAME TO HEARKEN, NAMED RHODA."

The composition is:

1. The Grace of God always and without exception has as its pivot point the Cross of Christ.

2. This means that the Cross of Christ alone makes all Grace possible (Gal. 2:21).

THE HOME OF MARY

The phrase, *"And as Peter knocked at the door of the gate,"* tells us somewhat the type of home this was.

In those days, houses of wealthy families, which here seems to be the case, were built around a courtyard, in which were planted beautiful flowers, etc. In other words, the house would have been somewhat like a horseshoe, with a gate at the entrance to the courtyard.

As we have stated, this tells us that the family of Mark was quite well off financially, even able to employ servants, as we shall see.

If all of this is correct, it might explain why Mark deserted Paul and Barnabas on Paul's first missionary journey, even at a critical juncture when he was the most needed. Having been raised in comfort, he was not too accustomed to such hardships.

On Paul's second missionary journey, Barnabas wanted to give Mark a second chance in going with them, feeling that the past situation would not be repeated. However, Paul was not of the same frame of mind and refused to take him. This caused a rift between Paul and Barnabas, with even Barnabas not going and being replaced by Silas (Acts 13:5, 13; 15:35-41).

However, as we shall later see, Paul ultimately changed his mind about Mark and actually sent for him (II Tim. 4:11).

RHODA

So, Peter stood outside the courtyard gate knocking because it was locked.

The phrase, *"A damsel came to hearken, named Rhoda,"* pertains to this lady who was a servant in this house, with a part of her duties being to welcome the guests.

The name *"Rhoda"* actually has two meanings in the Greek Text: *"Rhode,"* meaning *"a rose,"* and *"Rode,"* referring to her as a servant girl.

Every indication is that she was a Believer and would have the distinct privilege of having her name mentioned in the Word of God, of which there could not be a higher honor. Thus, the Holy Spirit honors both the wealthy family of Mark and this lowly servant girl, beautifully portraying the Gospel of Jesus Christ and what it is all about.

What if Rhoda had had little concern about what was happening, even as many Believers, and would not have bothered being in this prayer meeting, especially considering that this was probably between 3 and 6 a.m.? She would have missed out on one of the greatest happenings in history and the great reward given her by the Lord for the simple task of going to the door (gate), thereby, proving her faithfulness.

NOTES

SERVICE FOR CHRIST

Any and all Believers must set themselves to the idea that they are going to be in every single Church service that is humanly possible. Understanding that some must miss some services due to their employment, still, otherwise, they must not miss a service. Christians who attend only on Sunday mornings, thereby, ignoring all other services, must be concluded as spiritually lukewarm, therefore, unfaithful! There is no other conclusion that can be drawn. Their love for the Lord must be labeled as tepid, at best! But yet, many who call themselves *"Believers"* fall into that category.

The only answer that one could give concerning these people is that they have little concern about the Lord or His Work. In other words, their hearts and affections are somewhere else. They attend Church or serve the Lord only enough that they may call themselves *"Believers."* In reality, such people have very little, if any, experience with the Lord, and to be frank, most in this category actually are not saved.

(14) "AND WHEN SHE KNEW PETER'S VOICE, SHE OPENED NOT THE GATE FOR GLADNESS, BUT RAN IN, AND TOLD HOW PETER STOOD BEFORE THE GATE."

The exegesis is:

1. The phrase, *"And when she knew Peter's voice,"* tells us that the wall and gate were tall, with the visitor unable to be seen by those in the courtyard. However, when she asked for identification, which was the normal manner, Peter spoke up, with her instantly recognizing who he was.

2. As one might understand, these were dangerous times, and a knock in the night was ominous most of the time.

3. The phrase, *"She opened not the gate for gladness,"* presents that which is understandable.

4. It seems that Peter was very close to this family, with every evidence being that he had won Mark to the Lord, as well as possibly the entire family (I Pet. 5:13).

5. Also, it is almost certain that Peter

NOTES

collaborated greatly with Mark in the writing of Mark's Gospel. In other words, the account of all the Miracles of Christ, plus other things Jesus did, was told to Mark by Peter, thereby, providing eyewitness and firsthand information.

6. So, Rhoda was so thrilled and happy at the hearing of Peter's voice that in her excitement she failed to even open the gate and let him in.

7. The phrase, *"But ran in, and told how Peter stood before the gate,"* presents her message as being so astounding as to be unbelievable!

(15) "AND THEY SAID UNTO HER, YOU ARE MAD. BUT SHE CONSTANTLY AFFIRMED THAT IT WAS EVEN SO. THEN SAID THEY, IT IS HIS ANGEL."

The synopsis is:

1. Everything we receive from God, and I mean everything, all and without exception is made possible by the Cross.

2. To receive these benefits, this means that we must, without fail, place our Faith exclusively in Christ and what He did for us at the Cross.

NOTHING IS IMPOSSIBLE WITH GOD

The phrase, *"And they said unto her, You are mad,"* places the emphasis on the pronoun *"You."* In other words, they not only did not believe her but concluded that she was losing touch with reality.

Almost all commentators judge this prayer meeting as faithless. They reason that these early Believers were praying for Peter's deliverance, but yet, would not believe it when it happened. However, I think that such judgment is harsh! I am not certain if we would have done any better. Several things should be noted here:

• The Lord can answer prayer at times so astoundingly and so miraculously that it is simply beyond the comprehension of the Believer to grasp it all. However, that does not note a lack of Faith, but only that God is so far above us that we are left speechless at some of the things He does.

• Irrespective of how much Faith a Believer has, the Lord always takes one beyond his Faith. Actually, this is the very nature of Faith!

If the Lord took us only to the limit of our Faith, I am not so sure that it would be proper for us to even call it Faith. By its very nature, Faith reaches out to the impossible, meaning past our comprehension and understanding. Faith always takes the Believer into uncharted territory. That is the reason Paul said, *"Now unto Him Who is able to do exceeding abundantly above all that we ask or think, according to the power that works in us"* (Eph. 3:20).

THEY WERE NOT FAITHLESS

• No! I do not believe these people were faithless. Had they been, they would not have been seeking God around the clock for Peter's deliverance. They knew the Lord could do great things. Actually, they lived in the very time of the greatest Outpouring of the Spirit the world had ever known. People who do not have Faith do not pray! That is an obvious conclusion!

I believe they expected Peter to be delivered, and so he was! However, the manner in which it was done was simply beyond their ability to grasp, and I think it would be the same with us.

In truth, Peter himself at first was not so sure as to what was happening. His deliverance was likewise beyond anything he could ask or think!

It bothers me somewhat when Believers flippantly talk down about people such as these. When they get to the place they are able to see what these people saw, then maybe they can venture an opinion.

PRAYING AND CONFESSION

• Some others presently say that these people should not have been praying at all, but rather confessing Peter out of prison. They would also state that if Peter had had the right confession, he would have never been put in prison in the first place.

This error is so compounded that it borders on the edge of blasphemy. It shows an utter lack of knowledge of the Word of God and, as well, a false interpretation of what little is known.

While a proper confession is certainly important and Biblical, still, people and situations are not changed by a formula of confession, but rather by seeking God.

Is there any evidence in the Bible, be it Old or New Testament, that people confessed things into existence?

No! The silence is deafening!

However, the Word of God is replete, all the way from Genesis through the Book of Revelation, of people seeking God, oftentimes with bitter tears, in respect to particular needs, etc. (Gen. 18:23-33; 20:17; Num. 11:2; 21:7; Deut. 9:26; I Sam. 1:10; II Ki. 6:17; 19:15; II Chron. 32:20; Neh. 1:4; Jonah 2:1; 4:2; Mat. 26:39; Lk. 9:18; 22:32; Acts 4:31; 6:6; 8:15; 9:40; 13:3; 14:23; 16:25; 20:36; 21:5; James 5:18).

If the Bible is to be our criterion, then I think my point should be well taken!

"But she constantly affirmed that it was even so," pertains to her claim as being more and more of conviction. They kept saying *"no,"* and she kept saying *"yes,"* but yet, stronger than their *"no!"*

"Then said they, It is his Angel," proclaims a belief in that day that all Jews had a guardian Angel. They also believed that the guardian Angel could take a person's form (Horton). However, there is no Scriptural basis for such thinking.

(16) "BUT PETER CONTINUED KNOCKING: AND WHEN THEY HAD OPENED THE DOOR, AND SAW HIM, THEY WERE ASTONISHED."

The exegesis is:

1. The phrase, *"But Peter continued knocking,"* certainly proclaims that someone was at the gate. As well, they should have known that if indeed it was an Angel, he would not knock at a gate but simply appear before them, etc.

As well, the *"continued knocking"* refers to Peter knocking ever harder.

2. *"And when they had opened the door, and saw him, they were astonished,"* means they were speechless, even to the extent of putting them in a daze.

3. It was Peter and, as well, flesh and blood Peter!

(17) "BUT HE, BECKONING UNTO THEM WITH THE HAND TO HOLD THEIR PEACE, DECLARED UNTO THEM HOW THE LORD HAD BROUGHT HIM OUT OF THE PRISON. AND HE SAID, GO SHOW THESE THINGS UNTO JAMES, AND TO THE BRETHREN. AND HE DEPARTED, AND WENT INTO ANOTHER PLACE."

NOTES

The synopsis is:

1. Without the Cross, nothing could be received from the Lord.

THE DECLARATION

The phrase, *"But he, beckoning unto them with the hand to hold their peace,"* no doubt, means that they all, ever how many there were, quickly regained their composure and were shooting questions at him as fast as they came to their minds, and all at one time. He then held up his hand for them to be silent for a moment.

"Declared unto them how the Lord had brought him out of the prison," presents Peter giving all credit and praise to the Lord and none to his great Faith, or that of anyone else for that matter. While the praying of these people certainly availed much (James 5:16), still, it was the Lord Who did the work, as it is always the Lord Who does the work. It is by His Power that these things are brought to pass, with our intercession and petition only serving as the trigger. Of course, the Lord does not even need that, but through His Grace allows us to be a part of what He does.

The truth is, He does not need us at all, but we need Him for all things!

Did all these Miracles pass away with the Apostles as many contend?

No, they did not! There is no hint of such in the Word of God, only in the word of unbelieving men. In fact, the Scripture teaches the very opposite (Jer. 33:3; Mat. 21:21; Mk. 11:24; 16:15; Jn. 12:15, etc.).

GO TELL OTHERS

"And he said, Go show these things unto James, and to the brethren," referred to the Lord's half-brother and the Elders of the Church in Jerusalem, plus any other of the Twelve who may have been in Jerusalem at that time.

Whether it is true or not is not known, but tradition says that Peter, James (son of Zebedee), and John selected James, the Lord's half-brother, to be the Pastor (Bishop) of the Church in Jerusalem, which

NOTES

was according to the Will of God.

In fact, such does contain a ring of truth, inasmuch as James would never have placed himself in this position. Considering that he had not at all served Jesus in His earthly Ministry and, in fact, did not even believe in Him, he in no way considered himself worthy of anything. Actually, even though he definitely was an Apostle, neither he nor his brother Jude would refer to themselves as such at the opening of their two Epistles, but rather as *"a servant of God and of the Lord Jesus Christ"* (James 1:1), with Jude simply saying *"the servant of Jesus Christ, and brother of James"* (Jude, Vs. 1).

The evidence is that Jesus Personally appeared to James after the Resurrection, with His half-brother immediately accepting Him as Lord and Saviour (I Cor. 15:7). It is said that James then immediately won his brothers to the Lord, with them fervently serving Jesus until they died.

JAMES THE JUST

Tradition says that the name of *"James the Just"* was given to him by the Apostles, and that he prayed so much that his knees had calluses like those of a camel.

There is some disagreement as to how James died. Some say that he was stoned to death in A.D. 61, while others say that enemies hurled him down from off the pinnacle of the Temple. If this is true, it would have happened in about A.D. 62 or 63.

Tradition further says that by his preaching, James alienated Piobsata from her husband Ananus, the Roman governor of Jerusalem. Ananus, therefore, inflamed the Jews against James, with them hurling him from the Temple pinnacle.

The phrase, *"And he departed, and went into another place,"* proclaims such being done almost immediately by Peter, knowing that by dawn, Herod's men would be searching for him and would undoubtedly come there.

The evidence is that he did not tell anyone where he was going, so they could say honestly that they did now know where he was (Horton).

DID PETER GO TO ROME?

The Catholic church claims that Peter was the first Pope. Of course, for him to be the first Pope, he would have had to go to Rome; however, there is no evidence that Peter visited Rome before his death. He may have, but the Bible doesn't say so, and neither does history.

In I Peter 5:13, the great Apostle mentions Babylon, where he seems to have stayed for a period of time. It is, in fact, believed that he was the Pastor of the Church in Babylon. Some claim that he was actually speaking of Rome when he mentioned Babylon; however, there is no proof whatsoever of that. In fact, the proof is the other way.

When Paul wrote his great Epistle to the Romans and closed it out with a benediction containing many names, he did not mention Peter. It stands to reason that if Peter had been in Rome at this time, Paul definitely would have mentioned him. In fact, Paul would have mentioned him first.

According to the Catholic Catalog of Bishops in Rome, Peter was in Rome at this particular time. It is obvious, however, that he wasn't there, so this makes the very foundation of apostolic succession by our Catholic friends fall to the ground.

While Peter, at some particular time, may have gone to Rome, there is no Biblical or historical evidence that he did.

(18) "NOW AS SOON AS IT WAS DAY, THERE WAS NO SMALL STIR AMONG THE SOLDIERS, WHAT WAS BECOME OF PETER."

The exegesis is:

1. The phrase, *"Now as soon as it was day,"* pertains to the two guards awakening, who had been chained to Peter.

2. The phrase, *"There was no small stir among the soldiers, what was become of Peter,"* is certainly understandable, due to the fact that losing their prisoner meant for them certain death.

3. I wonder what their story was to Herod.

(19) "AND WHEN HEROD HAD SOUGHT FOR HIM, AND FOUND HIM NOT, HE EXAMINED THE KEEPERS, AND COMMANDED THAT THEY SHOULD BE PUT TO DEATH. AND HE WENT DOWN FROM JUDAEA TO CAESAREA, AND THERE ABODE."

NOTES

The pattern is:

1. The phrase, *"And when Herod had sought for him, and found him not,"* simply means that he sent for Peter, intending for him to be brought by the guards.

2. The Passover week had ended, and now he was ready to put forth his great spectacle of having a mock trial regarding Peter, and then executing him before thousands of onlookers. Considering that he had been advertising this all over Jerusalem for several days, his anger knew no bounds when he was told that Peter could not be found. One can almost hear the screaming rage as he demanded answers.

3. *"He examined the keepers,"* means that he did not believe their story at all, such as it was.

4. Actually, they did not have much of a story. All they knew was, they went to sleep the night before, with both chained to Simon Peter. When they awakened the next morning, Peter was not there, and, as well, none of the guards standing at the doors had seen him or heard anything.

5. The word *"examined"* actually means that Herod tortured the guards. Evidently he thought someone had bribed them; therefore, he was attempting to extract the truth when, in reality, he had already been given the truth, at least as it was known by them.

6. *"And commanded that they should be put to death,"* pertains to him being so disgusted, as well as embarrassed, that he ordered the execution of these men, which could have numbered six or more.

7. *"And he went down from Judaea to Caesarea, and there abode,"* has reference to the fact that he had been embarrassed before the people, not being able to put forth his spectacle concerning Peter. So, he left Jerusalem, it seems, almost immediately and went to Caesarea.

8. Concerning him going from Jerusalem to Caesarea, it says, *"He went down."* However, this does not refer to geography as, in fact, he actually went up, inasmuch as Caesarea is not too much short of 100 miles northwest of Jerusalem. It is speaking of topography, inasmuch as Jerusalem is about 3,000 feet above sea level, whereas Caesarea is only a few feet, considering that it is on the Mediterranean Coast.

(20) "AND HEROD WAS HIGHLY DISPLEASED WITH THEM OF TYRE AND SIDON: BUT THEY CAME WITH ONE ACCORD TO HIM, AND, HAVING MADE BLASTUS THE KING'S CHAMBERLAIN THEIR FRIEND, DESIRED PEACE; BECAUSE THEIR COUNTRY WAS NOURISHED BY THE KING'S COUNTRY."

The pattern is:

1. The phrase, *"And Herod was highly displeased with them of Tyre and Sidon,"* gives us no clue for the reason of this displeasure. As well, the reason is not found in any of the historical accounts.

2. However, it probably had something to do with trade between these two city states and Judaea. Evidently the leaders of these two cities had done something that greatly angered him. The anger was of such magnitude that he would have gone to war if Rome had allowed such. However, both were under Roman supremacy, which meant they must settle their disputes some other way than war.

3. The phrase, *"But they came with one accord to him,"* concerns the leaders of these two cities because the situation stood to fall out to great harm to Tyre and Sidon.

4. These two cities had very little land suitable for agriculture, consequently, they were dependent on Judaea for much of their food supply. The food was exchanged for cedar and fir trees, as well as other things, and had continued between these two countries for somewhat over 1,000 years (I Ki. 5:10-11).

5. As well, there is a good possibility that the famine spoken of by the Prophet Agabus (Acts 11:28) was now upon this part of the world, even affecting Tyre and Sidon greatly, thereby, making their situation even more perilous.

6. However, the Holy Spirit could have well orchestrated these events in order that Herod be taken up with other things, consequently, stopping the persecution of the Church, which seems to be what happened, at least for the time being.

7. *"And, having made Blastus the king's chamberlain their friend, desired peace,"* pertains to their soliciting the help of one

NOTES

of the king's confidential advisers. Using his influence, they asked for peace for themselves.

8. *"Because their country was nourished by the king's country,"* pertains to the trade agreements regarding food, which we have just mentioned.

(21) "AND UPON A SET DAY HEROD, ARRAYED IN ROYAL APPAREL, SAT UPON HIS THRONE, AND MADE AN ORATION UNTO THEM."

The order is:

1. The phrase, *"And upon a set day Herod,"* speaks of the agreement being made between Judaea and the twin cities. This *"set day"* was to be a time of great festivity and celebration, with hundreds of people coming from the twin cities, as well as the locals, in order to celebrate this occasion. It was probably conducted in the outdoor theater at Caesarea, from whence the king, raised above the rest of the audience on a platform, could both see the games and make his speech to the people.

2. The phrase, *"Arrayed in royal apparel,"* speaks of great pomp and ceremony, as King Herod appeared before the people in his royal robes.

Horton said, *"According to the Jewish Historian Josephus, the outer robe was of silver (either adorned with silver or actually woven of silver threads)."* Josephus also added that the sun's rays were reflected brilliantly from Herod's silver robe.

3. *"Sat upon his throne,"* does not refer to his kingly throne but, as stated, to a raised platform, which became a makeshift throne. All of this was done with great fanfare and ceremony.

4. *"And made an oration unto them,"* concerns him speaking with great pride about this agreement, making it appear that he was the savior of Tyre and Sidon.

(22) "AND THE PEOPLE GAVE A SHOUT, SAYING, IT IS THE VOICE OF A GOD, AND NOT OF A MAN."

The exegesis is:

1. The phrase, *"And the people gave a shout,"* means that whatever he was saying greatly pleased them. As stated, many of these people were probably from Tyre and Sidon, with most of the shouting, it seems, coming from them. It is highly unlikely that Jews, irrespective of their spiritual declension, would have used the type of terminology said here.

2. *"Saying, It is the voice of a god, and not of a man,"* means they kept shouting this over and over!

3. Herod in no way attempted to stop them, actually, it seems, encouraging them to continue.

4. Someone has said, his pride, so deflated by Peter's escape, was greatly puffed up again by the flattering cries of these people who called him a god. Furthermore, he not only accepted their worship but actually encouraged it.

(23) "AND IMMEDIATELY THE ANGEL OF THE LORD SMOTE HIM, BECAUSE HE GAVE NOT GOD THE GLORY: AND HE WAS EATEN OF WORMS, AND GAVE UP THE GHOST."

The way is:

1. God can only meet with sinful man at the foot of the Cross.

2. Sinful man can only meet God at the foot of the Cross.

THE ANGEL OF THE LORD

The phrase, *"And immediately the Angel of the Lord smote him,"* presents such being carried out for several reasons.

When he laid his hands on James and then attempted the same with Peter, he, at the same time, touched the Lord. No one touches in a negative way that which belongs to God without touching God! As well, it is a battle that no person can win, irrespective as to whom he may be.

In doing this, he was attempting to aid the Sanhedrin who had crucified Christ and, as well, to stop the Work of God respecting the Early Church. At that moment, he set himself on the road to destruction.

GIVING GOD THE GLORY

The phrase, *"Because he gave not God the glory,"* speaks of several things:

• Herod considered himself to be a great practitioner of Judaism, consequently, knowing God. However, he did not know the Lord, not in the slightest!

When an individual enters into a profession

NOTES

of religion of some sort, he automatically places himself in a different category. In other words, he is held far more responsible, which accounts for much judgment.

Jesus, speaking of the Pharisees and Sadducees in comparison to Pilate, said of these religious leaders, *"Therefore he who delivered Me* (speaking of the Pharisees and Sadducees) *unto you* (Pilate) *has the greater sin"* (Jn. 19:11).

Herod had committed the *"greater sin."*

• Herod had no spiritual mind whatsoever because he had no knowledge of God. And yet, due to his Judaistic leanings, in his mind, he was somewhat killing two birds with one stone. He was nurturing his political position as well as his spiritual position, or so he thought! In reality, he was doing neither, but actually the very opposite.

• In his blustering position, he now filled up the cup by accepting the praises of these heathen, in other words, taking the glory that belonged only to the Lord.

In fact, this sin, which should be readily understood as serious indeed, is committed to a far greater degree in the church world than most people realize. Actually, the failure to give God the glory is committed constantly!

At this present time, almost the entirety of America gives the glory for our prosperity to everything other than God. Politicians are lauded, along with major universities, etc. However, glory is seldom given to God from Whom all Blessings flow!

Believers too often do the same thing, thinking it is their ability, their prowess, their intelligence, their education, their methods, etc. If the Lord is given any credit at all, it is only in passing.

JUDGMENT

Due to the word *"immediately,"* the phrase, *"And he was eaten of worms,"* meant that he was stricken by the Angel even while these people were praising him.

Josephus said that he lingered for five days with agonizing pains in his stomach. This agrees with the Biblical account.

"And gave up the ghost," means he died. This took place in A.D. 44.

Being king helped him not at all, and neither did the beautiful garments he wore or the accolades of the crowd. It is so easy for fallen man to come to the place that he thinks very highly of himself, hence, mighty Nebuchadnezzar saying, *"Is not this great Babylon, that I have built for the house of the Kingdom by the might of my power, and for the honor of my majesty?"* (Dan. 4:30).

Consequently, he was cut down and lived in insanity for seven years.

This problem is acute in all, but to a much greater degree in those who claim religion! That is the reason the greatest atrocities are committed in the Name of God. That is the reason there is nothing more godly than the Church, and there is nothing more wicked than the Church!

(24) "BUT THE WORD OF GOD GREW AND MULTIPLIED."

The composition is:

1. Without the Cross, Salvation was not possible and the Lord be true to His Nature.

2. While Jesus being God as well as man was absolutely necessary, still, He became Man for one purpose, and that was to go to the Cross.

THE CHURCH

Verse 24 is an exclamation that is somewhat different than what one would normally say, but yet, it totally gives us the Mind of the Spirit.

The Holy Spirit through Luke does not say that the *"Church grew,"* or even the Apostles or Believers. Instead, the *"Word of God"* is held up as *"growing and multiplying."*

This means that every single thing done for the Lord must be based squarely on the Word. When this is done, the tremendous benefits of the Word begin to be brought about, which results in many people being saved, healed, baptized with the Holy Spirit, and blessed in every conceivable way.

If the *"Word of God"* does not grow and multiply, nothing is accomplished for the Lord. The reason is simple: The Holy Spirit will only anoint Truth, which is the Word (Jn. 17:17).

So Herod, having proposed an ignominious death for Peter, himself suffered one much more ignominious. His word perished, but God's Word grew and multiplied (Williams).

THE WORD OF GOD AND THE CROSS OF CHRIST

Unless one has a proper understanding of the Cross of Christ, at the least in its elementary form, one simply cannot understand the Word as one should. A proper understanding of the Cross of Christ pulls everything into focus. In fact, I think one can say without fear of contradiction that the Cross of Christ is the key that unlocks every door.

If it is to be noticed, the statements of Paul lend heavy credence to this of which I say. The great Apostle said:

"Christ sent me not to baptize, but to preach the Gospel, not with wisdom of words, lest the Cross of Christ should be made of none effect" (I Cor. 1:17).

In fact, in this particular Verse, we are told what the Gospel actually is; it is the Cross of Christ. Yes, the meaning of the word *"Gospel"* is *"good news."* So, this also says that the Cross of Christ was and is good news for a lost and dying world.

POWER

The great Apostle then said, *"For the preaching of the Cross* (word of the Cross) *is to them who perish foolishness, but unto us which are saved it is the Power of God"* (I Cor. 1:18).

How is it that the Power is in the preaching of the Cross?

Actually, the Power is in the Holy Spirit (Acts 1:8). However, the Holy Spirit is able to perform His Work within our lives, thereby, using His Almighty Power because of what Jesus did at the Cross, which was to atone for all sin, past, present, and future, at least for all who will believe (Jn. 3:16).

JESUS CHRIST AND HIM CRUCIFIED

Then the great Apostle said, *"For I determined not to know anything among you, save Jesus Christ, and Him Crucified"* (I Cor. 2:2).

Paul preached the Cross because it alone can set the captive free. Nothing else can, only the Cross.

NOTES

WISDOM

The Apostle then said, *"But we speak the Wisdom of God in a mystery, even the hidden wisdom, which God ordained before the world unto our glory"* (I Cor. 2:7).

The Cross of Christ was the greatest display of the Wisdom of God given to us in the Word of God. The great Plan of Redemption is greater than all the Plan of Creation and all the Plan of the Operation of the Universe. That which the Lord did through the Cross in the Redemption of humanity knows no equal as it regards the Wisdom of God.

Let me say it again:

The Word of God cannot be understood as it ought to be understood without a proper understanding of the Cross of Christ, not only as the Cross refers to Salvation respecting the unredeemed but, as well, the Believer respecting our Sanctification. Without a proper understanding of the Cross, there will be an improper understanding in some way of the Word of God. In fact, it cannot be otherwise.

Every lamb that was offered up in Old Testament Times, at least as a sacrifice unto the Lord, presented itself as a Type of Christ and what He would do for us at Calvary's Cross. This means that untold millions of types and shadows of the Cross are given to us in the Word of God. In fact, I think that one can say that the Cross of Christ is so placarded before our very eyes all throughout the Word of God, that man is left with no excuse as it regards the understanding of the greatest Work that God ever carried out for the human race.

THE EARLY CHURCH AND THE APOSTLES

A lady asked me once, *"If the Cross of Christ is so important, why did not the Apostles preach it in the Early Church?"* She was right in that the Apostles little preached the Cross of Christ, that is, at the beginning of the Early Church.

Why?

The reason is obvious. They didn't know anything about the Cross. They preached what they knew, and that was that Jesus

NOTES

Christ had been raised from the dead, and of that they were certain. The Message of the Cross would not come along until the Lord gave this great Truth to the Apostle Paul, which Paul gave to us in his 14 Epistles. One must understand that Jesus Christ is the New Covenant.

This means that He does not merely have the understanding of the New Covenant but, in fact, is the New Covenant. The Cross of Christ is the meaning of that New Covenant, the meaning of which, as stated, was given to Paul. As is obvious, Paul preached the Cross. He gave to us in detail this great Plan of God, which saves the human race, at least for those who will believe. That's the reason the great Apostle said:

"But God forbid that I should glory (boast) *save in the Cross of our Lord Jesus Christ, by Whom the world is crucified unto me, and I unto the world"* (Gal. 6:14).

Here the great Apostle tells us that the only thing that we as Believers can boast about is the Cross of Christ. If boasting is effected in any other manner, it gives glory to self and not to God, which is a travesty. It is only Faith in Christ and what He did for us at the Cross of which we should boast. Anything else is a sin!

(25) "AND BARNABAS AND SAUL RETURNED FROM JERUSALEM, WHEN THEY HAD FULFILLED THEIR MINISTRY, AND TOOK WITH THEM JOHN, WHOSE SURNAME WAS MARK."

The direction is:

1. The phrase, *"And Barnabas and Saul returned from Jerusalem,"* proclaims such happening, but does not tell us exactly when.

2. Some claim that they were in Jerusalem at the time of Peter's great deliverance; however, there is no proof of that.

3. More than likely, they had returned to Antioch from Jerusalem before these events took place. To have been there at this time would have been of little service, at least tending to business, inasmuch as the Church was in turmoil, with possibly most of the Apostles gone. So, these things probably happened after Paul and Barnabas left.

4. *"When they had fulfilled their ministry,"* speaks of the offerings brought to Jerusalem from the Saints in Antioch, and possibly elsewhere as well.

5. The indication is that they did not tarry long, finishing their mission and then returning.

The word *"ministry,"* as used here, in the Greek Text is *"diakonia,"* and means *"to function as a servant."*

When this was done, the indication is that they returned to Antioch immediately, with but one excursion.

6. *"And took with them John, whose surname was Mark,"* proclaims them going by the home of this young man, which seems to have contained the largest house Church in that city, with possibly several hundreds of other similar gatherings.

The choice of Mark shows that they saw in him a desire for ministry and calling that they wanted to nurture and develop.

7. Jesus had set a precedent for this type of training by selecting the Twelve to be with Him and to be trained by Him. Consequently, Mark would now begin, but not with too much success immediately, as we shall soon see. But yet, it would conclude well!

8. What a privilege this young man had to be associated with both Paul and Barnabas. What an opportunity was his! How so much the Lord favored him by opening this door.

"My heart is fixed Oh God on Thee,
"No more my feet shall go astray,
"I caught a glimpse of Calvary,
"And now I walk with Christ today."

CHAPTER 13

(1) "NOW THERE WERE IN THE CHURCH THAT WAS AT ANTIOCH CERTAIN PROPHETS AND TEACHERS; AS BARNABAS, AND SIMEON WHO WAS CALLED NIGER, AND LUCIUS OF CYRENE, AND MANAEN, WHICH HAD BEEN BROUGHT UP WITH HEROD THE TETRARCH, AND SAUL."

The form is:

1. The Message of the Cross is the Word of God.

2. Jesus Christ is the New Covenant,

while the Cross is the meaning of that covenant.

THE TAKING OF THE GOSPEL TO THE WORLD

This Chapter deals with the beginning of Paul's first missionary journey, which took him to Cyprus, Perga, and Antioch in Pisidia. Actually, about three-quarters of the Chapter is given over to Paul's ministry in Antioch, where he was attempting to reach the Jews. He had some success but, as a whole, he was opposed greatly from this quarter. As should be understood, this is a different Antioch than the Antioch of Verse 1.

This concludes Chapter 13, but with that first missionary journey continuing on through Chapter 14. Actually, it lasted for about three years, with Paul seeing many souls saved and Churches established. However, the opposition and persecution were fierce to say the least. Actually, had it not been for the protecting Hand of the Lord, they would have lost their lives.

As we study the account of the establishment of Churches in various cities of the Roman Empire, to the unspiritual heart, these things are of little interest. However, to those who are led by the Spirit, the study of these accounts will not only be of great interest but will actually bring forth a rapture of joy, and for many reasons:

A WORK OF THE HOLY SPIRIT

- All of this being done was a Work of the Holy Spirit, which should be of utmost interest to all believers.
- These Churches established, representing many people coming to Christ, would bring *"light"* into the world such as it had never known before.
- The march of this missionary journey brought the Gospel of Jesus Christ ever closer to you and me, which is the single greatest thing that could ever happen to a person—to be saved by the Blood of Jesus. If Paul had not carried out this task (and in the way the Holy Spirit directed), this great Gospel may not have made its way to us.

So, what is done in these accounts should be of utmost interest to the believer and, as well, of absolute utmost significance, as should be obvious.

NOTES

If one only sees history in this study, then one misses the point entirely. In essence, we now begin the march of the Gospel, which would ultimately envelope the entirety of the Earth and, as stated, would ultimately come to our hearts.

THE CHURCH AT ANTIOCH

The phrase, *"Now there were in the Church that was at Antioch,"* presents information of vast significance.

For various reasons, the Holy Spirit, even as we shall see, shifted the emphasis from Jerusalem to this Syrian city. The following may provide some reasons this was done:

- As we have previously stated, Antioch of Syria was the third most prominent city in the Roman Empire, eclipsed only by Rome itself and Alexandria in Egypt. As well, it was strategically located to reach all points of the Roman Empire.
- There was a large colony of Jews in Antioch; still, this was a Gentile city, which made it much more favorable in reaching the Gentile world.
- Even though the Church in Jerusalem was always of great significance, and for obvious reasons, it continued to have great difficulty in breaking loose from its Jewish past. In other words, the Law of Moses, which Jesus fulfilled in totality, and which was meant to be laid aside, proved to be very difficult for the Jerusalem Church to carry out. It seems there were strong factions in that Church who sought to attach grace to law, which, of course, is impossible!

Even after the great council in Jerusalem concerning this very issue, which we will study in Chapter 15, the problem from this source seems somewhat to have continued, even though James addressed it correctly, at least as far as it went. Therefore, as is plainly obvious, the Holy Spirit shifted the emphasis to Antioch.

In this which the Holy Spirit would do, we will find three distinct parts to the great foundation of the Gospel, which will be obvious:

THE MESSAGE, THE MESSENGER, AND THE MINISTRY

1. The message: it is the Gospel of grace,

centered up in Jesus Christ as the crucified, risen Lord (Eph. 2:8-9).

2. The messenger: We will see the Church as a collective body playing a tremendously important part in this greatest of all endeavors; however, its role is that of support as God calls individual men to carry forth this message. In other words, when the Holy Spirit speaks, even as we shall see, He speaks to a man or woman, thereby, placing in their hearts the burden of that which He has called them to do. He does not speak to committees, boards, denominations, etc. However, these things are not wrong within themselves, providing they serve in a supporting role as God intends.

The tragedy is that man has turned it upside down from God's true intention. In most religious circles, the man or woman serves in a supporting role for the committees, boards, etc. Consequently, the Holy Spirit is able to function little, if any at all, with the efforts then becoming totally man-instituted and man-directed.

3. The ministry: As we will plainly see, the Ministry of the Holy Spirit, at least as it regards priority, is the taking of the Message of Jesus Christ, as it is given to His called Messengers, to the entirety of the world. This is not a by-product of the Holy Spirit but is plainly the emphasis and priority. For those who do not know what Jesus did at Calvary and the Resurrection, as far as that person is concerned, Jesus came to this world and died in vain.

So, whatever thrust is made by any ministry, priority must always be the taking of the Gospel worldwide.

CERTAIN PROPHETS AND TEACHERS

The phrase, *"Certain Prophets and Teachers,"* proclaims the ministry given by the Holy Spirit to these men. This is of extreme importance.

The offices of *"Prophet"* and *"Teacher"* cannot be bestowed by men, Churches, committees, etc. These are offices given totally by the Holy Spirit.

The title *"Prophet"* in the Greek text as given here is *"Propheteuo"* and means *"to foretell events by inspiration and divine power."*

NOTES

This is not the same as the gift of prophecy outlined in I Corinthians 12:10, which *"speaks unto men to edification, and exhortation, and comfort"* (I Cor. 14:3). As we have previously stated, all who stand in the office of the Prophet (Eph. 4:11) definitely have the gift of prophecy (to forthtell), as well as the ability to *"foretell"* as the Spirit of God moves upon them. However, only a very few who have the *"gift of prophecy,"* which any Spirit-filled believer can have, also stand in the office of the Prophet.

Actually, both *"Prophets"* and *"Teachers"* are part of the fivefold ministry calling (Eph. 4:11).

The office of the *"Teacher"* presents a special calling to individuals who are helped by the Holy Spirit to explain the Word of God in a more definitive way.

As well, the other four offices or callings of *"Apostles, Prophets, evangelists, and pastors"* are able to teach as well! However, the one who is specifically called of God to the office of the *"Teacher"* will, as a whole, be able to open up the Scriptures to a greater degree (Rom. 11:13; 12:4; I Tim. 3:1).

"Prophets" are listed before *"Teachers,"* but I think it unwise to place too much emphasis on the order of listing, unless the emphasis is obvious.

THE FIRST AND THE LAST

For instance, one would be unwise to say that the Tenth Commandment, *"You shalt not covet,"* is of little significance because it is listed last (Ex. 20:17). As well, each calling of the fivefold ministry (Eph. 4:11) is just as important as the other in its own way.

The problem is that men arbitrarily ignore or even deny certain callings, such as *"Apostles," "Prophets,"* etc., claiming they were only for the early Church, etc. As a result, I am concerned that these sectors of the Church, wherever it may be and whoever it may be, actually have no calling at all, at least that which is of the Lord. Most who deny certain parts of the Word of God, claiming that it passed away with the early Church or Apostles, are also to be found denying the Holy Spirit according to Acts 2:4. Accordingly, they are denied the benefit of all that He does, leaving them

NOTES

with that which is totally of human origin and, consequently, of no service to the Lord, despite its vast array of religious machinery.

CERTAIN BRETHREN

The phrase, *"As Barnabas, and Simeon who was called Niger, and Lucius of Cyrene, and Manaen, which had been brought up with Herod the Tetrarch, and Saul,"* pertains to those who were *"Prophets and Teachers."*

The emphasis on the Text seems to be that some were *"Prophets"* and some were *"Teachers."* However, the Greek text does not exclude all being both!

It is believed by some that *"Simeon,"* who was also called *"Niger,"* could have been Simon of Cyrene who carried the Cross for Christ (Mk. 15:21; Lk. 23:26). However, that is speculative at best!

"Lucius of Cyrene," could have been one of the first who brought the Gospel to Antioch (Acts 11:20).

"Manaen" was brought up with Herod Antipas, who murdered John the Baptist. The Greek for *"brought up"* means *"foster brother."* Even though *"Manaen"* was brought up in Herod's court, even favored by Herod, at some point, he gave his heart and life to Christ, which means that he forsook that court.

Some believe that John the Baptist may have influenced him, with him later accepting Christ. It is also possible that he was among those present on the Day of Pentecost when the Holy Spirit was first poured out.

(2) "AS THEY MINISTERED TO THE LORD, AND FASTED, THE HOLY SPIRIT SAID, SEPARATE ME BARNABAS AND SAUL FOR THE WORK WHEREUNTO I HAVE CALLED THEM."

The composition is:

1. At this stage, Paul already had the great meaning of the New Covenant, which was and is the Cross.

2. Now would begin the missions effort to take the Gospel elsewhere, which ultimately would change the world.

THEY MINISTERED TO THE LORD

The phrase, *"As they ministered to the Lord,"* proclaims to us a pattern, which should be the norm for the modern Church as well.

The word *"ministered"* in the Greek text is *"leitourgeo"* and means *"to perform certain tasks helping others, in other words His Hands extended."* However, it also means *"to worship."* So, in essence, it says two things:

1. Whenever the believer performs a service for others, irrespective as to what that service may be, whether preaching, teaching, or simply showing kindness, we are here told that the Lord calls this *"worship."* Actually, *"worship"* is what we are, while *"praise"* is what we do. All praise is worship, while all worship is not actually praise.

2. It also refers to one or more worshiping the Lord in prayer and praise, in other words, a prayer meeting. In fact, this is what the word *"ministered"* refers to in this particular passage.

These people were seeking God because, in some manner, the Holy Spirit had informed them that a very special work was about to begin. Consequently, they were seeking the Lord as to what that work would be. In fact, it was Paul's first missionary journey.

By the use of the title *"Lord,"* the Holy Spirit is telling us that the leaders of the Church in Antioch had no personal agenda of their own, but rather sought the Lord earnestly concerning what He wanted. This is to be the criterion for the modern Church as well!

Too oftentimes, men make their plans and then ask God to bless those plans. However, those types of man-instituted plans can never be blessed by God.

The idea is that we allow the Lord to make the plans, which we see being carried out in this episode, and then the plans are guaranteed of blessing. In other words, Jesus is *"Lord,"* i.e., *"the Head of the Church."*

FASTING

The words, *"And fasted,"* leave no clue as to how long, and may have varied with the different men listed here.

They wanted to know the Mind of God, which indicates, as we have stated, that the Holy Spirit had already informed them that something wonderful was about to be done. This would be the beginning of the Gospel of Jesus Christ, the Message of the Cross, taken to the entirety of the world. Of course, it would take a long time for this to take place, but this was the beginning; consequently, there is no way that you and I can understand the significance of this particular time. I feel that the believers in Antioch sensed this, knew this, and understood this, at least as far as a poor human being can understand such. That for which Jesus had died, the great price that He paid, and the benefits of the Cross were now about to be given to others, who would ultimately touch the world for Christ. The indication of the Text is that this time of seeking God was far more than routine, but rather directed by the Holy Spirit for a particular purpose and reason. That purpose and reason was for world evangelism and was the single most important thing happening at that time in the entirety of the world. Of course, had Rome known of such, they would not have given it a second glance.

Prayer and fasting are the only means God has given us to discern His Purposes. Of course, the Word of God plays a paramount role in all of this; however, without proper intercession before the Lord, the Word of the Lord cannot be rightly divided.

And yet, some have tried to force the attribute of *"fasting"* into an unscriptural position. For instance, some preachers are claiming that if one fasts so many days, this will give them victory over sin, victory over the flesh, etc. While fasting will definitely help in any capacity, still, it is unscriptural to think that fasting so many days will give one victory over the world, the flesh, and the devil. There is only one factor that will function, and function correctly, as it regards victory over the world, and that is the Cross of Christ and our faith in that finished work.

It was at the Cross where Satan plus every minion of darkness were defeated. It was at the Cross where all sin was atoned, past, present, and future, at least for all who will believe (Jn. 3:16). To reap the eternal consequences of what Jesus did at the Cross, all that it takes as it regards mankind is faith; however, it must be faith in Christ and what Christ has done for us at the Cross. If our faith is placed in Jesus minus the Cross, the Holy Spirit through Paul labeled such as another Jesus, another spirit, and another gospel (II Cor. 11:1-4). We must ever understand that the Cross of Christ is the means for all victory. In fact, there is no victory outside of the Cross. That's the reason that Paul said:

"For I determined not to know anything among you, save Jesus Christ, and Him Crucified" (I Cor. 2:2).

NOTES

THE HOLY SPIRIT SAID

The phrase, *"The Holy Spirit said,"* proclaims Him, as is obvious, giving direction.

The Holy Spirit is a Person, actually, the third Person of the Triune Godhead. In essence, He carries out everything on Earth ordered by the Godhead. Jesus plainly said of Him, *"When He, the Spirit of Truth, is come* (and He has already come), *He will guide you into all Truth: for He shall not speak of Himself; but whatsoever He shall hear, that shall He speak: and He will show you things to come."*

Jesus then said, *"He shall glorify Me: for He shall receive of Mine, and shall show it unto you"* (Jn. 16:13-14).

Jesus Christ is the Head of the Church (Eph. 1:20-23), but it is the Holy Spirit Who carries out His instructions.

The Holy Spirit in Acts gives commandments (1:2), gives power (1:8), speaks (1:16), fills believers (2:4), is poured out (2:18), is received (2:33), is a Gift (2:38), discerns lies (5:3), can be tempted (5:9), witnesses (5:32), gives wisdom (6:3), gives faith (6:5), can be resisted (7:51), gives direction (8:29), comforts (9:31), speaks (10:19), anoints (10:38), falls on people (11:15), baptizes (11:16), signifies (11:28), sins (13:4); and, in John, convicts and reproves (16:8), guides into all truth (16:13), glorifies Christ (16:14), etc.

WHO IS THE HOLY SPIRIT?

Christians confidently affirm the existence of one God, Who exists eternally in three Persons. The Father and the Son are the most familiar to most Christians;

however, that is certainly not the way it ought to be. That which the Bible teaches about the Holy Spirit is rich indeed, and something every believer ought to know. While the focus of our faith is rightly on Jesus, our Saviour, it is the Holy Spirit Who brings us all the benefits won for us by Christ.

In reference to Who the Holy Spirit is, the Scripture is plain and simple that He is God. Personal pronouns used of Him prove such (Jn. 16:7-15).

A clear distinction is made between the Son Who prays, the Father to Whom He prays, and the Holy Spirit for Whom He prays (Jn. 14:16).

Another clear distinction is made between the Son on the right Hand of the Father, the Father on the left Hand of the Son, and the Holy Spirit Who is sent from the Father and the Son (Jn. 14:16-17, 26; 15:26; 16:7-15; Acts 2:33-36; 7:56).

In other words, the Father is God; the Son is God; the Holy Spirit is God. Even though They are three different, distinct Personalities, They are *"One"* in essence, purpose, and direction, but are indivisible. The Holy Spirit is God, but He is not the Father, and neither is He the Son. As well, these two Divine Persons of the Trinity are not the Holy Spirit. Each is distinct regarding personality but are one in unity and essence.

Even though we have already given statements respecting the Holy Spirit in this volume, and even though there will be some repetition in the following, this subject is of such significance that I think it would be impossible to overstate the case. So, I would pray that you would carefully peruse the following:

THE HOLY SPIRIT SAID

As to how the Holy Spirit delivered this message, we aren't told; however, it, no doubt, came through a word of prophecy or tongues and interpretation. At any rate, the group at the Church at Antioch now had the Mind of the Spirit as it regarded the ministry of Barnabas and Paul. In fact, this was the secret of the New Testament Church, better referred to as the *"early Church."* It was a Church that was empowered by the Spirit, led by the Spirit, and guided by the Spirit.

NOTES

SEPARATE ME BARNABAS AND SAUL

The phrase, *"Separate Me Barnabas and Saul for the work whereunto I have called them,"* expresses a strong command or demand, in other words, it is not a suggestion.

A PERSONAL EXPERIENCE

Years ago while preaching a meeting in Kansas City, Missouri, a brother came up to me after the service on Sunday afternoon, asking for guidance.

He told me how that some months earlier an individual had prophesied over him and his family that they should move to Kansas City, etc.

On the strength of this so-called prophecy, he had quit his job, uprooted his family, and moved to this city. He then said, *"Brother Swaggart, everything has gone wrong! I can't find a job, and we are quickly in the process of losing everything we have."*

He then said, or words to this effect, *"Why would the Lord want me to do such a thing?"*

I asked him, *"Had the Lord previously dealt with you about moving to Kansas City?"*

"No!" he answered.

"In other words," I said, *"you uprooted your family and moved here strictly on the strength of someone prophesying over you?"*

He answered in the affirmative.

I then said to him, *"Brother, the Lord did not tell you to do this thing. If the prophecy given to you was valid, the Lord would have previously dealt with you, with the prophecy verifying what you already knew."*

The Holy Spirit does not work in that manner. He is perfectly capable of speaking to an individual Himself. Many of these foolish things are done simply because some people love to tell others what to do, and sadly, some people love to be told what to do.

This direction given to Paul and Barnabas definitely came from the Holy Spirit, but it was not a surprise. The Holy Spirit had been dealing with them for quite some time concerning this very thing. Consequently, when the Spirit spoke this particular time, they knew in their hearts it was time to put into action what He was saying. Paul would now begin his first missionary journey.

The Holy Spirit personally, directly, and pointedly *"called"* Paul and Barnabas for this special mission, which was so very important to the Kingdom of God. This tells us that the Lord not only calls particular people to the office of the *"Apostle, Prophet, Evangelist, Pastor, or Teacher,"* but, as well, calls them for a specific work.

So, individuals are called by God for special offices. They do not call themselves. As well, after they are called for these particular offices, they are not to attempt to chart their own course or to allow denominations (or anyone else for that matter) to designate their sphere of operation. Once again, this is solely of the Spirit.

Many preachers, genuinely called of God, have weakened or even destroyed their ministries by allowing men to dictate when and where they should minister. This is exclusively the domain of the Holy Spirit and is never to be abrogated by man. It is to never be forgotten that if the individual wants the Anointing and Blessing of the Holy Spirit, he will have to be led and guided exclusively by the Holy Spirit. The Holy Spirit will not place His Anointing or Approval upon that which is man-instituted and, consequently, man-directed.

Whenever the Spirit of God specified the ministry that Paul and Barnabas were to carry out, they did not check in with Jerusalem for approval. Please believe me, if there had ever been a time in history that such would have been appropriate, this would have been the time. All of the original Apostles, other than James, were still alive. However, Paul and Barnabas, even though respecting these men greatly, did not and, in fact, would not submit to anyone else for approval that which God had directed. They would seek their prayers and counsel but would not seek their approval!

(3) "AND WHEN THEY HAD FASTED AND PRAYED, AND LAID THEIR HANDS ON THEM, THEY SENT THEM AWAY."

The exegesis is:

1. The phrase, *"And when they had fasted and prayed,"* probably proclaims several days or even weeks.

2. Now that they had direction, they wanted to make certain that they had the Mind of the Lord in all things concerning this extremely important effort. There was only one way for this to be secured, and that was for continued praying and fasting. What an example for us presently!

3. The phrase, *"And laid their hands on them,"* proclaims several things:

a. It was recognition of what the Lord had already done.

b. It signified the blessings of the Church upon Paul and Barnabas.

c. It signified that the Church was standing behind these two men with their prayers and support.

4. *"They sent them away,"* represents, as far as is known, the very first missionary trip to new places for the expressed purpose of planting new Churches.

5. Up to this moment, the Gospel was mostly carried to new places by those who were scattered abroad by persecution.

(4) "SO THEY, BEING SENT FORTH BY THE HOLY SPIRIT, DEPARTED UNTO SELEUCIA; AND FROM THENCE THEY SAILED TO CYPRUS."

The synopsis is:

1. All false doctrine begins with an improper understanding of the Cross.

2. A proper understanding of the Cross of Christ will ward off most deception.

SENT FORTH BY THE HOLY SPIRIT

The phrase, *"So they, being sent forth by the Holy Spirit,"* presents the Spirit not only calling them, but sending them as well.

I am positive that the student of the Bible is made very much aware of the significance of this. Even though I am repetitive even to the point of being tedious, I must emphasize, and continue to do so, that the success of the early Church was in being led by the Spirit. Satan will fight this as nothing else, seeking to gain control over the ministry. He does so, not by the tentacles of the world oftentimes, but by the tentacles of religion.

This of which we read here in Verses 2 through 4 would be applauded by most Church leaders, that is, if they believe the Bible, but in practice, many of these individuals do the very opposite, seeking to control preachers and preaching.

The phrase, *"Departed unto Seleucia,"* represents a port city on the Mediterranean, about 15 miles from Antioch. In fact, Seleucia was looked at as the harbor for Antioch, as we have stated, one of the greatest cities in the Roman Empire.

SAILED TO CYPRUS

The phrase, *"And from thence they sailed to Cyprus,"* represented a journey of approximately 100 miles. As well, Cyprus was the boyhood home of Barnabas, where he, no doubt, still had many friends (Acts 4:36).

So, they would begin their missionary endeavor in friendly territory, at least for Barnabas, which, without a doubt, would signal one of the greatest moments in human history. The light of the Gospel of Jesus Christ, which alone can change hearts and lives, would now make steady progress until ultimately, it would touch the entirety of the globe. No wonder the Holy Spirit was so prominent! The salvation of every single person who has ever named the Name of Jesus, in a sense, began on the day that the Spirit of God touched Paul and Barnabas in the taking of this great salvation to mankind.

Jesus bled, suffered, and died on a hill called Golgotha in order to redeem man from the terrible clutches of Satan. However, for that which He did to be made known, someone had to go tell the story. In effect, Paul and Barnabas were the first on this long, long road from Pentecost until now. In their train have followed thousands, even tens of thousands, and it was all for the purpose of bringing the light to the darkness.

When they boarded the sailing vessel in Seleucia, I wonder if Paul and Barnabas understood the magnitude of what was happening.

These two men were so close to the Lord that if it were possible for them to understand, they did! However, I personally do not think it would have been possible for any person to have fully understood the significance, the magnitude, and yes, the glory of what was happening.

As I dictate these words, I sense the Presence of God. I know and realize, at least as much as a poor mortal can, that today I am saved and washed in Calvary's cleansing flow, with my name written down in the Lamb's Book of Life, and it all started on a hill far away. But yet, the story, as grand as it was and is, had to be told, and, in essence, its telling began that day with Paul and Barnabas. How thrilled I am that it reached even me, and how thrilled you must be as well!

NOTES

(5) "AND WHEN THEY WERE AT SALAMIS, THEY PREACHED THE WORD OF GOD IN THE SYNAGOGUES OF THE JEWS: AND THEY HAD ALSO JOHN TO THEIR MINISTER."

The way is:

1. The phrase, *"And when they were at Salamis,"* speaks of one of the principle cities on the island of Cyprus.

2. *"They preached the Word of God in the synagogues of the Jews,"* proclaims immediately a practice that Paul would continue, at least as long as it was possible to do so. They went to the Jew first and then to the Gentiles. However, their Message of Jesus Christ was intended for all. We are not told here exactly what success they had. Nevertheless, *"They preached the Word of God."*

Salamis had a large population of Jews and as a result, a number of synagogues.

However, the city was destroyed some years later by Trajan as a result of a terrible insurrection of the Jews, in which they massacred 240,000 of the Gentile population. Consequently, no Jew was ever after allowed to land in Cyprus.

3. *"And they had also John to their minister,"* speaks of John Mark, who wrote the book of the Four Gospels that bears his name.

4. The word *"minister"* here in the Greek text is *"huperetes"* and means *"an assistant or subordinate."* In other words, he was to help Paul and Barnabas any way that he could.

5. As well, inasmuch as Mark had been an eyewitness of the Arrest, Death, and Resurrection of Jesus, he was a valuable asset to the Work of God regarding this missionary trip.

6. Incidentally, he could well have been the young man mentioned in Mark 14:51-52.

(6) "AND WHEN THEY HAD GONE

THROUGH THE ISLE UNTO PAPHOS, THEY FOUND A CERTAIN SORCERER, A FALSE PROPHET, A JEW, WHOSE NAME WAS BAR-JESUS."

The composition is:

1. The phrase, *"And when they had gone through the Isle unto Paphos,"* presents the capital of Cyprus. The place, as most areas of the Roman Empire, was given over to idolatry.

2. The indication of the Text is that they ministered in some or all of the towns on the way to Pathos from Salamis.

3. It seems that Paul changed his method somewhat after this, selecting (no doubt by the Leading of the Holy Spirit) major cities in which to plant Churches, and then would spread out accordingly.

4. *"They found a certain sorcerer, a false Prophet, a Jew, whose name was Bar-jesus,"* points to one who was able to perform certain types of so-called magic tricks, and who claimed to be of God but, in reality, was of Satan.

Inasmuch as the Holy Spirit through Luke labeled him a *"false Prophet,"* it seems his ambition was of greater magnitude than merely sustaining himself, but rather to attract a large following. He called himself the *"son of Joshua."*

5. Such is somewhat understandable when one considers that the world of that day had precious little light of the Gospel, if any. However, sadly and regrettably, the practitioners of black arts, claiming to be of God, abound presently, despite the proliferation of the light of the Gospel. This tells us two things:

a. It proclaims the total depravity of the human heart.

b. It also says that despite the great claims of religion, and even those who claim to be Christian, the truth is, there is not much true Gospel being preached.

Millions presently go from America and other countries of the world to a spot in former Yugoslavia to visit a hilltop, where someone is supposed to have had a vision of the Virgin Mary. All of this is of Satan just as surely as this man who was confronted by Paul.

(7) "WHICH WAS WITH THE DEPUTY OF THE COUNTRY, SERGIUS PAULUS, A PRUDENT MAN; WHO CALLED FOR BARNABAS AND SAUL, AND DESIRED TO HEAR THE WORD OF GOD."

The synopsis is:

1. The phrase, *"Which was with the deputy of the country,"* speaks of the sorcerer.

This *"deputy"* was the *"Roman proconsul"* (governor) of the island of Cyprus.

2. Hervey says, *"This is an instance of Luke's great accuracy. Cyprus had become a Proconsular Province in the reign of the Emperor's Provinces governed by a Legatus."*

3. The phrase, *"Sergius Paulus, a prudent man,"* signifies a man of knowledge and superior intelligence and understanding.

4. He was named twice by Pliny in his books and quoted respecting accounts of the heavenly bodies and prognostications from the sun, moon, stars, etc.

5. Consequently, there can be little doubt that Sergius Paulus had this sorcerer with him so that he might learn from him such matters as might be useful for the book that he was writing, etc. Being a pagan, he did not know or understand the difference in sorcery or that which was legitimately of God.

6. *"Who called for Barnabas and Saul, and desired to hear the Word of God,"* evidently means that something aroused his curiosity. No doubt, it was the *"Word of God"* preached by Paul and Barnabas, which told of the Life, Death, and Resurrection of Christ. They were probably ministering in one or more of the synagogues.

It would be an astounding thing for someone to claim a Resurrection from the dead, especially considering that Mark had been an eyewitness. Then, to claim that Jesus was God, which they no doubt did, would have been of tremendous interest to this man. Consequently, he sent for *"Barnabas and Saul."*

(8) "BUT ELYMAS THE SORCERER, FOR SO IS HIS NAME BY INTERPRETATION, WITHSTOOD THEM, SEEKING TO TURN AWAY THE DEPUTY FROM THE FAITH."

The pattern is:

1. The phrase, *"But Elymas the sorcerer, for so is his name by interpretation, withstood them,"* seems to have come about for obvious reasons.

NOTES

2. These types of people (sorcerers) not only claimed to impart information that could not be received elsewhere but, as well, sought to gain a psychological hold on the person in question. The sorcerer saw this hold slipping away from Sergius Paulus as Paul and Barnabas witnessed to him about the Lord. Consequently, he began to oppose them by any means at his disposal.

3. The phrase, *"Seeking to turn away the deputy from the faith,"* means simply that the governor was believing the Message of Jesus Christ as presented by Paul and Barnabas.

(9) "THEN SAUL (WHO ALSO IS CALLED PAUL,) FILLED WITH THE HOLY SPIRIT, SET HIS EYES ON HIM."

The direction is:

1. The phrase, *"Then Saul (who also is called Paul),"* presents here the change of name, by which he would be referred from then on. Incidentally, Paul is the Roman derivative of the Hebrew Saul.

2. I think the indication is clear that the change of name was brought about by the Holy Spirit. Even though Paul continued to preach to Jews every opportunity that presented itself, still, his major thrust was always to the Gentiles. Consequently, the Holy Spirit would impress upon him the necessity of the use of his Roman name.

3. Also, some have said this was his Church name, signifying what the Lord was now doing. *"Saul"* represented something that had been wonderful and beautiful but now had come to a conclusion. I speak of the Law of Moses and Judaism as a whole.

4. Thus is introduced the Apostle Paul, and this was his first missionary journey—a journey, we might quickly add, that would do more to advance the Cause of Christ and civilization than anything else in history.

5. *"Filled with the Holy Spirit,"* not only speaks of an ongoing state but seems to imply a special new anointing, resulting from a special new filling.

6. Once again, the Holy Spirit is held up as the Teacher, Leader, and Guide, and above all, the One Who empowers.

7. *"Set his eyes on him,"* means that Paul did so according to the Leading of the Holy Spirit. In fact, all that was done was according to what the Holy Spirit desired.

8. It seems that these men constantly sought the Lord for leading and guidance, a prayer which was always answered!

(10) "AND SAID, O FULL OF ALL SUBTILTY AND ALL MISCHIEF, YOU CHILD OF THE DEVIL, YOU ENEMY OF ALL RIGHTEOUSNESS, WILL YOU NOT CEASE TO PERVERT THE RIGHT WAYS OF THE LORD?"

The direction is:

1. To properly understand the Gospel, one has to properly understand the Cross of Christ.

2. Basically, this refers to the believer understanding the Cross for sanctification exactly as it is understood for salvation.

NOTES

A CHILD OF THE DEVIL

The phrase, *"And said, O full of all subtilty and all mischief, you child of the devil, you enemy of all righteousness,"* proclaims, according to some, Paul using the gift of *"discerning of spirits"* (I Cor. 12:10).

However, while this gift, plus others, for Paul had them all, may have come into focus here, I think the spiritual status of this person was obvious to anyone who truly knew the Lord. Even though this sorcerer claimed spiritual gifts, as many of this ilk do, once placed beside those who were truly of God, it was instantly obvious as to what this person was, *"a child of the devil."*

The question, *"Will you not cease to pervert the right ways of the Lord?"* glaringly proclaims that this sorcerer had claimed to be of God; therefore, his alleged miracles and prognostications were claimed to be from the same source. The *"deputy,"* not knowing God, was easily deceived.

It is obvious that this man knew some of the *"ways of the Lord"* simply because, being a Jew, he was familiar with the Old Testament. However, he perverted those ways, as millions even do presently!

For instance, all the Gifts of the Spirit (I Cor. 12:8-10) are exactly as it says of the Holy Spirit, and are to be used by the Spirit through Spirit-filled believers as He wills and not according to what man wills (I Cor. 12:11). Sadly, many have perverted these gifts!

WHAT GOOD DOES THE FOLLOWING DO ANYONE?

I do not find any evidence in the Word of God that lends any legitimacy to these gifts when they are used service after service to impress people by someone claiming such gifts, telling them how much money they have in their pockets, on what street they reside, etc. While the Lord certainly may do something such as this occasionally, such is not normally done, and for obvious reasons.

What good does that do anyone?

As well, I have problems with those who use what they purport to be Gifts of the Holy Spirit as some type of sideshow attraction by doing certain things, such as blowing on people or flicking the hand, with individuals then falling to the floor, supposedly of the Spirit.

While God definitely uses His Power very often to such an extent that at times people are unable to stand, I cannot see from the Scriptures where it is ever turned into a carnival attraction, etc. One must ever understand that Satan's counterfeits are always very similar to that which is truly of God. The very purpose of the counterfeit is similarity, and for the purpose of deception. Many Pentecostals and Charismatics, I am afraid, are too often deceived by that which looks to be of God but actually is not.

HOW IS ONE TO KNOW?

If one is truly filled with the Spirit and consequently led by the Spirit, the false will quickly become obvious because the Word of God is being violated in some manner (Mat. 7:15-20; Jn. 16:7-15).

Respecting such, Satan generally works in two ways:

1. Knowing that a great Move of God is coming, Satan will attempt to preempt that move by first of all sending the false. As stated, it will be so near the genuine that many will be deceived.

2. When the Move of God truly does come, in whatever capacity, Satan will attempt to counterfeit that which is truly of the Lord.

This problem, which has always existed, is going to increase dramatically in these last days.

NOTES

Paul said, *"Now the Spirit speaks expressly, that in the latter times some shall depart from the faith, giving heed to seducing spirits, and doctrines of demons"* (I Tim. 4:1).

The word *"pervert"* in the Greek text as given in Verse 10 is *"diastrepho"* and means *"to distort, misinterpret, or corrupt."* It also means to *"turn away from the truth,"* corresponding with II Timothy 4:3-4.

Even though the statement I now make is strong, I fully believe it to be the truth.

PERVERSION

Most preachers pervert the truth. In fact, only a few truly preach the Word with the Anointing of the Holy Spirit.

How do I know that?

There is no fruit to their ministries, which is the criterion demanded by Christ (Mat. 7:15-20). What do we mean by fruit?

I speak of souls being saved, believers being baptized with the Holy Spirit, bondages being broken, lives being changed, and sick bodies truly being healed. Even though grandiose claims are made at times respecting this of which I speak, the truth is, at least for the far greater majority, there is no real fruit! The Holy Spirit can never bless or condone error, and neither can He anoint one with unconfessed and, thereby, unrepentant sin within his heart and life. He can only anoint *"truth"* and a cleansed vessel, i.e., cleansed by the Blood of the Lord Jesus Christ.

(11) "AND NOW, BEHOLD, THE HAND OF THE LORD IS UPON YOU, AND YOU SHALL BE BLIND, NOT SEEING THE SUN FOR A SEASON. AND IMMEDIATELY THERE FELL ON HIM A MIST AND A DARKNESS; AND HE WENT ABOUT SEEKING SOME TO LEAD HIM BY THE HAND."

The form is:

1. Without the Cross, Christianity is little more than a vapid philosophy.

2. With the Cross, Christianity becomes a living dynamo.

THE HAND OF THE LORD IS AGAINST YOU

The phrase, *"And now, behold, the Hand of the Lord is upon you,"* would have been better translated, *"Is against you!"*

Even though the Scripture gives little detail, it seems the opposition by this man against Paul and Barnabas was acute and lasted for some period of time.

As well, that which Paul did here was carried out only after the Holy Spirit had given instructions. Such must never come from one's own mind or feelings. In fact, it is a very dangerous thing to take matters of judgment into one's own hands. Considering that we find such carried out very little in the Book of Acts, we should understand accordingly that the Lord seldom gives such latitude to believers.

The phrase, *"And you shall be blind, not seeing the sun for a season,"* indicates that this limitation in time is an indication that there was place for repentance. In other words, it was a remedial chastisement.

Elymas personated the nation of Israel. He opposed Christ and the Gospel and for a season, darkness blinded their moral vision.

As well, it is remarkable that this was the moment chosen by the Holy Spirit to introduce Paul's new name.

A MIST AND A DARKNESS

How long this *"season"* lasted, we are not told.

The phrase, *"And immediately there fell on him a mist and a darkness,"* was used thusly by the Holy Spirit in order to teach this man that his message and his way were both *"darkness."*

Such not only pertains to Israel, but actually, to the whole of humanity that does not know Christ. Therefore, it must be remembered that it is impossible to show a blind man anything. So, to make an effort to reach men intellectually is a waste of time.

To be frank, those who do not have salvation have absolutely no idea as to Who God is or His Son the Lord Jesus Christ. Actually, a little 4-year-old girl, who has just given her heart and life to Jesus Christ, knows far more about God than the most brilliant professor teaching in one of the greatest universities in the land, who is not saved. That is a strong statement, but it is true.

Consequently, as with Paul, we must have the Holy Spirit functioning within our hearts and lives, Who alone can penetrate the darkness as the Word of God is preached. Sadly and regrettably, even then, only a few will truly accept the *"light"* (Mat. 7:14).

The phrase, *"And he went about seeking some to lead him by the hand,"* seems to indicate that he now had no followers due to the fact that he had been shown up for what he truly was, an impostor! Consequently, no one desired to be seen with him, or especially to help him, for fear that the same thing might happen to them!

(12) "THEN THE DEPUTY, WHEN HE SAW WHAT WAS DONE, BELIEVED, BEING ASTONISHED AT THE DOCTRINE OF THE LORD."

The diagram is:

1. It was at the Cross where the believing sinner came in.

2. It is at the Cross where the consecrated Christian stays in.

FAITH

The phrase, *"Then the deputy, when he saw what was done, believed,"* simply means that he accepted the Lord Jesus Christ as his Saviour.

The word *"believed"* in the Greek text is *"pisteuo"* and means *"to have faith in, upon, or with respect to, a person or thing,"* in this case Christ.

As well, his faith was not in the miracle that was performed, but rather to Whom the miracle pointed. In other words, the miracle verified what Paul was saying about Christ concerning His Death, Burial, Resurrection, and Ascension.

Even though Luke does not mention such, every evidence is that this man was also baptized in water and with the Holy Spirit with the evidence of speaking with other tongues.

The criterion had already been laid down that all new converts must be baptized in water (Acts 2:38; 8:12; 9:18; 10:47).

Considering that one of these accounts (Acts 9:18) pertained to Paul's own baptism in water, we know that he continued this practice, even though Luke, as was his custom, did not all the time relate everything that happened, even as here (Acts 19:5).

As well, the evidence is clear that the

NOTES

baptism with the Holy Spirit with the evidence of speaking with other tongues was also preached to all new converts. This is so clear and concerns the precedent being set that when the account of the great Move of God under Philip took place in Samaria, and the Apostles learned that even though these people had accepted Christ as their Saviour, they had not yet been baptized with the Holy Spirit, they immediately sent Peter and John, *"Who, when they were come down, prayed for them, that they might receive the Holy Spirit"* (Acts 8:14-17).

SCRIPTURALLY IGNORANT

As well, one of the problems in the Church at Corinth was the lack of knowledge concerning tongues, prophecy, and the other gifts, which was rectified by the Apostle Paul (I Cor., Chpt. 14).

The evidence is overly abundant and, therefore, obvious that the early Church preached salvation by the shed Blood of Jesus Christ, the baptism with the Holy Spirit with the evidence of speaking with other tongues, divine healing according to the Word of God, and the victorious, overcoming Christian life.

As well, they preached the Rapture (Resurrection) of the Church and the Second Coming. So, anything that differs from that, whether by addition or deletion, constitutes that which is man-induced and, therefore, of Satan. The Holy Spirit laid down the pattern as is given to us in the Book of Acts and the Epistles and means for it to be followed in totality. Man has no authority to change it in any way, and if done so, invites judgment.

THE DOCTRINE OF THE LORD

The record is clear in the Book of Acts that Jesus alone is held up as the Source of salvation, that all believers were baptized in water, and that the baptism with the Holy Spirit with the evidence of speaking with other tongues was preached and taught to all new converts, whether they received or not! Concerning water baptism, archaeologists have found evidence that the daughter of Sergius Paulus and her son were baptized believers.

NOTES

The phrase, *"Being astonished at the Doctrine of the Lord,"* speaks to the fact that this *"doctrine"* was not mere rhetoric but was, as well, accompanied by power.

The word *"astonished"* is used four times in the Book of Acts and every time concerns the Power of God (Acts 9:6; 10:45; 12:16; 13:12).

If the Holy Spirit is properly allowed to lead the Church, He will do things that will bring astonishment. Whenever this Roman governor saw the Power of God in operation, especially as it was compared to the fakery of Elymas, it quickly became obvious as to what was true and what was false.

(13) "NOW WHEN PAUL AND HIS COMPANY LOOSED FROM PAPHOS, THEY CAME TO PERGA IN PAMPHYLIA: AND JOHN DEPARTING FROM THEM RETURNED TO JERUSALEM."

The structure is:

1. The phrase, *"Now when Paul and his company loosed from Paphos, they came to Perga in Pamphylia,"* presents them going back to the mainland from the island of Cyprus. It was a distance of approximately 100 miles.

2. They would have gone to Attalia first, inasmuch as it was a harbor, and then would have gone to Perga, some eight or nine miles southeast and six miles inland. Perga was the capital of Pamphylia and engaged in constant trade with Paphos, the capital of Cyprus.

3. Two great things happened to Paul at Paphos:

a. As we have stated, his name was changed to *"Paul."*

b. The Holy Spirit now made him the leader, with his name being first in most accounts that followed.

4. Even at the very time that Paul came to Christ, it was told him that he would *"bear the Name of Jesus before the Gentiles, and kings, and the children of Israel"* (Acts 9:15). That had been about 12 or 13 years before. During this time, the Lord had prepared Paul for the great task that lay before him. Now that this task had begun in earnest, the Holy Spirit would put Paul in the position of leadership, which was welcomed by Barnabas, as is obvious.

5. As we have previously said, there

have been few men in Christian history as noble as Barnabas, and as used of God, we might quickly add! What an honor was his to have been so used by the Lord to help prepare Paul.

6. *"And John departing from them returned to Jerusalem,"* speaks of Mark who wrote the Gospel that bears his name.

7. We are given no information at all at this time as to why Mark did this, but we know from later happenings that his departure had caused hardships on this missionary team (Acts 15:37-39).

8. Some have ventured that Mark, being young, had gotten homesick and, therefore, went back to Jerusalem. Others have suggested that the hardships and rigors of this trip were many and that Mark, unaccustomed to such, went back to the comforts of his home.

Also, others say, which very well could have been true, that Mark did not go along with Paul on the Message of the Cross but was still trying to cling to the Law.

Irrespective, and for whatever reason, Mark deserted his post at that time; however, thankfully, he would see the error of his ways, and Paul, as well, would see the quality that was in this young man.

9. Thankfully, Mark would ultimately turn out to be—and recognized by Paul as well—a great man of God.

(14) "BUT WHEN THEY DEPARTED FROM PERGA, THEY CAME TO ANTIOCH IN PISIDIA, AND WENT INTO THE SYNAGOGUE ON THE SABBATH DAY, AND SAT DOWN."

The overview is:

1. The phrase, *"But when they departed from Perga, they came to Antioch in Pisidia,"* proclaims another Antioch, other than the Antioch of Syria, where the home Church was located (Acts 13:1). Actually, there were 16 Antiochs, all founded by Seleucus Nicator and named after his father, Antiochus. This Antioch was about 100 miles due east from Perga. Even though it was now a Roman colony, still, the road was difficult and dangerous. It was infested with robbers (II Cor. 11:26), was mountainous and rugged, and passed through an untamed and half-savage population. Pisidia was part of the province of Galatia.

NOTES

2. *"And went into the synagogue on the Sabbath day, and sat down,"* tells us that their route, at least for now, seemed to have been determined by the locality of the Jewish population, which was always their first object and their door of access to the heathen. The Lord had also said of Paul that he was not only to be an Apostle to the Gentiles but, as well, to the Jews (Acts 9:15). However, as we shall see, regarding the whole of the Jewish population, Paul's efforts among them would become more and more difficult, with their rejection of Christ becoming virtually total.

3. The short phrase, *"And sat down,"* has reference to special seats, thus intimating, as was the custom in the synagogue, that they were willing to speak, if invited (Williams).

(15) "AND AFTER THE READING OF THE LAW AND THE PROPHETS THE RULERS OF THE SYNAGOGUE SENT UNTO THEM, SAYING, YOU MEN AND BRETHREN, IF YOU HAVE ANY WORD OF EXHORTATION FOR THE PEOPLE, SAY ON."

The exegesis is:

1. The phrase, *"And after the reading of the Law and the Prophets the rulers of the synagogue sent unto them,"* proclaims the custom of the synagogue.

The order of the synagogue service was first the prayers, offered while the people were standing.

2. Then came the reading of a portion of the Law, with the interpretation or comments generally offered by someone else.

Next came the same thing, with reading from one of the Prophets, along with comments.

3. Last of all came the *"midrash,"* or sermon, which Paul delivered at the invitation of the ruler of the synagogue.

Actually, this was the same thing done by Jesus at Nazareth (Lk. 4:20).

4. The phrase, *"Saying, You men and brethren, if you have any word of exhortation for the people, say on,"* seemed to register that which was quite common, the inviting of a special guest to speak, whether prearranged or on the spot, as here.

5. As stated, this was generally the

NOTES

manner in which Paul began his evangelism in any given area. He would first go to the Jewish synagogue and then to the Gentiles.

(16) "THEN PAUL STOOD UP, AND BECKONING WITH HIS HAND SAID, MEN OF ISRAEL, AND YOU WHO FEAR GOD, GIVE AUDIENCE."

The composition is:

1. The phrase, *"Then Paul stood up, and beckoning with his hand said,"* seems to mean that he spoke from the area where the chairs or seats for visiting speakers were located.

2. The phrase, *"Men of Israel, and you who fear God, give audience,"* addresses both Jews and Gentiles.

3. Gentiles who attended Jewish synagogues and were given a particular place to sit were called *"God-fearers."*

4. These were not proselytes to the Jewish faith, for whatever reason, but were devotees to the God of Israel, Whom they saw as greatly superior to the many gods of their heathen religions.

5. Paul let these Gentiles know, which would become very obvious in his message, that they were very much included in that which he had to say.

6. The following gives us the gist of Paul's message, with Luke going into some detail, which probably represented most messages preached of this nature in Jewish synagogues. Thus, the Book of Acts does not go into such detail in the record of later sermons.

(17) "THE GOD OF THIS PEOPLE OF ISRAEL CHOSE OUR FATHERS, AND EXALTED THE PEOPLE WHEN THEY DWELT AS STRANGERS IN THE LAND OF EGYPT, AND WITH AN HIGH ARM BROUGHT HE THEM OUT OF IT."

The account is:

1. Every person that's ever been saved was saved simply because of what Jesus did at the Cross and their faith in Christ and His finished Work.

2. The Cross of Christ is forever the means of all that we receive from the Lord.

PAUL'S MESSAGE

The phrase, *"The God of this people of Israel chose our fathers,"* presents Paul beginning his message much as had Stephen those years before. Evidently, Stephen's message had made a great impression upon Paul, even though he did not at that time yield to Christ.

However, his message would take a different turn in that he would present Jesus as Saviour, while Stephen would present Jesus as having been rejected by Israel. In both cases, the Holy Spirit would steer the message according to what he desired respecting the audience.

Immediately, Paul lay down the foundation that God raised up Israel for the purpose of bringing the Messiah, the Saviour of men, into the world. While they were a *"chosen"* people, they were chosen for a particular purpose, but a purpose they would not recognize!

The phrase, *"And exalted the people when they dwelt as strangers in the land of Egypt,"* proclaims their *"exaltation,"* not because of who they were but because of their purpose.

Sometimes, the Church forgets that as well! We are chosen but for one purpose, and that is to glorify Christ. When we fail to do that, of necessity, we must be set aside exactly as Israel of old.

The way that one can know that God has set certain parts of the Church aside is when the Holy Spirit no longer works in its confines. Along with many other things, the Holy Spirit will always *"glorify Christ"* (Jn. 16:14).

THE MANNER OF THEIR DELIVERANCE

The phrase, *"And with an high arm brought He them out of it,"* proclaims the manner of their deliverance.

It was done in such a way as to get the attention of the world in that day, and to be sure, that it did!

When Pharaoh finally buckled to the demands of Jehovah through Moses, every god worshiped by Egypt had been laid low. As well, the firstborn of every home lay dead, which struck at the very heart of Egypt's primary religion.

This was the cult of Osiris, with his wife, Isis, and son, Horus.

The tradition was that Osiris was

NOTES

murdered by his wicked brother, Seth, who was avenged by his son, Horus, who, with the support of his mother, Isis, gained his father's kingship on Earth. The Egyptian could identify himself with Osiris through his firstborn, thereby, revivified in his kingdom of the hereafter (after death). So, the life and success of the firstborn guaranteed eternal dividends for the father and was repeated with each succeeding generation. With the early and untimely death of the firstborn, the afterlife of the father was greatly hindered, etc.

So, when the children of Israel were delivered, and considering that the firstborn in every Egyptian home lay dead, the eternal hopes of all were dashed. Of course, we know these hopes were false anyway.

Therefore, when Paul used the phrase, *"High arm,"* it spoke not only of the opening of the Red Sea and the death of Pharaoh but, as well, the destruction of the national hope.

(18) "AND ABOUT THE TIME OF FORTY YEARS SUFFERED HE THEIR MANNERS IN THE WILDERNESS."

The way is:

1. The phrase, *"And about the time of forty years,"* refers to the length of time spent in the wilderness because of Israel's unbelief.

2. The phrase, *"Suffered He their manners in the wilderness,"* in effect, has a double meaning:

a. To give an example of God's Patience in dealing with Israel during this time, the Book of Numbers gives us examples of what happened.

In Numbers, Chapter 11, their complaints had to do with appetite, the *"lust of the flesh."* In Numbers, Chapter 12, it was *"jealousy."* In Numbers, Chapter 13, it was *"unbelief,"* called the *"provocation in the wilderness."* In Numbers, Chapter 14, it was *"presumption."* In Numbers, Chapter 15, it was *"high-handedness"* that rebelled against God's Laws. In Numbers, Chapter 16, it was *"mutiny."* So, the word *"suffered"* aptly describes God's Endurance with these people.

b. The word *"suffered,"* in another variation, has reference to Deuteronomy 1:31, and means that He did bear or carry Israel during this time, even as a nursing father carries his child.

And that he did, despite their rebellion, stubbornness, wickedness, and unbelief!

(19) "AND WHEN HE HAD DESTROYED SEVEN NATIONS IN THE LAND OF CANAAN, HE DIVIDED THEIR LAND TO THEM BY LOT."

The way is:

1. The phrase, *"And when He had destroyed seven nations in the land of Canaan,"* referred to the Canaanites, Hittites, Girgashites, Amorites, Hivites, Perizzites, and Jebusites.

These seven nations were not destroyed until their cup of iniquity was full (Gen. 15:16).

2. One archaeologist stated that the God of the Israelites (as he put it) did the world and future generations an untold service when He gave instructions for these particular tribes or nations in the land of Canaan to be completely exterminated. He went on to speak of the incest, bestiality, homosexuality, and pedophilia that had become pandemic among these people.

3. *"He divided their land to them by lot,"* speaks of the Urim and Thummim.

These things, which mean *"lights and perfections,"* were carried in the ephod of the high priest's garment. However, exactly what they were is not known.

Used by the high priests, they gave direction according to the Will of God, hence, their meaning as just given.

Some think they were two flat objects, each with a *"yes"* side and each with a *"no"* side; however, as to exactly how they worked, the Old Testament is silent.

4. Irrespective, it was with the *"Urim and Thummim"* that the land was divided out among the various tribes. In other words, the Holy Spirit parceled out the land according to each tribe, with some evidence that even the families were allotted their own special position within the confines of the territory of each tribe (Josh., Chpts. 13-22).

(20) "AND AFTER THAT HE GAVE UNTO THEM JUDGES ABOUT THE SPACE OF FOUR HUNDRED AND FIFTY YEARS, UNTIL SAMUEL THE PROPHET."

The form is:

NOTES

1. Ninety-nine percent of the entirety of the Bible is given over to telling us how to live for God.

2. The Cross of Christ and only the Cross of Christ is the answer to that question.

JUDGES

The phrase, *"And after that He gave unto them judges,"* speaks of 16 deliverers raised up by God during times of oppression by the Philistines and other nations the Israelites were supposed to have driven out, but did not.

Samuel was the last of these judges, and the only judge who was able to unite all twelve tribes and through his Prophetic ministry, bring a spiritual revival (I Sam. 7:3-9).

"About the space of four hundred and fifty years, until Samuel the Prophet," does not present confusion as some claim.

From the time the children of Israel entered Canaan under Joshua through the life and ministry of Samuel, the last judge, it has been guessed at as a period of time anywhere between 250 and 750 years. The reason for the discrepancy is the attempts to correlate the various periods of time respecting various judges, etc.

All confusion is eliminated, however, when one understands that the periods during which the judges ruled overlapped in many cases.

FOUR HUNDRED AND FIFTY YEARS

For instance, a careful comparison of Bible passages shows that the Ammonites oppressed Israel from the east, while Philistines oppressed them from the west; and the judgeships of Jephthah, Samson, and Eli overlapped, each one exercising leadership in a different part of Israel, it seems! (Horton).

As well, we must come to the conclusion that Paul, as others during his time, had access to information respecting time factors, etc., which we do not presently have. So, when he gave the number, *"about four hundred and fifty years,"* it was that which he knew to be true.

Regrettably, many modern believers show little interest in Old Testament history, claiming that such is a bygone era and holds no present validity. However, it should be quickly noted that such thinking is a sure road to spiritual leanness.

One should take a lesson from the message here preached by Paul, wondering how the Gentiles present could have had interest in such, considering that it was the history of Israel.

To be sure, they had great interest, even as the Text portrays (Acts 13:42), and for the obvious reasons.

Israel was raised up by God as a benefit to the entirety of the world in that Jesus would come through these people as the last Adam; consequently, nothing could be more important! Therefore, as this was an interest to them of that day, it should be an interest to all presently, and even more so if possible!

Actually, to not know the Old Testament is to have an improper understanding of the New. That is the reason that many Charismatics come up with unscriptural doctrines, etc.

(21) "AND AFTERWARD THEY DESIRED A KING: AND GOD GAVE UNTO THEM SAUL THE SON OF CIS, A MAN OF THE TRIBE OF BENJAMIN, BY THE SPACE OF FORTY YEARS."

The lot is:

1. The phrase, *"And afterward they desired a king,"* is given as an account in I Samuel, Chapters 8 through 21, as well as I Chronicles, Chapter 10. They desired a king to be like other nations.

In fact, the Lord had promised them a king (Num. 23:21). Actually, David was to be the first king of Israel (I Sam. 16:1).

However, Israel, as so many presently, jumped ahead of the Lord, demanding a king before it was God's Time. Even as the Lord said to Samuel, *"They have not rejected you, but they have rejected Me, that I should not reign over them"* (I Sam. 8:7).

2. As a result of getting ahead of God, they suffered greatly, even as all suffer who jump ahead or lag behind.

3. *"And God gave unto them Saul the son of Cis,"* represents a work of the flesh, even though selected by God.

4. Israel was like a spoiled child, who stamps his feet demanding certain things.

NOTES

While the Lord did allow them to have what they wanted, it did not help them at all, even as it could not help them. To be frank, this scene is repeated constantly.

5. Religious men demand things that are unscriptural, and oftentimes the Lord will give such to them. Consequently, as Israel of old, they are then led to believe that what they are doing is blessed by God. However, that which is not *"born of the Spirit"* cannot be blessed by the Spirit.

6. Men make their plans and desire that God bless them, just as Israel! The true way is to let God make the plans, and they are guaranteed of blessing!

7. *"A man of the tribe of Benjamin,"* by his very description could not be God's King.

8. The one chosen by the Lord had to come from the tribe of Judah, which had been prophesied long before by Jacob (Gen. 49:10). David fulfilled that prophecy, being of the tribe of Judah (I Sam. 16:1; II Sam. 2:4).

9. *"By the space of forty years,"* presents the only account we have as to the length of the reign of Saul. The first 20 or 30 years of his reign after the rescue of Jabesh-gilead are passed over in absolute silence. The narrative from I Samuel, Chapters 13 to 21, relates only to about the last 10 years of his life.

(22) "AND WHEN HE HAD REMOVED HIM, HE RAISED UP UNTO THEM DAVID TO BE THEIR KING; TO WHOM ALSO HE GAVE TESTIMONY, AND SAID, I HAVE FOUND DAVID THE SON OF JESSE, A MAN AFTER MINE OWN HEART, WHICH SHALL FULFIL ALL MY WILL."

The composition is:

1. All false doctrine in the Bible is the result of an improper interpretation of the Cross.

2. Every Bible Doctrine is based squarely on the Cross of Christ.

DAVID

The phrase, *"And when He had removed him,"* presents the Lord as the ruling hand behind every throne and, in effect, every person. Men rule, while God overrules!

The phrase, *"He raised up unto them David to be their king,"* presents God's Choice, as Saul was the people's choice. Consequently, the former was of the Spirit, while the latter was of the flesh.

The phrase, *"To whom also He gave testimony,"* tells us why He chose David!

While God is Sovereign, thereby, able to do whatever He desires, still, His Sovereignty will never take Him beyond His Nature and Character. Every implication is that God chooses people for leadership on the basis of the two conditions given in the next phrase. It was a valid *"testimony"* then, and it is a valid *"testimony"* now! God does not change!

The phrase, *"And said, I have found David the son of Jesse, a man after My own Heart, which shall fulfill all My Will,"* gives us the two conditions:

1. *"A man after Mine own Heart"*: Such does not mean that David was perfect because he was not. It does mean that despite his failures and difficulties, his heart was after God. He had no personal agenda of his own, and neither did he have self-will, which is the bane of most believers.

2. *"Which shall fulfil all My Will"*: his heart was to do the Will of God at all costs.

THE WILL OF GOD

As is obvious, he did not always succeed, but this one thing he did do: when he erred, he did not blame others but only himself, and always took the matter to the Lord (II Sam. 22:22; Ps. 18:21-24).

It is incumbent upon the believer to find the Will of God and to fulfill it in totality.

Believers make terrible mistakes when they place God last, if at all.

Decisions are too often made with a personal agenda in mind, which reeks with self-will, with God given little thought. Such is the sure road to disaster.

As stated, the believer must ardently seek the Will of God for all things, even that which seems to be insignificant, and once that Will is ascertained, then set about to carry it out in totality. Paul said, *"That you may prove what is that good, and acceptable, and perfect, Will of God"* (Rom. 12:2).

A PROPER RELATIONSHIP WITH CHRIST

Even as I sit behind my desk holding a

dictaphone in my hand, I sense the Presence of God. My heart's desire is to do the Will of God, and to do it in its totality. I have learned in my years of attempting to live for God and to represent the Lord Jesus Christ, which I feel I have done so poorly, that God has a perfect Will for every single believer. That means every single thing in our lives, even that which we consider to be small and insignificant. In other words, He wants us to seek Him ardently about everything.

If we do not know the Will of God, it is best to wait where we are until His Will is revealed unto us. If we earnestly seek Him, He will let us know what to do.

Having said that, I emphasize the fact that knowing, having, and doing the Will of God is absolutely impossible without a proper relationship with Christ, which can only be brought about by a proper prayer life and knowledge of His Word. Sadly, these are the two commodities that most believers simply do not have. Consequently, most do not know and have the Will of God, therefore, even as Saul of old, accrue to themselves great difficulties.

(23) "OF THIS MAN'S SEED HAS GOD ACCORDING TO HIS PROMISE RAISED UNTO ISRAEL A SAVIOUR, JESUS."

The composition is:

1. The phrase, *"Of this man's seed,"* speaks of David through whom would come the second Man Who would be the last Adam, Who would succeed where the first Adam failed!

Of the fact that the Messiah would be the Son of David, Israel was in agreement, but that Jesus was that *"Seed,"* they were not in agreement at all!

Thus, we see how that Paul, step-by-step, gave the reason for Israel's existence, which proclaimed her deliverance from Egypt and then the kingdom of David. All were preparatory to the actual coming of the Son of David, the Messiah, to save His People Israel.

2. The phrase, *"Has God according to His Promise,"* speaks of the Davidic Covenant, at least one of the greatest covenants in the Bible. It is found in II Samuel 7:12-16; Psalm 132:11; and Isaiah 9:6.

David wanted to build a temple for the Lord, but the Lord told him that He had

NOTES

something in mind for him much greater than the temple. In fact, through David's family, i.e., his seed, would come the promised Redeemer.

Nevertheless, this *"promise"* began in the Garden of Eden (Gen. 3:15).

3. The phrase, *"Raised unto Israel a Saviour, Jesus,"* proclaims the Apostle now introducing the One Who is the cause and reason for everything. I speak of the *"Saviour,"* the Lord Jesus Christ, the Son of God, the Saviour of man. There is no other; He alone fills that role!

4. However, sadly, Israel did not want a Saviour, but rather a conqueror! She did not recognize her true need, as most do not recognize their true need presently.

Plainly, clearly, even dogmatically, Paul announced in no uncertain terms that this of which God had promised had been fulfilled in *"Jesus."*

5. I wonder what the reaction was of the rulers of the synagogue when Paul made this statement concerning Jesus, and made it without apology or doubt. I think that the implications of what was being said were so great that it was probably impossible for them to digest all at one time.

6. This being true, Judaism, even as Paul declared, had fulfilled its role. It was raised up for the expressed purpose of bringing the Messiah into the world and now that He had come, there was no more need for all that Judaism represented, such as the temple, the sacrifices, the feast days, circumcision, Sabbaths, etc., at least at this time.

7. The record will show that when Paul's message was finished, most of the Jews would rebel against him and the message.

The King, exactly as God had promised David, had come, but they did not want this King, telling Pilate they preferred Caesar instead (Jn. 19:15). Caesar they got, and it has proven to be the saddest choice ever made by any people, anytime, anywhere, and any place.

(24) "WHEN JOHN HAD FIRST PREACHED BEFORE HIS COMING THE BAPTISM OF REPENTANCE TO ALL THE PEOPLE OF ISRAEL."

The way is:

1. The phrase, *"When John had first*

preached before His coming," speaks of the Baptist being the forerunner of Christ.

2. Considering that John was the first Prophet since Malachi, a period of about 400 years, his life and ministry were well-known everywhere.

3. Actually, John was raised up for the very purpose of announcing the Messiah to Israel and of preparing the way for Him. In other words, his mission was so described and obvious that there was absolutely no doubt as to his purpose and reason.

4. That the spiritual leadership of Israel would not accept him or the One he announced was not for lack of evidence, for there was evidence in every shape and form. As stated, his mission was obvious, so Israel was without excuse!

5. The phrase, *"The baptism of repentance to all the people of Israel,"* presents that which was an absolute necessity before the Messiah could be introduced. In other words, Israel desperately needed to repent (from the top down), but, regrettably, the leadership would not repent, as leadership seldom repents!

6. Paul used the term *"baptism of repentance,"* which adequately described John's message. This did not mean that the ceremony of water baptism constituted repentance, as many believe, but rather that the ceremony was because repentance had already been engaged, of which the baptism was a symbol.

7. The water baptism was not the cause of repentance, but rather the result of repentance.

8. As we have stated, the phrase as used by Paul, *"All the people of Israel,"* means that repentance was needed, even desperately needed, from the top down.

(25) "AND AS JOHN FULFILLED HIS COURSE, HE SAID, WHOM DO YOU THINK THAT I AM? I AM NOT HE. BUT, BEHOLD, THERE COMES ONE AFTER ME, WHOSE SHOES OF HIS FEET I AM NOT WORTHY TO LOOSE."

The way is:

1. The phrase, *"And as John fulfilled his course,"* refers to his short ministry raised up for the expressed purpose of introducing the Messiah of Israel and the Saviour of mankind.

NOTES

2. The question, *"He said, Whom do you think that I am?"* was asked in order that all would know exactly who he was and his purpose.

3. Luke states that all men were musing in their hearts of John whether he were the Christ or not (Lk. 3:15).

4. The phrase, *"I am not He,"* tells us that John wanted no mistake made whatsoever as to who he was. He was not the Messiah, but rather the one to introduce the Messiah.

5. *"But, behold, there comes One after me, Whose shoes of His Feet I am not worthy to loose,"* answers this question in such a way as to leave no room for misunderstanding.

6. John declared that his position and that of Christ were not even close.

7. Irrespective of the lauding of John and even many falsely thinking that he was the Messiah, the truth was that he (John) did not think himself worthy even to be a slave of Jesus Christ. How true that was!

8. But yet, in His Humanity, though never ceasing to be God, Jesus was so fully human that it was difficult for men to accept Him for Who He really was. They could not see the deity for the humanity.

9. Despite the greatest array of miracles the world had ever known, even to the raising of the dead, and despite His Words of life, which, in fact, no man had ever uttered before Him, still, the religious leadership of Israel could not see past His Humanity, despite the fact that He was the only perfect Human Who has ever lived.

Therefore, they called Him an impostor and a blasphemer!

(26) "MEN AND BRETHREN, CHILDREN OF THE STOCK OF ABRAHAM, AND WHOSOEVER AMONG YOU FEARS GOD, TO YOU IS THE WORD OF THIS SALVATION SENT."

The exegesis is:

1. Jesus Christ came to this world for the express purpose of going to the Cross.

2. In order to do this, He would have to become Man, which He did.

CHILDREN OF THE STOCK OF ABRAHAM

The phrase, *"Men and brethren, children of the stock of Abraham,"* pertains to the Jews.

For the entirety of his ministry, Paul kept trying to reach the Jews with the great Gospel of Jesus Christ, but most of the time to no avail. This is so sad considering that these were God's chosen People; however, Jesus was to them *"a Stone of stumbling, and a Rock of offence"* (I Pet. 2:8).

Why?

The spiritual leadership of Israel at the time of Christ was abominable to say the least! But yet, people generally get the type of leadership they deserve, at least for the most part.

The common people heard Jesus gladly, with some few of the wealthy as well, but mostly, He was rejected.

We can say they failed to follow the Word, which is certainly true. We can also say that His Humanity was so pronounced that they balked at accepting this Peasant as their Messiah, especially considering that they expected someone entirely different. The expectation of someone different is closer to the truth, I think, than with all the other excuses.

SELF-RIGHTEOUSNESS

When people become lifted up in pride, as Israel of long ago, they look at everything in a warped, twisted way, especially that which is of God. This is especially true as it pertains to the Lord. I am speaking of spiritual pride, i.e., self-righteousness. In other words, their spiritual pride keeps them from rightly dividing the Word of Truth. As well, everything they see is clouded by their self-deception. Not only do they not walk right, they do not think right, do not see right, and do not come to right conclusions. Regrettably, much, if not most, of the modern Church falls into the same category.

That is the reason Jesus said, *"Blessed are the poor* (broken) *in spirit: for theirs is the kingdom of heaven"* (Mat. 5:3).

Instead of being *"poor"* or *"broken"* in spirit, the modern Church is rather saying, *"I am rich, and increased with goods, and have need of nothing."*

Jesus then said, *"And you do not know that you are wretched, and miserable, and poor* (spiritually bankrupt), *and blind, and naked"* (Rev. 3:17).

NOTES

So, the *"stock of Abraham,"* even after bringing the Messiah into the world, rejected Him of Whom the Prophets spoke and, in effect, rejected the fruit of their own womb.

The phrase, *"And whosoever among you fears God,"* was directed at the Gentiles in the synagogue, of which there were almost always some, and were called *"God-fearers."*

THE WORD OF THIS SALVATION

The phrase, *"To you is the word of this salvation sent,"* presents Paul, without apology, including the Gentiles in this great plan of salvation. Actually, he was emphatic in his statement respecting the pronoun *"you"* that it include both Jews and Gentiles.

Now, Paul, after laying the foundation of his message, would preach Jesus and would pull no punches whatsoever! Preachers should take a lesson from his approach, which, in fact, was the approach of the Holy Spirit.

Paul did not soft-pedal anything, leaving absolutely no doubt as to what he was saying. There is a reason for that:

People must be dealt with in love; however, true love will tell the truth for the simple reason that it is true love, i.e., *"the love of God."*

A brother wrote me a short time ago, which we have received untold thousands of such letters through the years.

He was accusing me of being too hard on Catholics.

I answered him, thanked him for his letter, and stated that it was not Catholics who I opposed, but rather Catholic doctrine, which I know to be grossly unscriptural and accordingly, has led untold millions into eternal darkness. In other words, if we truly love people, we will tell them the truth. The feelings of people are very important, but their souls are of far greater worth.

(27) "FOR THEY WHO DWELL AT JERUSALEM, AND THEIR RULERS, BECAUSE THEY KNEW HIM NOT, NOR YET THE VOICES OF THE PROPHETS WHICH ARE READ EVERY SABBATH DAY, THEY HAVE FULFILLED THEM IN CONDEMNING HIM."

NOTES

The synopsis is:

1. The phrase, *"For they who dwell at Jerusalem, and their rulers,"* pinpoints the murderers of Christ. This lays the blame squarely at the feet of the religious leadership of Israel.

2. *"Because they knew Him not,"* implies a willful ignorance, which brought about a willful blindness. In other words, they could have known simply because the proof was abundant before them, but they did not desire to know.

3. Some have claimed that by this phrase, *"Because they knew Him not,"* Paul was absolving them of blame because of ignorance; however, his following statements prove otherwise.

4. The phrase, *"Nor yet the voices of the Prophets which are read every Sabbath day,"* proclaims the fact that even though they read the Scriptures, and even discussed them constantly, still, they did not know them. They did not believe what they said, especially concerning the Messiah, but put their own spin or twist to what the Prophets had originally said.

Such is indicative of untold numbers of preachers and people. They read the Bible and claim to believe what it says; however, they attempt to conform the Bible to their beliefs instead of conforming their beliefs to the Bible!

5. Of course, it is obvious, as should be understood, that despite the great profession of religion and the constant occupation in its service, these men (the leadership of Israel) really were not saved. In fact, they did not know God. Such epitomizes most of Christianity presently!

6. *"They have fulfilled them in condemning Him,"* proclaims within itself a statement so startling that it defies description.

7. Even as they read the Scriptures, they were so spiritually blind that they did not really know they were fulfilling what the Prophets had said concerning the Messiah. Chapter 53 of Isaiah is a case in point. They fulfilled its predictions in totality but did not know they were doing so. Jesus proclaimed what they were.

He said, *"Let them alone: they be blind leaders of the blind. And if the blind lead the blind, both shall fall into the ditch"* (Mat. 15:14).

(28) "AND THOUGH THEY FOUND NO CAUSE OF DEATH IN HIM, YET DESIRED THEY PILATE THAT HE SHOULD BE SLAIN."

The exegesis is:

1. The phrase, *"And though they found no cause of death in Him,"* means that they opposed Him from the very beginning. In other words, they did not at all give Him or His Message a chance. They heard Him with closed minds, and as a result, closed their ears.

2. During all of this time, they sought diligently to find fault with Him or His Message, or both! However, despite their constant nit-picking, they could not scripturally fault His Message and, as well, could find no sin within His Life.

3. Irrespective, they wanted Him dead!

4. The flesh always opposes the Spirit. Cain must kill Abel, and Esau must try to kill Jacob. As well, Joseph's brethren must do the same to him, or attempt to do so!

Saul must try to kill David, and Israel must kill the Son of David!

5. *"Yet desired they Pilate that He should be slain,"* speaks of His Trial and their demand for His Death, even though Pilate plainly said that he found no fault in Him. The charges were trumped up, and the accusations were false. Never in history has there been such a travesty of justice!

(29) "AND WHEN THEY HAD FULFILLED ALL THAT WAS WRITTEN OF HIM, THEY TOOK HIM DOWN FROM THE TREE, AND LAID HIM IN A SEPULCHRE."

The synopsis is:

1. The phrase, *"And when they had fulfilled all that was written of Him,"* pertained to that which the Prophets had predicted.

Did they not know or understand what they were doing?

Did they not know the Word of God well enough to see that they were actually fulfilling these things predicted of Him?

When they beat Him, they were fulfilling Isaiah 50:6 and 53:5.

In their mockery as they bowed the knee, they portrayed the fact that Jesus is the King of kings and Lord of lords and before Him every knee shall bow, thus fulfilling Isaiah 45:23.

The entire comportment of His Trial, Death, and Burial fulfilled Isaiah, Chapter 53.

His being crucified outside the city walls fulfilled the typology of the sin offering on the great Day of Atonement, fulfilling Leviticus 16:27.

When the soldiers cast lots for His clothes, they were fulfilling the great prophecy of Psalm 22:16-18.

THEY TOOK HIM DOWN FROM THE CROSS

The phrase *"They took Him down from the tree,"* speaks of the Cross and the manner in which they demanded that He die. This was done for reason:

The Law of Moses stated, *"For he who is hanged is accursed of God"* (Deut. 21:23).

Consequently, His being crucified would picture Him to the people of Israel as being cursed by God. They reasoned in their wicked minds that if He was truly what He said He was, God would not allow such. Hence, they tormented Him on the Cross, saying, *"If You be the Son of God, come down from the Cross"* (Mat. 27:40).

In their blindness, they did not understand that He was made a curse by God, but not for His sins, for He had none. He was made a curse as our substitute and as such, suffered the penalty we should have suffered.

In a short time, Paul would write, *"Christ has redeemed us from the curse of the Law, being made a curse for us."*

He then said, *"That the blessing of Abraham might come on the Gentiles, through Jesus Christ; that we might receive the Promise of the Spirit through faith"* (Gal. 3:13-14).

"And laid Him in a sepulchre," proclaims such being done by Nicodemus and Joseph of Arimathea, who were both members of the Jewish Sanhedrin.

Paul did not mention their great kindness shown to Christ at this time, probably because they were unknown to the people at Antioch.

It is certain that these Jews in Antioch of Pisidia had heard all about the Ministry of Christ, how He was crucified, etc. So, I wonder what their thoughts were at the moment Paul was making these statements.

(30) "BUT GOD RAISED HIM FROM THE DEAD."

The exegesis is:

1. As Paul proclaimed the Crucifixion of Jesus, he now proclaimed His Resurrection.

2. Evil men, even evil religious men, crucified Him, but God performed the impossible and raised Him from the dead.

3. Of course, the Jews denied this, claiming that the disciples had stolen Him away, etc.

4. However, it was difficult to make that story stick, considering that Roman soldiers were guarding the tomb constantly. None are so blind as those who will not see!

(31) "AND HE WAS SEEN MANY DAYS OF THEM WHICH CAME UP WITH HIM FROM GALILEE TO JERUSALEM, WHO ARE HIS WITNESSES UNTO THE PEOPLE."

The pattern is:

1. The phrase, *"And He was seen many days of them which came up with Him from Galilee to Jerusalem,"* concerns a number of appearances over a timespan of some 40 days.

2. This speaks of His Appearances to His Disciples, as well as some of the women and others, most from Galilee. Actually, there were appearances in both Jerusalem and Galilee, as well as the road to Emmaus (Lk. 24:13).

3. The phrase, *"Who are His witnesses unto the people,"* numbered well over 500 (I Cor. 15:3-8).

Paul was making the case that there were too many appearances for His Resurrection to be denied, at least with any degree of honesty!

4. So, the Jews were faced with a dilemma. They must admit that He had indeed been raised from the dead, of which there was a mountain of evidence, but which admittance would give veracity to His claim of being the Son of God. It would, as well, admit that they had actually crucified their Messiah!

As most, they would not do such a thing, so they had to hold to their ridiculous story that He really was not resurrected but spirited away by His Disciples.

(32) "AND WE DECLARE UNTO YOU GLAD TIDINGS, HOW THAT THE PROMISE WHICH WAS MADE UNTO THE FATHERS."

The overview is:

1. The phrase, *"And we declare unto you glad tidings,"* speaks of the good news of the Gospel and that it is available to all, both Jews and Gentiles. It speaks of salvation for all, at least all who will believe (Jn. 3:16).

2. *"How that the promise which was made unto the fathers,"* had its beginning in Genesis 3:15, when the Lord promised that the Seed of the woman would bruise the head of Satan. To be sure, this was done at Calvary.

3. However, the *"promise,"* of which Paul here speaks, was first made to Abraham and then to Isaac and Jacob. The *"promise"* was also given to Moses, to Isaiah, as well as David, etc. (Gen. 12:1-3; Deut. 18:15; Ps. 16:10; Isa. 7:14; 9:6; 11:1; 42:1-5; 61:1).

(33) "GOD HAS FULFILLED THE SAME UNTO US THEIR CHILDREN, IN THAT HE HAS RAISED UP JESUS AGAIN; AS IT IS ALSO WRITTEN IN THE SECOND PSALM, YOU ARE MY SON, THIS DAY HAVE I BEGOTTEN YOU."

The structure is:

1. Satan fights the Cross of Christ as he fights nothing else.

2. The Evil One knows that all victory is found in the Cross.

3. That's the reason for his opposition.

PROMISES KEPT

The phrase, *"God has fulfilled the same unto us their children,"* means simply that the Lord did exactly what He had promised.

Even though the ones to whom such was promised did not see this great thing happen, the sending of Jesus, their ancestors did!

"In that He has raised up Jesus again," simply refers to the Resurrection.

Jesus was given to the world, namely to Israel, in effect, raised up by the Lord. When He was crucified, He was *"raised up again."*

"As it is also written in the Second Psalm, You are My Son," refers to the incarnation when the second Person of the Divine Trinity took a perfect human body in order that it would be offered up as a sacrifice to redeem humanity (Isa. 7:14; 9:6; Phil. 2:5-11).

THE REASON FOR THE INCARNATION

The phrase, *"This day have I begotten You,"* concerns the time when Jesus was born of the Virgin Mary (Mat. 1:18-25; Lk. 1:35; Jn. 1:14). To redeem the lost sons of Adam's fallen race, God would have to become Man, which, in fact, the Lord had predicted almost immediately after the fall (Gen. 3:15).

The Son of God would have to be born of a virgin, or else, He would be born in original sin as all other babies are born. Due to the fact that Adam was the federal head of the human race, all of humanity, theoretically, was in his loins; this means that all who were born after the fall were born in the likeness of Adam instead of the likeness of God (Gen. 5:3).

In effect, Jesus was the *"last Adam"* (I Cor. 15:45). This means that there will never have to be another one because Jesus carried out to completion everything that needed to be done. Where the first Adam disobeyed, Jesus obeyed in every respect.

JESUS AND HIS DEATH

While everything that Jesus did was of utmost importance, meaning that it played a part in our salvation experience, the main purpose for which He came was to die. Had He stopped short of death, irrespective of His virgin Birth, His perfect Life, and His Miracles and Healings, still, we could not have been saved. It was His Death on Calvary's Cross that effected our salvation, and did so completely (Gal. 1:4).

As should be obvious, God, as a Spirit-being, cannot die. So, in order for God to die, He would have to become Man, which He did! He died as our substitute, which demanded the incarnation. For the terrible sin debt to be paid, God would have to bring about a perfect human body for our Lord, which would be a fit subject for a perfect sacrifice (Heb. 10:5). God could accept no less than perfection. So, when Jesus died on the Cross, with His life's Blood being shed, it was from a perfect body that had never sinned, and neither had it known sickness or disease. He died that we might live.

The giving of this perfect body in sacrifice presented that which God, in His perfect Righteousness and Holiness, could accept, which He definitely did.

THE CROSS!

J. C. Ryle, who lived in the 1800s, made the following statements concerning the Cross. They are certainly worth repeating.

He said, *"There is no Doctrine in Christianity so important as the Doctrine of Christ Crucified. At the same time, there is none in which the devil tries so hard to destroy. There is none which is so needful for our own peace to understand. The death of Christ made a full, perfect, and complete satisfaction to God for the ungodly, and that through the merits of that death all who believe in Him are forgiven all their sins, however many and great, entirely and forever.*

"The Doctrine of Christ Crucified is the grand peculiarity of the Christian Faith. Religions have laws and moral precepts, forms and ceremonies, rewards and punishments; but religion cannot tell us of a dying Savior: They cannot show us the Cross. In fact, the Cross is the crown and glory of the Gospel; this is the special comfort which belongs to it alone. Miserable indeed is that religious teaching which calls itself Christian and yet contains nothing of the Cross. A man who teaches in this way might as well profess to explain the solar system, and yet tell his hearers nothing about the Sun.

"The Cross of Christ is the only lever which has ever turned the world upside down hitherto, and made men forsake their sins; and if this will not, nothing will."

(34) "AND AS CONCERNING THAT HE RAISED HIM UP FROM THE DEAD, NOW NO MORE TO RETURN TO CORRUPTION, HE SAID ON THIS WISE, I WILL GIVE YOU THE SURE MERCIES OF DAVID."

The diagram is:

1. A crucified Saviour will never lay upon me anything that is not good for me.
2. The Cross tells us that Jesus is a mighty, loving, and ready Saviour.

NO CORRUPTION

The phrase, *"And as concerning that He raised Him up from the dead, now no more to return to corruption,"* tells us several things:

- It proclaims the Resurrection of Jesus from the dead, but in greater form than when He went into that place. He died with a regular human body, although perfect, but was raised with a glorified body.
- Death was so totally and absolutely defeated by Jesus that this particular battle will never have to be fought again. He will *"no more have to return to the place of corruption, i.e., 'death.'"*

His Body was so pure and perfect, having never known sin, that, in fact, it could not die in the sense that we know and understand death. Consequently, Jesus said concerning His Life, *"No man takes it from Me, but I lay it down of Myself. I have power to lay it down, and I have power to take it again"* (Jn. 10:18).

So, when He died on Calvary, it was not from the torture or the wounds, but that He simply breathed out His Life; consequently, the approximate 100 pounds of spices applied to the Body of Jesus by Nicodemus was a wasted effort for two reasons (Jn. 19:39):

A WASTED EFFORT

1. Jesus was going to be resurrected.
2. His Body could not corrupt due to it being absolutely sinless and perfect.

Some may argue that He took our sins and, therefore, became polluted for our sakes, etc.

However, this is error because of an improper understanding of II Corinthians 5:21. The Scripture says, *"For He has made Him to be sin for us, Who knew no sin,"* but should have been translated, *"For He has made Him to be a sin-offering for us, Who knew no sin."*

He took the penalty for our sins but did not take our sins. Had He done so, His Body would not have been a proper sacrifice and could not have been acceptable to God.

Paul wrote plainly, *"Who knew no sin,"* and in that context, He was able to offer up Himself as a perfect sacrifice, acceptable unto God.

So, His perfect Body could not have corrupted in the grave.

NOTES

"He said on this wise, I will give you the sure mercies of David," actually refers to the Lord Jesus Christ, Who embodies all of these great *"mercies"* and refers to Isaiah 55:3.

Solomon also mentioned this when he dedicated the temple and said, *"O LORD God, turn not away the face of Your Anointed: remember the mercies of David Your Servant"* (II Chron. 6:42). *"Your Anointed"* refers to the Messiah.

THE SURE MERCIES OF DAVID

More perfectly, this speaks of God becoming Man, i.e., the Messiah, through the family of David, which was anchored in the Davidic Covenant. In that covenant the Lord said to David, *"But My Mercy shall not depart away from Him* (Jesus, as the Son of David), *as I took it from Saul, whom I put away before you.*

"And your house and thy kingdom shall be established for ever before you: your throne shall be established for ever" (II Sam. 7:15-16).

As Paul used this statement, he presented Jesus, the Son of David, as the fulfillment of that covenant, given to the entirety of the world, both Jew and Gentile, in which mercy will never cease. In other words, this great plan of salvation in Jesus was what God always promised and now is given and will never change, for He said, *"And I will stablish the throne of His Kingdom for ever"* (II Sam. 7:13).

These *"Mercies"* of Christ are *"sure,"* meaning they will never fail. On a sepulchral monument dated 1427 were the words, *"Beat at the door of God's Mercy."* I might quickly ask, *"Are there any of us who have not had to beat at that door again and again?"*

Jeremiah said, *"It is of the LORD's mercies that we are not consumed, because His compassions fail not.*

"They are new every morning: great is Thy faithfulness" (Lam. 3:22-23).

Even as I dictate these notes, I strongly sense the Presence of God! No wonder the Psalmist said, *"O give thanks unto the LORD; for He is good: for His Mercy endures forever"* (Ps. 136:1), and so he said in all 26 verses of this Psalm.

(35) "WHEREFORE HE SAID ALSO IN ANOTHER PSALM, YOU SHALL NOT SUFFER YOUR HOLY ONE TO SEE CORRUPTION."

NOTES

The composition is:

1. Error on outward points is only a skin-deep disease, so to speak. Error about the Cross is a disease of the heart.

2. Every believer should sincerely glory in the Cross of Christ (Gal. 6:14).

THE HOLY ONE

The phrase, *"You shall not suffer Your Holy One to see corruption,"* refers to the Man, Christ Jesus, as in the incarnation, but, as well, refers to Him as deity.

The One the Pharisees and religious leaders of Israel called an impostor and a blasphemer, God speaks of Him as the *"Holy One!"*

Even though Jesus bore the penalty of our sins by becoming a curse for us, and in the doing so, gave up His own Life, and even though He went into the grave with all its attendant horror, still, there was absolutely nothing of sin, death, or Satan that clung to Him.

Corruption in the Greek text is *"diaphthora"* and means *"to decay."* Consequently, this shoots down the *"Jesus died spiritually"* doctrine.

In brief, this doctrine teaches that Jesus became more than a *"sin-offering,"* but actually, on the Cross became a sinner Himself and, consequently, died lost and went to hell. It concludes this erroneous doctrine by saying that He was born again in hell, etc.

SIN OFFERING

There is not a shred of scriptural evidence to support such fallacy. Actually, such teaching is rank heresy, even bordering on blasphemy.

As we have stated, Jesus could not have been suitable as a *"sin-offering"* had He not been perfect. The very premise of such an offering demanded perfection on the part of the sacrifice. Hence, the lambs that were offered accordingly under the Law of Moses, which served as types of the coming *"Holy One,"* had to be inspected carefully that there be no blemish about them.

It is even said that once the little animal was killed with the skin removed from its body, the priest would lay open the flesh with a sharp knife and inspect it minutely for any type of discoloring or blemish. This was necessary for obvious reasons.

As well, the very product of sin is *"corruption,"* and in every capacity. Jesus did not see *"corruption"* because He contained no seedbed of corruption, which is sin.

So, the idea that He died lost as a sinner is rank heresy.

As well, the teaching that He went as a sinner down into the burning side of hell and was born again there is also fiction in totality.

In fact, Jesus did go down into paradise, which is actually a part of hell (Lk. 16:19-31; Eph. 4:8-9). The Scripture does say, *"For You will not leave My Soul in hell,"* referring to Jesus. However, as stated, this refers only to the paradise side and not the burning side of the pit (Ps. 16:10; Lk. 16:19-31).

(36) "FOR DAVID, AFTER HE HAD SERVED HIS OWN GENERATION BY THE WILL OF GOD, FELL ON SLEEP, AND WAS LAID UNTO HIS FATHERS, AND SAW CORRUPTION."

The pattern is:

1. The phrase, *"For David, after he had served his own generation by the Will of God, fell on sleep,"* simply refers to David's death.

2. The intimation is that David was the blessing to his own generation that God intended and carried out the *"Will of God"* for his own life and for Israel. Considering that this was said by the Holy Spirit, we know without question that it is correct.

3. The phrase, *"And was laid unto his fathers, and saw corruption,"* simply means that even though David was greatly and mightily used of God, still, the great Davidic Covenant pertained to the greater Son of David. David, as a mortal, died *"and saw corruption,"* proving that he was not the *"Holy One"* of Psalm 16:10.

(37) "BUT HE, WHOM GOD RAISED AGAIN, SAW NO CORRUPTION."

The way is:

1. This speaks of the greater Son of David, Who did fulfill the prophecies and was the *"Holy One,"* and as a result, was raised from the dead and, thereby, *"saw no corruption."* This is the Lord Jesus Christ.

2. If one studies Peter's message in Acts, Chapter 2, he will find it the same as preached by Paul.

3. Some in the recent past and, no doubt, down through the centuries, as well, have attempted to make a claim that Paul preached a different message than Peter, etc. Nothing could be further from the truth, at least as it refers to the subject at hand. As Peter, Paul was attempting to convince these Jews, as well as the Gentiles present, that Jesus Christ died on the Cross and was raised from the dead by the Power of God.

4. The Holy Spirit was the Author of both messages as preached by both Apostles. If one studies the content, it will become abundantly clear that there is no difference in the messages, as there could not be any difference in the messages.

5. When people attempt to pick and choose in the Bible, it shows they have a very improper understanding of the Word of God, actually, not even comprehending the basic fundamentals. The Holy Spirit is the Author of the entirety of the Word of God from Genesis through the Book of Revelation, and He does not contradict Himself.

(38) "BE IT KNOWN UNTO YOU THEREFORE, MEN AND BRETHREN, THAT THROUGH THIS MAN IS PREACHED UNTO YOU THE FORGIVENESS OF SINS."

The exegesis is:

1. The phrase, *"Be it known unto you therefore, men and brethren,"* proclaims Paul about to give an altar call, so to speak.

2. The phrase, *"That through this Man is preached unto you the forgiveness of sins,"* presents Jesus as having paid the price for man's redemption and through Him alone can be *"forgiveness of sins."*

3. If one is to notice, Paul completely ignored the sacrifices, Sabbath-keeping, and circumcision as playing any part at all in one's salvation.

4. It should be obvious that the people in this synagogue had never heard a message of this magnitude. Their history had been that of sacrifices and Law-keeping. So,

NOTES

NOTES

it should have been the greatest news they had ever heard, especially considering that Paul proclaimed this message and Jesus as the fulfillment of all the prophecies. Even on the surface, his simple statements concerning Jesus and the forgiveness of sins, etc., evoke a joy and gladness which Christ alone can afford. Paul made it clear that it is *"through Jesus alone"* that this great redemption and forgiveness can be carried out.

5. The word *"forgiveness"* in the Greek text is *"aphesis"* and means *"a dismissal, or release."* The Greek text further proclaims that it is more, much more, than merely *"forgetting or forgiving,"* but rather *"a suspension of the just penalty."* In other words, it did what the old Law could not do!

The next verse will explain it even further.

(39) "AND BY HIM ALL WHO BELIEVE ARE JUSTIFIED FROM ALL THINGS, FROM WHICH YOU COULD NOT BE JUSTIFIED BY THE LAW OF MOSES."

The way is:

1. The Doctrine of Christ Crucified is the grand center of union among true Christians.

2. Without Christ Crucified in her pulpits, a Church is little better than a dead carcass.

ALL WHO BELIEVE

The phrase, *"And by Him all who believe are justified from all things,"* proclaims so much with so few words.

First of all, the words *"by Him"* once again place Jesus and what He did as the source of all salvation.

As well, Paul gave us the requirement on the part of the sinner. He must *"believe!"* It is not all who are baptized and confirmed, who partake of the Mass, or live a life of carnal holiness, but it is all who simply repose in faith their sin stained souls upon an atoning and ascended Saviour.

The word *"justified"* means *"to be declared innocent."* That is even far greater, as would be obvious, than being declared *"not guilty!"*

The latter in no way declares the person innocent but simply that he could not be proven guilty. Being declared *"innocent"* not only means that one is not guilty but, in fact, that the crime or sin never was committed.

Here is the great problem of the Gospel message. How can a righteous God declare guilty men innocent? (Rom. 4:5). The Epistle to the Romans resolves that problem.

Let never so great a list of sins be presented to the believer as having been committed by him that he cannot, whilst sorrowfully confessing them and turning in shame from them, write the divine Words across them, *"Justified from all things,"* even as Paul here declared.

FAITH, NOT WORKS, THE MEANS OF JUSTIFICATION

The word *"believe,"* as used by Paul, gives us the means or condition of justification (Rom. 3:22, 25-28). *"Faith"* or *"believing"* rests upon the pure Grace of God and is itself, therefore, His Gift (Eph. 2:8). Making faith the only instrument of justification is not arbitrary, but being the receptive attitude of the soul, it is in the nature of the case the only avenue through which divine blessing can come.

The Gifts of God are not against or opposed to laws of the soul that God has made, but rather are in and through those laws. Faith is the hand outstretched to the Divine Giver, Who, though He sends rain without our consent, does not give salvation except through an appropriate spiritual response.

WHAT TYPE OF FAITH?

This faith is not simply belief in historical facts, though this is presupposed as to the atoning Death (Rom. 3:25) and the Resurrection of Jesus (Rom. 10:9), but is a real heart reception of the gift and is, therefore, able to bring peace in our relation to God (Rom. 5:1)

THE OBJECT OF THIS FAITH

The object of this faith must without fail be Jesus Christ and what He did for us at the Cross (Rom. 3:22). That's why Paul said, *"We preach Christ crucified"* (I Cor. 1:23). It is through Jesus that comes the gift of righteousness and the reigning in life (Rom. 5:17)—not Mary, not angels, not doctrine, and not the Church, but Jesus only.

This, to be sure, does not exclude God the Father as an object of faith, as the redeeming act of Christ is itself the Work of God (II Cor. 5:19), Whose Love expressed itself toward us in this way (Rom. 5:8).

Faith in the only one God is always presupposed (I Cor. 8:6), but it was the apostolic custom rather to refer repentance to God and faith to Christ (Acts 20:21), and for some obvious reasons.

However, the Oneness of God the Father and Christ the Son in a work of salvation is the best guarantee of the Divinity of the latter, both as an objective fact and as an inner experience of the Christian, all done by the Holy Spirit, thereby, engaging the entirety of the Trinity.

JUSTIFICATION BY FAITH

Justification being by faith is not by works or even by love, or by both in one. It cannot be by the former because they are lacking either in time, amount, or quality, nor can they be accepted in any case until they spring from a heart renewed, for which faith is the necessary presupposition.

It cannot be by the latter (love), for it exists only where the Spirit has shed it abroad in the heart (Rom. 5:5). So, *"works"* or *"love"* cannot come about until faith has first been exhibited.

This does not mean that the crown of Christianity is not love, for it is (I Cor. 13:13); it means only that the root upon which love is built is faith.

As well, love cannot be foisted in as a partial condition of justification on the strength of the word often quoted for that purpose, *"Faith working through love"* (Gal. 5:6). The Apostle was speaking here only of those who were already *"In Christ,"* and he said that over against the Galatian believers bringing in a lot of legal observances. The only availing thing was not circumcision or its lack, but faith energizing through love.

Martin Luther said, *"Faith is a Divine Work within us which changes and renews us in God according to John 1:13, 'Who were born not of blood, nor of the will of the flesh, nor of the will of man, but of God.'*

"This destroys the old Adam and makes new creatures of us in heart, will, disposition, and all our powers. Oh, Faith is a living, active, jealous, mighty thing, inasmuch as it cannot possibly remain unproductive of good works."

NOTES

THE LAW OF MOSES

The phrase, *"From which you could not be justified by the Law of Moses,"* dogmatically and without apology sets aside the Law of Moses as being empty of any ability to justify one with God. This is where the rubber meets the road.

The great truth of *"justification by faith,"* and faith alone, was given to Paul while in Arabia, which occurred very shortly after his conversion (Gal. 1:17). How long he remained there is not known!

This statement as given by Paul in Verse 39 is so simple, but yet, that which the early Church did not approach with confidence. Many desired to attach the works of the *"Law of Moses"* to *"faith,"* which Paul staunchly rejected. To be sure, and sadly so, the battle waxed hot! Men, even believing men, do not give up their own works easily, nor do they admit quickly their spiritual bankruptcy. I am afraid the problem continues to exist, and in a much more pronounced way than most would dare to believe.

PETER AND PAUL

A comparison of Peter's first sermon with Paul's first sermon, to which we have already alluded, shows that the one object of both was the Lord Jesus; the one subject, the forgiveness of sins; the one authority, the Bible; and the one warning, the wrath of God—and a personal testimony was added.

If those who claim to be their successors, whether of the Roman Church or those who claim to be God-called, would preach the same doctrine, direct men's attention to the one Saviour, and add a personal testimony of His saving Power, the moral Kingdom of God would be a present-day reality to a far greater extent than at the present!

(40) "BEWARE THEREFORE, LEST THAT COME UPON YOU, WHICH IS SPOKEN OF IN THE PROPHETS."

The overview is:

1. The phrase, *"Beware therefore, lest*

NOTES

that come upon you," speaks of the judgment of God and plainly says that it will come upon rejecters of truth.

2. *"Which is spoken of in the Prophets,"* refers back to the Word of God, in this instance, the Old Testament.

3. So, the idea of judgment, as proclaimed by the Prophets in the Old Testament, has not been declared null and void because of the entrance of the New Covenant, as many people believe! Paul plainly tells us here that every threat of judgment against sin and Christ-rejecters is as apropos now as it was the day it was given.

4. To be frank, and to which we will address ourselves more freely further on in this volume, the judgment of God is far more pronounced presently under the Covenant of Grace than it ever was during the Old Covenant. In other words, it is the very opposite of what most people think.

(41) "BEHOLD, YOU DESPISERS, AND WONDER, AND PERISH: FOR I WORK A WORK IN YOUR DAYS, A WORK WHICH YOU SHALL IN NO WISE BELIEVE, THOUGH A MAN DECLARE IT UNTO YOU."

The diagram is:

1. All the intellectual sermons in the world will never make up for the absence of sermons about the Cross of Christ.

2. Such sermons may amuse some, but they will feed none.

DESPISERS

The phrase, *"Behold, you despisers, and wonder, and perish,"* plus the remainder of this verse, is taken from Habakkuk 1:5.

Habakkuk's prophecy was directed against the Jews who did not believe that judgment was going to come upon them through the Babylonians, who would destroy Jerusalem and Solomon's Temple. Inasmuch as they were God's chosen People, they simply did not believe, despite what the prophecies said, that God would allow such a thing to happen to them, no matter how sinful they became.

Even though the prophecy was directed against Israel, probably during the time of Jeremiah, still, Paul broadened it to include all of humanity and for all time.

The *"despisers"* pertains to anyone who ignores the Word of God for any purpose or reason. To disbelieve, set at nought, deny, or ignore the Word of God is the stupidest thing that any individual could ever do. God says what He means and means what He says!

At this present time (as this volume is being written), the Lord is helping us to touch a good part of the world with *"The Message of the Cross."* There is an *"offense to the Cross,"* and that offense comes mostly from the Church. This means that people reject it, and one might quickly ask, *"How could anyone reject the Cross of Christ?"*

Let me say that the Cross of Christ is the means and the only means by which we are given anything and everything from God. In other words, without the Cross, there is no salvation, no baptism with the Holy Spirit, no divine healing, no blessings from the Lord, no communion with God, no answers to prayer, etc. Everything, and I mean everything, comes through the Cross of Christ. So, if the Cross is denied, this shuts off the individual from God, for the only place that God can meet with sinful man is the Cross, and the only place that sinful man can meet with God is the Cross. And yet, the modern Church little preaches the Cross, despite the fact that *"Jesus Christ and Him Crucified"* is actually the story of the entirety of the Bible.

HOW IS THE CROSS OF CHRIST AN OFFENSE?

It is an offense because it lays waste all of man's efforts, exposing such for what it really is, *"a waste."* Religious man does not enjoy being told that what he's doing is not going to bring about any righteousness and will bring about nothing from God. He bridles at such a statement because it lays waste all of his works and efforts. We might quickly add that every direction, other than the Cross of Christ, always and without fail leads to self-righteousness. We must remember, it was self-righteousness that nailed Jesus Christ to the Cross.

We must also remember that works and legalism are very dear to the heart of religious man. As an example, Ishmael was a work of the flesh, the product of the scheming of Abraham and Sarah. There came a

NOTES

day after Isaac was born that the Lord spoke to Sarah and said, *"The bondwoman and her son have to go."* Abraham loved Ishmael because he was the product of their labor and their work, but God said he had to go. Abraham obeyed the Lord, but it didn't come easily, as it never comes easily.

WONDER AND PERISH

About 600 years before Christ, the people of Jerusalem ignored the prophecies of Jeremiah and Habakkuk; therefore, that which God said through the Prophets would happen came to pass exactly as stated. Jerusalem was destroyed and the temple razed to the ground. Untold thousands died simply because they would not believe the Word of God.

To be sure, it is the same presently. Most of the world ignores God's Word, and most of the world *"perishes."*

The word *"wonder"* in the Greek text is *"thaumazo"* and means *"to marvel."* The idea is this:

The *"despisers"* of the Word of God will one day marvel, whether now or at the Great White Throne Judgment, at the exactness of the Word of God being carried out and fulfilled in totality. However, that *"wonder"* will not save them, for they will *"perish,"* i.e., be eternally lost!

These words as proclaimed by Paul are fearful indeed! It says that all who despise God's great Plan of Salvation through Jesus Christ and what He did for us at the Cross will perish. Jesus Christ and the Cross is the focal point, is the Door, is the Way, is the Truth, and is the Life. There is no salvation other than through Jesus. Jesus is Salvation!

I WORK A WORK

The phrase, *"For I work a work in your days,"* speaks, as stated, of the work of judgment directed against Israel because of her departure from God.

However, the Holy Spirit broadened the content from Israel only to the whole of humanity who rejects Jesus Christ. This work of judgment is pronounced and is as certain as God Himself!

The phrase, *"A work which you shall in no wise believe, though a man declare it unto you,"* predicts the unbelief of mankind respecting Jesus Christ as the Source of all salvation. While some few do believe, that number in comparison to the whole is minuscule.

It is, no doubt, correct that Luke only gave a compendium of Paul's message. However, he gave that which the Holy Spirit desired, which, no doubt, formed the foundation of all that was said.

It is interesting to note that Paul, as he was led by the Holy Spirit, closed his message with words of awful warning. Immediately, that throws out most preaching that specializes only in a positive note. We should take our lesson from the Bible.

It is the business of the preacher of the Gospel to lift up Jesus Christ as the only answer for man's dilemma and, as well, to warn man that if Christ is rejected, there remains only an awful doom!

However, as then, such a message makes men angry. The trouble is, most modern preaching makes no one angry, but neither does it save souls or change lives!

(42) "AND WHEN THE JEWS WERE GONE OUT OF THE SYNAGOGUE, THE GENTILES BESOUGHT THAT THESE WORDS MIGHT BE PREACHED TO THEM THE NEXT SABBATH."

The overview is:

1. The phrase, *"And when the Jews were gone out of the synagogue,"* by association with the following text, seems to say that unbelieving Jews grew angry at Paul's statements and left en masse immediately after Paul had finished. They were angry! However, we shall see that some Jews believed what Paul said and remained in the synagogue.

2. The phrase, *"The Gentiles besought that these words might be preached to them the next Sabbath,"* speaks of the God-fearers, which were prevalent in most synagogues.

3. For the first time, these Gentiles heard a beautifully simple message, properly outlining Jesus Christ as the Way of salvation. To receive this, they did not have to become a proselyte Jew or try to keep the Law of Moses, but simply *"believe"* what Paul said about Christ. Their hungry hearts wanted

NOTES

to hear more; therefore, they would importune Paul and Barnabas to remain among them and to speak again on the following Sabbath.

4. As we shall see in the next verse, every evidence is that Paul gave an invitation for both Jews and Gentiles to accept Christ as their Saviour, which it seems that some, if not many, did.

(43) "NOW WHEN THE CONGREGATION WAS BROKEN UP, MANY OF THE JEWS AND RELIGIOUS PROSELYTES FOLLOWED PAUL AND BARNABAS: WHO, SPEAKING TO THEM, PERSUADED THEM TO CONTINUE IN THE GRACE OF GOD."

The composition is:

1. The phrase, *"Now when the congregation was broken up, many of the Jews and religious proselytes followed Paul and Barnabas,"* seems to speak of Gentiles who had converted to Judaism, i.e., *"proselytes."*

2. So, if that is the case, it seems there were three types of people in the synagogue that day—Jews, Gentile proselytes, and Gentiles who were not converts to Judaism but did revere the God of Abraham, Isaac, and Jacob.

3. These people, ever how many there were, followed Paul and Barnabas outside of the synagogue, desiring to hear more. They were hungry for God!

4. *"Who, speaking to them, persuaded them to continue in the Grace of God,"* tells us several things:

a. As stated, it seems as if Paul had given an altar call, with some responding and accepting Christ.

b. They were told by Paul and Barnabas that not only must they accept Christ, which they had done, but, as well, must continue in Christ. The idea is that if they attempted to attach the Law of Moses (works) to the Grace of God, they would lose that which they had just received.

Consequently, this shoots to pieces the unscriptural doctrine of unconditional eternal security. This statement by Paul and Barnabas is foolish if there is no possibility of failure in the Grace of God (Gal. 1:6; 5:4; Heb. 12:15).

5. The word *"persuaded"* in the Greek text is *"peitho"* and means *"to convince by argument"* or *"to assent to evidence or authority,"* in this case, the Scriptures.

6. These simple statements tell us that it is possible to be converted—born-again—and yet, depart from the Grace of the Lord. It is possible to be a part of the Church, the Body of Christ, and yet, cease to believe in Jesus and what He did for us at the Cross. If this were not so, as we have stated, there would be no point to these warnings. Hebrews 2:3 was speaking to Christians when it said, *"How shall we escape, if we neglect so great salvation."*

(44) "AND THE NEXT SABBATH DAY CAME ALMOST THE WHOLE CITY TOGETHER TO HEAR THE WORD OF GOD."

The exegesis is:

1. The phrase, *"And the next Sabbath day,"* represents an entire week, during which time, it seems, the new converts quickly spread the message of the Gospel of grace through Jesus Christ. As well, Paul and Barnabas, no doubt, spent the entirety of the week explaining the Gospel to all who desired to hear.

2. Pisidian Antioch was a center of Greek culture and a prosperous commercial center. It was also the center for Roman civil and military administration for the southern part of the province of Galatia.

3. It had a large number of Roman colonists among its chief citizens. Jewish colonists had also settled there for over 200 years, primarily for business and commercial reasons. So, the synagogue was, no doubt, well known to most all in the city.

4. The phrase, *"Came almost the whole city together to hear the Word of God,"* presented a crowd many times larger than the small synagogue could contain. This portrays the hunger of the people for the Word of God, both Jews and Gentiles.

5. As we shall see, when the *"Word of God"* is faithfully proclaimed, it will always bring beautiful, wonderful, and miraculous results. However, it will also arouse the devil as nothing else, causing great disturbance and even persecution. If Satan hates anything, he hates the Word of God.

(45) "BUT WHEN THE JEWS SAW

THE MULTITUDES, THEY WERE FILLED WITH ENVY, AND SPOKE AGAINST THOSE THINGS WHICH WERE SPOKEN BY PAUL, CONTRADICTING AND BLASPHEMING."

The synopsis is:

1. The phrase, *"But when the Jews saw the multitudes, they were filled with envy,"* tells us that the Jews did not expect this size crowd.

2. The word *"envy"* in the Greek text is *"zelos"* and actually means *"jealousy."* The distinction lies in this: envy desires to deprive another of what he has, while jealousy desires to have the same or the same sort of thing for itself.

3. The unbelieving Jews were opposed to Paul, Barnabas, and the Christ they preached. As well, they were jealous of the influence these two men had, which seems to have touched the entire city, far outpacing the activity of the synagogue. So, they saw in this a double-barreled threat.

4. Also, they had no love at all for all of these Gentiles, which probably made up the greater number of the multitude, who they considered to be nothing relative to the religion of Judaism. In other words, they called them *"Gentile dogs!"*

5. *"And spoke against those things which were spoken by Paul, contradicting and blaspheming,"* seems to indicate that Paul and Barnabas were outside of the synagogue with the multitude, addressing them concerning the Grace of God. The unbelieving Jews then attempted to contradict what they were saying and even resorted to blaspheming both Paul and Christ.

6. As here, the greatest hindrance to the *"Word of God"* has always been that which labels itself as *"Church," "religious leaders,"* etc. It was the problem then, and it is the problem now!

(46) "THEN PAUL AND BARNABAS WAXED BOLD, AND SAID, IT WAS NECESSARY THAT THE WORD OF GOD SHOULD FIRST HAVE BEEN SPOKEN TO YOU: BUT SEEING YOU PUT IT FROM YOU, AND JUDGE YOURSELVES UNWORTHY OF EVERLASTING LIFE, LO, WE TURN TO THE GENTILES."

The pattern is:

NOTES

1. The Doctrine of Christ Crucified is the foundation of the prosperity of the Church.

2. Without the Cross of Christ, no good will ever be done.

BOLDNESS

The phrase, *"Then Paul and Barnabas waxed bold,"* tells us:

- There was no fear of the Jews in their hearts.
- They were given great boldness by the Holy Spirit to say what He desired to be said.

Actually, the Greek word for *"bold"* is *"parrhesiazomai"* and means *"to speak boldly, or freely."*

The manner in which it is said here concerns the freedom of speech they had and means that the Holy Spirit anointed them mightily at this time. In the first place, truth carries with it its own power. As well, when preachers are totally consecrated to the Will and Word of God, this makes for fertile ground for the Holy Spirit to work.

As Verse 48 proclaims, the multitude of Gentiles made up much of the audience and was witness to the exchange, of which Paul and Barnabas came out on top, and greatly so!

THE WORD OF GOD

The phrase, *"And said, It was necessary that the Word of God should first have been spoken to you,"* proclaims that which God ordained, and for purpose and reason.

As I have said many times in these volumes, the Lord raised up Israel from the loins of Abraham for a specific purpose:

- They were to give the world the Word of God, which they did.
- They were to serve as the womb of the Messiah, which they did as well!
- They were to evangelize the world.

Actually, the very first promise given to Abraham by the Lord contained all three provisions.

He said, *"And in you shall all families of the Earth be blessed"* (Gen. 12:3).

In the purpose of world evangelism and under the ministry of Paul, who, of course, was Jewish, along with the other Apostles, they did evangelize the world of that day and made it possible for the Gospel to ultimately spread to the entirety of the world.

The phrase, *"But seeing you put it from you,"* means that these Jews in Pisidia, Antioch, would not accept the Gospel, i.e, the Lord Jesus Christ.

Israel was the only nation in the world that was monotheistic. In other words, they worshiped one God, which was correct and right, for there is only one God. The other nations of the world worshiped many gods, but gods of their own making, which were, in reality, no gods at all! Inasmuch as the Word of God was given to Israel and Israel alone, it placed them to a far greater advantage over other nations; however, there were conditions attached to this.

CONDITIONS

They must obey the Word that was given. Tragically, this they did not do, despite repeated warnings.

They not only would not obey the Word, but they greatly added to it, so that by the time of Christ, over 600 laws had been added by the religious leadership of Israel to the original Law of Moses. Of course, these 600 laws were man-devised, which meant they were unacceptable to God. Jesus completely ignored that part of the Jewish law, which incensed the religious leadership of Israel. Jesus said of them and to them, *"You have made the Word of God of none effect through your tradition"* (Mk. 7:13).

The phrase, *"And judge yourselves unworthy of everlasting life,"* proclaims them serving as their own judge.

At the trial of Christ, Pilate said, *"I am innocent of the Blood of this Just Person: see you to it.*

"Then answered all the people, and said, His Blood be on us, and on our children" (Mat. 27:24-25), thereby, serving as their own judge and passing sentence upon themselves.

Despite overwhelming, abundant proof of the innocence of Christ, they *"cried out, Away with Him, away with Him, crucify Him. Pilate saith unto them, Shall I crucify your King? The chief priests answered, We have no king but Caesar"* (Jn. 19:15).

Once again, they served as their own judge and passed sentence upon themselves.

NOTES

So, they only had themselves to blame!

WE TURN TO THE GENTILES

The phrase, *"Lo, we turn to the Gentiles,"* proclaims a statement of such far-reaching magnitude that it literally defies description:

- Due to the spiritual blindness of these unbelieving Jews, they had absolutely no conception of the Gospel being taken to Gentiles. In fact, at worst, they hated Gentiles, and at best, they tolerated them. That God had always intended for the Gospel to go to the entirety of the world, even as the Lord had said to Abraham in the very beginning (Gen. 12:3), had long since been lost in their self-righteousness.
- That Gentiles, or Jews for that matter, could be saved simply by believing Christ was beyond their thinking. Salvation had become a very cumbersome process with the Jews at this time. They were wrapped up in the Law of Moses, but more particularly, in their own glosses on the Law. So, simple faith in Christ, which completely gutted their entire system, was not only beyond their thinking but incurred their total wrath.
- Even though Paul would continue to try to reach Jews wherever he went, still, the far greater thrust was now toward the Gentiles, which he had known it would be from the beginning (Acts 9:15).

(47) "FOR SO HAS THE LORD COMMANDED US, SAYING, I HAVE SET YOU TO BE A LIGHT OF THE GENTILES, THAT YOU SHOULD BE FOR SALVATION UNTO THE ENDS OF THE EARTH."

The pattern is:

1. The phrase, *"For so has the Lord commanded us,"* speaks not only of his personal call but, as well, of the prophecy given by Isaiah.

If one is to notice, the words *"commanded us"* are used concerning the Gospel being given to Gentiles, which means it is not a suggestion.

The word in the Greek text is *"entellomai"* and means *"to give a charge,"* which is actually a military term and is meant to be obeyed in its exactness.

2. The phrase, *"Saying, I have set you to be a Light of the Gentiles,"* is taken from

Isaiah 49:6 and refers to the Messiah, the Lord Jesus Christ, and clearly means that He was not to be the Jewish Messiah only but, as well, the world's Saviour. Furthermore, Jehovah said, *"I have set You,"* speaking of Christ, meaning this is God's Plan, and to oppose that Plan is to oppose God.

SALVATION

3. The phrase, *"That you should be for salvation unto the ends of the Earth,"* presents that which is unmistakable in its meaning. The salvation afforded by Christ is intended for the entirety of the world. Consequently, the Jews could not deny their own Prophet, so they stood condemned.

4. To buttress this, when Jesus was brought to the temple as a Baby, the godly Spirit-led Simeon also recognized Him as *"a Light to lighten the Gentiles, and the Glory of Your people Israel"* (Lk. 2:32) (Horton).

5. From this prophecy given by Isaiah and here quoted by Paul, we know that priority with God is the taking of the Gospel message to the entirety of the Earth. Of all the other things in which the Church is engaged, everything else pales by comparison to this great and overwhelming task.

6. That is what God has called THE SONLIFE BROADCASTING NETWORK to do. Twenty-four hours a day, seven days a week, we are to take the Gospel to the world, which we are doing. It is the business of every single believer to have a part in this undertaking. For every person in the world who doesn't know Jesus Christ or even about Jesus Christ, as far as that person is concerned, Jesus died in vain. The Holy Spirit is insistent that every person have the opportunity to hear, whether they accept Christ or not. To be sure, every last believer is going to answer to God at the JUDGMENT SEAT OF CHRIST concerning this very thing. As Paul said, *"I am debtor"* (Rom. 1:14).

7. I personally believe that when we stand before God, every believer is going to be judged primarily regarding his faithfulness or the lack thereof concerning this all-important task. To be frank, many things that we look at now as very important will be given there no shift at all.

8. The only question that will be important to the believer, and the only thing that will really matter, is our role (if any) in taking the Gospel *"unto the ends of the Earth."*

NOTES

(48) "AND WHEN THE GENTILES HEARD THIS, THEY WERE GLAD, AND GLORIFIED THE WORD OF THE LORD: AND AS MANY AS WERE ORDAINED TO ETERNAL LIFE BELIEVED."

The account is:

1. The phrase, *"And when the Gentiles heard this, they were glad,"* presents such for all the obvious reasons.

2. In the hearts of many Gentiles of that day, there was a hunger for reality. The vapid, senseless religions of paganism satisfied not at all the hunger and thirst of the soul. Consequently, quite a number of Gentiles of that time frequented Jewish synagogues, sensing that what the Jews taught about God was right. But yet, all the ceremonial obligations, and especially that added by the Jews to the original Law of Moses, made things very difficult. So, when they now heard Paul and Barnabas proclaim salvation by simple trust in Christ, it gladdened their hearts, even as it should have!

3. *"And glorified the Word of the Lord,"* means that they accepted this that was said by Paul and Barnabas as *"the Word of the Lord,"* thereby, ensuring themselves of salvation.

4. *"And as many as were ordained to Eternal Life believed,"* simply means that God has appointed and provided Eternal Life for all who will believe (Jn. 3:15-20; Rom. 1:16; 10:9-10; I Tim. 2:4; II Pet. 3:9; Rev. 22:17).

5. Despite the claims of some, it does not mean that by God's predetermined decree certain ones are to be saved, and certain others are to be lost simply upon the basis of God's choice alone.

6. Man's choice is always involved in the salvation process (Rev. 22:17). This means that predestination always refers to the plan and never to the individual who will conform or not conform to that plan. All who conform to the Plan of God, which is Jesus Christ and Him Crucified, are predestined to be saved (Jn. 3:16). If the Plan of God is rejected, the person will be

lost, no matter how religious he might be. It's just that simple!

7. If it is to be noticed, it did not say that God *"ordained them,"* but that *"He ordained,"* which means that He has *"ordained"* or *"predestined"* His Plan, which says, *"And whosoever will, let him take the water of life freely"* (Rev. 22:17).

8. In truth, *"whosoever will"* is the standing invitation for all! It is not merely *"whosoever God wills,"* for He *"wills that all should come unto repentance"* (II Pet. 3:9). So, in reality, it's up to the individual whether that person will be saved or not. It is *"whosoever will!"*

(49) "AND THE WORD OF THE LORD WAS PUBLISHED THROUGHOUT ALL THE REGION."

The way is:

1. Considering the great number of Gentiles, and even some Jews, who had given their hearts to Christ, the news quickly began to spread far and wide.

2. *"And the Word of the Lord was published,"* means it spread quickly by word of mouth. They normally were not allowed to have Church buildings in those days, as we think of such, but that proved to be of little hindrance.

3. The early Church met in people's homes, caves, or wherever it was convenient.

4. So, I think it is obvious that Paul and Barnabas, at least for a period of time, were kept very busy.

5. The phrase, *"Throughout all the region,"* speaks of South Galatia, of which *"Pisidian Antioch"* had become the new Gospel center.

6. This means that Churches were springing up in towns and villages *"throughout all the region."*

(50) "BUT THE JEWS STIRRED UP THE DEVOUT AND HONOURABLE WOMEN, AND THE CHIEF MEN OF THE CITY, AND RAISED PERSECUTION AGAINST PAUL AND BARNABAS, AND EXPELLED THEM OUT OF THEIR COASTS."

The form is:

1. The Doctrine of Christ Crucified is the secret of all missionary success.

2. The Cross of Christ is the weapon that has won victories over hearts of every kind and in every quarter of the globe.

NOTES

GREAT OPPOSITION

The phrase, *"But the Jews stirred up the devout and honorable women, and the chief men of the city,"* seems to indicate female Gentile proselytes.

It seems these women were very prominent and, consequently, held some sway over the civil rulers of Antioch. Evidently, though *"devout and honorable,"* they had not accepted Christ but had remained on the side of the unbelieving Jews.

So, we are faced here with the fact that proper devotion and honor, although very commendable, does not save anyone. Neither will it keep one from false doctrine.

For all their devotion and honor, these women went down in history as those who attempted to hinder the Move of God in their city and region.

Evidently, they believed the lies told them by the unbelieving Jews of the synagogue. This is one of Satan's greatest weapons.

If he can get so-called good people, even good Church people, to oppose that which is truly of God, he has greatly strengthened his hand. Sadly, he is very successful in this effort.

At this present time, it could probably be said, and without fear of contradiction, that most of the *"good and honorable people"* in most Churches are opposed to that which is truly of God. They work hard at their devotion and honor, but, in reality, it is not of faith but of works, hence, these women opposing Paul and Barnabas, even as many, if not millions, do the same presently.

PERSECUTION

The phrase, *"And raised persecution against Paul and Barnabas,"* means, as stated, that they believed the lies told them about these two.

The word *"persecution"* in the Greek text is *"diogmos"* and comes from the root *"dioko"* and means *"to press forward."* In other words, the persecution was intended to drive them out of the area.

I suspect that these *"devout and honorable women"* felt they were truly doing God a service by ridding their area of these undesirables. Deception is a terrible thing. It blinds the individual so severely that up is down and down is up; good is evil and evil is good.

Satan's object was that if these *"devout and honorable women"* were opposed to Paul and Barnabas, even to the extent of working diligently to expel them from the area, then there must be something badly wrong with these men, which is what he wanted the people to believe.

The phrase, *"And expelled them out of their coasts,"* presents a strong term.

The word *"expelled"* in the Greek is *"ekballo"* and means *"to eject or put forth."* In other words, they were not merely requested to leave but forcibly ejected. There is no evidence of physical violence but definite evidence that physical violence was threatened.

How so awful to go down in history, and by the Holy Spirit at that, attempting to stop the Work of God, while at the same time attempting to be *"devout and honorable."*

How so easily deceived is man!

(51) "BUT THEY SHOOK OFF THE DUST OF THEIR FEET AGAINST THEM, AND CAME UNTO ICONIUM."

The construction is:

1. The phrase, *"But they shook off the dust of their feet against them,"* presents that which Jesus commanded His Disciples to do under these circumstances (Mat. 10:14; Mk. 6:11; Lk. 9:5; 10:11). The force of the gesture as presented by Christ is powerful.

By rejecting Paul and Barnabas, or any true Servant of the Lord, at the same time is rejecting Christ.

2. The shaking of the dust off their feet spoke of the deadly effects of their rebellion and sin, and meant that these people had broken every bond with God and His true People.

3. However, there is every evidence that faithful believers would carry on the Work of the Lord. Actually, this opposition against Paul was liable to happen at any time and in any place. Consequently, one can be sure that Paul, even with the short time allotted him in some cases, would seek greatly to ground new converts properly in the faith in order that they might carry on without him.

NOTES

The Holy Spirit, no doubt, greatly helped him and the people in this.

4. One must understand that in those days, Churches were planted in the midst of raw heathenism. As a result, there were no preachers, other than those the Lord raised up immediately after conversion, but remarkably, the evidence is abundant that the Lord preserved His People and His Church.

5. One must ever understand that it is a very holy thing for God to appoint someone such as Paul and Barnabas to take the Gospel to a particular area. The acceptance or rejection of God's Messengers either spells blessing or a curse, depending on the response. Consequently, believers should be very careful what they reject or accept!

6. *"And came unto Iconium,"* presents a Phrygian city in the southern part of the Roman province of Galatia. It was about 60 miles east and a little south of Pisidia Antioch. It was a key city on the border between Phrygia near Lycaonia. It was also a center from which five Roman roads radiated (Horton).

(52) "AND THE DISCIPLES WERE FILLED WITH JOY, AND WITH THE HOLY SPIRIT."

The direction is:

1. This passage tells us that the Holy Spirit was directing the Apostles, and that it was His Will that Iconium be their next stop.

2. As well, the phrase, *"And the disciples were filled with joy,"* tells us that the Holy Spirit informed them that the problem in Antioch was not their fault.

3. Whenever something of this nature happens, one has a tendency to second guess everything that has happened, ascertaining if there has been a lack of wisdom, etc. The Holy Spirit grandly informed the Apostles that all they had done had been exactly according to the Spirit, which now brought them great joy.

4. The phrase, *"And with the Holy Spirit,"* means that the Spirit of God was the Author of this *"joy."*

Horton said, *"One should notice how being filled with Joy and being filled with the Spirit go together in the Scriptures."*

As well, one should note that this *"joy"* and refilling *"with the Holy Spirit"* took place in the midst of persecution (Acts 5:41; Heb. 10:34; James 1:2).

"To him that overcomes the foe,
"White raiment shall be given;
"Before the angels he shall know,
"His name confessed in heaven.
"Then onward from the hills of light,
"Our hearts with love aflame,
"We'll vanquish all the hosts of night,
"In Jesus' conquering Name."

CHAPTER 14

(1) "AND IT CAME TO PASS IN ICONIUM, THAT THEY WENT BOTH TOGETHER INTO THE SYNAGOGUE OF THE JEWS, AND SO SPOKE, THAT A GREAT MULTITUDE BOTH OF THE JEWS AND ALSO OF THE GREEKS BELIEVED."

The order is:

1. The phrase, *"And it came to pass in Iconium, that they went both together into the synagogue of the Jews,"* presents them continuing with their custom of going to the Jews first.
2. Despite the Jew's rebellion, this portrays to us that God in His Mercy, Grace, and Love was still continuing to attempt to reach these who were His Chosen. As usual, some few of the Jews seemingly would believe, thereby, accepting Christ.
3. As well, using the Jewish synagogue in each place, at least as long as possible (which was not very long in most cases), served as a springboard for reaching the entire city.
4. *"And so spoke,"* infers that Paul basically preached the same message that he had in Antioch of Pisidia. Paul preached essentially the same message everywhere concerning Christ and the forgiveness of sins, which did not require works of the Law, etc.
5. *"That a great multitude both of the Jews and also of the Greeks believed,"* once again portrays to us that this synagogue, as usual, had a number of Gentiles attending.
6. The word *"believed"* strongly implies and actually guarantees that they believed in Christ.
7. The *"great multitude"* who came to the Lord speaks of a period of time of several months, or even longer.

NOTES

(2) "BUT THE UNBELIEVING JEWS STIRRED UP THE GENTILES, AND MADE THEIR MINDS EVIL AFFECTED AGAINST THE BRETHREN."

The diagram is:

1. There is no doctrine in Christianity so important as the Doctrine of Christ Crucified.
2. As well, there is none that the devil tries so hard to destroy.

UNBELIEVING JEWS

The phrase, *"But the unbelieving Jews stirred up the Gentiles,"* tells us that some Jews did accept Christ. However, the unbelieving group resorted to their usual tactics of trying to turn the Gentiles of the city against Paul and Barnabas.

The word *"unbelieving,"* as used here, speaks of an obstinate rebellion, in other words, a settled fact.

These particular Jews heard Paul's message concerning Christ and were, no doubt, heavily convicted by the mighty anointing of the Holy Spirit. During this time, some accepted Christ as the Holy Spirit was moving upon all. However, those who refused to believe not only repudiated the message and the messengers but, as well, set about to stop Paul and Barnabas, using any tactic at their disposal.

As we have already stated, Satan hates the Gospel. To be sure, he has no problem whatsoever with that which is brought forth by most preachers, actually being the author of much of what they say. However, he hates with a passion the Gospel that truly liberates men and sets captives free, and will do anything within his power to bring it to a halt. As well, almost always, as here, he uses professed followers of the Lord to carry forth his bidding.

MINDS EVIL AFFECTED

The Jews whom God had raised up from the loins of Abraham for the very purpose of shedding the Gospel light abroad, here, as in most all places, do everything they can to oppose that *"light."* Many modern religious denominations, although beginning in the fire of the Holy Spirit, sadly and regrettably, follow suit. As those Jews, their major effort now is to stop the Gospel, to which they devote all of their energy.

The Gentiles here who were stirred up evidently were not of the ruling class of the city as it had been in Antioch of Pisidia; therefore, it seems they were not successful in immediately expelling the Apostles from the city.

"And made their minds evil affected against the brethren," included all the Believers, as well as Paul and Barnabas. In other words, war of sorts was declared, as is usually the case!

To *"evil affect the minds"* of the Gentiles, they used any tactic at their disposal, in other words, any lie they could tell. However, none of this affected the moving and operation of the Holy Spirit in this place, actually, as it never affects such.

(3) "LONG TIME THEREFORE ABODE THEY SPEAKING BOLDLY IN THE LORD, WHICH GAVE TESTIMONY UNTO THE WORD OF HIS GRACE, AND GRANTED SIGNS AND WONDERS TO BE DONE BY THEIR HANDS."

The diagram is:

1. There is no doctrine so needful as the Cross of Christ as it regards our own peace and understanding.
2. By *"Christ Crucified,"* I mean the doctrine that Christ suffered death on the Cross to make atonement for our sins.

SPEAKING BOLDLY IN THE LORD

The phrase, *"Long time therefore abode they speaking boldly in the Lord,"* tells us several things:

- They could have stayed there for several months or even as much as a year or more.
- The Greek word for *"boldly"* is *"parrhesiazomai"* and means *"to be frank in utterance and confident in spirit and demeanor."*

However, that which gave them this frankness and confidence was the Holy Spirit Who anointed them to preach the Gospel, and to do so powerfully. One could probably say without any fear of exaggeration that there is no persuasive power like that which is generated by the Holy Spirit in anointing a man or woman to preach the Gospel of Jesus Christ. It carries with it a force that is absolutely unmistakable, which is totally of another world.

- This anointing of the Holy Spirit was so powerful because they were constantly lifting up Jesus. He was their message, strength, power, and cause for all good things.

Unmistakably, they preached salvation by the blood of Jesus and Faith in that Name, healing by His mighty Power, the baptism with the Holy Spirit with the evidence of speaking with other tongues, the Gifts of the Spirit, and the overcoming, victorious Christian life in Christ. They also preached the Rapture, which is the Resurrection, and the Second Coming of the Lord.

How do we come to this conclusion when all of these things mentioned are not related at this time?

THE WORD OF HIS GRACE

As an example, I am positive that Paul preached strongly the mighty baptism with the Holy Spirit with the evidence of speaking with other tongues, even though it is not mentioned in the Text. I am sure that most were filled everywhere he went, at least those who accepted Christ. An example is found in his insistence that the Ephesian Believers know about and receive the Holy Spirit (Acts 19:1-7).

We know he preached all the other great doctrines, as well, due to the amount of information given us concerning these things in his Epistles.

The phrase, *"Which gave testimony unto the Word of His Grace,"* presents a beautiful way in which to describe the Gospel.

What was that *"Word of His Grace?"*

It speaks of God's unmerited Favor in sending Jesus to save us from our sins. *"For by grace are you saved through Faith; and that not of yourselves: it is the Gift of God:*

"Not of works, lest any man should boast" (Eph. 2:8-9).

SIGNS AND WONDERS

The phrase, *"And granted signs and*

wonders to be done by their hands," presents here the *"testimony,"* which is the proof of the Gospel. The *"signs and wonders"* were, no doubt, healings, miracles, and astounding things the Lord did, and of whatever capacity.

The Holy Spirit is saying here that if the true Gospel of Jesus Christ is truly preached, this *"testimony"* of *"signs and wonders"* will surely follow (Mk. 16:17-18).

The Lord anointed the Apostles to do these things by the Power of the Holy Spirit, i.e., *"done by their hands."*

The question should be asked here, *"Is this 'testimony' present in the Church you now attend?"*

Much of the modern Church world has argued that these things ceased with the Apostles, etc. However, there is nothing in the Word of God that substantiates such a claim, and, in fact, the Word of God mitigates against such thinking (Mat. 21:22; Mk. 11:24; 16:17-18; Jn. 14:14; 15:7; etc.).

(4) "BUT THE MULTITUDE OF THE CITY WAS DIVIDED: AND PART HELD WITH THE JEWS, AND PART WITH THE APOSTLES."

The exegesis is:

1. Through the merits of the death of Christ, those who believe in Him are forever forgiven of all their sins entirely, however many and however great they may be.

2. The Doctrine of Christ Crucified is the grand peculiarity of the Christian Faith.

BIBLE CHRISTIANITY

The phrase, *"But the multitude of the city was divided,"* presents the norm when the Gospel is truly preached. Some accept while some reject!

This message, though grace is its keynote, causes dissension and disrupts families, communities, and nations.

Due to a *"great multitude both of Jews and also of the Greeks* (who) *believed,"* the entire city, more or less, was impacted.

Of all the religions in the world, none has this power or impact as Bible Christianity. The reason is obvious:

When Jesus is accepted, the individual who accepts Him makes Him paramount in his life. Everything, and we mean everything, must be subservient to Christ. Ways change, friends change, and direction changes, with the person actually entering into a new culture. Even though the Believer does not initiate or desire such disruptions and, for the most part, is grieved because of such, still, the very nature of good and evil demands such a rupture. The evil and unrighteousness in the unconverted automatically oppose the righteousness of the Believer. Jesus warned against such by saying, *"Do you suppose that I am come to give peace on Earth? I tell you, No; but rather division"* (Lk. 12:51).

Actually, the Lord initiates this division for the simple reason that the Believer now belongs to Him exclusively. However, at the same time, the greatest cause of such division is the unabated anger that unrighteousness holds against righteousness. This is the cause of all persecution of the saints.

THE JEWS AND THE APOSTLES

The phrase, *"And part held with the Jews, and part with the Apostles,"* proclaims to us the extent of this division and, as well, that the Holy Spirit refers to Barnabas, as well as Paul, as an Apostle. In fact, the Lord is still giving to the Church *"Apostles,"* as well as *"Prophets, Evangelists, Pastors and Teachers"* (Eph. 4:11) He has continued to do so from the Day of Pentecost.

I think that Paul and Barnabas would not have set very well in most of that which presently calls itself *"Church."* Everywhere Paul went, the Spirit of God moved, with many people being saved, baptized with the Holy Spirit, healed, and delivered by the Power of God. As should be obvious, such constitutes a direct invasion upon Satan's territory, even as Jesus intended (Mat. 12:28-29). When this happens, Satan becomes very angry. Most of the time, it resulted in Paul suffering bodily harm, etc.

The modern Church pretty well has most things backward. Most of the time, it places its seal of approval upon that which is not opposed by Satan at all. The reason is obvious: what is being promoted is not of God.

However, if something is truly of the Lord, it will never have the plaudits of the world, but rather its opposition and, as well, the opposition of most of the Church. Satan does not oppose that which is causing him little or no difficulty. Consequently, he opposed Paul greatly, and continues to do so to this moment to all who are truly of the Lord.

Our defense against him is Christ and the Cross, which then gives the Holy Spirit the latitude to work in our hearts and lives. The Holy Spirit works exclusively within the parameters of the Finished Work of Christ and will not work outside of those parameters. That's the reason that Paul also said:

"For the Law of the Spirit of Life in Christ Jesus, has made me free from the Law of Sin and Death" (Rom. 8:2).

(5) "AND WHEN THERE WAS AN ASSAULT MADE BOTH OF THE GENTILES, AND ALSO OF THE JEWS WITH THEIR RULERS, TO USE THEM DESPITEFULLY, AND TO STONE THEM,"

The synopsis is:

1. The phrase, *"And when there was an assault made both of the Gentiles, and also of the Jews with their rulers,"* means that plans were being made to stone Paul and Barnabas, with the consent and approval of the civil rulers of the city.

2. The Text seems to imply that before now, the opponents had not had the support of the civil rulers, but now, with that support, they would take bold steps.

3. The phrase, *"To use them despitefully, and to stone them,"* constitutes their plans, but with Paul and Barnabas leaving before those plans were put into motion.

4. The word *"despitefully"* implies in the Greek text that they desired to insult and humiliate them before the stoning. Exactly what this meant is not known, except to hold them up to ridicule and humiliation.

5. Whereas these plans of humiliation came from both the Gentiles and Jews, the *"stoning"* was Jewish entirely.

6. They were claiming that Paul and Barnabas had blasphemed the Law of Moses, etc., which was punishable by stoning. However, Paul and Barnabas had not said anything contrary to the Law of Moses, much less blaspheming. The truth is, it was the Jews who were blaspheming Christ and God, as well as the Law of Moses.

There are none so blind as those who will not see!

(6) "THEY WERE MADE AWARE OF IT, AND FLED UNTO LYSTRA AND DERBE, CITIES OF LYCAONIA, AND UNTO THE REGION THAT LIES ROUND ABOUT."

The order is:

1. Religions have laws and moral precepts and forms and ceremonies, but they cannot show us the Cross.

2. The Cross of Christ is the crown and glory of the Gospel.

EITHER CAUSED OR ALLOWED BY THE LORD

The phrase, *"They were made aware of it,"* means they were informed of the plot. This information, no doubt, was brought about by the Holy Spirit. Why would the Lord bring about the provision of such information that would spare the Apostles great suffering and at other times not do so?

Actually, that question could possibly be asked about any and all situations respecting the Believer. And yet, as someone has said, and I suspect it's closer to the truth than we realize, *"Biblical Faith, which is Faith in Christ and the Cross, has no questions."*

The Believer must conclude that every single thing that happens to him, irrespective of the direction from which it comes, is always, and without exception, either caused or allowed by the Lord. While the Lord certainly does not cause a Believer to sin, fail, etc., still, He definitely does allow such, along with the consequences.

Respecting adverse circumstances such as the proposed stoning of Paul and Barnabas, some would contend that all of these things are predicated strictly on one's Faith or the lack thereof.

In other words, such false Teachers claim that proper Faith will forestall all adverse and hurtful circumstances. Some even advocate that if Paul had had Faith as strong as theirs, he would not have had to undergo the adverse things that came his way. To be frank, such is so silly that it is hardly worth a response.

While one's Faith is definitely of vast significance and the lack thereof the cause

NOTES

of many problems, still, the simple matter of having Faith or not having Faith does not answer the question.

Were that the case, Faith would be bigger than God, which is exactly what some people have made it out to be.

GOD'S WORD CAN NEVER BE USED AGAINST HIMSELF

The Believer must understand the words of our heading, which states that *"God's Word can never be used against Himself."* In other words, Mark 11:24 and other such Scriptures cannot be used to circumvent the Will of God. Many have taken these Scriptures and claimed outlandish things. However, they are not going to receive such simply because such things are not in the Will of God for that person.

It is the business of the Holy Spirit to help us pray *"according to the Will of God"* and not according to our wills (Rom. 8:26-27).

All Believers must understand that even while it may be the Will of God for certain things to come our way that are good, the wisdom of God knows that it would not be good for us at the present.

So, the point is that the Lord, even though delivering Paul and Barnabas here, at times allowed them to suffer greatly, etc. The latter was not because of a lack of Faith but because it was the Will of God for such to be suffered by His choice Apostles.

Why would He want that?

Of course, the Lord does not bother to explain everything to us, and neither should He. However, the flesh and self-will are so dominant, even in the best of God's People, that adverse circumstances are at times needed to keep us on our faces before God and, thereby, remain broken before Him. That is one of the reasons that Solomon wrote, *"Give me neither poverty nor riches; feed me with food convenient for me:*

"Lest I be full, and deny You, and say, Who is the LORD? or lest I be poor, and steal, and take the name of my God in vain" (Prov. 30:8-9).

THE INSTRUCTIONS OF THE LORD

The phrase, *"And fled unto Lystra and Derbe, cities of Lycaonia,"* does not mean that Paul and Barnabas were afraid, but that these were the instructions of the Lord.

Lystra was about 18 miles west of Iconium, with Derbe about 20 miles south of Lystra.

Lystra was a Roman military colony and had the responsibility of safeguarding the interests of Rome and guarding the Roman roads. It was completely Gentile, with no Jewish population and, therefore, no synagogue. It was the same in Derbe.

So, Paul would depart from his usual method of going first to the synagogue, but would broach the subjects of Christ and salvation to pagans who had absolutely no knowledge of God in any capacity. They were idolaters with all its attendant ignorance. However, the Holy Spirit, as we shall see, was perfectly equal to the task.

The phrase, *"And unto the region that lies round about,"* referred to smaller towns and villages in the area of these twin cities. So, the Apostles must have remained there for several months, etc.

(7) "AND THERE THEY PREACHED THE GOSPEL."

The direction is:

1. Miserable indeed is the teaching that calls itself Christian, and yet, contains nothing of the Cross.

2. A man who teaches the Bible and ignores the Cross is like someone trying to explain the solar system, but yet, says nothing about the sun.

THE PREACHING OF THE GOSPEL

This and this alone is the method chosen by God to reach people, irrespective of the locality or their circumstances, and I am calling attention to the preaching of the Gospel.

Many missionaries foolishly think that one has to learn the culture of a particular native people before one can be effective in ministering to them. Such could not be further from the truth.

First of all, the culture of the entirety of the world is demented, to say the least! Consequently, the problem is the same. All men are sinners.

As well, even as the problem is the same the world over, the solution also is the same.

It is the Gospel of Jesus Christ and Him Crucified.

Paul did not change his way or message wherever he went, irrespective as to whom he spoke. He preached the Good News of Jesus Christ and His Power to save.

In many years of conducting giant citywide crusades all over the world, I have had the privilege of working with some godly missionaries. However, I have also been forced to work with some who knew more about psychology than they did the Gospel of Jesus Christ. Almost without exception, these individuals would claim that I could not be effective because I did not properly know the culture of the area, etc.

They would always be dumbfounded whenever the Lord would help us to pack the stadiums to capacity, having upwards of 100,000 people a night, and consequently, seeing untold thousands brought to a saving knowledge of Jesus Christ. In their erroneous thinking, they did not understand how this could happen, but, of course, the answer is simple.

THE PROBLEM AND THE SOLUTION

As stated, man's problem the world over is sin, and man's solution the world over is the Gospel of Jesus Christ, irrespective of color, creed, nationality, etc.

I remember one missionary informing me that I could never be effective in France due to the fact that the French were very sophisticated. I guess he was informing me that I did not have much sophistication.

He then informed me that his son was serving as a missionary in France and was reaching the French by his ability to play classical piano.

I asked him how many people had been saved as a result of his son's ministry of classical piano.

"Well none," he stated, *"but some are interested!"*

A short time after that, we had the privilege of going on television in France and immediately began to see people saved, even a great harvest of souls.

The truth is, the Frenchmen are like all others, sophisticated or not. They are sinners and need a Saviour.

NOTES

When men conduct themselves in a manner that seems to indicate that they know more than God, they have just crossed the boundaries, which means they will see absolutely nothing done for Christ. God's Methods are those designed by the Holy Spirit, and they are the only methods that will work to bring the lost to Jesus. That method is the preaching of the Gospel under the anointing of the Holy Spirit, whether to one person or thousands.

(8) "AND THERE SAT A CERTAIN MAN AT LYSTRA, IMPOTENT IN HIS FEET, BEING A CRIPPLE FROM HIS MOTHER'S WOMB, WHO NEVER HAD WALKED."

The construction is:

1. The phrase, *"And there sat a certain man at Lystra, impotent in his feet,"* seems to indicate that Paul was preaching in the open air, and most probably, in an open space by the city gates, which Verse 13 seems to portray.

2. In many of these cities at that time, there was a gathering place where speakers addressed particular subjects to an ever-present crowd. This was most probably that type of place.

3. *"Being a cripple from his mother's womb, who never had walked,"* presents this man whom the Lord would choose to be a recipient of grace.

(9) "THE SAME HEARD PAUL SPEAK: WHO STEADFASTLY BEHOLDING HIM, AND PERCEIVING THAT HE HAD FAITH TO BE HEALED."

The order is:

1. The phrase, *"The same heard Paul speak,"* has reference to the fact that the Gospel began to penetrate the heart of this pagan.

From what little description we do have, Paul would have had to begin his message with an explanation as to Who exactly was God. Pagans worshiped many gods and had no concept of one God.

2. He would then have told the great and beautiful story of Jesus and how He came to this Earth and died on Calvary in order to save men. He would, as well, have told about the Resurrection and Ascension, plus the Holy Spirit being sent on the Day of Pentecost.

NOTES

In this explanation, he would have told how Jesus not only could save but could heal as well! This is evident in the reaction respecting the crippled man.

3. So, we learn from this that Paul preached Jesus, Who could not only save but could heal.

4. *"Who steadfastly beholding him,"* presents Paul being drawn to this man by the Holy Spirit for a distinct purpose and reason, as we shall see.

5. The phrase, *"And perceiving that he had Faith to be healed,"* means that as he heard Paul preach, he began to believe the things he heard. The entrance of the Word, if accepted, always gives light. With it comes Faith!

(10) "SAID WITH A LOUD VOICE, STAND UPRIGHT ON YOUR FEET. AND HE LEAPED AND WALKED."

The direction is:

1. The phrase, *"Said with a loud voice,"* presents Paul still looking intently at the man, and then, with a very loud voice, giving him a command. This would have been heard by everyone there, which was the intention of the Holy Spirit.

2. The phrase, *"Stand upright on your feet,"* presents the greatest words this man had ever heard.

Whenever Paul gave this command, the Power of God responded to the man's Faith, with him experiencing an instant healing.

3. *"And he leaped and walked,"* proclaims him being healed immediately. Considering that he had never walked, one might say that two miracles were performed here at the same time.

4. The man, never having walked, normally would have had to learn to do so, but not on this occasion. He not only *"walked,"* but, as well, he began to *"leap."*

5. This shows even greater Faith on his part than the cripple at the gate called beautiful, who had never walked either. There, Peter took him by the hand and lifted him up, but no hand was needed for this man. He just simply began to *"leap and walk,"* all on his own!

(11) "AND WHEN THE PEOPLE SAW WHAT PAUL HAD DONE, THEY LIFTED UP THEIR VOICES, SAYING IN THE SPEECH OF LYCAONIA, THE GODS ARE COME DOWN TO US IN THE LIKENESS OF MEN."

The construction is:

1. The phrase, *"And when the people saw what Paul had done,"* presents an astonishment that gripped the crowd, with many of them probably being acquainted with this former cripple, or at least they knew him. Consequently, they knew this was not a hoax, but rather the result of some mysterious power.

2. Oftentimes the Lord uses healings and miracles of this nature to get the attention of people, as well as being of great benefit to the recipient of such.

3. *"They lifted up their voices, saying in the speech of Lycaonia,"* presents their native language.

4. Greek was the common language spoken by all at that particular time, but with most knowing their native language, as well, which meant they were bilingual, and in some cases, trilingual.

5. However, Paul being able to use the Greek language, which was understood by all, made it much easier to preach the Gospel. I have preached countless times with interpreters, which causes no problem at all for the Holy Spirit. However, due to the complexity of languages, it is easier and better if no interpreter is needed, as should be obvious.

6. The phrase, *"The gods are come down to us in the likeness of men,"* despite being so very wrong, still, was somewhat natural for these people to believe.

Greek mythology pointed to many gods and of their coming down to Earth in human form. As well, the images of their Greek gods were in human form. So, it was natural for them to think such of Paul and Barnabas, especially considering that they had never seen a miracle.

(12) "AND THEY CALLED BARNABAS, JUPITER; AND PAUL, MERCURIUS, BECAUSE HE WAS THE CHIEF SPEAKER."

The form is:

1. The phrase, *"And they called Barnabas, Jupiter; and Paul, Mercurius,"* presents their two principle gods.

Zeus (Jupiter) was the Greek god, who

NOTES

was king of gods and men.

Mercury was the god of markets and trade, but the Lycaonians here thought of him in his principle character of herald and messenger of the gods and, hence, the god of eloquence and speech.

There was a legend among these people that Jupiter and Mercury paid a visit to an aged couple, Philemon and Baucis, in the neighboring province of Phrygia, and that they were supposed to have come down to visit Lycaonia, from whence the Lycaonians derived their name.

In the works of Ovid, Homer, Virgil, and other poets, there are many such visitations described. These, no doubt, are corruptions of the many angelic appearances to men recorded in Scripture.

2. Jupiter and Mercury were the gods that the heathen believed visited men more than others. Jupiter was pictured as large and old, while Mercury was pictured as small and young. So, in the minds of these poor heathen, Paul and Barnabas were thought to be these two gods, especially considering there had been a great healing.

3. The phrase, *"Because he was the chief speaker,"* gives us the Will of the Lord, as well as the type of education that Paul had received. The word *"lawyer"* would have probably better described him.

4. His manner of presenting a subject was both defensive and offensive at the same time. His way of constructively building a message also carried within it, at least to some degree, a refutation of opposing arguments.

(13) "THEN THE PRIEST OF JUPITER, WHICH WAS BEFORE THEIR CITY, BROUGHT OXEN AND GARLANDS UNTO THE GATES, AND WOULD HAVE DONE SACRIFICE WITH THE PEOPLE."

The way is:

1. The phrase, *"Then the priest of Jupiter, which was before their city,"* speaks of the temple, which was constructed just outside the gates.

The lame man had probably sat near the gates through which men were passing in and out. As stated, there was most likely a square or open space immediately inside the gates that served as a type of forum, which was where Paul probably spoke.

2. The phrase, *"Brought oxen and garlands unto the gates,"* signals that the priest of Jupiter had been told almost immediately about the miracle and the two men who were responsible.

In the next few minutes, he gave instructions that oxen, which were the most costly victims that could be used, be brought and offered in sacrifice to Paul and Barnabas. The garlands (wreaths of flowers) draped over the horns signified that the animal was special and was to be used in sacrifice to one of the gods.

3. *"And would have done sacrifice with the people,"* spoke of offering up the animals and actually worshiping Paul and Barnabas.

This was of far greater moment than meets the eye. This would make their city famous and their temple one of the greatest in the Roman Empire. In fact, an entire industry could be built up around this visitation, with craftsmen making small idols of Jupiter and Mercury in the likeness of Paul and Barnabas.

4. Considering that such a miracle had been performed, there was no limit to where this could go, at least in the minds of these pagans devoted to these gods.

(14) "WHICH WHEN THE APOSTLES, BARNABAS AND PAUL, HEARD OF, THEY RENT THEIR CLOTHES, AND RAN IN AMONG THE PEOPLE, CRYING OUT."

The account is:

1. The phrase, *"Which when the Apostles, Barnabas and Paul, heard of,"* probably means (with the people speaking in their native language) that the Apostles at first did not know what was happening. Upon inquiry, someone must have related to them in the Greek language what was about to be done.

2. *"They rent their clothes, and ran in among the people, crying out,"* shows the utter horror registering upon them of what these people were about to do.

3. Despite the fact that most Jews opposed Christ and His Followers, still, by this incident, we are made to realize how much good the Jewish synagogues had done wherever they were built. They taught one true God and high moral standards. The

Gentiles who attended knew the Word. They had heard the prophecies. They knew God worked through men *"of like passions,"* for they heard the stories of Moses, Elijah, etc.

4. In most of the places they were constructed, they had enough influence on the community around them so that no one would ever have interpreted miracles the way these people at Lystra did. There being no synagogue at Lystra, the people here had no knowledge of God whatsoever; consequently, they interpreted this miracle according to their own pagan ideas.

Wherever the Bible stands, the intelligence of all is vastly improved and superstition checked!

(15) "AND SAYING, SIRS, WHY DO YOU THESE THINGS? WE ALSO ARE MEN OF LIKE PASSIONS WITH YOU, AND PREACH UNTO YOU THAT YOU SHOULD TURN FROM THESE VANITIES UNTO THE LIVING GOD, WHICH MADE HEAVEN, AND EARTH, AND THE SEA, AND ALL THINGS THAT ARE THEREIN."

The pattern is:

1. The Doctrine of Christ Crucified is the strength of the preacher.

2. The Cross is the only lever, so to speak, that has ever turned the world upside down and made men forsake their sins.

WHY WOULD THEY DO SUCH A THING?

The question, *"And saying, Sirs, why do you these things?"* of course, is already understood by Paul and Barnabas as to why these heathen did such things. So, this question applies not only to those in Lystra but, as well, to the entirety of the world for all time.

Why do people in India bathe in the filth of the Ganges River, which is a veritable cesspool, thinking that such will guarantee them some type of Eternal Life, etc.?

Why do many in Africa smear cow dung over their bodies and work themselves into a frenzy as someone beats a drum?

The other day, I saw a documentary on a particular sect in India that worshiped rats. Actually, a giant temple was built many, many years ago in order to worship the rat god. Why do they do such a thing?

NOTES

Sometime back, while in Guatemala, I had the opportunity of seeing the Mayan ruins, which portrayed an extensive engineering ability, etc. What happened to these people?

It is believed that they may have literally sacrificed themselves to death. In other words, they sacrificed so many of their young men and young ladies that the population could not sustain itself and, consequently, was ultimately exterminated.

Why would they do such a thing?

THE ANSWER

The answer to all of these questions, plus a myriad of others not asked, is because these people did not and do not know God. So, they make up their own religions, which are actually instigated by demon spirits, even though the people, much of the time, would not be aware of such.

As we have already stated, these people in Lystra were rank pagans, which means they had no knowledge of the true God whatsoever! Consequently, they lived in superstition, fear, and darkness, which pushed them in terrible directions.

In the phrase, *"We also are men of like passions with you,"* Paul and Barnabas disavowed the ridiculous claims of these people.

In looking at this situation, modern similarities are very quickly brought to mind. Millions of young people the world over idolize certain rock stars, almost to the point of deity. Others do the same thing respecting the product of Hollywood. Sports stars fall into the same category! To be frank, so do some preachers!

Actually, millions of young people literally sacrifice themselves to death on the altars of passion, greed, and lust in honor of these rock stars, etc. Many adults do the same thing, at least in some measure, to sports stars.

So, the problem did not perish with the passing of the generation of Paul's day. It is very much alive and well at present!

EMPTY NOTHINGS

In fact, many preachers should tell their followers, and plainly so, even as Paul and Barnabas, *"We also are men of like passions with you."* Maybe all of us fall into that category in one way or the other. True, this man was instantly healed even as Paul preached, but it was not Paul or Barnabas who brought about this great miracle, but God alone!

"And preach unto you that you should turn from these vanities unto the living God," presents everything else in comparison to God. Paul called these things *"vanities,"* which means *"empty nothings!"*

I wonder what these pagan priests thought when Paul referred to their main religion and its type of worship as *"vanity,"* i.e., *"empty nothings"*? One thing is certain, Paul never minced words. No one had any trouble knowing of what he spoke or whether it was right or wrong! He *"preached"* unto them this Word of turning unto the living God because that was their only hope. It was not merely one of several ways but, in fact, the only way. Consequently, Paul would have been looked at in today's modern society as very narrow.

While that is true, there is a reason that it is true.

As an example, man's interpretation of mathematics has literally already been decided for him. In other words, the interpretation is very narrow and definitely will not tolerate any exceptions. The reasons are obvious!

If architects or engineers deviate from that narrow interpretation, airplanes will not fly, bridges will fall, and nothing will work. So, the engineers are not criticized for being so narrow in their interpretation but are actually demanded that they remain narrow.

It is the same with God! He demands that we be narrow in our interpretation of the Word of God because if such is not maintained, souls will die lost and lives will go deeper into satanic bondage.

For instance, it is not possible for the teachings of Catholicism to be right, that is, if the Bible is right.

In answer to that, some would argue their sincerity; however, an engineer being sincerely wrong does not alleviate the situation. The bridge he is working on will fall. So, sincerity, good motives, or other things are not the criteria, but the Word of God.

NOTES

GOD THE CREATOR

The phrase, *"Which made heaven, and Earth, and the sea, and all things that are therein,"* presents Paul going all the way back to Creation.

He did not speak to these people of the Law of Moses, or any of the patriarchs of the Bible for that matter, because these people would not have known what he was talking about. They did not know there was such a thing as a Bible or the things that God had done in this Earth. Likewise, they did not know Jesus as the Saviour of man, except what little they had heard regarding the message brought to them by Paul and Barnabas.

However, to be introduced to One Who is the Creator of all things puts *"the living God"* far above the fake luminaries of their own imagination who, in fact, were mere myths. Due to the great miracle recently performed, they were forced to give audience to Paul and Barnabas, with some small evidence that they did.

There was something universally common in these false religions of that day and continues to carry over even unto the present. The people feared these mythical gods. So, what they did in offering sacrifice to them or other things was meant to appease the anger of these fake deities.

A PERSONAL EXPERIENCE

Years ago, I posed a question to a woman in Haiti, the wife of one of, if not the most, notorious witch doctors on that island nation. I asked her why they engaged in such sordid practices as drinking chicken blood, etc. Her answer was interesting.

She said, *"We are afraid not to do these things for fear of what the spirits will do to us."* People who practice these heathenistic religions are ruled by fear.

God does not function on that basis, but rather on the foundation of love (Jn. 3:16). Of course, we are to fear God, but not in the cringing manner engaged by the heathen concerning their fake deities.

In fact, even as Paul would portray, God does not work with humanity or approach humanity—irrespective as to how evil they

NOTES

may be—on the basis of fear, but rather of love. This is overwhelmingly obvious in all that He does. Paul would later write, *"But God commends His Love toward us, in that, while we were yet sinners* (opposed to God), *Christ died for us"* (Rom. 5:8).

(16) "WHO IN TIMES PAST SUFFERED ALL NATIONS TO WALK IN THEIR OWN WAYS."

The synopsis is:

1. A man may preach with a perfect knowledge of Greek and Hebrew, but he will do little or no good among his hearers unless he knows something of the Cross.

2. Never was there a minister who did much for the conversion of souls who did not dwell much on Christ Crucified.

ALL NATIONS

The phrase, *"Who in times past,"* pertains to the manner in which God dealt with the entirety of the human family, at least the Gentiles, until the first advent of Christ. With His Coming, constituting His Life and Ministry, the price paid at Calvary, plus His Resurrection and Ascension, God's Manner of dealing with the Gentile world changed. In effect, even though this period has been the time of grace, God deals much more stringently and much more exact than previously (Acts 17:30).

The phrase, *"Suffered all nations to walk in their own ways,"* needs some explanation.

Before Noah, God dealt with the human family through their conscience. Even then, man was taught the principles of the sacrificial offering and what it represented, which was the way to God (Gen. 4:4-7).

However, man overrode his conscience until it was darkened, when the Lord said of him, *"The wickedness of man was great in the Earth, and that every imagination of the thoughts of his heart was only evil continually"* (Gen. 6:5). This is what Paul was speaking of when he said, *"When they knew God, they glorified Him not as God, neither were thankful; but became vain in their imaginations, and their foolish heart was darkened."*

He then said, *"Wherefore God also gave them up to uncleanness through the lusts of their own hearts, to dishonor their own bodies between themselves."*

And then, *"Who changed the truth of God into a lie, and worshipped and served the creature more than the Creator, Who is blessed for ever. Amen"* (Rom. 1:21-25).

GOD GAVE THEM UP

The key is contained in the words, *"God also gave them up,"* which means He allowed them to have their perfidious ways; however, that was only for a time, approximately 1,600 years. Consequently, we see the Lord in Genesis, Chapters 1 through 11, dealing with the world as a whole but, as stated, to no avail!

While the flood rid the Earth of this terrible debauchery, in effect, giving man a new beginning, it really did not solve the problem.

Horton said, *"In Genesis, Chapter 12, the Lord, as we see, rather begins to deal with one man, Abraham, instead of dealing with the whole of mankind. Through him and his descendants would come the Greater Seed of Abraham, the Lord Jesus Christ. However, during the approximate 400 years from the flood to the time of Abraham, the world was in rank idolatry. According to Jewish tradition, Abraham's father Terah was actually an idol-maker."*

From Abraham would come the Jewish people, raised up for the express purpose of bringing the Messiah into the world, who would be the Saviour of all mankind, at least those who would believe. As we have previously stated, the Jews were to reach out to the Gentile world, but this they did not do. However, that did not stop the Plan of God to reach the entirety of the world, which was to be done through Jesus Christ, which Paul and others were now doing.

(17) "NEVERTHELESS HE LEFT NOT HIMSELF WITHOUT WITNESS, IN THAT HE DID GOOD, AND GAVE US RAIN FROM HEAVEN, AND FRUITFUL SEASONS, FILLING OUR HEARTS WITH FOOD AND GLADNESS."

The synopsis is:

WITNESS

The phrase, *"Nevertheless He left not Himself without witness,"* pertains to that which Paul wrote in Romans 1:19-20. He said, *"Because that which may be known of God is manifest in them; for God hath showed it unto them.*

"For the invisible things of Him from the Creation of the world are clearly seen, being understood by the things that are made, even His Eternal Power and Godhead; so that they are without excuse."

The idea is that Creation, functioning in its prescribed order, is a witness to anyone that such could not be on its own but, of necessity, the work of a Creator, i.e., *"God."* That is what makes evolution, even in our modern times, so absolutely unbelievable.

However, a *"witness"* within itself, as powerful as Creation may be, is not a Saviour. So, even though this *"witness"* should point men toward God, it within itself will not save men.

The phrase, *"In that He did good,"* proclaims God's Actions toward a fallen race who had rebelled against their Creator.

God, Who is Omnipotent, had the power to do whatever He so desired. Especially considering that virtually all of the human family had rebelled against Him, actually throwing in their lot with the Evil One, God's Restraint is within itself beyond the pale of human understanding.

EVERYTHING GOD DOES IS GOOD

I realize that some would claim that sending a flood, which God did, is not exactly *"good!"* However, that is a completely erroneous view.

In truth, everything God does is *"good."* Had He not taken out humanity with the flood (with the exception of Noah), mankind would have totally destroyed itself.

Evil cannot improve within itself. Such is impossible! It can only degenerate and regressively grow worse. It steals, kills, and destroys because that is its nature (Jn. 10:10).

So, the act of God in sending the flood is the same as a doctor surgically removing a cancer from a patient. Even though it does cause pain, suffering, and great discomfort, still, the doctor is not faulted for doing such a thing, but rather praised, as he should be. Therefore, the acts of judgment performed by God were, in the long run, for the betterment of the human family and not its destruction. God is a Creator, not a destroyer, as Satan. Everything He does is *"good"* because that is His Nature, and He never goes against His Nature.

NOTES

However, Satan has been very adept at making people believe that God is a despot and a dictator, consequently, destructive toward the human race, etc. Nothing could be further from the truth!

The phrase, *"And gave us rain from heaven, and fruitful seasons, filling our hearts with food and gladness,"* presents the goodness of God even extended to those who hated Him.

Horton said, *"In fact, God put man originally into an environment where everything was "very good," perfectly suited to man's needs, provided with every opportunity for man's growth and development. Then, even after man fell, He continued to provide good things to enjoy."*

Horton also said, *"He sets us an example of how to treat unbelievers who oppose us by making His Sun to shine on the evil and on the good and by sending rain on the just and on the unjust"* (Mat. 5:44-48).

GOD IS LONGSUFFERING

In fact, God is longsuffering, so much, in fact, that in some cases, men even claim He does not exist.

The flood, as I think is obvious, was so grievous to God, even though He had to do such a thing, that He promised to all of mankind that He would never do such again. The sign of that promise or *"covenant"* is the rainbow. He said, *"And I will look upon it, that I may remember the everlasting covenant between God and every living creature of all flesh that is upon the Earth"* (Gen. 9:13-17).

In fact, God never sends judgment until every warning is exhausted, and there is simply no other choice.

If people truly want to know what God is like and Who God is like, they need but to look at Jesus. He answered Philip's request, *"Lord, show us the Father,"* by saying:

"Have I been so long time with you, and yet have you not known Me, Philip? He that has seen Me has seen the Father" (Jn. 14:8-9).

(18) "AND WITH THESE SAYINGS SCARCE RESTRAINED THEY THE PEOPLE, THAT THEY HAD NOT DONE SACRIFICE UNTO THEM."

The exegesis is:

1. The phrase, *"And with these sayings scarce restrained they the people,"* means several things.

2. As we have stated, the idea that two of their gods had come down to them in the form of men was very enticing indeed! From now on, their city would be famous. The prosperity of the region would be greatly increased due to the flock of visitors and the selling of replicas of these gods, etc. With the former cripple testifying as to the power that healed his legs, which was witnessed by many, the conclusion that would be drawn by all was that Jupiter and Mercurius had favored them greatly by appearing in their midst and doing this great deed.

3. However, with Paul and Barnabas resisting these efforts so strongly, and considering that many of them still believed that these two were gods, they were somewhat fearful of not heeding them.

4. *"That they had not done sacrifice unto them,"* means they were on the verge of killing the oxen, thereby, initiating the sacrifice. They were restrained at the last moment.

5. We are not given further information as to exactly what happened at this time, but with what little is said here, along with the information given in Acts, Chapter 16, we know that a Church was planted in this city. Actually, Timothy was a native of Lystra. How wonderful is the grace of our God! Truly, even as Paul said, *"He is good."*

(19) "AND THERE CAME THITHER CERTAIN JEWS FROM ANTIOCH AND ICONIUM, WHO PERSUADED THE PEOPLE, AND, HAVING STONED PAUL, DREW HIM OUT OF THE CITY, SUPPOSING HE HAD BEEN DEAD."

The structure is:

1. Never was there a minister who did much for the conversion of souls who did not dwell much on Christ Crucified.

2. Luther, Rutherford, Whitfield, and M'Cheyne were all most imminently preachers of the Cross.

NOTES

OPPOSITION FROM THE JEWS

The phrase, *"And there came thither certain Jews from Antioch and Iconium, who persuaded the people,"* evidently took place some days or even weeks after the situation concerning the proposed sacrifice.

For these *"Jews"* in Antioch and Iconium to have heard what was happening at Lystra, which caused them to come to that city, there must have been many people giving their hearts to the Lord and, as well, baptized with the Holy Spirit. No doubt, there were other miracles as well! Actually, I think it is obvious that Timothy's conversion must have occurred at this time (Acts 14:21; 16:1-3; II Tim. 3:10-11).

These Jews were able to *"persuade"* some of these people to turn against Paul and Barnabas by using various arguments.

The Apostles were branded as troublemakers and definitely not gods as previously thought. Still smarting from that, many of the people were easily influenced the other way.

It is amazing, yet true to form, that the Jews made no effort to build a synagogue in this city but would do everything within their power to stop Paul and Barnabas. They had no complaint of these pagans worshiping heathen gods, thereby, steeped in idolatry, but took great umbrage at them turning to Christ, and more particularly, under Paul and Barnabas.

It is sad, but yet similar, that I meet preachers constantly who refer to themselves as religious leaders, etc., who will not lift a finger to try to get people to Christ, but will do everything within their power to stop me from preaching a crusade and winning souls.

Why?

The same spirit that propelled those Jews of Paul's day propels these of which I speak as well.

Was Paul and Barnabas infringing on the *"territory"* of these Jews?

ACUTE PERSECUTION

No, they were not! In truth, there is no *"territory"* off limits as far as the salvation of souls is concerned. However, as stated, there was no synagogue in Lystra and no cause for these Jews to be concerned, irrespective of how wrong their concern was to begin with. As one sees constantly in the Book of Acts, the greater part of opposition against the true Work of God always came from organized religion. In other words, the very ones who should have been attempting to help were instead attempting to hinder, even to the point of murder, as we shall see. It has changed no less presently.

The phrase, *"And, having stoned Paul,"* tells us they considered Paul the leader, with Barnabas being spared, or at least not handled as severely.

Stoning, as previously stated, was the method of the Jews, telling us that they had fomented this satanic effort. The message is not only hated, but the messenger, as well, and more particularly, the messenger.

The phrase, *"Drew him out of the city,"* seems to imply that he was dragged outside the walls.

"Supposing he had been dead," means he was very near death but did not actually die, as some have claimed.

He was unconscious and must have been severely bruised all over his body. Undoubtedly, he had broken bones as well.

In II Corinthians 11:25, Paul mentions this *"stoning"* between beatings and shipwrecks as calamities he endured. He did not mention that he died because he had not.

Horton said, *"In Galatians 6:17, he mentions the scars and marks left on his body because of these stonings and beatings, and calls them 'the marks of the Lord Jesus.'"*

ANOTHER JESUS

What these men suffered, especially Paul, to take the Gospel to lost humanity is, I think, beyond the comprehension of most modern Believers. The last several decades, I'm afraid, have ushered in that which Paul, I think, would call, *"Another Jesus, whom we have not preached ... another spirit ... or another gospel"* (II Cor. 11:4).

This *"other gospel"* tells us that if we have enough Faith, we can escape all of these difficulties faced by Paul, etc. Some of these false Teachers are so bold as to say that if Paul had their Faith, he could have escaped these things.

NOTES

No! Paul was not stoned because of a lack of Faith, but rather because of great Faith!

Regrettably, this silly drivel, and drivel it is, espoused by these people is believed by many because it appeals to pride and a false prosperity.

In fact, Jesus perfectly outlined the Church Age when He answered the question posed by His Disciples, *"Tell us, when shall these things be? and what shall be the sign of Your coming, and of the end of the age?"* (Mat. 24:3).

In Matthew 24:4-14, Jesus described the Church Age.

He began in Matthew 24:4 by warning of deception.

In Matthew 24:6-8, He spoke of the world continuing to be subjected to wars, earthquakes, etc., because Israel had refused the invitation of the Kingdom (Mat. 4:17). To be sure, they wanted the *"Kingdom,"* but they did not want the *"King."*

THE PRINCE OF PEACE REFUSED IS THE KINGDOM REFUSED

When Jesus was refused, the Kingdom was refused, as well, with these *"sorrows"* continuing, which they do unto this hour and will until His Second Coming.

In Matthew 24:9-10, He spoke of great persecution that would come to Believers.

Actually, such persecution began immediately by the Jews, even as we here see, and then was taken up by the Romans. Untold thousands of Christians died in the Roman arenas, torn limb from limb, even as Jesus predicted.

Regrettably and sadly, beginning with the second century, the Church began to apostatize, which was almost total by the fourth and fifth centuries.

With Rome now gutted by its own corruption, the *"Catholic Church"* took up where the pagans had left off. The *"Church,"* having totally left the Word of God, attempted to build a kingdom on Earth, and do so by force. It was called *"the Dark Ages."* Untold hundreds of thousands, if not millions, died on the Catholic torture racks up unto the 14th century.

With the beginning of the Reformation, the persecution intensified for a time, but the light of the Gospel began to break through, which gradually broke the power of the Catholic Church.

Beginning in the 1600s, even though there was still persecution, the light of the Gospel began to make itself felt all over the world. Great moves of God took place in the 1700s and 1800s, more particularly in America and England, but in other parts of the world as well. Then, at the turn of the 20th century, the world experienced the beginning of the great outpouring of the latter rain of the Holy Spirit prophesied by Joel and quoted by Peter on the Day of Pentecost. From that time, millions have been baptized with the Holy Spirit with the evidence of speaking with other tongues, with great power invested in the Church, resulting in the touching of the entirety of the world with the Gospel.

THE APOSTASY

However, this is the most dangerous time of all. Jesus spoke of this time in Matthew 24:11-14. With persecution almost a thing of the past, at least for now, the Church has entered into the age of apostasy. It is the time of *"false Prophets"* and *"acute deception."*

So, this time in which we now live is the greatest and, at the same time, the worst. The Scripture is plain, I think, with the promise of the greatest outpouring of the Holy Spirit the world has ever known, which will happen, I believe, at this time (Acts 2:17-21).

As well, the Scripture is clear and plain concerning the apostasy, actually, the greatest of all (II Tim. 3:1-5; 4:3-4).

To be sure, the *"false Prophets"* are going to be so subtle in their approach, sounding like God, looking like God, and claiming to be of God, that Jesus said, *"Because iniquity* (unrighteousness) *shall abound, the love of many* (most) *shall wax cold"* (Mat. 24:12).

Even though the greatest number in history will profess Christ, only those who truly push close to the Lord, are anchored in His Word, and are being constantly led by the Holy Spirit are going to spiritually survive!

(20) "HOWBEIT, AS THE DISCIPLES STOOD ROUND ABOUT HIM, HE ROSE UP, AND CAME INTO THE CITY: AND THE NEXT DAY HE DEPARTED WITH BARNABAS TO DERBE."

NOTES

The overview is:

1. The phrase, *"Howbeit, as the disciples stood round about him,"* speaks of those who had come to Christ in the last few days or weeks. There is actually a possibility that Timothy, newly won to Christ, was standing there with the others beside Paul. I have to believe they were praying and seeking God respecting Paul's condition.

2. *"He rose up,"* indicates that ever how serious the situation was, he was instantly healed. If, in fact, there were broken bones, this means they were instantly healed as well. This, no doubt, was a happy moment for all who were there, noting the miracle-working Power of God.

3. *"And came into the city,"* means that Paul's detractors had now left, thinking he was dead. So, Paul and Barnabas, along with others, came back into Lystra, probably shielded by the converts and, therefore, unnoticed by the persecutors.

4. The phrase, *"And the next day he departed with Barnabas to Derbe,"* presents a distance of about 40 miles. It lay southeast of Lystra (all in modern Turkey).

(21) "AND WHEN THEY HAD PREACHED THE GOSPEL TO THAT CITY, AND HAD TAUGHT MANY, THEY RETURNED AGAIN TO LYSTRA, AND TO ICONIUM, AND ANTIOCH."

The diagram is:

1. The phrase, *"And when they had preached the Gospel to that city,"* proclaims their evangelism as not having slowed at all.

Apparently, there was no synagogue in Derbe either, and with little opposition, it seems, since Paul's enemies thought he was dead.

2. The phrase, *"And had taught many,"* refers to a considerable period of time, with people being saved and then instructed more perfectly in the Word of God. Actually, they could have remained in Derbe for several months.

3. *"They returned again to Lystra, and to Iconium, and Antioch,"* presents them retracing their steps, but for a particular reason, as we shall see.

4. It would seem they were taking their lives in their hands when they did this; however, the Holy Spirit was directing them

in all they did, which, as well, guaranteed His Protection.

5. No, His Protection did not mean that they were spared all difficulties and problems, even as we have just seen, but it does mean that Satan could not kill them until their work was finished.

(22) "CONFIRMING THE SOULS OF THE DISCIPLES, AND EXHORTING THEM TO CONTINUE IN THE FAITH, AND THAT WE MUST THROUGH MUCH TRIBULATION ENTER INTO THE KINGDOM OF GOD."

The overview is:

1. Whatever the preacher gives to the people, he must give them the Cross of Christ.

2. The Cross of Christ is the Gospel. Everything else is about the Gospel. There is a vast difference.

THE DISCIPLES

The phrase, *"Confirming the souls of the disciples,"* pertained to the new converts in these areas. In fact, every time the word *"disciple"* is used in the Book of Acts, it always refers to followers of Christ, meaning that they are saved, i.e., *"born again."*

I think that Paul did not do much evangelizing on this particular trip but mostly spent the time teaching the saints. As well, they must have spent several months in these three cities.

One can see Paul and Barnabas (either together or going in different directions) meeting almost every night with a house full of saints. How the hearts of these people must have warmed as these two Apostles proclaimed to them the Word of God. The people were hungry for God, and Paul and Barnabas were hungry to give them the Gospel.

The word *"confirming"* in the Greek is *"episterizo"* and means *"to support, reestablish, confirm, and strengthen."*

So, they spent this time instructing the saints more perfectly.

"And exhorting them to continue in the Faith," as should be obvious, shoots to the ground the unscriptural doctrine of unconditional eternal security.

The Greek word for *"continue"* is *"emmeno"* and means *"abide in, stand by, or continue in."*

Regrettably, many, if not millions, make a start in the Faith and are genuinely born again but do not *"continue."*

The phrase, *"And that we must through much tribulation enter into the Kingdom of God,"* proclaims firsthand (and by no less than Paul) that Satan is not in sympathy with anyone entering into the Kingdom of God, as should be obvious, and will do all within his power to stop any and all.

TRIBULATION

The word *"tribulation"* in the Greek is *"thlipsis"* and means *"affliction, anguish, burden, persecution, tribulation, and trouble."*

As well, this shoots down the claims by many that proper Faith will eliminate all of these difficulties. The actual truth is that proper Faith is that which brings on these difficulties.

That is the reason that one must walk closely to God, have a strong prayer life, be anchored in the Word, and have his Faith ever in Christ and the Cross. Anything less, that is, if the person is truly in the Kingdom, will spell disaster.

I might quickly add, as well, that many so-called, professing Believers suffer very little if any tribulation simply because they actually do not belong to the Lord, or else, they have so compromised their walk with God that they are of no threat to Satan. I greatly suspect that the latter is all too often the case.

Why would Satan desire to hurt or harm any Believer who has compromised his testimony?

E. M. Bounds was once asked the question as to whether all Christians suffer great tribulation, etc.

His answer was somewhat revealing. He said, *"Only the Believers who are giving Satan problems will experience his wrath!"*

He then said, *"I seriously doubt that Satan knows that most Christians are alive. They harm him or his kingdom of darkness not at all."*

(23) "AND WHEN THEY HAD ORDAINED THEM ELDERS IN EVERY CHURCH, AND HAD PRAYED WITH

NOTES

NOTES

FASTING, THEY COMMENDED THEM TO THE LORD, ON WHOM THEY BELIEVED."

The overview is:

1. Jesus Christ is the New Covenant.
2. The Cross of Christ is the meaning of the New Covenant.

THE ORDAINING OF ELDERS

The phrase, *"And when they had ordained them elders in every Church,"* gives us an idea of the method of Church government of that particular time. Let's take it step-by-step, especially considering that it is the Holy Spirit Who is the Author of these proceedings.

The word *"ordained"* in the Greek text is *"cheirotoneo"* and means *"to vote by the raising of the hand, or to select or appoint."* Consequently, there is a wide disagreement among commentators and Greek scholars, as well, as to whether the people voted on the *"elders," i.e., "Pastors,"* by the raising of their hands, or whether they were simply appointed by the Apostles.

One Greek scholar said, *"It cannot possibly refer to voting by the people,"* due to the structure of the Greek word used here.

However, due to the fact that the word can refer to voting by a show of hands, other commentators have jumped to that conclusion as the manner in which this was done.

I think if we look at the manner in which Paul addressed himself to these specifics in his Epistles, we will get an idea as to how these elders were ordained or appointed.

Paul was very strong regarding the independence of God-called preachers, etc. For instance, he said, *"Paul, an Apostle, not of men, neither by man, but by Jesus Christ, and God the Father"* (Gal. 1:1). So, he plainly said here that man has no part in these callings, but that they are strictly from the Lord (Eph. 4:11-12).

And yet, the record is clear that Paul considered the local Church to be the highest spiritual authority. Of course, that must be qualified.

THE LOCAL CHURCH

By the term *"highest spiritual authority,"* we simply mean that the local Church must run its own affairs and not be overruled by an outside authority. We know this from Jesus addressing His Letters directly to the seven Churches of Asia, and more particularly, to the Pastors of these Churches (Rev., Chpts. 2-3). If the mother Church in Jerusalem had exercised authority over these Churches (or any other Churches for that matter), Jesus would have simply addressed the letter to the mother Church. However, this He did not do, and for the reasons given. To be sure, these Churches were in fellowship one with the other, but no one Church ruled.

The local Church being the highest spiritual authority does not in any way weaken or curtail the spiritual authority held by Apostles, Prophets, Evangelists, Pastors and Teachers (Eph. 4:11). However, when we address *"spiritual authority,"* we must understand two or three things:

1. Every Believer in the world has spiritual authority and, of course, there are some, such as Apostles, Prophets, Evangelists, etc., who have more than others.
2. However, we must always understand that this spiritual authority is never over other people, only over Satan, demon spirits, and fallen angels.

The idea of all of this is, even as Paul set the example: he would recommend to Churches that which the Lord had given to him respecting doctrine or problems in local Churches; however, he constantly used terms such as, *"I beseech you," "That I might know the proof of you, whether you be obedient in all things,"* etc. (Acts 21:39; 26:3; Rom. 12:1; 15:30; 16:17; I Cor. 1:10; II Cor. 2:8-9; Gal. 4:12).

In other words, Paul would not force a position upon the local Church, nor could he do so. To take that position is to abrogate Christ as the Head of the Church (Eph. 1:22-23).

APPOINTED

Consequently, attempting to arrive at a conclusion by example, I believe that Paul, by the guidance of the Holy Spirit, personally chose and appointed the *"elders"* in each Church. I believe he then presented these *"elders,"* whom he had already appointed to the Church, for their approval, which was

NOTES

done by uplifted hands. The entirety of the body in this manner is allowed to participate, which I think is scriptural.

I cannot conceive of Paul taking no hand whatsoever in the selection of these people and leaving it all up to the congregation. As well, I cannot conceive that any congregation would desire to enter into these very important proceedings without having the advice and counsel of one such as Paul.

The word *"elders,"* as it is used here, means the same thing as *"presbyter," "bishop," "shepherd,"* or *"Pastor."* In other words, they all refer to the *"Pastor"* of a local Church.

None of these designations, offices, or titles caused any problems in the early Church because they all referred to the Pastor (bishop) of the local Church, which was independent, but yet, in fellowship with other Churches. Only when men attempted to add to the government of God by changing the meanings did problems arise.

BISHOP

I speak of the title *"bishop"* as it is presently used in some circles, referring to one man being in authority over an entire area containing any number of Churches, etc. There is no trace in the early Church of Church government by a single bishop, and I again speak of one man over many Churches.

So, these *"elders"* were to be (in our terminology) the Pastors of local Churches. Actually, there were several bishops in the single congregation at Philippi (Phil. 1:1), and may well have been in many of the Churches, but with one serving as the senior.

At the present time, any Church of any size will have several Pastors, even as we do at Family Worship Center. This is in keeping with the New Testament pattern.

PRAYER AND FASTING

The phrase, *"And had prayed with fasting,"* proclaims the seeking of God by Paul and Barnabas and the congregation regarding the Lord's Will as to His Choice concerning *"elders."* This must ever be the criterion in any and all Churches, that is, if the Lord's Will is desired.

"They commended them to the Lord," referred to seeking the Lord for the appointment and then the Lord's Blessings after the appointment.

The phrase, *"On Whom they believed,"* refers to the Apostles and the congregation trusting the Lord to guide them in this very important endeavor.

The idea here is not who Paul or the congregation desired respecting the *"elder"* or *"elders,"* but rather who the Lord desired!

Far too often, Churches make decisions based on outward appearance, which most if not all the time is wrong, instead of allowing the Lord to select.

Incidentally, where there were several *"elders"* or *"Pastors"* in one Church, of necessity, one would be set there by the Holy Spirit as the leader or senior, with the others submitting to him. Peter said, *"Likewise, you younger* (elders), *submit yourselves unto the elder* (senior)*"* (I Pet. 5:5).

(24) "AND AFTER THEY HAD PASSED THROUGHOUT PISIDIA, THEY CAME TO PAMPHYLIA."

The overview is:

1. Antioch would have been their last stop in the ordaining of elders, with Paul and Barnabas now going through the district of Pisidia to Perga, a distance of about 75 or 80 miles. Perga is located very near the Mediterranean coast.

2. Pamphylia is southwest of Pisidia.

(25) "AND WHEN THEY HAD PREACHED THE WORD IN PERGA, THEY WENT DOWN INTO ATTALIA."

The exegesis is:

1. The phrase, *"And when they had preached the Word in Perga,"* presents the capital of Pamphylia, as Antioch was capital of Pisidia.

2. Some three years before, Paul and Barnabas had come through Perga when they left Paphos; however, there is no record that they preached there at that particular time.

3. They would now minister in Perga, but with no information given in Scripture as to exactly what were the results.

4. *"They went down into Attalia,"* presents the harbor town on the Mediterranean coast, about seven or eight miles from

NOTES

Perga. There is no record that they ministered there.

(26) "AND THEN SAILED TO ANTIOCH, FROM WHENCE THEY HAD BEEN RECOMMENDED TO THE GRACE OF GOD FOR THE WORK WHICH THEY FULFILLED."

The construction is:

1. The phrase, *"And thence sailed to Antioch,"* refers back to Antioch, Syria, from where they had originally come. This would have probably been a distance of about 300 miles.

2. The phrase, *"From whence they had been recommended to the grace of God for the work which they fulfilled,"* tells us several things:

a. The word *"recommended"* in the Greek is *"paradidomi"* and means *"to surrender or entrust."* The idea is twofold:

i. The Spirit of God chose them, which was obvious to the Church.

ii. They surrendered to do that which the Lord had called them to do.

b. The *"grace of God"* pertains to the foundation of all that is done in taking the Gospel to the world. It was God's Grace given to hell-deserving sinners. These were people who did not know God and really had no desire for God, as most, if not all, sinners. So, it could only be grace that would put itself out to take a message of life to such people. However, that is true of all!

c. Paul and Barnabas felt that they had fulfilled what the Spirit of God desired that they do because they had followed His Leading.

(27) "AND WHEN THEY WERE COME, AND HAD GATHERED THE CHURCH TOGETHER, THEY REHEARSED ALL THAT GOD HAD DONE WITH THEM, AND HOW HE HAD OPENED THE DOOR OF FAITH UNTO THE GENTILES."

The structure is:

1. The phrase, *"And when they were come, and had gathered the Church together,"* implies that they somehow gathered all the people in one spot. This was not normal since there were no Church buildings in those days, with the people mostly worshiping in houses, etc.

2. One can well imagine the excitement of the people in welcoming Paul and Barnabas home but, as well, how they were desiring to hear what the Lord had done respecting this first missionary journey.

3. *"They rehearsed all that God had done with them,"* proclaims Paul and Barnabas giving God all the glory for the many souls won. Here, and in the following Chapter, God is stated some 15 times to have been the Worker in this first missionary journey.

4. The phrase, *"And how He had opened the door of Faith unto the Gentiles,"* presents, without a doubt, one of the greatest statements ever made.

5. The *"door of Faith"* pertains to *"salvation by Faith"* without all the accouterments of the Mosaic Law, or anything else for that matter. Without ceremony, without ritual, and without works of any nature, all the person has to do, whether Jew or Gentile, is simply *"believe in Christ, and what He has done for us"* (Jn. 3:16). In essence, this is the greatest *"door"* the world has ever known, and it is open to all!

(28) "AND THERE THEY ABODE LONG TIME WITH THE DISCIPLES."

The direction is:

1. This speaks of the Church at Antioch, Syria, which, without a doubt, had become one of the most important Churches of all time. From here, the Gospel would go to much of the civilized world, with Paul taking the leadership in this great thrust.

2. The *"long time"* here mentioned has been estimated at anywhere from several months to five years. Inasmuch as the Scripture gives no more clues, anyone's guess is as good as the other.

"Arise, my soul, arise! Shake off your guilty fears;
"The bleeding Sacrifice in my behalf appear.
"Before the Throne my surety stands;
"My name is written on His Hands,
"My name is written on His Hands."

CHAPTER 15

(1) "AND CERTAIN MEN WHICH CAME

DOWN FROM JUDAEA TAUGHT THE BRETHREN, AND SAID, EXCEPT YOU BE CIRCUMCISED AFTER THE MANNER OF MOSES, YOU CANNOT BE SAVED."

The form is:

1. Anything given preeminence except the Cross of Christ is instantly rejected by the Lord (I Cor. 1:17).

2. Everything we have from God is made possible by the Cross of Christ, and I mean everything (I Cor. 1:18).

CERTAIN MEN

The phrase, *"And certain men which came down from Judaea taught the brethren,"* presents the greatest crisis of the early church.

These *"certain men"* from *"Judaea"* were from the mother church in Jerusalem but without the authority they claimed to have (Acts 15:24). Consequently, irrespective of who they were, this gave them legitimacy, and for all the obvious reasons. All of the original Twelve apostles considered the Jerusalem church their church home and attended there when they happened to be in the city. The weight of this credibility was awesome, to say the least.

However, this in no way implies that the *"Twelve"* were involved in this *"false doctrine."* Even though it would ultimately have an effect even on Peter (Gal. 2:11-14), they were not its originators.

In this scenario, it is my opinion that James, the Lord's Brother, who served as the pastor or bishop of the church in Jerusalem, did not take the stand at the beginning that he should have taken respecting this false doctrine. Consequently, it made it very difficult for the Apostle Paul and was actually the cause of this first council conducted at Jerusalem respecting church doctrine.

To James' credit, the evidence will show that he properly followed the Lord respecting what was decided at that council. Still, it seems that this problem plagued the church throughout the account given to us through the entirety of the Book of Acts. I feel that James should have included the Jews in his statement that gave freedom to the gentiles. However, it seems that James, as well as all of the other believers in the church in Jerusalem, including all the elders, were trying to wed Christ and the grace of God to the Law of Moses, which could not be done. As stated, it caused untold problems for Paul in world evangelism.

PETER

It must ever be known that Satan does his best work inside the church rather than from without.

If the views broached by these Judean Christians had prevailed, the whole character of Christianity would have been changed and its existence cut short.

In fact, some think that Paul's confrontation with Peter, to which we have just alluded, may have taken place before the council at Jerusalem and could have even precipitated this momentous occasion (Gal. 2:11-14).

Some think that Peter accepting Paul's rebuke preceded him and Barnabas and prepared the way at Jerusalem for the solution ultimately decided.

Indeed, Peter's words at Jerusalem, as we shall see, are almost an echo of Paul's words addressed to him at Antioch.

CIRCUMCISION

The phrase, *"Except you be circumcised after the manner of Moses, you cannot be saved,"* squarely describes the *"Law/grace"* issue. As we have stated, this was the first doctrinal controversy.

The gist of this doctrinal error was that to be saved, the person, be he Jew or gentile, had to accept Jesus Christ as Saviour plus keep the Law of Moses. Whether the proponents of this error understood it or not, in effect, this was saying that the price paid by Christ at Calvary was not enough, and man, consequently, had to add something to that price. In other words, it was saying that Christ's Work was not a finished work, but rather an incomplete work. Of course, there could be no greater insult tendered toward the Lord than that.

However, this problem has persisted from then until now in various and different directions. For instance, many presently believe that in order to be saved, one has to accept Christ plus be baptized in water.

Others claim that one has to accept Christ

NOTES

plus speak in other tongues.

Still others claim that one has to accept Christ plus join their particular church, etc.

All of this, in whatever direction it may take, is identical to the problem that faced the early church. Individuals were attempting to add to the Finished Work of Christ, in this case, the Law of Moses.

A PERSONAL EXPERIENCE

I was speaking once with a preacher, and he happened to mention that a particular denomination punished their preachers in a certain way if a particular preacher failed the Lord in some manner.

I heard him out, and then I said to him, *"In other words, they are saying that Jesus did not suffer enough punishment on the Cross, so other punishment has to be added to what He has already done. In other words, what He did was not a 'Finished Work.'"*

He wheeled around and looked at me very intently for a short period of time and then said, *"I have never thought of that."*

However, that's exactly what their process was doing, claiming that Jesus did not pay the full price and that something has to be added to what He has already paid. There could be nothing more unscriptural than such a position, which I am sure angers God greatly. For anyone to say or even think that what Jesus did at the Cross was insufficient borders on blasphemy, if not blasphemy outright.

WHAT IS THE LAW OF MOSES?

The giving of the Law is found in the Books of Exodus and Leviticus in the Old Testament. However, the balance of the Old Testament, as well as the Four Gospels, proclaims to us Israel's participation in the Law and their terrible failure.

The Law of Moses was actually the Law of God. It was the greatest legislation the world had ever known and, in fact, was the only perfect legislation the world ever knew, addressing itself to every facet of life and living in Israel.

To be sure, there were many laws in the world before the Law of Moses, but they were all devised by man and, consequently, seriously flawed!

The Law, as given to Moses, dealt with every single aspect of human life. It dealt with man's relationship to God, his relationship to his fellowman, and even to the animal kingdom and the environment. It left absolutely nothing undone respecting a pattern for living.

Actually, the Law could be divided into three parts:

1. The moral Law: this included the Ten Commandments.

2. The ceremonial Law: this included the sacrificial system, along with the feast days, the Sabbath, etc.

3. The social Law: this pertained to how Israel dealt with her fellowman in every capacity.

ISRAEL FAR AHEAD OF OTHER NATIONS

This which God gave placed Israel far ahead of all the other nations of the world. Actually, this was the only Law which told man how to live. As stated, it addressed every single part of his existence. It was totally fair, objective, impartial, and straightforward. It did not favor a few while placing an undue burden on others. It was the same for the king as it was the poorest person in Israel.

LAW AND COVENANT IN ISRAEL

In Old Testament history and theology, covenant preceded Law. God made His historic Commitment to Abraham some 430 years before the Law was introduced at Sinai, and the Law made no basic change in the covenant.

It is the covenant that stands as the basis of Israel's relationship with the Lord, and it is the covenant with Abraham to which God will remain faithful.

Law was introduced to meet a need that existed within the context of the covenant. God acted in covenant faithfulness to bring Israel out of Egypt, but Israel's unresponsiveness to God demonstrated that this people needed guidance and structure.

At Sinai, God provided the needed structure. He established guidelines for Israel for living with Him and with others and, as stated, as individuals and in the community. God also made clear the consequences of obedience and disobedience (Deut., Chpt. 28).

The individual or generation that lived in harmony with the divine teaching would receive blessing. The individual or generation that wandered away from the path marked out by Law would be disciplined.

THE FUNCTION OF THE LAW

The Law was designed by God to carry out several things:

• The Law was to show man God's Standard of Righteousness. If it is to be noticed, this Standard is wrapped up in the Ten Commandments. To be sure, these Commandments are so very simple, but despite that, we now find where the next situation comes into play.

• Despite the simplicity of the Law, despite its simple commands, and despite the simplicity of the Ten Commandments, man simply could not keep the Law no matter how hard he tried. So, the Law was given in order to show man how inadequate he was.

Why?

Paul said:

"And if Christ *be* in you *(He is in us through the Power and Person of the Spirit [Gal. 2:20])*, **the body *is* dead because of sin** *(means that the physical body has been rendered helpless because of the Fall; consequently, the Believer trying to overcome by willpower presents a fruitless task)*; **but the Spirit *is* life because of Righteousness** *(only the Holy Spirit can make us what we ought to be, which means we cannot do it ourselves; once again, He performs all that He does within the confines of the Finished Work of Christ)*" **(Rom. 8:10).**

Unfortunately, man refuses to believe that he is incapable of keeping the simple Laws, such as the Ten Commandments; however, the truth is, due to the Fall, which rendered man helpless, the best of us present our lack of capability in carrying out this task. As someone has said, *"The Law is like a mirror which shows man what he is but has no power to change man."*

THE LAW WAS EVER MEANT TO BE TEMPORAL

The Law of Moses, *"the Law of God,"* was given to Israel and meant to last until the coming of the Messiah, which it did.

NOTES

A perfect example of the fading of the Law, even as it was meant to be, is the face of Moses, which did shine after he had been with the Lord (Ex. 34:44). Moses, the Scripture says, *"Put a veil on his face,"* so the people could look at him. Otherwise, his face did shine so brightly that it brought fear to the hearts of the people.

Paul used that experience, and rightly so, and added something that was not given in the Book of Exodus. He said:

"And not as Moses, which put a veil over his face, that the Children of Israel could not steadfastly look to the end of that which is abolished" (II Cor. 3:13).

As the glory on Moses' face faded, such was meant to show that the Law would fade, as well, which it did with Christ, Who fulfilled it all. That is proven by the word *"abolished."*

Paul had several things to say about the Law.

They are:

• **"*Forasmuch as you are* manifestly declared to be the Epistle of Christ ministered by us, written not with ink** *(not as the Law)* **but with the Spirit of the Living God; not in tables of stone** *(the Law)*, **but in fleshly tables of the heart" (II Cor. 3:3).**

He then said:

• **"Who has made us able Ministers of the New Testament** *(the New Covenant)*; **not of the letter** *(the old Law of Moses)*, **but of the Spirit** *(Holy Spirit)*: **for the letter kills** *(refers to the Law; all the Law can do is kill)*, **but the Spirit gives life** *(and does so through Christ, due to what Christ did at the Cross)*" **(II Cor. 3:6).**

He also said:

• **"But if the ministration of death** *(the Law of Moses)*, **written *and* engraved in stones, was glorious** *(and it was)*, **so that the children of Israel could not steadfastly behold the face of Moses for the glory of his countenance; which *glory* was to be done away** *(the glory on Moses' face faded, just as the Law faded as it was intended to when Christ came)*" **(II Cor. 3:7).**

• **"For if that which is done away *was* glorious** *(the Law)*, **much more that which**

remains *is* glorious *(this pertains to the Gospel of Christ, which is forever)*" **(II Cor. 3:11).**

The Law was meant to remain until Christ. When Christ came, He fulfilled the Law in totality and in every capacity. Concerning this, Paul also said:

"For Christ *is* the end of the Law for Righteousness *(Christ fulfilled the totality of the Law)* **to everyone who believes** *(Faith in Christ guarantees the Righteousness which the Law had, but could not give)*" **(Rom. 10:4).**

IT IS CHRIST WHO HAS DELIVERED US

We understand that the Law and faith are opposing principles, which cannot be mixed. Paul insisted that it is for freedom that Christ has set us free (Gal. 5:1).

One who seeks to be justified (to become or to be declared righteous) by the way of Law has been alienated from Christ (Gal. 5:4).

Richards said, *"In effect, Paul is threatening the loss of Salvation. He teaches that the source of Righteousness is known through intimate relationship with and dependence on Jesus. To turn to Law as a path to Righteousness is to turn away from Jesus, which constitutes the loss of the soul."*

Each of these passages develops a common view:

Law must be seen as a total system and evaluated as a system. In other words, one has to accept all of the Law or none of the Law. This was a rebuttal against the Jews attempting to mix Law with grace. It cannot be done!

If the Law is accepted by modern believers as a total system, which it must be if it is to be accepted at all, the following must be understood:

- The Law cannot give life.
- It is opposed to faith as an approach to a relationship with God.
- It actually energizes man's sin nature and produces sin.
- It cannot produce righteousness.

So, to accept that system is to accept a system that was never designed to give salvation. If it could not give salvation under the old covenant, how does one think it can bring salvation under the new?

NOTES

As we have stated, the teeth of Paul's remarks are that if a modern believer is going to attempt to force a part of the Law into grace, he is obligated to take on the whole system. In other words, he must go back to offering sacrifices and keeping the Sabbath, feast days, etc. Of course, he is going to have great difficulty in doing this, considering that it first must be done in Jerusalem, and second, it must be done at and in the Temple. That is going to be difficult considering that there is no Temple.

MODERN LAW AND THE LAW OF MOSES

When law is mentioned, most Christians would automatically state that *"we are now living in the time of grace,"* and the Law is not part of our system. In a sense, they are correct; however, the problem is, virtually every one of these Christians is living in law and by Law and really do not realize it. Let me explain.

If the believer doesn't understand the Cross of Christ as it refers to sanctification, in other words, how we live for God, how we order our behavior, and how we attain to victory over the world, the flesh, and the devil, then such a believer is going to be under the law whether he or she realizes it or not. There are only two places for the believer to be, and that is law or grace. You cannot be in both. Either one cancels out the other. Now, because it's so very important, let me say it again:

For the believer to understand grace and to live under grace, which we are intended to do, such a believer must understand the Cross of Christ as it refers to sanctification. What does that mean?

It means that our faith is to be exclusively in Christ and what Christ did for us at the Cross. In fact, we are admonished by the Lord to *"take up the Cross daily"* (Lk. 9:23). We are to understand that every single thing we receive from the Lord is because of what Jesus did at the Cross. When we speak of the Cross, we aren't speaking of the wooden beam on which Jesus died, but rather what He there did.

He atoned for all sin at the Cross, past, present, and future, at least for all who will believe (Jn. 3:16). In the doing of this, He defeated Satan, all the fallen angels, and all demon spirits (Col. 2:14-15). Knowing we could not do this thing ourselves, God has done it for us by the giving of His Son as a perfect Sacrifice, which gives the Holy Spirit latitude to work in our lives, that is, if our faith is properly placed in Christ and the Cross.

MODERN LAW!

Whenever law is mentioned, most Christians automatically think of the Law of Moses, which they should; however, anything in which we place our faith, in other words, make as the object of our faith, other than Christ and the Cross, is turned into law. To say it another way, things which aren't law within themselves become law whenever we make them the object of our faith.

Many Christians think they can have victory over sin by fasting so many days. While fasting is scriptural, if we try to force it in the position for which it was never designed, that is to give us victory over sin, we turn it into a law. This stops the action of the Holy Spirit, which guarantees failure on the part of the believer. Let me say it again:

Fasting is scriptural. It will bless anyone who functions in this capacity in the right way; however, once the believer tries to force it into a position for which it was never intended, then it becomes a law, which God cannot bless.

One can even turn prayer, the Lord's Supper, water baptism, etc., into a law. Sadly, that's where most believers are.

Now, think about it. Many Christians have been told by some preacher that if they will purchase a Jewish prayer shawl, this will help them to pray more effectively, and God will bless them to a greater degree.

That is pure superstition, which means it's not of God and, in effect, is a sin. Christians are putting their faith in such, which God can never accept. Please allow me to say it again:

God can only accept His Son Jesus Christ and what our Lord has done for us at the Cross. With that being done, the Holy Spirit will work mightily within our lives (Rom. 6:1-14; I Cor. 1:17-18, 23; 22; Gal. 6:14; Col. 2:10-15).

NOTES

HOW DOES THE HOLY SPIRIT WORK?

He will not work in the realm of law. He will only work in the realm of the Cross, which is where the price was paid.

To be sure, we as believers must have the power and the help of the Holy Spirit to live this life. We are facing powers of darkness which are far stronger than we could ever think of being by our own efforts. It is the Holy Spirit alone Who can do in our hearts and lives what needs to be done, but this is something most believers don't know or understand.

If the question were asked to most believers, and when I say most, I mean virtually all, *"How does the Holy Spirit work within our lives?"* most would look at you blankly. They would get a puzzled look on their faces, and if they said anything, it would be, *"Well, He just works."* No, He doesn't just work.

The Holy Spirit is God, meaning that He can do anything; however, He works under a set of guidelines, which will never impugn His Character or His Nature. In other words, He will speak to us, move upon us, and deal with us, but He will never force the issue. To say it another way, if a Christian wants to do something stupid, while he will be warned, that's as far as the Holy Spirit will go. He will allow us to do stupid things if we are so minded to do so, and we will have to pay the consequences.

Before the Cross, the Holy Spirit could not work in the hearts and lives of any believer for any period of time. While He could come into the hearts of certain individuals, such as prophets, etc., to function and help them do what they were called to do, when the work ended, He would vacate the premises, so to speak. In a sense, He was with all believers, but He definitely was not in all believers, at least permanently.

Consequently, due to the fact that the blood of bulls and goats could not take away sins, when believers died, the terrible effects of original sin were still with them, and they were not allowed to go into heaven in their soul and spirit form, but went down into paradise (Lk., Chpt. 16).

However, when Jesus died on the Cross, He paid the total price for the fallen sons of

NOTES

Adam's lost race. He then went down into paradise and delivered all of those who were there, which refers to all Old Testament saints, and brought them out of that place and took them with Him to heaven. Now, due to the Cross, when a believing sinner comes to Christ, instantly, the Holy Spirit comes in, there to abide forever (Jn. 14:16). As well, when the believer dies, his soul and spirit instantly go to heaven because the terrible sin debt (original sin) was erased when Jesus died on the Cross, and such a person accepted Christ as his personal Saviour.

So, the Holy Spirit works exclusively within the parameters of the Finished Work of Christ and will not work outside of those parameters. So, that means that the believer must have as the object of his faith at all times Christ and the Cross.

Paul said, *"For the Law of the Spirit of Life* (Holy Spirit) *in Christ Jesus* (what Christ did for us at the Cross), *has made me free from the Law of Sin and Death"* (Rom. 8:2).

JESUS SATISFIED THE LAW IN EVERY RESPECT

Jesus came to this world as our Representative Man and as our Substitute. That's the reason He was referred to by the Apostle Paul as the *"second Man"* and the *"last Adam"* (I Cor. 15:45-47).

As our Representative Man, Jesus came to do what we could not do for ourselves, which was keep the Law in every capacity. That He did! In the entirety of His Life and Living, He never broke the Law in any capacity, not one single time. We say it again, *"He did this altogether for you and me."*

He then went to the Cross to satisfy the demands of the broken Law, which had been broken by all who had ever lived. He did that by giving Himself as a perfect Sacrifice, which paid the price that God accepted as *"paid in full,"* at least for all who will believe (Jn. 3:16). So, as stated, He was our Representative Man in every respect, doing for us what we could not do for ourselves. Now all that is needed to gain the great victory that He won for us, in effect, to gain all that He did for us, is to exhibit our faith in Him and what He did for us at the Cross, ever making Christ and the Cross the object of our faith. That's the reason Paul said:

"Christ sent me not to baptize, but to preach the Gospel: not with wisdom of words, lest the Cross of Christ should be made of none effect" (I Cor. 1:17).

He also said, *"For the preaching of the Cross is to them who perish foolishness; but unto us who are saved it is the Power of God"* (I Cor. 1:18). That's the reason He said as well, *"For I determined not to know any thing among you save Jesus Christ, and Him Crucified"* (I Cor. 2:2).

It was at the Cross where all victory was won and where all victory is had. In fact, God can meet with sinful man no place other than the Cross, and sinful man can meet with God no place other than the Cross.

The Law was satisfied by our Lord by His Life, and above all, by His Death. That means it is no more, and we are to look at it in the same way.

BUT WHAT ABOUT THE TEN COMMANDMENTS

The Ten Commandments, sometimes referred to as the *"Ten Words,"* constitute the righteousness of God. They are moral and, therefore, cannot change. If it was wrong to lie, cheat, steal, etc., 3,500 years ago, its wrong today. The moral Law of God does not change, as it cannot change, because it is moral. So, yes, the moral Law of God is most definitely incumbent upon us at this present time, but there's a difference in the way that it is kept.

When the believer places his or her faith exclusively in Christ and what Christ has done for us at the Cross, then the Holy Spirit works within us in that the moral Law of God is kept in totality without the believer even having to think about it.

Now, consider the following:

Sin is abhorrent as it regards any believer. In other words, every true believer hates sin and hates it in every capacity. While the flesh may want something that's wrong at times, the inner man doesn't (Rom. 7:22). That's the wonderful thing about the Cross that the Law could never do. Where the Law stimulated sin, the Cross of Christ takes away the desire for sin. Please believe me,

NOTES

there is a vast difference between the two.

How does the Law stimulate sin?

It tells the believer not to do something but gives no power to conduct himself as he should. The Spirit gives power, but again I state, the Holy Spirit works entirely within the parameters of the Cross of Christ, which demands that it ever be the object of our faith.

Under the Law, the only thing that believers had in those days to oppose sin was *"will power,"* which was woefully inadequate. Now, we have the Holy Spirit; however, you must remember, and I state it again, the Holy Spirit does not just work automatically, but rather He functions entirely within the confines of Christ, which demands that Christ and the Cross ever be the object of our faith (Col. 2:10-15; Rom. 8:1-11). The sad fact is, most believers have the help of the Holy Spirit precious little simply because their faith is in something else other than Christ and the Cross. Such a direction is the sure road to spiritual disaster. For such a person, the sin nature is going to rule that person, which makes life miserable. Sadly, due to the fact of not understanding the Cross of Christ relative to our sanctification, most believers are, in fact, ruled by the sin nature (Rom. 6:1-14).

FAITH

The medium of exchange, one might say, that God recognizes is the medium of faith. He will recognize no other.

Paul said, *"For by grace are you saved through faith"* (Eph. 2:8).

He also said: *"Therefore being justified by faith..."* (Rom. 5:1).

He then said, *"By Whom* (the Lord Jesus Christ) *also we have access by faith into this grace"* (Rom. 5:2).

As it regards Law and faith, Paul also said, *"Therefore by the deeds of the Law there shall no flesh be justified in His Sight"* (Rom. 3:20).

He then said, *"But now the Righteousness of God without the Law is manifested... Even the righteousness of God which is by faith of Jesus Christ, unto all and upon all them who believe* (who have faith)*"* (Rom. 3:21-22).

In fact, God is a faith God. What do we mean by that?

Paul also said, concerning this very thing, *"Through faith we understand that the worlds were framed by the Word of God, so that things which are seen were not made of things which do appear"* (Heb. 11:3). In other words, God did not create the universe out of material that was already there, for there was nothing there. By faith, He literally spoke the universe into existence.

That's the reason that the free market system works where socialism will not work. The free market works on faith, while socialism has no faith attached to it whatsoever. So, it simply will not work. Actually, every human being in the world has faith. To be sure, virtually all of it is in the wrong object; nevertheless, they have faith. Even the atheist has faith. Actually, it is faith in himself, but he does have faith.

Of course, none of this faith will God honor. In fact, He honors only one type of faith and that is faith in Christ and what Christ did for us at the Cross (Rom. 6:1-14; 8:1-11; I Cor. 1:17-18, 23; 2:2; Gal. 6:14; Col. 2:10-15).

THE CORRECT OBJECT OF FAITH

As we've just stated, Christ and the Cross must be the object of our faith, and ever the object of our faith. Some would immediately retort and state, *"Well, my faith is in the Word of God."* That is certainly a correct statement and exactly where one's faith ought to be. However, we need to understand what that actually means.

The story of the Bible is the story of *"Jesus Christ and Him Crucified."* John wrote and said:

"In the beginning was the Word, and the Word was with God, and the Word was God" (Jn. 1:1).

This tells us that the entirety of the Word of God is Jesus Christ and what He has done for us. So, if one's faith is truly in the Word of God, it will be in the fact of Jesus Christ and what He did for us at the Cross, which, as stated, is the entirety of the story of the Word of God.

God always honors faith, but it must be faith in Christ and what Christ has done for

NOTES

us at the Cross. That's the coin that spends, so to speak, in the economy of heaven. As we've already stated, every single thing that anyone receives from God, no matter what it is, all and without exception is made possible by the Cross of Christ. Again I state, when I speak of the Cross, I am not speaking of the wooden beam on which Jesus died, but rather what He there accomplished for us. Let us say it one more time:

Every single blessing that comes to the believer from God comes from Christ as the source and the Cross as the means, all superintended by the Holy Spirit (Rom. 8:2).

Jesus Christ satisfied the Law in every respect, and He did it as our Substitute and our Representative Man. Simple faith in Him gives us that for which He has paid the price. I might quickly add, He will not tolerate something else held up to take the place of faith in Christ and the Cross, no matter what the something else is.

Unfortunately, the modern church, and perhaps it's always been that way, jumps from one erroneous fad to the other. It believes anything and everything except that which it ought to believe, which is Christ and Him Crucified. It was to the Apostle Paul that this great truth was given (Gal. 1:1-12). Paul was a very educated man, perhaps the most educated of anyone who wrote the sacred Texts, but he rejected all of that and plainly stated, *"For I determined not to know any thing among you, save Jesus Christ, and Him Crucified"* (I Cor. 2:2).

The Greek word for *"determined"* is *"krino"* and means *"to distinguish, to decide mentally or judicially."*

In other words, it seems that Paul may have had a struggle with this thing, but the Spirit of God got through to him that the only solution for man's dilemma is the Cross of Christ. Understanding that, the great apostle determined not to go in other directions but to give and to keep giving the people that which would set them free, which is *"Jesus Christ and Him Crucified."*

ANOTHER JESUS, ANOTHER SPIRIT, AND ANOTHER GOSPEL

Paul said:

"For if he who comes preaching another Jesus, whom we have not preached, or if you receive another spirit which you have not received, or another gospel, which you have not accepted" (II Cor. 11:4).

What did he mean *"another Jesus, another spirit, and another gospel?"*

He meant that if Jesus is preached outside of the Cross, in other words, the Cross is eliminated and Jesus only is proclaimed, such would be *"another Jesus, which produces another spirit, which plays out to another gospel."* Sadly and regrettably, that is where the majority of the modern church presently is. The modern church is ignoring the Cross, whether out of ignorance or whether out of a deliberate rejection. Consequently, the Jesus they hold up is not the Jesus of the Bible, but rather a Jesus of their own manufacture. In fact, the world has ever tried to replace God with a god of their own making. Regrettably, the church has ever tried to replace the Cross with a sacrifice of their own making.

AND FINALLY

Some would ask the question, *"Brother Swaggart, aren't we supposed to keep the Ten Commandments?"*

We most definitely are!

Its not a question of should they be kept, but how they are to be kept is the great question.

If any believer sets out to try to keep the Ten Commandments, which means he is reverting to law, he will fail every single time simply because the Holy Spirit will not condone such.

When we accept Christ, we have accepted everything that He did for us at the Cross. What does the Word of God say about the Ten Commandments and, in fact, the entirety of the Law?

Paul also wrote: *"Blotting out the handwriting of ordinances that was against us, which was contrary to us, and took it out of the way, nailing it to His Cross."*

He then said: *"And having spoiled principalities and powers, He made a show of them openly, triumphing over them in it"* (Col. 2:14-15).

So, Jesus has kept the Law perfectly and in every respect. When we make Him the

Lord of our lives, we don't really have to worry about any law or law of any kind because our faith is exclusively in Christ. That being done, the Holy Spirit will automatically keep the Ten Commandments and every other thing that we ought to do as well. We have Him as our constant Helper, and please understand, the Holy Spirit is God, and He can do anything.

I never get up in the morning and wonder how I'm going to keep the Ten Commandments that day. They never cross my mind. But yet, I do keep them because my faith is exclusively in Christ and the Cross. This great thing is done and carried out in my life by the Holy Spirit and through my faith in Christ without my having to do anything else other than exhibit faith.

(2) "WHEN THEREFORE PAUL AND BARNABAS HAD NO SMALL DISSENSION AND DISPUTATION WITH THEM, THEY DETERMINED THAT PAUL AND BARNABAS, AND CERTAIN OTHER OF THEM, SHOULD GO UP TO JERUSALEM UNTO THE APOSTLES AND ELDERS ABOUT THIS QUESTION."

The pattern is:

1. When it comes to Bible doctrine, the Cross of Christ must always be understood as the foundation of all Bible doctrine.

2. All false doctrine begins with a false interpretation or ignoring of the Cross of Christ.

NOTES

NO SMALL DISSENSION

The phrase, *"When therefore Paul and Barnabas had no small dissension and disputation with them,"* seems to indicate that these men came to Antioch not long after Paul and Barnabas had returned from their first missions tour.

They evidently began to teach the doctrine of adding Law to grace, even being very explicit, and denying Salvation to all who did not comply.

The word *"dissension"* in the Greek text is *"stasis"* and means, at least in this instance, *"a strong controversy."*

The word *"disputation"* in the Greek text is *"suzetesis"* and means, *"to investigate, question, and dispute."*

When this false doctrine began to be promoted by these teachers, it was immediately contested by Paul and Barnabas. However, inasmuch as these men had come from Jerusalem, this gave them a certain status and legitimacy. Nevertheless, irrespective of its source, Paul knew this teaching to be false and if allowed to make inroads, could greatly subvert the cause of Christ, and would actually greatly weaken and ultimately destroy all for which Jesus had died at Calvary.

Why was it that the Jewish segment of the church at that time seemed determined to hold onto the Mosaic Law?

SIXTEEN HUNDRED YEARS OF LAW

It was very difficult for some of them to admit or to understand that the great Mosaic Law was no longer needed. For about 1,600 years, Israel, i.e., Jews, had a monopoly on the Word of God. In other words, if any gentile wanted the Lord, he had to go through the Jews, i.e., the Mosaic Law, to obtain that which he desired. Now that the Jews, along with their Temple rituals and ceremonies, were no longer needed, such did not set very well. The Law, or their perverted versions, was the totality of their lives and existence. Now, to suddenly be told that all of this, which figured so minutely in every single thing they did, was to be set aside and, in effect, play no part whatsoever was more than most could handle.

Had they treated the Law as it should have been treated, understanding that all of its rituals and ceremonies pointed to Christ and were actually symbolic of Him and, therefore, made void by His Coming, they would have had little difficulty. However, they had made salvation out of the Law, or had attempted to do so; consequently, they had lost all understanding as to what the Law really was.

AN IMPROPER UNDERSTANDING OF JESUS

It seems in some way that some of these teachers were willing to forego some of the Law. For instance, the Law required that all sacrifices must be offered up in Jerusalem and more particularly, at the Temple. Consequently, this would have made it well

NOTES

nigh impossible for most gentiles then, with some living 1,000 or more miles away from that city. So, it seems that some of them may have been willing to forego some parts of the Law but maintain other rituals, such as circumcision or Sabbath-keeping.

This shows that they not only had an improper understanding of Jesus and Who He was and what He had done, but that they little understood the Law as well! The very nature of *"law"* demands that all of it be kept, or else, the person is a lawbreaker. One was not free to pick and choose as one is not free to pick and choose regarding obedience to any law. Nevertheless, strong elements in the Jerusalem church were still trying to hold onto the Law, or at least some parts of it, and to force gentiles to comply.

Also, it should be quickly noted that the task of contending for the faith seemed to have pretty much been laid at the feet of Paul. It is not a pleasant task to disagree with someone, even strongly so, as this Text implies. Enemies are made this way. Consequently, most preachers simply will not take a stand. Whatever is popular, they bend to that wind.

CONFRONTING ERROR

However, irrespective as to how unpopular it may be, how many enemies one may make, or how distasteful the situation, it is incumbent upon God-called men and women to confront error and to do so boldly and without compromise. One must ever understand that we are dealing with the eternal souls of men, and as such, the true way of salvation must never be weakened.

Most of the time, false doctrine comes into the church on the back of truth. Actually, that is the most lethal of all. Had these men totally repudiated grace, which meant to repudiate Christ, they would not have had many takers, but when they held up Christ as the Saviour of man, which they seemed to have done, it gave legitimacy to their error.

However, it is impossible to trust Christ and works at the same time. Either Christ paid it all, or He paid it not at all!

It is the same with modernistic psychology. Men can claim to believe and trust Christ, but if they resort to this humanistic approach, attempting to wed Christ and psychology, they always conclude with a psychologized Christ, who is, as Paul said, *"Another Jesus"* (II Cor. 11:4).

The phrase, *"They determined that Paul and Barnabas, and certain other of them, should go up to Jerusalem unto the apostles and elders about this question,"* no doubt, refers to the trip mentioned by Paul in Galatians 2:1-10.

WENT UP BY REVELATION

This tells us that this particular problem was widespread and beginning to make strong inroads into the churches. Some even think that these Judaizers had also made a sweep through Galatia, which necessitated Paul writing the Book of Galatians sometime after his return from this all-important trip to Jerusalem.

It was very necessary that this council be conducted in Jerusalem about this matter in order that it be settled once and for all. If the original Twelve did not go along with the message of grace without additions, Paul knew that his task would be all but impossible.

I believe that Paul sought the Lord earnestly concerning this very important matter, with the Lord revealing to him the necessity of this council. That is why he said, *"And I went up by revelation, and communicated unto them that Gospel which I preach among the gentiles"* (Gal. 2:2).

The pronoun *"they"* of Verse 2 speaks of the elders in the church at Antioch deciding along with Paul and Barnabas as to the necessity of this trip.

Titus went with them and possibly others as well (Gal. 2:3).

(3) "AND BEING BROUGHT ON THEIR WAY BY THE CHURCH, THEY PASSED THROUGH PHENICE AND SAMARIA, DECLARING THE CONVERSION OF THE GENTILES: AND THEY CAUSED GREAT JOY UNTO ALL THE BRETHREN."

The pattern is:

1. The phrase, *"And being brought on their way by the church,"* simply means that the church at Antioch paid the expenses of the brethren respecting this trip.

2. The phrase, *"They passed through*

Phenice and Samaria," would have taken them due south, pretty close to the coast of the Mediterranean, through Sidon and Tyre. They probably then journeyed to Ptolemais and then to Caesarea, turning southeast to go into Samaria and then to Jerusalem.

3. *"Declaring the conversion of the gentiles,"* indicates that they stopped to visit churches all along the way.

Of all the things Paul related in these churches, the conversion of the gentiles seemed to be the main theme. He, no doubt, told how they came to Christ, were baptized in water, and were baptized with the Holy Spirit.

The churches in Phoenicia were mostly made up of Jewish believers, with those in Samaria made up of Samaritans who thought of themselves as part Jewish.

4. The phrase, *"And they caused great joy unto all the brethren,"* seems to indicate that the Judaizers had not brought their false doctrine to these churches. They probably reasoned that inasmuch as Paul had not planted these particular churches, they believed exactly as they (the Judaizers) believed. This referred to all gentiles becoming Jews, that is, if they were to be saved. However, these Jews and Samaritans met Paul's testimony of gentile conversions with *"great joy."* In other words, they did not at all question the grace of God.

(4) "AND WHEN THEY HAD COME TO JERUSALEM, THEY WERE RECEIVED OF THE CHURCH, AND OF THE APOSTLES AND ELDERS, AND THEY DECLARED ALL THINGS THAT GOD HAD DONE WITH THEM."

The way is:

1. The phrase, *"And when they had come to Jerusalem, they were received of the church,"* indicates they were received with open arms.

2. It seems these Judaizers (Acts 15:1), with whom Paul and Barnabas had strongly disputed respecting the Law/grace issue, had not returned back to Jerusalem but had gone on into Galatia, etc. Even though there were other Judaizers present, as we shall soon see, the original group was not there.

3. The phrase, *"And of the apostles and elders,"* undoubtedly referred to the Twelve minus James, the brother of John, who had been martyred. If all were present, and it seems they were, this would have been the only occasion of such a gathering when Paul was present (Gal. 2:9).

NOTES

4. When one thinks of this meeting, irrespective of the doctrinal questions addressed, with the simple presence of all the Apostles of our Lord and then Paul, it is well nigh impossible to fully understand the contribution this group has made to our lives and civilization in general! Of all the great men who have ever lived, with all the feats of arms, the contribution made by these apostles to the whole of humanity, and for all time, has no equal! There is one overriding factor in all of this, which far supersedes who these men were, and that is Who had chosen them and of Whom they had witnessed. I speak of Jesus, the Son of the Living God! Even though Paul's experience with Christ had been of short duration, with him saying, *"And last of all He was seen of me also, as of one born out of due time,"* still, that one Appearance would change him for time and eternity (I Cor. 15:8). When one understands that these Twelve had walked with Jesus for at least an approximate three and one-half years, but above all, had been witnesses of His Resurrection, then the magnitude of this meeting begins to register.

The *"elders"* were the pastors of the many house churches throughout Jerusalem and surrounding areas.

5. *"And they declared all things that God had done with them,"* no doubt, represented a survey of their recent missions trip into Cyprus, Pisidia, and Pamphylia.

6. Considering the following verse, Paul and Barnabas, with Barnabas probably taking the lead because he was well known in Jerusalem, no doubt, related the conversion of the gentiles by simple faith in Christ. With some there, this would not set well, as we shall see!

(5) "BUT THERE ROSE UP CERTAIN OF THE SECT OF THE PHARISEES WHICH BELIEVED, SAYING, THAT IT WAS NEEDFUL TO CIRCUMCISE THEM, AND TO COMMAND THEM TO KEEP THE LAW OF MOSES."

NOTES

The account is:

1. This meeting that was attended by Paul and Barnabas had as its foundation the Cross of Christ.

2. Was the Cross sufficient upon simple faith to proclaim man as justified?

THE PHARISEES

The phrase, *"But there rose up certain of the sect of the Pharisees which believed,"* refers to them as having accepted Christ as their Saviour. They were in the church at Jerusalem.

As we have stated, there could have been as many as 50,000 believers at that time in Jerusalem, and possibly even more, who had accepted Christ as their Saviour. As well, virtually all of these people were continuing to honor the Law of Moses respecting circumcision, Sabbaths, feast days, and, no doubt, sacrifices, in other words, the entirety of the Law of Moses.

"Saying, That it was needful to circumcise them, and to command them to keep the Law of Moses," presents that which was the great controversy.

The testimony which Paul and Barnabas had given to the apostles and elders was absolutely phenomenal, to say the least. The testimony was respecting the thousands of people who had come to Christ, mostly gentiles, with a number of churches planted in these respective areas. Even though the salvation of these people had caused heaven to shout, it seems not to have had that effect upon these Judaizers, but rather the opposite. They began to find fault with their conversion, claiming they must also become proselyte Jews. This is the manner of false doctrine.

What the Lord has done and is doing is of little consequence to those who have turned their eyes away from Jesus onto peripheral matters. False doctrine has that effect on people. They lose sight of that which is really important and begin to major on minors.

These Pharisees thought Christianity should be added to the Law, but the reverse is true. As Galatians 3:19 indicates, the Law was added to the promise, not the other way around. As well, it was added only temporarily *"Till the Seed should come to whom the promise was made."* That Seed is Christ.

It being blatantly obvious that these people were adding to the Finished Work of Christ, the question must be asked if they were genuinely saved.

The same question could be asked of those presently who would add water baptism, the Lord's Supper, tongues, etc.

This question becomes even more significant when one realizes that Paul, addressing this very issue, was inspired by the Holy Spirit to write, *"Christ is become of no effect unto you, whosoever of you are justified by the Law* (attempt to be justified by the Law); *you are fallen from grace"* (Gal. 5:4).

Regarding individual salvation, the answer to this all-important question must be left up to the Lord. Only He knows the hearts of men. As well, He is very patient with all of us, and thank God a thousand times over that He is. If not, I don't know where any of us would be!

LEAVEN

However, Paul labeled false doctrine as *"leaven."* If that *"leaven"* is allowed to remain, it will ultimately corrupt the whole. He said, again concerning this very issue, *"A little leaven leavens the whole lump"* (Gal. 5:9).

When the Lord gives light to any believer, as He always does, He expects that believer to walk in that light, pointing out false doctrine, plus many other situations as well. If the light is ignored, even as it is by many, it will ultimately be withdrawn. Light rejected is light removed.

However, the believer, who is now believing wrong, never remains static but, as well, loses what little light he has previously had. Jesus graphically described this in the parable of the talents.

The man who had one talent and hid it in the ground lost even that talent, for it was taken from him and given to the one who had the most (Mat. 25:14-30).

For instance, the *"leaven"* of unconditional eternal security has been embraced by our Southern Baptist friends for many, many years. This *"leaven"* has now corrupted the whole until that is about all that remains. They were once great soul-winners, and, of course, some few still are; however, for the most part, what light they did have has been removed as well.

HUMANISTIC PSYCHOLOGY

The same could be said for our United Pentecostal friends, who have tried to make works a part of salvation by demanding that certain things be added to the Finished Work of Christ, such as water baptism by a particular baptismal formula, speaking with other tongues, etc. Due to this *"leaven,"* about all that is left among these good people is legalism.

From an entirely different perspective, most of the other Pentecostal denominations, such as the Assemblies of God, the Church of God, etc., have embraced the *"leaven"* of humanistic psychology. Little by little, that's about all that is left in the Church of God and is fastly going in that direction respecting the Assemblies of God.

I would hope the reader would understand that these remarks are meant to be constructive and not the opposite. To call attention to error is not pleasant and, to be sure, gains no popularity. To be factual, this stand has pretty well turned the entirety of the church world against me, and on a very personal basis I might add. Consequently, I am very familiar with the statement of the Apostle Paul, *"At my first answer no man stood with me, but all men forsook me: I pray God that it may not be laid to their charge"* (II Tim. 4:16).

TO OPPOSE FALSE DOCTRINE

I realize that most think other things were the cause. No, that was the excuse. The real reason was what I preached and that for which I stood and continue to stand!

As I have stated, to oppose false doctrine, even though one attempts to do so most congenially, seldom brings any accolades, but rather the very opposite. Satan never stops. Two thousand years ago, it was the Law of Moses which was the issue. Down through the centuries and presently, it is a variation on that same demand or other things; nevertheless, the intention of Satan is always the same, and that is to compromise the Gospel of Jesus Christ. Thank God for Paul and others like him, who have been willing to take a stand, irrespective of the cost.

NOTES

One day we all will stand before God, and to be sure, at that time, it will not matter what men thought, but what God thought, for it is to Him that all must answer.

This was the third time Paul visited Jerusalem (Acts 9:26; 11:30).

(6) "AND THE APOSTLES AND ELDERS CAME TOGETHER FOR TO CONSIDER OF THIS MATTER."

The diagram is:

1. This meeting by the *"apostles and elders"* was surely to be one of the most important meetings ever conducted. As we have stated, if Satan could weaken the early church with false doctrine, the *"leaven"* would ultimately corrupt the whole. So, *"this matter"* of adding the Law of Moses to the grace of God was of utmost significance. It was an issue that had to be faced and addressed and, thankfully, was. Part of the responsibility of being an *"apostle and elder"* is to address these very important issues. As well, the criterion for all such things must ever be the Word of God.

2. As is obvious, I think, this was not a closed meeting, but rather played out before many believers.

3. It seems that the proponents for the Law of Moses stirred up all to their side whom they could, which would possibly have made the crowd quite large.

4. Also, it is very good, at least in matters of this nature, to make it all public. Everyone then has their say with nothing hidden.

(7) "AND WHEN THERE HAD BEEN MUCH DISPUTING, PETER ROSE UP, AND SAID UNTO THEM, MEN AND BRETHREN, YOU KNOW HOW THAT A GOOD WHILE AGO GOD MADE CHOICE AMONG US, THAT THE GENTILES BY MY MOUTH SHOULD HEAR THE WORD OF THE GOSPEL, AND BELIEVE."

The form is:

1. The entirety of this meeting was to answer the question, *"Is the Cross of Christ enough, or is something else needed?"*

2. In fact, that is the situation as it

involves all doctrine.

MUCH DISPUTING

The phrase, *"And when there had been much disputing,"* simply means much questioning and discussion. The idea from the Greek text does not seem to be that of argument, but rather a sincere desire from all concerned to find a scriptural answer to this question.

Consequently, the Word of God regarding faith and the Law of Moses must have been discussed strongly.

As well, it seems that both Peter and Paul remained silent during the time of the discussion, which was quite lengthy. That way, everything could be laid on the table with all having their say.

The phrase, *"Peter rose up, and said unto them,"* portrays the apostle in the position of leadership, at least at this particular meeting. I should think the necessity of this should be obvious.

SIMON PETER

This does not mean that the Holy Spirit favored him above all others, but that he had been chosen by the Spirit even from the beginning as a spokesman for the Twelve. So, in this climate, it was proper for him to speak first, which the Holy Spirit, no doubt, instigated.

"Men and brethren, you know how that a good while ago God made choice among us, that the gentiles by my mouth should hear the Word of the Gospel, and believe," harks back some 10 to 12 years to Peter's experience with Cornelius (Acts, Chpt. 10).

It seems that in all of this time, no one had referred to Cornelius, which tells us that the church in Jerusalem had not put the proper interpretation on that great moment, nor did they realize its implications. In fact, if they had, this meeting would not have been necessary.

So, they evidently thought that this was merely a personal experience with Peter, consequently, having no bearing on the overall plan of God. How so blind are most of us concerning the things of God! How so obvious they are at times, and yet, so hard for us to see!

NOTES

PAUL'S STAND FOR THE TRUTH

This shows us that before Acts, Chapter 10, gentiles had not been given the Gospel, and basically, only by Paul and Barnabas after then and up to this point. It also seems that Peter had not followed through as he should after the vision experience in Acts, Chapter 10.

The situation which took place at Antioch with the false teachers coming in (Acts 15:1), to which we have already alluded, very well could have been the time of which Paul spoke when he confronted Peter *"to the face"* (Gal. 2:11).

While Peter did not come with these *"certain men"* (Acts 15:1), already being there when they arrived it seems, still, he was greatly influenced, and in the wrong direction we might quickly add, by their false teaching. In fact, Barnabas was adversely affected as well (Gal. 2:13).

Nevertheless, both Peter and Barnabas, thankfully, responded favorably to Paul's admonition and repented of their false direction. In fact, this confrontation, as stated, could very well have caused the council at Jerusalem.

THE CHRONOLOGY

Peter, accepting Paul's rebuke, could have preceded him and Barnabas to Jerusalem and prepared the way, causing James to have everything in preparation for the time Paul and Barnabas would arrive.

Actually, Peter's words now given are very similar to Paul's words addressed to him at Antioch (Gal. 2:14-21).

If the chronology is correct concerning Peter, this shows us the humility of this man who could take a rebuke from Paul, even publicly before all others (Gal. 2:14), and not allow such to harbor and fester within his heart. As well, every evidence is that he not only accepted Paul's rebuke but, as well, fully embraced the truth which Paul expounded.

So, it was necessary, as stated, that Peter speak first in that Paul may not have been accepted otherwise.

Peter's expression, *"That the gentiles by my mouth should hear the Word of the*

Gospel," seems to imply, as well, that he realized he had not been as faithful to follow up with this as he should have. If so, the church in Jerusalem possibly would not have been in this quandary. As well, he would not have been so easily persuaded as he was at Antioch by these false teachers.

When God gives us something, it must be acted upon, or it will die!

(8) "AND GOD, WHICH KNOWS THE HEARTS, BEAR THEM WITNESS, GIVING THEM THE HOLY SPIRIT, EVEN AS HE DID UNTO US."

The overview is:

1. Even though we have stated the case, still, due to its significance, it must be understood that the Cross of Christ is really the basis of the argument.

2. Did Jesus pay it all, or was something left to be desired?

GOD KNOWS THE HEART

The phrase, *"And God, which knows the hearts,"* speaks of this action being of the Lord and not of Peter, or any other human being for that matter!

The idea is that God searches the hearts of people, basing His decisions and actions on this factor, and not on particular man-made rules and regulations, etc. As well, the Lord did not ask Israel, the early church, or Peter for that matter, as to what He could do. Neither does He ask anyone today! The idea is that we follow Him, not that He follow us. For us to do anything less is to abrogate the headship of Christ regarding the church. It is sad, but most preachers (and I think I exaggerate not) look little to the Lord, but rather to men.

The phrase, *"Bear them witness,"* has to do with that which God deems as evidence. The evidence of most is approval by men, while with God, it is the moving and operation of the Holy Spirit.

WILL RELIGIOUS MEN ACCEPT THIS WITNESS

Sadly and tragically, most do not! In truth, the moving and operation of the Holy Spirit is the very witness they do not want. In other words, they bitterly oppose this witness.

The reason the Pharisees opposed Christ was because of the moving and operation of the Holy Spirit within His Life and Ministry. That is the reason much of the modern church world opposes the true church; it is because of this *"witness."*

Concerning the leaders of some Pentecostal denominations, I once thought that if they would just come to our meetings, they would see that the Lord was present and, consequently, would not oppose us so greatly. However, I finally came to realize that the moving and operation of the Holy Spirit was the very reason they were opposing us.

In truth, this is the dividing line for the entirety of the church. Irrespective of other excuses projected, it boils down to the Holy Spirit. Some few want Him, while most do not! Actually, even many of those who claim to want Him, in truth, do not!

THE HOLY SPIRIT

The phrase, *"Giving them the Holy Spirit, even as He did unto us,"* means that the Holy Spirit being given according to Acts 2:4 proved that they had truly been born-again. The simple fact looms large that the Holy Spirit cannot abide a Temple which has not been thoroughly cleansed and washed by the precious blood of Jesus. In other words, the unbeliever cannot receive the Holy Spirit (Jn. 14:17).

Even though the Holy Spirit definitely comes into the heart and life of the believer at conversion, which is the regeneration process, still, this is not that of which Peter spoke. Had it stopped there, the Jews in the early church could have easily denied what Cornelius and his household actually received. However, inasmuch as they were also baptized with the Holy Spirit with the evidence of speaking with other tongues, the same that happened on the Day of Pentecost, this was concrete proof that they had truly been saved, and without all of the Jewish rituals and ceremonies. Consequently, it was hardly possible for anyone to deny the experience of Cornelius and the others.

Even though I dare not take this too far, still, considering that such was done by the Holy Spirit, I want to press the point that if the believer does not go on and be baptized with the Holy Spirit, his spiritual growth is

NOTES

NOTES

going to be considerably hindered, as should be obvious. As well, the baptism with the Holy Spirit is always with the evidence of speaking with other tongues. To ignore this great gift freely supplied to us by the Lord is a travesty indeed!

(9) "AND PUT NO DIFFERENCE BETWEEN US AND THEM, PURIFYING THEIR HEARTS BY FAITH."

The order is:

1. The Cross of Christ is the Gospel (I Cor. 1:17).

2. If one properly accepts the Cross, one has properly accepted the Gospel.

NO DIFFERENCE

The phrase, *"And put no difference between us and them,"* tells us plainly that the Lord now deals with both Jews and gentiles alike. Actually, He deals with the entirety of the world on the same basis, irrespective of race, nationality, color, gender, etc.

While looking at the two words *"no difference,"* I think we should look at some of the modern efforts, such as *"Jews for Jesus,"* or other such like efforts.

On the surface, such does not seem to be wrong; however, to make a distinction solely on the basis of race, nationality, or color is unwise.

The early church, which is our pattern, had people of all sorts in its confines, as it should be. In other words, slaves sat by the side of wealthy landowners, etc. All were one, as all should be one. Paul said, *"Where there is neither Greek nor Jew, circumcision nor uncircumcision, barbarian, Scythian, bond nor free: but Christ is all, and in all"* (Col. 3:11).

So, for modern Jews, even though they have accepted Christ, to have meetings exclusively for Jews simply because they are Jews is an abrogation, I think, of these very words of Paul.

For persons to meet of similar nationality because of language barriers is understandable; however, otherwise, it presents a message to the world, whether we realize such or not, which, in effect, says there are several different types of salvation, or that God deals with some differently than others, which is false! The body of Christ is one body and made up of all types of people from every different background.

PURIFYING THEIR HEARTS BY FAITH

That is one reason that all the myriad of denominations are wrong. While I realize this will not be remedied until the return of Christ, still, the various interpretations of the Word of God have caused great problems in the church, as should be obvious. Paul's great question still looms large, *"Is Christ divided?"* (I Cor. 1:13).

The phrase, *"Purifying their hearts by faith,"* simply means this is the only way the evil hearts of men can be purified.

Purity of the heart and not ceremonial washing of the body is what God requires and what this new covenant provided. The idea is this:

To be purified by faith means that one trusts Christ respecting what He did at Calvary and the Resurrection. He paid the price for our sins, in effect, satisfying that terrible debt.

Understanding that all of this was done for sinners and knowing that we could not do such for ourselves, having faith in Christ and what He wondrously did automatically purifies the heart. With the unrighteousness being taken away, the Lord instantly imputes His Righteousness to the believing sinner (Jn. 3:16).

If one attempts to purify the heart in any other way, such as good works, religious ceremonies, or even the rightful ordinances of the church, such as water baptism or the Lord's Supper, the heart will not be purified because there can be no purity on that basis. It is all by faith in Christ (Eph. 2:8-9).

Consequently, that shoots down circumcision, Sabbath-keeping, or anything else one may do.

(10) "NOW THEREFORE WHY TEMPT YOU GOD, TO PUT A YOKE UPON THE NECK OF THE DISCIPLES, WHICH NEITHER OUR FATHERS NOR WE WERE ABLE TO BEAR?"

The direction is:

1. The beginning of the question, *"Now therefore why tempt you God...?"* presents a question that is serious indeed!

2. The word *"tempt"* in the Greek Text

is *"peirazo"* and means *"to put to the test, because of unbelief."*

3. It is actually the calling into question that which God has done, and more importantly, the greatest act of all, the Finished Work of Christ.

God had already made known His Will respecting what He did for Cornelius and his household. Why does the situation have to be approached again? In other words, this meeting in Jerusalem was very, very necessary; however, it was necessary only because of the unbelief of some. Had they taken God at His Word, this question of forcing the gentiles to enter into the Law of Moses would never have arisen.

As the songwriter said, *"Oh what needless pain we bear."*

3. The conclusion of the question, *"To put a yoke upon the neck of the disciples, which neither our fathers nor we were able to bear?"* was not meant by Peter to speak disparagingly of the Law of Moses.

4. The idea is that even though the Law of Moses was from God and, as such, was wonderful, righteous, and holy, still, its demands were beyond the ability of any human being to meet. So, why saddle the gentiles with something that the Jews could not do themselves and, in fact, was now completely unnecessary?

5. Why is it that some believers enjoy attempting to make Christianity a hard yoke to bear? Jesus plainly said, *"For My yoke is easy, and My burden is light"* (Mat. 11:30).

(11) "BUT WE BELIEVE THAT THROUGH THE GRACE OF THE LORD JESUS CHRIST WE SHALL BE SAVED, EVEN AS THEY."

The construction is:

1. As we study this controversy in the Book of Acts, which is of great significance, we come to realize, as previously stated, that the argument, whether realized or not, is always concerning the Cross.

2. When anything is exposed for what it really is, we find that the question is always about the Cross, whether realized or not.

THE GRACE OF GOD

Verse 11 records the last words of Peter recorded in the Book of Acts.

NOTES

There are several key words in this statement which serve as the very foundation of the Gospel. They are as follows:

- *"Believe"*: the Greek word for *"believe"* is *"pisteuo"* and means *"to have faith in or to put in trust with."* This is the very key to Christianity.

However, as it is extremely significant that a person *"believe,"* it is even more important *"what"* one believes. Actually, this was the very reason for this council in Jerusalem.

Some were believing that the Law had to be added to grace in order for one to be saved. Peter, as Paul, proclaimed this error as a faulty faith structure. Actually, the situation was far more critical than appears on the surface.

The Judaizers were maintaining that the Law had to be added to grace, while, in essence, the apostles were saying that this not only didn't have to be done, but, in fact, if this adding of Law was done, or anything else for that matter, salvation was forfeited.

- *"Grace"*: the Greek word for *"grace"* is *"charis"* and means *"divine favor granted without works or merit."* However, even though such is available to all, it cannot be triggered without faith. In essence, faith unlocks this door of grace, but we must quickly add, it must be faith in Christ and what He has done for us at the Cross.

Understanding that, we see how that it is literally impossible for Law or any type of works to be added. In fact, if such is done, it is no longer grace but merit, which God cannot accept. Paul would later write, *"And if by grace, is it no more of works: otherwise grace is no more grace"* (Rom. 11:5-6).

GRACE ON THE PART OF GOD

God has no more grace presently under New Testament guidelines than He did under Old Testament guidelines. The situation was not the degree of grace but the fact that original sin, which could not be addressed by the blood of bulls and goats, hindered the dispensing of such. And yet, God showed grace and gave grace in Old Testament times whenever and wherever He could. The Cross of Christ, of which we will say more directly, changed everything.

God delights in doing good things for His Children. He delights in blessing us and giving to us, which is grace in operation.

JESUS AND GRACE

Jesus is the One Who has made all grace possible in that He opened the door wide by the Sacrifice of Himself on the Cross of Calvary. The Cross is what made it possible for God to grant grace presently in copious quantities, which He could not do in Old Testament times. It is ever the Cross! The Cross! The Cross!

Whereas the blood of bulls and goats could not take away sins (Heb. 10:4), the Cross, in fact, did take away all sin, past, present, and future. That's what John the Baptist was talking about when he said to Jesus:

"Behold the Lamb of God which takes away the sin of the world" (Jn. 1:29).

The Cross of Christ removed the terrible sin debt, paid the price in full, and satisfied the demands of a thrice-Holy God, thereby, opening the door for *"whosoever will."* It broke down the barrier between Jew and gentile, between rich and poor, and between great and small. It is the Cross which made the difference, and which makes the difference.

Whenever the believer comes before the Father in the name of Jesus, due to what the Name represents and what our Lord has done for us at the Cross, such a person is instantly given admittance to the very throne of God. That's the reason that John the Beloved wrote in closing out the great Book of Revelation:

"And the Spirit and bride say, Come. And let him who hears say, Come. And let him who is athirst, come. And let whosoever will, let him take the water of life freely" (Rev. 22:17).

What a sweeping statement! What a sweeping invitation! The Holy Spirit extends an invitation to the entirety of the world and the bride of Christ, which incorporates every single believer, and says *"Whosoever will, let him take the water of life freely."* It's an open-ended invitation. It doesn't matter who the person is, what the person has done, or how evil and black the sins, Calvary covered it all! Let us say it again:

It is the Cross of Christ that makes the grace of God possible.

Even in the Old Testament times, still, every iota of grace was extended on the premise of faith in what the sacrifices represented. Having faith in that lamb that was slain, and the blood that was shed from that little animal, really could not effect anything, but faith and trust in what that represented most definitely could bring about the covering of sin. While it could not take sin away, it could cover it. It took the blood of Jesus Christ at Calvary's Cross to *"take all sin away."* That's the reason that we can say:

"The believer has no past, while Satan has no future."

If we try to divorce the Cross of Christ from the dispensing of grace, we have just closed the door to grace. Unfortunately, most modern believers little understand the part the Cross plays in the grace of God.

THE DISPENSATION OF GRACE

Many believers think because this is the Dispensation of Grace, and it definitely is, that such is automatic with God. In other words, He just automatically dispenses grace because it is the Dispensation of Grace. Nothing could be further from the truth. Please notice what Paul said:

"I do not frustrate the Grace of God; for if righteousness come by the Law, then Christ is dead in vain" (Gal. 2:21).

What does it mean to *"frustrate the grace of God?"*

The word *"frustrate"* in the Greek is *"atheteo"* and means *"to neutralize or violate, to disannul, to bring to naught."*

That simply means that the grace of God stops toward such a person.

Why?

That which Paul was addressing concerned the Galatians who were listening to false teachers and were trying to add something to the Cross of Christ, such as Law. If our faith is in anything other than Christ and the Cross, we frustrate the grace of God. We must never forget the following: every single thing we receive from God comes through Jesus Christ as the Source, and we mean everything, but all of it is made possible by the Cross. In other words, were it not for the Cross, God could not even look at us, much less give us an audience into the very throne room of grace. If the believer doesn't understand the Cross of Christ respecting sanctification, in other words, how we live for God and how we order our behavior, then such a person is going to frustrate the grace of God. He will do so because his faith is in something other than the Cross. His situation may be because of lack of knowledge, or it may be because of rebellion, but the end result will be the same—frustrating the grace of God.

FALLING FROM GRACE

Paul also said:

"Christ has become of no effect unto you, whosoever of you are justified by the Law; you are fallen from grace" (Gal. 5:4).

WHAT DOES IT MEAN TO FALL FROM GRACE

It means to fall from the position of grace to the position of law, which no sane person wants to do.

To make the explanation short, falling from grace refers to the believer placing his or her faith in something other than Christ and the Cross, and it doesn't really matter what the *"other"* is.

Unfortunately, most Christians believe that when a fellow Christian sins, he falls from grace. Nothing could be further from the truth. Were that the truth, then every believer, because there are no perfect believers, would be in a fallen state, which, of course, is basely incorrect. Let us say it again:

The grace of God is given to believers, even though grossly undeserving, simply because of what Jesus did at the Cross on our behalf and our faith in that Finished Work. As long as our faith remains in Christ and what He did for us at the Cross, the pipeline of grace, so to speak, will ever be full flowing. It is the believer placing his or her faith in something else that frustrates the grace of God and places such a believer in a fallen position. The something else can be anything else other than Christ and the Cross. It doesn't matter what it is.

NOTES

DOES IT MEAN SUCH A BELIEVER IS LOST?

No!

If it did, virtually every Christian in the world would now be lost because most have placed their faith in something other than the Cross. This is due to the fact that they do not understand the Cross relative to sanctification, While they aren't fallen, such a person is in a serious situation. This means the sin nature is ruling such a person, which means he is failing on every hand, no matter how hard he tries to stop the downward process. Such a person's faith is in Christ for his salvation, but it's in himself for his sanctification, thinking he can bring about such by his own actions. He cannot!

Living for the Lord is the most gracious, fruitful, abundant, and glorious life. It is the most abundant life that anyone could ever live, providing its done the way that it should be done, which is by faith in Christ and the Cross.

Let us say it again:

The grace of God and the Cross of Christ are tied together indivisibly, which means they cannot be separated. To guarantee a constant flow of grace, which means we do not frustrate such, it only remains for us to evidence faith in Christ and the Cross, and maintain our faith in Christ and the Cross. If the believer does this, he or she is guaranteed a steady flow of the grace of God, which, in fact, all of us have to have, that is, if we are to live a righteous life of any degree. Grace is simply the goodness of God freely given to undeserving people. The only requirement is faith, but as we have repeatedly stated, it must be faith in Christ and the Cross (Rom. 6:1-14, 8:1-11; I Cor. 1:17-18, 23; 2:2; Gal. 6:14; Col. 2:5-15).

WE SHALL BE SAVED

The idea of the phrase, *"Shall be saved,"* is that we have been saved, are being saved, and shall be saved. In essence, it means that one must keep believing in order to keep on being saved.

Horton says, *"Both the present tense*

'believing' and the future tense 'shall keep on being saved' are continuous tenses representing continuous action. The idea is that the Grace is continuous if the action of believing is continuous."

So, this refutes the unscriptural doctrine of unconditional eternal security.

As well, it was a warning to the Judaizers that they could lose their salvation if they ceased to believe solely in Jesus Christ and what He had done for them at the Cross. It is a warning to us as well!

The short phrase, *"Even as they,"* means that all, both Jew and gentile, are saved in the same manner, *"Through the Grace of the Lord Jesus Christ."*

(12) "THEN ALL THE MULTITUDE KEPT SILENCE, AND GAVE AUDIENCE TO BARNABAS AND PAUL, DECLARING WHAT MIRACLES AND WONDERS GOD HAD WROUGHT AMONG THE GENTILES BY THEM."

The exegesis is:

1. The phrase, *"Then all the multitude kept silence,"* no doubt, refers to the introduction to the audience of both *"Barnabas and Paul."*

The audience had heard many things of these two men, especially Paul, so they were probably very anxious to hear them.

2. *"And gave audience to Barnabas and Paul,"* notes Barnabas listed first, who, no doubt, spoke first as well.

3. He was well known to the church in Jerusalem, which, with him speaking first, would have given even more credence to that which would be said by Paul.

4. The phrase, *"Declaring what miracles and wonders God had wrought among the gentiles by them,"* seems to indicate that neither Barnabas nor Paul sought to improve on what Peter had said respecting salvation by grace, but rather testified of the *"miracles and wonders,"* which authenticated the *"grace"* message.

5. In essence, by the recounting of these *"wonders,"* they were saying that God would not have done such a thing if they had been preaching error. At the same time, they were also saying that *"miracles and wonders"* do not accompany the false doctrine of Law added to grace. It was a telling argument.

(13) "AND AFTER THEY HAD HELD THEIR PEACE, JAMES ANSWERED, SAYING, MEN AND BRETHREN, HEARKEN UNTO ME."

The synopsis is:

1. Works can never be accepted by God as payment for blessings.

2. God honors only one thing, and that is faith; however, it must, without fail, be faith in Christ and what He has done for us at the Cross.

JAMES

The phrase, *"And after they had held their peace,"* speaks of Barnabas and Paul concluding their remarks.

"James answered, saying, Men and brethren, hearken unto me," presents the Lord's Brother as the presiding elder of the church in Jerusalem.

As well, the evidence is that James did not arise immediately upon Barnabas and Paul concluding their remarks, but waited some moments in order that someone else may speak if they so desired. In this, we see the humility of this man, as well as his dependence on the Holy Spirit.

Also, the entirety of Chapter 15 is a remarkable testimony against papal supremacy as claimed by the Catholic Church. James was in charge here, not Peter.

Concerning Rome, there is no scriptural or historical evidence that Peter was ever in Rome.

As Paul closed out the Book of Romans, he mentioned many people. In fact, Romans, Chapter 16, consists of little more than a lengthy list of those he greeted there. According to the papal catalog of bishops of Rome, Peter was in Rome at this time. Amazingly, however, Paul did not send greetings to Peter!

Since Peter was not mentioned here by Paul, it can be concluded with some certainty that he was not there at that time! This, of course, undermines the very foundation of the claimed apostolic succession of the Roman bishops.

If Peter had been in Rome as bishop (as the Roman Catholic Church claims), he would have been the first one to whom Paul would have referred! It is, therefore, a waste of time to consider such a groundless theory.

To be frank, it is unlikely that Peter ever even saw the city of Rome in his lifetime!

We do know a number of things about Simon Peter, however. He was one of the Twelve. He was a native fisherman of Bethsaida when the Lord called him. He was a married man (Mat. 8:14; I Cor. 9:5). He had no headship over the entire church.

PETER

He ministered primarily to Jews (Gal. 2:7). It seems he was not even the head of the Jewish sector of the church, even as we see in Chapter 15 of Acts, much less of the gentiles (II Cor. 11:28; Gal. 2:6-21).

Peter was only one elder among many (I Pet., Chpt. 5). As previously mentioned, there is not the slightest indication that he ever set foot in Rome.

Instead of traveling west (toward Rome), we find Peter in the east, writing an Epistle from Babylon (I Pet. 5:13). Furthermore, we know nothing of his death—other than the prophecy given in John 21:18-19.

Some claim that Peter's reference to Babylon in I Peter actually refers to Rome. This is a ridiculous assertion, however. The city of Babylon still existed when Peter wrote this. It was home to many Jews and was well-known as a major city on the Euphrates River.

The great historian Josephus wrote of Babylon during this same period. Why then would Peter send salutations from Babylon if he was actually in Rome? This would be as irrational as a person today claiming he was in San Francisco when he was really in New York City. Sad to say, Catholic assertions about this do not hold water when exposed to the facts of the case.

(14) "SIMEON HAS DECLARED HOW GOD AT THE FIRST DID VISIT THE GENTILES, TO TAKE OUT OF THEM A PEOPLE FOR HIS NAME."

The exegesis is:

1. The phrase, *"Simeon has declared how God at the first did visit the gentiles,"* refers to the conversion of Cornelius and his household. Here, James proclaims this event, which transpired some 10 years before, as definitely being of God. However, as we have previously stated, there seems to have been little headway made by the Jerusalem church respecting this all-important plan of God, other than what had been done by Paul and Barnabas.

2. *"To take out of them a people for His Name,"* presents this as the plan of God, which it surely was! In truth, almost all of the *"people for His Name"* are gentiles, which have numbered hundreds of millions from that time. Actually, the church is virtually all gentile!

NOTES

(15) "AND TO THIS AGREE THE WORDS OF THE PROPHETS; AS IT IS WRITTEN."

The pattern is:

1. That which James did was exactly that which should be done in all situations of this nature.

2. While we are only given a compendium of what actually was said, we find that Peter proclaimed his experience, which was telling indeed.

3. Barnabas and Paul then related how the Lord did mighty things among the gentiles, in essence, verifying the Word of God.

4. James now sealed the entirety of the discussion by appealing directly to the Word of God, which verified all that had been said (Isa. 11:10; 42:1, 6; 49:6, 22; 60:3; 66:19; Amos 9:10-11; Mal. 1:11; Rom. 9:25-33).

(16) "AFTER THIS I WILL RETURN, AND WILL BUILD AGAIN THE TABERNACLE OF DAVID, WHICH IS FALLEN DOWN; AND I WILL BUILD AGAIN THE RUINS THEREOF, AND I WILL SET IT UP."

The composition is:

1. The more I study the Word of God, the more the Cross of Christ takes center stage.

2. Everything, and I mean everything that comes from God to believers, all and without exception is made possible by the Cross of Christ.

I WILL RETURN

The phrase, *"After this I will return,"* is an addition to Amos 9:11-12 and speaks of the Church Age and the Second Coming of the Lord.

By now, some 12 years after the Day of Pentecost, it was becoming quite obvious what the Church Age would be like. How

NOTES

long it would last, of course, they did not know, and neither does anyone else. However, all of the apostles were very much aware of the words of Jesus respecting His Second Coming and events leading up to that time, as given in the Sermon on the Mount (Mat., Chpt. 24). So, James knew that Jesus was not coming back until after the Church Age, which he here plainly said by using the words, *"After this."*

"And will build again the Tabernacle of David, which is fallen down; and I will build again the ruins thereof, and I will set it up," speaks of the restoration of Israel in the coming Kingdom Age, which all the prophets declared (Isa. 9:6-7; Dan. 7:13-14; Hos. 3:4-5; Lk. 1:32-33; Rev. 11:15; 20:1-10; 22:4-5).

There is a strong movement afoot in the church at present, mostly from the charismatic sector, claiming Israel is no more and that the State of Israel has no relativity to Bible prophecy. They claim that Israel's crucifixion of Christ sealed their doom, with the nation being totally destroyed in A.D. 70, and never rising again. Consequently, the prophecies of Daniel and John regarding the Book of Revelation are now relegated to history, as it regards these teachers.

THE CHURCH AND ISRAEL

This teaching claims that the church has taken the place of Israel. They also deny the Rapture of the church and the coming Great Tribulation, once again claiming that the Great Tribulation was fulfilled in A.D. 70, or else, they mystify that period.

They also claim that the world is getting better and better, with the church on the verge of ushering in the Millennium. One of their proponents claims that he will stand on the Mount of Olivet and welcome Jesus back, etc.

There have always been wild speculations respecting the teaching of the Word of God concerning end-time events; however, this is probably the most widespread effort to date. Even though it goes under various names, the most popular is probably *"kingdom now."* It is fueled, as well, by the *"greed message.*

It is difficult to understand how such a philosophy could be accepted in the church, especially considering the mountain of Biblical evidence otherwise!

This which James gave here is about as clear as possible concerning the future of Israel. He plainly quoted Amos that the *"Tabernacle of David"* will be restored.

What does that mean?

ISRAEL

Due to Israel's rejection of Christ, the nation, by its own volition, took itself out from under the hand of God and placed itself into the hands of Caesar (Jn. 19:15).

In A.D. 70, they were by and large destroyed as a nation and were actually scattered all over the world, exactly as the prophets said (Jer. 30:11; Ezek. 34:6; 36:19; Joel 3:2; Zech. 1:19).

This *"scattering"* lasted for about 1,900 years, with Israel once again becoming a nation in 1948, as a direct result of the fulfilling of Bible prophecy. That was the beginning of the regathering, which will not begin in earnest until the Second Coming (Isa. 11:11; 14:1; 43:5-6; Jer. 16:14-16; 23:5-8; 33:6-26; Ezek. 20:33-44; Chpt. 37; Hos. 3:4-5; Joel, Chpt. 3; Obad., Vs. 21; Mic. 5:3-15; Zech. 2:8-13; 10:6-12; 12:1-14:21; etc.).

The Great Tribulation coming upon the world immediately after the Rapture of the church will serve many purposes, but primarily, it will be to bring Israel ultimately to repentance (Jer. 30:7; Dan. 9:27; Rev., Chpts. 6-19).

The Battle of Armageddon will conclude the Great Tribulation, with Israel in dire straits. They will then begin to call for the Messiah as never before. He will not disappoint them! It is the Second Coming, which will be the most dramatic event in the annals of human history.

THE SECOND COMING

Jesus foretold this in His Sermon on the Mount, when He spoke of false messiahs coming toward the close of the Great Tribulation. He warned Israel not to be fooled by these deceivers (Mat. 24:23-26), stating that when He truly does come, no one will have to guess Who He is. All will know, *"For as the lightning cometh out of the east, and shines even unto the west; so shall also the coming of the Son of Man be"* (Mat. 24:27).

His Coming will be accompanied by the greatest display of heavenly fireworks the world has ever known (Mat. 24:29-30).

According to the Prophet Zechariah, Israel will finally accept Jesus of Nazareth as her Messiah (Zech. 12:10-14; 13:1-6; Chpt. 14).

According to Ezekiel, Israel will then be fully restored, accepting their rightful place as the leading nation in the world, actually a nation of priests, which God intended all along (Ezek., Chpts. 40-48).

Then, the Tabernacle of David will be fully restored, just as the Prophet Amos said, and James quoted.

Actually, the *"Tabernacle of David"* refers to his throne and kingdom, which are now fallen. They were overthrown in 616 B.C. and have been fallen down ever since. However, when that Tabernacle shall be raised up again, as it shall be at the beginning of the coming Kingdom Age, David will actually become the king of Israel under the Messiah (Isa. 9:6-7; 16:5; Jer. 30:9; Ezek. 34:23-24; 37:24-25; Hos. 3:4-5).

(17) "THAT THE RESIDUE OF MEN MIGHT SEEK AFTER THE LORD, AND ALL THE GENTILES, UPON WHOM MY NAME IS CALLED, SAYS THE LORD, WHO DOES ALL THESE THINGS."

The synopsis is:

1. The phrase, *"That the residue of men might seek after the Lord,"* is actually the same as spoken by Amos, *"That they may possess the remnant of Edom."* Horton said, *"Actually, the Hebrew should have been translated "mankind" instead of 'Edom.' However, one should note that 'Edom' in Amos is parallel to the heathen, and referring to the Gentiles."*

2. *"And all the gentiles,"* according to its structure, refers to gentiles or heathen, with Israel over the entirety of the world.

3. *"Upon whom My Name is called, saith the Lord,"* refers to how large the church will be that is called after His Name. In other words, the Jews refused to seek after the Lord, but literally hundreds of millions of gentiles the world over took their place.

4. *"Who does all these things,"* refers to the power of God in performing this, i.e., the building of the church (Mat. 16:18).

5. The reader is not to misinterpret the Text as the Lord turning to the gentiles upon Israel's rebellion, but rather that this was God's Plan all along. Actually, Israel was supposed to evangelize the gentiles but refused to do that and rejected their Messiah as well!

6. However, their rejection and rebellion did not stop the plan of God concerning salvation for all of mankind, but rather only abrogated their part in that Plan, at least for a period of time. However, as stated, they will be restored!

(18) "KNOWN UNTO GOD ARE ALL HIS WORKS FROM THE BEGINNING OF THE WORLD."

The exegesis is:

1. In the last nearly 100 years, the church has so little preached the Cross that anymore, modern believers are Cross illiterate.

2. That's like saying that a lawyer knows nothing about law, or an airplane pilot knows nothing about airplanes.

NOTES

FROM THE BEGINNING OF THE WORLD

Regarding the human family, the plan of God was known, even as James said, *"From the beginning of the world."*

The Bible is the revelation of that Plan, and that is the reason believers ought to take the opportunity of mastering its contents, at least as far as is possible. Of course, such cannot be done through a mere intellectual pursuit, but rather must be done by revelation from the Holy Spirit.

The Bible speaks of seven dispensations of man between the restoration of the Earth from chaos (Gen. 1:3-2:25) and the new heavens and the new Earth:

1. Dispensation of Innocence (Gen., Chpt. 3): it is not known how long this period lasted, but it is certain that it was a short period of time, perhaps about 40 days. It ended with the fall of Adam and Eve in the Garden.

2. Dispensation of Conscience (Gen., Chpts. 4-8): this period lasted about 1,600 years and culminated in the Flood. During this time, God dealt with the entirety of the

NOTES

human family, but without much success. Actually, from Adam up to Noah, only two people in all of this 1,600 years are recorded as being right with God. That was Abel, who was killed by his brother Cain, and Enoch (Gen. 4:4; 5:21-24).

3. Dispensation of Human Government (Gen., Chpts. 9-11): this was approximately 400 years in length and lasted from Noah to Abraham. As well, human government did not turn out and necessitated being scattered all over the world.

4. Dispensation of Promise (Gen. 12:1–Ex. 12:36): this period was about 400 years, as well, and lasted from Abraham to Moses. During this dispensation, God began to deal with just one man, Abraham, to whom He gave a promise.

5. Dispensation of Law (Ex. 12:37–Mat., Chpt. 3): this period lasted for about 1,600 years, spanning from Moses to Christ. God gave the Law to Moses and governed Israel accordingly.

6. Dispensation of Grace (Mat. 3:1–Rev. 19:21): this period has lasted now for nearly 2,000 years and represents the tremendous price paid by Jesus at Calvary, and that men can be saved by simply having faith in Him and what He did. This dispensation will end at the Second Coming of Christ.

7. Dispensation of Divine Government, or sometimes referred to as the Millennium (Rev. 20:1-15): this period will last for 1,000 years, with Jesus personally ruling from Jerusalem and, as a result, the world experiencing the greatest time of prosperity and peace it has ever known.

As stated, the Bible plainly tells us of all of these great *"works"* of the Lord. Considering how absolutely significant they are, the believer should devote as much attention to learning the Word as he does his own natural food (Mat. 4:4).

(19) "WHEREFORE MY SENTENCE IS, THAT WE TROUBLE NOT THEM, WHICH FROM AMONG THE GENTILES ARE TURNED TO GOD."

The status is:

1. The phrase, *"Wherefore my sentence is,"* would have probably been better translated, *"I think it good."*

2. It is obvious here that James was president of the council and, therefore, gave the final sentence.

This was James, the Lord's Brother.

3. It is safe to conclude that when James is referred to without any designation as *"brother of John," "Son of Zebedee,"* or *"Son of Alphaeus,"* that James, the Brother of our Lord, is meant (Acts 12:2, 17; 15:13; 21:18; I Cor. 15:7; Gal. 1:19; 2:9, 12; James 1:1; Jude, Vs. 1). It is believed that he was martyred in A.D. 62.

4. The phrase, *"That we trouble not them,"* presents a beautifully simplistic way of reducing a very complex subject down to its lowest possible common denominator.

5. In other words, *"These gentiles have accepted the Lord, and let's not add useless trivia to their experience in Christ."*

6. *"Which from among the gentiles are turned to God,"* carries the idea, that it does not make any sense to demand certain other things of them, claiming such things are needed in order to be saved, when, in fact, the people are already saved!

7. Should not the modern church take a cue from this word of wisdom given by James?

8. How silly it is to demand other things on top of one's faith in Christ. Such shows terrible spiritual and scriptural ignorance! At the moment the sinner sincerely trusts Christ, asking for salvation, that person is saved (Jn. 3:16; Rom. 10:9-10).

(20) "BUT THAT WE WRITE UNTO THEM, THAT THEY ABSTAIN FROM POLLUTIONS OF IDOLS, AND FROM FORNICATION, AND FROM THINGS STRANGLED, AND FROM BLOOD."

The overview is:

1. In the modern church, the Cross of Christ has no part at all.

2. Consequently, virtually nothing is done for the Lord in these churches because without the Cross, all that is left is a vapid philosophy.

FOUR COMMANDS

The phrase, *"But that we write unto them,"* pertains to particulars after their salvation, which means it is a result and not the cause.

The four commands spoken by James are

NOTES

of far greater magnitude than meets the eye. In fact, everything demanded by God of the human family is proclaimed in these four statements. They are as follows:

ABSTAIN FROM POLLUTIONS OF IDOLS

This speaks of man's relationship to God and that he must have no other gods. Almighty God is the Creator of all things, and He alone is to be worshiped.

Even though modern man little bows to the idols of old, still, the problem is just as acute presently as then. Men, even Christians, make idols out of sports, money, pleasure, education, religion, etc. That is why John, writing to the church, said, *"Little children, keep yourselves from idols"* (I Jn. 5:21).

AND FROM FORNICATION

This is the sin against oneself, one's own body, the temple of the Holy Spirit. It includes all types of immorality. To sin against God's Temple is to sin grievously against God.

Paul said, *"Know you not that your bodies are the members of Christ? shall I then take the members of Christ, and make them the members of an harlot? God forbid."*

He then said, *"What? know you not that he which is joined to an harlot is one body? for two, says He, shall be one flesh."*

And finally, *"Flee fornication. Every sin that a man does is without the body; but he that commits fornication sins against his own body"* (I Cor. 6:15, 18).

AND FROM THINGS STRANGLED

When animals were strangled, the blood remained in their bodies contrary to Leviticus 17:10-14.

The idea is that Jesus shed His life's Blood in order that man may be saved. Consequently, to eat things strangled symbolically says that man is not a sinner and does not need a Saviour. In other words, this hits at the very heart of man's condition, which is sin, and God's Solution, the shed blood of Jesus Christ.

Spiritually speaking, all over the world in tens of thousands of churches, people hear preachers proclaim another salvation other than the shed Blood of the Lamb, which symbolically is the same as *"eating things strangled."*

AND FROM BLOOD

This pertains to dealing (relationship) with other human beings and God's Prohibition against murder.

At the beginning, God said, *"Whoso sheds man's blood, by man shall his blood be shed: for in the Image of God made He man"* (Gen. 9:6).

This is God's approval for capital punishment for capital crimes and is upheld in the New Testament in Romans 13:1-7.

Contrary to what some think, this severe penalty exacted by God concerning cold-blooded murder is not meant as a deterrent to crime, but rather that man's life must be respected in that he is made in the image of God.

So, in this fourfold admonition, the Holy Spirit through James dealt with man's relationship to God, his relationship with himself, his relationship with Christ, and his relationship with his fellowman.

(21) "FOR MOSES OF OLD TIME HAS IN EVERY CITY THEM THAT PREACH HIM, BEING READ IN THE SYNAGOGUES EVERY SABBATH DAY."

The status is:

1. Any preacher who doesn't understand the Cross of Christ relative to sanctification simply does not know how to tell believers how to live for God.

2. That's the reason that virtually the entirety of the modern body of Christ, no matter how sincere, simply doesn't know how to live for God.

THE LAW OF MOSES

The phrase, *"For Moses of old time has in every city them that preach him,"* speaks of Jewish synagogues and the Law of Moses read and studied every Sabbath.

"Being read in the synagogues every Sabbath day," in essence, is saying that the Law of Moses would not be weakened by the decision made concerning gentiles.

As is obvious, and as we have attempted to delineate, the Holy Spirit prompted that decision, and it was right. However, at the

NOTES

same time, we see James attempting to hold on to the Law of Moses respecting Jewish believers. So, even though the problem was solved respecting gentiles that they did not have to mix Law with grace in order to be saved, the statement did not address the Jews and, in fact, left them continuing to attempt the wedding of Law and grace, as proven in Verse 21.

JEWISH CHRISTIANS

It seems to me that James, even though deciding correctly regarding gentile converts, was still attempting to maintain the old system of Judaism for Jewish Christians. Actually, this was improper and unscriptural, which greatly weakened the Jewish sector of the church until it was finally destroyed. If James had extended his statement to cover Jews as well as gentiles, it would have greatly strengthened the work of God and would have been an untold blessing to Jews in general.

Whenever Jewish Christians attempted to hold onto the Law of Moses as well as embracing Christ, which they did for the most part, it ultimately destroyed the church at Jerusalem, which was made up exclusively of Jews. It hindered Jews elsewhere from being solidly anchored in Christ as well. This is one of the reasons that Paul bluntly wrote, *"Whosoever of you* (referring to both Jews and gentiles) *are justified by the Law* (or attempt to be justified by the Law, which cannot be done); *you are fallen from grace* (salvation is forfeited)*"* (Gal. 5:4).

In truth, I think Paul is one of the very few who fully saw this situation exactly as it was. Actually, his writings tell us this. Even after this council at Jerusalem, where the correct decision had been made concerning gentiles, still, the Law/grace issue continued to be a great problem, which Paul had to address over and over again. As I have already said, if James had taken a firm stand, making his decision binding on both Jews and gentiles, he would have done his own people a tremendous service, as well as the work of God.

However, because of an improper understanding of the Law, it seems even godly men such as James (and he was godly) were loath to turn loose of this system, which had been replaced by Christ.

Other than Paul, most seemed to have great difficulties in understanding that the Law of Moses, while serving as a pattern for living, which it did, was in its greatest power a symbol of Christ. Now that the Symbol has come, the symbolism is no longer needed. However, I think the record is clear that the Jerusalem church, even though embracing Christ, continued to offer up sacrifices at the Temple. This served no rhyme or reason, especially considering that Jesus, to Whom the sacrifices had pointed, had now made further sacrifices unnecessary. He did this by the offering up of His own Body on the Tree, Actually, this is the very reason that the Book of Hebrews was written. It delineated perfectly what I am here attempting to say, concerning the new covenant replacing the old.

It is my feeling that the Lord was greatly displeased by the continuance of this action. He was so displeased, in fact, that He would have the Temple completely destroyed in A.D. 70, making it impossible to offer up further sacrifices.

While it is true that Paul oftentimes went to Jerusalem on the feast days, etc., I think the record will show that his reasons for attending these feasts had nothing to do with their original purpose, which was made unnecessary after the advent of Christ.

(22) "THEN PLEASED IT THE APOSTLES AND ELDERS, WITH THE WHOLE CHURCH, TO SEND CHOSEN MEN OF THEIR OWN COMPANY TO ANTIOCH WITH PAUL AND BARNABAS; NAMELY, JUDAS SURNAMED BARSABAS, AND SILAS, CHIEF MEN AMONG THE BRETHREN."

The status is:

1. The phrase, *"Then pleased it the apostles and elders, with the whole church, to send chosen men of their own company to Antioch with Paul and Barnabas,"* proclaims that all the churches in Jerusalem, or at least the far greater majority, totally agreed with what James had said respecting gentiles and the Law of Moses.

2. The apostles and elders felt that it would make a greater statement, which it did,

NOTES

if they would do more than simply write a letter but, as well, would send chosen delegates to Antioch to personally confirm what had been decided.

3. The phrase, *"Namely, Judas surnamed Barsabas, and Silas, chief men among the brethren,"* names the two chosen.

4. Some think that Judas Barsabas was the brother of Joseph Barsabas, the one who, along with Matthias, was proposed as a possible substitute for Judas the traitor (Acts 1:23). However, this cannot be proven.

5. As we shall see, Silas, called Silvanus by Paul, was to play a very important part as a companion of Paul in the evangelism of that day (Acts 15:40-41; 16:19-29; 17:4-15; 18:5).

6. As well, he would deliver the first Epistle written by Peter to the churches in Asia Minor (I Pet. 5:12).

7. Silas, as well as being a Jew, was also a Roman citizen (Acts 16:37-39).

(23) "AND THEY WROTE LETTERS BY THEM AFTER THIS MANNER; THE APOSTLES AND ELDERS AND BRETHREN SEND GREETING UNTO THE BRETHREN WHICH ARE OF THE GENTILES IN ANTIOCH AND SYRIA AND CILICIA."

The order is:

1. The phrase, *"And they wrote letters by them after this manner,"* presents that of great significance, which should be obvious. Truly, the Spirit of the Lord had His Way that day, at least as far as gentiles were concerned.

2. The letters were, no doubt, written in Greek, which was the major language of the gentile-speaking world of that day.

3. *"The apostles and elders and brethren send greeting unto the brethren which are of the gentiles in Antioch and Syria and Cilicia,"* presents the salutation, and what a salutation it was! I sense the presence of God even as I dictate these words.

4. The key is found in the word *"brethren."* By giving the gentiles this recognition as fellow brothers in the Lord, they were recognizing their salvation, putting it on the same par with theirs, and without qualifications.

This means that they were no longer strangers and foreigners to the promises of God; they were brothers. Paul enlarged on this thought in Ephesians 2:11-22.

Concerning this, Horton said, *"These Gentiles were once outside of Christ, aliens separated from the Commonwealth of Israel, strangers cut off from the Covenants of Promise, having no hope, and without God in the world. But now, through the Blood of Christ, they are no longer foreigners but fellow citizens with the Saints."*

5. Do not misunderstand, even if the brethren in Jerusalem had not recognized the salvation of these gentiles, that would have made them no less saved in the eyes of God. However, the recognition, which was right, was of tremendous benefit to the work of God all over the world of that day.

6. One's true salvation in Christ, whether recognized by man or not, is no less valid with God, Who alone counts. Nevertheless, for believers to fail to recognize what God is doing does a great disservice to the work of God and, in effect, is sin. Paul addressed this by saying, *"For whatsoever is not of faith is sin"* (Rom. 14:23).

(24) "FORASMUCH AS WE HAVE HEARD, THAT CERTAIN WHICH WENT OUT FROM US HAVE TROUBLED YOU WITH WORDS, SUBVERTING YOUR SOULS, SAYING, YOU MUST BE CIRCUMCISED, AND KEEP THE LAW: TO WHOM WE GAVE NO SUCH COMMANDMENT."

The status is:

1. The phrase, *"Forasmuch as we have heard, that certain which went out from us have troubled you with words, subverting your souls,"* evidently speaks of those mentioned in Verse 1.

2. Evidently these false teachers gave the impression that their doctrine was sanctioned by the leadership of the mother church in Jerusalem, which is here denied.

3. The word *"subverting"* in the Greek text is *"anaskeuazo"* and means *"to upset or reverse."* In other words, these false teachers were reversing what Paul and others had taught at Antioch and elsewhere. The gentiles had been told that simple faith in Christ guaranteed salvation. The false teachers, in effect, reversed this, telling them that they had to also keep the Law of Moses to be saved. In other words, they were telling

NOTES

them they were not saved.

4. *"Saying, You must be circumcised, and keep the Law: to whom we gave no such commandment,"* specifies exactly what the error was. As stated, the claims of these people were emphatically denied.

5. They were not sent by the church in Jerusalem, nor were they given any commandment to teach any type of false doctrine.

(25) "IT SEEMED GOOD UNTO US, BEING ASSEMBLED WITH ONE ACCORD, TO SEND CHOSEN MEN UNTO YOU WITH OUR BELOVED BARNABAS AND PAUL."

The diagram is:

1. The phrase, *"It seemed good unto us, being assembled with one accord,"* proclaims the unity of the brethren in Jerusalem, which included all of the apostles and elders, respecting this decision. However, this was a unity brought about by the Holy Spirit, and it was unity concerning correct doctrine.

2. The idea of having unity with all types of doctrines which oppose each other, with many being grossly unscriptural, is never the type of unity brought about by the Holy Spirit, but always by man.

3. The favorite plea of these people is that we overlook our differences and come together. However, such is not scripturally possible. The only *"accord"* that the Holy Spirit will sanction is that which is truth. He will not, and neither can He, place His Seal of approval on that which is not truth.

4. So, the idea that Catholics can come to Christ and then remain in the error of the Catholic Church has no scriptural foundation, but rather the opposite. In fact, the same could be said regarding those who have been baptized with the Holy Spirit! To remain in a church which teaches the opposite of the Acts 2:4 experience can never be sanctioned by the Holy Spirit, except possibly in some very unusual circumstances.

5. *"To send chosen men unto you with our beloved Barnabas and Paul,"* places a gracious and kind endearment toward Paul and Barnabas, which, as well, spoke volumes. However, this is what should have been said, which showed that there was no schism or division in the church.

(26) "MEN THAT HAVE HAZARDED THEIR LIVES FOR THE NAME OF OUR LORD JESUS CHRIST."

The composition is:

1. The phrase, *"Men that have hazarded their lives,"* speaks of what they did.

This would have included the stoning that Paul endured of Acts 14:19, plus many other dangers, toils, and snares, which were not specified. To be sure, this type of consecration is rare!

2. The phrase, *"For the Name of our Lord Jesus Christ,"* tells us for Whom it was done!

3. The idea is that men will not normally go to these lengths to proclaim false doctrine. Someone who literally lays down his life for the cause of Christ must be very sure of his doctrine, exactly as were Paul and Barnabas. Precious few men are willing to die for the truth, much less for error!

(27) "WE HAVE SENT THEREFORE JUDAS AND SILAS, WHO SHALL ALSO TELL YOU THE SAME THINGS BY MOUTH."

The overview is:

1. The phrase, *"We have sent therefore Judas and Silas,"* presents two of their leaders, who would verify all that was being said in this letter.

2. *"Who shall also tell you the same things by mouth,"* would seem at first glance to be over precautionary.

3. However, knowing the wiles and subtlety of Satan, James, along with the apostles and elders, was, no doubt, led by the Holy Spirit in this action.

4. With these two men accompanying this letter and verifying its contents, no false prophet could claim that the letter was forged, etc.

5. Considering how utterly significant these proceedings were, there is no doubt, as stated, that the Holy Spirit guided them in these precautionary measures.

(28) "FOR IT SEEMED GOOD TO THE HOLY SPIRIT, AND TO US, TO LAY UPON YOU NO GREATER BURDEN THAN THESE NECESSARY THINGS."

The diagram is:

1. The phrase, *"For it seemed good to the*

NOTES

Holy Spirit, and to us," proclaims, without a doubt, that the Holy Spirit led and guided in all of these proceedings.

2. If one is to notice, the Holy Spirit is lauded here, and not James or Peter, etc.

3. *"To lay upon you no greater burden than these necessary things,"* refers to Verse 20.

When men leave the Word of God, they get into a lot of *"unnecessary things,"* which characterizes much of the modern church.

4. When the Holy Spirit leads, it is only *"necessary things"* which are stipulated and are based squarely on the Word of God.

5. When men lead without the guidance of the Holy Spirit, they always make the *"burden"* much *"greater!"* How so much the modern church needs to read this one Scripture and take it to heart.

(29) "THAT YOU ABSTAIN FROM MEATS OFFERED TO IDOLS, AND FROM BLOOD, AND FROM THINGS STRANGLED, AND FROM FORNICATION: FROM WHICH IF YOU KEEP YOURSELVES, YOU SHALL DO WELL. FARE YE WELL."

The composition is:

1. The phrase, *"That you abstain from meats offered to idols, and from blood, and from things strangled, and from fornication,"* is explained in commentary on Verse 20.

2. *"From which if you keep yourselves, you shall do well. Fare ye well,"* simply admonishes the keeping of these four stipulations.

3. As stated, if these rulings were properly understood, which they, no doubt, were, the significance of their salvation would become even more pronounced.

4. The benediction of *"Fare ye well,"* meant simply, *"Make yourselves strong"* or *"may you prosper."*

(30) "SO WHEN THEY WERE DISMISSED, THEY CAME TO ANTIOCH: AND WHEN THEY HAD GATHERED THE MULTITUDE TOGETHER, THEY DELIVERED THE EPISTLE."

The structure is:

1. The phrase, *"So when they were dismissed, they came to Antioch,"* refers to them being sent away with great love. The group consisted of Paul, Barnabas, Judas, and Silas. As well, it could have included Titus and maybe even others (Gal. 2:1).

2. *"And when they had gathered the multitude together, they delivered the Epistle,"* concerns the entirety of the church at Antioch, Syria.

3. Inasmuch as the church there, as elsewhere, was mostly home churches, in other words, many homes being used over the area, it is not exactly known as to what accommodations they used in gathering the entirety of the multitude together.

4. How large the church was at Antioch at this time, we are not told. However, it could have well numbered several thousands of people, or at least many hundreds.

5. Gathering all of these people together could well have been conducted in the open air at the outskirts of the city.

(31) "WHICH WHEN THEY HAD READ, THEY REJOICED FOR THE CONSOLATION."

The exegesis is:

1. The phrase, *"Which when they had read,"* pertains to the Epistle sent from Jerusalem and was, no doubt, heard with great interest and thanksgiving.

2. *"They rejoiced for the consolation,"* tells us that the Law/grace issue had been very serious. In other words, the Judaizers had made some inroads into the thinking of the people. Now, this settled the dispute once and for all.

3. To be sure, and as stated, whatever the letter stated added nothing to their salvation, nor did it remove anything, for man does not have that prerogative, irrespective as to whom he may be. However, the letter definitely was a great boon to the work of God. A split between the church at Antioch and Jerusalem would have been disastrous, which is what Satan was trying to bring about, but without success we might quickly add!

(32) "AND JUDAS AND SILAS, BEING PROPHETS ALSO THEMSELVES, EXHORTED THE BRETHREN WITH MANY WORDS, AND CONFIRMED THEM."

The synopsis is:

1. The phrase, *"And Judas and Silas, being prophets also themselves,"* means that they stood in the office of the prophet (Eph. 4:11).

2. *"Exhorted the brethren with many words, and confirmed them,"* presents them addressing the *"multitude"* with words of great encouragement, which tended to heal the confusion brought about by the Judaizers.

3. The word *"confirmed"* means that the Holy Spirit evidently used them in a prophetic utterance, which confirmed all that had been done.

4. This, no doubt, was a happy day for the church at Antioch and for the work of God in general, spanning even unto this present hour.

(33) "AND AFTER THEY HAD TARRIED THERE A SPACE, THEY WERE LET GO IN PEACE FROM THE BRETHREN UNTO THE APOSTLES."

The pattern is:

1. The phrase, *"And after they had tarried there a space,"* refers to a period of time in which they evidently continued to minister and be a blessing to the church.

2. *"They were let go in peace from the brethren unto the apostles,"* refers to returning to Jerusalem.

3. The idea seems to be, at least when Verse 34 is added, that there were either others with Judas and Silas, or that both Judas and Silas made preparation to leave, with Silas changing his mind at the last minute.

(34) "NOTWITHSTANDING IT PLEASED SILAS TO ABIDE THERE STILL."

The account is:

1. Some claim that Silas did go back with Judas but soon returned to Antioch. However, the Text does not seem to imply such.

2. It seems that the Holy Spirit was dealing with Silas about remaining in Antioch, knowing the controversy which would arise shortly between Paul and Barnabas, and that Silas would then be greatly needed.

3. Of course, Silas did not know any of this at that particular time, but nevertheless, he knew that for some reason, the Holy Spirit desired that he stay, which he did! The reason would become obvious very shortly!

(35) "PAUL ALSO AND BARNABAS CONTINUED IN ANTIOCH, TEACHING AND PREACHING THE WORD OF THE LORD, WITH MANY OTHERS ALSO."

NOTES

The way is:

1. The phrase, *"Paul also and Barnabas continued in Antioch,"* proclaims them, no doubt, led by the Holy Spirit to do so. As well, if one is to notice, Paul's name is first once again.

2. This is of little consequence but does refer to leadership, and leadership, we might quickly add, designated by the Holy Spirit.

3. The phrase, *"Teaching and preaching the Word of the Lord,"* refers to two particulars:

a. *"Teaching the Word"*: inasmuch as most all the leadership in Antioch, as well as other churches at that particular time, was raised up locally, much teaching was needed. To be sure, these people could not have had any better teachers than these two apostles. What an honor to have sat under either one of them.

b. *"Preaching the Word"*: along with teaching the Word to believers, they also continued to evangelistically preach the Gospel, which brought sinners to Christ. This should be the criterion for all churches.

Preaching proclaims the truth, while teaching explains the truth.

If believers are never taught, they cannot grow in the Lord. As well, if evangelistic type messages are not preached, new converts are little brought to salvation. Every church should have this balance.

4. The phrase, *"With many others also,"* refers to other preachers and teachers as well!

(36) "AND SOME DAYS AFTER PAUL SAID UNTO BARNABAS, LET US GO AGAIN AND VISIT OUR BRETHREN IN EVERY CITY WHERE WE HAVE PREACHED THE WORD OF THE LORD, AND SEE HOW THEY DO."

The form is:

1. The phrase, *"And some days after Paul said unto Barnabas,"* referring to the Greek, leaves us with little idea as to exactly the time frame, but it was probably as much as a year.

2. *"Let us go again and visit our brethren in every city where we have preached the Word of the Lord, and see how they do,"* refers to the churches they had planted on the first missionary journey.

This would have been on the island of Cyprus, Antioch, Pisidia, Iconium, Lystra, and Derbe. On the way back, they also *"preached the Word in Perga."*

3. Paul constantly felt, as is obvious, the burden of these churches even after they were planted. Knowing how easy it was for false doctrine to make inroads, and knowing the persecution that many of these churches suffered, his repeated visits or Epistles were very necessary.

4. To understand Paul's concern, one need only read his Epistles, which portray him correcting doctrine and dealing with problems, some very severe! Actually, his second letter to Corinth expresses great consternation that the Work there might even be lost due to false doctrine, etc. However, it was salvaged, which brought Paul great joy. In all of this, he constantly showed a shepherd's heart, which ever portrayed concern for the flock.

5. Perhaps there have been few examples as Paul! His consecration, manner, and devotion are hardly equaled, if ever! Almost single-handedly he demanded the purity of the new covenant.

This in no way is meant to take away from the original Twelve. Actually, each of them contributed mightily to the work of God at that time, ministering over much of the Roman Empire, with all, tradition says, other than John, dying a martyr's death. However, it was Paul who the Holy Spirit used to spearhead this thrust of that which we now know as the early church.

(37) "AND BARNABAS DETERMINED TO TAKE WITH THEM JOHN, WHOSE SURNAME WAS MARK."

The construction is:

1. As we remember, Mark had left Paul and Barnabas on the first missionary journey at Pamphylia almost at the beginning of the trip, going back to Jerusalem. Inasmuch as he was very much needed, this created a hardship on both Paul and Barnabas. Why Mark did this, we do not know. It could have been homesickness or whatever! Some have even ventured that it may have been the Law/grace issue.

2. During the past approximate four or five years since the episode of Mark leaving them, there had, no doubt, been some dialogue between Mark and Barnabas concerning this situation, with Mark assuring him that if given another opportunity, he would not fail again. Mark had eventually come up from Jerusalem and was now in Antioch. Incidentally, Mark and Barnabas were cousins.

3. Whatever happened, Barnabas was convinced that Mark would prove his metal the second time and *"determined"* that he should go.

4. The word *"determined"* in the Greek text is *"boulomai"* and means *"a deliberate action, or deliberate determination."*

5. It seems that Barnabas had a closed mind on the subject, determined to take him, with Paul determined not to take him!

(38) "BUT PAUL THOUGHT NOT GOOD TO TAKE HIM WITH THEM, WHO DEPARTED FROM THEM FROM PAMPHYLIA, AND WENT NOT WITH THEM TO THE WORK."

The direction is:

1. The phrase, *"But Paul thought not good to take him with them,"* coupled with the next phrase, seems to indicate that there was more here than meets the eye.

2. The phrase, *"Who departed from them from Pamphylia,"* suggests a rupture.

3. The word *"departed"* in the Greek is *"aphistemi"* and means *"to remove, or to instigate to revolt."*

4. It has been suggested, but without proof, that Mark was leaning somewhat toward Judaizing views and, consequently, was not in complete sympathy with Paul's doctrine of grace.

5. The phrase, *"And went not with them to the work,"* in effect, says, *"He did not go with them to the work to which God called them as he ought to have done."*

6. So, whatever the problem those several years before, I think it is obvious that it was more than homesickness or youth on the part of Mark, but something of far greater magnitude, even as suggested here.

(39) "AND THE CONTENTION WAS SO SHARP BETWEEN THEM, THAT THEY DEPARTED ASUNDER ONE FROM THE OTHER: AND SO BARNABAS TOOK MARK, AND SAILED UNTO CYPRUS."

NOTES

NOTES

The status is:

1. Unless the believer understands the Cross of Christ relative to sanctification, such a believer cannot really understand the Word of God as one should.

2. Upon understanding the Cross relative to sanctification, one will find that the entirety of the Word of God begins to fall into place to a greater degree than ever.

CONTENTION

The phrase, *"And the contention was so sharp between them,"* suggests far more than a mere disagreement.

The word *"contention"* in the Greek text is *"paroxusmos"* and means, at least in this case, *"to dispute to the point of anger."*

This Greek word also has the same sense of our English word *"paroxysm"* and means *"an increase or recurrence of symptoms, until it is at the point of violent emotion or action, even rage."*

The phrase, *"That they departed asunder one from the other,"* tells us that ever how severe the contention was, it created an abrupt and severe rupture.

The word *"asunder"* in the Greek is *"apochorizo"* and means *"to rend apart,"* the point being, whether we like to say it or not, their separation was not amicable.

BARNABAS AND MARK

The phrase, *"And so Barnabas took Mark, and sailed unto Cyprus,"* seems to indicate that he was determined to visit some of the same churches, as well, but with Paul going in another direction.

This is a very interesting turn of events in the narrative, with its record allowed by the Holy Spirit for reason.

Who was right in this contention, Paul or Barnabas?

It is obvious that Luke took Paul's side and threw the blame of the quarrel, or at least of the separation, upon Barnabas.

In reading behind various expositors and commentators, it seems, at least of the ones I have read, that they are just about evenly divided. Some claim that Barnabas was in the right due to the fact that Paul later asked Timothy to bring Mark with him because he was useful for ministry (II Tim. 4:11). That may very well have been the case.

However, inasmuch as Luke sided with Paul, with the church at Antioch seemingly doing the same, or at least not taking sides, I suppose I would have to come down on the side of Paul.

Others have contended that with this separation, a greater work for God was now accomplished due to the fact that two missionary teams were now at work. However, I'm not so sure of the validity of that thought.

THE WILL OF GOD

A work for God has little to do with numbers, but rather the will of God, which alone can have the anointing and help of the Holy Spirit. However, this we do know, God does not work from *"if only,"* but rather *"what is!"*

Mark was with Peter when that apostle went to Babylon, where he wrote his first Epistle (I Pet. 5:13).

Most scholars believe that Mark's Gospel bears the heavy imprint of Simon Peter. In other words, Mark gleaned most of his information from Peter, which enabled him to write this Gospel, thereby, giving to the world one of the most beautiful presentations of the life and ministry of Jesus ever written. In its beautiful simplicity, which bears all the marks of Peter, it stands out with a grace that puts it in a league all by itself. Once again, that is Peter!

I guess I am saying that whoever was in the right or wrong respecting this disagreeable situation between Paul and Barnabas, the Lord, working from *"what is,"* used Mark to give us this most beautiful Gospel according to St. Mark. Had there not been the separation, with Mark then thrown with Peter, his uncle incidentally, the great Gospel according to Mark may never have come to us.

BARNABAS

So, here we leave *"Barnabas,"* who will not again be mentioned in the great Book of Acts. And yet, one has to say, as one should say, that there are few men in history who equaled this man.

As I have previously stated, had there

not been a Barnabas, there may not have been a Paul. It was Barnabas who stood up for Paul at the very beginning when the elders at Jerusalem were afraid of Paul. As well, it was Barnabas who sought him out whenever the great move of God took place at the church in Antioch, in effect, bringing Paul into the ministry.

It was Barnabas who risked his life with Paul on the first missionary journey, and Barnabas, as well, who battled with Paul the great Law/grace controversy, which threatened the early church.

The church, even unto the present, owes this man much!

Beautifully enough, Paul's friendly mention of him in I Corinthians 9:6 shows both that he continued his labors as an apostle and that the estrangement between him and Paul had passed away.

Concerning my own thoughts respecting the situation, I personally think that Paul was in the wrong by not wanting to take Mark on the second missionary journey. However, at the same time, I think Barnabas was wrong in leaving Paul.

"The Holy Spirit said, Separate me Barnabas and Saul for the work whereunto I have called them" (Acts 13:2).

That takes precedence over our feelings. So, in one sense of the word, it looks to me as if both of these men were wrong in the decisions they made. Nevertheless, the Lord continued His Work, but I think it would have gone better had it gone as the Holy Spirit originally intended.

(40) "AND PAUL CHOSE SILAS, AND DEPARTED, BEING RECOMMENDED BY THE BRETHREN UNTO THE GRACE OF GOD."

The order is:

1. The phrase, *"And Paul chose Silas, and departed,"* proclaims the beginning of the second missionary journey of Paul.

2. As well, the Greek structure of the Text tells us that Paul's choice of Silas was after the contention with Barnabas. In other words, it had not been in Paul's mind whatsoever regarding the taking of Silas. However, the Holy Spirit knew this rupture between Paul and Barnabas would come about and moved upon Silas to remain in Antioch, as we have previously stated, with now the reason being revealed (Acts 15:34).

3. *"Being recommended by the brethren unto the grace of God,"* seems to indicate that the church at Antioch was not affected in a negative sense toward either Paul or Barnabas respecting the dissension. Every evidence is that they gave Paul a great send-off and heartily approved of his choice respecting Silas.

4. Even though Silas was not a part of the church at Antioch, they recognized his maturity and recommended him strongly. He would be an excellent partner with Paul respecting the great Gospel of the *"grace of God."*

5. Silas, being an outstanding member of the Jerusalem church, would be helpful in showing the Galatian churches that there was unity between Paul and the Jerusalem leaders. Horton said, *"This would further put to rest the arguments of the Judaizers and would confirm the statements of Paul in Galatians 2:1-10 (where he said those Leaders accepted his Gospel as the same one they were teaching and gave him the right hand of fellowship)."*

6. Some think, as well, that Silas may have even personally heard Jesus teach and preach and, as well, that he saw Him after His Resurrection.

7. If that is correct, then Silas would have been of immense help to Paul for the obvious reasons.

(41) "AND HE WENT THROUGH SYRIA AND CILICIA, CONFIRMING THE CHURCHES."

The exegesis is:

1. While Barnabas and Mark caught a ship to Cyprus, Paul went overland to Cilicia.

2. Actually, this second missionary journey in Acts, Chapters 15 through 18, would take them to the following cities:

a. From Antioch, through Syria and Cilicia, to Derbe, Lycaonia (15:41-16:1).

b. Lystra and Lycaonia (16:1).

c. Iconium, Lycaonia (16:2-4).

d. Through Phrygia, Galatia, and Mysia to Troas (16:6-8).

e. Across the Aegean Sea to Samothracia and Neapolis (16:11).

f. Philippi, Macedonia (16:12-40).
g. Through Amphipolis, Apollonia, to Thessalonica, Macedonia (17:1-9).
h. Berea, Macedonia (17:10-14).
i. Athens, Greece (17:15-34).
j. Corinth, Greece (18:1-17).
k. Cenchrea, Greece (18:18).
l. Back across the Aegean Sea to Ephesus, Asia Minor (18:19-21).
m. Caesarea, Samaria (18:21-22).
n. Jerusalem (18:22).
o. Back to Antioch, Syria (18:22).

"Out of my bondage, sorrow, and night,
"Jesus, I come! Jesus, I come!
"Into Thy Freedom, Gladness, and Light,
"Jesus, I come to Thee!
"Out of my sickness into Thy Health,
"Out of my want and into Thy Wealth,
"Out of my sin and into Thyself,
"Jesus I come to Thee."

CHAPTER 16

(1) "THEN CAME HE TO DERBE AND LYSTRA: AND, BEHOLD, A CERTAIN DISCIPLE WAS THERE, NAMED TIMOTHEUS, THE SON OF A CERTAIN WOMAN, WHICH WAS A JEWESS, AND BELIEVED; BUT HIS FATHER WAS A GREEK."

The construction is:

1. To fully understand the Word of God, one must have a working knowledge of the Cross of Christ as it refers to our sanctification.
2. One must understand that everything revolves around the Cross.

PAUL'S SECOND MISSIONARY JOURNEY

The phrase, *"Then came he to Derbe and Lystra,"* begins Paul's second missionary journey, concluding with Acts 18:22. It would be a most momentous journey, which, undoubtedly, would have greater effect on civilization than anything that has ever happened, other than the First Advent of Christ.

NOTES

From this trip would ultimately spring that of which we refer to as western civilization. Understandably, it would be many centuries in coming, but the seedbed of the greatest freedoms and prosperity the world has ever known would be planted then.

The trip overland from Antioch to Derbe and Lystra would take Paul and Silas through the Taurus Mountains by way of a famous pass called the Cilician Gates. As stated here, Derbe would be their first stop. The church here had been established toward the end of the first missionary journey, probably about two years before.

A church had been established in Lystra, as well, actually, immediately preceding the church at Derbe, a distance of about 10 miles. This was where Paul and Barnabas were thought to be the Greek gods *"Jupiter and Mercurius"* after the healing of the cripple.

TIMOTHY

The phrase, *"And, behold, a certain disciple was there, named Timotheus, the son of a certain woman, which was a Jewess, and believed,"* speaks of him and his mother as being followers of Christ. Her name was Eunice, and the Scripture says that his grandmother Lois was also a godly believer (II Tim. 1:5; 3:14-15). They were probably saved when Paul preached the meetings in Lystra about two years before.

The phrase, *"But his father was a Greek,"* lends some small support to the idea that he was a man of means. As well, it seems he was not a believer.

Paul was strongly attracted to Timothy, evidently seeing something in him that was quite extraordinary. I speak primarily of his consecration to the Lord. Consequently, he would add him to his party, perhaps as a substitute for John Mark, whom he had refused to take.

This choice appears to have had other endorsement, for Paul later referred to prophetic utterances, which confirmed Timothy being set apart for this work (I Tim. 1:18; 4:14). It seems he had received, at this time, a special endowment for his mission, communicated through the laying on of the hands of the elders and of Paul (I Tim. 4:14; II Tim. 1:6). To allay any needless opposition from local Jews, Timothy was circumcised before setting out on this journey with Paul.

THE MINISTRY OF TIMOTHY

He was first entrusted with a special commission to Thessalonica to encourage the persecuted Christians. He is associated with Paul and Silas in the greetings of both Epistles directed to that church, and was present with Paul during his time at Corinth (II Cor. 1:19).

He is next heard of during the apostle's Ephesian ministry, when he was sent with Erastus on another important mission to Macedonia, whence he was to proceed to Corinth (I Cor. 4:17).

If we are reading Timothy correctly, he seems to have been a young man of some timid disposition, for Paul urged the Corinthians to set him at ease and not to despise him (I Cor. 16:10-11).

From the situation which resulted in Corinth (II Corinthians), Timothy's mission, it seems, was not successful, and it is significant that, although his name was associated with Paul's in the greeting in this Epistle, it was Titus and not Timothy who had become the apostolic delegate. However, Timothy accompanied Paul on his next visit to Corinth, for he was with him as a fellow-worker when the Epistle to the Romans was written (Rom. 16:21).

LOYALTY

Timothy also went with Paul on the journey to Jerusalem with the collection (Acts 20:4-5) and is next heard of when Paul, then a prisoner, wrote Colossians, Philemon, and Philippians. In the later Epistle, he is warmly commended and Paul intended to soon send him to them in order to ascertain their welfare.

When the apostle was released from his imprisonment and engaged in further activity, as the Pastoral Epistles indicate, it would seem that Paul left Timothy at Ephesus (I Tim. 1:3) and commissioned him to deal with false teachers.

Although Paul evidently hoped to rejoin Timothy, the fear that he might be delayed occasioned the writing of the first letter to him. This was followed by another when

NOTES

Paul was not only rearrested but on trial for his life. Timothy was urged to hasten to him, but whether he arrived in time cannot be ascertained. Of his subsequent history, nothing definite is known.

It seems he was an affectionate young man (II Tim. 1:4) but somewhat fearful (II Tim. 1:7), needing not a few personal admonitions from his father in the faith. He was warned not to give way to youthful lusts (II Tim. 2:22) and not to be ashamed of the Gospel (II Tim. 1:8).

Yet, no other of Paul's companions were so warmly commended for his loyalty (I Cor. 16:10; Phil. 2:19; II Tim. 3:10).

It is fitting that Paul's concluding letter should be addressed so affectionately to this almost reluctant successor, whose weaknesses are as apparent as his virtues.

(2) "WHICH WAS WELL REPORTED OF BY THE BRETHREN WHO WERE AT LYSTRA AND ICONIUM."

The pattern is:

1. Timothy's consecration is obvious here. Quite possibly, he had felt the call to preach almost immediately after his conversion approximately two years earlier. As well, to whatever degree was his ministry at that time, he seemed to be well known in both Lystra and the neighboring city of Iconium.

2. Paul, noting the young man's consecration, evidently inquired about him, already feeling led of the Lord to add him to their party.

3. Timothy received a most favorable report!

(3) "HIM WOULD PAUL HAVE TO GO FORTH WITH HIM; AND TOOK AND CIRCUMCISED HIM BECAUSE OF THE JEWS WHICH WERE IN THOSE QUARTERS: FOR THEY KNEW ALL THAT HIS FATHER WAS A GREEK."

The synopsis is:

1. The phrase, *"Him would Paul have to go forth with him,"* concerns that which was undoubtedly a Leading of the Spirit.

2. *"And took and circumcised him because of the Jews which were in those quarters,"* needs some explanation.

3. Even though his father was a Greek, his mother, as stated, was a Jewess, but for some reason, did not see fit to circumcise

NOTES

him when he was born, which strongly violated Jewish custom. Nevertheless, his mother being Jewish, he was labeled such, as well, despite his father being a Greek.

Jews still go by the custom of children being Jewish if their mother is Jewish.

As well, in some manner, it was known that he was not circumcised.

4. *"For they knew all that his father was a Greek,"* implies that there may have been a dispute over circumcision between his Jewish mother and Greek father when he was born. To keep peace, his mother acquiesced to her gentile husband, that is, if we are correct in our assumption.

5. Inasmuch as Paul seemed to have many enemies among the Jews, had he taken a young Jewish helper with him and his party with him not being circumcised, the detractors would have spread such far and wide, making it even more difficult for him to reach the Jews. So, he would have him circumcised, even though it meant nothing concerning his walk with the Lord.

6. We learn from this and other things that Paul did not go against the cultural norms of the people to whom he ministered unless those norms were immoral or idolatrous. In fact, this was excellent wisdom, as should be obvious (I Cor. 9:20-23).

7. However, on the other hand, Paul refused to circumcise Titus, who was a gentile. Under the circumstances, at least at that time, to circumcise him would have meant yielding to the Judaizers who said gentiles must become Jews in order to keep their salvation (Gal. 2:3-5).

8. As stated, Paul would do all that he could to appease people, but not at the expense of compromising the Gospel of Jesus Christ.

(4) "AND AS THEY WENT THROUGH THE CITIES, THEY DELIVERED THEM THE DECREES FOR TO KEEP, THAT WERE ORDAINED OF THE APOSTLES AND ELDERS WHICH WERE AT JERUSALEM."

The structure is:

1. The phrase, *"And as they went through the cities,"* referred to Phrygia and south Galatia.

2. Some claim that Paul by now had already written the Book of Galatians (Epistle), which dealt strongly with the Law/grace issue, with copies being given to all the churches in that region. However, it is most probable that it was not written until the beginning of the third missionary journey, which would have been several years later.

3. The phrase, *"They delivered them the decrees for to keep,"* pertained to copies of the decision concerning the Law/grace issue, which came out of the council at Jerusalem. Evidently, they had transcribed a number of copies, with each church to keep one on record, respecting this all-important doctrine.

4. The phrase, *"That were ordained of the apostles and elders which were at Jerusalem,"* signifies that this came from the very highest authority. However, I remind the reader that this authority was vested by the Holy Spirit in apostles and pastors, who had been chosen by the Lord. In fact, the *"apostles"* named here were the Twelve personally chosen by the Lord Jesus Christ, who had been by His Side for the entirety of the approximate three and one-half years of His public Ministry. As is obvious in the Book of Acts and the Epistles, such authority continues to be vested in the fivefold calling (Eph. 4:11).

5. Regrettably, when the apostles and elders of that first century gradually died off, little by little the church began to apostatize. It did so as men gradually usurped authority over the government of God, inserting their own government instead.

6. The Book of Acts and the Epistles are our pattern and standard for church government. There is absolutely nothing in these books that lends any type of credence to the idea that preachers and delegates from local churches are to elect some preacher by popular ballot to serve in a capacity of leadership over the church as a whole! Such simply does not exist, at least in the Word of God! But yet, such is pandemic in the modern church. Consequently, offices are established which have no scriptural credence. The will of these offices is imposed upon the church, with the word or the will of God given little place, if any at all! And yet, these offices can be a blessing if no

NOTES

spiritual connotation is attached to them.

7. So, these *"decrees"* were the result of God's divine Order of government and not that of the whims of man, which constitutes most decrees presently!

(5) "AND SO WERE THE CHURCHES ESTABLISHED IN THE FAITH, AND INCREASED IN NUMBER DAILY."

The pattern is:

1. The phrase, *"And so were the churches established in the faith,"* refers not just to faith, but *"the faith."* This was the truth of the Gospel with its teachings and precepts.

2. In other words, *"the faith"* was the whole body of truth that was preached and believed.

3. In fact, as should be obvious, this is the foundation of the work of God on Earth. The Holy Spirit can only bless *"the faith,"* which is *"Jesus Christ and Him Crucified"* (I Cor. 1:23).

Understanding that it's what Jesus did at the Cross that gives us the blessings of heaven, and that our faith must be anchored solidly in Christ and the Cross and maintained in that posture, this is called *"the faith."*

4. As well, if one is to notice, the Holy Spirit through Luke says, *"the churches,"* which speaks in the plural sense and not *"the church."* This denotes the fact that each church was independent and, therefore, not controlled by any outside ecclesiastical force. And yet, there was a great fellowship between these churches, and even Jerusalem, based on *"the faith,"* on which all true fellowship must be based. If the common bond is ecclesiastical force or hierarchy other than *"the faith,"* in the strict sense of the word, there is no fellowship.

7. Considering that these *"decrees"* came from Jerusalem and that they were *"ordained of the apostles and elders,"* if there was ever a time to establish a hierarchy, this would have been the time. However, nothing like that was established because it was not the will of God for such to be.

These *"decrees"* were definitely the Word of God and were meant to be obeyed, as is all of the Word of God. Nevertheless, such must be voluntary, or else, it is not a true acceptance, as should be obvious.

8. When Jesus Christ is allowed to be the Head of the Church and, in essence, *"the churches,"* the Holy Spirit can then lead, guide, and direct. However, once control is taken away from Christ, churches then become man-directed, with the Holy Spirit unable to function in such a climate. Sadly, such is the case in most modern churches.

8. The phrase, *"And increased in number daily,"* portrays growth, and more importantly, the right kind of growth.

9. It was growth established on *"the faith,"* which is the work of the Holy Spirit.

(6) "NOW WHEN THEY HAD GONE THROUGHOUT PHRYGIA AND THE REGION OF GALATIA, AND WERE FORBIDDEN OF THE HOLY SPIRIT TO PREACH THE WORD IN ASIA."

The exegesis is:

1. If the Cross of Christ is neglected, then whatever it is that is proposed is not the Gospel.

2. It is only when the Cross of Christ is held up that the Holy Spirit will then begin to do His Work.

STRENGTHENING THE CHURCHES

The phrase, *"Now when they had gone throughout Phrygia and the region of Galatia,"* implies a time frame of probably several months. As well, it implies that they were in the center of God's Will but with the direction, as we shall see, about to change. The time spent, as one might say, was well spent and constituted the strengthening of the elders (pastors) in the various churches and teaching the Word of God to the people.

We find here, which, of course, should be obvious, how necessary it is that believers know and understand the Word of God. For the Spirit of God to use these apostles in this manner, especially considering the ability that Paul had to raise up new churches, it lets us know how significant the teaching of the Word of God actually is.

One must remember that Bibles were not as proliferated then as now. Actually, for one to have had the Bible in those days, which consisted of Genesis through Malachi, it would have cost quite a sum of money, causing it to be out of reach for most people. Each Book of the Bible was written on long scrolls made of animal skins and copied

NOTES

laboriously by hand. It is quite certain that many, if not virtually all, believers had copies of some Books (the Law, the Psalms, the prophets), but probably precious few had all the Books of the Old Testament.

At this particular time frame, approximately 20 years after the Day of Pentecost, most probably the Books of Matthew and James were the only two of the New Testament which had been written by now. It is thought that Matthew was written in A.D. 37, with James written about A.D. 45. However, these dates are speculative at best.

FORBIDDEN OF THE HOLY SPIRIT

The phrase, *"And were forbidden of the Holy Spirit to preach the Word in Asia,"* refers to the area now known as northwestern Turkey. Asia is used here in its restricted sense of that district on the western coast of Asia Minor, of which Ephesus was the capital. It seems that Paul may have been on his way to Ephesus at this time with the purpose in mind of planting a church, which he later did do. The second missionary journey was not exclusively a visit to churches planted sometime before, but was also meant to plant new churches as well!

The word *"forbidden"* in the Greek text is *"koluo"* and means *"to stop by word or act."* Consequently, as is obvious, it is a strong word.

Why did not the Holy Spirit desire Paul to go to this area at this time?

From this we learn several things which are extremely important to the Child of God:

• The apostles were sent by the Holy Spirit wherever they were to go, meaning that they did not go anywhere of their own accord.

• The preacher of the Gospel must find the Mind of the Lord respecting his place of ministry. He must not be sent by man or according to his own desires, but rather according to the mind of God.

• Sadly, most preachers presently are sent by man. Consequently, I think it should be obvious as to the fallacy of such action.

What would have happened had Paul and Silas not had the leading of the Holy Spirit respecting their direction?

I think the answer should be obvious; they would have accomplished little or nothing for the Lord, and that is exactly what happens with any preacher who functions accordingly.

The preacher of the Gospel is supposed to be called by the Lord. As such, the ministry in which he is engaged is not his in the strict sense of the word, but rather that which belongs entirely to God. Accordingly, he is to seek the Face of the Lord extensively respecting leading and direction, and not move until that leading and direction are forthcoming.

FAMILY WORSHIP CENTER

The year, if I remember correctly, was 1980. I had felt led of the Lord to begin a church in Baton Rouge, Louisiana, even though I was gone almost constantly in those days in crusades all over the world. Nevertheless, the Holy Spirit began to deal with me greatly. After ascertaining that this definitely was the Lord, I set out to do what He had told me to do, wondering in my mind how in the world this could be accomplished, considering my extensive schedule.

Our beginnings were very small, actually using the facilities of a local Holiday Inn. However, in a short time, we purchased property at the outskirts of Baton Rouge on which the ministry complex was to be constructed. At the rear of that property, we built a small metal building and moved the *"church"* into that structure.

As mentioned, I was gone almost constantly, with the church pretty much left in the hands of associates, etc.

However, the Lord began to bless, with people being saved and baptized with the Holy Spirit, with the church growing.

The Lord then began to deal with me extensively about the construction of a larger facility, actually, a facility which would hold several thousands of people, even though at the time our attendance was probably only about 400 or 500, if that!

I engaged an architect, with work proceeding on the drawing of the plans, when I began to have doubts about the construction of this particular building, etc. Was I being foolish erecting a building 15 times the size of our present congregation?

NOTES

THE DREAM

During this time, I asked the architects to stop work on the drawings. With a renewed effort, I began to seek the Lord respecting the certitude of this direction. Was I certain that I had the Mind of the Lord?

I suppose it must have been several weeks after I had stopped the architects when the Lord gave me a dream.

In the dream, I saw the church exactly as it now stands, in other words, completely finished. However, it was more than that.

In the dream, I saw shafts of light streaming from heaven directly onto the church. That was all! However, when I awakened the next morning, I knew beyond the shadow of a doubt that I was on the right track and that the Lord was leading me in what I was doing. I gave notice to the architects to finish the drawings, with the new structure of Family Worship Center finished in 1984.

However, the point I wish to make in all of this concerns the leading of the Holy Spirit. It is absolutely imperative that the man of God have that leading, and nothing but that leading! Of course, this is where Satan fights the hardest.

If he can swing the leadership away from the Lord to self-will or other men, he has accomplished his purpose and task. The thing then becomes man-originated, therefore, man-instituted and man-led. As such, which comprises almost all of that which goes under the guise of Gospel presently, little or nothing is done for the Lord.

After the leading of the Holy Spirit is obtained, meaning that the individual is certain that what he is doing is the will of God, that leading must never be presented to anyone for approval. It is quite proper to ask for advice and counsel of other brothers and sisters in the Lord, with it being very proper to submit what one believes that God has told him (or her). Still, if one is absolutely certain that one has the mind of God, men must never be allowed to circumvent such leading or direction.

LED BY THE SPIRIT

Above all, I do not want the reader to think that we are advocating a Lone Ranger mentality because, in essence, we are actually saying the very opposite. What I am saying is this:

Many, if not most, modern Pentecostal denominations have long since ceased to follow this scriptural pattern. These hierarchies (and hierarchies they are) make their own plans, little heeding that which someone says that God has called them to do. In fact, and I know what I say is true, some of them take delight in doing the very opposite.

If the preacher and church are led exclusively by the Holy Spirit, such always constitutes a unity, with all having part in that which God is doing. Otherwise, it is limited to the hierarchy, which it mostly now is!

In truth, the Lone Ranger mentality, which religious hierarchies are fond of applying to others, is exactly what they are themselves.

It must be ever understood that the Lord does not use hierarchies, boards, committees, etc. He uses individuals exclusively. I do not know anywhere in the Bible that it mentions the Lord speaking to a board, committee, etc. He always speaks to a lone individual!

THE WAYS OF GOD

However, when He does this, He will, as well, speak to the church body in one way or the other, whether by gifts of the Spirit, a general feeling, etc. In truth, the Word of God is never *"of any private interpretation"* (II Pet. 1:20). One sees this pattern beautifully so in Acts 13:1-4.

The ways of God are beautiful, fair, equitable, and obvious, at least to those who are truly attempting to follow the leading of the Holy Spirit. It is only when man attempts to insert his own ways into this perfect way of God that problems arise!

The Holy Spirit stopped Paul and Silas from going into Asia at this time because He knew that these people were not ready yet to accept the Gospel. He also knew that the place He would now send Paul, which was Macedonia, was ready!

Of course, at this stage, the question could be asked as to why Paul and Silas did not have this particular leading at the

NOTES

beginning of the mission. As we have already stated, it seems that Paul had intended to go to Ephesus at this time, having previously believed this was the leading and direction of the Holy Spirit. Was he wrong at that time of this assessment?

At this time, I think it would be very proper to address ourselves to the finding of the will of God, which is the single most important thing in a believer's life.

Paul said, *"I beseech you therefore, brethren, by the Mercies of God, that you present your bodies a living sacrifice, holy, acceptable unto God, which is your reasonable service.*

"And be not conformed to this world: but be ye transformed by the renewing of your mind, that you may prove what is that good, and acceptable, and perfect, will of God" (Rom. 12:1-2).

Consequently, we know from this passage, plus many others which we will address, that God has a *"perfect will"* for any and all of His Children. As well, it is absolutely imperative, and I pray I am using the strongest language possible, that the believer *find* the will of God and *do* the will of God.

A PERMISSIVE WILL OF GOD?

As it regards believers, there is no such thing in the Word of God as a *"permissive will of God."*

Some have said that God has a perfect will for a person and, as well, a permissive will. No, He does not!

Such error is probably based on Israel's demand for a king when it was not the will of God that they have a king, at least at that time, but finally permitting them to do so, hence, the permissive will of God.

To attempt to base one's direction on error, even as this demand by Israel was, is foolishness indeed!

THE HOLY SPIRIT AND THE WILL OF GOD

The Holy Spirit will operate only in or toward the perfect will of God. It is impossible for Him to settle for anything else.

Paul wrote, *"And He* (our Heavenly Father) *Who searches the hearts knows what is the Mind of the Spirit* (knows what He has told the Spirit to do), *because He* (The Holy Spirit) *makes intercession for the Saints according to the Will of God"* (Rom. 8:27).

Consequently, we know and understand from this that the Holy Spirit will not intercede for us respecting anything less than the perfect will of God.

A PERFECT WILL FOR YOUR LIFE

God has tailor-made a plan of life and godliness for each and every believer, which constitutes His Will for that particular person (Lk. 22:42). Consequently, it is up to the believer to find God's Will and to do such. As well, it is not difficult for that to be done, that is, if the believer has a proper consecration to the Lord. Sadly, many, if not most, believers have no idea whatsoever as to what the will of God is for them. They live almost exclusively in their own will instead of the will of God.

Actually, this is the very reason that Jesus told His Disciples, and all others who would follow Him, as well, *"If any man will come after Me, let him deny himself* (deny his own will), *and take up his Cross daily, and follow Me"* (Lk. 9:23).

The *"Cross"* is a place of death, of crucifixion, if you will, and refers to dying to self, self-esteem, self-will, and self-aggrandizement in order that Christ may live within us. In other words, the greatest hindrance to the will of God being carried out in a believer's life is self-will.

Once again, as the Cross is the place of death, death to the old man, it is also the place of life, actually more abundant life (Jn. 10:10). While the Cross of Christ takes something from us, self-will, it also gives us something, which is God's Will, and that is the greatest place in which a person can find himself or herself.

Unless the believer knows and understands the Cross of Christ relative to our sanctification, in other words, how we live for God, and how we order our behavior, such a believer cannot really know the will of God. The will of God is always wrapped up in the Cross of Christ. If the believer places his or her faith exclusively in Christ and what Christ has done for us at the

NOTES

Cross, then the Holy Spirit, Who works exclusively within the parameters, so to speak, of the Cross of Christ, i.e., *"the Finished Work of Christ,"* then the Holy Spirit will work mightily within our lives. Let me say it again:

It is absolutely impossible for the believer to have, to know, and to do the will of God if that believer does not understand the Cross of Christ relative to sanctification. Once again, the Cross is the place where self-will dies, and it is the place where God's Will is brought about in our hearts and lives.

THE CROSS OF CHRIST
AND THE WILL OF GOD

Can a believer find the will of God without properly understanding the Cross of Christ relative to sanctification? Yes, a believer can because God loves us and always seeks our good. However, the fact remains, if one wants to consistently find and have the will of God to where the Holy Spirit can speak to him accordingly, just as He spoke to Paul and Silas, he must take up the Cross daily (Lk. 9:23).

The Lord is not sitting up in heaven waiting for a believer to take a misstep so He can swat him down. That's not the God that we serve. He loves us! Consequently, He will do with us and for us all that is possible for Him to do under the circumstances. But again, if we want the perfect will of God for our lives, we are going to have to understand the Cross of Christ as it regards our everyday life and living. Regrettably, most believers don't have the slightest idea how the Cross plays into their everyday life and living. They understand the Cross regarding salvation but not sanctification!

Please note the following, and I think it will help you to understand even more of this which we are attempting to say.

• Jesus Christ is the Source of all things we receive from God (Jn. 1:1-3, 14, 29; 14:6, 20).

• While Jesus is the Source, the Cross of Christ is the means, and the only means, by which all of these wonderful things are given to us (I Cor. 1:17-18, 23, 2:2).

• With Jesus as the Source and the Cross as the means, then our faith must be exclusively in Christ and the Cross. This is extremely important. The object of our faith must be the Cross of Christ (Rom. 6:1-14; Col. 2:10-15).

• With this being done, the Holy Spirit, Who works exclusively within the parameters of the Finished Work of Christ, will then work mightily on our behalf (Eph. 2:13-18; Rom. 8:1-11).

In brief, what we have just given you is God's Plan and the way and means to know His Will at all times.

(7) "AFTER THEY WERE COME TO MYSIA, THEY ASSAYED TO GO INTO BITHYNIA: BUT THE SPIRIT SUFFERED THEM NOT."

The structure is:

1. The phrase, *"After they were come to Mysia, they assayed to go into Bithynia,"* represented the area that was east of the Ephesus area.

Bithynia was another important Roman province, which lay along the Black Sea. It had important Jewish settlements, especially in the Greek-speaking cities of Nicaea and Nicomedia. I Peter 1:1 shows that Bithynia was later evangelized by others. About 50 years later, the Roman writer Pliny the Younger reported that there were a great many Christians there.

2. *"But the Spirit suffered them not,"* once again proclaims the door being closed to Paul and Silas, at least at this time.

One can see in this scenario the apostles attempting to find the mind of God respecting direction, but which did not come immediately.

Why?

That is a good question!

To properly understand this of which we speak, one has to understand two things:

1. The ways of God

2. These ways are tailored for each particular believer. In other words, there is no set formula for the leading and guidance of which we speak.

The Lord wants us to constantly look to Him about all things. Consequently, He, at times, as here, only gives us information sparingly, which causes us to continue to seek Him for further direction. Actually, that is the idea!

NOTES

The Lord wants us to totally depend on Him in every capacity and for everything.

VEERING OFF COURSE

The constitution of man is such, even believing man, that we will veer off course at the slightest opportunity, and that goes for even the most consecrated. If one is to notice, the Lord, at least at this stage of the game, told the apostles where not to go but did not tell them where to go. This, no doubt, took place while Paul and Silas were in prayer seeking God's Help and Guidance respecting all they were doing. The Holy Spirit would have simply spoken to their hearts, which let them know that these doors were closed. Consequently, they would keep seeking the next place of ministry until direction would come, which it did.

The most wonderful thing in the world is to be led by the Holy Spirit in this fashion. Such takes deep consecration and, as should be obvious, a strong prayer life. Let us say it again:

Sometimes the will of God is not easy to find. Sometimes we wonder what the Lord is doing; however, if our faith is in His Will and not our personal will, ultimately, we will find, we will see, and we will have the Mind of the Lord, the perfect will of God, even as did Paul and Silas.

(8) "AND THEY PASSING BY MYSIA CAME DOWN TO TROAS."

The diagram is:

1. There is some indication in the Text that Paul thought that the Holy Spirit possibly wanted him in *"Mysia,"* but the Spirit said *"no"* to that city as well!

2. Even though the Spirit told him to go to *"Troas,"* he was to find the door to ministry closed there also. As we have hopefully emphasized, all of this indicates the total moving and operation of the Holy Spirit in Paul's life and ministry respecting leading and guidance. Even at the risk of being overly repetitive, I would strongly emphasize to the reader that this lesson given here by the Holy Spirit is not meant to be a mere emphasis on geography, but rather how imperative it is that every believer have the absolute mind of God respecting direction. The Lord seeks that type of involvement in our lives concerning everything. If our relationship with the Lord is what it ought to be, it will soon become obvious, even as here with Paul and Silas, as to what is His perfect Will! To do otherwise is to fail completely because God cannot bless that which He has not directed. Sadly, that means that most believers have little Blessing from the Lord simply because they have little leading!

(9) "AND A VISION APPEARED TO PAUL IN THE NIGHT; THERE STOOD A MAN OF MACEDONIA, AND PRAYED HIM, SAYING, COME OVER INTO MACEDONIA, AND HELP US."

The overview is:

1. The major thrust of Paul's message was the Cross of Christ (I Cor. 1:23).

2. In fact, the Gospel is the Cross of Christ (I Cor. 1:17).

THE VISION

The phrase, *"And a vision appeared to Paul in the night,"* now proclaims the Holy Spirit telling Paul exactly where He wanted him to go.

As we have already stated, the Leading of the Lord is generally a step at a time, even as here. Such develops trust and causes one to continue seeking the Lord respecting what is to be done.

As well, this statement portraying the *"vision"* given to Paul by the Lord expresses another way in which the Lord communicates with His Children.

In fact, *"visions"* and *"dreams"* have been, and continue to be, used to impart information. The only difference in a vision and a dream is that the former is given while awake, with the latter being given while asleep (Joel 2:28; Acts 2:17).

The phrase, *"There stood a man of Macedonia,"* presents the northern part of modern Greece from the Adriatic to the Hebrus River. It is centered on the plains of the Gulf of Thessalonica, running up the great river valleys into the Balkan Mountains. It was famous for timber and precious metal.

This province included six Roman colonies, of which Philippi, Paul's first stop, was one.

Despite this area being a part of Greek culture, which actually has influenced the entirety of the world even unto this hour, due to Roman subjugation, many of the people were in a state of privation and want. II Corinthians 8:1-5 bears this out!

The *"man"* who Paul saw in the vision was a pagan who needed God. Whether he was a particular person who Paul later recognized upon going to the area or representative of all pagans is not known. At any rate, Paul now had direction.

COME OVER INTO MACEDONIA AND HELP US

The phrase, *"And prayed him, saying, Come over into Macedonia, and help us,"* presents the heart's cry of the lost who do not know the way and, within themselves, cannot find the way. Someone must help them find Jesus!

If it is to be known, how many at this very moment all over the world are crying in the very same manner? Sadly, there are precious few, if any, to help them!

Great segments of the church, although claiming to be Spirit-filled, are attending seminars where they will be told how to get rich. Many others, also in the Pentecostal realm, are wandering in confusion, following wrong shepherds, and, therefore, cannot hear the call. Countless others fall into the category of apathy. They simply have little or no concern at all for the lost.

Also, I wish to emphasize the fact that only those who are baptized with the Holy Spirit according to Acts 2:4 can be used in such a fashion. Without this great *"Helper,"* the believer can be little led by the Lord, if at all! So, virtually all of the true missions work that has been done in this century has been done exclusively by Spirit-filled believers (Acts 1:8).

So, Satan seeks to keep believers from being baptized with the Holy Spirit. If he cannot succeed in that, he seeks to divert those who are truly Spirit-filled to other pursuits which have little meaning and, in fact, are unscriptural. For the most part, he succeeds!

THE SIGNIFICANCE OF THE MACEDONIAN CALL

Concerning this Macedonian Call, Hervey said, *"Thus was ushered in the most momentous event in the history of the world, the going forth of Paul to take the Gospel to the Nations of the West."* As we have already stated, this is the beginning of what is presently referred to as *"western civilization."* Consequently, the Apostle Paul, at least as far as a messenger is concerned, was the greatest contributor to this all-important aspect of civilization, with the message of Jesus Christ being the actual foundation.

As well, considering something of this significance, the greatest in the history of the church to date, and maybe for all time, it should be understood that Satan would do everything within his power to hinder such an Operation of the Spirit. That may very well be why it was so difficult for Paul and Silas to find the mind of God. We cannot know or realize the war that must have been going on in the spirit world as Satan tried his best to hinder or even stop the Spirit of God from this great work. However, evil spirits and fallen angels did not succeed because Paul and Silas were adamant in their efforts to find the mind of God, which they did. I am persuaded that many times the Spirit of the Lord cannot have His Way because the individual or individuals with whom he is trying to work will not persevere as Paul and Silas did.

And yet, the east was not left without a witness, especially the witness of the other apostles, with Paul going there later himself.

There is strong tradition that the Apostle Thomas went to south India, had a great ministry, and was martyred there near Madras. However, as is obvious, it would be the west which would open its heart more so to the Gospel of Jesus Christ. Even then, Satan made great inroads in his attempt to stop the message by the apostasy of the church, with it ultimately sinking into that which is presently known as Catholicism. However, there was always a remnant which held true.

With the coming of the Reformation in the 16th century, the way was ultimately prepared for the great Latter Rain Outpouring (Joel 2:28-29; Acts 2:17-18), which commenced at the turn of the 20th Century and continues to this hour.

(10) "AND AFTER HE HAD SEEN THE

NOTES

NOTES

VISION, IMMEDIATELY WE ENDEAVORED TO GO INTO MACEDONIA, ASSUREDLY GATHERING THAT THE LORD HAD CALLED US TO PREACH THE GOSPEL UNTO THEM."

The overview is:

1. The phrase, *"And after he had seen the vision, immediately we endeavored to go into Macedonia,"* proclaims by the pronoun *"we"* that Luke, the writer of the Book of Acts, now joined Paul here at Troas.

2. He would travel with Paul, Silas, and Timothy to Philippi, but seemingly went no further regarding this second missionary journey. However, on the third missionary trip, he seems to have joined Paul there again (Acts 20:5-6).

3. Acts 21:1 finds Luke still with Paul and going with him to Jerusalem and then to Caesarea. It seems he remained there all the time Paul was a prisoner in that city (Acts 27:1). As well, Luke accompanied Paul on the voyage to Rome, which is the last place where we hear of Paul (Acts 27:2-3; 28:2, 11, 14-16).

4. It is believed by some that Luke wrote the Gospel which bears his name during this time of Paul's imprisonment at Caesarea, and did much work on the Book of Acts as well.

Very little information is given about Luke, or even how he came to know Paul.

LUKE

It is quite characteristic of the Holy Spirit to relate things at times without any explanation. Hence, the simple pronoun *"we"* speaks of Luke's presence.

Irenaeus, who lived in the second century after Christ, is the first person to refer clearly to Luke and to name him as the author of the third Gospel and Acts. Tradition also says that he came from Antioch in Syria, which, in a sense, was Paul's home church. It is said that he was not married and, therefore, had no family. He died at the age of 84 in Boeotia; however, that cannot be proven.

Paul mentioned him in his last Epistle, saying, *"Luke alone is with me"* (II Tim. 4:11). Consequently, this confirms the close link between the two men.

The phrase, *"Assuredly gathering that the Lord had called us to preach the Gospel unto them,"* proclaims an instant obedience to the Macedonian Call.

So, they left Troas with a definite objective in mind, anxious to begin their work of proclaiming the Gospel in that area. They had every confidence that it would be gladly received!

(11) "THEREFORE LOOSING FROM TROAS, WE CAME WITH A STRAIGHT COURSE TO SAMOTHRACIA, AND THE NEXT DAY TO NEAPOLIS."

The composition is:

1. *"Samothracia"* is a small island in the Aegean Sea. This sea is actually a part of the Mediterranean Sea, which separates Europe from Asia.

2. This island, though small, has a 5,000 foot mountain which, in clear weather, guided them on a straight course, and was a little short of being halfway to Neapolis.

3. *"Neapolis"* was actually the harbor of Philippi, which was about 10 miles away.

4. All of this is extremely important for several reasons:

a. They were answering the Macedonian Call, which was a direct admonition of the Holy Spirit.

b. This would be the very first presentation of the Gospel on European soil, which would have such a bearing on what is presently referred to as *"western civilization."*

c. There would be a great harvest of souls in this area now known as Greece, resulting in the planting of several churches.

(12) "AND FROM THENCE TO PHILIPPI, WHICH IS THE CHIEF CITY OF THAT PART OF MACEDONIA, AND A COLONY: AND WE WERE IN THAT CITY ABIDING CERTAIN DAYS."

The way is:

1. The phrase, *"And from thence to Philippi, which is the chief city of that part of Macedonia,"* proclaims Paul's destination.

2. The Scripture is not clear if the Holy Spirit directed the apostles to Philippi, or if they went there simply because it was the chief city, which seems to have been the case. The message in the vision simply was, *"Come over into Macedonia, and help us."*

3. The phrase, *"And a colony,"* simply

refers to Philippi being a colony of Rome. It had gold mines, plus other things, and as a result, it was now, as Paul said, the chief city of the area.

It received the name of Philippi from Philip, the father of Alexander the Great, who extracted a great revenue from its gold mines. Its great historical celebrity arose from the battle in the plain of Philippi, in which Antony and Octavian fought against Brutus and Cassius, with the former winning this conflict. This was 42 B.C.

4. Its prominence was enhanced further when, after the battle of Actium in 31 B.C. in which Octavian defeated the forces of Antony and Cleopatra, the town received a settlement of Italian colonists, with privileges conferred upon them, which gave them the same rights as if their land were part of Italian soil.

5. The phrase, *"And we were in that city abiding certain days,"* represents tremendous hardships they were forced to undergo, as we shall see, but, as well, the Lord moved mightily on their behalf, with a church established.

(13) "AND ON THE SABBATH WE WENT OUT OF THE CITY BY A RIVER SIDE, WHERE PRAYER WAS WONT TO BE MADE; AND WE SAT DOWN, AND SPOKE UNTO THE WOMEN WHICH RESORTED THITHER."

The synopsis is:

1. The phrase, *"And on the Sabbath we went out of the city by a river side, where prayer was wont to be made,"* evidently meant there was no synagogue in the city.

2. Synagogues were generally built next to a river or a body of water of some type, if such were available. Inasmuch as there evidently were not enough Jews in Philippi to have a synagogue, the few Jews there, plus interested gentiles, obviously met on the Sabbath at this particular place. This river was probably a small stream called the Ganges or Gangites, which is crossed by the Via Egnatia, about one mile out of Philippi.

3. *"And we sat down, and spoke unto the women which resorted thither,"* seems to tell us that no men were present other than Paul and his party.

4. Evidently there were some Jewish women present, plus proselytes to Judaism, or at least interested parties.

5. Obviously Paul had inquired if there was any meeting place of this type in the city, especially respecting synagogues, and was evidently informed of this meeting place.

6. As was ever Paul's method, at least where possible, he always went to the Jews first because of this obvious burden for his own countrymen.

(14) "AND A CERTAIN WOMAN NAMED LYDIA, A SELLER OF PURPLE, OF THE CITY OF THYATIRA, WHICH WORSHIPPED GOD, HEARD US: WHOSE HEART THE LORD OPENED, THAT SHE ATTENDED UNTO THE THINGS WHICH WERE SPOKEN OF PAUL."

The form is:

1. Without understanding the Cross of Christ as it refers to salvation and sanctification, a person cannot really understand the plan of God, at least as one should.

2. When Jesus said, *"It is finished,"* that means the terrible sin debt which hung over all of humanity was totally and completely eradicated, at least for all who will believe (Jn. 19:30).

LYDIA

The phrase, *"And a certain woman named Lydia, a seller of purple, of the city of Thyatira,"* indicates a businesswoman.

"Thyatira" was a city in what is now Asiatic Turkey, in other words, in the very area where Paul had intended to go before being directed to Macedonia by the Holy Spirit. In fact, a church would later be planted there, being one of the seven churches of Asia to which Jesus directed seven letters (Rev. 2:18-29).

It was not only an important point in the Roman road system, for it lay on the road from Pergamum to Laodicea, it was also an important center of manufacture, with dyeing and garment-making being a part of its prosperity.

"Lydia" was probably the overseas agent of a Thyatiran manufacturer; she may have been arranging the sale of dyed woolen goods, which were known simply by the name of the dye. This *"purple"* was obtained from the madder root and was produced in

NOTES

NOTES

the district under the name *"Turkey red."* It was a luxurious and expensive product!

The phrase, *"Which worshipped God,"* proclaims her as a gentile who had probably begun visiting a Jewish synagogue in Thyatira. Now, on being transferred to Philippi, if, in fact, that was the case, she continued her worship.

The words *"heard us"* referred to the fact that Paul evidently was asked to speak to these women, thus proclaiming the story of Jesus Christ and His Resurrection.

AN OPEN HEART

The phrase, *"Whose heart the Lord opened,"* presents her hungry for God, which I think is obvious, or she would not have been at this prayer meeting.

As the Holy Spirit anointed Paul to speak, the Lord, at the same time, began to deal with the heart of this wealthy businesswoman.

Actually, this is the method of the Holy Spirit in reaching souls. The Gospel is presented, with the Holy Spirit anointing its presentation by anointing the preacher and, at the same time, convicting the individual for whom the Gospel is intended. However, the structure of the Text implies that the Holy Spirit moved upon *"Lydia"* to a greater degree than normal. This, as well, shows the state of her heart. She was hungry for God.

However, the heart of the person is not arbitrarily opened by the Lord but is done so only if the person freely yields. Otherwise, it is hardened! The Gospel always has that type of effect. It either softens the heart or hardens the heart, all dependent upon the person's free moral agency. It is like the sun which softens wax and hardens clay. The result is in the material, not the sun.

ATTENTION TO THE WORD OF GOD

The phrase, *"That she attended unto the things which were spoken of Paul,"* refers to her eagerly grasping the great and grand story of Jesus Christ. The word *"attended"* in the Greek text is *"prosecho"* and means *"to hold the mind, or to have regard."*

One can only imagine the thoughts of her heart, the feelings of her soul, and the grasping of her very being upon hearing the grandest story ever told, especially considering that she had never heard it before! It was like water for a thirsty soul or bread for a hungry heart.

Why is it that some few respond in this manner, with most refusing and rebelling?

I suppose God alone would know the answer to that question. Once again, even though the Holy Spirit moves upon and convicts the sinner, still, the person's free moral agency, in other words, his free will, is never violated. The decision to accept Christ or reject Him is always the decision of the individual.

(15) "AND WHEN SHE WAS BAPTIZED, AND HER HOUSEHOLD, SHE BESOUGHT US, SAYING, IF YOU HAVE JUDGED ME TO BE FAITHFUL TO THE LORD, COME INTO MY HOUSE, AND ABIDE THERE. AND SHE CONSTRAINED US."

The exegesis is:

1. Due to the fact of the modern church little preaching the Cross in the last 50 or more years, the modern church is basically Cross illiterate presently.

2. This simply means, if one doesn't understand the Cross of Christ relative to sanctification, then, simply put, one doesn't know how to live for God.

WATER BAPTIZED

The phrase, *"And when she was baptized, and her household,"* seems to imply a particular period of time. In other words, it seems that all of this did not take place immediately upon Lydia hearing the message the first time.

At some point, she was baptized in water, as well as the entirety of her household, which, no doubt, included servants and associates who had evidently come to Christ as a result of her testimony.

Consequently, the very first convert in Europe was a woman, and the very first church established was in this woman's house. Once again, we see the tremendous part played by women in the realm of the Gospel.

"She besought us, saying, If you have judged me to be faithful to the Lord, come into my house, and abide there," seems to have a twofold application.

This tells us that she must have had quite

NOTES

a large residence, which evidently speaks of her station in life. In other words, she was successful!

She wanted Paul and his party to make her house their headquarters while they were in Philippi and, as well, to establish the church in her house.

LYDIA, THE SELLER OF PURPLE

The phrase, *"And she constrained us,"* means at first, they did not acquiesce, feeling perhaps that it may be an imposition on her. However, her continued assurance to them otherwise brought about their acquiescence. This, no doubt, was a great help to Paul respecting not only very suitable accommodations but, as well, a place to establish the church.

However, this woman's generosity and kindness were of far greater import than she could ever begin to imagine. Little did she realize at the time that this noble deed would be remembered forever. How could she know that what she did would become a part of the Word of God, and would be read by literally hundreds of millions of people down through the centuries!

Of course, those things were not in her mind and, in fact, could not be; however, that was not the point anyway. She was obeying God in what she did and would have the privilege of helping to establish the very first church in Europe.

What an honor that was bestowed upon *"Lydia, the seller of purple!"* And yet, the idea is that every believer should conduct himself or herself accordingly. To be sure, exactly as this record was kept of this noted lady, likewise, it is kept of all that is done for Christ, which will have eternal consequences.

Incidentally, according to Verse 40, men were soon added to the church.

(16) "AND IT CAME TO PASS, AS WE WENT TO PRAYER, A CERTAIN DAMSEL POSSESSED WITH A SPIRIT OF DIVINATION MET US, WHICH BROUGHT HER MASTERS MUCH GAIN BY SOOTHSAYING."

The construction is:

1. There are enemies to the Cross of Christ (Phil. 3:17-19).

2. What is the end result of such a position? It is destruction! (Phil. 3:19).

THE SPIRIT OF DARKNESS

The phrase, *"And it came to pass, as we went to prayer,"* does not exactly tell us where this was, but it does specify a certain place. However, it could very well have been in the home of Lydia, who had opened her house, as stated, to church services.

The phrase *"A certain damsel possessed with a spirit of divination met us,"* tells us that the girl was demon possessed. She gave advice and predicted futuristic events; evidently, she occasionally got some things right. This was done by a *"familiar spirit."*

Fortunetelling and all of its many forms are prevalent today. If individuals who practice such get anything right, it is all done by demon spirits and will ultimately result in wreckage.

Jesus said that the thief comes not but for to steal, kill, and destroy (Jn. 10:10).

"Which brought her masters much gain by soothsaying," pertains in the Greek to ventriloquism.

Evidently this spirit spoke through the girl, using a voice other than hers, claiming to give advice and counsel, which brought in quite a sum of money to her owners.

Various types of fortunetelling, astrology, and spiritism (or spiritualism) were common in all the ancient heathen religions of the Middle East and Europe. Isaiah 47:12-14 shows how all of this was part of the heathenism of ancient Babylon and was of no profit to these people, having its origin in the powers of darkness.

These things, as should be obvious, are part of the powers of darkness and must never under any circumstances be a part of anything that pertains to believers in the Lord.

MARY AND CATHOLICS

Believers are to receive guidance through the Spirit of God, Who will always guide us according to the Word of God. If it is not according to the Word of God, irrespective as to how religious it may be, it is not of God but of the Evil One.

For instance, all the many alleged

sightings of Mary by Catholics is a case in point.

Is this really Mary who is being seen?

No! It is a familiar spirit (demon spirit) imitating Mary, which is quite common respecting such spirits of darkness. This is obvious simply because there is no foundation for such in the Word of God. As well, the Mary worship of the Catholics being totally unscriptural fosters and nurtures operations by demon spirits, which is always the case in such unscriptural circumstances.

If one is to notice, Mary worship and sightings have exacerbated greatly since Pope John Paul II gained that particular office. One of the reasons is that he claimed that Mary appeared to him many years ago, telling him that he would be pope, etc. Actually, this situation has become so acute that feelers have been put out from the Vatican to various Catholic bishops and cardinals all over the world, respecting this pope speaking ex cathedra, thereby, proclaiming Mary as a co-redemptress with her Son, the Lord Jesus Christ. The answer has come back that the pope and the powers that be should cool such ideas, inasmuch as it is felt to be extreme. To be sure, that's an understatement!

DEMON SPIRITS

The idea that anyone would even remotely consider such a thing as making Mary co-redemptress is not only grossly unscriptural, but is obviously the leading of demon spirits as well!

Consequently, where does this leave Protestant preachers who proclaimed this pope as a *"godly man," "the greatest leader yet of Christianity,"* etc.?

To be frank, this, and such like, is the greatest sin in the modern church and is rife in modern church circles.

As well, where does that leave the multiple tens of thousands of modern believers who claim to be Spirit-filled, who pour tens of millions of dollars into so-called Christian enterprises, which espouse these very lies of darkness that I have just mentioned?

Such people are not Spirit-filled, or at least not Spirit-led (meaning led by the Holy Spirit) irrespective of their claims, and, in truth, they're the greatest hindrance to the true work of God in the world today.

NOTES

RELIGION

Most do not think of demon spirits operating in the realm of religion. However, this is the greatest domain of the world of darkness. Satan has damned more people to hell through religion than he has all the vices of the world put together a thousand times over.

If the truth be known, that which fuels such apostasy is the same thing that fueled the soothsaying of Paul's day. As this demon possessed girl brought much monetary gain to her masters, likewise, much monetary gain is presently brought to the modern purveyors of blasphemy.

A short time ago, I personally observed over one of the so-called Christian television networks a Christian leader, again so-called, who was touting the efforts of a so-called Christian entertainer, who was supposedly reaching the rock'n'roll crowd by singing their songs, walking their walk, and talking their talk!

If this apostasy was not bad enough, the audience, applauding this blasphemy, made it even worse!

Many who claim to be Christians are going to stand before God ultimately and find out that what they were supporting with their money and promotion was not really the work of God after all, despite its claims, but rather the work of Satan. That is a strong statement, but I know it to be true!

(17) "THE SAME FOLLOWED PAUL AND US, AND CRIED, SAYING, THESE MEN ARE THE SERVANTS OF THE MOST HIGH GOD, WHICH SHOW UNTO US THE WAY OF SALVATION."

The way is:

1. The phrase, *"The same followed Paul and us,"* implies that this went on for some time, even as the next verse proclaims, possibly for several weeks, etc.

2. The words, *"And cried,"* proclaim this demon spirit screeching through her the message she was to deliver. It was, no doubt, a very weird and strange sound, which used the vocal cords of this girl, but was actually the voice of the demon spirit that possessed her.

NOTES

3. *"Saying, these men are the Servants of the most high God,"* was somewhat that which the unclean spirits cried out concerning Jesus, *"You are the Son of God"* (Mk. 1:23-26; 3:11; Lk. 4:34-35).

Even though she was telling the truth in this instance, still, two things are made obvious here:

a. Respecting the Godhead, the Holy Spirit will not accept praise or acknowledgement in any capacity from evil spirits. This is one of Satan's greatest efforts in that he attempts to commingle the two, which is exactly that of which I have just spoken respecting the Catholic worship of Mary and the Protestant approval.

b. *"The most high God,"* would not have meant the same thing to the Greeks and Romans as it did to believers. They might have supposed she was talking about one of their gods, such as Zeus or Jupiter.

Inasmuch as they worshiped many gods, Satan was using this tactic to discredit Paul's message, actually making it the same as all the other messages received by the people from the world of darkness.

4. *"Which show unto us the way of salvation,"* should have been translated, *"A way of salvation,"* because the word in the Greek has no definite article. It reads *"a way,"* rather than *"the way,"* and should have been translated accordingly!

5. Even today, many heathen are willing to call the Gospel *"a way"* of salvation, but they are not at all willing to concede that the Gospel is *"the way,"* that is, the only way.

(18) "AND THIS DID SHE MANY DAYS. BUT PAUL, BEING GRIEVED, TURNED AND SAID TO THE SPIRIT, I COMMAND YOU IN THE NAME OF JESUS CHRIST TO COME OUT OF HER. AND HE CAME OUT THE SAME HOUR."

The status is:

1. Every believer is saved simply because of what Jesus Christ did at the Cross.

2. Every believer who is baptized with the Holy Spirit is such because of what Christ did at the Cross.

THE DELIVERANCE OF THIS GIRL

The phrase, *"And this did she many days,"* brings up the question as to why Paul allowed this to go on as long as he did.

Her actions must have drawn unwanted attention to Paul and his party and, as well, created a spectacle everywhere they went, or at least the times she was following them, which seems to have been spasmodic.

The only answer that can be given to this question is that for whatever reason, up to now, the Holy Spirit did not give him the latitude to cast this demon out. Why the delay, we are not told!

"But Paul, being grieved, turned and said to the spirit," proclaims Paul addressing himself to this evil spirit and not directly to the girl.

He was *"grieved"* for her terrible plight, for the torment of such a one is literally unbearable. As well, in the word *"grieved,"* there seems to be the idea that Paul had wanted to cast this thing out long before now but, for whatever reason, as we have stated, had not been given latitude by the Holy Spirit to do so. However, now that changed!

"I command you in the Name of Jesus Christ to come out of her," is in fulfillment of Mark 16:17. As well, every Spirit-filled believer has the authority to do the same thing, for the Scripture says, *"And these signs shall follow them that believe."*

"And he came out the same hour," means that the spirit came out instantly, which became very obvious within a short period of time.

WHAT ARE DEMON SPIRITS?

They are disembodied spirits that seek to inhabit human beings, or even animals for that matter (Mk. 5:1-13).

Even though they literally fill the atmosphere around the Earth (Eph. 2:2), even to the extent that their presence can be felt by Spirit-filled believers, still, they cannot successfully carry out their ungodly activities unless they possess a human being.

This is why the Gospel of Jesus Christ is so very, very important! The only Power that can overcome these spirits of darkness, which *"steal, kill and destroy"* (Jn. 10:10), is the name of Jesus exhibited by the believer through the Person and agency of the Holy Spirit (Acts 1:8).

That is the reason all the social or

educational programs in the world do precious little good alleviating the problems of mankind. These things, although of some small help, do not really address the true problem, which is actually demon spirits promoting and controlling their victims, respecting terrible acts of violence, deception, murder, destruction, etc. That is the reason that despite the pouring of billions of dollars into particular programs and efforts, the federal government cannot solve the drug problem, the crime problem, etc. These are spiritual problems, which definitely have an effect in the social, domestic, physical, and economic realm, but cannot be addressed in that respect. The problem is solved only when the Gospel of Jesus Christ is presented, accepted, and received by the sinner. Then the problem is addressed, and it is solved!

This is the basic reason that the church has little effect with all of its abortion marches, attempting to solve the problems of the nation by political means, etc. God's Way is the proclamation of the Gospel by Spirit-filled preachers, bringing forth the Gospel by the anointing of the Holy Spirit, which alone deals with the problem at hand.

WHERE DO DEMON SPIRITS COME FROM?

The Bible does not really tell us of the origin of demon spirits.

Some claim they are fallen angels; however, that is incorrect in that there is no indication in the Bible whatsoever of angels, be they good or bad, possessing anyone. In fact, all angels, whether the righteous or unrighteous variety, have spirit bodies and, as such, do not and, in fact, cannot possess anyone.

Some think that these are the disembodied spirits of a pre-Adamic creation on this Earth, which threw in their lot with Lucifer when he rebelled against God at some point in the distant past. To say it another way, it would have been before Genesis 1:2 and actually would have caused that upheaval, etc. However, there is not enough scriptural authorization to guarantee such a claim, meaning that it is speculative at best. This we do know:

NOTES

God did not originally create these spirits in their present evil, disembodied state. Everything He creates is good (Gen. 1:31; James 1:17). In fact, James said that not only do all good things come from God but, as well, *"With Whom is no variableness, neither shadow or turning."* In other words, in the distant past, He did not, and in the distant future, He will not suddenly turn and change respecting that which He does, because He will never go against His Nature and Character.

These spirits, which are of every description, help Satan carry out his work of rebellion against God and are the cause of so much misery and heartache.

WHAT DO THEY DO?

Jesus said they *"steal, kill and destroy,"* which means that is their end result. As we have stated, they seek to inhabit human beings, whom they can use to carry out their evil designs.

I think if the truth be known, demon spirits are the cause of all sickness, bondage, and aberrant behavior.

That does not mean that every cold or sickness of any nature is directly caused by demon spirits. However, it definitely does mean they are the originators of these illnesses and sicknesses that are such a liability to the human family.

This one thing is certain: God did not originate sickness and disease. If He did, Jesus would have been in rebellion by healing all who came to Him, etc. Actually, the Scripture plainly tells us that the liabilities of sickness, disease, and bondage are all with the devil, for it says, *"How God anointed Jesus of Nazareth with the Holy Spirit and with Power: who went about doing good, and healing all who were oppressed of the devil; for God was with Him"* (Acts 10:38).

As stated, this plainly tells us where sickness, bondage, and oppression come from!

These spirits are given various names in the Bible. They are called *"unclean spirits"* (Mk. 1:26), *"a dumb spirit"* (Mk. 9:17), *"the foul spirit"* (Mk. 9:25), *"a dumb and deaf spirit"* (Mk. 9:25), *"a spirit of infirmity"* (Lk. 13:11), *"a spirit of divination"* (Acts 16:16), *"the evil spirit"* (Acts 19:15), *"the spirit of bondage"* (Rom. 8:15), *"the spirit of the world"* (I Cor. 2:12), *"familiar spirits"* (Lev. 19:31), and *"a lying spirit"* (II Chron. 18:21).

CAN A BELIEVER BE DEMON POSSESSED?

In a word, *"No!"*

However, a believer definitely can be oppressed by demon spirits, which can cause sickness, bondage, etc. Jesus said, *"And ought not this woman, being a daughter of Abraham, whom Satan has bound, lo, these eighteen years, be loosed from this bond on the Sabbath day?"* (Lk. 13:16).

So, this tells us that Satan had caused this terrible physical problem in this woman, who definitely was a believer, even according to the words of Jesus. She was not possessed by the devil but was definitely oppressed by Satan, as is obvious!

In fact, there are hundreds of thousands, if not millions, of believers who definitely love the Lord, are definitely born-again, and many of them are Spirit-filled, but they are oppressed by demon spirits in the form of sickness, or even bondage in some cases. They need deliverance, which can only be brought about by the power of God.

THE CROSS OF CHRIST

Christians are in trouble, that is, if they are, because they do not understand the Cross of Christ relative to sanctification. By that, I am speaking of how we order our behavior, how we have victory over the world, the flesh, and the devil, in other words, how we live for God. The tragedy is, most believers simply do not know how to live for the Lord. Most will not believe that, but it is true.

Every demon power of darkness was defeated at the Cross of Christ. In regard to this very thing, Paul said:

"Blotting out the handwriting of ordinances that was against us which was contrary to us, and took it out of the way, nailing it to His Cross; and having spoiled principalities, and powers, He made a show of them openly, triumphing over them in it" (Col. 2:14-15).

Pure and simple, the Holy Spirit through Paul tells us in the passage just quoted that every power of darkness, which includes demon spirits, fallen angels, and Satan himself, were all defeated at the Cross of Calvary. That's the reason that Satan fights the Cross as he fights nothing else.

The believer must understand that everything we receive from God comes from Jesus Christ as the Source because He paid the price at Calvary's Cross. Having said that, let us make it clearer by saying that the Cross of Christ is the means, and the only means, by which we receive all of these wonderful things from the Lord. It is Christ and what He did at the Cross that makes it all possible.

Every believer must understand that we are facing the terrible powers of darkness, and there is only one thing that can defeat these powers, and that is the name of Jesus according to what He did at the Cross.

Listen again to Paul:

"For we wrestle not against flesh and blood, but against principalities, against powers, against the rulers of the darkness of this world, against spiritual wickedness in high places" (Eph. 6:12).

To be sure, nothing that man has can overcome these things, only the power of God registered in the Holy Spirit.

HOW THE HOLY SPIRIT WORKS

The Holy Spirit is God. As such, He can do anything, as should be obvious.

However, there's one thing about the Holy Spirit that we must know. It is the following:

The Holy Spirit works exclusively within the parameters, so to speak, of the Finished Work of Christ. In fact, the Holy Spirit will not work apart from the Cross of Christ. That's what gives Him the legal means to do all that He does for us. Paul said:

"For the Law of the Spirit (Holy Spirit) of Life in Christ Jesus (what Jesus did for us at the Cross) has made me free from the Law of sin and death" (Rom. 8:2).

The Holy Spirit does not demand much of us, but He does demand one thing, and on that He will not bend.

He demands that our faith be exclusively in Christ and what Christ did for us at the Cross (Rom. 6:1-14; 8:1-11; I Cor. 1:17-18,

NOTES

23; 2:2; Gal. 6:14; Col. 2:10-15). If our faith is properly placed, the Holy Spirit can easily overcome these powers of darkness; otherwise, we are on our own. To be sure, as we have stated, without the Holy Spirit, we cannot do anything. That's the reason that so many believers, although loving the Lord, still function in bondage, which makes life miserable.

HUMANISTIC PSYCHOLOGY

This is why it is so terrible for so-called church leaders to refer believers with problems, of whatever nature, to a psychologist, who has no spiritual understanding whatsoever of the problems involved. If the truth be known, these people, who only have the learning of the world, not only cannot help the person but actually make the situation worse.

Laying aside the spiritual and looking at aberrant behavior from a strictly practical sense, it should be understood that the field of psychology has no wonder or miracle drug that they can dispense to someone respecting behavior problems, fears, etc. Such does not exist for that purpose.

All they can do is talk to the person and have the person talk to them. When it is all said and done, that is the extent of psychology. Now I will make this statement:

The problem that besets humanity, which is a spiritual problem and was caused by the Fall, can only be addressed by the power of God through the name of Jesus, with our faith in Christ and the Cross, which then gives the Holy Spirit latitude to work within our lives.

We must understand that this problem is so severe that even God could not talk man's problems away. To be sure, He was able to speak light into existence and actually frame the worlds, respecting all of His Creation, strictly by His Word (Gen., Chpt. 1; Heb. 11:3).

However, when He came to the salvation of man, He could not speak redemption into existence. He had to literally become man and die on a cruel Cross, thereby, paying the price of the terrible sin debt and, consequently, breaking the grip of sin in the human family.

NOTES

OMNIPOTENT, OMNISCIENT, AND OMNIPRESENT

Now, if God being all of these things listed in our heading could not speak man's redemption and deliverance into existence, how in the world does one think a mere human being can do such?

No! There is no help for man from this source, only harm!

However, there is help, and there is a solution. That solution is Jesus Christ and His Power to save through what He did for us at the Cross and our faith in that Finished Work.

While believers feel the impact of demon spirits constantly and observe their evil handiwork on every hand, no believer need ever fear these powers of darkness, providing his faith is anchored in Christ and the Cross. The reason is very simple: *"You are of God, little children, and have overcome them: because greater is He Who is in you, than he who is in the world"* (I Jn. 4:4).

(19) "AND WHEN HER MASTERS SAW THAT THE HOPE OF THEIR GAINS WAS GONE, THEY CAUGHT PAUL AND SILAS, AND DREW THEM INTO THE MARKETPLACE UNTO THE RULERS."

The construction is:

1. The *"flesh,"* as Paul used the word, pertains to that which is indicative to human beings. It is our education, motivation, talents, ability, self-will, will power, etc.

2. Due to the Fall, man has been weakened to the extent that he cannot hope to live for God by the means of *"the flesh."* He can only do so by the power of the Holy Spirit.

ILL GOTTEN GAINS

The phrase, *"And when her masters saw that the hope of their gains was gone,"* implies that it quickly became obvious that the demon spirit no longer possessed the girl. Consequently, when people came to her for fortunetelling, etc., she not only could not tell them anything about the future, her entire demeanor and nature were completely changed. Even though the Scripture is silent, there is some implication, as well, that the girl gave her heart to the Lord Jesus Christ upon her deliverance. Consequently, she was of no more service whatsoever to these who had used her bondage, as hurtful as it was to her, to bring in monetary gain to themselves.

How so much this pictures the majority of the world. A few grow filthy rich providing drugs to those who are hopelessly bound by this power of darkness. The same goes for alcohol, etc.

As well, states fill their coffers with gambling money that is provided mostly by the poorest of the poor, who can ill afford the lottery tickets they purchase, hoping to strike it rich. In fact, one can probably say that much of the *"gain"* of this world comes from the unfortunate disposition of the ignorant and the dispossessed, in other words, those who can little help themselves.

In fact, their only answer, even as illustrated in this 16th chapter of Acts, is the Lord Jesus Christ.

A PERSONAL EXPERIENCE

Having ministered in parts of Africa, I have a love for these people and a concern for what happens in these particular countries.

Just a short time ago, I observed over the news, as did most of the world, the change of government in a particular African country. The people were dancing in the streets for joy, but yet, I knew they were merely replacing one tyrant with another. Off of their backs, he will become a billionaire, with no thought of alleviating their suffering.

No, the answer is not found in politics, education, money, or any other thing that could be named, at least that is in this world, but only in Jesus. While these other things certainly are significant, still, they cannot address themselves to the real problem of humanity, which can only be done through and by the Gospel of Jesus Christ. That is the reason He said that we should *"go into all the world, and preach the Gospel to every creature"* (Mk. 16:15).

The phrase, *"They caught Paul and Silas, and drew them into the marketplace unto the rulers,"* implies several things:

After realizing the girl could no longer be used in the fashion of divination, they set about to lay hold on Paul and Silas. The implication is that they laid wait for them, apprehending them at a particular time.

NOTES

Also, it seems that *"her masters"* must have been well known in the city, holding sway with particular magistrates. Quite possibly, upon hearing the complaint, these *"rulers"* may very well have told these people that if Paul and Silas could be brought before them, they would take the necessary steps. In other words, it was what is presently referred to as a kangaroo court.

(20) "AND BROUGHT THEM TO THE MAGISTRATES, SAYING, THESE MEN, BEING JEWS, DO EXCEEDINGLY TROUBLE OUR CITY."

The pattern is:

1. The phrase, *"And brought them to the magistrates, saying,"* pertained to Romans appointed by Rome. Consequently, their power and authority were beyond that which would be normal.

2. The next phrase states, *"These men, being Jews, do exceedingly trouble our city."* If it is to be noticed, it does not mention the real reason they were there, which was the girl being set free. So, they would cloud the issue, leveling general charges against Paul and Silas, which little could be proven either way.

As well, the manner in which the word *"Jews"* was used implies contempt.

Long since being away from God, Jews, who had previously been a great blessing to all, now seems to have been the very opposite, except those who named the name of Jesus.

The name *"Jews"* was now used as a slur and, unfortunately, continues unto this present hour.

Such is very sad because it is not only very hurtful to the Jews but, as well, deprives people of the blessings of God. It is true that the Jews have long since departed from their service to God and, worse still, have murdered their own Messiah in the Person of Jesus Christ. Still, the Word of God means exactly what it says in the promise given to Abraham, *"I will bless them who bless you, and curse him who curses you"* (Gen. 12:3).

3. From that one passage, I believe that God means exactly what He says. Any people who bless the Jews, irrespective of their spiritual state, will be blessed by God. That is one of the reasons, I think, for the

prosperity in America.

Conversely, any nation in the world who curses the Jews, as many have, will ultimately find themselves on the rocks, facing certain destruction. It may be awhile in coming, but come it shall!

Paul and Silas were accused of exceedingly troubling the city of Philippi but, in reality, had only troubled those who were making gain from someone else's terrible misfortune.

(21) "AND TEACH CUSTOMS, WHICH ARE NOT LAWFUL FOR US TO RECEIVE, NEITHER TO OBSERVE, BEING ROMANS."

The synopsis is:

1. The phrase, *"And teach customs, which are not lawful for us to receive, neither to observe,"* blatantly presented a gross untruth. Actually, Judaism was a legal religion in the Roman Empire. Paul and Silas were not teaching Judaism, but rather Jesus. However, because they were Jews, these Romans would not have been able to distinguish the difference.

2. Actually, they could not have cared less about these *"customs,"* only that the girl was no longer making them money, and they blamed Paul and Silas for this.

3. The words, *"Being Romans,"* imply superiority. In other words, they considered themselves in every way to be superior to the Jews. After all, were they not the masters of the whole world?

(22) "AND THE MULTITUDE ROSE UP TOGETHER AGAINST THEM: AND THE MAGISTRATES RENT OFF THEIR CLOTHES, AND COMMANDED TO BEAT THEM."

The exegesis is:

1. The phrase, *"And the multitude rose up together against them,"* proclaims the judgment seat as probably being out-of-doors, at least the part where the people stood, as well as a part of the marketplace. Consequently, there was always a crowd of people at these proceedings, which, at times, provided sport for the spectators, etc.

2. As well, there is a possibility that the owners of this delivered girl may well have sent people into the crowd to stir them up, which did not take much agitation anyway, considering that the ones on trial were Jews.

4. *"And the magistrates rent off their clothes, and commanded to beat them,"* is recalled by Paul in I Thessalonians 2:2.

5. Scourging under Roman law was a most brutal and cruel punishment. Many died under its torture.

6. Paul and Silas must have been given superhuman strength to have endured it.

They then had to suffer the added torture of the stocks in the inner prison, which usually was a noisome and wet dungeon without any light. As well, the stocks were frequently so placed that the unhappy prisoner's shoulders lay on the wet stone floor, and his feet, drawn as far apart as possible, were fastened high up to the wall.

(23) "AND WHEN THEY HAD LAID MANY STRIPES UPON THEM, THEY CAST THEM INTO PRISON, CHARGING THE JAILOR TO KEEP THEM SAFELY."

The pattern is:

1. The phrase, *"And when they had laid many stripes upon them,"* refers to the fact that the lictors were egged on by the mob, with the apostles beaten almost to death.

2. While the Mosaic Law did allow scourging, 40 stripes were the limit. However, Rome had no such law, consequently, they could lash the whip as long as they desired.

3. *"They cast them into prison,"* proclaims such as being beyond the pale of modern thinking. If prisons are bad now, they were awful then! Prisoners had no rights and could be treated any way that was desired, which they usually were.

4. *"Charging the jailor to keep them safely,"* contains the implication that Paul and Silas were desperados and, consequently, must be watched closely.

(24) "WHO, HAVING RECEIVED SUCH A CHARGE, THRUST THEM INTO THE INNER PRISON, AND MADE THEIR FEET FAST IN THE STOCKS."

The account is:

1. The Cross of Christ portrays the love of God in a fashion that man cannot deny, at least if he is to be honest!

2. When Jesus poured out His Life on the Cross by the shedding of His own precious Blood, He atoned for all sin, at least for all who will believe.

TORTURE

The phrase, *"Who, having received such a charge,"* implies their notoriety and that he could use any means at his disposal to continue the punishment, which he did!

"Thrust them into the inner prison," pertained to that which was escape-proof and, as well, was reserved for the most violent of criminals.

"And made their feet fast in the stocks," not only presented a means of guaranteeing security, but also was an extremely torturous device.

The legs were pulled wide apart, with the feet fastened in the stocks, which, after a few moments, caused the muscles in the legs to begin constriction. In a very short period of time, the pain would have been unbearable.

As we have stated, it is almost certain that their shoulders, which had been beaten raw, lay on the wet stone floor. This added to the pain and misery, that is, if it was possible for such to be increased.

Considering that the Lord would send an earthquake a short time later, which would effect their release, why would He allow them to suffer this terrible pain and indignities? Understanding that He is able to do whatever is needed, why was the deliverance after the terrible torturous beating and not before?

WHY?

We know that Paul was one of the godliest and most consecrated men to the Lord who ever lived. Considering that and the power of God manifested in his ministry, and considering that the Lord is able to do anything, it is incumbent upon us to plumb these depths, at least as far as is possible, to see what the Holy Spirit is saying.

Some in the modern so-called faith ministry have claimed that Paul suffered these terrible things because his faith was insufficient. They have even gone as far as to say that if he had possessed their degree of faith, all of these torturous indignities could have been avoided.

To be frank, such drivel, and drivel it is, is hardly worth dignifying with a response.

NOTES

However, I do believe that it would be very profitable in a spiritual sense, even as we have stated, to investigate this extremely important matter.

While we cannot understand all the reasons that God would do certain things, I am positive that His Reasons, or at least some of them, will become obvious.

THE BELIEVER'S RELATIONSHIP WITH THE LORD

The believer must understand that nothing can happen to a believer but that the Lord either causes it or allows it (Job, Chpts. 1-2).

Of course, the Lord does not cause a believer to sin, with all its attendant misery. However, He does allow such and its attendant consequences! As well, He did not cause these people to treat Paul and Silas in the manner in which they were treated, but He did allow them to do this dastardly thing, even though He had the power to stop it instantly.

The Scripture plainly says, *"There has no temptation taken you but such as is common to man: but God is faithful, Who will not suffer you to be tempted above that you are able; but will with the temptation also make a way to escape, that you may be able to bear it"* (I Cor. 10:13).

The believer must understand that Satan can only do what he is allowed to do. He is even held in restraint by God regarding the unsaved, much less believers! In other words, and I say again, he can only do what the Lord allows him to do.

To not understand that limits God's Power and makes Him subject to Satan instead of otherwise. Of course, we know that all answer to God!

So, these things which happened to Paul and Silas, and have happened to untold numbers of believers down through the many centuries, were allowed by the Lord for a purpose and a reason (Heb. 11:36-38).

IS IT POSSIBLE THAT A LACK OF FAITH COULD PLAY A PART IN SUCH DIFFICULTIES?

It certainly is true that a lack of faith definitely plays a part in some difficulties and problems experienced by believers. Still, even as we have stated, to conclude Paul as lacking in faith and, consequently, having to suffer these indignities for that reason is beyond conjecture and could be labeled only as silly!

Of course, faith plays an extremely important part in all that we do, but at the same time, the idea that one can have enough faith and, consequently, be spared all tribulations and difficulties is simply not taught in Scripture. At the same time, and as stated, all problems are not necessarily because of a lack of faith (Ps. 34:19).

WHY DOES THE BELIEVER NEED CERTAIN DIFFICULTIES?

Despite thoughts to the contrary, none of us, no matter how consecrated, are as holy as we think we are. Also, even in the life of the strongest believer, flesh and self-will are far more prominent than any of us would like to believe, even in the life of one such as the Apostle Paul.

As well, even as Paul mentioned, if we are given certain things by the Lord, we have a tendency to very quickly become puffed up, in other words, getting our eyes off the Lord onto our own abilities and so-called righteousness (II Cor. 12:7-12).

Consequently, the more that one is used of the Lord, the more difficulties and problems it seems are allowed, and for the very reasons mentioned.

These things have a tendency to keep the believer on his knees when, otherwise, such might not be the case. In other words, if we do not have something to pray about, even something severe, there is a good possibility that we will not pray at all!

Yes, the Lord allows certain difficulties to come our way, even some very severe, but all for the purpose of our good and never for our harm.

IT IS THE LORD'S INTENTION THAT WE TURN THESE DIFFICULTIES INTO A SACRIFICIAL OFFERING!

In other words, we are not to consider these things as a penalty or punishment, which Satan traps many believers into thinking, but rather as an offering before the Lord, which then brings it into the Spirit of Christ. As we shall see, this is exactly what happened with Paul and Silas.

NOTES

As well, if one is to notice, when Paul was placed in prison, he referred to himself as *"Paul, a prisoner of Jesus Christ,"* which meant that he was not a prisoner of Nero (Phile. 1:1).

He knew the Lord could have easily stopped his being placed in prison or could have delivered him anytime He so desired. However, for whatever reason, incidentally, a reason not known to Paul, the Lord wanted Paul in prison at this time. Consequently, Paul referred to himself, as stated, as a *"prisoner of Christ and not Caesar."*

THE OFFERING OF SACRIFICE

In doing this, he submitted this dilemma and himself as an offering of sacrifice unto the Lord, which is what the Lord intended all along.

Unfortunately, in many of these situations, Satan has been very successful in making Christians believe a lie, in other words, that they have suffered their particular problem because of a lack of faith, that God is punishing them for something which happened in the past, etc.

None of that is correct! God does not work in that fashion. In fact, if a believer has sinned, and that believer earnestly and honestly repents before the Lord, the sin is washed away, and the penalty as well (I Jn. 1:9). While it certainly may be true that some fellow believers may attempt to exact their pound of flesh, which, regrettably, often happens, still, that is not the Lord, but rather the evil in these particular people, whomever they may be.

Even then, the Lord has to allow them to do such a thing, which will not really hurt their intended victim, that is, if total trust is placed in the Lord. However, to be sure, such action will definitely hurt the perpetrator, and for the obvious reasons.

No, the far greater majority of adverse situations that happen to the believer is allowed by the Lord for particular reasons, and is meant for our good and not for our harm. While it may seem grievous for the time being, it will ultimately bring forth good fruit (Jn. 15:2).

(25) "AND AT MIDNIGHT PAUL AND SILAS PRAYED, AND SANG PRAISES UNTO GOD: AND THE PRISONERS HEARD THEM."

The account is:

1. The Cross alone can effect humility in the heart and life of the believer.

2. More than anything else, as it regards the believer, the Cross of Christ deals with self (Lk. 9:23).

MIDNIGHT

The phrase, *"And at midnight Paul and Silas prayed,"* does not mean that they began praying at midnight, but rather that they were still praying at midnight, having begun sometime earlier.

As well, the word *"prayed"* in the Greek text is *"proseuchomai"* and means *"to supplicate and worship."*

The manner of their praying, as is evident here, tells us their frame of mind, which registered no complaint against God at all.

Because of the difficulties experienced, if there was ever a time for them to think that the Macedonian Call was just a bad dream and that they must be out of the will of God, this was the time they could have thought such. However, they knew the opposite was true.

Unfortunately, due to the unfavorable climate at the present time regarding erroneous teaching respecting faith, many believers have been led to think that if any difficulty arises, that means something is wrong, etc. Quite the contrary is true!

I think one can safely say that if no problems arise in our work for God, this is a sure sign that we are out of the will of God. Satan does not oppose that which is causing him no problem, however, to be sure, he will oppose, and deadly so, that which is truly of God.

WHAT DOES IT TAKE TO ROB THE BELIEVER OF HIS VICTORY?

In other words, we know that the terrible beating that both of these men suffered, plus the terrible torture of being fastened in the stocks, in addition to being thrown in prison, did not get their victory. In other words, they could still praise God, and they could still worship God without the slightest hint of complaint or self-pity.

That should be a lesson to us, considering that some who read these words lose their victory at the slightest provocation, even if the car immediately ahead does not accelerate as quickly as we think it should upon the light turning green.

This lesson given to us here and played out by Paul and Silas should be taken very seriously for the following reasons:

It is no problem whatsoever for any of us to pray and sing praises unto God whenever things are going our way. With good health, our pockets full of money, and the well-wishes of others, it is very easy to do these things. However, this which Paul and Silas faced is where the rubber meets the road. When one can pray and sing under these circumstances, one has victory that Satan and all the hordes of hell cannot take. Considering these circumstances, what a joy to heaven and what a disappointment to the Evil One!

SANG PRAISES UNTO GOD

To pray and worship the Lord, as wonderful as that might be, especially considering these circumstances, still is not the ultimate, that being the song that now filled the hearts of these two apostles.

As well, they did not sing complaints or something gloomy or melancholy. In other words, they were not singing the blues! They were singing praises to God!

This meant they were singing of His Might and Power to deliver, even though they had not yet experienced any deliverance. Now, if one wants to give a definition of faith, the singing praises unto God in the midst of this terrible situation is the greatest definition I know!

What Psalm were they singing, if, in fact, it was a Psalm?

Of course, only the Lord knows the answer to that. However, they could have been singing the following:

"I will extol You, my God, O King;
"And I will bless Your Name forever and ever.
"Every day will I bless You;

"And I will Praise Your Name forever and ever.
"Great is the LORD, and greatly to be praised;
"And His greatness is unsearchable" (Ps. 145:1-3).

"And the prisoners heard them," actually means the other prisoners were listening to them. I'm sure those prisoners had never heard anything like this before. How in the world could somebody sing when his back was cut to pieces by the lictors lash, etc.?

Considering this moment, Hervey said, *"What a scene! The dark inner dungeon; the prisoners fast in the stocks, their backs still bleeding and smarting from the stripes; the companionship of criminals and outcasts of society; the midnight hour; and not groans, or curses, or complaints, but joyous trustful Songs of Praise ringing through the vault! While their companions in the jail listened with astonishment to the heavenly sound in that place of shame and sorrow."*

This was something these *"prisoners"* had never heard in all of their lives. These types of circumstances normally precipitated cursing, swearing, and blasphemy, but now, they were hearing someone praising God in both prayer and song. As well, it was accompanied by a mighty moving of the Holy Spirit.

Even though this day had begun for all of these prisoners under very dire circumstances, it would end in the greatest moment they had ever experienced. Whether any of them accepted Christ or not, we are not told. However, I find it difficult to believe that they experienced this tremendous miracle, which was about to happen, without any of them giving their hearts to Christ.

No! I believe that many of them, if not all, said *"yes"* to Jesus!

Incidentally, we know what these prisoners heard from Paul and Silas! What are they hearing from us?

(26) "AND SUDDENLY THERE WAS A GREAT EARTHQUAKE, SO THAT THE FOUNDATIONS OF THE PRISON WERE SHAKEN: AND IMMEDIATELY ALL THE DOORS WERE OPENED, AND EVERY ONE'S BANDS WERE LOOSED."

NOTES

The account is:

1. The phrase, *"And suddenly there was a great earthquake,"* presents something that is quite common through the Mediterranean region, for one of Earth's great earthquake zones runs through that area.

2. However, I think that when we closely inspect the Text, we will find this was no ordinary earthquake. In fact, there has probably never been an earthquake quite like this one, at least up to that time, as I think we shall see.

3. The phrase, *"So that the foundations of the prison were shaken,"* presents the Lord as the Instigator of this upheaval, and not a normal force of nature.

4. Anything that is strong enough to shake the foundations of a structure, which this did, will also at the same time destroy most everything above the foundation, unless it is completely supernatural. In this case, the foundations shook, but the walls did not fall because, in doing so, the prisoners would have been harmed, which the Lord did not desire to do.

5. *"And immediately all the doors were opened,"* presents another miracle!

6. In a normal earthquake, some doors are opened in a structure, and some are jammed shut. All of these were opened without a single wall falling, which could only have been done by the miracle-working power of God.

7. *"And every one's bands were loosed,"* presents another miracle!

8. These prisoners were not only locked in a cell but, as well, were chained to the walls. Not only did all the doors open, but all the chains fell loose from the walls, which would not have been possible to happen normally. Again, such may have happened to one or possibly several, but not all! In that it did, it shows us the miracle-working power of God.

9. As well, and even greater, not only did the chains come loose from the walls, but the word *"loosed"* implies that they fell from the hands and feet of the prisoners also! No earthquake within itself could have done such a thing. It was God Who did this thing!

(27) "AND THE KEEPER OF THE PRISON AWAKING OUT OF HIS SLEEP,

AND SEEING THE PRISON DOORS OPEN, HE DREW OUT HIS SWORD, AND WOULD HAVE KILLED HIMSELF, SUPPOSING THAT THE PRISONERS HAD BEEN FLED."

The account is:

1. The phrase, *"And the keeper of the prison awaking out of his sleep,"* proclaims such being brought about, as is obvious, by the earthquake. That which would await him was to be the greatest thing he would ever know, the salvation of his soul. However, at that moment, he saw nothing but the opposite! His house was evidently next to the prison.

2. The phrase, *"And seeing the prison doors open,"* means that it automatically caused him to assume that all the prisoners had fled. As bad as prisons were, he could not imagine that such would not be the case!

3. *"He drew out his sword, and would have killed himself, supposing that the prisoners had been fled,"* means that he as the jailer was responsible for the prisoners, even under the penalty of death, for such was Roman law.

4. Rather than face the shame and public humiliation, along with certain death, and even the destruction of his family, he would commit suicide. Perhaps he would try to do it in such a way that his superiors would think that one of the escaping prisoners had killed him, which, hopefully, would at least spare his family.

(28) "BUT PAUL CRIED WITH A LOUD VOICE, SAYING, DO YOURSELF NO HARM: FOR WE ARE ALL HERE."

The exegesis is:

1. The phrase, *"But Paul cried with a loud voice,"* proclaims the apostle, as is obvious, seeing what the jailer was about to do to himself.

2. Exactly as to how Paul could see, we are not told, and neither do we know how the prison was constructed in order that Paul might have this viewpoint. However, it is certain that the Lord stayed this man's hand until he was visible to Paul.

3. Considering that it was shortly after midnight, it must have been that there was some type of torch burning in the hall outside the cells, which was probably caused to burn all night long. It would seem that it would have had to be something of this nature for Paul to be able to see the man.

4. The phrase, *"Saying, Do yourself no harm: for we are all here,"* tells us that none of the prisoners took the opportunity to escape. This tells me that some, if not all of them, had now given their hearts to the Lord, or would shortly do so!

5. Considering that all the doors were open, and all the chains and fetters were loosed, the normal instinct of any person in prison, especially during those times, would be to escape. The fact that they did not do such tells us that they would rather have been close to Paul and Silas and the presence of God than to have their so-called freedom. Actually, and in no uncertain terms, they were now free in their spirit, which is the greatest freedom of all.

(29) "THEN HE CALLED FOR A LIGHT, AND SPRANG IN, AND CAME TREMBLING, AND FELL DOWN BEFORE PAUL AND SILAS."

The account is:

1. The phrase, *"Then he called for a light,"* tells us that someone else, perhaps a member of his family, had now come upon the scene, or else, one of the prisoners brought a light.

2. *"And sprang in, and came trembling,"* proclaims that something powerful was happening to this man, even over and above the shock of the earthquake and his thoughts of suicide.

3. I believe the power of God was so strong in the prison at that particular time that it could obviously be felt and experienced by all! This had to be the case, considering that none of the prisoners desired to escape and, as well, the reaction of the jailer.

4. The phrase, *"And fell down before Paul and Silas,"* proclaims that his action was precipitated by much more than Paul calling out to him as he was about to take his own life.

5. The jailer treated Paul with great brutality, but Paul treated him with great humanity.

6. The testimony of the damsel and the preaching of the apostles must have become

NOTES

NOTES

common knowledge, for many weeks had evidently gone by since their arrival. The great question he would ask them, as given in the next verse, shows that he knew something about salvation, which he could only have learned from Paul and Silas.

7. So, whatever had happened, including the earthquake, all the prisoners' shackles falling off, and then none taking the opportunity to escape, he knew was tied to Paul and Silas. He did not know everything, but he knew that all that had happened was centered around these two. Hence, he fell down before them!

(30) "AND BROUGHT THEM OUT, AND SAID, SIRS, WHAT MUST I DO TO BE SAVED?"

The synopsis is:

1. The phrase, *"And brought them out,"* seems to imply Paul and Silas only! What steps were taken regarding the other prisoners, we are not told; however, they were probably made secure.

2. The question, *"And said, Sirs, what must I do to be saved?"* presents terminology which shows some familiarity with the Gospel.

3. As we have previously said, Paul, Silas, Timothy, and Luke had been in the area for some weeks, constantly preaching and teaching, with the church already established in the house of Lydia, the seller of purple. Somehow it seems that some part of the Gospel preached by Paul had gotten to the ears of this jailer. Terminology, such as *"saved"* or *"lost,"* is not really in the vocabulary of unbelievers, especially pagans who have had no knowledge of God whatsoever. So, I think it is obvious that this man, as well as many others in the city, had been previously exposed somehow to Paul's message of redemption through Jesus Christ.

4. Without a doubt, the question, *"What must I do to be saved?"* is the greatest question that could ever be asked by anyone. It speaks to the eternal destiny of the person and proclaims that one has come to the place that he knows he is lost! As someone has well said, *"One has to understand one is lost before one can understand one needs to be saved."*

5. Whatever had happened in the past few weeks concerning this pagan jailer, and especially what had just transpired with the earthquake and the prisoners remaining in their cells when they could have easily escaped, had all worked together to bring this man to a knowledge of his lost condition. In other words, and putting it simply, he wanted what Paul and Silas had!

6. Even though that certainly will not be the case all the time, and probably not most of the time, still, it should be the case at least some of the time. The men who were using the girl to bring in money through her divination did not at all desire what Paul and Silas had, even though there was a perfect example in front of their very eyes regarding the deliverance of the girl. The same could be said for most of the Jews who heard Paul preach. However, in some cases, even as this jailer, some saw Christ to such an extent in Paul, and even those with him for that matter, that as the jailer, they desired the Lord.

What a testimony!

(31) "AND THEY SAID, BELIEVE ON THE LORD JESUS CHRIST, AND YOU SHALL BE SAVED, AND YOUR HOUSE."

The account is:

1. The object of our faith must without fail be the Cross of Christ, or else, its not faith that God will recognize.

2. Faith and the Cross are so intertwined, so melded together, and so one in essence, one might say, that when one begins to fully understand the Cross, then faith is likewise understood.

WHAT DOES IT MEAN TO BE SAVED?

One is saved from something to something. In the case of Biblical salvation, it speaks of God, *"Who has delivered us from the power of darkness, and has translated us into the Kingdom of His dear Son"* (Col. 1:13).

Actually, the words *"salvation,"* or *"saved,"* are not mere technical theological terms, but rather denote *"deliverance,"* exactly as stated in Colossians 1:13. Also, it refers to deliverance in any sense the word can have.

The words *"deliver,"* or *"deliverance,"*

imply a state or position from which the one delivered could not, under any circumstances, deliver himself, but deliverance which is effected by the power of God.

In this one word *"deliverance,"* we learn that man is not slightly maladjusted or is he partially lost, but rather totally and completely lost without God, in fact, held in the clutches of Satan and a virtual slave to that monster. Unregenerate man is so totally lost that within himself, he has no knowledge of God and no way to reach God. As well, he is so deceived that he has little knowledge, if any at all, as to how bad his situation really is.

Consequently, salvation, as it is offered by God, has its origination in God totally and not at all in man. As well, the entirety of the initiative of salvation toward the sinner is on the part of God, reaching out for the lost, hence, John 3:16.

Only when the sinner is lifted out of this world of darkness by the power of God to the realm of salvation does he finally know and understand how lost he really was and now how saved he really is!

BIBLE SALVATION

Salvation is historical. The Old Testament view of salvation, as effected through historic, divine intervention, is fully honored in the New Testament.

In other words, salvation has always been through Jesus Christ, to Whom the Old Testament sacrifices pointed, and Calvary and the Resurrection fulfilled. Consequently, man is saved by God's Action in history in the Person of Jesus Christ (Rom. 4:25; 5:10; II Cor. 4:10; Phil. 2:6; I Tim. 1:15; I Jn. 4:9-10, 14).

While the birth, life, and ministry of Jesus are definitely not unimportant, the stress, however, falls upon His Death and Resurrection, which, in effect, purchased man's redemption (I Cor. 15:5). We are saved by *"the Blood of His Cross,"* and more perfectly, faith in what He did at Calvary (Acts 20:28; Rom. 3:25; 5:9; Eph. 1:7; Col. 1:20; Heb. 9:12; 12:24; 13:12; I Jn. 1:7; Rev. 1:5; 5:9).

As this message of Jesus Christ and Him Crucified is proclaimed, and men hear and

NOTES

come to respond in faith, God's Salvation is brought to them (Rom. 10:8-14; I Cor. 1:18-25; 15:11; I Thess. 1:4).

FALSE WAYS OF SALVATION

To be sure, false ways of every description abound, which is Satan's greatest method of bringing men to eternal damnation.

For instance, as previously stated, concerning the statements the girl following Paul made before her deliverance, she said, *"These men are the Servants of the most High God, which show unto us the way of salvation"* (Acts 16:17).

As we explained, the original Greek says, *"A way"* instead of *"the way,"* and should have been translated accordingly.

The idea is that all kinds of ways of salvation abounded in the pagan world of that day, and actually still do. However, without the Word of God as the guide, most of the world has not known, nor does it know presently, what salvation actually means.

One who does not know he is lost, at the same time, will not know when he is saved. So, salvation, as explained and understood outside of the Bible, has no reference whatsoever to real salvation, which is always the Bible way.

The Gnostics of old, in the teaching of Gnosticism, taught that man is saved by wisdom, which is not so.

As well, many, if not most, in Israel came to believe that Judaism, i.e., the Law of Moses, effected salvation, which was gross error. In other words, they came to believe that man was saved by moral and religious merit, which John the Baptist, and Jesus most of all, struck down in totality. This aroused the anger of the religious leaders of Israel to a fever pitch.

In the Hellenistic mystery cults, which includes the modern Catholic Church, as well as Mormonism and others, man was and is taught that he is saved by a technique of religious practice, which is gross error!

In Paul's day, Rome taught that salvation was equated with political order and liberty, etc. Of course, once again, this and all other types of would-be salvation miss the mark totally, in fact, not even addressing the problem much less the solution!

NOTES

WHAT DOES BIBLE SALVATION NOT INCLUDE?

Even though it is not desirable, still, it is important to indicate the negative implications of this, i.e., what Christian salvation does not include.

Salvation does not guarantee material prosperity or worldly success (Acts 3:6; II Cor. 6:10).

While it is definitely scriptural that the Lord abundantly blesses His People in the material sense, still, the Bible does not teach that this is a *"right"* of every believer and if not enjoyed, a sign of lack of faith, etc.

As well, salvation does not promise or guarantee physical health until the believer dies. While the Lord definitely heals and performs miracles, with even such as gifts of the Spirit given to the church, still, perpetual divine health will not be a fact until the Resurrection (II Cor. 12:7-9; Phil. 2:25; I Tim. 5:23; II Tim. 4:20).

Further, salvation does not include deliverance from all physical hardship and danger, even though at times the Lord does grandly deliver from these things (I Cor. 4:9-13; II Cor. 11:23-28).

As well, salvation does not absolve one from social injustice and ill-treatment, as proven abundantly in the lives and ministries of the apostles and others in the New Testament (I Cor. 7:20-24; I Pet. 2:18-25).

Satan is very successful in making salvation mean less than it is, and with others, more than it is, or rather claiming things that are not fully promised at this particular time, but which will definitely come about in the future, i.e., the Kingdom Age.

SALVATION IS NOT ONLY PRESENT BUT FUTURE AS WELL!

I felt that I must address myself to the negatives concerning what salvation does not promise at the present time, at least in totality. Having said that, the great danger in the church is definitely not in believing for too much but for too little! In other words, in too many cases, the church does not even begin to live up to its full potential respecting that which was paid for at Calvary by our Lord.

If one is to notice, Jesus did not mention the word *"salvation"* very much, and there was a reason for that.

His central category was the Kingdom of God, the manifestation of God's sovereign Rule. In Revelation 12:10, however, salvation and the kingdom are virtually equated because that is the way the Lord looked at the situation.

Referring to salvation, the corresponding pattern laid down by Christ is spoken of as life under the reign or government of God, or, as in the witness of the fourth Gospel, Eternal Life. Salvation, therefore, gathers up all the contents of the Gospel. It includes deliverance from sin and all its consequences, and positively the bestowal of all spiritual blessings in Christ (Eph. 1:3), the gift of the Holy Spirit, and the life of blessedness in the future age. In other words, we are not saved just for now, as important as that is, but for eternity.

This future perspective is crucial (Rom. 8:24; 13:11; I Cor. 5:5; Phil. 3:20; Heb. 1:14; 9:28; I Pet. 1:5, 9). Actually, all that is known of salvation now, even as grand and glorious as it presently is, in fact, is but a preliminary and foretaste of the fullness which awaits the coming kingdom at the second advent of Christ.

WHAT DOES IT MEAN TO BELIEVE ON THE LORD JESUS CHRIST?

In its simple form, it means that one must believe that Jesus is the Son of God, and that He came down to this world, took upon Himself a human body, and offered it up in sacrifice to settle the terrible sin debt owed by all of humanity. In other words, He paid for us what we could not pay for ourselves.

If we believe that and put our trust and faith in Him, salvation is instant, total, and complete (Jn. 3:16; Rom. 5:8; 10:9-10, 13; Eph. 2:8-9).

All of this is spelled out as *"salvation by faith,"* which amounts to that of which we have just spoken. However, even though the Lord does require faith in respect to what we have said, He does not require, at least at the outset, that the believing sinner understand all the things concerning that of

NOTES

which he believes. In fact, I do not think anyone totally understands all that Jesus did for us at Calvary. In other words, it is a glorious subject which never ceases to expand.

FAITH

Of all the teaching on faith throughout the entirety of the Word of God, which is the foundation of the Gospel and the manner in which God deals with humanity, Paul, more than all, I think, expanded this all-important subject. For Paul, faith was the typical Christian attitude. For instance, in Romans 1:16, he speaks of the Gospel as *"the power of God for salvation to everyone who believes"* (has faith).

If one is to notice in Paul's writings, he stresses the point over and over that Christianity is more than a system of good advice. It not only tells men what they ought to do but gives them power to do it, which no other system in the world can do.

Again and again Paul contrasts mere words with power, always with a view to emphasizing that the power of the Holy Spirit of God is seen in the lives of Christians, that is, if they are truly walking with the Lord.

However, Paul makes it crystal clear that this Power becomes available to man only when he believes. In other words, there is no substitute for faith. However, we must always understand that when we speak of faith, we are speaking of faith in the correct object, which is Christ and the Cross. In fact, God will honor no other type of faith, but only that which is anchored in the Cross of Christ (Gal. 6:14).

PAUL'S DISPUTE WITH THE JUDAIZERS

The Judaizers insisted that it was not enough for Christians to believe in Christ solely as a basis for salvation, but they must also be circumcised (the little boys) and thus admitted to Judaism, with an endeavor to keep the whole of the Mosaic Law. In other words, they made obedience to the Law a necessary precondition of salvation, at least in the fullest sense of that term.

Paul would have none of that! He insisted that men can do nothing, nothing at all, to bring about their salvation, except to evidence faith in Christ and what Christ has done for us at the Cross. That means that all has been done by Christ, and no man can add anything to the perfection and Finished Work of Christ, which took place at the Cross.

So it is that Paul insisted that men are *"justified by faith"* (Rom. 5:1). Actually, the doctrine of *"justification by faith,"* which is actually what he was saying to the Philippian jailer, lies at the very heart of his message. However, whether with this terminology or not, he was always putting the idea forward.

Paul vigorously combated any idea of the merit of good deeds. *"A man is not justified by works of the Law but through faith in Jesus Christ,"* he wrote to the Galatians and proceeded, *"even we have believed in Christ Jesus, in order to be justified by faith in Christ, and not by works of the Law."* He added resoundingly, *"because by works of the Law shall no one be justified"* (Gal. 2:16).

Clearly, for Paul, faith meant the abandonment of all reliance on one's ability to merit salvation. It is a trustful acceptance of God's Gift in Christ, and a reliance on Christ and Christ alone, as to what He did for us at the Cross of Calvary for all that salvation means.

As well, as I am sure by now is overly obvious, faith in Christ and believing in Christ are virtually the same.

THE WORK OF THE HOLY SPIRIT

Another outstanding feature of Paul's theology is the very large place the apostle gave to the work of the Holy Spirit. He thought of all Christians as indwelt by the Spirit (Rom. 8:9, 14), and he connected this too with faith. Thus, he wrote to the Ephesians concerning Christ, *"You also, who... have believed in Him, were sealed with the Promised Holy Spirit, which is the guarantee of our inheritance"* (Eph. 1:13-14).

Sealing represented the mark of ownership, a metaphor readily understood in an age when many could not read.

The Spirit within believers is God's Mark of ownership, and this mark is put on men

NOTES

only as they believe. The apostle went on to speak of the Spirit as *"the Guarantee of our inheritance."* Paul employed here a word which in the first century meant a down payment, i.e., a payment which at one and the same time was part of the agreed price and the guarantee that the remainder would be forthcoming.

Thus, when a man is baptized with the Holy Spirit, which is one of the great purposes and reasons for salvation (Eph. 2:22), that is an assurance that the remainder will infallibly follow. This speaks of all the attributes of the Holy Spirit and, above all, the Kingdom Age to come! In other words, the Spirit of God is involved in our salvation from beginning to end, and, in fact, with the Spirit, there will never be an end.

THE PRINCIPLE AND FOUNDATION OF FAITH

The writer of the Epistle to the Hebrews, who I believe was Paul, saw that faith had always been a characteristic of the people of God. In his great portrait gallery in Hebrews, Chapter 11, he reviewed the worthies of the past, showing how one by one they illustrated the great theme that *"without faith it is impossible to please God"* (Heb. 11:6).

He was particularly interested in the opposition of faith to sight. Faith is the assurance of things hoped for, the conviction or substance of things not seen (Heb. 11:1).

He emphasized the point that men, who had nothing in the way of outward evidence to support them, nevertheless, retained a firm hold on the promises of God. In other words, they walked by faith and not by sight.

And yet, the faith that God honors, and the only type of faith which God honors, is faith in Christ and what Christ has done for us at the Cross (Rom. 6:-14; 8:1-11; I Cor. 1:17-18, 23; 2:2).

THE TRUTHS ON FAITH GIVEN BY JAMES

Of the other writers in the New Testament, we must notice James, for he has often been held to be in opposition to Paul in this matter, which, of course, is totally incorrect!

Where Paul insisted that a man is justified by faith and not by works, James said *"that a man is justified by works, and not by faith alone"* (James 2:24), which seems on the surface to be a contradiction. We must always compare what is said by any of the Bible writers, that is, if we are to properly understand what they were saying. Therefore, when we compare all that James said on this subject, the kind of *"faith"* that he was opposing was not the personal trust in a living Saviour of which Paul spoke. It was a faith which James himself described: You believe that God is One; you do well. Even the demons believe—and tremble (James 2:19).

James had in mind an intellectual assent to certain truths, an assent which was not backed up by a life lived in accordance with those truths (James 2:15).

So far was James from opposing faith in the full sense that everywhere, he presupposed it.

Right at the beginning of his Epistle, he spoke naturally of *"the testing of your faith"* (James 1:3), and he exhorted his readers, *"Show no partiality as you hold the faith of our Lord Jesus Christ, the Lord of Glory"* (James 2:1).

He criticized a wrong faith, even as he should have done, but assumed that everyone would recognize the need for a right kind of faith, which always produces fruit.

Moreover, by *"works,"* James did not mean what Paul meant by that term. Paul thought of obedience to the commands of the Law as being regarded as a system whereby a man might merit salvation. For James, the Law was *"the law of liberty"* (James 2:12). His *"works"* looked uncommonly like *"the Fruit of the Spirit"* of which Paul spoke.

They are warm deeds of love springing from a right attitude to God. They are the fruits of faith. What James objected to was the claim that faith is there when there is no fruit to attest it.

FAITH IS RELIANCE ON GOD

Faith is clearly one of the most important concepts in the entirety of the Bible. Everywhere it is required and its significance insisted upon.

Faith means abandoning all trust in one's own resources. Faith means casting oneself unreservedly on the mercy of God. Faith means laying hold on the promises of God in Christ, relying entirely on the Finished Work of Christ for salvation, and on the Power of the indwelling Holy Spirit of God for daily strength.

Faith implies complete reliance on the Lord and full obedience to the Lord.

The phrase, *"And your house,"* does not mean that the jailer's household would be saved simply because the jailer was. Neither did he mean that the jailer's salvation would guarantee theirs.

In essence, Paul was saying that the offer of salvation was not limited merely to the jailer but, as well, to the entirety of his family, that is, if they would meet the conditions of faith in Christ required of them. If they would believe, they too would be saved.

During Paul's day, there were particular cults popular among the Romans, which were composed of men only. As well, some cults catered to certain classes. However, this of which Christ has afforded is for all, male and female, great and small, young and old, and of every race, color, and nationality. Also, we must understand that the Holy Spirit works entirely within the parameters, so to speak, of the Finished Work of Christ. This means that our faith must have as its object, and on a constant basis, Christ and the Cross. Christ is the Source of all wonderful things we receive from God the Father, while the Cross is the means, and the only means, by which all of these things are given to us. However, as stated, we must have faith in Christ and the Cross, ever making Christ and the Cross the object of our faith. This is of vital significance (I Cor. 1:17-18, 23; 2:2; Col. 2:10-15).

(32) "AND THEY SPOKE UNTO HIM THE WORD OF THE LORD, AND TO ALL THAT WERE IN HIS HOUSE."

The account is:

1. The phrase, *"And they spoke unto him the Word of the Lord,"* pertained to a fleshing out of the answer given in Verse 31, explaining what believing in Christ really meant.

NOTES

2. The moral effect of salvation by faith in contradistinction to salvation by works may be recognized by contrasting the conduct of the jailer and that of the rich young ruler who approached Christ (Mk. 10:17-22).

3. The man asked, *"What shall I do that I may inherit Eternal Life?"* which tells us by the way his question was framed that he thought good works constituted salvation.

4. However, Jesus addressing him on the level of works, showed him that he did not measure up there despite his thoughts to the contrary. Jesus showed by His answer to the man that salvation cannot be gained by works.

5. Trying to obtain salvation by this method, he found he did not measure up and left, while the jailer accepted salvation on the principle of faith. Consequently, he opened his purse and his house, which the rich young ruler would not do to the shamefully entreated preachers of the Word of God.

6. *"And to all that were in his house,"* presents this service being conducted sometime after midnight, which resulted in all of his family giving their hearts to Christ. What a beautiful night it turned out to be!

(33) "AND HE TOOK THEM THE SAME HOUR OF THE NIGHT, AND WASHED THEIR STRIPES; AND WAS BAPTIZED, HE AND ALL HIS, STRAIGHTWAY."

The synopsis is:

1. The phrase, *"And he took them the same hour of the night, and washed their stripes,"* speaks of the terrible beating they had suffered a short time before.

2. As we have already alluded, Roman scourgings were fearsome to say the least. Consequently, the backs of Paul and Silas would have been lashed raw, even with deep cuts. They had, no doubt, lost a lot of blood and then had been forced to lie prone on their backs on the floor with their feet made fast in the stocks, which greatly exacerbated the already serious wounds.

3. However, if one is to notice, Paul and Silas first preached the Gospel to these people, with them accepting Christ, even before their backs were cleaned and treated. They must have been in terrible pain, but first of all, the Gospel had to be preached, which it

NOTES

was to hungry hearts.

4. Washings of this nature during that day and for these purposes, at times, had certain types of olive oil mixed with ointments as a part of the water. This would aid in the healing process.

Whether this was done at this time is not known. However, it probably was!

5. *"And was baptized, he and all his, straightway,"* was probably done in a pool in the courtyard of the house. Such pools were not uncommon in the larger Roman-style homes of those days, as archaeology now shows.

As well, water baptism took place the very same night in which these people were saved. Water baptism then and water baptism now is very significant to the Christian faith, as should be obvious.

6. It represents the death, burial, and resurrection of the Lord Jesus Christ and of the believer, as well, in a spiritual sense. Consequently, it is *"the answer of a good conscience toward God, by the Resurrection of Jesus Christ"* (I Pet. 3:21).

7. And yet, water baptism does not save one or contribute anything to one's salvation. It is always the result of salvation and never the cause!

(34) "AND WHEN HE HAD BROUGHT THEM INTO HIS HOUSE, HE SET MEAT BEFORE THEM, AND REJOICED, BELIEVING IN GOD WITH ALL HIS HOUSE."

The overview is:

1. The phrase, *"And when he had brought them into his house, he set meat before them,"* proclaims, as is obvious, a meal prepared for them.

2. It is easy to see that this prison would have a different jailer from now on! Kindness, courtesy, and feelings for others were not very common at that time, or any other time for that matter! However, now that Jesus was in this man's heart, it is positive that cruelty toward prisoners, which was common in those days, was instantly stopped. In other words, this prison now had a brand-new jailer, one who now had the love of God.

3. *"And rejoiced, believing in God with all his house,"* presents the jailer as being Pentecostal as, actually, were all of the converts in the early church.

4. The word *"rejoicing"* in the Greek text is *"agalliao"* and means *"to jump for joy, and to rejoice greatly."*

5. Even though the Scripture does not say, it is most probable that this convert, and the entirety of his household, as well, were baptized with the Holy Spirit with the evidence of speaking with other tongues (Acts 2:4). This is often the occasion of not only great joy to the heart but demonstrative joy as well!

6. Regarding water baptism, some have attempted to read into this account that babies and little children were present and were also baptized, hence, promoting infant baptism. However, there is no proof of that whatsoever.

7. In the first place, if there were babies and little children in the house, they surely were asleep at this time of night. As well, there is a possibility, and was probably the case, that the jailer was of mature years, with any children he and his wife would have had now grown.

8. So, this is no case for infant baptism, which, in fact, is unscriptural! There is no record of such in the New Testament!

(35) "AND WHEN IT WAS DAY, THE MAGISTRATES SENT THE SERJEANTS, SAYING, LET THOSE MEN GO."

The structure is:

1. The phrase, *"And when it was day, the magistrates sent the serjeants,"* refers to lictors who beat with rods. These were probably the same men who had administered the beating to Paul and Silas.

2. *"Saying, Let those men go,"* speaks of something out of the ordinary.

3. The Codex Bezae says that the magistrates came into court that morning, feeling that their treatment of Paul and Silas had brought on the earthquake. They were right!

4. Due to the wide sweep of paganistic religions, most of the people were extremely superstitious. They knew that Paul and Silas were preachers of the Gospel but, of course, had little understanding of what that meant. Nevertheless, knowing that it had something to do with God, especially considering the girl who had been delivered of demon spirits, they felt they may have

offended deity by beating the apostles.

5. Most definitely, that was true! They had definitely offended God! As well, there is no doubt that it was God Who sent the earthquake. Exactly how much damage it did in the city, if any, is not known. However, these magistrates probably thought there could be more to follow if they did not take steps immediately in attempting to rectify the situation.

(36) "AND THE KEEPER OF THE PRISON TOLD THIS SAYING TO PAUL, THE MAGISTRATES HAVE SENT TO LET YOU GO: NOW THEREFORE DEPART, AND GO IN PEACE."

The pattern is:

1. The phrase, *"And the keeper of the prison told this saying to Paul,"* means that Paul did not meet with the sergeants at this time but was given the information by the jailer who had seen these messengers.

2. *"The magistrates have sent to let you go,"* carries in its phrasing a note of thanksgiving by the jailer. In other words, all charges were dropped!

3. *"Now therefore depart, and go in peace,"* does not mean that the newly converted jailer desired that Paul and Silas leave but that they were free to go anytime they so desired.

4. As well, they were to understand that no further charges would be made, and they could, therefore, *"go in peace."*

(37) "BUT PAUL SAID UNTO THEM, THEY HAVE BEATEN US OPENLY UNCONDEMNED, BEING ROMANS, AND HAVE CAST US INTO PRISON; AND NOW DO THEY THRUST US OUT PRIVILY? NAY VERILY; BUT LET THEM COME THEMSELVES AND FETCH US OUT."

The status is:

1. The glad tidings of the Gospel exist in the declaration that for all who by faith in Christ died and rose with Him, there is no person and no thing that can condemn them.

2. In Christ, there is now no condemnation.

A ROMAN CITIZEN

The phrase, *"But Paul said unto them, They have beaten us openly uncondemned, being Romans,"* presents a scenario that puts an entirely different complexion on the entirety of the matter.

Evidently, Silas was a Roman citizen as well as Paul.

This is of special interest to the Bible student because of the Apostle Paul's relation to it. It was one of his qualifications as the apostle to the gentiles.

Luke showed him in Acts as a Roman citizen, who, though a Jew and a Christian, received, for the most part, some justice and courtesy from Roman officials, and more than once successfully claimed its privileges. He himself declared that he was a citizen of Tarsus (Acts 21:39). He was not only born in that city but had a citizen's rights in it, which gave status.

Due to a particular series of events, Tarsus received the position of an independent and duty-free state respecting the Roman Empire. This privileged status was confirmed by Augustus after the victory of Actium had made him sole master of the Roman Empire. This was in 31 B.C.

It did not by itself bestow Roman citizenship on the Tarsians, but doubtless, there were many natives of the city to whom Pompey, Caesar, Antony, and Augustus granted that honor for themselves and, as a consequence, for their descendants. Evidently, this included the family of Paul, for his father possessed this coveted privilege (Acts 22:28), which was passed down to him.

What his family might have done to warrant this privilege is not known!

IMMUNITIES AND RIGHTS

So, over and above Paul's Tarsian citizenship was the Roman one, which availed for him certain privileges, not in one city only, but throughout the Roman world. This Roman citizenship secured for him everywhere certain immunities and rights.

Precisely what all of these were, we are not certain. However, we know that by the Valerian and Porcian laws, exemption from shameful punishments, such as scourging with rods or whips, and crucifixion, was secured for every Roman citizen. Also, the right of appeal to the emperor with certain limitations was another privilege.

This sanctity of person had become

almost a part of Roman religion so that any violation was esteemed a sacrilege.

As well as appealing to the emperor, the Roman citizen had the right to be sent to Rome for trial before the emperor himself when charged with capital offenses (Acts 22:25-29; 25:11).

"And have cast us into prison," presents another manner in which the magistrates had broken the law. They had sent Paul and Silas to prison without a trial.

At least one of the reasons instigating Paul's remarks, and a very important reason at that, was the welfare and growth of the new church in Philippi. If the people were allowed to think that Paul and Silas were the troublemakers they were accused of being, persecution for the new believers would, no doubt, have resulted and would have hindered others in the city from accepting their witness. So, Paul made these protests in the manner in which he did to clear up this matter.

THE MAGISTRATES

I cannot imagine that Paul did not attempt to inform the magistrates of his Roman citizenship before the beating. Evidently, they did not believe him, or else, in their haste to condemn him and Silas, they did not hear what he said.

In that event, it is quite possible that someone informed the magistrates of Paul's claims after the episode had taken place, which occasioned the hurried command the next morning for them to be released.

The question, *"And now do they thrust us out privily?"* means as common criminals!

The phrase, *"No verily; but let them come themselves and fetch us out,"* means that they had been thrown publicly into prison with the whole crowd looking on, and, as well, they should come themselves and release the apostles publicly. In this way, the city of Philippi would know that the charges were false.

As we have stated, I think it is conclusive that Paul had his mind more so on the new church in this city rather than himself.

(38) "AND THE SERJEANTS TOLD THESE WORDS UNTO THE MAGISTRATES: AND THEY FEARED, WHEN THEY HEARD THAT THEY WERE ROMANS."

The way is:

1. Either the magistrates did not know that Paul and Silas were Romans, or else, the *"serjeants"* verified what they had previously heard.

2. At any rate, the situation of the law being broken by the magistrates was far more serious than one might realize. If Paul and Silas desired to do so, as we have already stated, they could appeal to Rome regarding this treatment, with severe measures taken regarding these officials. Romans were zealous in protecting their citizens.

(39) "AND THEY CAME AND BESOUGHT THEM, AND BROUGHT THEM OUT, AND DESIRED THEM TO DEPART OUT OF THE CITY."

The pattern is:

1. The phrase, *"And they came and besought them, and brought them out,"* refers to the fact that the *"magistrates"* themselves now came to Paul and Silas. As well, they came to the prison, for it seems that the apostles had by now gone back to the prison in order that the jailer would not be charged with dereliction of duty respecting prisoners not properly handled, etc.

The phrase, *"And desired them to depart out of the city,"* has reference to the fact that they were pleading with the apostles not to bring charges against them.

Horton said, *"They were asking them to leave the city, but not because they were offended at their Gospel, but rather that they were afraid that the sympathies of the people would now swing to Paul and Silas, and, therefore, against them, because of the unjust beating. So they asked the apostles to leave for the sake of peace in the city."*

The Codex Bezae says that they came with many of their friends, pleading for the men to leave before another mob rose up, but this time against them (the magistrates).

(40) "AND THEY WENT OUT OF THE PRISON, AND ENTERED INTO THE HOUSE OF LYDIA: AND WHEN THEY HAD SEEN THE BRETHREN, THEY COMFORTED THEM, AND DEPARTED."

The diagram is:

1. The phrase, *"And they went out of*

the prison, and entered into the house of Lydia," presents them somewhat the worse for wear in the physical sense, but yet, greatly encouraged in the spiritual sense. The Lord had graciously performed miracles, turning this situation around, which would help guarantee the strength of the Philippian church.

2. The phrase, *"And when they had seen the brethren, they comforted them, and departed,"* refers to them, no doubt, relating what had happened in the prison with the conversion of the jailer, his relatives, and servants. Undoubtedly, these new converts became a part of the Philippian church.

3. The word *"brethren,"* at least as it was used by the Jews, referred to both men and women. However, it does let us know that whereas the church began with women only, men had now been added.

4. When Paul and Silas *"departed,"* even though Timothy went with them, it is obvious that Luke did not. In the first verse of the next chapter, he used the pronoun *"they"* instead of *"we,"* as he normally did when he was travelling with the party.

5. Luke was undoubtedly left by Paul and Silas in Philippi in order to oversee the new church. Horton said, *"His teaching and guidance is undoubtedly another reason why there were so few problems in this Assembly."*

6. It is actually believed by some that Luke remained there for some six or seven years.

"My faith has found a resting place,
"Not in device nor creed;
"I trust the Ever-living One,
"His Wounds for me shall plead."

"Enough for me that Jesus saves,
"This ends my fear and doubt;
"A sinful soul I come to Him,
"He'll never cast me out."

"My heart is leaning on the Word,
"The written Word of God,
"Salvation by my Savior's Name,
"Salvation through His Blood."

"My great Physician heals the sick,
"The lost He came to save;
"For me His precious Blood He shed,
"For me His Life He gave."

"I need no other argument,
"I need no other plea,
"It is enough that Jesus died,
"And that He died for me."

NOTES

CHAPTER 17

(1) "NOW WHEN THEY HAD PASSED THROUGH AMPHIPOLIS AND APOLLONIA, THEY CAME TO THESSALONICA, WHERE WAS A SYNAGOGUE OF THE JEWS."

The overview is:

1. The phrase, *"Now when they had passed through Amphipolis and Apollonia,"* concerns two towns of considerable importance in size but with no Jewish synagogue. Amphipolis was about 30 miles west of Philippi, and Apollonia was about 25 miles south of Amphipolis. Evidently, Paul would leave these two cities to be evangelized by the church at Philippi, which was now probably under the leadership of Luke.

2. *"They came to Thessalonica,"* presents Paul's destination, apparently directed here by the Holy Spirit.

Thessalonica was about 40 miles west of Apollonia and contained about 60,000 citizens. Its ancient name was Therma, but it took the name of Thessalonica under the Macedonian kings.

It continued to grow in importance under the Romans and was the most populous city of the whole of Macedonia. Actually, it was the capital of Macedonia Secunda under the division by Aemilius Paulus.

From its situation and great commercial importance, it was virtually the capital of Greece, Macedonia, and Illyricum.

If one is to notice, the Holy Spirit seemed to direct Paul to the major centers of an area and there establish a church. From this mother church, all the surrounding areas would be evangelized, with other churches planted.

To be sure, if that was the method of the Holy Spirit then, it is His method now!

NOTES

3. During the last two or three years we were with a major Pentecostal denomination, I felt led of the Lord to do the same thing of erecting large churches in major cities in certain foreign countries, which could branch out to the surrounding areas. Those churches, thanks to the Lord, continue to thrive and grow. How much they are presently thrusting out to other areas in nearby towns and villages, of that, I am not aware. Nevertheless, the opportunity presents itself, and if the present leaders continue to follow the leading of the Holy Spirit, the Book of Acts pattern will be followed, and always with excellent results.

4. *"Where was a synagogue of the Jews,"* presents Paul once again taking the Gospel first of all to the Jews. Thankfully, some few would heed, while, sadly, most would not!

(2) "AND PAUL, AS HIS MANNER WAS, WENT IN UNTO THEM, AND THREE SABBATH DAYS REASONED WITH THEM OUT OF THE SCRIPTURES."

The diagram is:

1. The phrase, *"And Paul, as his manner was, went in unto them,"* should have been translated, *"As his custom was."*

2. *"And three Sabbath days reasoned with them out of the Scriptures,"* proclaims the foundation of Paul's ministry, the Word of God. It must be remembered that all they had at this particular time was the Old Testament.

3. He reasoned with them about what?

4. Horton said, *"The next Verse plainly tells us, but it should be stated that Paul did not deal with the human theories of ethics, economics, or politics, etc. He did not lecture them out of philosophy or out of the teachings of his former Professor, Gamaliel."*

5. Man's original problem was not money. If it had been, God would have sent an economist. As well, man's original problem was not physical. If so, God would have sent a physician. Man's original problem was not in engineering. If so, the Lord would have sent an engineer. As well, man's original problem was not education. If so, God would have sent an educator.

Man's original problem was sin and in response to that problem, God sent a Saviour. That Saviour is the Lord Jesus Christ.

6. The modern ministry must never forget that! If we as preachers are ever so versed in human theories and are able to expound perfectly on these particular subjects, the help that man so desperately needs, he will not receive at all. This is sadder still when one realizes that much, if not most, of modern preaching is more psychology even than it is the Word of God. As such, man will not be helped, even though the subject matter may be very titillating.

This is the reason that it is difficult for God to use those who are highly educated. In fact, the Holy Spirit through Paul would later say, *"How that not many wise men after the flesh, not many mighty, not many noble, are called"* (I Cor. 1:26).

Paul did not say that God did not call any of this nature, but rather not many! Actually, Paul had been in this category of worldly wisdom himself before his Damascus Road experience.

7. By these statements, we surely do not mean that God places a premium on ignorance. We do mean that very educated preachers are too often guilty of feeding men worldly wisdom instead of the beautiful, simple message of Jesus Christ and Him Crucified. That is the only message that will help humanity! So, Paul opened up the Scriptures to these Jews (I Cor. 2:2).

(3) "OPENING AND ALLEGING, THAT CHRIST MUST NEEDS HAVE SUFFERED, AND RISEN AGAIN FROM THE DEAD; AND THAT THIS JESUS, WHOM I PREACH UNTO YOU, IS CHRIST."

The exegesis is:

1. All victory for the Child of God is found exclusively in the Cross of Christ.

2. This means that the believer should place his or her faith exclusively in Christ and what Christ has done for us on the Cross, and maintain it there accordingly.

OPENING AND ALLEGING

The phrase, *"Opening and alleging,"* proclaims the foundational method of proper Biblical interpretation.

The word *"opening"* in the Greek text is *"dianoigo"* and means *"to open thoroughly and to expound."* In this case, to open up

NOTES

thoroughly the Scriptures pertaining to Who and what the Messiah would be and do.

It is not enough to say that the Word of God reinforces one's belief. To do such is to go astray. The idea is that our belief conforms to the Word of God.

Many believers attempt to make the Word of God fit their particular doctrine or doctrines, instead of making their doctrine or doctrines fit the Word of God.

Paul, of course, as all true believers, had allowed the Word of God to form his doctrines, as in this case, about Jesus, and now he opened up the Old Testament Scriptures respecting the doctrine of Christ.

The word *"alleging"* in the Greek text is *"paratithemi"* and means *"to present, to place alongside and to set before."*

So, after securing the particular passages reflecting the Messiah, he then *"set before"* his listeners the contention that Jesus fulfilled all of these passages and was indeed the Messiah!

As stated, this is the way to interpret the Word of God, actually, the way given by the Holy Spirit, which guarantees the truth.

In interpreting Scripture respecting any doctrine or contention, all Scriptures on that subject, whether from the Old or New Testament, must harmonize and agree. It is quite possible to pull Scriptures out of context and make them seem to support a contention, which is an improper manner of interpretation. As stated, all Scriptures on any given subject must agree and harmonize.

BIBLE INTERPRETATION

The science of scriptural interpretation is generally known as *"hermeneutics,"* while the practical application of the principles of this science is known as *"exegesis."*

In nearly all cases, Biblical interpretation has in mind the thoughts of another, and then further, these thoughts are expressed in another language than that of the interpreter. In other words, the Bible writers did not originally write in English or any other language, with the exception of Hebrew in the Old Testament and Greek in the New.

While Bible translations are not supposed to be interpretations, still, as should be obvious, some interpretation must of necessity be a part of the translation. Therefore, our understanding of Scripture must take into account the language translation, which is actually unavoidable. In this sense, interpretation is used in Biblical research.

THE INTERPRETATION OF THE THOUGHTS OF ANOTHER

A person has interpreted the thoughts of another when he has in his own mind a correct reproduction or photograph of the thought as it was conceived in the mind of the original writer or speaker. It is accordingly a purely reproductive process, involving no originality of thought on the part of the interpreter. In other words, to properly interpret Scripture, we are not to add to what the writer has said or take away from what the writer has said.

The moment the Bible student has in his own mind what was in the mind of the author or authors of the Biblical Books when these were written, he has interpreted correctly the thought of the Scriptures.

THE HUMAN ELEMENT IN THE BIBLE

The Scriptures are a divine and human product combined. That the holy men of God wrote as they were moved by the Spirit is the claim of the Scriptures themselves. Just where the line of demarcation is to be drawn between the human and the divine factors in the production of the Sacred Text materially affects the principles of correct interpretation of these Writings. To do that, one must have a proper understanding of inspiration as well. However, we will not address ourselves to that subject at this time.

That the human factor was sufficiently potent to shape the form of thought in the Scriptures is evident on all hands.

Paul does not write as Peter does, nor John as James; the individuality of the writer of the different Books appears not only in the style, choice of words, etc., but in the whole form of thought also.

For instance, there are such things as a Pauline (Paul), a Johannine (John), and a Petrine (Peter) type of Christian thought, although there is only one body of Christian truth underlying all types.

MORE RULES OF INTERPRETATION

Insofar as the Bible is exactly like other books, it must be interpreted as we do other works of literature, etc., however, only so far as it is like other books.

The Scriptures are written in Hebrew and in Greek, and the principles of forms and of syntax that would apply to the explanation of other books written in these languages and under these circumstances must be applied to the Bible as well.

Again, the Bible is written for men, and its thoughts are those of mankind and not of angels or creatures of a different or higher spiritual or intellectual character. Accordingly, there is no specifically Biblical logic, rhetoric, or grammar, at least as it applies to that.

The laws of thought and of the interpretation of thought in these matters pertain to the Bible as they do to other writings.

INTERPRETATION PECULIAR TO THE BIBLE

However, in regard to the material content of the Scriptures, matters are different, and the principles of interpretation must be different than our interpretation of other books, etc. God is the Author of the Scriptures, which He has given through human agencies. Hence, the content of the Scriptures, to a great extent, must be far above the ordinary concepts of the human mind.

For instance, when John declares that God so loved the world that He gave His only begotten Son to redeem it, the interpreter does not do justice to the writer if he finds in the word *"God"* only the general philosophical conception of the Deity and not of God Who is our Father through Christ; for it was the latter thought of *"Father"* that was in the mind of John when he penned these words.

Concerning the prayer which we commonly refer to as the *"Lord's Prayer,"* it is a false interpretation to find in *"our Father"* anything but this specifically Biblical conception of God. As well, it is not possible for anybody but a believing Christian to utter this prayer (Mat. 6:9) in the sense which Christ, Who taught it to His Disciples, intended.

NOTES

HARMONY

Again, the example of Christ and His Disciples in their treatment of the Old Testament teaches the principle that the explanation of a scriptural passage is to be interpreted as decisive as to its meaning.

For instance, in the approximate 400 citations from the Old Testament found in the New Testament, there is not one in which the mere *"it is written"* is not regarded as settling its meaning.

Whatever may be a Bible student's theory of inspiration, the teachings and the examples of interpretation found in the Scriptures are in perfect harmony in this matter. Actually, the Bible should always be taken literally where possible. When it's not possible, such as Matthew 5:13-14, we should understand the truth being conveyed.

WHAT GOD INTENDED

These latter facts, too, show that in the interpretation of the Scriptures, principles must be applied that are not applicable in the explanation of other books.

As God is the Author of the Scriptures, He may have had, and, as a matter of fact, in certain cases, did have in mind more than the human agents through whom He spoke themselves understood. In the New Testament, persons like Aaron and David, institutions like the Law, the sacrificial system, the priesthood, and the light, are interpreted at face value as to what they are, regarding their practical application.

However, until we get into the New Testament, we cannot really know and understand the true significance of the Levitical system, etc., which can only be found in the light of New Testament fulfillment. Therefore, God had much more in mind than the mere system that He gave, etc.

As someone has well said, *"The Old Testament is the New Testament concealed, while the New Testament is the Old Testament revealed."*

In fact, one cannot properly understand the New Testament unless he properly understands the Old, and he cannot have a true understanding of the Old until it is revealed in the New.

NOTES

THE PRINCIPLE OF PARALLELISM

Parallelism is simply that which pertains to resemblance. In other words, a recurrent similarity which is introduced for effect.

For instance, when Moses smote the rock and water came out, Paul said, *"And that Rock was Christ"* (I Cor. 10:4).

Paul was drawing a parallel. He did not mean that the rock was literally Christ, but as the water came out of the smitten rock, which satisfied the physical thirst of the Israelites in the desert, likewise, Jesus was smitten on the Cross, which effected the shedding of His precious Blood, and all who partake by faith in Him will satisfy their spiritual thirst. As stated, Paul was using a parallel, of which many are found in Scripture.

The Scriptures represent only one body of truth; however, it is presented in a variety of forms.

For instance, a statement on a particular subject in one place can be accepted as in harmony with a statement on the same subject elsewhere. In short, in all of these characteristics in which the Scriptures are unlike other literary productions, the principles of interpretation of the Scriptures must also be unlike those employed in any other cases.

THE RULE OF FAITH AND LIFE

The Reformation, with its principle that the Bible and the Bible alone is the rule of faith and life, made the correct grammatical interpretation of the Scriptures an absolute necessity, which, of course, God intends!

Nothing is more important than the Bible, and nothing is more important than a correct interpretation of the Bible, which should be obvious!

This is the reason, I believe, that THE EXPOSITOR'S STUDY BIBLE is so very, very important. It is orthodox in every respect, meaning it holds true to the interpretation of Scripture as laid down by the fathers of many centuries past, even back to the early church. In fact, as I dictate these notes, the Lord has instructed me to place this Bible (incidentally, it is King James) into the hands of every pastor in the world where the door is opened, and that's what we are attempting to do.

It deals with every Scripture in the Word of God, but the foundation of the interpretations pertains first of all to the Cross of Christ, then the Holy Spirit, and then Bible prophecy. As it regards these all important subjects, I believe that the notes open up the Word of God in this respect as possibly has not been opened up since the time of the early church. To be sure, as it regards the standard doctrines of the Word of God as it regards the foundation of the church, this information was given by the Holy Spirit first of all to the Apostle Paul, who gave it to us in his 14 Epistles.

The Word of God is the only revealed truth in the world today and, in fact, ever has been. Actually, a proper understanding of the Word of God is the single most important thing as it regards any and every believer.

Consequently, every believer should avail himself or herself of any aid that comes their way to help them understand the Word to a greater degree. That's the reason that every single believer, no matter how many Bibles they presently have, need desperately a copy of THE EXPOSITOR'S STUDY BIBLE. The Holy Spirit told us to carry out this task of developing this study Bible, He showed us how to do it, and then He helped us to carry it out.

If one does not rightly divide the Word of Truth, not only will the desired effects not be received, but the individual will be led down a completely erroneous path, which never leaves one static but actually worse!

THE HOLY SPIRIT AND INTERPRETATION

The Bible unequivocally teaches that proper interpretation of the Scripture cannot be brought about by educational or mental processes alone. The Holy Spirit must be involved, and not only involved, but rather serving as the Leader, Teacher, and Guide. The Scripture plainly says, *"Howbeit when He, the Spirit of Truth, is come, He will guide you into all Truth: for He shall not speak of Himself; but whatsoever He shall hear, that shall He speak: and He will show you things to come"* (Jn. 16:13).

John also wrote, *"But the Anointing which you have received of Him* (Holy Spirit) *abides in you, and you need not that any man teach you* (tell you something contrary to Scripture): *but as the same Anointing teaches you of all things* (tells you if what you are hearing is right or wrong), *and is Truth, and is no lie* (the Holy Spirit will not tell you something contrary to Scripture), *and even as it* (the Anointing of the Holy Spirit) *has taught you, you shall abide in Him* (abide in Jesus, and you cannot abide in Him unless you are properly led by the Spirit, Who will always lead you according to the Word of God)*"* (I Jn. 2:27).

Many in the church attempt to understand the Word of God without the help, leading, and instruction of the Holy Spirit, which guarantees a carnal interpretation, which will always be error. For the Word of God to be rightly divided and properly understood, the Holy Spirit must be looked to as the prime Agent in this process. To do otherwise is to court disaster!

THE CROSS OF CHRIST

The phrase, *"That Christ must needs have suffered, and risen again from the dead,"* proclaims from the Old Testament that which Christ would do and, in fact, did do! Among many other passages, Isaiah, Chapter 53, graphically describes the *"suffering of Christ."*

As well, the Levitical Law of the cleansing of the leper in the use of two birds beautifully described the death and resurrection of Christ. The one bird was killed, typifying His Death, with the other one turned loose, typifying His Resurrection (Lev. 14:1-7).

Also, Paul would have quoted David as he said, concerning the resurrection of Christ, *"For You will not leave My Soul in hell; neither will You suffer Your holy One to see corruption"* (Ps. 16:10).

Plus, of course, all the myriad of sacrifices, which numbered hundreds of millions, represented the death of Christ on the Cross of Calvary.

THE OPENING

All of this pertains to the *"opening,"* as Luke used the word in Verse 3 of this Book of Acts.

NOTES

The phrase, *"And that this Jesus, Whom I preach unto you, is Christ,"* pertains to the *"alleging."* To say it again:

In this verse, the *"opening"* was showing from the prophets that the Messiah was to die and rise again; the *"alleging"* was that Jesus was that very Christ.

The Jews at this time had some strange and vague ideas as to Who and what the Messiah would be. Actually, the scholars had deduced from Daniel's writings, and rightly so, that the Messiah was to come at about the time that Christ was born (Dan. 9:24-26). As well, they knew He was to be in the lineage of David, hence, the appellative, *"the Son of David"* (II Sam., Chpt. 7; Gen. 49:10).

However, it seems that very few in Israel at that time had deduced from the Scriptures, as they should have, that the Messiah would be God (Isa. 7:14).

They thought He might be an Incarnation of one of the prophets of old, such as Elijah or Jeremiah, which, of course, is totally unscriptural.

Whoever and Whatever He would be, all thought that He would be extremely charismatic and would lead Israel once again to a place of glory, power, and prominence. Consequently, this is why the chosen Twelve constantly referred to Jesus ushering in the Kingdom at that time. However, two things were wrong:

1. His Disciples, at least before the advent of the Holy Spirit, did not really understand Who He was.
2. They had little understanding as to what He would do.

That is the reason that Jesus asked them, *"But Whom say you that I am?*

"And Simon Peter answered and said, You are the Christ, the Son of the Living God" (Mat. 16:15-16).

Due to an improper understanding as to Who and What He was according to the Scriptures, Israel did not recognize Him when He actually did come. So, Paul clearly and plainly shows from the Scriptures What He would be and Who He would be!

(4) "AND SOME OF THEM BELIEVED,

AND CONSORTED WITH PAUL AND SILAS; AND OF THE DEVOUT GREEKS A GREAT MULTITUDE, AND OF THE CHIEF WOMEN NOT A FEW."

The synopsis is:

1. Due to repeated failure, many have come to believe that total victory is not possible in this life.

2. However, the Holy Spirit through Paul loudly debunks this erroneous thought by declaring that victory is possible now!

3. It is through and by the Cross of Christ, with our faith anchored in that Finished Work, which then gives the Holy Spirit latitude to work in our hearts and lives (Rom. 6:1-14; 8:1-11; I Cor. 1:17-18; 2:2; Col. 2:10-15).

SOME BELIEVED

The phrase, *"And some of them believed,"* speaks of believing the Word of God as Paul and Silas had preached. In other words, they accepted Christ as their Lord and Saviour.

Regrettably, all did not believe, as all seldom do. Also, this was probably over a period of several months.

As well, it should be noted that irrespective of the extremely harsh treatment experienced by Paul and Silas in Philippi, they did not at all temper their preaching of Christ, not in the least! Regrettably, if there is the slightest opposition and problem, far too often, some preachers compromise their message and, as a result, are of no more effect for the Kingdom of God.

What we preach is never to be tempered, irrespective of the fallout, that is, if we truly have the mind of God!

I have had some experience in this capacity, knowing that the Lord had laid heavily on my heart certain things to preach, which would definitely arouse the ire of certain people. To be sure, it did, despite my efforts to be as diplomatic as possible. However, we must remember, the Gospel of Jesus Christ is not a diplomatic effort, but rather an ultimatum. We must not forget that!

Due to the fact that we had a worldwide television audience, at least to a certain extent, the fallout was strong, to say the least! In seeking the Lord constantly about the situation, the Spirit of the Lord plainly informed me that I was to trust Him respecting His Protection of the ministry and even my person. As well, I was to continue preaching exactly as I had been.

NOTES

In the midst of it all, great numbers of people were brought to Christ with, I think, some of the most remarkable testimonies of deliverances, which the Lord alone can bring about. However, it was at a price, but that is what Jesus meant when He spoke of the opposition (Lk. 9:23; 14:27).

THE PREACHER OF THE GOSPEL

Paul said, *"That I may know Him, and the power of His Resurrection, and the fellowship of His Sufferings, being made conformable unto His Death"* (Phil. 3:10).

The business of the preacher of the Gospel is to hear from the Lord and deliver what is heard. The preacher is not responsible for the fallout, the opposition, or the effect. Now, please understand, I am speaking here of preaching the Gospel. I am not speaking of the preacher responding with anger and insulting those whom he would attempt to reach. That is not the way.

If there was anybody in the world who did not have an easy time preaching the Gospel, it was the Apostle Paul. He suffered much, even as anyone knows who has even an elementary knowledge of the Book of Acts and his Epistles. However, irrespective of the suffering and to whatever degree it may have been, even to near death as it happened at times, he never one time tempered his message even in the slightest, but was faithful to carry out that which God gave him to give to the people. What an example for the cause of Christ! What an example we should follow.

Too many preachers are attempting to please people instead of pleasing God. Actually, the pulpit is full of people pleasers. I speak of seeker sensitive churches, which, in reality, are no churches at all, at least according to the Word of God. And yet, far too many preachers are compromising the Word of God in order to get money and numbers. As one of them said, *"It sells!"*

Yes, it sells, but it is not the Gospel, and such preachers will one day stand before God and will give an account, and the end result will not be pretty.

My prayer is that God will help me to be a preacher who will not bend or bow to that which is unscriptural, irrespective as to what the cost may be! One day when I stand before the Lord, even as all preachers of the Gospel, I will be judged totally and completely on my faithfulness to deliver God's Word and to do it in the way that He wanted it done. What people thought, did, or liked will be of no consequence whatsoever! My Commander-in-Chief is the Lord Jesus Christ, and it is Him Whom I must obey, and it is Him Whom I will obey by His Help and Grace!

So, the *"some who believed"* in Thessalonica were the result of Paul's fearless, uncompromising stand, respecting the great and glorious Gospel of Jesus Christ, irrespective of the cost to him personally.

DOCTRINE, DISPOSITION, AND DIRECTION

The phrase, *"And consorted with Paul and Silas,"* speaks of common purpose, in other words, *"to associate with."*

As the first phrase says, they believed the Gospel as preached by Paul and Silas concerning Christ; consequently, they threw in their lot with them. A further account is found in I Thessalonians 2:1-13.

In the Book of Acts, it becomes more and more apparent as to how the Lord works in the building of His Church. The Head of the church is Jesus Christ, and a very active Head at that (Eph. 1:20-23). However, the *"Head"* works through the Holy Spirit regarding doctrine, disposition, and direction, hence, the Words of Jesus, *"Hear what the Spirit says unto the churches"* (Rev. 2:7, 11, 17, 29; 3:6, 13, 22). As is obvious here, Jesus said this seven times respecting the seven churches of Asia.

Inasmuch as He said it seven times, He was telling us that the church can only have perfect doctrine, disposition, and direction, as that which is said by the Holy Spirit, as given to Him by Christ, is followed minutely.

The Holy Spirit in His directing the church does so through apostles, prophets, evangelists, pastors, and teachers (Eph. 4:11-12).

NOTES

SIX

If this order, as laid down by the Lord, is abrogated in any way, whether by denominations, denominationalism, or denominational hierarchy, according to the amount of that abrogation, to use a play on words, the *"seven,"* which is perfection, will degenerate to a *"six,"* which is man's number (Rev. 13:18). The number *'six'* always represents imperfection, incompleteness, and confusion for that matter!

However, when we speak of *"perfection,"* we are only speaking of that which is done by the Lord. Due to the human equation, even the godliest of the godly, such is always a work in progress, in other words, less than perfect.

So, I have said all of that to say this: the order laid down by the Holy Spirit in the Book of Acts is that believers follow someone whom God has called, such as these followed Paul and Silas, as they follow Christ (I Cor. 4:16; Lk. 11:1; Phil. 3:17; I Thess. 1:6; II Thess. 3:7, 9).

However, even the following of those whom God has definitely called must be done with the understanding that Christ is the One we are actually following. To have strife or contention over particular preachers was roundly condemned by Paul (I Cor. 1:12-13). Believers are to be fed and strengthened by all whom God has truly called (Eph. 4:12). All of the fivefold calling are to contribute to the saints and is the order laid down by the Holy Spirit (Eph. 4:11-12). However, to place any preacher in a godlike category is improper and unscriptural (I Cor. 1:10-13).

MANY PEOPLE SAVED

The phrase, *"And of the devout Greeks a great multitude,"* proclaims the success of Jewish synagogues in these pagan cities to influence the heathen toward the knowledge of the true God. As we have already explained, some of these gentiles became Jewish proselytes, with others not embracing Judaism totally but definitely worshiping the true God. As Paul ministered in these synagogues, it seems that these particular gentiles heeded the message of Jesus Christ to a far greater degree, at least as a whole, than the Jews.

However, it should be understood, as it is obvious, that the foray of gentiles into Judaism did not save them. It did greatly benefit them as they were pulled away from paganistic superstition toward the true God, but this within itself did not and, in fact, could not save. They were saved only when they accepted Christ!

The phrase, *"And of the chief women not a few,"* could have referred to the wives of some of the civil rulers in the city, or at least wives of influential men.

So, we see in the founding of the church in Thessalonica that some Jews came to Christ, as well as gentiles and some influential people. However, it is obvious that the Jews were in the minority!

(5) "BUT THE JEWS WHICH BELIEVED NOT, MOVED WITH ENVY, TOOK UNTO THEM CERTAIN LEWD FELLOWS OF THE BASER SORT, AND GATHERED A COMPANY, AND SET ALL THE CITY ON AN UPROAR, AND ASSAULTED THE HOUSE OF JASON, AND SOUGHT TO BRING THEM OUT TO THE PEOPLE."

The synopsis is:

1. Was it possible for Jesus to have sinned?

2. Yes! He had to be a man like all other men, or else, His Work and function would be to no avail.

3. That's why He was referred to as *"the last Adam"* (I Cor. 15:45).

NOTES

UNBELIEVERS

The phrase, *"But the Jews which believed not, moved with envy,"* presents a perfect example of religious people who refuse the light of the Gospel and then set about to stop the propagation of that light.

These kinds are seldom satisfied to simply disagree, but with few exceptions, seek to hinder or stop if possible the ways of the Lord. As such, and I think church history will prove me out, this has been the greatest hindrance to the Gospel of all! When religious leaders do not follow the Word of God, they, at the same time, develop a protective mentality. In other words, the Lord, as regarding the Jewish synagogues of that particular time, was no longer the Head of these religious efforts. They had become a man-instituted and man-directed effort, who would go to any lengths to protect what they considered to be their territory.

Conversely, the true man of God with the Lord as his head looks to the Holy Spirit to protect or safeguard the work.

JEWS

These particular *"Jews"* were envious of the people heeding the message of Jesus Christ, which they knew would diminish their numbers and would impact their finances as well! Several things are incumbent in these types of situations which need to be observed:

- These Jews, and countless others like them, did not have the Spirit of God and were jealous of anyone who did.
- In these situations, the spirit of control is always very strong. In other words, religious man who is not following the Bible loves to control other people. If the person or persons cannot be controlled, even as the Pharisees could not control John the Baptist and Jesus, and as these Jews could not control Paul and Silas, they will always attempt to destroy what they cannot control.
- As we have already stated, a protective spirit is involved in these things, as well, simply because such religious leaders look at their particular work, or whatever they are in, as belonging to them personally, which, in a way, it does! It does not belong to God anymore, that is, if it ever did, so it belongs to human beings.

As well, one would be surprised, at least in most cases, how that money enters into these situations. When Jesus ran the moneychangers out of the Temple, the Sadducees became very angry because the profits from this merchandise went to them. All of this looks to individuals who, in effect, are not trusting God.

So, such religious leaders, who seem to abound in the world and, in fact, ever have, are the greatest hindrance of all to the work of God.

THE POWERS OF DARKNESS

The phrase, *"Took unto them certain*

NOTES

lewd fellows of the baser sort, and gathered a company, and set all the city on an uproar," proclaims these Jews as being unable to scripturally counter Paul's message, so now they resort to other measures. In truth, they would rather see these gentiles die eternally lost without God, thereby, going to hell, rather than find the Lord through the message of Jesus Christ as preached by Paul and Silas. Please believe me, even though the statement just made is strong indeed, their modern counterparts are identical in spirit. While the modern versions would not necessarily oppose the message of Jesus Christ, they do oppose it being preached by anyone except those who fall into their sphere of approval.

We are not speaking of religious leaders opposing that which is unscriptural, false, or fraudulent, which should be opposed by all, but rather those whom they cannot control. This is true despite the fact that the right message is being preached, evident by the anointing of the Holy Spirit, which brings many to Christ!

"And assaulted the house of Jason, and sought to bring them out to the people," evidently refers to where Paul and his associates were staying.

This mob spirit, as stirred up by the Jews, once again, as we shall see, had resorted to accusing Paul of violating Roman law, which, of course, was ridiculous!

Some feel that the Jason mentioned here is the same person as the Jason of Romans 16:21. Even though that may be correct, there is no proof, for Jason, a Roman derivative of the name *"Jesus, or Joshua,"* was common in those days.

More than likely, church services were now being conducted in the house of Jason as well!

(6) "AND WHEN THEY FOUND THEM NOT, THEY DREW JASON AND CERTAIN BRETHREN UNTO THE RULERS OF THE CITY, CRYING, THESE THAT HAVE TURNED THE WORLD UPSIDE DOWN ARE COME HERE ALSO."

The exegesis is:

1. The phrase, *"And when they found them not,"* gives us no indication as to whether Paul, Silas, and Timothy had been there but escaped, or were not there at all, at least at that time, which seems to have been the case.

2. *"They drew Jason and certain brethren unto the rulers of the city,"* proclaims this mob determined to take their anger out on someone, if not Paul! So, now they would charge Jason and others it seems!

3. *"Crying, These that have turned the world upside down are come here also,"* tells us that the Jews had prepped certain people in this mob thoroughly.

4. In effect, the Jews and the mob were right and, at the same time, wrong. In truth the world was upside down because of the Fall in the Garden of Eden. However, since the advent of Jesus Christ and, as a result, the presentation of His Gospel, the world, at least in a spiritual sense regarding those who believe, is at last right side up.

5. However, such is always a traumatic thing, as the presentation and acceptance of the Gospel always is. It actually changes everything, but for the best, and by far the best! In truth, the acceptance of Jesus Christ as one's Lord and Saviour is the most cataclysmic, revolutionary thing that could ever happen to anyone at anytime!

(7) "WHOM JASON HAS RECEIVED: AND THESE ALL DO CONTRARY TO THE DECREES OF CAESAR, SAYING THAT THERE IS ANOTHER KING, ONE JESUS."

The composition is:

1. The phrase, *"Whom Jason has received,"* refers to them charging Jason as being a part of the alleged conspiracy. So, it was guilt by association!

2. *"And these all do contrary to the decrees of Caesar, saying that there is another King, one Jesus,"* presents that which is blatantly false, and the Jews knew it was false.

3. In the first place, Jesus as a King, which He was and is, had nothing to do with an earthly kingdom. They perfectly well knew that!

4. Also, the pretension of these Jews to be concerned over Caesar and the laws of the Roman Empire is so absurd as to be ludicrous! They were known the world over for their hatred of the Roman Empire, and Caesar in particular. So, for them to accuse

Paul and Jason of high treason presents hypocrisy and deception of the highest sort!

(8) "AND THEY TROUBLED THE PEOPLE AND THE RULERS OF THE CITY, WHEN THEY HEARD THESE THINGS."

The way is:

1. That which *"troubled"* the *"rulers"* was the extent of this accusation, especially considering that such had not come to their ears before now.

2. When one considers that one or more of the *"chief women"* mentioned in Verse 4 may well have been the wife of one or more of these rulers, or at least of some very influential men in the city, they were, no doubt, troubled at these implications, as would be obvious. However, the rulers had not heard of such sedition simply because none existed. All of this was a trumped-up charge on the part of the Jews, which, as well, was not something new.

3. This is the very charge that the Sanhedrin leveled against Jesus when He was brought before Pilate. According to their claims, He was declaring Himself King in opposition to Caesar. So, Satan continued his same old tricks, although at a different stand.

(9) "AND WHEN THEY HAD TAKEN SECURITY OF JASON, AND OF THE OTHER, THEY LET THEM GO."

The composition is:

1. The phrase, *"And when they had taken security of Jason,"* probably means that Jason put up a security bond of some sort. To be sure, if the authorities had taken these charges seriously, they would have taken much sterner measures.

2. *"And of the other,"* probably referred to a guarantee on the part of Jason and others that Paul and his party would leave the city so as not to cause problems, even though they were not to blame.

3. *"They let them go,"* implies that the authorities were now satisfied.

4. It is becoming very obvious that every time Paul went into a new city, he first went into the Jewish synagogue, that is, if one was available. It was also obvious that most of the time, there erupted a great fight and disturbance regarding his testimony of Jesus Christ. One then wonders why he

NOTES

kept trying to reach these people.

5. Paul had a tremendous burden for them, as would be obvious! No group of people has ever forfeited so much as the Jewish people. To be the very people through whom the Redeemer of mankind would come, and actually raised up for this very purpose, and to speak of it for some 1,600 years, and do so constantly, and then not know Him when He actually did come is beyond words! However, if that were not bad enough, to murder Him as an impostor or blasphemer places this dastardly deed as the crime of all crimes! And yet, that is exactly what happened!

6. So, Paul would attempt to reach them at whatever cost, and he did reach some.

7. Even if Paul had ignored the synagogues, the ire of these people would have been aroused no less. They would still have risen up against him, using the same tactics. As it was, he did get some of them to Christ.

(10) "AND THE BRETHREN IMMEDIATELY SENT AWAY PAUL AND SILAS BY NIGHT UNTO BEREA: WHO COMING THERE WENT INTO THE SYNAGOGUE OF THE JEWS."

The status is:

1. The phrase, *"And the brethren immediately sent away Paul and Silas by night unto Berea,"* presents this town, which is about 50 miles from Thessalonica.

2. To keep peace, the brethren felt it would be best for Paul and Silas to leave at the present time. Timothy is not mentioned here, but he was probably with them.

3. *"Who coming there went into the synagogue of the Jews,"* presents, as we have just been discussing, Paul's custom, but which, at this time for a change, would turn out much better.

4. As someone has said, no amount of ill usage from the Jews could weaken Paul's love for *"his brethren, his kinsmen according to the flesh"* (Rom. 9:3); and no amount of danger or suffering could check his zeal in preaching the Gospel of Christ to them, at least where possible!

(11) "THESE WERE MORE NOBLE THAN THOSE IN THESSALONICA, IN THAT THEY RECEIVED THE WORD WITH ALL READINESS OF MIND, AND

SEARCHED THE SCRIPTURES DAILY, WHETHER THOSE THINGS WERE SO."

The order is:

1. Unless the admonition of Romans, Chapter 8, is followed regarding the work of the Holy Spirit, the flesh will triumph.

2. In other words, the believer fails despite the fact that he does not want to do so and is trying with all his strength not to do so.

MORE NOBLE

The phrase, *"These were more noble than those in Thessalonica,"* presents Paul using the word *"noble"* in a different manner than its regular aristocratic meaning.

He was not speaking of anything of the world, whether of education or high birth, but rather the dedication and devotion to the Scriptures evidenced by these Jews in Berea. So, in essence, we learn from this exactly who God labels as *"noble!"*

The influential, famous, powerful, rich, and highly educated of the world are seldom, if ever, looked at by God as the world looks at such. God's Nobility refers to fidelity to His Word.

"In that they received the Word with all readiness of mind," presents something, especially among Jews, of which Paul was not accustomed to seeing.

As he opened up the Scriptures to them, explaining Who and what the Messiah would be, and how that Jesus had met the criteria in every respect and was indeed the Messiah, he found them receiving this Word without hesitation. What a joy that must have been to the apostle.

The phrase, *"And searched the Scriptures daily, whether those things were so,"* tells us why they so eagerly accepted the message of Jesus Christ.

THE WORD OF GOD

The answer for all things pertaining to life and godliness is found in the Word of God. The reason that people will not believe the truth and will accept a lie is because they do not know the Word of God. This is the cause of all false doctrine, the cause of all error, and, actually, in essence, the cause of the loss of every soul.

NOTES

If a believer does not properly know the Word of God, he is prone to reject that which is definitely of God and to accept that which is not. The only frame of reference is the Bible. So, believers either follow the Bible or they follow men who claim to be leading them according to the Word of God, but some are actually appealing to the base desires in their hearts and lives.

One must understand that Satan is so clever in counterfeiting that which is truly of God that it takes someone who is well versed in the Scripture to tell the difference. Satan does this in a variety of ways; however, his two greatest ways are false doctrine and false manifestations.

The only way one can know that which he needs to know is to *"search the Scriptures daily, whether those things were so."* Four things are told us in Verses 2, 11, and 12:

1. Sincere study of the Bible leads to faith in Christ.

2. All are to search the Scriptures, whether layperson or preacher.

3. All are to exercise private judgment as to whether the teaching they receive from the minister is scriptural.

4. No faith can be said to be a living faith that does not result from personal conviction based upon the Scriptures.

(12) "THEREFORE MANY OF THEM BELIEVED; ALSO OF HONORABLE WOMEN WHICH WERE GREEKS, AND OF MEN, NOT A FEW."

The direction is:

1. The phrase, *"Therefore many of them believed,"* states, as it does over and over, that faith in Jesus Christ is the criterion for salvation. As it was then, so is it now! The *"many"* spoken of here were Jews.

2. The phrase, *"Also of honorable women which were Greeks,"* once again speaks of gentiles who attended the Jewish synagogue, thereby, worshiping the God of Abraham, Isaac, and Jacob. As well, they were *"honorable,"* meaning they were women of influence and status in the city.

3. The phrase, *"And of men, not a few,"* implies that these were gentiles as well!

(13) "BUT WHEN THE JEWS OF THESSALONICA HAD KNOWLEDGE THAT THE WORD OF GOD WAS

PREACHED OF PAUL AT BEREA, THEY CAME THERE ALSO, AND STIRRED UP THE PEOPLE."

The construction is:

1. Here we go again!

2. The phrase, *"But when the Jews of Thessalonica had knowledge that the Word of God was preached of Paul at Berea,"* insinuates that Paul and Silas were able to spend probably several weeks in this place before the news got back to Thessalonica of the goodly number of people who had been saved. So, these Jews in Thessalonica, not content with what they had done in their city, now attempted to stop that which was happening in Berea. They would succeed up to a point.

3. *"They came there also, and stirred up the people,"* shows how effective a lie can be. Actually, the *"lie"* is Satan's greatest weapon.

2. There is seldom a defense, at least one that is satisfactory, against a lie. Whether accepting all of the lie or not is one thing; however, even though not believed, a residue, most, if not all of the time, is left in the minds of the hearers.

3. So, the good people in Berea would be left with a lingering thought that Paul and Silas just might be engaged in some small way respecting sedition against Caesar. It was difficult, at least for some of the people in Berea, to believe that people would go to all of this trouble to spread a lie. However, people do such everyday! Actually, people of this nature tell a lie so much that they come to the place that they actually believe it themselves.

(14) "AND THEN IMMEDIATELY THE BRETHREN SENT AWAY PAUL TO GO AS IT WERE TO THE SEA: BUT SILAS AND TIMOTHEUS ABODE THERE STILL."

The form is:

1. The phrase, *"And then immediately the brethren sent away Paul to go as it were to the sea,"* speaks of the Aegean, which was about 17 miles from Berea. From there, either Pydna or Dium, Paul caught a ship for Athens.

2. Due to the opposition by the Thessalonian Jews, the converted Jews and gentiles at Berea thought it best that Paul leave immediately, which he did! It seems that the greatest animosity was directed against Paul, which it was, because he was the leader.

3. Why Paul went to Athens, we are not told! However, I am sure the Lord was leading him ultimately to Corinth, where a great church would be established.

4. The phrase, *"But Silas and Timotheus abode there still,"* refers to them remaining in Berea.

5. Inasmuch as the new believers in that city were well versed in the Word of God, there was not as much danger of them being sidetracked as many others who had come to Christ. As well, Silas and Timothy would continue to instruct and teach them, which, of course, was a tremendous help!

(15) "AND THEY WHO CONDUCTED PAUL BROUGHT HIM UNTO ATHENS: AND RECEIVING A COMMANDMENT UNTO SILAS AND TIMOTHEUS FOR TO COME TO HIM WITH ALL SPEED, THEY DEPARTED."

The way is:

1. The Cross of Christ is the very heart of the Gospel, the very life of our souls.

2. By trusting ourselves to that great Sacrifice, the dread of punishment will fade from our hearts.

ATHENS

The phrase, *"And they who conducted Paul brought him unto Athens,"* presents the chief city of Greece, famed for its learning.

The implication is that the Bereans who were with Paul at this time, as well, accompanied him to Athens. The Text also slightly indicates that these men, ever how many there were, feared a possible ambush of Paul by the Thessalonian Jews and, therefore, stayed with him to give protection.

"And receiving a commandment unto Silas and Timotheus for to come to him with all speed, they departed," gives credence to the thought that when Paul left Berea, he and the men with him were not sure as to exactly where they were going. Once Athens was decided upon, he sent the message back with these men that Silas and Timothy were to come to Athens as quickly as possible.

From I Thessalonians 3:1-2, we learn that when Timothy did arrive, Paul sent him

NOTES

from Athens back to Thessalonica. This was probably done because Paul feared that the new church at Thessalonica might not be able to stand up under the persecution. Timothy would be of some help, most of all, because he was a close associate of Paul.

From I Thessalonians 3:6, we learn that Timothy stayed there for a period of time and then joined Paul at Corinth, where the Epistles to the Thessalonians were written.

THE NEW CHURCHES

One can see in all of this several things:

First of all, Paul, as would be obvious, had a deep and abiding concern for these new churches, hence, his attempting to spread his party thin in order to utilize both Silas and Timothy. As we have stated, it seems that Luke remained at Philippi.

Also, there were not very many men, at least at this stage, who Paul could trust to send to these respective places. Actually, as further information will reveal, he was very jealous that only his handpicked people be sent. He would later say while in prison in Rome, and speaking of the church at Philippi, *"But I trust in the Lord Jesus to send Timotheus shortly unto you, that I also may be of good comfort, when I know your state.*

"For I have no man like-minded, who will naturally care for your state.

"For all seek their own, not the things which are Jesus Christ's" (Phil. 2:19-21).

Not only was there the problem of acute persecution, but, as well, the Judaizers would soon begin their attempts to compromise the Gospel of grace and, as well, to demean the person of Paul. One thing is certain, it was not easy for Paul to carry out that which the Lord had called him to do.

No wonder, even at the time of his conversion, the Lord spoke to Ananias, *"For I will show him how great things he must suffer for My Name's sake"* (Acts 9:16).

(16) "NOW WHILE PAUL WAITED FOR THEM AT ATHENS, HIS SPIRIT WAS STIRRED IN HIM, WHEN HE SAW THE CITY WHOLLY GIVEN TO IDOLATRY."

The account is:

1. The phrase, *"Now while Paul waited for them at Athens,"* proclaims to us an intensely interesting episode respecting the life and ministry of this great apostle. The time waiting for Silas and Timothy was probably in the neighborhood of two or three weeks. The brethren with him had to sail back to Berea, with Silas and Timothy then going to Athens. Even though the time spent there was very short, I am certain that Silas and Timothy put each hour to good use in teaching these new converts at Berea.

2. The phrase, *"His spirit was stirred in him, when he saw the city wholly given to idolatry,"* means it was full of idols!

About 500 years before the time of Paul, Athens was at the zenith of its power. It was famous for its culture and the great philosophers like Plato and Aristotle. However, after the Roman conquest of Greece, Athens became a part of the Roman Empire. And yet, according to particular treaties, it paid no taxes to Rome and had internal judicial autonomy, which meant it was ruled by Greeks.

3. Of the three great university cities, Athens, Tarsus, and Alexandria, Athens was the most famous. However, its great fame was now history, with Alexandria of Egypt overshadowing its present glory.

Yet, it still nurtured the memory of its past. Its temples, such as the Acropolis, were still beautiful examples of the best in Greek architecture. And yet, the Athenians had made gods out of their philosophical fame of the past, hence, the city full of monuments, statues, and idols! In effect, their god was culture, wisdom, and learning. However, their culture was jaded, their wisdom was sensual, and their learning was error!

May it ever be said that he who does not know God, though he knows everything else, in truth, really knows nothing!

(17) "THEREFORE DISPUTED HE IN THE SYNAGOGUE WITH THE JEWS, AND WITH THE DEVOUT PERSONS, AND IN THE MARKET DAILY WITH THEM THAT MET WITH HIM."

The pattern is:

1. The phrase, *"Therefore disputed he in the synagogue with the Jews,"* proclaims him once again doing what was his custom. His message would have been the same as

NOTES

always, proving Who and What the Messiah would be according to the Scriptures, and then proving that Jesus Christ met all of these specifications and fulfilled all Scriptures.

2. *"And with the devout persons,"* singles out the Jews who really seemed to be devoted to the Scriptures. These were people who were consecrated to God, at least as much as they knew how to be.

3. *"And in the market daily with them that met with him,"* pertained to the busiest section of the city. It was near the Pnyx, the Acropolis, and the Areopagus.

4. This *"marketplace"* was said to be the central seat of commercial, forensic, and philosophic intercourse, as well as the busy idleness of the loungers.

5. So, Paul met with the Jews and proselytes on the Sabbath and ministered every other day to the gentiles in the marketplace.

6. How many Sabbaths he ministered in the synagogue is not stated. It could have been only one, but probably three at the most! All of this was going on, as stated, while he was waiting for Silas and Timothy.

(18) "THEN CERTAIN PHILOSOPHERS OF THE EPICUREANS, AND OF THE STOICKS, ENCOUNTERED HIM. AND SOME SAID, WHAT WILL THIS BABBLER SAY? OTHER SOME, HE SEEMS TO BE A SETTER FORTH OF STRANGE GODS: BECAUSE HE PREACHED UNTO THEM JESUS, AND THE RESURRECTION."

The pattern is:

1. Jesus Christ was a Man, fully Man, total Man, absolute Man, *"The Man Christ Jesus."*

2. However, even though He willingly laid aside His expression of Deity, not for a moment did He lay aside His possession of Deity.

NOTES

THE PHILOSOPHERS

The phrase, *"Then certain philosophers of the Epicureans, and of the Stoicks* (Stoics), *encountered him,"* gives us an idea as to what some part of this marketplace was all about.

Not having the modern methods of entertainment now available, its greatest form in those days consisted of particular speakers holding forth at a given place in the market. When one speaker finished after having espoused his particular philosophy on whatever subject, another would instantly take his place. The crowd would either agree, disagree, or just simply be amused! As stated, this was a great part of their entertainment and was attended, more or less, by many people, especially considering that it was in the midst of the marketplace. In this mix, Paul took his turn in order to minister to the crowd. As should be known, these people were rank pagans, with no idea whatsoever as to the existence of the true God.

THE EPICUREANS AND STOICS

The *"Epicureans"* were followers of Epicurus, who lived in 342-279 B.C.

He taught his followers not to believe in any gods except in name. They denied that these gods exercised any government over the world or its inhabitants. They held that the chief good consisted in gratification of the appetites and that pleasure was the only end in life.

Actually, this philosophy was the seedbed of the 1960s, *"If it feels good, do it!"*

The *"Stoics"* were the followers of Zeno, who had lived about 270 B.C.

He believed in gods but taught that all human affairs were governed by fate or blind chance. He also taught that there was no good which came from these various so-called deities!

They held that no supreme good was virtue, and that man should be free from passion and moved by neither joy or grief, nor pleasure or pain. Consequently, they were the opposites of the Epicureans.

Actually, they were the fatalists and pantheists of that day.

GREEK PHILOSOPHY

During an approximate 500 years before Christ, especially the last 200 years, Greek thought spread so widely that it came to dominate the cultured thought of the world into which Christianity entered. As a result, it was addressed in some of Paul's Epistles.

THE PHILOSOPHY OF SOCRATES

In the first stage of its development,

from Thales to Socrates, philosophy was concerned almost entirely with attempts to explain the nature of reality by reducing the striking events of the world, such as war, the elements, etc., into another direction. In effect, Socrates changed its center of gravity, and by that, I refer to its focal point. Pushing these great phenomena aside, he raised the problems of morality and knowledge to the position of first importance. Basically, that was the kernel of Socrates' philosophy.

THE PRINCIPLES OF PLATO

The principles of Socrates were developed by Plato into a complex and many-sided system, which, more than any other, has influenced all subsequent thought, at least that which is outside of Christianity.

He united ultimate reality and the highest good into one supreme principle or idea, which he called *"the good,"* or *"God."* His thinking, at least in the world of that day, was the essence, archetype, and origin of all wisdom, goodness, and beauty. It communicated itself as ideas to produce all individual things. Consequently, at least in his thinking, all the formative principles of all existence were moral and spiritual.

So, we can see how these thinkers of old were casting about for an answer to all things, but without God. As such, the answers are impossible. As well, man cannot reach God from his own initiative. God has to reveal Himself to man, which He has done through His Word given to the prophets and apostles.

THE BIG PROBLEM WITH SOCRATES AND PLATO

Inasmuch as these philosophers did not start with God because they could not start with God, having no knowledge of Him, their ideas had to be formed out of preexisting matter, which is essentially evil, at least as they judged it, and which, therefore, was hostile to the good. That is why they could not make their philosophy produce a perfect world.

Plato's system was, therefore, rent by an irreconcilable dualism of mind and body, spirit and matter, and good and evil, with all of his great ideas unable to bridge this gulf. He could see the ideal, but he could not bring it to pass.

NOTES

THE PHILOSOPHY OF ARISTOTLE

Aristotle was Plato's disciple, as Plato had been Socrates' disciple.

He began with Plato's principles of the *"good"* and *"God,"* at least as Plato defined God, which, of course, was erroneous, and then endeavored to transcend the dualism that stopped Plato. While the good was present, at least as they defined good, so was the evil. The problem was how to stop the evil.

He thus applied himself to a closer and more accurate study of actual experience and added much to the knowledge of the physical world.

In effect, Aristotle created the science of logic, which, in the Christian Middle Ages, became the chief instrument of the great systematic theologians of the church. However, it was earthly wisdom and, therefore, sensual and devilish, which was almost the ruin of the church.

Aristotle tried to bring Plato's ideas *"down from heaven,"* and to represent them as the creative and formative principles within the world, which he conceived as a system of development, rising by spiritual gradations from the lower to the higher forms, and ultimately culminating in God, Who is the uncaused Cause of all things.

However, underneath all the things he said, still, there remained the problem of *"evil,"* for which he had no answer, and which he rather concealed than solved. Of course, it could not be solved except by Jesus Christ.

ENTER THE EPICUREANS AND STOICS

These two groups, the Epicureans, whose philosophy was pleasure, and the Stoics, whose philosophy was fatalism (*"what will be, will be!"*), were both derived from the so-called moral principles of Socrates. That is interesting, understanding that they are divergent views. However, now entered subjective truth, which, in reality, is no truth at all!

SUBJECTIVE TRUTH

Man's philosophies can only produce

subjective truth, which simply means that the understanding and explanation of truth is subject to whatever someone desires or thinks it to be. Consequently, in that type of thinking, which is the ruination of the world, what is truth for one will not be truth for another!

Man's philosophies can only produce subjective truth for the simple reason that it does not begin with the first cause, Who is God. Man attempts to build upon a series of events and thinking toward God, Who cannot be reached or understood in that manner. All knowledge of God must come from God to man and then only does man have objective truth, which never changes because it is built on the first cause, Who is God.

The Bible, which is the Word of God, is the standard for all law, right and wrong, in other words, the standard for everything. As such, and as stated, it is objective truth simply because it changes not, as truth does not need to change.

Man's philosophies change constantly because they begin with man, who holds no answers within himself.

PHILO, THE JEWISH PHILOSOPHER OF ALEXANDRIA

He was probably born about 10 years before Christ and died at about 60 years of age. He was a native of Alexandria, Egypt. His relatives were wealthy and prominent, with him receiving the very best Jewish education. He was also trained in much gentile learning, hence, the philosophies of the Greeks.

He attempted to reconcile Greek intellectualism with Jewish belief. He taught there were two meanings in Scripture, a *"lower"* meaning obvious in the literal statements of the Text, and a *"higher"* or hidden meaning perceptible only to a few.

He taught that Greek thought exhibited the *"hidden"* meaning. Despite this obvious contradiction, he insisted that he was thoroughly true to the Old Testament.

He was a perfect example of attempting to understand the Scriptures by natural means. There is a good possibility that it is to this philosophy that Paul directed his

NOTES

statement, *"But the natural man receives not the things of the Spirit of God: for they are foolishness unto him: neither can he know them, because they are spiritually discerned"* (I Cor. 2:14).

JESUS CHRIST

Not accepting Jesus Christ, Philo reasoned that God is, and of that he was fully persuaded, but what He is, no man could ever tell, or so he said!

Accordingly, the conclusion of the whole matter is that he never saw how the divine and the human can be united. Having rejected Jesus Christ, there remained no way for man to be united with God, therefore, the salvation of Philo was a salvation basically of intellectualism, which was no salvation at all!

Regrettably, this snare has engulfed untold numbers from his time until now.

Jesus Christ is the Door to the Father, not intellectualism, knowledge, science, mysticism, etc.

God has set about to reveal Himself to the human family, but He has done so exclusively and entirely through His Son, the Lord Jesus Christ. The sacrifices pictured Jesus! The covenants pictured Jesus! The Law pictured Jesus! The Tabernacle and the Temple pictured Jesus! The prophecies pictured Jesus!

Jesus plainly said, *"I am the Door: by Me if any man enter in, he shall be saved, and shall go in and out, and find pasture"* (Jn. 10:9).

So, the Answer to all philosophy is Jesus! The Answer to all seeking is Jesus! The Answer to all needs is Jesus! The Answer, as given by God, is Jesus!

BABBLER?

The question, *"And some said, What will this babbler say?"* presents the highest insult of which they could think.

The word *"babbler"* in the Greek text is *"spermologos"* and means *"seed-picker or chatterer."*

The "seed-picker" was a small bird which lived by picking of seeds with its beak. It was applied to those who gathered information from gossip. In other words, they were saying that Paul had no philosophy of

NOTES

his own, but rather scraps here and there, which he had stolen from others! Of course, one wonders as to exactly how they could have come up with this conclusion, especially considering that what Paul was saying, they had never heard before!

In essence, as is plainly obvious to the believer, he was answering all the questions that their noted philosophers of the past and present could not answer. That for which Socrates, Plato, and Aristotle had searched, he now provided the answers, but they were too lifted up in themselves, and too puffed up by their own self-importance to properly hear him. After all, were they not the Greeks, the thinkers of the great philosophies! The facts were, they were *"ever learning,* (but) *never able to come to the knowledge of the Truth"* (II Tim. 3:7).

Sadly, with the demise of these self-pronounced philosophers, the breed did not die! It is alive and well presently!

THE BEGINNING OF WISDOM

However, even though they held Paul in contempt, in essence, calling him a *"babbler"* and his message *"babbling,"* the truth was and is that it was the other way around. Paul was actually educated to a far greater degree than these detractors. He not only was very learned in these philosophies which they exhibited, but, as well, and of that which is all-important, he knew the Lord. In regard to that, the Scripture says, *"The fear of the LORD is the beginning of wisdom"* (Prov. 1:7). The idea is this:

All types of philosophies abound and, in fact, ever have done so! However, they are all man-originated, which guarantees error, and gross error at that!

On the other side of all of these philosophies is Bible Christianity. In respect to that, Peter said:

"According as His Divine Power has given unto us all things that pertain unto life and godliness, through the knowledge of Him Who has called us to glory and virtue:

"Whereby are given unto us exceeding great and precious promises: that by these we might be partakers of the Divine Nature, having escaped the corruption that is in the world through lust" (II Pet. 1:3-4).

The philosophies of men, even as profound as they may seem, in truth, answer no questions and provide no solutions. The great sadness is that billions have died eternally lost, coming to death and finding no way across that dark void. However, the solid rock of Jesus Christ ever holds true!

PHILOSOPHY

The word *"philosophy"* simply means *"a pursuit of wisdom, the purpose of life and a search for truth."* However, because it originates with man, this quest can never find the answers. In fact, man cannot reach God or know God by intellectual pursuit. It simply does not work in that fashion. The ingredient upon which God has built the entirety of the structure of His Dealings with man is through faith (Heb., Chpt. 11). Consequently, all the answers begin with God and not man. As well, the truth that He provides and is wrapped up in the person of Jesus is objective truth, which can never change. Philosophies change by the day, while God never changes simply because, being perfect, He does not have to change!

STRANGE GODS?

The phrase, *"Other some, He seems to be a setter forth of strange gods,"* contains the idea of gods who were foreign to Greek thought and philosophy. In their minds, anything outside of Greek philosophy was of no consequence whatsoever.

The word *"gods"* in the Greek text, at least as it is used here, is *"xenos daimonion"* and means *"foreign demons."*

The phrase, *"Because he preached unto them Jesus, and the Resurrection,"* presented that which was greatly offensive to them, and for several reasons:

THE RESURRECTION

First of all, as stated, if it was outside of Greek thought, and Jesus definitely was, then it was of no consequence, and not only of no consequence, but rather harmful! Also, if, in fact, Paul was introducing a new divinity, this was forbidden both in Rome and in Athens.

As well, the *"Resurrection"* was not something they desired whatsoever.

They took the position that life was hard enough without having to do it all over again, whether in reincarnation or being raised from the dead, etc. So, even though they despised death, seeing it as an aberration, which is correct, still, on the other side of the coin, death was an escape from the hardships and rigors of this life, which, to them, was desirable!

So, the idea of a resurrection was not something they met with joy, especially considering that they had no understanding whatsoever of the type of Resurrection of which Paul spoke.

To be resurrected as we now are has little point; however, to be resurrected in glory, in other words, a glorified body, is something else altogether. To retain the corruption and mortality serves no purpose. However, if, in fact, which is the case, *"The dead shall be raised incorruptible, and we shall be changed,"* then resurrection takes on a brand-new perspective.

Regarding this, Paul further said, *"For this corruptible must put on incorruption, and this mortal must put on immortality"* (I Cor. 15:52-53).

(19) "AND THEY TOOK HIM, AND BROUGHT HIM UNTO AREOPAGUS, SAYING, MAY WE KNOW WHAT THIS NEW DOCTRINE, WHEREOF YOU SPEAK, IS?"

The synopsis is:

1. What is the flesh?
2. It is that which is indicative to a human being.
3. It pertains to our education, motivation, personal talent and ability, personal strength, will power, etc.

THE SUPREME COURT IN ATHENS

The phrase, *"And they took him, and brought him unto Areopagus,"* refers to Mars Hill, which faces the Acropolis. This was the Supreme Court in Athens.

In the 5th and 4th centuries B.C., Athens was famous for its culture, the home of the great dramatists and great philosophers, like Plato and Aristotle. After the Roman conquest of Greece, Athens became a city linked to Rome by treaty, but yet, was entirely independent of the governor of Achaia, the province of its location, paying no taxes to Rome, and with internal judicial autonomy.

Of the three great university cities, Athens, Tarsus (the home of Paul), and Alexandria, Athens was the most famous. Philo the Alexandrian said that the Athenians were the keenest-sighted mentally of the Greeks. Athens was also famous for its temples, statues, and monuments.

Though the Athenians were religious and eager to discuss religion, as is evidenced by them hearing Paul, their spiritual level was made up almost entirely of superstition.

The truth is, the entirety of the world is mostly made up of superstition as it regards religion, which has been the case since the very beginning. In fact, all superstition, in one way or another, has its origin in religion.

RELIGION

Religion is that which is conceived by man, birthed by man, and instituted by man. It claims to reach God or to better oneself in some way. It is not of God. Christ and the Cross constitute God's Way.

Some years ago, I had the occasion, along with Frances and a number of others, to stand on this very spot in Athens. Actually, we taped a short television piece there.

If I remember correctly, I attempted to make the point in my short message that all of the glory, power, and greatness, which once made Greece the center of world learning, are now gone. Consequently, Greece, only able to look back at former glories, sits like a drowsy beggar watching the hands of a broken clock.

Then I attempted to make the point that its greatness and glory are gone because it was built on a lie. However, the Jesus Whom Paul preached has changed this world, with Him inhabiting the hearts and lives of untold millions, because He is Truth.

The question, *"Saying, May we know what this new doctrine, whereof you speak, is?"* presents Paul facing the Supreme Court justices of Athens.

The question posed by these men was polite and carried no direct implications. It was, even as they said, *"This new doctrine."*

Of all the thousands of times this court had convened on this very spot, the proceedings of this day would be by far the most

NOTES

important that were ever there convened, even though little realized by these justices. For the first time, despite all the philosophies of the past and present, they would now hear the truth! That for which they had long searched would now be presented to them. However, as we shall see, it would be refused, at least for the most part!

(20) "FOR YOU BRING CERTAIN STRANGE THINGS TO OUR EARS: WE WOULD KNOW THEREFORE WHAT THESE THINGS MEAN."

The exegesis is:

1. The phrase, *"For you bring certain strange things to our ears,"* puts a different spin on what is being said.

2. It is strange that these self-appointed philosophers would label that taught by Paul as no more than babblings or scraps, but yet, would think them important enough that he be taken before the highest court in Athens! Blessed consistency!

3. So, not only were they questioning the origin of what Paul was saying but, at the same time, called it *"strange,"* meaning something they had never heard before.

4. As well, Paul, it seems, was given no time whatsoever to prepare his defense, which caused no problem. The Holy Spirit was helping him constantly, and, as well, he knew his Gospel inside out, backwards and forwards.

And yet, when it was all said and done, I'm not so sure that Paul was happy with what he had preached that day. Beside the point that what he did preach was powerful and, of course, was the truth, still, he really did not preach the Cross that day, but rather the Resurrection, etc. I'm not so sure that he was happy with the results of what he brought to the people, even though it was most definitely the truth.

He left Athens and went to Corinth and there made the declaration, *"I determined not to know any thing among you save Jesus Christ and Him Crucified"* (I Cor. 2:2).

I personally feel that this statement came from a soul searching as it regarded Athens.

5. The phrase, *"We would know therefore what these things mean,"* presents a noble request to Paul and an unparalleled opportunity! To be sure, Paul was ready!

NOTES

(21) "FOR ALL THE ATHENIANS AND STRANGERS WHICH WERE THERE SPENT THEIR TIME IN NOTHING ELSE, BUT EITHER TO TELL, OR TO HEAR SOME NEW THING."

The structure is:

1. The phrase, *"For all the Athenians and strangers which were there,"* presents Luke establishing several things as he wrote this account.

There seemed to be no great philosophers in Athens at this time, such as Socrates, Plato, and Aristotle of the past. So, present Athens was attempting to live off the glory of former times.

Horton said, *"In truth, even though Athens had once been the greatest of the learning centers of the world, other places such as Ephesus, Alexandria, Antioch and Tarsus had by now far surpassed it as learning centers. It had lost its drive and creativity. It was filled with curiosity seekers and with philosophical speculation that was without depth."*

2. *"Spent their time in nothing else, but either to tell, or to hear some new thing,"* seemed to speak, however, to that which fit their mold. To be sure, what Paul was saying was definitely a *"new thing,"* at least to them, and in a magnitude they had not previously known.

3. No doubt, this caused them to give him audience to begin with in the marketplace, but soon so impacted their own philosophy, even in a negative sense, that they grew perturbed.

4. As well, which was, no doubt, the case, they were unable to refute Paul's arguments or to counter them with their own philosophy. Consequently, they did what most do in these situations. They attacked not only his message, but him personally! So now, he stood before their Supreme Court!

5. In truth, these people were the very thing of which they had accused Paul, *"babblers."*

(22) "THEN PAUL STOOD IN THE MIDST OF MARS' HILL, AND SAID, YOU MEN OF ATHENS, I PERCEIVE THAT IN ALL THINGS YOU ARE TOO SUPERSTITIOUS."

The composition is:

1. The phrase, *"Then Paul stood in the midst of Mars' hill, and said,"* presents the continued fulfillment of Paul standing *"before the gentiles,"* as predicted! (Acts 9:15).

2. *"You men of Athens, I perceive that in all things you are too superstitious,"* has been debated from then until now as to exactly what Paul said.

3. Referring to all the many gods they worshiped, some scholars claim he was referring to their superstition as desiring not to offend any of these alleged deities. Considering that they thought of themselves as most highly educated and not given over to superstition, if, in fact, that was what Paul said, they would have been highly insulted.

4. Others claim the word, as used here, refers to them being very religious, and if that is the way it was used by Paul, it would have probably been looked at as a mild compliment.

5. It is my thought that the manner in which Paul used the word, it was definitely not a compliment. In fact, even if it meant religious, such is the source of more superstition than anything else in the world. Consequently, his statement was derogatory, and meant to be that way, whether they understood it accordingly or not!

6. (All religion originates with man, and is by and large a system of do's and don'ts, a code of ethics, if you will! Bible Christianity is not a religion or anything close to such. It is actually a Person, and that Person is the Lord Jesus Christ. To add to that, Catholicism is a religion and so is Mormonism. Jehovah's Witnesses, Church of Christ, and Seventh Day Adventism would fall into the same category. As such, they are not Christian, despite their claims! In fact, every believer must be very careful that they do not sink down to that level. If such happens, Paul said, *"You are fallen from grace"*) (Gal. 5:4).

(23) "FOR AS I PASSED BY, AND BEHELD YOUR DEVOTIONS, I FOUND AN ALTAR WITH THIS INSCRIPTION, TO THE UNKNOWN GOD. WHOM THEREFORE YOU IGNORANTLY WORSHIP, HIM DECLARE I UNTO YOU."

The overview is:

NOTES

1. It is clear that in the Old Testament, it was recognized that death was the penalty for sin (Ezek. 18:20).

2. However, God graciously permitted the death of a sacrificial animal to substitute for the death of the sinner (Heb. 9:22).

IDOL GODS

The phrase, *"For as I passed by, and beheld your devotions,"* has reference to their objects of worship.

The truth was and is painfully obvious that despite all these gods to whom the Greeks had built monuments, they did not feel close to any god. They went from god to god, from altar to altar, hoping that somehow they could be helped, etc. Thus, despite their education and highly-developed culture, they were, in fact, without God and without hope, which generated superstition and fear.

Horton said, *"Of course there was no help from these sources, because these gods did not exist, and were all figments of men's imagination. In fact, their ancestors had long since forsaken God, putting self on the throne; consequently, they were soon worshiping gods of their own making, gods they thought they could manipulate to do their will."*

But yet, for all this devotion and building of monuments, etc., there was no answer from these sources, and for the simple reason that the lesser is always made by the greater. In other words, how could something made by their own hands, which, of necessity, was less, be of any help to them? And yet, man continues along this same path.

He thinks his education will lead him into the Promised Land, not stopping to realize that much modern education is error, therefore, the product of man's mind. Again, anything that man can make is, of necessity, less than its maker. Consequently, how can it lead man to a higher spiritual plane?

IGNORANT WORSHIP

Psychology is another case in point! It is devised by man in totality, therefore, of necessity, it is less than he is, so how can it solve his problems?

For man to be saved and consequently

taken to a higher spiritual plane, something outside of himself must be the first cause. Of course, that first cause is God Who, through His Son, the Lord Jesus Christ, has lifted man out of this hopeless abyss!

The phrase, *"I found an altar with this inscription, TO THE UNKNOWN GOD,"* proclaims the direction that Paul would go respecting his message. So, they could not claim that he was preaching a foreign god to them, but rather making known to them one whom they had already included in their devotions without knowing Him.

They could hardly go against their own monument, but the facts were, God was truly *"unknown"* to them!

The phrase, *"Whom therefore you ignorantly worship, him declare I unto you,"* refers to them acknowledging that maybe they did not have the last word on gods! Actually, they did not have any word at all!

So from this *"altar,"* Paul would present to them the One of Whom this inscription spoke. As stated, this was to be the greatest moment of their lives, but yet, a moment they could not see simply because they were spiritually blind.

(24) "GOD WHO MADE THE WORLD AND ALL THINGS THEREIN, SEEING THAT HE IS LORD OF HEAVEN AND EARTH, DWELLS NOT IN TEMPLES MADE WITH HANDS."

The diagram is:

1. Every believer is importuned by the Lord to live the Resurrection life, but how do we do that?

2. Paul tells us. He said, *"For if we have been planted together in the likeness of His death* (the Cross), *we shall be also in the likeness of His Resurrection"* (Rom. 6:5).

3. In other words, the Resurrection life depends exclusively upon the Cross of Christ and our faith in that Finished Work.

THE CREATOR

The phrase, *"God Who made the world and all things therein,"* presents an entirely different tact than that normally used by Paul in his ministry to the Jews. However, there was no point in Paul beginning his message with the Prophecies and Promises of the Messiah when he was dealing with gentiles who did not know or believe the Bible.

We can be assured that he was led by the Holy Spirit; therefore, he would begin his message portraying God as Creator of all things!

Consequently, and even immediately, he debunked all the many gods worshiped by the Greeks, who were each supposed to be in charge of various parts of the world and the universe, etc.

If man does not understand God as Creator, and of all things at that, then he has no basis for knowing God. That is the reason evolution is the insult of all insults toward God!

THE DOCTRINE OF CREATION

No idea of Creation can now be taken as complete, which does not include all that was, but, as well, all that now is.

We must ever understand that God creates nothing but that it is totally dependent upon Him. In other words, His Creation cannot exist independently of Him. His preserving Agency is inseparably connected with His creative Power. He not only creates, but His Creation must have His continued Care, or else, it does not function properly.

Those who truly know their Bibles have long since ceased to think of God's Creation as a machine, completely made, left to its own automatic working. Such is not only incompatible, it is impossible!

GENESIS AND PHYSICAL SCIENCE

If one is to notice, God, at the beginning of His Word, makes no attempt to explain Himself, but rather takes it for granted that the sensible Creation knows and understands that He is the Creator. The reason is simple. Creation demands a Creator.

As well, the early chapters of the Book of Genesis were, of course, not given to reveal the truths of physical science, but they recognized Creation as marked by order, continuity, law, power of productiveness in the different kingdoms, unity of the world, and progressive advance, but they advance only under the tutelage and care of man's unity with God. In other words, God has so created things in this world that it will experience digression instead of progression unless superintended, cultivated, and nurtured by man. This is the manner in which God created these things, and this is the manner of dominion given to man by God (Gen. 1:28-31). Consequently, this law, and it is a law, debunks evolution in totality!

Even at the beginning, the Old Testament presents the real emphasis, which is on the energy of the Divine Word, which brought all things into existence that did not heretofore exist (Heb. 11:3).

NO ETERNAL MATTER BEFORE CREATION

The Old Testament and the New Testament, in their doctrine of Creation, recognize the existence of no eternal matter before Creation. The writer of Hebrews said, *"Through faith we understand that the worlds were framed by the Word of God, so that things which are seen were not made of things which do appear"* (Heb. 11:3).

The meaning of that is extremely complicated and, at the same time, extremely simple.

The idea is that no material existed before Creation, with God actually speaking these things into existence—that is to say that all were done by His divine Word or originative Will.

THE WISDOM OF GOD

In the Old Testament Books, as the Psalms, Proverbs, and Jeremiah, the Creation is expressly declared to be the work of wisdom—a wisdom not apart from goodness, we might quickly add, as is yet more fully brought out in the Book of Job.

The heavens declare the glory of God as the world manifests or reveals Him to our experience, which is taken up and interpreted by our consciousness. This is what Paul was speaking of when he said, *"Because that which may be known of God is manifest in them; for God has showed it unto them.*

"For the invisible things (His Glory and Power) *of Him from the creation of the world are clearly seen, being understood by the things that are made, even His Eternal Power and Godhead* (Deity); *so that they* (unbelieving humanity) *are without excuse"* (Rom. 1:19-20).

NOTES

However, due to the fall of man in the Garden of Eden and the necessary acute diminishing of his powers of comprehension and understanding, fallen man does not see God in Creation. Proper interpretation comes about only by the sinner making Christ his Saviour, and then by faith, he begins to understand Who and What is God.

Such faith is the by-product of salvation, which comes about through the Word of God.

In Creation, God is but expressing or acting out the conscious Godhood that is in Him. In it, the thought of His absolute Wisdom is realized by the action of His perfect Love.

It is absolutely necessary to maintain that God, as the absolute Being, must find the end of Creation in Himself, and only in Himself.

GOD IS GREATER

What the consciousness of the believer is concerned to maintain is the absolute freedom of God in the creation of the universe, and the idea that He is so much Greater than that which He has created, which should be obvious! The Scriptures are, from first to last, shot through with this truth.

GOD AS THE FIRST CAUSE

The characteristic of deity, as the Creator, is that He is the Cause of the existent universe—cause of its being, not merely of its evolution or present arrangements. The doctrine of His being the Creator implies, that is to say, that He is the real and the exclusive Agent in the production of the world, and all Creation for that matter. For, as one has said, the thought of the Creator is the most fruitful of all our ideas.

As Creator, God is the unconditioned and the all-conditioning Being. The universe is thus dependent upon Him as its Creator.

In all His Work as Creator, there is nothing that comes from without Him, but rather from within Him.

This creative action of God is portrayed in Christ—by Whom Were all things created, in the heavens and upon the earth, things visible and things invisible, whether thrones or dominions or principalities or powers; all things have been created through Him, and unto Him (Col. 1:16).

(Most of the thoughts on God as Creator were derived from the writings of James Orr, J. Iverbach, S. Harris Bowne, G. B. Fisher, and James Lindsay.)

PRECISION

It is my understanding that when the astronauts go out of Earth's atmosphere, and they seek to come back in, they have to be at a certain place at a certain time. As well, they have to depend on the rotation of the Earth being absolutely perfect. If it's off by even a millisecond, they will not be able to enter into Earth's atmosphere. This means they are dependent totally, even for their lives, on the precision of God's Creation. I might quickly add, that precision never fails. So, as we have said, Creation demands a Creator and, as well, a Creator Who is greater than that which He has created. That's the reason that Moses wrote:

"In the beginning God ..." (Gen. 1:1).

HE IS LORD OF HEAVEN AND EARTH

The phrase, *"Seeing that He is Lord of heaven and Earth,"* proclaims Him not only as Creator but, as well, the constant Manager of all that He has created. As we have previously stated, His Creation is done in such a way that it requires His constant Maintenance. In other words, Creation did not come into existence without Him, and is not and, in fact, cannot be maintained without Him!

"Dwells not in temples made with hands," proclaims a striking instance of Paul's unflinching boldness and fidelity to the truth that he should expose the hollowness of heathen worship, especially considering that he was standing within a stone's throw of the Parthenon and the Temple of Theseus, and the countless other temples of gods and goddesses, which were the pride and glory of the Athenian people.

Actually, the Athenians were the most highly cultivated and artistic people in the ancient world, and their art and philosophy are today regarded as standards in the greatest centers of learning.

NOTES

However, they did not know God and, hence, in speaking to them, the apostle had to come down to the lowest step on the ladder of truth. He set forth the unity of God; His Glory as Creator; man's relationship to Him; God's just Right as Creator to judge His Creatures; His manifestation of Himself in Christ; the resurrection of Christ; and the delegation of future judgment to Him as Son of Man. In effect, He preached Jesus as being God.

THE CROSS

As stated previously, it is my personal opinion that when the service at Mars' Hill ended, Paul left the place with very little satisfaction. While the message he preached was excellent, to say the least, and while he told these people things they desperately needed to hear, still, he did not preach the Cross. In fact, he preached the Resurrection, but not the Cross of Christ. Regarding some of the things he said a little later to the church at Corinth, I personally feel that he resolved from then on that wherever he went, he would preach the Cross (I Cor. 2:2).

While the message of God as Creator is that which everyone should know, and while the message of the Resurrection is of equal glory, as well, still, man is saved in only one way, and that is by and through what Jesus did for us at the Cross. Without the Message of the Cross, there is very little, if any, salvation. Man must be made to see that he is a sinner, and man must be made to understand that there is only one salvation from sin, and that is due to what Christ did at the Cross on our behalf and our faith in that Finished Work. That's the reason that the Holy Spirit through John said:

"For God so loved the world, that He gave His only Begotten Son, that whosoever believes in Him should not perish, but have everlasting life" (Jn. 3:16).

(25) "NEITHER IS WORSHIPPED WITH MEN'S HANDS, AS THOUGH HE NEEDED ANY THING, SEEING HE GIVES TO ALL LIFE, AND BREATH, AND ALL THINGS."

The status is:

1. The phrase, *"Neither is worshipped with men's hands, as though He needed*

anything," tells us several things:

a. Man does not worship God, and, in fact, is absolutely forbidden to worship God, by the making of statues, images, etc. purportedly of Him, or some such thing!

As well, He cannot be worshiped through buildings, in the sense of an architectural design of some churches, with their stained glass, etc. In other words, when people claim that such makes them feel God (the religious tone of some church buildings), they have, in effect, made an idol out of a building, which is very displeasing to the Lord.

b. The Lord must be worshiped *"in Spirit and in Truth"* (Jn. 4:24).

This means that we worship Him with our spirit, which must be done according to the Word of God, and is accordingly aided and helped by the Holy Spirit.

Such, consequently, has no need of outside benefits or attractions, such as buildings, ceremonies, rituals, etc. So, that means that most which goes under the guise of *"worship,"* in reality, is not worship at all, at least that which is recognized by God!

c. God does not need anything! That means He does not need a house, for how could such contain Him? In actuality, He needs absolutely nothing that man has! God is free of any dependence on anything and, as such, is eternally existent within Himself. We as creatures need Him and need Him desperately, while He as Creator needs nothing! In fact, He does not even need our worship.

While He does seek such, it is for our benefit and not His (Jn. 4:23).

The phrase, *"Seeing He gives to all life, and breath, and all things,"* presents His Creation needing what He provides, which is provided by no other source.

(26) "AND HAS MADE OF ONE BLOOD ALL NATIONS OF MEN FOR TO DWELL ON ALL THE FACE OF THE EARTH, AND HAS DETERMINED THE TIMES BEFORE APPOINTED, AND THE BOUNDS OF THEIR HABITATION;"

The order is:

1. What is the Law of the Spirit of Life in Christ Jesus?

2. It is the manner in which the Holy Spirit works.

NOTES

3. It is the Cross of Christ that gives the Holy Spirit all latitude (Rom. 8:2).

ONE BLOOD

The phrase, *"And has made of one blood all nations of men for to dwell on all the face of the Earth,"* proclaims all having their origin in Adam. Consequently, no one should have any room for pride of ancestry or pride of race. Even though there are five color groups in the world, red, yellow, brown, black, and white, still, they all spring from the same source.

Even though these five color groups exist, but yet, spring from one source, still, God looks at the entirety of the human family as divided into two groups. The first group dwells in the kingdom of darkness, with Satan as their head, while the second group dwells in the Kingdom of Light, with Jesus as their Head (Col. 1:13), which has no bearing on their race, gender, culture, etc. In other words, there are only two groups of people with God, and those are the ones who are saved and the ones who aren't saved.

THE BOUNDS OF THEIR HABITATION

The phrase, *"And has determined the times before appointed, and the bounds of their habitation,"* pertains to particular parts of the world and those who occupy these areas. In other words, as is obvious, certain races or types of people occupy certain parts of the world. Even though there is overlapping and mixing, the Far East has its type of people (Orientals), while Western Europe and America, along with other nations, are occupied basically by white Caucasians, but with much mixing, especially in America. Mexico, Central America, and South America fall into their own category, occupied mostly by those of brown skin, etc.

Irrespective of the mixing, as does occur in many countries, the various races of the world are pretty well ensconced in the *"bounds of their habitation."*

"Appointed" in the Greek text is *"protasso"* and means *"to pre-arrange." "Bounds"* in the Greek text is *"horothesia"* and means *"the placing of limits or a boundary line."*

NOTES

Some have attempted to prove segregation of the races from this passage; however, I do not think this is the intention of the Holy Spirit. The statement, *"Hath made of one blood all nations of men,"* eliminates any type of racial superiority, etc. As well, it is natural for those of like color and culture to group together. But yet, it is not displeasing to the Lord, I think, for one to live among others of another race, etc. Of course, the believer should desire to be exactly where God wants him and should be led by the Holy Spirit accordingly!

Inasmuch as we are directing attention toward certain aspects of the race question, perhaps the following would be of some help:

IS INTERRACIAL MARRIAGE A SIN?

No, it is not!

The following contains that which we believe the Bible teaches concerning this very important subject:

Before I proceed in more depth, please allow me to say this—especially to my critics. There is no interracial marriage in my family, of which I am aware, so I do not have a personal position to defend. As I have stated, I will attempt to approach this important question from the position of the Bible, exclusive of else.

ONE BLOOD, BUT FIVE RACES (ACTS 17:26)

By five races, I mean the five distinct color groups of the human family: brown, black, white, yellow, and red.

The different colors and types of men, it seems, came into existence after the Flood. Until the Flood, all men were white, for there was only one family line—Noah's, who was white and in the line of Christ, being mentioned in Luke 3:36, with his son Shem.

Through Noah's three sons, Japheth, Shem, and Ham, the entire Earth was populated and the various colors, it seems, were originated at that time. As to how the colors originated, no one knows, for the Bible is silent on the subject. However, this much we do know:

From the sons of Japheth came the white and yellow races, which populate Europe, modern Russia, the Persian Gulf area, Asia, and, ultimately, much of North America.

The sons of Shem were also white, with the possibility of some yellow. They constitute mostly the Jews and the Arabs, plus some of the tribes of Asia Minor.

The sons of Ham make up the black, brown, and red races. They settled mostly in Africa and India. Canaan, which was later populated by the Israelites, was also settled by the sons of Ham. However, the Canaanites were close relatives to the Egyptians.

WHERE DID THE NORTH AMERICAN INDIANS COME FROM?

"And unto Eber were born two sons: the name of the one was Peleg; because in his days the Earth was divided..." (I Chron. 1:19).

Peleg was the great-grandson of Noah, and it says, *"In his days the Earth was divided,"* which placed it probably about 200 to 300 years after the Flood.

In Peleg's time, it seems that a catastrophic event took place with gigantic earthquakes breaking apart the continents. This would explain the presence of North American Indians, as well as the Indians in Central and South America.

Today, there is mounting evidence that the continents of the world were at one time joined together. It is said that the continents could be fitted together like a jigsaw puzzle. The east coast of South America matches the west coast of Africa, with the rounded corner of Brazil fitting into the Gulf of Guinea. Facing coasts of the United States and Europe can also be fitted together, and so forth.

Some scientists even now are predicting that ultimately, a giant earthquake will split off part of California, pushing it out 50 to 100 miles into the Pacific Ocean, forming an island about the size of Cuba.

It seems that scientists are now beginning to accept as fact what the Bible recorded as truth about 4,000 years ago.

From these predictions, we see that the obscure statement found in I Chronicles is not so far-fetched after all.

Acts 17:26 says that God determined the bounds of the habitation of the races, and, despite minor scattering, those bounds of habitation remain the same today.

However, as stated, this does not mean that it is sinful or wrong for Africans to move to North America or North Americans to move to Asia, or vice versa. It just means that there are certain areas designated for certain people, and it seems it will remain that way.

RACISM

Due to sin, wickedness, and ungodliness, the terrible evil of racism grips almost all of mankind.

The basic reason for the beginning of World War II was racism. The Japanese felt they were a superior people.

Of course, the whole world is very well aware of Adolph Hitler's master-race policy. In carrying out his evil policy, he slaughtered 6,000,000 Jews, whom he considered to be subhuman, plus millions of other innocents.

As another example, the terrible problems of South Africa have primarily been because of racism. In some cases, certain whites considered members of the black race to have no souls and, consequently, to be the same as animals. Hence, much of the time, they were treated as animals.

Racism is a belief that race is the primary determinant of human traits and capacities, and that racial differences produce an inherent superiority of a particular race.

Such belief produces bias, prejudice, and discrimination. It is wicked in the eyes of God!

In Israel, the Jews of Jesus' Day hated Samaritans, who were only part Jewish. Yet, Jesus ministered to them just as readily when the occasion presented itself.

Much of the evil of the world is caused by racism, which spreads its tentacles into every facet of human life. It produces class consciousness and social superiority.

RACISM AND DENOMINATIONALISM

In religion, denominationalism is very much akin to racism, claiming that membership in its particular group produces a spiritual superiority. That is hated by God because it is *"a proud look"* and *"a lying tongue"* (Prov. 6:17).

Congress has endeavored to erase the

NOTES

problems of bias, prejudice, and discrimination by passing laws. Although such aims are commendable, the true nature of the heart is not affected by the passing and enforcing of laws.

Jesus Christ is the only Answer for bias, prejudice, or discrimination. The heart of man, which is wicked, evil, and deceitful, must be changed. It cannot be changed externally; it must be changed internally, and that can only be done by the power of the Lord Jesus Christ.

Actually, the true New Testament Christian way erases all national culture and institutes in its evil place the culture of the Bible. Jesus summed it up in two statements:

- *"You shall love the Lord your God with all your heart, and with all your soul, and with all your mind.*
- *"You shall love your neighbor as your self"* (Mat. 22:37-40).

A lawyer, who was, no doubt, a Pharisee, asked Jesus, *"Who is my neighbor?"* (Lk. 10:29).

Jesus gave him the parable of the *"good Samaritan"* (Lk. 10:30-37).

The moral of that story: anyone who is in need should be helped, irrespective of his race or nationality, and we should be glad to accept help from anyone, irrespective of his race or nationality.

MARRIAGE

As we have stated, there is nothing in the Bible that prohibits interracial marriage. Moses, who was one of the greatest men of God who ever lived, married an Ethiopian woman (Num. 12:1). This woman was a Midianite and not a member of the Negro race, as some think, but still not a Jewess.

While it was certainly true that Jews were forbidden to marry outside of their nationality, except in certain cases, even as we have just mentioned, that was for the purpose of keeping the lineage pure for the coming Messiah. The Davidic line through which Jesus was to come, which reached all the way back to Adam, was not to be blurred and, of course, spoke of the Incarnation.

Regrettably, most complaints against racial intermarriage are brought about because of bias or prejudice and have no spiritual basis. This, within itself, is wicked in the sight of God because when Jesus died, He died for the whole world (Jn. 3:16).

SOCIAL IMPLICATIONS

Nevertheless, interracial marriage will definitely bring social implications. It should not, but it does! Unfortunately, we have to live with the situation as it is, not with what it should be. Consequently, the children of such a union will probably suffer even more than the parents. Therefore, all of these things should be taken into consideration before such a union is established.

Marriage already has enough strain without adding more difficulties that an interracial union would add. Among the problems causing tremendous divorce rates now is the strain placed on marriages by various factors even before the ceremony. Too many people have the abominable idea that if their marriage does not work out, they will get a divorce and try it again. Such thoughts are the blueprints for disaster.

IS IT THE WILL OF GOD?

Now, that is the question!

A young man came to see me sometime ago who was contemplating an interracial marriage. My answer to him was in the following vein:

"Even though the color of one's skin definitely has social implications (whether we like it or not) *and can certainly have an impact on the children of such a marriage, that is really not the question."*

I went on to say to him:

"Is it the Will of God that I marry this young man or young lady?" That should be the question!

It does not really matter what the color of the skin is. Is the Lord pleased with such a union? If it is the will of God, it will work, that is, if both parties attempt to follow the Lord! If not, it will not work regardless of race, color, nationality, or religion! Too few really seek the will of God in such matters and as a consequence, very shortly, most couples find themselves in severe trouble.

In the eyes of God, marriage is a very permanent thing. Except under certain prescribed circumstances, it is *"until death do us part."* It was that way from the very beginning (Mk. 10:2-9).

NOTES

To sum up, there is no passage in the Bible of which I am aware that forbids interracial marriage. Therefore, that is not the real question.

The real question pertains to seeking the will of God, irrespective of race, creed, or religion.

Only then can the right direction concerning marriage be ascertained.

(27) "THAT THEY SHOULD SEEK THE LORD, IF HAPLY THEY MIGHT FEEL AFTER HIM, AND FIND HIM, THOUGH HE BE NOT FAR FROM EVERY ONE OF US."

The order is:

1. It is impossible to have Resurrection life without first understanding and accepting the *"Cross life."*

2. Paul said, *"If we have been planted together in the likeness of His Death, we shall also be in the likeness of His Resurrection"* (Rom. 6:5).

SEEKING THE LORD

The phrase, *"That they should seek the Lord,"* presents the chief end of all God's Dealings with men (I Pet. 2:24; II Pet. 3:9; Jn. 3:15-20; Rev. 22:17).

This passage, as Paul used the statement, has a different implication than normal.

"Seek" in the Greek text is *"zeteo"* and means *"a search for knowledge,"* and came to indicate philosophical investigation. The word was used in the Septuagint in phrases indicating a turning to God. The person seeking the Lord focused his attention on God, on worship, and on obedience.

However, the manner in which Paul used the word, at least in this instance, can only apply to philosophical investigation.

Fallen man in his depraved state cannot really initiate any advance toward God except in the philosophical sense, in which God cannot actually be found! The idea is this:

Paul was encouraging the Athenian philosophers to use common sense in their seeking after deity. In their vast philosophical quests, it should be sensibly understood that the hand which makes something is, of necessity, greater than that which is made. In other words, these little gods they were

NOTES

worshiping were made by them and, of necessity, were far less than their human creator and, as a result, of no use!

LOGIC

All the Athenians had to do was to follow the logic of Aristotle, one of their own philosophers.

Logic is a sequence of facts or events when seen as inevitable or predictable. In other words, if it rains, it is logical that something will be wet.

Anything and everything created must, of necessity, have a creator. As well, he, of necessity, must be greater than that which he creates! Logic demands that!

The same could be said presently respecting evolution. Some scientists (falsely called) attempt to explain evolution, but admit that they have no knowledge whatsoever of the first or original cause. In other words, some claim that Creation began hundreds of millions or even billions of years ago as the result of a *"fire mist."* Others claim that Creation began as the result of a *"cold cloud."* However, none pretend to know where the *"fire mist"* or *"cold cloud"* came from. Consequently, without a proper origin, evolution is not logical, as evolution cannot be logical! It is logical that Creation have a creator!

Why is it that men, even very intelligent men, will use good common sense, plus proper investigation, respecting many other things, but will not use such with God or His Word?

The Athenians, plus most of mankind, and for all time, *"Worshipped and served the creature more than the Creator, who is blessed for ever"* (Rom. 1:25).

FINDING THE LORD

The phrase, *"If haply they might feel after Him, and find Him,"* proclaims the fact that, though God was very near to every man and had not left Himself without abundant witness in His manifold Gifts, yet through the blindness of the heathen, they had to feel their way uncertainly toward God. In this fact lies the need of a revelation, as it follows in Verse 30.

The passage, as Paul used it, does not mean that the heathens can initiate within their own depraved hearts a desire for God and a reaching out after Him. Such can come about only as a result of revelation, which pertains to the Word of God being preached, even as Paul was here doing, and the moving and operation of the Holy Spirit upon that Word.

GROPING

But yet, in their *"groping,"* for that is what the word *"feel"* means, Paul continued to use the action of logic and common sense. At least, there would be rationale as to what they were doing, which would stop the senseless worship of *"corruptible man, and to birds, and fourfooted beasts, and creeping things"* (Rom. 1:23).

"Though He be not far from every one of us," speaks of the Creator being very close to His Creation.

God is not hard to find, not at all! The problem with man is that he does not know Who or What God actually is! How can one know Who God is when he worships rats, as many do in India, or snakes, or statues, as do many Catholics?

The only answer to this dilemma of one truly finding God is as Paul would write, *"God, Who commanded the light to shine out of darkness, has shined in our hearts, to give the light of the knowledge of the glory of God in the face of Jesus Christ"* (II Cor. 4:6).

In other words, Jesus is the only way through Whom one may find God!

(28) "FOR IN HIM WE LIVE, AND MOVE, AND HAVE OUR BEING; AS CERTAIN ALSO OF YOUR OWN POETS HAVE SAID, FOR WE ARE ALSO HIS OFFSPRING."

The order is:

1. The phrase, *"For in Him we live, and move, and have our being,"* proclaims God as the Source of all life (Heb. 1:3). Actually, this statement used by Paul is a quotation from one of the ancient poets, possibly Minos or Epimenedes of Crete. Paul used these quotations, not because they were inspired, for they were not, but because they were true. God is indeed the Source of our existence and is near us.

2. *"As certain also of your own poets have said, For we are also His Offspring,"*

NOTES

presents a direct quote from Aratus of Tarsus, Paul's own country.

3. As he had just defended himself from the accusation of introducing foreign gods by referring to an Athenian altar, so now, he quotes one of their own Greek poets for the same purpose.

(29) "FORASMUCH THEN AS WE ARE THE OFFSPRING OF GOD, WE OUGHT NOT TO THINK THAT THE GODHEAD IS LIKE UNTO GOLD, OR SILVER, OR STONE, GRAVEN BY ART AND MAN'S DEVICE."

The direction is:

1. God and man are hopelessly estranged by man's sin, and there is no way back from man's side.

2. However, God has provided the way. That Way is *"Jesus Christ and Him Crucified."*

THE OFFSPRING OF GOD

The phrase, *"Forasmuch then as we are the offspring of God,"* is offered by Paul in the sense of Creation. It does not mean the *"Fatherhood of God and the brotherhood of man,"* as many contend.

The fatherhood and brotherhood claims pertain to God being the Father of all men and all men being brothers, etc. However, that is grossly incorrect and, therefore, untrue!

Even though God is the Creator of all, due to the Fall in the Garden of Eden, the original intention of God concerning Adam and Eve, as well as all others, of bringing sons and daughters of God into the world has been wrecked. Since the Fall, man has only been able to bring offspring into the world in the likeness of Adam with all its inherent corruption, which is the cause of all the problems respecting humanity (Gen. 5:3). Not able to bring offspring into the world in the image of God, man now can reproduce only after his own corrupt image. This speaks of the fallen state, which, in essence, makes men children of Satan, unless they are born-again! Jesus said concerning the Pharisees, and all unbelievers for that matter, *"You are of your father the devil, and the lusts of your father you will do"* (Jn. 8:44).

Due to this fact, the new birth is an absolute necessity, so much so, in fact, that Jesus also said to Nicodemus, *"Except a man be born-again, he cannot see the Kingdom of God"* (Jn. 3:3).

THE GODHEAD

The phrase, *"We ought not to think that the Godhead is like unto gold, or silver, or stone, graven by art and man's device,"* contains the simple meaning that if man is the offspring of God by Creation, which he is, of necessity, this would mean that God is similar to His Offspring. As a result, He is not some type of precious metal or stone, and, as well, He is not a device of man.

The philosophers of Athens and much of the world, and for all time for that matter, have turned the situation upside down by making themselves the creators of God instead of the creation of God.

This stems from the Fall and man desiring to be God!

The word *"graven"* in the Greek text is *"charagma"* and means *"a sculptured work such as images or idols."*

The word *"device"* in the Greek text is *"enthumesis"* and means *"a thought or contrivance,"* in other words, something out of one's own mind but not from God.

The word *"Godhead"* in the Greek is *"Theios"* and means *"that which is uniquely God's and proceeds from Him."*

As a result, Satan's greatest effort is to get men, especially religious men, to change the Word, in essence, adding their own thoughts, ideas, etc. Actually, *this* is the great apostasy of the church! Men change that which is uniquely of God, either adding or subtracting, which can only steal, kill and destroy (Jn. 10:10).

(30) "AND THE TIMES OF THIS IGNORANCE GOD WINKED AT; BUT NOW COMMANDS ALL MEN EVERY WHERE TO REPENT."

The construction is:

1. In Christ's Death, He took our place, and His holy Soul shrank from this identification with sinners.

2. In other words, He took the penalty for sin, even though He never sinned. That penalty was death.

THE TIMES OF IGNORANCE

The phrase, *"And the times of this*

ignorance God winked at," does not reflect that such ignorance was salvation, for it was not!

It simply means that before the advent of Christ, due to the Fall, there was very little knowledge of God in the world. As a result of this ignorance, the Lord, with some exceptions, withheld judgment regarding particular acts of sin, even though the people were sinners and, in fact, died eternally lost.

As we have stated, ignorance is not salvation! Were ignorance salvation, then the best way to guarantee salvation for all would be to eliminate every vestige of the Gospel in the world. Of course, such thinking is absurd!

The only times before Christ that God stepped in with judgment was when the situation became so intolerable that if allowed to continue, it would have destroyed all of mankind. I speak of Sodom and Gomorrah! As well, I speak of God's Threat against the people of Nineveh, but who repented at the preaching of Jonah.

Even after the Promise given to Abraham concerning possession of the Promised Land, the Lord said that it could not be realized until the fourth generation. The reason was that *"the iniquity of the Amorites is not yet full"* (Gen. 15:16).

So, God expelled these people from the Promised Land only when their wickedness became intolerable!

REPENTANCE

The phrase, *"But now commands all men every where to repent,"* tells us something extremely important.

The judgment of God on this world and the manner and way in which it operates is totally opposite of what most believers think.

Most believers have the idea that God poured out judgment continually in Old Testament times, with such judgment being withheld since the advent of Christ due to this being the time of grace. As stated, the opposite is true!

With Jesus dying on Calvary, thereby, satisfying the sin debt of humanity, at least for those who believe, the Holy Spirit could then come into the world and literally inhabit the hearts and lives of believers, which He does. As a result, the proliferation of the Gospel has made steady inroads.

NOTES

Due to this proliferation of the Gospel, God demands far more of mankind after Christ than before Christ! So, there is far more judgment under grace than before grace! Jesus said, *"For unto whomsoever much is given, of him shall be much required"* (Lk. 12:48).

The world has been given much light since Christ, and much is required now of the world!

The word *"repent"* means to turn away from the worship of idols and all other types of rebellion against God.

The Old Testament indicates that idolatry came to full flower after the Flood, probably by the time of the Tower of Babel (Babylon). At least, it seems that the Tower of Babel became the model for the temple towers or ziggurats of Babylonia. This was about the first 1,700 years of man's existence.

THE LIGHT OF THE GOSPEL

The Flood came approximately 1,600 years after Adam, and is another sign of the situation being so intolerable that God was forced to take drastic measures, which He did! It was either that and start over with Noah and his family, or else, let the gross sin and iniquity continue, which would have shortly destroyed itself through corruption.

After the Flood, the Lord gave a promise unto Abraham concerning the coming Redeemer, which allowed more light into the world. About 400 years after Abraham, Moses was given the Law, which, as well, brought a far greater degree of light.

Of course, the greatest light of all was the advent of Christ, Who was the Fulfillment of all the Promises! Since this advent, God holds the entirety of the world much more accountable, as should be obvious!

Men may seek to eliminate such close scrutiny by rejecting Bible Christianity and accepting other religions, such as Buddhism, Islam, etc. However, that absolves man of no responsibility whatsoever! All are going to answer to Jesus Christ, whether they believe He is the Son of God or not!

Before Christ, the problem was *"ignorance!"* Since Christ, the problem is *"unbelief!"*

NOTES

(31) "BECAUSE HE HAS APPOINTED A DAY, IN THE WHICH HE WILL JUDGE THE WORLD IN RIGHTEOUSNESS BY THAT MAN WHOM HE HAS ORDAINED; WHEREOF HE HAS GIVEN ASSURANCE UNTO ALL MEN, IN THAT HE HAS RAISED HIM FROM THE DEAD."

The construction is:

1. To preach Jesus in any other capacity than the Crucified, Resurrected One is to preach another Jesus (II Cor. 11:4).

2. What did Paul mean by *"another Jesus?"*

3. He was speaking of Jesus minus the Cross (I Cor. 1:17-18).

THE GREAT WHITE THRONE JUDGMENT

The phrase, *"Because He has appointed a day,"* refers to the coming Great White Throne Judgment outlined in Revelation 20:11-15. This is the final judgment!

However, this does not mean that God is not constantly judging sin presently. Today, His Judgment takes place in the form of war, disease, the elements, etc. Actually, Paul also said, *"For the wrath of God is revealed from heaven against all ungodliness and unrighteousness of men, who hold the truth in unrighteousness"* (Rom. 1:18).

The Great White Throne Judgment will take place at the end of the Millennium (Mat. 12:36; Jn. 5:22; Rom. 2:16; Rev. 20:7-15).

As well, the word *"appointed"* in the Greek text is *"histemi"* and means *"is predestined."* However, several things are predestined, as spoken in this statement:

- A coming judgment is predestined.
- This judgment will take place on a certain day.
- The righteousness (self-righteousness) of the world will be judged relative to Jesus Christ.
- Jesus Christ will be the Judge!

JUDGE THE WORLD IN RIGHTEOUSNESS

The phrase, *"In the which He will judge the world in Righteousness,"* refers to God's Standard of Righteousness and not man's!

God's Righteousness, which the world does not have, pertains to the Righteousness of God that is freely given to the sinner upon faith in Christ. At that time, all self-righteousness, works righteousness, and relative righteousness will be severely judged! The standard as always will be the Righteousness of God. As well, all who will be at this judgment will be lacking in the Righteousness of God, which means all will be lost!

THE LORD JESUS CHRIST

The phrase, *"By that man Whom He has ordained,"* speaks of Jesus Christ.

He is now the Saviour and, in fact, always has been and, as well, the only Saviour! However, at the time of which we speak, He will then be the *"Judge."*

So, every single thing regarding salvation and man's preparation to meet God is wrapped up totally and completely in Jesus Christ. It is *"that Man"* to Whom one must answer!

As well, this speaks of the Incarnation, God literally becoming Man, in which He purchased back that which the first Adam lost.

He, as the last Adam, was born without sin as a result of not being born by natural procreation, thereby, freeing the believing sinner from original sin, but not yet from all its negative results. This will take place totally at the Resurrection.

In His 33 and one half years of Life and Ministry, He, as well, walked perfectly before God and the world, satisfying every claim of the Law of Moses. In other words, He was and is our Representative Man. Upon faith in Christ, the believer is free from the demands of the Law.

At Calvary, He died, freely giving up His own Life, thereby, becoming the perfect Sin-Offering, which satisfied the claims of heavenly justice. By faith, the sinner died in Him but did not have to suffer the penalty of the broken Law, with Jesus taking that penalty on our behalf.

THE RESURRECTION

As well, we were in Him when He was buried in the tomb, thereby, for the believing sinner, proclaiming that the old man is dead and buried and, therefore, exists no more!

When Jesus was resurrected from the dead, we were resurrected in Him into newness of life, thereby, a new Creation, i.e., *"born-again"* (Rom. 6:3-11; II Cor. 5:17-19).

The word *"ordained"* in the Greek text is *"horizo"* and means *"to decree, declare, and determine."* In other words, it was ordained or appointed in eternity past that God would become Man and carry out the plan of redemption (I Pet. 1:18-21).

The phrase, *"Whereof He has given assurance unto all men, in that He has raised Him from the dead,"* refers to the Resurrection ratifying that which was done at Calvary and is applicable to all men, at least all who will believe!

As well, the fact of God raising Jesus from the dead proves that Jesus is Divine and that His Teaching and Salvation are true. He will be the Judge and will judge in righteousness as He said and as the prophets declared (Isa. 9:7; 11:4).

WHAT THE BIBLE SAYS
ABOUT JUDGMENT

God appears in the Old Testament very commonly in the role of *"Judge of all the Earth"* (Gen. 18:25), or more generally, as a *"God of justice"* (Deut. 1:17; 32:4; Ps. 9:8; 94:2; 97:2; Isa. 30:18; 41:1; 61:8; Jer. 12:1; Ezek. 7:27; Mic. 6:1; Mal. 2:17).

Judgment does not simply imply an impartial and detached weighing up of good and evil, but rather the thought of vigorous action against evil. It is on this understanding that the people of God are summoned to exercise judgment in turn (Isa. 1:17; Mic. 6:8; Zech. 8:16).

THE JUDGMENT OF GOD

The Judgment of God is not impersonal, the operation of some undeviating principle; it is a strongly personal notion. It is closely linked to the thought of God's Character of mercy, loving kindness, righteousness, truth, etc. (Ps. 36:5, Ezek. 39:21, Hos. 2:19).

It is the working out of the mercy and wrath of God in history and in human life and experience. Thus, the judgment of God can bring deliverance for the righteous, as it often has and often does (Deut. 10:18; Ps. 25:9-10), as well as doom for the wicked (Ex. 6:6; Num. 33:4; Deut. 32:41; Isa. 4:4; Jer. 1:10; 4:12; Ezek. 5:10; 23:10; 28:22).

Judgment is a particularly rich idea in the Old Testament with a variety of other terms used with this meaning (Gen. 30:6; Ex. 23:2; I Sam. 2:25; Ps. 43:1; 106:30; Isa. 1:18; Jer. 14:10; 51:47; Mic. 6:2).

As the Old Testament draws toward its close, the thought of God's Judgment becomes increasingly bound up with the eschatological (future) expectation of the coming Day of the Lord (Joel 2:1; Amos 5:18; 8:9; Obad., Vs. 15; Zeph. 1:7, 14; Mal. 4:1).

THE NEW TESTAMENT AND
THE JUDGMENT OF GOD

The New Testament, as we should expect, continues the Old Testament stress upon judgment as belonging to the nature of God and as part of His essential Activity (Rom. 1:18; Heb. 12:23; I Pet. 1:17; 2:23; Rev. 16:5).

As in the Old Testament, God's Judgments are not confined totally to the future but are already at work in man's life in the present age (Jn. 8:50; Rom. 1:18, 22, 24, 26, 28; Rev. 18:8). Judgment is associated even now with Christ, Who exercises the Father's Judgments (Mat. 3:11; 10:34; Jn. 3:19; 5:30; 8:12, 16; 9:39).

The light of God's Word is already shining into the world through His Self-revelation in man's moral experience and supremely in the incarnate Word, Jesus Christ. The judgment of men is, therefore, already in operation, for they show by their evil deeds that they *"love darkness rather than light"* (Jn. 3:19).

GOOD WORKS

Particular difficulty has been found with respect to the account as given by Jesus of the judgment of the nations at His Second Coming (Mat. 25:31-46).

Most completely misinterpret these Passages in one of two ways:

First of all, in this passage, Jesus is not speaking of charitable efforts or benevolence. That's not His meaning at all.

He is speaking of the nation of Israel and how the nations of the world treated Israel, especially during the time of the Great Tribulation. These nations will be judged on that basis.

Secondly, some have attempted to derive from this account that there is such a thing as *"anonymous Christians."*

NOTES

NOTES

This expresses the notion that there are some people who are Christians but who are unknown. This includes atheists who have spurned God and His witness to them, agnostics who aspire to sit on the fence with respect to God's Witness to them, and men and women of other so-called faiths who have repudiated to a greater or lesser degree Christian claims for Christ.

Understand, because some of them feed the hungry, visit inmates in prisons, minister to the needy, and maybe even fight in wars of liberation from political oppression, some claim that they are unconsciously followers of Christ and will be acquitted at the end. They believe that because of ministering to the needy in this way, they have actually ministered to Christ, etc.

FALSE PROPHETS

Such interpretations, however, suffer from a crucial weakness. These false prophets require us to interpret this teaching of Jesus on the judgment of the nations in a manner which yields conclusions at plain variance with many other clear sections of the Bible in general and the teaching of Jesus in particular.

Conversely, if we are able to interpret this account in a manner which does not involve any basic contradictions, but which enables it to be integrated harmoniously into Jesus' other Teaching, then clearly that ought to be the course to follow on any sound explanation of Scripture.

It is never proper to take a Scripture out of context, therein, to prove a doctrine. All of the Scriptures on any given subject must be in harmony with each other and, in fact, will be in harmony with each other. In other words, people are not saved because they engage themselves in benevolence or good works, as helpful as those good works might be. A person is saved only by accepting Christ as his personal Saviour (Jn. 3:3, 16; Rom. 10:9-11).

All of this is not to deny the fact that many non-Christians perform deeds of love and mercy, or even that Christians are sometimes put to shame by the *"good works"* of these who are unbelievers. These works, however, need to be evaluated Biblically.

Actually, they are evidences of God's *"common Grace,"* so to speak, operating within fallen society, which restrains evil and promotes goodness. We ought to give thanks for this to God and identify our Christian compassion where possible with all such efforts for the well-being of our human neighbors.

Such action, however, as noble as it might be, even when carried to the limits of self-sacrifice, cannot claim to have any atoning or justifying effect. There is only one way of salvation, and that is the acceptance of Jesus Christ as one's Saviour and one's Lord. He is the One Who died on the Cross of Calvary in order that the terrible sin debt be paid, at least for all who will believe. He is the One Who gave Himself and did so unreservedly, satisfying the justice of a thrice-Holy God in order that we might be saved. So, there is no other name under heaven given among men whereby we might be saved. It is only the name of Jesus (Acts 4:12).

THE PSYCHOLOGIZING OF THE CHURCH

Man today rejects out of hand the idea that he must one day render account for his life and its decisions. His loss of conviction concerning an afterlife, combined with the erosion of the notion of moral responsibility on the basis of popular understanding of psychological and psycho-analytical theories, has contributed to the moral indifference and pragmatism of our times.

Psychology teaches that man is the victim rather than the cause concerning aberrant behavior, etc. As such, the idea of being judged for one's actions, especially considering that psychology teaches basically that man is not responsible for his actions, is totally opposite of modern thinking. Regrettably, the church has by and large been so psychologized that this great doctrine of a final judgment, plus other great doctrines, as well, are being soft-peddled, if mentioned at all!

The truth is that it is impossible to mesh the theories of psychology with the Word of God. When this is attempted, and it is being attempted today in most churches, one does not conclude with a watered-down psychology, but rather a watered-down Gospel! As the two are opposites, there is no way to make them agree. In other words, either one cancels out the other.

JUDGMENT IS INEVITABLE

In the teaching of psychology, moral issues, insofar as they matter at all, relate only to the present moment and to considerations of personal happiness. The thought that they might relate to some divine dimension, or that all men will one day be inescapably summoned to accept responsibility for these very moral decisions in the all-seeing Presence of their Creator, is anathema to psychological thinking.

Unfortunately, for modern man, it happens to be true. Judgment is inevitable and awaits us all. In face of this modern tendency to dismiss future judgment, there is the greater and more urgent responsibility placed upon the Christian church to tenaciously maintain these great Biblical perspectives.

To sum up, the truth is that man must allow his sins to be judged at Calvary, with the judgment in that case falling upon Christ instead of the perpetrator, or else, he will be judged at the Great White Throne Judgment. Therefore, man has a choice:

He can trust Christ today as Saviour, or he will face Him tomorrow as Judge (Rev. 20:11-15).

At the latter, there will be no reprieve!

(32) "AND WHEN THEY HEARD OF THE RESURRECTION OF THE DEAD, SOME MOCKED: AND OTHERS SAID, WE WILL HEAR YOU AGAIN OF THIS MATTER."

The diagram is:

1. The phrase, *"And when they heard of the Resurrection of the dead, some mocked,"* presents that which is twofold:

a. Their *"mocking"* was caused by sheer unbelief. In other words, these mockers simply did not believe what Paul was saying. The idea that Jesus was raised from the dead and, in fact, that all men will ultimately be raised from the dead, whether at the first Resurrection of Life or the second Resurrection of damnation, was preposterous to these people!

NOTES

The Epicureans, who lived for pleasure, placed no stock at all in any type of afterlife. It did not fit whatsoever with their thinking. Their lifestyle consisted of the pleasure of the moment with no concern for tomorrow! So, they surely would have fallen into this group of *"mockers!"*

b. The greater thinking of that day repudiated any idea of a resurrection from the dead. The idea was that life was hard enough as it was, so why would anyone want to come back to this?

Of course, their understanding was faulty. They were quite right in not necessarily wanting to do this all over again; however, the resurrection of which Paul preached was totally different than anything they had ever heard. Actually, the saint of God will be raised in glorified form, which speaks of a human body that cannot age or die, and neither can it grow sick, etc. In other words, the dimension is totally different than that which is presently known.

2. Even with all of Paul's explanation in I Corinthians, Chapter 15, John would later write, and rightly so, *"Beloved, now are we the Sons of God, and it does not yet appear what we shall be: but we know that, when He shall appear, we shall be like Him; for we shall see Him as He is."*

He then said, *"And every man that has this hope in him purifies himself, even as He is pure"* (I Jn. 3:2-3).

3. So, the Resurrection, as spoken of by Paul to the Athenians, was of such magnitude that it defied description. However, most of the Athenians would not listen and, therefore, lost the greatest opportunity they would ever have respecting the receiving of Eternal Life. They rejected Jesus and, therefore, they rejected life!

4. The phrase, *"And others said, We will hear you again of this matter,"* means that some that day were definitely touched by the Spirit of God regarding Paul's message but, sadly and regrettably, procrastinated, as do so many!

5. The truth is, they would never hear him again, thus, losing their great opportunity.

6. How so much this should be a lesson to us all! When God speaks, He must be

heeded forthwith!

7. The writer of Hebrews said, *"Today if you will hear His Voice, harden not your hearts"* (Heb. 3:15).

8. Paul also said, *"Behold, now is the accepted time; behold, now is the day of salvation"* (II Cor. 6:2).

(33) "SO PAUL DEPARTED FROM AMONG THEM."

The status is:

1. The statement has a double meaning:

a. They had ascertained that he had broken none of their laws, so he was free to go, which he did!

b. However, his leaving them had far greater spiritual portent, which was all-important. For the first time, they had heard the truth—a truth, we might quickly add, which cut through all of their philosophical janglings like a knife through hot butter. Never had something been put to them in such a manner or way! In a few words, Paul showed them the senselessness of their logic.

In fact, their so-called logic, of which they gloried, was shown to be no logic at all.

2. As we have stated, was it logical that these idols, which they had made with their own hands, were greater than their makers and something to be worshiped? The truth is, the lesser cannot make or create the greater, only the greater can create the lesser!

3. So, he departed, and they would never hear him again, at least of which there is a record.

4. Quite possibly, some who are mentioned in the next verse, who became believers that day, would have continued opportunity to witness to the others. If so, that would probably be their only hope to once again hear the Gospel.

5. What will the judgment, which Paul has just mentioned, be like for those who have had unlimited opportunities to hear the Gospel, but yet, refuse to heed, in comparison to those who have had little opportunity, such as these Athenians, as well as some who have no opportunity at all?

(34) "HOWBEIT CERTAIN MEN CLAVE UNTO HIM, AND BELIEVED: AMONG THE WHICH WAS DIONYSIUS THE AREOPAGITE, AND A WOMAN NAMED DAMARIS, AND OTHERS WITH THEM."

NOTES

The form is:

1. The phrase, *"Howbeit certain men clave unto him, and believed,"* presents the fact that these believed wholeheartedly, recognizing in Paul the true words of life.

2. The word *"clave"* in the Greek text is *"kollao"* and means *"to glue, to join self and to keep company."*

Even though it seems only a few did believe, still, it seems they believed all the way and without any reservations.

3. *"Among the which was Dionysius the Areopagite,"* portrays this man as a member of the great court of Athens, which evidently pertained to one of the judges or justices.

4. As well, it is said that in order to hold one of these positions, one had to have a high post in civil government.

5. Some claim that Paul did not establish a church in Athens. However, contrary to that thought is some evidence that he did. Even among the few converts listed in Verse 34, such were a sufficient nucleus for a church.

6. One of the church fathers, Eusebius, said, *"We are told by an ancient writer, Dionysius the Pastor of the Church of Corinth, that his namesake Dionysius the Areopagite, of whom Luke says in the Acts that he was the first who embraced the Faith after Paul's discourse in the Areopagus, became the first Pastor* (Bishop) *of the Church in Athens."*

It is further said that Dionysius suffered a cruel martyrdom.

The phrase, *"And a woman named Damaris, and others with them,"* gives us no clue as to who this woman was, with the exception that the Greek text seems to imply that she was a person of prominence.

"Love divine, all loves excelling,
"Joy of heaven, to Earth come down;
"Fix in us Your humble Dwelling;
"All Your faithful Mercies crown."

"Jesus, You are all Compassion,
"Pure, unbounded Love You are;
"Visit us with Your Salvation;
"Enter every trembling heart."

"Breathe, O breathe Your loving Spirit,

"Into every troubled breast!
"Let us all in You inherit,
"Let us find the promised rest;"

"Take away our love of sinning;
"Alpha and Omega be;
"End of faith, as its beginning,
"Set our hearts at liberty."

CHAPTER 18

(1) "AFTER THESE THINGS PAUL DEPARTED FROM ATHENS, AND CAME TO CORINTH."

The status is:

1. If the believer, although Spirit-filled, does not understand the Cross of Christ relative to our sanctification, such a believer cannot live a victorious life.

2. In other words, a believer can be baptized with the Holy Spirit with the evidence of speaking with other tongues, and even be used by the Holy Spirit in a great way, but still live a life of spiritual failure, that is, if he doesn't understand the Cross of Christ relative to sanctification.

CORINTH

The phrase, *"After these things Paul departed from Athens,"* seems to imply that he departed alone, with Silas and Timothy joining him later at Corinth.

How long Paul stayed at Athens, we are not told; however, joining together the things which were done, it seems he must have stayed there at least a month, or maybe longer!

The phrase, *"And came to Corinth,"* presents a distance of about 50 miles.

Corinth was now a Roman colony and, as well, the capital of the province of Achaia and the residence of the Roman proconsul. It was, as well, a great commercial city, the center of the trade of the Levant and, consequently, a great resort of the Jews. It also had a very large Greek population.

Ancient Corinth had been destroyed by Mummius, surnamed Achaicus, in 146 B.C., and it remained waste for many years.

Julius Caesar founded a Roman colony on the old site, consisting principally of freed men, among whom were great numbers of the Jewish people.

NOTES

IDOLATRY AND LICENTIOUSNESS

Corinth was also a center of idolatry and licentiousness. It is said that no city in Greece, or in the Roman Empire for that matter, was more corrupt. It was filled with Greek adventurers, Roman merchants, lustful Phoenicians, sharp-eyed Jews, ex-soldiers, near-philosophers, sailors, slaves, and agents of every kind of vice.

The town was dominated by the Acrocorinth, a steep, flat-topped rock surmounted by the Acropolis, which, in ancient times, contained a temple of Aphrodite, goddess of love, whose service gave rise to the city's proverbial immorality.

Actually, the vice and immorality at Corinth were of such magnitude and so much known far and wide that the term, *"to be corinthianized,"* became a byword concerning those who dipped deep into the swill of immorality.

The city was also famous for the Corinthian Order of Architecture, which continues even unto this day. According to the testimony of Chrysostomus, Corinth had become in the second century of our era the richest city in Greece and was well on its way at the time of Paul. Its monuments, public buildings, and art treasures are described in detail by historians.

It seems at first that Paul had no intention of making this city a base of operations, for it seems he wished to return to Thessalonica. However, his plans were changed by a revelation, which we will see in this chapter, with the Lord commanding him to speak boldly, remaining in the city some 18 months. Consequently, a great church was founded, which occasioned Paul later writing two Epistles regarding particular problems in the church, and almost certainly a third Epistle, and even maybe a fourth, of which we have no record of the latter two.

(2) "AND FOUND A CERTAIN JEW NAMED AQUILA, BORN IN PONTUS, LATELY COME FROM ITALY, WITH HIS WIFE PRISCILLA; BECAUSE THAT

CLAUDIUS HAD COMMANDED ALL JEWS TO DEPART FROM ROME: AND CAME UNTO THEM."

The order is:

1. Christ's Cross is the end of the Law as ceremonial.

2. Paul's position held that Christ's Coming put the whole system of Law out-of-date because it fulfilled it all.

AQUILA AND PRISCILLA

The phrase, *"And found a certain Jew named Aquila, born in Pontus, lately come from Italy, with his wife Priscilla,"* pertains to a husband and wife who became very close friends to Paul.

Aquila was a Jew from a family of the Roman province of Pontus, located in northern Asia Minor, east of Bithynia on the Black Sea.

It seems that when the Romans took Pontus, his family was captured and sold as slaves in Rome.

Priscilla was not Jewish and seems to have been a Roman lady of one of the upper classes of society. It is even thought that she may have been the daughter of Aquila's former master. Whatever the case, it seems likely that Aquila may have helped her to believe in the one true God, the God of Israel. When he was set free, they then married, or so it may have been!

The phrase, *"Because that Claudius had commanded all Jews to depart from Rome,"* probably occurred, it is believed, in about A.D. 49 or 50. That would have meant that Paul arrived in Corinth in A.D. 50.

Suetonius mentioned the expelling of the Jews from Rome by the Emperor Claudius but, unfortunately, did not say in what year of Claudius' reign it took place.

It seems that the cause of this expulsion was the disturbances among the Jews, which by and large consisted of unbelieving Jews attacking Christian Jews, similar to that which had happened in Jerusalem and elsewhere! However, the Romans did not discriminate between Jews and Christian Jews and so expelled all of them. Therefore, Aquila and Priscilla, victims of this expulsion, found themselves now at Corinth. However, as is obvious, the Holy Spirit was directing things in totality, even though at first, possibly not recognized as such!

NOTES

PAUL

There is every indication that both Aquila and Priscilla were already Christians on meeting Paul in Corinth. As we shall see, when Paul finally left, they accompanied him as far as Ephesus, where they received and assisted to a fuller faith the very influential Apollos. Actually, they were still at Ephesus, and a church was meeting in their house when the Book of I Corinthians was written.

However, it seems at some point, they may have gone back to Rome (Rom. 16:3). Perhaps they were taking advantage of relaxations toward Jews after the death of Claudius. Furthermore, this passage in Romans shows how widely this ever-hospitable couple were known and loved in the gentile churches.

The phrase, *"And came unto them,"* pertains at first, at least, to their tent-making craft, as explained in the next verse. However, it was definitely no chance meeting but was orchestrated totally and completely by the Holy Spirit.

In most places, Paul had no means of support, with the exception of plying his tent-making, which he was now compelled to do.

We learn elsewhere in Paul's writings that churches at times supported him, but that seems to have been at a later date. At this particular time, he seems not to have had any support at all from the church at Antioch, or even those he had recently planted.

(3) "AND BECAUSE HE WAS OF THE SAME CRAFT, HE ABODE WITH THEM, AND WROUGHT: FOR BY THEIR OCCUPATION THEY WERE TENTMAKERS."

The form is:

1. The phrase, *"And because he was of the same craft, he abode with them, and wrought,"* evidently means that Paul had inquired concerning those involved in this occupation, and upon coming to them, seems to have found that they were working out of their home.

2. Evidently, they invited him to take up residence with them, joining his hands with

theirs respecting their craft. This must have been a delightful time for Paul, especially having the company of those who were as congenial as these two and, above all, considering their consecration to the Lord!

3. Some commentators have ventured that this pair was not believers at this particular time but were quickly won to the Lord by Paul. While that is certainly possible, from the manner in which Luke treats this subject, it is my thought that they already were believers in Christ.

4. *"By their occupation they were tentmakers,"* presents that which was common with the Jewish people. Every Jewish boy was compelled to learn a trade. This was their culture and custom. For parents not to teach their sons a particular trade was considered disreputable.

5. The rabbis said, *"Whosoever does not teach his son a trade is as if he brought him up to be a robber."*

6. The word *"tentmaker,"* as it was used of Paul, was perhaps not exactly the best translation. Actually, most of Paul's labor in this capacity involved the repairing of tents. Quite possibly, the apostle had the knowledge and understanding of how to make tents, but, in reality, as he attempted to support himself in various places, he rather repaired tents instead of the wholesale manufacture of these items (Acts 20:34; I Cor. 4:12; II Cor. 9:8-9; II Thess. 3:8).

7. In the midst of all of this, it is very obvious that the apostle did not consider himself to be above menial labor.

(4) "AND HE REASONED IN THE SYNAGOGUE EVERY SABBATH, AND PERSUADED THE JEWS AND THE GREEKS."

The synopsis is:

1. The phrase, *"And he reasoned in the synagogue every Sabbath,"* portrays Paul following his usual custom. As well, Aquila and Priscilla, no doubt, accompanied him in all of these meetings.

2. *"And persuaded the Jews and the Greeks,"* once again points to gentiles, of which every synagogue seemed to have a complement.

3. The words, *"Every Sabbath,"* imply a number of weeks, evidently, with the people wanting to hear more of what Paul was teaching. Here, as in other places, this would be the beginning of the church in Corinth.

4. In the mid 1980s, Frances and I, along with others, had the opportunity to visit the ruins of Corinth. It is still possible to locate the approximate position of the Judgment seat of Gallio. As well, the beauty of the landscape is obvious, but yet, as stated, during the time of Paul, it was one of the most wicked cities in the world.

5. And yet, this is exactly where the Lord desired that Paul plant a church. They that sat in darkness were to see great light! As well, Satan would fight atrociously, seeking to hinder that which God would do.

(5) "AND WHEN SILAS AND TIMOTHEUS WERE COME FROM MACEDONIA, PAUL WAS PRESSED IN THE SPIRIT, AND TESTIFIED TO THE JEWS THAT JESUS WAS CHRIST."

The exegesis is:

1. In the Cross is the judgment of this world, and by it is the prince of this world cast out.

2. Satan holds men captive by ignorance of God, but the Cross reveals him by the lie that sin was a trifle and teaches us its gravity and power.

THE PRESSURE OF THE HOLY SPIRIT

The phrase, *"And when Silas and Timotheus were come from Macedonia,"* probably means that Silas had come from Berea, with Timothy coming from Thessalonica. Macedonia was a province that included both these places.

How long this was after Paul had arrived in Corinth is not said; however, it was probably a period of several weeks.

"Paul was pressed in the spirit, and testified to the Jews that Jesus was Christ," lends credence to the idea that the Holy Spirit was greatly pressuring Paul at this time concerning his ministry in this synagogue. He was to strongly bear down on the great truth that Jesus was indeed the Jewish Messiah, fulfilling all the prophecies and, as well, was the Redeemer of mankind.

How strongly Paul bore down on this fact at the beginning of his ministry in the

NOTES

NOTES

synagogue is not clear! The situation could have gone in two ways:

TWO WAYS

1. The possibility exists, as stated, that he gradually brought the Jews, as well as the Greeks, to a place of scriptural understanding respecting the many prophecies concerning the Messiah. At this stage, he would not have, as of yet, revealed to them that Jesus was the Fulfillment of these prophecies, as he now would do.

If that is the case, the Holy Spirit was strongly pressing upon him the absolute necessity of now revealing Jesus as the Christ, i.e., the Messiah.

2. Quite possibly, with the very first service in the synagogue, he began preaching Jesus to them as the Fulfillment of the prophecies. Desiring to hear more, he was allowed to continue.

However, at some point, opposition rose up with the demand that Jesus be eliminated from the preaching and teaching. If this is what happened, which is probably the case, the Holy Spirit was strongly urging him, even to the point of force, to bear down even harder that *"Jesus is the Christ!"*

The word *"pressed"* in the Greek text is *"sunecho"* and means *"to compel."*

This is that which the Holy Spirit demands of all preachers. The man who trims his sails to catch the popular breeze, consequently, preaching what the people want to hear, is a hireling and, therefore, not of God. And yet, virtually all fall into that category. Only a precious few are of the stripe of Paul.

SEEKER SENSITIVE?

It is not the business of the preacher to ascertain, or even attempt to do so, what the people want to hear, but rather what *"thus saith the Lord!"* The preacher is to hear from the Lord and then deliver to the people what the Lord has given.

Even though he strongly desires that they heed the message, still, that is not his responsibility. The only responsibility he has is to be faithful to deliver the Word. Sometimes the response will be extremely negative and sometimes positive; however, the message must not change irrespective of the response.

Regrettably, much modern ministry has degenerated in many circles to the place of a mere profession or avocation. Precious few are truly God-called, and then sadly, many who have been genuinely called of God have long since compromised their message. They bow to the dollar or public opinion!

The apostolic message of the Book of Acts was *"A proclamation of the Death, Resurrection and Exaltation of Jesus that led to an evaluation of His Person as both Lord and Christ, confronted man with the necessity of repentance, and promised the forgiveness of sins."*

DIVINE COMPULSION

I think the most prominent feature in New Testament preaching is the sense of divine compulsion. In Mark 1:38, it is reported that Jesus did not return to those who sought His healing Power but pressed on to other towns in order that He might preach there also—*"for that is why I came."*

Peter and John replied to the restrictions of the Sanhedrin with the declaration, *"We cannot but speak the things which we have seen and heard"* (Acts 4:20).

Paul said, *"Woe is me if I do not preach the Gospel"* (I Cor. 9:16).

This sense of compulsion is the seal of true preaching. Preaching is not the relaxed recital of morally neutral truths; it is God Himself breaking in and confronting man with a demand for decision. This sort of preaching, of necessity, meets with opposition. In II Corinthians 11:23-28, Paul lists his sufferings for the sake of the Gospel.

THE TRANSPARENCY OF MESSAGE AND MOTIVE

Another feature of apostolic preaching was its transparency of message and motive. Since preaching calls for faith, it is vitally important that its issues not be obscured with eloquent wisdom and lofty words (I Cor. 1:17; 2:1-4).

Paul refused to practice cunning or to tamper with God's Word but sought to commend himself to every man's conscience by the opened statement of truth (II Cor. 4:2).

NOTES

The radical upheaval within the heart and consciousness of man, which is the new birth, does not come about by the persuasive influence of rhetoric but by the straightforward presentation of the Gospel in all its simplicity and power.

In fact, there is no power in the world greater than that which accompanies Holy Spirit-anointed preaching. That is the reason that the great religions of the world cannot even remotely compete with Bible Christianity. And yet, sadly, the anointing and power of the Holy Spirit is absent from most preaching due to the fact that most do not even believe in the Holy Spirit, at least in this capacity! However, preaching compels only when the power is present—the power of the Holy Spirit!

THE ESSENTIAL NATURE OF PREACHING

In the Gospels, Jesus is characteristically portrayed as One Who came *"heralding the Kingdom of God."* In Luke 4:16-21, He interprets His Ministry as the fulfillment of Isaiah's prophecy of a coming Servant-Messiah through Whom the Kingdom of God would at last be realized.

This Kingdom is best understood as God's *"Kingly Rule"* or *"Sovereign Action."* Only secondarily does it refer to a realm or people within that realm. That God's eternal Sovereignty was now invading the realm of evil powers in winning the decisive victory was the basic content of Jesus' Preaching.

THE CHANGE FROM THE GOSPELS TO THE EPISTLES

When we move from the Gospels into the rest of the New Testament, we note a significant change in terminology. Instead of the *"Kingdom of God,"* we find *"Christ"* as the Content of the preached message. This is variously expressed as *"Christ Crucified"* (I Cor. 1:23), *"Christ ... raised"* (I Cor. 15:12), *"the Son of God, Jesus Christ"* (II Cor. 1:19), or *"Christ Jesus as Lord"* (II Cor. 4:5).

This change of emphasis is accounted for by the fact that Christ *is* the Kingdom. The Jews anticipated the universal establishment of the sovereign reign of God respecting His Kingdom. The death and resurrection of Jesus Christ was the decisive act of God whereby His eternal Sovereignty was realized in human history.

With the advance of redemptive history, the apostolic church could proclaim the Kingdom in the more clear-cut terms of decision concerning the King. In other words, to preach Christ is to preach the Kingdom because Christ is the Kingdom!

TRUE PREACHING AND REVELATION

True preaching is best understood in terms of its relation to the wider theme of revelation.

Revelation is essentially God's Self-disclosure apprehended by the response of faith. Since Calvary is God's supreme Self-revelation, the problem is, how can God reveal Himself in the present through an act of the past?

The answer is, through preaching—for preaching is the timeless link between God's redemptive Act and man's apprehension of it. It is the medium through which God portrays His historic self-disclosure in Christ and offers man the opportunity to respond in faith.

The message of the preacher is greater than the man because it is from God. As such, it must never be compromised in any fashion!

As well, the great theme in this is, and must be, the preaching of the Cross. Jesus Christ is the New Covenant, which means that He doesn't merely have the New Covenant but, in reality, is the New Covenant, the meaning of which was given to the Apostle Paul, which Paul gave to us in his 14 Epistles (Gal., Chpt. 1).

If the preacher is not preaching the Cross, he's really not preaching the Gospel. This means that the Cross of Christ must ever be the undergirding factor in all of our preaching. If that is the case, the people will understand the source of their salvation and their walk with God. The Cross of Christ is the solution, and the only solution.

SIN AND THE CROSS

The problem is sin! The problem has always been sin, and the problem now is

NOTES

sin. The only answer for sin, and we mean the only answer, is the Cross of Christ. Due to man's condition, the Cross of Christ is the only place in which God can meet with sinful man. To turn it around, the Cross of Christ is the only place that sinful man can meet with God.

We live in what is presently referred to as the *"Seeker Sensitive Age."* The Cross of Christ does not bow to that dictum, even as it cannot bow to that dictum.

Paul said that it did not really matter if the Cross of Christ was a stumbling block to the Jews and foolishness to the Greeks (gentiles), still, the Cross must be preached because it is the answer, and the only answer, for man's dilemma. Let us say it again:

If the preacher doesn't preach the Cross, whatever it is that he is preaching is not the Gospel. In fact, the Cross of Christ, as stated, is the meaning of the New Covenant and is the Gospel (I Cor. 1:17).

(6) "AND WHEN THEY OPPOSED THEMSELVES, AND BLASPHEMED, HE SHOOK HIS RAIMENT, AND SAID UNTO THEM, YOUR BLOOD BE UPON YOUR OWN HEADS; I AM CLEAN: FROM HENCEFORTH I WILL GO UNTO THE GENTILES."

The order is:

1. In some cases, man is made to believe that sin is unforgivable, but the Cross brings pardon for every transgression and cleansing for every stain.

2. By the Cross, the world is a redeemed world, at least those who will believe (Jn. 3:16).

BLASPHEMY

The phrase, *"And when they opposed themselves, and blasphemed,"* proclaims the response of the Jews to the claim of Christ as Messiah.

The word *"themselves"* has reference to the fact that the rulers of the synagogue, who normally prompted others to do such, now loudly took the lead themselves in their denunciation of Paul.

The word *"blasphemed"* refers to vilifying Paul! In other words, pandemonium broke loose in the synagogue that day, almost to the point of a riot! To be sure, Paul's type of preaching would also not have set well in many modern circles. The response he tendered here was violent, to say the least. Of course, a watered-down, compromised message will arouse no such anger but, as well, sees no one saved!

Some claim that the true Gospel is positive only! Therefore, they say that they preach only a positive message. However, for something to be truly positive, it must at the same time be negative.

In fact, Paul's message that *"Jesus was Christ"* is about as positive as anything could ever be. However, it had an extremely negative effect on the Jews, as is obvious!

Conversely, at times, a negative Gospel, as the Gospel also is, will have a positive effect.

For example: on the Day of Pentecost, Peter said to the great throng of Jews in the Temple, *"Therefore let all the house of Israel know assuredly, that God hath made that same Jesus, Whom you have crucified, both Lord and Christ"* (Acts 2:36).

FAITHFUL TO THE WORD

To place the responsibility of the crucifixion of Christ squarely on the Jews, as Peter did, is about as negative as anything could ever be. However, it elicited an extremely positive response.

The Scripture says, *"Now when they heard this, they were pricked in their heart, and said unto Peter and to the rest of the apostles, Men and brethren, what shall we do?"* (Acts 2:37).

Again, we emphasize the fact that the preacher is to be faithful to the Word, preaching that which God has given him to preach. While he must not be negative for the sake of such, and certainly not harsh or cruel, still, at the same time, he must deliver, without fail, the Word of God exactly as it is given to him by the Holy Spirit.

In fact, the Holy Spirit will anoint only that which He has given and never that which is conjured in the minds of men.

The phrase, *"He shook his raiment, and said unto them, Your blood be upon your own heads; I am clean,"* proclaims him having done exactly what God told him to do. In other words, what he said and the way it was said was led, guided, and directed by the Holy Spirit.

Paul's action here portrayed that of Ezekiel.

The warning is clear from both Ezekiel and Paul that if God gives the man the message, and he refuses to deliver it, *"His* (their) *blood will I require at your hand"* (Ezek. 3:18).

This means that an awful lot of preachers are going to have the blood of untold numbers of souls on their hands when they stand before God.

I AM CLEAN

Even if the message is not delivered even though commanded, the people will still die in their sins. However, the compromising preachers will answer to God!

Conversely, if the message is properly delivered, as here with Paul, even though rejected, the responsibility now passes from the preacher to the intended recipient. Their blood is now upon their own heads, and they will not be able to say that they were not warned! When Paul said, *"I am clean,"* he was simply meaning that he had delivered the Word of God exactly as required. He was free from responsibility (Ezek. 3:17-21; 33:1-6).

How many preachers today can say the same thing concerning the Word of God and its uncompromised delivery, *"I am clean"*?

Only God knows the answer to that, but I am persuaded that the number is infinitesimally small regarding preachers who are faithful, at least in comparison to the total number of preachers!

The phrase, *"From henceforth I will go unto the gentiles,"* does not mean that he would no longer minister to Jews if given the opportunity, which he did do at Ephesus (Acts 19:8), but that the thrust would be toward the gentiles. Consequently, the churches more and more would be gentile and less and less Jewish! Paul addressed this very succinctly in Romans, Chapters 9 through 11.

The reader should understand the following:

If light is given and then rejected, not only does the person, church, or people forfeit what they could have had, but, as well, they lose what they already have! This law, and I think it is a law, is obvious throughout the entirety of the Word of God. It is boldly evidenced in the parables given by Jesus of the *"pounds"* (Lk. 19:13-25) and *"talents"* (Mat. 25:15-28). This is obvious in much of the church world respecting the last day outpouring of the Holy Spirit.

NOTES

The Lord wondrously used many preachers of the past who had not been baptized with the Holy Spirit with the evidence of speaking with other tongues. However, once the Holy Spirit began to be outpoured at about the turn of the 20th century, fulfilling the prophecy of Joel concerning the Latter Rain (Joel 2:23), more and more light on this all-important work of God began to be manifested. As that light began to shine brighter and brighter, literally with hundreds of thousands being baptized with the Holy Spirit, then all were held accountable.

REJECTING LIGHT

In other words, many preachers in particular denominations were brought to the place that they either had to accept the Holy Spirit according to the Word of God or reject Him! To be sure, many did accept and were gloriously filled with the Holy Spirit. However, regrettably, most in these denominations did not accept and then forcibly rejected this all-important experience.

When one rejects light, even as the Jews of old, most of the time, they then begin to violently oppose that which is of God, with every determination of stamping it out and using every method at their disposal. To be sure, it does not stop the move of God, despite their efforts, but it does spiritually destroy them.

As far as any move of God is presently concerned, one will have to look long and hard at these particular denominations to find anything at all! Not only have they forfeited what God desired to do, but, as well, they lost what little they actually did have! The same can be said for many Pentecostal denominations. Little by little, many of them have turned away from the Word of God and the moving and operation of the Holy Spirit as He glorifies Christ, rather turning to the wisdom of this world, i.e., humanistic psychology, etc. As well, they are forfeiting what God could do and, also, losing what little they do have, if anything!

Faith must ever follow God, and if it is true faith, it will follow the Lord! To not do so is sin, thereby, throwing one in reverse (Rom. 14:23).

So, as should be obvious, Israel no longer has any semblance of God whatsoever and has been that way for many centuries.

(7) "AND HE DEPARTED THENCE, AND ENTERED INTO A CERTAIN MAN'S HOUSE, NAMED JUSTUS, ONE WHO WORSHIPPED GOD, WHOSE HOUSE JOINED HARD TO THE SYNAGOGUE."

The exegesis is:

1. The phrase, *"And he departed thence, and entered into a certain man's house, named Justus,"* refers to a meeting place for church and not him moving from the home of Aquila and Priscilla regarding his immediate domicile, as some have suggested.

2. Some have also suggested that his full name was Gaius Titius Justus, which meant that he was a Roman citizen and, as well, the Gaius mentioned by Paul in Romans 16:23 and I Corinthians 1:14.

3. The phrase, *"One who worshipped God, whose house joined hard to the synagogue,"* evidently points to Justus in the recent past as having accepted Christ under Paul's ministry.

4. Even though he could have been Jewish, the evidence seems to indicate that he was a gentile who had been attending the synagogue, as did many gentiles in those days! At any rate, he freely offered his home to Paul in order to conduct services.

5. At this stage, it seems that he fully understood the animosity among the Jews which this would create; nevertheless, he was willing to take a bold stand, which is not characteristic of too very many at the present time. This man had found Christ; consequently, he would do whatever it took to further the cause of Christ, even at the risk of harm to himself. What a beautiful statement concerning Justus and sanctioned by the Holy Spirit, *"one who worshipped God!"*

(8) "AND CRISPUS, THE CHIEF RULER OF THE SYNAGOGUE, BELIEVED ON THE LORD WITH ALL HIS HOUSE; AND MANY OF THE CORINTHIANS HEARING BELIEVED, AND WERE BAPTIZED."

NOTES

The status is:

1. The phrase, *"And Crispus, the chief ruler of the synagogue, believed on the Lord with all his house,"* presents a startling statement!

2. This must have been galling to the Jews to have their chief ruler of the synagogue converted to Christ!

3. In effect, the chief ruler of the synagogue was exactly what his title implied. He presided over the services and gave the final judgment in connection with disputes. He also performed marriage ceremonies and even issued divorces.

4. *"And many of the Corinthians hearing believed, and were baptized,"* speaks of many gentiles now being saved.

5. The word *"hearing"* proclaims Paul's preaching of the Gospel, which generated faith in the hearts of these gentiles. Hence, the Bible says, *"So then faith comes by hearing, and hearing by the Word of God"* (Rom. 10:17). Actually, that is the method of all being saved!

The Word of God must be preached, and must be preached under the anointing of the Holy Spirit (Acts 1:4, 8; Lk. 4:18).

6. They were then baptized in water! Both I Corinthians 1:14 and 16 portray that Paul personally baptized in water both Crispus and Gaius (Justus), as well as the *"household of Stephanas."* It seems these were the only ones he personally attended!

The very manner in which the Holy Spirit caused Luke to use the name *"Corinthians"* speaks glowingly of the grace of God. As we have stated, the very name *"Corinthian"* spoke of vice, immorality, licentiousness, and wickedness, and was known as such all over the Roman world.

However, the great and glorious Gospel of Jesus Christ so miraculously changed many of these *"Corinthians"* that the name now took on a completely new meaning. How wonderful and beautiful is the grace of God! How so much so this epitomizes that which God alone can do! He turns the darkness into light, sin into salvation, unrighteousness into righteousness, impurity into purity, in effect, hell into heaven, so much so, in fact, that the former is no longer recognized or present! That is the reason the message of Jesus Christ is the *"greatest story ever told!"*

(9) "THEN SPOKE THE LORD TO PAUL IN THE NIGHT BY A VISION, BE NOT AFRAID, BUT SPEAK, AND HOLD NOT YOUR PEACE."

The exegesis is:

1. The Cross was the manner in which our Lord spoiled all of the kingdom of darkness.

2. The phrase, *"He made a show of them openly,"* means that what Jesus did at the Cross was in the face of the whole universe (Col. 2:15).

THE VISION

The phrase, *"Then spoke the Lord to Paul in the night by a vision,"* does not clarify as to whether Paul saw the Lord or only heard Him speak. It being a *"vision"* implies that he was awake.

"Be not afraid, but speak, and hold not your peace," gives us some indication as to what was happening at this time in Paul's heart and life.

The command of Jesus to *"be not afraid"* spoke to the situation at hand. There was fear in Paul's heart regarding the tremendous opposition against him. He was either afraid that he would have to leave the city as he had been forced to do so in other places, or else, even fearful for his life. Probably both were the case.

Some would take Paul to task, claiming that he was lacking in faith; however, such was not correct!

Great faith does not always mean a total lack of fear. It does mean that one continues to believe God and obey Him despite the fear! In fact, many modern preachers have literally made a god out of faith. In other words, they have created their own rules and regulations, ignoring that which is the Bible. They claim that if one has enough faith, one will never be sick, one will never lack for money, and all persecution and opposition will cease as well.

FAITH

While faith certainly does play a part in all that happens to us, still, while the Lord definitely does heal, at times the believer is not healed, and it is not because of a lack of faith. God does bless and prosper financially; however, sometimes believers are not blessed accordingly, and it is not because of a lack of faith. The same could be said for persecution, opposition, etc.

In Hebrews, Chapter 11, the writer lists a number of men and women who by faith were able to see great miracles performed and mighty things done. However, at the same time, he also spoke of those who were not delivered from prison, persecution, or even destitution (Heb. 11:35-38). As well, these people did not suffer these things because of a lack of faith, but rather because they did have faith, and great faith at that!

The writer of Hebrews said, *"And these all* (speaking of those who saw the miracles and those who did not), *having obtained a good report through faith* (God gave a good report to both groups, marking all of them down as having great faith)*"* (Heb. 11:39).

Whenever great delivering or blessing faith is placed as the barometer for all things, which it is in many circles, control is then wrested out of the hands of God. Of course, God will never allow such! Great faith, or any faith for that matter, is always subject to the will of God (Rom. 12:1-2).

Some have even gone so far as to say that if Paul had the amount of faith that they possess (modern preachers), he would not have had to suffer hardships, imprisonment, etc.

To find the right vocabulary to address such stupidity, referring to such thinking being what it actually is, I am afraid is beyond the pale of my ability. Only gross ignorance would make such a stupid remark, and stupid it is!

No! Paul did not suffer these things because of a lack of faith, but rather because of great faith!

Consequently, the Lord told him to keep preaching in Corinth and not be silent, in other words, not even begin to be silent (Horton).

(10) "FOR I AM WITH YOU, AND NO MAN SHALL SET ON YOU TO HURT YOU: FOR I HAVE MUCH PEOPLE IN THIS CITY."

The structure is:

1. The phrase, *"For I am with you, and*

no man shall set on you to hurt you," speaks to the idea that Paul had threats on his life, threats, we might quickly add, which were not empty, but rather deadly serious.

2. This is not the idea that Paul held his life as dearer than the presentation of the Gospel, but rather the very opposite. His striving was for the will of God, not for his own protection, etc.

3. Due to his call of taking the Gospel to the world of that day, he did not want to waste his life by being cut short. Consequently, he was, no doubt, at this time, earnestly seeking God as to what he should do about the situation, whether stay or go! If he had the mind of the Lord, he then knew that whatever happened would be the will of God, and that is what he desired, and that only!

In view of that, the Lord gave him direction and assurance!

4. *"For I have much people in this city,"* concerns the great church which would be raised up at Corinth.

This is the reason that one must follow the Lord in all things. He alone knows the end from the beginning and can function accordingly. If we have His Will in any matter and follow that Will, we then know the situation will come out as it should.

However, in no way does this mean that all difficulties and problems will instantly cease or that opposition will cease. In fact, it may even increase! Nevertheless, if we are in the center of God's Will, irrespective of the opposition or its severity, victory will ultimately be ours.

(11) "AND HE CONTINUED THERE A YEAR AND SIX MONTHS, TEACHING THE WORD OF GOD AMONG THEM.

The form is:

1. The phrase, *"And he continued there a year and six months,"* records the longest time that Paul spent any place other than Ephesus, where he spent some three years.

2. During this time, he wrote the Books of I and II Thessalonians. This was probably about A.D. 51 or 52.

3. The phrase, *"Teaching the Word of God among them,"* presents that which is so very, very important! Paul was not only a preacher but a teacher as well. Preaching proclaims truth, while teaching explains truth.

NOTES

4. So, the people at Corinth were so very blessed to sit under the teaching of Paul for this period of time. They would have learned much about the Word of God. And yet, as Paul's two letters to this church make evident, problems still arose. Judaizers came in after Paul left, attempting to subvert the Gospel of grace, and other problems came about as well. However, they were ultimately all settled for the glory of God.

5. Considering the tremendous opposition that Satan brought against this church, it is quite possible that had not Paul spent this 18 months grounding the people in the Word of God, the church, in fact, would have been lost!

(12) "AND WHEN GALLIO WAS THE DEPUTY OF ACHAIA, THE JEWS MADE INSURRECTION WITH ONE ACCORD AGAINST PAUL, AND BROUGHT HIM TO THE JUDGMENT SEAT,"

The exegesis is:

1. The phrase, *"And when Gallio was the deputy of Achaia,"* gives us no clue in the Text as to when this was; however, an inscription at Delphi makes it virtually certain that he was proconsul in A.D. 52-53.

2. His full name was Lucius Junius Gallio Annaeanus, and he was appointed by the Roman Senate to govern the province of Achaia, which was all of Greece, south of Thessaly.

3. He was the brother of the famous Stoic philosopher, Seneca, who was Nero's tutor.

4. It is said that he was a very wise ruler, known for his great personal charm and easygoing manner.

5. As per the inscription, he did not serve very long in this position and was executed by Nero's order in A.D. 65.

6. *"The Jews made insurrection with one accord against Paul,"* gives us little clue as to exactly when this was, but yet, if the inscription previously mentioned is correct, it, as stated, would have been in A.D. 52 or 53.

7. *"Insurrection"* in the Greek text speaks of a well thought-out plan, which, as usual, attempted to incorporate the civil government. However, these Jews seemed not to have been quite as smart as some of the others in that they did not accuse Paul of insurrection against Caesar, but rather against

the Law of Moses. That was a mistake in Paul's favor, as we shall see!

8. They were evidently jealous of Paul and the many people he was winning to Christ; consequently, unable to compete with his Gospel, they resorted to the age-old tactic, *"If you cannot defend against the message, attack the messenger!"*

9. *"And brought him to the judgment seat,"* speaks of a platform on which the judge sat between the accused and the accuser on two other platforms in the court.

The Jews had no power to sentence a person to death and carry out the execution. That authority rested solely with the Romans. To be sure, if the Jews had had that authority, they definitely would have killed Paul. Such is religion!

(13) "SAYING, THIS FELLOW PERSUADETH MEN TO WORSHIP GOD CONTRARY TO THE LAW."

The synopsis is:

1. Man thinks he is only slightly maladjusted and can be quickly rehabilitated.

2. The truth is, due to the Fall, man is totally incapable of bettering, much less, redeeming himself. It can only be done by the Lord.

PAUL AND THE JEWS

The phrase, *"Saying, This fellow persuades men,"* tells us several things:

- They held Paul in great contempt. The word *"fellow"* was inserted by the translators, with the accusers merely using the word *"this,"* speaking of Paul, and it was said in a very derogatory manner.

Then, as now, to fail to use someone's name but to refer to them by an epithet, as here, was, as stated, highly insulting, which it was intended to be!

- But yet, their charge against Paul respecting his ability to *"persuade men"* contradicts their insult. If he was not worthy to even be called by name, why were they bringing him before the proconsul?

The truth was, they could not compete with him respecting his knowledge of the Law of Moses, and especially his ability to proclaim Jesus as the Fulfillment of all the prophecies. In other words, they were helpless before his argument!

NOTES

- As well, they accused him of *"persuading men,"* meaning that his Gospel was not a mere philosophy. He was after converts to Christ and used every argument to bring men to the foot of the Cross.

In reality, this is the great battleground and always has been! The souls of men are at stake! Sadly, Satan's greatest snare is not from the world, but rather from that which calls itself *"the church!"*

CONTRARY TO THE LAW

The phrase, *"To worship God contrary to the Law,"* does not pertain to Roman law as some claim, but rather the Law of Moses. We know this from what Gallio said in Verse 15.

Their accusation was baseless. As we have already stated, Paul was probably the greatest scholar of his day in Levitical Law. As well, he never considered Christianity as a new religion, or any religion at all for that matter! He proclaimed it as the continuation and fulfillment of God's Plan and Promises revealed in the Old Testament. In other words, the New was a fulfillment of the Old, with both, in essence, *"one."*

In Ephesians 3:9-11, he speaks of a mystery hidden in God in Old Testament times, *"To the intent that now unto the principalities and powers in heavenly places might be known by the church the manifold wisdom of God.*

"According to the eternal purpose which He purposed in Christ Jesus our Lord."

That is, what God is doing through the church is not something different from what He revealed in the Old Testament, but actually its fulfillment, with all as a part of His eternal Purpose.

Everything in the Old Testament pointed to Jesus. The very first promise given by God concerning a Redeemer was made almost immediately after the Fall, thereby, setting the stage for what was to come (Gen. 3:15).

JESUS AND THE LAW

As well, the sacrifices which the Lord taught Adam, as evidenced by Abel (Gen. 4:1-5) and continued by the patriarchs, all spoke of Jesus. The lamb, an innocent victim, represented Christ Who would give His

NOTES

Life as a Sin-Offering for lost humanity. In fact, Abraham was an altar builder. It all pointed to Calvary, and all pointed to Jesus.

About 2,000 years after the Fall, God gave to Moses the Law, which was a portrayal of Jesus in every capacity. Every sacred vessel in the Tabernacle pictured Jesus. All the sacrifices pictured Jesus. All the Feast Days pictured Jesus, as did the keeping of the Sabbath, circumcision, etc.

The entirety of the plan of God was the bringing into the world the Redeemer of mankind, at least for those who would believe, with everything He did regarding the promises, the prophecies, and the covenants, all, and without exception, pointing to Christ.

So, Jesus was a Fulfillment of all this, even as Paul constantly preached, and, actually, without Him, the whole of the Old Testament was meaningless.

What Paul was doing was in no way contrary to the Law but, in fact, totally obedient in every respect to the Law of Moses. In truth, it was the Jews who were worshiping wrongly by their denial of Christ. By denying Him, they were virtually denying the Law of Moses!

(14) "AND WHEN PAUL WAS NOW ABOUT TO OPEN HIS MOUTH, GALLIO SAID UNTO THE JEWS, IF IT WERE A MATTER OF WRONG OR WICKED LEWDNESS, O YOU JEWS, REASON WOULD THAT I SHOULD BEAR WITH YOU."

The construction is:

1. The phrase, *"And when Paul was now about to open his mouth,"* refers to him waiting for his accusers to cease their tirade against him, and he would now defend himself.

2. *"Gallio said unto the Jews,"* proclaims the proconsul interrupting Paul.

3. Quite possibly, the Jews thought that the new governor would be easily persuaded to their cause, but they reckoned wrongly!

4. Horton said, *"Gallio was born in Cordova, Spain, and grew up in the midst of Philosophers, Poets, and Orators in Rome. He was a man of intelligence and wit, highly educated, and made it his business to know what was going on in the Province he had been sent to govern."*

5. *"If it were a matter of wrong or wicked lewdness, O you Jews, reason would that I should bear with you,"* proclaims the governor putting everything in its proper perspective immediately! He instantly saw through the Jews, knowing that they did not have a case, and that they were trying to use him to do what they were not able to do for themselves.

6. First of all, he detected that Paul was no threat to Caesar or Roman law of any nature.

7. Secondly, he saw that the accusations contained no moral charge, such as stealing, fraud, etc. Were there charges pertaining to those matters, he would hear them out and let the case run its course; however, he would not go on with this charade any longer!

(15) "BUT IF IT BE A QUESTION OF WORDS AND NAMES, AND OF YOUR LAW, YOU LOOK TO IT; FOR I WILL BE NO JUDGE OF SUCH MATTERS."

The synopsis is:

1. The phrase, *"But if it be a question of words and names, and of your Law, you look to it,"* in effect, told them to settle this thing themselves because it had no place in a Roman court. How right he was!

2. As we have stated, the Jews were trying to get him to do what they could not do themselves, which was to get rid of Paul! I want to say, and to which I have alluded, had they taken another tact, accusing Paul of treason against Caesar, which was the usual accusation, they may have had more success; however, I really think not! This governor was not of the usual stripe, it seems, not at all political. Irrespective of the charges, I think he would have dismissed them out of hand, quickly seeing through the real intentions.

3. The phrase, *"For I will be no judge of such matters,"* in essence, says, *"You will not use a Roman court to carry forth your personal schemes!"*

4. It is not often that one sees a Roman proconsul such as Gallio! How refreshing in a sea of perfidy, calumny, politics, and subterfuge!

(16) "AND HE DROVE THEM FROM THE JUDGMENT SEAT."

The exegesis is:

1. When one goes beyond the Cross, one

loses one's way.

2. Is it Who He was, or what He did?

3. It was both!

THE ACTION OF GALLIO

Several things are here said:

- This implies the ignominious dismissal of the case without its being even tried or further heard!
- The word *"drove"* implies, as well, that the Jews did not immediately obey the dismissal, probably continuing to argue, with the governor giving instructions to the lictors to drive them away. The lictors were soldiers with whips.
- Horton said, *"Sir William Ramsay, noted British Historian and Archaeologist gave much credence to this decision by the Roman Governor Gallio, calling it 'The Charter of Christian Freedom.' He claims it set a precedent that would keep the Jews from ever trying to use the Roman Government or Roman Power against the Christians again."*

I think it is obvious that this decision definitely helped Paul in many ways; however, I do not think it was quite the help that Sir Ramsay claims! For instance, Acts 25:1-9 portrays the Jews up to their old tricks again.

Whatever the help, I wonder if Gallio sensed at all the significance of what was taking place before him that day. Did he think it just another nuisance, or did he somehow catch the significance of the moment?

It is ironic, in the entirety of the world at that time, this was the single most important thing that was happening, but almost no one would have understood that. To prove the point, even though Gallio had powerful friends in Rome, with even his brother, the noted philosopher Seneca, being private tutor to Nero, still, history records almost nothing of his life, with this Biblical account supplying more information by far than any other source. This tells us that only what is done for Christ will last.

THE GREATNESS OF THE WORK OF GOD

In fact, even though mighty Rome ruled the world of that day, it is mentioned by the Holy Spirit only as it impacts the work of God, which was then paramount under Paul. To the believer, the reasons are obvious:

All technological advancement, as well as social, economic, political, and religious freedoms, can be laid at the doorstep of the moving and operation of the Holy Spirit in the lives of believers. No! It does not mean that Spirit-filled believers are necessarily scientists, etc., but it does mean that the *"light,"* which makes all of this possible, is derived exclusively from the advent of the Holy Spirit.

So, what Jesus did at Calvary and the Resurrection performed the great task of satisfying the claims of heavenly justice in respect to paying the awesome sin debt, which broke the grip of sin and Satan. As well, it made possible the advent of the Holy Spirit in an entirely new dimension respecting believers but, also, to the enlightenment of the world (Isa. 11:2; Jn. 14:17; Acts 2:4).

(This pertains primarily to Joel's prophecy, Joel 2:23, concerning the Former and Latter Rain, with the latter commencing at approximately the turn of the 20th century and, as well, the fulfillment of Daniel's prophecy concerning the increase of knowledge in the last days) (Dan. 12:4).

(17) "THEN ALL THE GREEKS TOOK SOSTHENES, THE CHIEF RULER OF THE SYNAGOGUE, AND BEAT HIM BEFORE THE JUDGMENT SEAT. AND GALLIO CARED FOR NONE OF THOSE THINGS."

The way is:

1. At the Cross, Jesus atoned for all sin past, present, and future, at least for all who will believe (Jn. 3:16).

2. Sin provides the legal means that Satan has to hold man captive; however, with all sin atoned, which Jesus did at the Cross, this removed the legal right that Satan had to hold anyone in bondage.

THE CHIEF RULER OF THE SYNAGOGUE

The phrase, *"Then all the Greeks took Sosthenes, the chief ruler of the synagogue,"* presents the man who took the place of Crispus, who had given his heart to the Lord under the ministry of Paul.

NOTES

Beautifully enough, even though no account is given here, it seems that Sosthenes soon accepted the Lord, as well, and is, no doubt, the same brother mentioned by Paul in I Corinthians 1:1. This must have been especially galling to the unbelieving Jews in Corinth, considering that two of their rulers of the synagogue had given their hearts to Christ, if, in fact, this Sosthenes is the same one mentioned in I Corinthians 1:1.

The phrase, *"And beat him before the judgment seat,"* gives us little clue as to why this was done, unless they had refused to disassemble.

THE JEWS AND CIVIL AUTHORITIES

It does seem that the Jews in Corinth got along poorly with the civil authorities. For instance, due to what he said in Verses 14 and 15, it seems that Gallio, although governor only a short time when this scene with Paul and the Jews occurred, had already had some negative experience with the Jews, or else, had been warned about them.

For the most part, it seems that they had great difficulty in getting along with the powers that be, irrespective of where they were. In most places, there was tension between them and the authorities, with the recent expulsion of all Jews from Rome being but an example! So, what the Jews had hoped to happen respecting Paul, instead happened to them. They were greatly humiliated, with great grievance taken out on Sosthenes.

As well, the Lord had promised Paul, *"For I am with you, and no man shall set on you to hurt you"* (Vss. 9-10). As should be obvious, the Lord was speaking only of Corinth, at least concerning *"hurt."*

The phrase, *"And Gallio cared for none of those things,"* means that he considered the whole matter outside his jurisdiction. As stated, he seems to have been a man who could not be politically persuaded, but rather sought the truth of the matter and, thereby, acted thereon!

(18) "AND PAUL AFTER THIS TARRIED THERE YET A GOOD WHILE, AND THEN TOOK HIS LEAVE OF THE BRETHREN, AND SAILED THENCE INTO SYRIA, AND WITH HIM PRISCILLA AND AQUILA: HAVING SHORN HIS HEAD IN CENCHREA: FOR HE HAD A VOW."

The account is:

1. Jesus Christ is the New Covenant.
2. The meaning of the Cross is the meaning of the New Covenant, which meaning was given to the Apostle Paul (Gal. 1:12).

PAUL LEAVING CORINTH

The phrase, *"And Paul after this tarried there yet a good while,"* could have referred to several months.

Some contend that this particular period of time, ever how long it was, was in addition to the 18 months of Verse 11. However, I do not think there is any credence for that, with the situation with Gallio taking place sometime during the 18 months and not after! This much is sure: after the decision by the Roman proconsul, Paul would have had little opposition at all from the Jewish quarter in Corinth.

"And then took his leave of the brethren," was done strictly according to the Timing of the Lord.

Paul ever sought the will of God in all that he did, which should be obvious! That referred not only to where he would go but, as well, what and how he would do after arriving, and then staying and leaving according to the Lord's Timetable. This is where most Christians fall down.

GOD'S WILL

Most do not seek God's Face respecting His Will for their lives, and I speak of totality. Many believers take the position somewhat like the Stoics of old, which is a fatalist's view, in other words, *"What will be, will be!"* Nothing could be further from the truth!

The believer must seek the Lord constantly respecting leading, guidance and direction. As well, a person merely saying that is what they want is not enough. I suppose that most, if not all, would fall into that category.

Knowing that it is Satan's business to confuse the issue and that he works tirelessly to this end, every believer must have a strong prayer life and a strong habitual study of the Word of God. Regrettably, of those who fall into that category, the number is small

NOTES

indeed! So, the truth is that most believers only partially realize the will of God in their lives, which causes them to forfeit untold blessings.

Then again, many believers have been taught in the last few years the erroneous message of what passes for *"faith teaching,"* which pretty much centers up on *"things."* In other words, the relationship with the Lord is mostly believing Him for money, etc. This is such a travesty!

One's personal relationship with Christ, and I speak of one really knowing Who Jesus is, is far beyond *"things"* He gives us. We short-change ourselves terribly so if the Lord is reduced to the level of a glorified bellhop!

PRISCILLA AND AQUILA

The phrase, *"And sailed thence into Syria, and with him Priscilla and Aquila,"* presents Luke placing Priscilla first, even as he usually did concerning this couple, which probably means that she was the stronger of the two relative to the work of God. However, in no way is this meant to take away from Aquila because there is not the slightest indication in the Text that he was weak or of little consecration, but rather the very opposite. One need only notice Paul's statement about this couple in Romans 16:3-4 in order to understand their worth to the Kingdom of God.

The idea of the woman taking the lead in spiritual matters, as is obvious here, in fact, is the case many times. To be sure, the husband should take the lead in spiritual matters and, in fact, is ordained by God to do so; however, if for whatever reason that is not the case, no violence is done to Scripture whatsoever for the wife to stand in that place, as is here evidenced by Priscilla and Aquila. However, having said that, every woman who finds herself in the place of Priscilla should take extra care that her husband as the head should be recognized as such in every way possible (I Cor. 11:3).

THE VOW

Syria mentioned here was not Paul's first stop, that being Ephesus, at least after leaving Greece. He would ultimately go to Jerusalem, with Israel then looked at as a part of Syria. In other words, this was his ultimate destination respecting this trip.

The phrase, *"Having shorn his head in Cenchrea: for he had a vow,"* actually speaks of the port of Corinth. There was a church at Cenchrea, as well, probably founded by Paul during his stay at Corinth, or else, by others after he had departed (Rom. 16:1).

There is some controversy over what type of *"vow"* of which Luke spoke! Some say it was the vow of a temporary Nazarite as described in Numbers, Chapter 6. Others say it was not!

Trying to put together the little information which we do have, it seems that the vow was concluded in Jerusalem (Acts 18:21).

To come up with an educated guess, I suppose I would say that it was some type of partial temporary Nazarite vow; however, inasmuch as this was a part of the old Levitical Law, it is hard for me to see Paul doing such, especially considering his claims, and rightly so, that Jesus had fulfilled all of the old Law, with it no longer binding upon believers.

Consequently, we have to come to the conclusion that if the Holy Spirit had wanted us to know more, He would have told us.

(19) "AND HE CAME TO EPHESUS, AND LEFT THEM THERE: BUT HE HIMSELF ENTERED INTO THE SYNAGOGUE, AND REASONED WITH THE JEWS."

The account is:

1. The New Covenant cannot fail because it is all in Christ.

2. Christ is both God and Man, so He fills both roles.

EPHESUS

The phrase, *"And he came to Ephesus,"* pertains to his first stop after sailing across the Aegean Sea, a distance of about 300 miles. Approximately two years before, the Holy Spirit had forbidden Paul to minister in this very important city, no doubt, because they were not yet ready. However, the situation had now changed, with a great church to be built.

Ephesus was the most important city in the Roman province of Asia. It was situated on the west coast of what is now Asiatic Turkey. It was situated at the mouth of the

NOTES

Cayster River between the mountain range of Coressus and the sea.

There was a magnificent road lined with columns that ran down through the city to the excellent harbor, which served both as a great export center and, also, as a natural landing point from Rome. The city, now uninhabited, has been undergoing excavation for many years and is probably the most extensive and impressive ruined site of Asia Minor. Actually, the city died because of the silting up of the harbor, which took several centuries but, ultimately, made it unusable.

During the time of Paul, the city was large, perhaps as much as approximately 300,000 in population.

THE CHURCH AT EPHESUS

Under Roman rule, it became a center of the emperor cult and eventually possessed three official temples, thus, qualifying thrice over for the proud title of *"Temple-Warden."*

It is remarkable that Paul had friends, as we shall see, among the officers of the imperial cult.

The temple of Artemis itself had been rebuilt after the great fire of 356 B.C., and ranked as one of the seven wonders of the world until its destruction by the Goths in A.D. 263. This temple had been the largest building in the Greek world. It contained an image of the goddess Artemis which, it was claimed, had fallen from heaven. Indeed, it may well have been a meteorite originally. Silver coins from many places show the validity of the claim that the goddess of Ephesus was revered all over the world (Acts 19:27).

There was a large colony of Jews at Ephesus, and they had long enjoyed a privileged position under Roman rule. This visit by Paul is the earliest reference of Christianity as it pertained to the city.

Even though a church was begun at this particular time, one could say, it still would not flower until Paul's third missionary journey. He would then make it the base for evangelization of the whole province of Asia. It was then that Colossae and the other cities of the Lycus Valley were evangelized. It also served as Paul's headquarters for most of the time of the Corinthian controversy respecting Judaism, etc. (I Cor. 16:8).

The city was later the headquarters of John the Beloved, with it being listed first of the seven leading churches of Asia addressed in the Apocalypse.

According to Irenaeus and Eusebius, Ephesus was also the home of John the Beloved. A generation after his time, Ignatius wrote of the continuing fame and faithfulness of the Ephesian church.

The phrase, *"And left them there,"* has to do with Priscilla and Aquila and their remaining in Ephesus when Paul left some days later.

REASONING WITH THE JEWS

The phrase, *"But he himself entered into the synagogue, and reasoned with the Jews,"* has no reference to the previous phrase, simply speaking of Paul's usual custom of ministering to the Jews first of all, at least if there was a synagogue. No doubt, Priscilla and Aquila were with him during this meeting, with the foundation of the church now being laid.

Paul's *"reasoning"* with the Jews basically referred to the information given in the Old Testament concerning the Messiah and what He would do! He would then present Jesus as the Fulfillment of all of these prophecies.

As should be obvious, Paul little concerned himself with other topics, as important as they may have seemed at the time. His message strictly was Jesus and Him crucified and raised from the dead (I Cor. 2:2; 15:1-23).

(20) "WHEN THEY DESIRED HIM TO TARRY LONGER TIME WITH THEM, HE CONSENTED NOT."

The account is:

1. These Jews at Ephesus seemed now to be entirely different than most, actually, similar to the ones in Berea; however, the future would prove them as hateful as any!

2. They were so interested in what he was saying, at least now, that they wanted him to tarry longer with them, which he, at that time, seemingly could not do! As stated, Priscilla and Aquila remained with them, with at least some teaching and instruction continuing.

(21) "BUT BADE THEM FAREWELL, SAYING, I MUST BY ALL MEANS KEEP THIS FEAST THAT COMES IN JERUSALEM: BUT I WILL RETURN AGAIN UNTO YOU, IF GOD WILL. AND HE SAILED FROM EPHESUS."

The synopsis is:

1. The only way to God is through Jesus Christ (Jn. 14:6).
2. The only way to Jesus Christ is by the Cross (Lk. 14:27).
3. The only way to the Cross is a denial of self (Lk. 9:23).

THE FEAST

The phrase, *"But bade them farewell,"* speaks of Priscilla and Aquila, as well as possibly some few Jews who had accepted Christ as their Saviour.

The phrase, *"Saying, I must by all means keep this feast that comes in Jerusalem,"* is said by some to refer to the Feast of Passover, with others claiming it was Pentecost. It is thought that if it was not specifically identified, as here, it was speaking of the Passover, for this was the most important Jewish feast.

Once again, we are not given any information concerning Paul's insistence that he *"keep this feast!"*

There were seven feasts given in the Mosaic Law, with, as stated, the Passover being the most important! All of these feasts typified Jesus in His atoning, intercessory, and mediatorial Work. However, with this being done, which it was in Christ, there was no more purpose for these feasts, even as there was no more purpose for the sacrifices, etc.

Actually, the entirety of the functions of the Temple had now become a moot point! So, once again, we are faced with the question as to why Paul would continue to be this involved. He would later write in the Epistle of the Galatians, *"Stand fast therefore in the liberty wherewith Christ has made us free, and be not entangled again with the yoke of bondage"* (Law of Moses) (Gal. 5:1). Comparing the keeping of the feasts, plus other similar things, with such like statements just given, seems to present a contradiction. However, the following may throw some light on this very important subject.

NOTES

THE WISDOM OF PAUL

It is believed that Paul by now had written only two of his Epistles, I and II Thessalonians. In these two Epistles, he little mentioned the problem of the Judaizers as he did strongly in I and II Corinthians, as well as other Epistles. The reason was simple: they were only now beginning their efforts in this respect concerning gentile churches.

As well, Paul was still trying to do all within his power, which he would continue, it seems, even unto the very end, not to allow this problem to cause a split in the church or to hinder the process of evangelism.

The major problem was the church in Jerusalem. It was, as is obvious, the first church, actually having begun on the Day of Pentecost. There were many thousands associated with this church, all Jews with the exception of some few proselytes. Also, the Twelve Apostles attended this church, that is, when they were in Jerusalem.

Even though the first council recorded in Acts, Chapter 15, and held at Jerusalem, had been a grand success relative to this very subject, the indication seems to be that the Jerusalem church was still promoting the Law of Moses (Acts 21:21-24).

DETRACTORS

That Paul had many detractors becomes overly obvious once all of Acts and the Epistles are joined together. These detractors were Jews who had accepted Christ but insisted on the Law being continued. In other words, they tacked Jesus Christ onto the Law, which was exactly the problem in Acts, Chapter 15. So, even though the question was settled concerning gentiles, it seems to have been settled precious little regarding the Jews. How they thought there could be one type of salvation for gentiles and another for Jews is anyone's guess! It would seem that even a superficial knowledge of the Word of God would have exposed such error!

PAUL THE APOSTLE

If the message cannot be refuted, one of the age-old methods of defense is to then

NOTES

attack the messenger. This was basically their method of operation with Paul.

Some claimed he was not an apostle, hence, him constantly referring to himself as such was for the obvious reasons. Were he not an apostle, which means in its most simple form, *"One who is sent,"* then Paul's entire contention falls down. He was the one given the all-important Gospel of grace, and for that to be done, it would necessitate him being an apostle.

THE LAW

For some 1,600 years, the Law of Moses had more or less guided Israel and, in fact, was by far the greatest legislation the world had ever known. The simple reason is that it was totally God-instituted! This gave Israel something that was had by no other people on the face of the Earth. As a result, it actually made them superior, but they allowed superiority to destroy them through pride.

Even though the Law of Moses was given by God and, therefore, perfect in every respect concerning what it was intended to do, it in no way contained salvation and, in fact, was meant to be temporal, only until Jesus would come, Who was the Fulfillment of the Law in every respect. In fact, everything in the Law pointed to the coming Redeemer, Who would bring salvation. Nevertheless, the Jews somehow lost sight of this glorious One Who was to come, at least as the Scripture actually portrayed Him (Isa., Chpt. 53), but rather fixated on the Law. This took the whole thing out of focus, causing them to become acutely self-righteous, which ultimately destroyed them.

At any rate, they were loath to give up that which had been theirs for 1,600 years, and especially to lay it aside as something not needed anymore, having served its purpose! So, they conveniently tacked Jesus, so to speak, onto the Law. This meant that as well as accepting Christ as one's Saviour, one also had to keep the Law, which, in effect, nullified grace, making it a religion of works. This they could not seem to see. As a result of this, the evidence seems to be that Paul, due to his insistence on faith alone, was not very much appreciated. By that, I do not speak of the Twelve Apostles, but rather others in Jerusalem.

PAUL'S GREAT EFFORTS

In all of this, as evidenced here, Paul, it seems, did everything he could to portray to Jerusalem that he was not opposing the Law, but rather attempting to show that it had gloriously served its purpose. In doing this, he would bend as far as possible, attempting to prove this point.

Paul never looked at Christianity as different and apart from Judaism, but rather, as stated, the fulfillment of Judaism, which it was! Everything in the Old Testament pointed to one Person, the Lord Jesus Christ, and one purpose, the redemption of mankind. So, the Lord Jesus Christ and the New Testament fulfilled all of that which the Old Testament promised (Gen. 3:15; 12:3; 49:10; Ex., Chpt. 12; Lev., Chpts. 1-5; II Sam. 7:11-18; Isa. 7:14; Chpt. 53; Zech. 13:6).

Actually, the very manner in which the New Testament begins portrays beautifully this truth of Christianity being a fulfillment of Biblical Judaism, *"The Book of the Generation of Jesus Christ, the Son of David, the Son of Abraham"* (Mat. 1:1).

The phrase, *"But I will return again unto you, if God will,"* portrays the manner in which all believers should conduct everything. We do whatever we do if it is according to the will of God!

Of course, we could ask the question, *"Did not Paul know at this stage if it was the will of God for him to return to Ephesus?"*

I am sure that he felt he knew, but his action here portrays to believers that it seems at this stage the Lord had not been specific. As a result, Paul could not be specific.

If the Lord has been specific to us regarding direction, it is perfectly proper for us to be specific, as well; however, if not, it would pay us to say as Paul said, *"If God will!"*

The phrase, *"And he sailed from Ephesus,"* places him on his way to Jerusalem, with his first stop at Caesarea, a distance of approximately 500 miles.

(22) "AND WHEN HE HAD LANDED AT CAESAREA, AND GONE UP, AND SALUTED THE CHURCH, HE WENT DOWN TO ANTIOCH."

The synopsis is:

1. The phrase, *"And when he had landed at Caesarea,"* puts him about 65 miles northwest of Jerusalem.

Caesarea was the military capital of the Roman province of Judaea, of which Felix was procurator at this time. From here, roads spread out to Egypt on the south, to Tyre, Sidon, and Antioch on the north, and eastward to Nablus, Jerusalem, and the Jordan.

Who was with Paul at this time, if anyone, we are not told!

2. The phrase, *"And gone up, and saluted the church,"* without a doubt, refers to the mother church at Jerusalem.

No doubt, he was received officially by the apostles, at least those who were there, represented by James and the elders and the church. He would have given a formal account of the result of his second missionary journey, and of the great event of the introduction of the Gospel into Macedonia and Achaia (Greece).

3. As well, this is the time and place his vow was to be fulfilled, but of which we are given no information. Quite possibly, the reason for this lack, as we have attempted to portray, is because these things held very little spiritual significance, if any!

ANTIOCH

The phrase, *"He went down to Antioch,"* refers to Antioch, Syria, from where he had launched both missionary journeys, and which now concluded the second. It had lasted approximately three years and, without a doubt beyond words to express, it had been significant beyond comprehension.

The Gospel, as a result of this second missionary journey, had been taken first of all to Europe, from where it ultimately spread over the centuries to the entirety of the western world. Hence, as stated, this was actually the birth of what is presently referred to as *"western civilization."*

The journey from Jerusalem to Antioch, Syria, was north and approximately 400 miles. Consequently, when Luke referred to this trip and used the word *"down,"* he must have been referring to topography instead of direction. (Jerusalem is about 2,500 feet above sea level.)

NOTES

(23) "AND AFTER HE HAD SPENT SOME TIME THERE, HE DEPARTED, AND WENT OVER ALL THE COUNTRY OF GALATIA AND PHRYGIA IN ORDER, STRENGTHENING ALL THE DISCIPLES."

The exegesis is:

1. The phrase, *"And after he had spent some time there, he departed,"* portrays the beginning of his third missionary journey. Once again, who was with him, we are not told!

2. It is believed that this was the fall of A.D. 53.

The following is a list of the places in the Book of Acts he visited on this trip:

- He went by land again through Syria, Cilicia, Galatia, and Phrygia (Acts 15:41-16:6; 18:23).
- Ephesus, Ionia, Asia Minor (Acts 19:1-41).
- Macedonia (tour of churches, Acts 20:1).
- Greece (tour of churches, Acts 20:2).
- Macedonia (tour of churches, Acts 20:3).
- Philippi, to Troas, Mysia, across the Aegean to Asia Minor (Acts 20:4-12).
- Assos, Mysia (Acts 20:13).
- Mitylene, Isle of Lesbos (Acts 20:14).
- Trogyllium (Acts 20:15).
- Miletus, Caria, Asia Minor (Acts 20:15-38).
- Isle of Coos (Acts 21:1).
- Isle of Rhodes (Acts 21:1).
- Patara, Syria (Acts 21:1).
- Tyre, Phoenicia (Acts 21:2-6).
- Ptolemais, Galilee (Acts 21:7).
- Caesarea, Samaria (Acts 21:8-14).
- Back to Jerusalem (Acts 21:15–23:30).

The phrase, *"And went over all the country of Galatia and Phrygia in order, strengthening all the disciples,"* seems to indicate that this journey probably lasted about six months. Incidentally, it is believed that Timothy, Erastus, Gaius, and Aristarchus may have been Paul's traveling companions at this time. Some have thought that Titus may have been included as well! (Acts 19:22, 29; II Cor. 1:1). However, there is no proof of this, but it is almost certain that Paul was not traveling alone.

As far as we know, this would be Paul's

NOTES

last visit to Antioch. He, no doubt, loved this church and its people very dearly, considering that it had been the launching point of all of his missionary trips.

If one is to notice, Paul constantly felt the need of reinforcing the churches that had been planted and *"strengthening the disciples."* This portrays to us the constant necessity of teaching the Word of God. It is impossible for the saint of God to have too much teaching of this all-important instruction but so easy to have too little!

As well, it should be overly obvious that the people in these particular churches were undoubtedly thrilled at Paul's visits, especially considering that they were so few and far between.

This journey would have taken, as stated, approximately six months, and would have covered about 1,500 miles. Considering the manner of travel in those days, especially in landlocked areas, which was walking, at least for Paul and his companions, the hardships of such a journey should be obvious. Consequently, for Paul to be able to visit these churches at all was no easy task.

(24) "AND A CERTAIN JEW NAMED APOLLOS, BORN AT ALEXANDRIA, AN ELOQUENT MAN, AND MIGHTY IN THE SCRIPTURES, CAME TO EPHESUS."

The status is:

1. Even though Jesus was *"very Man,"* at the same time, He was also *"very God."*

2. As someone has well said, *"While Jesus laid aside the expression of His Deity, He never for a moment lost possession of His Deity."*

APOLLOS

The phrase, *"And a certain Jew named Apollos,"* introduces a man whom Paul came to hold in high esteem. Other than this passage, he is mentioned in Acts 19:1; I Corinthians 1:12; 3:4-6, 22; 4:6; 16:12; Titus 3:13, all in a positive sense. From these incidents in the Book of Acts, even as of Apollos, we learn certain things:

Even though the Twelve Apostles, plus others, were doing great things for the Lord at this particular time elsewhere in the Roman Empire, still, the major thrust of the Holy Spirit, as should be obvious, was with Paul. Some of the reasons are:

Paul, as no other man, held up the true Gospel of Jesus Christ, which meant that it was distinct and apart from the Law and, as well, was attempting to take this great message to the furthermost frontiers. Consequently, anyone who became a part of this in any way was honored greatly by the Lord, even as Apollos.

This is certainly not to say that other things which were happening at the time, even to which we have alluded, were not important. In fact, they were! However, beginning with Chapter 13 of Acts, the emphasis is with Paul.

PAUL

I think we should learn from this that those who helped Paul in this greatest of all endeavors would be greatly honored and blessed by the Lord. That should be obvious! As well, it should be obvious that those who attempted to hinder Paul would not be looked at favorably at all by the Lord!

The moral is that the believer must make an effort to find out exactly what the Lord is doing around the world. To be sure, that will not be difficult if one will only seek the Lord and inspect the fruit.

When that direction is ascertained, the believer in the will of God should support it financially, prayerfully, and personally wherever possible!

The tragedy is, even as with Paul, the detractors abound, while those who help are in short supply.

Regrettably, many, if not most, believers follow or support certain things simply because it is the policy of their particular religious denominations. Others follow or support someone simply because of circumstances, whatever they may be.

All of these reasons are wrong simply because all such direction is man-instituted and, therefore, man-directed! Only the Spirit of God can properly lead a person regarding the particulars of which I speak.

Paul was a controversial person. He minced no words in exclaiming the Gospel of Jesus Christ, which infuriated the Jewish Sanhedrin, etc. At the same time, it seems the mother church in Jerusalem was not nearly so bold respecting Jesus Christ and His Power to save. It is not my intention to take away from the Twelve Apostles or even of James, the pastor of the church in Jerusalem, because these men were some of the godliest who have ever lived. However, I think it is obvious in Scripture that the mother church in Jerusalem little knew what to do with Paul. It is my personal thought that if it had not been for the Apostle Paul, the proper message of Jesus Christ would have been ultimately so weakened and diluted that it would have soon been of no consequence!

ALEXANDRIA

As a result, it is not easy or simple, at least for most believers, to support a man like Paul. As stated, he was controversial, having problems with the authorities almost everywhere he went and, as well, suffered terribly for the cause of Christ.

However, he saw untold thousands of souls brought to a saving knowledge of Jesus Christ, plus baptized with the Holy Spirit, as well as bondages of every nature broken by the power of God. He pushed the darkness, at least in some places, to the very extremity of the Roman Empire, but, regrettably, most looked at the obvious controversy but not so much at the obvious fruit!

The phrase, *"Born at Alexandria,"* proclaims the mightiest city in the Roman Empire at that time, other than Rome itself. It was located in Egypt on the Mediterranean Sea about 100 miles northwest of modern Cairo.

It was built by Alexander the Great under the direction of Dinocrates, the celebrated architect of the temple of Diana at Ephesus. Ptolemy Soter founded the famous academy here called *"The Museum,"* in which learned men devoted themselves to philosophical studies. Some of the most celebrated schools of antiquity flourished here.

One of the Seven Wonders of the Ancient World was located at Alexandria. It was the Tower of Pharos. The Septuagint, which is the Greek version of the Old Testament, was translated here in 285 B.C.

The phrase, *"An eloquent man, and mighty in the Scriptures, came to Ephesus,"* gives us no reason as to why he came, but, at the time, whether he knew it or not, he was being led by the Holy Spirit.

NOTES

The word *"eloquent"* in the Greek text is *"logios"* and means *"to be fluent, i.e., an orator."* Such demands that he was trained in the Alexandrian schools. He was well educated, probably to the extent of an earned doctorate in our modern recognition system. Above that, he was a scholar, as well, in the Scriptures, at least according to the light he presently had! However, that light was about to be greatly increased!

(25) "THIS MAN WAS INSTRUCTED IN THE WAY OF THE LORD; AND BEING FERVENT IN THE SPIRIT, HE SPOKE AND TAUGHT DILIGENTLY THE THINGS OF THE LORD, KNOWING ONLY THE BAPTISM OF JOHN."

The form is:

1. The phrase, *"This man was instructed in the Way of the Lord,"* refers to the Lord Jesus Christ. However, his knowledge, although proficient as far as it went, was greatly limited respecting grace and the Baptism with the Holy Spirit.

2. However, whatever he had learned about Jesus was evidently from those who were deficient themselves. In other words, they told him all they knew, which obviously blessed him greatly, but it seems their knowledge was limited. Consequently, if he had been excited heretofore with only a partial knowledge of Christ, that joy was about to multiply manyfold.

3. *"And being fervent in the spirit,"* spoke of his own spirit and not necessarily the Holy Spirit.

4. As stated, he was so thrilled by what he did know about Jesus, which evidently spoke of His Birth, Life, Ministry, Death, and Resurrection, that he could not help but proclaim what he did know with great exuberance.

5. *"He spoke and taught diligently the Things of the Lord, knowing only the baptism of John,"* speaks of repentance and water baptism.

6. While he certainly was saved, as should be obvious, and, as well, was consecrated to the Lord, still, he, as millions of others, could make precious little advancement

spiritually due to not being baptized with the Holy Spirit.

(26) "AND HE BEGAN TO SPEAK BOLDLY IN THE SYNAGOGUE: WHOM WHEN AQUILA AND PRISCILLA HAD HEARD, THEY TOOK HIM UNTO THEM, AND EXPOUNDED UNTO HIM THE WAY OF GOD MORE PERFECTLY."

The order is:

1. To attempt to understand the Trinity, the *"Father"* is *"God"* but not first God.

2. The *"Son"* is *"God"* but not *"second God."*

3. The *"Holy Spirit"* is *"God"* but not *"third God."*

4. There is only one God but manifested in three distinct Persons, God the Father, God the Son, and God the Holy Spirit.

THE MINISTRY OF APOLLOS

The phrase, *"And he began to speak boldly in the synagogue,"* proclaims the style and method of most synagogues.

In most, if not all, synagogues, a special place was set aside for guests who desired to minister or felt they had something to say. The ruler of the synagogue could invite the guest to speak, which they did most of the time.

Apollos boldly and grandly portrayed Jesus Christ from the Scriptures, at least as far as he knew.

"Whom when Aquila and Priscilla had heard," presents that which was all in the providence of God. The Lord knew the hunger of this brother's heart and so would arrange this divine appointment, for that is what it was!

The phrase, *"They took him unto them, and expounded unto him the way of God more perfectly,"* pertained, no doubt, to the full complement of salvation by the grace of God exclusively, correct water baptism, and the Baptism with the Holy Spirit with the evidence of speaking with other tongues.

THE WAY OF GOD MORE PERFECTLY

How many presently, and, in fact, have always existed, who desperately need to know the *"way of God more perfectly"*? As Apollos, they are saved but can little grow in grace because of a lack of scriptural knowledge, or mostly, the problem of erroneous teaching respecting the Baptism with the Holy Spirit.

Satan, of course, does everything within his power to keep people from hearing the Gospel of Jesus Christ. If they do have the privilege of hearing the good news, he will do all he can to keep them from accepting free salvation as offered by the Lord.

However, if they do accept Christ, he will do all within his power to stunt their spiritual growth by causing them to hear and believe false teaching and error, or else, to not hear the total message of salvation by faith in Christ and the Baptism with the Holy Spirit with the evidence of speaking with other tongues (Eph. 2:8-9; Acts 2:4).

If he can succeed in doing this, he knows that the leaven of error, if not rooted out, can never remain static but must enlarge until it ultimately corrupts the whole!

Thankfully, despite all of his education and eloquence, Apollos had a humble, teachable spirit, which received readily from God's Messengers, Aquila and Priscilla.

(27) "AND WHEN HE WAS DISPOSED TO PASS INTO ACHAIA, THE BRETHREN WROTE, EXHORTING THE DISCIPLES TO RECEIVE HIM: WHO, WHEN HE WAS COME, HELPED THEM MUCH WHICH HAD BELIEVED THROUGH GRACE."

The synopsis is:

1. Other than the absolute absurdity and stupidity which characterizes the vapid philosophy of evolution, the sheer affront to God as Creator by the propagation of this lie, and a lie it is, is the greatest insult of all.

2. Actually, evolution is an insult to intelligence in any capacity.

3. The idea that something on its own can be brought out of nothing is the beginning of this lie. In other words, evolution has no explanation for the first cause. We know what the first cause is, *"In the beginning God..."* (Gen. 1:1).

RECEIVING APOLLOS

The phrase, *"And when he was disposed to pass into Achaia,"* refers to Greece, which was across the Aegean Sea, and Corinth in particular!

"The brethren wrote, exhorting the disciples to receive him," tells us that despite the fact that Paul had only been able to minister in the synagogue in Ephesus for probably one service before leaving, at least the seed of a church was now established in Ephesus. It seems obvious that Priscilla and Aquila were very instrumental in the growth here, which is evident. It would have hardly been possible for the word *"brethren"* to be used were there not a goodly number of men already in the faith, even though continuing in the synagogue.

As well, Apollos probably stayed for some time, maybe even several months, and was, no doubt, a great help in further establishing the work.

So, when he felt led of the Lord to go to Corinth, the *"brethren"* would recommend him, and rightly so.

THROUGH GRACE

The phrase, *"Who, when he was come, helped them much which had believed through grace,"* tells us several things:

- It seems that Apollos had understood precious little, if anything at all, at the outset, respecting the grace of God, which is the foundation of salvation in Christ. However, upon having this great doctrine expounded to him, he was now very proficient in this most excellent message. It seems that Priscilla and Aquila had done their work well.
- As a result of what he had learned, especially considering his background, he could be of great blessing, which he was, to the believers at Corinth.
- Quite possibly, the first efforts by the Judaizers may already have begun at Corinth in attempting to add Law to grace. We do know that just a little later, this became an extensive problem at Corinth, and elsewhere as well! Consequently, new converts, as well as others who were not too well versed in the Word, could easily be swayed, which some were.

So, I think it is obvious that the Holy Spirit directed Apollos to this church because of this very need, in which he was a tremendous help.

How beautiful is the working and administration of the Holy Spirit! As well, how wonderful it is when perplexing problems are so easily solved when the Holy Spirit has His Way, and people, such as Apollos, can be led and directed according to the will of God!

(28) "FOR HE MIGHTILY CONVINCED THE JEWS, AND THAT PUBLICLY, SHOWING BY THE SCRIPTURES THAT JESUS WAS CHRIST."

The synopsis is:

1. The phrase, *"For he mightily convinced the Jews, and that publicly,"* more than likely, had reference to ministering in their synagogue.
2. *"Showing by the Scriptures that Jesus was Christ,"* actually says that Jesus was the Messiah.
3. *"He mightily convinced,"* means he overwhelmed with argument, and continued to do so, proving from the Scriptures, and without any doubt, that Jesus was the Messiah. So, he bore down all opposition.

Actually, he used the same line of preaching as did Paul when addressing Jews. No doubt, Aquila and Priscilla patiently explained to him Paul's method, which was probably given by the Holy Spirit. (Up to this time, Paul had not personally met Apollos.)

4. It is remarkable that the success of Apollos at Corinth seems to have been chiefly among the Jews, who had opposed themselves so vehemently to Paul. This tells us that if one preacher cannot reach a particular group of people, quite possibly another can.
5. It is one of the many proofs of the singleness of eye and simplicity of purpose of the great apostle that the success of this novice, where he himself had somewhat failed, did not excite the least jealousy (I Cor. 16:12).
6. As well, Luke, as he recounted these occasions, even though Paul's great friend and biographer, spoke here of the powers and work of Apollos with no stinted measure of praise.

What a beautiful spirit was resident within both Paul and Luke!

"O for a thousand tongues to sing,
"My great Redeemer's praise,
"The glories of my God and King,
"The triumphs of His Grace."

"My gracious Master and my God,
"Assist me to proclaim,
"To spread through all the Earth abroad,
"The honors of Your Name."

"Jesus! The Name that calms our fears,
"That bids our sorrows cease;
"'Tis music in the sinner's ears,
"'Tis life, and health, and peace."

"He breaks the power of canceled sin,
"He sets the prisoner free;
"His Blood can make the foulest clean;
"His Blood availed for me."

"Hear Him, ye deaf; His praise, ye dumb,
"Your loosened tongues employ;
"Ye blind, behold your Saviour come;
"And leap, ye lame, for joy."

CHAPTER 19

(1) "AND IT CAME TO PASS, THAT, WHILE APOLLOS WAS AT CORINTH, PAUL HAVING PASSED THROUGH THE UPPER COASTS CAME TO EPHESUS: AND FINDING CERTAIN DISCIPLES."

The exegesis is:

1. The church, in essence, began with the Message of the Cross.
2. Jesus Christ is the New Covenant, while the Cross of Christ is the meaning of that covenant.

EPHESUS

The phrase, *"And it came to pass, that, while Apollos was at Corinth,"* pertains to Verse 27 of Acts, Chapter 18. Apollos had felt led of the Lord to go to Corinth, which he did, and was a tremendous blessing.

The phrase is given to us to show that Apollos was not present in Ephesus when Paul finally returned.

"Paul having passed through the upper coasts came to Ephesus," refers back to Verse 23 of Acts, Chapter 18, with the apostle *"going over all the country of Galatia and Phrygia in order, strengthening all the disciples."* As stated, Paul visited all the churches in these areas, or at least many of them, that he had recently planted, which, undoubtedly, was a tremendous blessing to these particular people.

NOTES

As should be understood, these works were raised up out of rank paganism. As such, most of the people, other than the Jews who had been saved, had little or no knowledge of God whatsoever previous to their conversion. As well, Bibles, which then consisted of the Old Testament, were not at all proliferated as they are presently. Without a doubt, many, if not all, of the believers sought the help of the converted Jews in securing scrolls of various different Books of the Old Testament. However, due to these having to be copied laboriously by hand and, therefore, expensive, as stated, they, no doubt, were not in abundant supply!

As well, and that to which we have previously alluded, the pastors of these churches were, for the most part, people out of their own ranks whom God had called. Even though this call of God placed these individuals, whomever they may have been, in a different category, still, most, if not all, were woefully inadequate in the Scriptures. Due to this, it was very easy for false doctrine to spring up, which Paul corrected during these visits, hence, their significance!

Having finished this tour, Paul was now back in Ephesus. It had probably been about one year since his very brief visit there, which was actually the beginning of the church in this city (Acts 18:19-21). Much had happened in the meantime!

CERTAIN DISCIPLES

The phrase, *"And finding certain disciples,"* tells us by the use of the word *"disciples"* that these were followers of Christ but were deficient in their understanding.

Some believe these were disciples of John the Baptist; however, everywhere else in the Book of Acts, the use of the word *"disciples"* means *"Disciples"* of Jesus, in other words, believers in Jesus.

Some think these men had been won to the Lord by Apollos before his being instructed more perfectly in the Word of God by Priscilla and Aquila. That very

NOTES

well could have been the case because they, as we shall see, referred to John's baptism exactly as did Apollos (Acts 18:25). However, whether that is correct or not, many questions remain unanswered.

For instance, if they had been in Ephesus any time at all, would not Apollos or Priscilla and Aquila have instructed them more perfectly? Possibly they had just arrived in Ephesus, and Apollos had already left and maybe even Priscilla and Aquila.

At any rate, whatever the case, these particular disciples had not yet come into the Fullness of the Spirit, even though they had accepted Christ as their Saviour.

As we shall see, even though there was by now the nucleus of a church in Ephesus, it continued to be associated with the Jewish synagogue and had not really separated out on its own as it would shortly. As a result, and as would be obvious, it did not have nearly the strength at present that it shortly would have.

(2) "HE SAID UNTO THEM, HAVE YOU RECEIVED THE HOLY SPIRIT SINCE YOU BELIEVED? AND THEY SAID UNTO HIM, WE HAVE NOT SO MUCH AS HEARD WHETHER THERE BE ANY HOLY SPIRIT."

The structure is:

1. Wherever the *"light"* shines, the powers of darkness are destroyed, and man is bettered in every conceivable way possible.

2. Of all the people delivered by Christ, one might could say that being delivered from the bondage of religion is the greatest deliverance of all.

THE HOLY SPIRIT

The question, *"He said unto them, Have you received the Holy Spirit since you believed?"* in the Greek is literally, *"Having believed, did you receive?"*

Horton said, *"The whole impression of this verse is that since these Disciples claimed to be Believers, the Baptism with the Holy Spirit should have been the next step, incidentally a distinct step from the believing."*

Every Christian receives the Holy Spirit of Sonship (Rom. 8:14-16) and, consequently, has Him when converted (Rom. 8:9), but that is not what Paul was referring to here. As we have said elsewhere in this volume, there is a vast difference in being born of the Spirit than being baptized with the Spirit.

This which Paul was asking had nothing to do with the new birth by the Holy Spirit (Jn. 3:1-5) in that these individuals were already saved. It was the enduement of power for service (Lk. 24:49; Acts 1:4-8; 2:38-39; 5:32).

In essence, John's disciples could receive baptism in water, but Christ's Disciples could receive the Baptism with the Holy Spirit, which is separate and distinct from conversion, hence, the inquiry of Paul.

Actually, this of which Paul spoke was the same thing, in essence, spoken to Apollos by Priscilla and Aquila in Acts 18:26.

HAVING BELIEVED

The Greek word for *"having believed"* or *"since you believed"* is *"pisteusantes."* The idea is that these men had already believed in the Lord Jesus Christ and, as a result of that believing, had been saved (Jn. 3:16). However, even though they were now spiritually ready to be baptized with the Holy Spirit due to having their sins washed away by the precious Blood of Jesus Christ, they had not gone on and received. The reason was, as their answer portrayed, they knew nothing about this Baptism with the Holy Spirit with the evidence of speaking with other tongues!

However, the entirety of the emphasis in this Text is the absolute necessity of the believer being baptized with the Holy Spirit. The need for the believer to be baptized with the Holy Spirit is for many and varied reasons.

In fact, why is the Baptism with the Holy Spirit so important?

Before I attempt to answer that, allow me to deal with the answer given by these men to Paul in respect to his question.

The phrase, *"And they said unto him, We have not so much as heard whether there be any Holy Spirit,"* does not mean that they did not know of Whom Paul was speaking. They knew of the existence of the Holy Spirit, but they were not aware that the Age of the Spirit had come and that believers could be literally baptized with Him! Let's

NOTES

look now at this great experience:

WHAT PAUL'S QUESTION TEACHES US

These passages glaringly tell us that one is not baptized with the Holy Spirit at conversion. One may be filled with the Spirit immediately thereafter, as were Cornelius and his household, but this Baptism of which Paul spoke is not an automatic part of conversion as many teach.

Regrettably, much of the Christian world teaches that there is no such thing as a separate experience of being baptized with the Holy Spirit after salvation. If that is so, Paul's question and actions in this instance make no sense.

No, the Scripture is replete that the Baptism with the Holy Spirit is an experience separate and apart from salvation, actually made possible because of salvation, but for which one must ask (Lk. 11:13).

TONGUES

As well, the Scripture is replete, as we shall see, that all believers, without exception, speak with other tongues upon being baptized with the Spirit (Acts 2:4; 10:46; 11:17; 19:6). In other words, speaking with other tongues (which are languages known somewhere in the world, but not by the speaker) is the initial physical evidence that one has been baptized with the Holy Spirit (Acts 2:4). To state it another way: if one has not spoken with other tongues, one has not been baptized with the Holy Spirit! It is just that simple!

No, there is nothing in Scripture that teaches that some are baptized with the Holy Spirit with tongues and some without tongues. The Scripture says, *"And they were all filled with the Holy Spirit, and* (all) *began to speak with other tongues, as the Spirit gave them utterance."*

EQUIPS FOR SERVICE

While faith in what Christ did at Calvary and the Resurrection saves one from sin (Jn. 3:16), the Baptism with the Holy Spirit equips one for service. In other words, without being baptized with the Holy Spirit, very little, if anything, is going to be done for God. There may be much religious activity and machinery, which fools many people into thinking that much is being done, but, in reality, nothing can be truly done for God unless it is done through and by the person, agency, leading, guidance and power of the Holy Spirit (Acts 1:8).

WORSHIP

Without being baptized with the Holy Spirit, the believer really cannot worship God. He may engage himself in things which he labels worship but really is not worship, at least that which is recognized by God and, indeed, cannot be. Jesus said, *"And they who worship Him must worship Him in spirit and in truth"* (Jn. 4:24).

While the word *"spirit"* is here speaking of the spirit of man, still, such can only be energized and empowered by the Holy Spirit.

If one is to notice, all Spirit-filled people basically worship alike, at least if they are scriptural, irrespective of the church affiliation. It is because the Holy Spirit is the One Who orchestrates the worship, as only He can do!

In churches where the opposite of what I am here saying is taught, one will look in vain for any type of worship. With some few exceptions, there is precious little praise to God, if any, with most thinking that their mere presence in church constitutes worship.

Such certainly can be correct at times, but not in the manner in which we are here speaking. Most of these people, whomever they may be, are not worshiping God but are merely showing up in a physical sense.

WORKS OF GOD

Without being baptized with the Holy Spirit, none of the works of God can be carried out (Lk. 4:18). I speak of the anointing of the Holy Spirit upon preachers to preach, as well as all to witness, prayer for the sick in order that they may be healed, powers of darkness broken in people's lives according to the laying on of hands, etc. When one reads the Four Gospels, this is what we find Jesus doing, as well as His Disciples, and then it continuing in the early church, as recorded in the Book of Acts.

As I have said previously, if our churches are not copies of the churches in the Book

NOTES

of Acts and with all their earmarks, that tells us the Holy Spirit is not present, at least in the manner in which we speak. This is actually what occasioned Paul's question of this verse. If He is present and allowed to have His Way, these things will take place!

GIFTS OF THE SPIRIT

Without the Baptism with the Holy Spirit, the gifts of the Spirit are not present, consequently, depriving the Body of Christ of that which is so desperately needed (I Cor. 12:1-13).

FRUIT OF THE SPIRIT

Without the Baptism with the Holy Spirit, the Fruit of the Spirit cannot be developed (Gal. 5:22-23). This is Christlikeness, which only the Holy Spirit can bring about. To deny this experience as taught in the Bible is to deny all of His Attributes as well!

OBVIOUS!

After being around these individuals at Ephesus for a very short period of time, it was very obvious to Paul that even though they were saved, therefore, followers of Christ, they were not baptized with the Holy Spirit.

Is it that obvious?

Yes, it is! So, if it is that obvious, this shows us how all-important this great work of grace actually is to the believer.

What does the reader think would have happened to these men, and I speak of the spiritual sense, if after hearing Paul explain this vital work of the Holy Spirit, they had rejected this plain, scriptural necessity?

After hearing the truth and then rejecting the truth, it is my thought that these people would have ultimately lost out with God. To refuse to walk in the light as it is given forfeits not only that light but, as we have previously said, even the light one presently has (Mat. 25:28-30; Lk. 19:24-26).

It is quite one thing to not have light on a particular Bible subject, but something else altogether to be presented the light and then reject the light!

WHY WOULD ANY BELIEVER REJECT THE LIGHT OF THE HOLY SPIRIT?

Of course, only the Lord knows the answer to that question. However, I think one can say without any fear of contradiction or exaggeration that it is spiritual pride which stands in the way of most.

Many old-line denominations have so strayed from the Word of God that they make little pretense anymore at having much of anything in the spiritual sense! Therefore, it is not too difficult to show them this great truth, or any Bible truth for that matter, and have them to receive. They do not profess very much in the first place anyway; therefore, there is very little, if any, spiritual pride with many of these people.

However, with those who make great claims of knowing the Lord and believing all of the Bible, etc., such as the holiness groups, the fundamentalists, and many modern Pentecostals for that matter, great spiritual pride oftentimes is involved. As a result, many will not admit that there is something from God which they do not have.

OPPOSITION

As well, many of these people, especially the preachers who fall into this category, are not content to merely reject the Baptism with the Holy Spirit, but they feel they must also stop the propagation of this message and will pretty well resort to any tactics to carry out these efforts. Such opposition oftentimes goes into blasphemy, claiming that anyone who speaks in tongues is of the devil, etc. Then, as well, not content to attack only the message, they extend the opposition to the messenger!

Actually, it is impossible for one to be given Biblical light on any subject and to remain static if that light is refused. As we have repeatedly stated, a regression instantly begins to take place and does not stop until nothing is left, at least as far as the Lord is concerned.

That is the position presently of most old-line denominations, as well as some Pentecostal denominations.

PENTECOSTALS?

To reject the light is one thing, but to have the light and then forsake it is worse still! Regrettably and sadly, that is the state of some modern Pentecostal denominations!

NOTES

Prefixing or carrying the name *"Pentecostal"* does not at all mean that one actually is that of which one claims. The Pentecostal way is not a religious denomination, or even certain groups of people, etc. The Pentecostal way is a way of life and is actually that which is characterized in the Book of Acts and the Epistles.

So, as we have already stated, if one does not have the earmarks of this New Testament account, despite claims, one cannot truly be Pentecostal. It is a *"way"* far more than it is a doctrine.

MANY WHO SPEAK IN TONGUES ARE NOT, IN FACT, PENTECOSTAL!

This is actually the great controversy in some modern Pentecostal denominations at present. The Pentecostal experience in some circles has by and large been reduced to merely speaking with other tongues. While speaking in tongues is certainly Biblical, it by no means claims the full experience.

To be sure, if the Pentecostal way is reduced to merely speaking in tongues, after awhile, even that will fall by the wayside. Tragically, in the two major Pentecostal denominations, the Assemblies of God and the Church of God, I am told that less than one-half of their adherents even claim the Pentecostal experience. Consequently, these denominations, at least if they are to be honest with themselves, cannot really even claim anymore to be Pentecostal!

WHAT IS THE PENTECOSTAL WAY?

Joel is the Old Testament prophet quoted by Peter on the Day of Pentecost (Acts 2:16-21); therefore, he can be concluded as the Holy Spirit prophet of the Old Testament, even though other prophets spoke greatly of this subject as well!

According to his prophecies, which we see carried forth in the Book of Acts and the Epistles, in brief, the following is the description of this *"way"*:

The description of this Pentecostal way as given by Joel, at the beginning, is described more so as a state of affairs rather than an action of affairs. By that, I mean this:

In his description of the outpouring of the Holy Spirit on this Earth, Joel describes it in the sense of the *"Former Rain"* and the *"Latter Rain"* (Joel 2:23).

Even though these were terms describing weather elements, as is obvious, Joel uses them to describe the moving and operation of the Holy Spirit.

The *"Former Rain"* began on the Day of Pentecost and continued throughout the early church. The *"Latter Rain"* speaks of the Outpouring of the Spirit beginning approximately at the turn of the 20th century and continues unto this hour. Although some were filled with the Spirit during the intervening centuries, the greatest outpourings by far refer to this of which we have spoken.

THE SOUND OF ALARM

If one is to notice, the destruction of Jerusalem and Israel as a nation followed the outpouring of the *"Former Rain"* and took place in A.D. 70. Likewise, this latter outpouring, even as the Bible declares, will immediately precede the coming Great Tribulation, which will be worse than anything the world has ever known (Mat. 24:21).

Joel described this *"state"* of the Pentecostal way by saying, *"Blow you the trumpet in Zion, and sound an alarm in My Holy Mountain: let all the inhabitants of the land tremble: for the Day of the Lord comes, for it is near at hand"* (Joel 2:1).

So, even as the *"Former Rain,"* this *"Latter Rain outpouring"* is meant to serve as a sign to the entirety of the world that time is about up, and great tribulation is right around the corner. As we have stated, it begins with a *"state of affairs"* rather than the *"action of affairs,"* which now follows.

FASTING AND PRAYER

The Pentecostal way is a way of fasting and prayer (Joel 2:12-17).

Intercession and travail are hallmarks of Spirit-filled believers, that is, if they are truly Pentecostal. This is important beyond words!

Everything done for God on this Earth has its beginnings in fasting and prayer. Every move of God begins in this fashion!

As well, I must quickly add that this of which I speak cannot be confessed into existence, as is taught by many. Revival, and any move of God for that matter, is brought about as someone intercedes and cries to God!

If one carefully studies the Book of Acts, it will be overly obvious as to the action of these attributes.

Actually, the Day of Pentecost was preceded by 10 days of prayer and seeking God, and fasting, no doubt, as well!

At the beginning of Chapter 3, Peter and John were on their way to the Temple in order to pray when the great miracle of the cripple occurred.

Chapter 4 of Acts concludes with the people praying and the place being shaken by the power of the Holy Spirit.

When the Lord spoke to Ananias concerning Paul, He said of the former persecutor, *"He prays"* (Acts 9:11).

As well, when the Gospel was first presented to the gentiles, it first began with Peter praying (Acts 10:9).

Need I give more examples?!

GLADNESS AND REJOICING

The Pentecostal way is a way of gladness and rejoicing (Joel 2:21-27). Only the Holy Spirit can impart such joy and gladness in the hearts and lives of believers. Without Him, such does not exist!

As a result, there will be demonstrations as people grandly worship! This is what makes church different than anything else in the world. To be frank, without the Holy Spirit, church is little more than a meeting of the Kiwanis Club, etc. However, when the Holy Spirit is present and working, there will be shouting, praising, worship, even dancing before the Lord, etc.

It will not stop there, resulting, at times, in great laughter and being slain in the Spirit, all which produces an exuberance that the world can in no way give.

THE OUTPOURING OF THE SPIRIT

The Pentecostal way is the way of the Outpouring of the Spirit, resulting in the gifts of the Spirit going into operation (Joel 2:28-29).

Without the Holy Spirit, and I speak of the Baptism with the Spirit with the evidence of speaking with other tongues, the Lord can little reveal Himself to His People. With the Holy Spirit resident in the believer's heart and life and the believer yielding to Him, allowing Him to control our actions, great revelation is given to the church through prophecy, dreams, and by other means. This is the Way of the Spirit, and to be sure, He is gloriously active when given preeminence as He should be!

NOTES

SIGNS AND WONDERS

The Pentecostal way is a way of signs and wonders (Joel 2:30).

I speak of *"wonders"* such as the healing of the sick, the working of miracles, and great deliverances as the Lord breaks the bondages of humanity. True Pentecostal people believe in a God Who can and will do great and mighty things. As well, they believe that He will do it now (Mk. 16:17).

SALVATION OF SOULS

The Pentecostal way is the way of the salvation of souls as they are brought to Jesus as a result of the Word of God being preached in fullness and power, with Holy Spirit Conviction settling upon the lost, thereby, bringing them to salvation (Joel 2:32). In other words, without the Holy Spirit, the harvest cannot be gathered!

In all of this, the Holy Spirit wondrously and gloriously lifts up Jesus. He glorifies Jesus, magnifies Jesus, presents Jesus, and makes real all that Jesus has done for us through the Cross (Jn., Chpt. 16).

Actually, the great victories won by Christ at Calvary literally cannot be realized in the life of the believer without the work, power, and leading of the Holy Spirit (Rom., Chpt. 8).

THE COMING OF THE LORD

Joel spoke of all this leading up to the Coming of the Lord (Joel 2:31). Actually, the *"Latter Rain"* outpouring is meant to precede the Second Coming and is the greatest sign of that coming glorious time.

So, the *"Pentecostal way"* is also a proper understanding of Endtime events. Jesus is coming! When He comes, the world will then know peace as never before. As well, His Coming will be accompanied by the greatest heavenly display ever known (Mat. 24:27-31). True Pentecostals are not in doubt about the future. They know who holds tomorrow.

This in brief is the Pentecostal way, and is carried forth in the Book of Acts and the Epistles, and is meant to be carried on in our modern churches as well! Otherwise, it is not of God!

(3) "AND HE SAID UNTO THEM, UNTO WHAT THEN WERE YOU BAPTIZED? AND THEY SAID, UNTO JOHN'S BAPTISM."

The account is:

1. The question, *"And he said unto them, Unto what then were you baptized?"* proclaims Paul having asked about the Holy Spirit Baptism and being met somewhat with a blank stare. He now inquired as to where they actually were in their following of Christ.

2. *"And they said, Unto John's baptism,"* proclaims them, as stated, as possibly being followers of Apollos up to now.

3. These men, even as millions today, believed that Jesus was the Son of God and that He died for our sins and rose from the dead. In the believing of this and the accepting of Him, which is so vitally important, they were, of course, saved! (Jn. 3:16; Rom. 10:9-10).

However, as I have so laboriously attempted to proclaim, if the believer stops there, a terrible injustice is done to Christ respecting all He has done for us. If we think that the only purpose of salvation is to save our souls, as important as that surely is, we greatly misunderstand what salvation is all about.

While the salvation of the soul is of such magnitude that its significance cannot be overemphasized, still, that is only the beginning. The Lord intends for the believer to be *"a habitation of God through the Spirit"* (Eph. 2:22). The Holy Spirit indwelling the believer is the manner, and, in fact, the only manner, in which the work of God can be carried out in this world. As we have repeatedly stated, this does not happen at salvation but is an experience separate and apart from the salvation experience.

The sealing of the Holy Spirit (Eph. 1:13), i.e., the regeneration of the Holy Spirit (Titus 3:5), which takes place at conversion, is not to be confounded with the miraculous outpouring of the Holy Spirit upon believers, which is so remarkable a feature of the Book of the Acts of the Apostles, and which is promised to all believers (Mk. 16:17; Acts 1:4; 2:39).

NOTES

(4) "THEN SAID PAUL, JOHN VERILY BAPTIZED WITH THE BAPTISM OF REPENTANCE, SAYING UNTO THE PEOPLE, THAT THEY SHOULD BELIEVE ON HIM WHICH SHOULD COME AFTER HIM, THAT IS, ON CHRIST JESUS."

The order is:

1. The only way that Christlikeness in every manner can be carried out in the life of the believer is that we have a correct interpretation of the Cross.

2. This refers to what Jesus did in that great Sacrifice and our placing all of our trust in that Finished Work.

THE BAPTISM OF REPENTANCE

The phrase, *"Then said Paul, John verily baptized with the baptism of repentance,"* in effect, was all that could be done at that particular time.

Before Jesus came to this Earth and paid the price for man's redemption on Calvary's Cross, repentance was the limit of one's spirituality.

This was signified by John the Baptist in baptizing the repentant ones in water. In other words, after they had truly repented before God, that was to serve as a type of the Baptism with the Holy Spirit, which only Jesus could give (Mat. 3:11).

Water baptism, as John carried it out, was new to Israel, at least in this fashion! Consequently, it had nothing to do with one's salvation, as that gift came about through the covenants as one repented before God and evidenced faith in their substitutionary offering, which was a Type of the coming Christ.

As stated, the water baptism offered by John was meant to serve as an example or a type, if you will, of the Baptism with the Holy Spirit, which could not come until Jesus took our sins away. This He did by His Death on Calvary's Cross.

So, this was John's Baptism!

BELIEVE ON CHRIST JESUS

The phrase, *"Saying unto the people, that they should believe on Him which should come after him, that is, on Christ Jesus,"* proclaims John lifting up Jesus as the Saviour of mankind!

In other words, he was saying that his water baptism could not save anyone, but that salvation was afforded only by one's faith in Christ Jesus. In fact, salvation has always been on that basis and that basis alone! From the time of the Fall in the Garden of Eden, there has never even been any other type, manner, or way of salvation.

As we have stated, even though no one knew Jesus before His first Advent, still, they did know that God had promised a Redeemer, Who, in effect, would be Jesus (Gen. 3:15). So, it was faith in that coming Redeemer, Who was promised in the covenants (Gen. 3:21; 12:1-3; 15:1-15; 22:13-14; 49:10), which guaranteed salvation!

From this description as given by Paul, we see that the major contrast here is not between John and Jesus, and neither is it between John's baptism and the baptism commanded by Jesus in Matthew 28:19. Rather, it is between John's baptism in water and the Baptism where Jesus is the mighty Baptizer, the Baptism with the Holy Spirit.

This is the contrast Jesus Himself made in Acts 1:5 and that to which Peter drew attention in Acts 11:16.

THE FIGURE OF WATER BAPTISM

So, for God to give this beautiful figure of water baptism to John the Baptist in order to serve as a type of the coming Baptism with the Holy Spirit, and then for men to reject it, is serious indeed!

To be sure, water baptism, as it was then offered, was a fit and beautiful example of the Baptism with the Holy Spirit. The person put down into the water until it totally covers him is meant to explain the indwelling of the Holy Spirit.

Even though this is the closest thing that could be given as an example, still, even this example falls woefully short of what really happens to the believer upon being baptized with the Holy Spirit.

NOTES

In water baptism, the person is in the water, and the water is all around the person. However, that is as far as it can go because if the water went into the person, the person, of course, would drown.

However, when one is baptized with the Holy Spirit, one is not only completely immersed totally in the Spirit, with the Spirit totally on the believer, but, as well, the Spirit is actually in the believer, which, of course, water baptism could not do (John 14:17).

The word *"baptism"* in its truest sense in the Greek text is *"baptizo"* and means *"to dip, immerse, to overwhelm, to saturate."* Consequently, in its simplest form, it means that the person is literally into the object into which he is baptized, and the object is literally in the person.

(5) "WHEN THEY HEARD THIS, THEY WERE BAPTIZED IN THE NAME OF THE LORD JESUS."

The account is:

1. The phrase, *"When they heard this,"* characterizes these men as instantly believing and accepting what Paul had said, and then desiring that which he had said.

2. The phrase, *"They were baptized in the Name of the Lord Jesus,"* in no way means baptism saved them because they were already saved. Paul undoubtedly explained to them how that Christian baptism is a testimony to one's identification with Jesus in His Death and Resurrection.

3. As water baptism by John was meant to serve as a type or example of the mighty Baptism with the Holy Spirit, likewise, Christian water baptism is meant to serve as a type or example of what Jesus did at Calvary and the Resurrection, which makes possible the Baptism with the Holy Spirit.

When the person is standing in the water, that's a type of being crucified with Christ. When the believer is put under the water, that's a type of all of our sins and the *"old man"* being buried with Jesus. Whenever the Believer is brought out of the water, that's a type of our resurrection in Christ as a new man.

4. Horton said, *"'In the Name' means they were Baptized into the worship and service of the Lord Jesus, making Him truly the Lord and Master of their lives. By this*

NOTES

also they declared themselves publicly as members of the Body of Christ.

5. As well, *"In the Name of the Lord Jesus,"* means, *"By the Authority of the Lord Jesus."* The formula Paul used was, *"In the Name of the Father, and of the Son, and of the Holy Spirit"* (Mat. 28:19).

6. Without going into great detail, Matthew 28:19 is the only formula given in the Word of God regarding water baptism. As well, it is only by and through the authority of Jesus Christ, due to our faith in Him regarding what He did at Calvary and the Resurrection, which gives us access to the Father and makes it possible for believers to be baptized with the Holy Spirit.

The statement used by Paul in Verse 5, *"In the Name of the Lord Jesus,"* is a little different from Acts 2:38, *"In the Name of Jesus Christ,"* and different still in Acts 10:48, *"In the Name of the Lord."*

7. If the Holy Spirit had intended for the name of Jesus only to be used in water baptism, He would have given it identically each time instead of the variations. As stated, the only formula for water baptism in the Bible is found in Matthew 28:19 and is given by none other than the Lord Jesus Christ Himself!

(6) "AND WHEN PAUL HAD LAID HIS HANDS UPON THEM, THE HOLY SPIRIT CAME ON THEM: AND THEY SPOKE WITH TONGUES, AND PROPHESIED."

The direction is:

1. If the Cross was that to which He came, and that's exactly why He came, then it was the Cross in which the need of humanity was met.

2. It is impossible to exhaust the potential of the Finished Work of Christ.

THE LAYING ON OF HANDS

The phrase, *"And when Paul had laid his hands upon them,"* constitutes a Biblical principle that is also mentioned in Acts 8:17; 9:17-18; Heb. 6:2.

Even though the *"laying on of hands"* is, as stated, a viable Bible doctrine (Heb. 6:2) and can be used in praying for the sick (Mk. 16:18) and for believers to be baptized with the Holy Spirit, as here, still, people can be healed and filled without this particular physical manifestation, even as important as it is.

For instance, the believers on the Day of Pentecost were all baptized with the Holy Spirit without anyone laying hands on them. To the contrary, Peter and John laid hands on the believers in Samaria in order that they might receive (Acts 8:17). It was the same with Paul (Acts 9:17). However, with Cornelius and all who were with Him, there was no laying on of hands (Acts 10:44).

THE HOLY SPIRIT

The phrase, *"The Holy Spirit came on them,"* refers to their being baptized with the Holy Spirit. In this one short statement, we have a wealth of meaning.

It is certainly true that the Holy Spirit plays a vital part in our conversion, which pertains to regeneration (Titus 3:5). However, many teach that there is no such thing as a second experience which one can receive. If one is automatically baptized with the Holy Spirit at conversion, then the phrase, *"the Holy Spirit came on them,"* makes no sense at all! Even though they were saved as are all believers and, as well, the Holy Spirit had performed His office Work respecting regeneration, still, they had not yet been baptized with the Holy Spirit. This is something that all believers can have, and upon this event, without fail, one speaks with other tongues as the Spirit gives the utterance (Acts 2:4).

For those who will not believe despite the light given to them, I suppose it can be said, *"There are none so blind, as those who will not see!"*

TONGUES

The phrase, *"And they spoke with tongues, and prophesied,"* proclaims the tongues as the initial physical evidence that one has been baptized with the Holy Spirit. Sometimes there is prophesying at this time and sometimes not.

On the Day of Pentecost, they spoke with tongues, but nothing is said about them prophesying. It was the same with the Samaritans (Acts 8:17). As well, nothing is said about Paul prophesying when he was baptized with the Holy Spirit (Acts 9:17).

Neither does it say that Cornelius and those with him prophesied (Acts 10:46).

So, prophesying upon one being baptized with the Holy Spirit may or may not happen, but when looked at honestly, the evidence is clear that all do speak with other tongues (Acts 2:4; 10:46; 19:6).

(7) "AND ALL THE MEN WERE ABOUT TWELVE."

The account is:

1. It seems that no women were involved at this particular time. As well, Luke said, *"About twelve,"* meaning it could have been 11, or 13 for that matter.

2. The important thing is that they had the receiving of the Holy Spirit explained to them, and that all of them believed and all were filled. Wouldn't it be wonderful if all believers presently yielded to the Word of God in like manner?

3. When one considers how readily these men believed and received, one is made to realize how sinful and wicked it is for modern believers to be faced with such an abundance of information respecting the Holy Spirit, and then continue to believe error and reject that which is so clear and plain! It is a sin God cannot overlook. As well, to reject this, as important as it is, even as the Scripture plainly declares, can only lead to severe spiritual anemia and even the loss of one's way.

(8) "AND HE WENT INTO THE SYNAGOGUE, AND SPOKE BOLDLY FOR THE SPACE OF THREE MONTHS, DISPUTING AND PERSUADING THE THINGS CONCERNING THE KINGDOM OF GOD."

The direction is:

1. If the believer does not base everything on the Cross and in the capacity of the Cross, and we mean everything, thus denying a proper foundation, all else believed will be somewhat skewed as well!

2. The total plan of redemption demanded not only death by Crucifixion but, as well, a perfect sacrifice, which no human being, other than Christ, could fulfill.

THE SYNAGOGUE

The phrase, *"And he went into the synagogue, and spoke boldly for the space of three months,"* presents Paul picking up where he had left off approximately one year before.

NOTES

As well, this tells us that whatever foothold had been made respecting a church in Ephesus was still tied to the synagogue. In other words, it seems that the dispute up to now regarding Jesus as the Messiah had not been brought to a head as of yet, as it shortly would, with all continuing to worship in the synagogue.

It is not known at the moment if Priscilla and Aquila were still in Ephesus. However, whatever time they had been there, or if still there, it seems that they had not pressed the issue very strongly as Paul always did. Maybe they did not feel led of the Lord to push quite so hard respecting Jesus as the Fulfillment of all the Law, waiting for Paul to arrive, which he now had.

Due to the word *"brethren"* used in Acts 18:27, we know that some people had accepted Christ.

Irrespective of what had happened during this past approximately 12 months, Paul had now returned and a mighty church would be established, but with the usual opposition, etc.

So, for three months, Paul proclaimed mightily in the synagogue the truth of Christ. This was probably only on Sabbath days.

"Disputing and persuading the things concerning the Kingdom of God," presents a compendium description of Christian doctrine.

Horton said, *"He would have brought reasonable proofs from the Old Testament Scriptures to show that the Kingdom (rule, authority) of God is revealed in Jesus, Who is now ascended to the Right Hand of the Father, seated at the Father's Throne (Acts 2:30-33)."*

THE KINGDOM OF GOD

Exactly what was Paul speaking of when he referred to the *"Kingdom of God"*?

If one will notice in the New Testament, two terms are used, *"The Kingdom of Heaven"* and *"The Kingdom of God."*

Is there a difference in these two designations?

Yes, there is a difference, although they are at times used interchangeably.

NOTES

"The Kingdom of God": the Kingdom of God consists of everything, for God is the Creator of all. That speaks of heaven and Earth, as well as all the planetary bodies. It speaks of all of humanity, all the angels, even including Satan and demon spirits, etc.

In the Kingdom of God, most of humanity is in rebellion against God, as well as one-third of the angels. Of course, the fallen angels would include Satan, all demon spirits, etc.

There will come a day that this rebellion will be put down, and once again, God will be *"All in All"* (I Cor. 15:24-28).

THE KINGDOM OF HEAVEN

"The Kingdom of Heaven": the Kingdom of Heaven is a lesser term than the Kingdom of God. It is the earthly sphere of the universal Kingdom of God, and in this respect, the two terms have almost all things in common.

The Kingdom of Heaven is not now the literal reign of heaven over the Earth but is presently in the sphere of profession. It covers only the part of humanity called *"Christendom."* At the present, it takes in both good and bad, or anyone who professes to be a child of the future Kingdom (Mat., Chpt. 13).

However, in the next dispensation, the Millennium, the Kingdom of Heaven will cease to be a mere sphere of profession and will become the real, literal Kingdom of the Son of Man, which was rejected by the Jews at the beginning of this dispensation of grace, but who will then accept Him.

Now, the Kingdom of Heaven is only in the hearts and lives of believers, but then, at the Second Coming of Christ, it will be literal as well!

FUTURE HAPPENINGS

Then Jesus will rule with a rod of iron to put all enemies under His Feet, whether they profess to be real sons of the Kingdom or not.

As stated, the Kingdom of Heaven will then be brought down to Earth (the Millennium) because Jesus will be ruling personally on Earth. To be frank, Jesus is the Kingdom. In other words, you cannot have the Kingdom of Heaven without having Jesus.

At the end of the Kingdom Age, Satan will be loosed out of the bottomless pit. Then he will attempt once again to raise an insurrection against Christ and the saints but will be put down in short order. At that time, Satan and all fallen angels, etc., will then be put in the Lake of Fire, where they will remain forever and forever (Rev. 20:7-15).

Then, according to Revelation, Chapters 21 and 22, the Lord will transfer His Headquarters from heaven to Earth, with the New Jerusalem being brought down to this planet, and then the Kingdom of God and the Kingdom of Heaven will be one and the same, with no more rebellion anywhere in God's Creation.

THE GOSPEL OF THE KINGDOM

The New Testament tells us that Jesus came preaching the Gospel of the Kingdom.

What was His Good News?

Was that early Word of the Kingdom only for Israel, or does it have meaning for us today?

The many references in the Gospels to the Kingdom of Heaven and to the Kingdom of God make one thing clear: Jesus shares significant truth with us when He speaks of the Kingdom, and due to this, we realize that, in a sense, the *"Kingdom"* is what it is all about!

THE KINGDOM IN THE OLD TESTAMENT

In modern thought, a kingdom is a specific geographical area with national identity. In the Old Testament, however, *"kingdom"* is best expressed by the idea of reign or sovereignty. One's kingdom is the people or things over which he or she has authority or control.

In the Old Testament, *"kingdom"* is most often used in the secular sense to indicate the sphere of authority of human rulers. However, the Bible does speak of God's Kingdom in two significant ways:

GOD'S KINGDOM

First, the entire universe (or rather universes) is God's Kingdom, for He exercises sovereign rule over all things, due to Him being Creator of all things.

Psalm 103:19 affirms, *"The LORD has established His Throne in heaven, and His Kingdom rules over all."*

Similarly: *"They will tell of the glory of Your Kingdom and speak of Your might, so that all men may know of Your mighty acts and the glorious splendor of Your Kingdom. Your Kingdom is an everlasting Kingdom, and Your dominion endures through all generations"* (Ps. 145:11-13).

The same theme is developed in Nebuchadnezzar's praise after he recovered from a madness given as divine judgment: *"How great are His* (God's) *signs, how mighty His wonders! His Kingdom is an Eternal Kingdom; His Dominion endures from generation to generation"* (Dan. 4:3).

The overarching sovereignty of God may not always be expressed in mighty acts. It also operates in quiet providence as history marches toward God's intended End, but all is God's Kingdom, and He is the ultimate Ruler of all (II Chron. 13:8; Dan. 4:17; 5:21; 6:26-27).

THE FORWARD LOOK TO THE KINGDOM

The Old Testament looks forward to a future expression of God's now-disguised Sovereignty. Then the Kingdom will have a visible, earthly form.

Daniel speaks of a time when *"the God of heaven will set up a Kingdom that will never be destroyed, nor will it be left to another people. It will crush all other Kingdoms and bring them to an end, but it will itself endure forever"* (Dan. 2:44).

Essentially, the same vision is repeated in Daniel, Chapter 7, and the establishment of God's visible Kingdom is again foretold. In fact, Old Testament prophecy uniformly and consistently pictures a time when Earth will be ruled by the Messiah, when *"the Kingdom will be the LORD'S"* (Obad., Vs. 21).

In the Old Testament, therefore, God is seen as the present, though often unacknowledged, Ruler of the universe. The universe and everything in it constitute His Kingdom, for He exercises sovereign control over all beings.

At the same time, the Old Testament anticipates a day when God will establish a visible Kingdom on Earth and speaks often through the prophets of that coming time. In that day, His Sovereignty will be recognized, and His Authority will be acknowledged by all.

THE KINGDOM IN THE NEW TESTAMENT

The import and fuller meaning of *"kingdom"* in the New Testament is derived from Old Testament thought, rather than from Greek culture, which then prevailed in New Testament times.

A kingdom is a realm in which a king exerts control and authority. The *"Kingdom of Heaven,"* rather than being a place, is the realm in which God is in control.

The Old Testament draws attention to two aspects of God's Kingdom. As King of the created universe, God is always at work, actively shaping history's flow according to His Will. This expression of the Kingdom of God is usually hidden. Only at times, as at the Exodus, has God visibly broken into time and space to set His unmistakable imprint on events.

However, the Old Testament looks forward to a time when God's Messiah will step boldly into history. Then, with raw power, He will act to establish God's open Rule over the entire Earth.

Then Israel's enemies will be shattered, the Davidic successor established on the throne in Jerusalem, and God will enforce peace on all people.

JESUS AND THE KINGDOM

In Jesus' Day, Israel lay under Roman rule. Rome was only the latest in a centuries-long series of pagan overlords because of Israel's departure from the Word of God. Consequently, the Lord took the scepter of world power out of the hands of the faltering kings of Judah and placed it into the hands of the gentiles, where it has remained ever since.

Understandably, Israel longed for the Kingdom the prophets graphically foretold. No wonder Jesus was looked to at first as the One Who would establish the prophesied Kingdom. Jesus' own Disciples, even late

NOTES

in His Ministry and even after His Resurrection, expected Him to establish the visible Kingdom soon (Mat. 20:21-23; Acts 1:6-7).

So, when Jesus came, at first preaching the *"Gospel of the Kingdom,"* it was natural that He was understood and, at the same time, not understood!

His listeners' perceptions were shaped by their vision of the Kingdom to come. They could not grasp the fact that Jesus actually spoke, not of one of the two Old Testament forms of the Kingdom, but of another expression of God's Rule, yet another way in which God would act in human affairs.

In reading the New Testament, it is important to remember the basic meaning of *"kingdom."* It refers to the realm in which a ruler acts to carry out his will. If we operate from this basic definition, Scripture will break down our stereotypes, as well, and reveal an exciting aspect of the Kingdom of Heaven that Christians too often miss.

THE GOOD NEWS OF THE KINGDOM

When it was time for Jesus to begin His public Ministry, John the Baptist began to preach, *"Repent, for the Kingdom of Heaven is at hand"* (Mat. 3:2). God was about to break into history and to act in a bold, fresh way. This message, which was also the theme of Jesus' early Ministry (Mat. 4:17; Mk. 1:15), is *"the good news of the Kingdom"* (Mat. 4:23).

Jesus' Message was stronger than that of John. In a sense, John said the Kingdom was shortly coming, while Jesus announced that it had arrived!

Confronting men who accused Him of doing His Miracles by Satan's power, Jesus said, *"If I drive out demons by the Spirit of God, then the Kingdom of God has come upon you"* (Mat. 12:28; Lk. 11:20).

In fact, most of Jesus' Miracles belonged to this time period, the time of His preaching the Gospel of the Kingdom. The King had come and had demonstrated His Power to act, revealing His Authority over every natural and supernatural power.

In the New Testament, the Kingdom and Jesus are inseparable, even as the concept of kingdom is meaningless apart from the person of the king.

NOTES

THE KINGDOM MUST FOCUS ON THE PERSON OF JESUS

In a significant sense then, any announcement of the Gospel of the Kingdom must focus on the Person of Jesus, promising that He is, or soon will be, present and able to act in all His sovereign Power.

There seems to have been two periods of time when this particular message was presented:

1. The first is seen in Jesus' own historic Announcement of His Presence when, in effect, He offered the Kingdom to Israel at that time.

In other words, Israel was called on to acknowledge the heavenly King and thus, by faith, step into that realm in which He would freely exercise His Power for them (Mat. 3:2; 4:17, 23; 9:35; 10:7; Mk. 1:15; Lk. 4:43; 8:1; 9:2, 11, 60; 10:9, 11).

Jesus summed up this era by saying, *"The Law and the prophets were proclaimed until John. Since that time, the good news of the Kingdom of God is being preached"* (Lk. 16:16).

Of course, it is a moot point, but had Israel then accepted Him, with the understanding that they would have to accept Him in the manner that was correct and right, the Kingdom of Heaven would then have come to the Earth. However, Jesus was denied.

Israel possibly would have accepted Him, but it had to be on their terms, which, of course, Jesus could not accept. Were that the case, it would have been their kingdom instead of God's Kingdom.

It is all conjecture, but had that been, Israel would have been a far worse tyrant than ever dared Rome. I speak of religious rule and ruin!

THE ENDTIME

Of course, they did not accept, even as God through foreknowledge knew they would not accept. As a result, their refusal of their Messiah subjected the world to further war, bloodshed, hate, sin, and iniquity. Because of His Kingdom being rejected, the Earth has been soaked with blood enumerable times, which will not cease until the Prince of Peace actually does come and

NOTES

institute His Kingdom, which He shall! (Rev., Chpt. 19).

2. The second time that Jesus spoke of the Kingdom pertained to His Second Coming. It is outlined in Matthew, Chapter 24.

This chapter records Jesus' Answer to His Disciples' questions about history's end. Jesus reviewed Old Testament prophecy and said of that future time: *"This Gospel of the Kingdom shall be preached to the whole world as a witness to all nations, and then shall the end come"* (Mat. 24:14).

So, in essence, He was saying that despite the fact that Israel rejected her King and, therefore, the Kingdom, still, the Gospel of the Kingdom will be preached just the same, and to the entirety of the world, which it has!

As well, when this happens, as, in effect, it already has and continues to do so, that within itself serves as an announcement to all that Jesus is again about to appear on Earth.

Incidentally, this *"Gospel of the Kingdom"* is to be preached to *"all nations,"* and not necessarily all people.

WHAT IS THIS GOSPEL OF THE KINGDOM?

This Gospel of the Kingdom, which, in essence, means the Gospel of the King, the Lord Jesus Christ, is expressed fully in the Book of Acts and the Epistles.

It is the good news that Jesus saves and that His Salvation is by faith and according to grace (Eph. 2:8-9).

As well, the Gospel of the Kingdom is that since the Day of Pentecost, believers can now be baptized with the Holy Spirit, which is a wonder of wonders. This could only come about after Jesus satisfied the sin debt at Calvary, therefore, removing Satan's claim on the human family. Now, the sinner can be made clean and pure by the precious Blood of Jesus, with all sins not only being covered but, in essence, being taken away (Jn. 1:29; Acts 2:1-21).

The Gospel of the Kingdom is also power given to believers through the Person, office, and agency of the Holy Spirit in the use of the name of Jesus to heal the sick and cast out demons (Mk. 16:16-18).

As well, the Gospel of the Kingdom is the urgent, consistent, and powerful presentation that the King is soon to come, when the Kingdom then will not only be in the hearts and lives of believers, but will cover the world in every aspect. This will include the political, economic, physical, material, and above all, spiritual worlds. Jesus will then reign personally from Jerusalem.

That is what the Prophet Malachi was saying when he uttered the words, *"But unto you who fear My Name shall the Sun of Righteousness arise with healing in His Wings* (the healing rays or beams which will extend from Christ to heal all men on Earth)*"* (Mal. 4:2).

THE PRESENT KINGDOM

While Jesus was on Earth, He taught much about an expression of the Divine Kingdom that was unrecognized in the Old Testament.

When it was clear that Israel would not accept Christ as Messiah/King, Jesus began to speak of the Kingdom in parables, and He began to speak of His Death. When asked why He used parables, He told the disciples that *"the knowledge of the secrets of the Kingdom of Heaven has been given to you, but not to them* (religious leaders of Israel)*"* (Mat. 13:11).

Matthew points out that Jesus' Use of parables fulfilled the Old Testament: *"I will open My Mouth in parables, I will utter things hidden since the creation of the world"* (Mat. 13:35; Mk. 4:10-13).

It is best to take this *"secret"* as a previously unrevealed expression of the Divine Kingdom—a way in which God acts in man's world that is not known from the Old Testament.

The New Testament has much to say about this form of the Kingdom, for this is the Kingdom in which you and I are called to live today.

THE PRESENT KINGDOM IN THE EPISTLES

Most of what the Epistles have to say about the Christian life does not mention the Kingdom. Yet, it is clear that believers have been rescued by the Father from the domain of darkness and have been brought *"into the Kingdom of the Son He loves"* (Col. 1:13).

In Hebrews 12:28, Paul uses the Kingdom in a present tense, *"We are receiving a Kingdom that cannot be shaken."*

A number of passages speak of inheriting the Kingdom (I Cor. 6:9-10; 15:50; Gal. 5:21; Eph. 5:5; James 2:5).

With the possible exception of James 2:5, the matter of inheritance is viewed in the context of Roman law. In that law, at birth, a child became an heir and had an established right to the possessions controlled by his father.

Clearly, the New Testament presents another Kingdom in addition to:

- The universal rule of God through providence.
- The yet-future Kingdom of prophecy (Rom. 14:17; I Cor. 4:20; Col. 1:12-13; 4:11; I Thess. 2:12; II Thess. 1:5; Rev. 1:6; 5:10).

Still, the Epistles say less than the Gospels do about this other Kingdom, possibly because it was necessary for Jesus to speak in Kingdom terms before the language of resurrection could be established by His Death and coming to life again.

All of this speaks of the Kingdom of God, which now rules in the hearts and lives of believers, and is a present established fact. However, once again, we emphasize that this which we now have in our hearts is preparing us for the day when the Kingdom will rule in every aspect on this Earth, and not just in the hearts of believers.

KINGDOM LIFESTYLE IN THE GOSPELS

A number of extended passages in the Gospels explore life in Jesus' present Kingdom. Using Matthew's Gospel as a framework, we see these major teaching passages.

Matthew, Chapters 5 through 7: the Sermon on the Mount has been interpreted in a number of ways.

- Is it a salvation message?
- Was it given to show Christians how they ought to live?
- Is it a picture of life in Jesus' future and coming Kingdom?
- Is it a combination of the above?

In view of the nature of the Kingdom, it seems best to understand this sermon as Jesus' Statement of how people of every age live when they abandon themselves to God's Will. In other words, while the Sermon on the Mount is definitely a picture of Jesus' future and coming Kingdom, it is also a picture of His present Kingdom within our hearts and lives.

Matthew 5:3-12: the Beatitudes describe the values of a person living a Kingdom lifestyle. Jesus then gave a series of illustrations, showing how inner values find expression in lifestyle (Mat. 5:17-42).

As King, Jesus acts to transform the character of His Subjects.

Jesus in the present Kingdom is working in our inner selves to change our outward behavior. Jesus went on to show how we can experience this transforming power. We focus on our *"in secret"* relationship with the Lord, not on visible piety, which He condemns, in other words, merely an outward show (Mat. 6:1-18).

We give priority to seeking God's Kingdom and Righteousness, and we trust our Father to supply our material needs (Mat. 6:19-33).

Matthew 7:1-14: we relate to other Kingdom citizens as brothers and sisters and reject every claim of a right to judge or control them. Instead of relying on human leaders, we rely on the simple words of Jesus and commit ourselves to obey them (Mat. 7:15-27).

Matthew, Chapter 13: Jesus explained in parables how the present form of the Kingdom compares with and yet differs from the expectant, prophetic vision of God's direct Rule on Earth.

Matthew, Chapters 18 through 20: Jesus explained how one becomes great in God's present Kingdom.

THE CROSS

What Jesus is portraying in these chapters, regarding Matthew, is Kingdom lifestyle. However, it cannot be properly approached in one's heart and life until the Cross of Christ becomes a fact. The Cross alone deals with the problems of mankind and makes it possible for the believer to be what he ought to be in Christ. Without the Cross of Christ, there cannot be victory in one's life. One can look at these statements made by Christ with a longing in his heart

NOTES

but never realize them outside of the Cross. Of course, when Jesus uttered these words, the Cross was yet future. So, the truth is, believers can now live the Kingdom life within their own hearts. Even though we have not yet come to the place to where this world presents itself as the Kingdom of Heaven, that will come shortly. However, in spirit, due to the Cross and the Holy Spirit within our hearts and lives carrying out that which must be done, the Kingdom life is now possible for believers, but only in spirit.

Any believer who thinks he can live this life as it ought to be lived, take to himself the great blessings of God as they ought to be taken, and walk this walk as he should walk this walk, without his faith exclusively in Christ and the Cross, is foolish indeed! In other words, if one thinks he can live the Kingdom life now as much as possible but without the understanding of the Cross, he is sadly mistaken. It is the Cross of Christ that gives the Holy Spirit latitude to work within one's life. In fact, everything hinges on the Cross. The blessings of God are abundant and are meant for us to have. We can have that for which Jesus paid such a price, but only if we do so God's Way. Paul gave us that way, and it is the Cross of Christ. The Cross must be the object of our faith, and I am not speaking of the wooden beam on which Jesus died, but rather what He there did. Faith properly placed, and we speak of Christ and the Cross, then gives the Holy Spirit the latitude to work mightily within our hearts and lives, bringing about this Kingdom life.

THE LORD'S PRAYER

For instance, we read in the Lord's Prayer: *"Your Kingdom come. Your Will be done on Earth as it is in heaven"* (Mat. 6:10).

In context, this is no prayer for the end of time, but rather that we may pray for His Kingdom to come as quickly as possible. However, until it comes, it is the believer's request that God will give us the ability to do His Will now, here on this present Earth, even as it is done in heaven, which can only be done, as stated, by the power of the Cross (I Cor. 1:18).

The kingdom is the realm in which the king acts with sovereign power. In Christ, you and I can experience that Kingdom here and now within our hearts and lives. We can know God's Power at work in our own lives as we adopt the lifestyle of the Kingdom over which our Saviour rules. However, it can be done only by the means of the Cross of Christ.

THE BIBLICAL BASIS FOR THE PRESENT KINGDOM

It is clear that God's sovereign touch rules the universe now and always. So, the present Kingdom of Jesus does not supersede or replace providence. Yet, in speaking of the still-future Kingdom over which Jesus will rule visibly, Scripture introduces a unique expression of the Divine Kingdom.

God's providential Supervision of the universe usually leaves Him hidden. In the future, however, His Rule on Earth will be unmistakable and visible, and, of course, we are speaking of the Second Coming.

The New Testament's introduction of a Kingdom currently ruled by Jesus presents another unique expression of the Divine Kingdom: a mode in which God has chosen to act and through which His Control will be expressed. This is to be done within our lives presently, in other words, with us presently living the Kingdom life. However, as we have previously stated, this can only be done by and through the means of the Cross of Christ.

THE KINGDOM AND THE NEW BIRTH

The theological basis for Jesus' Action in the present form of His Kingdom is laid in the new birth. *"No one can see the Kingdom of God until he is born-again"* and *"No one can enter the Kingdom of God unless he is born of water and the Spirit"* (Jn. 3:3, 5).

The new birth gives entrance into the Kingdom—the realm in which Jesus' sovereign Power is translated into action on behalf of His People. This is the reason for the stress as expressed by Jesus on being born-again.

When a person is born-again, Jesus enters his or her life, and there He takes up permanent residence. Now and for all time, Jesus is present in His People—in each believer and in the corporate Body of Christ.

In a mystical but real way, Jesus is present on Earth in us, hence, His Kingdom within our hearts.

He is the Key to release of the power needed to transform us and to shape the events that affect our lives according to His Will.

The Kingdom is here now because Jesus is here now, at least in this context relative to our hearts and lives. Because Jesus is here in that capacity, the possibility of a new kind of life is laid open before us. It is the Kingdom life.

THE COMING KINGDOM

The New Testament never rejects the Old Testament's portrait of the future. Exactly as the Old Testament proclaims, the Kingdom of Heaven on Earth will portray Jesus ruling over it in Person, which will take place, as stated, at His Second Coming. It will be, and is, a literal Kingdom with a literal King, and that literal King, of course, is Jesus. In fact, He will be King of kings and Lord of lords of the entirety of the Earth.

Even though the New Testament does not say very much about this, for the simple reason that the Old Testament is replete with these prophecies, Jesus Himself confirms the Old Testament vision of history's end (Mat. 8:11-12; 16:28; 20:21; 25:1, 34; 26:29; Mk. 11:10; 14:25; 15:43; Lk. 13:28-29; 14:15; 17:20; 19:11; 21:31; 23:43, 51; Acts 1:6-7).

In other words, all of the promises by the prophets in the Old Testament that concerned the restoration of Israel will come about exactly as foretold by the prophets. This includes the promise of Israel finally taking her place on the Earth as God originally intended as the priestly nation of all the Earth.

As well, the glorified saints of God will help Christ rule and reign in this glorious and wonderful Kingdom. This will include every single person who has ever been saved from the very beginning to the Second Coming!

IN SUMMARY

When we read the word *"kingdom"* in the

NOTES

Bible, we must not import modern notions of a geographical area. The word simply indicates a realm in which a king exercises his power to act and control.

The Old Testament knows two different forms of God's sovereign Rule or Kingdom:

1. There is a universal Kingdom. God controls all events in the universe but does so nearly always through providence, so that His Rule is somewhat hidden.

2. There is to be a visible earthly Kingdom, which is yet to come. In the future, Jesus will return to Earth to rule in Person over the whole world, which will then not be providential, but rather very visible. In other words, as stated, a very real and literal Kingdom, covering every strata of society, be it spiritual, domestic, material, physical, or economic, and in entirety.

THE PROPHETIC KINGDOM

The New Testament adds another previously unknown form of the Divine Kingdom. This form, like that of the prophetic kingdom, as evidenced in the Old Testament, is intimately linked with Jesus, for He is its King. When Jesus was on Earth, this Kingdom existed here. However, He did not take up earthly political power at that time (Jn. 18:36), although His Miracles He performed showed His Authority over every competing power.

Sadly and regrettably, Jesus the King was rejected and then crucified. His enemies, which, in effect, were His own People, struggled to force His Kingdom out of history.

However, Jesus' Death was not the end. During His Days on Earth, Jesus explained what life under His Rule (in His Kingdom) would be like.

It is best to take most Gospel descriptions of the Kingdom of Heaven and the Kingdom of God as explanations of life in Jesus' present Kingdom. Here we are given powerful insights into how we can live today as Jesus' Subjects and experience His Power.

THE KINGDOM OF GOD

Because the new birth brings us into union with Jesus and brings Jesus in a unique way into our experience here on Earth, we live in a day in which the King is

NOTES

present in our hearts, though, in some fashion, still disguised. However, because He is present, the unmatched power of God can find supernatural expression in and through our lives, consequently, changing them into the image of the heavenly.

And yet, we believers, enjoying this privilege of the Kingdom of God within our hearts, at the same time, causes us to long for this Kingdom to be totally over the entirety of the Earth, knowing that it, or rather *"He,"* is the only Solution to the problems that plague this Earth and all its inhabitants.

That is the reason we pray, *"Your Will be done on Earth as it is in heaven,"* respecting not only our personal lives, for which we surely do pray, but, as well, for the entirety of the world and all of mankind.

In fact, believers are the only people on Earth, who know what this coming Kingdom will be like, because we know what it has done in our own hearts and lives!

So, this is somewhat of that which Paul was explaining in the synagogue in Ephesus when he was *"disputing and persuading the things concerning the Kingdom of God."*

(9) "BUT WHEN DIVERS WERE HARDENED, AND BELIEVED NOT, BUT SPOKE EVIL OF THAT WAY BEFORE THE MULTITUDE, HE DEPARTED FROM THEM, AND SEPARATED THE DISCIPLES, DISPUTING DAILY IN THE SCHOOL OF ONE TYRANNUS."

The diagram is:

1. The grace of God is the goodness of God freely given to undeserving saints.

2. The grace of God always functions through, by, of, and within the Cross of Christ, i.e., *"the Finished Work of Christ on the Cross."*

UNBELIEF

The phrase, *"But when divers were hardened, and believed not,"* could have been translated, *"Divers* (many of all kinds) *believed not, and were hardened!"*

It was the act of refusing to believe, which occasioned the hardened heart.

Why is it that some believe and some do not?

Many, not understanding this, claim that predestination is the answer to that question. However, even though predestination is a viable Bible doctrine, providing it is understood correctly, it has nothing to do with one's acceptance or rejection of Jesus Christ.

The only answer that one can give is the free moral agency of man. In other words, man has a free will, created that way by God. Even though God deals with people, with Satan doing so, as well, still, it is the individual who has the power of choice and ultimately chooses. The Scripture plainly says, *"And whosoever will, let him take the water of life freely"* (Rev. 22:17). The spirit of that Text runs through the entirety of the Bible, all the way from Genesis through the Book of Revelation.

The reason that one person chooses one way, and another the other, has to do with many factors. Self-will greatly enters into people's decisions, as well as pride, etc.

WHY DO SOME REJECT AND OTHERS ACCEPT?

In truth, all begin on the same level and the same playing field, so to speak! The Psalmist said, concerning the manner in which God created men, *"He fashions their hearts alike"* (Ps. 33:15). In other words, God does not create some men with a heart of rebellion and others the opposite. All begin alike, at least respecting free choice. Of course, as we have already stated, a person's choice is affected by many things as life progresses, whether good or bad.

The word *"fashions"* in the Hebrew is *"yatsar"* and means *"to mold into a form,"* and in the case of men's hearts, all forms are alike at the beginning.

The word *"hardened"* in the Greek text is *"skleruno"* and means *"to render stubborn."* However, the stubbornness, as mentioned here, is not in the hearts of people at birth but becomes that way, as stated, because of unbelief.

That is the reason some people can sit in church with the power and presence of God prevalent in the service, with scores of others being greatly moved, and them moved not at all! Their hearts are hardened, and, therefore, the door is closed to the Spirit of God. It is a terrible state in which to be.

The word *"believed not"* in the Greek text is *"apeitheo"* and means *"to disbelieve willfully and perversely."* In other words, the individual refuses to believe, despite the fact of a mountain of evidence to the contrary. It is a conscious, deliberate decision which, in effect, says, *"It does not matter what the Bible says or what type of proof you place before me, I will not believe!"*

In a sense, as it relates to God and His Creation, every person who has died lost falls into this category.

While it is true that some people are given much greater opportunity than others, still, unbelief plays a great part in all that is done, at least that which is opposite of God.

THAT WAY

Horton says, *"'But spoke evil of that Way before the multitude,' means they spoke against what Paul was teaching to everyone who would hear, implying that they spread their insults and vile comments through the whole community at Ephesus."*

The words *"that Way"* were used quite often during the times of the early church as a manner to describe Christianity (Acts 9:2; 18:25-26; 19:23; 22:4; 24:14, 22).

The phrase includes the whole of Christian teaching and comprehends all that Christianity and the Gospel mean. It is truly the one and only way of salvation.

The phrase, *"He departed from them, and separated the disciples,"* proclaims the break with the synagogue. It was something which had to come sooner or later!

The word *"departed"* implies a withdrawal and separation from fellowship with these members of the synagogue who were opposed to Christ.

Even though the church had actually begun a little over one year earlier when Paul preached his first message in the synagogue, it did not come into full flower, so to speak, until now!

CHRISTIAN SEPARATION

Separation, as it refers to believers, never means isolation! If the route of isolation is taken, as it has been by many in the past, there is no way for the light of the Gospel to shine to darkened hearts. So, separation does not imply isolation of the Christian from his or her culture and society or from the lost neighbor, providing the believer does not have to compromise the Word of God.

NOTES

As Jesus' Representatives in the world, we are called to live within our society and in the company of sinful people.

In its most significant sense, our separation is to God. We are to be different from those around us, not withdrawn from them. The distinction that God seeks to draw in and through our lives is simply that we are to walk as Jesus walked when He was here (I Jn. 2:6).

As Jesus sought and helped the lost, so will we. As Jesus suffered the accusations of those who criticized His Association with the sinners of His Day, so we may suffer the accusations of the religious among us when we reach out to draw others with and to God's Love. However, let us state it again, the Gospel must never be compromised.

SEPARATE LIFESTYLES

Paul said, *"Be not unequally yoked together with unbelievers: for what fellowship has righteousness with unrighteousness? and what communion has light with darkness?"* (II Cor. 6:14).

This means that a believer should not enter into marriage with an unbeliever. As well, the believer must be very careful about entering into business deals with unbelievers!

Actually, the entirety of the spirit of this world is opposed to that which is of God. Even though we as believers are in the world, we must never be of the world.

It is the same as a ship sailing on the ocean. As long as it is sailing on the water, it can be of great profit and benefit, but the moment the water gets into the ship, then the ship is no longer of any service. So, we as believers are in the world, with the world actually all around us; however, that is as far as it should go. The world must never be allowed within us. If so, it will have the same effect as water does in a ship.

This is one of the reasons it is so foolish for so-called Christian musicians and singers to think they can win the lost of this world by playing the music of the world.

Even an elementary believer should know better than that!

We do not win the drunk by drinking with him, the gambler by gambling with him, the addict by taking drugs with him, etc. We as believers are separate from these things.

We ought to love all people but not with the idea of joining in with their sin. That is ridiculous, to say the least!

To be frank, the more separate (not isolated), but yet, loving the believer actually is, the more the unsaved will be won to Christ. If one is firmly separate but beautifully loving, the light will shine all the brighter. However, whenever the believer adopts the ways of the world, the light is then clouded and ultimately extinguished.

SEPARATION FROM FALSE DOCTRINE

Paul said, *"Having a form of godliness, but denying the power thereof: From such turn away"* (II Tim. 3:5).

Back in the early 1980s, I felt distinctly led of the Lord to address myself to particular situations which were then rife in the Christian community.

As an example, I speak of the Catholic charismatic community, which was big in those days, with some so-called Pentecostal leaders encouraging these people to remain in the Catholic Church.

Unequivocally, the Lord spoke to my heart that I should tell them, and I speak of our telecast, which then covered a large part of the world, that these Catholics who had truly been born-again, with some even being baptized with the Holy Spirit, must leave the Catholic Church forthwith!

To be sure, my statements drew fire from many directions. One Pentecostal leader wrote me and stated, *"You have destroyed with one message what it has taken me years to build."* He was a strong advocate of saved Catholics remaining in that doctrine under the pretext that they could win other Catholics to the Lord, etc.

While I do not doubt that many of these people had truly been saved, with even some being baptized with the Holy Spirit, I do know that once this is done, the Holy Spirit will not allow them, or anyone else for that matter, to remain in gross false doctrine. To be sure, all Catholic doctrine, and I said all, is unscriptural!

NOTES

THE HOLY SPIRIT GUIDES INTO ALL TRUTH

The Holy Spirit leads into truth and not error (Jn. 16:13). That is actually His strong Forte! If allowed to have His Way, He will lead the believer, as should be obvious, in the opposite direction of false doctrine.

As well, there is no way that one can properly lead others to the Lord by practicing error and continuing to do so. As stated, the Holy Spirit, Whom we must have in order to do anything for God, cannot in any shape or form help or anoint anyone to lead people toward continued wrong direction.

Some may take the position that if the Lord leads them to leave such churches, they will do so, but not before! However, through His Word, the Lord has already told us what to do. We must turn away from that which is false and, thereby, error.

The truth is, if the person continues to remain in that which is wrong, thereby, ignoring the constant checks of the Holy Spirit, ultimately, the Holy Spirit will leave. He cannot abide in such, especially if the believer will not heed His warnings. If one puts a live chicken under a dead hen, ultimately, both will be dead!

WHAT WILL SEPARATION COST ME?

Now, that is the question!

In truth, it will cost one everything, and that is exactly what Jesus demands of His Followers. We are to forsake all in order to properly follow Him. There is no other way. Jesus plainly said, *"If any man will come after Me, let him deny himself, and take up his Cross, and follow Me."*

He then said, *"For whosoever will save his life shall lose it: and whosoever will lose his life for My Sake shall find it"* (Mat. 16:24-25; Mat., Chpt. 10; Lk. 9:23-24).

I have every confidence that when Paul knew there was no other choice but to leave the synagogue, his decision divided families and friends; however, there was absolutely no other choice then, as there is absolutely no other choice now! To stay in the synagogue, they would have to compromise

NOTES

their message, which the Holy Spirit could not tolerate.

I suspect, if the truth is known, that the pride factor enters into many of these decisions.

Because of family and friends, as well as other particulars, many desire to continue to say, *"I am Catholic"* or *"whatever!"* It is a reproach to say, *"I am Pentecostal,"* at least it once was! Regrettably, the Pentecostal message has been so compromised in many quarters that there remains little reproach anymore.

Even though it was Paul who was the instrument of this separation in Ephesus, still, it was and is the Holy Spirit Who is actually the Instigator of such!

The phrase, *"Disputing daily in the school of one Tyrannus,"* is thought to have been the lecture hall of a Greek philosopher.

This being the first time, at least that is recorded, that a church had a meeting place other than people's houses, etc., lends some credence to the thought, as proposed by some, that the decision favorable to Paul, made by the Roman governor Gallio at Corinth, guaranteed a modicum of freedom, at least for a particular period of time (Acts 18:12-16).

(10) "AND THIS CONTINUED BY THE SPACE OF TWO YEARS; SO THAT ALL THEY WHICH DWELT IN ASIA HEARD THE WORD OF THE LORD JESUS, BOTH JEWS AND GREEKS."

The form is:

1. The believer must place his or her faith exclusively in the Cross and leave his faith in the Cross.

2. The believer must understand, as well, that all things we receive from God come through what Jesus did for us on the Cross.

THE WORD OF THE LORD JESUS

The phrase, *"And this continued by the space of two years,"* probably referred to most every night and during the day at times as well! Actually, Paul spent a total of three years in Ephesus (Acts 20:31).

It seems that he also went from house to house at times, holding services (Acts 20:20).

The phrase, *"So that all they which dwelt in Asia heard the Word of the Lord Jesus, both Jews and Greeks,"* does not refer to every single person, as should be obvious, but rather to people from all walks of life and from all surrounding areas. There is some small indication that Philemon, a somewhat wealthy landowner from Colossae, came to the services in Ephesus and was saved.

As the Scripture plainly speaks of both Jews and Greeks (gentiles), it has long been obvious, even beginning graphically with Peter as he took the Gospel to Cornelius, the Roman centurion, that the Lord had opened the Gospel to all. But yet, most of the Jews continued to rebel against Christ, attempting to hold onto Judaism, which had now run its course simply because it had fulfilled all that God intended for it to do.

It was always God's intention, as we have previously said, that the Gospel go to the entirety of the world (Gen. 12:3). Actually, from the loins of Abraham, the Lord raised up these people for that particular purpose. The Gospel was not meant at all to go to Jews only, or that the nation of Israel was to be the only recipient of the Blessings of the Lord. It was ever God's intention that all would hear and all would know!

THE JEWS

However, Israel turned inward, thereby, becoming sectarian, holding themselves as better than anyone else. As a result of their self-righteousness, they denied the Gospel to gentiles, except under most limited circumstances, actually calling them *"dogs!"* Consequently, when Jesus came, born of the Virgin Mary, even though fulfilling all the prophecies to the letter, still, they rejected Him and even crucified Him.

Therefore, less than 20 years after this particular time of Paul in Ephesus, the Lord literally made it impossible for Judaism to continue, at least to any degree of the manner in which it had been.

In A.D. 70, Titus, the Roman general, completely destroyed Jerusalem and the Temple, making it impossible to offer sacrifices any longer, to keep the feast days, or anything pertaining to the Temple for that matter, which, in effect, was the core of Judaism.

However, in the early church, which, at

its very beginning, was made up totally of Jews, the Gospel of grace was not readily received. This was even after the Lord had wondrously used Peter, respecting Cornelius, without all the fanfare of Judaism.

There is no record that any of the original Twelve opposed Paul in any way respecting this issue, with Peter graphically siding with the apostle, as Acts, Chapter 15, portrays. As well, with Peter generally being the spokesman for the Twelve, it means they felt the same way also.

However, it seems that James, the Lord's Brother, somehow tried to mesh Judaism with grace, at least where Jews were concerned, which, of course, could not be done, and which caused Paul many difficulties.

THE CHURCH

Paul, even as we shall later see, bent over backwards to try to appease the situation without compromising the Gospel. I am sure that he feared, and every evidence points in that direction, that the church as a whole would split, with one section attempting to keep the Law and the other pointing exclusively to grace. I think it is obvious that Paul succeeded in shoving this thrust aside, but not without great price!

As we study the Book of Acts, it becomes quite obvious that Satan's greatest efforts are always from within and not without. Even though Rome at times gave Paul problems, it was those who professed to be believers who proved to be the greatest hindrance of all. To be sure, such has continued unchecked from that moment until now.

Actually, mighty Rome did not destroy the church, despite slaughtering multiple thousands in the Roman arenas for the sport and pleasure of the jaded mobs, but the early church gradually apostatized over a period of time as it compromised its message. In other words, it was greatly weakened, if not destroyed, from within! It gradually sank to the far lower level of a man-instituted organization that came to be called the *"Catholic Church,"* which continues unto this hour.

However, all through the Dark Ages, which was brought on by apostasy, the Lord always had a remnant who served Him, even though at times it meant their lives. Then in the 16th century, the Lord brought about the Reformation, as well, at great price, with many giving their lives for the cause of Christ. Nevertheless, it pushed toward the ultimate outpouring of the Holy Spirit at approximately the turn of the 20th century, beginning to fulfill the prophecy of Joel concerning the Latter Rain (Joel 2:23). However, apostasy is presently rife in the modern church and actually will intensify with the advent of the Antichrist.

NOTES

JESUS

Of this one can be sure, and as the Scripture plainly states, whenever people came to the church in Ephesus, or anywhere that Paul was preaching the Gospel, they heard *"the Word of the Lord Jesus."*

That speaks of His Birth, Life, Death, Resurrection, and Exaltation! In other words, Jesus saves, Jesus baptizes with the Holy Spirit, Jesus heals, Jesus is the Overcomer, and Jesus is coming again! This is the Gospel of Jesus Christ. In other words, Paul preached the Cross!

If Jesus is removed or side-tracked in any way, Christianity becomes just another philosophy, which is of no more use than the religions of the world, at least as far as saving souls is concerned. The message must ever be *"Jesus Christ and Him Crucified!"* (I Cor. 1:23).

(11) "AND GOD WROUGHT SPECIAL MIRACLES BY THE HANDS OF PAUL."

The status is:

1. The righteousness of any believer comes directly from God because of the believer's faith in Christ and what Christ did for us at the Cross.
2. Works, while important in their own right, do not earn the believer anything with God.
3. It is faith alone that accomplishes the task (Heb. 11:5-6).

SPECIAL MIRACLES

In Verses 10 and 11, we have the order laid down by the Holy Spirit respecting His Manner of operation.

As stated, *"The Word of the Lord Jesus,"* i.e., the preaching of the Gospel, came first.

Horton said, *"Then, the Lord did*

NOTES

extraordinary miracles and manifestations of Divine Power, by the hands of Paul. The Greek literally means the Lord made mighty miracles an everyday occurrence in Paul's ministry in Ephesus."

However, it was the *"Word of the Lord Jesus"* that Paul preached, which produced faith in the hearts of the people, making possible these *"miracles,"* etc. In other words, Paul preached that Jesus could not only save from sin but could heal, as well, even to the doing of mighty things which were impossible within themselves. To be sure, this attracted thousands of people from all over that part of Asia.

Is such ministry to continue unto this hour, or did it all stop with the original Twelve Apostles and Paul, as many teach?

MIRACLES TODAY?

We must use the Bible as our answer to this question, and any other question for that matter, that has to do with spiritual things.

There is absolutely nothing in the Word of God that lends any credence whatsoever to the erroneous teaching that miracles ceased with the apostles, etc. To be sure, the purveyors of this error, and gross error it is, attempt to pull one or two Scriptures out of context to prove their contention. However, in doing this, they are guilty of attempting to make the Word of God fit their particular beliefs, instead of allowing the Word of God to mold their beliefs, as it is intended to do.

Some are fond of quoting I Corinthians 13:8-11, which says, *"Charity never fails: But whether there be prophecies, they shall fail; whether there be tongues, they shall cease; whether there be knowledge, it shall vanish away.*

"For we know in part, and we prophesy in part.

"But when that which is perfect is come, then that which is in part shall be done away.

"When I was a child, I spoke as a child, I understood as a child, I thought as a child: But when I became a man, I put away childish things."

In their contentions, they claim that the gifts of the Spirit are not for us today, but only love.

They fail to understand, it seems, that Paul was telling us that whatever gifts from the Lord we may have, if we do not have love, all the others will be of no consequence. He was not demeaning the gifts or denying them but merely putting everything in its proper perspective.

They also claim that prophecies and tongues shall cease and, in fact, have already ceased, having done so when John the Beloved died, the last apostle of the original Twelve.

PERFECT

However, they never mention *"knowledge,"* which Paul also listed! Blessed consistency!

Paul in these passages was merely comparing this present life with that which is to come. It is that simple! A proper rendering of the associating Texts unequivocally prove this.

Many of these people contend, as well, that the passage, *"But when that which is perfect is come,"* refers to the completing of the Canon of Scripture, which was done by John the Beloved with the writing of the Book of Revelation. They contend that with all the Word of God now given to us, these things, such as miracles, gifts of the Spirit, etc., are no longer needed!

Once again, such manner of interpretation of Scripture is silly, to say the least!

With the word *"perfect,"* Paul was not referring to the Word of God or its completion by John, which would later take place, but rather the life to come.

A CHILD?

Others contend that the phrase, *"When I was a child,"* refers to immature Christians who need, in their childishness, such things as miracles, etc.

Once again, Paul was merely comparing this present life to what is to come, which is the same as comparing a child to an adult. Adulthood is so far advanced beyond childhood as to be on another plane entirely.

So, when all the saints are glorified, which will take place at the coming first Resurrection of Life, the advancement, as I think should be obvious, will be astronomical!

It is amazing the lengths people will go, especially in twisting Scripture, to attempt to prove their point.

The Bible says concerning miracles, etc., *"These signs shall follow them that believe; in My Name they shall cast out demons; and they shall speak with new Tongues;*

"They shall take up serpents (put away demon spirits)*; and if they drink any deadly thing, it shall not hurt them* (Divine protection by the Lord, in that Satan would kill every Child of God if he could, but thank the Lord he cannot)*; they shall lay hands on the sick, and they shall recover"* (Mk. 16:17-18).

Luke wrote, *"The former treatise have I made, O Theophilus, of all that Jesus began both to do and teach"* (Acts 1:1).

What Jesus *"began"* to do, believers are to continue!

GIFTS

Paul spoke of the gifts of the Spirit, which should be given to believers, as outlined in I Corinthians 12:8-10.

The idea that these *"gifts"* were to be given only until John finished the Book of Revelation, which took place at about the turn of the First Century, is silly indeed! No, they are meant for all Spirit-filled believers presently and include miracles, healings, etc.

Also, one need only read the words of Jesus Himself in Matthew 21:21-22; Mark 11:22-24; John 14:14; 15:7, to name just a few!

The truth is, people who presently deny the miracle-working power of God, along with the gifts of the Spirit, etc., in fact, have denied the Holy Spirit, for these things, as they are done in the name of Jesus, are a Work of the Spirit (Acts 1:8). This means that entire religious denominations have cut themselves off from most all things which God does, making their efforts no more than that which is man-concocted, man-instituted, man-led, and man-directed! Let me quickly say that all such efforts are of no consequence to God whatsoever!

Yes! We are still serving a God Who answers prayer and performs miracles, in fact, to a far greater degree than any of us realize.

THE WORD OF THE LORD

Sometime back, as I was writing commentary on the Gospel of Mark, the Lord dealt with me greatly in respect to the subject of *"miracles."*

He spoke to my heart that day, I believe, and said, *"I am performing miracles for My Children constantly, and to a degree that most have never imagined."*

He then said, *"All the miracles which I perform are not always obvious or observable."*

Then He concluded by saying, *"Every time I answer prayer for any of My Children, I must perform miracles in one way or the other in order to bring the situation to pass."*

When the Lord spoke these things to my heart, I then began to understand things in a different light. It is not that He performs possibly one or two miracles during our lifetimes, whatever that may be, but that He is constantly doing such. Just because we do not see them, it does not mean they have not happened.

In fact, if each people holding this book in their hands will stop and think of the times the Lord has brought things to pass in their lives, then they must understand that a miracle, or even a series of miracles, was brought about for this thing to be done, whatever it may have been. These were things which they knew to be from God, and which only He could have done. Satan sets about to stop our prayers from being answered, and he will use any tactic at his disposal. To overcome that, the Lord performs miracle after miracle, most of the time, in ways which we do not even see or know. Nevertheless, the miracles are performed!

As well, as these miracles were brought about by God, using the hands of Paul, this tells us that God uses human instrumentation.

As one studies the Bible, one finds that the Lord does very little without using a man or woman to carry out the task. God is the Author as we believers are the instruments.

Consequently, this plainly tells us that God does not use committees, boards, or church denominations. He certainly does use people on committees or boards and in religious denominations, but the emphasis is always on the person and never on the organization in general. There is no such

NOTES

NOTES

thing as a religious hierarchy in the Bible.

(12) "SO THAT FROM HIS BODY WERE BROUGHT UNTO THE SICK HANDKERCHIEFS OR APRONS, AND THE DISEASES DEPARTED FROM THEM, AND THE EVIL SPIRITS WENT OUT OF THEM."

The order is:

1. Believers cannot fast or pray their way to victory, as important as these twin attributes are.

2. Sin can be addressed only in one way, and that is the Cross of Christ.

3. When we place our faith exclusively in Christ and the Cross, then the Holy Spirit, Who is God, can do anything and will grandly and greatly help us.

HANDKERCHIEFS AND APRONS

The phrase, *"So that from his body were brought unto the sick handkerchiefs or aprons,"* tells us several things:

• These were items that had touched his skin, such as a sweat cloth which he used to wipe his face while working at his tent-making occupation, or types of aprons which are worn by carpenters, etc.

• There is no indication in the Text that he purposely sent these things out, although he definitely may have. It seems that people on their own simply picked up these items and took them to the diseased or demon-possessed. They evidently placed the cloth on those in need, with them receiving healing and/or deliverance.

Every evidence is that not only were many people being saved and baptized with the Holy Spirit, but, as well, the sick were being brought from many surrounding areas to this lecture hall where Paul was ministering. Then, for those who were too sick to come, or for whatever reason, these pieces of cloth were taken to them.

• One preacher likened such examples of faith as a *"point of contact,"* and rightly so! It is not that God needed handkerchiefs or such, or anything for that matter, in order to heal people; however, such things are needed by many and perhaps, at least in some way, by us all, referring to our faith.

That is at least one of the reasons we are told to anoint with oil when praying for the sick (James 5:14). It is not that the oil has any magic properties in it, for it does not, or that God needs such, for He does not. Even though the oil is a symbol, in a sense, of the Holy Spirit, as well, it is a point of contact, as well as is the laying on of hands, etc. Also, even though oil can be used and is scriptural, still, the Lord heals at times without such being applied.

A POINT OF CONTACT

As another example, whenever we hear of God doing some great thing somewhere else or for someone else, that serves as a point of contact for us to believe Him for the same thing for ourselves, etc. Whenever someone testifies of being healed, that also encourages faith, serving as a point of contact.

Anything that will help a person to believe, even as these handkerchiefs and aprons did, is sanctioned by the Lord, providing it does not go into superstition or merchandising.

By merchandising, I am referring to the practice of some who put a price tag on that which God does. As well, even the hint of such is wrong! Isaiah said, *"Ho, every one who thirsts, come to the waters, and he who has no money; come, buy, and eat; yes, come, buy wine and milk without money and without price"* (Isa. 55:1). (The word *"buy"* means it has been paid for by someone else, in this case, Jesus.)

The phrase, *"And the diseases departed from them, and the evil spirits went out of them,"* proclaims that when these items were placed on the physical bodies of these individuals, they were instantly healed and delivered.

To be sure, it was not these items that brought about healing, and neither was it Paul for that matter, who was just a channel through whom the Spirit of God flowed. It was God Who carried out the healings and deliverances but, as stated, working through human instrumentation.

This human instrumentation would have included not only Paul, but the ones who secured these pieces of cloth as well!

(13) "THEN CERTAIN OF THE VAGABOND JEWS, EXORCISTS, TOOK UPON THEM TO CALL OVER THEM WHICH HAD EVIL SPIRITS THE NAME OF THE

NOTES

LORD JESUS, SAYING, WE ADJURE YOU BY JESUS WHOM PAUL PREACHES."

The direction is:

1. The phrase, *"Then certain of the vagabond Jews, exorcists,"* speaks of individuals who practiced divination, who were not of God but rather of Satan.

"Exorcists" in the Greek text is *"exorkistes"* and means *"one that binds by an oath or spell."* In plain everyday English, it means that the person (exorcist) performs some type of incantation over the one who is supposedly demon-possessed, with the demon or demons supposedly going out, etc.

2. There are Catholics, who claim to be exorcists, and do such by holding up a cross before the possessed, or some such paraphernalia, plus reciting some incantation, etc.

None of this is of God and, accordingly, there are no true deliverances, even if they use the name of Jesus. It is as those vagabond Jews of Paul's day, who tried to use the name of Jesus but did not know Him as Lord and Saviour.

To be frank, most of the modern so-called exorcisms are extracted from Hollywood, therefore, having absolutely no scriptural veracity whatsoever!

Any believer who is Spirit-filled can use the name of Jesus to cast out demons (Mk. 16:17). They do not have to have any special gift to do so, or calling, etc.

"Took upon them to call over them which had evil spirits the Name of the Lord Jesus," presents these people who evidently visited the services where Paul was ministering and observed him praying for the sick and casting out demons. They evidently noted that he used *"the name of Jesus,"* which had a powerful effect, even to the setting of captives free, respecting the demon-possessed, etc.

However, they did not know or understand that the use of that Name within itself carried no special power. In other words, it could not be used as some type of magic incantation, etc. There had to be a personal relationship with Christ in order for the use of the Name to be effective, and that relationship, these people did not have.

3. The phrase, *"We adjure you by Jesus who Paul preaches,"* seems to be their own formula or incantation they had cooked up by observing Paul. Not only, as we shall see, was it a formula that God would not recognize, but, as well, He would not recognize the men!

(14) "AND THERE WERE SEVEN SONS OF ONE SCEVA, A JEW, AND CHIEF OF THE PRIESTS, WHICH DID SO."

The construction is:

1. The phrase, *"And there were seven sons of one Sceva, a Jew,"* probably represents a title more so than a name.

2. In the understanding of the Jewish rituals, it could have been a form of *"Sheba,"* which means *"oath."*

3. It is said that the title was used of those belonging to one of the high priestly families, especially if they belonged to or were associated in some way with the Sanhedrin. However, *"Sceva"* could also be used in other capacities of the Jewish order of worship respecting the Temple.

4. The phrase, *"And chief of the priests, which did so,"* implies that this man may have been a member of the Jewish council at Ephesus.

However, it is also believed that Sceva had taken this title of Jewish high priest in order to impress gentiles who knew little or nothing about God, and would hire out himself or members of his family to perform incantations, exorcisms, etc.

5. Due to God doing great things for the Jews in centuries past, and with this knowledge known somewhat by the gentiles, there was a mystique about these people, which would have impressed the gentiles. So, they evidently made a good living by playing upon the superstitions and fears of the heathen.

(15) "AND THE EVIL SPIRIT ANSWERED AND SAID, JESUS I KNOW, AND PAUL I KNOW; BUT WHO ARE YOU?"

The form is:

1. Someone has said that the *"doing of religion"* is the most powerful narcotic there is.

2. Please understand, it is the *"doing"* that makes one feel religious.

THE EXISTENCE OF EVIL SPIRITS

The phrase, *"And the evil spirit answered and said,"* points to a man who was demon-possessed, and some or all of these seven sons had been hired to exorcise this spirit.

If one is to notice, it is the evil spirit who actually answers, using the vocal chords of the man who it possessed.

There are only a few references in the Old Testament regarding evil spirits.

The first is found in Deuteronomy 32:17, which speaks of the rebellious generation of Israelites who died in the wilderness: They sacrificed to demons, which are not God—gods they had not known, gods that recently appeared, gods your fathers did not fear.

The second is found in II Chronicles 18:18-22, and speaks of an evil spirit in heaven, which volunteered to be *"a lying spirit in the mouth of all his* (Ahab's) *prophets."*

The Lord granted him permission to do that, which resulted in the death of Ahab.

Some may not understand the idea of demon spirits being in heaven; however, evil spirits and fallen angels, as well as Satan himself, regularly appear before the throne of God to give account of their activities. This is found in Job, Chapters 1 and 2, as well as II Chronicles, Chapter 18.

There will come a time when they will be allowed no more access, with Satan actually cast out, because of being near the end of this dispensation (Rev. 12:7-9).

Psalms 106:36-37 says, They worshipped their idols, which became a snare to them. They sacrificed their sons and their daughters to demons.

Both of these passages suggest that real demonic beings existed behind the gods and goddesses of the pagans. This is, in fact, something that Paul affirms in I Corinthians 10:20, saying that *"the sacrifices of pagans are offered to demons."*

While the Old Testament does not say very much about evil spirits, it does contain prohibitions against all spiritism (delving into the spirit world through witchcraft of any sort) and magic, which were linked with the demonic in every ancient culture (Deut. 18:9-12). There are other hints in such passages as I Samuel 28:13 and Isaiah 8:19.

The basic concentration of the Old Testament is instead on God, the Creator and Redeemer, Who is Sovereign over every power—natural and supernatural.

NOTES

EVIL SPIRITS RELATIVE TO THE GOSPELS

Although the Old Testament is relatively silent concerning evil spirits, the Gospels are full of references to demonic activity. This is because of several things:

Israel was extremely religious, but yet, a religion of their own making, having forsaken the God of Abraham, Isaac, and Jacob, even though they strongly professed such.

Whenever great religious activity is found, one will also find great demonic activity. The simple reason is that religion is Satan's greatest area of activity and the means through which he has destroyed most of humanity.

As well, a strong display of the power of God, which Jesus displayed the greatest of all, always exposes demon activity that may possibly be somewhat hidden otherwise.

Some have suggested that when Jesus walked the land of Israel, Satan's kingdom concentrated unusual forces in order to hinder Him. However, I seriously doubt that Satan would have attempted such, knowing the Power resident within Christ.

This we do know: the level of demonic activity was of far greater magnitude during Jesus' Day than ever before.

These references to demon spirits show them possessing and oppressing human beings (Mat. 8:16, 28, 33; 9:32; 12:22-28; Mk. 1:32; 5:16-18; Lk. 4:33-35; 8:27-29, 36; 9:42).

Such demonic influence was expressed in various sicknesses and even in madness. Consequently, the Gospels plainly picture demons as living beings with malignant powers. They are personal beings, not impersonal influences (Mat. 8:31).

Jesus demonstrated His total Mastery of demons by expelling them with His Word. He is the *"Stronger,"* being of His own Illustration, able to *"attack and overpower"* the demons even in their own realm (Lk. 11:21-22).

However fearsome demons may be, the person who walks with Jesus has nothing to fear from them.

DEMONS IN THE EPISTLES

Even though some demonic activity is

NOTES

reported in Acts and the Epistles, nevertheless, after Jesus returned to heaven, it was greatly lessened! Acts, Chapters 5, 8, and 19 mention evil spirits. The Epistles do not; however, the Epistles are not normally accounts of happenings, but rather teaching and instruction. In that capacity, some direction is given.

Romans 8:38 established a dichotomy between angels and demons. In I Corinthians 10:20-21, Paul warns that demonic beings are the spiritual realities behind the facades of idolatry.

In I Timothy 4:1, Paul suggests that demons distort truth and encourage the spread of twisted doctrines of their own. Aside from brief views of increased demonic activity at history's end, which is given in the Book of Revelation, this is approximately all that the New Testament has to say about demons!

A POINT TO CONSIDER!

Of particular note in the Epistles, there is comparative silence on the demonic in the fact that in many passages that deal with Christian life and ministry, none speak of demons. There are no guidelines for the casting out of these things, except the use of the name of Jesus (Mk. 16:17). There are no warnings against demon possession. There is no hint of terror or awe and no suggestion that we should fear or pay special attention to these unseen evil powers.

Why this silence?

This does not mean there is no demon activity at the present time or that it has not continued through the ages. However, what Jesus did at Calvary and the Resurrection has greatly diminished the power and control of evil spirits in this Earth, especially as they relate to believers.

When Jesus died on Calvary, the Scripture plainly tells us, and I quote directly from THE EXPOSITOR'S STUDY BIBLE:

"*And* having spoiled principalities and powers *(Satan and all of his henchmen were defeated at the Cross by Christ atoning for all sin; sin was the legal right Satan had to hold man in captivity. With all sin atoned, he has no more legal right to hold anyone in bondage)* **He** *(Christ)* **made a show of them openly** *(what Jesus did at the Cross was in the face of the whole Universe)*, **triumphing over them in it.** *(The triumph is complete and it was all done for us, meaning we can walk in power and perpetual victory due to the Cross)*" **(Col. 2:15).**

These *"principalities and powers"* constituted Satan himself, all demon spirits, and all fallen angels. This was and is the power of the Cross and the reason that demon activity is not nearly as prevalent now as it was before the Cross.

CHRIST AND THE CROSS

After the defeat of all powers of darkness at the Cross, this greatly lessened demon activity throughout the entirety of the world. Even though demon spirits continue to be active, nevertheless, their activity is not nearly with the power they evidenced before the Cross.

After the Cross and the exaltation of Christ, with Him seated at the Right Hand of the Father, He truly is the Head over all things for the church, which is His Body. He is *"far above all rule and authority, power and dominion"* (Eph. 1:21).

To be sure, in this exalted position, and due to Satan being totally defeated at Calvary and the Resurrection, the rule and authority once exercised greatly by these spirits of darkness have been greatly lessened.

Instead of dwelling on demon spirits, believers should dwell on Christ! We should understand that *"all power is given unto Me* (Jesus) *in heaven and in Earth"* (Mat. 28:18).

In view of that, and considering that believers are now baptized with the Holy Spirit, or else, should be, John says, *"You are of God, little children, and have overcome them: because greater is He that is in you, than he that is in the world"* (I Jn. 4:4).

KNOW

The question, *"And said, Jesus I know, and Paul I know; but who are you?"* represents two different and distinct Greek verbs regarding the word *"know."*

The verb *"know,"* referring to Jesus, in effect, says, *"Jesus I well know,"* or *"Jesus indeed, I know,"* implying fear!

The verb *"know"* referring to Paul is a

NOTES

different type of verb, representing much less action.

In effect, the evil spirit was saying, *"I am acquainted with Paul,"* which presents the evil spirit placing Jesus and Paul in two entirely different categories altogether. This is not brought out in the English translation. There is knowledge of Paul but to a far less degree than Jesus and, as well, a different type of knowledge respecting Jesus. The former (Paul) speaks of acquaintance, while the latter (Jesus) speaks of fear!

One thing is sure, this evil spirit did not know the seven sons of Sceva. The reasons are obvious: these people did not know Jesus.

It is only those who really and truly know Jesus Christ and are baptized with the Holy Spirit, thereby, believing that God is able to do all things, who are truly known by demon spirits. To be frank, most so-called believers, preachers or otherwise, are not known by evil spirits at all simply because they present no threat whatsoever to that kingdom of darkness.

From investigating the Scriptures very carefully for many, many years, it is my belief that for one to truly be a threat to Satan and his spirits of darkness, one must not only be saved but, as well, baptized with the Holy Spirit (Acts 2:4). I believe that the religious denominations which discount the Holy Spirit, actually refusing this great gift of God, are of no threat whatsoever to the world of darkness.

THE HOLY SPIRIT

As well, regarding those who embrace the doctrine of the Baptism with the Holy Spirit with the evidence of speaking with other tongues (Acts 2:4), unless the Holy Spirit has proper control, very little will even then truly be done for the Lord. Into the category of which Paul is placed in Verse 15, very few occupy this position.

Actually, a goodly number of laypersons around the world would fit this description, although unknown to most of the church. Of course, some preachers also fit this category; however, considering the great number who profess Christ, the number of which I speak is infinitesimally small.

And yet, it is this small number, whomever they may be, or wherever they may be, who shakes the powers of darkness to its core by destroying the works of Satan (I Jn. 3:8).

There are two places in which I desire to be known. First and foremost, I want to be known to God. As well, I want to be known by the spirits of darkness as a great threat to their evil kingdom.

Even as I dictate these words, I strongly sense the presence of God! To be known by man, even the church, in whatever capacity, is one thing; however, that serves little purpose, whether right or wrong. To be known of God is that which is altogether paramount.

As someone has said, *"The stands may cheer, or the stands may jeer, but it is the man in the striped suit who calls the game."*

In other words, men, or even the church, may say or do whatever, but it is God Who decides the outcome!

(16) "AND THE MAN IN WHOM THE EVIL SPIRIT WAS LEAPED ON THEM, AND OVERCAME THEM, AND PREVAILED AGAINST THEM, SO THAT THEY FLED OUT OF THAT HOUSE NAKED AND WOUNDED."

The form is:

1. The phrase, *"And the man in whom the evil spirit was leaped on them,"* proclaims this spirit of darkness taking control of the man and actually exerting superhuman strength through him, which is quite common in such cases.

2. *"And overcame them, and prevailed against them,"* probably speaks of all seven of the sons.

3. Some claim that one of the Greek words here used in the original *"amphoteron"* actually means *"both."* However, words then changed in meaning even as they now do at times, and, in fact, by New Testament times, that word had come to mean *"all."* Thus, it is most probable that all seven sons were involved.

4. The phrase, *"So that they fled out of that house naked and wounded,"* probably means their outer garments were torn off, and that they suffered wounds severe enough to affect them for awhile, as the Greek text indicates.

(17) "AND THIS WAS KNOWN TO ALL

THE JEWS AND GREEKS ALSO DWELLING AT EPHESUS; AND FEAR FELL ON THEM ALL, AND THE NAME OF THE LORD JESUS WAS MAGNIFIED."

The way is:

1. When we place our faith in the Cross, and the Cross exclusively, knowing that everything we receive from the Lord comes from this source, the Holy Spirit can then help us.

2. In fact, the Holy Spirit will not give us victory over the world, the flesh, and the devil any other way.

JESUS MAGNIFIED

The phrase, *"And this was known to all the Jews and Greeks also dwelling at Ephesus,"* tells us several things:

- In order for this situation to be so well known in the city, the possibility definitely exists that these sons of Sceva, charlatans that they were, had an audience when they attempted this exorcism. Evidently, they felt, with the addition of the name of Jesus to their bag of tricks, they would be able to create quite a spectacle.

This they did, to be sure, but not in the way they had first thought! Consequently, those who were witnesses of this spectacle began to relate it all over the city.

Inasmuch as they heard the evil spirit speak and saw the results of this aborted effort, such would have provided quite a conversation piece, to say the least!

- As well, the word *"all"* does not mean every single person, but rather quite a number.
- In all of this, as we shall see, the Lord would get great glory!

FEAR

The phrase, *"And fear fell on them all,"* proclaims the desired effect.

In this episode, these bystanders were made to realize that the Gospel of Jesus Christ is no trifling matter. As such, they were given a glimpse into both worlds, the world of light and the world of darkness. It becomes painfully obvious that both are very, very real!

How much these people knew about demon possession is anyone's guess. However, due to events, they knew this world of darkness was not a figment of one's imagination. Seeing how this evil spirit controlled the man and gave him great physical power, it was painfully obvious as to the reality of this part of the spirit world.

And yet, having seen Paul cast these things out and, thereby, observing great bondages broken, all of this was taken far beyond the weirdness and superstition normally associated with the spirit world as these pagans understood such. They had come face-to-face with the Power of the Gospel of Jesus Christ and now knew beyond the shadow of a doubt that what Paul was doing was genuine! Consequently, it created a fear in the hearts of them all, and rightly so!

Too much of the modern world has lost the fear of God, and I wonder if it is due to a lack of delivering power on the part of the church.

The phrase, *"And the name of the Lord Jesus was magnified,"* presents the constant idea of the Holy Spirit in that Jesus will always be glorified.

Even though there was a very negative response from the demon spirit respecting the name of Jesus, at least as it was used by these sons of Sceva, still, it fell out to a positive result, with this spirit exhibiting reverence and fear at the mention of that Name! As well, the Name used by the proper people brought, and still does, amazing, even miraculous, results.

THE NAME OF JESUS

According to the speech attributed to Peter on the Day of Pentecost, as Luke wrote the account, the significance of the Resurrection was that God had made Jesus, Whom the Jews crucified, to be both Lord and Christ (Acts 2:36).

This Text gives the key to the development of all the Titles of our Lord. The Resurrection was the decisive event which led the followers of Jesus to a new evaluation of His Person, and this was confirmed for them by the Gift of the Holy Spirit coming from the exalted Jesus (Acts 2:33).

Jesus' Claims to be the Jewish Messiah had now been vindicated by God in raising

NOTES

Him from the dead and, thereby, attesting the truth of these claims.

KING IN A DEEPER SENSE

The One Who died under Pilate's sarcastic placard as *"the King of the Jews"* had now been shown to be a King in a deeper sense. The actual title of *"King"* does not seem to have been used overmuch. It is true that the *"King"* replaced the *"Kingdom"* in apostolic preaching, but the word *"Kingdom"* was probably politically dangerous (Acts 17:7) and, consequently, the use of it was restrained (Rev. 17:14; 19:16). Note, however, that the title of *"Lord,"* which was equally dangerous, at least in a political sense, due to Caesar having been made *"god"* by the Roman Senate, still, was in frequent use. Actually, untold thousands of Christians died in the Roman arenas, torn by wild beasts and dispatched by every other torturous means possible, simply because they would not refer to Caesar as *"lord!"* Consequently, *"Lord"* is the title referred to most of all in the New Testament respecting Jesus.

MESSIAH!

The word *"Messiah"* is actually a Hebrew word and was replaced not so much by *"King"* as by *"Christ,"* which means *"Anointed"* or *"Anointed One."*

Actually, the title *"Christ"* is particularly used in statements about the death and resurrection of Jesus (Rom. 5:6, 8; 6:3-9; 8:34; 14:9; I Cor. 15:3-5; I Pet. 3:18).

It was the One Who died and rose again, Who was *"Jesus* (Saviour)," and was the *"Christ* (Anointed).

Although *"Christ"* tended to become more and more a name for Jesus rather than a title, it continued to have a sense of dignity about it, so that it was scarcely ever used alone with the title *"Lord,"* i.e., *"the Lord Christ,"* but rather in the form of *"the Lord Jesus Christ."*

THE NAME AS IT LOOKED TOWARD THE END OF THIS AGE

In Acts 3:20, Jesus is represented as the One Who is designated to appear as the Christ at the end of this age. Accordingly, it has been claimed that the earliest controversy of the church was concerned with the future coming of Jesus, and that the various titles of *"Son of Man," "Christ,"* and *"Lord"* were originally used to indicate what His Function will be at that coming day. Only later (though still within this period) was it realized that the One Who would come as Christ and Lord at the end was already Christ and Lord by virtue of His Death at Calvary, His Resurrection and Exaltation (and that the Resurrection and Exaltation confirmed an existing status).

Consequently, Jesus is not the Messiah-designate but is already the Messiah. In fact, it was because of the resurrection of Christ and what it implied concerning the Person of Jesus that the early church could look forward with confidence to His future Appearance as the Son of Man. It was, accordingly, the Death and Resurrection which established the meaning of the term *"Christ."* The Christian message in Paul's view was exclusively oriented to *"Christ Crucified"* (I Cor. 1:23; 2:2), ever proclaiming the glory and power of the Cross.

THE TITLE *"LORD"*

The other title which figures in Acts 2:36 is *"Lord."* By the Resurrection, God had demonstrated that Jesus was indeed the Lord, and the early church applied the words of Psalm 110:1 to Him in virtue of this event: *"The LORD said to My Lord, Sit at My Right Hand, till I make Your enemies a stool for Your Feet"* (Acts 2:34-35).

This Text had already been used by Jesus when He taught that the Messiah was David's Lord (Mk. 12:36) and in His reply to the high priest at His Trial (Mk. 14:62).

If Jesus was now Lord, it followed that the task of the early church was to lead people to recognize the status of Jesus. New converts became members of the church by acknowledging Jesus as Lord. If you confess with your mouth that Jesus is Lord and believe in your heart that God raised Him from the dead, you will be saved (Rom. 10:9; I Cor. 12:3).

THE GREAT SIGNIFICANCE OF THE TITLE *"LORD!"*

The great significance of this confession

is seen in Philippians 2:11, where the climax of God's Purpose is that all Creation will ultimately acknowledge Jesus Christ as Lord of all. As we have stated, in this confession of Jesus as Lord, there may well be a political note since it places Jesus over against other *"lords"* recognized by heathenistic worshipers of idols, etc.

Certainly Jews recognized only one God and Lord, but pagans worshiped *"gods many and lords many."* Over against them both, Christians acknowledged *"one God, the Father... and one Lord, Jesus Christ"* (I Cor. 8:6).

As we have stated, the Roman emperor too was acclaimed as lord by his subjects, and successive emperors increasingly claimed and demanded their total allegiance. This was to lead to keen conflicts of conscience for Christians at a later stage.

THE SON OF GOD

The final term to be discussed in this section is *"Son of God."* It may well have been especially associated with the preaching of Paul. It is significant that Acts 9:20 links the title with his preaching, and that it appears only once elsewhere in the Book of Acts, namely in a citation of Psalm 2:7 in Paul's sermon in Pisidian Antioch (Acts 13:33).

Here the promise, *"You are My Son, today I have begotten You,"* is applied by Paul to the Resurrection, which is regarded as the begetting of Jesus in the Incarnation to a new life.

The thought, however, is not that Jesus became God's Son by being raised from the dead, but rather that because He was His Son, God raised Him from the dead.

The same thought reappears in Romans 1:3-4, generally regarded as a pre-Pauline formula, where Jesus is said to have been declared to be Son of God with Power by the Resurrection from the dead.

In I Thessalonians 1:9-10, the Sonship of Jesus is again connected with the Resurrection, and this fact has made the basis for the hope of His future coming.

JESUS ALWAYS AS THE SON?

Two further elements appear to be associated with the title of *"Son"* in this early period. One is the thought of the preexistence of the Son. A number of Texts speak of God sending His Son (Jn. 3:16-17; Rom. 8:3; Gal. 4:4; I Jn. 4:9, 14), and clearly presuppose that the Son came into the world from being with the Father.

This line of thought is expressed quite explicitly without the actual use of the term *"Son"* in Paul's statement of Philippians 2:6-11.

Here, Jesus is a Divine Figure, existing in the image of God and equal with God, Who exchanged His heavenly mode of existence for a human, earthly form of existence in humility.

This statement by Paul speaks of His *"emptying Himself"* so that He exchanged the form of God for that of a slave. However, the fact that Paul regarded Jesus as God's Son during His Life and Death indicates that he did not interpret his statement as meaning that Jesus surrendered His Divine Nature in order to become incarnate.

Rather, *"He emptied Himself in that He took the servant's form...;"* and this necessarily involved an eclipsing of His Glory as the Divine Image in order that He might come in human flesh as the image of God incarnate. In this capacity, Jesus is the *"Son of God"* and, in fact, became such when He divested Himself of His Glory, in effect, losing the expression of deity, while never losing its possession.

As well, as the Son of God, He can be designated *"Emmanuel,"* which means, *"God with us,"* with His Presence on Earth tantamount to that of God Himself!

THE BOOK OF HEBREWS

The Book of Hebrews is perhaps the most distinctive in its use of titles concerning Christ. Thus, it reverts to the use of the simple *"Jesus"* to designate the One Who suffered humiliation and death, and yet, has been exalted by God (Heb. 2:9; 13:12). It also refers to Him simply as *"Lord"* (Heb. 2:3; 7:14) or as *"Christ"* (Heb. 3:6, 14).

As well, the writer, who I think was Paul, was conscious that Christ means *"Anointed"* (Heb. 1:9). Paul used it more as a name, which needs to be explained by other titles.

NOTES

He described Jesus as a *"Pioneer,"* if you will, of salvation and faith (Heb. 2:10; 12:2), using a phrase which may have had a wider usage in his day (Acts 3:15; 5:31).

However, above all, Paul thought of Jesus as the High Priest and expounded His Work in terms of this category drawn from the Old Testament sacrificial legislation. If this term is more a description than a title of Jesus, the term *"Son"* is the significance which underlies it. It was only after he had established the identity of Jesus as the Son of God, exalted above the angels and Moses, that he went on to demonstrate how this position qualified Jesus to be the High Priest and Mediator between God and man. Paul made careful use of Psalm 2:7 (Heb. 1:5; 5:5) and 110:4 to define the status of Jesus.

Consequently, he stressed the enormity of rejecting the salvation achieved by so exalted a Saviour (Heb. 6:6; 10:29).

THE PERSON OF JESUS AND TITLES

The teaching of the New Testament about the Person of Jesus is not confined to what is expressed by the titles, Whose use has been rapidly sketched in this short dissertation. We should also need to take into account what is said about the character and activity of Jesus, both during His earthly Life and in His heavenly State. It is also important to consider the kinds of statements which were created to express His Significance.

Nevertheless, the titles themselves sum up much of New Testament teaching. Study of them enables us to see how the thinking of the disciples was molded and formed by their first contact with Jesus during His Lifetime, then decisively fixed by their experience of Him as the risen Lord, and finally, elaborated in the course of their evangelism and teaching at that particular time.

In differing ways, the titles express the supreme worth of Jesus as the Son of God, His saving Function as Messiah and Saviour, and His honorable Position as Lord. However, in no way do these titles give these attributes to Jesus, but rather His Actions and, in effect, Who He was, gave rise to the titles. The titles not at all added to Who and What He was and is. They only designate that which is already obvious!

NOTES

The early church drew on a rich source of material to explain Who Jesus was. Basically, it took its material from the Old Testament, which it saw as the divinely-given prophecy of the coming of Jesus, but, at the same time, it did not shrink from using titles which would be meaningful in the wider world.

Some titles proved less adequate than others, but collectively, they all bear testimony to the fact that in Jesus, God has acted decisively to judge and save the world. They summon all to acknowledge that this Jesus is indeed one with God and Worthy of the worship that is fitting for God Himself.

(Information on names and titles of Jesus was derived from F. H. Borsch, *"The Son of Man in Myth and History"*; W. Bousset, Kyrios Christos, O. Cullmann, *"The Christology of the New Testament."*)

(18) "AND MANY WHO BELIEVED CAME, AND CONFESSED, AND SHOWED THEIR DEEDS."

The status is:

1. The position which Christianity takes in reference to the whole matter is to maintain that Christ has conquered the kingdom of evil by His Death on the Cross.

2. As well, no man owes this kingdom of evil any fear or obedience if he will only hold fast by his Lord and maintain his faith in that great Finished Work.

MANY BELIEVED

The phrase, *"And many who believed came,"* speaks of those who had already trusted the Lord for salvation but, as of yet, had not given up particular sins, etc.

The phrase, *"And confessed, and showed their deeds,"* concerns the Holy Spirit now leading these believers to holiness and righteousness, even as He had led them to salvation previously!

Upon salvation, the Holy Spirit immediately sets about to perform the necessary work within hearts and lives, which will be indicative, as stated, of holiness and righteousness. While it is true that these twin attributes are imputed to believing sinners upon faith in Christ, still, the *"condition"* of the saints must now be brought up to the *"position"* of the saints.

In effect, this is the road to true Biblical holiness. Once the sinner becomes a believer in Christ, the Holy Spirit immediately begins to move and operate in the realm of leading and guidance. This leading and guidance deals with every part of our lifestyles, and in every capacity (Rom., Chpt. 8).

The idea of true holiness is not necessarily to subscribe to a particular set of rules and regulations, which by and large is no more than law, but rather that we be led by the Spirit. He knows exactly what we need and what we should do. In other words, He sets the standard and not some man-devised organization.

However, in the setting of this standard, which He always does, at least if given the opportunity, He will never run contrary to His Character and Nature. So, the idea is that we allow Him to lead us, and we not try to lead Him.

(19) "MANY OF THEM ALSO WHICH USED CURIOUS ARTS BROUGHT THEIR BOOKS TOGETHER, AND BURNED THEM BEFORE ALL MEN: AND THEY COUNTED THE PRICE OF THEM, AND FOUND IT FIFTY THOUSAND PIECES OF SILVER."

The order is:

1. In the Cross is the judgment of the world, and by it is the prince of this world cast out.
2. Jesus has taken away the power of these evil influences that have been so mighty among men.
3. It was all done at the Cross!

CURIOUS ARTS

The phrase, *"Many of them also which used curious arts brought their books together, and burned them before all men,"* gives us direction respecting what happened then and the manner and operation of the working of the Holy Spirit:

- The pronoun *"them"* refers to the believers of Verse 18 and speaks of the change that came to their lives as a result of their acceptance of Christ.
- We are told here, to which we have already alluded, how the Holy Spirit began to deal with these believers concerning things in their lives which were wrong. It is the same with all believers respecting the Holy Spirit.
- *"Curious arts"* in the Greek text is *"periergos"* and means *"the practicing of magic."*

Here the idea is that of pretending by incantations to raise the dead, coerce spirits to reveal the unknown, foretell events, heal, inflict diseases, counteract evil by amulets or charms, interpret dreams, calculate sex of children before birth, and foretell by the planets one's daily life.

In other words, it is pretty much the same as now respecting horoscopes, readings, the Zodiac, fortunetelling of psychics, etc. All of this is evil and comes from the world of darkness, and must never be consulted by believers. That's why the Holy Spirit called them *"curious!"*

Actually, Ephesus was a center for the practice of magical arts, especially the putting of spells on people or things, etc. As would be obvious, before coming to Christ, some of the believers had practiced this magical spiritism.

MONEY

The phrase, *"And they counted the price of them, and found it fifty thousand pieces of silver,"* referred to the so-called worth of these books and paraphernalia.

It is said that *"fifty thousand pieces of silver"* would be the equivalent of the yearly wage of about 200 laborers. In today's money that would amount to approximately $4,000,000.

This was done publicly and was engaged by hundreds of people, which greatly impacted the city, as we shall see!

I might quickly add that many modern believers need to have a bonfire exactly as the believers did in Ephesus, regarding things which are not pleasing to God.

I speak of many musical recordings, which are not Christlike and need to be burned. I speak of certain types of drugs prescribed by doctors and given for emotional disturbances, but which only lead to addiction. I speak of certain types of books or magazines, which are not proper for believers and can only lead downward.

These passages, as Luke related to us, tell us plainly that there are some things

NOTES

believers ought not to do. It completely refutes the idea that one can have Christ and the world at the same time.

The truth is, when the bartender gets saved, he quits tending bar. When the dancer gets saved, he or she quits dancing in the chorus lines, etc. When the gambler gets saved, he quits gambling. When the entertainer gets saved, he leaves the entertainment business.

While the believer is in the world, the believer must never be a part of the world.

(20) "SO MIGHTILY GREW THE WORD OF GOD AND PREVAILED."

The direction is:

1. Satan held men captive by ignorance of God, but the Cross reveals him by the lie that sin was a trifle and teaches us its gravity and power.

2. Some 750 years before Christ, the Prophet Isaiah beautifully and wondrously prophesied what would take place when Jesus suffered the dire penalty on the Cross.

THE KINGDOM OF DARKNESS AND THE KINGDOM OF LIGHT

Whenever the sinner comes to Christ, he actually comes from the kingdom of darkness, headed up by Satan, to the Kingdom of God, headed up by the Lord Jesus Christ. As such, every single thing we do must come under the scrutiny of the Word of God. The Word is always the standard and must never be twisted, perverted, or compromised.

The Word of God plainly prohibited any dealings with the world of darkness respecting fortunetelling, etc., which made up the warp and woof of the lives of pagans. Their whole world revolved around their gods and all of the witchcraft which surrounded such involvement. This is one of the reasons that God demanded that Israel be a separate people and not involve themselves with the surrounding heathen. Israel was to look to God for all leading, guidance and help! So, they must not take upon themselves the ways of the heathen.

When the gentiles came to Christ, the admonition was the same! The Word of God that applied to Israel of old also applied to the early church and to us presently, as should be obvious!

NOTES

The Old Testament, which was the Bible of the early church, but with the New Testament added shortly, forbade the following heathen practices:

HEATHEN PRACTICES

- Enchantments—the practice of magical arts (Ex. 7:11, 22; 8:7, 18; Lev. 19:26; Deut. 18:10; II Ki. 17:17; 21:6; II Chron. 33:6; Isa. 47:9, 12; Jer. 27:9; Dan. 1:20).
- Witchcraft—practice of dealing with evil spirits (Ex. 22:18; Deut. 18:10; I Sam. 15:23; II Ki. 9:22; II Chron. 33:6; Micah 5:12; Nahum 3:4).
- Sorcery—same as witchcraft (Ex. 7:11; Isa. 47:9, 12; 57:3; Jer. 27:9; Dan. 2:2; Mal. 3:5).
- Soothsaying—same as witchcraft (Isa. 2:6; Dan. 2:27; 4:7; 5:7, 11; Micah 5:12).
- Divination—the art of mystic insight or fortunetelling (Num. 22:7; 23:23; Deut. 18:10-14; II Ki. 17:17; I Sam. 6:2; Jer. 14:14; 27:9; 29:8; Ezek. 12:24; 13:6-7, 23; 21:22-29; 22:28; Micah 3:7; Zech. 10:2).
- Wizardry—same as witchcraft. A wizard is a male and a witch is a female who practices witchcraft. If found out in Israel, both were to be executed (Ex. 22:18; Lev. 19:31; 20:6, 27; Deut. 18:11; I Sam. 28:3, 9; II Ki. 21:6; 23:24; II Chron. 33:6; Isa. 19:3).
- Necromancy—divination by means of pretended communication with the dead (Deut. 18:11; I Sam., Chpt. 28; I Chron. 10:13; Isa. 8:19).
- Magic—any pretended supernatural art or practice (Gen. 41:8, 24; Ex. 7:11, 22; 8:7, 18-19; 9:11; Dan. 1:20; 2:2, 10, 27; 4:7, 9; 5:11).
- Charms—to put a spell upon. Same as enchantment (Deut. 18:11; Isa. 19:3).
- Prognostication—to foretell by indications, omens, signs, etc. (Isa. 47:13).
- Observing times—same as prognostication (Lev. 19:26; Deut. 18:10; II Ki. 21:6; II Chron. 33:6).
- Astrology and star gazing—divination by the stars (Isa. 47:13; Jer. 10:2; Dan. 1:20; 2:2, 10; 4:7; 5:7-15).

DEMON SPIRITS

All of the above practices were and still are carried on in connection with demons,

NOTES

called familiar spirits. All who forsook God and sought help from these demons were to be cut off from God (Lev. 19:31; 20:6; Deut. 18:11; I Sam., Chpt. 28; II Ki. 21:6; 23:24; I Chron. 10:13; II Chron. 33:6; Isaiah 8:19; 19:3; 29:4).

Of course, the same prohibitions are in the New Testament as the Old.

I must quickly add that modern psychology is very little removed from these forbidden practices in the Word of God. To be frank, both the magical arts and modern psychology have their roots in the power of darkness.

There is only one cure for aberrant behavior or sin of any nature, and that is the Lord Jesus Christ.

If everything is brought under the judgment of the Word of God, as it certainly must be, the Word of God will then mightily grow in the hearts and lives of believers because it prevails over all else!

In truth, the struggle in the believer's life is whether the Word of God will prevail or evil passions and worldly wisdom.

(21) "AFTER THESE THINGS WERE ENDED, PAUL PURPOSED IN THE SPIRIT, WHEN HE HAD PASSED THROUGH MACEDONIA AND ACHAIA, TO GO TO JERUSALEM, SAYING, AFTER I HAVE BEEN THERE, I MUST ALSO SEE ROME."

The order is:

1. One must understand that the Word of God must stand as the criterion for all faith and belief.

2. Agreeing upon that, our next task is to rightly divide the Word of Truth.

IN THE SPIRIT

The phrase, *"After these things were ended,"* actually means *"were fulfilled."* It will also include the happenings in the remainder of this chapter.

The idea is that from this moment, Paul, led by the Holy Spirit, was making plans to leave Ephesus, which would take place probably in the next two or three months. All in all, he spent three years in Ephesus (Acts 20:17-31).

He had raised up a great church in Ephesus, but at great price!

Referring to this time, he said that he fought with the *"beasts"* at Ephesus (I Cor. 15:32). Some have claimed that he was referring to the Roman arenas where he was pitted against wild animals, etc. However, there is no indication of such, with him probably referring to men who were so filled with the devil that they acted like beasts.

He also said that he suffered such affliction in Asia, but referring to Ephesus, he stated that he despaired even of his life but was thankfully delivered by the Lord (II Cor. 1:8-10).

AT GREAT PRICE

So, as we have stated, the great victories had come at great price, as do all great victories. These problems and difficulties cannot be confessed away, as some claim, and neither can a person reach a particular faith principle and, thereby, ward off all adversity.

To be frank, these things came upon Paul, not because of a lack of faith, but rather because of his great faith.

Satan little opposes that which little opposes him. However, to be sure, he opposes greatly that which greatly opposes him!

The phrase, *"Paul purposed in the Spirit,"* refers here to the Holy Spirit. It means the Lord had been dealing with him for some time concerning his next move—a move, we might quickly add, which would ultimately take him to Rome as a captive of the Roman government!

It should be obvious by now that Paul sought the Lord earnestly about all things. He ever wanted and sought the perfect will of God.

The word *"purposed"* in the Greek Text is *"tithemi"* and means *"a passive or horizontal posture."* It speaks of coming to a particular purpose or position, at least in this case, by being totally submissive to the will of God, actually seeking only His Will with no addition of his personal will.

This short phrase gives us the attitude of this apostle and shows us how totally he desired the will of God, and he was determined to do nothing else but the will of God.

In this context, as we shall see in later chapters, danger, persecution, or nothing for that matter, must impact the carrying out of that Will.

NOTES

ROME

The phrase, *"When he had passed through Macedonia and Achaia, to go to Jerusalem,"* concerned churches already planted and, in some cases, flourishing, but which needed the attention and care that Paul could provide.

Macedonia consisted of the northern part of modern Greece, while Achaia consisted of its southern portion.

This spoke of the churches at Philippi, Thessalonica, and Berea, as well as Corinth, and, no doubt, others! Also, Paul desired to be in Jerusalem for the Feast of Pentecost (Acts 20:16).

The phrase, *"Saying, After I have been there, I must also see Rome,"* lays to rest the idea that Paul was out of the will of God by going to Jerusalem and finally to Rome.

While it is true that the Spirit of God would warn him all along the way of the dangers which awaited him, even as we shall see, still, this was only that the saints would pray mightily for him at this very dangerous time, which they, no doubt, did!

Horton said, *"With the words, 'I must also see Rome,' the Greek indicates a Divine necessity laid upon Paul. He did not know how God would get him to Rome, but this one thing was certain, from this point Rome is the objective in view."*

(22) "SO HE SENT INTO MACEDONIA TWO OF THEM WHO MINISTERED UNTO HIM, TIMOTHY AND ERASTUS; BUT HE HIMSELF STAYED IN ASIA FOR A SEASON."

The construction is:

1. The phrase, *"So he sent into Macedonia two of them who ministered unto him, Timothy and Erastus,"* concerned preparations they would make in the churches for Paul's visit a short time later.

The idea was to alert them that he was coming, with them, no doubt, ministering as well.

Erastus is mentioned here for the first time. It is believed he is the same one mentioned by Paul in Romans 16:23 and II Timothy 4:20.

It is probable that he was one of Paul's Corinthian converts who had gone with him from Corinth to Jerusalem and Antioch, and then had accompanied him through Phrygia and Galatia to Ephesus.

It is believed that Silas, who had been Timothy's companion on the former visit to Macedonia, may have left Paul possibly at Jerusalem, from whence he (Silas) originally came (Acts 15:22, 32, 34). It seems he may have then begun traveling with Peter (I Pet. 5:12).

The phrase, *"But he himself stayed in Asia for a season,"* probably refers, as stated, to two or three months.

The passage seems to indicate that Paul was forced to stay in Ephesus a while beyond his original intention. The reason may have been the incident which took place and is recorded in the remainder of this chapter concerning the Ephesian games, which were celebrated at Ephesus in May. These games brought a large number of Ionians to Ephesus. It was at this time, doubtless, that the principal sale of *"silver shrines of Diana"* took place, which implies that the sales were not as large as normal, with the blame laid on Paul. So many had given their hearts to the Lord that the market for those little idols had been seriously weakened!

(23) "AND THE SAME TIME THERE AROSE NO SMALL STIR ABOUT THAT WAY."

The form is:

1. *"That way"* is the *"Pentecostal way,"* which characterizes the entirety of the Book of Acts, and which was so very obvious anywhere and everywhere Paul ministered.

2. Satan now would work through one of the economic arms of the city, relative to the making of idols, etc. Many people had given their hearts to the Lord, and as a result, they ceased to purchase these figurines. Evidently, some of the craftsmen who made these things were put out of work, which caused animosity against Paul. Satan would use this to stir up trouble.

(24) "FOR A CERTAIN MAN NAMED DEMETRIUS, A SILVERSMITH, WHICH MADE SILVER SHRINES FOR DIANA, BROUGHT NO SMALL GAIN UNTO THE CRAFTSMEN."

The way is:

1. The phrase, *"For a certain man*

named Demetrius, a silversmith," presents this man possibly as the guild master of the silversmiths' guild or trade union.

Actually, the Roman world of that day had unions as we have now. Many unions are mentioned on papyri discovered in Egypt.

The phrase, *"Which made silver shrines for Diana,"* speaks of miniatures of the temple of Diana, with the goddess in the middle of the temple background. All types of these statues were made, some large and some small. It was believed that carrying a small replica of this goddess as a charm would bring good luck.

2. The temple was 220 years in its construction. It was a monstrous building, some 425 feet long and 220 feet wide, and had 127 columns, each 60 feet high, with the entirety of the temple adorned by beautiful statues. It was one of the Seven Wonders of the Ancient World.

3. It was built in 550 B.C. of pure white marble and rebuilt in 355 B.C., with still greater splendor. It contained, it is said, incredible wealth.

The goddess in question had the form of a many breasted woman, emblematic of the abundance of nature, and was claimed to have fallen from heaven.

4. Silver models for sale were made, as stated, of this temple and of the goddess, and were believed to bring prosperity to houses in which they were placed. Ephesus was devoted to this divinity, and however people might speak lightly of other divinities, no one dared to disparage Diana.

5. I might quickly add that similar models are made today of the Virgin Mary, in whatever type of setting, and are believed to convey spiritual grace.

6. It is stated that in places where Catholicism is strong, blasphemy against God might be tolerated, but an attack upon the Virgin would bring swift retribution on the perpetrators, possibly even death.

7. The common people believed these images of Diana to be gods. The more intelligent people used them as aids to devotion, thinking somehow they might bring good luck. Such is exactly the same in many Catholic Churches all over the world but, as stated, of Mary.

NOTES

8. The phrase, *"Brought no small gain unto the craftsmen,"* speaks of those who were members of this union of silversmiths who made their living, and it seems a good living at that, crafting these little idols and charms.

(25) "WHOM HE CALLED TOGETHER WITH THE WORKMEN OF LIKE OCCUPATION, AND SAID, SIRS, YOU KNOW THAT BY THIS CRAFT WE HAVE OUR WEALTH."

The account is:

1. The phrase, *"Whom he called together with the workmen of like occupation,"* refers to those who were members of this particular guild or union. This included not only the *"craftsmen"* but, as well, any and all who had any interest whatsoever in this particular shrine trade.

2. *"And said, Sirs, you know that by this craft we have our wealth,"* tells us that their chief concern was not the worship or the honor of this goddess but their own prosperity. Horton said, *"Their attachment to the goddess was simply to make it a means of gain for themselves."*

3. Due to some modern teaching on prosperity, I am concerned that many in Christendom fall into the same category. While the Lord definitely does bless His People, still, when money becomes the primary object of one's message, then it becomes perversion and, in effect, *"another gospel"* (II Cor. 11:4).

4. Paul warned Timothy about the *"gain is godliness"* doctrine! (I Tim. 6:5). Many have ignored that warning.

5. Paul called on us to turn away from such teachers to real godliness, which makes Christ the Center of all things, instead of using Him as a means to an end.

6. Warning against riches, he said, *"Godliness with contentment is great gain."*

He then said, *"For we brought nothing into this world, and it is certain we can carry nothing out.*

"And having food and raiment let us be therewith content.

"But they that will be rich fall into temptation and a snare, and into many foolish and hurtful lusts, which drown men in destruction and perdition."

NOTES

Finally, he said, *"For the love of money is the root of all evil: which while some coveted after, they have erred from the faith, and pierced themselves through with many sorrows."*

Then bluntly, he unequivocally said, *"But you, O man of God, flee these things; and follow after righteousness, godliness, faith, love, patience, meekness"* (I Tim. 6:6-11).

(26) "MOREOVER YOU SEE AND HEAR, THAT NOT ALONE AT EPHESUS, BUT ALMOST THROUGHOUT ALL ASIA, THIS PAUL HAS PERSUADED AND TURNED AWAY MUCH PEOPLE, SAYING THAT THEY BE NO GODS, WHICH ARE MADE WITH HANDS."

The pattern is:

1. *"Now if any man have not the Spirit of Christ, he is none of His,"* actually refers to the Holy Spirit.

2. Some have thought that the *"Spirit of Christ"* referred to Christ's personal Spirit; however, that is incorrect.

A POWERFUL TESTIMONY

The phrase, *"Moreover you see and hear,"* presents, as we shall see, a powerful testimony from an enemy, no less, to the power and effectiveness of Paul's labors and message.

The results of that message of Jesus Christ could be seen all over respecting a change of lifestyle in the hearts and lives of possibly thousands.

Also, it seems about all that one heard in those days was something about Paul or the Gospel he preached! As we have stated, what a testimony to the power of the Gospel of Jesus Christ.

In fact, none of these places had ever seen anything like the miracles being performed, and neither had they heard anything like the message being preached concerning the Lord Jesus Christ. In fact, this is the way the Gospel is to be at all times. It is to be a miracle-working Gospel, with life-changing power and properties. Anything else is not truly the Gospel of Jesus Christ!

PAUL

The phrase, *"That not alone at Ephesus, but almost throughout all Asia, this Paul has persuaded and turned away much people,"* presents what had happened and the anger it aroused.

To be sure, this is the type of Gospel which Satan hates and will do anything within his power to bring it to a halt, or at least attempt to do so.

Paul was able to *"persuade"* people simply because his message was anointed by the power of the Holy Spirit, and it was followed by miracles. Such is a powerful combination, but yet, that which God intends for all preachers to have and do.

NO GODS

The phrase, *"Saying that they be no gods, which are made with hands,"* proclaims that which Paul had preached, and which the people, or at least many of them, had come to believe, and rightly so!

Common sense tells one, or at least should, that what is made is less than the one who made it.

The Prophet Isaiah, even with sarcasm and tremendous irony, pictured a rich man hiring a workman to cast and shape an image and then hiring a goldsmith to overlay it with gold. Then he had silver chains made to hold it up. After all, a rich man would not want his gold-plated god to fall over!

The poor man, as Isaiah continued, could not afford a gold-plated god, so he cut down a tree and had a wooden god made with a broad base so it would not fall over (Isa. 40:18-20).

At the present time, millions bow down to the god Buddha. Untold millions follow suit in the worship of Mary, which has no validity whatsoever in the Word of God.

Islam is idol-worship, pure and simple, although in a little different style. In effect, people worship that particular religion and all of its rudiments. Actually, religion worship is pandemic all over the world. In fact, religion is that which originates with man, in other words and in a sense, *"that which is made with hands."*

(27) "SO THAT NOT ONLY THIS OUR CRAFT IS IN DANGER TO BE SET AT NOUGHT; BUT ALSO THAT THE TEMPLE OF THE GREAT GODDESS DIANA SHOULD BE DESPISED, AND HER MAGNIFICENCE SHOULD BE DESTROYED,

WHOM ALL ASIA AND THE WORLD WORSHIPS."

The exegesis is:

1. The phrase, *"So that not only this our craft is in danger to be set at nought,"* follows the idea that it would fall into disrepute.

2. Although Paul probably said little if anything directly concerning the goddess Diana, still, the evidence is strong that Paul loudly proclaimed that anything which could be made by the hands of men was obviously no god. Verse 26 proclaims this statement! Consequently, it was very easy for the people to understand what he was talking about.

3. The phrase, *"But also that the temple of the great goddess Diana should be despised, and her magnificence should be destroyed,"* tells us two things:

a. Whenever men truly come to Christ, finding in Him everything their heart craves, these phony things of the past are then despised, which makes the silversmith right in what he said.

b. If the goddess Diana was so great as claimed, how could her magnificence be destroyed?

The truth is, the entirety of these religions, even as today, play off ignorance and superstition.

"Whom all Asia and the world worships," presents somewhat of an exaggeration.

While this temple to Diana was indeed one of the Seven Wonders of the Ancient World, still, the worship was more localized than anything else.

4. This Ephesian goddess actually had no relation to the other Artemis, the Artemis of Greece known as the maiden huntress and identified by the Romans with their goddess Diana.

5. Horton said, *"The Artemis of Ephesus was worshiped primarily in that city (despite the claims otherwise), and was not at all like the Roman goddess Diana or the Greek Artemis. The names were the same, but the goddesses were different."*

(28) "AND WHEN THEY HEARD THESE SAYINGS, THEY WERE FULL OF WRATH, AND CRIED OUT, SAYING, GREAT IS DIANA OF THE EPHESIANS."

NOTES

The structure is:

1. The phrase, *"And when they heard these sayings, they were full of wrath,"* proclaims these accusations by the man called Demetrius as having the desired effect. The crowd primarily turned into a mob!

2. *"And cried out, saying, Great is Diana of the Ephesians,"* presents the devotion to their goddess.

3. Diana is pictured as being covered all over with breasts from the shoulders to the feet, and in other images, with breasts to the bottom of the abdomen and the legs covered with heads of animals.

4. She was supposed to be the mother and nourisher of all Creation. Some identify her with Semiramis, the queen of Babylon and wife of Nimrod, from whom all licentiousness in ancient worship proceeded.

5. Horton said, *"Actually, the great wealth and prominence of the city of Ephesus was largely due to its great Temple of Diana. So proud were the Ephesians of the Temple that when Alexander the Great offered to rebuild it after a fire if his name could be inscribed over its entrance, its Priests refused and the Ephesians rebuilt it at their own expense."*

6. Consequently, the livelihood of many depended on making people believe that Artemis of the Ephesians was great.

(29) "AND THE WHOLE CITY WAS FILLED WITH CONFUSION: AND HAVING CAUGHT GAIUS AND ARISTARCHUS, MEN OF MACEDONIA, PAUL'S COMPANIONS IN TRAVEL, THEY RUSHED WITH ONE ACCORD INTO THE THEATRE."

The composition is:

1. The phrase, *"And the whole city was filled with confusion,"* proclaims such being done because of the rhetoric of Demetrius and now the stirring up of the mob.

2. *"And having caught Gaius and Aristarchus, men of Macedonia,"* proclaims two of Paul's associates.

3. More than likely, even though *"Gaius"* was a common name at that time, still, this is probably the same man mentioned in Acts 20:4; Romans 16:23; and I Corinthians 1:14.

Aristarchus was a Thessalonian (Acts 20:4).

In Acts 27:2, where we find him

accompanying Paul from Caesarea to Rome, he is described as a *"Macedonian of Thessalonica."*

In Colossians 4:10, he is Paul's *"fellow-prisoner,"* as voluntarily sharing his prison, and in Philemon, Verse 24, he is his *"fellow-labourer."*

4. His history, therefore, is that having been converted under Paul's ministry in Thessalonica, he attached himself to Paul as one of his missionary staff, and continued with him through good report and evil report, through persecution, violence, imprisonment, shipwreck, and bonds, even to the latest moment on which the light of Bible history shines. Blessed servant of Christ! Blessed fellow-servant of the Lord's chief Apostle!

5. *"Paul's companions in travel,"* proclaims that Paul's company seemingly was considerably larger on this missionary journey than on his earlier travels.

6. *"They rushed with one accord into the theatre,"* presents that which was a common place of resort for all great meetings. However, the amphitheater at Ephesus of which *"ruins of immense grandeur"* still remain, is said to be the largest of which we have any account. It would seat upwards of 25,000 people.

7. These amphitheaters were used for all types of athletic contests modeled after the Olympic and Isthmian Games of Greece. They were also used for drama and intellectual contests, as well as a place for other types of amusement.

Evidently, this mob came upon *"Gaius and Aristarchus,"* and recognizing them as Paul's associates, dragged them into the amphitheater.

8. The mob, no doubt, was looking for Paul, possibly going to the school of Tyrannus where he had been holding services. There finding only the two associates, they seized them!

(30) "AND WHEN PAUL WOULD HAVE ENTERED IN UNTO THE PEOPLE, THE DISCIPLES SUFFERED HIM NOT."

The synopsis is:

1. The phrase, *"And when Paul would have entered in unto the people,"* speaks of the apostle now hearing about the situation and determining to go into the theater and address the mob, or at least attempt to do so!

NOTES

2. It is one thing to address a crowd, but something else altogether to attempt to address a mob, and this crowd had turned into a mob!

3. *"The disciples suffered him not,"* refers to the believers who were a part of the church at Ephesus.

4. These people, who were citizens of Ephesus, knew the temperament of the people even more than Paul did. Though they believed with Paul that the Lord would protect him, still, they felt, and rightly so, that Paul would be endangering his life needlessly.

The implication is, realizing the danger, they were adamant in their demands regarding the apostle.

6. It is thought by some that when these decisions were being made, Paul was at the home of Aquila and Priscilla. If so, that would explain Romans 16:3, where he says that to shield him, they laid down their own necks, i.e., they risked their lives.

(31) "AND CERTAIN OF THE CHIEF OF ASIA, WHICH WERE HIS FRIENDS, SENT UNTO HIM, DESIRING HIM THAT HE WOULD NOT ADVENTURE HIMSELF INTO THE THEATRE."

The overview is:

1. The phrase, *"And certain of the chief of Asia,"* referred to men who were called *"Asiarchs"* in the Greek.

2. These officers, or Asiarchs, were 10 in number and were men of high rank and great wealth. They were chosen to preside over all sacred rites and to provide at their own expense the public games in honor of the gods and of the deity of the emperor. Actually, Ephesus was also one of the great centers of Caesar worship.

3. *"Which were his friends,"* presents another striking proof of the enormous influence of Paul's preaching in Asia.

4. For the Scripture to say they were his *"friends"* gives us insight into these very wealthy men and the respect they had for Paul. It does not say that they became believers, but it does say that the Gospel had made such a penetration into their hearts that they now knew the fallacy of these so-called gods. Whether they later accepted

Christ or not is not known, but they now knew there was only one Lord, and that was *"the Lord Jesus Christ."*

5. *"Sent unto him, desiring him that he would not adventure himself into the theatre,"* seems to mean that they sent Paul word but did not come to him in person.

6. There seems to be some indication that they were telling him that they would do everything they could to guarantee his protection, that is, if he stayed away from this mob. However, if he went into the theater, the implication is that there was very little, if anything, they could do!

(32) "SOME THEREFORE CRIED ONE THING, AND SOME ANOTHER: FOR THE ASSEMBLY WAS CONFUSED; AND THE MORE PART KNEW NOT WHEREFORE THEY WERE COME TOGETHER."

The diagram is:

1. The phrase, *"Some therefore cried one thing, and some another,"* pretty well presents the actions and mannerisms of a mob. They were stirred up, but most did not know what about!

2. *"For the assembly was confused; and the more part knew not wherefore they were come together,"* means that a few were agitating the many. The whole thing was in an uproar, but most did not know why!

3. In this verse, however, is a perfect example of the spirit of the world and the Spirit of God.

The word *"assembly"* in the Greek text is *"ekklesia"* and means, or rather originally meant, *"a called-out assembly,"* referring to the church. It is used about 112 times in the New Testament in this fashion.

The only time the word *"assembly"* is used otherwise is in this chapter, where it refers to a confused mob.

4. Consequently, we have two groups mentioned here, the believers of Ephesus, which constituted the true church, and this unruly mob. The first group are citizens of heaven, while the latter group were citizens of Rome. The former was of righteousness and holiness, with the latter being of confusion and unrighteousness!

5. So, men have a choice! They can be a part of the *"Assembly"* of God or of the *"assembly"* of the world. They cannot be both!

NOTES

(33) "AND THEY DREW ALEXANDER OUT OF THE MULTITUDE, THE JEWS PUTTING HIM FORWARD. AND ALEXANDER BECKONED WITH THE HAND, AND WOULD HAVE MADE HIS DEFENSE UNTO THE PEOPLE."

The pattern is:

1. The phrase, *"And they drew Alexander out of the multitude, the Jews putting him forward,"* proclaims the Jews being fearful that the mob would think they were confederate with Paul, inasmuch as he was a Jew, and turn on them as, in fact, had been done many times in other cities of the Roman Empire.

2. Exactly who this Alexander was is not clear. Some think he is the same man as in I Timothy 1:20 and II Timothy 4:14. That may well be the case, and probably is.

3. *"And Alexander beckoned with the hand, and would have made his defense unto the people,"* presents that which was to no avail.

4. If this man was *"Alexander the coppersmith,"* of whose conduct Paul complained so bitterly, then this may explain why the Jews put him forward as their spokesman. As a fellow metal worker, he would be known by the silversmiths who had started this riot and hopefully might be able to influence them away from the Jews.

However, being a Jew, it is very unlikely that he would have engaged in the making of any type of idols, etc.

(34) "BUT WHEN THEY KNEW THAT HE WAS A JEW, ALL WITH ONE VOICE ABOUT THE SPACE OF TWO HOURS CRIED OUT, GREAT IS DIANA OF THE EPHESIANS."

The pattern is:

1. Satan coming as a roaring lion is overly obvious and does not pertain to deception (I Pet. 5:8).

2. However, his coming as a *"serpent"* definitely does pertain to deception (II Cor. 11:3), but he is most dangerous as *"an angel of light"* (II Cor. 11:14).

THE JEW

The phrase, *"But when they knew that he was a Jew,"* proclaims the reason for their outbursts which followed.

NOTES

They knew that Jews did not subscribe to the worship of the goddess Diana or any of the other gods of the Roman Empire, but rather admitted to only one God, Jehovah. So, they had little or no interest whatsoever in what Alexander had to say.

"All with one voice about the space of two hours cried out, Great is Diana of the Ephesians," seems on the surface to present great strength. However, this gathering, as well as all of the clamor, for all its show was rather that of weakness. The Gospel of Jesus Christ had come up against this heathenistic superstition, with it ultimately overcome in totality.

Previously, people came to Ephesus from outlying towns and districts and would purchase the charms or silver shrines. No matter where their homes were located, they would take the idols with them when they left as good luck charms or even to worship this goddess. They considered these miniature temples as *"holy ground."*

THE GOSPEL OF JESUS CHRIST

However, thousands were now coming to Ephesus from all over Asia, not for this goddess Diana, but rather to attend services where Paul was ministering, with many of them finding Jesus as Lord and Saviour. Consequently, they took the Gospel back with them to their homes, wherever that may have been. As stated, it is thought that Philemon, the wealthy businessman from Colossae, found Jesus at these meetings.

History records that from this time forward, worshipers of the goddess Diana came in ever fewer numbers, while the church in Ephesus continued to flourish. It is said that the Apostle John spent the last years of his life there, writing his Gospel and Epistles from that place.

In A.D. 262, this beautiful temple of Diana again burned, but this time was never rebuilt. Its influence was gone. By contrast, Ephesus became such a prominent Christian city that in A.D. 341, a great council of the church was held there.

So we learn that despite the shouts of the mob as to how great Diana was, in fact, she was not great at all, but rather a figment of someone's imagination. How so much like all the vain philosophies of this world, which seem great for the moment, but soon begin to fade. By contrast, the Lord Jesus Christ stands astride history, with everything more and more looking to Him. Today He stands taller than ever, and then at history's end, He is the only One Who will remain. The reason is simple: Jesus Christ is God!

JESUS CHRIST

The Gospels present to us in Jesus the Image of the flawless character—in the words of the writer to the Hebrews, *"Holy, guileless, undefiled, separated from sinners"* (Heb. 7:26).

The ideal of perfect Holiness regarding Christ in the Gospels has fascinated the conscience of Christendom for nearly 20 centuries. As well, the critics cannot claim the church invented such a thing because it was not the church—least of all, such a church—that created Christ, but Christ that created the church.

THE SINLESSNESS OF CHRIST ASSURED

The sinlessness of Jesus is a given in the Gospels. Over against a sinful world, He stands as a Saviour, Who is Himself without sin, which, of course, was an absolute necessity if, in fact, He would redeem humanity, which He did!

His is the one Life in humanity in which is presented a perfect knowledge and unbroken fellowship with the Father, undeviating obedience to His Will, unswerving devotion under the severest strain of temptation, and suffering to the highest ideal of goodness.

The ethical ideal was never raised to so absolute a height as it is in the teaching of Jesus, and the miracle is that, high as it is in its unsullied purity, the character of Jesus corresponds with it and realizes it.

Word and Life for once in history perfectly agree. Jesus, with the keenest sensitiveness to sin in thought and feeling as in deed, is conscious of no sin in Himself, confesses no sin, disclaims the presence of it, and speaks and acts continually on the assumption that He is without it, which even His most strident enemies could not refute.

Those who knew Him best declared Him to be without sin (II Cor. 5:21; I Pet. 2:22; I Jn. 3:5).

HOW DO WE EXPLAIN SUCH?

How is this phenomenon of a sinless personality in Jesus to be explained?

The only answer is that it is itself a miracle and can only be made credible by a creative miracle in Christ's origin. It may be argued that a virgin birth does not of itself secure sinlessness, but it will hardly be disputed that at least a sinless personality implies a miracle in its production, which the Incarnation is all about!

It is precisely because of this that modern thought feels bound to reject it.

However, in the Gospels, it is not the virgin birth by itself which is invoked to explain Christ's sinlessness, but the supernatural conception by the Holy Spirit (Lk. 1:35). It is because of this conception that the birth is a virgin one. No explanation of the supernatural element in Christ's Person is more rational or credible.

SINLESSNESS AND THE MESSIANIC CLAIM

If from the first Jesus was conscious of Himself as without sin, and if as the converse of this, He knew Himself as standing in an unbroken filial fellowship with the Father, He must have become conscious of His special vocation early and learned to distinguish Himself from others as One called to bless and save them.

Here is the true germ of His Messianic Consciousness from which everything subsequently is unfolded. He stood in a rapport with the Father, which opened His Spirit to a full, clear revelation of the Father's Will regarding Himself, His Mission, the Kingdom He came to found, His Sufferings as the means of salvation to the world, and the Glory that awaited Him when His earthly Work was done.

In the light of this revelation, He read the Old Testament Scriptures and saw His Course there made plain. When this hour had come, He went to John for baptism, and His brief, eventful Ministry, which should end on the Cross, actually began. This is the reading of events which introduces consistency and purpose into the life of Jesus.

NOTES

Jesus was and is God, actually very God, while at the same time being Man, even very Man! As we have said repeatedly, at the Incarnation, He laid aside the expression of deity, while never for a moment losing the possession of His Deity. He never ceased to be God while being Man, but yet, performed every miracle not as God, but as a Man, in effect, the Man Christ Jesus, filled with the Holy Spirit (Jn. 1:33-34).

So, there is only One Who is truly *"Great,"* and that is Jesus, in essence, the Lord Jesus Christ.

(35) "AND WHEN THE TOWNCLERK HAD APPEASED THE PEOPLE, HE SAID, YOU MEN OF EPHESUS, WHAT MAN IS THERE WHO KNOWS NOT HOW THAT THE CITY OF THE EPHESIANS IS A WORSHIPPER OF THE GREAT GODDESS DIANA, AND OF THE IMAGE WHICH FELL DOWN FROM JUPITER?"

The diagram is:

1. *"Or another gospel, which you have not accepted,"* refers to a gospel that is man-devised, which repudiates the Cross.

2. If another gospel is preached, it is because another Jesus is being presented, and done so by another spirit (II Cor. 11:4).

THE TOWNCLERK

The phrase, *"And when the townclerk had appeased the people,"* presents an office of influence, seeing he was the chief registrar, who had the responsibility of drafting the laws and the custody of the archives.

Actually, there were three orders of these scribes or town clerks, with a great difference in the political rank of each.

Evidently this *"townclerk"* was of the highest political rank, especially considering that he was responsible as the official contact or liaison with the Roman government. Thus, if the mob broke the law, the responsibility would be on his back, hence, his attempting to *"appease the people,"* which he did!

"He said, You men of Ephesus," proclaims the mob quieting down after some two hours of chanting, etc. Now, he would talk at least some sense of reason to them.

NOTES

The question, *"What man is there who knows not how that the city of the Ephesians is a worshipper of the great goddess Diana, and of the image which fell down from Jupiter?"* appeals to the alleged greatness of this goddess.

The idea is that Ephesus was the proud possessor of this goddess, of which no other city in the world could boast, hence, the chant, *"Great is Diana of the Ephesians."*

EPHESUS

Ephesus was the most important city in the Roman province of Asia, on the west coast of what is now Asiatic Turkey. It was situated at the mouth of the Cayster River, between the mountain range of Coressus and the sea. The magnificent road, some 33 feet wide, lined with columns, ran down through the city to the fine harbor, which served both as a great export center at the end of the Asiatic caravan route and also as a natural landing point from Rome.

The main part of the city, with its theater, baths, library, agora, and paved streets, lay between the Coressus ridge and the Cayster, but the temple for which it was famed lay over two kilometers to the northeast. As stated, this site was originally sacred to the worship of the Anatolian fertility goddess, later identified with Greek Artemis and Latin Diana.

Ephesus was a city of religious importance under Roman rule. It became a center of the emperor cult and eventually possessed three official temples, thus qualifying thrice over for the proud title of *"temple-warden,"* which spoke of the emperors, as well as being a city devoted to the goddess Diana (Acts 19:35). It is remarkable that Paul had friends among the temple officers, whose primary function actually was to foster the imperial cult.

The earliest reference to the coming of Christianity to Ephesus was in A.D. 52, when Paul made a short visit and left Aquila and Priscilla there (Acts 18:18-21). Paul's third missionary journey had Ephesus as its goal, and he stayed there over two years (Acts 19:8, 10).

His work was at first based on the synagogue. Later, he debated in the lecture hall of Tyrannus, making Ephesus a base for the evangelization of the whole province of Asia.

Paul used every means at his disposal to spread the Gospel. While there was much opposition, irrespective as to what that opposition was, how debilitating or how offensive, he let nothing stop him from this all-important task. The reason?

The souls of men were and are at stake. We must take the message of salvation in Christ Jesus to the world.

(36) "SEEING THEN THAT THESE THINGS CANNOT BE SPOKEN AGAINST, YOU OUGHT TO BE QUIET, AND TO DO NOTHING RASHLY."

The exegesis is:

1. The phrase, *"Seeing then that these things cannot be spoken against,"* appealed to the pride of these individuals, regarding Diana being so great, that whatever anyone said would have had no consequence.

2. This *"townclerk"* may have been in agreement with Paul's statements concerning the falsity of these gods made by the hands of men, even as the next verse hints. Still, he was, no doubt, more concerned than anything about this mob getting out of hand, which would then be his responsibility. So, he appealed to their pride!

3. *"You ought to be quiet, and to do nothing rashly,"* represents good advice, even though coming from a heathen.

(37) "FOR YOU HAVE BROUGHT HITHER THESE MEN, WHICH ARE NEITHER ROBBERS OF CHURCHES, NOR YET BLASPHEMERS OF YOUR GODDESS."

The synopsis is:

1. The phrase, *"For you have brought hither these men,"* speaks of *"Gaius and Aristarchus."* The idea is that they had brought them forcibly and, in effect, had broken the law.

2. *"Which are neither robbers of churches,"* actually speaks of plunderers of temples. In other words, not a single Christian, much less these two men, had ever done any harm whatsoever to the temple of Diana.

3. *"Nor yet blasphemers of your goddess,"* means that Paul had not directed attention to this particular idol. However, I think it is conclusive that he had stated, probably many times, the fallacy of that

which men referred to as god, but which was made by their own hands (Acts 19:26).

4. It is doubtful that Demetrius would have attributed such a statement to Paul had the apostle not said such. Anyway, the terminology is hardly that which this heathen would have fabricated.

5. As well, by this *"townclerk"* using the term, *"Your goddess,"* it implies that quite possibly he too had been greatly influenced by Paul's preaching and in his heart had renounced this foolishness as nothing more than mere superstition, which it was!

(38) "WHEREFORE IF DEMETRIUS, AND THE CRAFTSMEN WHICH ARE WITH HIM, HAVE A MATTER AGAINST ANY MAN, THE LAW IS OPEN, AND THERE ARE DEPUTIES: LET THEM IMPLEAD ONE ANOTHER."

The pattern is:

1. The phrase, *"Wherefore if Demetrius, and the craftsmen which are with him, have a matter against any man, the law is open,"* reflects the common sense of the town clerk. In other words, the way to file a complaint was not through the actions of a mob, but rather in open court.

2. *"And there are deputies: let them implead one another,"* refers to the governor appointed by the Roman Senate for provinces under Roman jurisdiction. (Deputies are plural but generally does not mean there were more than one at a time.)

3. In other words, he was saying that if Demetrius really had a case against Paul and those with him, he should pursue it in open court.

(39) "BUT IF YOU ENQUIRE ANY THING CONCERNING OTHER MATTERS, IT SHALL BE DETERMINED IN A LAWFUL ASSEMBLY."

The order is:

1. The phrase, *"But if you inquire any thing concerning other matters,"* in effect, is saying, *"If there are other complaints against Paul than that mentioned, it should be addressed correctly and not by mob action."*

2. *"It shall be determined in a lawful assembly,"* refers to complaints filed in a proper way and done so in a lawful assembly, i.e., open court!

NOTES

(40) "FOR WE ARE IN DANGER TO BE CALLED IN QUESTION FOR THIS DAY'S UPROAR, THERE BEING NO CAUSE WHEREBY WE MAY GIVE AN ACCOUNT OF THIS CONCOURSE."

The construction is:

1. The phrase, *"For we are in danger to be called in question for this day's uproar,"* refers to *"Pax Romana,"* or Roman peace.

2. The Romans at this time were very proud of the law and order they brought to every conquered province. They did not tolerate any kind of uprising, rebellion, or rioting, whatever the cause. They looked at all such action as directed against the Roman government, whether it was or not, and treated everything of this nature as political and as a breach of Roman peace. They would not understand, or even care, that this riot was over a purely religious matter but would take it as a breach of Roman law.

3. *"There being no cause whereby we may give an account of this concourse,"* proclaims the *"townclerk"* wondering how this mob action could be explained.

4. The action this day had put the city in danger of having a charge of sedition, rebellion, or revolution brought against it. This kind of uprising would run a very real risk of having the Roman government crack down on them.

5. To have explained it as a religious controversy would have made the situation even worse. The Roman authorities would have concluded that the appointed officials, who, incidentally, were natives, were not capable of proper administration and, consequently, might need martial law, which would greatly hinder their freedoms.

So now, the danger had passed from Paul to the inciters of this mob action.

(41) "AND WHEN HE HAD THUS SPOKEN, HE DISMISSED THE ASSEMBLY."

The pattern is:

1. The phrase, *"And when he had thus spoken,"* indicates that common sense now prevailed. Obviously, Gaius and Aristarchus were released forthwith.

2. *"He dismissed the assembly,"* proclaims the situation now properly under control.

3. With regard to this great tumult, it is

NOTES

certain that Luke has by no means exaggerated its importance.

4. In his second Epistle to the Corinthians, written from Macedonia shortly after his departure from Ephesus, Paul spoke as one still smarting under the severity of his sufferings. In the language of trust, yet of trust sorely tried, he spoke of the Father of Mercies, *"Who comforts us in all our tribulation."*

5. He spoke of the sufferings of Christ as abounding in him. Then, referring directly to the trouble which came upon him in Asia, he said, *"We were pressed out of measure, above strength, insomuch that we despaired even of life:*

"But we had the sentence of death in ourselves, that we should not trust in ourselves, but in God which raises the dead:

"Who delivered us from so great a death" (II Cor. 1:4-10).

6. It was, no doubt, this occasion of which Paul spoke! It is also very probable, which we have related, that it was on this occasion that Aquila and Priscilla may have saved Paul's life, even at the risk of their own (Rom. 16:3-4).

7. So, it is certain that the riot and the danger to Paul's life were even greater than we should have inferred from Luke's narrative alone.

8. As well, it is believed that the first Epistle to the Corinthians was written at this time from Ephesus (I Cor. 16:8, 19).

"All hail the pow'r of Jesus' Name!
"Let Angels prostrate fall:
"Bring forth the royal diadem,
"And crown Him Lord of all."

CHAPTER 20

(1) "AND AFTER THE UPROAR WAS CEASED, PAUL CALLED UNTO HIM THE DISCIPLES, AND EMBRACED THEM, AND DEPARTED FOR TO GO INTO MACEDONIA."

The exegesis is:

1. The phrase, *"And after the uproar was ceased,"* speaks of the danger which was now past. Whatever Satan had planned in this effort, as is obvious, did not materialize. The Lord used a *"town clerk"* to appease the situation.

2. *"Paul called unto him the disciples, and embraced them,"* speaks of some of the believers of the church in Ephesus. He loved these people even more than words could ever begin to say.

3. When Paul came to this city some three years before, most of these people were rank heathen. Due to their acceptance of the Gospel of Jesus Christ, their lives had been gloriously and wondrously changed. They were now members of the Body of Christ, having been made that way through their faith in the shed blood of the Lamb.

4. Paul, embracing these, not only portrays the heart of a shepherd for the sheep, but, as well, it pictures the great family of God. These people now, or at least most of them, were far closer to each other and to Paul than even some of their blood relatives who did not know Jesus. It continues to be the same presently.

5. *"And departed for to go into Macedonia,"* pertained to his care for the churches in that region.

6. There is a possibility that Aquila and Priscilla left Ephesus at about the same time or soon after. The Epistle to the Romans, which Paul wrote just a little later, found them again at Rome (Rom. 16:3-4).

7. This was probably the last time that Paul would see this body of believers. Sometime later, while on his way to Jerusalem, he would stop at Miletus and from there, send for the Ephesian elders, requesting that they meet him, which they did, but he did not go to Ephesus itself.

(2) "AND WHEN HE HAD GONE OVER THOSE PARTS, AND HAD GIVEN THEM MUCH EXHORTATION, HE CAME INTO GREECE."

The synopsis is:

1. We are saved solely because of what Jesus Christ did at the Cross.

2. We are baptized with the Holy Spirit simply because of what Christ did at the Cross.

CARE OF THE CHURCHES

The phrase, *"And when he had gone over*

those parts," no doubt, included Philippi, Thessalonica, and Berea. How many associates he had traveling with him at this time, we are not told.

That which Paul wrote in II Corinthians 2:12-13 is believed to speak of this time. If that is correct, Paul would have gone from Ephesus to Troas, where he hoped to find Titus, who could give him some information concerning the church at Corinth, as well as other churches, no doubt! However, Titus was not at Troas.

At this time, it seems that the Judaizers were making every effort to circumvent the great Gospel of grace as preached by Paul. These people, who, for the most part, were from Jerusalem, now made it a point to go to many of the churches that Paul had planted and attempt to do two things:

1. They maligned the person of Paul, claiming that he really was not an apostle, etc.

2. They insisted that the Law of Moses must be kept, as well as accepting Jesus Christ, in order for one to be saved. It seems they were not willing to abide by the decision which had been made in Jerusalem about this very thing and is recorded in Acts, Chapter 15. However, it is my thought that this decision, as it was handed down by James and sanctioned by all of the apostles (the original Twelve), even though correct, did not go quite far enough. As we have previously stated, the decision pertained mostly to gentiles and not Jews!

JEWS AND GENTILES

In other words, the gentiles, who were being won to Christ, did not have to add to their faith the keeping of the Law of Moses. James had said, *"Wherefore my sentence is, that we trouble not them, which from among the gentiles are turned to God"* (Acts 15:19).

However, that *"sentence"* said nothing about Jews and, thereby, gave, I think, rise to the very thing now happening, which was to ignore what James had said and impose the Law upon gentiles. It was the greatest attack by Satan to split the church at that time, with some holding to the Law and some not!

I personally feel that if the *"sentence"* handed down by James and agreed to by all had been extended to cover the Jews, many, if not all, of these problems concerning the Law of Moses would have then been solved. This should have been done, and it was what Paul really wanted. While Paul was thrilled about what had been done regarding the gentiles and the great Gospel of grace, I believe that he knew in his heart that the decision fell short of what it should have been. Consequently, the situation had now become acute.

Concerning this very issue, the implication is that when he left Ephesus, he did so with a heavy heart.

News had come to him of the terrible problems concerning the church at Corinth, and other churches, no doubt, as well!

THE CHURCH AT CORINTH

Leaving Troas and going on into Macedonia, he said, *"Our flesh had no rest, but we were troubled on every side; without were fightings, within were fears"* (II Cor. 7:5). However, Titus did eventually get to him with good news concerning the church at Corinth.

Paul had written the Epistle of I Corinthians, dealing with many problems, and in the doing of that, he had made many strong statements. Even though he was inspired by the Holy Spirit in all that he wrote, he was very, very concerned that the church at Corinth might not accept his statements, or at least a strong faction would fall into this category, thereby, causing a split in the church, which is exactly what Satan wanted.

However, the Holy Spirit, having told Paul what to write, used it extensively so. This brought about repentance, which Paul mentioned in II Corinthians 7:8-16.

I realize that many modern preachers would criticize Paul severely, even as they have done in principle, respecting his great consternation regarding the church at Corinth. They would claim that it showed a lack of faith, etc. However, nothing could be further from the truth.

First of all, concern is not a lack of faith, even extensive concern. As well, an attack by Satan against Paul regarding this problem at Corinth, and that is exactly what it

NOTES

was, does not, as well, translate into a lack of faith (II Cor. 1:8-11). In effect, this attack was so severe that he despaired even of his life, as he plainly stated in these passages. Satan always takes full advantage of these types of things, wanting to kill Paul at this time, as should be obvious, but such was not allowed by the Lord.

FAITH

In today's charismatic church climate, few would want to follow a man such as Paul, especially with him confessing that he was *"troubled on every side; without were fightings, within were fears"* (II Cor. 7:5). For somebody to say as he did, *"We were pressed out of measure, above strength, insomuch that we despaired even of life"* (II Cor. 1:8), it would be constituted as a bad confession, etc.

However, the problem with the modern church is Monday morning quarterbacks and armchair generals. In other words, too many preachers are writing books on how to win the victory when they have never even been in a battle! I will gladly follow a man like Paul because he has been there and has come through victorious. I have little interest in the others.

EXHORTATION

The phrase, *"And had given them much exhortation,"* as is obvious, refers to the teaching of the Word of God.

"Exhortation" in the Greek text is *"to implore, or to recommend strongly, to console, which refers to encouragement, to exhort, or to serve in an advisory role,"* which speaks of teaching the Word of God, at least in this case.

The teaching of the Word, even on a constant basis, as should be obvious, is ever so important respecting Christian and Bible growth. In other words, the believer should be constantly learning in this respect because in the Word of God is found the answer and solution to every single problem that one may have regarding life and godliness. As well, it is impossible to exhaust the Word; consequently, the Holy Spirit, irrespective of how much we have previously learned, always has more to impart.

NOTES

The phrase, "He came into Greece," probably refers to a repeat visit to Athens, Corinth, and Cenchrea, as well as other places.

(3) "AND THERE ABODE THREE MONTHS. AND WHEN THE JEWS LAID WAIT FOR HIM, AS HE WAS ABOUT TO SAIL INTO SYRIA, HE PURPOSED TO RETURN THROUGH MACEDONIA."

The diagram is:

1. In certain religious circles, the Cross of Christ is repudiated. Such is the road to disaster.

2. It must be understood, if one wants to live the Resurrection life, which the Lord intends, he or she must understand that the Resurrection is built on the Cross. In other words, if there is no Cross, there is no Resurrection (Rom. 6:5).

JEWS FIGHTING CHRISTIANS

The phrase, *"And there abode three months,"* probably pertains to most of that time spent at Corinth (I Cor. 16:6). The problem seems to have been more acute in that particular church, therefore, claiming more of Paul's attention. Some believe it was during this time that he wrote the Book of Romans. As well, the date of these happenings is placed at approximately A.D. 56, or maybe as late as A.D. 58.

"And when the Jews laid wait for him, as he was about to sail into Syria," apparently pertains to a plot laid against Paul, evidently to take his life. These were most probably Jews from the synagogue at Corinth.

These people had rejected the Gospel of Christ and, as such, now saw Paul as a great threat to Judaism, but it also included jealousy and envy. There is no hatred like religious hatred!

These Jews who were fighting Christianity were, nevertheless, a perfect example of what happens in much of Christendom. Most preachers are not content to merely disagree with particular doctrines, but, at the same time, also feel they must stop the propagation of whatever it is with which they disagree.

As well, many will use any tactic at their disposal to carry out this particular crusade. Even though what I am about to say is strong, I know it to be true.

NOTES

OPPOSITION

The only thing that keeps some preachers from literally killing or murdering other preachers, exactly as Stephen was stoned to death, is the law of the land. In other words, murder is in their hearts.

Then again, many Christians have the idea that if a preacher disagrees with a particular doctrine, at the same time, he is fighting the person propagating such doctrine, whatever it may be.

However, that is not necessarily true. To oppose an erroneous doctrine, or at least that which one believes to be erroneous, is not necessarily to oppose the person preaching that doctrine. Actually, Jesus forbade such by answering the question of the servant, *"Will You then that we go and gather them up* (root them up)*?"*

However, He said, *"No; lest while you gather up the tares* (uproot them)*, you root up also the wheat with them."*

He then went on to say that at the time of the end, He would handle the separation Himself (Mat. 13:28-30).

If one is to notice, Jesus did *not* say, *"Beware the Pharisees and the Sadducees,"* but rather, *"beware of the leaven of the Pharisees and of the Sadducees"* (Mat. 16:6).

SEARCH THE SCRIPTURES

Freedom of religion, as one of the constitutional planks of the United States, is right and scriptural. As a believer, I have the right and the responsibility to *"search the Scriptures daily, whether those things be so,"* concerning what others preach and teach (Acts 17:11).

However, even if I disagree, at the same time, I will fight for their right to preach or teach what they think is right, whomever they may be. The same privilege I demand must be extended to others also!

However, those who are not right with God, irrespective as to what they may claim, not only demand the right to say and preach whatever they desire but, as well, demand the right to stop anyone else who does not agree with them. Such is unscriptural and, therefore, ungodly, as should be obvious! To be frank, it would shock most true believers in this country to know how many preachers, and laypersons for that matter, fall into the category of these Jews. If the truth be known, they desired to kill Paul in the name of the Lord, and would have done so if the occasion had presented itself.

As I have said repeatedly, Satan does his best work from within!

PRESUMPTION?

The phrase, *"He purposed to return through Macedonia,"* basically presents the opposite direction, actually to Philippi, from where he would then turn toward Syria.

I realize that many may misunderstand Paul's actions, concluding such as a lack of faith. In other words, the Lord could have easily taken care of him respecting this plot concerning the Jews.

That is true, but only if the Lord had purposely told Paul to go in that particular direction. That not being the case, Paul ignoring the warnings would have constituted presumption, which is not faith, and which has no promise of anything from God. Regrettably, many believers have never learned the difference between faith and presumption.

The believer must not be foolhardy, claiming God's Protection in any and all things, which many do. Evidently, the Lord left this matter of direction up to Paul, or else, instructed him, which is probably the case, to go toward Philippi rather than taking a ship from Cenchrea. This was probably his original plan. Following that admonition, he was now guaranteed God's Protection.

(4) "AND THERE ACCOMPANIED HIM INTO ASIA SOPATER OF BEREA; AND OF THE THESSALONIANS, ARISTARCHUS AND SECUNDUS; AND GAIUS OF DERBE, AND TIMOTHEUS; AND OF ASIA, TYCHICUS AND TROPHIMUS."

The exegesis is:

1. According to some, the phrase, *"And there accompanied him into Asia,"* indicates that these seven men took the ship as originally planned but without Paul; however, that is not necessarily the case. They could have easily gone to Philippi with Paul and then preceded him to Troas, which is

NOTES

probably what happened.

2. The phrase, *"Sopater of Berea,"* is probably one of Paul's converts from the meetings and resultant church at Berea (Acts 17:10-11).

3. *"And of the Thessalonians, Aristarchus and Secundus,"* as well, spoke of converts from that city (Acts 17:1-4). Aristarchus was with Paul at Ephesus and was seized by the mob there.

4. The phrase, *"And Gaius of Derbe, and Timotheus,"* proclaims two converts from Paul's meetings in Derbe, referring to his first missionary journey (Acts 14:20-23; 16:1-3). This would have been several years before.

As well, *"Gaius"* was also one of Paul's associates seized by the mob at Ephesus.

There are some who claim that the *"Gaius"* of Acts 20:4 is not the same Gaius of Acts 19:29. That may be true, but not necessarily so.

Even though Acts 19:29 speaks of Gaius as a man of Macedonia, it doesn't mean he could not be the same person of Derbe. It is possible that Gaius had ministered extensively in Macedonia, causing him now to be associated with that area.

Timothy, as stated, was converted by Paul on his first trip. He was part Jew and part Greek. He was also ordained as the first bishop (pastor) of Ephesus (I Tim. 1:3). So, Timothy probably stayed in Ephesus for awhile before going to meet Paul in Macedonia or Greece.

It is believed by some that he was Paul's scribe in writing Hebrews and Galatians.

5. *"And of Asia, Tychicus and Trophimus,"* no doubt, as well, speaks of converts from that area.

"Tychicus" is mentioned in Ephesians 6:21; Colossians 4:7; II Timothy 4:12; and Titus 3:12, which indicates that he continued to be in constant attendance to Paul. However, exactly where in Asia he was from is not mentioned, unless it was Ephesus.

Trophimus was called *"an Ephesian"* (Acts 21:29) and, therefore, of Ephesus.

It is believed by some expositors that some of these men were chosen by various churches to take their offerings for the poor to Jerusalem (Acts 19:29; 27:2; Rom. 15:25-28; I Cor. 16:3; II Cor. 8:19-23; 9:12-13; Eph. 6:21-22; Col. 4:10; II Tim. 4:20).

(5) "THESE GOING BEFORE TARRIED FOR US AT TROAS."

The synopsis is:

1. By the use of the pronoun *"us,"* Luke indicated that he had once again joined Paul and his party.

2. In Acts 16:11, we find Luke joining Paul at Troas. He went with him to Philippi (Acts 16:12), and there he appears to have remained until Paul returned there in his third missionary journey, as Acts 20:6 states. Luke continued with Paul on to Jerusalem, where Paul was ultimately arrested. We again find Luke with Paul at Caesarea while he was a prisoner there (Acts 27:1). He, as well, accompanied him on the voyage to Rome, which is the last we hear of him (Acts 27:2-3; 28:2, 11, 14-16).

3. The seven men listed in Verse 4, as stated, had already gone to Troas from Corinth, or else, they left Philippi ahead of Paul and Luke, preceding them to Troas.

4. Troas was across the Aegean Sea from Philippi, actually, southeast of that city.

(6) "AND WE SAILED AWAY FROM PHILIPPI AFTER THE DAYS OF UNLEAVENED BREAD, AND CAME UNTO THEM TO TROAS IN FIVE DAYS; WHERE WE ABODE SEVEN DAYS."

The overview is:

1. Being baptized with the Holy Spirit actually guarantees much, but more than all, portrays the potential of what can be.

2. All victory is found in the Cross of Christ. It is the Cross in which the Holy Spirit works, and, in fact, He will not work outside of the Cross (Rom. 8:2).

THE DAYS OF UNLEAVENED BREAD

The phrase, *"And we sailed away from Philippi after the days of Unleavened Bread,"* speaks of the Passover week. Even though three feasts came about in this week, *"Unleavened Bread, Passover, and Firstfruits,"* it was all referred to as *"Passover."*

As we have previously stated, the Lord originally gave all of these feasts in the Mosaic Law. They were seven in number and were meant to be celebrated at specific times throughout the year as a portrayal of the work which Christ would carry out at His Coming, which He did! Consequently, even though most Christian Jews then continued to keep these feasts, more or less, in truth, their role had been fulfilled, as had all of the Law of Moses by the coming of Christ. The continuing to keep the symbol was not really pleasing to the Lord, I think, inasmuch as the One Who was symbolized had come.

In effect, the continuance of these things made an adverse statement respecting Christ, insinuating that possibly He was not the Messiah or that He did not fully finish the work. This and this alone was, no doubt, the greatest hindrance to the great Gospel of grace that Paul faced. Men do not break religious habits easily!

However, it should be noted that Luke used these designations regarding the feasts mostly as a point of reference.

Fifty days from Passover was the Feast of Pentecost, when Paul desired to be in Jerusalem. So, we know it took this many days, counting the stopovers, to make the trip.

It was to the church at Philippi that Paul wrote his Epistle, which was toward the end of his first imprisonment in Rome. This Epistle was partly in response to a gift sent by the Philippian church and brought by Epaphroditus (Phil. 4:10). Paul also recognized that they had sent him gifts, which were obviously much needed, on other occasions.

The phrase, *"And came unto them to Troas in five days,"* evidently portrays the length of time it took to make the voyage by ship. Inasmuch as it was only about 150 miles, they must have encountered unfavorable winds, etc.

The phrase, *"Where we abode seven days,"* proclaims, according to the next verse, the last day of the seven, a Sunday.

They must have arrived on the preceding Monday, having left Neapolis, the port for Philippi, on the preceding Thursday.

During the seven days, other than Sunday, which was the final day of the seven, there is no record as to where Paul ministered.

(7) "AND UPON THE FIRST DAY OF THE WEEK, WHEN THE DISCIPLES CAME TOGETHER TO BREAK BREAD, PAUL PREACHED UNTO THEM, READY TO DEPART ON THE MORROW; AND CONTINUED HIS SPEECH UNTIL MIDNIGHT."

NOTES

The overview is:

1. *"The death of the Cross"* indicates the climax of Christ's Self-abasement, for it was the most ignominious of all the modes of death then known.

2. Thus, the Cross was surrounded by the deepest shame (Heb. 12:2).

THE MEANING OF THE OLD JEWISH SABBATH

The phrase, *"And upon the first day of the week,"* proclaims important evidence of the keeping of the first day of the week, referred to as the *"Lord's Day,"* which replaced the Jewish Sabbath, which was Saturday. This was evidently done by the Holy Spirit simply because Christ rose from the dead on the first day of the week, which, in a sense, signified a new beginning.

As we have just stated, the Jewish Sabbath was Saturday and was meant strictly to be a "day of rest." In fact, the keeping of the Sabbath was the Fourth Commandment given by God to Moses regarding the Ten Commandments. And yet, we find the New Testament church not keeping the old Jewish Sabbath, but rather the first day of the week, which was Sunday (Mat. 28:1; Mk. 16:9; Jn. 20:1, 19, 26; Acts 20:7; I Cor. 16:2; Rev. 1:10).

Why did the Holy Spirit abolish the old Jewish Sabbath keeping of Saturday and institute in its place Sunday, the first day of the week, as the day of worship?

Everything in the Law of Moses, including the Sabbath, and especially the Sabbath, pointed strictly to Christ. In other words, whatever laws, rules, regulations, or ceremonies were given in that Law, they were all meant to point in some way to the atoning, mediatorial, and intercessory work of Christ. When we say everything, we mean everything, and in every capacity.

Please see our two Commentaries on Exodus and Leviticus concerning a study of the Tabernacle and all its appointments, along with the sacrificial system.

A DAY OF REST

As we have stated, the Sabbath referred to a day of rest more than anything else. In fact, there were no synagogue services on Saturday or anything else of that nature. The people of God were supposed to rest on this particular day, and rest completely.

This *"rest"* was meant to point totally to Christ and the *"rest"* that believers would find in Him and in Him alone.

That's why Jesus said:

"Come unto Me *(is meant by Jesus to reveal Himself as the Giver of Salvation)*, **all *you* who labor and are heavy laden** *(trying to earn Salvation by works)*, **and I will give you rest** *(this 'rest' can only be found by placing one's Faith in Christ and what He has done for us at the Cross [Gal. 5:1-6])*.

"Take My yoke upon you *(the 'yoke' of the 'Cross' [Lk. 9:23])*, **and learn of Me** *(learn of His Sacrifice [Rom. 6:3-5])*; **for I am meek and lowly in heart** *(the only thing that our Lord Personally said of Himself)*: **and you shall find rest unto your souls** *(the soul can find rest only in the Cross)*.

"For My yoke *is* easy, and My burden is light *(what He requires of us is very little, just to have Faith in Him and His Sacrificial, Atoning Work)*" **(Mat. 11:28-30).** (What He requires of us is very little, just to have Faith in Him and His Sacrificial, Atoning Work.)

THE SUBSTITUTE AND THE SUBSTANCE

The Jewish Sabbath was a substitute, or rather a type of Christ, Who would come and Who alone could give *"rest."* To be sure, there was a modicum of *"rest"* found in the keeping of the Jewish Sabbath, that is, if they understood what it meant and placed their faith accordingly. However, the facts portray that Israel little knew or understood at any time, with, of course, some few exceptions, what all these ceremonies actually meant. So, more and more, she looked to the ceremony itself, which, in reality, provided no *"rest"* whatsoever.

Concerning this, Paul said:

"And to whom swore He that they should not enter into His rest, but to them who believed not? *(Israel lost everything because of unbelief, and the modern Church is doing the same, which is the very reason that Paul wrote the Epistle to the Hebrews.)*

"So we see that they could not enter in because of unbelief *(and if the modern Believer registers unbelief toward Christ and the Cross, the results will be the same as with Israel of old)*.

"Let us *(modern Believers)* **therefore fear** *(refers to the fact that Salvation can be lost if the Believer ceases to believe)*, **lest, a Promise being left *us* of entering into His rest** *(the Promise of Salvation)*, **any of you should seem to come short of it.** *(This proves it is possible for such to be done, which means the loss of the soul.)*

"For unto us was the Gospel preached, as well as unto them *(there is only one Gospel, and that is 'Jesus Christ and Him Crucified')*: **but the Word preached did not profit them** *(if the Cross is abandoned as the object of Faith, Christ will profit no one anything [Gal. 5:2])*, **not being mixed with faith in them who heard *it*.** *(The Israelites had faith, but not in the right object. It must be Faith in Christ and the Cross, or it's not valid faith.)*

ENTERING INTO REST

"For we which have believed do enter into rest *(proclaims unequivocally that faith is the key, but let it be understood that it's Faith in Christ and the Cross)*, **as He said, As I have sworn in My Wrath, if they shall enter into My rest** *(the condition is Faith)*: **although the works were finished from the foundation of the world** *(this refers to this great Plan of Salvation through Christ and the Cross having been formulated even before the world was created [I Pet. 1:18-20])*.

"For He *(God)* **spoke in a certain place of the seventh *day* on this wise** *(Gen. 2:3)*, **and God did rest the seventh day from all His Works.** *(God ceased from the Work of Creation, simply because the Creation was finished.)*

"And in this *place* again *(Ps. 95:7-11)*, **If they shall enter into My rest** *(conditions are to be met)*.

"Seeing therefore it remains that some

must enter therein *(speaks of the New Covenant and the Church)*, **and they to whom it was first preached entered not in because of unbelief** *(proclaims from Verse 2 that the Israelites of old had the same Gospel preached unto them as we do, but to no avail)*:

"Again, He *(God)* **limited a certain day** *(proclaims in no uncertain terms that even though the Call of God is unlimited, the opportunity to accept that Call is definitely limited)*, **saying in David, Today, after so long a time** *(the Holy Spirit said 'Today' then, and He is continuing to say 'Today' at present, referring to the fact that tomorrow may be too late)*; **as it is said, Today if you will hear His Voice, harden not your hearts** *(once again, refers to unbelief)*.

JESUS

"For if Jesus *(should have been translated 'Joshua')* **had given them rest** *(refers to the fact that even though Joshua was able to lead Israel into the Land of Canaan by the Power of the Holy Spirit, this was only a symbol of the true Rest which was to come, namely, the Lord Jesus Christ)*, **then would He** *(God)* **not afterward have spoken of another day** *(meaning the Law could not bring about what was desired, but definitely did point to that which was to come, namely, the Lord Jesus Christ)*.

"There remains *(what the Law couldn't do, Christ would do)* **therefore a Rest to the people of God.** *(This is found only in Christ and through what He did at the Cross, to which everything in the Old Testament pointed.)*

"For he who has entered into His *(God's)* **rest** *(due to what Christ did at the Cross, anyone can enter into this 'Rest')*, **he also has ceased from his own works** *(we enter in by Faith, which refers to Faith in Christ and what He did at the Cross)*, **as God** ***did*** **from His.** *(God rested on the seventh day when Creation was finished. And we can rest in Christ because the Plan of Redemption is finished, of which God's Rest was a Type.)*

"Let us labour therefore to enter into that Rest *(could be translated 'Let us hasten therefore to enter into that Rest')*, **lest any man fall after the same example of unbelief** *(This tells us that the root cause of the 'fall' of any Believer is unbelief, and it refers to unbelief in the Cross, which was the true Mission of Christ, which alone gives 'Rest')"* **(Heb. 3:18-19; 4:1-11).**

NOTES

JUSTIN MARTYR

The phrase, *"When the disciples came together to break bread,"* presents a Hebraism, which means *"to dine in company"* (Deut. 26:14; Job 42:11; Jer. 16:7; Ezek. 24:17; Hos. 9:4; Mat. 14:19; 15:36; Lk. 24:30, 35; Acts 27:33-36).

The belief entertained by some that this was the Catholic Mass, or by others that it was what is now called the *"Lord's Supper,"* is without foundation. However, it is certainly possible that they did celebrate the *"Lord's Supper"* at this time, but it is not guaranteed in the Text.

In fact, the following is a description given by Justin Martyr in his second apology to Marcus Aurelius of the church assemblies in his day, which was less than 100 years after Paul's day.

He said:

SUNDAY

"On the day which is called Sunday, all Christians who dwell either in town or country come together to one place. The memoirs of the Apostles and the writings of the Prophets are read for a certain time, and then the President of the meeting, when the reader has stopped, makes a discourse, in which he instructs and exhorts the people to the imitation of the good deeds of which they have just heard.

"We then all rise up together, and address prayers to the Lord; and when our prayers are ended, bread and wine and water are brought, and the President, to the best of his ability, offers up both prayers and thanksgivings, and the people assent, saying 'Amen.'

"And then the distribution of the bread and wine, over which the thanksgivings have been offered, is made to all present, and all partake of it."

He added that the elements (bread and wine) are carried to the absent by the deacons, and that collections are made for poor widows, orphans, sick, and prisoners.

PAUL PREACHING UNTIL MIDNIGHT

The phrase, *"Paul preached unto them, ready to depart on the morrow; and continued his speech until midnight,"* proclaims him ministering possibly for several hours.

Paul, no doubt, dealt with many problems, even answering their questions. For this length of time, he could well have dealt with the subject of the gifts of the Spirit, the Resurrection, and the second coming of Christ, as well as the Law/grace issue, etc.

To have the privilege to hear the Apostle Paul was a privilege unexcelled. I think it can be said that no man at that particular time knew more about the Gospel of Jesus Christ than Paul.

And yet, I am certain that the accounts given of the life and ministry of Jesus by the original Twelve Apostles were, of necessity, unexcelled in their glorious blessing, especially considering that it was firsthand information about Christ. So, the statements we make about Paul, which are extremely positive, and should be, are no way meant to take away from the contribution of the original Twelve, which, in fact, could not be done, even if someone tried. Nothing, and I mean absolutely nothing, supersedes firsthand information about Jesus, as I think should be obvious!

EYEWITNESS ACCOUNTS OF JESUS

How blessed anyone would have been to have had the privilege to hear the Apostle Paul, but again, how blessed to have been able to hear eyewitness accounts of Jesus. No wonder John the Beloved is reputed to have said, *"When I am gone, there will be no one left alive who saw Him, who touched Him, and who heard Him!"*

Even now as I dictate these words, I greatly sense the presence of God. That of which we speak concerning both Paul and the Twelve is of such magnitude as to defy all description. By that, I do not mean what we say, and clumsily so I might quickly add, but rather these august happenings concerning the great Gospel of Jesus Christ and those He called to observe and take that Gospel to the world.

NOTES

Some say that Paul's Message that night was the longest sermon on record, lasting perhaps from six to ten hours. He had much to say to these people and only that night in which to say it, as he would leave the following day.

(8) "AND THERE WERE MANY LIGHTS IN THE UPPER CHAMBER, WHERE THEY WERE GATHERED TOGETHER."

The construction is:

1. The phrase, *"And there were many lights in the upper chamber,"* evidently spoke of a third story room, as will later be revealed, believed to hold approximately 200 to 300 people.

2. The phrase, *"Where they were gathered together,"* probably refers to the fact that this was the meeting place or church in Troas.

3. Why Luke would have mentioned the *"many lights"* is not immediately obvious. Perhaps there were far more in the room than normal and were olive oil lamps, as was common in those days.

4. The idea seems to be that they knew Paul was going to speak to them, and they wanted the room well lit so that all could easily see and be seen. Many times in those days, questions were asked of the speaker concerning what had been taught, with convenient light making it easier to do so.

(9) "AND THERE SAT IN A WINDOW A CERTAIN YOUNG MAN NAMED EUTYCHUS, BEING FALLEN INTO A DEEP SLEEP: AND AS PAUL WAS LONG PREACHING, HE SUNK DOWN WITH SLEEP, AND FELL DOWN FROM THE THIRD LOFT, AND WAS TAKEN UP DEAD."

The status is:

1. The phrase, *"And there sat in a window a certain young man named Eutychus, being fallen into a deep sleep,"* presents an open window, which was common in those days. In other words, a wooden shutter covered the window and could be easily opened, which they were in the summer, to admit breeze, etc.

2. As Paul had probably ministered for several hours, and it was now approaching midnight, the young man simply fell asleep.

3. *"And as Paul was long preaching, he sunk down with sleep,"* is not meant in the

NOTES

Text to find fault with Paul or the young man who fell asleep. Luke was just simply stating what happened, with no inference to be drawn from the statements.

Some have claimed that the Lord allowed him to fall because of not paying attention to the Word of God, but there is nothing in the Text to substantiate such a thought.

4. *"And fell down from the third loft,"* means that the upper chamber where the people gathered was the third story. It was probably over 20 feet from the street or courtyard below, which was undoubtedly paved with stone. This would have caused his death!

5. *"And was taken up dead,"* was written by Luke, a physician, who was an expert in such matters.

6. As well, the Greek clearly indicates that the boy was dead and not just thought to be, as some claim.

7. Here, the Greek is the same as is used elsewhere when people were actually dead. He was a lifeless corpse. In the natural, there was no hope for him.

8. Obviously, everyone's attention was on Paul as he was ministering to them, with no one noticing the boy sitting in the window having fallen asleep. Sitting in such a window constituted no danger normally; however, to fall asleep did constitute great danger, as is here obvious.

(10) "AND PAUL WENT DOWN, AND FELL ON HIM, AND EMBRACING HIM SAID, TROUBLE NOT YOURSELVES; FOR HIS LIFE IS IN HIM."

The exegesis is:

1. The phrase, *"And Paul went down,"* does not indicate in the Text that he was the first one to reach the boy. Actually, there is indication that a number of others arrived first, ascertained that he was dead, and began to weep, and to do so loudly.

2. *"And fell on him, and embracing him,"* presents the example of Elijah in this, which is probably what Paul intended.

3. In I Kings 17:17-21, when the widow's son died, Elijah came and stretched himself over the child three times and prayed. The Hebrew indicates that Elijah did not put any of his weight on the child, but rather bent over him as an expression of faith in prayer. The emphasis is clearly on prayer, which Paul undoubtedly engaged.

4. Elisha had a similar experience when the son of the wealthy Shunammite woman died (II Ki. 4:34-35).

5. The phrase, *"Said, Trouble not yourselves; for his life is in him,"* in effect, makes two statements:

a. The phrase, *"Trouble not yourselves,"* implies that many had begun weeping, even uncontrollably, which, in a situation of this nature, would be understandable. Paul now told them they could stop the weeping, etc.

b. The phrase, *"For his life is in him,"* does not mean, as some claim, that the boy had merely been knocked unconscious, but rather that he had been dead and that Jesus had infused life back into him.

"Life" in the Greek is *"psuche,"* which also means *"soul"* or *"person,"* but, in this case, means physical life.

In effect, Paul here calmed the rising sobs and wailings of the people standing around the body of Eutychus, by saying, *"Do not wail over him as dead, for Jesus has restored his life to him."*

Even though the Scripture is silent regarding this moment, it is obvious that the weeping, at least for sorrow, instantly subsided, with shouts of praises to the Lord filling the air. What a moment that was!

(11) "WHEN HE THEREFORE WAS COME UP AGAIN, AND HAD BROKEN BREAD, AND EATEN, AND TALKED A LONG WHILE, EVEN TILL BREAK OF DAY, SO HE DEPARTED."

The order is:

1. The debt that was owed by man was not owed to Satan, but rather to God.

2. While the Cross definitely defeated Satan and all powers of darkness, it was not actually instituted to address the problem according to Satan, but rather according to God.

3. As stated, this debt was owed to God, and it was to God that this debt must be paid, which it was paid by the Cross.

BIBLE CHRISTIANITY

The phrase, *"When he therefore was come up again, and had broken bread, and eaten,"* presents a joyous occasion of fellowship. What a delightful time that must have been!

These people had the Word of God imparted to them as possibly they had never heard before. As well, they had seen a demonstration of the power of God as few human beings have ever seen, a boy actually raised from the dead, and right in front of their very eyes.

There is nothing in the world, and I mean absolutely nothing, which can compete with Bible Christianity. Everything else, irrespective of its wealth or numerical status, is man-devised and, therefore, man-instituted, consequently, of no spiritual purpose, regardless of its claims. Tragically and sadly, much of Christianity falls into that category as well!

Only when the Holy Spirit is properly allowed control in the believer's life can Jesus be properly glorified and the work of God carried out as it should be. However, for all the hundreds of millions who claim Christ around the world, most, regrettably, are not even saved. In other words, they are merely religious and not born-again. They are like Nicodemus of old. Although a respected teacher of the Bible in the Israel of Jesus' Day, nevertheless, he was not saved. Hence, Jesus told him, *"Verily, verily, I say unto you, Except a man be born-again, he cannot see the Kingdom of God"* (Jn. 3:3).

NICODEMUS

Sadder still, the far greater majority will not even remotely come up to the status of Nicodemus although claiming Christ.

Again, of the hundreds of millions who are truly saved, many have been taught erroneously that the mighty Baptism with the Holy Spirit (Acts 2:4) is not for this present time, having passed away with the Apostles, or some other such type foolishness. The Holy Spirit is the One Who carries out the work of God in our lives; consequently, without Him, nothing is done. Through false doctrine, Satan has effectively shut down this very large segment of the Christian community.

Even of those who claim the Baptism with the Holy Spirit with the evidence of speaking with other tongues, there are only a precious few who are really truly led and guided by the Spirit of God. This is because of self-will, lack of consecration, erroneous teaching, etc.

All of this which I have mentioned is obvious by the lack of spiritual fruit within the lives of these people, whomever they may be (Mat. 7:15-20).

THE PHILOSOPHY OF CHRISTIANITY

Hundreds of millions around the world have accepted the philosophy of Christianity but have never had a relationship with Christ. In other words, they are not saved, even though most would probably claim to be. These individuals, and their numbers are overly large, subscribe to some type of Christian *"golden rule,"* which makes them feel righteous but, in effect, is a religion of their own making. The transforming power and nature of Christ has never been empowered to their lives simply because they have never been regenerated by the power of God.

These people function by a list of rules pretty much of their own making. They judge their lives according to a Brownie point system, which compares the good with the bad, etc. Of course, they always judge their *"good"* greater than their *"bad,"* never seeming to realize that this is not the basis at all on which God judges humanity, irrespective as to how good their good may be. However, it deceives many in the world.

CHURCH MEMBERSHIP

The far greater number of these people belong to a church of some nature and attend spasmodically, if not regularly. In fact, their church actually becomes a part of the whole scheme.

Years ago in Baton Rouge, Louisiana, a young man came to the Lord who had been a professional ballplayer with one of the major league teams. He came to my door one Saturday morning, one of the rare times that Frances and I were home because we were traveling almost constantly in those days. He introduced himself and told me that he wanted to be baptized with the Holy Spirit.

I found out that he was a member of one of the major old-line churches in the city and had just given his heart and life to the Lord.

I explained to him how that the Baptism with the Holy Spirit was a different experience apart from salvation and was meant to give the believer power, etc. (Acts 1:8), and I prayed for him to be filled. It being some years ago, I do not remember if he was filled that day or later, but I do remember that he did ultimately receive this wondrous Gift from the Lord.

Seeing him sometime later and discussing the situation, I happened to refer to the church to which he belonged.

He instantly stated, *"Brother Swaggart, I do not attend that church anymore."*

He then said with a chuckle, *"I began to tell others in the church how the Lord had saved me and filled me with the Holy Spirit, which prompted me being called into the pastor's office."*

"After a short conversation regarding my experience, he said to me, 'John (not his real name), *I think you might be happier in another church!'"*

He laughed again and said, *"Brother Swaggart, when I was staying drunk half the time, strung out on drugs, and engaging in every type of immorality one could think, with my life coming apart, as well as my marriage and family, I was a member in good standing in this church."*

He then said, *"Now that Jesus has saved my soul and baptized me with the Holy Spirit, which has occasioned a total change in my lifestyle, which has saved my home, my marriage, and everything I hold dear, I am now no longer welcome in this church."*

Regrettably, this is not an isolated case, but rather the norm in most church circles which deny the Baptism with the Holy Spirit. In other words, they are left with a mere philosophy of Christianity, which will actually save no one.

JESUS!

Without Jesus, and I mean Jesus as paramount, supreme, total, absolute, and the center and circumference of all things, Christianity is reduced to a mere religion. In fact, Jesus and Him Crucified is true Christianity, at least that which is according to the Bible.

NOTES

Of the hundreds of millions who fall into this category of having only the philosophy of Christianity, Jesus Christ is merely a part of the religious mix. He is looked at as Someone Who lived a long time ago and was a good Teacher, etc. Others in this false way may even claim that He is the Son of God, but simply believing that is not enough, at least as it falls into a mere mental assent. In other words, they have never really had a life-changing experience with Christ, which, in fact, can come about by one simply trusting Him, thereby, giving one's heart and life to Him.

Again, many, if not most, of these people would claim the very thing I have just said, but, as stated, the fruit of their lives show otherwise!

THE BAPTISM WITH THE HOLY SPIRIT

I strongly maintain that the reason for this, at least for the most part, is because of erroneous doctrine respecting the Baptism with the Holy Spirit. In other words, these preachers, who lead these congregations by the hundreds of thousands, claim that this of which I speak (Acts 2:4) passed away with the apostles, with some of them even going so far as to say that it is of the devil, etc. Consequently, they have closed the door to the Holy Spirit, Who leads us into all things pertaining to God and His Word, even though professing to believe. However, the Holy Spirit in these individuals is totally silent with absolutely no part or parcel in anything that is done. As a theological doctrine, they accept the Holy Spirit, but only as a doctrine, with Him playing no role whatsoever in anything they do regarding the Lord and His Word. As a result, almost all, if not all, that is done in these circles is man-devised and not Spirit-led.

As a result, most of the people in these respective churches are not even saved, and the few who are saved stay on the edge of spiritual anemia because they have been told the Holy Spirit, as an experience in one's life, is not valid at this time. Therefore, they are depriving them of the only One Who can give them all the things that true Christianity actually provides.

THE LATTER RAIN OUTPOURING!

Some may attempt to counter my statements by referring to men who were used greatly by the Lord in long years past, but yet, did not teach the Baptism with the Holy Spirit as I am here proclaiming (Acts 2:4). However, if one is to notice, they only point to those in the past but to precious few, if any, at the present! The reason is simple:

These men of whom they speak, such as D. L. Moody, etc., were walking in all the light they presently had. As a result, the Lord used them greatly. The light on the Holy Spirit began to be spread abroad in the world at approximately the turn of the 20th century. This was fulfilling Joel's prophecies concerning the *"Latter Rain"* (Joel 2:23-32; Acts 2:15-21), which actually began with the *"Former Rain"* on the Day of Pentecost. Even though continuing to be patient as always, the Lord expected that *"light"* to be responded to favorably.

Thankfully, it was responded to favorably by literally hundreds of thousands in old-line churches. However, most, if not almost all, of the so-called leadership in these particular denominations rejected it out of hand. Consequently, they have not only lost the *"light"* which they could have had but rejected, but lost what little light they did have, leaving them with basically a hollow religious shell.

I realize that my statements are strong, but again, the fruit, I think, will bear me out.

When the Lord gives *"light,"* He expects people to walk in that light. Actually, this is what Paul said, *"And the times of this ignorance God winked at; but now commands all men every where to repent"* (Acts 17:30).

SPIRIT-FILLED PEOPLE?

As revolutionary as salvation is to the sinner, as revolutionary will be the Baptism with the Holy Spirit to the believer.

Someone has said that salvation separates the believing sinner from the world, while the Baptism with the Holy Spirit separates the believer from dead, cold, religious ritual.

However, having said that, I must also point to millions who have, in fact, been baptized with the Holy Spirit but have allowed Him precious little latitude within their lives. Consequently, they receive precious little of what He can actually do. However, that is not the Spirit's fault, but rather their fault!

One could say, and rightly so, that after one is *"Spirit-filled,"* one must allow the Holy Spirit to bring one to the place to where one is Spirit-controlled. That is the problem! He does not have much control in many lives, with all of us, to be frank, desperately needing to yield to His Leading more than we presently do.

The very first thing, and the most important thing, the Holy Spirit will do is to begin to glorify Jesus in the believer's heart and life. His primary objective is to make Jesus more and more real, and active I might quickly add! Christ becomes paramount in all things. As someone has said, and rightly so, *"The greatest thing which will happen to the Spirit-filled believer is not speaking in tongues, as great and wonderful and helpful as that is, but rather the Holy Spirit placing a love in one's heart for Christ as one has never had before, thereby, establishing a relationship which can be obtained no other way."*

Again I emphasize, everything done by the Lord and for the Lord in this world, and I mean every single thing, comes through the person, agency, office, and ministry of the Holy Spirit. In fact, it has always been that way (Gen. 1:2). So, if the Bible pattern of the Holy Spirit is denied, all His Services are forfeited, with the effort then being totally man-directed, which will accomplish no work for the Lord.

HOW THE HOLY SPIRIT WORKS

When asked as to how the Holy Spirit works within their lives, most believers will respond with a blank stare. Most think that whatever it is that he does, it's just automatically done. Nothing could be further from the truth.

If the Holy Spirit just functioned automatically, then not a single believer would ever fail the Lord in any capacity. The Holy Spirit would simply step in and stop the wrongdoing, whatever it is; however, we

NOTES

know that this doesn't happen.

And yet, the Holy Spirit is God, which means that He can do anything; however, He will never violate our free moral agency. He'll speak to us, deal with us, and move upon us, but He will not force the issue. So, how is it that He works within our lives and uses His mighty Power on our behalf?

The Holy Spirit works entirely within the confines, so to speak, of the Cross of Christ. In other words, it's the Cross that gives the Holy Spirit the legal means to do all that He does within our hearts and within our lives. Paul said:

"For the Law of the Spirit of Life in Christ Jesus, has made me free from the Law of sin and death" (Rom. 8:2).

The Holy Spirit does not demand much of us, but He does demand one thing, and on that He will not bend. He demands that our faith ever be in Christ and what Christ has done for us at the Cross. That being the case, the Holy Spirit will then work mightily on our behalf, doing for us what we cannot do for ourselves, and will do so wondrously.

Every believer must understand that we are facing in the spirit world fallen angels and demon spirits, which seek to steal, kill, and destroy. In our own education, ability, personal strength, will power, etc., we are simply unable to overcome these powerful forces. That's the reason that Paul said:

"We wrestle not against flesh and blood, but against principalities, against powers, against the rulers of the darkness of this world, and against spiritual wickedness in high places" (Eph. 6:12).

Using the *"flesh"* as Paul often put it, we are helpless before these powers. However, we are not helpless if we use the mighty name of Jesus and, thereby, place our faith exclusively in Christ and what He has done for us at the Cross. As stated, the Holy Spirit will then work mightily with us and for us. However, most modern Christians have no idea whatsoever as to how the Holy Spirit works.

Even though what we have given you is very brief, it is to the point and will help you to understand simply how to live for God, at least if you will heed what we have said.

The Answer of the Lord to demon spirits and to sin of any nature always and without exception is the Cross of Christ.

NOTES

A SPIRITUAL PROBLEM

Man's problem is a spiritual problem. It is not economical, agricultural, intellectual, or educational. Inasmuch as it is spiritual, the things which must be done to address these terrible problems cannot be done in the natural or by natural means, but only by the power of God registered in the life of the believer through and by the power of the Holy Spirit. That is the reason Jesus *"commanded"* His Followers to be filled with the Spirit first before they attempted to do things for Him (Acts 1:4). The reason is simple! Without the Baptism with the Holy Spirit, none of these things can be done. Incidentally, He does not come automatically at conversion but is a separate and distinct experience other than salvation.

I will say it again: without the Holy Spirit, and I might quickly add, the manner in which He is portrayed in the Bible, Christianity pretty much becomes little more than a philosophy. That is why the Holy Spirit through Paul addressed these *"last days"* and stated, in essence, that much of the church would *"have a form of godliness, but deny the power thereof."*

He then said, *"From such turn away"* (II Tim. 3:1-5).

The phrase, *"And talked a long while, even till break of day,"* portrays, as we have stated, this one message lasting some six to ten hours. It was interrupted only by the raising of the boy from the dead and the meal which was served a little after midnight.

"So he departed," refers, of course, to him and his associates leaving the city but, more importantly, leaving the people with great and grand things that had happened. They had experienced, as stated, the teaching of the Word of God, of which there could be nothing more important. As well, they had experienced the mighty power of God in the raising of the boy from the dead. It was a momentous occasion to say the least!

Whenever the man or woman of God does depart, in whatever capacity, may the Lord help all of us to leave the people, as we go to

NOTES

other fields of endeavors, as Paul left those believers at Troas.

(12) "AND THEY BROUGHT THE YOUNG MAN ALIVE, AND WERE NOT A LITTLE COMFORTED."

The construction is:

1. The phrase, *"And they brought the young man alive,"* probably refers to him being in his teens, with the people exultant over what the Lord had done, even physically examining him, in a sense, to see that there was no trace left in his physical body regarding this terrible fall, which had actually taken his life.

2. *"And were not a little comforted,"* certainly presents that which is understandable but, from the word *"comforted,"* it more so proclaims the doctrine of the Resurrection.

3. Paul used the same word in his description of the Rapture or Resurrection by saying, *"Wherefore comfort one another with these words"* (I Thess. 4:13-18).

4. Along with being overjoyed that the boy had been raised from the dead, they were, as well, thrilled at this example of the coming Resurrection, which Paul, no doubt, had explained and demonstrated to them graphically so that night.

5. As well, this young man would have something to tell people for the balance of his life, which, no doubt, included many years.

(13) "AND WE WENT BEFORE TO SHIP, AND SAILED UNTO ASSOS, THERE INTENDING TO TAKE IN PAUL: FOR SO HAD HE APPOINTED, MINDING HIMSELF TO GO AFOOT."

The synopsis is:

1. If one were to ask most Christians, even preachers, how the Holy Spirit works in our hearts and lives, one would probably be met with a blank stare.

2. The answer is: He works exclusively by and through the Cross of Christ, which demands the faith of every believer (Rom. 8:2).

FOLLOWING THE LEADING OF THE LORD

The phrase, *"And we went before to ship,"* refers to Luke and the men of Verse 4, but not Paul, as we shall see. Actually, it seems they may have left even before Paul finished his teaching to the gathered congregation. More than likely, the ship was leaving at daylight, or possibly even a little before, and to catch the ship, they had to leave early.

"And sailed unto Assos," presents a short distance around Cape Lectum of about 40 miles.

The phrase, *"There intending to take in Paul: for so had he appointed, minding himself to go afoot,"* presents a distance by land of about 20 miles.

Why Paul wanted to walk this distance alone, we are not told!

Some have ventured that the Holy Spirit, through various different means, had related to Paul extensively the terrible trials which were just ahead. Actually, he would relate this to the Ephesians just a short time later (Acts 20:22-24).

Knowing these things, it is possible that he desired to walk this distance alone in order that he may settle it with the Lord whether it was truly His Will for him to continue on this trip.

THE LEADING OF THE LORD

If we follow closely the experiences of the Apostle Paul, plus others in the Word of God as well, we soon come to the conclusion that finding the mind of the Lord is not always as easy as some have claimed. While at times the believer knows beyond the shadow of a doubt what the Lord wants, at other times, it is not so clear and simple.

For instance, and to which we have already alluded, when Paul left on his second missionary journey, he left with every intention of going in a certain direction. I am positive he was thinking that he had the Mind of the Lord. However, as the Scripture portrays, he was to find after the journey began that this was not exactly the case. Even after the trip had begun, the Holy Spirit stopped him at the time from preaching the Word in Asia. It also says, *"They assayed to go into Bithynia: but the Spirit suffered them not."*

However, the Lord would then give Paul direction regarding the Macedonian call (Acts 16:6-10).

It is certain that Paul earnestly sought the Lord, no doubt, as well as the entirety of

NOTES

the church at Antioch, regarding this trip, thinking that they knew exactly what the Lord wanted. So, why did the Lord function in this capacity?

CONSTANT SEEKING OF THE LORD

I believe the Scripture is clear that the manner in which the Lord functions is designed, among other means, to keep the believer constantly seeking Him. One has to walk very close to the Lord in order to ascertain the will of God.

The truth is, man is so construed in his spirit and will, which is a symptom of the Fall, that if given the slightest opportunity, he will veer off course spiritually. He will take God for granted, automatically assuming that he knows the Mind and Will of the Lord at all times, which is not the case! So, to counter this constant danger, even in the choicest such as Paul, the Lord ladles out information to us very sparingly at times. This keeps us seeking Him and constantly depending on Him.

The danger always is, as stated, that we cease to depend on the Lord and rather on ourselves. Many times we think our dependence is in God when it really is not.

Self is a very deceitful, egotistical, and personal seeking part of our physical, emotional, mental, and spiritual make-up.

Someone has said, and rightly so, that Jesus died on Calvary not only to deliver man from sin but, as well, from self! Consequently, one is to *"deny himself, and take up his cross, and follow Me"* (Mk. 8:34).

Actually, self must be crucified on a daily basis (Lk. 9:23). How is that to be done?

It means that on a daily basis, we look to Christ and the Cross for all that we need, which the Holy Spirit will then supply. The key in all of this is the Cross of Christ. Any other way or means of trying to live for God other than the Cross brings glory to self, which God can never honor. When the believer places his or her faith exclusively in Christ and the Cross, then the Lord in totality receives the glory for all that is done, whatever it is.

Paul also said: *"That you may prove what is that good, and acceptable, and perfect Will of God"* (Rom. 12:2).

(14) "AND WHEN HE MET WITH US AT ASSOS, WE TOOK HIM IN, AND CAME TO MITYLENE."

The synopsis is:

1. The phrase, *"And when he met with us at Assos,"* seems to indicate that they arrived there before Paul, which was, no doubt, the case.

2. *"We took him in, and came to Mitylene,"* presented another approximate 40 mile trip by ship. This was the capital of the island of Lesbos, about 40 miles, as well, from the Asia Minor coast (modern Turkey). The Romans had made this island a favorite vacation spot. Its excellent harbor faced the coast of Asia Minor and, thus, it was a convenient place for the ship to stop.

3. Even though the Scripture is silent on the subject, I think we would have to assume that Paul had settled this thing with the Lord, knowing he was in God's Will respecting this trip to Jerusalem, irrespective of the hardships he would face. Even as we have stated, for one to know beyond the shadow of a doubt that he has the mind of God in a particular thing is a most comforting feeling, and one which brings about a deep settled peace. However, such does not mean that the problems will go away, but it does mean the Lord will see us through, whatever the situation.

(15) "AND WE SAILED THENCE, AND CAME THE NEXT DAY OVER AGAINST CHIOS; AND THE NEXT DAY WE ARRIVED AT SAMOS, AND TARRIED AT TROGYLLIUM; AND THE NEXT DAY WE CAME TO MILETUS."

The exegesis is:

1. The phrase, *"And we sailed thence, and came the next day over against Chios,"* presents another island about the size of Lesbos. It lay due west of both Smyrna and Ephesus, about 100 miles in distance.

2. *"And the next day we arrived at Samos,"* presents about 100 miles distance, as well, for that day's travel and another large island, which was southwest of Ephesus. It had been made a free state by the Roman Emperor Augustus. However, it doesn't seem that they stopped at Samos.

3. *"And tarried at Trogyllium,"* presents

a narrow strait between the island of Samos and the promontory point at this area, which made the channel here barely a mile wide.

4. Evidently, they came on past Samos and anchored for the night at Trogyllium, not getting off the ship. During those days, this channel was evidently too dangerous to navigate at night.

5. *"And the next day we came to Miletus,"* presents a trip about 20 miles from where they had spent the night. Miletus was about 30 miles south of Ephesus.

6. This city was founded by the Ionian Greeks and was very prosperous until it was destroyed by the Persians in 494 B.C. Though it was rebuilt, it never regained its past glories.

7. Some believe this is the same place mentioned by Paul in II Timothy 4:20, and spelled *"Miletum,"* which is probably the case.

(16) "FOR PAUL HAD DETERMINED TO SAIL BY EPHESUS, BECAUSE HE WOULD NOT SPEND THE TIME IN ASIA: FOR HE HASTED, IF IT WERE POSSIBLE FOR HIM, TO BE AT JERUSALEM THE DAY OF PENTECOST."

The overview is:

1. The phrase, *"For Paul had determined to sail by Ephesus,"* means that he would not stop there because of a lack of time. However, he would see the Ephesian elders, as we shall see.

2. *"Because he would not spend the time in Asia,"* tells us, I think, having settled this thing with the Lord respecting this eventful trip, he did not want to tarry.

3. *"For he hasted, if it were possible for him, to be at Jerusalem the Day of Pentecost,"* distinctly marks this time. Paul was at Philippi at the time of the Passover and hoped to reach Jerusalem by Pentecost, which was 50 days after the Passover. It is obvious from the Text that even though this matter was settled with the Lord respecting the trip, it still weighed heavily on Paul's mind.

It was almost as if he must haste lest he tarry, for if he did tarry, he might not go at all, considering the terrible hardships of which the Holy Spirit had already warned him and would continue to do so.

NOTES

(17) "AND FROM MILETUS HE SENT TO EPHESUS, AND CALLED THE ELDERS OF THE CHURCH."

The status is:

1. The only way that Christlikeness can be carried out in the life of the believer is that we have a correct interpretation of the Cross.

2. This refers to what Jesus did in that great Sacrifice, understanding our part in that and why it was done, and placing all of our trust in this Finished Work.

THE ELDERS OF THE CHURCH

The phrase, *"And from Miletus he sent to Ephesus,"* does not tell us how this was done. It was about 30 miles to Ephesus and would have taken a full day for a messenger to arrive and a full day to return.

Paul probably reasoned that this would be quicker than going to Ephesus himself, inasmuch as the elders there, and in other churches nearby, as well, would, no doubt, press him greatly to spend time with them, which he, of course, longed to do. However, two factors were involved, as we have mentioned:

1. As stated, he wanted to be in Jerusalem by Pentecost.

2. Once again, I think he may have feared that if he became involved in ministering in these churches to any extent, he would forfeit the trip to Jerusalem altogether.

Even though I am attempting to read Paul at this time, we certainly do not desire to misdirect. And yet, I think the weight of the Text lends integrity to the things I have said.

The phrase, *"And called the elders of the church,"* speaks of the pastors of that church.

PASTOR

Terms such as elder, bishop, overseer, shepherd, and presbyter, all indicate the one office of pastor. There was no such thing as a Diocesan Episcopate then and did not come about but gradually as the church began to apostatize.

As we have repeatedly stated, during the times of the early church, nothing held greater authority than the local church, the government of which the Holy Spirit instituted, we might quickly add. In other words, there was no headquarters anywhere that controlled churches, etc., not even Jerusalem.

HIERARCHY

It is not wrong to have a central headquarters in order to facilitate the carrying out of the work of God around the world, providing that spiritual authority over the local church is not abrogated. If it is, which it almost always is at the present time, the ways of God are then replaced by the ways of man, with the work of God being seriously hindered.

The Lord does not do things by proxy, at least as it pertains to His Leading and Guidance. He does not speak to a hierarchy, with them filtering down His Word to others, but this is mostly the case presently. In that case, His Voice is silent.

The Lord always speaks directly to the person in question concerning His Leading and Guidance, and will only speak to others regarding the same matter after He has first spoken to the principal, and then only for confirmation.

One will look in vain in the New Testament for any type of religious hierarchy, or any outside leader for that matter, who exercised any type of spiritual authority over the local church. They simply did not exist.

To be sure, if the Holy Spirit had wanted such, this would certainly have been the time to institute this program, especially considering that most of the original Twelve were still alive and that the Jerusalem church was powerful and strong. As well, Paul would have been an excellent candidate for such. However, even though the apostle constantly gave advice to the local churches, and mostly to those he had planted himself, still, he never exercised authority over those churches, which, in fact, he had every right to do.

It was only later after the death of the apostles that the church gradually began to drift from the ways of God to the far lower level of the ways of man, thereby, creating religious offices, such as *"bishop,"* etc., which have no spiritual foundation. Men love to rule, and religious men especially love to rule!

NOTES

APOSTASY

As the church gradually apostatized, creating offices of their own making, the Roman bishop and the pope came to dominate the western world, which ultimately plunged the world into the Dark Ages, from which it did not begin to arise until the Reformation.

Actually, the address, as we shall see, to the elders at Ephesus destroys the figment of the historic episcopate (the government of the church by bishops or by a hierarchy).

Paul had no successor. He did not commend the Ephesian brethren to Timothy, to the Twelve, to a church organization, or to a body of tradition. He commended them to God and to the Bible, assuring them that such a provision amply sufficed for all their spiritual necessities, whether as a church or as individuals. All official resource, as is obvious, he set aside, and rightly so.

(18) "AND WHEN THEY WERE COME TO HIM, HE SAID UNTO THEM, YOU KNOW, FROM THE FIRST DAY THAT I CAME INTO ASIA, AFTER WHAT MATTER I HAVE BEEN WITH YOU AT ALL SEASONS."

The status is:

1. The phrase, *"And when they were come to him,"* probably represents two or three days from the time the messenger was originally sent.

2. Even though the round trip was approximately 60 miles, which they probably walked, they saw it as no imposition, especially considering the opportunity to be in the presence of Paul once again. With most of these people having been brought to Christ under his ministry, he was, in effect, their spiritual father.

3. Considering the manner in which he addressed them, the apostle seemed to feel that he would not see them again, which the record seems to indicate.

4. *"He said unto them, You know, from the first day that I came into Asia,"* took them back to the very beginning of the church at Ephesus. Actually, Paul, by the guidance of the Holy Spirit, founded most, if not all, the churches in Asia Minor. Consequently, this would have included the

seven churches of Asia addressed by Christ (Rev., Chpts. 2-3).

5. *"After what manner I have been with you at all seasons,"* indicates his nurturing them with the Gospel of Jesus Christ, which had not changed simply because perfection cannot change, and neither does it need to change.

(19) "SERVING THE LORD WITH ALL HUMILITY OF MIND, AND WITH MANY TEARS, AND TEMPTATIONS, WHICH BEFELL ME BY THE LYING IN WAIT OF THE JEWS."

The order is:

1. If the Cross is that to which He came, and that's exactly why He came, then it is the Cross in which the need of humanity was met.

2. The Cross must be the starting place and the stopping place for all believers.

HUMILITY

The phrase, *"Serving the Lord with all humility of mind,"* presents that which is the very opposite of the Judaizers and other false teachers who were attempting to draw a following after themselves.

The word *"humility"* in the Greek text is *"tapeinophrosune"* and means *"a lowliness or humiliation of mind … without pride."*

Studying the life of Paul and, thereby, understanding the toughness which he rightly exhibited respecting the proper Gospel of Jesus Christ, we learn that humility is not softness or weakness, and neither is it a lack of resolve or determination.

We are told in this statement by Paul, *"Humility of mind,"* that this which the Spirit of God seeks to bring about, only He can do.

Concerning the *"mind,"* as it refers to *"humility,"* Paul said, *"Let this mind be in you, which was also in Christ Jesus:*

"Who, being in the form of God, thought it not robbery to be equal with God:

"But made Himself of no reputation, and took upon Him the form of a servant, and was made in the likeness of men:

"And being found in fashion as a man, He humbled Himself, and became obedient unto death, even the death of the Cross" (Phil. 2:5-8).

NOTES

So, the only way to have humility of mind is to have the mind of Christ Jesus.

THE IMPORTANCE OF HUMILITY

The importance of this virtue springs from the fact that it is found as part of the character of God. In Psalms 113:5-6, God is represented as being incomparably High and Great, and yet, He humbles Himself to take note of the things which are created, while in Psalm 18:35 and II Samuel 22:36, the greatness of God's Servant is attributed to the humility (gentleness) which God has displayed toward him.

HUMILITY IS PRAISED

Wherever this quality of humility is found in the Old Testament, it is praised (Prov. 15:33; 18:12) and God's Blessing is frequently poured upon those who possess it.

Moses was vindicated because of humility (Num. 12:3), while Belshazzar was reproved by Daniel, and in a most stringent way (Dan. 5:22), because he had not profited by the experience of Nebuchadrezzar before him, which might have brought him into an attitude of humility. II Chronicles in particular makes it the criterion by which the rule of successive kings was to be judged.

THE PRODUCING OF HUMILITY

The term is closely connected with affliction, which is sometimes brought upon men by their trials and sometimes attributed directly to the purpose of God, but is always calculated to produce humility of spirit.

Similarly, in the New Testament, at Matthew 23:12 and parallels, the same word is used to express the penalty for arrogance (abasement) and the prerequisite of preferment (humility). In the first case, it is a condition of low estate, which will be brought about through the judgment of God.

In the second, it is a spirit of lowliness, which enables God to bring the blessing of advancement. Paul, too, in Philippians 4:12, used it to describe his affliction, but went on to make clear that the virtue lies in the acceptance of the experience so that a condition imposed from without becomes the occasion for the development of the corresponding attitude within.

NOTES

As we have already stated, in the same Epistle (Phil. 2:8), he cites as an example to be emulated the humility of Christ, Who deliberately set aside His divine Prerogative and progressively humbled Himself, receiving in due time the exaltation which would, without fail, follow.

SIMULATED HUMILITY

Like all virtues, humility is capable of being simulated (faked), and the danger of this is particularly plain in Paul's letter to the Colossians. Whatever may be the true rendering of the difficult passage in Colossians 2:18, it is clear that here and in Colossians 2:23, the reference is to a sham.

Despite all the appearances of humility, these false teachers were really puffed up with a sense of their own importance. Setting their own speculative system over against the revelation of God, they denied the very thing which, by their asceticism, they seemed to proclaim.

Paul warned his readers against this pseudo-humility and went on in Philippians 3:12 to exhort them to the genuine thing.

GOD AND HUMILITY

In the Old Testament, as well as in the New, humility is an essential characteristic of true piety, or of the man who is right with God. God humbles men in order to bring them to Himself (Deut. 8:2-3), and it is when men humble themselves before Him that they are accepted (I Ki. 21:29; II Chron. 7:14); to *"walk humbly with your God"* completes the divine requirements (Micah 6:8).

GREEK THOUGHT CONCERNING HUMILITY

The Greek word *"tapeinophrosune,"* which Paul here used, is not found in classical Greek. In the New Testament, with the exception of I Peter 5:5, it is Pauline.

In Greek pre-Christian writers, humility was, with a few exceptions in Plato and Platonic writers, used in a bad or inferior sense—as denoting something evil, unworthy, and, therefore, undesired.

While the modern world, which has been heavily influenced by Christianity, would not go that far, still, without God, humility cannot be produced in the heart and life of the worldling. This is the reason that ego, self-will, self-importance, and the self-made idea is so prominent in the world and characteristic of the world. In other words, it is the very opposite of that which is demanded by the Lord.

The prominence of humility gained in Christian thought indicates the new conception of man in relation to God, to himself, and to his fellows, which is due to Bible Christianity.

WHAT HUMILITY ACTUALLY MEANS

As stated, it is the *"mind of Christ"* respecting the realm of lowliness. In fact, one of the meanings of *"humility"* is *"a river that runs low."* As would be obvious, a river that runs high destroys everything in its path, while a river that runs low destroys nothing.

However, this *"mind of Christ"* by no means implies slavishness or servility, and neither is it inconsistent with a right estimate of oneself, one's gifts and calling of God, or with proper self-assertion when called for, as evidenced in the life and ministry of Paul.

However, the habitual frame of mind of a child of God is that of one who feels not only that he owes all his natural gifts, etc., to God, but that he has been the object of undeserved redeeming love, and who regards himself as being not his own but God's in Christ.

HUMILITY, THE OPPOSITE OF SELF-EXALTATION

The true believer, that is, if he rightly understands the Word of God and who he actually is in Christ, cannot exalt himself, for he knows that he has nothing of himself. The humble mind is, thus, at the root of all other graces and virtues. Self-exaltation spoils everything. There can be no real love without humility.

"Love," said Paul, *"Vaunts not itself, is not puffed up"* (I Cor. 13:4). As Augustine said, *"Humility is first, second and third in Christianity."*

JESUS AS THE SUPREME EXAMPLE

Jesus not only strongly impressed His

Disciples with the need of humility, but was in Himself its supreme Example. He described Himself as *"meek and lowly in heart"* (Mat. 11:29), which, in effect, was the only thing He ever said of Himself personally.

The first of the Beatitudes was to *"the poor in spirit"* (Mat. 5:3), and it was *"the meek"* who should *"inherit the Earth."*

Humility is the way to true greatness: he who should *"humble himself as this little child"* should be *"the greatest in the Kingdom of Heaven"; "whosoever shall exalt himself shall be humbled; and whosoever shall humble himself shall be exalted"* (Mat. 18:4; 23:12; Lk. 14:11; 18:14).

To the humble mind, truth is revealed (Mat. 11:25; Lk. 10:21). Jesus revealed a touching example of humility in His washing His Disciples' feet (Jn. 13:1-17).

NOTES

THE CHARACTERISTICS OF TRUE BIBLICAL HUMILITY

It is not genuine humility when we humble ourselves with the feeling that we are greater than others, but only when we do not think of self at all.

It is not the sense of sin alone that should create the humble spirit: Jesus had no sin. It belongs not merely to the creature, but even to a son in relation to God.

There may be much self-satisfaction where sinfulness is confessed. We may be proud of our humility. However, if that is the case, it is necessary, also, to always beware of *"the pride that apes humility,"* which, in reality, is a *"false humility."*

HUMILITY AND THE CROSS OF CHRIST

Jesus said that if we were going to come after Him, we must deny ourselves (which is the first step toward humility), and take up the Cross daily and follow Him (Lk. 9:23). In fact, it is impossible for anyone to know Bible humility without taking up the Cross, even on a daily basis. The Cross of Christ, which was the greatest example of humility, figures prominently in our experience. Paul said:

"Let nothing be done through strife or vainglory; but in lowliness of mind (humility) *let each esteem other better than themselves.*

"Look not every man on his own things, but every man also on the things of others (humility).

"Let this mind be in you which was also in Christ Jesus:

"Who being in the form of God, thought it not robbery to be equal with God:

"But made Himself of no reputation, and took upon Him the form of a servant, and was made in the likeness of men:

"And being found in fashion as a Man, He humbled Himself, and became obedient unto death, even the death of the Cross.

"Wherefore, God also has highly exalted Him, and given Him a Name which is above every name" (Phil. 2:3-9).

Due to the Cross of Christ being so little preached at present, at least by the whole of the church, sadly, one would have to say, *"There is less humility present today in Christendom than at any time since the Reformation."*

Let us say it again: the Cross of Christ refers to the sanctification process, meaning that every single thing we receive from God, all and without fail, is made possible by what Jesus did at the Cross. In fact, pride is the reason that the Cross is so readily rejected. It exposes man for what he really is, and men do not like that, and religious men most of all do not like that.

Without fail, a way chosen other than the Cross leads to self-righteousness. Please notice the following:

- The only way to God is through Jesus Christ (Jn. 14:6).
- The only way to Jesus Christ is by the way of the Cross (Lk. 9:23).
- The only way to the Cross is a denial of self (Lk. 14:27).

ONE MORE WORD ABOUT PAUL!

Seeing and understanding that humility is the state to which the Holy Spirit is striving to bring the believer, and noting the difficulty of the flesh in obeying the Spirit in this capacity, I think a great truth is brought out in the life of Paul, which is an example for us all.

Even though Paul experienced things

from the Lord as few men ever had, even to which he alluded (II Cor. 12:1-3), still, he said that he would not glory in such, as wonderful as they were, but rather, *"but in my infirmities"* (II Cor. 12:5-6).

Why?

He said, *"And lest I should be exalted above measure through the abundance of the Revelations, there was given to me a thorn in the flesh, the messenger of Satan to buffet me, lest I should be exalted above measure"* (II Cor. 12:7).

Alongside the great revelations given to him, which included the meaning of the New Covenant, the meaning of which was the Cross, with him writing about one-third of the New Testament, at the same time, Paul experienced suffering, hardship, difficulties, and problems as few men in history. He was almost beaten to death several times, suffered stonings, shipwreck, and tremendous opposition by many preachers who claimed to be in Christ (II Cor. 11:23-28).

Knowing the power of God, why was it necessary that the Lord subject Paul to these terrible hardships?

PAUL ANSWERS THAT QUESTION HIMSELF

He said, *"And lest I should be exalted above measure through the abundance of the Revelations"* (II Cor. 12:7).

In other words, the flesh is so susceptible to dependence on self, a boastful ego, or the desired self-esteem of which so many boast, that it is only through these great difficulties, it seems, can man, even the godliest such as Paul, be brought to a place of *"humility of mind."*

So, that makes much of the modern gospel, such as the so-called *"prosperity message,"* spurious to say the least! The idea that one can confess away all difficulties and problems, or even that one should be able to, flies in the face of Scripture, which is so overly obvious. Yes, the Lord does abundantly bless! He does abundantly prosper His Children! He does give wonderful and good things to those who believe Him! However, if the end result becomes those things, we have graphically stepped outside of the revealed will of God.

NOTES

THE GOAL OF THE HOLY SPIRIT

Even though these blessings are desirable and, in a measure, given to all believers, still, the goal of the Holy Spirit is not to bring the believer to a trouble-free existence, a bigger car than he is presently driving, etc., but rather to *"humility of mind."* In other words, if this is the goal of the Holy Spirit, and I think the Scripture is abundantly clear that it is, then this should be our objective as well!

Most all believers hardly think of the flesh as the danger it really is! Much that we call faith is really only the boasting of the flesh. Covering it with Scriptures makes it no less flesh and no less evil!

Incidentally, the flesh is that which is indicative to the human being. It pertains to our education, motivation, talent, ability, expertise, will-power, etc. As stated, it is that which is indicative to a human being.

While these things within themselves are not sinful, the fact is, we cannot live for God by the means of the flesh. It was so weakened at the fall in the Garden of Eden that it rendered man incapable of doing what needs to be done. So, the Lord has provided a way, and that way is *"Jesus Christ and Him Crucified"* (I Cor. 1:17-18, 23; 2:2).

Man's way is *"the flesh,"* while God's Way is *"faith."* However, for it to be faith that God will recognize, it must have as its object the Cross of Christ.

I maintain that according to the Scripture, it is very difficult for the Holy Spirit to bring the believer to the desired place without at least some of the difficulties to which we have alluded. No! It is not the difficulties or the hardships themselves which bring about the humility of mind, but rather that these things drive us to our knees and to an even greater dependence on Christ.

HARDSHIPS

This is certainly not to mean that believers are to ask for such hardships, for that would be foolishness indeed, for as we have stated, it is not those things that bring humility of mind. In fact, even as Paul, we should ask the Lord to remove any type of hindrance of this nature. But yet, if the

Lord knows it is necessary for some things to be, even as with Paul, we, as well, should then look at the situation not as a lack of faith, as some have accused Paul, but rather the words of Christ, *"My Grace is sufficient for you: for My Strength is made perfect in weakness"* (II Cor. 12:9).

The phrase, *"And with many tears,"* tells us something else about Paul as well!

We understand that people's emotions are different and that all do not respond in the same manner. However, once again, I think the example of Paul as recorded here should help us to understand that of which he spoke and that of which I speak. It is beyond mere emotion, but rather the very soul and spirit of the believer.

Were we speaking of a mere philosophy, that would be different. However, we are speaking here of one's relationship with Christ and service for the Lord. We are speaking, as well, of the Holy Spirit, Who lives within our hearts and lives even for the express purpose of glorifying Christ. Consequently, as stated, these are not mere philosophies, but divine Beings Who have, as well, brought us from death to life. Properly understanding this, our emotions, even to the very depths of our being, are powerfully affected.

PAUL

I believe it was D. L. Moody who said, and I repeat as best as I can recollect, *"If a Preacher or any Believer for that matter, cannot weep over the lost, something is missing in that person's life."*

Paul wept as he sought to bring sinners to Christ. As well, he wept over the needs of the believers. When he preached judgment, it was not from a sarcastic, accusing spirit, but rather out of a broken heart full of love for the people with whom he was dealing. His tears flowed from the Love and Compassion of Jesus that flooded his own soul, which should flood ours as well.

As stated, understanding that the emotions of people are different, still, I do not understand how any preacher can preach the Gospel, understanding the import of that which he is doing, and not be moved in some way from the very depths of the entirety of his being!

NOTES

Someone said that we must weep over the lost and shout with the redeemed, and that is right. How could we do less?

The trouble with much of the modern ministry is that it is a dry-eyed ministry, which, in fact, is not much of any ministry at all! It too much has not experienced what it sometimes preaches.

The phrase, *"And temptations,"* in the Greek text is *"peirasmos"* and means *"tests, trials and adversity, but also a solicitation or provocation to deal with the situation outside of the Way of the Lord."* Consequently, the word *"temptations,"* as it is used here by Paul, is of far greater weight than a mere test or trial.

The phrase, *"Which befell me by the lying in wait of the Jews,"* gives us a greater understanding of that which he meant, and which, if properly understood, will be a valuable lesson.

The constant plots against Paul by the Jews were never ceasing, whether to accuse him before civil authorities, to besmirch his character, inflict bodily harm upon him, or even to take his life.

As well, when he spoke of *"Jews,"* he was speaking not only of those in the synagogues who had blatantly rejected Christ, but also, the Judaizers who professed Christ but also insisted that believers must keep the Law of Moses in order to be saved. To be frank, this latter group was far more harmful to the work of God, and possibly even to Paul, than the former.

Consequently, the word *"temptations,"* as it is used here, not only pertained to the tests and trials caused by these Jews, but, as well, there was a constant temptation, which Satan used against Paul, that he take matters into his own hands in this regard instead of leaving it with the Lord. This is extremely important to the child of God, with hopefully this lesson not being lost upon us.

Whenever we are wronged by others, whether unbelievers or believers, the temptation of the flesh is always to defend ourselves, strike back, etc. However, to do such takes it out of the Hands of the Lord. The Holy Spirit through Paul plainly said and

NOTES

was that which Paul practiced, although the temptation was ever constant to do otherwise, *"Dearly beloved, avenge not yourselves, but rather give place unto wrath: for it is written, Vengeance is Mine; I will repay, saith the Lord"* (Rom. 12:19).

It is not easy at times for us not to make the attempt to avenge ourselves, but it is always wrong and for many reasons.

First of all, irrespective of what has been done to us by others, we are not qualified to serve as the judge and the jury. James makes that very plain (James 4:12).

As well, when we take vengeance into our own hands, even as Paul was tempted to do at times, and all of us have been tempted to do, we, at that time, take the vengeance out of the hands of God.

We are to give the thing to the Lord, whatever it is, and whoever the person is, and do what the Spirit through Paul said to do, *"If your enemy hunger, feed him; if he thirst, give him drink: for in so doing you shall heap coals of fire on his head.*

"Be not overcome of evil, but overcome evil with good" (Rom. 12:20-21).

THE WAY OF THE LORD

Someone put on my desk the other day the following statement, which I think is well worth repeating. Regrettably, the author is unknown, so I have no way to give credit. However, it said:

"Keep about your work that God has given you. Do not flinch because the lion roars; do not stop to stone the devil's dog; do not fool away your time chasing the devil's rabbits. Do your work. Let liars lie, let corporations resolve, let the devil do his worst; but see to it that nothing hinders you from fulfilling the work that God has given you.

"He has not commanded you to get rich. He has never bidden you to defend your character. He has not set you at work to contradict falsehood about yourself which Satan and his servants may begin to peddle.

"If you do those things, you will do nothing else; you will be at work for yourself and not for the Lord. Keep at your work.

"Let your aim be as steady as a star. You may be assaulted, wronged, insulted, slandered, wounded and rejected. You may be abused by foes, forsaken by friends, and despised and rejected of men. But see to it with steadfast determination, with unfaltering zeal, that you pursue the great purpose of your life and object of your being until at last you can say, 'I have finished the work which You gave me to do.'"

(20) "AND HOW I KEPT BACK NOTHING THAT WAS PROFITABLE UNTO YOU, BUT HAVE SHOWED YOU, AND HAVE TAUGHT YOU PUBLICKLY, AND FROM HOUSE TO HOUSE."

The order is:

1. The phrase, *"And how I kept back nothing that was profitable unto you,"* means, in essence, that he did not allow the onslaught of Satan, discouragement, plots by Jews, or denial of the Gospel of grace by many to silence his voice respecting these great doctrines.

2. Even though *"the preaching of the Cross to them that perish is foolishness,"* Paul did not allow that to stop him. Even though to *"preach Christ crucified* (was), *unto the Jews a stumblingblock, and unto the Greeks foolishness,"* he did not allow that to deter his message at all.

3. As well, even though *"not many wise men after the flesh, not many mighty, not many noble, are called"* (not many of these kinds would accept), again, Paul did not allow that to deter him (I Cor. 1:26).

All of the Gospel of Jesus Christ is a reproach to the world. Part of the Gospel of Jesus Christ is a reproach to part of the church simply because it is not believed. I speak of the Baptism with the Holy Spirit with the evidence of speaking with other tongues, etc. I speak of the Message of the Cross, which is an affront to many. To those who do such things, the delivering power of Christ is simply a reproach to them, and they feel much more comfortable appealing to the wisdom of the world.

However, thank God for the preachers who will keep back nothing that is profitable for the Body of Christ, irrespective of the ridicule or persecution. Those are the men and women who touch the world!

The phrase, *"But have showed you,"* speaks of a double meaning:

a. It means that Paul plainly explained the Word of God to the people. It was done succinctly, tediously, forthrightly, and courageously, with Paul going over it again and again in order that it may be fully and completely understood.

b. Paul showed them not only by the Word but, also, by example. What he preached, he had experienced, and it was meant for the people to experience it as well.

4. *"And have taught you publickly, and from house to house,"* refers to public meetings where all would come together at one time, such as our modern churches, and, as well, discuss the Gospel *"from house to house."* The following should be said:

Every evidence is that when Paul met with people, whether it was one person or many, the conversation was little on the fashions of that particular time, the latest gossip from the sporting arenas, or anything of the world for that matter, but rather on the Word of God.

I am afraid that at this time, and it has possibly always been a problem, too much conversation of modern believers is on things other than the Lord. While it is certainly not wrong to discuss these things, still, our conversation should be far more taken up with the things of the Lord, as should be obvious!

(21) "TESTIFYING BOTH TO THE JEWS, AND ALSO TO THE GREEKS, REPENTANCE TOWARD GOD, AND FAITH TOWARD OUR LORD JESUS CHRIST."

The account is:

1. The reader must understand that everything in pre-Christ's history strained toward the Cross, while everything now strains from the Cross.

2. If the believer does not base everything on the Cross, all else believed will be skewed as well!

THE TESTIMONY

The phrase, *"Testifying both to the Jews, and also to the Greeks,"* specifies that the Gospel is the same for all. This is why, as I have already related, that I feel that James did not go quite far enough in his sentence or statement respecting the Law/grace issue. He did not hold the gentiles to the Law of Moses, which was right; however, he gave some credence, I think, to the Jews continuing to try to keep the Law although professing Christ (Acts 15:19-21).

NOTES

To be sure, that which James did do constituted a tremendous victory for the cause of Christ and was certainly the will of God. However, making a division somewhat between gentiles and Jews, as he seems to have done, I think was not pleasing to the Lord as this continued to cause problems, and great problems at that.

However, having said that and knowing the tendencies of men, even godly men, the verdict handed down concerning this problem was, no doubt, a miracle within itself.

Naturally, the Law problem was no issue at all with gentile converts simply because they had never known anything about it to start with. However, with Jews, the Law of Moses had more or less guided their destiny for about 1,600 years. It seems to have been very difficult for them to lay it all aside, fully understanding that Jesus had fulfilled it in totality. While we criticize them, possibly we have the same problem in holding to things which are spiritually injurious to us as well!

REPENTANCE

The phrase, *"Repentance toward God, and faith toward our Lord Jesus Christ,"* actually presents the Gospel in the proverbial nutshell.

This which Paul has said proclaims in few words the very fundamentals of salvation, even as it applies to all, Jews and gentiles alike. Let's address it briefly:

"Repentance toward God": as all are born in original sin, all are lost until *"born-again"* (Jn. 3:3). However, I do believe the Scripture also teaches that all babies and children below the age of accountability are protected by the Lord respecting their soul's salvation, should they die at that age (Mat. 18:3; 19:14; Mk. 9:36; 10:15). The age of accountability varies with different children according to many factors. From the moment the person reaches the age of accountability, whatever that may be in each particular case, he is expected to accept the Lord or be eternally lost.

Inasmuch as man is a sinner, he has greatly offended God, whether he realizes it or not. Because of his rebelling against God, Who is his Creator, and actually serving as a child of Satan (whether realized or not), he owes God a great apology.

When the Gospel is preached under the anointing of the Holy Spirit, the Word of God strikes the heart of the sinner and makes him realize his lost condition and that it means lost respecting God. Every unbeliever at *this stage*, at least in some fashion, realizes his offense against God and is moved to repentance.

TO THINK DIFFERENTLY, TO CHANGE ONE'S MIND

The word *"repentance"* in the Greek text as presented here is *"metanoeo"* and means *"to think differently, to change one's mind."* In other words, it means to change one's mind about God and to turn from sin to God.

Repentance is not so much the exact words which are spoken, but rather a state of being or a position of the heart.

The individual is sorry for his sin and rebellion and realizes his sin and rebellion have greatly offended God! The Word of God, by the power of the Holy Spirit, causes him to come to this place, without which, he cannot come.

Regrettably, many in the modern church claim that *"repentance"* is an Old Testament doctrine and, consequently, is not applicable to this day of grace.

It is taught in some circles presently that when believers sin, they do not have to confess that sin and, thereby, do not have to repent. What does the Bible say?

John wrote, and I quote from the EXPOSITOR'S STUDY BIBLE the following:

"If we say that we *('we' refers to Believers)* **have no sin** *(refers to 'the sin nature')*, **we deceive ourselves** *(refers to self-deception)*, and the truth is not in us. *(This does not refer to all truth as it regards Believers, but rather the Truth of the indwelling sinful nature)*.

"If we confess our sins *(pertains to acts of sin, whatever they might be; the sinner is to believe [Jn. 3:16]; the Saint is to confess)*, **He** *(the Lord)* **is faithful and just to forgive us** *('us' refers to Believers)* **our sins** *(God will always be true to His own Nature and Promises, keeping Faith with Himself and with man)*, **and to cleanse us from all unrighteousness.** *('All' not some. All sin was remitted, paid for, and put away on the basis of the satisfaction offered for the demands of God's Holy Law, which sinner's broke when the Lord Jesus died on the Cross.)*

"If we say that we have not sinned *(here, John is denouncing the claims of sinless perfection; he is going back to Verse Eight, speaking of Christians who claim they have no sin nature)*, **we make him a liar** *(the person who makes such a claim makes God a liar, because the Word says the opposite)*, **and His Word is not in us.** *(If we properly know the Word, we will properly know that perfection is not in us at present, and will not be until the Trump sounds.)*" **(I Jn. 1:8-10).**

Some erroneously claim that John is not speaking here of believers, but rather unbelievers. However, the Greek tenses plainly tell us that John is here speaking to believers and not to unbelievers. So, if the Holy Spirit through him stated that we believers must confess our sins before the Lord, which can be done instantly in a moment's time, this is what we must do.

THE WORDS OF JESUS

Once again dealing with the claim as given by some that believers are not to ask forgiveness for sins, etc., let us look at the words of our Lord.

In Jesus addressing the seven churches of Asia, which included the entirety of the church world for all time, it is overly obvious that He was speaking to believers.

To five of the churches of Asia, He demanded repentance (Rev. 2:5, 16, 22; 3:3, 19).

When a believer sins, that believer is to immediately confess his sin to God, rather admitting that he has sinned, and ask forgiveness from the Lord, which will always be granted.

WHAT ABOUT BELIEVERS WHO DO NOT CONFESS THEIR SINS TO THE LORD?

Such a believer will find his or her heart

little by little becoming more hardened (Heb. 3:13). If a believer stays on that path, little by little becoming more and more hardened, such a person can come to the place that he no longer believes in the sacrifice of Christ.

WHAT ABOUT BELIEF IN THE INTERCESSION OF CHRIST?

Paul wrote:

"Wherefore He *(the Lord Jesus Christ)* **is able also to save them to the uttermost** *(proclaims the fact that Christ alone has made the only true Atonement for sin; He did this at the Cross)* **who come unto God by Him** *(proclaims the only manner in which man can come to God)*, **seeing He ever lives to make intercession for them.** *(His very Presence by the Right Hand of the Father guarantees such, with nothing else having to be done [Heb. 1:3])*" **(Heb. 7:25).**

This means that the very presence of Jesus Christ at the throne of God guarantees the Mercy, Grace, and Forgiveness of our Lord extended to believers. The *"intercession"* here made is not for unbelievers, but rather for believers.

While *"repentance"* is certainly an Old Testament doctrine, it is, as should be overly obvious, a New Testament doctrine as well! The reason is simple:

Man's offense against God does not change from the Old to the New Covenant. The problem remains the same, and the solution is the same and, in fact, always has been. The truth is, every single person who has ever been saved, and that means from the very beginning, has always engaged in repentance of some sort, whether they realized it or not. In fact, the Old Testament sacrifices were a form of repentance. In totality, Jesus' Death on the Cross was a form of repentance ensconced in the Atonement, which was done not for His Part, because He had nothing about which He needed to repent, but it was on our part. However, that great repentance, in a sense, which was effected toward God on our behalf, cannot be realized on the part of the sinner unless the sinner has faith in Christ, which is the second point.

In looking at this as Paul has stated the case, is it possible to engage in *"repentance toward God,"* but not have faith in Jesus Christ, and still be saved?

No!

Hundreds of millions of Muslims each day, in fact, five times a day, offer up a form of repentance toward God, but it effects no salvation simply because of having no faith in Jesus Christ as God manifest in the flesh, Who purchased man's redemption at Calvary's Cross.

The same goes for hundreds of millions of others who in some way recognize God but not Jesus Christ. In truth, it is not really even possible to know God at all except by and through Jesus Christ. Only through Him is the Father revealed (Jn. 10:7; 17:1-5). In fact, Jesus said, *"No man comes unto the Father, but by Me"* (Jn. 14:6).

FAITH TOWARD OUR LORD JESUS CHRIST

The faith toward Christ represents a belief in Who Jesus is, the Son of the living God, God manifest in the flesh, and what He has done, the atoning, vicarious, efficacious, Finished Work of Redemption on the Cross.

Even though men repent toward God, which is absolutely necessary, still, at the same time, they must realize that it is Jesus Christ, God's Son, Who came down to this world and died on the Cross in order that the great sin debt against man could be paid. That He did and then rose from the dead, with faith in that guaranteeing salvation.

So, the two, repentance toward God and faith toward the Lord Jesus Christ, go hand in hand and constitute salvation.

WHAT DOES IT MEAN TO HAVE FAITH IN CHRIST?

It is really not complicated, especially considering that the Holy Spirit will help the sinner who truly desires to come to the Lord.

In its simplest form, faith in Christ means that we believe that He is God manifest in the flesh, and that He died to redeem man from sin, in effect, taking our place. He then rose from the dead on the third day to ratify what had been done at Calvary. It is that simple!

While the believing sinner may not

NOTES

understand very much about what he believes, at least at the beginning, the Lord will always honor anyone who comes to Him in any capacity, providing it is based on faith in what Jesus did (Jn. 6:37).

Sometimes, preachers make faith something very difficult to come by. However, faith is simply believing the Word of God. That does not mean that one has total understanding, but it does mean that the person believes everything that God has said. That is faith, as simple as it may be.

However, at the same time, it is impossible to have faith without the Word of God in some form being given to such a person. That is the reason that Paul wrote, *"So then faith comes by hearing, and hearing by the Word of God,"* which simply means that we hear the Word of God when it is preached and taught, and we believe it (Rom. 10:17).

FAITH, THE MANNER IN WHICH GOD OPERATES

In dealing with humanity, God has chosen the principle of faith in order to bring this about. There are reasons for that.

God is a faith God. In other words, all of His Creation was carried out *"through faith."*

The Holy Spirit through Paul said, *"Through faith we understand that the worlds were framed by the Word of God, so that things which are seen were not made of things which do appear"* (Heb. 11:3).

In other words, God spoke these things into existence, having such faith in His Word that these things came into being. As an example, He said, *"Let there be light: and there was light"* (Gen. 1:3).

In fact, the entirety of Chapter 1 of Genesis, dealing with the Creation, proclaims God speaking these things into existence. So, the principle of faith is the underlying principle of all that God does. Consequently, He deals with man in the same capacity.

This is the reason that socialism or communism won't work. It takes away the faith principle. That is the reason that capitalism does work; it is because it is based on faith. True, it's not faith that God recognizes, but, nevertheless, it is faith. That is what has made America at least one of the greatest nations in the world. Our system encourages faith. Unfortunately, there are powerful voices in America at present that are trying to steer the nation away from the faith principle toward socialism or even communism. We should have enough sense to look at Russia, which tried the experiment of communism for some 70 years, which totally bankrupted the nation and subjected its people to a subsistent form of living. However, once again, capitalism will not thrive and, in fact, cannot thrive in an atmosphere lacking Bible Christianity. So, in truth, the reason for America's problems at present (2014) is because there is very little faith in the church at present. In fact, it is impossible to properly have faith in God without an understanding of the Cross of Christ. Regrettably, the modern church has long since ceased to preach the Cross, and until the church, at least with a modicum of direction, comes back to the Cross of Christ, the situation in America is going to steadily grow worse.

NOTES

JESUS AND FAITH

As stated, the manner in which God deals with man is the manner of faith. The reason is clear and simple.

God's dealings with man after the Fall in the Garden of Eden have strictly been on the basis of man as a lost soul and, furthermore, with no way to rectify this situation within himself. Man is not just lost, he is hopelessly lost. In effect, he is without God and without hope, at least as far as effecting his own salvation is concerned.

Considering that, if God had demanded anything from man to assuage the terrible sin debt piled up against him, such as good works, merit, etc., man simply could not have paid the account. It was literally and is literally impossible. As a result, he would have remained forever lost.

To address this terrible situation, God became Man and paid the debt by the offering of His own Life in sacrifice on Calvary's Cross, which was the only payment that heaven could accept in all honesty.

Sinful man must understand that God did all of these things for man simply because man could not do them for himself. It was all done by the Love and grace of God

NOTES

(Jn. 3:16). Consequently, to receive this which the Lord has amply and adequately provided for all regarding salvation, all man has to do is simply believe that which was done in Jesus Christ (Rom. 10:9-13). He doesn't have to pay anything or do anything except simply believe in what God has done.

BELIEVING

Upon believing, which is faith, the Lord erases the terrible sin debt for that particular sinner and freely imputes righteousness, a perfect, spotless righteousness, the righteousness of God, to the believing sinner (Gen. 15:6; Jn. 3:16; Rom. 4:3, 6; Gal. 3:6; James 2:23). This is a righteousness that man cannot earn, no matter what he does, but is freely given to him upon simple faith exhibited by him in Christ and what Christ has done for us at the Cross.

Man could in no way have saved himself, irrespective of any merit he may have had, simply because the debt was of such magnitude to have made such impossible. In view of that fact, it displeases God greatly for man to approach Him on the basis of merit, social standing, high birth, good works, or wealth (Gen. 4:5; Eph. 2:8-9). At the same time, it pleases Him greatly when we approach Him the proper way by faith (Heb. 11:5-6).

Man's problem has always been, and continues to be, that he attempts to replace God's Way, which is by faith, with his own way, which God understandably cannot accept. Please understand, it must be faith in Christ and what Christ has done for us at the Cross. To eliminate the Cross out of faith completely sidetracks the plan of God, making it impossible for God to accept or receive such. That's why Paul said, *"We preach Christ Crucified"* (I Cor. 1:23). As well, he said, I determined to know nothing among you save Christ and Him Crucified (I Cor. 2:2). He also said, God forbid that I should boast save in the Cross of our Lord Jesus Christ, by which I was crucified to the world, and the world unto me (Gal. 6:14).

So, the worst sinner in the world can throw himself at the Feet of the world's Redeemer, having faith in what Jesus did at Calvary and the Resurrection, and be instantly made perfectly righteous. That is what Jesus said when He spoke of the publican who was a criminal and traitor, who smote upon his breast, saying, *"God be merciful to me a sinner."*

THE RESPONSE OF CHRIST TO THE PUBLICAN

Jesus said, **"I tell you, this man went down to his house justified *rather* than the other** *(the Pharisee who refused to humble himself and admit what he truly was)*: **for every one who exalts himself** *(offers anything other than Faith in Christ)* **shall be abased** *(rejected by God)*; **and he who humbles himself** *(trusting in what Christ has done for him)* **shall be exalted** *(accepted by the Lord, Justified and made Righteous, and instantly)*" **(Lk. 18:13-14).**

JUSTIFICATION BY FAITH

Justification by faith is simply the Lord awarding a pure, spotless righteousness, the righteousness of God, to an obviously guilty sinner, thereby, cleansing him from all sin simply on the basis of faith in the Lord exhibited by that believing sinner. As stated, such a person doesn't have to know too very much about God or what Jesus did at Calvary. He simply has to believe. When this is done, every sin is washed away, with such a person then declared *"not guilty."* In fact, the only way that a person can be justified before God is by simple faith in Christ and what Christ has done for us at the Cross. God will accept no other type of faith (Rom. 5:1).

(22) "AND NOW, BEHOLD, I GO BOUND IN THE SPIRIT UNTO JERUSALEM, NOT KNOWING THE THINGS THAT SHALL BEFALL ME THERE."

The exegesis is:

1. The phrase, *"And now, behold, I go bound in the Spirit unto Jerusalem,"* refers to the Holy Spirit.

2. Horton says, *"'Spirit' referring to the Holy Spirit, should have been capitalized in the King James' Version, but was not. The original Greek uses the definite article here, and this normally indicates the Holy Spirit when this is done."*

3. The entire Text, I think, bears out that this is indeed the Holy Spirit. Consequently,

despite the forthcoming problems, Paul made it clear that he definitely had the Mind of the Lord respecting this very important trip. In other words, if he was to obey God, despite the potential problems, he had to go to Jerusalem.

4. The entirety of this scenario tells us how Paul obligated himself to the Leading of the Spirit. Everything he did was in conjunction with what the Lord directed. What a lesson this should be for us.

5. We must seek God constantly respecting His Will, taking nothing for granted. God has a perfect way for all concerned, and it is up to the believer, even as we have repeatedly stated, to ascertain that Will and not let go until clear direction is forthcoming, at least as far as is possible.

TRUST IN THE LORD

The phrase, *"Not knowing the things that shall befall me there,"* tells us that even though Paul was in the direct center of God's Will regarding this trip, still, that did not mean that everything would be smooth and problem free. Actually, even as the Spirit of God repeatedly told him, it would be the very opposite.

As well, just because one is in the center of God's Will, it does not mean that the Lord will explain all things to us or tell us why respecting certain problems. He does not owe us that, but we do owe Him total allegiance and trust, having confidence that whatever He does allow will ultimately fall out for our good (Rom. 8:26-28).

(23) "SAVE THAT THE HOLY SPIRIT WITNESSES IN EVERY CITY, SAYING THAT BONDS AND AFFLICTIONS ABIDE ME."

The synopsis is:

1. All life is in Christ.

2. Without Christ, there is no life, only death, *"spiritual death"* (Jn. 1:3-5).

THE WITNESS OF THE SPIRIT

The phrase, *"Save that the Holy Spirit witnesses in every city,"* proclaims to us that such happened, but it does not give us any illustrations, at least up to this time. (An example is given to us in Acts 21:10-11.)

As well, we are not told the manner in which the Holy Spirit did this. However, considering the manner in which it is said, it is almost certain that it was through prophecy or tongues and the interpretation of tongues (I Cor. 12:10).

"Saying that bonds and afflictions abide me," proclaims what was going to happen to Paul, which actually did happen.

WHAT WAS THE PURPOSE OF THE HOLY SPIRIT IN GIVING THESE WARNINGS?

As we have stated, it was not as some think, to tell Paul not to go, for the Holy Spirit had already strongly committed Paul to this direction. So, the will of God was not now in question.

I think the Holy Spirit primarily did this for two major purposes:

These constant warnings by the Spirit in the various cities would serve as a tendency to put Paul high on everyone's prayer list. In other words, by doing this, the Spirit of God was telling the people that Paul must be carried in prayer constantly.

From this we learn that the Lord has purposely given the church, His Body, an amazing responsibility and latitude respecting the carrying out of His Will. He is God, and as such, He needs nothing or no one; therefore, His using the Body of Christ in this fashion is for our benefit and not for His.

However, the purposeful giving of such responsibility to believers should leave us in utter awe! In other words, the Lord allows us to have a major part in the bringing about of His Will. As well, along with this responsibility is the possibility of failure.

RESPONSIBILITY

By that, I mean that if the responsibility is not taken seriously, and the church falls down on what it should do, in this case, prayer, oftentimes the Lord will not step in and salvage the situation. The Scripture plainly says, *"Where there is no vision, the people perish"* (Prov. 29:18). For instance, the Lord told Ezekiel to warn the people. However, if he did not warn them, *"The same wicked man shall die in his iniquity; but his blood will I require at your hand"* (Ezek. 3:18).

Jesus said, *"Verily I say unto you, Whatsoever you shall bind on Earth shall be*

NOTES

bound in Heaven: and whatsoever you shall loose on Earth shall be loosed in Heaven."

He further stated, *"Again I say unto you, That if two of you shall agree on Earth as touching any thing that they shall ask, it shall be done for them of My Father which is in Heaven"* (Mat. 18:18-19).

However, it must not be forgotten that *"whatsoever"* or *"anything"* are predicated on His Will and not our capriciousness.

THE AUTHORITY OF THE BELIEVER

All of this speaks to the *"authority of the believer,"* an authority I might quickly add, that is given freely by the Lord Jesus Christ (Mat. 21:21-22; Mk. 11:24; Jn. 14:12-14; 15:7). The word *"authority"* speaks of delegated power, in this case, from the Lord Jesus Christ, and means *"power to influence or command thought, opinion, or behavior."* However, this authority is never over other people, but rather over Satan, fallen angels, and demon spirits (Mk. 16:17-18; Lk. 10:19; Jn. 14:12; I Jn. 3:8).

APOSTLE

Many were saying at this time that Paul was not an apostle, hence, the reason he constantly claimed that office, and that his revelations of the great Gospel of grace were not from God. These accusations occasioned much of II Corinthians, as well as many other statements in Paul's other Epistles.

In view of this, many, no doubt, would have pointed, or did point, toward the terrible problems which Paul would encounter, even being imprisoned, as proof that if he was really of the Lord, the Lord would not allow these things to happen, etc.

It is unbelievable at present that anyone would question Paul's apostleship, but to be sure, it was held up with contempt by some from Jerusalem (not by James or the Twelve).

So, from many and varied sources and in many different churches, the Holy Spirit witnessed this which was to come, which would help to allay the accusations and criticism.

NOTES

(24) "BUT NONE OF THESE THINGS MOVE ME, NEITHER COUNT I MY LIFE DEAR UNTO MYSELF, SO THAT I MIGHT FINISH MY COURSE WITH JOY, AND THE MINISTRY, WHICH I HAVE RECEIVED OF THE LORD JESUS, TO TESTIFY THE GOSPEL OF THE GRACE OF GOD."

The synopsis is:

1. Man knows that something is wrong, but due to having no *"light,"* he does not know exactly what it is.

2. He continues to think it can be corrected by education, money, or various different philosophies.

THE PRISONER OF JESUS CHRIST

The phrase, *"But none of these things move me,"* proclaims Paul putting himself entirely in the Hands of the Lord. In other words, his only concern was the will of God and not his own safety, convenience, protection, or welfare. This is a man who had given himself totally and completely to the Lord Jesus Christ. Hence, he would refer to himself, and rightly so, as a *"prisoner of Jesus Christ"* (Eph. 3:1; 4:1). That is what all of us should do as well.

How many today can say as Paul that they are interested in nothing whatsoever except that which the Lord desires?

PAUL'S LIFE

The phrase, *"Neither count I my life dear unto myself,"* refers to the fact that he had already given himself to the Lord, and that included his life and its duration, whether long or short.

He would not unnecessarily put himself in danger, but if called upon to do so, which he often was, he did not flinch from its direction. He knew that the Lord would protect him, but if not, he would gladly forfeit his life for the Cause of Christ.

"So that I might finish my course with joy," was harking back in the mind of Paul to the manner in which Israel was divided by the Spirit of God under Joshua, relative to the portions given to each Tribe, even down to each family (Josh. 18:10).

In other words, the Children of Israel did not necessarily pick and choose where their portion of Canaan would be, but rather that which the Holy Spirit gave them. It was done through the high priest who then had

NOTES

the Urim and Thummim (Ex. 28:30), which were contained in his breastplate.

This is what David was referring to when he said, *"The LORD is the portion of mine inheritance and of my cup: You maintain my lot.*

"The lines are fallen unto me in pleasant places; yea, I have a goodly heritage" (Ps. 16:5-6).

THE COURSE

In essence, David was saying that the lines that the Lord had drawn respecting his life's work were drawn in pleasant places.

From this we learn that the Lord has drawn out the portion of ministry, in whatever capacity, for each and every believer. It is our responsibility to find that place and position, which can easily be done by seeking the Lord, and then to carry out that which the Lord has designed for us to do. Paul was speaking of this *"course"* designed by the Holy Spirit especially for him, and he was determined to finish that course with joy!

So, if that *"course"* included difficulties, imprisonment, or even death, which it eventually would, that mattered not at all.

Despite these adverse things, Paul was saying, even as David of old, that he was thankful to the Lord for the particular *"course"* drawn for him, and that he was privileged to work and function in this capacity, irrespective of the difficulties involved. He looked at it as a *"joy"* that would be total when the *"course"* was finished.

"And the Ministry which I have received of the Lord Jesus, to testify the Gospel of the grace of God," proclaims basically what this *"course"* actually was.

In effect, Paul was the Moses of the New Testament. As Moses was given the covenant of the Law, Paul was given the meaning of the covenant of *"the Gospel of the grace of God,"* i.e., the Cross.

He gave an abbreviated account of this in Galatians 1:6-12 and II Corinthians 12:1-7.

WHAT IS THE GOSPEL OF THE GRACE OF GOD?

In brief, the Gospel of the grace of God is the manner in which God deals with the human family through His Son, the Lord Jesus Christ. It refers to man's salvation, which is given to believing man freely upon faith, and is done so by *"grace."*

WHAT IS GRACE?

While grace is *"unmerited favor,"* the Biblical concept is much greater than is suggested in that common definition. *"Grace"* is a word that expresses a radical view of life and of relationship with God.

Grace teaches that God's attitude toward us is one of acceptance and love. Knowing God's Heart, we can *"approach the Throne of Grace with confidence"* (Heb. 4:16) with every sin and need. I like to refer to grace as *"God giving good things to unworthy individuals."*

A DRAMATIC STATEMENT

Grace is a dramatic statement about the human condition. Each person is helpless, trapped in sin and incapable, at least within himself, of pleasing God or winning His Favor.

Grace is a proclamation. It is the triumphant announcement that God in Christ has acted and has come to the aid of all who will trust Him for their eternal salvation.

A WAY OF LIFE

Grace is a way of life. Relying totally on Jesus to work within us, we experience God's own unlimited Power, vitalizing us and enabling us to live truly good lives.

The message of grace found in the New Testament, as given by Paul, calls us to a completely different outlook on relationship with God and on spiritual achievement than is found in any religion of human invention.

Understanding the nature of grace, we decisively reject any confidence in ourselves, and we trust ourselves totally to Jesus. He alone is able not only to declare us truly righteous men and women of God but, also, to make us so.

THE BASIS OF PAUL'S DOCTRINE OF GRACE

The word *"grace"* has a prominent place in the opening greetings and the closing benedictions of the Epistles, being added

NOTES

to the conventional Jewish greeting of *"peace,"* as given to Paul. Actually, the basis of Paul's doctrine regarding grace is found in Romans 1:16-3:20. Man is shown as a sinner, and a totally hopeless sinner at that, but by grace, he is justified (Rom. 3:21-4:25), i.e., God in His Grace treats him, though guilty, as if he had never sinned. This comes about by faith evidenced on the part of the believing sinner.

THE PROPER RESPONSE

Faith is the human response to divine grace and, actually, that which God intends (Rom. 5:2; 10:9; Eph. 2:8). This faith is the gift of God (Eph. 2:8).

Paul sought to point out that the word *"faith"* must not be thought to imply some independent action on the part of the believer. Although it implies that there is no salvation through the Law, this faith is not unethical. Faith is morally vital by itself. It works *"through love"* (Gal. 5:6).

The believer's position in grace is explained, not by anything in himself, but by the will of God.

The doctrine of election has two functions, that is, if properly understood:

First of all, it checks human independence and self-righteousness. Second, it shows that in bestowing favor, God is perfectly free (Eph. 1:1-6; II Tim. 1:9; Titus 3:5). However, the grace of God does not go into motion until the sinner wills this favor and has faith for its reception (Rev. 22:17).

Actually, every step in the process of the Christian life is due to grace (Gal. 1:15; Eph. 2:8-9; II Tim. 2:25).

THE DIVINE AGENCY

In Romans 8:28-30, Paul surveys the divine agency from the call to the final glory of the redeemed, which is all predicated on faith and grace. He does not, however, overlook man's responsibility. Obedience (Rom. 1:5; 6:17) is a moral attitude and cannot be made anything else. A man of himself turns to the Lord (II Cor. 3:16), but as the Lord draws him, not against his will.

Predestination or election never chooses one against his will, with Romans, Chapter 10, proclaiming that rejection by God is due to unbelief and disobedience. Grace cannot and will not override unbelief and disobedience. The grace of God is always predicated on a willing heart (Rev. 22:17).

One might say that predestination pertains to the particular plan of God. In other words, while at times the plan might be delayed, whatever that plan is, it will never stop but will always ultimately come to fruition. However, as to who will be in that plan pertains to *"whosoever will"* (Jn. 3:16; Rev. 22:17).

GRACE AS IT IS SEEN BY GOD

Grace is an attitude on God's Part that proceeds entirely from within Himself, and that is conditioned in no way by anything in the objects of His Favor. So, in Romans 4:4, if salvation is given on the basis of what a man has done, then salvation is given by God as the payment of a debt, which, of course, God cannot do.

However, when faith is reckoned by what it is not, i.e., righteousness, there is no claim on man's part, and he receives as a pure gift something that he has not earned and, in fact, cannot earn.

CONTROVERSIES

Most of the discussions of the Biblical doctrine of grace, it is said, have been faulty in narrowing the meaning of *"grace"* to some special sense and then endeavoring to force this special sense on all the Biblical passages.

For instance, Roman Catholic scholars, starting with the meaning of the word *"grace"* in II Corinthians 12:9, have made Romans 3:24 state that men are justified by the infusion of divine holiness into them, brought about by particular works. This is an interpretation that utterly ruins Paul's argument that justification is exclusively by faith. In other words, our Roman Catholic friends teach that grace comes partly by works.

On the other hand, some protestant extremists have tried to reverse the process and have argued that grace cannot mean anything except favor as an attitude, with results that are equally disastrous from correct Biblical interpretation.

NOTES

Actually, a rigid definition is hardly possible respecting grace, but, still, a single conception is usually present in almost every case where *"grace"* is found.

That conception is that all a Christian has, or is, is centered exclusively in God and Christ and depends utterly on God through Christ. The Kingdom of heaven is reserved for those who become as little children, for those who look to their Father in loving confidence for every benefit, whether it be for the pardon so freely given or for the strength that comes from Him Who works in them both to will and to do.

GRACE AND THE CROSS OF CHRIST

That which man must know and understand is that the grace of God is made possible in totality by the Cross of Christ (I Cor. 1:17-18, 23; 2:2; Gal. 6:14; Col. 2:10-15). This is why the Cross of Christ is so very, very important. Please understand, God has no more grace now than He did before the Cross, but the fact remained that the blood of bulls and goats could not take away sins, so that meant that the sin debt remained (Heb. 10:4). So, God did what He could before the Cross, but He, at that time, was limited.

Now that the Cross of Christ is a fact, this means that all sin has been atoned. This means that God can give to man everything that man needs, and He does so without payment or merit. In other words, there is nothing that God has that is for sale. Everything He has is a gift, which means it is freely given.

However, we must ever understand that it is the Cross of Christ which has made all of this possible. While Jesus Christ is the Source of all things we receive from God, it is the Cross of Christ that is the means, and we might quickly add, the only means by which all of these wonderful things are given to us. It is the Cross! The Cross! The Cross! It is according to our understanding of the Cross that the grace of God can come to us in an unlimited manner. While grace most definitely is free and is gained exclusively by faith on the part of the individual, it must never be forgotten that a tremendous price was paid for this which we so readily enjoy.

God does not demand much of the human race, but there is one thing that He does demand, and that is that we would have faith. Now, what does He mean by that?

He means that the believing sinner must exercise faith in Christ, believing that He is the Son of God, and that He paid the price on Calvary's Cross in order that man might be saved, and that God raised Him from the dead. When the believing sinner exercises faith in that of which I have stated, then the door is wide open for God to give that person everything that heaven has, and we speak of Eternal Life. In fact, grace and the Cross are so intertwined as to be indivisible.

(25) "AND NOW, BEHOLD, I KNOW THAT YOU ALL, AMONG WHOM I HAVE GONE PREACHING THE KINGDOM OF GOD, SHALL SEE MY FACE NO MORE."

The pattern is:

1. It is the Cross alone that deals with sin (Heb. 9:28).
2. If man tries to deal with sin any other way than the Cross, the sin remains (I Cor. 1:17).

THE KINGDOM OF GOD

The phrase, *"And now, behold, I know that you all, among whom I have gone preaching the Kingdom of God,"* presents Paul's message that the Holy Spirit had given him, which is to be preached by all!

In a sense, Paul showed that the Gospel of the grace of God is the same as the preaching of the Kingdom of God and, therefore, is the same as the Gospel of the Kingdom.

It is by God's Grace that we are brought under the rule and authority of God through our Lord Jesus by His Death and Resurrection. The evidence of that rule is the righteousness, peace, and joy that are given by the Holy Spirit (Rom. 14:17).

Horton said, *"In effect, there is only one Gospel, and it includes the present rule of God as well as the future rule when Jesus will establish His Kingdom on Earth, as He most certainly shall."*

WHAT IS THE KINGDOM OF GOD?

Even though we have dealt with this subject elsewhere in these volumes, please allow us an abbreviated sketch:

The phrases, *"Kingdom of God"* and *"Kingdom of Heaven,"* are used at times interchangeably in the Four Gospels. In fact, as we have previously said, Jesus did not speak too very often in the Gospels about being *"saved,"* but rather mostly preached the *"Kingdom of Heaven"* or the *"Kingdom of God."* There was a reason for that:

He had come to present the Kingdom to Israel, who was due the first offer, which was for many reasons. Had they accepted, it would have changed the entirety of the complexion of the world. However, they did not accept, which subjected the world to continued war, bloodshed, sickness, death, suffering, etc. Even though all believers presently have the Kingdom abiding in their hearts, it will not come in totality until two things transpire:

JESUS MUST RETURN

Jesus must first be present on Earth, and Israel must accept Him as Lord and Messiah for the Kingdom to commence in totality, which will take place at the Second Coming.

Concerning all that Jesus purchased for us in the Atonement at Calvary, we now only have *"the earnest of our inheritance* (a down-payment on what is coming) *until the Redemption of the purchased possession* (the Resurrection of Life), *unto the Praise of His Glory"* (Eph. 1:14).

PROVISIONS OF THE ATONEMENT

Many people misunderstand the provisions of the Atonement (what Jesus did at the Cross), thinking they are spiritual only. While the spiritual sets the tone for all else, as should be obvious, literally, not only was salvation provided, but healing, prosperity, peace, righteousness, and the Baptism with the Holy Spirit, plus many other things too numerous to mention. However, now, even as Paul has said, we have only been given an *"earnest"* of what is yet to come. Then the Kingdom of God will be realized in totality concerning believers (Rom. 8:23).

Even though Jesus paid the full price at Calvary for our salvation, regrettably, because we still live in this body of clay that is saddled with the sin nature, Christians, at times, still sin. However, that does not mean we are not saved. As well, Christians, at times, still get sick, but that doesn't mean Jesus does not heal. As stated, all that He provided has not even remotely been realized yet.

NOTES

EARNEST EXPECTATION

Paul also said, *"For the earnest expectation of the creature* (the down-payment we have already received) *waits for the Manifestation* (Resurrection) *of the Sons of God* (when the Believer will come into full Glory)*"* (Rom. 8:19).

As we have previously stated, the Kingdom of God covers the entirety of God's Creation, even including Satan, fallen angels, and demon spirits, who, incidentally, were not originally created in this manner and are now in rebellion against God.

The *"Kingdom of Heaven,"* which can be translated, *"the Kingdom from Heaven,"* does not include the satanic world of spiritual darkness. However, it does include professing believers on Earth, who are actually not saved. In other words, they profess but do not possess (Mat. 13:24-33).

THE KINGDOM OF HEAVEN

When Jesus returns, the Kingdom of Heaven will then be transferred to Earth and Kingdom rule will commence with Jesus serving as the Premier (King of kings and Lord of lords) of the entirety of the world and all its government, which Isaiah, as well as the other prophets, spoke of constantly (Isa. 9:6-7; 11:1-12).

At the end of that age, which will be one thousand years (Rev. 20:1-6), there will be one more short conflict with Satan as he is released from the bottomless pit, with him and all of his cohorts then being cast into the Lake of Fire, where they will remain forever and ever (Rev. 20:7-15).

According to Peter, the Earth will then be renovated by fire (II Pet. 3:10-13), with the Lord at that time transferring His Headquarters from Heaven to Earth. This is what John spoke of when he said, *"And I John saw the Holy City, New Jerusalem* (perpetually new), *coming down from God out of Heaven, prepared as a bride adorned for her husband"* (Rev., Chpts. 21-22).

NOTES

ALL THINGS

Paul said, *"Then comes the end, when He* (Jesus) *shall have delivered up the Kingdom to God, even the Father; when He* (Jesus) *shall have put down all rule and all Authority and Power"* (I Cor. 15:24).

Then, Paul said, *"And when all things shall be subdued unto Him* (Jesus), *then shall the Son also Himself be subject unto Him* (the Father) *Who put all things under Him* (Jesus), *that God may be all in all"* (I Cor. 15:28).

Then the *"Kingdom of God"* and the *"Kingdom of Heaven"* shall be one and the same, with the terrible satanic rebellion forever ended, with God, as Paul said, *"All in All."*

As surely as it is spoken, it will come!

The phrase, *"Shall see my face no more,"* tells us, I think, that the Holy Spirit had told Paul that due to events, they would not see him again this side of Glory.

Knowing how Paul loved these people—they were his converts—this must have been a very painful time for both the apostle and the Ephesian elders.

Some claim that Paul did come back to Ephesus after his first imprisonment, but there is no Biblical or historical proof of such. We had best follow and believe the Text exactly as Luke wrote.

(26) "WHEREFORE I TAKE YOU TO RECORD THIS DAY, THAT I AM PURE FROM THE BLOOD OF ALL MEN."

The composition is:

1. The phrase, *"Wherefore I take you to record this day,"* presents a strong statement and is meant to be that way. In other words, Paul is saying, *"The heavenly record will show...."*

2. *"That I am pure from the blood of all men,"* means that he had delivered the Gospel to everyone who heard him preach exactly as it was given to him by the Lord. Irrespective of the anger it aroused toward him, the reproach he endured, or the threats of bodily harm and even death, he never soft-pedaled or compromised the message in any way.

3. By the manner in which Paul used this phrase, *"The blood of all men,"* he was undoubtedly referring back to Ezekiel, and all others for that matter, when the Lord told that prophet, *"Son of man, I have made you a Watchman unto the House of Israel: therefore hear the Word at My Mouth, and give them warning from Me"* (Ezek. 3:17).

4. He then said to the prophet, *"And* (when) *you give him* (the wicked) *not warning, nor speak to warn the wicked from his wicked way, to save his life; the same wicked man shall die in his iniquity; but his blood will I require at your hand"* (Ezek. 3:18).

5. How many preachers are going to stand before God one day with the blood of many on their hands, because they did not faithfully preach the Word of God and would not deliver what the Lord told them to deliver? To be sure, and sadly so, it will probably be the far greater majority.

(27) "FOR I HAVE NOT SHUNNED TO DECLARE UNTO YOU ALL THE COUNSEL OF GOD."

The construction is:

1. One might say that before the Incarnation, Jesus was a perfect Expression of a perfect essence of God the Father.

2. Essence is the properties or attributes by means of which something can be placed in its proper class or identified as being what it is.

THUS SAITH THE LORD

The phrase, *"For I have not shunned to declare unto you,"* refers to the fact that the temptation was always there to trim the message. Knowing the animosity that the Gospel would produce and the anger it would arouse, his concern always was never for himself, but rather for the souls of men. Hence, the word must not be compromised, weakened, diluted, or abbreviated. It must always be, *"Thus says the Lord,"* and whatever that entails must be faithfully delivered, irrespective of the outcome.

This story is told of John Bunyan, who lived and ministered in Bedford, England:

As he was imprisoned by the authorities for preaching the Gospel, his wife and little child were visiting him in this prison when the child asked him, *"Daddy, when are you coming home?"*

It broke his heart to hear this plea, with no answer forthcoming.

NOTES

After his wife and child left, the authorities came into him immediately, informing him that they had overheard the exchange.

They said to him, *"We are not unreasonable men. If you will promise to stop preaching, you may walk out of this prison now and go home to your family."*

It is said that Bunyan sat there for a moment and then slowly stood and said, *"Gentlemen, if you let me out of Bedford Prison today, I will be preaching in Bedford Square tomorrow!"*

It is only those of this caliber who touch the world. The message must never be compromised!

TO HEAR FROM GOD

It is the responsibility of the preacher to hear from God and to deliver what the Lord has given, and in no uncertain terms. His responsibility is not popularity but rather faithfulness.

Only the Lord knows the preachers, the press, entire denominations, and, actually, most of the church world who have done everything within their power to stop my voice. Leaders of major Pentecostal denominations (Pentecostal in name only) vowed to get me off of television, saying, *"We will do anything we have to do to accomplish this task!"*

Why?

I realize that the world and most of the church thinks the actions of the so-called church were because of my own personal problems, but that is not so. It was because of what I preached!

What was that?

ALL THE COUNSEL OF GOD

The phrase, *"All the counsel of God,"* pertains to all of the Word of God.

That means to preach the precious shed blood of Jesus as the only cleansing for sin and faith in that which He did as the only vehicle, so to speak, of justification. When the Lord told me to preach that to the Catholics over our telecast, which then went into a major part of the world, and to pull no punches, that did not set well at all. However, I think I had more opposition from Pentecostals and Charismatics regarding this situation even than from the Catholics themselves. To be sure, we saw untold numbers of Catholics brought to a saving knowledge of Jesus Christ.

"All the counsel of God," also includes the Baptism with the Holy Spirit with the evidence of speaking with other tongues (Acts 2:4). I was to tell the denominational, non-Pentecostal, church world that without the Holy Spirit, their denominations would spiritually die. To be sure, that did not set well either!

I was also to tell the Pentecostal denominations and Charismatics that they must return to dependence on the Holy Spirit, which, in effect, means to return to the Word of God.

The Lord warned me, even as He warned Paul and, no doubt, many others through the ages, of the great opposition that would come. He said to me, *"If you preach what I tell you to preach, you may well lose everything."*

He then said, *"Your own* (Pentecostals) *will turn against you."*

All of this has come to pass exactly as He said, and, as stated, it is because of what I preached.

This I can say: I have had to fall at the feet of the world's Redeemer countless times, even with hot tears bathing my face, because of coming short of the glory of God and, thereby, begging His Mercy and Grace. However, by the grace of God, I know I can say as Paul, *"I am pure from the blood of all men ... for I have not shunned to declare unto you all the counsel of God."*

ALL, NOT JUST A PART

If one is to notice, the Holy Spirit through the Apostle said, *"All the counsel of God,"* not just a part!

The problem of the church is and always has been that it compromises the message. Even though I am blunt, this I must say:

If the preacher of the Gospel who claims to be God-Called does not preach all of the things of God, then he is not declaring "all the counsel of God." He must preach, *"By grace are you saved through faith"* (Eph. 2:8-9), the Baptism with the Holy Spirit with the evidence of speaking with other

NOTES

tongues (Acts 2:4), and the divine healing and miracle-working power of God presently manifest among us (Mk. 16:17-18). As well, and above all, one might say, he must *"preach the Cross,"* the victorious Christian life in Jesus, Who saves us from sin and not in sin (Rom. 8:2), the Resurrection of the body at the trump of God, i.e., the Rapture of the church (I Thess. 4:16-18), and the soon imminent return of our Lord and Saviour, Jesus Christ (Rev., Chpt. 19). Again I say, if he is not preaching all of these things, he is not declaring *"all the counsel of God!"*

I realize that is blunt, but it is meant to be that way.

The Holy Spirit demands that *"all"* of this counsel be preached and not just part. As well, the proper *"Fruit"* will always follow the preached total counsel of God.

Souls will genuinely be saved, believers will be baptized with the Holy Spirit, sick bodies will be healed, and bondages will be broken in hearts and lives when this great Gospel is preached in its fullness. In fact, the Holy Spirit, I maintain, will only anoint that which is *"all the counsel of God."* He will not anoint a partial Counsel!

(28) "TAKE HEED THEREFORE UNTO YOURSELVES, AND TO ALL THE FLOCK, OVER THE WHICH THE HOLY SPIRIT HAS MADE YOU OVERSEERS, TO FEED THE CHURCH OF GOD, WHICH HE HAS PURCHASED WITH HIS OWN BLOOD."

The structure is:

1. There is one God, which means the Godhead cannot be separated as it regards deity, but yet, manifested in three Persons.
2. Those three Persons are, *"God the Father, God the Son, and God the Holy Spirit."*

TAKE HEED

The phrase, *"Take heed therefore unto yourselves and to all the flock,"* presents a double-barreled thrust.

The word *"heed"* in the Greek text is *"prosecho"* and means *"to be cautious about or to have regard."*

These elders (pastors) were to be cautious about their own experience with the Lord. The preacher of the Gospel can only give the people what is already in his own soul. Many have the erroneous idea that it is not so important respecting the consecration of the man of God, but only what he preaches.

THE MAN AND HIS MESSAGE

While his message is certainly of singular significance, still, the Holy Spirit has so intertwined the man and the message that they are actually inseparable. In other words, if the man is not consecrated to God, the message, irrespective as to how truthful it may be, will not be anointed by the Holy Spirit and will reap precious few results.

So, the preacher of the Gospel is not only to seek the Lord constantly that his own life stay clean before God but, as well, that he stay close to God in order that the Holy Spirit may have full latitude. If one is to notice, the warning concerning the preacher comes before the warning respecting the *"flock."*

All of this can be done only if the preacher understands the Cross of Christ not only as it refers to salvation but, as well, to sanctification. In other words, we are speaking of how we live for God, how we order our behavior, and how we grow in grace and the knowledge of the Lord. Regrettably, most modern preachers have little or no knowledge whatsoever of the Cross of Christ and the great part it plays in the sanctification process. What we are about to give is this great truth, which makes up basically the entirety of the Bible.

THE WORD OF GOD IN BRIEF

- Jesus Christ is the Source of all things that we receive from God (Jn. 1:1-3, 14, 29; 14:20; Col. 2:10-15).
- While Jesus Christ is the Source, the Cross of Christ is the means, and the only means by which all of these wonderful things from God are given to us (Rom. 6:1-14; I Cor. 1:17-18, 23; 2:2).
- Jesus Christ being the Source and the Cross being the means, the object of our faith must always be, and without fail, *"Jesus Christ and Him Crucified."* The Cross of Christ ever being the object of our faith is extremely important.
- With Jesus as the Source and the Cross

as the means, and the Cross of Christ the object of our faith, the Holy Spirit will then work mightily on our behalf. The Holy Spirit is God but for Him to do all within our hearts and lives that He can do, which we must have, the Cross of Christ must, without fail, be the object of our faith. That being the case, the Holy Spirit will work grandly for us, overcoming every vestige of darkness (Rom. 8:1-11; Gal. 6:14; Col. 2:10-15).

THE FLOCK

The second *"heed"* has to do with the church body itself, which is the responsibility of the preacher of the Gospel.

The preacher is to preach the truth to *"the flock"* and, as well, to love them, even as Christ loves the church.

The *"flock"* cannot rise any higher than the man who stands behind the pulpit. If the love of God fills his heart, his people will have that same spirit. If there is a burden for souls on his part, a hunger for the moving of the Holy Spirit, some of his people will most certainly follow course.

Sadly and tragically, if it is otherwise, that, too, will inculcate itself in those who sit under his particular ministry, whomever he may be.

THE HOLY SPIRIT

Sometime ago, one young man made the statement to me that since he had been coming to our church, he had seen the anointing and moving of the Holy Spirit as he had not seen it before. Then he said, *"Brother Swaggart, sometimes now I will go back to churches where I thought the Spirit of God was actually moving, and now I see that much of what I thought was the Spirit was really nothing more than the flesh."*

He had been exposed to the true Spirit of God, and, regrettably, in many churches, it is little more than noise or activity that passes for the Spirit. Because the people are so spiritually dull, they do not really know what is or isn't the Spirit of God.

I do not mean to insinuate that our church is the only church in our city that has the Spirit of God, for that is not so. However, to be sure, there are not many churches anywhere, which truly have the

NOTES

moving and operation of the Holy Spirit within the services. Regrettably, they are few and far between!

OVERSEERS

The phrase, *"Over the which the Holy Spirit has made you overseers,"* speaks of pastors. As we have said, and as is obvious in Acts and the Epistles, the titles of *"elders, bishops, overseers, shepherds, and presbyters,"* all mean the same thing, *"pastor."*

As well, as one should notice, it was the *"Holy Spirit"* and not Paul Who called these men. To be sure, the Holy Spirit does so under the leadership of the Head of the church, the Lord Jesus Christ (Eph. 1:22-23).

While Paul advised and counseled, even as here, by the Commandment of the Lord, as is obvious, still, he never took a position, even as he should not have, to force these particular individuals to do anything. It was the Holy Spirit Who was to do the doing. He alone was the final Authority.

SPIRITUAL AUTHORITY

It is here where Satan has made his greatest headway in the church, and I speak of spiritual authority. So-called spiritual leaders want to exercise this authority over others and, in fact, do so constantly; however, such always abrogates the headship of Christ. Spiritual Authority, as invested in those called by God (Eph. 4:11), never refers to authority over people, but rather demon spirits.

As we have repeatedly stated, the Lord gives *"some, apostles; and some, prophets; and some, evangelists; and some, pastors and teachers;*

"For the perfecting of the Saints, for the work of the ministry, for the edifying of the Body of Christ" (Eph. 4:11-12). However, in that *"perfecting"* and *"work,"* there are strict guidelines to be followed, which are overly obvious in the Book of Acts and the Epistles, that the headship of Christ never be abrogated. I will give one example, and to be sure, this is not an isolated case but actually the norm.

UNSCRIPTURAL AUTHORITY

A pastor friend of mine was called by

NOTES

the Lord to go to a certain city and plant a church. The year was 1969.

The Lord helped him to build, which, over the course of years, saw many people saved and lives changed.

In 1995, there was a minor problem in the church that involved, among a few other minor things, the color which a particular item was painted. (Yes, I said it was over the color of some paint!)

Through carnality among some of the church members, the situation became heated until finally, there was a voting in the church, that is, if I remember the situation correctly, with about 85 percent of the people voting in favor of the pastor, etc.

Irrespective of that, a small nucleus appealed to the headquarters in that particular state regarding that denomination, with the ultimate decision by these so-called spiritual authorities being that this pastor must resign, which he did.

This particular denomination takes the position, as do most Pentecostal denominations, that *"preachers are a dime a dozen,"* to quote one verbatim; consequently, irrespective of the situation, almost all of the time, they demand that the preacher leave, irrespective as to the right or wrong.

The truth is, preachers are a dime a dozen, but only of the stripe of which they speak. Those who are truly God-called and anointed by the Holy Spirit, even as is my friend, are as scarce as the proverbial hen's teeth.

Whether right or wrong, no outside influence has any scriptural right to override the authority of the pastor in any church. Such is always unscriptural, and sadly, that is the reason, among other things, that these denominations are spiritually dying.

Incidentally, the reason they gave him for demanding his resignation was that he was *"inefficient as a pastor."*

WAS THAT CORRECT?

Were that so, which it was not, why did it take them 26 years to find out?

The Bible way is that God called this man to this place, even as the Lord calls all, at least those who are truly sent by Him. Under the leadership of the Holy Spirit, and that of no one else I might quickly add, he should attempt to carry out the work that the Lord has called him to do in that particular place.

No, even as I have repeatedly said, it is not scripturally wrong to have a denominational headquarters, or something of this nature. The wrong comes whenever headquarters usurps authority over the pastor and the local church.

I emphasize again, this is not an isolated case of which I have spoken, but rather the norm. In other words, it goes on constantly.

The laity may read this and take the position that these are matters which are of little interest to them. However, I remind the laity that such religious control, which is so abjectly unscriptural, in fact, does affect them greatly! That is the reason many churches in these respective denominations are saddled with preachers who are man-led and not God-led. Consequently, everyone suffers!

Some would read this and argue, even as a man told me just the other day, *"Oh, but we must have discipline!"*

DISCIPLINE

In fact, he is exactly right, but whose discipline?

The scriptural pattern is that the Lord exert such discipline, with that being the reason for what Paul said concerning these elders, *"Over the which the Holy Spirit has made you overseers,"* i.e., *"pastors."*

That does not mean that the Holy Spirit calls individuals and then turns the discipline over to other men. No!

He calls, He guides, He leads, He empowers, He anoints, and He disciplines, and it is Him alone!

AN UNSCRIPTURAL POSITION ALWAYS LEADS TO UNSCRIPTURAL RESULTS

Actually, this of which we here speak is what ultimately caused the spiritual declension of the early church. The apostles were led by the Holy Spirit and, therefore, used mightily of God to establish the church in the world of that day.

However, after their deaths and those who had followed them, carnal men gradually began to usurp authority over the Holy

Spirit and, in actuality, the headship of Christ over His Church. Thus, they formed religious offices which had no scriptural validity, thereby, they gradually took control of the church from the Lord. The end result of that, even though it took several hundreds of years to come about, was the Catholic Church, which is now, and has been for many centuries, total apostasy.

To be frank, if Jesus would tarry, present Pentecostal denominations, and even others who have little or no denominational affiliation, would mostly follow and, in fact, are following in the same identical manner as that of the Catholic Church. Spiritual declension is suffered accordingly.

THE SCRIPTURAL POSITION

Everything must be done according to the Word of the Lord. When men make up their own religious rules, obviously, the rules are not that which are of God. The idea of the church on Earth is its heavenly origin. Every part and parcel must be scriptural. Even though the Lord definitely uses men and women to carry out this great work, still, it is always to be done under scriptural guidelines.

Church government can be a godly and holy thing, if it is held to the Word of God, for the simple reason that such government is God's Government. However, when man begins to insert his own government, which is, of necessity, out of his own mind and of the world, then it simply is not of God, irrespective of the good intentions. This is true regardless of how much he may cover it with religious overtones.

GOD'S GOVERNMENT

The Lord will never work outside of His framework of government, which is outlined perfectly in the Word of God and leaves religious man with no excuse. God's Method is to speak to men and women, not committees, boards, hierarchies, organizations, denominations, etc. He then expects these men and women to carry out what He has called them to do.

To be sure, it is wise and scriptural to submit to others of like faith and confidence what one thinks the Lord has instructed one to do; however, the submitting of such is not meant to be for approval, but rather prayer and proper counseling. If the Lord has truly told a person to do something, He certainly means for that person to carry out that calling. In fact, there are guidelines respecting this, but, as we shall see, these guidelines never abrogate the call of God in its proper order.

NOTES

SUBMISSION

Peter discussed submission respecting the local church in Chapter 5 of his first Book.

He began the chapter by addressing *"elders,"* who are pastors. He admonished them to *"feed the flock of God which is among you..."* He then told how that was to be done.

He then addressed the younger pastors in that local church by saying, *"Likewise, you younger* (other preachers who labor under the elder or main pastor), *submit yourselves unto the elder"* (I Pet. 5:1-6).

However, this submission of which Peter spoke is confined to that local church and does not include some mythical headquarters elsewhere, etc. Of course, this means submitting oneself to that which is scriptural. If the senior pastor seeks to do something that is not scriptural, and it is obviously that way, the younger preacher must not submit to such, as ought to be obvious.

Actually, Peter always fell back to the proper type of submission as laid out by the Holy Spirit by saying, *"Yea, all of you be subject one to another, and be clothed with humility."*

Other than younger preachers submitting to the head pastor in the local church, submission, as laid down by the Holy Spirit, is always on a horizontal level and never vertical, other than all submitting totally to the Lord and His Word. Paul said, *"Submitting yourselves one to another in the fear of God"* (Eph. 5:21).

As stated, submitting one to another is horizontal submission and not vertical submission, which is demanded, unscripturally I might quickly add, by those who would be *"lords over God's Heritage,"* which is especially forbidden (I Pet. 5:3).

The submission of which I speak has to

do with the church, with another type of submission demanded by the Holy Spirit regarding civil authorities, which is totally different (Rom. 13:1-7; I Pet. 2:13).

As well, there is a marital submission as addressed by Paul, which, of course, must be followed (Eph. 5:22).

God's Ways are the only ways, and they are meant to be followed, and if followed, will bring forth beautiful and wonderful results. To do otherwise, irrespective of the good intentions, will never lead to that which is good.

GUIDELINES OF HONESTY

Going back to previous statements, the believer, be he preacher or otherwise, should always *"try the spirits"* as to the veracity of what he thinks the Lord is telling him (I Jn. 4:1). Concerning this very thing, Paul said, *"Satan himself is transformed into an angel of light"* (II Cor. 11:14), meaning that he attempts to deceive people constantly by claiming what they are hearing is from the Lord when, in reality, it is not.

Just because someone has said the Lord has told him to do something does not at all mean that the Lord has actually done that. Everything must be judged scripturally, irrespective of the claims. If it is scriptural, it will be obvious; consequently, it will, as well, abide by guidelines of honesty and integrity with all fairness to others. The idea that the Lord has told someone to do something that will obviously hurt others could not truly be of the Holy Spirit.

When the Holy Spirit calls someone to do certain things, it is always done not only with that particular work in mind but, as well, the entirety of the Body of Christ.

Down through the years I have had many people to write me concerning the following:

AN EXAMPLE

The Lord had just baptized them with the Holy Spirit, but they were attending a church which did not subscribe to the Pentecostal experience. Some claimed that the Lord had told them to stay there and do *"missionary work,"* etc.

Almost all of the time my answer to them would be, *"No!"*

NOTES

If the pastor of that local church is not in favor of the Pentecostal doctrine, even though that doctrine is right and that pastor is wrong, still, it is his church, and no one else has the right to usurp authority over him, teaching that of which he does not approve. To do such is ethically wrong concerning practice, even though the one who has been recently baptized with the Holy Spirit is scripturally right concerning doctrine. The Holy Spirit will never condone such!

If the pastor is not in sympathy with what is being done, irrespective of how right it may be, that person should find another church to attend.

In view of that, it must be emphasized that to be right scripturally also means to be right regarding integrity and ethics. As well, the Lord can never bless a right thing which is done in a wrong way.

The following is an article written by Dr. Bernard Rossier, a former professor at World Evangelism Bible College.

Even though some of the things said will be repetitive according to what we have already stated, I feel personally that the detail given is excellent and will be of great scriptural and spiritual benefit to the Bible student.

WHAT IS NEW TESTAMENT SUBMISSION?

The New Testament term for *"submission"* (hupotasso) is used in a plethora of different ways:

- Of believers being subject to civil authorities (Rom. 13:5; Titus 3:1; I Pet. 2:13);
- Of Creation being subjected to vanity or frustration because of the fall of mankind into sin in the Garden of Eden (Rom. 8:20);
- Of the spirits of the prophets being subject to the prophets (I Cor. 14:32);
- Of women submitting regarding particular conduct in the church (I Cor. 14:34);
- Of Jesus submitting to Mary and Joseph (Lk. 2:51);
- Of slaves submitting to their masters (Titus 2:9; I Pet. 2:18);
- Of younger preachers in the local church submitting to the elder pastor (I Pet. 5:5);

NOTES

• Of Christians submitting to God (James 4:7);

• Of the submission of all things to Christ (I Cor. 15:27-28; Eph. 1:22; Heb. 2:8; I Pet. 3:22);

• Of wives submitting to their husbands (Eph. 5:22; Col. 3:18; Titus 2:5; I Pet. 3:1, 5);

• Of the refusal of Israel to submit to God's Righteousness (Rom. 10:3);

• Of the impossibility of the carnal mind submitting to God (Rom. 8:7);

• Of the church submitting to Christ (Eph. 5:24);

• Of believers submitting one to another (I Cor. 16:16; Eph. 5:21).

ECCLESIASTICAL AUTHORITIES OUTSIDE THE LOCAL CHURCH

It is interesting that the New Testament says nothing about submitting to ecclesiastical authorities outside the local church.

Why?

The reason is that there were not any ecclesiastical authorities in the early church. The local assemblies did respond to appeals from people like the Apostle Paul, even as they certainly should have, but none of the apostles occupied hierarchal positions as we know them today.

As noted above, believers generally submitted to one another within local assemblies. In fact, the Epistle we know as Ephesians was written to instruct the Body of Christ on the way it should operate.

THE PURPOSE OF THE CHURCH

It begins by specifying that the New Testament church has one particular purpose and reason for its existence, and that is to worship God (Eph. 1:6, 12, 14). After dealing with salient topics that relate to the operation of the New Testament church, the Apostle Paul treated the matter of submission.

Verse 21 of Ephesians, Chapter 5, serves as the introductory and the controlling verse for the entire section, which continues through Ephesians, Chapter 6, Verse 9.

This introductory verse literally reads, *"Being subject to one another in fear of Christ."* Therefore, this regulating verse contains a qualifier that the submission must be out of reverence for Christ. Actually, this type of qualifier can be seen throughout the passage.

For example, Verse 22 of Ephesians, Chapter 5, instructs wives to submit to their husbands *"as unto the Lord."* Also, the first verse of Ephesians, Chapter 6, requires children to obey their parents *"in the Lord."*

In other words, in this matter of submission, God does not expect Christian wives to do things that would be unscriptural just because their husbands say so.

Even Christian children would not be required by God to disobey the Bible just because their parents say so.

When Peter and John were commanded by the Sanhedrin not to speak or teach any longer in the name of Jesus, even though they were the rulers of Israel, the apostles implied that they would obey God rather than men (Acts 4:18-20).

Shortly thereafter, the apostles were issued a similar command by the Sanhedrin, which, incidentally, was the religious ruling body of Israel, but they responded with the same basic answer (Acts 5:27-29).

VOLUNTARY SUBMISSION

It is important to note that the emphatic word in Ephesians 5:21 is the participle *"submitting"* (hupotassomenoi). In the Greek structure, because this is what is referred to as a *"middle voice participle,"* it indicates a *voluntary* submission, not one forced as if the participle were active voice or one that emphasizes a passive acquiescence.

It is also crucial to notice that Verse 23 of Ephesians, Chapter 5, designates Christ as the *"Head of the church"* (kephale tes ekklesias). This phrase means that He is the Operating Head, not just a Figurehead!

THE NEW TESTAMENT CHURCH HAD NO ECCLESIASTICAL HIERARCHY

The New Testament church does not indicate an ecclesiastical hierarchy. In fact, it indicates the very opposite.

When Paul gave his farewell address to the Ephesian leaders, he first labeled them as *"elders"* or *"presbyters"* (Presbuterous—Acts 20:17). Later in the passage, he called the same people *"overseers"* or *"bishops"*

(Episkopous—Acts 20:28).

Also in this latter verse, he told them *"to shepherd"* (poimainein), the Greek word from which we derive *"pastor."*

Therefore, he named the same people *"presbyters," "bishops,"* and *"pastors."*

In Philippians 1:1, the address is to all the saints in Christ Jesus at Philippi, with the bishops and deacons. Since this was a formal salutation in an official Epistle, it seems unlikely that the order of presbyters would be disregarded, that is, if there indeed was an official order at that point in time.

The qualifications for bishops and deacons are listed in I Timothy, Chapter 3, where the author did not mention any intermediate order between bishops and deacons. Instead, he passed without a break from the characteristics needed by bishops to those needed by deacons.

In the same Epistle, Paul referred to presbyters (I Tim. 5:17-19) and ascribed to them functions similar to those discharged by bishops (I Tim. 3:4; 5:17). In the opening chapter of Titus, there is even clearer identification of bishops and presbyters. In other words, these designations all refer to the *"pastor"* of the local church (last sentence mine).

No scriptural data exists to point to any ecclesiastical hierarchy outside the local church.

WHERE DID THE CHURCH COME UP WITH ALL THE UNSCRIPTURAL OFFICES WHICH SEEM SO PREVALENT PRESENTLY?

If many of these modern, man-devised, religious offices did not come from the early church, which they did not, when did such begin to develop, and from where did it originate?

It is evident that a monarchical episcopacy began to surface by the beginning of the second century. Ignatius, who wrote noncanonical letters early in the second century, was the first definite proponent of the threefold order of bishops, presbyters, and deacons, although this form of church polity did not become widespread for another 50 years.

Throughout his writing, Ignatius designated the bishop as supreme, ascribing to him all the powers the apostles previously possessed.

Irenaeus, who probably wrote toward the end of the second century, also was one of the architects of the monarchical episcopacy.

The monarchical episcopacy was the standard pattern, regrettably so, of church government by the end of the second century. (This gradually went into the Catholic Church as man wrested control of the church from the Holy Spirit.)

Although they use different terminology, many Protestant denominations have adopted similar arrangements and usurped the authority that God labeled as belonging to the local church. In other words, this type of church polity began because some people did exactly what Peter said not to do when he warned against lording it over God's People (I Pet. 5:3).

Actually, Jesus used the same Greek term when He cautioned against hierarchies of importance, or *"lording it down"* over other people (Mat. 20:25). *"Down"* comes from the prefix of the word and indicates a mind-set of feeling more important than other people. Jesus said not to do it because it is the world's way (Mat. 20:25-26). Instead, He said that we should serve one another.

FINALLY

In conclusion, it is quite obvious that the New Testament emphasizes a submission among believers in local assemblies, but it does not authorize ecclesiastical structures that appropriate to themselves the authority belonging exclusively to the local body.

New Testament churches cooperated with each other, but they were not controlled by any outside governing agency.

They practiced submission, but it was a voluntary submission among the members of a local assembly, and it was a submission that recognized Christ as its Operating Head.

The church needs to get back to following Jesus' Instructions about self-abnegation for the benefit of other people (Mat. 20:27-28; Mk. 10:43-45). Where would we be if Jesus had exalted Himself instead of submitting to the will of the Father and giving Himself as the perfect Sacrifice for our sins?

NOTES

NOTES

Once again, Paul said, *"Let this mind be in you, which was also in Christ Jesus..."* (Phil. 2:5-8).

The phrase, *"To feed the church of God,"* proclaims, as is obvious, the responsibility of the preacher of the Gospel.

Even though each of the fivefold callings of the ministry has its different functions and responsibilities (Eph. 4:11), still, believers must be spiritually fed. That simply means that the Word of God, undiluted, uncompromised, and preached and taught with the power and anointing of the Holy Spirit must be given to the people.

FEED THE FLOCK

The word *"feed"* in the Greek text is *"poimaino"* and means *"to tend as a shepherd."* There are two things which must be said about this:

The preacher of the Gospel must have it settled in his mind that the Lord through *"His Divine Power has given unto us all things* (through the Gospel) *that pertain unto Life and Godliness, through the knowledge of Him* (Jesus) *Who has called us to Glory and Virtue"* (II Pet. 1:3).

PSYCHOLOGY?

One of the greatest dangers at this present time to this of which I have just said is the modern philosophy of humanistic psychology. (I say modern in that this philosophy basically began approximately 150 years ago with Sigmund Freud.) Unfortunately, this has made great inroads in the church and is the total opposite of the Gospel of Jesus Christ.

Despite the claims of many, psychology, at least that which pertains to psychoanalysis, is not a science and in no way can be construed as such. Its practitioners stumble from one foolish fad to the other. It is worldly wisdom pure and simple and, as such, holds no answers for mankind. James said, *"This wisdom descends not from above, but is earthly, sensual, devilish"* (James 3:15).

The few statements I will make should be obvious to all. However, much of the modern church world has opted for this lie of man because they have forsaken the Word of God. Jeremiah said, and rightly so, *"For My people have committed two evils; they have forsaken Me the fountain of living waters, and hewed them out cisterns, broken cisterns, that can hold no water"* (Jer. 2:13).

About 2,600 years ago, Jeremiah portrayed this modern evil perfectly.

THE CAUSE

Modern psychology has no knowledge of the cause of man's problems or the cure. If anyone will take the time to peruse the variant causes which are projected, plus the foolish recommendations for so-called help, the conclusion, at least if honestly approached, could only be negative.

In truth, psychology is a master at symptoms. Because it is a master in this respect, it fools many people. However, as stated, it does not take a genius to know that Pavlov's dog is going to respond the same each time. So, someone telling a person their symptoms, and even being accurate, is no solution to the problem. However, that is the gist of psychological knowledge—symptoms. From humanistic wisdom, they do not know the cause of man's problems or the cure.

ONLY TALK

Humanistic psychology has no antibiotics, miracle drugs, or any type of medicine whatsoever that they can prescribe respecting particular problems. However, through the medical profession, they have prescribed mood-altering drugs, which address the real problem not at all, and have probably done more to exacerbate the approximately six million prescription addicts in America than anything else. The only thing that psychology has is *"talk."*

I must remind the reader that if it is possible for one to talk away aberrant behavior, sin, or anti-social activities, which actually strike at the very heart of the human problem, then Jesus wasted His Time coming down to this sin-sodden world to die on Calvary in order to redeem humanity.

I must remind the reader that even God, Who is Omnipotent (All-powerful), Omniscient (All-knowing), and Omnipresent (Everywhere), Who could speak Creation into existence (Gen., Chpt. 1), could not speak man's salvation and redemption into being and be true to His Nature. Now, I ask this question:

If even God could not speak a cure into existence for the very problems of which we are discussing, how in the world do poor, frail mortals think they can do so?

THE WORLD

One can well understand why the world would resort to such. They do not know God, so they have to try to address these problems some way, but sadly, it will help not at all.

However, it is something else altogether for the church, which ought to know better, to resort to such foolishness and, in many cases, outright blasphemy. The only way such can be done is to forsake the Word of God. It is not possible to mesh heavenly wisdom and worldly wisdom, and neither should it be tried.

As Peter said, *"If believers will totally turn to Jesus Christ and learn of Him, respecting behavior problems, bad habits, anti-social habits, or any other spiritual problem, He will continue to do in hearts and lives presently as He has done with millions in the past."* Jesus Christ can change men and women, and, in fact, He alone can change men and women.

RELIANCE ON JESUS

However, for that change to be brought about, there must be a total and complete dedication to Him and a reliance upon Him. The answer that Christ provides is the answer of the Cross. It is the Cross that has dealt with sin, and the Cross alone that has dealt with sin. It was there that Jesus atoned for all sin, past, present, and future, at least for all who will believe (Jn. 3:16). Even with Christians, if they do not understand the Cross of Christ relative to one's sanctification, then the believer is going to face problems that he cannot solve. The Cross alone is the answer. The Cross of Christ relative to sanctification is that which was given to the Apostle Paul, and he gave to us in his 14 Epistles.

As we've already stated, Jesus Christ is the Source of all things we receive from God. As well, the Cross of Christ is the means and the only means by which all of these wonderful things are given to us. That being the case, Jesus Christ and Him Crucified must be the object of our faith. In fact, the entirety of the story of the Bible from Genesis 1:1 through Revelation 22:21 is *"Jesus Christ and Him Crucified."* So, when one places one's faith exclusively in Christ and Him Crucified, one is placing his faith exclusively in the Word of God (Rom. 6:1-14; 8:1-11; I Cor. 1:17-18, 23; 2:2; Col. 2:10-15). All victory is found in the Cross of Christ, and if the Cross is ignored, there is no victory.

We must understand that the Holy Spirit, Who brings all of this to pass within our lives, works exclusively within the parameters, so to speak, of the Finished Work of Christ. In other words, it is the Cross of Christ that gives the Holy Spirit the legal right to do as He does, which is to use His mighty Power on our behalf (Rom. 8:2).

He doesn't demand much of us, but He does demand one thing, and that is that our faith be exclusively in Christ and the Cross (Rom. 6:1-14; Eph. 2:13-18). That's why Paul said:

"For the preaching of the Cross is to them who perish foolishness, but unto us who are saved, it is the Power of God" (I Cor. 1:18).

HOW IS THE CROSS OF CHRIST THE POWER OF GOD?

In fact, there was no power in the wooden beam on which Jesus died. There is really no power in death itself. The power is in the Holy Spirit (Rom. 8:1-11). It is the Cross which has given the Holy Spirit the legal means to do all that He does, hence, Paul also stating:

"The Law of the Spirit of Life in Christ Jesus, has made me free from the law of sin and death" (Rom. 8:2).

Unfortunately, many Christians have tried to use means other than Christ and the Cross to bring about victory, which always fails. For instance, many have thought that the answer was in the laying on of hands, which, within itself, is a viable, scriptural doctrine, but they have found that it does not solve all the problems. Don't

NOTES

misunderstand, we lay hands on people every week at Family Worship Center, praying for them. As stated, it is scriptural. However, it cannot take the place of the great victory won by Christ at the Cross. Let us say it again:

Many, if not most, believers have an understanding of the Cross of Christ as it regards the salvation experience. However, they basically have no knowledge at all as it regards the Cross and our sanctification experience, which refers to how we live for God, how we order our behavior, and how we grow in grace and the knowledge of the Lord. The Cross of Christ is that which makes all of this possible.

PURCHASED WITH HIS OWN BLOOD

The phrase, *"Which He has purchased with His own Blood,"* is the latter portion of Verse 28 of the chapter of our present study. This speaks of the Cross, exactly that which we have been addressing.

The price of the Cross is of such magnitude that I think it would be impossible for even the godliest to fully comprehend or understand all that was done in the most unselfish act that humanity would ever know, the redemption of mankind by Jesus Christ. When we understand that He gave not only His best, but actually Himself, how can we do less than give Him our best?

To be sure, all of us have failed, and failed miserably, but at the same time, God help us to at least be going in the right direction, especially considering that the *"Way"* through the Word of God is Christ and the Cross.

(29) "FOR I KNOW THIS, THAT AFTER MY DEPARTING SHALL GRIEVOUS WOLVES ENTER IN AMONG YOU, NOT SPARING THE FLOCK."

The status is:

1. The only way that Christlikeness can be carried out in the life of the believer is that we have a correct interpretation of the Cross of Christ.

2. *"The death of the Cross"* indicates the climax of Christ's Self-abasement, for it was the most ignominious of all the modes of death then known.

NOTES

PAUL

The phrase, *"For I know this, that after my departing,"* has to do with the phrase concerning these Ephesian elders, *"Shall see my face no more"* (Acts 20:25).

Even though Paul's life span would continue for several years yet, as we have stated, there is no record that he ministered again in this particular part of the world. Whatever the case, whether absence or his ultimate going on to be with the Lord, the Ephesians, plus all others under his sphere of influence, would no longer be privileged to have the tremendous ministry afforded in the person of Paul. Very shortly, he would be imprisoned in Caesarea and then in Rome.

From this imprisonment, it is believed by some that he was released in about A.D. 63. Some claim that he then went to Spain and even back to the Aegean area again before his re-arrest and death at the hands of Nero, which some believe was in the year A.D. 67. However, except for the death of Paul by Nero, these particulars are more speculation than anything else.

GRIEVOUS WOLVES

The phrase, *"Shall grievous wolves enter in among you, not sparing the flock,"* presents a perfect description of those who merchandise the Body of Christ in whatever way. This is done by preachers, whether pastors or evangelists, who have their own agenda and not that of the Holy Spirit. It can refer to the leadership of entire religious denominations respecting church government, etc.

"Wolves" do not always come in the stripe of unscrupulous preachers but, at times, with a very religious direction.

The word *"grievous"* in the Greek text is *"barus"* and means *"oppressive or burdensome."* In other words, the agenda is personal greed in one way or the other, making great demands on the people, etc.

"Wolves" in the Greek text is *"lukos"* and means *"a wolf with whitish hair,"* which leaves the inference and is actually present in the Text of *"wolves in sheep's clothing."*

Even though that was the problem then and continued to be a problem in the church down through the centuries, it is more acute today than ever and, in fact, will worsen!

This present time is the very age of apostasy and deception, even as we are warned by the Holy Spirit and the Lord Himself (Mat. 24:11-14; II Tim. 4:3-4).

(30) "ALSO OF YOUR OWN SELVES SHALL MEN ARISE, SPEAKING PERVERSE THINGS, TO DRAW AWAY DISCIPLES AFTER THEM."

The account is:

1. The scriptural truth is that the only manner of victory which God has prescribed is our faith in what Christ has done at the Cross on our behalf.

2. Consequently, the three main ingredients regarding the Christian's life and walk are *"the Cross," "our faith,"* and *"the Holy Spirit."*

OF YOUR OWN SELVES

The phrase, *"Also of your own selves shall men arise, speaking perverse things to draw away disciples after them,"* not only has to do with *"grievous wolves"* from *without*, but that Satan will attempt to raise up individuals *within* the local church, who will have their own agenda and not the mind of God. So, Paul's warnings present a double threat, that from without and that from within.

The word *"perverse"* in the Greek text is *"diastrepho"* and means *"to distort, misinterpret, and turn away."*

In one sense of the word, this latter is more serious than the former. To be sure, they both come from the same source, which is an agenda that is not of the Lord, but the latter is the cause of most church splits.

DIVISION

While the occasion may arise that a division is needed, the necessity of the division, if, in fact, such exists, never justifies unethical practices in the carrying out of what should be done.

I think I can say without fear of exaggeration or scriptural contradiction that it is never right for an associate pastor or preacher in the local church to participate in such a thing in any capacity. Concerning any church that God has ordained, which means it was instituted by the Holy Spirit concerning its functions, the Lord will never place a seal of approval on anyone attempting to cause that church harm in any way. That should go without saying! The Lord does not oppose Himself.

This means that when a local church has problems, nothing must be done by anyone to take advantage of such problems. Instead, every member of that church, plus all of its leadership, should seek the Lord earnestly in order for the problems to be handled.

If, in fact, the leadership takes an unscriptural position, which is plainly obvious from the Word of God, such could definitely occasion a division. However, even then, one must be very, very careful about what one does in such situations.

Just because a man or woman of God may temporarily get off base, it gives no one any right whatsoever to take advantage of that for their own benefit.

JUSTIFICATION?

One may seek to justify his actions, as almost all do, by claiming that the leadership has done something wrong; therefore, that gives license for the party in question to do what he desires by drawing away people after himself, etc. However, two wrongs never make a right. Irrespective of what happens, no wrongdoing on the part of others ever justifies unethical actions. A case in point is David and his son Absalom.

There is no one who reads his Bible but that it is known of David's terrible sin with Bath-sheba and the murder of her husband Uriah. The situation was so awful that it defies description. Of course, David suffered immeasurably for this sin, as all sin brings about.

THE ABSALOM SPIRIT

However, at the same time, this gave Absalom no right whatsoever to attempt to take the kingdom from David's hands. God is the One who set up David, and it was God's Responsibility to do with him what He desired, not what others desired. David's sin in no way justified Absalom's actions, nor could it justify those actions. Irrespective of the circumstances, whenever anyone for

NOTES

any reason lays his hand on the one who is God-called, he has just come face-to-face with the Lord. Consequently, whatever they do cannot have the blessings of God.

Paul plainly referred to the *"overseers,"* whom the Holy Spirit had instituted. Consequently, they were the Holy Spirit's responsibility, and His responsibility alone. For anyone to abrogate that order, ultimately, his conclusion will be exactly that of Absalom.

Once again, I emphasize that this does not mean that anyone is to condone sin or wrongdoing in any manner. However, the manner in which any action is taken regarding those called of God must be made certain as to its scripturality and, as well, the ethics of those actions, if indeed there are actions. Permit me again to use David as an example:

SAUL

Even an elementary perusal of the life of Saul, the first king of Israel, proclaims the evil and unscripturality of almost all of the reign of this man. However, even that being the case, David never lifted a hand against him or engaged in any insurrection of any nature. In fact, David said, regarding the question of killing Saul when he had the opportunity, *"Destroy him not: for who can stretch forth his hand against the LORD's anointed, and be guiltless?"*

David then said, *"As the LORD lives, the LORD shall smite him; or his day shall come to die; or he shall descend into battle, and perish"* (I Sam. 26:9-10).

By the use of the word *"anointed,"* David was not insinuating that Saul was anointed by the Holy Spirit, for he was not! He was simply meaning that the position of king in Israel fell into that category, irrespective as to whom the man was. As such, this was God's Territory, and, consequently, He must be the One Who would take action, which He ultimately did.

Now, we surely should understand, if this was right concerning Saul, and it definitely was, then how much more wrong is it for someone to touch one who is definitely of God, called by God, and anointed by the Lord?

To be sure, such will never go unnoticed by the Lord. Due to the tremendous seriousness of the action, judgment always awaits those who ignore God's warnings.

JESUS

The idea of all ministry is to draw disciples to Jesus Christ and not oneself!

Now, what does that mean?

Some people think it means drawing them to a particular religious denomination; however, nothing could be further from the truth.

In drawing people to Jesus, we do just that! We draw them to the Word of God, knowing they have been bought with a price and, consequently, are very special in the eyes of the Lord.

As preachers of the Gospel, we are to never draw people to ourselves concerning our support, our benefit, or to carry out our agenda.

As an example, the Lord has called me for a particular ministry of world evangelism. To be sure, I need literally hundreds of thousands of people to help me carry out this task. As such, I want these people and need them, as would be obvious. However, other than praying for God to move on hearts, I will not go further than that. If I feel that there is interest, I may even go so far as to ask for their help. However, the bottom line always is that the Body of Christ is exactly that, the *"Body of Christ,"* and not the body of Jimmy Swaggart or anyone else, including religious denominations. As such, I want only those whom the Lord has appointed to this work. To obtain them, I will pray and, as stated, at times, solicit, but that is all!

CHURCH

Regarding our church, which should go for any church, I want those to come to my church whom the Lord desires to come. I believe He has a church for every single person. In fact, I know He does! The regret is that most people are not going to the church the Lord desires, even though they may think they are.

Most are going because of the denominational name on the door or because of other reasons which are not scriptural.

NOTES

The Lord would have you to attend a church where you can truly get your soul fed by the Word of God. As well, there will be a moving and operation of the Holy Spirit present in the services. Consequently, the criteria always is the *"Word"* and *"the Spirit of God."* Everything else is spurious!

Unfortunately, there are preachers who make little or no attempt at all to win souls or to truly feed the flock. They prey on those won by others. They have a personal agenda, which, by its very nature, is not of the Lord. They have no true burden for souls, but rather a carrying out of benefit to themselves in some way. In the next verse, Paul gives us further information concerning this.

(31) "THEREFORE WATCH, AND REMEMBER, THAT BY THE SPACE OF THREE YEARS I CEASED NOT TO WARN EVERY ONE NIGHT AND DAY WITH TEARS."

The form is:

1. The manner in which the Holy Spirit works is to energize the great truths of Calvary to the heart and life of the believer.

2. This will bring him to his full potential that he may realize this great victory purchased by Christ at the Cross.

SPIRITUAL SLEEP

The words, *"Therefore watch,"* simply mean to be spiritually vigilant. *"Watch"* in the Greek text is *"gregoreuo"* and means *"to keep awake."*

That is what Paul was speaking of when he said, *"Therefore let us not sleep, as do others; but let us watch and be sober"* (I Thess. 5:6).

After over one-half century of preaching the Gospel, it is my feeling, and I believe correct, that this of what Paul has said is extremely important, as should be obvious. Many believers are simply not wary enough of potential problems in this direction. They too easily believe the lies of false apostles or follow after those who are only attempting to enrich themselves. Too many do not soberly understand the dangers.

That means that every single believer should know the Word of God well enough that he can spot false doctrine when it is preached. To be sure, if the person is truly wanting to follow the Lord and is truly seeking to walk in the right direction, the Holy Spirit within that person will inform him concerning right and wrong doctrine. John said, *"Let that therefore abide in you, which you have heard from the beginning"* (I Jn. 2:24).

John was referring to the Gospel which brought the person to Christ and the fullness of the Spirit, which could not have been done were it error.

He is then saying, *"This is the promise,"* meaning the true Word of God (I Jn. 2:25).

SEDUCTION

He then said, *"These things have I written unto you concerning them who seduce you"* (I Jn. 2:26), referring again to wolves in sheep's clothing.

To be sure, the danger is always present, but if we are truly following the Lord and remaining in the Gospel even as John said, then we have the promise of the Lord that, *"The anointing which you have received of Him abides in you ...* (and) *teaches you of all things, and is truth, and is no lie"* (I Jn. 2:27).

So, even though all believers should study all of the Word of God diligently, actually making it a life's work, still, no one has to be a Bible scholar to be led by the Spirit. If one is truly hungering after the Lord, desiring to be led by the Spirit, the Spirit will do exactly that because His Business is to guide into all truth. As well, in the doing of that, He will also point out error (Jn. 16:13).

Sometime ago, a dear lady friend of both Frances and me, who, incidentally, has been living for the Lord a long time, began to listen to a particular preacher over television with whom I am acquainted. I know the man very well and regard him highly as a man. However, I also know that he does not believe in the Baptism with the Holy Spirit with the evidence of speaking with other tongues. As such, I personally feel he is not preaching all the counsel of God, and, as a result, those who sit under his teaching will be seriously hindered in their walk with the Lord.

She remarked to me how she had been listening to him for several weeks and how much she enjoyed the teaching, etc.

NOTES

I did not say anything to her, thereby, not responding.

Sometime later, she mentioned that in one of this man's messages, he began to denigrate the Baptism with the Holy Spirit, with his statements coming as a shock to our friend. However, knowing what he believed, or else, she should have known, she should not have been surprised at his statements.

The statement I'm going to make I realize is strong. However, I believe I am right, and I believe that it is good scriptural advice.

THE BAPTISM WITH THE HOLY SPIRIT

First of all, I do not feel I can truly receive much spiritual benefit from any preacher who does not believe in the Baptism with the Holy Spirit with the evidence of speaking with other tongues. I realize that some may take issue with that, but it is my feeling and belief after all these many years that those who preach that type of doctrine are not preaching, as stated, all the counsel of God. Inasmuch as everything done on this Earth by the Lord is done through the person, office, agency, and ministry of the Holy Spirit, I just simply feel that even though their words may be right in some cases, little benefit will accrue.

As well, there are scores of preachers who claim the Baptism with the Holy Spirit, as I have mentioned, but whom I feel are of little benefit as well. I feel that some of these come under the heading of *"grievous wolves,"* irrespective of how they may outwardly look. I believe others are into false doctrine and, as such, it has no benefit for me. I feel others have a personal agenda and it comes through. So, what I am saying is this:

I am very careful as to whom I hear preach the Gospel! In fact, Jesus said to His Disciples, and all others for that matter, *"Take heed what you hear"* (Mk. 4:24).

FALSE PROPHETS AND THE TRUE GOSPEL

"And remember, that by the space of three years I ceased not to warn every one night and day with tears," presents a side of the Gospel which many preachers deny.

In essence, Paul was saying that he not only preached the truth of the Word, which was *"repentance toward God, and faith toward our Lord Jesus Christ"* (Acts 20:21), but, as well, warned of, and pointed out, false doctrine and false apostles.

Many claim that one is to only preach the truth, not referring to the error, which, within itself, will handle the error. Unfortunately, that is not true!

While the preacher most definitely must proclaim the good news of the Gospel constantly, which is truth and does have its powerful effect, as should be obvious, still, the corrective warnings must be given constantly respecting false ways as well!

It is not enough to warn believers that those things exist; at the same time, they must be spelled out.

To be sure, it is not a pleasant thing to be corrective. Among other things, it makes enemies. However, in view of the fact that this Gospel is the most serious thing there could ever be, the true watchman must be willing to take the heat. To be sure, it is only the preacher who truly loves the people, who, at the same time, will warn them, even though, at times, he knows it is not what they want to hear. It is the hireling who seeks to tell people only what they want to hear and not what they need to hear.

THE WORD OF GOD

In fact, if one properly studies the Word of God, one will find that there is at least as much warning given concerning error as it is instruction concerning truth.

Considering that Paul made this a part of his ministry for the entirety of the time he was in Ephesus, as well as all other places, it tells us how vitally important all of this really is.

As well, he felt, and rightly so, that the matter was so serious that the warning was given *"with tears,"* showing the extreme emotion of the situation. Also, it was done *"night and day."* The reason is simple:

That of which we speak is the single most important thing known to man, the salvation of one's soul. Most of the human family, even from the very beginning, has died lost simply because *"they should believe a lie...*

(and)... be damned" (II Thess. 2:11-12).

So, the stakes are high!

(32) "AND NOW, BRETHREN, I COMMEND YOU TO GOD, AND TO THE WORD OF HIS GRACE, WHICH IS ABLE TO BUILD YOU UP, AND TO GIVE YOU AN INHERITANCE AMONG ALL THEM WHICH ARE SANCTIFIED."

The overview is:

1. Some have claimed that God created man because He wanted or needed fellowship.

2. God has never needed anything, much less fellowship.

3. No! He created man simply and totally from a position of love, and, as such, He would *"crown him with glory and honor"* (Ps. 8:5).

NOTES

I COMMEND YOU TO GOD

The phrase, *"And now, brethren, I commend you to God,"* has reference to the fact that Paul had had to give this warning, even though, as usual, it was distasteful, and now he could turn to that which was positive. As well, this statement says something else:

Paul was stating that he had given these people the pure Gospel. It had been all the counsel of God. He would not be with them again, which means they would have to stand on what had been given them. So now, he entrusted*"to God"* this most prized possession, these believers, for whom Jesus died. Inasmuch as they came in on the true Gospel and were anchored in the firmness of the Word of God as given by the apostle, I believe if the truth be known, very few, if any, of these people were lost in the coming years. Actually, I think that in a collective sense, that is borne out. In a personal sense, I feel it is correct as well! They were sufficiently grounded in the faith.

THE WORD OF HIS GRACE

The phrase, *"And to the Word of His Grace,"* proclaims the foundation of the New Covenant.

In this, Paul was saying that the Law of Moses has no place. It has been fulfilled, and, as such, it gives way to that which was intended all along, the great *"Word of grace."*

In brief, what is that Word?

It is found in all the promises of the Old Testament and proclaimed grandly in the New Testament, which would be obvious! However, I will use only one passage:

- *"The blessing of Abraham"*: this is justification by faith. Abraham simply believed God, and without works, God *"counted it to him for righteousness"* (Gen. 15:6; Gal. 3:14). Paul further said, *"Therefore it is of faith, that it might be by grace"* (Rom. 4:16).
- The blessing of Abraham also includes *"receiving the promise of the Spirit through faith"* (Gal. 3:14).

This speaks of the Baptism with the Holy Spirit with the evidence of speaking with other tongues (Acts 2:4).

In other words, the *"promise of the Spirit through faith could not come to believers until Jesus effected the Work at Calvary, thereby, taking away the sin of believing man"* (Jn. 1:29; 7:37-39).

To nullify the latter, as many in the modern church have, nullifies a great part of the provision of the blessing of Abraham. To not take full advantage of all that Jesus did for sinners at Calvary and the Resurrection is, to say the least, to do *"despite unto the Spirit of grace"* (Heb. 10:29).

BUILT UP IN THE FAITH

The phrase, *"Which is able to build you up,"* suggests that man has been ruined as a result of the Fall, which has wrecked his body, soul, and spirit, and which must be repaired and made new again by the *"habitation of God through the Spirit."* Actually, the Holy Spirit is doing this constantly!

When anyone comes to Christ, I full well believe that every faculty of one's being is bettered. I believe that one's intelligence is increased, even with the physical body experiencing improvement, because the Spirit is now regenerated. Actually, salvation is explained as *"regeneration"* (Titus 3:5).

In truth, this great salvation offered by Jesus Christ is the only thing that can truly *"build one up."* All else is of no consequence.

Back in 1986 (I believe it was), one of the dearest friends I had in this world was given three months to live. He was eaten up with cancer, plus all types of other physical problems, with any one of them being

NOTES

lethal. At that time, he gave his heart and life to the Lord Jesus Christ. He lived some 15 years more, with the doctors calling him the *"miracle man."*

The other day, I spoke to another friend who was pretty well in the same condition when he began to attend Family Worship Center. At that time, Jesus Christ became more real in his heart and life than he had ever known before. Despite some physical problems which still remain, these past five years have seen the Lord literally *"build him up."* In truth, this is the case with all who truly come to Christ.

THE INHERITANCE

The phrase, *"And to give you an inheritance among all them which are sanctified,"* refers to the inheritance of Christ, which every believer is privileged to share. At the moment of conversion, all believers become *"heirs; heirs of God, and joint-heirs with Christ"* (Rom. 8:17).

In fact, the Holy Spirit, with the outward evidence of speaking with other tongues, is the earnest or first installment of our inheritance that will fully come when the Trump sounds (Eph. 1:13-14).

However, even though the entirety of one's *"inheritance"* is guaranteed, still, only a small part is initially received at the time of salvation. Paul also said, *"For the earnest* (down-payment) *expectation* (that which we expect to come) *of the creature* (all of God's Creation including man) *waits* (looks forward with great anticipation to that coming time) *for the manifestation* (to be Glorified) *of the Sons of God"* (Rom. 8:19).

It's true that we as believers do not have all of our inheritance yet and, as stated, actually only a small part at the present. Still, without fail, the time is coming, which will be at the Resurrection of Life, when the entirety of the inheritance will then be received.

SANCTIFIED

The word *"sanctified,"* as it is used here, in the Greek text is *"hagiazo"* and means *"to make holy."*

This refers to the work that is done automatically at conversion. In other words, it comes with salvation.

At conversion, spiritually speaking, one is *"washed"* (made clean by the blood of Jesus), *"sanctified"* (instantly made holy), and *"justified"* (declared as legally holy in the sight of God) (I Cor. 6:11).

However, there remains a final step to salvation regarding the believer being *"glorified."* That remains yet to be done and will take place, as stated, at the first Resurrection of Life (Rom. 8:17-18).

Even though all believers are now completely saved (Rom. 8:14-16), the believer does not yet have all the benefits or results of salvation, which will come at the Resurrection of Life, as stated!

(33) "I HAVE COVETED NO MAN'S SILVER, OR GOLD, OR APPAREL."

The diagram is:

1. Paul was making this statement to show the comparison between him, and what any true preacher of the Gospel should be and do, by comparison to these *"grievous wolves."* In fact, their motive was money!

2. He was telling these people plainly that his desire was never in that capacity, but always to build them up in the Lord.

3. At times, Paul did make strong appeals for funds, even as II Corinthians, Chapters 8 and 9, portray; however, these appeals were not for himself personally but actually for the situation in Jerusalem (thousands of believers deprived because of their testimony of Christ).

4. The word *"covetousness"* is brought into play here because this is what underlies personal greed, which Paul condemns.

(34) "YEA, YOU YOURSELVES KNOW, THAT THESE HANDS HAVE MINISTERED UNTO MY NECESSITIES, AND TO THEM THAT WERE WITH ME."

The synopsis is:

1. The phrase, *"Yea, you yourselves know, that these hands have ministered unto my necessities,"* most likely referred to Paul's tent-repairing or tent-making business (Acts 18:3).

2. *"And to them that were with me,"* referred to the seven men of Verse 4; this number probably fluctuated from time to time. At any rate, some or all of these evidently worked with Paul respecting the

meeting of their daily needs.

3. As well, this *"business"* of tent-repairing evidently was a hands-on situation, which seems to be obvious from the Scripture.

One must remember that Paul did all of these things while conducting services daily.

6. Paul seemingly took this tact because he was dealing with new converts. Whereas the heathen temples in these cities constantly demanded quite healthy gifts of money from their devotees, Paul desired to show that the Gospel of Jesus Christ was not a gospel for money, etc. So, he made no demands at all on the new converts, portraying to them that he was there not for their money, but rather for their souls.

7. However, when it came to settled, established churches, Paul even recommended that the *"elders"* (pastors) who ruled well should be given a double honorarium, *"for the laborer is worthy of his hire"* (I Tim. 5:17-18).

8. So, the established pattern was to be that the pastors would be cared for by the flock, at least when the church became established, in order that the pastor may be able to give all of his time to the spiritual care of the people.

9. In fact, Paul addressed himself to this thing respecting his own personal experience. Even though his statement is made with some sarcasm, in effect, he told the church at Corinth that he may have been wrong in not asking more of them (II Cor. 12:13). This much is sure, neither Paul nor any of the people who traveled with him were ever a burden to any of the believers. What an example for all to follow.

(35) "I HAVE SHOWED YOU ALL THINGS, HOW THAT SO LABOURING YOU OUGHT TO SUPPORT THE WEAK, AND TO REMEMBER THE WORDS OF THE LORD JESUS, HOW HE SAID, IT IS MORE BLESSED TO GIVE THAN TO RECEIVE."

The exegesis is:

1. The phrase, *"I have showed you all things,"* means that this particular aspect of unselfishness, along with all else that Paul taught, is to serve as an example.

2. In the words of Paul, the phrase, *"How that so laboring you ought to support the weak,"* portrays that everything the believer does is to set a spiritual example and, in fact, does do so, whether good or bad. It is not the idea that believers set an example because, of necessity, such will be done, but rather what type of example it is.

3. *"And to remember the words of the Lord Jesus, how He said, 'It is more blessed to give than to receive,'"* is not recorded in the Bible. In fact, only a part of all that Jesus said and did, as would be obvious, was reported in the Word of God. Possibly Peter, or any one of the other apostles who was with Jesus, related this to Paul.

4. Actually, John said concerning Jesus, *"And there are also many other things which Jesus did,"* insinuating that all was not recorded, as would be obvious (Jn. 21:25). However, this statement by Paul concerning Christ is no less inspired than all written in the Four Gospels concerning Jesus. Even though not there recorded, it is absolutely certain that a greater blessing accompanies the giving than is found in the receiving.

5. In fact, the very economy of God, the way He operates His Business, is based on the principle of *"giving."* John also wrote, *"For God so loved the world, that He gave . . ."* (Jn. 3:16). As such, and having the Lord as our supreme Example, the believer must follow suit regarding this all-important principle.

6. When the believer comes to Christ, he enters into the economy of God, in which giving is a part. However, as stated, *"It is impossible to out give God."* When the believer begins to liberally give, God automatically places into motion His Economy of giving to His Children. Paul also said, concerning this very thing, *"But this I say, He which sows* (gives) *sparingly shall reap* (receive) *also sparingly; and he which sows* (gives) *bountifully shall reap* (receive) *also bountifully"* (II Cor. 9:6).

By contrast, the economy of God is diametrically opposed to its opposite, the economy of the world, which is one of greed and covetousness.

(36) "AND WHEN HE HAD THUS SPOKEN, HE KNEELED DOWN, AND PRAYED WITH THEM ALL."

The direction is:

NOTES

NOTES

1. The words, *"And when He had thus spoken,"* represented the last time they would ever hear him preach or speak to them in any manner respecting the Word of God. What a special moment this was, and yet, they were so saddened by the thought that they would not see him again.

2. *"He kneeled down, and prayed with them all,"* concerns, as well, the last time he would pray with them, even though continuing to pray for them.

3. Even though we are not told what he said in this prayer, one can be certain that he asked the Lord to keep them, even as Jesus had prayed shortly before the Crucifixion that which is recorded in John, Chapter 17.

(37) "AND THEY ALL WEPT SORE, AND FELL ON PAUL'S NECK, AND KISSED HIM."

The account is:

1. The phrase, *"And they all wept sore,"* concerns their great love for the apostle, especially considering that he was leaving them.

2. When one enters by conversion to Christ into the Family of God—and what a family it is—the other members of that family actually become closer to the Child of God than one's own flesh and blood relatives who do not know Jesus Christ.

3. *"And fell on Paul's neck, and kissed him,"* shows us a love beyond the normal love, if it could be called that, of the Family of God.

4. Paul was the spiritual father of these people. It was because of his love, burden, and consecration to the Lord, and great sacrifices we might quickly add, that they had the privilege of hearing the Gospel of Jesus Christ. If Paul had not brought that Gospel to them, quite possibly, no one else would have, and they would have died eternally lost. Consequently, what they owed him was literally beyond comprehension, as would hold true for anyone who falls into the same category presently.

5. It is one thing to pastor people in the sense of feeding the flock, and something else altogether to be the first one to take the Gospel to them, whomever they may be.

In addressing this very thing, Paul said to Philemon, the wealthy land-owner or businessman of Colossae, *"You owe unto me even your own self besides"* (Philemon, Vs. 19).

The gift of salvation is the greatest gift of all and certainly is given by our Lord and Saviour Jesus Christ; however, that gift must be brought to dying humanity and can only be done so in some way by preachers of the Gospel.

(38) "SORROWING MOST OF ALL FOR THE WORDS WHICH HE SPOKE, THAT THEY SHOULD SEE HIS FACE NO MORE. AND THEY ACCOMPANIED HIM UNTO THE SHIP."

The order is:

1. The phrase, *"Sorrowing most of all for the words which he spoke,"* does not mean at all that the words were negative, but rather that they were his last words unto them. They now knew how much they meant and how much they would be missed in the future.

2. *"That they should see his face no more,"* seems to have been the case. So far as is known, the apostle never saw these Ephesian brethren again, at least this side of Glory. However, to be sure, they are all now together and, as well, with Christ!

3. *"And they accompanied him unto the ship,"* concerns the port at Miletus.

It is certain that these *"elders"* stood waiting on the shore while Paul and his associates boarded the ship for the journey ahead. As well, I am certain they stayed there and waited until the ship sailed, finally going over the horizon.

4. It is my thought that as long as they could see the apostle and he them, they stood waving before starting the approximate 30-mile journey back to Ephesus.

5. It was said by Hervey, *"It is impossible to part with this most touching Narrative, of such exquisite simplicity and beauty, without a parting word of admiration and thankfulness to God for having preserved to His Church this record of Apostolic wisdom and faithfulness on the one hand, and of loving devotion of these Pastors to their Great Chief on the other."*

He then said, *"As long as the stones of the Church are bound together by such strong mortar, it can defy the attacks of its enemies from without."*

"God be with you till we meet again;
"By His Counsels guide, uphold you,
"With His sheep securely fold you;
"God be with you till we meet again."

"Till we meet, till we meet,
"Till we meet at Jesus' Feet;
"Till we meet, till we meet,
"God be with you till we meet again."

CHAPTER 21

(1) "AND IT CAME TO PASS, THAT AFTER WE WERE GOTTEN FROM THEM, AND HAD LAUNCHED, WE CAME WITH A STRAIGHT COURSE UNTO COOS, AND THE DAY FOLLOWING UNTO RHODES, AND FROM THENCE UNTO PATARA."

The exegesis is:

1. The phrase, *"And it came to pass, that after we were gotten from them, and had launched,"* represents the parting, which, as we have already stated, was not easy.

2. The phrase could be translated, *"Having torn ourselves away,"* which refers to one unwillingly torn away from friends and loved ones. In other words, it denotes a painful separation wrung from them by necessity.

3. In this scenario, one sees the love projected here that is to a degree that the world cannot emulate. It is love that only comes from God and can only be generated by God. It is love He freely gives to His Children.

4. This type of love is what should characterize all of God's Children. Actually, the lack of such is a terrible aberration that deprives itself of the great fundamental of the Christian faith. That is the reason John said, *"We know that we have passed from death unto life, because we love the brethren. He who loves not his brother abides in death"* (I Jn. 3:14).

5. *"We came with a straight course unto Coos, and the day following unto Rhodes, and from thence unto Patara,"* probably represented about 100 miles on the first leg to Coos, with a little shorter distance to Rhodes.

6. Rhodes is an island, even as is Coos. It is somewhat large, about 45 miles long and 20 miles wide. On this island was built a brazen image of Apollo, which was one of the ancient wonders of the world. This image was said to be over 100 feet high, with its legs spread so far apart that ships could pass between its legs. It was destroyed by an earthquake in 224 B.C., after standing for approximately 66 years.

6. Rhodes also was a great commercial center, primarily because it was where the great commercial sea routes crossed.

7. Patara, a little over 100 miles from the island of Rhodes, was located on the west coast of Lucia and Pamphylia.

(2) "AND FINDING A SHIP SAILING OVER UNTO PHENICIA, WE WENT ABOARD, AND SET FORTH."

The pattern is:

1. In those days, ships normally hugged the coastline, which lengthened the journey greatly at times. However, Paul and his associates found a ship about to leave that was going to go straight across the Mediterranean from Patara to Tyre in Phoenicia. Consequently, it cut many days off their trip.

2. By Luke using the pronoun *"we,"* it is known that he remained with Paul all the way to Rome.

(3) "NOW WHEN WE HAD DISCOVERED CYPRUS, WE LEFT IT ON THE LEFT HAND, AND SAILED INTO SYRIA, AND LANDED AT TYRE: FOR THERE THE SHIP WAS TO UNLADE HER BURDEN."

The pattern is:

1. The phrase, *"Now when we had discovered Cyprus, we left it on the left hand,"* means they did not stop at this island.

2. The sight of Cyprus as he sailed by must have brought to the apostle's mind many and various memories of Barnabas, Serguis Paulus, Elymas, and many others. I am sure that Paul would have loved to have stopped and spent some time in this area. Actually, the island of Cyprus was the first ministry stop on the first missionary journey (Acts 13:4).

3. *"And sailed into Syria, and landed at Tyre: for there the ship was to unlade her burden,"* now found Paul and his party in

NOTES

NOTES

Phoenicia, with Tyre as its principle seaport.

4. In 332 B.C., Alexander the Great laid siege to the island port of Tyre for seven months and captured it only by building a mole to the island fortress. Despite heavy losses, the port soon recovered under Seleucid Patronage.

5. Herod I rebuilt the main temple, which would have been standing when the Lord visited the district bordering Tyre and Sidon (Mat. 15:21-28; Mk. 7:24-31). Actually, people of Tyre heard Him speak (Mk. 3:8; Lk. 6:17), and He cited Tyre as a heathen city that would bear less responsibility than those Galilean towns, which constantly witnessed His Ministry (Mat. 11:21-22; Lk. 10:13-14).

6. There were believers at Tyre during this time of Paul's visit, as we shall see. The scholar Origen was buried there in A.D. 254.

(4) "AND FINDING DISCIPLES, WE TARRIED THERE SEVEN DAYS: WHO SAID TO PAUL THROUGH THE SPIRIT, THAT HE SHOULD NOT GO UP TO JERUSALEM."

The synopsis is:

1. The only way the saint is going to have victory over the *"Law of Sin and Death"* is by allowing the Holy Spirit to bring about this victory, which He always does through our faith in the Finished Work of Christ.

2. The *"Law of Sin and Death"* is so strong that it is not possible to be defeated in any other manner.

DISCIPLES

The phrase, *"And finding disciples,"* implies that the group was small and not easily found. As well, it is almost certain these were gentiles exclusively because there is no mention of a synagogue. As usual in Acts, the word *"disciples"* means followers of Christ.

"We tarried there seven days," proclaims the fact that Paul was given a little extra time due to the ship cutting straight across from Patara to Tyre.

It seems obvious that the believers there impressed upon Paul strongly to stay with them as long as he could, with this seven days, no doubt, being for them a tremendous time of instruction and learning as Paul opened the Word of God. How blessed and fortunate they were!

BY THE HOLY SPIRIT

The phrase, *"Who said to Paul through the Spirit, that he should not go up to Jerusalem,"* seems at first glance to imply that the Spirit of the Lord was telling Paul this. However, that is not the case!

Actually, the Greek text does not mean that the Spirit did not want Paul to go to Jerusalem. The Spirit was, in fact, constraining Paul to go (Acts 20:22). Perhaps the following will clear it up somewhat.

IN CONSEQUENCE OF THE SPIRIT

Horton said, *"The word 'through' is not the word used in previous Passages for the Direct Agency of the Holy Spirit. Consequently, the Greek would have been better translated, 'Who said to Paul in consequence of the Spirit,' that is, because of what the Spirit said."*

The idea is this: due to what the Spirit of God was portraying to these believers concerning the coming problems in Jerusalem, the individuals themselves, proven by the word *"who,"* were voicing their own feelings that he should not go.

It is almost certain that this came about as a result of the gifts of the Spirit relative to prophecy and tongues and interpretation of tongues (I Cor. 12:8-10).

As well, it is obvious that these gifts were operative in most, if not all, the churches, as evidenced in Acts 20:23; 21:4, 11. It is impossible, I think, to understand these happenings and not recognize that these churches were thoroughly Pentecostal. The Holy Spirit was very active, and, as such, they operated in the gifts.

Again, I maintain that if modern churches do not have the earmarks of the churches in the Book of Acts, then they are really not following the Lord and cannot actually even be labeled as *"church,"* at least as recognized by the Lord.

The Spirit of God is, in essence, the Preacher, the Instigator of worship, the Proponent of praise, and the thrust of evangelism, which should be overly obvious. He anoints, convicts, empowers, leads, guides,

NOTES

and directs. In other words, the Holy Spirit is very active.

It is this activity that makes church *"church."*

(5) "AND WHEN HE HAD ACCOMPLISHED THOSE DAYS, WE DEPARTED AND WENT OUR WAY; AND THEY ALL BROUGHT US ON OUR WAY, WITH WIVES AND CHILDREN, TILL WE WERE OUT OF THE CITY: AND WE KNEELED DOWN ON THE SHORE, AND PRAYED."

The pattern is:

1. When the Holy Spirit dominates the believer, it is only when the believer has freely given control to the Spirit.

2. The Holy Spirit will never take control without the free volition of the believer.

PAUL'S JOURNEY

The phrase, *"And when he had accomplished those days, we departed and went our way,"* even though abbreviated, tells us that Paul had been a tremendous blessing to these people in the past seven days, and they were now reluctant to see him go.

I have every confidence that they had previously heard of Paul, but now, knowing that he had been with them this number of days, it must have been very, very special to these people, as is obvious.

"And they all brought us on our way, with wives and children, till we were out of the city," shows the love and affection for Paul that was gained in these last few days, even down to the children.

Paul had to take a strong stand against false doctrine, which angered many people, even with many claiming that he really was not an apostle. As a result, he became one of the most controversial figures of his time. No one took the heat that Paul took, not even the Twelve. Almost alone, except those who had been saved under his ministry, Paul stood against the encroachment of error, demanding the pure grace of the Gospel of Jesus Christ.

Despite these very necessary things, the Text abundantly proves that the apostle was a very warm, kind, generous, and loving individual, who beautifully epitomized a Christlike spirit. The love that people had for him, even after a short time, as exhibited here, wondrously portrays this fact.

Paul was a scholar, but he was not cold! He was the Moses of the New Testament, but broken, loving, and humble!

He wrote about one-third of the New Testament, but yet, never evidenced any attitude or spirit of superiority. He was used by God as few men in history have ever been used, and yet, I think, he was totally unpretentious!

THE GREAT POWER OF THE APOSTOLIC AGE

Not at all taking away from the tremendous contribution of Peter, as well as others of the Twelve, I think it is clear, at least in my own mind, that Paul was spiritually the great power of the apostolic age. Deissmann the historian said, *"Paul is first after Jesus."*

Feine said, *"Paul grasped the essence of the Ministry of Christ as none other."*

To seek to explain Paul as a result of heredity or environment presents a wrong direction and fails of conclusion. Put simply, Paul was what he was because of his experience with Jesus Christ.

More than all, Paul portrayed water baptism and the Lord's Supper not as magical sacraments producing some type of new life, but rather symbolic pictures of death to sin and new life in Christ, which the believer has already experienced. This shows his tremendous understanding of Who and What Jesus was and is.

THE HEBREW SCHOLAR OF HIS TIME

The Judaism which Paul knew and practiced was pure, in fact, as he gives it to us in Philippians 3:5. He was a Jew of the stock of Israel, of the Tribe of Benjamin, which gloried in the fact that that Tribe remained with Judah at the time of the division after the death of Solomon. He was a Hebrew, of the seed of Abraham (II Cor. 11:22). He shared in full all the Covenant blessings and privileges of his people (Rom. 9:1-5), whose crowning glory was that Jesus, the Messiah, came from them. In other words, it was Jesus Who glorified Israel instead of Israel glorifying Jesus.

Paul was proud of the piety of his ancestors (II Tim. 1:3) and made progress as a student of Judaism ahead of his fellows (Gal. 1:14).

His ancestry was pure, Hebrew of the Hebrews (Phil. 3:5), and so his family preserved the native Israeli traditions in Tarsus.

His name *"Saul"* was a proof of loyalty to the Tribe of Benjamin as his change of name *"Paul"* was evidence of his Roman citizenship but, above all, his Christian citizenship.

In his home, he was taught the Law by his mother (Gal. 1:14), as was true of Timothy's mother and grandmother (II Tim. 1:5). In Tarsus, he attended the synagogue also.

We know little of his father, save that he was a Roman citizen and so a man of position in Tarsus and possibly of some wealth. That Paul was a tentmaker leaves no clue as to the direction of his father for the simple reason that all Jewish sons were taught a trade by their fathers, whatever their rank in life. So, that occupation in no way gives us a clue as to the place and position of his parents.

HIS BRINGING UP

He was brought up a Pharisee (Acts 23:6) and was sent at a young age to Jerusalem to study at the feet of one of the great Jewish scholars, Gamaliel (Acts 22:3).

He was known in Jerusalem as a student. He knew Aramaic as well as Greek (and probably Latin), and could speak it so as to attract the attention of Jewish audiences (Acts 22:2).

It seems that Paul was fortunate in having his great teacher Gamaliel, who was liberal enough to encourage the study of Greek literature. However, Gamaliel's liberality in defending the apostles against the Sadducees in Acts 5:34-39 must not be misinterpreted in comparison with the persecuting zeal of his brilliant pupil Paul against Stephen (Acts 7:58).

Stephen was in opposition to the Pharisees themselves, and there is no evidence that Gamaliel made a defense of Stephen against the lawless rage of the Sanhedrin, which resulted in Stephen losing his life.

It is believed that Paul was the most brilliant student of Gamaliel and, as some think, probably the hope of his heart for the future of Judaism.

Harnack said, *"Pharisaism fulfilled its mission in the world when it produced Paul."* He was their hope!

NOTES

Unfortunately, Pharisaism did not die. In truth, it has never died, not even from Christianity, but young Paul was the crowning glory of Pharisaism.

A VISION OF JESUS

With this type of background, it is easy to understand that a mere philosophy of some other stripe could never pull Paul from this position of dedicated Judaism and Pharisaism. He was sold to the image in every respect.

Nevertheless, the cataclysmic, traumatic, and life-changing experience with Jesus on the road to Damascus would forever change Paul for time and eternity. It was not years of philosophic training, but one glimpse of Jesus! It was a leap from religion to relationship. It was instantaneous! Paul was changed instantly in every capacity, and from then on, he could never see anything or anyone but Jesus.

In later years, after this glorious meeting with Jesus, Paul told how he struggled in vain against the curse of the Law (Rom. 7:7), and that, it seems, was after his conversion. Even though he grandly knew Jesus from the moment of the Damascus revelation, still, Who and what Jesus was and did took time for Paul to learn simply because of the weaknesses of the flesh.

One scholar has said that the conversion of Paul is a psychological and ethical problem which cannot be accounted for save by Paul's own interpretation of the change wrought in him. He plainly saw Jesus and surrendered to Him. As well, his surrender was instantaneous and complete: *"What shall I do, Lord?"* (Acts 22:10).

When he saw the glory of Jesus Christ, the god of this world could blind him no longer. He had seen Jesus, and all else had lost charm for Paul.

Hence, Paul is the man who, under God, in the Name of the Lord Jesus Christ, and by the power of the Holy Spirit, would do more to change the world through the Gospel than any other man who has ever lived. He alone stands as the great contributor to what is presently referred to as *"western civilization,"* although many have built upon his efforts.

HE PRESENTED JESUS AS NO OTHER HUMAN BEING

It was not that Paul did anything or contributed any part thereof respecting the great miracle-working power of God, for he did not. His life and ministry were spent in the effort of telling the grandest story ever told and demanding its purity, undiluted by speculative philosophies or past glories of Judaism. That was his contribution!

Jesus did the work, but it was Paul who introduced Jesus. In his introduction, we find the power of a consecrated life that Jesus or His Message not be diluted but presented whole. In effect, the message was secondary to the person of Christ, which stands alone in the annals of human history.

The world glories in its philosophies and gives credit to the philosopher; however, if there is any good, it is the philosophy that glorifies the philosopher.

With Jesus Christ, it is the exact opposite. He glorifies the message, and Paul knew this as no other man. That is the reason he demanded that the message be kept pure, simple, and undiluted by the Law of Moses, which pointed to Jesus, and which Jesus literally fulfilled.

So, this simple message of redemption brought about by faith in Christ was the introduction to the all-powerful Christ Himself Who performed the work and, in fact, had already performed it at Calvary and the Resurrection.

JESUS EVER SUPREME

However, let not the reader think that it was Paul who in any way lustred Christ, but it was the very opposite. It was Christ Who made Paul shine! It was Christ Who empowered the apostle through and by the Holy Spirit. He perfectly hides behind that Name and continually puts it forth.

That is the reason I say, as have others, that Paul knew Jesus as no man ever knew Him. That is the reason he cried, *"I count all things but loss for the excellency of the knowledge of Christ Jesus my Lord: for Whom I have suffered the loss of all things, and do count them but dung, that I may win Christ"* (Phil. 3:8).

NOTES

My prayer is that in the years that God further allows to me, somehow I can know Jesus as Paul knew Him; that somehow, I can experience Him even as Paul; and that somehow I may evermore know His Message, but more so His Person!

The phrase, *"And we kneeled down on the shore, and prayed,"* concerns their parting, but more so the type of parting it was.

As should be obvious by now, Paul soaked everything in prayer. Here they would pray because God answers prayer. It is the greatest privilege of the Child of God, the privilege of speaking to one's Heavenly Father.

(6) "AND WHEN WE HAD TAKEN OUR LEAVE ONE OF ANOTHER, WE TOOK SHIP; AND THEY RETURNED HOME AGAIN."

The form is:

1. The phrase, *"And when we had taken our leave one of another, we took ship,"* proclaims the same type of spirit and atmosphere as it did back at Miletus with the Ephesian elders.

2. The phrase, *"And they returned home again,"* proclaims somewhat in the Greek text a full and beautiful moment.

3. Even though parting was hurtful, still, they had been so blessed in Paul's visit, and there is every evidence that they knew and realized that God had indeed blessed them in a beautiful and wonderful way. So, these believers at Tyre returned to their homes, but with a full heart and an exercised soul. They had wondrously seen Jesus in Paul!

(7) "AND WHEN WE HAD FINISHED OUR COURSE FROM TYRE, WE CAME TO PTOLEMAIS, AND SALUTED THE BRETHREN, AND ABODE WITH THEM ONE DAY."

The pattern is:

1. The phrase, *"And when we had finished our course from Tyre, we came to Ptolemais,"* actually proclaims the end of Paul's voyage by ship. It was only about 30 miles from Tyre.

2. Ptolemais was the Old Testament Accho mentioned in Judges 1:31 and is now called Acre or Akka. In the division of the land after Joshua's conquest, the city was assigned to the Tribe of Asher, but they never actually took possession of it.

It remained under the dominion of Tyre and Sidon until the Assyrians took it in about 70 B.C. About 200 B.C., its name was changed to Ptolemais, probably in honor of Ptolemy Philadelphus.

3. In New Testament times, it was an important seaport for trade with Galilee, the Decapolis, and Arabia.

4. *"And saluted the brethren, and abode with them one day,"* proclaims believers, as is obvious, but no account is given of how Ptolemais was evangelized. Perhaps the Gospel was first preached there to the Jewish colony by those who traveled *"as far as Phenice"* after *"the persecution that arose about Stephen"* (Acts 11:19).

(8) "AND THE NEXT DAY WE WHO WERE OF PAUL'S COMPANY DEPARTED, AND CAME UNTO CAESAREA: AND WE ENTERED INTO THE HOUSE OF PHILIP THE EVANGELIST, WHICH WAS ONE OF THE SEVEN; AND ABODE WITH HIM."

The account is:

1. To be properly led by the Lord demands proper faith in Christ and the Cross.

2. With proper faith in the Cross of Christ, there will be a broken and contrite spirit.

3. The Cross generates such!

PAUL'S COMPANY

The phrase, *"And the next day we who were of Paul's company departed, and came unto Caesarea,"* proclaims a journey of approximately 60 miles. Paul and his associates evidently walked this distance.

How large *"Paul's company"* was at this time is not clear, unless it was the seven of Acts 20:4, plus Luke, and adding Paul for a total of nine.

The phrase, *"And we entered into the house of Philip the evangelist,"* presents the same Philip of Acts 8:40.

Inasmuch as the Holy Spirit prompted the designation of *"evangelist"* by Luke of Philip, this gives unto us one of the fivefold ministry gifts (Eph. 4:11).

The Greek word for *"evangelist"* is *"evangelists"* and means *"one who brings good news,"* i.e., the Gospel. Actually, this word is used only here, at least in this fashion. (Timothy was told to *"do the work of an evangelist"*) (II Tim. 4:5).

NOTES

WHAT IS THE MINISTRY OF THE EVANGELIST?

The evangelist is primarily a preacher of righteousness. While there definitely will be a teaching aspect to his ministry, even as it is all good ministries, still, the business of the evangelist is to *"proclaim"* the Gospel. The business of the teacher is to *"explain"* the Gospel already presented.

As the evangelist engages in his God-given calling, there is a greater thrust of the Holy Spirit to engage the lost and to bring them to a life-changing experience in Christ.

The ministry of the evangelist carries within it the thundering tones of the prophets of old, along with the proclamation of the Good News. The evangelist must bring the person to a decision. If he is preaching on healing, he expects to see people healed. If he is preaching on the Baptism with the Holy Spirit, he expects to see people filled. If he is preaching to the lost, he expects to see people saved. He is primarily a gatherer of the harvest.

While pastors can definitely preach evangelistically, and should, even as Paul told Timothy, still, there is nothing that can take the place of the calling of the evangelist, as the evangelist cannot take the place of the other callings of apostle, prophet, pastor, and teacher (Eph. 4:11).

THE FIRE OF THE CHURCH

The type of harvest gathered by the evangelist is that designed by the Holy Spirit. It is the penetrating message that pierces the very hearts of the listeners, revealing their sin and lost condition. As well, it opens up the lives of believers and strikes them with conviction as the Lord draws them closer to Himself. So, the work and ministry of the evangelist is not only to the lost soul but, as well, to the church.

Whenever the church begins to lose its way, consequently, spiritually dying, the very first ministry to be abandoned is the evangelist. In the spiritual coldness, which threads toward intellectualism, the evangelist becomes an anachronism, in other words, an embarrassment. Consequently, the church dies!

Yes, I meant exactly that!

Without the ministry of the evangelist, the church will suffer accordingly. It is a calling by the Holy Spirit that others can attempt but never successfully imitate.

A DECISION NOW

In no way is the ministry of the evangelist meant to abrogate the office of pastor. Actually, the pastor oftentimes, at least if he is led by the Holy Spirit, sets everything up in a spiritual sense for the evangelist. Pastoral preaching, at least the Biblical kind, gets things ready for the harvest in the spiritual sense, with the evangelist then reaping that harvest.

Whenever a church is on fire for God, and I speak of entire denominations, it will be rife with evangelists. Otherwise, it is the opposite!

The ministry of the evangelist is different because it demands a decision now. True evangelistic preaching is always heavily anointed by the Holy Spirit, which within itself is an unparalleled factor. As the Holy Spirit brings forth conviction, the die is cast for the sinner to come to Christ.

At such times, I have seen literally hundreds and even thousands run down aisles or grassy corridors in vast stadiums around the world as the Spirit of God would deal with their souls, and they would hurry to find Christ. That is the ministry of the evangelist. Whether preaching to a few or to many, the results should be the same.

THE MESSAGE OF THE EVANGELIST

As stated, it is the good news of the Gospel, but, as well, it is the ministry of the *"watchman"* (Ezek. 3:17).

The evangelist must preach the great doctrines of the Bible. He must preach about the horrible subject of hell and make it so real, even as Jesus did, Who was the consummate Evangelist, that it will seem as if people can see the fire and feel the flame. That is exactly what the Holy Spirit will do!

The evangelist must preach the mighty Baptism with the Holy Spirit with the evidence of speaking with other tongues (Acts 2:4). In fact, the Holy Spirit plays an obvious, even visible, role in the ministry of the evangelist.

NOTES

The evangelist must preach justification by faith, and, as well, the miracle-working power of God Almighty!

The evangelist must preach the Cross, that is, if he wants to preach the Gospel. He must understand the Cross of Christ not only as it refers to salvation but, as well, to sanctification.

The evangelist must preach love and faith to such an extent that men will dare to believe God for mighty things, even at that very moment. He must also stress the fact that our faith must have as its object the Cross of Christ (Rom. 6:1-14; 8:1-11; I Cor. 1:17-18, 23; 2:2; Col. 2:10-15).

Above all, the evangelist must preach Jesus. Jesus must permeate, riddle, saturate, and literally exhaust all that is presented. Considering his earlier ministry, the Scripture says that Philip *"went down to the city of Samaria, and preached Christ unto them"* (Acts 8:5).

Even though it seems that Philip was somewhat remiss at that time for not preaching the Baptism with the Holy Spirit as well, such was soon rectified by Peter and John (Acts 8:14-17). However, by the time of Paul's visit, which we are studying here, the Holy Spirit proves that by the very designation of Philip as *"an evangelist"* that this problem had now been rectified.

In other words, Philip was not only a great preacher to the lost, bringing sinners to Christ, but now, as well, a great proclamator of the great Pentecostal experience of the Baptism with the Holy Spirit accompanied by the evidence of speaking with other tongues (Acts 2:4).

THE REACH OF AN EVANGELISTIC MINISTRY

Inasmuch as there is a fivefold calling, such could be explained by the holding up of one's five fingers (Eph. 4:11).

If one is to notice, the middle finger, which symbolizes the evangelist, is longer than all other fingers. Of course, in a physical sense, it is done so for purpose.

In the spiritual sense, the thrust remains the same. There is a greater influence, at least as far as the harvest of souls is concerned,

NOTES

than with any other calling of the ministry.

I think it can be said without fear of contradiction that when Paul went into any new city to plant a church, it was in the role of the evangelist, even though all other of the callings manifested themselves in Paul's life at one time or the other. However, the initial stages, I think, were always in the realm of the evangelist, even though Paul most definitely was an apostle. In fact, the calling of the apostle included all of the five-fold ministry gifts as they were needed.

After the people were brought to Christ, the teaching then commenced, bringing in another ministry calling, and we continue to speak about Paul. The fish must be caught, and then they must be cleaned.

While signs and wonders should follow all of the five designated callings, still, it is to the evangelist that these gifts, I think, are of greater import. The reasons should be obvious!

The evangelist should see the sick healed, lives changed, miracles performed, bondages broken, believers filled and, above all, sinners saved.

THE EVANGELIST AND HIS APPEARANCE

Evangelists are not entertainers and neither are they showmen. Even though they may be flamboyant at times, their appearance must always be reckoned by the Holy Spirit. God is to move and, in fact, must move. As He does so, wondrous and glorious things will be done in the mighty Name of Jesus.

In my own personal life and ministry, I am so thankful that the Lord so constructed my beginning days by having me to come in contact with one of the great evangelists of that particular time, although relatively unknown to the world. I speak of A. N. Trotter, who, in my opinion, had one of the heaviest anointings of the Holy Spirit of any preacher I have ever heard. As well, his knowledge of the Word of God was absolutely unexcelled.

Sometime back, after having just landed at the airport at a particular African city and waiting for all of our baggage to come through customs, I happened to ask some missionaries standing by if they were acquainted with the brother I have just mentioned.

In one of the Campmeetings in which I was privileged to minister with him, I knew he was to go to this very city immediately after that Camp, which he did. That was back in 1962.

One of the missionaries, who had been there for many years, quickly turned his head toward me and said, *"Oh yes, I knew Brother Trotter very well."* Then he said:

"Of all the hundreds of churches built in this part of Africa, almost all of the pastors were baptized with the Holy Spirit in Brother Trotter's meetings conducted here in the early 1960s."

I had the pleasure to tell him that I was ministering with him just before he had come to that part of the world at that time.

THE HOLY SPIRIT

I stood there that day looking at the missionary as he began to tell me of the hundreds in those meetings who came through to the mighty Baptism with the Holy Spirit with the evidence of speaking with other tongues. He said, *"Brother Swaggart, those meetings revolutionized this part of Africa."*

He then said, *"Without those times, it is my belief that very few churches would have been built. But after those meetings, hundreds of young Africans, freshly baptized with the Holy Spirit, began to build churches by the scores, with literally thousands of people being brought to a saving knowledge of Jesus Christ."*

The Lord was so kind and gracious to place me under that man. How much I learned, I do not know, but this I do know:

I learned of the value of the mighty power of the Holy Spirit. I learned of His Anointing. I learned to shout with the redeemed and weep over the lost.

THE WAY OF THE HOLY SPIRIT

Whatever it is the Lord has helped us to do around the world in bringing men to Christ, I owe at least a great part of that to the ministry of the evangelist whom I have mentioned.

That is the way of the Holy Spirit. In respect to that *"way,"* I pray that God, that is, if Jesus tarries, will help me to influence and touch others who feel the call of that mighty work of the Holy Spirit, the call of the evangelist. No higher accolade could have been paid Philip than for the Holy Spirit to say, *"Philip the evangelist."*

The phrase, *"Which was one of the seven,"* harks back to Acts 6:5.

Philip was then a deacon but concludes now as an evangelist.

The phrase, *"And abode with him,"* must mean that Philip's home was quite large in order to entertain Paul and the entirety, it seems, of his company. Horton says, *"It is probable that his home was the Chief Christian Center or Church in Caesarea and that an Assembly of Believers gathered there."*

Considering a house of this size, this would suggest that the Lord had blessed Philip materially.

It is also believed that Paul may have visited there on previous occasions when he had passed through Caesarea and that he was well-known to Philip.

Whether that is true or not is not known. However, it is clear that Philip at least knew Paul, if only by reputation, and now warmly welcomed him, along with his entire party, into his house. It would prove to be a very blessed time for the apostle, as evidenced by the length of his stay.

(9) "AND THE SAME MAN HAD FOUR DAUGHTERS, VIRGINS, WHICH DID PROPHESY."

The pattern is:

1. The Holy Spirit alone can bring that which is required of the believer, a life of righteousness and holiness (Rom. 8:1-11).

2. To make it easier to understand, it is impossible for the believer to sanctify himself, at least according to the New Covenant. That can only be done by the Holy Spirit.

FOUR DAUGHTERS

The phrase, *"And the same man had four daughters, virgins,"* although abbreviated, contains very weighty information.

The idea is that these girls were given over to perpetual virginity, meaning they would not marry, thereby, dedicating themselves exclusively to the service of the Lord. Of course, if, in fact, that was the case, Philip would have no one to carry on his name.

NOTES

Obviously, these young ladies, who were totally sold out to the Lord, had felt within their hearts that this was what the Lord would have them do. That being the case, Philip bowed to their wishes.

The phrase, *"Which did prophesy,"* proclaims two headings:

The word *"prophesy"* in the Greek text is *"propheteuo"* and means *"to foretell events and to speak under inspiration."*

This means that they had the gift of prophecy as designated in I Corinthians 12:8-10, as well as the call to preach the Gospel, in other words, evangelists as their father.

The Greek here does not actually call them prophetesses but uses an attributive participle in order to emphasize this fulfillment. In other words, they were *"four prophesying virgin daughters."*

As well, the Greek indicates they were regularly used by the Holy Spirit in this ministry of prophesying, whether the gift of prophecy or preaching the Gospel.

This flies in the face of those who claim that women preachers are not scriptural. The following says they are:

WOMEN PREACHERS

In the Gospels we read of several women messengers who proclaimed *"good news"* (Mat. 28:1-10; Lk. 24:9-11; Jn. 4:28-30; 20:16-18).

• In Acts 2:14-21 and Joel 2:28-31, God predicted and promised that He Himself would pour out His Spirit upon women, and they would prophesy.

To prophesy means to speak to men to edification, exhortation, and comfort (I Cor. 14:3).

"He who prophesies edifies the church" (I Cor. 14:4).

Prophesying is for the church and general public, which speaks, at least in this case, of preaching the Gospel (I Cor. 12:1-31; 14:1-6, 12, 24-26, 29-33).

• In Acts 21:8-9, it is clear that Philip's four daughters were preachers, that is, they were evangelists like their father. This is in perfect accord with Joel 2:28-29, which was fulfilled in the early church (Acts 2:16), and with Acts 2:17-18, which is fulfilled in the last days.

• In Romans, Chapter 16, we have record of a number of women servants of the Lord in various churches. Phebe (Rom 16:1-2), Priscilla (Rom. 16:3-5), Mary, Tryphena, Tryphosa, Persis, and Julia (Rom. 16:6-15) are mentioned as laborers in the Lord.

• In Philippians 4:2, Euodias and Syntyche are mentioned as being leaders of the church at Philippi.

USURP AUTHORITY

• Corinthian women prophesied and prayed in church (I Cor. 11:4-5), so the Scripture in I Corinthians 14:34-35 that is used to condemn women preachers does not refer to preaching but to disturbance in church services—asking or talking out to their husbands in church, as stated in I Corinthians 14:35.

Even so, with I Timothy 2:11-15, Paul was not condemning women preachers, as long as they keep their place and do not *"usurp authority over the man."* Both men and women at Corinth were permitted to pray and prophesy but were regulated by fixed laws in doing so (I Cor. 14:24-32).

• In I Corinthians, Chapter 12, Paul compares the church to a human body and mentions nine gifts of the Spirit, including the gift of prophecy, for all the members of the Body of Christ, men and women.

• Women were used of God in Old Testament days as prophetesses (Ex. 15:20; Judg. 4:4; II Ki. 22:14; II Chron. 34:22; Neh. 6:14; Isa. 8:3; Lk. 1:39-56; 2:36).

The Law of Moses made provision for women to make sacrifices, attend feasts, and make vows (Lev., Chpt. 27; Deut. 12:11-18).

I think it is very obvious that the home of Philip, the evangelist, was godly to a far greater degree than normal. What a testimony for the cause of Christ.

Church historian Eusebius (A.D. 260-340) quoted Papias as saying these daughters ultimately moved to Asia, lived long lives, and continued to minister and witness to the early church. Thus, they were used *"as the Spirit wills"* (In I Cor. 12:11, *"every man"* is literally *"each one,"* which includes both men and women.).

(10) "AND AS WE TARRIED THERE MANY DAYS, THERE CAME DOWN FROM JUDAEA A CERTAIN PROPHET, NAMED AGABUS."

NOTES

The exegesis is:

1. The phrase, *"And as we tarried there many days,"* evidently means that Paul and his party had made good time coming from Philippi, with some days to spare before the Feast of Pentecost.

2. As well, it is obvious that Paul enjoyed very much the company of Philip, with the evangelist, no doubt, giving Luke much information concerning the early days of the church at Jerusalem. These were facts which the Holy Spirit was able to direct Luke to use in writing the Book of Acts.

3. Also, it is quite possible and, no doubt, true that the Lord used Philip's daughters in the realm of prophecy during this time, with certain things given by the Holy Spirit which were a great encouragement to Paul. Actually, prophesying brings edification (that builds up spiritually and develops or confirms faith), exhortation (that encourages and awakens, challenging all to move ahead in faithfulness and love), and comfort (that cheers, revives, and encourages hope and expectation). Thus, by prophesying, these daughters were blessing, edifying, and building up spiritually all the believers who heard, and I think especially the Apostle Paul. The Holy Spirit, no doubt, did this in order to offset the very negative messages that had to be given, as well, and which would now continue also!

4, The phrase, *"There came down from Judaea a certain prophet, named Agabus,"* presents the second time this brother is mentioned (Acts 11:28).

5. Whether Agabus had heard that Paul was at Caesarea, or whether the Holy Spirit simply directed him to go, we are not told.

(11) "AND WHEN HE WAS COME UNTO US, HE TOOK PAUL'S GIRDLE, AND BOUND HIS OWN HANDS AND FEET, AND SAID, THUS SAYS THE HOLY SPIRIT, SO SHALL THE JEWS AT JERUSALEM BIND THE MAN THAT OWNS THIS GIRDLE, AND SHALL DELIVER HIM INTO THE HANDS OF THE GENTILES."

The diagram is:

1. The answer for which we seek is found in the Cross.

2. The answer for which we seek is found only in the Cross (I Cor. 1:17; 2:2; Gal. 6:14).

THUS SAYS THE HOLY SPIRIT

The phrase, *"And when he was come unto us,"* insinuates that he had been there awhile before this action took place. Quite possibly during this time, Paul and others were discussing the situation in Jerusalem. Maybe Paul even mentioned, which he, no doubt, did, the things the Spirit had thus far said concerning these coming days.

"He took Paul's girdle, and bound his own hands and feet," presents that which the Holy Spirit told him to do as an object lesson.

Paul's girdle was probably a wide belt made of linen cloth, long enough to be wrapped several times around the waist.

"And said, Thus says the Holy Spirit," proclaims the Word as coming directly from the Lord.

Even though the Holy Spirit is referred to as speaking, it is only through another party in which He does so.

EIGHT WAYS GOD SPEAKS TO INDIVIDUALS:

1. By prophecy (Acts 3:21; 11:27-28; 21:10; Heb. 1:1; II Pet. 1:21).
2. Tongues and interpretation (I Cor. 12:4-11; 14:1-40).
3. Still small voice (I Ki. 19:12).
4. Audible voice (Deut., Chpt. 5; Mat. 3:17; 17:5; Jn. 12:28; Acts 9:7).
5. By angels (Acts 8:26; 12:8; 27:23).
6. By visions (Ps. 89:19; Acts 10:3, 10; 11:5; 16:9; 18:9).
7. By dreams (Gen. 20:6; Dan. 2:19, 28, 45; Mat. 1:20; 2:12-22; Acts 2:17).
8. By impression upon one's spirit (Acts 17:16; 18:5; 19:21; Rom. 8:16; II Cor. 2:13; Eph. 4:30; I Thess. 5:19).

The manner in which the Holy Spirit works upon our hearts and lives is in varied and different ways. Sometimes it is by intuition and sometimes by impression.

The Holy Spirit is a Person. As such, and being God, He can move upon us in various different ways, which means that we should ever be sensitive to His Leading and Guiding.

The idea for the Spirit-filled believer is that the Spirit of God Who abides within, actually making the believer a temple, seeks to control the person in all that is done. However, it is control that the believer must freely give to the Holy Spirit, which He will never take by force, hence, the incoming of the Spirit being symbolized by a *"dove"* (Jn. 1:32). He is symbolized in several other ways, as well, such as *"fire, wind, water, and oil,"* but yet, He makes His entrance into the believer as a dove. This speaks of the gentleness, which characterizes His dealings with us.

THE PERSONALITY OF THE HOLY SPIRIT

It is of the greatest importance that we believe in the Divinity of the Holy Spirit and also His personality. It is only when we learn these truths that we can give Him the honor, adoration, and personal respect that we give to God the Father. We must learn that the Holy Spirit is not a mere Power that we need to have and use, but we must learn that He is a Person Who is infinitely wise, holy, just, and gracious, and Who seeks to quicken us and use us. We must become acquainted with Him as a Person and not merely as an influence or power derived from a person.

HIS WORK

In the Holy Spirit's relationship to men, He is spoken of as searching hearts, regenerating, sanctifying, helping, convicting, teaching, quickening, guiding, witnessing, interceding, revealing, working, hearing, speaking, communing, appointing, commanding, counseling, comforting, inspiring, assuring, calling, and in all ways, acting as a real Person, which He is—the third Person of the Triune Godhead, *"God the Father, God the Son, and God the Holy Spirit."*

THE HOLY SPIRIT IS NOT THE FATHER OR THE SON

- The Holy Spirit has been seen with the natural eye as a separate Person from the Father and the Son, although in symbolic form (Mat. 3:16-17; Lk. 3:21-22; Jn. 1:31-34; Rev. 4:5; 5:6).

In Revelation 1:4-6; 3:1; 4:5; 5:6, the

Spirit is symbolized by seven Lamps of Fire, seven Eyes, and seven Horns *"before the Throne,"* upon which God the Father is sitting, and *"upon the Lamb,"* which is a symbol of Jesus Christ.

The Spirit then could not be the person of God the Father sitting on the Throne or the Lamb, Who comes to the Father on the Throne and takes a seven-sealed book out of His right Hand. Thus, we have three Persons and each one is distinguished from each other: the Father on the Throne; the Son symbolized by the Lamb *"before"* the Throne; and the Spirit symbolized by seven Lamps, also *"before"* the Throne.

The fact that Christ and the Spirit are separate Symbols seen at the same time and at the same place, Both *"before"* God the Father on the Throne, proves that they are two separate and distinct Persons from each other as well as separate and distinct from the Father.

A symbol is something that stands for or represents something else. Inasmuch as the Father is seen on the Throne, Christ and the Spirit are symbolized by two separate Beings before the Throne; therefore, there must have been three separate and distinct Persons involved in the scenes that were observed by the eyes of John in his vision (Rev. 4:1).

HOW THE HOLY SPIRIT DWELLS IN MEN

The Holy Spirit dwells in men only in the sense of *"union with,"* but never by bodily entrance into the human body to live there like an incarnation.

Upon acceptance of Christ as one's Lord and Saviour, which means all sin has been washed away by the precious shed Blood of the Lord Jesus Christ, God and men can now be in perfect union and are considered as being one and dwelling in each other (Jn. 14:17, 20).

The phrase, *"So shall the Jews at Jerusalem bind the man who owns this girdle, and shall deliver him into the hands of the gentiles,"* presents nearly the same words as those in which our Lord foretold His own betrayal (Mat. 20:19; Mk. 10:33; Lk. 18:32).

One scholar said, *"The predictions as to what would happen to Paul if he persisted in going up to Jerusalem, were doubtless designed to test his resolution to obey the inward voice which bound him to go, even as Elijah tested Elisha."*

NOTES

Irrespective, the Text is clear that Paul was in the direct will of God, and irrespective as to what happened, that was all that mattered.

(12) "AND WHEN WE HEARD THESE THINGS, BOTH WE, AND THEY OF THAT PLACE, BESOUGHT HIM NOT TO GO UP TO JERUSALEM."

The overview is:

1. To walk after the Spirit simply means that the believer places his or her faith exclusively in Christ and what Christ did for us at the Cross (I Cor. 1:17-18, 23; 2:2).

2. To *"walk after the flesh"* refers to the believer placing his or her faith in anything except Christ and the Cross (Rom. 8:1).

SPOKEN BY THE LORD

The phrase, *"And when we heard these things,"* presents that spoken by the Lord and was taken to be as from the Lord, which it surely was.

Back in the late 1900s, the Holy Spirit through utterances in tongues and interpretation, as well as prophecy, began to give forth situations which are just now coming to pass at Family Worship Center. To be sure, the Holy Spirit, Who spoke that day at the house of Philip the evangelist, is the same Holy Spirit Who spoke to us, as well as countless others around the world.

Even as far back as 1992, one morning in prayer meeting, the Lord moved greatly upon my heart, telling me, *"I'm going to start a move at Family Worship Center that will girdle the globe."* I knew that what I was told was from the Lord. I had no doubt about that. There are some things that we think are from the Lord, and there are some things we know are from the Lord. This was one of the latter.

Now (2014), I am watching this beginning to come to pass exactly as that which was given that morning in prayer meeting those long years ago. The Lord has told us to develop a television network, which actually began in 2010 (THE SONLIFE

NOTES

BROADCASTING NETWORK). At the time of this writing (March, 2014), the television ministry now goes into some 300,000,000 homes worldwide. On top of that, it is growing almost daily.

In 1997, the Lord gave me the great revelation of the Message of the Cross. No, it was not anything new, but actually, that which was given to the Apostle Paul, which he gave to us in his 14 Epistles. However, it has revolutionized my life and my ministry, and it's beginning to revolutionize the church, at least those who will believe.

It is ironic that the early church was begun on the Message of the Cross. Anyone who knows anything about the Apostle Paul understands that (I Cor. 1:17-18, 23; 2:2; Gal. 6:14; Col. 2:10-15). After the apostles and those who knew them passed on to Glory, little by little the church began to go into spiritual declension, until it finally morphed into what came to be known as the Catholic Church. This plunged the world into the Dark Ages, and then in the early 1500s, the Reformation began to take place, which was definitely from God. This was followed by the great Holiness meetings, instigated in England, Scotland, Wales, etc. Then, at the turn of the 20th century, the great outpouring of the Holy Spirit took place, which helped to touch the entirety of the world. I know because we were privileged to have a great part in that, sending television programming of the Gospel all over the world. Now, sadly, it seems that this move is weakening, but with the Holy Spirit bringing back the Cross. In fact, this means that the entirety of the church has come full circle.

The Holy Spirit came on the Day of Pentecost in a brand-new dimension in order that He may empower the church. He has remained ever since. It is the Cross of Christ which gave and gives the legal means to the Holy Spirit to do all that He does (Rom. 8:2). To be sure, as much as the Holy Spirit was needed in the times of the early church, He is needed now, which should be glaringly obvious!

To be frank, without the Holy Spirit in this capacity, irrespective as to what it is called, it is no longer church, at least in the eyes of God. It is the Holy Spirit Who leads the church, gives guidance and direction, and empowers the church, which enables it to carry out the works of Christ, and above all, Who lifts up and glorifies Jesus. So, without a proper understanding of the Spirit and the acceptance of all that He does, church becomes a man-instituted effort, which can never be recognized by God. With Him, there is life, while without Him, there is nothing!

THE PLEA TO PAUL

The phrase, *"Both we, and they of that place, besought him not to go up to Jerusalem,"* places everyone there, even Luke, attempting to persuade Paul to cancel this trip to Jerusalem. Consequently, there are several things here which we should notice:

These people, who, as stated, included Luke and Philip the evangelist, all seemingly took this prophecy to mean that Paul should not go in the direction of Jerusalem. However, if one notices carefully the Text, the Holy Spirit did not tell Paul not to go, but rather what would happen to him when he went. Actually, in recent days, the Holy Spirit had spoken thusly a number of times.

In view of this, we presently must be careful that we correctly interpret what the Lord is saying. As should be obvious, even the strongest in the Lord, who, without a doubt, were at this gathering at this time, can easily arrive at a wrong conclusion.

I am attempting to say that not only must we seek the Lord that He speak to us in this fashion but, as well, that we have His Help in properly interpreting what has been said. The Spirit of God must be involved in every aspect of our leading and understanding, and we must seek the Lord accordingly.

This incident portrays to us that we must follow the Lord and not men, even godly men, and do exactly what He says.

Of course, the motives of Philip, Luke, and all that were there that day were totally right toward God, so this is not meant to impugn their otherwise godly demeanor. It is meant to say this:

THE LEADING OF THE LORD

When the Lord gives leading, and we

NOTES

know beyond the shadow of a doubt that it is the Lord, even as Paul had previously tested this, the Lord must be obeyed without question. This is true irrespective of what others say, even the godliest. Jesus Christ is the Head of the church, not man! To be frank, this is one of the reasons for the present spiritual declension. Too many men are following men instead of God.

Of course, relative to the things I have just said, the person who does this, even as Paul, will be labeled as a *"lone ranger,"* who will not submit to proper authority, demanding to do his own thing, etc. Nothing could be further from the truth!

The idea is that the Lord does the leading and that He be followed without question. As the Head of the church, He has the right to demand that, as should be overly obvious.

While I love my brothers and sisters in the Lord and greatly value their counsel, prayers, and advice, still, my total objective is to do what God says and not man. As well, even if all men turn against me, I still must obey God, for this I know:

If all men are for me, and God isn't, then my ministry has just ended. Conversely, if God is for me, even though all men may be against me, I know the situation will come out right, and that is all that matters.

(13) "THEN PAUL ANSWERED, WHAT MEAN YOU TO WEEP AND TO BREAK MY HEART? FOR I AM READY NOT TO BE BOUND ONLY, BUT ALSO TO DIE AT JERUSALEM FOR THE NAME OF THE LORD JESUS."

The composition is:

1. The phrase, *"Then Paul answered,"* presents that which the Holy Spirit seeks in all lives. Our answer must be His Answer!

2. The question, *"What mean you to weep and to break my heart?"* proclaims that their request of Paul was not mere verbiage, but they kept on trying to persuade him, becoming quite emotionally distraught, with some of them weeping.

3. I do not want it to seem as if the people in this house were attempting to get Paul to disobey the admonition of the Spirit of God, for that was not the case at all. These people wanted the will of God as much as did Paul. They were just not certain, I think, that this actually was the will of God for him, especially in view of what the Holy Spirit had just said. As well, they loved him dearly and even beyond that, they recognized what the church would suffer if he was killed.

I AM READY

The phrase, *"For I am ready not to be bound only, but also to die at Jerusalem for the Name of the Lord Jesus,"* proclaims the consecration, which had already been settled in Paul's heart and mind respecting these coming events.

As we have stated, Paul did not go unnecessarily into danger, but if given directions by the Lord, he would place himself in any position, trusting the Lord to protect him as he so desired. This statement by the apostle proclaims a man who has truly given everything to the Lord. He no longer holds his welfare or life as dear. Both have been given to the Lord. Whatever the Lord wanted, that is what Paul desired as well!

Paul's statement proclaims to us that he knew tremendous difficulties were coming; however, he did not know if it would be imprisonment or death, but seemingly, definitely felt it would be one or the other. Irrespective, he was prepared to face either!

(14) "AND WHEN HE WOULD NOT BE PERSUADED, WE CEASED, SAYING, THE WILL OF THE LORD BE DONE."

The composition is:

1. The phrase, *"And when he would not be persuaded, we ceased saying,"* presents that which most cannot stand up against. Strong persuasion generally turns the heads of men. However, it must be quickly said that there is only one persuasion which really matters, and that is the persuasion of the Lord.

The phrase, *"The will of the Lord be done,"* means that all had now come to the place that they realized what Paul was doing and the direction he was going was, indeed, the will of God.

2. All of these people in the home of Philip wanted the will of God just as much as Paul. They just wanted to make certain it was the will of God, which is understandable.

3. God's Way is sometimes a hard way, but it is always the best way!

4. Whenever the Lord gives directions, it is not only for the individual involved but is actually for the entirety of the Body of Christ. In other words, everything must fit, but cannot fit unless the Lord is followed in totality. When all are in the will of God, everything is right. Again, I emphasize the fact that all believers must earnestly seek the will of God in all things, and then seek diligently to follow that will in totality. Nothing else could be more important!

5. As well, one must be willing to follow at any and all costs. In fact, the *"cost"* must never be the significant factor, if any factor at all, but rather to obey the Lord.

(15) "AND AFTER THOSE DAYS WE TOOK UP OUR CARRIAGES, AND WENT UP TO JERUSALEM."

The structure is:

1. The phrase, *"And after those days we took up our carriages,"* referred to their baggage, whatever that may have been.

2. Inasmuch as they had arrived here by ship, the baggage had not heretofore been a problem. Now they must walk or ride horses to Jerusalem, which was a distance of approximately 60 miles. They probably walked.

3. *"And went up to Jerusalem,"* refers to topography or altitude and not direction. Actually, Jerusalem was southeast of Caesarea.

4. So, the die was now cast. In a matter of hours, Paul would be in Jerusalem.

(16) "THERE WENT WITH US ALSO CERTAIN OF THE DISCIPLES OF CAESAREA, AND BROUGHT WITH THEM ONE MNASON OF CYPRUS, AN OLD DISCIPLE, WITH WHOM WE SHOULD LODGE."

The exegesis is:

1. The phrase, *"There went with us also certain of the disciples of Caesarea,"* meant that the party was now quite large, possibly numbering 15 to 20 people, or even more.

Incidentally, the word *"disciples,"* as used in the Book of Acts, always refers to followers of Christ.

2. *"And brought with them one Mnason of Cyprus,"* means that he was originally from Cyprus but now lived in Jerusalem or nearby.

3. Horto said, "*'An old Disciple,' does not necessarily mean old in age, but thought by some to mean that he was one of the original number Baptized with the Holy Spirit on the Day of Pentecost. That being the case, which it well could have been, some believe also that Luke's reference to Mnason as one of the original Disciples implies that he spent time with him and used him to check up on the events of the early part of the Book of Acts.*"

4. *"With whom we should lodge,"* simply means that Mnason had invited Paul and his party to stay at his home while in Jerusalem.

It being the Feast of Pentecost, the city would be glutted with people, with accommodations at a premium; therefore, I am certain this was greatly welcomed by Paul.

Also, we should learn from this that a common courtesy to the people of God is always rewarded by the Lord in great ways. Because of this hospitality, Mnason would have his name, plus the account of his generosity, forever inscribed on the eternal pages of the Word of God. What an honor!

(17) "AND WHEN WE WERE COME TO JERUSALEM, THE BRETHREN RECEIVED US GLADLY."

The synopsis is:

1. The phrase, *"And when we were come to Jerusalem,"* constituted the single most important thing on the face of the Earth of that particular time. All of this pertains to the furtherance of the Kingdom of God, to which Rome and all its mighty power must give way.

2. As should be obvious, God's Work on Earth is the single most important thing there is, by far eclipsing the pomp and ceremony of governments, plus all other happenings relative to the ways of the world. Of course, this is known only to the Lord and some few believers, with the world taking no notice whatsoever.

3. Nevertheless, what the true people of God do as they follow the Lord impacts the world in a very favorable way, even though not realized by the world. Conversely, what the world does is not supposed to impact the church whatsoever. In other words, the ways of the true church are not the ways of the world, and though greatly inconvenienced at times by those ways, we must

NOTES

never allow them to affect the outcome of what the people of God are called to do.

4. *"The brethren received us gladly,"* indicates some of the saints in Jerusalem, but not necessarily the leaders of the church at this particular time. That would come the next day.

(18) "AND THE DAY FOLLOWING PAUL WENT IN WITH US UNTO JAMES; AND ALL THE ELDERS WERE PRESENT."

The pattern is:

1. The Cross of Christ is the end of the Law as ceremonial.

2. Paul's position holds that Christ's Coming put the whole system out-of-date because it fulfilled it all.

JAMES

The phrase, *"And the day following Paul went in with us unto James,"* refers to James, the Lord's Brother, who was the senior pastor of the church in Jerusalem. It seems that Luke, as well as the entire party of Paul, ever how many, were present at this meeting.

"And all the elders were present," refers to the many associate pastors who served with James concerning the care of all the house churches in Jerusalem plus the environs.

The church in Jerusalem at this time, no doubt, was the largest in the world. It probably had as many as 20,000 to 50,000 members. They were not allowed any type of large buildings, so, as stated, the *"church"* was scattered all over Jerusalem, with people meeting in homes or wherever they could.

As well, the word *"elders"* did not include the original Twelve, for it seems that none were present at this time. (James, the brother of John, was now dead.) Tradition says they were scattered all over the Roman world of that day, taking the Gospel to far-flung fields of labor.

For instance, it is believed that Andrew was martyred in Scythia, or else, Greece, with Thomas martyred in India. Actually, it is thought that all of the original Twelve died martyr's deaths in various far-flung areas of the world, with the exception of John the Beloved, who, it is said, died a natural death

NOTES

in Ephesus at about 100 years of age.

PAUL

In view of the fact that these were the original Twelve who had been with Jesus (Matthias having been chosen to take the place of Judas), and considering the tremendous contribution they made to the work of God, as should be obvious, why did the Holy Spirit single out Paul as the guiding light of the early church, in fact, making him the masterbuilder of the church? While it is certainly true that Peter was given prominence during the first few years, it was Paul who, at a given point in time after his conversion, was given the reigns of leadership by the Spirit.

I do not think the answer lies in the fact of personal consecration, for I think it is obvious that all of these men loved the Lord supremely and ultimately paid with their lives. Therefore, the answer must lie in the direction given by the Holy Spirit, and I speak of the meaning of the Cross, or one might say, the Covenant of Grace, which was the meaning of the Cross that was given to Paul.

Due to the fact that the Law of Moses had run its course, having been fulfilled by Jesus Christ, it was now replaced by grace, to which the Law had pointed for nearly 1,600 years. However, this transition would not be simple or easy. Even though Peter, as recorded in Acts, Chapter 10, was given the beginning thrust of grace and its inclusion of gentiles, it was to Paul that the meaning of all of this was given in totality.

As we have previously stated, even then, the Jewish segment of the church gave up dependence on the Law very grudgingly, seemingly attempting to mesh it with grace. Of course, such was impossible and had it succeeded, it would have destroyed the church.

THE GOSPEL OF GRACE
MUST NOT BE DILUTED

It was Paul who stood his ground, even against what looked like insurmountable odds, in order that the Gospel of grace not be diluted and weakened by erroneous amalgamation. He went so far as to bluntly say,

"But though we, or an angel from heaven, preach any other gospel unto you than that which we have preached unto you, let him be accursed (damned)*"* (Gal. 1:8).

No! Even accounting for the tremendous consecration of the original Twelve, as well as their tremendous contribution, it is doubtful, and I think obvious, that none of them could have stood the onslaught which Paul suffered respecting this all-important task. In doctrine, I think the evidence is abundantly clear that all of these men (the Twelve) agreed with Paul one hundred percent respecting the Covenant of Grace. However, regarding a pure, undiluted message, I am not certain that any one of them would have had the courage and strength to stand as Paul stood!

Harmony in the Gospel is one thing, while a defense of that Gospel is something else altogether.

Then again, even though in perfect harmony with grace, I do not think that the Twelve understood this covenant quite as clearly as did Paul. For instance, in addressing himself to this very subject, Peter said, *"Even as our beloved brother Paul also according to the wisdom given unto him has written unto you;*

"As also in all his Epistles, speaking in them of these things; in which are some things hard to be understood ..." (II Pet. 3:15-16).

So, the major thrust of the great Gospel of grace was left primarily with Paul, and I think for the reasons given!

(19) "AND WHEN HE HAD SALUTED THEM, HE DECLARED PARTICULARLY WHAT THINGS GOD HAD WROUGHT AMONG THE GENTILES BY HIS MINISTRY."

The synopsis is:

1. The phrase, *"And when he had saluted them,"* refers to Paul greeting all the elders and probably introducing all who were with him, etc.

2. *"He declared particularly what things God had wrought among the gentiles by his ministry,"* proclaims, no doubt, an account, which was quite lengthy, of his second and third missionary journeys, with the planting of many churches.

NOTES

3. He would probably have related in detail the Macedonian Call, with the Gospel making its first thrust into Europe. He would have told of all the miracles and healings which the Lord had wrought by his hands, as well as enumerable conversions of miraculous power.

In looking at this, one stands amazed!

Paul did these things without a printed Bible and without the help of modern advertisement, transportation, or communication. As well, it was carried out under the threat or actual fact of violence, even in the face of tremendous opposition. There was and is only one answer, and that is the Spirit of God. This should tell us something!

4. While all the things mentioned, such as modern mass communication, transportation, etc., are definitely helpful in this great task, still, none of that ensures any type of success at all. It was the Holy Spirit Who empowered Paul with leading, guidance, and the anointing. By Him and Him alone can these things be done. However, much of the modern church totally ignores the Holy Spirit, rather depending upon the other things mentioned. This, in fact, may create a lot of religious machinery but, in truth, will do nothing for Jesus.

5. The preacher, and every believer for that matter, must be filled with the Spirit, led by the Spirit, guided by the Spirit, empowered by the Spirit, and as such, controlled by the Holy Spirit. Only then can a work for God be carried out, brought about, and accomplished. That and that alone is the secret.

(20) "AND WHEN THEY HEARD IT, THEY GLORIFIED THE LORD, AND SAID UNTO HIM, YOU SEE, BROTHER, HOW MANY THOUSANDS OF JEWS THERE ARE WHICH BELIEVE; AND THEY ARE ALL ZEALOUS OF THE LAW."

The pattern is:

1. The Jesus that Paul preached, *"Christ and Him Crucified,"* sets captives free.

2. It saves souls while at the same time destroying the powers of darkness.

THE LAW OF MOSES

The phrase, *"And when they heard it, they glorified the Lord,"* speaks of a continual praising of the Lord for this which had been done. So far, so good!

"And said unto him, You see, brother, how many thousands of Jews there are which believe," was probably spoken by James and refers to the church in Jerusalem, as stated, made up exclusively of Jews and numbering many thousands.

All of these converts had accepted Jesus as their Messiah, Lord, and Saviour, but yet, they were still eagerly devoted to the Law of Moses, actually, ardent observers of the Law.

"And they are all zealous of the Law," refers to the following:

The word *"zealous"* in the Greek text is *"zelotes"* and means *"enthusiast."* In other words, their new-found faith in Christ stirred them up to serve the Lord with a new zeal, which they channeled in the direction of attempting to obey the Law of Moses even to a greater degree than ever. They had merely tacked Jesus onto the Law, in effect, becoming more religious.

To be frank, even though the Jerusalem church retained tremendous authority, for all the obvious reasons, still, one now sees why the Holy Spirit shifted the thrust of world evangelism away from the mother church in Jerusalem to Antioch, and even other places (Acts 13:1-2). In this of which we speak lies a tremendous danger in more ways than one.

SALVATION BY THE BLOOD OF JESUS

The acceptance of Christ into one's heart and life is meant by the Holy Spirit to have but one purpose, and that is to establish a constant relationship between the believer and Jesus. However, many believers instead simply become more religious. In other words, they miss the great Point of conversion, Who is Jesus, and instead, go in the opposite direction. Then the mechanics of religion become paramount. They have a tendency to push one toward self-righteousness, with *"works"* becoming paramount. Relationship with Christ, which is the very foundation of salvation, actually what it is all about, is then placed on hold, with little true spiritual progress being made. It is the business of the Holy Spirit to glorify Christ and not more religion (Jn. 16:14).

NOTES

So, as the Jerusalem Christians were *"zealous"* for the wrong thing, so are many modern Christians! Zealousness for Christ must be the criterion, and zealousness for Christ alone!

THE SCHISM

Once again, I go back to the ruling handed down by James at the first council as recorded in Acts, Chapter 15. That ruling stated that the Law of Moses was no longer binding upon gentiles. Had that ruling been extended to Jews, which it certainly should have been, many of these problems would have been avoided, with the presentation of the Gospel made much easier. As it was, Satan took full advantage of this schism, causing Paul to have to spend much time and effort correcting the situation.

Were these Jerusalem Jews truly saved who were attempting to mix Law with grace, which Paul had strongly opposed? (Gal. 5:1-6).

Yes, they were saved, and for the simple reason that they had accepted Christ.

An acceptance of Christ does not necessarily mean a perfect doctrine; however, at the same time, at the moment of conversion, the Holy Spirit goes to work to correct and rectify. That, among other things, is His Business: to guide believers into all truth (Jn. 16:13). According to the manner in which the believer yields to the Spirit, spiritual growth will come about.

However, if one insists upon continuing in false doctrine, the *"leaven,"* as small as it may initially be, will, as Paul said, ultimately corrupt the whole (I Cor. 5:6-8). The leaven of false doctrine must be rooted out!

THE MIXING OF THE LAW AND THE GOSPEL

Mixing anything with the Gospel of grace, such as the Law of Moses, church membership, good works, etc., does despite to the spirit of grace and actually makes a corrupt form of Christianity. In truth, either one nullifies the other.

Concerning this problem at Jerusalem at this time, Judaism and Christianity could not function together for they were opposites.

Even though all of the Law had been

totally fulfilled in Christ, which was meant to be all the time, still, many Jewish believers insisted on continuing in the Law plus Christ. It was impossible for such to continue!

The Lord is very patient with us all and, therefore, tolerated the Jews continuing, at least for a time, with all their Mosaic rituals. However, the Lord brought all of that to an abrupt end in A.D. 70 with the Romans destroying Jerusalem and the Temple. As would be obvious, this destruction made it impossible for Jewish rituals to continue.

AN EXAMPLE WE SHOULD HEED!

While the Law of Moses is of little consequence presently to modern believers, still, other things have taken its place and have the same effect on believers.

I speak of Catholics who make the *"church"* and *"Mary"* a part of salvation along with Christ. However, that *"leaven"* has been there so long until it now corrupts the whole, with Jesus in the Catholic Church no more than a mere figurehead, if that. It is now the *"church"* and *"Mary"* held up as the way of salvation.

As well, many other church groups are following in the same path of Catholicism, making their church a part of the salvation mix. In other words, they teach either directly or by inference that to be saved, one must accept Christ plus be associated with their particular church or one of its ordinances, etc.

ONLY JESUS

In other words, the Church of Christ teaches that one must be baptized in water and, accordingly, into the Church of Christ in order to be saved. So, they have made water baptism plus their church a requirement for salvation, which is the very opposite of the Word of God (Eph. 2:8-9).

To be frank, millions of Baptists believe the same thing! If one is truly saved, they say, one will be a Baptist, etc. Many Oneness claim that one has to be baptized in water, be baptized according to a certain formula, a formula, incidentally, which they have devised themselves, plus speak in tongues in order to be saved.

However, let it ever be known, *"Neither is there salvation in any other: for there is none other name under heaven given among men, whereby we must be Saved"* (Acts 4:12). That Name is Jesus!

To add anything to that Name or the Finished Work of Christ, which, in essence, cannot be done, is to fall from grace. Either Jesus' Work is a Finished Work, meaning that nothing needs to be added, or it is nothing at all! Either He paid the full price, never needing more to be paid, or else, He paid no price whatsoever!

In the eyes of God, to attempt to add anything to the great Covenant of Grace must be a sin of unprecedented proportions. In effect, it calls God a liar and claims by example that Christ did not pay the full price at Calvary. What travesty! What blasphemy! What arrogance!

THIS SIMPLE TRUTH

It would seem, would it not, that this simple truth of salvation solely in and through Christ would be eagerly embraced by all! And yet, this is where Satan makes the greatest inroads.

I think we can say that such error has its roots in the Fall in the Garden of Eden. In that perfect environment, man fell simply because he desired to add to the Word of God, thereby, inserting his own way, which, in fact, was the cause of the Fall! Nevertheless, this spirit of disobedience has inculcated itself in every human being from that time until now. It is hard for man to fall at the feet of Jesus, for there, he must throw himself totally and completely on the mercy and grace of God. As well, he must admit that he is nothing within himself and can do nothing to save himself. As such, he must also rely totally upon Christ and what He has done for us at the Cross. Most are loath to admit that! As a result, despite the fact of much of the world being very religious, most are lost!

(21) "AND THEY ARE INFORMED OF YOU, THAT YOU TEACH ALL THE JEWS WHICH ARE AMONG THE GENTILES TO FORSAKE MOSES, SAYING THAT THEY OUGHT NOT TO CIRCUMCISE THEIR CHILDREN, NEITHER TO WALK AFTER THE CUSTOMS."

NOTES

The pattern is:

1. Peter said, *"Who verily was foreordained before the foundation of the world, but was manifest in these last times for you,"* which refers to the fact that the Godhead deemed it necessary for man to be redeemed by the means of the Cross.

2. This was done before the foundation of the world (I Pet. 1:18-20).

TWIN DIRECTIONS

The phrase, *"And they are informed of you,"* now concerns itself with charges against Paul relative to what he was teaching. In a sense, the charges were true and, at the same time, untrue, which we will attempt to explain.

The question is, *"What was the position of James in this all-important controversy?"*

I do not think anyone could read this account without coming to the conclusion that James was still holding somewhat to twin directions. In other words, he, in effect, was subscribing one salvation for gentiles and another for the Jews, which, of course, is woefully wrong. As we have previously stated, the Jews, even those who had accepted Christ, were loath to give up the Law of Moses.

The phrase, *"That you teach all the Jews which are among the gentiles to forsake Moses,"* is not correct, at least in the manner in which it is being said.

Paul had never told anyone, whether Jews or gentiles, to forsake Moses. In fact, Paul preached almost exclusively from the Old Testament, holding up all that it stated as pointing to Christ. It was not a matter of forsaking Moses but properly understanding Moses.

OLD TESTAMENT

The Old Testament is the Word of God. In that, it serves as the foundation of all that we presently have. It is the story of God's Redemption Plan, respecting the Law of Moses, as well as the admonitions of the prophets.

Paul taught the veracity of all these things and how they were given by God in order to ultimately lead men to Christ.

When Christ came, He was the Fulfillment of all these promises, covenants, and laws. They were meant to point to Him, explain Him, and portray Him, which they beautifully did, that is, if they were properly interpreted. They were the means to an end but by no means insignificant, as should be overly obvious.

NOTES

But yet, by the time of Christ, Israel had attempted to make salvation out of the keeping of the Law, which was not possible, but only tended to breed an acute self-righteousness. In effect, it was a salvation by works, which, of course, could never be, and which God could never accept.

Men love to think that their religious activity makes them holy, especially when it is activity concerning that which has been truly given by God, even as the Law of Moses.

THE LAW AND ITS TRUE MEANING

It was in this context in which Paul held up the Law. To understand its true meaning made Christ even more real, but trying to maintain that which had already been fulfilled only tended to breed more self-righteousness. Why is the symbol necessary when the reality has come?

The phrase, *"Saying that they ought not to circumcise their children,"* once again, was not exactly what Paul was saying.

He taught in his Epistles, and rightly so, as given by the Holy Spirit, that circumcision did not save the soul and *"by the deeds of the Law no flesh shall be justified"* (Rom. 3:20-31; 4:21; Gal. 3:19-25).

So, we have the subtle difference, and sometimes not so subtle, of Jews believing that circumcision, which, of course, was a part of the old Law, had something to do with the salvation of one's soul. Paul was emphasizing that no trust should be put in these things, for they had already served their purpose in pointing to the coming Christ. Israel was to be a separated people from the world, which circumcision implied, and for special reasons. However, now that these particular reasons had been realized in the coming of Christ, it was the circumcision of the heart that was now required, and not circumcision of the flesh, etc. (Rom. 2:29; Phil. 3:3). Of course, circumcision of the heart is a spiritual experience.

In fact, neither circumcision nor the Law

NOTES

of Moses, nor any part thereof, ever saved anyone and was never intended to save anyone. It was meant to show God's Standard of Righteousness and to show man how unable he is to keep even the simplest of Laws. He was then to turn to the sacrifices, in effect, to what the sacrifices pointed, namely Christ. Salvation has always been in the Cross, symbolized by the sacrifices, and is now a fact. Salvation is received simply by one believing, and I speak of believing in Christ and what He has done for us at the Cross (Jn. 3:16; Rom. 10:9-13; Rev. 22:17).

THE LAW FULFILLED IN CHRIST

Paul was not attempting to destroy the Law or even to ban the Law, but rather that the Law represented mere forms and ceremonies, which were fulfilled in Christ. Paul's contention was, and rightly so, that one should not depend on these forms and ceremonies for salvation. In actuality, this is what Israel had done, with even the Jewish segment of the early church, even though accepting Christ, still continuing, at least in part, to look to the Law in this fashion.

Consequently, these matters were of far greater significance than one might at first think. Actually, the adding of Christ to the Law was probably Satan's greatest thrust at that present time, and he was using the mother church in Jerusalem, to a certain extent, to further his cause. Almost all of the false teachers who advocated the continuance of the Law of Moses plus Christ came out of the Jerusalem church. So, instead of the mother church being greatly used to take the Gospel to the world, at least some parts of it were busy trying to preserve Law-keeping, even among the gentiles, and especially among the gentiles. Of course, James had no part of this relative to the gentiles, but it is my feeling, as stated, that his segregation of the Jews respecting Law-keeping only exacerbated the problem.

(22) "WHAT IS IT THEREFORE? THE MULTITUDE MUST NEEDS COME TOGETHER: FOR THEY WILL HEAR THAT YOU ARE COME."

The account is:

1. The question, *"What is it therefore?"* represents, I think, that James was not settled on the matter himself respecting Paul.

2. One commentator claimed that the elders recognized that these accusations against Paul were false and merely wanted them clarified. Perhaps that is true to a certain extent, but I think not altogether. I believe the evidence is somewhat clear that the problem continued to persist in respect to one way for gentiles and another way for the Jews, which was wrong. It was impossible for this problem not to continue as long as this dichotomy remained.

3. The phrase, *"The multitude must needs come together: For they will hear that You are come,"* seems to imply that the gathering could be somewhat volatile because of this very issue.

If, in fact, that was the case, it is easily observable as to how Satan had done his work well.

As is obvious, Paul was one of the greatest men of God in the world of that day, possibly seeing movings and operations of the Holy Spirit, even to the raising of the dead, as few, if any, had ever experienced. To hear him speak and to give account of all the great things that had happened was an opportunity and privilege unparalleled! And yet, the reason for the proposed gathering of the people seems to have been little in that vein.

Due to this erroneous doctrine of Law/grace, most in Jerusalem did not place Paul in the same position as he was placed by the Holy Spirit. Again, this is Satan's greatest effort.

For those whom God has called and used extensively so, the Evil One does all he can to denigrate their person in the eyes of believers in order that they not receive of the benefits given by the Holy Spirit through the called one. Satan is a master at making men believe that what is of God isn't, and what isn't of God is!

So, it seems that few of the people had a desire to hear of the great things of God, but rather wanted to argue over these particular questions!

(23) "DO THEREFORE THIS THAT WE SAY TO YOU: WE HAVE FOUR MEN WHICH HAVE A VOW ON THEM."

The way is:

1. If you were to ask most Christians, even preachers, how the Holy Spirit works in the heart and life of the believer, most would probably give you a blank stare.

2. The Holy Spirit works exclusively within the parameters, so to speak, of the Finished Work of Christ, which requires the Cross of Christ to be the object of our faith (Rom. 8:2).

WHAT DOES THIS MEAN?

The phrase, *"Do therefore this that we say to you,"* proclaims a plan which it seems that James thought might defuse the situation, but yet, a plan, I think, which was little from the Lord.

I do not seek to attribute more to the situation than we should, but, as well, we should not attribute less than what is obvious.

Considering the tens of thousands of Jews coming into Jerusalem for the Feast of Pentecost, possibly James saw a situation that could erupt into mob riot, consequently, causing the church in Jerusalem great difficulties. In other words, if the Jews who paid no allegiance to Christ, who, incidentally, were in the great majority, even remotely thought that their customs of the Law of Moses were being attacked in any way, the situation could turn ugly very fast. So, James seemed to be very concerned about what Paul might say and do, which he thought might precipitate great problems.

However, whatever it was in James' mind, and whatever problems were now accruing, in my thinking, were due to him not taking a stand at the very beginning some years before. He was attempting to function as Jews had always functioned, heavily involved in the Law of Moses, and as a result, a part of Jewish life, but with the addition of Christ. However, such was an untenable situation.

When Paul went into new places to plant a church, he always went to the Jewish synagogue first of all, at least if there was one in the city. However, after awhile, continued meetings in the synagogue would be impossible for the simple reason that many, if not most, of the Jews rejected Christ, forcing a division regarding those who did accept Him, whether Jew or gentile. In other words, it simply was not possible for converted Jews to continue in the previous posture; therefore, to fully follow Christ, they would have to turn their backs upon all they had previously known. Actually, Jesus had said that it would be this way and, in fact, must be this way (Mat. 10:16-42).

A BOLD STAND

However, it seems to me that James was attempting to continue in Jewish life, which, in essence, amounted to a terrible compromise of the Gospel. He would have been better off at the outset to have renounced Judaism as a means of salvation and go all out for Christ, Who, in reality, was a Fulfillment of Judaism. So, accepting Christ was not really rejecting Judaism, but rather giving it credit for a job well done. Consequently, to reject Christ, in effect, was to reject Judaism, as its very role was to point to Christ.

If James had taken a bold stand at the beginning, it definitely would probably have increased the persecution. However, it would have also made a statement and would have solved the Law/grace issue at the very outset instead of Paul having to deal with the thing constantly and, at times, with great hurt.

Luke does not tell us what Paul said or what type of answer was forthcoming. The Scripture is silent!

PAUL'S POSITION

Many have taken Paul to task concerning his actions at this time, claiming that he compromised the Gospel. However, I think not.

Paul knew Satan's plans to divide the church and to do so over the Law/grace issue. Above all, he was attempting to circumvent Satan's efforts. So, I think what he did was done to ameliorate the situation as far as possible, and I must believe that Paul had the mind of the Lord regarding the entirety of this situation. I cannot imagine that he would have done otherwise!

PAUL AND THE LAW

As we have previously stated, Paul was probably the greatest Hebrew scholar in the world at that time regarding the Law of Moses. In other words, no one knew the

Law better than this man. This very well could have been one of the reasons the Lord chose him for this task.

In knowing the Law as he did, it would be easier for the Holy Spirit to open up to him the pointed thrust of the Law, which was to point to the coming Redeemer, the Lord Jesus Christ.

In doing what James suggested, even though it would little help the situation, at the same time, it could not hurt.

Paul had never taught that keeping any part of the Law at this time was wrong. The actual thrust of his message was that there was now no spiritual benefit either way in its rituals and ceremonies. In other words, keeping the Law added no spiritual benefit, while not keeping the Law fell into the same category. So, him carrying forth this vow, as we shall see, carried no spiritual portent whatsoever (Rom. 2:28-29; Gal. 2:16; 5:6).

THE VOW

The phrase, *"We have four men which have a vow on them,"* pertained to the Nazarite vow.

The Nazarite vow was instituted after God set apart the Levites to serve the Tabernacle and the family of Aaron as priests.

Desiring that all of the Tribes should grow closer to Jehovah, the Lord instituted the Nazarite vow, which was available to all. Not only did it pertain to all the Tribes, but to men and women also. In other words, it was completely nondiscriminatory.

Usually, the vow was taken for a limited period of time. During the time they were observing the vow, they were not to cut or trim any of the hair on the head. By this, they declared that God's Will was more important to them than any human custom.

As well, they were not to drink wine or even grape juice, or even eat grapes or raisins. The grapevine had become a symbol of human pleasures, so they put everything connected with it aside in order to declare that God was their chief Joy.

Also, those who had taken upon themselves the Nazarite vow were not to touch any dead human body. This was because that death was the wages of sin, and actually the very opposite of all that pertained to God, Who is Life.

NOTES

At the close of the period they had chosen for the vow, and the length of time was up to their choosing, expensive sacrifices were to be offered, including a male and female lamb, a ram, and other offerings. Then they would shave their heads as a sign the vow was completed (Num. 6:14-20).

(24) "THEM TAKE, AND PURIFY YOURSELF WITH THEM, AND BE AT CHARGES WITH THEM, THAT THEY MAY SHAVE THEIR HEADS: AND ALL MAY KNOW THAT THOSE THINGS, WHEREOF THEY WERE INFORMED CONCERNING YOU, ARE NOTHING; BUT THAT YOU YOURSELF ALSO WALK ORDERLY, AND KEEP THE LAW."

The form is:

1. Walking after the Spirit simply refers to the believer placing his or her faith exclusively in Christ and the Cross (Rom. 8:1-2).

2. Walking after the flesh refers to the believer placing his or her faith in anything other than Christ and the Cross (I Cor. 1:17).

THE PURIFICATION PROCESS

The phrase, *"Them take, and purify yourself with them, and be at charges with them, that they may shave their heads,"* tells us two things.

1. Paul was having to pay for all of these sacrifices for four men and himself out of his own pocket, which, in 2014 dollars, would amount to at least $3,000.

I have no idea why James insisted on Paul paying for these sacrifices, unless he felt it would make a statement concerning Paul's fidelity to the Law of Moses.

2. Not only would he pay for all the sacrifices, but, as well, he was to join in with the purification process, which was to last some seven days.

It is suggested that Paul entered into a Nazarite vow some weeks earlier, as recorded in Acts 18:18, and intended to complete the vow at Jerusalem. That may well have been the case!

Inasmuch as these parts of the Law pertained to consecration to the Lord, in effect, making a statement, perhaps these types of things continued to be a part of Paul's consecration and worship.

NOTES

Knowing how strong Paul was relative to the Law having no part in one's salvation, one has to conclude that there were nuances about the Law, which spoke of consecration, that continued to hold a spiritual application.

THE THINKING OF JAMES

The phrase, *"And all may know that those things, whereof they were informed concerning you, are nothing,"* probably, in some way, would serve that purpose. The thinking was that if Paul was as opposed to the Law as it was claimed, he certainly would not be in the Temple carrying out a Nazarite vow, which was a part of the Mosaic Law.

The phrase, *"But that you yourself also walk orderly, and keep the Law,"* presents a very difficult situation, but with only silence on the part of Paul, at least regarding any recorded statements.

There is no way that one could say that Paul kept the Law inasmuch as such would have meant the continuing offering of sacrifices, plus Sabbath observance, circumcision, etc.

Perhaps Paul justified this action in his own mind in that, in fact, he did keep the Law through accepting what Jesus had done in that respect. In other words, no one ever really kept the Law of Moses, other than Christ. However, upon faith in Him, His perfect Law-keeping Victory is then given freely to the believer. Through Christ, the believer then becomes a Law-keeper. In truth, the Law is not dead, even presently, but the believer is dead to the Law through Christ (Rom. 7:4).

CHRIST AND THE FULFILLMENT OF THE LAW

Looking at the whole testimony of the Gospels, we can see how it was that Christ fulfilled the Law. He fulfilled the moral Law by obeying, by bringing out its fullness of meaning, and by showing its intense spirituality, and He established it on a surer basis than ever as the eternal Law of Righteousness.

He fulfilled the ceremonial and typical Law, not only by conforming to its requirements, but by realizing its spiritual significance. He filled up the shadowy outlines of the types, and thus fulfilled, they passed away, and it is no longer necessary for us to observe the Passover or kill the daily lamb: we have the substance in Christ.

Jesus kept the Law as our Representative Man by never breaking it one single time and, thereby, keeping it perfectly all the days of His Life.

As well, not only did He keep the Law by living the Law, but He also answered the charges of the broken Law, which was incumbent upon every human being. The penalty for that was death, which referred to eternal separation from God, which refers to hell itself.

When He gave Himself as the perfect Sacrifice to die on the Cross of Calvary, He offered Himself as a Sacrifice, a perfect Sacrifice if you will, which was accepted by the Godhead. This made it possible for any and every Lawbreaker in the world to accept Christ as Saviour, which then erased and erases the terrible death sentence hanging over the head of every Lawbreaker in the world. In other words, Calvary paid it all.

HE CLEARED UP THE MYSTERY

Jesus also cleared the Law from the traditional excesses, which had gathered around it under the hands of the rabbis and especially the Pharisees. He showed that the ceremonial distinction between meats, clean and unclean, was no longer necessary but showed the importance of true spiritual purity (Mat. 15:11; Mk. 7:18-23).

Jesus taught His Disciples those great principles when, after His Resurrection, *"Beginning from Moses and from all the prophets, He interpreted to them in all the Scriptures the things concerning Himself"* (Lk. 24:27).

CHRIST OPENED THEIR MINDS

As He opened their minds that they might understand the Scriptures, He declared, *"These are the Words which I spoke unto you, while I was yet with you, that all things must be fulfilled, which were written in the Law of Moses, and in the Prophets, and in the Psalms, concerning Me"* (Lk. 24:44).

John sums this up in his pregnant phrase,

"The Law was given through Moses; grace and truth came through Jesus Christ" (Jn. 1:17).

The grace was in contrast to the condemnation of the moral Law; the truth was the concrete foundation of the shadowy outline of the types and ceremonies of the Law. In other words, Jesus fulfilled all the Law, which no one else could ever do, and then through His Grace, which is truth, He awarded this great victory of Law-keeping to believing sinners. Thus, the Law was fulfilled and completed, which it was ever meant to be in Christ.

THE LAW OF MOSES AND THE BELIEVER

In Christ, it is possible for the believer to say that the Law remains as a rule of life. Thus, the Law is not abrogated in the sense of failure. It remains as the Standard of Righteousness, and, of course, we are speaking of the moral Law, the Ten Commandments, which ought to be the *"rule of life"* for believers in Christ.

The utmost holiness to which the believer can attain under the influence of the Holy Spirit is still the *"righteousness,"* which the Law requires but gave no power to bring about.

Actually, the believer in Christ has found the true principle of obedience to the Law. He has entered into the true spirit of the Holy Law. That is all summed up in love, and he, having received the love of Christ, living in His Love, sees the Law not as a stern taskmaster condemning, but as a bright vision alluring.

He indeed sees the Law embodied in Christ, and the imitation of Christ involves obedience to the Law, but he fulfills the Law not simply as a standard outside, but as a living principle within.

Acting according to the dictates of the love begotten at the Cross, the believer's life is conformed to the image of Christ, and insofar as conformed to the Law—*"Love therefore is the fulfillment of the Law"* (Lk. 10:27; Rom. 13:10).

When one accepts Christ, the Holy Spirit within such a person makes one into the image of Christ, which fulfills all of the moral Law in totality, which is the only way it can be kept. In other words, it's the Cross that makes all victory possible, all forgiveness of sin, and all victory over sin. It's the Cross! The Cross! The Cross!

NOTES

THE PASSING AWAY OF THE LAW

The great general principles of the Law were not transitory but abiding and reappear under the Gospel dispensation. Otherwise, however, in those particulars, whether ceremonial or civil, in which it was adapted to merely passing needs, the Law passed away when Christ came because He fulfilled it in total.

However, it is not always realized that before Christ came, it had already begun to pass away.

THE ARK OF THE COVENANT

The whole rationale of the Levitical worship consisted in its being based upon the covenant made at Sinai, and the symbol of the covenant was the Ark containing the Tables of the Law and surmounted by the Mercy Seat.

Therefore, one of its most significant acts was the sprinkling of the blood of the sin-offering within the Veil upon the Mercy Seat, or without the Veil, but yet, before the Mercy Seat. However, this most significant act could no longer be performed when, after the Babylonian captivity, there was no longer either Ark or Mercy Seat.

When Nebuchadnezzar broke into the Holy of Holies upon his invasion of Israel in Jerusalem, there was no Ark there. Some say that Jeremiah took it and hid it in a cave, where it remains until this day.

Also, when the Romans broke into the Holy of Holies in Herod's Temple, this room, which should have contained the Ark, was empty.

JESUS

In effect, Jesus was the true Brazen Altar, Brazen Laver, Table of Shewbread, Golden Lampstand, Altar of Incense, and Ark of the Covenant. He alone is the true Mercy Seat, upon which His own Blood was spilled.

To be sure, the ceremonies and rituals of the Law were beautiful to behold, in a sense,

NOTES

because, most of all, of what they represented. The elaboration of the performance of the priests, along with the divinely-given ordinances and rituals, presented a work which pointed toward the coming redemption of mankind through the Lord Jesus Christ.

However, the beautiful ritual of the Law, in a sense, became a snare for the simple reason that religious men delighted in its practice even though it was never fully kept. Doing religion seems to serve as a spiritual narcotic. This has lulled untold millions into the eternal sleep of spiritual death, with the people thinking all the time that it brings righteousness when, in fact, works can never bring true righteousness, only self-righteousness.

So, when Jesus came, born of the Virgin, but yet, a Peasant, Israel could not equate Him with all the glory of the Temple and its accouterments. Hence, Jesus said that He was greater than the Temple, but yet, a *"greatness"* that Israel could not see because of their unbelief (Mat. 12:6).

FAITH

Faith was intended by God to be the instrument that spoke of Christ. In other words, it was not so much what the Law was but to Whom all its ceremony and ritual pointed. That Person was Christ! However, Israel lost sight of the coming One as they fixated on the beauty of the ceremonies and rituals. In other words, they made a *"religion"* out of the Law, which God never intended. It was to ever be a type, a symbol if you will, and a stop-gap measure, which would suffice until the coming Reality. That Reality was Christ! However, He was a *"Stone of stumbling, and a Rock of offence"* (I Pet. 2:8).

Despite His virgin Birth, His Miracles, and His claims, still, there was no beauty that one should desire Him; therefore, He was refused (Isa., Chpt. 53).

So, when James said, *"That you yourself also walk orderly, and keep the Law,"* as he referred to Paul, it was agreed to by Paul, but probably not in the same capacity or direction as understood by James.

(25) "AS TOUCHING THE GENTILES WHICH BELIEVE, WE HAVE WRITTEN AND CONCLUDED THAT THEY OBSERVE NO SUCH THING, SAVE ONLY THAT THEY KEEP THEMSELVES FROM THINGS OFFERED TO IDOLS, AND FROM BLOOD, AND FROM STRANGLED, AND FROM FORNICATION."

The way is:

1. The phrase, *"As touching the gentiles which believe,"* refers to followers of Christ.

2. *"We have written and concluded that they observe no such thing,"* released gentiles from obligation to the Mosaic Law, in other words, from having to become Jews in order to be saved, but, still, continued to present a dichotomy, which I think was not pleasing at all to the Lord.

3. *"Save only that they keep themselves from things offered to idols, and from blood, and from strangled, and from fornication,"* no doubt, constituted that given to James and the apostles by the Holy Spirit. In other words, it was right. (Please see Commentary on Acts, Chpt. 15.) However, this should have been the ruling for Jews as well!

4. As is obvious, at its very beginning, the early church consisted only of Jews, save for a few gentile proselytes. Despite the terrible opposition against Christ, with the Jewish leadership having bloody hands, multiple thousands in Jerusalem flocked to the banner of Christ, giving Him their hearts and lives, signifying that they believed He was really and truly the Messiah and had risen from the dead.

5. However, the Jewish part of the early church in Jerusalem slowly weakened and ultimately died simply because most were not willing to separate themselves from Jewish life, thereby, cutting all shorelines, which Jesus demanded, hence, the great Law/grace issue. As a result, even as is here obvious, the church ultimately became almost totally gentile and remains so unto this very day.

(26) "THEN PAUL TOOK THE MEN, AND THE NEXT DAY PURIFYING HIMSELF WITH THEM ENTERED INTO THE TEMPLE, TO SIGNIFY THE ACCOMPLISHMENT OF THE DAYS OF PURIFICATION, UNTIL THAT AN OFFERING SHOULD BE OFFERED FOR EVERY ONE OF THEM."

NOTES

The pattern is:

1. The phrase, *"Then Paul took the men,"* means that he acquiesced to the request of James, not only to go through the purification process but, as well, to stand good for the expenses of all the sacrifices which would be offered at the conclusion of the seven days.

2. I think one could say that Paul did this in the same capacity in which he circumcised Timothy (Acts 16:3), so as not to offend the Jews. As should be obvious, there was no spirituality in the circumcision.

3. Both the circumcision, which stood for separation, and the purification process of the Nazarite vow had no power within themselves to bring about true separation of the heart or purity of the heart. However, as symbolism in the Law of Moses, they served their purpose, as did all the other rudiments of the Law of Moses, by pointing to One Who would be able to do all of these things. As should be obvious, rituals and ceremonies have no power within themselves to bring about any type of change.

In effect, the Law of Moses, among all its other aspects, was beautiful in its application of symbolism, beautifully portraying the One Who would be able to effect these miraculous changes in the hearts and lives of men, which the Law could never bring about. However, as we have repeatedly stated, now that the Reality has come, the shadow is no longer needed, having served its purpose.

4. *"And the next day purifying himself with them entered into the Temple, to signify the accomplishment of the days of Purification,"* presents something which Paul had, no doubt, done many times in the past. But yet, I wonder what was going through his mind at this particular time. He must have had a heavy heart, realizing that the Jews in Jerusalem, who had accepted Christ as their Saviour, still, in a sense, did not seem to fully realize all that Jesus had actually done for them, and the whole of humanity for that matter. He fulfilled the Law in every respect, actually making its practical application unnecessary.

5. Why continue to offer up sacrifices when Jesus had already fulfilled the type by becoming the great Sacrifice?

6. Why laboriously continue to keep the Sabbath when the One Who the Sabbath represented had now come and provided a true rest for the people of God?

Nevertheless, so as not to broaden the schism that was already in the church, Paul would acquiesce to that of which James requested.

7. *"Until that an offering should be offered for every one of them,"* speaks of the sacrifices that were to be offered at the conclusion of the seven days. However, as we shall see, Paul never entered into that phase of the purification process due to the fact that he was arrested shortly. (Whether these four men followed through with the sacrifices, we are not told. As well, unless Paul had already paid for the sacrifices, quite possibly, they would now have to pay for their own.)

(27) "AND WHEN THE SEVEN DAYS WERE ALMOST ENDED, THE JEWS WHICH WERE OF ASIA, WHEN THEY SAW HIM IN THE TEMPLE, STIRRED UP ALL THE PEOPLE, AND LAID HANDS ON HIM."

The synopsis is:

1. The phrase, *"And when the seven days were almost ended,"* had to do with the seven days of preparation rather than the entirety of the days of the whole Nazarite vow. The *"vow,"* as stated, could be any length of time, even as the participant felt it should be.

2. *"The Jews which were of Asia,"* represented some of those who came from all over the Roman world of that day to keep the feasts in Jerusalem. This area of *"Asia"* would have included Ephesus, etc. Not only in this city, but others, as well, the Lord had helped Paul to build great churches, which angered the Jews very much. Of course, we are now speaking of the Christ-rejecting Jews and not the church in Jerusalem, which was also made up of Jews, but believers in Christ.

3. *"When they saw him in the Temple, stirred up all the people, and laid hands on him,"* speaks, as is obvious, of Paul being recognized by these people.

4. I wonder, *"Did it not cross Paul's*

NOTES

mind before he entered into the Temple that this possibly may happen?" Of all people, he knew of the tremendous influx of Jews from all over the Roman Empire, and that some of them surely would be from the very areas in which he had planted churches, and with great confrontation at times, I might quickly add!

5. Their laying their hands on him means that they bodily seized him.

(28) "CRYING OUT, MEN OF ISRAEL, HELP: THIS IS THE MAN, WHO TEACHES ALL MEN EVERY WHERE AGAINST THE PEOPLE, AND THE LAW, AND THIS PLACE: AND FURTHER BROUGHT GREEKS ALSO INTO THE TEMPLE, AND HAS POLLUTED THIS HOLY PLACE."

The structure is:

1. *"After the Spirit"* is a way of life (Rom. 8:1).

2. Romans 8:1 should have been translated, *"For they who are dominated by the flesh do mind the things of the flesh; but they who are dominated by the Spirit the things of the Spirit."*

THE TUMULT

The phrase, *"Crying out, Men of Israel, help,"* speaks of Paul and the others, all men, being in the innermost Court. Actually, the Temple in those times was surrounded by three Courts.

The innermost Court, as stated, was the Court of Israel. Here, the men could come as Israelites and offer sacrifices required by the Law. However, that was as far as the men could go. Only the consecrated priests could enter the Temple building itself, and only the high priest could enter into the inner sanctuary of the Temple proper, which, in effect, was the Holy of Holies. The high priest could then go into the Holy of Holies only on the great Day of Atonement. However, by this time, the great Day of Atonement was no longer kept because the Ark of the Covenant no longer occupied the Holy of Holies. In fact, it had been lost about 600 years before when Nebuchadnezzar took Jerusalem and destroyed the Temple. Some say that the Prophet Jeremiah took the Ark before the arrival of Nebuchadnezzar and hid it, where it remains unto this day; however, it has never yet been found.

THE COURT OF THE WOMEN

The second Court was the Court of the Women, so called because it was as far as women could go. Actually, the whole family could gather in this Court for prayer and worship, but if the men desired to go further into the inner Court, they must go alone, their wives not being able to follow them. Only Jews were allowed in these two Courts.

The outer Court was called the Court of the Gentiles because it was as far as gentiles could go. Actually, there was a barricade or low wall that separated the Court of Gentiles from the other Courts, and if any gentile ventured into the two Courts reserved for Jews only, he could be executed summarily.

This is what Paul was speaking of when he wrote, *"For He is our Peace, Who has made both one* (Jews and gentiles one in Christ), *and has broken down the middle wall of partition between us"* (Eph. 2:14). In other words, due to what Christ did at Calvary and the Resurrection, all, both Jews and gentiles, may now come to Christ, even into the Holy of Holies, so to speak.

"This is the man, who teaches all men every where against the people, and the Law, and this place," once again portrays one of Satan's favorite tactics of twisting what has actually been said to make it mean something else entirely.

Paul had not taught anyone anywhere against the Jews, the Law, or the Temple. That was not the idea at all!

If the truth be known, he did the very opposite. He always made it clear as to how important the Jews were in the great plan of God (Rom. 3:1-2) and how the Law had served its great and noble purpose (Rom. 7:7). As well, Paul held up the Tabernacle and the Temple as a *"Figure"* of the One Who was to come, Who would fulfill everything the Tabernacle and Temple represented (Heb. 9:8-9, 24). Actually, the Temple and the Law were only *"a shadow of good things to come"* (Heb. 10:1).

So, no one could rightly accuse Paul of denigrating these things, but rather portraying them in the best possible light, as having completed their task and served their purpose upon the arrival of the One they represented, the Lord Jesus Christ.

No, the anger of these Jews was not because of these things they were saying, but rather because of their hatred for Jesus Christ, Who Paul lifted up as the Messiah and the Fulfillment of all the prophecies and predictions.

THE LIE

The phrase, *"And further brought Greeks also into the Temple, and has polluted this Holy Place,"* was a false accusation entirely, even as the next verse reveals.

However, they little cared about the truth but only desired to say something that would enflame the people against Paul. Now it begins: all the things of which the Holy Spirit has warned Paul.

If one is to notice, these accusations leveled against Paul by these unbelieving Jews, at least in part, were very similar to the accusations leveled against him by the believing Jews of Verse 21. This, within itself, should serve notice as to how wrong all these charges were on both counts.

(29) "FOR THEY HAD SEEN BEFORE WITH HIM IN THE CITY TROPHIMUS AN EPHESIAN, WHOM THEY SUPPOSED THAT PAUL HAD BROUGHT INTO THE TEMPLE."

The overview is:

1. The phrase, *"For they had seen before with him in the city Trophimus an Ephesian,"* pertains to one of Paul's traveling associates as listed in Acts 20:4.

2. *"Whom they supposed that Paul had brought into the Temple,"* presents that which was totally wrong.

3. Just because he had been with Paul in the city the day before, it did not mean he was with him now, which he was not! Of course, in their thinking, to even be seen with a gentile was a serious breach of Mosaic principles, which, actually, it wasn't.

(30) "AND ALL THE CITY WAS MOVED, AND THE PEOPLE RAN TOGETHER: AND THEY TOOK PAUL, AND DREW HIM OUT OF THE TEMPLE: AND FORTHWITH THE DOORS WERE SHUT."

The account is:

1. The phrase, *"And all the city was moved,"* proclaims the news spreading like wildfire, claiming that Paul had brought a gentile into the innermost Court.

2. This tells us that Paul was very well known. Of course, that would be obvious, considering that he had ministered in many of the synagogues in Asia and Europe. As well, he was very controversial, being the focal point of much disturbance—disturbance, we might quickly add, which he did not foment, but was fomented by the Jews themselves as they rejected his message.

Why he was not recognized in the Temple until these seven days were almost complete is not known.

3. *"And the people ran together: and they took Paul, and drew him out of the Temple,"* actually means they dragged him out, beating him as they did so. He was dragged into the Court of the Gentiles, which was the outer Court.

4. *"And forthwith the doors were shut,"* referred to the doors between the Court of the Gentiles and the Court of Women. So, most probably, they would have dragged him from the inner Court through the Court of Women into the Court of Gentiles. However, it seems that no one noticed that no gentile was with him!

5. The gate mentioned here was probably the gate of Nicanor or the *"Beautiful Gate."* Horton said, *"It was the gift of a wealthy Alexandrian Jew named Nicanor. It was solid Corinthian bronze, some 75 feet high and 60 feet wide. It was beautifully carved and glittered like gold. From it, steps led down into the Court of the Gentiles."*

(31) "AND AS THEY WENT ABOUT TO KILL HIM, TIDINGS CAME UNTO THE CHIEF CAPTAIN OF THE BAND, THAT ALL JERUSALEM WAS IN AN UPROAR."

The way is:

1. The phrase, *"And as they went about to kill him,"* once again presents the twisted thinking of these people.

They would not kill Paul in the inner Court or the Court of Women because such would have defiled those Courts. However, they would feel no compunction whatsoever about killing him in the Court of the Gentiles because it was polluted already, inasmuch as it was reserved for gentile worshipers. They

NOTES

NOTES

did the same with Jesus.

2. The accusing Jews would not enter Pilate's Judgment hall on the Day of Passover because they would have been defiled in doing so. However, they could stand outside, screaming for the life of Christ, actually murdering Him, and feel no pang of conscience!

Such is religion! Such is why religion is so damnable!

3. Their whole world was wrapped up in rituals and ceremonies, which affected their hearts not at all, even as most of the world presently. Religion, which is *"rituals and ceremonies and rules and regulations,"* cannot effect a change in anyone simply because it deals with the outward. However, the problem of man is inward and does not really pertain to environment, geography, or association. Only Jesus can change the part of man which really needs changing, the heart.

4. These people fully intended to kill Paul and evidently were trying to do so by beating him. In other words, they were trying to beat him to death.

5. *"Tidings came unto the chief captain of the band, that all Jerusalem was in an uproar,"* pertained to the Roman Tribune, who commanded a cohort of approximately 1,000 soldiers, who were stationed in the tower of Antonia on the northwest side of the Temple, where the guards could overlook the Temple area. These soldiers were stationed there for the very purpose of preventing riots, which tells us that the Temple was ever a source of contention of one thing or the other.

(32) "WHO IMMEDIATELY TOOK SOLDIERS AND CENTURIONS, AND RAN DOWN UNTO THEM: AND WHEN THEY SAW THE CHIEF CAPTAIN AND THE SOLDIERS, THEY LEFT BEATING OF PAUL."

The account is:

1. The phrase, *"Who immediately took soldiers and centurions, and ran down unto them,"* probably represented about 200 men. A centurion was over 100 men, and as the plural is used, it must have been at least 200, which would have made quite a show of force.

2. At the time of the feasts, which took place three times a year (Passover, Pentecost, and Tabernacles), Jews came from all over the Roman Empire, with as many as 2,000,000 filling the city at these times. As well, Herod the Great had doubled the size of the Temple Courts, making room for all, which could probably hold several hundreds of thousands of people. It was during these times that Rome feared an uprising or disturbance of any sort, especially considering the great number of people involved. Consequently, they were quick to engage with force any disturbance that they feared could spread over the entirety of the city in a very short time.

3. Actually, Rome probably had more difficulties with the Jews than anyone else in their far-flung empire. So, they were quick to step in at the slightest hint of trouble.

4. *"And when they saw the chief captain and the soldiers, they left beating of Paul,"* no doubt, saved Paul's life.

5. These people ceased the beating of the apostle immediately because they knew the chief captain would take any steps he thought necessary to restore peace and order.

(33) "THEN THE CHIEF CAPTAIN CAME NEAR, AND TOOK HIM, AND COMMANDED HIM TO BE BOUND WITH TWO CHAINS; AND DEMANDED WHO HE WAS, AND WHAT HE HAD DONE."

The diagram is:

1. The phrase, *"Then the chief captain came near, and took him,"* pointed to Paul as the cause, or at least the principal figure, in this uprising.

2. *"And commanded him to be bound with two chains,"* simply refers to him being bound to a soldier on each side.

3. *"And demanded who he was, and what he had done,"* proclaims the captain seeking to find out what had happened.

4. The questions are logical: *"Who is Paul, and what has he done?"*

(34) "AND SOME CRIED ONE THING, SOME ANOTHER, AMONG THE MULTITUDE: AND WHEN HE COULD NOT KNOW THE CERTAINTY FOR THE TUMULT, HE COMMANDED HIM TO BE CARRIED INTO THE CASTLE."

The overview is:

1. The phrase, *"And some cried one thing, some another, among the multitude,"* generally proclaims the conduct of a mob,

for this is what the crowd now was!

2. Most of the people had no idea what had happened or was happening. This much is sure: had it not been for the Roman captain, these people would have beaten Paul to death.

3. However, the Lord was overseeing the situation in its entirety, as He always does respecting any or all of His Children. In other words, nothing can happen to a Child of God but that the Lord either causes it or allows it. Of course, the Lord did not cause the murderous hatred in the hearts of these Jews, but He did allow their actions, at least up to a certain point.

4. *"And when he could not know the certainty for the tumult, he commanded him to be carried into the castle,"* presents pandemonium, which is obvious, and from which the Roman captain could make little sense. Consequently, he gave instructions for Paul to be taken into the fortress or tower of Antonia.

(35) "AND WHEN HE CAME UPON THE STAIRS, SO IT WAS, THAT HE WAS BORNE OF THE SOLDIERS FOR THE VIOLENCE OF THE PEOPLE."

The synopsis is:

1. The phrase, *"And when he came upon the stairs,"* represents the stairs from the Temple area at the northwest corner to the castle of Antonia.

2. *"So it was, that he was borne of the soldiers for the violence of the people,"* represents the fact that the mob was pushing at Paul to such an extent, actually seeking to kill him, that in order to protect him, the soldiers were forced to lift him up, possibly even above their heads.

(36) "FOR THE MULTITUDE OF THE PEOPLE FOLLOWED AFTER, CRYING, AWAY WITH HIM."

The structure is:

1. The phrase, *"For the multitude of the people followed after,"* presents an extremely ugly situation, as is obvious.

2. *"Crying, Away with him,"* basically presents the cry of those who had thirsted for the blood of Jesus Christ (Lk. 23:18).

In looking at this scenario, one is presented with a perfect description of religion. In fact, these people who wanted to kill Paul were extremely religious. As well, the Temple and many of its functions were originally ordained by God. In fact, these very people, the Jews, had once been called *"God's chosen People"* (I Chron. 16:13; Ps. 33:12; Isa. 41:8).

So, what had happened?

3. The simple truth is that Israel gradually forsook the Lord and His Ways, which left them with nothing but a hollow shell of religion, which was actually satanic. This spiritual degeneration took place despite the Lord sending the prophets to them, even with repeated warnings.

4. Finally, despite the prophesying of Jeremiah, Judah went into total apostasy, with the Babylonians becoming their rulers. At that time, the scepter of world power passed from the faltering hands of the kings of Judah, in which that power had originally been placed by God, and was transferred to the gentile monarch, Nebuchadnezzar. From then on, a time period of approximately 600 years unto Christ, Israel remained under the gentile yoke and then continued under the Romans until they were destroyed as a nation in A.D. 70.

5. The crowning horror of their spiritual declension was, as is obvious, the Crucifixion of their Messiah and our Lord and Saviour, Jesus Christ. And yet, the Lord through the ministry of Paul at this time, even as we shall see, would give them one more opportunity to repent, but to no avail!

(37) "AND AS PAUL WAS TO BE LED INTO THE CASTLE, HE SAID UNTO THE CHIEF CAPTAIN, MAY I SPEAK UNTO YOU? WHO SAID, CAN YOU SPEAK GREEK?"

The composition is:

1. The phrase, *"And as Paul was to be led into the castle,"* undoubtedly presents the Holy Spirit speaking to Paul relative to what will now transpire.

2. The question, *"He said unto the chief captain, May I speak unto you?"* presents Paul speaking to the captain in the Greek language, which was actually the major language of the Roman Empire, and known by most, along with their own local language or dialect.

3. The question, *"Who said, Can you speak Greek?"* should not have been a surprise to the Roman captain. However, the next

NOTES

NOTES

verse probably explains his question.

(38) "ARE YOU NOT THAT EGYPTIAN, WHICH BEFORE THESE DAYS MADE AN UPROAR, AND LED OUT INTO THE WILDERNESS FOUR THOUSAND MEN WHO WERE MURDERERS?"

The composition is:

1. The beginning of the question, *"Are you not that Egyptian which before these days made an uproar...?"* portrays the mistaken identity of Paul by this captain.

2. Somehow, he had it in his mind that Paul was an Egyptian insurrectionist, who claimed to be a prophet, and who told his followers that the walls of Jerusalem would fall before them if they would help him attack the city, thereby, dislodging the Romans.

3. He is said to have attracted a following of approximately 30,000 Jews but was quickly overcome when the Roman governor suddenly came upon him with a large army of Roman soldiers, both infantry and cavalry. In this scrimmage, about 400 were killed and some 200 were taken prisoner, with the Egyptian and some of his associates escaping. Evidently, the Roman captain thought that the Egyptian could not speak the Greek language, hence, his question to Paul.

4. The conclusion of the question, *"And led out into the wilderness four thousand men who were murderers?"* seems to be the number among his 30,000 followers who proposed to storm the wall, etc.

(39) "BUT PAUL SAID, I AM A MAN WHICH AM A JEW OF TARSUS, A CITY IN CILICIA, A CITIZEN OF NO MEAN CITY: AND, I BESEECH YOU, SUFFER ME TO SPEAK UNTO THE PEOPLE."

The exegesis is:

1. The phrase, *"But Paul said, I am a man which am a Jew of Tarsus, a city in Cilicia, a citizen of no mean city,"* presents an entirely different scenario to the Roman captain, inasmuch as Tarsus was famous for philosophy and learning, and was regarded by many as equal in culture to Athens and Alexandria.

2. *"And, I beseech you, suffer me to speak unto the people,"* proclaims Paul, no doubt, impressed by the Holy Spirit to do this.

3. Knowing the Gospel of Jesus Christ as he did and being possibly the greatest Old Testament scholar in the world of that day, Paul, probably as no other man, knew the thin ice on which Israel was now standing as a nation. The shadows were long, and judgment was just over the horizon, a judgment, incidentally, which would be absolutely horrifying in its conclusion. Israel would literally cease to be a nation!

4. Consequently, Paul, no doubt feeling this, sensed that he must try to reach them some way, which he probably knew would be to no avail.

(40) "AND WHEN HE HAD GIVEN HIM LICENCE, PAUL STOOD ON THE STAIRS, AND BECKONED WITH THE HAND UNTO THE PEOPLE. AND WHEN THERE WAS MADE A GREAT SILENCE, HE SPOKE UNTO THEM IN THE HEBREW TONGUE, SAYING."

The account is:

1. The phrase, *"And when he had given him licence,"* means simply that the Roman captain allowed Paul to address the crowd.

2. The phrase, *"Paul stood on the stairs, and beckoned with the hand unto the people,"* presents, at least as far as is recorded, the last time the Holy Spirit would appeal to Israel as a nation.

3. *"And when there was made a great silence,"* speaks of more than the ordinary. I think it is obvious that the Holy Spirit was at work, moving upon the people in that which would be said, which would be of such great consequence. But yet, as we shall see, it would be rejected!

4. *"He spoke unto them in the Hebrew tongue, saying,"* probably represented the Syro-Chaldaic, which was the vernacular of the Hebrew Jews at that time, being the language the Jews brought back from Babylonia after their exile there in the sixth century B.C. Aramaic and Hebrew are closely related, actually belonging to the same branch of the Semitic family of languages.

5. However, it is possible that Paul was actually speaking in the ancient Biblical Hebrew, which was read every week in the synagogues.

6. So, it is entirely possible that the Holy Spirit addressed this last Message to Israel in their ancient native tongue. In other words, they had now come full circle.

"The sands of time are sinking,
"The dawn of Heaven breaks,
"The Summer morn I've sighed for,
"The fair sweet morn awakes:
"Dark, dark has been the midnight,
"But Dayspring is at hand,
"And Glory, Glory dwells in Emmanuel's Land."

"Oh, Christ He is the Fountain,
"The deep, sweet well of Love!
"The streams on earth I've tasted,
"More deep I'll drink above.
"There, to an ocean-fullness,
"His Mercy doth expand,
"And Glory, Glory dwells in Emmanuel's Land."

"With Mercy and with Judgment,
"My web of time He wove,
"And aye the dews of sorrow
"Were lustred with His Love.
"I'll bless the hand that guided,
"I'll bless the heart that planned,
"When throned where Glory dwells in Emmanuel's Land."

"The Bride eyes not her garment,
"But her dear Bridegroom's face:
"I will not gaze at Glory,
"But on my King of Grace
"Not at the crown He gives,
"But on His pierced Hand:
"The Lamb is all the Glory of Emmanuel's Land."

CHAPTER 22

(1) "MEN, BRETHREN, AND FATHERS, HEAR YOU MY DEFENCE WHICH I MAKE NOW UNTO YOU."

The pattern is:

1. The phrase, *"Men, brethren, and fathers,"* presents the beginning of Paul's final address to Israel, at least of which we have record, which would culminate the next day with the Sanhedrin. One might say and be totally correct that it was the last message given by the Holy Spirit to Israel.

2. This word would culminate that which began with Abraham approximately 2,000 years before. From his loins, God raised up a great nation for the purpose of giving the world the Word of God and to serve as the womb of the Messiah, the Redeemer of mankind. Israel, as well, was to evangelize the gentiles, for it was always God's Plan that all, the entirety of the world, be given the great Gospel message.

During this some 2,000 years, God worked miraculously and mightily with these people. He nurtured them into a great nation, who reached their zenith under David and Solomon, with both men being types of Christ. However, as checkered was Israel's past before David, as checkered would be her future!

3. In the closing days of the ministry of the Son of God, Israel's Messiah and the world's Redeemer, He said, *"O Jerusalem, Jerusalem, you who killed the prophets, and stoned them which are sent unto you, how often would I have gathered your children together, even as a hen gathers her chickens under her wings, and you would not!*

"Behold, your house is left unto you desolate" (Mat. 23:37-38).

The desolation of which Jesus spoke was now only about 10 years away.

4. But yet, even in that dire announcement, Jesus spoke of a coming glad day when Israel will finally be restored. He said, *"For I say unto you, you shall not see Me henceforth, till you shall say, 'Blessed is He who comes in the name of the Lord'"* (Mat. 23:39).

5. That great prediction has not yet been fulfilled but definitely will be at the Second Coming. At His First Coming, they cursed Him and crucified Him; however, at the Second Coming, they will *"bless"* Him!

6. Despite the treatment of Paul by his own countrymen, with them even desiring to kill him, he would address them with dignity and respect.

7. The phrase, *"Hear you my defence which I make now unto you,"* presents at least one of the greatest words they would ever hear, words I might quickly add, which haunt them unto this day, and which will do so forever. As stated, Paul was the instrument but the Holy Spirit was actually the Speaker.

NOTES

NOTES

(2) "AND WHEN THEY HEARD THAT HE SPOKE IN THE HEBREW TONGUE TO THEM, THEY KEPT THE MORE SILENCE: AND HE SAID."

The way is:

1. The phrase, *"And when they heard that he spoke in the Hebrew tongue to them,"* automatically demanded attention due to the language. Even though the ones trying to kill Paul knew he was a Jew, and knew it very well, most of the people in that huge crowd of thousands that day had little knowledge of what was actually happening. They may have even thought that Paul was a gentile who was desecrating their Temple. However, they now knew that was not the case!

2. *"They kept the more silence: And he said,"* spells a moment that was beyond the actual happenings of what was taking place. In brief, it was the Holy Spirit Who moved upon these proceedings, which brought about this *"silence,"* due to what Paul was about to say. So, as should be obvious, the Holy Spirit was working here in a powerful way, still trying to reach these people, who were on the very crumbling edge of doom.

(3) "I AM VERILY A MAN WHICH AM A JEW, BORN IN TARSUS, A CITY IN CILICIA, YET BROUGHT UP IN THIS CITY AT THE FEET OF GAMALIEL, AND TAUGHT ACCORDING TO THE PERFECT MANNER OF THE LAW OF THE FATHERS, AND WAS ZEALOUS TOWARD GOD, AS YOU ALL ARE THIS DAY."

The form is:

1. The entirety of the story of the Bible is the story of Jesus Christ and Him Crucified (Jn. 1:1-2, 14, 29).

2. Every Old Testament sacrifice pictured and portrayed the Lamb of God, Who would ultimately come into this world, and would die on a Cross for the sins of man.

PAUL'S DEFENSE

The phrase, *"I am verily a man which am a Jew, born in Tarsus, a city in Cilicia,"* presents Paul, I think, as proud of his native city, *"The famous capital of a Roman province,"* which was watered by the *"swift stream of the Cydnus,"* and looked down upon by the snowy summits of Mount Taurus.

"Yet brought up in this city at the feet of Gamaliel," automatically gave Paul credibility with the Jews.

First of all, Gamaliel, who had passed on by now, had been a member of the vaunted Sanhedrin, the civil and religious ruling body of Israel. As well, he was one of the best known, if not the most popular, rabbi of his day.

According to the Jewish Talmud, he was the grandson of the famous rabbi Hillel, who was also considered by many as one of the most outstanding rabbis in the history of the Pharisees.

The manner in which Paul used the term *"brought up"* could well mean that he came to Jerusalem in his early youth, possibly in his early teens, for the purpose of studying under Gamaliel. This alone tells us that the possibility at least existed that Paul's parents were of the wealthy class.

THE LAW OF THE FATHERS

The phrase, *"And taught according to the perfect manner of the Law of the fathers,"* lends much credence to the fact that Paul was a Mosaic Law scholar, that Gamaliel trained him not only in the Law of Moses but, as well, in all the traditions of the scribes and Pharisees.

Consequently, as we have stated, Paul was undoubtedly the most noted Hebrew scholar in the world of that day regarding the Law of Moses. In other words, his credentials, at least in that capacity, were impeccable.

"And was zealous toward God," proclaims his consecration, dedication, and zeal perhaps as no other, but for all his religious training at that time, he did not know God. Such characterizes so many in the modern church as well! To be religious, even very religious, in no way means that one is right. To study about God constantly in no way means that one knows God. Actually, the Lord cannot be found in that manner, even as Paul would traumatically come to see.

However, as a result of his upbringing, his training, and his zeal, he, as possibly no other man, knew what the Jews were doing, and he understood their opposition to Christ.

As we have previously stated, it is believed by some that Paul was looked at by Gamaliel, as well as other Jewish scholars, as the last great hope of Pharisaism, but was forever interrupted on the road to Damascus as Paul had a vision of Jesus.

A ZEAL FOR GOD

The phrase, *"As you all are this day,"* proclaims a zeal for God, even though lacking knowledge (Rom. 10:2).

Again, we emphasize that millions fall into this category presently. They are religious, even as the Jews of old, but are not truly born-again for the simple reason that a relationship with Christ does not come about by works, but rather by faith, and more particularly, faith in Christ and what He has done for us at the Cross.

Much religion, with all of its accouterments, activity, movement, business, and demands, makes men feel righteous, but sadly, it is a self-righteousness, which God can never accept.

It is bad enough to be an atheist and die lost, but worse still to talk about God constantly, be involved in what one thinks is His Work, and yet, die eternally lost. However, this is exactly the case with many who claim the Lord, even as the Jews of old!

In their own minds, the idea that they were not righteous and holy was totally preposterous! Considering that they were the chosen people of God, the people of the prophets, and the people of the Book, in their thinking, they were the righteousness of the world, and yet, they were lost!

How is it possible to be so immersed in that which is thought to be the things of God, and yet, not know Him?

How is it possible to be so deceived?

Actually, *"deception"* is the word! Satan has used this killer as no other, bringing about an unimagined harvest of lost souls, even though religious!

DECEPTION

There are several different Greek terms associated with the idea of deceit. The most common is *"planao,"* which means *"to lead astray or deceive by words or behavior."*

The New Testament almost always uses this word when speaking of the influence of false teachers. It is also the word chosen to speak of Satan's final effort to deceive at history's end. When the New Testament warns, *"Don't be deceived,"* this statement expresses the writer's concern, as inspired by the Holy Spirit, that we might be led away from the true ways of God.

Deception sometimes comes from within as our desires impel us to deceive. However, in the New Testament, deceit is more often error urged by external evil powers or by those locked into the world's way of thinking.

FALSEHOOD

There are some 15 different Greek words in the New Testament built on the root *"pseudo,"* which means *"to be false."* A verb of that root *"pseudomai"* means *"to deceive by lying."*

The concept underlying the truth-falsehood dichotomy in Scripture is important, particularly to those who live in a relativistic (what is relative) world that can erroneously speak of something as being *"true for you"* (that which is labeled subjective truth) while denying absolute (objective) truth.

OBJECTIVE TRUTH

The Bible clearly affirms objective truth, and it grounds that belief in the Biblical concept of God. God is Truth. (Objective truth is that which does not change simply because truth cannot change.)

All that God says is in strict accord with reality. His Words are, therefore, firm and trustworthy.

By contrast, we human beings are trapped in illusion. We struggle to understand the meaning of the world around us and of our experiences. However, unaided, we cannot distinguish between the real and the counterfeit, the truth and the lie.

Only reliance on God's Word, which is truth, and, in reality, the *"truth,"* enables us to build our lives on a firm foundation.

WHAT DECEPTION IS

Deception is anything that is the opposite of truth, with the most dangerous deception of all being that which contains truth, even much truth, but yet, with some error. Because of the obvious truth, it is swallowed eagerly by most! However, that which is error, even as small as it may be, and which Paul labeled as *"leaven,"* if not rooted out completely, will ultimately overtake and corrupt the whole (I Cor. 5:6-8).

DECEPTION AND SELF-WILL

As should be obvious, deception always springs from that other than God. In other words, there is no deception whatsoever in God, which should be overly obvious. However, there is deception in all else, irrespective of how religious it may be.

Self-will is the springboard for all deception, which speaks of a personal agenda or anything that is not instituted by the Lord. That is the reason Paul said, *"Let this mind be in you, which was also in Christ Jesus"* (Phil. 2:5).

It speaks of the *"mind"* of humility and a resultant obedience to God (Phil. 2:8). In essence, one can say that people are deceived simply because they want to be deceived. Their self-will pulls them in that direction, which speaks of that which is outside the Will of God.

Deception is always subtle because that is its very nature. The spirit of deception makes one think that the way is right when all the time, it is wrong. Hence, Solomon said, *"There is a way which seems right unto a man, but the end thereof are the ways of death"* (Prov. 14:12).

THE CAUSE OF THE FALL OF MAN

The reason man is so easily deceived, especially in the spiritual realm, is because this is the means by which Satan brought about the Fall. Paul wrote, *"But I fear, lest by any means, as the serpent beguiled* (deceived) *Eve through his subtilty* (subtlety), *so your minds should be corrupted from the simplicity that is in Christ"* (II Cor. 11:3).

Even as deception was the manner of the Fall, deception continues to plague the entirety of the human family. However, its true picture is not that man is plagued by deception, which he is, but that actually man is deception. In other words, deception inculcates itself through the entirety of man's spirit, soul, and being. That is at least

NOTES

one of the reasons that man cannot be won to Christ through the intellect, but instead, only by a revelation of Jesus Christ to the soul. Everything about man is deception, and consequently, he can do nothing but practice deception.

Man believes a lie because he is a liar! He deceives because he is deception! To be sure, that deception is so deep, so all encompassing, and so total, and in every capacity, that within himself, there is no way that man can climb out of this dilemma. In fact, he does not even know he is deceived, thinking all the time that what he is doing is right, or at least claiming he can change anytime he so desires. Of course, it is all a lie, but unredeemed man actually believes it is truth because he is deceived!

RELIGION THE GREATEST DECEIVER OF ALL

Even though deception springs from every pore of man's spirit and being, still, it is religion that deceives more than all. For most of the world that believes there is a God of some sort, almost all also believe they are saved, or else, they are on the plus side, whatever that is. Religion is the answer, they think, whether formulated by Satan or out of the deceitful hearts of men. Nevertheless, the end result is the same, deception!

In fact, all the great religions of the world, such as Islam, Buddhism, Shintoism, Confucianism, Hinduism, etc., are all and without exception *"a lie,"* i.e., *"deception."*

Even in the ranks of that which calls itself *"Christianity,"* deception oftentimes rules! That is what Paul addressed when he spoke of *"another Jesus, another spirit, or another gospel"* (II Cor. 11:4).

That means that these brands of religion, whatever they may be, are preaching *"Jesus,"* or at least some of them, but it is not the *"Jesus"* of the Bible. They have a *"spirit,"* but it is not the *"Holy Spirit."* As well, they present a *"gospel,"* but it is not the true *"Gospel"* of the Word of God.

For instance, hundreds of millions of Catholics speak of Jesus, but it is not the *"Jesus"* of the Bible. The same could be said for Mormonism, so-called Christian

Science, Jehovah's Witnesses, etc.

As well, even for those of us who claim to believe the Word of God in its entirety, with the proper fruit to prove those claims, still, we must ever be on guard against the subtlety of self-will, which automatically leads to self-righteousness, which God cannot accept.

THE CROSS, PROTECTION AGAINST DECEPTION

The Cross of Christ is actually the only real defense against the terrible blight of deception. That and that alone is the true Gospel of Jesus Christ (I Cor. 1:17).

Sometime before the creation of the universe, before the creation of this world, and, thereby, before the creation of man, God knew through foreknowledge that He would create all these things, and He knew that man would fall. So, it was determined by the Godhead in eternity past, before the foundation of the world, that man would be redeemed by God becoming man and, thereby, going to the Cross. There the sacrifice would be made, and the price would be paid for man's redemption. That makes the Cross of Christ the oldest doctrine in the Bible, actually, the foundational doctrine of all things that are holy. That means every Bible doctrine is built squarely on the foundation of the doctrine of the Cross (I Pet. 1:18-20).

Any doctrine that is spurious, that is specious, and that doesn't hold to the Cross, always and without exception, is in error. That means that all false doctrine begins with a wrong understanding of the Cross, an ignoring of the Cross, or an outright rejection of the Cross (Rom. 6:1-14; I Cor. 1:17-18, 23; 2:2; Col. 2:10-15; Gal. 6:14).

In fact, that is the reason so much false doctrine is rampant in the world today. It is because there has been so little preaching of the Cross that the church world, for all practical purposes, is presently Cross illiterate. This means they don't understand very much about the Bible because a proper understanding of the Cross is also a proper understanding of the Bible. The story of the Bible is the story of *"Jesus Christ and Him Crucified."* In fact, the *"Message of the Cross"* is that which the Holy Spirit is presently saying to the churches. That's the reason Jesus said, *"He who has an ear, let him hear what the Spirit says unto the churches"* (Rev. 2:11, 17, 29; 3:6, 13, 22).

NOTES

(4) "AND I PERSECUTED THIS WAY UNTO THE DEATH, BINDING AND DELIVERING INTO PRISONS BOTH MEN AND WOMEN."

The construction is:

1. The phrase, *"And I persecuted this way unto the death,"* proclaims this way of worshiping God, the Christian way of life (Acts 9:2; 18:25-26; 19:9, 23; 22:4; 24:14, 22).

2. It is believed by some that Paul's persecution of followers of Christ was much more severe than many have been led to believe. He used the word *"death"* as it related to that time in his life, linking it to the persecution he leveled against believers. So, the idea is that his persecution of many consisted of much more than just imprisonment, but that many, or at least some, paid with their lives.

Even though he may not have been the one who actually threw the stone or administered the fatal blow, still, he was responsible! The idea is there were many empty places at many tables, and all because of Paul.

3. The phrase, *"Binding and delivering into prisons both men and women,"* proclaims that he showed no mercy.

4. How can religious men kill people in the name of the Lord, actually believing that what they are doing is of the Lord?

Once again, the answer is *"deception!"*

5. Paul laid the groundwork for what he would say by acknowledging that where these Jews presently were, desiring to kill him, in that place, that very place, he once was, as well! So, he could empathize with them, and hopefully, they would now more so understand him.

(5) "AS ALSO THE HIGH PRIEST DOES BEAR ME WITNESS, AND ALL THE ESTATE OF THE ELDERS: FROM WHOM ALSO I RECEIVED LETTERS UNTO THE BRETHREN, AND WENT TO DAMASCUS, TO BRING THEM WHICH WERE THERE BOUND UNTO JERUSALEM, FOR TO BE PUNISHED."

NOTES

The status is:

1. The phrase, *"As also the high priest does bear me witness,"* is not clear exactly if Paul was referring to the high priest at the time of his conversion or now at the time of this mob action. He was probably speaking of the high priest now, who would, of course, have knowledge of that which happened to Paul, even though it had been approximately 25 years before.

2. *"And all the estate of the elders,"* speaks of the Jewish Sanhedrin, made up of some 71 members.

3. *"From whom also I received letters unto the brethren,"* speaks of that recorded in Acts 9:1-2.

These *"letters"* were given by the Sanhedrin to Paul and granted him authority to do whatever was necessary to apprehend the followers of Christ.

4. *"And went to Damascus,"* proclaims that which did not turn out as Paul had expected.

5. This foray to Damascus proclaimed Paul, at that time Saul, branching out from Jerusalem, showing that this crusade was deadly serious and was meant to stop *"this Way,"* and he was to use any means necessary to accomplish the task.

6. *"To bring them which were there bound unto Jerusalem, for to be punished,"* referred to being beaten or incarcerated, or both, or possibly even executed.

(6) "AND IT CAME TO PASS, THAT, AS I MADE MY JOURNEY, AND WAS COME NIGH UNTO DAMASCUS ABOUT NOON, SUDDENLY THERE SHONE FROM HEAVEN A GREAT LIGHT ROUND ABOUT ME."

The order is:

1. The phrase, *"And it came to pass, that, as I made my journey,"* would turn out to be a journey of unprecedented proportions, a visitation from the Lord of such magnitude that it would change Paul for time and eternity. He would draw near to Damascus as a hater of the Lord Jesus Christ, and then go the last short distance into the city as a totally changed man, a follower of the Lord as possibly there has never been in history.

2. What could change a person to this extent and this quickly?

As we shall see, the answer is Jesus!

3. The phrase, *"And was come near unto Damascus about noon,"* presents that which was high noon to Paul, and he would be the one to bite the dust, to use a modern vernacular.

4. *"Suddenly there shone from heaven a great light round about me,"* would be later described by him as brighter than the noonday sun (Acts 26:13).

5. Without a doubt, these people must have wondered what could have changed Paul so dramatically from that which he had been unto that which he was now.

6. This testimony is the answer to that question. This is an appearance of Christ in His Glory, which is the same Glory in which He will return to this Earth (Mat. 24:27).

(7) "AND I FELL UNTO THE GROUND, AND HEARD A VOICE SAYING UNTO ME, SAUL, SAUL, WHY DO YOU PERSECUTE ME?"

The direction is:

1. The phrase, *"And I fell unto the ground,"* presents the power of God so strong that Paul could not maintain his feet. This was the same power that filled the Temple when it was dedicated about 1,000 years before *"so that the priests could not stand to minister because of the cloud* (in other words, they fell): *for the Glory of the LORD had filled the House of the LORD"* (I Ki. 8:11).

2. Even though there has been abuse concerning this which I am about to say, still, that does not take away from the reality of the power of God moving upon people to such an extent, even at this present time, that they simply fall, unable to stand!

3. The question, *"And heard a voice saying unto me, Saul, Saul, why do you persecute Me?"* portrays the following:

a. When those who belong to God are opposed, it is the same as God being opposed! During those times, Paul did not for a moment consider himself to be opposing God; however, he did consider himself opposing the Lord Jesus Christ, Whom he believed to be an impostor. Regrettably, many follow in his footsteps, opposing that which is of God, thinking all the time they are doing

NOTES

the very opposite.

(8) "AND I ANSWERED, WHO ARE YOU, LORD? AND HE SAID UNTO ME, I AM JESUS OF NAZARETH, WHOM YOU PERSECUTE."

The exegesis is:

1. The question, *"And I answered, Who are You, Lord?"* was not meant as a mere expression of respect on the part of Paul, but rather that this appearance was of such trauma that Paul knew that it was deity to Whom he was speaking, hence, the appellative *"Lord!"*

2. *"And He said unto me, I am Jesus of Nazareth,"* describes the Lord using the very name hated so much by Paul. However, so that no mistake would be made, the Lord used the full name, *"Jesus of Nazareth."* Consequently, He pointedly identified Himself as the very One they crucified a short time before.

3. As well, when Paul related his testimony to this great crowd and then plainly and clearly used the name *"Jesus of Nazareth,"* Whom they hated as much as he had hated Him before, such proclaimed that Paul was not at all ashamed of that name, but rather gloried in its expression and wonder, irrespective of what anyone thought.

4. *"Whom you persecute,"* proclaims the Lord making this statement the second time. When men persecute Christians, they persecute Christ (Mat. 19:29).

(9) "AND THEY THAT WERE WITH ME SAW INDEED THE LIGHT, AND WERE AFRAID; BUT THEY HEARD NOT THE VOICE OF HIM WHO SPOKE TO ME."

The synopsis is:

1. The phrase, *"And they that were with me saw indeed the light, and were afraid,"* tells us that all of Paul's testimony could be confirmed by witnesses.

2. When men have a revelation of the Lord in some manner, even as here, it always strikes fear to their hearts. The reason is simple!

3. God is a thrice-Holy God, and man is sinful. As a result, perfect holiness automatically strikes fear to the sinful heart. This is a result of the fallen nature of man, meaning that he little more represents his Creator, but now, the Evil One himself, Satan!

4. The absolute holiness of God has very little representation on Earth, even among those who are truly His. As a result, man quickly loses his fear of God, until there is a demonstration, as it was that day, on the road to Damascus.

5. As well, even though these men saw the light, they did not actually see Jesus. Paul saw both the light and Jesus (I Cor. 15:8).

6. In this, we see the power of the Lord Jesus Christ. All the intellectual arguments in the world could not have changed Paul's mind regarding Jesus; however, one glimpse of Him would change this man instantly for time and eternity.

7. Far too many people see only the church or preachers, or maybe they have seen a philosophy or a religion, but none of these things will slake the spiritual thirst of man, and neither can they do so. However, a revelation of Christ to the soul will forever change one. Paul saw Jesus, and he would never be the same again!

8. The phrase, *"But they heard not the voice of Him Who spoke to me,"* seems to be a contradiction, for the account in Acts 9:7 says, *"And the men which journeyed with him stood speechless, hearing a voice, but seeing no man."* However, the seeming contradiction is cleared up when we understand that *"sound"* and *"voice"* are the same word in Greek.

9. It should have been translated, *"They did not hear what the voice said, they only heard the sound."*

(10) "AND I SAID, WHAT SHALL I DO, LORD? AND THE LORD SAID UNTO ME, ARISE, AND GO INTO DAMASCUS; AND THERE IT SHALL BE TOLD YOU OF ALL THINGS WHICH ARE APPOINTED FOR YOU TO DO."

The status is:

1. Who Jesus was (the Son of God) and what He did (the Cross) were both necessary in order for man to be saved.

2. Man is saved because Jesus Christ was the perfect Sacrifice offered up on Calvary's Cross.

WHAT SHALL I DO LORD?

The question, *"And I said, What shall I do, Lord?"* tells us several things:

• Inasmuch as Paul now called Jesus *"Lord,"* with full knowledge of Who He was, it makes it clear that he immediately accepted Jesus as the divine Lord and, also, as the Lord of his life. In other words, that is the moment that Paul was *"born-again."*

• Immediately and forever Paul placed himself in the hands of Jesus for the Lord to do with him as He liked! He never veered from that for the rest of his life.

• In the manner in which Paul related this glorious incident, he, in effect, was telling the crowd of Jews that day that Jesus Christ, the One they crucified, was, in fact, the Jehovah of the Old Testament.

"Lord" was the title the Jews used to refer to God the Father in their reading of the Scriptures and in their worship in the synagogues. This does not mean that Paul was identifying Jesus as the same Person as God the Father, but it does mean he was recognizing Jesus as God, as divine.

THE LORD SPOKE TO PAUL

Horton said, *"'And the Lord said unto me, Arise, and go into Damascus,' is so structured in the Greek, that it refers to everything set in motion by the Lord concerning Paul. In other words, it had been appointed, ordered, and commanded for him in advance, and, in fact, continued to be so even unto the end of his life."*

"And there it shall be told you of all things which are appointed for you to do," proclaims the plan of God for Paul's life and ministry, with that plan now being put into motion.

In fact, this was not only true for Paul, but it is true for all believers. In other words, God has a plan for every single believer that is tailor-made for one's life and ministry. Yes, every believer has a ministry.

David said, concerning this very thing, *"The Lord is the portion of my inheritance and of my cup: You maintain my lot.*

"The lines are fallen unto me in pleasant places; yea, I have a goodly heritage" (Ps. 16:5-6).

The *"lines"* concern the blueprint for David's life as designed by the Lord. It is the same for all believers!

NOTES

GOD'S PLAN

The idea is that the believer earnestly seek the Lord in order that God's Plan be revealed to the individual, which it certainly shall be if one will only ask and seek.

The most beautiful, wonderful, and fulfilling life is to ascertain God's Plan for one's life and to function in that plan, carrying out that which the Lord has ordained. The sadness is that many, if not most, believers not only do not properly function in that which the Lord has designed for them, but most do not even know what that plan is. That is such a shame when a little diligence and consecration will cause it to be revealed (Ps. 37:23; 119:33; Acts 20:24; I Cor. 3:16).

Even though we briefly dealt with this in Acts, Chapter 20, this subject of the plan of God for each and every believer is so very important that, hopefully, some small repetition will stress its significance to an even greater degree.

(11) "AND WHEN I COULD NOT SEE FOR THE GLORY OF THAT LIGHT, BEING LED BY THE HAND OF THEM WHO WERE WITH ME, I CAME INTO DAMASCUS."

The status is:

1. The phrase, *"And when I could not see for the glory of that light,"* presents connotations of the Shekinah, the divine manifestation of glory and light in the Old Testament. In other words, this was similar to the *"fire"* or *"light"* which covered the Tabernacle at night while the children of Israel were in the wilderness. It was unmistakably the power of God and something which could not be refuted. Paul knew this was the Lord beyond the shadow of a doubt!

2. This *"light"* represented not only His Power and Glory but, as well, the true illumination which only the Truth, Who is Jesus Christ, can bring forth.

3. The phrase, *"Being led by the hand of them who were with me, I came into Damascus,"* presents Paul coming into the city in an entirely different posture than he had heretofore reckoned.

4. What a sight this must have been! This lion of the Law, this former hater of Christ, who was coming to hail the saints to prison or worse, was now led by the hand,

totally helpless, the posture to which he had been reduced.

5. The world is full of men pitting themselves against God, with all, sooner or later, humbled in one way or the other. Regrettably, most do not even understand that it is God Who does the humbling, but, to be sure, that in no way lessens His involvement.

6. Even though it is not related here, we are told in Acts, Chapter 9, that Paul went to a street called *"Straight"* and was taken into the house of one called Judas (Acts 9:11).

7. Who this Judas was, we are not told. As well, how Paul knew to go to this place, we are uninformed, that is, unless he was led there by the Lord, which very well could have been the case.

(12) "AND ONE ANANIAS, A DEVOUT MAN ACCORDING TO THE LAW, HAVING A GOOD REPORT OF ALL THE JEWS WHICH DWELT THERE."

The order is:

1. The phrase, *"And one Ananias, a devout man according to the Law,"* presents this man as chosen by the Lord for a tremendously important task and, as well, a follower of Christ. (This is not the Ananias of Acts 5:1-8 but the same one as in Acts 9:17-18).

2. *"Having a good report of all the Jews which dwelt there,"* specifies one who it seems was accepted by all. In other words, he was a follower of Christ but still was loved and respected by the Jews who were not friendly to Christ.

(13) "CAME UNTO ME, AND STOOD, AND SAID UNTO ME, BROTHER SAUL, RECEIVE YOUR SIGHT. AND THE SAME HOUR I LOOKED UP UPON HIM."

The construction is:

1. The phrase, *"Came unto me, and stood, and said unto me, Brother Saul, receive your sight,"* presents Paul being healed, and it seems he was also baptized with the Holy Spirit at this time with the evidence of speaking with other tongues (Acts 9:17).

2. *"And the same hour I looked up upon him,"* reflects his eyes being completely healed. Acts 9:18 says, *"There fell from his eyes as it had been scales."*

3. Quite possibly, the Lord placed the scales over Paul's eyes in order to shield them from the great light which did shine and would have blinded him otherwise.

4. Incidentally, from the manner in which Ananias addressed Paul as *"brother,"* it shows us that these terms *"brother"* and *"sister"* were already becoming meaningful to Christians. They recognized that whether they were Jew or gentile, they were in the family of God, which is the greatest family in the world.

(14) "AND HE SAID, THE GOD OF OUR FATHERS HAS CHOSEN YOU, THAT YOU SHOULD KNOW HIS WILL, AND SEE THAT JUST ONE, AND SHOULD HEAR THE VOICE OF HIS MOUTH.

(15) "FOR YOU SHALL BE HIS WITNESS UNTO ALL MEN OF WHAT YOU HAVE SEEN AND HEARD."

The structure is:

1. Before man could be redeemed, God had to become Man, and He had to do so for the purpose of going to the Cross.

2. It was the Cross alone which made redemption possible.

CHOSEN

In the two verses above, we are given the fivefold commission of the Apostle Paul. It is very revealing that this part of the account was not given in Acts, Chapter 9, and neither did Paul mention it in the account given in Acts 26:13-18. This fivefold calling is as follows:

"And he said, The God of our fathers has chosen you":

The word *"chosen"* in the Greek text is *"procheirizomai"* and means *"to handle in advance or to purpose."*

It actually refers to the Lord having chosen Paul for a particular task even before he was born and, to be frank, probably in eternity past. In a sense, this is predestination but necessary of qualification.

God does not predestine anyone respecting a violation of his will. However, He does predestinate according to foreknowledge. In other words, the Lord, Who is Omniscient (All-knowing), has the ability to look down through time and foreknow what an individual will do without tampering with his will. In this sense, the Lord predestined Paul for this cause and purpose, knowing through foreknowledge that Paul would acquiesce to the heavenly vision and immediately set himself to do that which the Lord wanted and desired.

THE CALLING

So, his *"calling"* was decided in the high counsels of heaven, as is every God-called person, with no human instrumentation involved. Consequently, we are speaking of the highest calling that one could ever have, which speaks of being called by God in whatever capacity.

When Ananias used the title *"fathers,"* he was actually saying that Paul's calling was in line with all the predictions of the prophets and, in fact, not only did not violate the Word of God, but rather fulfilled that great and glorious Word.

So, Paul was not only not operating outside of the great predictions of the prophets of old, but rather was instrumental under God in fulfilling these prophecies.

TO KNOW THE WILL OF GOD

The Lord had a *"will"* for Paul's life exactly as He has for every single believer who has ever lived.

It was absolutely imperative that Paul learn what the will of God was. To be frank, there is absolutely nothing more important than this. Each believer, that is, if he is not already aware what God's Will actually is, should earnestly seek the face of the Lord until it is abundantly clear as to exactly what the Lord wants.

There is such a thing as a *"permissive will,"* but not for human beings. For instance, when Satan led his revolution against God, the Lord permitted him to do this for reasons of His Own. However, when it comes to believers, God has only one will, and that is a perfect will.

The Scripture plainly says, *"That you may prove what is that good, and acceptable, and perfect, will of God"* (Rom. 12:2).

We are told here that it is only the *"perfect will of God"* that is *"good and acceptable."*

The ultimate goal of any believer is to know the will of God for his or her life and then to carry out that will by the help and grace of God.

NOTES

THE LORD JESUS CHRIST

"And see that Just One":

Jesus Christ was to be the Focal Point, the Intersection, the Foundation, and the Epitome of all that Paul would see and know.

The idea of the appellative *"Just One"* refers to Jesus Christ and Jesus Christ alone!

This type of phraseology would not be used of deity but only of a man, not just any man, but rather *"the Man, Christ Jesus."*

In other words, Jesus is the only *"Just One"* Who has ever lived. There is no other!

It is to be ever understood that Christianity is not a philosophy, but rather a Man, the Lord Jesus Christ. Consequently, the preacher must preach Jesus. He must preach Jesus as the Saviour, the Baptizer with the Holy Spirit, the Healer, the Miracle-Worker, the Overcomer, the Victory, the Power, the Grace, and the Glory. He must, as well, preach Jesus as coming again!

However, the preacher cannot preach Jesus in these capacities, in fact, in any capacity, until he first knows Jesus as Saviour and Lord. I speak of relationship. To know Him is one thing; to know Him in a very personal, intimate way is something else again.

THE VOICE OF HIS MOUTH

The appearance of Jesus to Paul was not a dream, a vision, etc. Jesus, in literal, bodily form, appeared to him and spoke with him. This means that Jesus came to Paul in just as real and literal a way as He did to the other apostles after His Resurrection. This made Paul a witness to His Resurrection on the same level as those who saw Him alive before His Ascension.

As well, this was not the only time that Jesus would appear to Paul. Actually, He would do so again not long after Paul's conversion, even as Verses 17 and 18 proclaim. Also, Paul would see Jesus again very shortly after this particular address to the Jews (Acts 23:11).

HIS WITNESS

"For you shall be His Witness unto all men of what you have seen and heard": this

NOTES

speaks of his great commission to take the Gospel to the world of that day, which he did! This meant both Jews and gentiles.

It should be obvious that Paul had *"seen"* something and had *"heard"* something, hence, he was to proclaim, which he did, what he had *"witnessed."*

Our problem presently is, and perhaps always has been, that too many preachers have not *"seen"* anything or *"heard"* anything. Consequently, they are not much of a witness, which should be overly obvious.

Any person who has *"seen"* the Lord in some way, whether literal, visible, or merely a moving of the Holy Spirit upon one's heart and life, at the same time, will always *"hear"* something. The Lord never moves upon people but that He brings a message of vast significance.

My cry is to *"see"* Him and to *"hear"* Him, for then and then only will I have something to say!

The answer of Peter and John to the Sanhedrin when commanded to cease preaching or teaching in the name of Jesus, was, *"For we cannot but speak the things which we have seen and heard"* (Acts 4:20).

It should be obvious here that Paul had a revelation and an experience, which are sorely needed, rather than more theological degrees behind preachers' names, which speak to the situation not at all.

(16) "AND NOW WHY DO YOU TARRY? ARISE, AND BE BAPTIZED, AND WASH AWAY YOUR SINS, CALLING ON THE NAME OF THE LORD."

The diagram is:

1. Anything and everything that we as believers receive from the Lord, all and without exception are made possible by the Cross of Christ.

2. The Cross of Christ changed everything because it atoned for all sin, at least for all who will believe (Jn. 3:16).

WATER BAPTISM

The question, *"And now why do you tarry?"* pertains to Ananias, in essence, telling Paul that it was time to begin. He had already been saved, healed, and baptized with the Holy Spirit, and now he must be baptized in water as a symbol of his new-found Life in Christ.

The phrase, *"Arise, and be baptized, and wash away your sins, calling on the name of the Lord,"* refers to a present action, but being done because of a past action. In other words, one is not baptized in water in order to wash away sins, but rather because the sins have already been washed away by the precious Blood of the Lord Jesus Christ.

The idea of the Text is the same as Acts 2:38, which says, *"Repent, and be baptized every one of you in the name of Jesus Christ for the remission of sins ..."*

The word *"for"* in the Greek text is *"eis"* and means *"because of remission of sins."* In other words, you are to be baptized in water because your sins have already been remitted, i.e., *"washed away."*

The translation could have been, *"Be baptized, because your sins have been washed away as you called on the name of the Lord!"*

MORE ABOUT WATER BAPTISM

As it regards the New Covenant, water baptism is to the church somewhat as the Rite of Circumcision was under the Old Covenant. Circumcision was the physical sign of the Old Covenant, while water baptism is the physical sign regarding the New Covenant. However, we must always remember that the ceremony itself, irrespective as to how important the symbol might be, contains within its action no salvation.

In other words, Jews were not saved simply because they circumcised all the little baby boys at eight days old, with, of course, all the men also being circumcised. In fact, circumcision pointed to the Cross, which was to come. There was a cutting of the flesh, which symbolized separation from our own personal efforts and trusting entirely in Christ, and blood was shed, which typified the sacrifice of Christ, which, of course, was to come.

While the Rite of Circumcision pointed to that which was to come, water baptism, also a symbol, points to that which has already come.

In other words, while those in Old Testament times looked forward to a prophetic

Jesus, we look back to a historical Jesus.

Water baptism typifies the death, burial, and resurrection of Christ, and our death, burial, and resurrection, which portrays us *"in Christ"* (Rom. 6:3-5). As the Rite of Circumcision could not save, likewise, the ordinance of water baptism contains no salvation either! We must never get our eyes on the type, symbol, ordinance, or rite, but rather on the One Whom these things represent, namely, the Lord Jesus Christ.

AN IMPROPER UNDERSTANDING OF THE CROSS

Everything that we have in Christ comes to us exclusively through what He did for us at the Cross. No exceptions! While everything else that pertains to Christianity is certainly important, even as water baptism, still, it is faith in Christ and the Cross that brings about salvation and sanctification, with all of its overcoming victory.

Satan is a past master at shifting the faith of believers from the correct object of Christ and the Cross to other things. He doesn't too much care what those other things are, just as long as it isn't the Cross.

That's why Paul said the following:

"Is Christ divided? (Is there a Baptist Christ, a Pentecostal Christ, or a Holiness Christ? The answer is a solid *'No.'*) *Was Paul crucified for you?* (The apostle rebukes the partisanship which attached itself to his own name.) *or were you baptized in the name of Paul?* (This proclaims the idea that he had never attempted to draw away Disciples after himself, but rather to Christ.)

PAUL'S STATEMENT ABOUT WATER BAPTISM

"I thank God that I baptized none of you, but Crispus and Gaius (if water baptism were essential to salvation, as some claim, I hardly think Paul would have blatantly announced that he only had baptized these few, as he did here);

"Lest any should say that I had baptized in mine own name (nothing must be done to draw away allegiance from Christ).

"And I baptized also the household of Stephanas: besides, I know not whether I baptized any other (informs us that the inspiration of the apostles in writing the Scriptures involved none of the mechanical infallibility ascribed to them by popular dogma).

"For Christ sent me not to baptize (presents to us a cardinal truth), *but to preach the Gospel* (the manner in which one may be saved from sin): *not with wisdom of words* (intellectualism is not the Gospel), *lest the Cross of Christ should be made of none effect.* (This tells us in no uncertain terms that the Cross of Christ must always be the emphasis of the Message.) (I Cor. 1:13-17).

If water baptism was needed for one to be saved, I hardly think that Paul would have made the statements that he did. While it most definitely is important, it is never to be thought of as saving grace, which can only come by and through the Cross.

(17) "AND IT CAME TO PASS, THAT, WHEN I WAS COME AGAIN TO JERUSALEM, EVEN WHILE I PRAYED IN THE TEMPLE, I WAS IN A TRANCE."

The construction is:

1. The phrase, *"And it came to pass, that, when I was come again to Jerusalem,"* pertains to Acts 9:26.

In this account, Paul omitted his experience in Damascus immediately after his conversion, even with the Jews then wanting to kill him.

His account of Jerusalem here speaks of the time that *"Barnabas took him, and brought him to the apostles"* (Acts 9:27).

2. While he was in Jerusalem at that time, he now relates an experience which took place in the Temple, which was not mentioned by Luke in the Acts, Chapter 9, account.

3. The phrase, *"Even while I prayed in the Temple, I was in a trance,"* speaks of his high regard for the Temple and, at the same time, refutes the accusation of some of the Jews that he was now polluting the Temple, etc.

The word *"trance"* in the Greek text, as it is used here, is *"ekstasis"* and means *"a displacement of the mind, bewilderment, amazement or astonishment."*

It does not here refer to being unconscious of one's surroundings, as it can sometimes mean.

NOTES

4. Paul was overwhelmed by another appearance of Christ to him at this time and, as well, was seemingly somewhat chagrined concerning the message given to him by the Lord regarding the hatred of the Jews for him. He seemed to think, as we shall see, that considering what he had recently been regarding his opposition to Jesus, surely they would hear his message. However, he was to find out, that was not the case.

(18) "AND SAW HIM SAYING UNTO ME, MAKE HASTE, AND YOU GET QUICKLY OUT OF JERUSALEM: FOR THEY WILL NOT RECEIVE YOUR TESTIMONY CONCERNING ME."

The overview is:

1. When we speak of the Cross of Christ and what was there accomplished, we aren't speaking of the wooden beam on which Jesus died.

2. We are speaking of what He there accomplished, which was to atone for all sin, past, present, and future, at least for all who will believe, and, as well, defeat every power of darkness (Col. 2:10-15).

THE APPEARANCE OF CHRIST TO PAUL

The phrase, *"And saw Him saying unto me,"* represents Jesus appearing to Paul as he was praying in the Temple. As we have stated, this pertained to years before, which took place very shortly after his conversion.

During these times, I wonder what was in Paul's mind respecting Jesus, considering that the Lord had appeared unto him twice now in a matter of days, the first time being his conversion on the road to Damascus.

Experiencing the mighty power of God, plus the constant nearness of Jesus Christ, which fulfilled the cry of his soul as he had never known before, I am positive he must have wondered how he could have previously been so blind! Considering how real, wonderful, glorious, and how ever present that Jesus Christ was, and how obvious all of this now was, why did he not see it at the outset?

Now it was so clear to him how Jesus did fit all the prophecies of old, all the symbols of the Tabernacle and Temple, and especially of the Law of Moses. But yet, he was totally blind to these things, even as obvious as they were, before the great revelation of Christ, which resulted in his instant conversion.

NOTES

DECEPTION

In fact, why does almost all the world, and for all time, walk in spiritual darkness despite the preponderance of evidence reflecting Jesus Christ and His Deity?

As we have already stated, the answer is spiritual deception. It is such a powerful weapon in the hands of Satan and so all-encompassing in its darkness, in fact, far more powerful than anyone realizes.

As well, deception is fed by man's fallen condition. Man is altogether dead in trespasses and sins and, as such, has absolutely no true spiritual perception, irrespective of how much religion he may have as a covering.

However, even in a totally fallen state, still, there is a faint image of God left in man, which causes him to desire to worship in some capacity, although totally wrong. So, in this deception, he reaches out toward something which will appease his guilt and conscience because guilt is ever with him, which he cannot explain!

So, Paul was zealous in his Judaism, even as wrongly interpreted as it was, and even as much of the world in their own particular religions.

THE WORD OF GOD AND THE POWER OF THE HOLY SPIRIT

The only way that this spiritual darkness can be penetrated is by a revelation of Jesus Christ to the soul, brought about by the Word of God in some capacity, through the illumination and convicting power of the Holy Spirit. Then and then alone can man see his true spiritual condition, understanding that he is without God and without Hope!

Now, some may argue that Paul did not have the Word of God ministered to him at his conversion; however, that is totally incorrect.

Chapter 7 of Acts graphically describes the great message preached by Stephen, which caused him to be stoned to death. Paul heard that message! For a certainty, and especially considering that it was the

Word of God preached with a powerful anointing and moving of the Holy Spirit, there is no way that Paul could not have been greatly stirred and moved upon by what he had heard that day. As we have previously stated, as the convicting power of the Holy Spirit settled upon him, he responded, as many do, by fighting out, even to a greater degree, against that which is of the Lord. In other words, in his case, he went on a rampage against the followers of Christ (Acts 9:1-2). However, the Word had been given, and it would ultimately bring forth its fruit, irrespective of Paul's rebellion.

ANOTHER CASE IN POINT

Among all the myriad of examples of deception, the modern Catholic Church is a prime example.

Back in 1997, I believe it was, the leadership of the Catholic Church, headed up by the pope, strongly attempted to bring about the deification of Mary, claiming that she is a co-redemptorist with Jesus Christ, the Son of God. In effect, they were attempting to make, and in principle have already made, a quadrinity of deity versus the Biblical Trinity.

Worse still, and which is already being done in principle, the Catholic religious system, whether admitted or not, is made up of, *"God the Holy Mother, God the Father, God the Son, and God the Holy Spirit."*

Not only is Mary worship unscriptural and, therefore, ungodly, worse still, Mary is placed first.

Considering that there is not a shred of Biblical evidence concerning the Catholic worship and deification of Mary, where in the world do they get the idea that to be saved, one has to go to Christ through Mary?

It is certain that they do not get it out of the Bible. Therefore, they are simply making up these things about Mary out of whole cloth, even as the entirety of Catholicism is unscriptural.

How can they project such when the Bible plainly says, *"For there is one God, and one Mediator between God and men, the Man Christ Jesus; Who gave Himself a ransom for all, to be testified in due time?"* (I Tim. 2:5-6).

NOTES

They do such because they do not believe the Bible, despite their claims otherwise.

Regrettably, this example I have just given is only one among many traveling this road of deception and, consequently, leading millions astray and, regrettably, will only grow worse!

The only answer to all of this is exactly that which happened to Paul: we desperately need to see Jesus!

JERUSALEM

The phrase, *"Make haste, and you get quickly out of Jerusalem,"* proclaims the Lord once more indicting this city, even His City, but now in total rebellion against Him, even as He had said, *"O Jerusalem, Jerusalem, ... Behold, your house is left unto you desolate"* (Mat. 23:37-38).

The phrase, *"For they will not receive your testimony concerning Me,"* proclaims that the Jews would not only reject the message of Jesus Christ but, as well, would kill Paul, that is, if given the opportunity.

This statement as offered by Christ to Paul is of far greater magnitude than anyone could ever begin to imagine.

The very reason for the call of Abraham out of Ur of the Chaldees and the raising up of a nation out of his loins was Jesus Christ. He and He alone was the sole Purpose of the Jews. That was the only reason for their existence.

Inasmuch as they rejected Him, even crucifying Him, there is now no more purpose for their existence, at least until the end of this dispensation, which will bring in the Second Coming. Consequently, in A.D. 70, they would be completely destroyed as a nation, actually wandering as outcasts for nearly 2,000 years, suffering untold horror, and only finally becoming a nation again in 1948.

THE NATION OF ISRAEL

Their becoming a nation at that time was all in fulfillment of Bible prophecy concerning the restoration of these people, which most surely will come to pass. Then and only then can things be made as they ought to be regarding the nations of the world and, more particularly, Jesus reigning from

Jerusalem. This He will do at the Second Coming, with Israel then accepting Him as their Messiah, Lord, and Saviour.

However, they have one more extremely trying time yet to come, even more horrifying than anything in the past, which Jesus called *"great tribulation,"* and which Jeremiah called *"the time of Jacob's trouble,"* but they *"would be saved out of it"* (Mat. 24:21; Jer. 30:7).

However, not only would the Jews not receive the testimony concerning Jesus, but most of the world falls into the same category. To be frank, even most who call themselves *"Christians"* follow suit by rejecting part or all of the testimony concerning Christ.

(19) "AND I SAID, LORD, THEY KNOW THAT I IMPRISONED AND BEAT IN EVERY SYNAGOGUE THEM WHO BELIEVED ON YOU."

The status is:

1. The phrase, *"And I said, Lord,"* presents Paul looking to Jesus as his Lord and Master, in other words, the totality of his life. And yet, Paul, even as he would now say, had once greatly opposed Christ by opposing those who were His.

2. *"They know that I imprisoned and beat in every synagogue them who believed on You,"* gives us some idea as to the manner of life of the early Jewish believers in Christ.

3. At the beginning, these people in no way considered themselves as different from any other Jews, at least as far as Jewish life was concerned. They continued, even as they always had done, to look to the synagogue as the center of their life and activity. The only difference was that they had accepted Christ as their Saviour, whereas others in the synagogue had not done so, which ultimately would bring a division, with all believers in Christ forced out of that part of Jewish life.

4. Consequently, it was not difficult at all for Paul to locate these people. All he had to do was go to the synagogue, where they would be easily pointed out.

5. So, for a period of time, that is exactly what he did, and with great violence, even to the death of some of these people (Acts 22:4).

6. It is ironic that Paul, before his conversion, along with the Jewish Sanhedrin and Pharisees, etc., would physically beat believers in Christ, imprison, and even kill them, all in the name of the Lord. They were so blind that they did not see the total incongruity of such action.

7. Actually, the same was done respecting the Catholics and their terrible inquisitions in the Middle Ages. They tortured people to death, even hundreds of thousands, simply because they would not accept Catholicism. As stated, they did it all in the name of the Lord!

(20) "AND WHEN THE BLOOD OF YOUR MARTYR STEPHEN WAS SHED, I ALSO WAS STANDING BY, AND CONSENTING UNTO HIS DEATH, AND KEPT THE RAIMENT OF THEM WHO KILLED HIM."

The form is:

1. The phrase, *"And when the blood of Your martyr Stephen was shed,"* presents that this event undoubtedly had a lasting effect on Paul, as he now stated, and must have played a great part in his salvation.

The word *"martyr"* actually means *"witness"* in the Greek text.

2. In New Testament times, those who witnessed for Christ were risking their lives whether they were actually killed or not. Inasmuch as this *"witness"* of Christ led so many to their deaths, the word *"martyr"* came to be used of those who gave up their lives for Christ.

3. *"I also was standing by, and consenting unto his death,"* presents Paul as undoubtedly having heard the message which was preached by Stephen and, as well, having sensed the powerful anointing of the Holy Spirit that accompanied the message. Also, he saw how Stephen died, even calling upon the Lord to forgive those who were committing this horrible sin (Acts 7:60).

4. There is no way this could not have affected the man greatly. In his heart, even though it would not be admitted then, he knew that Stephen had something that he did not have. To be sure, and as previously stated, he responded to that conviction of the Holy Spirit, and great conviction I believe it was, by *"breathing out threatenings and slaughter against the disciples*

NOTES

NOTES

(followers) *of the Lord"* (Acts 9:1).

5. The convicting power of the Holy Spirit, which is an absolute necessity for one to be saved, brings about many and varied responses from the person under conviction. Some few yield immediately, saying *"yes"* to Christ, which is the intention of the Holy Spirit (Jn. 16:8-11).

Regrettably, many others do the very opposite, going deeper into sin, even as Paul did! Nevertheless, such response at times is caused by the Holy Spirit dealing with these people in order to ultimately bring them to a saving knowledge of Jesus Christ.

6. The phrase, *"And kept the raiment of them that slew him,"* made Paul a party to the death of this man, who actually was the first martyr for Christ.

(21) "AND HE SAID UNTO ME, DEPART: FOR I WILL SEND YOU FAR HENCE UNTO THE GENTILES."

The status is:

1. Sin provides the legal means that Satan has to hold man captive.

2. However, with all sin atoned, which Jesus did at the Cross, this removed the legal right that Satan had to hold anyone in bondage.

3. So, if there is bondage, this means the individual is not taking advantage of what the Lord has already done at Calvary.

THE WORD OF THE LORD TO PAUL

The phrase, *"And He said unto me, Depart,"* presents the Lord cutting Paul's argument short.

It was natural that Paul wanted to reach his own people, and for all the obvious reasons. He felt in his heart that no one could appeal to them exactly as he could simply because he had once been the champion destroyer of *"this Way."* All of them knew this and surely, at least in his thinking, would be interested in what he had to say.

However, at this early stage in Paul's following of Christ, he did not quite understand that *"reason"* would have little effect upon these rebels. Rather than hear what Paul had to say, they would have killed him in short order.

Blind rebellion against Christ is totally unlike any other type of response or rebellion that one could name. It is fueled by spiritual darkness and cannot be broken without a direct revelation of Jesus Christ to the soul, brought by the Holy Spirit, even as with Paul.

However, even though such a revelation is absolutely necessary, at least in one way or the other, still, that within itself in no way guarantees salvation, for many would little accept that either. As we have previously stated, the Lord revealed Himself to Paul even as He did simply because through foreknowledge, he knew that Paul would accept.

DEPART

So, the Lord bluntly told Paul to *"depart!"*

The phrase, *"For I will send you far hence unto the gentiles,"* proclaims this was the particular calling of Paul, even as he had been told by Ananias at the time of his conversion (Acts 9:15).

Paul was the apostle to the gentiles, meaning that he was called of God for this great task. Actually, the very word *"apostle"* in the Greek text is *"apostolos"* and means *"he who is sent."* However, it means one sent respecting a special mission, which has implications for the entirety of the Body of Christ. Paul's message was *"The Message of the Cross,"* or one might say, *"The Message of Grace."*

This is the way presently that apostles function, and it really doesn't matter if the individual refers to himself as an apostle or not, and probably won't. However, irrespective, the message he brings is an apostolic message, which means it is given by the Holy Spirit, and it's that which the church desperately needs. Such will affect the entirety of the Body of Christ in some way. And yes, the Lord is still setting apostles in the church.

GENTILES

Even though Paul continued to preach to the Jews, as is obvious in the Book of Acts, to preach and to write the revelation of God to the gentiles was his great work. To this end, we find him traveling in Judea, Samaria, Syria, Phoenicia, Arabia, Cilicia, Pisidia, Lycaonia, Pamphylia, Galatia,

Phrygia, Macedonia, Greece, Asia, the isles of the Mediterranean and the Aegean Sea, Italy, possibly Spain, and other lands.

No other preached, traveled, and labored like Paul. The Epistles of all the others are mainly Jewish, in which many of the revelations of the Lord to Christians are not found except in a minor way.

Paul was assigned by the Lord as the masterbuilder of the church. Of course, Jesus was the Foundation (I Cor. 3:10).

Horton said, concerning Paul, *"Yet this Apostle was not one of the special group of the Twelve Apostles Jesus first chose, and he never claimed to be. Consequently, he had no expectation of sitting on a Throne during the coming Millennium ruling one of the Twelve Tribes of Israel, even as the original Twelve will do (Mat. 19:28)."* Nevertheless, not taking away at all from the original Twelve, Paul's mission and ministry were the far more important regarding the Message of Jesus Christ and His Church, even as the Holy Spirit outlines it in the Book of Acts.

(22) "AND THEY GAVE HIM AUDIENCE UNTO THIS WORD, AND THEN LIFTED UP THEIR VOICES, AND SAID, AWAY WITH SUCH A FELLOW FROM THE EARTH: FOR IT IS NOT FIT THAT HE SHOULD LIVE."

The form is:

1. The phrase, *"And they gave him audience unto this word,"* speaks of the word *"gentiles."*

That word lashed their pride and prejudice into fury, although their own prophets largely predicted that the Messiah should reign over the gentiles.

Israel, at this time, looked at gentiles as if they were dogs. In other words, they felt very superior to all others, which was at least in part the reason that they killed Christ.

2. In their spiritual superiority or elitism, they could not even begin to think of themselves as needing to repent, even as John the Baptist and Jesus demanded. Of course, we speak primarily of the religious leadership of Israel, which, as well, included the Pharisees.

So, when Paul mentioned *"gentiles,"* they would tolerate his words no longer.

NOTES

3. *"And then lifted up their voices and said, Away with such a fellow from the Earth,"* actually means they wanted to kill him.

The word *"Away"* in the Greek text is *"airo"* and means *"take up, remove, take away, put away, do away."*

In this case, it means *"kill him."*

4. The phrase, *"For it is not fit that he should live,"* presents these people as claiming they were scriptural in their demands for Paul's life.

How could they think this?

5. They knew, or else, should have known, the truth that God cares about the gentiles, as is clear in the Old Testament. God's very Purpose in calling Abraham was to bring blessing to all the families of the Earth (Gen. 12:3), which, of course, included gentiles. As well, every time the promise was repeated to Abraham, Isaac, and Jacob, the same truth was reemphasized (Gen. 18:18; 22:18; 26:4; 28:14).

6. Horton said, *"In Galatians 3:6-8 Paul reminds us of this Promise and shows that Gentiles become heirs of the same Promise through Faith as the Jews. Then he goes on to show that Christ is the Seed of Abraham through Whom the Blessing comes to all who believe, both Gentiles and Jews (Gal. 3:16, 29)."*

7. Due to their religious prejudice, these people could not bear the idea of the gentiles, who, as stated, they considered to be no more than dogs, being admitted into the Kingdom of God, much less that all were to be admitted on the same basis of faith. It was a blow to their pride of exclusiveness.

8. The bringing up of the gentiles to this glorious position seemed to be as intolerable to them as the putting down of themselves, at least as they saw the situation (Isa. 1:10; Ezek. 16:45).

(23) "AND AS THEY CRIED OUT, AND CAST OFF THEIR CLOTHES, AND THREW DUST INTO THE AIR."

The status is:

1. The phrase, *"And as they cried out,"* presents the Jews in the Temple once again going into a frenzy.

2. *"And cast off their clothes, and threw dust into the air,"* was the greatest expression

NOTES

they could choose in order to portray their rejection of what Paul had said.

3. In other words, while they were screaming these insults at Paul, even demanding his life, they were taking off their outer garments and throwing them in the air while, at the same time, throwing dust. As stated, this was the ultimate insult!

4. If not for the Roman captain, they would have killed Paul then and there, no doubt, by stoning him or beating him to death.

5. This was their answer to the final appeal to their souls before the coming judgment.

6. It is no wonder the Holy Spirit through Solomon said, *"Because I have called, and you refused; I have stretched out My Hand, and no man regarded;*

"But you have set at nought all My Counsel, and would none of My Reproof:

"I also will laugh at your calamity; I will mock when your fear comes" (Prov. 1:24-26).

(24) "THE CHIEF CAPTAIN COMMANDED HIM TO BE BROUGHT INTO THE CASTLE, AND BADE THAT HE SHOULD BE EXAMINED BY SCOURGING; THAT HE MIGHT KNOW WHEREFORE THEY CRIED SO AGAINST HIM."

The account is:

1. The phrase, *"The chief captain commanded him to be brought into the castle,"* pertained to him now trying to find out the cause of this disturbance.

2. Inasmuch as Paul was speaking Hebrew, and the shouts of the mob against Paul were in the same language, the captain did not understand what was being said.

3. *"And bade that he should be examined by scourging,"* presents a common type of Roman punishment and was often used to extract the truth from the victim, etc.

Inasmuch as the mob had responded very violently to Paul's address, the captain was determined to know what Paul had said that instigated such a response.

Scourging was a most severe implement of flogging, under which many died. This was the same type of punishment to which Pilate had subjected Jesus (Jn. 19:1).

4. The phrase, *"That he might know wherefore they cried so against him,"* pertains, in a sense, to the Roman captain being responsible for any type of unrest, such as had just happened. Consequently, measures were always taken to find the instigator and to punish him accordingly.

(25) "AND AS THEY BOUND HIM WITH THONGS, PAUL SAID UNTO THE CENTURION THAT STOOD BY, IS IT LAWFUL FOR YOU TO SCOURGE A MAN WHO IS A ROMAN, AND UNCONDEMNED?"

The form is:

1. The phrase, *"And as they bound him with thongs,"* pointed to getting him ready for the beating, which would now be inflicted.

To prepare him for the scourging, the soldiers made him bend over and stretch forward, with some saying that what was now done was even more severe. In some cases, they hanged the victim by the thongs so that his feet dangled a few inches above the floor. They would then proceed with the whipping.

2. Paul was no stranger to torture. He had already been whipped by Jews five times and beaten with rods by the Romans three times (II Cor. 11:24-25). However, this type of punishment by the Roman scourge was so bad that it often crippled or killed, as stated, its victim. If Paul had experienced this beating, it would probably have killed him.

3. There are some who suggest that due to these beatings, the apostle's spine had been somewhat affected, with his legs bowing outward and, consequently, his living in constant pain.

Despite the great healings and miracles performed by the power of God by the hands of Paul, there is little doubt that this was true. He said at one time, *"But though our outward man perish, yet the inward man is renewed day by day."*

4. He then went on to refer to these terrible things as *"our light affliction"* (II Cor. 4:16-17).

5. And yet, at his conversion, the very first thing told to him by the Lord through Ananias was, *"For I will show him how great things he must suffer for My Name's sake"* (Acts 9:16).

6. Much of the modern Gospel has little similarity to that of which we speak here, even claiming that if Paul had proper faith, he could have warded off these things. Such

is, pure and simple, *"another gospel,"* and one could, as well, say, *"another faith."* In other words, such drivel is not of God!

7. The question, *"Paul said unto the centurion that stood by, Is it lawful for you to scourge a man who is a Roman, and uncondemned?"* puts an entirely different light on the situation, as we will now see!

8. At this point, Paul was, no doubt, stretched on the stake, or else, hung upward by his hands, ready to receive the scourging.

(26) "WHEN THE CENTURION HEARD THAT, HE WENT AND TOLD THE CHIEF CAPTAIN, SAYING, TAKE HEED WHAT YOU DO: FOR THIS MAN IS A ROMAN."

The pattern is:

1. Most of the modern church will agree that *"Jesus Christ is the Source of all things we receive from God."*

2. However, when we say that the Cross of Christ is the means, and the only means, by which we receive all these wonderful things from the Lord, that's where we have a problem. However, it most definitely is true!

THE ROMAN CENTURION

The phrase, *"When the centurion heard that, he went and told the chief captain,"* pertains to the great significance of what Paul had just said.

The phrase, *"Saying, Take heed what you do: For this man is a Roman,"* pertained to Roman law.

The rights of Roman citizens were guarded by Rome as something sacred. Consequently, great penalties would fall on those who disregarded those rights.

Valerian and Porcian laws provided that no judge or officer had the right to bind, scourge, or kill a Roman citizen without proper trial, hence, Paul mentioning that he was *"uncondemned."*

Horton said, *"At first this was the decision of the General Assembly of the Citizens of Rome, while later the power was transferred to the Emperor, to whom appeal could be made.*

All a person had to do to claim his rights was to say the words, 'I am a Roman Citizen,' even as Paul here does."

Consequently, in the providence of God, Paul was both a Jew and a Roman.

NOTES

ROMAN CITIZENSHIP

Roman citizens were divided into three classes socially. These three classes were

1. Senatorial.
2. Equestrian.
3. Plebeian.

Actually, the whole system of government harmonized with this triple division.

The *"senatorial"* class was composed of descendants of Roman senators and those upon whom the emperors conferred the privilege of wearing the tunic with broad purple border, the sign of membership in this elitist order.

The qualifications for membership in the senate were the possession of senatorial rank and property of the value of not less than 1,000,000 sesterces, which amounted to at least one million dollars, and even more in 2014 currency.

This senatorial class had judicial functions, setting as a court of justice for trying important criminal cases and hearing appeals in civil cases from the provinces.

The *"equestrian"* class was made up of those who possessed property of the value of approximately half of that of the senatorial rank.

Whereas the senatorial class could wear a tunic with a broad purple border, the *"equestrian"* class wore a narrow purple band on the tunic.

Of this group, the emperors filled many important financial and administrative positions, whether in Italy or the provinces under their control.

The *"plebeians"* were what one might call ordinary Roman citizens and made up the greater bulk of the population. They were either born into this position, had it conferred by edict from Rome, or purchased this privilege.

Paul was a member of this latter group, with this privilege probably conferred upon his family, or else, the entire city of Tarsus, or a certain part of the city, which sometimes happened.

(27) "THEN THE CHIEF CAPTAIN CAME, AND SAID UNTO HIM, TELL ME, ARE YOU A ROMAN? HE SAID, YES."

NOTES

The exegesis is:

1. The phrase, *"Then the chief captain came,"* points to that which was very serious. In fact, if this was true, that Paul was a Roman citizen, the chief captain had broken the law even by binding Paul.

2. The question, *"And said unto him, Tell me, are you a Roman?"* was taking this captain much further than he at first had dreamed possible.

3. Initially, he had Paul erroneously pegged as an Egyptian who had caused great trouble for Rome in the recent past. Then he found out that Paul was a Jew from the influential city of Tarsus. Now, he was told the apostle was a Roman!

4. The phrase, *"He said, Yes,"* is said without hesitation and in a conclusive manner, as if his status was not in doubt, which it was not!

(28) "AND THE CHIEF CAPTAIN ANSWERED, WITH A GREAT SUM OBTAINED I THIS FREEDOM. AND PAUL SAID, BUT I WAS FREE BORN."

The synopsis is:

1. The phrase, *"And the chief captain answered, With a great sum obtained I this freedom,"* proclaims one of the ways that Roman citizenship could be gained.

What Claudius Lysias meant by a *"great sum,"* we are not told.

3. Originally, the privileges of Roman citizenship were limited to all, other than slaves, living in the city of Rome itself. Later, citizenship was extended to a number of Italian tribes and cities, and then to most of Italy. Emperors kept adding to the places outside Italy that could have Roman citizenship. Often, individuals who had rendered some outstanding service to the empire would also receive citizenship for themselves and their families. Actually, it is thought that Paul's father or grandfather fell into this category because of some unusual service.

4. During the reign of Emperor Claudius, his wife and other court favorites were allowed to sell Roman citizenship, which they did, apparently as a means of lining their own pockets.

At any rate, the chief captain had paid a great sum for the Roman citizenship he now enjoyed.

5. The phrase, *"And Paul said, But I was free born,"* means, as stated, that Paul was born a Roman citizen, either through some service performed for Rome by his family, or else, because of living in the city of Tarsus.

6. It is claimed by some that Tarsus was a free city, and all its inhabitants were considered Roman citizens by a grant from Julius Caesar. However, there are some who say the historical evidence is against this.

(29) "THEN STRAIGHTWAY THEY DEPARTED FROM HIM WHICH SHOULD HAVE EXAMINED HIM: AND THE CHIEF CAPTAIN ALSO WAS AFRAID, AFTER HE KNEW THAT HE WAS A ROMAN, AND BECAUSE HE HAD BOUND HIM."

The synopsis is:

1. The phrase, *"Then straightway they departed from him which should have examined him,"* referred to those who were going to scourge Paul now quickly retiring.

2. *"And the chief captain also was afraid, after he knew that he was a Roman, and because he had bound him,"* clearly refers to this chief captain breaking the law. Consequently, had Paul so desired, he could have easily filed charges on this man, which could have caused him great problems. However, Paul had no desire to do such a thing.

(30) "ON THE MORROW, BECAUSE HE WOULD HAVE KNOWN THE CERTAINTY WHEREFORE HE WAS ACCUSED OF THE JEWS, HE LOOSED HIM FROM HIS BANDS, AND COMMANDED THE CHIEF PRIESTS AND ALL THEIR COUNCIL TO APPEAR, AND BROUGHT PAUL DOWN, AND SET HIM BEFORE THEM."

The synopsis is:

1. The weakness of the Law is that it merely commands but has no power or claims to have those commandments obeyed.

2. The Law is like a mirror, which shows a man what he is but gives him no power to change it.

THE ACTIONS OF THE CHIEF CAPTAIN

The phrase, *"On the morrow, because he would have known the certainty wherefore he was accused of the Jews,"* means simply that the chief captain took all restrictions off of Paul immediately, even though it would be the next day before he would know what the complaint of the Jews was all about. However, he did keep him in custody, probably because he felt that Paul's safety could be guaranteed that way. As well, he had the responsibility to give the Jews an opportunity to present their case.

"He loosed him from his bands," means that he was no longer restricted but, at the same time, held in custody.

"And commanded the chief priests and all their council to appear," spoke of the Jewish Sanhedrin, the highest Jewish council and ruling civil and religious body.

THE HISTORY OF THE SANHEDRIN

The history of this council is not clear at all points. Traditionally, it originated with the 70 elders who assisted Moses some 1,500 years before (Num. 11:16-24).

Ezra is supposed to have reorganized this body after the Exile. The Persians gave authority to the Jews in local affairs, with the governing body made up of that which resembled the later Sanhedrin (Ezra 5:5, 9; 6:7, 14; 7:25-26; 10:8, 14; Neh. 2:16; 4:14, 19; 5:7; 7:5).

THE ROMANS AND THE SANHEDRIN

Under the Romans, except for a short period under Gabinius, this body had wide powers. It was Julius Caesar who reversed the plan of Gabinius and extended the power of the Sanhedrin once again over all Judaea, although during the reign of Herod (37-4 B.C.), its powers were severely curtailed.

Under the procurators (A.D. 6-66), which was the time of Paul, the powers of the Sanhedrin were extensive, with the internal government of the country being in its hands.

According to Josephus and the New Testament, the high priest usually served as the president (Mat. 26:57; Acts 5:17; 7:1; 9:1; 22:5; 24:1). Thus, Caiaphas was president at the trial of Jesus and Ananias at the trial of Paul (Acts 23:2).

PAUL

"And brought Paul down, and set him before them," must have presented quite a moment.

NOTES

Even though it had been some 25 years before when the Sanhedrin had given Paul letters of authority concerning the arrest of the followers of Christ, surely some of the members were alive now who served at that particular time. Some have even suggested that Paul was a member of the Sanhedrin himself; however, there is no record of such, and, therefore, the matter is only speculative at best.

I greatly suspect that many, if not all, these men were very anxious to question Paul, although I am sure that most of them hated him. In their eyes, he was a traitor!

Even though many of the members of the Sanhedrin were Sadducees, even as we shall see, still, many of them were Pharisees, who had once held Paul as the great hope of Pharisaism, in other words, the savior of the Mosaic Law. But now, this man was threatening Judaism, or so they believed, as no other human being.

As well, he was the greatest champion of Jesus Christ, affirming everywhere he went that Jesus was indeed the Messiah, and above all, was raised from the dead and now sits exalted by the right hand of the Father. So, in this one man, they saw more threat to Judaism than any other human being on the face of the Earth. As we shall see, the meeting would not be uneventful.

"Jesus, the very thought of You
"With sweetness fills my breast;
"But sweeter far Your Face to see
"And in Your Presence rest."

"Nor voice can sing, nor heart can frame,
"Nor can the memory find,
"A sweeter sound than Your blest Name,
"O Saviour of mankind."

"O Hope of every contrite heart,
"O Joy of all the meek,
"To those who fall, how kind You are!
"How good to those who seek."

"But what to those who find? Ah, this
"Nor tongue nor pen can show,
"The Love of Jesus, what it is

"None but His loved ones know."

"Jesus, our only Joy be Thou,
"As You our prize will be;
"Jesus, be Thou our Glory now,
"And through eternity."

CHAPTER 23

(1) "AND PAUL, EARNESTLY BEHOLDING THE COUNCIL, SAID, MEN AND BRETHREN, I HAVE LIVED IN ALL GOOD CONSCIENCE BEFORE GOD UNTIL THIS DAY."

The synopsis is:

1. The phrase, *"And Paul, earnestly beholding the council, said,"* evidently speaks of all 71 members, with the high priest Ananias serving as its president.

2. *"Men and brethren, I have lived in all good conscience before God until this day,"* means that whatever he had been doing, he had thought it was right at the time, whether so or not.

3. In this statement, Paul pleaded conscience as his guide when imprisoning or killing saints, proving that conscience is not always a good guide. It can be seared and, in that state, is not normal (I Tim. 4:1-2). Actually, it cannot be a right rule unless enlightened and kept normal. In ignorance, it can burn saints at the stake, even as were many in the Dark Ages.

4. The accusation against Paul was that he was a traitor to the Law and to the nation, with him, correspondingly, beginning his defense most properly by stating that, as to such a charge, he had a good conscience before God. He declared his integrity and his loyalty in those relationships. He did not mean by this that he was sinless, for he was actually guilty of very grievous sin. However, all the time, he was thinking he was doing the right thing, even as wrong as it actually was, which was before his conversion. This attitude, as well, includes most of humanity.

(2) "AND THE HIGH PRIEST ANANIAS COMMANDED THEM WHO STOOD BY HIM TO SMITE HIM ON THE MOUTH."

The status is:

NOTES

1. The phrase, *"And the high priest Ananias,"* portrays this office, which once was of the Aaronic lineage and of God, now as no more than a political office, actually, only a political office.

2. This Ananias was well-known as an unscrupulous, greedy, and grasping politician. He had been appointed about nine years before this through political influence. He ruled like a tyrant in Jerusalem and according to the Jewish Talmud, he was a glutton.

3. He was killed by zealots in A.D. 66 for his pro-Roman sympathies.

4. *"Commanded them who stood by him to smite him on the mouth,"* gives us little clue as to why he did this thing.

5. Some suggest that he was angry because Paul had declared himself not guilty of any of the charges brought against him. Others suggest that Paul's statement about a *"good conscience"* was the cause.

6. While all of that may have had something to do with his attitude toward Paul, still, it is most probable that his great anger against the apostle was already in his heart when he was summoned to this meeting by the chief captain. As unscrupulous and ungodly as he was, he would have hated Paul, which is obvious!

(3) "THEN SAID PAUL UNTO HIM, GOD SHALL SMITE YOU, YOU WHITED WALL: FOR SIT YOU TO JUDGE ME AFTER THE LAW, AND COMMAND ME TO BE SMITTEN CONTRARY TO THE LAW?"

The form is:

1. The phrase, *"Then said Paul unto him,"* pertains to an answer that would be very strong, but yet, based somewhat on lack of knowledge.

Some believe that Paul's indignation was a failure in self-control, while others see the opposite.

2. The phrase, *"God shall smite you, you whited wall,"* in effect, says, *"You whitewashed wall."* Such was used to cover over that which was unsightly and unclean, constituting a strong rebuke.

3. As well, Paul's prediction concerning the high priest came true in that he became involved in a tumult, which was caused by his own son, who was caught hiding in an

NOTES

aqueduct and, according to Josephus, was murdered. Thus, God did *"smite him."*

4. The question, *"For sit you to judge me after the Law, and command me to be smitten contrary to the Law?"* presents Paul as knowing the Law of Moses to a far greater degree than any of these members of the Sanhedrin. To be frank, they cared little at all about the Law of Moses, either disbelieving most of it altogether, as this Sadducee high priest, or else, as the Pharisees, twisting it to their own desires.

5. In fact, it was the duty of the Sanhedrin to hold to the Law in totality, but, as stated, most of them little believed it, not unlike many modern preachers who do not believe the Bible.

6. To be frank, the Word of God, which was supposed to be the foundational criterion for all of Israel, was now little more than window-dressing, with lip service only, if that! In fact, there were very few people in Jerusalem, if any, whom God would have judged more wicked than the Sanhedrin. For the most part, they were scoundrels and murderers who, some 27 years earlier, whether these or others, crucified the Lord of Glory, the most heinous act in the annals of human history. So, Paul was standing in front of the very epitome of evil, for religious evil is the greatest evil of all!

(4) "AND THEY WHO STOOD BY SAID, DO YOU REVILE GOD'S HIGH PRIEST?"

The account is:

1. Paul held that Christ's coming put the whole system of the Law out of date because it fulfilled it all.

2. Inasmuch as we now have the reality, we do not need the shadow.

THE QUESTION

The question posed to Paul came as a surprise to him simply because he did not know this man was now the high priest.

The word *"revile"* in the Greek text is *"loidoreo"* and means *"to reproach or vilify."* It also has the connotations of *"a blackguard."*

Paul did not revile the high priest by his answer, or anyone for that matter.

His answer was strong, even as it should have been, which I do not feel compromised the Christlikeness in Paul whatsoever. These men were purporting to be keepers and guardians of the Law of Moses, so for the high priest or any member of this council to give instructions for Paul to be slapped on the mouth, especially considering his kind and gracious salutation, contained no rhyme or reason for such action.

In respect to this type of council or committee, etc., which much of the time is unscriptural anyway, I have noticed that it is quite common for some of its members at times to develop a god-like complex. Many of these people seem to think, especially in a group mentality, that whatever they do is right, irrespective as to what it is.

Actually, they will sometimes do things in a committee or council setting that are extremely injurious and hurtful, which they would not dare do as an individual person. They seem to think that several agreeing on any one thing somehow legitimizes it, irrespective as to what it might be or how ungodly!

WICKED AND UNGODLY

An acquaintance of mine, who served for many years in such a capacity in a major Pentecostal denomination, stated once he had retired, and I will quote as best I can from memory, *"Considering some of the hurtful things I did to other people while in that particular office, looking back, I am not even certain if I was saved!"*

He then said, *"It was like a spirit that was on me, controlling me, which did not leave until I was completely out of that position."*

The brother in question was in an unscriptural position because the office he held was man-instituted; consequently, these things he did do could be judged as none other than evil.

Irrespective as to what men may have thought, through the eyes of God, the Sanhedrin, the ruling religious body of Israel, was wicked and ungodly beyond compare. By contrast, Paul was one of the godliest men on the face of the Earth.

Far too often, organized religion finds itself in the same category as the Jewish Sanhedrin of old! To be frank, even as that council of old, the greatest hindrance to the work of God is organized religion. By

NOTES

that, I am not meaning that organization is wrong, for that is not the case. What I am addressing is that which is organized by man and, consequently, not according to the Word of God.

(5) "THEN SAID PAUL, I DID NOT KNOW BRETHREN, THAT HE WAS THE HIGH PRIEST: FOR IT IS WRITTEN, YOU SHALL NOT SPEAK EVIL OF THE RULER OF YOUR PEOPLE."

The construction is:

1. The debt that man owed was not to Satan, but rather to God.
2. It took the Cross of Christ to pay that debt, and it was paid in full.

THE HIGH PRIEST?

The phrase, *"Then said Paul, I did not know brethren, that he was the high priest,"* tells us that at this particular time, it was very difficult for a visitor to Jerusalem, as Paul was, to know who was high priest—for the Romans, as well as the Sanhedrin, made and unmade them at their pleasure.

Williams said, *"As a lawyer Paul was stung by the insult illegally ordered by the Judge; but if he was for a moment thrown off his guard (Christ never was), nothing can surpass the Grace and the frankness with which he expressed his sorrow; and so the manner in which he atoned for his error honored Christ."*

The phrase, *"For it is written, You shall not speak evil of the ruler of your people,"* is taken from Exodus 22:28.

In Paul's first address to the mob (Acts 22:1-21), he gave his credentials as a Jew. As he addressed this crowd, he spoke of things that every Jew understood and even went so far as to relate his persecution of Christians.

He then gave his testimony of his great conversion to the Lord Jesus Christ on the road to Damascus. Of course, the hatred of the Jews for Jesus caused them to reject everything he said. In fact, because of ignorance and prejudice, had he been a gentile, he would not have been accepted no matter what he said. However, considering who Paul was, it was hard for them to discount his testimony.

PAUL

Paul had actually been the darling of the Pharisees, the man who was being groomed to take the place of the great scholar, Gamaliel. This had been some years previously. At any rate, the Lord, in saving Paul and using him, presented the greatest argument that could ever be offered regarding the validity of the Message of Christ.

As Paul readily knew, the great nation of Israel was actually divided into primarily two groups, the Pharisees and the Sadducees. Paul had been a Pharisee, so he appealed to this group, and did so with telling conviction.

Evidently, he was led by the Holy Spirit to do this because the Pharisees, at least up to a point, took up his cause.

Annas, in reality, was not the high priest. He had been deprived of this office by the Romans and had been succeeded by Jonathan, after whose murder by Festus, there occurred a period of vacancy in this office. During this time, Annas somewhat took over the office, even though he had no official appointment as such.

When Paul stated that he did not know that this man was the true high priest, he was telling the truth. Even though Annas was referred to by his friends as the high priest, he really did not, as stated, hold an appointment to this office. Paul probably thought that he was the deputy of the high priest or someone acting in this capacity at that particular time.

(6) "BUT WHEN PAUL PERCEIVED THAT THE ONE PART WERE SADDUCEES, AND THE OTHER PHARISEES, HE CRIED OUT IN THE COUNCIL, MEN AND BRETHREN, I AM A PHARISEE, THE SON OF A PHARISEE: OF THE HOPE AND RESURRECTION OF THE DEAD I AM CALLED IN QUESTION."

The structure is:

1. Due to the Fall in the Garden of Eden, Satan legally had a claim on the entirety of the human race.
2. However, at the Cross, Jesus Christ took away that legal claim by atoning for all sin, past, present, and future, at least for those who will believe (Jn. 3:16).

PHARISEES AND SADDUCEES

The phrase, *"But when Paul perceived*

that the one part were Sadducees, and the other Pharisees," causes us to wonder how Paul came to this sudden realization.

Quite possibly, the Pharisees were opposed to the action of Ananias, a Sadducee, in ordering Paul to be struck, which indeed was a violation of the Law of Moses.

They quite possibly voiced their strong disapproval, knowing that the Sadducees had little regard for the Law of Moses at any rate, while they, the Pharisees, considered themselves to be guardians of the Law.

The Sadducees were a major religious/political party in Israel (mostly political), which controlled the high priesthood and many of the seats on the council of the 71.

Believing in only scattered parts of the Old Testament, they laid emphasis on free will but denied the afterlife and any future rewards or punishments. In other words, they did not believe in heaven or hell, and neither did they believe in miracles of any kind. As well, they had no room in their theology and traditions for any resurrection. They would have been called the modernists of this present time.

PHARISEES

By contrast, the Pharisees claimed to believe in all the Law of Moses and, by their traditions, often modified the Law to meet conditions not expressly mentioned.

They taught the immortality of the soul and emphasized the election of Israel. They also believed the hope of the resurrection was fundamental to the hope of Israel.

They would have been called the fundamentalists of our time because of their claims to believe all of the Bible. And yet, along with the Sadducees, they were bitter enemies of Christ and actually clamored for His Crucifixion as much or more than their sister party, the Sadducees.

THE COUNCIL

The phrase, *"He cried out in the council,"* probably means that an argument had ensued between the Pharisees and Sadducees on the council, which had become quite heated, etc. In view of this, Paul shouted out over the tumult in order to make himself heard.

THE PRESERVATION OF THE LAW OF MOSES

The phrase, *"Men and brethren, I am a Pharisee, the son of a Pharisee,"* expresses the party with which Paul had been associated before his conversion, with his father having been the same.

The manner in which it was said tells us that both the father and the son had taken great pride in this association.

As we have previously stated, it is believed by some that Paul, a student of the famous Gamaliel, was being heralded as the last great hope of Pharisaism. In other words, to him was being entrusted the preservation of the Law of Moses in the maintaining of its purity.

Paul was speaking only of his before conversion association. Even though he continued to maintain his core beliefs, but now greatly fleshed out by revelations from the Lord, that party affiliation held no meaning for him now. But yet, he would use it at the present, and for the obvious reasons.

RESURRECTION

The phrase, *"Of the hope and resurrection of the dead I am called in question,"* totally and completely presents that which is truth.

The whole Christian faith is built around Christ and what He did for us at the Cross, along with His bodily Resurrection. Without faith in both, men are lost (Rom. 10:9-10; I Cor. 15:1-23).

However, the Pharisees, who were members of the Sanhedrin and hearing Paul that day, would probably not have connected Jesus Christ with his statement concerning the Resurrection, but would have limited it to their own doctrines.

Some believe that Paul can be criticized for seizing on the controversy between the Pharisees and Sadducees to divert attention from himself. They say it was a mere stratagem, ducking the blow, and avoiding the issue. However, the real issue at stake was not his safety or protection, but rather the truth of the Gospel.

Farrar strongly blamed Paul regarding this incident, saying, *"The plan showed great knowledge of character ... but was it worthy of Paul? Could he worthily at this time say, 'I am a Pharisee'?"*

He further asked, *"Had he any right to enflame an existing animosity?"*

THE FUNDAMENTAL DOCTRINES OF PHARISAISM

However, Hervey, in answer to those questions, said, *"It could not be wrong for Paul to take advantage of the agreement of Christian Doctrine with some of the tenets of the Pharisees, to oppose the unbelief of the Sadducees."*

He went on to say, *"Paul had never thrown off his profession as a Jew, and if a Jew, then one of the straightest sect of the Jews, namely a Pharisee, which in the strict sense of the word was not unscriptural, at least as far as it went."*

Jesus never opposed or negated the great fundamental doctrines of Pharisaism for the simple reason that they were scriptural. He did oppose strongly, and rightly so, their gross additions and glosses to the Law and their elitist self-righteous attitude and spirit, which were repugnant in His Sight, as it should have been!

So, Paul was not wrong in the statement that he made and was, no doubt, led by the Holy Spirit in the tact he now took.

(7) "AND WHEN HE HAD SO SAID, THERE AROSE A DISSENSION BETWEEN THE PHARISEES AND THE SADDUCEES: AND THE MULTITUDE WAS DIVIDED."

The diagram is:

1. When Jesus poured out His Life on the Cross by the shedding of His own precious Blood, He atoned for all sin.
2. Because His Sacrifice of Himself was a perfect Sacrifice, God would accept it as payment in full, which He did.

LED BY THE HOLY SPIRIT

The phrase, *"And when he had so said,"* pertains to that, as stated, which I believe the Holy Spirit gave him to say. Knowing Paul, I have to believe that he was led totally by the Spirit respecting his dealings with the mob and now the Sanhedrin.

If the situation had not turned in this direction, a confrontation of sorts between the members of the Sanhedrin, it is anyone's guess as to what the chief captain would have done with Paul. However, as we shall see, we know that it was the will of the Lord for Paul not only to have testified of Jesus in Jerusalem but that he would do so in Rome as well.

In view of that, Paul was being led by the Holy Spirit respecting the Pharisee/Sadducee argument, which this council normally avoided when they met together.

"There arose a dissension between the Pharisees and the Sadducees," pertains to a continuation of religious bickering, which ever has been and ever shall be, at least until Jesus returns.

I remember preaching a city-wide meeting years ago in Louisville, Kentucky. Colonel Sanders of Kentucky Fried Chicken fame was in one of the services. He was asked to greet the crowd sometime before having professed Christ as his Saviour. His statements were very wise, but yet, somewhat humorous.

HOW RIGHT HE WAS!

After relating to the people how the Lord had given him the preparation secret of his brand of fried chicken, he then made mention of the fact of how many church groups and denominations there were in America.

I do not remember the number, but it was something like 4,000 to 5,000 different groups.

He then said, *"Most of these groups are teaching the very opposite of others, and common sense plainly tells us that all cannot be right."*

How right he was!

A Methodist layman said to me one time, *"Brother Swaggart, I am a man, I think, of at least average intelligence, but yet, it is not easy to discern what is right and wrong, especially considering that preachers oftentimes oppose each other in their doctrine."*

He then went on to ask, *"How do we know what is right and what is wrong?"*

That is a good question, especially considering that Satan has done his work well in cloaking the truth or in promoting outright lies, or worse yet, the truth mixed with a little leaven, i.e., error. However, the Holy Spirit is the Giver and Superintendent of all truth (Jn. 16:13-15).

THE APPEAL OF ERROR

All religious error always appeals to prurient interests, in other words, self-will, which in some way is selfish and wrong. For instance, millions look for a church that will make them feel comfortable in their sin and allow them to do pretty much whatever they want to do regarding sin, while all the time being led to believe they are saved. Many look for a church where the Holy Spirit is little, or not at all, present regarding His convicting Power. Of course, those types of churches are very easy to find.

So, for error to be accepted, it has to appeal to self-will, which is not God's Will.

TRUTH AND ERROR

Another of Satan's favorite ploys is to sprinkle a tiny bit of *"leaven"* (false doctrine) into that which is truth. Inasmuch as it is mostly truth, the bait is eagerly grabbed, with the people little cognizant of the error.

However, the error will not remain small for long because the very nature of *"leaven"* is to grow until it corrupts the whole, which is the intention to begin with (I Cor. 5:6).

JESUS AND FRUIT

Jesus said, *"Beware of false prophets, which come to you in sheep's clothing, but inwardly they are ravening wolves"* (Mat. 7:15).

In this scenario, Jesus points to the *"fruit"* as the identification of who they are (Mat. 7:20).

Regarding practicality, His definition and direction are very easy to comprehend and understand, that is, if we are looking at the situation, not according to self-will, but according to the Word of God.

He said that, *"A good tree cannot bring forth evil fruit, neither can a corrupt tree bring forth good fruit"* (Mat. 7:18).

Of course, the purveyors of false doctrine, whomever they may be, are going to claim all kinds of good fruit and in staggering numbers, etc. So, it remains for the believer to do some inspecting.

NOTES

If a preacher of the Gospel is scripturally right in that which he believes and teaches, and consequently, the Holy Spirit is working in him, certain things will be obvious.

First of all, souls will be saved, believers will be baptized with the Holy Spirit, bondages of darkness will be broken in human hearts and lives, and sick bodies will be healed. As well, the saints of God who sit under his ministry will grow in grace and the knowledge of the Lord, that is, if their hearts are right.

As well, if the preacher is preaching all of the Gospel and not just part of the Gospel, without fail, he will be preaching the Cross. Paul said:

"For the preaching of the Cross is to them who perish foolishness, but unto us who are saved it is the power of God" (I Cor. 1:18).

The tragedy is, while most preachers understand the Cross of Christ relative to salvation, they have little or no understanding of the Cross as it regards our sanctification, in other words, how we live for God and how we have victory over the world, the flesh, and the devil. So, whatever it is they are preaching, it may be correct as far as it goes, but if it does not include the Cross relative to everything we believe, then the listeners or viewers will not be hearing the entirety of the Gospel.

FALSE PROPHETS

Almost all false prophets will claim these things I have mentioned are in abundance. However, when looked for, they are little to be found, if at all! Sadly, many Christians believe everything they hear, irrespective!

Whenever the goal is money, as in the greed gospel, that tells us this is not the Gospel because there is nothing in the Word of God to substantiate such teaching. Yes, the Lord does bless people financially, but that is not the thrust of the Gospel, as should be overly obvious. In other words, *"money"* is not the *"fruit"* of which Jesus spoke.

When tuning in to many television ministries, which is a mirror of the church, most of the time, there is very little appeal for souls, very little appeal for believers to be baptized with the Holy Spirit, very little appeal for victory over particular bondages

NOTES

in the lives of believers, and very little appeal for righteousness and holiness. Oftentimes, the appeal is in the realm of gimmicks, with things being done which purport to be miracles but, in reality, are not!

Even though there certainly are some godly preachers, the truth is, they are few and far between.

The phrase, *"And the multitude was divided,"* speaks of the Sanhedrin itself but typifies the majority of the church world presently.

Many have attempted to address themselves to this difficulty of division by trying to force unity that is not based on correct doctrine, but which they say is love.

While the requirement certainly is that we love one another, still, the Word also says, *"Can two walk together, except they be agreed?"* (Amos 3:3).

So, it is not possible for true and false shepherds to have fellowship. It just simply cannot be done and, in fact, should not be done!

(8) "FOR THE SADDUCEES SAY THAT THERE IS NO RESURRECTION, NEITHER ANGEL, NOR SPIRIT: BUT THE PHARISEES CONFESS BOTH."

The overview is:

1. A believer can be forced by the powers of darkness to do things against his will if his faith is in anything other than the Cross of Christ (Rom. 7:19).

2. This means that Satan can override the will of a believer, forcing that believer to do things he should not do. Yes, such a person is responsible despite the fact that he's doing something he doesn't want to do (Rom. 7:18).

RESURRECTION

The phrase, *"For the Sadducees say that there is no resurrection, neither angel, nor spirit,"* well describes the doctrine of these people.

Actually, to sum up the doctrine of the Sadducees, they basically denied personal immortality. As well, they denied heaven and hell, and the spirit world, including angels, etc. Like some of the Greek philosophers, they considered body, soul, and spirit to be a unity so that one could not exist without the other. In other words, they did not believe that the soul and the spirit left the body at death, but that all went into nothingness.

In dealing with this question concerning the Sadducees, Jesus emphasized that God declared Himself to be the God of Abraham, Isaac, and Jacob, who, in fact, had died many, many years before.

Jesus addressed that by saying that God was not a God of the dead but of the living, meaning that there was no point in being God of something which, in fact, no longer existed! That would be silly!

So, the idea is that even though the physical bodies of Abraham, Isaac, and Jacob had long since gone back to dust, as had all of those who had previously died, still, their souls and spirits were not dead and were, in fact, alive to God (Mat. 22:23-33; Mk. 12:18-27; Lk. 20:27-40).

With this answer, Jesus blasted the chief argument of the Sadducees that souls and spirits do not exist apart from their bodies.

THE RESURRECTION, A CARDINAL DOCTRINE

As well, on this basis, Jesus proclaimed the resurrection, in which the soul and the spirit will be reunited with the body, which will be especially prepared by the Lord (I Cor. 15:38; I Thess. 4:16-17).

In fact, there was no reason for anyone who believed the Old Testament to be in the dark respecting the resurrection. Even though it was not as pronounced there as it later would be in the New Testament, still, it was clear in its teaching regarding this all-important subject.

Job's testimony is a perfect example, as he said, *"I know that my Redeemer lives, and that He shall stand at the latter day upon the Earth:*

"And though after my skin worms destroy this body, yet in my flesh shall I see God:

"Whom I shall see for myself, and my eyes shall behold" (Job 19:25-27).

THE WORD OF GOD

Psalm 16:10 shows the Messiah will be raised from the dead (Acts 2:24-32; 13:34-37). Psalm 17:15 shows a hope, not only of going

NOTES

to be with the Lord, but of a change when we are raised at Christ's Coming (I Cor. 15:51-52; I Jn. 3:2).

Psalm 73:23-26 shows faith in personal immortality to be ever with the Lord and implies the hope of the resurrection. Isaiah 53:8-12 also shows the Resurrection of the suffering Messiah, and Daniel 12:2 specifically prophesies two resurrections (Jn. 5:29; Rev. 20:4-5, 12-13).

The phrase, *"But the Pharisees confess both,"* proclaims the very opposite of the Sadducees and that which was actually scriptural, at least as far as it went.

However, it should be noted that to be scripturally correct is demanded, of course, but that alone will not suffice. In fact, the Pharisees, even though holding to the fundamentals of the faith, still hated Christ with a passion and were the chief instigators in His Crucifixion.

In other words, one can be right and still be wrong! Being Biblically correct can only come to its full potential as one, as well, makes Christ supreme within one's life.

(9) "AND THERE AROSE A GREAT CRY: AND THE SCRIBES THAT WERE OF THE PHARISEES' PART AROSE, AND STROVE, SAYING, WE FIND NO EVIL IN THIS MAN: BUT IF A SPIRIT OR AN ANGEL HAS SPOKEN TO HIM, LET US NOT FIGHT AGAINST GOD."

The composition is:

1. The phrase, *"And there arose a great cry,"* evidently pertained to pandemonium, which seems to have broken loose. To be frank, there is nothing quite like a religious argument!

2. *"And the scribes that were of the Pharisees' part arose, and strove, saying, We find no evil in this man,"* proclaims the situation being decided on the basis of doctrine and not on Paul personally per se. The Holy Spirit, no doubt, constructed this scenario.

3. Scribes were responsible for faithfully handing down the Hebrew Scriptures. They were actually the professional students of the Law and its defenders. As well, they transmitted unwritten legal decisions that had come into existence in their efforts to apply the Mosaic Law to daily life.

They were referred to at times as *"lawyers"* or *"teachers of the Law."*

For their services in the Sanhedrin, they were not paid.

4. They belonged mainly to the party of the Pharisees but, as a body, were distinct from them, albeit, joining on their side in this situation concerning Paul.

5. The phrase, *"But if a spirit or an angel has spoken to him, let us not fight against God,"* proclaims the scribes exerting their belief in the spirit world and, as well, at least after a fashion, siding with Paul.

6. To be frank, the argument was becoming very heated with tempers frayed.

(10) "AND WHEN THERE AROSE A GREAT DISSENSION, THE CHIEF CAPTAIN, FEARING LEST PAUL SHOULD HAVE BEEN PULLED IN PIECES OF THEM, COMMANDED THE SOLDIERS TO GO DOWN, AND TO TAKE HIM BY FORCE FROM AMONG THEM, AND TO BRING HIM INTO THE CASTLE."

The synopsis is:

1. In my opinion, the *"Message of the Cross"* is the most important message in the world today.

2. I believe it is what the Holy Spirit is presently saying to the churches.

THE DISSENSION

The phrase, *"And when there arose a great dissension,"* proclaims, as stated, the subject becoming very heated.

Jesus had silenced the Sadducees respecting this erroneous doctrine, but, as most, they refused to give it up. So, now they were attempting to defend their turf.

Actually, it was much easier for a Pharisee to become a Christian than it was a Sadducee. In fact, many Pharisees had become Christians, even as Paul.

However, for a Sadducee to become a Christian, he would have to give up being such altogether, as should be obvious. The same is true respecting many modern religions.

To become a Bible Christian, which, of course, refers to being a follower of Christ, one would have to give up any religion one may have, such as Islam, Buddhism, Hinduism, etc., as, of course, is obvious. However, to become a follower of Christ, one also

NOTES

would have to give up Catholicism, or Mormonism for that matter, and I mean in totality. This also includes scores of other sects, etc., that is, if one is to follow Christ. In other words, it is not possible for one to be a follower of Christ, at least according to the Word of God, and at the same time be a Catholic or a Mormon. The same would hold true for Christian Science, Jehovah's Witnesses, etc.

I realize that many would take issue with my statements concerning Catholicism; however, there is absolutely no way that Catholicism can be made to agree with the Word of God. It is totally outside the scope of Biblical salvation.

How could a Sadducee be a follower of Christ and at the same time deny the Resurrection, which, in effect, denies the Resurrection of Christ? Of course, the answer is obvious.

As well, how can a Catholic be a follower of Christ and at the same time continue to pray to Mary or to confess to a priest, of which there is not such in the New Covenant, other than Christ? Once again, the answer is obvious.

RESCUE PAUL

The phrase, *"The chief captain, fearing lest Paul should have been pulled in pieces of them, commanded the soldiers to go down, and to take him by force from among them, and to bring him into the castle,"* portrays that the situation had gotten completely out of hand.

From the manner in which the sentence is structured, it seems as if the Sadducees had become so heated that they were attempting to do Paul bodily harm, while the Pharisees and scribes were trying to defend him.

The state of things described here is exactly what the pages of Josephus and of Tacitus disclose as to the combustible state of the Jewish mind at this particular time.

Their rejection and crucifixion of Christ and continued rebellion against God, even though loudly trumpeting their faithfulness to Jehovah, had taken a deadly toll respecting the emotions of these people. Actually, *"dissension"* describes it mildly!

Such upheaval and tumult was always just beneath the surface, presenting, in fact, a constant agitation of mind and spirit, which could be flamed in a moment's time, even as here. To be frank, about the only safe place in Jerusalem at this time was the tower of Antonia, where Paul was to be taken. There he would be under the protection of Roman power. Of course, the ultimate power was of the Lord, Who was guiding and instructing all events.

(11) "AND THE NIGHT FOLLOWING THE LORD STOOD BY HIM, AND SAID, BE OF GOOD CHEER, PAUL: FOR AS YOU HAVE TESTIFIED OF ME IN JERUSALEM, SO MUST YOU BEAR WITNESS ALSO AT ROME."

The exegesis is:

1. The *"flesh"* refers to the fact that we cannot live for God by the same means that we do everything else as a human being.

2. In fact, we can only successfully live for the Lord in one way. That one way is that our faith be placed exclusively in Christ and what Christ has done for us at the Cross (Lk. 9:23).

THE APPEARANCE OF CHRIST TO PAUL

The phrase, *"And the night following the Lord stood by him,"* presents another appearance of Jesus Christ to Paul (Acts 22:8, 14, 18; I Cor. 9:1; 15:8; II Cor. 12:1-4).

Why did the Lord appear to Paul, and at this particular time?

The reasons are given to us in the remainder of the verse, and as they proved to be a tremendous help, strength, and encouragement to Paul, they will prove the same to all believers as well! Also, we will learn, I think, some things about the moving and operation of the Holy Spirit.

I might quickly ask the question, *"Was it possible that Paul struggled in his mind and spirit, wondering if he was doing the right thing by being here?"* If that did occasion to Paul, then the appearance of Christ would have laid the situation completely to rest. Simply stating, the Lord would not have appeared to Paul if Paul was out of the will of God. That should be obvious.

I want the reader to notice that the Lord *"stood by him,"* meaning that Israel had not stood by him, nor had the Sanhedrin, but

NOTES

Jesus did! The truth is this:

With some few exceptions, it has never been any different. If the person truly has Jesus standing by him, most of the time, he will not have the leadership of the church as a whole. It is tragic and sad that this is true, but regrettably, it seems to be the case most of the time.

For instance, it seems that Paul little had much support from the Jerusalem church, if any at all! No, I do not want to put words into the mouth of James or to build too much on silence. As well, the volatility of the situation in Jerusalem is surely obvious, which, of necessity, would limit what the church could actually do. We must not overlook that.

However, having said that, the silence of the church in Jerusalem, even during the two or more years of Paul's imprisonment in Caesarea, which was about 60 miles from Jerusalem, cannot help but be noticed. There is no record that anyone from the church at Jerusalem visited Paul whatsoever during this time.

And yet, on the other side of the coin, so to speak, the situation possibly could have been so volatile and so explosive that the church in Jerusalem simply could not do anything. There is definitely a possibility that this was the case.

So, as stated, Paul basically only had Jesus to stand by him, but that is more than enough.

BE OF GOOD CHEER

The phrase, *"And said, Be of good cheer, Paul,"* proclaims the fact, as should be obvious, that Paul was not of good cheer, and understandably so! In fact, he must have been terribly discouraged, considering all the adverse things that had happened, and, as well, what the future looked like it would hold.

Despite all the previous warnings given by the Holy Spirit and even the assurance as Paul had felt that he was in the will of God, Satan, no doubt, took advantage of this situation. He possibly used the circumstances to place doubts in Paul's mind. So, as stated, Jesus would appear to him with the assurance that what was happening was the will of God. This was not meaning that the Jews who would hurt or even kill Paul were in the will of God, for they certainly were not.

TESTIFIED OF JESUS IN JERUSALEM

The phrase, *"For as you have testified of Me in Jerusalem,"* proclaims the Lord as being pleased with what Paul had said to the mob, and to the Sanhedrin for that matter.

While it was true that there were no converts, at least at the present, still, Paul's conduct was right, what he said was right, and the direction was right as well.

All preachers of the Gospel delight in seeing very favorable results to their message, as should be understood. Still, the preacher is not responsible for the response, that is, if the invitation is offered correctly. Rather, he is responsible for hearing from the Lord, even as Paul had done, and then faithfully delivering what the Lord has given him to say. That is the responsibility of the man and woman of God.

Horton said, *"If one is to notice, there was absolutely no condemnation whatsoever in the Words of Jesus, only comfort and cheer."*

The phrase, *"So must you bear witness also at Rome,"* proclaims, without telling him how, that as he has testified in Jerusalem, so shall he do so in Rome as well!

This meant, as well, that despite the hatred of his enemies, the Jews in Jerusalem would not be able to kill Paul, no matter how hard they tried, which they did, and neither would such happen by the Roman authorities in Caesarea. In other words, Paul was going to Rome. Jesus had said it, and nothing would stop this being brought about.

(12) "AND WHEN IT WAS DAY, CERTAIN OF THE JEWS BANDED TOGETHER, AND BOUND THEMSELVES UNDER A CURSE, SAYING THAT THEY WOULD NEITHER EAT NOR DRINK TILL THEY HAD KILLED PAUL."

The pattern is:

1. We are to understand that every single thing we receive from the Lord, all and without exception, is made possible by what Jesus did at the Cross.

2. Understanding that, our faith must ever be in Christ and the Cross. Actually,

NOTES

the entirety of the story of the Bible is the story of *"Jesus Christ and Him Crucified."*

THE EFFORTS OF SATAN

The phrase, *"And when it was day,"* refers to the fact that these Jews who wanted to kill Paul had probably been up most of the night plotting what they would do. Consequently, one should look at the irony of the situation:

On that previous night, Jesus had stood by Paul, encouraging him and guaranteeing his protection, while these Jews had been plotting most, if not all, of the night to kill him.

Sadly, these Jews were supposed to be God's chosen People, and, as well, they were supposed to be carrying out the work of God on Earth. However, the very opposite was true!

Despite their efforts and their numerical superiority, this was a battle they could not win, but yet, one they would continue to fight. How awful it is to fight against God, for that is exactly what they were doing, even though they thought otherwise!

As we have repeatedly stated, this scenario continues to play itself out, more or less, in many and varied ways.

Both claim to be of God, but if the situation is similar to this, only one is, as should be obvious!

THE CURSE

The phrase, *"Certain of the Jews banded together, and bound themselves under a curse,"* somehow tended to make these men think that such would cause God to help them in this sordid, despicable act. In other words, their *"curse"* was a religious curse, which sought to put God in a position to where He would have to do their will.

However, such is never of God and, consequently, never recognized by God, except in a negative sense. In other words, it is impossible for one to use God's Word against Himself.

By that, I mean that one cannot take a certain passage of Scripture, using Mark 11:24 as an example, and bring about anything one selfishly desires. The believer can only bring about what God desires. As stated, He will not allow His Word to be used against His Will.

They were cursing Paul, in effect, attempting to place a religious curse upon him, while Jesus was blessing him.

THE WILL OF GOD?

The phrase, *"Saying that they would neither eat nor drink till they had killed Paul,"* implies that they thought God would help them do this dastardly thing, considering how serious they were. As someone said, *"They either broke their vow, or else died, because they did not succeed in killing Paul, as is obvious."* They did not at all have the help of the Lord, but rather His displeasure, and sore displeasure at that.

Even though we have asked the question repeatedly, due to its serious consequences, one has to wonder how that people could think they are doing the will of God in desiring to murder someone, even as these men wanted to kill Paul! What was being planned was cold-blooded murder! And yet, they somehow justified their actions in their own eyes and even thought the Lord was pleased with them regarding this evil, wicked effort.

Well, of course, the answer is obvious in that these men did not know God despite all their religious claims, and, as well, anyone who functions in such capacity does not know God. Being religious does not mean being godly, in fact, it means the very opposite!

(13) "AND THEY WERE MORE THAN FORTY WHICH HAD MADE THIS CONSPIRACY."

The synopsis is:

1. These *"forty"* here mentioned were probably at least some of the leading citizens of Jerusalem.

2. Horton said, *"In their minds they had conjectured that by Paul becoming a Preacher of Christ to the Gentiles, he had become a false prophet. They would have believed that he was enticing people to turn away from the Way in which the Lord their God had commanded them to walk, as Deuteronomy 13:5 warns when it commands the death penalty for all who do this. However, they were misreading the Text, even as many do.*

"Deuteronomy is dealing with false prophets who turn the people to the worship of false gods."

They placed their own interpretation on the Scripture, which is the plight presently of untold millions.

Once again, we have a serious misunderstanding of the Text, which, as well, characterizes all Biblical error.

(14) "AND THEY CAME TO THE CHIEF PRIESTS AND ELDERS, AND SAID, WE HAVE BOUND OURSELVES UNDER A GREAT CURSE, THAT WE WILL EAT NOTHING UNTIL WE HAVE KILLED PAUL."

The exegesis is:

1. The phrase, *"And they came to the chief priests and elders, and said,"* is meant to seek the coalition of certain members of the Sanhedrin, in other words, to make their effort official.

2. Many seem to think, even presently, that if they have some type of official acceptance or approval, regarding the leadership of religious denominations, such sanctions their actions, whatever those actions may be, with God, they think, on their side. However, wrongdoing in any capacity can never be sanctioned by God, irrespective of all the religious leadership in the world giving approval. To be frank, with some few exceptions, most religious leadership presently, and, in fact, has always been the case, is as evil and wicked as those who conspired against Paul nearly 2,000 years ago. If it is fighting God, as here, there is no way possible that it can be of God! God does not oppose Himself!

3. *"We have bound ourselves under a great curse, that we will eat nothing until we have killed Paul,"* pictures them not actually setting themselves against Paul, as they thought, but rather against God. This is a battle no one can hope to win!

4. To be frank, every believer should consider very seriously that which he favors or disfavors, respecting that which is of God, or purports to be. The believer should prayerfully seek that which is scriptural and then seek to follow accordingly, irrespective as to what others may say or do. In other words, the Word of God must be the only criterion.

NOTES

Too often (even one time is too often), believers tend to follow denominational policy, or else, the way the political wind is blowing, irrespective of what the Word of God says. Such can only lead to disaster, no matter how many people are traveling that particular road.

(15) "NOW THEREFORE YOU WITH THE COUNCIL SIGNIFY TO THE CHIEF CAPTAIN THAT HE BRING HIM DOWN UNTO YOU TO MORROW, AS THOUGH YOU WOULD ENQUIRE SOMETHING MORE PERFECTLY CONCERNING HIM: AND WE, OR EVER HE COME NEAR, ARE READY TO KILL HIM."

The overview is:

1. The phrase, *"Now therefore you with the council signify to the chief captain that he bring him down unto you to morrow,"* presents the plan.

2. More than likely, these were the Sadducee members of the Sanhedrin who were involved in this conspiracy. They hated Paul with a passion and seemed determined that he would not escape out of their hands.

3. *"As though you would enquire something more perfectly concerning him,"* now presents a lie to their conspiracy of murder.

4. *"And we, or ever he come near, are ready to kill him,"* proclaims the depth of infamy to which the religion of the carnal heart can sink cultured and religious people, of which this is a perfect example, and is repeated many times over in one way or the other.

(16) "AND WHEN PAUL'S SISTER'S SON HEARD OF THEIR LYING IN WAIT, HE WENT AND ENTERED INTO THE CASTLE, AND TOLD PAUL."

The direction is:

1. The phrase, *"And when Paul's sister's son heard of their lying in wait,"* presents Paul's nephew and all we know of his family other than references in Romans 16:7, 11, 21.

2. It is believed by some that this young man had come to Jerusalem from Tarsus to be educated, just as Paul had many years before. However, even though that may have been the case, there is no proof.

3. As well, Luke did not say if the young man was a Christian or not. It has been suggested that possibly he was not since

NOTES

in Acts, Luke usually identified those who were Christians by calling them disciples.

4. *"He went and entered into the castle, and told Paul,"* indicates that if there had been any differences between the young man and Paul, he laid them aside, going to his uncle and revealing this plot. In other words, the Lord used him.

5. How he came into this knowledge, we are not told. Evidently he somehow overheard people talking about the situation and was finally able to piece together the plot.

6. If, in fact, this is the way it did happen, this gives us at least some small clue to the idea that the young man was not a believer. If so, it is doubtful he would have been associating with these people in any manner.

(17) "THEN PAUL CALLED ONE OF THE CENTURIONS UNTO HIM, AND SAID, BRING THIS YOUNG MAN UNTO THE CHIEF CAPTAIN: FOR HE HAS A CERTAIN THING TO TELL HIM."

The form is:

1. The phrase, *"Then Paul called one of the centurions unto him, and said,"* presents that which is obvious. The Lord would have the Roman army to work for Paul and against this plot by the religious leaders of Israel.

2. *"Bring this young man unto the chief captain: for he has a certain thing to tell him,"* provides to us one of the beautiful ways in which the Lord works. Generally, it is exactly as this situation.

3. The Lord would have this young man, Paul's nephew, to overhear this plot, with the consequences being that the chief captain would now know and take suitable measures.

4. In living for the Lord well over one-half a century, I never cease to be amazed at the manner in which the Lord does things. That which seems so very complicated to us, He solves most of the time in an elementary way. Being God and knowing all things, able to do all things, and being everywhere, as well, nothing is hard for Him, as should be obvious. That is the reason that every believer ought to trust Him implicitly.

5. Nothing can happen to a Child of God unless it is caused or allowed by the Lord. We are not our own; we are bought with a price. We belong to Christ, and He takes that ownership very, very seriously.

6. As a result, John would say, *"There is no fear in love; but perfect love casts out fear"* (I Jn. 4:18).

(18) "SO HE TOOK HIM, AND BROUGHT HIM TO THE CHIEF CAPTAIN, AND SAID, PAUL THE PRISONER CALLED ME UNTO HIM, AND PRAYED ME TO BRING THIS YOUNG MAN UNTO YOU WHO HAS SOMETHING TO SAY UNTO YOU."

The account is:

1. The phrase, *"So he took him, and brought him to the chief captain, and said,"* presents Paul as not telling the centurion what he had been told, but asking that the young man would tell the chief captain personally.

2. *"Paul the prisoner called me unto him,"* presents a title that Paul came to cherish (Eph. 3:1; 4:1; II Tim. 1:8; Phile., Vs. 9).

However, Paul took it a step further, referring to himself as *"the prisoner of the Lord"* or *"a prisoner of Jesus Christ."* This meant that the Roman army, Nero, the Jews, or anyone for that matter, did not chart the course or decide the destiny of the apostle, that being the prerogative of Christ exclusively.

3. As well, every believer should understand that accordingly. We are not at the mercy of the world, Wall Street, congress, the Supreme Court, or any court or judge for that matter, or, in fact, anyone, but rather subject to Jesus Christ alone. That includes Satan and all his cohorts as well!

However, this in no way means that believers are exempt from the laws of the land, at least if those laws are moral and right, but it does mean that the Lord has the final say. In other words, men rule, but God overrules!

The phrase, *"And prayed me to bring this young man unto you, who has something to say unto you,"* presents all the plans of the plotters, as well as their hunger strike, as about to go out the window.

(19) "THEN THE CHIEF CAPTAIN TOOK HIM BY THE HAND, AND WENT WITH HIM ASIDE PRIVATELY, AND ASKED HIM, WHAT IS THAT YOU HAVE

NOTES

TO TELL ME?"

The rule is:

1. In God's Sight, faith justifies. In man's sight, work justifies.

2. However, there is a problem here that work cannot justify (Eph. 2:8-9).

ROMAN LAW

The phrase, *"Then the chief captain took him by the hand, and went with him aside privately,"* evidently presents Paul's nephew as asking for a private meeting and, also, as being quite young.

The question, *"And asked him, What is that you have to tell me?"* portrays an honest effort on the part of the chief captain to obtain the truth in all these matters.

One of the most important documentary legacies the Romans left behind was the law—the comprehensive body of statute and case law that some scholars consider one of the greatest legacies from ancient Rome.

The idea of written law as a shield—to protect individuals against one another and against the awesome power of the state—was a concept the Romans took from the Greeks. However, it was Rome that put this abstract notion into daily practice, and the practice is today honored around the world in many countries.

For instance, a Latin inscription at Harvard Law School conveys the idea precisely, *"Non sub homine sed sub deo et lege—it is not by men but by God and the law* (that we are governed)."

THE RULE OF LAW

The Romans, too, felt some ambiguity about the preeminence of law. The historian Tacitus observed—*"The worse the state, the more laws it has."* However, in the ongoing struggle between the ordinary people of Rome and the governing elites, the Plebeians (common people) decided they would much rather rely on laws than the all-too-human whims of their rulers.

Under pressure from this class or group, the governing class was repeatedly forced to issue written codes.

The first of these, the Twelve Tables, came out in 450 B.C., and the Romans continued to issue legal codes for the next 1,000 years.

Actually, the emperor Justinian's monumental compilation of the Digests, the Institutes, and the Revised Code, completed in A.D. 534, have served as the foundation of western law ever since.

THE EMPEROR AND THE LAW

A society with an all-powerful emperor who could kill at will, and a society with millions of slaves treated as human chattel, does not exactly meet our expectations for a lawful society. However, in many ways, despite that just said, Roman law, as it was practiced, would be very similar to our present law.

There were indictments and jury trials, hanging judges and soft-hearted ones, hard-hitting prosecutors and wily defense attorneys. The long-winded Cicero is a case in point. He was a man who perfected many defense techniques still in use today.

ROMAN LAW AND ESTABLISHED SAFEGUARDS

Two thousand years before the Miranda warnings, the Romans also established safeguards to assure the rights of the accused. We can see this process at work in the case against Paul, even as we are now studying.

In Chapter 22 of Acts, even as we have seen, Paul found himself before a Roman captain, with the suspicion on the part of the captain that he had provoked a riot. He was about to be beaten and jailed when Paul exclaimed his Roman citizenship. That changed everything, and he was put in protective custody for his own safety, pending a trial.

Later, as we shall see, the chief priests of Jerusalem complained to the Roman governor Festus about the failure to prosecute. Festus responded with a lecture on legal rights: *"It is not the Roman custom to hand over any man before he has faced his accusers and has had an opportunity to defend himself against their charges."*

As well, as we shall see, Paul again asserted yet another legal prerogative—his right to make an appeal directly to Caesar.

To show their respect for law, even after Augustus established one-man rule, in other words, a dictatorship, there was a tendency among the emperors to abide by legal dictates. To be sure, there was not much that people could do if a Nero or Caligula rode roughshod over the law, but, for the most part, even the emperors felt obliged to obey.

(20) "AND HE SAID, THE JEWS HAVE AGREED TO DESIRE YOU THAT YOU WOULD BRING DOWN PAUL TO MORROW INTO THE COUNCIL, AS THOUGH THEY WOULD ENQUIRE SOMEWHAT OF HIM MORE PERFECTLY."

The rule is:

1. The phrase, *"And he said, The Jews have agreed to desire you that you would bring down Paul to morrow into the council,"* refers to the Jewish Sanhedrin, the ruling body of Israel, both secular and religious. By using the name *"Jews,"* it does not refer to all of Israel but only to a designated leadership.

2. This depth of infamy to which the religion of the carnal heart can sink cultured and religious people is seen in the collusion of the chief ministers of Judaism with the assassins.

3. *"As though they would enquire somewhat of him more perfectly,"* posed what seemed on the surface a reasonable request, and probably would have been readily heeded by the chief captain had he not been warned by Paul's nephew.

What I am about to say, I realize is very strong, but yet, I believe it to be true.

4. Bible Christianity projects Jesus as the Head of the church (Eph. 1:20-23), and a very active Head at that. He does His Work through the person, office, and agency of the Holy Spirit, as the Third Person of the Godhead reveals the will of God to yielded men and women to be used as instruments (I Cor. 2:9-16).

However, for men and women to be such instruments, it demands a close walk with God, with most unwilling to pay the price.

5. As a result, carnal men in the church (whatever the church may be), at times, gradually gain the ascendancy, with the Word of God, which is to be the standard at all times, gradually set aside in favor of man's rules and regulations, etc. Men, and religious men most of all, love to lord it over others, and strangely enough, many preachers love being lorded over (Mat. 20:25-28).

NOTES

6. Once control is gained, these men, and regrettably, they are greatly in the majority, will do almost anything to maintain that control. As should now be obvious, the Lord is no longer serving as the Head of the church, with it now controlled by men, which is without a doubt the greatest hindrance to revival, a moving of the Spirit, and the work of God being carried out. In such atmosphere, the Holy Spirit will little work, with what little He attempts to do almost all the time quickly smothered by the *"lords"* of the church.

7. As we have said several times in the past, the only thing that stops many religious leaders from murder is the law of the land. If the law permitted, as it has countless times in history, many would torture and murder with gleeful self-righteousness, doing it all in the name of the Lord.

(21) "BUT DO NOT THOU YIELD UNTO THEM: FOR THERE LIE IN WAIT FOR HIM OF THEM MORE THAN FORTY MEN, WHICH HAVE BOUND THEMSELVES WITH AN OATH, THAT THEY WILL NEITHER EAT NOR DRINK TILL THEY HAVE KILLED HIM: AND NOW ARE THEY READY, LOOKING FOR A PROMISE FROM YOU."

The pattern is:

1. The Holy Spirit alone can bring that which is required of the believer, a life of righteousness and holiness (Rom. 8:1-11).

2. It is impossible for the believer to sanctify himself, at least according to the New Covenant (Rom. 8:10).

THE TRIBUNE

The phrase, *"But do not thou yield unto them,"* was not meant to tell the tribune what to do but would now follow up with an explanation.

The phrase, *"For there lie in wait for him of them more than forty men, which have bound themselves with an oath, that they will neither eat nor drink till they have killed him,"* immediately got the tribune's attention.

The taking of the law into one's own hands, or else, as here, the plot to commit cold-blooded murder, constituted a serious

NOTES

breach of Roman law, as should be obvious. Consequently, if such had succeeded, it would, no doubt, have cost many lives, with Roman power coming down heavily. As well, it could have caused the tribune great problems, even his own execution. However, the Lord was orchestrating these events respecting the overruling of the plans of evil men.

To be sure, such is not an isolated case. Men rule, while the Lord overrules. Against our own ministry, I can recall countless efforts by evil men, many of them religious, just as in Paul's time, who would attempt to cause great problems, but every time, the Lord has worked out the situation, just as He did for Paul.

WHY DID THESE JEWS HATE PAUL SO MUCH?

These people wanted to shut Paul's mouth. In other words, they wanted to stop him from preaching the Gospel. And yet, all claimed to be of God, even those who were plotting to kill Paul.

One might well ask the question that if the Lord was foiling the plots of these religious assassins, as He most certainly was, why did He not at the same time deliver Paul from the imprisonment he would soon face?

I realize the stock answer to that question is that the Lord wanted Paul in Rome, even as Verse 11 states, and would use this method to bring about that result. However, that answer begs the question!

God being God and able to do all things, He could have certainly gotten Paul to Rome any number of ways. Therefore, the only suitable answer is that the Lord, for whatever reason, wanted Paul imprisoned for this period of time, even as Paul himself stated (Eph. 3:1).

The Lord is not required to explain to His Children all the things He does. Actually, the very rudiment of Christianity is that the believer follow the Lord without question, and that perfect obedience does not really need an answer. It simply trusts, and that is enough!

The phrase, *"And now are they ready, looking for a promise from you,"* proclaims the plot set in motion, to which the tribune would probably have readily agreed had not the young man warned him.

(22) "SO THE CHIEF CAPTAIN THEN LET THE YOUNG MAN DEPART, AND CHARGED HIM, SEE YOU TELL NO MAN THAT YOU HAVE SHOWN THESE THINGS TO ME."

The diagram is:

1. The phrase, *"So the chief captain then let the young man depart,"* probably refers to this boy being in his mid-teens. Irrespective, he had made an impression upon the chief captain, with the tribune believing him.

2. *"And charged him, see you tell no man that you have shown these things to me,"* seems to imply a stronger command than usual, and was probably done so because of the youthfulness of the boy. However, I do not think the tribune had any need for concern.

3. It is believed, although not stated, that the young man went and related to Paul his ready acceptance by the tribune, which, no doubt, encouraged Paul greatly.

(23) "AND HE CALLED UNTO HIM TWO CENTURIONS, SAYING, MAKE READY TWO HUNDRED SOLDIERS TO GO TO CAESAREA, AND HORSEMEN THREESCORE AND TEN, AND SPEARMEN TWO HUNDRED, AT THE THIRD HOUR OF THE NIGHT."

The rule is:

1. The preaching of the Cross is the power of God (I Cor. 1:18).

2. The power is actually in the Holy Spirit; however, the Holy Spirit functions entirely within the parameters, so to speak, of the Finished Work of Christ. It is the Cross that gives the Holy Spirit the means to do all that He does (I Cor. 1:17).

CAESAREA

The phrase, *"And he called unto him two centurions, saying, Make ready two hundred soldiers to go to Caesarea,"* meant, as is obvious, 100 to the centurion.

This magnificent city was built by Herod the Great on the Mediterranean about 60 miles northwest of Jerusalem.

Named in honor of the Roman emperor

Caesar Augustus, it was the Roman metropolis of Judaea and the official residence both of the Herodian kings and the Roman procurators (governors).

It stood on the great caravan route between Tyre and Egypt and, thus, was a busy commercial center for inland trade.

However, Caesarea was also a celebrated maritime trading center. This was due largely to the 200 feet wide causeway of huge stones in water 60 feet deep in order to enclose an artificial harbor that was unusually large for that day, all built by Herod.

The city was lavishly adorned with palaces, public buildings, and an enormous amphitheater. One outstanding architectural feature was a huge temple dedicated to Caesar and Rome and containing large statues of the emperor.

If it is to be remembered, Caesarea was the abode of the centurion Cornelius and the locale of his conversion (Acts 10:1, 24; 11:11). As well, it was here at Caesarea that Peter gained greater insight into the nature of the Divine Kingdom by realizing that God had disrupted the barriers between gentile and Jewish believers (Acts 10:35), and had dispensed with such classifications as *"clean"* and *"unclean."*

SOLDIERS

The phrase, *"And horsemen threescore and ten, and spearmen two hundred,"* made a total of 470 men, counting the 200 soldiers.

The Romans sternly opposed rioting of any nature, seeing such as a strike against Roman peace. They already had frequent proofs of the turbulence of the Jews. Actually, Roman officers who permitted rioting, and who failed to protect Roman citizens, were usually put to death. So now, it becomes a little more understandable respecting this action taken by the tribune.

The phrase, *"At the third hour of the night,"* referred to 9:00 p.m.

The tribune rightly reasoned that they would be miles away from Jerusalem by daylight, and if somehow the Jews discovered the situation, the force was large enough to throw off any likely effort.

(24) "AND PROVIDE THEM BEASTS,

NOTES

THAT THEY MAY SET PAUL ON, AND BRING HIM SAFE UNTO FELIX THE GOVERNOR."

The diagram is:

1. The phrase, *"And provide them beasts, that they may set Paul on,"* probably placed the apostle next to one of the centurions in the very midst of the force.

2. *"And bring him safe unto Felix the governor,"* does not exactly present a man of kind disposition to whom Paul must answer.

3. Marcus Antonius Felix was governor of Judaea from A.D. 52 to 59. He was a freedman (former slave) of the emperor Claudius or of the emperor's mother.

4. He was a violent man who slaughtered many Jews as well as others. Tacitus, the Roman historian, wrote: *"He reveled in cruelty and lust, and wielded the power of a King with the mind of a slave."*

5. Suetonius said that he had three wives, each a daughter of a king.

6. So, by ruthlessness and friends in high places, he had clawed his way to this present position of governor. This was quite a promotion for a former slave.

7. Irrespective, the Lord would guide events while watching over Paul, no matter this cruel governor.

(25) "AND HE WROTE A LETTER AFTER THIS MANNER."

The overview is:

1. This tells us that the tribune did not accompany this show of force but entrusted Paul to the centurions, with this letter written by his hand to the governor.

2. There is conjecture as to how Luke knew the contents of this letter.

3. Some think that the centurion showed it to Paul, with him possibly even copying it, considering its brevity.

4. The phrase, *"After this manner,"* actually means, *"A type, pattern, or copy."* So, what follows is probably a word for word copy, with either Paul or Luke somehow coming into possession, or at least observance, of the letter.

(26) "CLAUDIUS LYSIAS UNTO THE MOST EXCELLENT GOVERNOR FELIX SENDS GREETING."

The composition is:

1. The name *"Claudius Lysias"* probably

represents the name taken by the tribune at the time he bought his Roman citizenship.

2. Lysias was a Greek name common in Syria, indicating the man was a Greek.

3. The phrase, *"Unto the most excellent governor Felix sends greeting,"* represents a good style of letter writing of that day.

(27) "THIS MAN WAS TAKEN OF THE JEWS, AND SHOULD HAVE BEEN KILLED OF THEM: THEN CAME I WITH AN ARMY, AND RESCUED HIM, HAVING UNDERSTOOD THAT HE WAS A ROMAN."

The structure is:

1. The phrase, *"This man was taken of the Jews, and should have been killed of them,"* immediately stressed the problem in order that the governor would have no doubt as to what was being said and done.

2. *"Then came I with an army, and rescued him, having understood that he was a Roman,"* is somewhat misleading, making the governor think that the rescue came upon learning that Paul was a Roman.

3. As is obvious, he omitted his proposed scourging of Paul, only stopping when Paul divulged the information concerning his Roman citizenship.

4. Nevertheless, what Lysias said in its simplicity was probably better than to have gone into too much detail.

(28) "AND WHEN I WOULD HAVE KNOWN THE CAUSE WHEREFORE THEY ACCUSED HIM, I BROUGHT HIM FORTH INTO THEIR COUNCIL."

The exegesis is:

1. The phrase, *"And when I would have known the cause wherefore they accused him,"* presented Paul in a good light. In other words, he was not jumping to conclusions.

2. *"I brought him forth into their council,"* refers to the Sanhedrin.

3. It is of note that most of the Roman officers who are described in the New Testament were well-disposed to the Jews, and later on, it seems, to the Christians. Actually, two centurions are mentioned by name. Cornelius at Caesarea worshiped God and became a believer in Christ and a recipient of the Holy Spirit, the first gentile to receive (Acts, Chpts. 10 and 11).

4. In Acts, Chapter 27, as we shall see, Julius, another centurion, conducted Paul to Rome and treated him with consideration and kindness.

NOTES

5. It also seems that other centurions believed and put their faith in Jesus. One of them, who Jesus described as having greater faith than anyone in Israel, was stationed at Capernaum (Mat. 8:5-10). The other centurion was guarding Jesus at the Cross, with every evidence being that he accepted Him as his Lord and Saviour (Mat. 27:54).

6. Horton said, *"It is an interesting sidelight that neither Jesus nor Peter nor Paul asked any of these soldiers to quit the army, proclaiming that they recognized the significance of Civil Government."*

(29) "WHOM I PERCEIVED TO BE ACCUSED OF QUESTIONS OF THEIR LAW, BUT TO HAVE NOTHING LAID TO HIS CHARGE WORTHY OF DEATH OR OF BONDS."

The synopsis is:

1. The phrase, *"Whom I perceived to be accused of questions of their Law,"* means, at the same time, that nothing was done by Paul which constituted a breaking of Roman law.

2. *"But to have nothing laid to his charge worthy of death or of bonds,"* presents a powerful testimony, considering that it came from the chief captain.

(30) "AND WHEN IT WAS TOLD ME HOW THAT THE JEWS LAID WAIT FOR THE MAN, I SENT STRAIGHTWAY TO YOU, AND GAVE COMMANDMENT TO HIS ACCUSERS ALSO TO SAY BEFORE YOU WHAT THEY HAD AGAINST HIM. FAREWELL."

The pattern is:

1. The Law of Moses was God's Standard of Righteousness.

2. However, it was a standard that man could not keep. And yet, it can be kept, but only in Jesus Christ and what He did for us at the Cross.

THE LETTER

The phrase, *"And when it was told me how that the Jews laid wait for the man,"* pertains, as is obvious, to Roman power protecting Paul from the Jews.

Actually, the entirety of this scenario is

a fulfillment of the words of Jesus when He said, *"And he that has no sword, let him sell his garment, and buy one"* (Lk. 22:36). This means that Christians were to accept the protection of an ordered government. The term *"sword"* means the power of the magistrate (Rom. 13:4).

It is ironic that true believers would need the protection of the government from others who call themselves believers as well! However, as stated, this situation continues unto this very hour, at least in one way or the other.

It is difficult to understand how that people who claim to be following Christ would at the same time resort to actions that could be described as none other than hatred, which many times is fueled by jealousy and envy. However, such is the case, so much so, in fact, that one is thankful for the law of the land that offers some protection.

A PERSONAL EXPERIENCE

Back in 1968, the Lord told me to go on radio, which we did in January, 1969. The program quickly expanded to approximately 600 stations daily. Preachers who did not believe in the Baptism with the Holy Spirit with the evidence of speaking with other tongues tried every method at their disposal to get us off the air. They were not successful, but it was not for lack of trying, and I speak of outright lies, etc. I know in my heart that if the law had permitted such, these men would have killed me, even in the name of the Lord, exactly as the Jews of old regarding Paul, etc.

In 1972, we went on television, with the Lord quickly blessing our efforts until the program was being aired in many nations of the world, translated into various languages. Regrettably and sadly, those of my own Pentecostal persuasion (they were Pentecostal in name only) attempted, as well, to get us off the air, even as we have previously stated. Again, I was thankful for the law of the land that protected us after a measure, for the hatred from this source was even more pronounced than the other. Actually, the Lord had told me in 1982, *"Your own will turn against you."*

It came to pass exactly as the Lord had spoken.

NOTES

THE GOVERNOR

I realize that most of the laity in the church, of whatever denomination, little understands that of which I speak, with the far, far greater majority not really believing what I say. However, even as Paul said, *"Now the things which I write unto you, behold, before God, I lie not"* (Gal. 1:20).

The phrase, *"I sent straightway to you,"* refers to the governor before whom this case should be tried.

"And gave commandment to his accusers also to say before you what they had against him," no doubt, refers to the tribune telling the Sanhedrin that they would now have to deal with the governor respecting Paul, for the apostle was now out of his jurisdiction.

The word *"farewell"* was the general benediction, as here given, representative of most letters of that day.

(31) "THEN THE SOLDIERS, AS IT WAS COMMANDED THEM, TOOK PAUL, AND BROUGHT HIM BY NIGHT TO ANTIPATRIS."

The account is:

1. The phrase, *"Then the soldiers, as it was commanded them,"* speaks of duty, including marching all of that night, which, no doubt, was not enjoyed very much. However, Roman discipline among its military was noted all over the world of that day and actually represented their great strength.

2. *"Took Paul, and brought him by night to Antipatris,"* represents a distance of about 40 miles, which means they must have marched without stopping for about 15 hours. As is obvious, this was quite a forced march.

3. A Roman garrison was headquartered at Antipatris, a small town on the plain of Sharon, with the centurions now feeling safe from a possible Jewish attack, hence, getting some rest.

(32) "ON THE MORROW THEY LEFT THE HORSEMEN TO GO WITH HIM, AND RETURNED TO THE CASTLE."

The way is:

Here the Infantry of some 400 soldiers, after a period of rest, returned to Jerusalem, while the cavalry, consisting of some 70 horsemen, marched the remaining approximate 26 miles to Caesarea, there handing Paul over to the viceroy.

(33) "WHO, WHEN THEY CAME TO CAESAREA, AND DELIVERED THE EPISTLE TO THE GOVERNOR, PRESENTED PAUL ALSO BEFORE HIM."

The form is:

1. The phrase, *"Who, when they came to Caesarea,"* presents, as we have stated, this city as the political capital and home of the governor instead of Jerusalem.

2. It must have been quite a sight to see these 70 horsemen coming into the city, with Paul, no doubt, riding beside their leader. The people viewing this procession undoubtedly thought this was someone of great note, which it was. Actually, there was no one in the Roman Empire who could equal the status of Paul and those of the Twelve who remained, plus others in the early church, at least in the eyes of God, Whose Eyes alone mattered!

3. The phrase, *"And delivered the Epistle to the governor,"* pertains to the letter of Verse 25.

4. *"Presented Paul also before him,"* seems to indicate that the cavalry leader waited for the governor to read the letter before he presented Paul.

(34) "AND WHEN THE GOVERNOR HAD READ THE LETTER, HE ASKED OF WHAT PROVINCE HE WAS. AND WHEN HE UNDERSTOOD THAT HE WAS OF CILICIA."

The form is:

1. The phrase, *"And when the governor had read the letter,"* presents the single most important document this man had ever read; however, he would have understood very little of its significance at this time.

2. That he had standing in front of him the foremost apostle of that day, a man who could open up the Gospel of salvation as possibly no other, was not readily understood at that time, if ever! Blind men cannot see, irrespective of the evidence presented unto them, and Felix was spiritually blind, as is most of the world, and for all time. Later on, under the testimony of Paul, he would have great opportunity to accept Christ but would let this all-important moment slip by, as do most.

3. The question, *"He asked of what province he was,"* pertained to Roman authority.

4. Horton said, *"Only if he came from a Roman Province could Felix, as a Roman Governor, take charge of Paul on his own authority (that is, without sending away to Rome to get the Emperor's permission)."*

5. The phrase, *"And when he understood that he was of Cilicia,"* means that it automatically gave the governor jurisdiction.

6. Cilicia was an important district or province in southeast Asia Minor between the Taurus Mountains and the Mediterranean Sea. It was separated from Syria on the east by Mount Amanas and was bound on the west by Pamphylia. The western part of the province is mountainous. The eastern part is a fertile, alluvial plain, with Tarsus, the birthplace of Paul, as its chief city.

7. The Romans took control of Cilicia beginning with Pompey's conquest about 66 B.C. Cicero, the famous Roman orator, was its governor for a short time in 51-50 B.C.

8. The fact that Paul was a Roman citizen from this important province meant that Felix could not ignore him.

(35) "I WILL HEAR YOU, SAID HE, WHEN YOUR ACCUSERS ARE ALSO COME. AND HE COMMANDED HIM TO BE KEPT IN HEROD'S JUDGMENT HALL."

The account is:

1. The phrase, *"I will hear you, said he, when your accusers are also come,"* pertained to members or representatives of the Jewish Sanhedrin. At that time, he would hear the accusations of these men, as well as Paul's defense.

2. *"And he commanded him to be kept in Herod's judgment hall,"* evidently was a part of the lavish palace built by Herod the Great. It served as the capitol building, as well as the official residence of the Roman procurators or governors.

3. Evidently, there were some prison cells attached to this *"judgment hall."*

"The Great Physician now is near,
"The sympathizing Jesus;
"He speaks the drooping heart to cheer,
"Oh hear the Voice of Jesus!"

"Your many sins are all forgiven,
"Oh! hear the Voice of Jesus;
"Go on your way in peace to Heaven,
"And wear a crown with Jesus."

"All Glory to the dying Lamb,
"I now believe in Jesus;
"I love the Blessed Saviour's Name,
"I love the Name of Jesus."

"And when to that bright world above,
"We rise to be with Jesus,
"We'll sing around the Throne of Love,
"His Name, the Name of Jesus."

CHAPTER 24

(1) "AND AFTER FIVE DAYS ANANIAS THE HIGH PRIEST DESCENDED WITH THE ELDERS, AND WITH A CERTAIN ORATOR NAMED TERTULLUS, WHO INFORMED THE GOVERNOR AGAINST PAUL."

The construction is:

1. The phrase, *"And after five days Ananias the high priest descended with the elders,"* probably represented members of the Sanhedrin who were Sadducees. It is unlikely that they would have brought any of the Pharisees, inasmuch as Paul had long been of that particular persuasion.

2. *"And with a certain orator named Tertullus, who informed the governor against Paul,"* simply means that he served as the lawyer or advocate for the Jews.

3. With Roman law and the Latin language being usual in the viceregal courts, advocates such as Tertullus were frequently employed by the Jews. Such men practiced in the provincial courts of law before proceeding to the great cities of the empire.

4. Horton said, *"Tertullus was a common Roman name. He was probably a Jew who was a Roman citizen trained in Roman oratory and legal methods. He was hired, no doubt, to counteract the effect of Paul's Roman citizenship as well as to impress Felix."*

(2) "AND WHEN HE WAS CALLED FORTH, TERTULLUS BEGAN TO ACCUSE HIM, SAYING, SEEING THAT BY YOU WE ENJOY GREAT QUIETNESS, AND THAT VERY WORTHY DEEDS ARE DONE UNTO THIS NATION BY YOUR PROVIDENCE."

The direction is:

1. The phrase, *"And when he was called forth, Tertullus began to accuse him,"* presents the manner in which this advocate approached his task. There were three parts to the oration.

a. Praise for the governor;
b. Accusation of Paul; and,
c. Narration of the charge.

2. The phrase, *"Saying, Seeing that by you we enjoy great quietness, and that very worthy deeds are done unto this nation by your providence,"* presents that which was mere flattery and actually the opposite of the truth.

3. In truth, Felix had incited robbers to assassinate the high priest, Jonathan, who had displeased him. Then he had many of the same robbers captured and crucified. His rule was one of cruelty and a tyrannical spirit.

4. Instead of there being *"great quietness"* as this orator claimed, the very opposite was actually the case. Felix had brought neither reforms nor great prosperity and success to the Jews. Instead, there was constant turmoil throughout his governorship.

5. Josephus said that even though he did suppress some of the robbers and murderers in Judea, he was himself *"more hurtful than them all."*

6. His brother Pallas was a favorite of the emperor Claudius, causing Felix to think he could basically do whatever he desired. The result was continuous revolts and constant dissatisfaction.

7. Actually, his governorship was an important factor leading up to the revolt of the Jews, which brought about the destruction of Jerusalem in A.D. 70.

(3) "WE ACCEPT IT ALWAYS, AND IN ALL PLACES, MOST NOBLE FELIX, WITH ALL THANKFULNESS."

The order is:

1. The phrase, *"We accept it always, and in all places,"* pronounces the flattery

NOTES

increasing to a ridiculous degree.

2. The phrase, *"Most noble Felix, with all thankfulness,"* was again, the very opposite of the attitude of the Jews and even those who stood there this very day. If we are to notice, Paul engaged in none of this rhetoric upon his turn to address the governor.

(4) "NOTWITHSTANDING, THAT I BE NOT FURTHER TEDIOUS UNTO YOU, I PRAY YOU THAT YOU WOULD HEAR US OF YOUR CLEMENCY A FEW WORDS."

The status is:

1. The phrase, *"Notwithstanding, that I be not further tedious unto you,"* has reference to the desire for brevity.

2. The phrase, *"I pray you that you would hear us of your clemency a few words,"* pertains to *"mildness, gentleness, and fairness,"* of which this man was the very opposite.

(5) "FOR WE HAVE FOUND THIS MAN A PESTILENT FELLOW, AND A MOVER OF SEDITION AMONG ALL THE JEWS THROUGHOUT THE WORLD, AND A RINGLEADER OF THE SECT OF THE NAZARENES."

The rule is:

1. The phrase, *"For we have found this man a pestilent fellow, and a mover of sedition among all the Jews throughout the world,"* presents in this verse three of the four accusations against Paul:

a. The Greek word for *"pestilent"* is *"loimos"* and means *"a plague."* It was a term used by current authors of a very bad or profligate man. He did not say that Paul was a pestilent fellow, as the Text seems to indicate, but actually, pestilence itself. As stated, there was hardly anything worse he could say about the apostle. However, Tertullus did not give any specific instance or any proof to uphold this accusation.

b. They accused him of stirring up sedition among all Jews, which he hoped would excite the anger of the Roman governor. To accuse someone of insurrection, especially considering the long record of Jewish revolts, was most likely to weigh heavily on the Roman procurator, or at least it was hoped.

c. They accused him, as well, of being a ringleader of heresy, a follower of Christ.

NOTES

d. As the next verse will show, he was also accused of being a defiler of the Jewish Temple.

2. As is obvious, the charges were strong but without any substance. In other words, there was no proof of what they were saying, or else, there was no wrong or harm in what was being done, such as Paul being one of the leaders among the followers of Christ.

3. The phrase, *"And a ringleader of the sect of the Nazarenes,"* presents the name coined by the Jews referring to followers of Christ.

4. Jews would not call them Christians, as this word was derived from the Greek word for Messiah, which they vehemently denied concerning Jesus.

5. The title *"Nazarenes"* simply meant followers of the Man of Nazareth.

(6) "WHO ALSO HAS GONE ABOUT TO PROFANE THE TEMPLE: WHOM WE TOOK, AND WOULD HAVE JUDGED ACCORDING TO OUR LAW."

The diagram is:

1. The phrase, *"Who also has gone about to profane the Temple,"* presents the most weighty charge, for the Romans permitted Jews to put anyone to death who profaned the Temple.

2. However, Paul did not profane the Temple in any way, and neither did he do anything that could have been misconstrued as such. He had not brought a gentile into the Temple as they had claimed (Acts 21:28-29), consequently, they could not produce such a gentile. In other words, their charges were pure fabrications.

3. The phrase, *"Whom we took, and would have judged according to our Law,"* presents that which is another outright lie. They had no intention of giving him a trial, as the word *"judge"* implies, but rather were attempting to beat him to death before he was rescued by the tribune.

4. Tertullus, however, pretended that Paul was arrested and was being judged by Jewish Law. He implied that they were doing what they had a right to do under the permission that the Roman government had given them.

(7) "BUT THE CHIEF CAPTAIN LYSIAS CAME UPON US, AND WITH GREAT

VIOLENCE TOOK HIM AWAY OUT OF OUR HANDS."

The synopsis is:

1. The phrase, *"But the chief captain Lysias came upon us,"* is meant to throw the Roman tribune in a bad light. It was a bad mistake on the part of Tertullus, considering that the governor had a letter from the tribune stating what the situation had been, which he was far more apt to believe.

2. *"And with great violence took him away out of our hands,"* fails to state that they were trying to kill Paul and that the *"great violence"* was actually on their part.

3. Felix knew of the constant turbulence of the Jews and that the Temple was one of the most volatile places of all. He also knew that the Roman tribune was responsible for keeping order in this place, and anywhere in Jerusalem for that matter, and would not have taken Paul from them if he had not felt it was right to do so. He had done his duty in rescuing Paul from the mob.

4. One can see here how the Holy Spirit orchestrated these events, causing this orator or advocate to overplay his hand.

5. Actually, we have personally had this very same thing to happen when we have been unjustly brought before particular courts. The Holy Spirit, at times, has caused the lawyers for the opposing side to make wild statements, which had a telling effect on the judge and fell out on our behalf.

(8) "COMMANDING HIS ACCUSERS TO COME UNTO YOU, BY EXAMINING OF WHOM YOURSELF MAY TAKE KNOWLEDGE OF ALL THESE THINGS, WHEREOF WE ACCUSE HIM."

The exegesis is:

1. The phrase, *"Commanding his accusers to come unto you,"* proclaims Tertullus declaring this to be wrong. He was now accusing the tribune.

2. Actually, some scholars claim that Tertullus meant that Lysias the tribune should be examined rather than Paul, with the apostle turned over to the Jews for trial, i.e., *"execution."* However, Felix knew from the letter that the Jews had attempted to wrest Paul from the custody of the chief captain, desiring to kill him, and actually planning to violate Roman law themselves.

NOTES

In truth, as is obvious, they, and not Paul, were the violators of Roman law!

3. *"By examining of whom your self may take knowledge of all these things, whereof we accuse him,"* refers to the fact that the situation was now in the court of the governor, even though the Jews did not think it should be there. For all of their plotting, they had not helped their cause.

(9) "AND THE JEWS ALSO ASSENTED, SAYING THAT THESE THINGS WERE SO."

The overview is:

1. The phrase, *"And the Jews also assented,"* refers to the high priest and those with him, who joined in with their voices of approval, respecting the statements of their hired advocate.

2. *"Saying that these things were so,"* means they kept affirming them over and over, seemingly thinking that such would impress the governor.

3. So now, they had made accusations not only against Paul but the Roman tribune, as well, which proved to be their undoing.

(10) "THEN PAUL, AFTER THAT THE GOVERNOR HAD BECKONED UNTO HIM TO SPEAK, ANSWERED, FORASMUCH AS I KNOW THAT YOU HAVE BEEN OF MANY YEARS A JUDGE UNTO THIS NATION, I DO THE MORE CHEERFULLY ANSWER FOR MYSELF."

The construction is:

1. The phrase, *"Then Paul, after that the governor had beckoned unto him to speak, answered,"* presents that which the Holy Spirit had said that Paul would do, *"To bear My Name before the gentiles, and kings, and the children of Israel"* (Acts 9:15).

2. However, lest anyone think of glamour, etc., the Holy Spirit quickly followed by saying (referring to Jesus), *"For I will show him* (Paul) *how great things he must suffer for My Name's sake"* (Acts 9:16).

3. The phrase, *"Forasmuch as I know that you have been of many years a judge unto this nation,"* presents the apostle referring to the long experience of the governor in Jewish affairs, making it a subject of his opening reference—a courteous and conciliatory reference in striking contrast with the false flattery of Tertullus.

4. Felix had been made governor in

A.D. 53, with it now probably being the year A.D. 58. But yet, the Roman historian Tacitus expressly stated that Felix was joint governor with Cumanus for some years, and, therefore, he had, in fact, been a judge to the Jewish nation even longer than the five years here represented. Consequently, Felix was somewhat knowledgeable concerning Jewish Law.

5. The phrase, *"I do the more cheerfully answer for myself,"* does not refer to mere rhetoric on the part of Paul, but was sincere.

6. There was no one in the world at that time who knew Mosaic Law any better than Paul. As well, being a Roman citizen, he was quite knowledgeable concerning Roman law.

7. So, even though the high priest, who was supposed to be the highest spiritual authority in Israel, could not answer for himself respecting these accusations, Paul could, and *"cheerfully so."*

(11) "BECAUSE THAT YOU MAY UNDERSTAND, THAT THERE ARE YET BUT TWELVE DAYS SINCE I WENT UP TO JERUSALEM FOR TO WORSHIP."

The synopsis is:

1. The phrase, *"Because that you may understand,"* is meant to proclaim to the governor the brevity of time and, consequently, the impossibility to foment insurrection, etc., in such a short period.

2. *"That there are yet but twelve days since I went up to Jerusalem for to worship,"* pertains to four days of the seven purifying himself in the Temple (Acts 21:27), and on the fifth day, giving his defense before the Sanhedrin (Acts 23:1-10). On the sixth day, the 40 Jews plotted to kill him (Acts 23:12-22), with the soldiers taking him that night to Antipatris (Acts 23:23-31). On the seventh day, he was brought to Caesarea and presented to Felix (Acts 23:32-35), and now, some five days later, he was on trial before Felix, thus, accounting for the entirety of the 12 days.

3. As stated, it should be obvious that there was no room for any type of insurrection or sedition as claimed by the Sanhedrin.

4. As well, Paul was telling the governor and all concerned that his only purpose for being in the Temple was to worship God.

NOTES

(12) "AND THEY NEITHER FOUND ME IN THE TEMPLE DISPUTING WITH ANY MAN, NEITHER RAISING UP THE PEOPLE, NEITHER IN THE SYNAGOGUES, NOR IN THE CITY."

The structure is:

1. If the heart of man is honest, earnest, and sincere, the Lord will reveal the truth to such an individual.

2. That truth in one way or the other will be, *"Jesus Christ and Him Crucified"* (I Cor. 1:23; 2:2).

PAUL'S STATEMENT

The phrase, *"And they neither found me in the Temple disputing with any man,"* means that he was not involved in an argument, a dispute, a misunderstanding, or anything that could be misconstrued as a defilement of the Temple. As stated, he was simply worshiping God.

The commotion had come about simply because some of the Jews there, actually from Asia, recognized Paul, and because they hated him to such an extent, they claimed that he had brought a gentile into the Temple with him, etc. Of course, all of that was a fabrication, with them unable to produce this alleged gentile or even tell who he was, and for the simple reason that he did not exist.

There was a commotion all right, which resulted in a near riot, but it was caused strictly by the Jews and not by Paul, unless his mere presence in the Temple constituted some type of breaking of the Law, which is absurd!

The phrase, *"Neither raising up the people,"* applies to the charge that he was stirring up sedition among the Jews. This was not true in any capacity!

The phrase, *"Neither in the synagogues, nor in the city,"* refers to the fact that absolutely nothing had been done that could be misconstrued in any way as it referred to these charges.

While it was true that in other cities there had been riots, or near so, just as here, it was not because of anything Paul had done, for he had only preached the Gospel. Disturbances had come about because of the reaction of Jews to the Gospel, which was,

NOTES

for the most part, very negative. However, their response was in no way his fault.

THE JEWS

As we have already stated, Rome probably had more difficulty with this province of Judea than any other province or area in the Roman Empire. There was a reason for that, which was little understood, if at all, by Rome.

Israel considered herself as the premier nation of the world and not Rome. In fact, this was true, in a sense, for approximately 400 years, especially under David and Solomon. In other words, Israel was decreed by God to serve as the leading nation of the world, with the Lord plainly telling them, *"And you shall lend unto many nations, but you shall not borrow.*

"And the LORD shall make you the head, and not the tail; and you shall be above only, and you shall not be beneath; if that you hearken unto the Commandments of the LORD your God, which I command you this day, to observe and to do them" (Deut. 28:12-13).

However, He also plainly told them that if they forsook the Law of God, *"The LORD shall bring a nation against you from far ... Therefore shall you serve your enemies which the LORD shall send against you"* (Deut., Chpt. 28).

Exactly what the Lord said would happen did happen, and now they attempted to regain their status by insurrection and war against Rome, which was not possible!

JESUS THE SAVIOUR

When Jesus came, Israel's Messiah, she would not recognize Him, irrespective that this was the very purpose for her existence. However, the few who did recognize Him thought surely He would restore Israel at that time to her rightful place and position. Of course, without a total change of heart, which Israel flatly refused, restoration was not then possible. In fact, the very purpose of the First Coming of Jesus, even as He was born of the Virgin Mary in order that He would become the Second Man and, therefore, the Last Adam, was to redeem the whole of mankind and not Israel only. Of course, Israel didn't even believe she needed redemption. However, such will change at the Second Coming when Israel will then repent, recognizing Jesus as her Messiah and Lord, and will then be restored to her rightful place in the world as the leading nation of all, even with Jesus Christ at her head. Then the blessings will flow out to the nations of the world through Israel as the Lord originally intended (Ezek., Chpts. 40-48).

DISPOSITION

Due to Israel's rebellion against God and subsequent self-righteousness, the spirit and attitude of these people had been severely warped and perverted. Consequently, they were extremely volatile, resorting to violence very quickly, especially considering that they believed that they were doing these things in the name of the Lord and, therefore, justified.

In fact, and I think I cannot be contradicted, they remain very contentious unto this hour, with some exceptions, of course. There is an adage among the Jews that says, *"No two Jews can even agree between themselves as to what day it is!"*

CHRISTIANS AND JEWS

Unfortunately, the Jews, at least for the most part, presently have an erroneous understanding as to who and what Christianity actually is, blaming it for all of their troubles. That is somewhat understandable, considering that they even thought of Adolf Hitler as a Christian!

Time and time again, I have spoken with various Jewish leaders, explaining to them that these people were not Christians, despite their claims. In fact, all Bible Christians, who, admittedly, aren't many, truly love the Jews, understanding that the roots of Christianity are in Judaism, as should be obvious.

However, it is very difficult for them to believe or accept the fact that most, if not all, the help for Israel that comes from congress is brought about because of the great number of true Christians in America. As well, they have great difficulty in understanding how that true Christians really love the Jews, and for the obvious reasons.

To them, a Jew is a Jew, and a Christian is a Christian.

While it may be true regarding what they say about themselves, or any other nationality for that matter, still, such does not hold true respecting Christians.

CHRISTIANS

A Christian is not a Christian simply because he claims to be such but, in truth, is a believer because he has truly accepted Jesus Christ as his Lord and Saviour. At the same time, this places a love in his heart that includes the Jews, and above all, the Jews!

So, there is no similarity respecting nationality and Christians. Being a Christian has nothing to do with nationality and, in fact, crosses all national boundaries.

If a person is a true Christian, his heart will be changed, causing the love of Christ to be predominant within his life, and he will be reaching out to others as well.

Actually, this was the very problem between Paul and his fellow Jews. They did not have the love of God in their hearts, while Paul did! Consequently, despite their claims, they were unregenerate people (save for those Jews who accepted Christ) and, therefore, conducted themselves as unregenerate people.

(13) "NEITHER CAN THEY PROVE THE THINGS WHEREOF THEY NOW ACCUSE ME."

The exegesis is:

1. No, they could not prove these accusations simply because they were baseless.

2. As well, Tertullus made his accusations in terms of generalities because he had no proof and could not specify any incident, with the exception of the Temple, and it, as well, was in generalities. He never said how Paul profaned the Temple because, in fact, Paul did not profane it in any way. They were all trumped-up charges.

(14) "BUT THIS I CONFESS UNTO YOU, THAT AFTER THE WAY WHICH THEY CALL HERESY, SO WORSHIP I THE GOD OF MY FATHERS, BELIEVING ALL THINGS WHICH ARE WRITTEN IN THE LAW AND IN THE PROPHETS."

The exegesis is:

NOTES

1. There is no real maturity in the Lord without a proper understanding of the Cross of Christ.

2. Every Bible doctrine is based squarely on the Cross of Christ, or else, it is specious.

PAUL'S DEFENSE

The phrase, *"But this I confess unto you,"* presents Paul not only defending himself against these baseless charges but, as well, taking the opportunity to proclaim the Gospel of Jesus Christ, which, in fact, was built on *"The Law and the prophets."*

So, the governor, as well as all others who were present, would hear the truth, some for the first time in their lives. How privileged they were, but yet, how little they took advantage of this, the single most important thing in their lives, the salvation of their souls.

At the Great White Throne Judgment (Rev. 20:11-15), this moment will be recalled by the Judge of all the ages, the Lord Jesus Christ, and presented to the governor, as well as the high priest and all others who were present that day. They will then know just exactly how significant this time was, but regrettably, they will know too late!

THE WAY

The phrase, *"That after the Way which they call heresy,"* presents Paul refusing to use the word *"sect"* as they had used it (Acts 24:5), but rather used the appellative *"the Way."*

Actually, the word *"sect"* does not necessarily have a negative meaning. In classical Greek, its secondary sense was a *"sect"* or *"school"* of philosophy, academics, etc.

Actually, the Jews applied it to their own different schools of thought. They also referred to the different parties in Israel as, *"The sect of the Sadducees," "The sect of the Pharisees,"* etc.

However, in Paul's Epistles (I Cor. 11:19; Gal. 5:20), it began to be used in a bad sense.

The Greek word for *"sect"* is *"hairesis"* and can mean *"heresy,"* even as Paul here alluded, and even though it originally denoted *"choice,"* it came to be used only in a bad sense, in other words, *"a bad choice."*

In essence, Paul was saying that

Christianity is not *"heresy,"* and so he would prove from the Scriptures.

The phrase, *"So worship I the God of my fathers,"* placed Christianity as the fulfillment of the great promises and predictions given to the *"fathers,"* i.e., all the Old Testament worthies.

Roman law forbade any man to introduce any new religion or object of worship. Consequently, Paul's reference to the *"God of my fathers"* was a defense for both judge and accusers to hear.

Paul insisted that by becoming a Christian, a follower of Christ, he had not been disloyal to Moses, the Law, the prophets, or to the manner and way of the fathers, but quite the contrary.

BELIEVE

The phrase, *"Believing all things which are written in the Law and in the prophets,"* pertains to the entirety of the Old Testament.

By his statement, the reader must understand that Paul was not advocating a continued keeping of the Law, but that the Law had pointed to Jesus as the Redeemer, and upon His Coming, it had served its purpose.

The word *"believe,"* as Paul used it here, implies a continued trust and obedience to God and His Word. Belief, in both the Old and New Testaments, always implies personal confidence and faithfulness, showing itself always in action, and not just a mental attitude.

In other words, if one's claims of *"believing"* and *"faith"* do not translate into action, in this case, the following of Jesus, one only has a mental attitude, which really serves little purpose. For one to truly believe, and we speak of Christ, one must take upon oneself the very Person of Christ, follow Him and, thereby, make Him the Lord of one's life.

By Paul using this statement as he did, concerning believing all that was written in the Law and the prophets, he was saying two things:

1. The Law and the prophets, as stated, pointed exclusively to Jesus Christ.

2. Despite their claims, the religious leadership of Israel did not believe what was written in the Law and the prophets, for if they did, they would have accepted Christ, to Whom the Law and the prophets pointed.

NOTES

(15) "AND HAVE HOPE TOWARD GOD, WHICH THEY THEMSELVES ALSO ALLOW, THAT THERE SHALL BE A RESURRECTION OF THE DEAD, BOTH OF THE JUST AND UNJUST."

The synopsis is:

1. Many think that because we're living in the day of grace, sin is excused; however, sin is never excused!

2. There is only one answer for sin, and that is the Cross of Christ.

HOPE

The phrase, *"And have hope toward God,"* contains a wealth of meaning.

Paul was, in essence, stating that the Law and the prophets were not complete within themselves, only pointing to the One Who was to come, Who would bring all of these things to pass, namely Jesus.

As well, Paul was also saying that this *"hope"* is still in force, and even though Jesus paid the full price for man's redemption at Calvary's Cross, still, even though believers are fully saved now, the final results or attributes of one's salvation will not be realized until the resurrection. The believer is now *"washed, sanctified and justified,"* but not yet *"glorified,"* which will take place at that coming glad day (I Cor. 6:11; Rom. 8:17).

Paul also referred to this *"hope"* as a *"blessed hope"* (Titus 2:13).

In essence, the only true *"hope"* in this world is the hope that is toward God. There is no hope in man or man's ways, and that is where the world is at cross-purposes with God. It claims, in one way or the other, that it can satisfy the craving and longing of the human heart. However, such is not to be, at least as it pertains to man.

EXACTLY WHAT WAS PAUL SPEAKING OF WHEN HE REFERRED TO HOPE?

When the word *"hope"* is presently used, it often has a wavering, uncertain sound. *"I hope I can make it,"* is said doubtfully.

However, the manner in which the Bible uses the word *"hope,"* at least in the realm of which we speak, focuses attention on God and fills the believer with eager expectation.

No one who learns to hope in a Biblical way will ever be overcome by disappointment but will be filled with patience, encouragement, and enthusiasm.

In other words, the word *"hope,"* as it is used in most cases in the Bible, contains no doubt whatsoever, but rather a guarantee that whatever is hoped for will definitely come to pass. The certitude of its action is not in question, only when it will be fulfilled, thereby, coming to fruition.

In its most basic way, the word *"hope"* is a relational term. It is a great affirmation of trust in God, not because the believer knows exactly what is ahead, but because God is known as wholly trustworthy.

HOPE AS USED IN THE OLD TESTAMENT

Each Hebrew word for *"hope,"* as it is used in the Old Testament, invites us to look ahead eagerly with confident expectation. Each also calls for patience, reminding us that the fulfillment of hope lies in the future. It focuses attention on what it is that awaits us.

In the Book of Job, perhaps the oldest Old Testament Book, Job expresses the sufferer's fears as tragedy shatters his sense of comfortable relationship with God. Job cried, *"If I wait, the grave is my house: I have made my bed in the darkness"* (Job 17:13).

He then said, *"And where is now my hope? as for my hope, who shall see it?"* (Job 17:15).

As Job faced his fears of the future, he rejected the suggestion of Eliphaz: *"Is not this your fear, your confidence, your hope, and the uprightness of your ways?"* (Job 4:6). Ultimately, he found the solution of the Psalmist: *"And now, Lord, what wait I for? My hope is in You"* (Ps. 39:7).

ALWAYS SOMETHING GOOD

In the New Testament, *"hope"* is always the expectation of something good. It is also something for which we must wait. In the New Testament, unlike the Old Testament, just what we hope for is carefully explained. The mystery that the Old Testament does not solve is untangled in the New Testament, and we are told about the wonders God has in store for us.

NOTES

THE RESURRECTION

The phrase, *"Which they themselves also allow,"* has reference to the prophets of old, and not to the Sadducees. In other words, Paul was saying that he believed the entirety of the Bible, which then pertained to the Old Testament, even as he alluded.

The phrase, *"That there shall be a resurrection of the dead, both of the just and unjust,"* proclaims, as is obvious, two resurrections.

As we have stated, the Sadducees did not believe in a resurrection at all, while the Pharisees believed only in the resurrection of the just (righteous); however, the Old Testament taught both (Dan. 12:2).

As well, Jesus clearly taught two distinct resurrections: one, a resurrection to life (eternal), and the other, a resurrection to damnation and judgment (Jn. 5:29).

Even though the prediction was given of the two resurrections in the Old Testament, nothing was said about the time element between the two, as is clearly outlined by John in the New Testament (Rev., Chpt. 20).

As well, in the Old Testament, the Lord did not reveal to the Old Testament prophets the time between the First and Second Comings of Christ, except somewhat in shadow.

For instance, Zechariah 9:9, tells of Christ's triumphal Entry into Jerusalem, which took place in connection with His First Coming. Zechariah 9:10, the very next verse, as is obvious, prophesies that His Dominion or Rule will be from sea to sea and from the river (the Euphrates) even to the ends of the Earth.

This applies to His Second Coming and shows that His Millennial Kingdom will not be limited to the territory promised to Abraham and his descendants, which was only from the river Euphrates to the river of Egypt (Gen. 15:18). Rather, it will cover the entire Earth.

However, the Lord did not tell Zechariah of the timespan between these two comings, which now has lasted for approximately 2,000 years.

WHY?

The timespan between the two comings

refers to the Church Age, which has no relationship to Israel. So, it was not mentioned in the Old Testament except, as stated, only in shadow (Isa., Chpt. 53).

In fact, all of the predictions concerning Israel as given to the Old Testament prophets pertained only to Israel and, as such, gave very little information concerning the Church Age.

For instance, when the Disciples asked Jesus when the Second Coming would be in what is referred to as the Olivet Discourse (Mat., Chpt. 24), He graphically outlined the future and what would lead up to that Coming. However, he never mentioned the church in this discourse, except only in shadow, because the Second Coming applies to national Israel and not the church. In fact, the church will be with Jesus, actually coming back with Him at the Second Coming (I Thess. 4:13-18; Rev., Chpt. 19).

(16) "AND HEREIN DO I EXERCISE MYSELF, TO HAVE ALWAYS A CONSCIENCE VOID OF OFFENCE TOWARD GOD, AND TOWARD MEN."

The composition is:

1. The true Gospel of Jesus Christ, which is the Message of the Cross, gets people saved, lives changed, bondages broken, sick bodies healed, and believers baptized with the Holy Spirit.

2. Any ministry that does not fit in somewhere with the things we have stated, which is a mirror of the Book of Acts and the Epistles, is not a true ministry.

PLEASING THE LORD

The phrase, *"And herein do I exercise myself,"* refers to diligence practiced by Paul constantly in order that his life and conduct please the Lord in all things. What a testimony for all!

The word *"exercise"* in the Greek text is *"askeo"* and simply means *"to train, even as an athlete would train."*

This was a 24-hour a day, 7 days a week lifestyle with Paul. It was not that he thought he could earn anything from the Lord by such a regimen. It was that he so wanted to please the Lord, and be what God wanted him to be, that he addressed this great Christian experience with the same concern and responsibility in the spiritual sense as an Olympic athlete does in the physical sense. This shows us a number of things:

Understanding the value of the soul and how important all of this is, Paul addressed it accordingly. As well, in view of what Jesus has done for the human family in coming from heaven, taking upon Himself the frailty of man, and then dying an ignominious death on the Cross of Calvary, such caused Paul to know how important all of this must be.

Also, he would never forget how close he had come in his bigotry to being eternally lost and, as well, his glorious conversion on the road to Damascus, which he would ever seek to relate.

THE SIGNIFICANCE OF ALL OF THIS

I think most believers, at least if we are to judge our feelings by our actions, little know or understand how lost we were and, now, how saved we are! Sadly, most spend far more time with hobbies, sporting activities, or other particulars than they do regarding their lives lived for God. The tragedy is, when these believers stand before the Lord at the Judgment seat of Christ, they will wish that they had been more diligent, even as Paul, in *"exercising themselves"* to a far greater degree in the things of God. This probably can be said for all of us.

The phrase, *"To have always a conscience void of offence toward God, and toward men,"* perfectly falls in line with the words of Jesus, *"You shall love the Lord your God with all your heart, and with all your soul, and with all your mind.*

"This is the first and great Commandment.

"And the second is like unto it, You shall love your neighbor as your self."

He then said, *"On these two Commandments hang all the Law and the prophets"* (Mat. 22:37-40).

In addressing this statement as given by Paul, one must understand exactly what he was saying. He was not meaning at all that he would compromise the Gospel in order to conciliate the differences in Christianity and Judaism so that he might win the approval of men, but rather that he would

NOTES

treat all men right respecting his conduct toward them. To be frank, to address one who is lost due to false doctrine, making him believe that everything is satisfactory, in no way shows love but, actually, the very opposite. To tell one the truth shows love, irrespective as to how distasteful the truth may be.

(17) "NOW AFTER MANY YEARS I CAME TO BRING ALMS TO MY NATION, AND OFFERINGS."

The rule is:

1. The phrase, *"Now after many years,"* probably refers to about six or seven years that Paul had been away from Jerusalem. Actually, his last visit was mentioned in Acts 18:22.

2. Since that time, he had spent a period at Antioch, had gone over all the country of Phrygia and Galatia, had come to Ephesus and stopped about three years there, had gone through Macedonia, had spent three months at Corinth, had returned to Macedonia, and from thence, had come to Jerusalem, this last journey, which took about 50 days.

3. This statement alone would tell Felix that he had not been plotting seditions regarding Jerusalem, especially considering that he had only arrived there some 12 days before.

4. *"I came to bring alms to my nation, and offerings,"* probably referred to those spoken of in II Corinthians, Chapter 8, and Romans 15:25-31.

5. These *"alms"* had to do with the Jerusalem church and the thousands who had lost their jobs and were, thereby, deprived of any means of support because of their acceptance of Christ.

6. The *"offerings"* referred to Paul proposing to pay for the sacrifices of the four Jews who accompanied him into the Temple, regarding the conclusion of their Nazarite vow (Acts 21:24).

7. The idea is that people who are plotting sedition and insurrection do not engage themselves in these types of things.

(18) "WHEREUPON CERTAIN JEWS FROM ASIA FOUND ME PURIFIED IN THE TEMPLE, NEITHER WITH MULTITUDE, NOR WITH TUMULT."

NOTES

The composition is:

1. The phrase, *"Whereupon certain Jews from Asia found me purified in the Temple,"* proclaims him as being engaged in something very correct, in fact, one of the very purposes of the Temple, consequently, the very opposite of the accusations.

2. As previously stated, these *"Jews from Asia"* were possibly from Ephesus and hated Paul because of the planting of the church in that great city. Without a doubt, some Jews who had formerly been active in the synagogue there had given their hearts to Christ, thereby, fueling the animosity of the rebels. As we have repeatedly stated, there is no hatred like religious hatred!

3. *"Neither with multitude, nor with tumult,"* refers to the fact that absolutely nothing was going on at that time which would have given any type of credence to these accusations.

4. The facts were, Paul was in the Temple, worshiping the Lord along with many others, when these particular Jews saw him. Fueled by hatred, they began to make wild accusations, claiming that he had brought a gentile into the Temple, and more particularly, to this place, *"the Court of Israel,"* hoping it would incense other Jews, which it did.

5. Horton said, *"Tertullus had not mentioned this because he wanted to give the impression that the Jews had arrested Paul to keep him from defiling the Temple."*

(19) "WHO OUGHT TO HAVE BEEN HERE BEFORE YOU, AND OBJECT, IF THEY HAD OUGHT AGAINST ME."

The account is:

1. The phrase, *"Who ought to have been here before you, and object,"* not only had to do with Roman law, but Levitical Law as well.

2. Actually, the Law of Moses demanded at least two or three witnesses in the case of any accusation of wrong for the matter to be established (Deut. 17:6-7; 19:15).

3. Jewish writings after Old Testament times also stressed that it was important that the witnesses be crossed-examined to be sure they were not false witnesses. This is also indicated in Deuteronomy 19:19. None of this was being done in this trial, and

neither had it been done the previous times Paul had faced the Jews.

4. The phrase, *"If they have ought against me,"* is, in effect, saying, *"Inasmuch as I am the subject of these proceedings, why aren't my accusers here as well?"*

(20) "OR ELSE LET THESE SAME HERE SAY, IF THEY HAVE FOUND ANY EVIL DOING IN ME, WHILE I STOOD BEFORE THE COUNCIL."

The pattern is:

1. The phrase, *"Or else let these same here say,"* now puts the high priest and those with him on the spot.

2. *"If they have found any evil doing in me, while I stood before the council,"* shifts the attention away from those not present to those who were present. It should be obvious that Paul was very sure of himself, as he had every right to be.

3. Of course, none of these present had been witnesses of anything that went on in the Temple, so the entirety of the scenario was no more than a farce, as should be obvious. All they had done was to bring with them a clever orator, who would hopefully dazzle the governor with his rhetoric, which probably had the opposite effect.

4. The high priest and those with him should have been grossly embarrassed, but most probably, their lives were such a sham anyway that they had long since passed any such feelings. If foiled in one of their fabrications, they evidently instantly set about to concoct another.

(21) "EXCEPT IT BE FOR THIS ONE VOICE, THAT I CRIED STANDING AMONG THEM, TOUCHING THE RESURRECTION OF THE DEAD I AM CALLED IN QUESTION BY YOU THIS DAY."

The way is:

1. The phrase, *"Except it be for this one voice, that I cried standing among them,"* now presents the only thing to which these Sadducees could honestly accuse Paul, at least as far as the accusation was concerned. Even then, their accusation was wrong concerning the resurrection, which they did not believe, and furthermore, it had only to do with Jewish Law, which interested the Romans not at all!

2. *"Touching the resurrection of the dead I am called in question by you this day,"* presents the only ground on which these accusers could stand, but yet, if they did so, it would expose their own sectarian attitude to Felix and would hurt their case.

NOTES

(22) "AND WHEN FELIX HEARD THESE THINGS, HAVING MORE PERFECT KNOWLEDGE OF THAT WAY, HE DEFERRED THEM, AND SAID, WHEN LYSIAS THE CHIEF CAPTAIN SHALL COME DOWN, I WILL KNOW THE UTTERMOST OF YOUR MATTER."

The rule is:

1. The phrase, *"And when Felix heard these things,"* presents that which was enough to set Paul free. However, the governor did not want to displease the powerful Jews who stood before him, therefore, he would take the political way out by referring to the coming of the chief captain.

2. Felix certainly should have set Paul free immediately, especially considering the evidence, or lack thereof, that was presented. However, irrespective of what Felix should have done, the Lord was working in all of these actions, with the long view in mind of Paul ultimately going to Rome.

3. *"Having more perfect knowledge of that Way,"* refers to Felix having far greater knowledge of Christianity than Tertullus and the Jews present at that trial were willing to give him credit.

4. Also, he knew enough about Mosaic Law to know that if he turned Paul over to these Jewish leaders, he would be condemning an innocent man.

5. *"He deferred them, and said,"* means simply that he refused to give a verdict at this time. His reasons were purely political. He was trying to play both ends against the middle, in essence, doing the same thing Pilate had done concerning Jesus.

6. He had already angered the Jews considerably on several occasions and was probably fearful that they would file a complaint against him in Rome, which he was confident he could have set aside but, nevertheless, would prove troublesome.

7. *"When Lysias the chief captain shall come down, I will know the uttermost of your matter,"* presents, as stated, only a delay tactic.

8. He already had the letter sent to him by Lysias, which gave all the pertinent information, and little else could be learned by his presence. Nevertheless, it was a good excuse to delay the matter, which he hoped would defuse the situation. Moreover, there is no record that he ever sent for Lysias.

(23) "AND HE COMMANDED A CENTURION TO KEEP PAUL, AND TO LET HIM HAVE LIBERTY, AND THAT HE SHOULD FORBID NONE OF HIS ACQUAINTANCE TO MINISTER OR COME UNTO HIM."

The way is:

1. The phrase, *"And he commanded a centurion to keep Paul, and to let him have liberty,"* tells us that Felix considered Paul as someone above the ordinary, hence, assigning a centurion to him rather than an ordinary soldier. As well, he had *"liberty"* to do many things, thereby, basically being only under house arrest. This tells us that Felix did not consider that Paul was guilty of any crime. He would have turned him loose but for two reasons:

a. To please the Jews

b. The hope of getting money from the apostle or his friends for his release, as we shall see in Verses 26 and 27.

2. *"And that he should forbid none of his acquaintance to minister or come unto him,"* simply meant that he could have as many visitors as he liked, with no restraint on such activity.

3. It is believed that Luke spent much time here with Paul, actually writing his Gospel at this particular time, as well as gathering much material for this Book of Acts.

4. Also, as Caesarea was the major port for Israel, multiple thousands of Jews passed through this city during the feast times, which, no doubt, included many friends of Paul. The news would have gotten out concerning his *"house arrest,"* and, no doubt, many visited him here, as well as many believers in the area of Caesarea proper.

5. Also, the word *"minister"* means that these people, whomever they may have been, were free to bring Paul anything they liked in the realm of food, clothing, or even money for that matter.

(24) "AND AFTER CERTAIN DAYS, WHEN FELIX CAME WITH HIS WIFE DRUSILLA, WHICH WAS A JEWESS, HE SENT FOR PAUL, AND HEARD HIM CONCERNING THE FAITH IN CHRIST."

NOTES

The pattern is:

1. The phrase, *"And after certain days, when Felix came with his wife Drusilla, which was a Jewess,"* gives us a little insight into the Roman world of that day, at least in this small part of the empire.

2. Drusilla was the young daughter of Herod Agrippa I, the Herod who had arrested James, the brother of John, and killed him with a sword (Acts 12:1-2). She was also the sister of both Herod Agrippa II and Bernice.

3. Felix had seduced her from her former husband, king Aziz of Emesa in the western part of Syria, by the means of a pretended Jewish magician.

4. Drusilla was actually the third wife of Felix, his first wife being the granddaughter of Marc Antony, the Roman orator and general, and Cleopatra, the queen of Egypt. His second wife was a princess.

Josephus mentioned that she and her son by Felix were consumed by an eruption of Mount Vesuvius.

Inasmuch as Drusilla was a Jewess, Felix would have probably learned a great deal about Jewish customs and laws.

5. The phrase, *"He sent for Paul,"* portrays the fact that the governor had been intrigued by the apostle, recognizing that this was no ordinary man.

6. In fact, the first phrase indicates that immediately after the hearing concerning Paul, the governor had left Caesarea for some days, when he may have inquired to a greater extent regarding Paul.

7. And yet, some claim that both Drusilla and Felix intended to entertain their curiosity by sending for Paul, with the situation not turning out quite as they had expected.

8. *"And heard him concerning the faith in Christ,"* seems to imply that the interest was sincere.

9. If one is to notice, the words, *"the faith,"* are used instead of *"his faith,"* implying that the governor and his wife were seeking more knowledge concerning Christianity in general, and especially of Christ.

(25) "AND AS HE REASONED OF RIGHTEOUSNESS, TEMPERANCE, AND

JUDGMENT TO COME, FELIX TREMBLED, AND ANSWERED, GO YOUR WAY FOR THIS TIME; WHEN I HAVE A CONVENIENT SEASON, I WILL CALL FOR YOU."

The direction is:

1. The Holy Spirit alone can bring that which is required of the believer, a life of righteousness and holiness (Rom. 8:1-11).

2. To make it easier to understand, it is impossible for the believer to sanctify himself, at least according to the New Covenant (I Cor. 1:17).

RIGHTEOUSNESS, TEMPERANCE, AND JUDGMENT TO COME

The phrase, *"And as he reasoned of righteousness, temperance, and judgment to come,"* deals with the great fundamentals of the faith and addresses itself to man's core problem.

RIGHTEOUSNESS

Paul would have proclaimed to the governor and his wife that due to the fall of man in the Garden of Eden, man, within himself, has no righteousness and, in fact, can in no way obtain such, at least within himself. He would have related to these people exactly how God became Man, the Man, Christ Jesus. He would have related to him, as well, the great price that Jesus paid at Calvary and how He was raised from the dead. He would then have strongly proclaimed that simple faith in Christ would guarantee that righteousness, the righteousness of God, would be instantly imputed to the believer.

TEMPERANCE

Paul would have dealt here with the bondages and vices which affect humanity, and which, within man's own strength and ability, he is unable to overcome and break. He would have proclaimed how that Jesus Christ alone can give man victory over these destructive forces.

He would have told how that abundant life is found only in Christ, and Christ alone, and how such life is not only abundant but eternal!

JUDGMENT TO COME

This speaks of every human being who must one day stand before God. If unsaved, consequently, without the righteousness of Christ, one will stand at the Great White Throne Judgment to give account. None will escape this reckoning, which is called the Second Resurrection of Damnation.

As well, he may have mentioned the Judgment seat of Christ, where every believer will stand. However, this will not be a judgment of the believers' sins, because that was done at Calvary, but rather a judgment of the believers' works and motives. Consequently, no believer will be lost regarding his soul, but many will lose rewards, and for the obvious reasons.

HOLY SPIRIT CONVICTION

The phrase, *"Felix trembled, and answered,"* proclaims tremendous Holy Spirit conviction.

In other words, while Paul was speaking, the Holy Spirit was working mightily upon both the governor and his wife, but especially the governor. When Paul came to the *"judgment to come,"* this account literally terrified the governor. The Greek word for *"trembled"* is *"emphobos"* and means *"afraid, affrighted, and even terrified."*

Felix knew that he was not ready to meet God, and the idea of standing at this coming judgment and giving account of his sins, which he knew were many, brought a chill over him that was obvious to all outward appearances. Consequently, this shoots down the idea that only positive preaching is proper.

It also shoots down the idea that it is improper to scare men into the Kingdom of God. The truth is that millions through the centuries have come to the Lord because the Holy Spirit allowed them to see, at least in some sense, the horrors of hell. In essence, the Lord, even as Paul preached, was hanging Felix over hell on a rotten stick, just as millions are in that very place at this very moment.

As well, and to which we have alluded, we are given an example here of the mighty convicting power of the Holy Spirit. Actually, this is absolutely imperative in the ministry of the evangelist, or any preacher for that matter, if people are to be saved.

NOTES

That is what Jesus was talking about when He said concerning the Holy Spirit, *"And when He is come, He will reprove* (convict) *the world of sin, and of righteousness, and of judgment"* (Jn. 16:8).

In fact, this is the only manner in which the sinner can be saved. As the Word is preached, as here, the Holy Spirit then anoints that Word, while, at the same time, convicting the sinner, which is a powerful factor.

This is the manner in which we have seen literally hundreds of thousands brought to a saving knowledge of Jesus Christ, and I exaggerate not. They came under powerful conviction, thereby, giving their hearts to Christ. As well, that is the reason I think I can say that most of these people have stood after coming to Christ and not gone back into the world.

A MORE CONVENIENT SEASON?

The phrase, *"Go your way for this time; when I have a convenient season, I will call for you,"* presents the sinner's excuse when under conviction and refusing to surrender.

It is not easy for men to give up their sins because, in fact, they love their sins. It is only when a person comes to Christ that he can see how absolutely terrible sin is and, consequently, hate it with a passion.

As well, Satan, of course, makes his play at this time, lying to the sinner who is under conviction, in fact, using any lie he can get him to believe.

It, no doubt, entered Felix's mind as to what all his friends would say if they knew he had given his heart to Christ. He imagined himself as the butt of every joke, the snicker of every conversation, and the end result being his ruin, at least as far as his position was concerned.

What would Rome say if they learned that he had become a Christian?

Without a doubt, all of these thoughts entered his mind, while, at the same time, he had little understanding as to what salvation in Christ really is or all the great things it provides. So, he put off this most important moment by speaking of a time that would be more *"convenient."* However, when the Gospel is preached, and the Holy Spirit moves, even as He did here, it is *"convenient"* and, in fact, will never be more *"convenient!"*

NOTES

(26) "HE HOPED ALSO THAT MONEY SHOULD HAVE BEEN GIVEN HIM OF PAUL, THAT HE MIGHT LOOSE HIM: WHEREFORE HE SENT FOR HIM THE OFTENER, AND COMMUNED WITH HIM."

The synopsis is:

1. The phrase, *"He hoped also that money should have been given him of Paul, that he might loose him,"* presents the greed which festered in the heart of the governor. If one could look closely, he would probably see that this was the cause that the man did not give his heart to the Lord.

2. The love of money ... What motivated him to think that money might be forthcoming is not known. However, knowing that Paul was innocent of any charges and maybe seeing the constant stream of believers who came to Paul regularly, he, no doubt, thought that a man with so many friends surely could get together a sizable sum.

3. However, there is no record that Paul ever paid bribes, etc. Even if the money was forthcoming, I seriously doubt that he would have done so because, for all practical purposes, such would not be right, I think, even in a case such as this.

4. I think it would be obvious that Paul took no delight in being kept in this place as a prisoner, but yet, he would put the situation in the hands of the Lord. Easily enough, and without bribes, if the Lord wanted him released, such would be very easy to come by. Otherwise, he would remain where he was until the Lord chose to change the condition.

5. The phrase, *"Wherefore he sent for him the oftener, and communed with him,"* portrays Felix as having a mixture of conviction with covetousness. Consequently, he sent for Paul many times, but with no record as to the extent of the conversations. As well, there is no record that he ever came to Christ.

6. As in other cases of double-mindedness, the convictions were doubtless stifled by the corrupt avarice, and so came to nothing.

(27) "BUT AFTER TWO YEARS PORCIUS

FESTUS CAME INTO FELIX' ROOM: AND FELIX, WILLING TO SHOW THE JEWS A PLEASURE, LEFT PAUL BOUND."

The way is:

1. The saving element of faith is our believing.

2. The evidential element of faith is our doing.

NOTES

TWO YEARS

The phrase, *"But after two years,"* gives us no hint as to what took place during this particular time. Quite possibly, and actually no doubt, Felix had many meetings with Paul during this intervening time. As well, there is evidence that Felix kept trying to extort Paul, which meant that had he paid a bribe, he could have been released the moment it was paid. However, this he would not do!

Even though this *"two years"* was, no doubt, freighted with many things, still, the Holy Spirit did not see fit to open it up to us, but only the nagging of the governor for money. This, no doubt, was a very trying time for the apostle. He must have reasoned in his heart many times as to what good he was doing for the work of the Lord cooped up in this place. To date, perhaps this was the worst time of all. But yet, the Lord had His Purposes, and I am positive that Paul knew and understood this. However, that did not stop the efforts and taunts of the Evil One.

FESTUS

The phrase, *"Porcius Festus came into Felix' room,"* means that Festus now became governor in the place of Felix. Josephus spoke of him as sent by Nero to be the *"successor"* of Felix.

Nothing is known of him from Tacitus or other Latin historians, and he appears from Josephus' account to have held the government for a very short time, probably less than two years, when he died in A.D. 61.

However, it seems he was a just and upright ruler, at least in some regards, in marked contrast to Felix, his predecessor, and his successors, Albinus and Gessius Florus.

It seems the reason that Felix was replaced was because of the increased unrest under his rule. It is said he was recalled by Nero, probably in A.D. 59. He was saved from proceedings instigated by the Jews, who filed many complaints on him, only through the influence of his brother Pallas, who was a close friend of the emperor. Of his later history, nothing is known.

PAUL

The phrase, *"And Felix, willing to show the Jews a pleasure, left Paul bound,"* presents a terrible travesty of justice.

In this very phrase, we see the handwriting on the wall respecting Felix. The Jews were more and more incensed with him, and their complaints to Nero now triggered his recall. Consequently, as one final act, he would attempt to curry favor with the Jews by leaving Paul bound, although he knew that Paul was innocent. His efforts would be in vain!

Josephus related, in point of fact, that the chief Jews in Caesarea sent an embassy to Rome to lodge a charge against Felix before Nero.

So, he lost not only his soul but, as well, the position that he craved so much.

How different would it have been had he accepted Christ?

To be sure, in that event, should it have happened, the position would, no doubt, have been lost, even as it was lost, but his soul would have been saved. The tragedy is, so many lose their souls attempting to hold on to certain things, but they ultimately lose the certain things anyway, as well as their souls.

The scene in this chapter is a very striking one, depicted with admirable simplicity and force:

- The bloated slave sitting on the seat of judgment and power, representing all the worst vices of Roman degeneracy.
- The heads of the sinking Jewish commonwealth, blinded by bigotry and nearly mad with hatred, forgetting for the moment their abhorrence of their Roman masters in their yet deeper detestation of the Apostle Paul. In other words, as much as they hated Rome, they hated Paul even more.
- The hired advocate with his fulsome

flattery, his rounded periods, and his false charges.

• And then, the great apostle, the noble confessor, the finished Christian gentleman, the pure-minded, upright, and fearless man, pleading his own cause with consummate force and dignity, and overawing his heathen judge by the majesty of his character.

It is a graphic description of a very noble scene.

"A mighty fortress is our God,
"A bulwark never failing;
"Our helper He, amid the flood,
"Of mortal ills prevailing:
"For still our ancient foe does seek to work us woe;
"His craft and power are great,
"And armed with cruel hate,
"On earth is not his equal."

"That word above all earthly powers,
"No thanks to them, abideth;
"The Spirit and the Gifts are ours
"Thro' Him Who with us sideth.
"Let goods and kindred go,
"This mortal life also;
"The body they makes ill,
"God's truth abideth still,
"His Kingdom is forever."

CHAPTER 25

(1) "NOW WHEN FESTUS WAS COME INTO THE PROVINCE, AFTER THREE DAYS HE ASCENDED FROM CAESAREA TO JERUSALEM."

The diagram is:

1. The phrase, *"Now when Festus was come into the province,"* refers to him taking the position of governor at Caesarea. No doubt, there would have been events of some sort in the amphitheater to celebrate the arrival of the new appointee by Nero.

2. *"After three days he ascended from Caesarea to Jerusalem,"* has to do with topography instead of geography. Jerusalem is about 2,500 feet above sea level, while Caesarea, situated on the coast, is just a few feet above this level of measurement. So, according to topography, he ascended, but according to geography, he descended, with Jerusalem being about 60 miles southeast of Caesarea.

3. Even though Caesarea was the seat of government, at least as it regarded Rome, Jerusalem was still the center as far as the Jews were concerned. There they carried on their religious government through the high priest and the Sanhedrin.

4. As well, Jerusalem was the city that fomented more unrest, hence, it demanded greater attention. Festus would begin his tenure in office attempting to placate these people who, in effect, had already signed their death warrant, at least as far as God was concerned. They were only marking time. So, this governor would find his task, at least as far as this task was concerned, as impossible as those before him, which would prove the same for those who followed him. Rome would finally lose patience, literally wiping the nation from the face of the Earth with a slaughter unparalleled, resulting in the death of one million plus Jews in Jerusalem alone!

(2) "THEN THE HIGH PRIEST AND THE CHIEF OF THE JEWS INFORMED HIM AGAINST PAUL, AND BESOUGHT HIM."

The overview is:

1. The phrase, *"Then the high priest and the chief of the Jews informed him against Paul,"* presents that which seemed to be high on their list. The Greek indicates that they began to besiege Festus with repeated accusations against Paul. Evidently they were still smarting concerning the failure of the plot of the 40 Jews to kill Paul some two years before.

2. The high priest at this time was no longer Ananias but Ismael, the son of Phabi, who was appointed by king Agrippa toward the close of Felix's government.

3. A little later, this high priest would go to Rome to appeal to Nero about a particular wall that the Jews had built to screen the Temple from being overlooked, and which Agrippa had ordered to be pulled down. However, he was not received too kindly in Rome, actually being detained as a hostage.

4. He was succeeded in the high priesthood by Joseph Cabi, the son of Simon.

5. The phrase, *"And besought him,"* speaks, as stated, of their continued besieging of the new governor regarding Paul.

6. As the next verse proclaims, they were already hatching up another plot to kill Paul, attempting to draw the governor into their web.

(3) "AND DESIRED FAVOUR AGAINST HIM, THAT HE WOULD SEND FOR HIM TO JERUSALEM, LAYING WAIT IN THE WAY TO KILL HIM."

The composition is:

1. The phrase, *"And desired favour against him,"* proclaims their feelings that they thought this was the opportune time to pressure the new governor. He evidently wanted to please them, or he would not have come to Jerusalem. However, they would find that he was not easily swayed.

2. *"That he would send for him to Jerusalem,"* simply means they wanted Festus to transfer Paul to Jerusalem, and they felt the new governor would comply.

3. *"Laying wait in the way to kill him,"* proclaims the idea, as thought by some, that this was to be done by the same 40 men who had originally made the vow to kill Paul (Acts 23:16).

Of course, they did not relate this to Festus and how Luke found out about this second plot is not known.

Quite possibly, the governor found out about it a little later and told Paul.

4. As stated at the close of the last chapter, *"The heads of the sinking Jewish commonwealth, blinded by bigotry and nearly mad with hatred,"* adequately describes these doomed people. They had forsaken God, and now God had forsaken them, but only because they no longer wanted Him.

(4) "BUT FESTUS ANSWERED, THAT PAUL SHOULD BE KEPT AT CAESAREA, AND THAT HE HIMSELF WOULD DEPART SHORTLY THITHER."

The structure is:

1. The phrase, *"But Festus answered, that Paul should be kept at Caesarea,"* means that the man, no doubt, saw through their ploy regarding Paul. Quite possibly, he had been informed of the previous plot to kill Paul and now was leery, even as he should have been. Even though two years had gone by, and the high priesthood had changed hands, still, their hatred burned just as fierce as ever toward Paul. They were fueled by Satan because they had given themselves over to Satan, despite their great religiosity.

2. In fact, the worst evil in the world is religious evil! That's the reason the separation of church and state is absolutely necessary, that is, if a modicum of freedom is to be enjoyed.

3. The phrase, *"And that he himself would depart shortly thither,"* seems to imply that the governor had about had his fill of the hatred and hypocrisy of these Jews.

(5) "LET THEM THEREFORE, SAID HE, WHICH AMONG YOU ARE ABLE, GO DOWN WITH ME, AND ACCUSE THIS MAN, IF THERE BE ANY WICKEDNESS IN HIM."

The exegesis is:

1. The phrase, *"Let them therefore, said he, which among you are able, go down with me, and accuse this man,"* in effect, says that Paul would get a fair hearing. Paul was a Roman citizen and must be treated as such.

2. And yet, this, these Jews going to Caesarea to accuse Paul, had already been done once. They had not been able to lodge any complaint, at least one that would stick. So, why should they be given another opportunity? In effect, this is what is referred to presently as *"double jeopardy."*

3. *"If there be any wickedness in him,"* is, no doubt, in answer to their accusation against Paul that he was greatly wicked.

(6) "AND WHEN HE HAD TARRIED AMONG THEM MORE THAN TEN DAYS, HE WENT DOWN UNTO CAESAREA; AND THE NEXT DAY SITTING ON THE JUDGMENT SEAT COMMANDED PAUL TO BE BROUGHT."

The synopsis is:

1. The phrase, *"And when he had tarried among them more than ten days, he went down unto Caesarea,"* probably means that he acquainted himself with the city during this time.

2. The phrase, *"And the next day sitting on the Judgment seat commanded Paul to be brought,"* speaks of him wasting no time,

NOTES

especially considering, as the next verse proclaims, that some Jews had accompanied him to Caesarea, or else, had come on their own, for the express purpose of testifying against Paul.

3. This action meant that the governor was calling for a new official trial. Festus could do this because Felix had never officially handed down a decision. He had only indicated he would carry out further investigation, which he did not do. Thus, Festus felt justified in calling this new trial.

4. Even though it is unstated, still, it is very obvious that these people were actually standing before the Judgment seat of God, even though they had no knowledge of such.

Festus thought he was acting as a governor, but actually, was only being political, or he would have instantly set Paul free.

The Jews were attempting to use this forum to silence Paul in some way, while Paul stood completely innocent of all charges.

Even though they would rule, God would overrule, as we shall see.

If men only realized that their every action is being judged by God, perhaps their actions would be different!

(7) "AND WHEN HE WAS COME, THE JEWS WHICH CAME DOWN FROM JERUSALEM STOOD ROUND ABOUT, AND LAID MANY AND GRIEVOUS COMPLAINTS AGAINST PAUL, WHICH THEY COULD NOT PROVE."

The pattern is:

1. The phrase, *"And when he was come, the Jews which came down from Jerusalem stood round about,"* refers to the new governor returning to Caesarea, with some of the Jews having come, as well, in order to voice their accusations against the apostle.

2. *"And laid many and grievous complaints against Paul, which they could not prove,"* undoubtedly, proclaims the same complaints they had registered some two years before, but with one new thing added.

3. Evidently the Jews, realizing that complaints concerning their own Law held little concern for the Roman governor, attempted to add another charge that would get the attention of the governor. In some manner, they charged that Paul had indeed violated Roman law. The next verse hints at this, but Luke did not specify.

4. At any rate, none of the charges, whether against Mosaic Law or Roman law, could be proven simply because they were not true.

The idea seems to be that they would throw out all types of charges, hoping at least one would stick respecting the governor, which basically is the tactic of liars.

(8) "WHILE HE ANSWERED FOR HIMSELF, NEITHER AGAINST THE LAW OF THE JEWS, NEITHER AGAINST THE TEMPLE, NOR YET AGAINST CAESAR, HAVE I OFFENDED ANY THING AT ALL."

The account is:

1. The statement made by James, *"Faith without works is dead,"* proclaims the point at which Law and grace are reconciled.

2. The New Testament way of life is not the Old Testament way.

3. We are saved by grace, but when grace saves, it produces in its place the fulfillment of the Law.

THE ANSWER AS GIVEN BY PAUL

The phrase, *"While he answered for himself,"* presents the apostle ably defending himself!

First of all, Paul was trained somewhat in the very manner in which lawyers are presently trained. In effect, it could be said, and without doing violence to the Text, that Paul could be looked at in this capacity—a lawyer.

As well, he knew Mosaic Law as probably no human being on the face of the Earth. Then, of course, he was saved and filled with the Holy Spirit, Who led and guided him in all of these matters, which meant that his defense was powerful indeed.

As well, even though it is not mentioned here, we know from Verse 19 that he strongly proclaimed Jesus in the midst of this defense.

"Neither against the Law of the Jews," presents his first statement.

In no way did Paul denigrate the Law of Moses. Actually, he, no doubt, testified to its veracity as no one else, for he understood it more than all. He knew that the Law was not God's conclusive Plan, but rather a

NOTES

NOTES

preparation for the very One to Whom the Law pointed, namely the Lord Jesus Christ. In other words, he taught that Jesus fulfilled the Law on every count, which meant that its continuance in its old form was no longer necessary.

THE JEWS

The trouble was, Israel had made the Law of Moses an end within itself. In other words, they tried to make salvation out of their efforts to keep the Law, which only tended to breed acute self-righteousness. That's exactly the state of those who try to live for God presently by means other than the Cross, acute self-righteousness. In other words, any faith making anything its object other than Christ and the Cross always and without fail leads to self-righteousness.

Most of the Jews of that day, at least the ruling hierarchy, had two problems:

1. They rejected Jesus Christ as the Messiah, thereby, rejecting the very purpose of the Law.
2. They wanted to continue in the Law, irrespective that it had already served its purpose.

THE TEMPLE

In no way did Paul denigrate the Temple, but again, he did preach and teach that it had served its purpose exactly as other parts of the Law, in that the *"greater than the Temple"* had come, and once again, the One to Whom the Temple had always pointed (Mat. 12:6).

What need was there of further sacrifices when Jesus, to Whom the sacrifices had always pointed, had, in fact, come and offered up Himself as the perfect Sacrifice, which satisfied all the claims of a thrice-Holy God? As well, the Table of Shewbread, along with the Golden Lampstand, were no longer needed, or the Altar of Incense for that matter, for they all pointed to Jesus, Who fulfilled the types with His Coming, making them no longer necessary.

Acceptance of Christ and believing what He did at Calvary and the Resurrection presents the believer in the mind of God as actually eating the flesh of the Son of God and drinking His Blood (Jn. 6:53, 63). It is not literal and was never meant to be literal. In view of this, the eating of the Shewbread by the priests is no longer needed due to the fact that the Bread of Life, Jesus Christ, has already come.

JESUS AND THE TEMPLE

The same can be said for all the other Sacred Utensils of the Temple, including the very Holy of Holies. Actually, when Jesus died, the Veil in the Temple, which separated the Holy of Holies from the Holy Place, was torn asunder by God, signifying that the way was now open to the very Throne of God. We might quickly add that it is open to everyone, both Jew and gentile, all made possible by what Jesus did at Calvary and the Resurrection.

So, it was not that Paul was opposed to the Temple, for his very actions spoke otherwise. It was the simple fact that such was no longer needed due to Jesus having come, Who is Greater than the Temple, and actually the One to Whom the Temple always pointed.

However, having rejected Jesus, the religious hierarchy would never admit to such. Consequently, the Lord made it impossible for the Jews to continue practicing the Law of Moses by destroying the Temple in A.D. 70. Without the Temple, everything fell to the ground respecting the Law because all in one way or the other was tied to the Temple.

A NEW RELIGION?

The phrase, *"Nor yet against Caesar, have I offended any thing at all,"* pertained to the Jews claiming that Paul had instigated a new religion, which, in effect, if true, would have been against Roman law.

Judaism was a recognized religion by Rome, consequently, constituting no illegality respecting its worship, etc. In effect, Paul considered Christianity to be an outgrowth of Judaism, which it was, having its roots of absolute necessity in the Law of Moses, etc.

So Paul argued that his worship of Christ in no way violated Roman law, inasmuch as Christ was the very Purpose for the Law and its fulfillment.

In effect, some believe that Paul's appearance before Nero concerning his first imprisonment in Rome, which would happen very shortly, actually clarified this issue, with Nero agreeing, at least at that time, that Christianity was indeed a product of Judaism and, therefore, no breach of Roman law.

The entire disposition of the ruling hierarchy of Israel was rooted in their hatred of Jesus Christ, which constituted their hatred of Paul as the great preacher of Christ. Their charges regarding the Law and the Temple, etc., were only excuses, which had no substance in fact.

(9) "BUT FESTUS, WILLING TO DO THE JEWS A PLEASURE, ANSWERED PAUL, AND SAID, WILL YOU GO UP TO JERUSALEM, AND THERE BE JUDGED OF THESE THINGS BEFORE ME?"

The synopsis is:

1. The phrase, *"But Festus, willing to do the Jews a pleasure, answered Paul, and said,"* means that the governor could not refute Paul's defense and, therefore, could not hand down a sentence of guilt of any nature. So, Festus was put between the proverbial rock and the hard place. He couldn't charge Paul, and yet, he wanted to pacify the Jews.

2. Festus feared these Jewish leaders, knowing that if they were willing to bring these types of false charges against Paul, they would not hesitate to do the same against him to Rome. So, he was not willing to set Paul free, despite his obvious innocence, but was casting about in order to do something that would pacify the Jews. He did not have the courage to do that which was right, which would have ensured the blessings of the Lord, but rather tried to play politics exactly as his predecessor Felix had done, as well as Pilate concerning Jesus.

3. Even in modern politics, this is the difference between the statesman and the politician. The politician seeks to please everyone and to do so by compromise, while the statesman attempts to do what is right, irrespective as to what the outcome may be. As should be obvious, as it was then, so it is now; there are not many statesmen.

4. The question, *"Will you go up to Jerusalem, and there be judged of these things before me?"* presents the compromise of the governor.

NOTES

In effect, this was already the second trial Paul had had, with him being vindicated both times, so why should he have to go through a third trial on the same identical charges? The further it went, the more ludicrous it became.

How would Jerusalem being the scene of the trial change anything? The charges would remain the same, and the lack of proof would be identical as well.

Festus attempted to soften the blow by indicating that he would serve as the judge in Jerusalem, which, in his mind, threw a sop to Paul, but once again, why?

Actually, the situation now had nothing to do with Paul, but rather the governor trying to placate these Jews.

(10) "THEN SAID PAUL, I STAND AT CAESAR'S JUDGMENT SEAT, WHERE I OUGHT TO BE JUDGED: TO THE JEWS HAVE I DONE NO WRONG, AS YOU VERY WELL KNOW."

The exegesis is:

1. One might say that the evidence of faith is in works, but it is works inspired by faith.

2. Works are the effect of faith and not the cause of it.

CAESAR

The phrase, *"Then said Paul, I stand at Caesar's Judgment seat, where I ought to be judged,"* proclaims the apostle readily seeing through this ploy, knowing that if he went to Jerusalem, the Jews would find some way to kill him. Actually, that was their purpose all along. They had no regard or concern about innocence or guilt. They wanted to kill the man simply because they saw him as a threat, but in what way, at least if honestly dealt with, they would be hard-put to explain.

In a spiritual sense, the Holy Spirit was, no doubt, leading Paul respecting his demand to be tried before Caesar, which was his right as a Roman citizen.

No, the Lord in the fulfillment of Paul's ministering in Rome, which Jesus had already told him he would do, in no way manipulated the Jews or the governor to do wrong in any fashion in order that this thing

NOTES

may be carried out. The wrongdoing on their part was theirs alone, as wrongdoing is always the responsibility of the perpetrator. God being God is not dependent on, or subject to, the doings of anyone, whether right or wrong. As God, He is able to bring about that which is predicted, and to do so in many and varied ways, without infringing upon the free moral agency of even one person.

So, even though the actions of the rebellious Jews and the decision of the governor played into the fulfillment of this prediction, it in no way absolved these people from responsibility. All would answer to God for their sins, as all always answer to God for their sins.

THE JUDGMENT SEAT

Even though Paul was speaking of the *"Judgment seat"* in Rome, actually, the Judgment seat of the procurator, who ministered judgment in Caesar's name and by his authority, in this case Festus, it was rightly called *"Caesar's Judgment seat."* Consequently, as a Roman citizen, Paul had a right to be tried there and not before the Sanhedrin. The pretense that he had offended against the Jewish Law and, therefore, ought to be tried by the Jewish court was a false one, as Festus well knew; for he had the record of the preceding trial before him.

The phrase, *"To the Jews have I done no wrong, as you very well know,"* proclaims that which was true, and which Paul hammered home, and rightly so! In effect, by using the strong term, *"As you very well know,"* Paul was somewhat rebuking the governor.

Before a Roman court, to which Paul insisted, he would be tried only according to Roman law. In that case, the only charge that could be brought against him, and it was baseless, pertained to Christianity being a new religion. Paul insisted that it was not new, but rather an outgrowth of Judaism, which was already recognized by Roman law. In effect, Gallio, the Roman governor at Corinth, had said the very same thing (Acts 18:12-16).

(11) "FOR IF I BE AN OFFENDER, OR HAVE COMMITTED ANY THING WORTHY OF DEATH, I REFUSE NOT TO DIE: BUT IF THERE BE NONE OF THESE THINGS WHEREOF THESE ACCUSE ME, NO MAN MAY DELIVER ME UNTO THEM. I APPEAL UNTO CAESAR."

The overview is:

1. The phrase, *"For if I be an offender, or have committed any thing worthy of death, I refuse not to die,"* in effect, proclaims Paul attempting not so much to save his life, but rather to declare his innocence. Actually, his statement has a far greater meaning than at first realized.

2. Even though he was addressing the governor and the Jews, he was, as well, addressing his entire state and position before the Lord. In other words, if, in fact, he was preaching erroneous doctrine, and all his experiences had been a lie, then he deserved to die. However, if not, which were the facts, he claimed the Lord's Guidance and Protection and, in fact, had both!

3. The phrase, *"But if there be none of these things whereof these accuse me, no man may deliver me unto them,"* means that the Lord would protect him from being delivered to the Jews.

So, he claimed his position as right, which it was, and, thereby, he claimed protection of the Lord, which he had.

4. The phrase, *"I appeal unto Caesar,"* I personally feel had something to do with our Lord's Appearance to Paul. The Lord had told him, *"Be of good cheer, Paul: For as you have testified of Me in Jerusalem, so must you bear witness also at Rome"* (Acts 23:11).

However, to knowingly walk into the presence of the Jews, knowing they had sworn to kill him, claiming God's Protection would not be faith, but rather presumption, which God would not honor.

The idea is, it was the will of God for him to appear before Caesar, whereas it was not the will of God for him to stand before the Jews, at least in this fashion.

(12) "THEN FESTUS, WHEN HE HAD CONFERRED WITH THE COUNCIL, ANSWERED, HAVE YOU APPEALED UNTO CAESAR? UNTO CAESAR SHALL YOU GO."

The account is:

1. The phrase, *"Then Festus, when he had conferred with the council, answered,"*

does not refer to the Jewish council or Sanhedrin, but rather to the legal advisory council of the governor, which evidently advised Festus to acquiesce to Paul because of Roman law. They made it clear that Paul was in his rights, and there was nothing Festus could do but send him to Caesar.

2. The question, *"Have you appealed unto Caesar?"* now presents Festus answering his own question, *"Unto Caesar shall you go."*

3. In essence, this took Festus off the hook. He could claim before the Jews that both of them would have to yield to the higher power of Roman law. Consequently, there was nothing the Jews or he could say!

4. As we have previously stated, this particular part of Roman law, regarding Roman citizens having the right of appeal to Rome, had come about over 500 years before Christ. However, addendums in 449 and 299 B.C. further reinforced this right.

5. The actual place of the trial, however, whether before the Roman Senate or the emperor, switched back and forth from time to time, but at this particular time, was being held before the emperor personally.

(13) "AND AFTER CERTAIN DAYS KING AGRIPPA AND BERNICE CAME UNTO CAESAREA TO SALUTE FESTUS."

The way is:

1. The phrase, *"And after certain days king Agrippa and Bernice,"* pertains to the second son of Herod Agrippa, who is mentioned in Acts 12:1.

At the death of his father, being only 17, he was too young to be king, or at least so thought Claudius, but in A.D. 50 Claudius gave him the kingdom of Chalcis.

His uncle, the husband of Bernice, had died two years before. Shortly after this, he was appointed the governorship of Abilene and Trachonitis with the title of king.

2. His relations with his sister Bernice were the occasion of much suspicion, with many believing that she was living in an incestuous intercourse with him.

She had been the wife of her uncle Herod, prince of Chalcis, and on his death, lived with her brother.

3. She then for awhile became the wife of Polemo, king of Cilicia, but soon returned to Herod Agrippa, her brother. It is said that she afterwards became the mistress of emperor Vespasian and then of emperor Titus in succession.

NOTES

4. It was this Herod who made Ismael the son of Phabi high priest, and who built the palace at Jerusalem, which overlooked the Temple and gave great offense to the Jews. He was the last of the Herods and reigned over 50 years.

5. He was strongly attached to the Romans and did all in his power to keep the Jews from rebellion. When they finally did rebel, he united his army with Titus and helped destroy Jerusalem.

6. He died in Rome in A.D. 100, still greatly honored as a *"praetor"* or *"high officer"* of Rome.

7. The phrase, *"Came unto Caesarea to salute Festus,"* simply means to pay their respects to the new governor.

(14) "AND WHEN THEY HAD BEEN THERE MANY DAYS, FESTUS DECLARED PAUL'S CAUSE UNTO THE KING, SAYING, THERE IS A CERTAIN MAN LEFT IN BONDS BY FELIX."

The rule is:

1. The phrase, *"And when they had been there many days, Festus declared Paul's cause unto the king, saying,"* proclaims such being carried out because Festus thought that Herod had a better understanding of Jewish Law than he did, which was true. Though Herod Agrippa II was educated in Rome, he was a Jew. As a result, the emperor Claudius had given him the government of the Temple in Jerusalem and the right to appoint the high priest, whereas Rome had previously held that right. Festus would seek his opinion regarding Paul for all the obvious reasons.

2. In fact, king Herod Agrippa never showed the sort of cold disdain that some of the other Herods had often shown in their treatment of their subjects. Actually, he had concern for his fellow Jews. It seems that his education in the emperor's palace did not turn him away from them or from Judaism.

3. The phrase, *"There is a certain man left in bonds by Felix,"* speaks, of course, of Paul! He would now have the opportunity to

NOTES

witness for Christ to this king, whose great uncle Herod Antipas had murdered John the Baptist, and who had a brief encounter with Jesus when the latter was sent to him by Pilate for judgment (Lk. 23:7). Jesus is recorded as having once described him as *"that fox"* (Lk. 13:32).

(15) "ABOUT WHOM, WHEN I WAS AT JERUSALEM, THE CHIEF PRIESTS AND THE ELDERS OF THE JEWS INFORMED ME, DESIRING TO HAVE JUDGMENT AGAINST HIM."

The status is:

1. The phrase, *"About whom, when I was at Jerusalem, the chief priests and the elders of the Jews informed me,"* speaks of bringing charges and accusations against Paul.

2. *"Desiring to have judgment against him,"* actually means that the Jewish leaders in Jerusalem did not really want another trial for Paul, but rather that Festus would accept their accusations at face value and pronounce the death sentence on Paul without any further trial or investigation.

(16) "TO WHOM I ANSWERED, IT IS NOT THE MANNER OF THE ROMANS TO DELIVER ANY MAN TO DIE, BEFORE THAT HE WHICH IS ACCUSED HAVE THE ACCUSERS FACE TO FACE, AND HAVE LICENCE TO ANSWER FOR HIMSELF CONCERNING THE CRIME LAID AGAINST HIM."

The order is:

1. According to most preachers, walking in victory is simply the believer having a resolute determination. Unfortunately, that is woefully insufficient.

2. There is only one way for the believer to walk in victory, and that is that his faith be exclusively in Christ and what Christ has done for us at the Cross. Then, the Holy Spirit, Who works exclusively within the framework of the Cross, will work mightily on behalf of such a believer (I Cor. 1:17-18; 2:2).

ACCUSERS

The phrase, *"To whom I have answered, It is not the manner of the Romans to deliver any man to die, before that he which is accused have the accusers face to face,"* presents this heathen as having a better sense of justice than the religious Jews, who, of all people, should have known better. However, by this time, the Jews, at least the majority of them, had become so hard in their hearts toward God and His Ways that they had no semblance left of any fairness, justice, or even shame.

They murdered the Lord Jesus Christ when Pilate repeatedly had tried to release Him. They also murdered Stephen, and did so in a rage. They were happy that Herod had killed James by the sword, and they were doing everything in their power to kill both Peter and Paul.

No! It was not justice the Jews wanted, but the apostle's life. What exactly must this heathen governor have thought about the blood lust of these Jews?

This is what Jesus meant when He spoke of an unclean spirit going out of a man, which was symbolic of the evil spirits going out of Israel as they were defeated by Christ, but with the evil spirit coming back and finding the place empty of the presence and power of God. That is what happened when Jesus went back to the Father. Having rejected Him, Israel was now *"empty, swept, and garnished."*

ISRAEL

As a result, this evil spirit *"takes with himself seven other spirits more wicked than himself, and they enter in and dwell there: and the last state of that man* (nation) *is worse than the first. Even so shall it be also unto this wicked generation* (Israel)*"* (Mat. 12:43-45).

Due to her rebellion against Christ and murdering Him, Israel was now seven times worse than before Jesus came. This is the reason for their hatred and murderous intent.

The phrase, *"And have licence to answer for himself concerning the crime laid against him,"* portrays the justice of the heathen government of Rome, with Israel, who was supposed to be God's Chosen, having no justice whatsoever.

It must ever be understood that for a person to be confronted by Christ, with Christ rejected, it never leaves the individual static, but rather much worse. Light refused is greater darkness entered.

(17) "THEREFORE, WHEN THEY WERE

COME HITHER, WITHOUT ANY DELAY ON THE MORROW I SAT ON THE JUDGMENT SEAT, AND COMMANDED THE MAN TO BE BROUGHT FORTH."

The direction is:

1. The phrase, *"Therefore, when they were come hither, without any delay on the morrow I sat on the Judgment seat,"* proclaims, as is obvious, the recounting of this episode to king Agrippa by Festus.

2. The idea is, as seems to be indicated in the Text, that he desired to quickly get this thing underway, perhaps out of curiosity to see what kind of man Paul was, especially considering the charges they had laid against him.

3. *"And commanded the man to be brought forth,"* proclaims that which this Roman governor never dreamed would be. I speak of the millions who have read this account from that day until now, with the governor basically known in history only for these incidents. Little did he realize that day what was happening before his very eyes, and that he was a part of eternal consequences.

4. In his mind, he probably thought this trial was little more than a nuisance. However, even though he little realized such, he had become a part of the single most important thing on Earth, the Gospel of the Lord Jesus Christ.

5. Regrettably and sadly, even as most, he missed the opportunity to accept Jesus and, thereby, to gain Eternal Life. As well, this scene plays out again and again, and in all types of varied ways, even unto the present time.

6. As we have previously stated, the nations of the world, irrespective of how rich or poor they may be, are judged by God only in the light as to how they affect His Body, the church. Even though other things are certainly important, still, all pales into insignificance in comparison to the work of God. Regrettably, most city fathers little know or realize that of which is in their midst, that is, if they are fortunate enough to have men and women of God in their community.

(18) "AGAINST WHOM WHEN THE ACCUSERS STOOD UP, THEY BROUGHT NONE ACCUSATION OF SUCH THINGS AS I SUPPOSED."

The direction is:

1. The phrase, *"Against whom when the accusers stood up,"* presents Festus thinking they would bring heavy charges against Paul, such as murder, fraud, theft, insurrection, etc., especially considering that they were demanding his life.

2. *"They brought none accusation of such things as I supposed,"* presents him as being somewhat baffled.

3. Festus was greatly blessed in that he had the opportunity and privilege of hearing the Apostle Paul, who, without a doubt, was one of the greatest men of God who ever lived. However, his meeting with the Jews, who were supposed to be God's chosen People, and were actually supposed to be serving the same God as Paul, would be anything but a blessing. In these two, Paul and the religious hierarchy, he, at the same time, saw the best and the worst. As is obvious, he had little understanding as to what was actually transpiring before his eyes. As we have previously stated, what he thought of the Jews is anyone's guess. However, setting aside the political ramifications, even as I think this Text implies, he must have held these religious leaders in utter contempt.

4. By comparison, I know that he was favorably moved upon by Paul and, no doubt, for the first time in his life sensed the presence of God when Paul spoke. I am convinced that it could have been no other way. But yet, as most, his place and position overrode the conviction, with him, as Felix, ultimately losing both his soul and his position.

(19) "BUT HAD CERTAIN QUESTIONS AGAINST HIM OF THEIR OWN SUPERSTITION, AND OF ONE JESUS, WHICH WAS DEAD, WHOM PAUL AFFIRMED TO BE ALIVE."

The form is:

1. What Christ did at Calvary was to effect a *"double work,"* or one might say, a *"double cure."*

2. The first part of Jesus dying for the sinner on Calvary is known by all true believers; however, the second Finished Work, one might say, presents victory for the

saint over the world, the flesh, and the devil (Gal. 6:14).

QUESTIONS

The phrase, *"But had certain questions against him of their own superstition,"* is not meant to present Judaism or Christ in a bad light. The word *"superstition"* in the Greek text, as it is used here, is *"deisidaimonia"* and actually has the same meaning as *"religion."* So, he was actually saying, *"Against him of their own religion."*

As well, knowing that king Agrippa was a Jew, Festus would not have made a statement that would have been derogatory toward the Jewish religion, which should be obvious.

The phrase, *"And of one Jesus,"* shows that Paul in his defense readily preached Jesus to the governor and these Jewish leaders. In fact, Luke probably only gave us a capsule sketch of all the things Paul said.

As well, from the way in which Festus spoke of Jesus, it seems that he had never heard of the Son of God, despite the greatest array of miracles performed during the Master's Ministry that the world had ever known. That may seem extraordinary to us presently, but due to the spirit of the times of that day, it is quite understandable that Rome paid little notice.

GOD?

There was at this time a plethora of claimants respecting deity. In other words, quite a number in the Roman Empire were claiming to be gods. In fact, even Nero had accepted the title *"lord,"* which his predecessors refused. So, another voice at this time would be little heard, especially from a province such as Israel.

And yet, one would think the great host of miracles would attract worldwide attention, but considering that communication and transportation were all but nonexistent in those days, at least as we compare them to the present, the lack of intelligence of Festus concerning Jesus becomes a little more understandable.

RAISED FROM THE DEAD

The phrase, *"Which was dead, Whom Paul affirmed to be alive,"* proclaims the Resurrection, which, in its manner, was the most astounding miracle the world had ever known.

Jesus had been crucified, which the Roman records could show, and Festus could check if he so desired. As well, the tomb was made secure by Roman soldiers. All of this, as stated, was a matter of record.

Consequently, due to the things mentioned, if one wanted to properly investigate, the Resurrection of Jesus Christ was absolutely uncontestable.

The way that Festus made the statement, *"Whom Paul affirmed to be alive,"* seemingly had made a powerful impression upon the governor.

To be sure, the doctrine of the Resurrection would have been something new and foreign to his thinking. However, he did not ridicule the idea the way that many did, but that is not to say that he accepted Paul's claim, for obviously, he did not. But yet, as a Roman, he knew how unlikely, or even impossible, it would have been for the body of Jesus to have been stolen out of that tomb. So, considering the fact of the empty tomb and with no plausible explanation, he must have pondered Paul's claim of Resurrection. As stated, the apostle's witness had undoubtedly made an impression upon the governor.

(20) "AND BECAUSE I DOUBTED OF SUCH MANNER OF QUESTIONS, I ASKED HIM WHETHER HE WOULD GO TO JERUSALEM, AND THERE BE JUDGED OF THESE MATTERS."

The way is:

1. The phrase, *"And because I doubted of such manner of questions,"* does not mean, as it seems, that Festus doubted the claims of Paul concerning Jesus, but that he was at a loss as to know how to decide such questions, which is understandable.

2. The phrase, *"I asked him whether he would go to Jerusalem, and there be judged of these matters,"* presents the governor as failing to relate to the king that the Jerusalem idea was done more so to please the Jews than anything else.

3. However, at the same time, it should be obvious that he was out of his depth,

NOTES

attempting to understand these things on which he was expected to pass sentence.

(21) "BUT WHEN PAUL HAD APPEALED TO BE RESERVED UNTO THE HEARING OF AUGUSTUS, I COMMANDED HIM TO BE KEPT TILL I MIGHT SEND HIM TO CAESAR."

The diagram is:

1. The phrase, *"But when Paul had appealed to be reserved unto the hearing of Augustus,"* presents the governor as using the title *"lord,"* as he referred then to Nero, and then to which Nero demanded to be referred. *"Augustus"* is a title which actually means *"the august, venerable, or lord."*

2. The title of *"Augustus"* was conferred by the Roman Senate upon Octavius Caesar in 27 B.C., whom we commonly designate *"Augustus* (or lord) *Caesar."* It became afterwards the distinctive title of the reigning emperor, with most of these men understanding their pitiful human frailties and, thereby, declining its use. However, Nero came to think of himself as a *"god,"* hence, demanding the use of that title, *"Augustus"* (lord), when addressed.

3. The original name of Nero was *"Lucius Domitius Ahenobarbus."* His mother, Agrippina, was the sister of the emperor Caligula and niece of the emperor Claudius.

4. His father died when Nero was three years old, and by intrigue, Agrippina married Claudius and had Nero adopted as his son. Claudius, sometime later, was poisoned, and Nero became emperor in A.D. 54. During the first five years of his reign, good advisors helped him to initiate many reforms; however, Nero himself began to indulge in all kinds of excesses, surrounding himself with profligate companions, and ultimately becoming a tyrant.

5. The phrase, *"I commanded him to be kept till I might send him to Caesar,"* in effect, says that Paul was still here in the palace, which excited the interest of king Agrippa and his wife Bernice, which we shall see.

(22) "THEN AGRIPPA SAID UNTO FESTUS, I WOULD ALSO HEAR THE MAN MYSELF. TOMORROW, SAID HE, YOU SHALL HEAR HIM."

The diagram is:

NOTES

1. The phrase, *"Then Agrippa said unto Festus, I would also hear the man myself,"* presents the greatest moment in the life of this king, but yet, a moment of which value he would not fully grasp or understand.

2. Inasmuch as Agrippa was a Jew, it is certain that he had heard of Christ, and Paul being one of the principal apostles of the Lord, his curiosity was, no doubt, whetted to hear him.

3. The phrase, *"Tomorrow, said he, you shall hear him,"* presents an appointment with destiny. If it is of God, it is always of destiny but seldom recognized by most, even as this king.

4. The soul of man is his single most important possession, so important that Jesus said, *"For what shall it profit a man, if he shall gain the whole world, and lose his own soul?"* (Mk. 8:36). Considering that there is no savior of the soul but Jesus, one can well imagine the significance of anyone having the opportunity to hear the Gospel, which literally means *"good news."* However, as we have seen, Felix trembled but would not accept, while Festus, it seems, did not get that far! King Agrippa, as we shall see, came closer, but not close enough. Once again, we hear the words of Paul, *"Not many mighty, not many noble, are called"* (accept the call) (I Cor. 1:26).

(23) "AND ON THE MORROW, WHEN AGRIPPA WAS COME, AND BERNICE, WITH GREAT POMP, AND WAS ENTERED INTO THE PLACE OF HEARING, WITH THE CHIEF CAPTAINS, AND PRINCIPAL MEN OF THE CITY, AT FESTUS' COMMANDMENT PAUL WAS BROUGHT FORTH."

The overview is:

1. The phrase, *"And on the morrow, when Agrippa was come, and Bernice, with great pomp,"* presents this man and his sister as the son and daughter of Herod Agrippa I. The pomp of their visit to Caesarea contrasts with the horrible death of their father in the same city some years before.

2. Agrippa's father, as we have stated, had been a persecutor of Christianity and had killed James with the sword. He proceeded to take Peter and would have killed him, also, but the apostle was delivered by an

angel (Acts 12:7-23). This evil king would have killed others, as well, had not he been removed by death, actually smitten by God (Acts 12:23).

3. So, his son Agrippa II had, no doubt, heard much about Christianity by this time.

4. *"And was entered into the place of hearing, with the chief captains, and principal men of the city,"* presents great pomp and display, with king Agrippa and his sister Bernice taking the opportunity to let the city of Caesarea see their glory. So, with great ceremony, they entered the palace where Paul was being kept, dressed in their royal robes, and with all their attendants, in a great show of magnificent pageantry.

5. With them were the tribunes of the Roman army, along with the leading men of the city and, no doubt, their wives.

6. Inasmuch as Caesarea was a cosmopolitan city, which included a great many gentiles, and especially a great number of Syrians, Agrippa was evidently attempting to make a great display of Jewish presence. However, his display would serve little purpose, with the Syrians venting their jealousy on the Jews a few years later by slaughtering hundreds. Actually, this was another act which brought on the revolt of the Jews in A.D. 67, ending with the nation and Jerusalem being destroyed in A.D. 70. After this, Titus, who had actually destroyed Jerusalem, celebrated the birthday of his brother Domitian by making 2,500 Jews fight with wild animals in the amphitheater.

7. The phrase, *"At Festus' commandment Paul was brought forth,"* presents that which the Lord had initially told Paul he would do, *"To bear My Name before the gentiles, and kings, and the children of Israel"* (Acts 9:15).

8. It is suggested that possibly Luke was in attendance this particular day, as well, and was a witness of all the proceedings.

(24) "AND FESTUS SAID, KING AGRIPPA, AND ALL MEN WHICH ARE HERE PRESENT WITH US, YOU SEE THIS MAN, ABOUT WHOM ALL THE MULTITUDE OF THE JEWS HAVE DEALT WITH ME, BOTH AT JERUSALEM, AND ALSO HERE, CRYING THAT HE OUGHT NOT TO LIVE ANY LONGER."

NOTES

The form is:

1. The will of man within itself is not able to throw off the powers of darkness.

2. This can only be done by the power of the Holy Spirit, Who operates solely within the parameters, so to speak, of the Finished Work of Christ.

3. This simply requires the faith of the individual being in Christ and the Cross exclusively (I Cor. 2:2).

PAUL

The phrase, *"And Festus said, King Agrippa, and all men which are here present with us,"* portrays quite an assembly of dignitaries from the king on down. It should be quickly noted that Israel had rejected her true King, the Lord Jesus Christ, and this is what they presently had, a man living in incest with his own sister, and for all practical purposes, having little knowledge of God. What a tragedy!

"You see this man," presents Paul evidently standing before this assemblage of dignitaries, etc.

Whether Festus was merely pointing to Paul as the subject of the discussion and the dilemma which had been handed to him by Felix, or whether he was meaning to point to Paul's diminutive appearance as one hardly likely to cause such a disturbance, and over much of the Roman world, as the Jews claimed, is not exactly clear. It could have been a little of both.

THE APPEARANCE OF PAUL

There is no actual proof of how Paul looked, but tradition says he was *"baldheaded, bowlegged* (probably brought about by the many beatings he had suffered), *strongly built, yet a man small in size, with meeting eyebrows, with a rather large nose, full of grace, for at times, as we have stated in a previous chapter, he looked like a man, and at other times, he had the face of an angel."*

And yet, other than the Lord of Glory Himself, as we have previously stated, not meaning to take away anything from the original Twelve, Paul, more than anyone else, I think, has proclaimed the great and glorious message of the Lord Jesus Christ.

As well, he pushed that message unto the furthest reaches of the Roman Empire, at least as far as he could. More than any other man, he was responsible for what we now refer to as *"western civilization,"* which is the result of true Bible Christianity. This has afforded every single prosperity and freedom that the world has ever known. I realize that is a bold statement, but I believe it to be true.

What has Islam, Buddhism, Shintoism, or Hinduism contributed to this world? The answer is obvious!

Islam has contributed violence, with Buddhism and Shintoism contributing a form of racism (superiority), and Hinduism contributing demonic bondage.

If true Bible Christianity were taken out of the world at present, even as it shall be in the coming Rapture of the church, there will be nothing left but hell, if the reader will pardon my bluntness. However, there is really no other way to describe what I have said.

THE RELIGIOUS WORLD

The phrase, *"About whom all the multitude of the Jews have dealt with me, both at Jerusalem, and also here, crying that he ought not to live any longer,"* pretty well describes the situation in a few words.

Also, this has ever been the response of the religious world to true people of God, especially one in whom the Spirit of God is mighty to work. If it is not possible to actually kill them, as laws in most countries forbid, they will at least attempt to kill their influence in any way possible.

In the words of Festus, we pretty much have the situation as it always has existed. The Roman world, typifying the world at all times, little thirsted for the life of Paul, however, the religious world, even as is blatantly portrayed here, is another matter altogether. This has always been Satan's greatest effort. Even when the state was instrumental in brutally murdering the saints of God, even as it was in the Dark Ages, still, the state was controlled then by the Catholic Church.

While Rome did greatly persecute Christians a little later, even as communism in our lifetime, still, the greatest effort of darkness has always come from that which calls itself *"the church!"*

NOTES

(25) "BUT WHEN I FOUND THAT HE HAD COMMITTED NOTHING WORTHY OF DEATH, AND THAT HE HIMSELF HAD APPEALED TO AUGUSTUS, I HAVE DETERMINED TO SEND HIM."

The synopsis is:

1. Salvation is all of God and none at all of ourselves.

2. It is easy to fall into the habit of preaching about the Gospel but not really preaching the Gospel itself.

HOLY SPIRIT CONVICTION

The phrase, *"But when I found that he had committed nothing worthy of death,"* proclaims the findings of this governor, but yet, with not enough moral courage to set the man free.

Regrettably, Festus had come to understand the legalities of this case, but he still little understood Paul's message, if at all! It is positive, even as we shall see, that the Holy Spirit dealt with him mightily, but he seemed to be little moved. And yet, both Felix and Agrippa, whose lives were much darker in a moral sense than that of Festus, were greatly moved, even though they would not accept.

How could this be?

Man's extremity is God's Opportunity!

Oftentimes a man's sin drives him to God. As most sin does, it begins as a lark but always ends in acute bondage, with all the attendant suffering and guilt. In that state, millions have turned to Christ simply because there was no other alternative.

That is at least one of the reasons that it is very difficult to get a so-called good moral person or an unconverted church member to turn to Christ. They equate their goodness and morality with salvation, when, in reality, it has nothing to do with salvation, at least in the strict sense of the word.

SALVATION

To be saved, all must come to Christ, understanding that they are sinners in desperate need of redemption and that Jesus alone can save. In that context, it is easy to convince the one who is morally bankrupt,

NOTES

and not so easy at all, if not next to impossible, to convince the morally self-righteous.

In truth, people mistake all types of things for salvation, such as wealth, education, place and position, religion, good works, and even race and nationality, when, in reality, none of these things have anything whatsoever to do with salvation.

Man is a lost sinner and must understand that. He is not lost because he has done certain bad or immoral things, but he was actually born that way in what is described as *"original sin."* Inasmuch as he was born a sinner, irrespective of good things he may attempt to do upon reaching the age of accountability, such does not change his status as a sinner in any degree. That can be changed only by accepting Christ as one's Saviour.

This means that one realizes and recognizes that Christ is God manifest in the flesh, and that He purposely died on Calvary's Cross in order to pay for our redemption, and then rose from the dead on the third day. In other words, Christ took our place in order that He may pay a debt that was impossible for us to pay—the debt of sin. If the sinner does not believe this, the sinner cannot be saved (Jn. 3:16; Rom. 10:9-10, 13).

To believe that Jesus actually lived and, consequently, was a good Man, even a Miracle Worker, or a great Teacher, Preacher, etc., is not enough. One must believe in Jesus as one's Saviour.

As we have stated, the phrase, *"And that he himself has appealed to Augustus,"* presents Festus referring to Nero as *"lord!"*

The phrase, *"I have determined to send him,"* had to do with Paul being a Roman citizen and, in effect, Festus declaring that the apostle had a right to this appeal.

(26) "OF WHOM I HAVE NO CERTAIN THING TO WRITE UNTO MY LORD. WHEREFORE I HAVE BROUGHT HIM FORTH BEFORE YOU, AND SPECIALLY BEFORE YOU, O KING AGRIPPA, THAT AFTER EXAMINATION HAD, I MIGHT HAVE SOMEWHAT TO WRITE."

The exegesis is:

1. The phrase, *"Of whom I have no certain thing to write unto my lord,"* once again refers to Nero.

2. The governor was complaining that he was going to send a man to Caesar for a trial, but he had no idea as to what to tell the emperor as to what he had done. What were his crimes? For what was he to be charged?

3. Paul had now had two trials, one before Felix and this last before Festus, with these two governors serving as judge on both counts. For neither one to know what Paul had done, even after hearing all the proceedings, full well proclaims what a farce these charges were.

4. The phrase, *"Wherefore I have brought him forth before you, and specially before you, O king Agrippa, that, after examination had, I might have somewhat to write,"* proclaims that he hoped the king, being a Jew, might be able to define the charges a little better. However, he would find that king Agrippa, as evil as he might have been, would come to no different conclusion than Festus.

(27) "FOR IT SEEMS TO ME UNREASONABLE TO SEND A PRISONER, AND NOT WITHAL TO SIGNIFY THE CRIMES LAID AGAINST HIM."

The status is:

1. The phrase, *"For it seems to me unreasonable,"* presents that which is exactly what it was. The whole thing was *"unreasonable!"* So, why didn't Festus do the right thing and set Paul free?

2. Once again, even as Pilate, he was attempting to play both ends against the middle. He did not want to be guilty of punishing Paul unjustly, but at the same time, he did not want to displease the Jews.

3. For one to do right, at times, angers others. However, one must do the right thing in the sight of God, irrespective of the price or the personal cost. And yet, if one is to know the truth, most people in the world, even most of those who call themselves *"Christians,"* conduct themselves in the same manner as this governor of so long ago.

4. As the great evangelist, Billy Sunday, once said, *"Knowing what is right is not man's problem; it's doing what is right which is the problem."* How right he was.

5. It is one thing to do right when many others are doing the same thing, but

something else altogether again to do such when precious few are, and to do so will exact a personal price. Most are not willing to pay that price.

6. So, when we come right down to the bedrock, most, even so-called Christians, are little different than Festus.

7. The phrase, *"To send a prisoner, and not withal to signify the crimes laid against him,"* does take a stretch of the imagination!

8. Once again I emphasize that the Roman world of that day found no fault in Paul, even as Pilate found no fault in Jesus, while the religious hierarchy screamed for the crucifixion of Jesus and for the life of Paul. What an irony!

9. Recently at Family Worship Center, I made mention in the message that the most dangerous place in town was not the bars, honky-tonks, or gambling casinos, but rather most churches.

I went on to say how that all knew that the places mentioned are those of infamy, while all churches claim to be places of righteousness, etc. The truth is, some few churches are godly; however, most are preaching and proclaiming a lie, and under the cloak of deception, cause many to be lost.

"Fill You my life, O Lord My God,
"In every part with praise,
"That my whole being may proclaim
"Your Being and Your Ways;
"Not for the lip of praise alone,
"Nor e'en the praising heart,
"I ask, but for a life made up
"Of praise in every part."

"Praise in the common words I speak,
"Life's common looks and tones,
"In fellowship at hearth or board
"With my beloved ones,
"Enduring wrong, reproach,
"Or loss with sweet and steadfast will,
"Loving and blessing those who hate,
"Returning good for ill."

"So shall each fear, each fret, each care,
"Be turned into song,
"And every winding of the way
"The echo shall prolong;

NOTES

"So shall no part of day or night
"From sacredness be free,
"But all my life, in every step,
"Be fellowship with You."

CHAPTER 26

(1) "THEN AGRIPPA SAID UNTO PAUL, YOU ARE PERMITTED TO SPEAK FOR YOURSELF. THEN PAUL STRETCHED FORTH HIS HAND, AND ANSWERED FOR HIMSELF."

The exegesis is:

1. The phrase, *"Then Agrippa said unto Paul, You are permitted to speak for yourself,"* proclaims Festus as the governor giving place to the king more out of courtesy than anything else. Rome looked to the governors to carry out Roman policy, while the kings in each country or nation were mostly to appease the population, in other words, a sop.

2. So, after the explanation by Festus, Agrippa said to the Apostle that he may begin.

3. The phrase, *"Then Paul stretched forth his hand, and answered for himself,"* proclaims the method of most public speaking in those days. However, it becomes dramatic when one realizes that quite possibly chains hung from his arms.

As stated, Luke was, no doubt, present.

4. Even though Festus had previously heard the Gospel at the mouth of Paul, the others in the room probably had never heard a presentation of Jesus Christ, but now would hear this eternal message from the lips of one of the greatest men of God who ever lived. There is no doubt that Paul was greatly anointed by the Holy Spirit as he began to address these notables. As stated, the room was filled with the principal men of the city, along with Roman tribunes, all dressed in their finest. The arms of Bernice, the sister of the king, would, no doubt, have been laden with jewels, with beautiful chokers of pearls or precious stones around her neck. All were there, for whatever purpose, but this day, they were to hear the Gospel of Jesus Christ.

NOTES

5. There is no record that any of them accepted the Lord, but one day, when they stand at the judgment, they will relive this moment in their lives, which was the single most important moment they would ever know. They would have an opportunity to accept Eternal Life, but sadly, to no avail!

6. These mighty and important people (important in the eyes of the world) had little or no purpose at all in life, even as all without God, whether rich or poor. Even though they did not have much purpose in life, Paul knew exactly who he was, where he was, and above all, Who he represented. He owed it all to Jesus!

(2) "I THINK MYSELF HAPPY, KING AGRIPPA, BECAUSE I SHALL ANSWER FOR MYSELF THIS DAY BEFORE YOU TOUCHING ALL THE THINGS WHEREOF I AM ACCUSED OF THE JEWS."

The structure is:

1. The phrase, *"I think myself happy, King Agrippa, because I shall answer for myself this day before you,"* is proclaimed in this fashion because Agrippa was a Jew. Consequently, he at least had some knowledge of Mosaic Law, which Festus did not have, nor Felix before him.

2. *"Touching all the things whereof I am accused of the Jews,"* immediately set before this assemblage the very question at hand. In other words, Paul knew why they were there and addressed himself accordingly.

3. As stated in previous Chapters, the Jews accused Paul of denigrating the Law of Moses and polluting the Temple. As well, they accused him of fomenting another religion, at least where they thought they could make it stick, which was the only part of their accusations that would have interested Rome whatsoever.

(3) "ESPECIALLY BECAUSE I KNOW YOU TO BE EXPERT IN ALL CUSTOMS AND QUESTIONS WHICH ARE AMONG THE JEWS: WHEREFORE I BESEECH YOU TO HEAR ME PATIENTLY."

The account is:

1. The phrase, *"Especially because I know you to be expert in all customs and questions which are among the Jews,"* was not offered as flattery. In fact, Agrippa's father, King Agrippa I, was zealous for the Jewish Law almost up to the end of his life. He was always very concerned with Jewish customs and especially the Temple. In fact, when the Emperor Caligula seemed determined to set up a statue of himself in the Temple, which, of course, would have been repugnant to the Jews, he persuaded the emperor not to do so. So, it would have hardly been possible for the son of this king not to have been somewhat knowledgeable, as well, respecting all of these things.

As stated, Paul was very pleased to be able to speak to someone who was at least somewhat knowledgeable in the customs of Mosaic Law instead of someone like Festus, who had little understanding of such matters.

2. *"Wherefore I beseech you to hear me patiently,"* presents a common form Paul used very much in his Epistles. The word *"beseech"* in the Greek Text is *"deomai"* and literally means *"to beg."*

3. I personally think this type of approach was used by the Apostle for several reasons. First of all, despite his hard-nosed attitude concerning the purity of the Gospel, which was an absolute necessity, Paul was a humble man. Even though he was constantly in the thick of trouble and difficulties, even to the point of riots, humility would have been an absolute necessity with this man.

4. As well, knowing the constant and terrible opposition against the message of grace, which, in effect, was the foundation of the New Covenant, it is almost as if Paul was pleading with his hearers, whether in person or reading his Epistles, to patiently hear what he had to say. He knew how important it was, but regrettably, most others did not, even many in the Church.

(4) "MY MANNER OF LIFE FROM MY YOUTH, WHICH WAS AT THE FIRST AMONG MY OWN NATION AT JERUSALEM, KNOW ALL THE JEWS."

The way is:

1. The phrase, *"My manner of life from my youth,"* presents the Apostle beginning his message by alluding totally to his Jewish upbringing. He would not mention his Roman citizenship or Tarsus, his city of note. He was appealing to a Jewish king, with these things having not nearly the importance as

it would with the Romans.

2. The phrase, *"Which was at the first among my own Nation at Jerusalem, know all the Jews,"* concerns Paul being immersed in Jewish ritual and Law from the time he was old enough to begin his advanced studies, which was probably at about 12 years of age.

3. Upon becoming a son of the Law at that time, some think he may have even remained in Jerusalem from that time forth, beginning immediately, or ultimately being taught by Gamaliel, the most renowned Mosaic scholar of that day.

4. In essence, Paul was saying that his Judaism was not something that was tacked on at a later time, but rather the very core of his being. Consequently, no one could accuse him of not knowing his subject, especially considering that after the death of Gamaliel, he was perhaps the greatest Mosaic scholar in the world of that day.

5. Therefore, he did not defend himself from the position of mere rhetoric, or even genuine experiences given by the Lord, even as he would here relate, but rather from a position of scholarship and experience in the Law of Moses. In other words, for anyone to attempt to make ridiculous claims against Paul regarding Mosaic Law (even as the religious leadership of Israel was now doing) only tended to portray their ignorance and not his.

6. In effect, he was saying that they knew of his learning and experience, or at least they should have known!

(5) "WHICH KNEW ME FROM THE BEGINNING, IF THEY WOULD TESTIFY, THAT AFTER THE MOST STRAITEST SECT OF OUR RELIGION I LIVED A PHARISEE."

The diagram is:

1. The phrase, *"Which knew me from the beginning,"* means simply that what he was saying could be easily proven. In other words, if the present religious hierarchy of Israel did not know that of which he spoke, they could easily be informed with a little inquiry.

2. *"If they would testify, that after the most straitest sect of our religion I lived a Pharisee,"* pertained to this group being the strictest in doctrines and moral practices.

3. Not only was he a Pharisee, but, as well, he was one of the leading lights of Pharisaism, and some believe he was the hope of that cause.

4. So, as stated, when Paul spoke about Jesus Christ and how He was the Fulfillment of the prophecies, and actually the One to Whom all of the Mosaic Law pointed, he was speaking of that which he knew from both scholarship and experience.

(6) "AND NOW I STAND AND AM JUDGED FOR THE HOPE OF THE PROMISE MADE OF GOD UNTO OUR FATHERS."

The account is:

1. The phrase, *"And now I stand and am judged,"* proclaims, as we shall see, the real reason for the hatred against the Apostle, which had nothing to do with crimes committed or wrongdoing of any nature. The reason Festus could not find anything with which to charge Paul was because there was nothing.

2. *"For the hope of the promise made of God unto our fathers,"* had to do with the coming Resurrection, which had been guaranteed by Jesus Christ in His being raised from the dead.

3. Even though Paul's defense addressed the claims of the Sadducees that there is no Resurrection, more than all it portrayed that all that Jesus did in His Virgin Birth, perfect Life, and Death on Calvary would have been in vain had there not been a Resurrection. As well, His Resurrection guaranteed the Resurrection of all the Saints. This great promise is found in Genesis 12:1-3; Job 19:26; Ps. 16:10; 17:15; Isa. 26:19; and Dan. 12:2.

(7) "UNTO WHICH PROMISE OUR TWELVE TRIBES, INSTANTLY SERVING GOD DAY AND NIGHT, HOPE TO COME. FOR WHICH HOPE'S SAKE, KING AGRIPPA, I AM ACCUSED OF THE JEWS."

The rule is:

1. The Cross alone is the answer for sin.

2. This means that Christ and the Cross must ever be the object of our Faith. In effect, that is what real Faith in the Word actually is.

TWELVE TRIBES

The phrase, *"Unto which promise our*

Twelve Tribes," proclaims that all of the tribes were in existence during Paul's day, with each Israelite actually knowing then to which tribe he or she belonged. (Presently, the Jews do not know their tribal affiliation.)

Paul was of the Tribe of Benjamin, while Anna (Lk. 2:36) was of the Tribe of Asher, one of the Ten Northern Tribes.

BRITISH ISRAELISM

I address this subject because there is a teaching called *"British Israelism,"* which claims that the British and American people are the Ten lost Tribes of Israel.

Some narrow it down, claiming that Britain is Ephraim and America is Manasseh, both originally sons of Joseph.

They claim that all the promises made to Israel are now being fulfilled with Britain and America, and never will be fulfilled with Jews.

THE ROYAL FAMILY OF ENGLAND

Some teach, as well, that the royal family of England constitutes the true legal heirs to the throne of David through Zedekiah's daughter, and that the throne of England is the throne of David.

Sometime back while in London and visiting Westminster Abbey where the kings and queens of England are crowned, I noticed under the chair where the crowning is performed a large stone about six or eight inches thick, approximately one foot wide, and maybe 18 inches long.

It is claimed that this is the stone that Jacob used for a pillar when he had the vision of the ladder that reached from Heaven to Earth. He, consequently, called the place *"Beth-el,"* meaning *"House of God"* (Gen. 28:10-22).

Regarding the stone, Jacob said, *"And this stone, which I have set for a pillar, shall be God's House"* (Gen. 28:22). Consequently, it was evidently believed by some in England that they are *"God's House."*

(Incidentally, this stone, which was taken from Scotland some centuries ago, was returned in the first part of 1997, if I remember correctly. So, there is no stone now under the throne chair at Westminster Abbey. As well, I have no idea what the present occupants of the throne of England believe concerning these things.)

Of course, all of this teaching is spurious, with not one hint of Scriptural validity.

THE DAVIDIC THRONE

The promises given by God of a Davidic throne were based upon obedience, and it was to be cut off until the Second Coming of Christ if that royal line went into sin, which it did (II Sam., Chpt. 7). Then, at the Second Advent, Judah and all Israel are to become one Nation again under the Messiah, Who will reign Personally from Jerusalem—not from London or anywhere else in the British Isles.

As well, there is nothing in Scripture that says that the Throne or Kingdom will be taken from the Tribe of Judah and given to the Ten Tribes, as some claim. Actually, the Holy Spirit through Jacob of old said, *"The Sceptre* (ruling power) *shall not depart from Judah, nor a Lawgiver from between his feet, until Shiloh* (Jesus) *come; and unto Him* (Jesus) *shall the gathering of the people be"* (Gen. 49:10).

To claim this Scripture was fulfilled with the First Advent of Christ is incorrect for the simple reason that the people were not gathered unto Him at that particular time. This waits to be fulfilled, which it shall be at the Second Coming when Israel will then be gathered to Him and will recognize Him as their Messiah and the Saviour of all mankind. In other words, the One they crucified actually was their Messiah and the Son of God, Who actually did rise from the dead and is coming again.

THE THRONE OF DAVID IN ISRAEL BEING CUT OFF

From the time of the Babylonian captivity, David's kingdom and throne were postponed because of sin, with such postponement to continue until the Second Coming of Christ (Hos. 3:4-5; Acts 15:13-18). There has been no such throne from then until now.

It was said to Jeconiah, the last ruler of David's line to be king in Judah, that no man of his seed should ever rule again on David's throne or rule in Jerusalem over Judah,

NOTES

that is, until Jesus comes the second time (Jer. 22:28-30).

Although Jeconiah (also called Coniah or Jehoiachin) had seven sons, none of them occupied the throne, with Zedekiah instead crowned as king of Judah. However, he was not of the royal line of David. Thus, the Davidic line of kings came to an end in Jehoiachin because he was cursed by God.

THE LORD JESUS CHRIST

And yet, the Messiah, the Eternal King of David's seed and of the royal Davidic family, came to be King of the Jews at His First Advent but was rejected by Israel. However, He will fulfill this role at His Second Advent.

Of course, the question must be asked, *"How can Christ succeed Jeconiah as King of the royal line if no man of that seed could ever reign anymore in Jerusalem and Judah due to the curse upon Jeconiah?"*

The answer is simple: Joseph, the husband of Mary, of whom the Christ was born, was of the seed of Jeconiah and the direct heir to the throne of David, which a son of his own begetting could not occupy, as stated, because of the curse. However, Christ was not begotten of Joseph but of God through Mary (who herself was of another line of David—Nathan's line). He could rightfully, in the reckoning of both God and man, occupy the throne and not violate the Scripture because by rights, He was and is not only the Son of David through the lineage but, as well, the Son of God. So, in that capacity, the curse did not extend to Him (Mat. 1:1-18; Lk. 1:23-38), Who will occupy that throne at the Second Coming, and do so forever.

RESTORATION

David's throne will be reestablished after the Church Age, for we read: *"And to this agree the Words of the Prophets; as it is written,*

"After this (after taking out of the Gentiles a people for His Name, and referred to as the Church) *I will return, and will build again the Tabernacle* (Throne) *of David, which is fallen down* (not which is built up and kept up by the kings of England)*; and I will build again the ruins thereof, and I will set it up"* (Acts 15:13-18; Amos 9:11-15).

NOTES

As well, it is in the original Promised Land of Israel (and not elsewhere) that all the Twelve Tribes will be gathered again to make an eternal Nation under the Messiah (Deut. 30:1-10; Isa. 11:10-16; 60:8-22; 66:19-21; Jer. 16:14-21; 23:3-8; 30:1-24; 31:18-40; 32:37-44; 33:6-26; 50:19-20; Ezek. 11:17-21; 20:33-44; 28:25-26; 34:11-31; 36:1-38; 37:1-28).

Also, all the Twelve Tribes will be restored in the coming Kingdom Age at the Second Coming because Jesus said that the Twelve Apostles will sit on Twelve Thrones judging the Twelve Tribes of Israel under David and Himself (Mat. 19:28; Lk. 22:28-30).

TWELVE TRIBES

All Twelve Tribes must be back in Israel when this happens, as it shall be when all Jews will be gathered from all over the world and brought to Israel, which will follow the Second Coming (Isa. 11:11-12; 14:1; 27:12; 43:5; 60:9; 66:20; Jer. 30:10; 31:1-14; 32:37; 33:7; 46:27; 50:4; Ezek. 16:53; 20:33-44; 34:11-16; 36:24; 37:11-19; 39:25; Hos. 3:4-5; Amos 9:13; Mic. 4:6; 5:7; 7:11; Zech. 2:6; 10:6, 9; Mal. 3:18; Mat. 24:31).

The phrase, *"Instantly serving God day and night, hope to come,"* refers to all Twelve of the Tribes of Israel, who in their zeal were attempting to serve God constantly, looking forward to the promise or the hope that is to come.

In no way did this mean that all the Jews were saved, for most were not. It simply meant that right or wrong, they all, more or less, were looking forward to the fulfillment of the prophecies.

In fact, Jesus Christ fulfilled all the promises and hopes of the Prophets and Israel, but Israel as a Nation would not recognize Him, and actually crucified Him. So, to be *"serving God day and night"* does not necessarily mean that one is saved. In fact, much of the world is acutely religious, with many doing exactly what Israel of old did but, nevertheless, on the wrong path. Sincerity and activity are not enough. Jesus Christ must be the center of all! (Jn. 3:16; Rom. 10:9-10, 13).

The phrase, *"For which hope's sake, King*

NOTES

Agrippa, I am accused of the Jews," now proclaims the divergence of direction.

All the *"Twelve Tribes"* were serving God, but only some were serving the Lord in His Way, with the others doing so from the position of self-will. Of course, we are speaking of Paul's day. It was this latter group, who made up the far greater majority of Israel, who were greatly opposing Paul because he said, and rightly so, that Jesus is the fulfillment of all the prophecies, and that He proved such by being raised from the dead.

(8) "WHY SHOULD IT BE THOUGHT A THING INCREDIBLE WITH YOU, THAT GOD SHOULD RAISE THE DEAD?"

The exegesis is:

1. In effect, the Jews were a miracle people. The Lord had brought them out of Egypt with a high and mighty hand, performing one miracle after the other, even to the opening of the Red Sea. All through the wilderness, He performed a series of miracles of every description.

2. Actually, the whole of Israel's existence was marked by a series of miracles respecting the mighty Power of God, which all Israelites knew very well.

3. Also, the ministry of Jesus for some three and one-half years had been the greatest times of miracles of every description, even to the raising of the dead, that had ever been known, seen, witnessed, or experienced.

4. Considering Israel's history and God's Dealings with them, and especially the Ministry of Christ, it should be obvious that God could raise the dead, even as He had already proven!

5. So, the idea that Paul believed that God was able to raise the dead should not have come as a great shock or surprise, much less something for which one should be imprisoned or even killed!

(9) "I VERILY THOUGHT WITH MYSELF, THAT I OUGHT TO DO MANY THINGS CONTRARY TO THE NAME OF JESUS OF NAZARETH."

The overview is:

1. The phrase, *"I verily thought with myself,"* proclaims the Apostle taking himself back to his dreadful time of unbelief.

2. The phrase, *"That I ought to do many things contrary to the Name of Jesus of Nazareth,"* puts the issue exactly where it really was—Jesus of Nazareth.

3. Even though the Sadducees did not believe in a Resurrection, this was actually not the issue. The issue was Jesus Christ as the Messiah of Israel, which they, as well as the Pharisees, denied, and more importantly, His being raised from the dead. If, in fact, He had really been raised from the dead, which He was, then beyond the shadow of a doubt He was the true Messiah of Israel, which meant they had doomed themselves by killing Him.

4. In effect, Paul here designated *"Jesus of Nazareth"* as the Lord of Glory, properly avowing himself a member of *"the sect of the Nazarenes."* As well, he used the same appellative, *"Jesus of Nazareth,"* which Jesus had Himself used when answering Paul's question, *"Who are You, Lord?"* (Acts 22:8).

5. As Jesus wanted Paul to know exactly Who He was, likewise, Paul wanted all to know and understand that it was *"Jesus of Nazareth,"* the despised One, of Whom he spoke. As is obvious, he was not ashamed of that Name, and one could tell by the way it was used that despite what others might think, he loved this One called Jesus to such an extent that he had given his all to follow Him.

(10) "WHICH THING I ALSO DID IN JERUSALEM: AND MANY OF THE SAINTS DID I SHUT UP IN PRISON, HAVING RECEIVED AUTHORITY FROM THE CHIEF PRIESTS; AND WHEN THEY WERE PUT TO DEATH, I GAVE MY VOICE AGAINST THEM."

The diagram is:

1. The Believer must understand that every single thing we receive from God is all made possible by the Cross.

2. When we speak of the Cross, we are speaking of what Jesus there did (I Cor. 1:18).

THE TESTIMONY OF PAUL

The phrase, *"Which thing I also did in Jerusalem,"* means that he began the persecution of the followers of Christ in this city and then branched out. This is to what Acts 9:1 refers, *"And Saul, yet breathing out threatenings and slaughter against the disciples of the Lord."* In other words, he meant business!

"And many of the Saints did I shut up in prison," proclaims only a part of his efforts of persecution. If one is to notice, the word *"Saints"* is used here, meaning that all true followers of Christ are labeled as *"Saints"* (Rom. 1:7).

Unfortunately, the Catholic Church has put an unscriptural connotation on the word *"Saint,"* which refers to the rules of the Church and not the Bible. Certain individuals are canonized or made *"Saints"* after death, that is, if they meet some certain requirements, which are probably impossible to truthfully trace after the fact. At any rate, when these people are made Saints, then members of the Catholic Church can pray to them, etc.

Once again, the criteria in the Catholic Church is not the Blood of Christ and Faith in what He has done, but rather man-made rules concocted by that Church, which are not recognized by God.

THE SANHEDRIN

The phrase, *"Having received authority from the chief priests,"* refers to the Sanhedrin.

They were not content with murdering Christ but they, as well, denied His Resurrection and now set about to imprison or kill all His Followers.

It is not a surprise that the Lord destroyed Jerusalem in A.D. 70, with the loss of over 1 million Jewish lives, but that He did not do such sooner!

The phrase, *"And when they were put to death, I gave my voice against them,"* presents the passage that some think is proof that Paul had been a member of the Jewish Sanhedrin. Even though that is a possibility, it is highly unlikely due to his young age at that time. If so, it does seem that Luke would have mentioned it or that Paul would, as well, have alluded to such a thing.

As stated, while such is possible, more than likely the Text means that inasmuch as he was the one who had arrested them, upon the vote by the Sanhedrin concerning their execution, he then lifted up his voice as a witness against them. This pretty well would have clinched the situation. At any rate, he was responsible for hurt, harm, and even death to many of the followers of Christ at that time. That's a heavy load to carry!

NOTES

(11) "AND I PUNISHED THEM OFT IN EVERY SYNAGOGUE, AND COMPELLED THEM TO BLASPHEME; AND BEING EXCEEDINGLY MAD AGAINST THEM, I PERSECUTED THEM EVEN UNTO STRANGE CITIES."

The form is:

1. The phrase, *"And I punished them oft in every synagogue,"* spoke only of Jerusalem at the moment. It is thought that there were over 400 synagogues in this city alone, with Paul attempting to raid each one, looking for Believers in Christ.

2. *"And compelled them to blaspheme,"* probably should have been translated, *"And attempted to compel them to blaspheme,"* because the Greek text implies that he was not successful in this effort. They would rather suffer imprisonment or even death.

3. The idea is that he attempted to make them blaspheme the Name of Jesus.

4. Surely, the manner in which these people died, holding the Name of Jesus sacred unto the end, must have left a mark on Paul. And yet, religious hardness is the worst sort of hardness, absolutely void of feelings, compassion, love, etc. The horrible thing is that such dreadful wickedness is always done in the Name of the Lord but, in reality, is the work of Satan, as is here blatantly obvious.

5. The phrase, *"And being exceedingly mad against them, I persecuted them even unto strange cities,"* indicates that Damascus was not the only city other than Jerusalem where Paul was practicing his deadly wares.

(12) "WHEREUPON AS I WENT TO DAMASCUS WITH AUTHORITY AND COMMISSION FROM THE CHIEF PRIESTS."

The status is:

1. The phrase, *"Whereupon as I went to Damascus,"* portrays the city to which he was headed and had almost arrived when a vision of Jesus would change his life forever.

2. Is there any reason the Lord chose Damascus as the place for this to happen?

NOTES

3. There probably is not! It was more than likely the time element that was important, rather than the place. He just happened to be on the road to Damascus when this great thing took place.

4. *"With authority and commission from the chief priests,"* proclaims his authority from the Sanhedrin, commissioning him to go into each synagogue and use Gestapo-type methods to ferret out the followers of Christ.

5. Whether the rulers of these synagogues had information or not that he was coming, we are not told. However, at any rate, it is most likely that most of the rulers of these synagogues were only too happy to supply Paul with the names of all the followers of Christ in each local congregation. It was only too easy then to arrest them, for which Paul evidently thought that God was well pleased. However, even as we shall see, Jesus was not pleased at all! It is impossible to oppose that which is of the Lord and, at the same time, be for the Lord. Such cannot be, as should be overly obvious!

6. With that being the case, and without going into detail, *most* of the Churches in the land are opposing Christ, while all the time they think they are aiding and abetting His Work. Such comes about because of a lack of knowledge of the Word of God, deception, false doctrine, and above all, an absence of the Holy Spirit. Regrettably and sadly, the Holy Spirit can little be found in virtually any Churches at the present time. Thank God for the few in which He is allowed to function.

(13) "AT MIDDAY, O KING, I SAW IN THE WAY A LIGHT FROM HEAVEN, ABOVE THE BRIGHTNESS OF THE SUN, SHINING ROUND ABOUT ME AND THEM WHICH JOURNEYED WITH ME."

The rule is:

1. The phrase, *"At midday, O king, I saw in the way a light from Heaven,"* proclaims one of the most dramatic Conversions the world has ever known.

2. This thing happened at midday, which precluded (whether fair or cloudy) any type of imaginary manifestations.

3. Paul had briefly alluded to his great persecution of Believers to portray to the king, and all present for that matter, that he was in no way predisposed toward Christ, but rather the very opposite, in fact, about as opposite as one could ever be. Consequently, what happened was of God, and of that there could be no doubt.

4. The phrase, *"Above the brightness of the sun,"* must mean that it was a fair day, with the sun shining brightly. Consequently, and especially at midday, the light that shone about Paul had to be of such brightness as to defy all description. Actually, this was the Glory of Jesus Christ.

5. *"Shining round about me and them which journeyed with me,"* means that Paul's associates saw the light, as well (Acts 22:9). Paul, along with being inspired by the Holy Spirit, may have had this occasion in mind when he said of Jesus, "*Who is the blessed and only Potentate, the King of kings, and Lord of lords;*

"Who only has immortality, dwelling in the light which no man can approach unto" (I Tim. 6:15-16).

(14) "AND WHEN WE WERE ALL FALLEN TO THE EARTH, I HEARD A VOICE SPEAKING UNTO ME, AND SAYING IN THE HEBREW TONGUE, SAUL, SAUL, WHY DO YOU PERSECUTE ME? IT IS HARD FOR YOU TO KICK AGAINST THE PRICKS."

The construction is:

1. Paul used the phrase, *"In Christ Jesus,"* or one of its derivatives, some 170 times in his 14 Epistles.

2. This describes the position of the Believer greater than any other phrase (Rom. 6:1-14).

THE VISION OF JESUS

The phrase, *"And when we were all fallen to the Earth,"* refers to the Power of God so strong at this time that none of these men, although all unsaved, could continue standing on their feet. Their knees buckled, and they fell!

This tells us that individuals being *"slain in the Spirit"* is Scriptural and, consequently, legitimate. Even though there has been some abuse in this area, still, a display of the Power of God often has this effect on people.

The phrase, *"I heard a voice speaking*

unto me, and saying in the Hebrew tongue, Saul, Saul," actually speaks of all hearing the voice, but only Paul knowing what was said (Acts 9:7).

In that the Lord spoke in the Hebrew language presents an additional detail not mentioned in Acts 9:4 or 22:8.

I think the Lord used this particular language because it was to Israel that He had given all the promises and prophecies, and this was their original language. And yet, sadly and regrettably, they had now rejected Him, but with God still loving them.

PERSECUTING THE LORD

The question, *"Why do you persecute Me?"* proclaims the fact that when we persecute those who belong to the Lord, we, in fact, persecute Jesus.

The phrase, *"It is hard for you to kick against the pricks,"* proclaims a common idiom of that day and even now.

When the oxen were harnessed for the pulling of the plow, sharp goads or sticks were fastened to the plow in such a way that if the ox kicked, attempting to kick off the traces, he would instead hit these sharp points, with the resultant pain meant to stop him from attempting again to kick off the traces.

As well, the insinuation in the Text is that Paul was under conviction by the Holy Spirit all the time he was doing these things (Jn. 16:8). Deep down in his heart, he saw the manner in which these people died, refusing to blaspheme the Name of Jesus, with him being unable to help knowing that this was reality. However, he attempted to smother this, which he knew in his heart to be true, by increasing his *"threatenings and slaughter."* As the oxen would kick against these sharp items, bringing pain, what Paul was doing was not only causing pain for the infant Church, but was causing him pain as well. However, it was something he would not at all admit, and probably could not have been stopped or turned without the great vision of Jesus Christ.

If one is to notice, the Lord did not ask Paul if it was hard for him to do these things, but rather made the statement that it was hard.

NOTES

(15) "AND I SAID, WHO ARE YOU, LORD? AND HE SAID, I AM JESUS WHOM YOU PERSECUTE."

The diagram is:

1. The question, *"And I said, Who are You, Lord?"* proclaims by the use of the title *"Lord"* that Paul knew that he was speaking to Deity.

2. *"And He said, I am Jesus Whom you persecute,"* proclaims the Lord using the Name that Paul hated the most—Jesus.

3. He was not ashamed to once again tell the story of his Conversion; and he used it as a sword to pierce the heart and conscience of the king, his sister, and all the exalted persons with them—all whom were living lives of abomination though professing forms of religion.

4. If one is to notice, the Apostle did not trouble to refute the charge of sedition. He confined himself rather to the one great subject of Salvation.

5. In Verses 14 through 18, Paul condensed into one embracing sentence various messages given to him by the Lord Jesus, so as to present at one view the nature of the commission given to him, and so help Agrippa to understand it.

6. Even though it may not be so dramatic or so powerful, still, in some way, every person must have a Damascus Road experience. There is no other way. The *"light"* must shine; the *"voice"* must be heard; the *"power"* must fall.

7. Too much, people have only become religious. Too much, they have looked to a Church or ceremony; and too much, they have relied on works. Nothing but a vision of Jesus will suffice. As was Paul, so are all!

(16) "BUT RISE, AND STAND UPON YOUR FEET: FOR I HAVE APPEARED UNTO YOU FOR THIS PURPOSE, TO MAKE YOU A MINISTER AND A WITNESS BOTH OF THESE THINGS WHICH YOU HAVE SEEN, AND OF THOSE THINGS IN THE WHICH I WILL APPEAR UNTO YOU."

The order is:

1. Jealousy is one of the Names of God (Ex. 20:5; 34:14; Nah. 1:2).

2. He is jealous of any infringement that is made by the world into the heart and life of the Believer, knowing that such will do

the Believer great harm (II Cor. 6:14-18).

THE WORDS OF THE LORD JESUS CHRIST

The phrase, *"But rise, and stand upon your feet,"* is very similar to that which the Lord had said to Job many years before, *"Gird up now your loins like a man; for I will demand of you, and you answer Me"* (Job 38:3).

The phrase, *"For I have appeared unto you for this purpose,"* specifies that the Lord has a work, a very important work, for Paul to do. As zealous as he had been in persecuting Jesus, he would now have to be just as zealous, and even more so, in laboring for Him. Hence, Paul would say in one of his Epistles, *"For I am the least of the Apostles, that am not worthy to be called an Apostle, because I persecuted the Church of God."*

However, then he said, *"But by the Grace of God I am what I am: and His Grace which was bestowed upon me was not in vain; but I laboured more abundantly than they all"* (I Cor. 15:9-10).

The phrase, *"To make you a Minister,"* refers to Paul being a Servant of Jesus Christ but, as well, an officer, who would be under the sole Authority of Christ. In other words, he, more than anyone, even the Twelve, would be given the responsibility of bringing this Gospel vessel called the Church through the tempestuous seas to that eternal shore.

THE COMMISSION

In this commission given to Paul, he was not placed under the authority of Peter, the Twelve, or anyone else for that matter, but answered directly to Jesus Christ. Even though he greatly respected Peter and the Twelve, and with his efforts toward the Church at Jerusalem always conciliatory, still, running like a thread through all of his Epistles is the unmistakable quality of this personal call by Christ. In writing to the Galatians, he said, *"Paul, an Apostle, (not of men, neither by man, but by Jesus Christ, and God the Father)"* (Gal. 1:1).

"And a witness both of these things which you have seen, and of those things in the which I will appear unto you," refers to the Damascus Road experience and the things the Lord gave him after that, which, in essence, among other things, was the New Covenant, the meaning of which is the Cross (II Cor. 12:1-12).

NOTES

The word *"witness"* in the Greek text is *"martus"* and actually means *"martyr, or one who gives his life in a particular cause."*

So, the word *"witness"* here does not merely mean having been a witness of something and then to convey that to others but, in fact, has reference to individuals literally giving their lives for that which they espouse, in this case, the Lord Jesus Christ. In effect, even hours after the Lord had appeared to Paul on the Damascus Road, He sent Ananias to give a message to Paul concerning certain particulars and then closed the message by saying, *"For I will show him how great things he must suffer for My Name's sake"* (Acts 9:16).

According to today's modern Gospel, this which the Lord told Paul was not exactly akin to the present health-and-wealth message.

One could say, I think, without fear of Scriptural contradiction, *"The greater the revelation, the greater the opposition by Satan!"* Regrettably, most of that opposition will come from those who claim to know the Lord, even as it did with Paul. In fact, it began with Cain murdering Abel.

(17) "DELIVERING YOU FROM THE PEOPLE, AND FROM THE GENTILES, UNTO WHOM NOW I SEND YOU."

The exegesis is:

1. The idea of this Verse pertains to the Lord protecting Paul from the Jews, for this is what the word *"people"* means, and from the *"Gentiles,"* which spoke of the Roman Empire. As should be obvious, the Lord had done that unto this hour, with Paul constantly facing those who thirsted for his life and, in fact, would have killed him were it not for the Lord.

2. However, this protection promised by the Lord did not guarantee protection from severe difficulties, such as imprisonment, beatings, stonings, etc. Hurtfully so, those things were present in Paul's life and ministry on a constant basis. So, when the Lord promises to deliver us, as He does in many and varied circumstances, and is buttressed

by His Word, we should understand exactly that of which He speaks. Regrettably, many have attempted to pull the coming Kingdom Age blessings over into the present, which is actually not possible. However, in that which He presently promises, He is Powerful and Mighty to save!

(18) "TO OPEN THEIR EYES, AND TO TURN THEM FROM DARKNESS TO LIGHT, AND FROM THE POWER OF SATAN UNTO GOD, THAT THEY MAY RECEIVE FORGIVENESS OF SINS, AND INHERITANCE AMONG THEM WHICH ARE SANCTIFIED BY FAITH THAT IS IN ME."

The way is:

1. The Incarnation of Christ was the way in which our Lord bound Himself to our woeful fortunes.

2. The Incarnation, which culminated in the Cross, carried to us the benefits with which He would enrich us. This means that His Death was for our sins and was endured that we might live.

THE COMMISSION GIVEN TO PAUL

This of which Paul spoke, in essence, is found in Isaiah 42:6-7 and 61:1-2, and was proclaimed by Christ, as well, at Nazareth when He said, *"The Spirit of the Lord is upon Me, because He has anointed Me to preach the Gospel to the poor; He has sent Me to heal the brokenhearted, to preach Deliverance to the captives, and recovering of sight to the blind, to set at liberty them that are bruised.*

"To preach the acceptable year of the Lord" (Lk. 4:18-19).

Paul in this statement actually proclaims the very purpose of the Gospel. It is as follows:

THE RECOVERY OF SPIRITUAL SIGHT TO THE BLIND

"To open their eyes, and to turn them from darkness to light": this says the same thing as spoken by Jesus, *"The recovery of sight to the blind."*

The Lord, as well as Paul, was not really speaking here of physical recovery or healing, but rather spiritual healing. This goes all the way back to the Fall and original sin.

Every person born is born a sinner and, thereby, spiritually blind. In other words, in this blinded state, the sinner does not know God and cannot know God or anything about the Lord, at least that which is correct. As well, it is impossible to effect any type of spiritual knowledge to the unsaved through the intellect. This is the reason that Preachers who attempt to deal with man's lost condition intellectually are doomed to failure. The simple reason is that a blind man cannot see anything, irrespective of how much you may show him.

THE GOSPEL AND THE HOLY SPIRIT

For spiritual eyes to be opened, the Gospel first has to be preached or proclaimed in some way, and then the Holy Spirit has to work His mighty Power on the Word of God as it is delivered to the sinner, thereby, awakening the sinner to his great spiritual need. Actually, this is one of the great office works and ministries of the Holy Spirit (Jn. 16:7-11).

Only then can the sinner understand his lost condition, with the Holy Spirit at that time presenting Jesus as the Saviour (and, in fact, the only Saviour) and man's need of Him.

There is only one *"light"* in the world, and that is the light of the Gospel of Jesus Christ. This means that Hinduism, Islam, Buddhism, Shintoism, Confucianism, and any other fake luminaries provide no light whatsoever. I emphasize again, the *"Light"* is actually Jesus. That means He not only has light but, in fact, is *"Light,"* i.e., *"the only source of light."* All else is *"darkness,"* irrespective of its claims or advertisement.

So, the Preacher must preach Jesus and nothing but Jesus.

FROM THE POWER OF SATAN UNTO GOD

In this, *"And from the power of Satan unto God,"* Paul points out that man is spiritually blind, enslaved, impure, morally poverty-stricken, and unholy, but that he can receive sight, liberty, forgiveness, true wealth, and holiness upon the principle of Faith in Christ.

As well, this tells us in no uncertain terms that every person in the world who does not know Christ as his own personal Saviour is controlled more or less by the power of Satan. Of course, the far greater majority would deny that, pointing to their alleged good morals or good works, which God will not accept. Despite these things, and even great religiosity in many cases, they are controlled by Satan.

If one is to notice, Paul mentioned the *"power of Satan."* This means that the sinner cannot break free of these clutches of darkness, at least within his own strength and abilities. It simply cannot be done. That is the reason that humanistic psychology (psychotherapy) is such a lie. It claims that it can rehabilitate man, which, in effect, says that man is not controlled by the powers of darkness but that his problems were caused by ill-treatment as a child, or a host of other suppositions. In other words, psychology denies man's true problem, which is sin, and the power of Satan, which energizes that sin.

THE POWER OF GOD

At this very moment, there are millions of alcoholics, drug addicts, homosexuals, hate-filled fanatics, and 100 other problems one might name, who do not want to be that way. They have tried repeatedly to change but have been unable to do so. It is because of the power of Satan.

However, the Power of God is much stronger than the power of Satan, so much stronger, in fact, that Satan has never been able to keep even one soul, no matter the degree of bondage, who earnestly and truly came to Jesus. Every single time, they have been gloriously and wondrously set free by the Power of God. Again I emphasize that it takes the Power of God to do these things, which cannot be done any other way. This is what makes the Holy Spirit so imperative. That is the reason Paul also said, *"For I am not ashamed of the Gospel of Christ: for it is the Power of God unto Salvation to every one that believeth"* (Rom. 1:16).

As well, please allow me to quickly add that of all the bondages of darkness, religion is the greatest bondage of all. It has caused more people to be eternally lost than probably all the vices of the world put together.

NOTES

The reason is deception.

Most people in bondages of vice know that it is wrong, while untold millions are steeped in religion, which has woven its tentacles around them, with them thinking they are saved when, in actuality, they are lost. It takes the Power of God to break that bondage just as much, and even more, than it does bondages of vice.

FORGIVENESS OF SINS

The Lord not only breaks the chains of darkness when He sets the captive free, but, as well, He forgives every single sin that the person has ever committed. Sin, within itself, is a burden that defies all description. This is one of the reasons that when a person comes to Christ, it seems like a weight has lifted off his shoulders, and, in reality, it is the weight of sin that has been lifted. With *"forgiveness"* comes the eradication of all guilt. It is like the whole world has become brand new, and, in fact, it has. Peace with God is instantly established, with all enmity removed. It is the single greatest thing that could ever happen to anyone.

Just this morning I was speaking with one of the men of our Church, and he was telling me how that alcohol and drugs had almost destroyed him. In that terrible condition, he found Jesus, and he stated, *"Brother Swaggart, all the things I had been looking for and trying to find in drugs and alcohol, in which it could not be found, I instantly found in Jesus. It was like all of Heaven had come down and filled my soul, and I knew I had found it at last."*

THE INHERITANCE

The phrase, *"And inheritance among them,"* speaks of the great inheritance in Christ, of which we now only have a down payment. Ultimately, all Saints of God who are now washed, sanctified, and justified, will also be glorified. This will take place at the First Resurrection of Life when all will be given a new body, which will not age or ever know disease. It is called Eternal Life, which we now have in principle, but will then have in fact. It is a future that is absolutely beyond the scope of human thinking or ability.

SANCTIFIED

In this statement, *"Which are sanctified by Faith that is in me,"* presents the Holy Spirit through Paul teaching us that these great Gifts of God are received by Faith. He even says our Sanctification comes by Faith, and what does he mean by that?

First of all, it means that the moment the sinner accepts Christ, he is not only washed but, at the same time, *"sanctified,"* which means to be *"made clean"* (I Cor. 6:11). That has to be done and is done instantly upon the sinner accepting Christ. This then makes it possible for the sinner to be justified, which is done instantly, as well. This means that he is then *"declared clean."* One has to be made clean before one can be declared clean.

As well, there is a sanctifying process which begins immediately in the new Believer's heart, with the Holy Spirit working mightily to bring the Believer's state up to his standing (what he is in Christ). This is called progressive Sanctification and is also a work of Faith (I Thess. 5:23).

THAT IS IN ME

The short phrase, *"That is in me,"* has Paul proclaiming the fact that the Lord gave him the actual meaning of Sanctification, which means to be set apart unto Christ. In fact, while Jesus Christ is the New Covenant, the Cross of Christ is the meaning of that New Covenant, the meaning of which was given to the Apostle Paul (Gal. 1:1-12).

(19) "WHEREUPON, O KING AGRIPPA, I WAS NOT DISOBEDIENT UNTO THE HEAVENLY VISION."

The way is:

1. The phrase, *"Whereupon, O King Agrippa,"* proclaims Paul addressing his remarks to the king, even though there were many other people present as well. It is obvious that this assemblage was for Agrippa; consequently, Paul addressing him as he did in no way was disrespectful to all the others who were present.

2. *"I was not disobedient unto the heavenly vision,"* proclaims that which every Preacher ought to say. Paul had faithfully carried out that which the Lord had called him to do, as is obvious. It is our responsibility to do the same as well.

3. To be sure, his enemies denied his vision and did everything possible within their power to stop his obedience. Regrettably, virtually all of the opposition came from the religious sector of that particular time, even as it continues to do so unto this very hour.

4. Then again, I think most Preachers have really never had a *"heavenly vision"* of any nature. Consequently, they have very little to say.

5. If one studies the Word of God, one will find that most, if not all, of the Bible Greats had an experience with God of some nature, which empowered them for the task. One could consider Abraham (Gen., Chpts. 12 and 15), Isaac (Gen., Chpt. 26), Jacob (Gen., Chpt. 32), Isaiah (Isa., Chpt. 6), and Ezekiel (Ezek., Chpt. 1), to name just a few.

(20) "BUT SHOWED FIRST UNTO THEM OF DAMASCUS, AND AT JERUSALEM, AND THROUGHOUT ALL THE COASTS OF JUDAEA, AND THEN TO THE GENTILES, THAT THEY SHOULD REPENT AND TURN TO GOD, AND DO WORKS MEET FOR REPENTANCE."

The diagram is:

1. Can the Believer reach a place to where there will be no more temptation?

2. No, we cannot, not until we die or the Trump sounds (I Cor. 15:53).

JESUS CHRIST, THE SON OF GOD

The phrase, *"But showed first unto them of Damascus,"* proclaims Paul, as recorded in Acts, Chapter 9, immediately after his Conversion beginning to preach the Gospel in the very synagogues in which he had at first thought to arrest followers of Christ. As well, he immediately preached *"Christ"* and declared that *"He is the Son of God"* (Acts 9:20).

One can well imagine what that might have done to the Sanhedrin when they got word of what had happened to their star pupil and their leading scholar of Pharisaism. I suspect that they hardly believed their ears, and then when they found out it was indeed true, their thoughts turned toward murder, which carries over unto this hour (Acts 9:23).

NOTES

THE GENTILES

The phrase, *"And at Jerusalem, and throughout all the coasts of Judaea,"* pertains to Paul going to Jerusalem immediately after Damascus, and then later, to other areas in Judaea.

The phrase, *"And then to the Gentiles,"* speaks of the far greater majority of his ministry, even up to this particular time. Even though he preached to Jews, even with a constant burden because of their terrible spiritual state, still, the greater part of his ministry was always to the Gentiles, for this was his major calling.

REPENTANCE

The phrase, *"That they should repent and turn to God, and do works meet for Repentance,"* proclaims *"Repentance"* as a requirement for all, both Jews and Gentiles.

If one is to notice, Paul did not normally say that much about Repentance, with most of his teaching centered up on Faith. There was a reason for that.

Repentance is something that must be engaged by every individual who comes to the Lord and, in fact, has been that way from the time of the Fall in the Garden of Eden. True heart-felt Repentance can be engaged in a variety of ways. It is not so much what one says or any particular ceremony, but rather an attitude of the heart, which realizes that we have sinned against God, and that we are sorry for that sin. Basically, that is Repentance, with its total power literally turning the person around, with him going in the opposite direction than he had previously been travelling, so to speak.

WORKS WHICH FOLLOW TRUE REPENTANCE

This is what Paul meant when he spoke of *"works meet for Repentance."* In other words, if an individual claims he has repented before God, and yet, is continuing in the same lifestyle, even the same sins, travelling the same road, etc., that is a sure sign that he really has not repented.

Anyone who truly repents will instantly begin to portray *"works"* of that Repentance by literally doing an about-face respecting his spiritual direction, which graphically affects his lifestyle (Jn. 3:19; I Jn. 2:15).

The repentant person will then truly seek the Kingdom of God, which literally means the Rule of God in one's life. As well, his life will be a perpetual seeking of the Righteousness of God (Mat. 6:33).

(21) "FOR THESE CAUSES THE JEWS CAUGHT ME IN THE TEMPLE, AND WENT ABOUT TO KILL ME."

The direction is:

1. The phrase, *"For these causes the Jews caught me in the Temple,"* refers back to Acts 21:28-32. In other words, Paul was saying that the hatred of the Jews against him was not because of the reasons they were saying but, in essence, because of his preaching Jesus.

2. *"And went about to kill me,"* in effect, says, *"O King Agrippa, I have spent my life in trying to persuade men to repent and turn to God, and for doing so, the Jews seek to kill me. Can this be right?"*

3. Why is it that those who oppose the message of the Power of God centered up in Jesus, at the same time, feel that they must stop not only the message but the messenger? Why aren't they content to just oppose the message?

4. The answer is simple but, at the same time, complicated.

The simple answer is that liars hate the truth. If one is to notice, those who preach the truth virtually never declare war on the messengers of error. Even though they may strongly point out the error, they leave these people to God because that is the way it should be done (Mat. 13:28-30).

5. However, as stated, the purveyors of error, exactly as the Jews of old, are not satisfied to merely oppose the message. At the same time, they feel they must destroy the messenger in some way.

(22) "HAVING THEREFORE OBTAINED HELP OF GOD, I CONTINUE UNTO THIS DAY, WITNESSING BOTH TO SMALL AND GREAT, SAYING NONE OTHER THINGS THAN THOSE WHICH THE PROPHETS AND MOSES DID SAY SHOULD COME."

The status is:

1. Within Israel at the time of Christ, there were found two major parties, one

NOTES

strict and the other lax in the observance of Mosaic Law.

2. The leaders of the former were the highly popular Pharisees, who, according to their name, were the *"separatists."* Their rivals, the Sadducees, were less fanatical in their observance of the demands of the Law and were more willing to compromise with the spirit of the time.

THE HELP OF GOD

Paul said, *"Having therefore obtained help of God, I continue unto this day, witnessing both to small and great."* This proclaims that God had sustained him through some very difficult times. In fact, if the Lord had not helped him, there is no way that he could have survived.

"Is God with us?" is the great question. Every Preacher in the world claims that God is with him, irrespective as to who he is or what he is doing. The truth is, the Lord is with only a few. So, how does one tell the difference?

Jesus told us how. He said: *"Beware of false Prophets which come to you in sheep's clothing, but inwardly they are ravening wolves."*

He then said, *"You shall know them by their fruits"* (Mat. 7:15-16).

But yet, there is a little catch to that also. Many Preachers, and we speak of the false ones, make great claims in order to deceive the people—great claims of healing, people being saved, etc.

But yet, if a person will look at the situation carefully, it's not too difficult to tell if the Preacher is telling the truth or not!

GREAT CLAIMS

Sometime back, I heard a so-called religious leader make the following statement:

He said, *"Last year, we had 2 million people saved,"* or figures that were similar.

I sat there and looked at him in astonishment, wondering what he was talking about. The man does not even really consider himself to be a Preacher, which means he does not give any Altar Calls, etc.

After awhile, I figured out what he was saying.

He was claiming that if the mayor of a city or the leader of a country got saved, or proposed to do so, irrespective as to where the country is, the city or the entirety of the country must be considered as saved, which, of course, is foolishness.

I doubt very seriously if the man in question had seen anyone saved in the entirety of the year, much less millions. So, this means that Believers should take very carefully what they hear with a grain of salt. If Believers believe a lie and then give money to support that lie, they have entered into the lie. Let me give you another example.

THE APOSTLE PAUL

Paul went into certain cities of the Roman Empire preaching the Gospel and, thereby, establishing Churches regarding the people who had been saved. He would stay there for a period of time and then go on to other fields of endeavor.

Almost all of the time, after he had left and gone to other areas, Judaizers would come into the Churches and flatter the people, while slowly tearing down Paul, hoping to get the people to embrace Law, i.e., *"the Law of Moses,"* which Jesus had already fulfilled. In fact, this is what occasioned much of the teaching in Paul's Epistles.

Now at times (or most all of the time), the people in these respective Churches who were taken in by these individuals would give them money, etc.

Do you think that God honored such giving? Of course, He did not!

These so-called Preachers were doing the work of Satan, not the Work of God. In fact, most opposition comes from within the Church instead of without. When money was given to these individuals, whomever they may have been, that's the same thing as supporting the work of Satan, which no sane person wants to do. But yet, when money is given to individuals who are preaching false doctrine or no doctrine at all, such a person, no matter his or her sincerity, is supporting the world of spiritual darkness. Check out the fruit! If you will do a little investigation and, as well, seek the Face of God as to what He would have you do, you will ultimately come out to the correct answer.

(23) "THAT CHRIST SHOULD SUFFER,

AND THAT HE SHOULD BE THE FIRST WHO SHOULD RISE FROM THE DEAD, AND SHOULD SHOW LIGHT UNTO THE PEOPLE, AND TO THE GENTILES."

The synopsis is:

1. The *"carnal"* mind is not a *"spiritual"* mind.

2. The *"carnal"* mind is that which depends on the flesh. The *"spiritual"* mind is that which depends on the Holy Spirit (Rom. 8:4-10).

THAT CHRIST SHOULD SUFFER

The phrase, *"That Christ should suffer,"* in essence, speaks of the Cross, actually, the very reason for which He came. This is proclaimed in Genesis 3:15; Psalms 16:10; and Isaiah, Chapter 53.

The Jews were looking for the Messiah at the time that Jesus came, but they were looking for a triumphant Messiah, Who would use His Power to deliver them from the Roman yoke. They refused to believe that they suffered a worse yoke, the yoke of sin. A suffering Messiah, they would not accept! So, they killed Him, thereby, fulfilling Scripture. They did so not because they were predestined, but simply because they willed such. Jesus said, *"For it must needs be that offences come; but woe to that man by whom the offence comes!"* (Mat. 18:7).

The phrase, *"And that He should be the First who should rise from the dead,"* refers to Jesus being the *"Firstfruits"* of the Resurrection and, therefore, the guarantee of the Resurrection of all men (I Cor. 15:1-23; Rev. 1:5). Jesus called it, *"The Resurrection of Life"* (Jn. 5:29).

In that Verse, He also mentioned *"the Resurrection of damnation,"* which will take place 1,000 years after the *"Resurrection of Life"* (Rev., Chpt. 20). It will include all Christ-rejecters, all the way from Adam and Eve up to and including the coming Kingdom Age. Actually, this Resurrection of damnation will take place after the 1,000-year Kingdom Age, with all in that Resurrection appearing at the Great White Throne Judgment (Rev. 20:11-15).

THE FIRST RESURRECTION OF LIFE

The First Resurrection of Life will actually be in five parts. They are as follows:

1. CHRIST AS THE FIRSTFRUITS

"Firstfruits" are basically a down payment of that which is to come, but with the guarantee that it will definitely come. While it is a *"down payment,"* it is more than that. It is the same as a businessman purchasing something with which he makes a down payment, and then he places the full amount in the bank, which guarantees payment in full. Paul said:

"But now is Christ risen from the dead and become the Firstfruits of them who slept" (I Cor. 15:20).

The Apostle went on to describe this momentous occasion, and I quote from THE EXPOSITOR'S STUDY BIBLE:

"For since by man came death *(refers to Adam and the Fall in the Garden of Eden, and speaks of spiritual death, separation from God)*, **by a man came also the Resurrection of the dead.** *(This refers to the Lord Jesus Christ, Who atoned for all sin, thereby making it possible for man to be united once again with God, which guarantees the Resurrection.)*

"For as in Adam all die *(spiritual death, separation from God)*, **even so in Christ shall all be made alive.** *(In the first man, all died. In the Second Man, all shall be made alive, at least all who will believe Jn. 3:16)"* **(I Cor. 15:21-22).**

2. AFTERWARD THEY THAT ARE CHRIST'S AT HIS COMING

This is the part of the Resurrection that is referred to as the Rapture (I Thess. 4:16-17; I Cor. 15:23). Actually, the Rapture and the Resurrection are one and the same. It is two words for the same event.

It somewhat amuses me to hear some Christians claim they do not believe in the Rapture. If, in fact, this is what they really believe, they do not believe in the Resurrection. I suspect that their statements are derived from a misunderstanding.

At this part of the Resurrection, every Saint who has ever lived and died, all the way from Abel to this very moment, will be resurrected. Paul said, *"The dead in Christ shall rise first."* He then said, *"Then we which are alive and remain shall be caught up together with them in the clouds*

NOTES

NOTES

(clouds of Saints), *to meet the Lord in the air: and so shall we ever be with the Lord"* (I Thess. 4:16-17).

So, this means that every Child of God, both the dead and those who are alive at that time, will be in the First Resurrection of Life (Lk. 21:34-36; Jn. 14:1-3; I Cor. 15:23, 51-54; II Cor. 5:1-8; Eph. 5:27; Phil. 3:11, 20-21; Col. 3:4; I Thess. 2:19; 3:13; 4:13-17; 5:9, 23; II Thess. 2:1, 7; James 5:7-8; I Pet. 5:4; I Jn. 2:28; 3:2).

3. 144,000 JEWS SAVED

This will take place in the first three and one-half years of the coming Great Tribulation. These Jews will be caught up (raptured) as the *"manchild"* in the middle of the Tribulation, or about three and one-half years before the Second Coming. Just exactly how these Jews will find Christ at this time, the Scripture does not say. However, one thing is certain: this which the Word of God predicts will most definitely take place (Isa. 66:7-8; Dan. 12:1; Rev. 7:1-8; 12:5; 14:1-5).

4. THE RAPTURE OF THE TRIBULATION SAINTS

There will be a tremendous number of people saved during the Great Tribulation (Rev., Chpts. 6:1-19:21).

The first martyrs of this period are told to rest until the others are killed, whomever they might be (Rev. 6:9-11).

Even those killed by the Antichrist in the last three and one-half years of the Great Tribulation (who are saved) will have part in the First Resurrection (Rev. 20:4-6).

This proves their Rapture or Resurrection in time for the Marriage Supper (Rev. 19:1-10) and in time to come back with Christ at the Second Coming, which they shall (Zech. 14:5; Jude, Vs. 14; Rev. 19:11-21).

There will be millions of people who call themselves *"Christian,"* and who are members of Churches but, nevertheless, have never been born again. Many of these people, no doubt, will come to Christ immediately after the Rapture of the Church. Many of them will be killed by the Antichrist, and, as stated, they too will be included in the Resurrection of Life.

5. THE TWO WITNESSES

These two witnesses will probably be Enoch and Elijah. These are the only two individuals who have never died. They will minister in Jerusalem the last half of the Great Tribulation until the Lord finally allows them to be killed; however, they will be raised from the dead three and a half days after being killed. As well, they will be raptured to glory at that time, which will be almost immediately before the Second Coming, and will be included in the First Resurrection of Life. In fact, their Resurrection will end the First Resurrection, which began with the Resurrection of Christ (Rev. 11:7-11).

LIGHT

The phrase, *"And should show Light unto the people* (Jews), *and to the Gentiles,"* refers, as stated, to the only *"Light"* there is. If that *"Light"* is rejected, Who is Jesus Christ, there remains no other spiritual illumination.

This should be understood as to how very serious this is. This means that if anything or anyone other than Jesus is projected, it is false and, consequently, its followers are lost!

It also means that Jesus Christ must be looked at and understood as exactly Who He is, the Son of God, God manifest in the flesh, the Redeemer of man, and the only Redeemer. This means all Catholics who faithfully follow their Church are lost simply because Mary and the Church are placed before Christ.

As well, it means that all Mormons are lost, inasmuch as in that religion, Jesus is relegated to the place merely of a good Teacher.

This means that all Muslims are lost simply because in that religion, Jesus is looked at merely as a Prophet and not the Son of God, Who and What He actually is.

This also means that many Protestants fall into the same category simply because they seek to add something to Faith in Christ. In other words, in order to be saved, they teach that one must accept Christ, plus belong to their particular Church denomination, be baptized in water, baptized with a particular formula, take the Lord's Supper, etc. If one does such, one simply is not saved, for Paul said, *"Christ is become of no effect unto you, whosoever of you are justified by the Law* (the Church, particular ordinances or ceremonies, etc.)*; you are fallen from grace"* (Gal. 5:4).

This certainly doesn't mean that Water Baptism, the Lord's Supper, etc., are wrong, but what is wrong is the trust in such for Salvation. It is Jesus only Who can save because He is the One Who paid the price at Calvary's Cross.

(24) "AND AS HE THUS SPOKE FOR HIMSELF, FESTUS SAID WITH A LOUD VOICE, PAUL, YOU ARE BESIDE YOURSELF; MUCH LEARNING DOES MAKE YOU MAD."

The synopsis is:

1. The phrase, *"And as he thus spoke for himself, Festus said with a loud voice,"* portrays terminology that leads one to believe that Luke was an eyewitness, which he, no doubt, was.

2. *"Paul, you are beside yourself; much learning does make you mad,"* portrays an excited interruption by Festus, showing that he was unable to accept the truth enunciated by the Apostle. The idea of a fulfilled prophecy, of the Resurrection of the dead, and of a crucified Jew giving light to the great Roman world were *"foolishness unto him"* because he lacked spiritual discernment. He thought the Apostle's glowing words must be the outcome of a disordered mind.

3. As a heathen, Festus could not understand, as Agrippa could, the great argument that the atoning Death and Resurrection of the Messiah fulfilled the predictions of the Prophets, and were necessary in order for the Salvation of sinful men.

4. Irrespective of the outburst of Festus regarding his unbelief, such portrays that he was under heavy conviction by the Holy Spirit. I believe one could say without any fear of contradiction that Paul's teaching and preaching were always freighted by the Power of God. To be sure, such will almost always elicit a reaction, whether positive or negative, even as here.

(25) "BUT HE SAID, I AM NOT MAD, MOST NOBLE FESTUS; BUT SPEAK FORTH THE WORDS OF TRUTH AND SOBERNESS."

The account is:

NOTES

1. The phrase, *"But he said, I am not mad* (insane)*, most noble Festus,"* presents Paul calmly answering the governor. Actually, the charge of insanity is quite often used by those such as Festus against the Preachers of truth. It is something they do not understand. At the same time, coming under the Power of the Holy Spirit, which most have never experienced before, they strike out, that is, if they do not accept Christ, which most don't.

2. *"But speak forth the words of truth and soberness,"* no doubt, presented the only *"truth"* that the governor, and the others for that matter, had ever heard, with the exception of Festus having heard Paul at least one other time.

3. All of these people had heard many things that were true, but they had never before heard *"Truth."*

4. Actually, *"Truth"* is not a philosophy, but rather a Person, the Man, Christ Jesus (Jn. 14:6).

5. As well, this *"Truth,"* which was the Word of God (Jesus is the Living Word), was delivered by Paul in a sober, responsible way. There were no sleight of hand tricks as employed by the magicians and soothsayers of that day, who often frequented the courts of both governors and kings. This was a sober presentation of the Gospel of Jesus Christ, which transcended all political orations, glib prattle of the comics, etc.

(26) "FOR THE KING KNOWS OF THESE THINGS, BEFORE WHOM ALSO I SPEAK FREELY: FOR I AM PERSUADED THAT NONE OF THESE THINGS ARE HIDDEN FROM HIM; FOR THIS THING WAS NOT DONE IN A CORNER."

The status is:

1. The maturity of the Believer cannot rise any higher than one's knowledge of the Cross.

2. While one can be saved, Spirit-filled, and even used by the Lord and not understand the Cross relative to Sanctification, one cannot be victorious in his own personal life without understanding the Cross of Christ.

THE WORD OF GOD

The phrase, *"For the king knows of these*

NOTES

things, before whom also I speak freely," spoke to Agrippa as a Jew, which he was! Paul knew that Agrippa was at least familiar with some of the things Paul was saying. Actually, this is the reason that Paul seemingly went into more detail than he usually did. Even though he was appealing to all who were there that day, he seemed to be making a special appeal to Agrippa in his message, which he, no doubt, was. The Holy Spirit was guiding him to do so.

In this, we can see the great contrast between the Jews and the Romans. The Jews had the Word of God for about 1,600 years, with the first five Books of the Bible being written by Moses. The Prophets and others had written the other Books, totaling the Old Testament. Consequently, they were the only people on the face of the Earth who had the *"light."* As well, they were the only people who worshiped one God.

By contrast, the balance of the world had no true light on any subject, and as a consequence, worshiped many gods, who, in actuality, were no gods at all, but rather demon spirits. So, the Jews were the spiritual and intellectual superiors of the world.

They had been subjugated by other nations and now by Rome simply because they had forsaken Jehovah, Who had given them this great light. The curses of Deuteronomy, Chapter 28, had come to pass exactly as the Lord through Moses said they would.

THIS THING WAS NOT HIDDEN

The phrase, *"For I am persuaded that none of these things are hidden from him,"* speaks of all things of which Paul had mentioned respecting Agrippa.

The phrase, *"For this thing was not done in a corner,"* primarily speaks of Jesus Christ.

It was certainly true that worldly Agrippa, although a Jew, may not have paid too much attention to that which was taught him as a child and a young man concerning the Word of God, which was taught all Jewish boys. Still, it would have been virtually impossible for him to have missed the three and one-half years of Jesus' public Ministry. With miracles being performed of every description, even to the dead being raised, and Jesus, at least for the first two years, being the topic of almost every conversation, it is not possible that Agrippa had not heard accounts of this, the greatest happening that Earth had ever known. This alone would have validated all that the Prophets had foretold and would surely have aroused the curiosity of this king, even as it had his evil father (Lk. 23:7-8).

As well, considering some 2,000 years of proliferation of the Word of God, true Bible Christianity is not something that can be dismissed lightly, *"It was not done in a corner."*

(27) "KING AGRIPPA, DO YOU BELIEVE THE PROPHETS? I KNOW THAT YOU BELIEVE."

The order is:

1. The question, *"King Agrippa, do you believe the Prophets?"* presents an Altar Call as given to this king and his sister, which drilled straight to the heart of this profligate Jew.

2. Having given thousands of Altar Calls myself, I personally believe that Paul asked this question of the king and then paused awaiting an answer.

3. At that moment, the silence would have been pregnant as it hung over the room. A man's soul was at stake, and the answer he would give would decide its destiny for all of eternity. The others, to be sure, fell into the same category, but Agrippa most of all.

4. Under other circumstances, Agrippa might have quickly said that he believed, inasmuch as he was a Jew, but knowing that Paul had presented Jesus Christ as the Fulfillment of that which the Prophets had predicted, if he now answered in the affirmative, he would, at the same time, be embracing Christ.

5. The phrase, *"I know that you believe,"* presents the Apostle finally answering for the king, which saved him further embarrassment.

6. The moment had come and now quickly waned, never to come again, at least in this fashion.

(28) "THEN AGRIPPA SAID UNTO PAUL, ALMOST YOU PERSUADE ME TO BE A CHRISTIAN."

NOTES

The form is:

1. The phrase, *"Then Agrippa said unto Paul,"* presents the king as finally breaking his silence, but with an answer that has been debated for centuries.

2. The phrase, *"Almost you persuade me to be a Christian,"* can be taken in two ways, for the original Greek text, especially considering that there was no punctuation then, gives little indication as to which is correct.

3. It can be looked at as a statement and, as such, would mean that he was coming close to yielding to the persuasion of Paul as the Holy Spirit moved upon him.

As well, it could have been stated in the form of a question, for the original Greek actually says, *"Me you persuade a Christian to become?"*

4. Considering Paul's answer in the next Verse, I personally believe that Agrippa was rather expressing surprise as he came to the conclusion that Paul was actually inviting him to be a Christian. So, he answered with some sarcasm!

5. However, in no way does that negate the Moving and Operation of the Holy Spirit upon him. In fact, it must have been extremely heavy, even as it possibly was upon Festus. Irrespective of the king's answer, he had heard the Word of God and had been given the opportunity of eternity. Sadly, he rejected but will relive this scene over and over, forever and forever, even as he is doing at this very moment. He would give the kingdom he once had a million times over for just one more opportunity to answer Paul. To be sure, his answer would be different the second time, but regrettably, there was no second time, and there will now never be a second time. First, second, and third opportunities are on this side of the grave. There is no other opportunity after death.

(29) "AND PAUL SAID, I WOULD TO GOD, THAT NOT ONLY YOU, BUT ALSO ALL WHO HEAR ME THIS DAY, WERE BOTH ALMOST, AND ALTOGETHER SUCH AS I AM, EXCEPT THESE BONDS."

The status is:

1. The phrase, *"And Paul said, I would to God, that not only you, but also all who hear me this day,"* presents the Apostle answering the king, and all others for that matter, and doing so in a kind and gracious way.

2. Hervey said of this moment, *"All acknowledge the extreme beauty and taste of this reply, combining the firmness of the martyr with the courtesy of the gentleman."*

3. The phrase, *"Were both almost, and altogether such as I am,"* presents the statement that I believe is the key to Agrippa's answer.

4. In effect, both Festus and Agrippa had somewhat ridiculed Paul's appeal. Festus accused him of being insane, and Agrippa lifted himself above the Apostle by claiming, in effect, that even though he was a Jew, he was too intellectual for such an appeal.

5. Paul countered by claiming his position in Christ as vastly superior, and as such, wished that these notables were such as he. How right he was!

6. *"Except these bonds,"* must have presented a dramatic moment when coupled with the majesty of his words. Paul lifted up his manacled hands, forming a picture of arresting grandeur.

(30) "AND WHEN HE HAD THUS SPOKEN, THE KING ROSE UP, AND THE GOVERNOR, AND BERNICE, AND THEY WHO SAT WITH THEM."

The account is:

1. The phrase, *"And when he had thus spoken, the king rose up,"* means that he did not want to hear anymore. So, he rose and thus closed the audience and silenced the brave confessor.

2. *"And the governor, and Bernice, and they who sat with them,"* presents them following Agrippa.

3. If Agrippa and his courtiers hoped to entertain themselves with the new religious views of this Jewish reformer, as they would account him, they were quickly undeceived, for the brave Preacher immediately raised moral and eternal issues and presented Christ to them as a Saviour from their sins.

4. Who they thought they would see, and what they thought they would hear is anyone's guess. However, whatever had been their thoughts, it had not turned out as they originally expected. They had been brought face-to-face with themselves and, above all,

with God. As such, they would never be the same again, even though they had rejected the appeal and the plea.

(31) "AND WHEN THEY WERE GONE ASIDE, THEY TALKED BETWEEN THEMSELVES, SAYING, THIS MAN DOES NOTHING WORTHY OF DEATH OR OF BONDS."

The structure is:

1. The phrase, *"And when they were gone aside, they talked between themselves, saying,"* presents the fact that all had been seriously affected by the message delivered by the Apostle. They were not cracking jokes or making fun of what they had heard. They could not deny what he had said, especially the way it had been presented to them. They had thought him to be on trial; but, in effect, they were on trial, with them now recognizing this truth.

2. *"This man does nothing worthy of death or of bonds,"* once again, declares Paul's innocence. Not only had he done nothing worthy of death, but he should not have even been imprisoned, for he had done nothing against the Jews, which even Agrippa admitted.

(32) "THEN SAID AGRIPPA UNTO FESTUS, THIS MAN MIGHT HAVE BEEN SET AT LIBERTY, IF HE HAD NOT APPEALED UNTO CAESAR."

The form is:

1. The phrase, *"Then said Agrippa unto Festus,"* presents the king as seemingly attempting to appease his conscience. In effect, he was saying that Festus had done wrong by not setting Paul free after the trial of some days before.

2. *"This man might have been set at liberty, if he had not appealed unto Caesar,"* seems to imply that the appeal had already been registered and now must be carried out.

3. Paul had long since settled it in his mind that the Lord desired that he go to Rome. Actually, Jesus had *"stood by him, and said, Be of good cheer, Paul: for as you have testified of Me in Jerusalem, so must you bear witness also at Rome"* (Acts 23:11).

4. This had been some two years before, but the Will of the Lord was the same now

NOTES

and actually would be set in motion very shortly.

"You servants of God, your Master proclaim,
"And publish abroad His wonderful Name;
"The Name all victorious of Jesus extol:
"His Kingdom is glorious, He rules over all."

CHAPTER 27

(1) "AND WHEN IT WAS DETERMINED THAT WE SHOULD SAIL INTO ITALY, THEY DELIVERED PAUL AND CERTAIN OTHER PRISONERS UNTO ONE NAMED JULIUS, A CENTURION OF AUGUSTUS' BAND."

The overview is:

1. The phrase, *"And when it was determined that we should sail into Italy,"* proclaimed the time as having arrived when Paul would now go to Rome. In a sense, he would do so as the guest of Caesar. Luke was with him, as evidenced by the pronoun *"we."* Evidently, he was given permission by Festus to make the trip and to serve Paul any way he could.

2. It had been over two years since the Lord had appeared to Paul, telling him, *"So must you bear witness* (of Me) *also at Rome"* (Acts 23:11). The delay of this period of time was the Lord's doing and evidently corresponded with His timetable.

3. When the Lord gives us information respecting certain things that will come to pass, whether telling us when or not, He, at the same time, is working out other situations of which we have no knowledge, but which will play a part or play into that of which He has told us.

Consequently, we are to wait on Him with patience, especially considering if He has not told us when certain things will come to pass. He told Paul that he must witness for Him in Rome but did not tell him when that would be. Therefore, the Apostle trusted the Lord to work out things in due time, which He did.

NOTES

4. *"They delivered Paul and certain other prisoners unto one named Julius, a centurion of Augustus' band,"* concerns a certain centurion who was stationed either in Caesarea or in a place called Bananaea, which was east of the southern end of the Sea of Galilee, which was in the territory of King Agrippa II.

5. Some have even speculated that Julius was present when Paul addressed King Agrippa, which he may well have been. Others speculate that he may have been acquainted some time before with the Roman centurion, Cornelius, who was saved and baptized with the Holy Spirit under Peter, as related in Acts, Chapter 10.

6. At any rate, he was very kind to Paul, which seems to indicate that he knew the Apostle, or at least knew of him.

7. This cohort or *"band"* called *"Augustus' band"* was an elite group directly responsible to the emperor.

8. There were five cohorts stationed at Caesarea, with at least four of them consisting of auxiliary troops (a cohort of which the majority of troops were not Italian). However, it is likely that this elite cohort commanded by Julius was all Italian, or at least was a majority.

(2) "AND ENTERING INTO A SHIP OF ADRAMYTTIUM, WE LAUNCHED, MEANING TO SAIL BY THE COASTS OF ASIA; ONE ARISTARCHUS, A MACEDONIAN OF THESSALONICA, BEING WITH US."

The rule is:

1. The phrase, *"And entering into a ship of Adramyttium, we launched, meaning to sail by the coasts of Asia,"* refers to the fact that most ships of that day kept the coast in sight, if at all possible, wherever they were going. Navigational abilities were limited. As well, even though the Mediterranean Sea was well known, the great sea beyond, now known as the Atlantic Ocean, was little known at all, save for the coastline, etc. This ship was probably home-based on the northwestern coast of Asia Minor, south of Troas, on the gulf opposite, which lies the island of Lesbos. Actually, Paul would sail on three different ships to Rome.

2. *"One Aristarchus, a Macedonian of Thessalonica, being with us,"* proclaims another of Paul's converts being with him, along with Luke. Consequently, Paul had two travelling associates, allowed by Festus. In other words, they were traveling at the expense of Rome.

3. This young man is first mentioned in Acts 19:29, and was one of Paul's associates at Ephesus. He was probably saved under Paul when the Apostle first visited Thessalonica.

4. We find him again with Paul on his last journey from Corinth to Asia (Acts 20:4), and we gather from the present notice of him that he kept with Paul till he arrived at Jerusalem, and even was with him in Caesarea. It seems from Colossians 4:10 that he also stayed with Paul throughout the two years of imprisonment at Rome.

5. From the way the situation is explained, knowing that Paul was innocent, it seems that Festus gave him much latitude of freedom in that he was not treated as other prisoners. For instance, as we have just observed, it was not common at all for prisoners to have associates travelling with them as Paul did. Therefore, in the midst of all the difficulties, the Lord gave the Apostle certain kindnesses, which made the situation much easier. To be sure, it was the Lord Who orchestrated this, moving upon the heart of the governor and whoever else was involved.

(3) "AND THE NEXT DAY WE TOUCHED AT SIDON. AND JULIUS COURTEOUSLY ENTREATED PAUL, AND GAVE HIM LIBERTY TO GO UNTO HIS FRIENDS TO REFRESH HIMSELF."

The composition is:

1. The phrase, *"And the next day we touched at Sidon,"* presents a port about 70 miles north of Caesarea. Evidently the ship stopped there to take on or take off cargo and was there at least a whole day, perhaps even two or three.

2. *"And Julius courteously entreated Paul,"* refers to the kindness of the centurion, and again, the special treatment afforded the Apostle.

3. *"And gave him liberty to go unto his friends to refresh himself,"* evidently speaks of Believers in Sidon.

4. This is the only mention of Paul

NOTES

stopping at Sidon. It seems quite clear that he did not establish the Church there, but, as well, it does seem that there was a well-established Church in the city. It also seems from the word *"friends,"* as it is used here, that Paul was acquainted with some of the Believers in this Church. Consequently, he, along with Luke and Aristarchus, were allowed to stay with these people until the ship sailed, ever how long that was.

5. To be sure, as stated, this was not the ordinary treatment at all concerning prisoners. So, we see that Paul was treated more so as a passenger than anything else.

6. Some commentators have endeavored to turn the word *"refresh"* into the idea that Paul was sick and needed care. However, there is nothing in that word or in the Text to suggest such. It simply referred to him enjoying the hospitality of these Sidonian Believers, and above all, to be able to discuss the Work of God with them, which was, no doubt, a time of special enjoyment. Paul may have even ministered unto them, although there is nothing in the Text to corroborate this.

(4) "AND WHEN WE HAD LAUNCHED FROM THENCE, WE SAILED UNDER CYPRUS, BECAUSE THE WINDS WERE CONTRARY."

The diagram is:

1. The phrase, *"And when we had launched from thence, we sailed under Cyprus,"* refers to the eastern side of the island, which took them a great distance out of the way. Normally, they would have sailed close to the western coast, with a straight shot to Myra, which was a little over 200 miles from Sidon. Myra is located on the coast of modern Turkey.

2. *"Because the winds were contrary,"* means they were the opposite of the direction the ship's captain desired. At this time of the year, the winds were normally westerly, with the captain needing the opposite. It was now September.

(5) "AND WHEN WE HAD SAILED OVER THE SEA OF CILICIA AND PAMPHYLIA, WE CAME TO MYRA, A CITY OF LYCIA."

The overview is:

1. The phrase, *"And when we had sailed over the Sea of Cilicia,"* brings Paul near his native province, with Tarsus lying due north, some 60 or 70 miles from this present position.

2. The phrase, *"And Pamphylia,"* concerns the province adjoining Cilicia and was due east.

3. *"We came to Myra, a city of Lycia,"* presents the next province (similar to our modern states).

4. Myra was built on a cliff about two and one-half miles from the seacoast. Its seaport was an important stopping place for ships from Egypt and Cyprus. Actually, it was a very prosperous city. It had been a Roman province since A.D. 53, with Myra, for a time, its capital.

(6) "AND THERE THE CENTURION FOUND A SHIP OF ALEXANDRIA SAILING INTO ITALY; AND HE PUT US THEREIN."

The composition is:

1. The phrase, *"And there the centurion found a ship of Alexandria sailing into Italy,"* speaks of the great port in Egypt, due south of Myra, across the Mediterranean Sea, a distance of approximately 400 miles.

2. The great city of Alexandria was founded in the year 332 B.C., and had an excellent harbor. Normally the grain ships would sail directly from its port to Puteoli on the north shore of the Bay of Naples in Italy. However, the same contrary westerly winds that caused Paul's ship to take the western side of Cyprus had probably, as well, forced this ship off its course so that it stopped at Myra.

3. We know from Verse 38 that it was carrying a cargo of wheat.

4. The phrase, *"And he put us therein,"* pertains to the second ship Paul and his associates would take on this journey to Rome.

5. As should be obvious, Rome paid the fares of the prisoners, for there were a number on board, and probably paid for Luke and Aristarchus, as well.

(7) "AND WHEN WE HAD SAILED SLOWLY MANY DAYS, AND SCARCE WERE COME OVER AGAINST CNIDUS, THE WIND NOT SUFFERING US, WE SAILED UNDER CRETE, OVER AGAINST SALMONE."

The structure is:

1. The phrase, *"And when we had sailed slowly many days,"* pertains to the winds continuing to be contrary. It seems it was blowing from the northwest, which was the very opposite of that which they needed.

2. The *"many days"* does not tell us exactly how many days, but at any rate, they had only travelled approximately 130 miles, which, under normal circumstances, could have been done in one 24-hour day.

3. The phrase, *"And scarce were come over against Cnidus, the wind not suffering us,"* pertains to them trying to reach this city but, due to the adverse winds, to no avail.

4. Cnidus was situated at the very end of a 90-mile-long peninsula that was considered the dividing point between the Aegean and Mediterranean Seas.

5. The phrase, *"We sailed under Crete, over against Salmone,"* pertains to them sailing south of the island when, in fact, they wanted to go north, even close to Achaea or Greece, but to no avail.

(8) "AND, HARDLY PASSING IT, CAME UNTO A PLACE WHICH IS CALLED THE FAIR HAVENS; NEAR WHEREUNTO WAS THE CITY OF LASEA."

The exegesis is:

1. The phrase, *"And, hardly passing it,"* simply means that it was very slow going. Due to the island giving some protection from the force of the northwesterly wind, they were spared that difficulty but left with another problem, no wind at all, or at least precious little.

2. The phrase, *"Came unto a place which is called the fair havens,"* presents mostly a place only to anchor the ship. There was nothing there in which they could replenish their stores, in other words, no town or settlement.

3. *"Near whereunto was the city of Lasea,"* presents the nearest town to Fair Havens, where they could replenish, and was about five miles to the east.

4. Crete is an island about 160 miles long, southeast of Greece. Fair Havens is located at Crete's most southerly point, about 100 miles from the western tip of the island.

(9) "NOW WHEN MUCH TIME WAS SPENT, AND WHEN SAILING WAS NOW DANGEROUS, BECAUSE THE FAST WAS NOW ALREADY PAST, PAUL ADMONISHED THEM."

NOTES

The synopsis is:

1. The phrase, *"Now when much time was spent,"* gives us no clue, but obviously spoke of several days. They still had no favorable winds.

2. Horton said, *"'And when sailing was now dangerous,' pertained to any time after September 14th. Storms were more frequent and the sky was so often overcast that they could not see the stars and navigation was difficult. Most ships therefore spent the winter in a safe harbor."*

3. However, they were presently in no harbor at all, only some place where the ship could anchor for awhile.

4. *"Because the fast was now already past, Paul admonished them,"* pertained to the Great Day of Atonement, and was actually a one day fast.

5. One expositor claims this was A.D. 59, while another claims it was A.D. 62. Most probably, the former is correct, and if so, the Great Day of Atonement fell on October 5.

6. Actually, this one day fast each year was the only fast commanded by the Law of Moses. However, by the time of Christ, the Pharisees had increased this to two fast days a week, making 104 for the year.

7. The admonishment given by Paul, as we shall see in the next Verse, evidently means that the Lord had already given him at least some information respecting the future of this trip.

(10) "AND SAID UNTO THEM, SIRS, I PERCEIVE THAT THIS VOYAGE WILL BE WITH HURT AND MUCH DAMAGE, NOT ONLY OF THE LADING AND SHIP, BUT ALSO OF OUR LIVES."

The pattern is:

1. An unsaved person cannot save himself by his works but can be saved only by having Faith in what Jesus did on the Cross (Jn. 3:16).

2. Likewise, the Christian cannot bring about a life of holiness, or any other desired result for that matter, by his works, but only by Faith.

PAUL

The phrase, *"And said unto them, Sirs, I*

perceive that this voyage will be with hurt and much damage," presents that which the Lord evidently had already given to Paul. As stated, the Lord did not inform him of everything, as would be later given in Verses 21 through 26, but did tell him enough that he knew they were in for great difficulties, that is, if they continued the voyage at this present time.

"Not only of the lading and ship, but also of our lives," would have to pertain to the ship being sunk.

Just exactly how or when the Lord conveyed this information to Paul, we are not told; however, it must have been in the last day or so.

Even though not much account is given in Acts or the Epistles, we know that Paul had a strong prayer life. In I Thessalonians 5:17, he said, *"Pray without ceasing."* As well, he was constantly imploring others to pray for him, even as he said in I Thessalonians 5:25, *"Brethren, pray for us."*

PRAYER

He would not have told others to *"pray without ceasing"* without doing such himself. By praying without ceasing, he simply meant that one should be in an attitude of prayer constantly.

Prayer and worship are the only methods that the Lord has chosen for the Believer to have communion with Him, other than His Word. Actually, prayer and the study of the Word go hand in hand.

If one prays but neglects the Bible, Satan will take advantage of such wrong direction and will gently push the Believer into an unscriptural mode. Of course, if he is successful in doing this, prayer then becomes ineffective.

By contrast, if we only study the Bible, not accompanying such with an ardent prayer life, the Word will cease to be vibrant, effective, and alive, and will degenerate into spiritual deadness. A strong prayer life is vital to the Believer relative to relationship with our Heavenly Father. I think it goes without saying that Paul had a tremendous relationship with the Lord.

Inasmuch as we are given very little information concerning Paul's family, we do not know if he had ever married, or that if married, his wife had left him when he gave his heart to Christ, which could have well been the case.

NOTES

We do know that his family seemed to forsake him after the Damascus Road experience, but of which he says almost nothing. The entirety of his life, as it was now lived, was for the Lord. Someone has said that he was the greatest example for Christ that Christianity had ever produced. It perhaps could be better said that he was the greatest example for Christianity that Christ ever produced.

(11) "NEVERTHELESS THE CENTURION BELIEVED THE MASTER AND THE OWNER OF THE SHIP, MORE THAN THOSE THINGS WHICH WERE SPOKEN BY PAUL."

The account is:

1. The phrase, *"Nevertheless the centurion believed the master and the owner of the ship,"* proclaims that the centurion was in charge. Evidently, he had weighed very carefully what Paul had said but was being pressured by the master of the ship, who was probably the pilot, and the owner, who also may have been the captain as well.

2. Actually, it would cost the owner much money for the ship to be tied up all of this time, especially in this place. Most of the time, these grain ships, which could be very large, even up to a capacity of over 1,200 tons, used the winter months for refitting, repairing, and cleaning the vessel. However, very little, if anything, could be done in this place (Fair Havens), that is, if they chose to stay here.

3. *"More than those things which were spoken by Paul,"* tells us that the master and owner won out, which would prove to be greatly to their dismay. The ship sank exactly as Paul had warned, and with great loss.

The centurion, no doubt, considered that the master and the owner knew far more about ships, as well as the weather and shipping, due to his many, many years of experience in this field, than did Paul; therefore, he took their advice. However, he did not realize that Paul was not merely giving advice or even sound judgment, but rather that which the Lord had told him. To be

NOTES

sure, if the owner of the ship had listened, he would have saved the ship and the cargo.

(12) "AND BECAUSE THE HAVEN WAS NOT COMMODIOUS TO WINTER IN, THE MORE PART ADVISED TO DEPART THENCE ALSO, IF BY ANY MEANS THEY MIGHT ATTAIN TO PHENICE, AND THERE TO WINTER; WHICH IS AN HAVEN OF CRETE, AND LIES TOWARD THE SOUTH WEST AND NORTH WEST."

The pattern is:

1. The phrase, *"And because the haven was not commodious to winter in, the more part advised to depart thence also,"* seems to indicate that others on the ship joined in with the master and the owner, respecting an attempt to reach a better harbor.

2. It was true that this place called Fair Havens was little more than an anchor and, as well, about five miles away from any type of town or settlement. Still, this was far better than losing the ship and the cargo.

3. *"If by any means they might attain to Phenice, and there to winter; which is an haven of Crete,"* pertains to a harbor which, in fact, was commodious, and where some imperial grain ships actually did tie up for the winter. It was about 50 miles west of Fair Havens.

4. *"And lies toward the southwest and the northwest,"* has been debated for centuries. It is supposed that Luke was in error respecting these directions.

5. It is claimed that this harbor opens to the southeast and to the northeast, which is actually the very opposite of the statements of Luke. They say that if it looked toward the southwest and the northwest, it would be exposed to the most furious of winter storms and, therefore, not be a very good place in which to winter. They, however, were wrong, and Luke was right.

6. Phenice was located in a harbor that had two openings divided by a little island. One opening, it is stated, was in the direction in which the southwest wind blows toward the northeast; the other opening was in the direction in which the northwest wind blows toward the southeast. It has recently been proven that the description given by Luke is the exact description of the haven of Phenice, Crete. So, Luke, after all, knew what he was talking about!

(13) "AND WHEN THE SOUTH WIND BLEW SOFTLY, SUPPOSING THAT THEY HAD OBTAINED THEIR PURPOSE, LOOSING THENCE, THEY SAILED CLOSE BY CRETE."

The form is:

1. The phrase, *"And when the south wind blew softly,"* pertains to a wind direction for which they had been waiting. They felt that this was their opportunity and would now take advantage of their good fortune. However, that which Paul had said was just as valid now as it would be some hours later.

2. *"Supposing that they had obtained their purpose, loosing thence, they sailed close by Crete,"* presents them hugging the shore, attempting to make the harbor at Phenice.

(14) "BUT NOT LONG AFTER THERE AROSE AGAINST IT A TEMPESTUOUS WIND, CALLED EUROCLYDON."

The overview is:

1. This is a type of storm somewhat akin to a hurricane.

2. Paul's prediction was now upon them, with them, no doubt, wishing they had listened to the Word of the Lord, for that is exactly what it was.

(15) "AND WHEN THE SHIP WAS CAUGHT, AND COULD NOT BEAR UP INTO THE WIND, WE LET HER DRIVE."

The account is:

1. The phrase, *"And when the ship was caught,"* refers to the wind taking the ship and literally tearing it away from its projected course toward Phenice.

2. *"And could not bear up into the wind, we let her drive,"* means that the helmsman simply could not hold the wheel for the force of the wind. He was trying to force the ship to go a certain direction, with the wind pushing powerfully so in another direction. Consequently, it became impossible to steer, and so the helmsman could do nothing but let it drive toward whatever direction the wind wanted it to go.

3. Luke's description of the entirety of this voyage, along with his use of nautical terms, tells us that he was well educated and well travelled.

(16) "AND RUNNING UNDER A

NOTES

CERTAIN ISLAND WHICH IS CALLED CLAUDA, WE HAD MUCH WORK TO COME BY THE BOAT."

The exegesis is:

1. The phrase, *"And running under a certain island which is called Clauda,"* points a little over 20 miles southwest of the island of Crete. Clauda, sometimes called *"Cauda,"* and now called *"Gaudho,"* is a very small island.

2. *"We had much work to come by the boat,"* implies that they possibly tried to drop anchor south of the island, which afforded a tiny bit of shelter, in order to take aboard a rowboat or skiff they were pulling. This was the custom in those days and actually remained so for hundreds of years. Evidently they were afraid it would break loose in the storm and would be lost.

3. However, even though the island did afford some protection, the turbulence was still so strong that they had great difficulty in trying to get the boat on board. As well, as the next Verse implies, they probably used the small boat, or attempted to do so, in undergirding the ship, but this proved tremendously difficult in the storm.

(17) "WHICH WHEN THEY HAD TAKEN UP, THEY USED HELPS, UNDERGIRDING THE SHIP; AND, FEARING LEST THEY SHOULD FALL INTO THE QUICKSANDS, STRUCK SAIL, AND SO WERE DRIVEN."

The synopsis is:

1. The phrase, *"Which when they had taken up, they used helps, undergirding the ship,"* probably means they had attempted to use the small boat to pass large cables around and under the hull, thus, undergirding it and saving it from strain, which resulted from the working of the mast in a storm.

2. In consequence of the extreme danger to which the ships of the ancients were exposed from leaking, it was customary to take to sea, as part of their ordinary gear, undergirders, which were simply large ropes for passing around the hull of the ship and, thus, preventing the planks or timbers from giving way.

3. *"And, fearing lest they should fall into the quick sands, struck sail, and so were driven,"* pertains to two gulfs on the north shore of Africa, full of shoals and sandbanks, called Syrtis Major and Syrtis Minor.

4. Actually, the wind was driving them straight toward the Syrtis Major. Another 24 hours of such a gale would bring them there, and if so, would quickly destroy the ship.

5. The words *"struck sail"* probably mean they took down the top sail, along with all of its attendant gear, including pulleys, ropes, etc. In other words, they were doing everything they could to enable the ship to go as near the wind as possible with as little straining and rolling as could be helped. The operation is called by sailors *"lying to."*

6. This way they would be driven by the wind, but with few or no sails stretched at all, they would be driven slowly, and hopefully, the wind would change before they were driven onto the shoals and sandbanks of North Africa.

(18) "AND WE BEING EXCEEDINGLY TOSSED WITH A TEMPEST, THE NEXT DAY THEY LIGHTENED THE SHIP."

The structure is:

1. The phrase, *"And we being exceedingly tossed with a tempest,"* proclaims the obvious fact that the storm had not abated, but if anything, had grown worse.

2. *"The next day they lightened the ship,"* refers to the fact that despite the undergirding, the storm was battering the ship to such an extent that it was taking on water, in other words, leaking. Consequently, they began to throw things overboard, such as the ship's furniture, and probably anything else that was not nailed down.

3. It does not mention that they sought to throw overboard the wheat. It was so valuable that it must not be jettisoned except as a last resort, which it was later.

(19) "AND THE THIRD DAY WE CAST OUT WITH OUR OWN HANDS THE TACKLING OF THE SHIP."

The composition is:

1. The phrase, *"And the third day we cast out with our own hands,"* pertains to the third day after leaving Clauda. As well, Paul, Luke, and Aristarchus, along with all other prisoners, were pressed into service to help any way they could. The boat was sinking, and all were fighting desperately,

attempting to save it and, as well, even their very lives. However, the Lord had told Paul that he would minister in Rome, and that meant he would not be killed on the way there. And yet, even as is glaringly obvious, Satan was doing all he could to hinder the Will of God, hopefully to stop it altogether. He would not succeed!

2. *"The tackling of the ship,"* evidently meant all the tools, ropes, etc., in other words, even the very things it was supposed that they had to have.

(20) "AND WHEN NEITHER SUN NOR STARS IN MANY DAYS APPEARED, AND NO SMALL TEMPEST LAY ON US, ALL HOPE THAT WE SHOULD BE SAVED WAS THEN TAKEN AWAY."

The account is:

1. In Genesis, Chapter 9, God says that man is not to eat flesh with blood in it because life is in the blood.

2. This means that blood is precious to God. It was given on the altar as an atonement for our souls during Old Testament times.

THE STORM

The phrase, *"And when neither sun nor stars in many days appeared,"* represented them having no way to ascertain their position, for the absence of the sun and stars kept them from shooting a course. In other words, they had no idea whatsoever as to where they were. It is believed now to have been about 11 days since they left Crete.

"And no small tempest lay on us," refers to the fact that the storm was still blowing full force.

"All hope that we should be saved was then taken away," speaks of a gloom that settled over the ship, with all, except Paul, Luke, and Aristarchus, believing they were going to die. Other than these three, all 273 others on the ship had no one to turn to, with their heathen gods unable to help, as, of course, is obvious, and for the simple reason that such gods really did not exist.

It is the same with all who do not know the Lord. Consequently, many, if not most, resort to alcohol or drugs, or something else of similar nature. However, the Child of God always has recourse in the Lord.

NOTES

To be sure, nothing can happen to a Believer, irrespective as to what Satan may attempt to do, unless the Lord wills such. We can always turn to Him for help, which He promises to be in any and all times of trouble.

Even though Paul, no doubt, was leaning heavily on what the Lord had told him some two years earlier, still, he along with Luke and Aristarchus, had been seeking the Lord constantly concerning this problem, and now would receive a direct answer from the Lord, as the next Verses indicate.

However, some modern Believers claim that if Paul had sufficient Faith, this storm could have been avoided. Is that true?

No! Paul was not in this situation because of a lack of Faith, but rather because of great Faith, of which we will say more momentarily.

ANOTHER FAITH?

Beginning approximately in the late 1960s, teaching on Faith became more and more pronounced, with the term *"Faith Teachers"* beginning to be heard throughout the land, with this message spreading rapidly.

In this particular teaching, much truth, even great truths were brought out, which was a tremendous blessing to the Church. In fact, it was a great blessing to me personally, respecting what Jesus had done for the human family in His Death, Resurrection, and Exaltation. Of this, many learned what and who they were in Christ, which afforded victory unparalleled and, as stated, was a great truth that the Church needed to learn. In fact, at that time, through our network of some 600 radio stations, I helped propagate this part of the Gospel on a daily basis. Probably at that particular time (1970-1973), at least as far as coverage is concerned, I was one of the strongest purveyors of this message.

DEVELOPMENT OR EXPLOITATION?

Sometime in 1973, I believe it was, the Lord began to deal with my heart concerning some of the things I was teaching respecting this message of Faith. To be sure, He had already told me some two or three

NOTES

years earlier that He would bless our ministry exceedingly so. However, He also told me that I must develop the people, anchoring them in the Word, and always pointing them to Jesus. He then said to me, *"If you ever exploit them, I will lift My Anointing from you."*

It was just that simple, but I got the message.

The Lord began to show me some of the things about this so-called message of Faith being propagated that were wrong. In fact, I was even helping to spread some of that which had gone into error.

What was that?

THE GIFT INSTEAD OF THE GIVER

Little by little, the Faith message ceased to be centered on Jesus, but instead, on the commodity of Faith itself. In other words, the attention was on the gift instead of the Giver, Who is Christ. Consequently, Faith became the all-important object, whereas the Scripture says, *"Looking unto Jesus the Author and Finisher of our Faith"* (Heb. 12:2).

In other words, the object of Faith, according to the Holy Spirit, must never be healing, money, or anything else for that matter, but rather Jesus and Him Crucified. It is Christ and the Cross, which the Faith message per se does not claim.

FAITH AS A BAROMETER

At that time, I noticed that many began to teach Faith as a barometer, meaning if they could get their Faith up to a particular height, they could in turn get great things, etc. In this, the Will of God is relegated to a secondary position, if any position at all, with the great man or woman of Faith automatically claiming to know what the Will of God is in any and all situations. In other words, they were teaching that whatever the Believer wanted constituted the Will of God.

Consequently, the leadership of the Holy Spirit has been replaced, with Him taking up a secondary role, in which He supplies all of these great things to the great Faith man or woman who reaches these desired heights of Faith. In effect, the Holy Spirit becomes a glorified bellhop or errand boy, carrying out the bidding of the Faith people.

LACK OF FAITH?

Many teach that all sicknesses, reverses, troubles, difficulties, and problems are because of a lack of Faith. In other words, if we have enough Faith, we can eliminate all of these things, bringing us into this great position of health and wealth at all times. Consequently, if one is sick and does not receive healing, it is always because of a lack of Faith, these teachers say, with these people shunted aside after a short period of time. In other words, there is no place in this camp for the sick, the hurting, etc. In effect, many of these teachers have taught that if Paul would have known and had the Faith that they have, he would not have had to undergo all of these great difficulties and problems, even as we are now studying. Of course, to follow that direction pretty well eliminates everyone in the Bible, even the great heroes of Faith of Hebrews, Chapter 11.

CONFESSION?

Confession is taught as the means that activates one's Faith. Consequently, if something is wrong, that means the confession is wrong, with the situation automatically cleaned up if the confession is made right. The confession of the Believer, that is, if it is a good confession, they teach, stirs God into action. Now anything becomes possible relative to one's confession, with Believers now confessing all types of things.

HEALTH AND WEALTH

In this teaching, money and health generally become the barometer of one's Faith. In other words, if one has great Faith, one will have plenty of money, and one will be totally healthy, without any sickness whatsoever. It is strange that the Lord is attempting to lead His People to holiness and Righteousness, while these so-called Faith teachers are attempting to lead people to money.

SCRIPTURES OUT OF CONTEXT

Scriptures are pulled out of context, with the idea that one can obtain whatever he

NOTES

wants or desires by using certain particular Scriptures in certain ways. In other words, whether they understand it or not, these people, much of the time, are attempting to use the Word of God against God.

They will take Scriptures such as Mark 11:24, which says, *"What things soever you desire, when ye pray, believe that you receive them, and you shall have them,"* and use them as some type of lever.

In their thinking, whatever they desire can be obtained, that is, if they have enough Faith. Consequently, these people come up with all types of things they desire, trying to force God into action on their behalf by claiming this Scripture or another and that it promises such to them.

They do not seem to realize that the Believer's desire must, at the same time, be the desire of the Holy Spirit. To be sure, the Holy Spirit has not been imparted to Believers in order to give us what we want but to give us what the Lord wants (Jn. 16:14-15).

THINGS?

Almost exclusively, this teaching has degenerated Faith to the level of mere things, in other words, *"stuff."* Actually, most of it is centered up on money, which completely ignores I Timothy 6:6-11. The hundredfold return is now brought into play, with Believers told that their giving will produce $100 to $1, or some such figure, that is, if their Faith is as it ought to be. Some of the Faith teachers claim that the Lord has given them the power to pray the hundredfold return on people, that is, if they will first *give*, preferably to them, the particular Faith teachers. Actually, some of them teach that the Lord will not give the hundredfold return unless they give to this teacher, etc.

Consequently, many sermons are preached on subjects such as *"Kmart Christians,"* implying that anyone who shops at *Kmart*, or some such like store, does not have proper Faith.

These are only a few of the topics of error that could be addressed, which the reader will have to admit, I think (that is, if he is honest with himself), constitutes obviously wrong directions. In other words, it is not scriptural, irrespective of the claims otherwise.

In fact, there is some truth in some of these claims, which, of course, makes it very palatable to the unknowing Believer. In other words, the little truth therein contained becomes the bait.

ERROR CANNOT RECEIVE ANYTHING FROM THE LORD

As this *"bait"* of wealth is dangled before Believers, appealing grossly to the flesh we might quickly add, such becomes greatly alluring, and for all the wrong reasons. However, the only ones who are going to get anything out of this, which, by now, has basically degenerated into money, are the Preachers. God simply cannot bless, anoint, or reward error in any nature, which certainly should be obvious. The Holy Spirit will guide only into all truth, not error (Jn. 16:13). In fact, the shores are littered with so-called Faith rejects, who are bitter and, in fact, have turned against God because they faced a crisis in their lives, as all do sooner or later, and this so-called Faith message simply did not work. However, one need not worry about the ranks being depleted because there is a fresh crop of gullibles waiting in the wings to take the place of the rejects.

In fact, many of the purveyors of this message claim that God has not called them to win souls, but rather to enlighten those already won. Consequently, they make little or no effort at all to bring people to Christ, instead serving as parasites.

Not only is there almost no one saved under these ministries, at least if you would call it that, at the same time, almost no one is baptized with the Holy Spirit. As well, precious few bondages are broken in hearts and lives, and precious few are truly healed, despite the outlandish claims. While there is an exception here and there, the greater thrust of this message centers up on money, with the other things mentioned only in passing. In other words, money is the priority and the goal, which this great Faith supplies.

Actually, in going to some of their meetings where other Preachers are present, there are some Preachers who will stop 25 or 30 miles short of their destination and rent a Mercedes if they cannot afford a Mercedes, etc. Thus, they drive to the meeting in the Mercedes, making the other Preachers think as to how successful they are and how great their Faith is.

Paul told Timothy, actually speaking of this very thing (money), *"But you, O man of God, flee these things; and follow after Righteousness, Godliness, Faith, love, patience, meekness"* (I Tim. 6:9-11).

So, I maintain that as Paul spoke of *"another Jesus," "another spirit,"* and *"another Gospel,"* this is *"another Faith"* (II Cor. 11:4).

THE FAITH OF PAUL

As stated, Paul did not face all of these difficulties because of a lack of Faith, but actually because of his great Faith.

All Faith must be tested, and great Faith must be tested greatly.

Paul's great Faith, which was centered up in Christ, guaranteed that he could run and finish this course, despite the things that Satan brought against him and, in fact, were allowed by the Lord. Actually, Paul had sought the Lord earnestly that all of these many difficulties would be removed, but Jesus said to him, *"My Grace is sufficient for you: for My strength is made perfect in weakness."*

Paul then said, *"Most gladly therefore will I rather glory in my infirmities, that the Power of Christ may rest upon me.*

"Therefore I take pleasure in infirmities, in reproaches, in necessities, in persecutions, in distresses for Christ's sake: for when I am weak, then am I strong" (II Cor. 12:8-10).

Of course, the modern Faith teachers would claim that Paul was exhibiting a bad confession when he admitted to being *"weak."*

However, Paul had learned the great lesson that as much as we dislike these difficulties and problems, sometimes they are necessary.

PRIDE

First of all, man is easily lifted up in his pride, and religious man most of all. If God blesses us even slightly, we instantly begin to think that we have had something to do with this and, therefore, if all others were like what we are, they too would have all of these great things. Consequently, we need, at least at times, these problems that tend to humble us and keep us on our face before God. Again I emphasize that the goal is Christlikeness instead of money, etc.

To stand these things, Paul had to have great Faith, and as all Faith is always tested, as stated, great Faith is always tested greatly.

No! Despite the fact that there is some truth in the modern Faith message, purely and plainly, as a whole, it is not scriptural, despite the claims to the contrary, but, in fact, is heresy.

HERESY

Paul also said, *"For the time will come when they will not endure sound Doctrine; but after their own lusts shall they heap to themselves teachers, having itching ears;*

"And they shall turn away their ears from the Truth, and shall be turned unto fables" (II Tim. 4:3-4).

The so-called Faith message is not *"sound doctrine"* because it appeals to the *"lusts"* (greed) of people. These *"false teachers,"* and that's what they are, listen carefully for those who would want such, and regrettably, there are many. They then give them what they want, thereby, turning away from the truth. In other words, exactly as Paul said, *"This message is a fable."*

THE CROSS

As well, and the worst thing of all, modern Faith teaching opposes the Cross in every capacity, referring to it as *"past miseries"* and the greatest weakness known to man. As a result, many of their Churches will not sing any songs at all about the Cross, about the Blood, about the Sacrifice of Christ, or about the Atonement, referring to that as *"defeatist teaching."* Consequently, they have ruled out the bedrock of all Biblical Christianity. The maturity of the Believer cannot go any higher than his understanding of the Cross, and we speak of the Cross as it relates both to Salvation and Sanctification.

Their position is strange when you consider that Paul said:

NOTES

"Christ sent me not to baptize, but to preach the Gospel, not with wisdom of words, lest the Cross of Christ should be made of none effect" (I Cor. 1:17).

He also said, *"For the preaching of the Cross is to them who perish foolishness, but to we who are saved, it is the Power of God"* (I Cor. 1:18).

He said to the Church at Corinth and to us, I determined to know nothing among you save Christ and Him Crucified (I Cor. 2:2).

As well, when we put Christ and the Cross first of all, we can be guaranteed the blessings of God, and that is in every capacity. However, when we put those things first instead of the Lord Jesus Christ, that is the sure road to disaster.

If you want to know the truth, the Message of the Cross is actually the only prosperity Gospel in the world today and, in fact, ever has been. Everything we receive from the Lord comes through the Lord Jesus Christ and is made possible by the Cross.

(21) "BUT AFTER LONG ABSTINENCE PAUL STOOD FORTH IN THE MIDST OF THEM, AND SAID, SIRS, YOU SHOULD HAVE HEARKENED UNTO ME, AND NOT HAVE LOOSED FROM CRETE, AND TO HAVE GAINED THIS HARM AND LOSS."

The rule is:

1. The phrase, *"But after long abstinence,"* does not refer to a two week fast as some claim, at least as Christians think of such.

2. There were 276 people on board, as Verse 37 tells us, with probably all of these people unsaved, with the exception of Paul, Luke, and Aristarchus. To be sure, they would not have been fasting for two weeks, as should be obvious.

3. Paul was speaking of the storm, which made it very difficult, if not impossible, to prepare meals. Consequently, they had to eat whatever they could that required no preparation, which was extremely scarce. One must understand that in those days, there was no abundance of fast foods and little means to keep food without spoilage, such as we have presently. Also, it is obvious that seasickness was rampant due to the violent motion of the ship, which destroyed appetites, even respecting what food they did have.

NOTES

4. *"Paul stood forth in the midst of them, and said, Sirs, you should have hearkened unto me,"* is not really meant as a reprimand by the Apostle, but rather to give foundation to what he was about to say.

5. *"And not have loosed from Crete, and to have gained this harm and loss,"* proclaims what happens when people go against the Word of the Lord.

6. This means that much loss could be avoided if people earnestly sought the Lord concerning all things, in which He has promised to give direction (James 1:5-8).

(22) "AND NOW I EXHORT YOU TO BE OF GOOD CHEER: FOR THERE SHALL BE NO LOSS OF ANY MAN'S LIFE AMONG YOU, BUT OF THE SHIP."

The exegesis is:

1. The phrase, *"And now I exhort you to be of good cheer,"* pertains to that which he had just heard from the Lord, and although not everything they would have desired to hear, still, it was great news concerning their lives.

2. *"For there shall be no loss of any man's life among you, but of the ship,"* told them plainly that the ship would be lost with its cargo of wheat, but that the Lord had told him that not a single man would lose his life, that is, if they did what Paul said to do.

Trying to stay with the ship in order to save it would result in loss of life.

(23) "FOR THERE STOOD BY ME THIS NIGHT THE ANGEL OF GOD, WHOSE I AM, AND WHOM I SERVE."

The account is:

1. The phrase, *"For there stood by me this night the Angel of God,"* presents the first time, at least that is recorded, that an Angel appeared to Paul. However, Jesus had personally appeared unto him three times (Acts 9:5; 22:17-18; 23:11).

2. Without a doubt, Paul, as well as Luke and Aristarchus, had been earnestly seeking the Lord for guidance and direction all of these past days and nights during the storm. Now the Lord had told Paul what to do by the sending of an Angel.

3. *"Whose I am, and whom I serve,"*

NOTES

proclaims the Apostle boldly proclaiming Christ to this heathen crew, along with the soldiers and other prisoners, but which he had, no doubt, done many times already.

(24) "SAYING, FEAR NOT, PAUL; YOU MUST BE BROUGHT BEFORE CAESAR: AND, LO, GOD HAS GIVEN YOU ALL THEM WHO SAIL WITH YOU."

The overview is:

1. If you were to ask most Christians, even Preachers, how the Holy Spirit works in the heart and life of the Believer, most would probably give you a blank stare.

2. The Holy Spirit works entirely within the framework, so to speak, of the Finished Work of Christ, i.e., *"the Cross."* This means that our Faith must be anchored in Christ and the Cross exclusively (Gal. 6:14).

PAUL AND FEAR

The phrase, *"Saying, Fear not, Paul,"* was said in this manner because there had been fear in Paul's heart, as well as everyone else on board.

Actually, the situation had now become totally desperate, with the captain and crew no longer able to do anything in order to save the ship and, above all, their lives. In other words, all had given up, with the exception of Paul, Luke, and Aristarchus.

I realize that many modern-day Preachers would take issue with my conclusion respecting Paul having fear; however, the structure of the Greek in the text lends credence to this conclusion. As well, the Angel of the Lord would not have addressed Paul in this fashion, plainly telling him to *"fear not,"* if, in fact, there was no fear.

Some may claim that the Angel addressed him thusly because Paul was fearing for the other people on board, but not necessarily for himself. However, that makes little sense because they were all in the same boat, literally speaking. As well, I do not think that Paul had the idea in his heart that the Lord would allow all of the others to drown but save only himself and his two associates. No, the Text clearly proclaims the opposite.

Then again, attempting to explain the storm in the light of the modern Faith message, some have, no doubt, said that the reason for this situation was the *"fear"* in Paul's heart. Again, that is not the case at all.

Also, some would attempt to claim that Paul did not really have any fear in his heart concerning the storm and their being saved, but rather the appearance of the Angel caused him to be fearful.

Again, the Greek text does not portray such, but rather fear in Paul's heart concerning their situation, and not because of the appearance of the Angel. As stated, Paul had seen the Lord some three times, and I am certain that those appearances were far more dramatic than this of the Angel.

PERFECT LOVE AND FEAR

Some would also claim that if, in fact, Paul actually had fear, this would mean that his love for God was not perfect, for John said, *"There is no fear in love; but perfect love casts out fear"* (I Jn. 4:18).

However, the type of *"fear"* of which John spoke was fear concerning God: fearful that God might do something that would cause hurt or harm to the person. This speaks of a very improper relationship on one's part, with the idea being that one who fears in this manner simply does not know the Lord as one should. If he did, there would be no such fear present in his heart because he would know that God looks after His Children.

Paul had no such type of fear concerning God, knowing Him as few have ever known Him.

As well, the type of fear here mentioned is not the *"spirit of fear,"* which Paul would later mention to Timothy (II Tim. 1:7).

THE TYPE OF FEAR

The type of fear of which the Angel spoke, and that which was in Paul's heart (and in all others, as well), is a natural and, in its purpose, beneficent feeling, arising in the presence or anticipation of danger and moving to its avoidance. In fact, all human beings have this type of fear, even the godliest men and women on the face of the Earth, even Paul, as here, said. People who claim they do not have such fear obviously do not know what they are talking about

NOTES

because if they are human, such is present, and gladly so!

Horton said, *"'You must be brought before Caesar,' is spoken by the Angel, not because of Paul's appeal to Caesar, or because of the charges brought against him by the Jews, but, rather, because of the Divine Plan."*

Once again, this tells us that Paul was in the Will of God respecting this journey.

THE WILL OF GOD

Many have the idea that if a person is in the Will of God, there will be no more problems or difficulties. Many times I have had people to write me and state, *"If God has really called you to World Evangelism as you say, you would never have to appeal for funds because they would be readily supplied,"* or words to that effect. However, the very opposite is actually the case.

At the very moment that God proclaims a course of direction for someone, Satan begins to hinder in every way possible. In fact, that should be obvious.

The truth is, having access to the Throne of God (Job, Chpt. 1), Satan, at times, knows certain things even before the Believer does. In other words, I am positive that he knows the call of God that rests upon a person sometimes even before that person is born.

SATAN AND THE WILL OF GOD

Having knowledge of such information, he will immediately set about to do whatever he can to hinder, even as he did Paul with this storm, and a hundred other ways one might quickly add. However, he has to obtain permission from the Lord for whatever he may attempt to do, with the Lord granting him only so much latitude (Job, Chpts. 1-2). The Lord allows such in order that we may constantly look to Him for guidance and deliverance, which teaches us trust, as well as many other things. Naturally, Satan means it for our destruction, while the Lord means it for the very opposite.

"And lo, God has given you all them who sail with you," proclaims the lives of all being saved, even as the Lord had spoken. This had to have been great news for the 276 people on this ship.

SAINTS AS A BLESSING

This portrays to us the tremendous blessing afforded all by the presence of a true Saint of God—that is, if that Saint is in the Will of God and not the opposite, as Jonah of old. Jonah, running from the Lord, would have brought about the destruction of the ship had he not been thrown overboard. By contrast, Paul's presence ensured the very opposite (Jonah later repented and was a great blessing to Nineveh).

Jesus referred to Believers as *"salt"* and *"light"* (Mat. 5:13-14).

In fact, if Paul, Luke, and Aristarchus had not been on board, this ship would, no doubt, have sunk with the loss of all hands; consequently, these people owed their lives to these three men, and especially Paul.

The blessing of God on any community, city, or nation can be directly attributed to the Saints of God in that city or nation. To be sure, it is for no other purpose. This is the reason for America's blessings—not Wall Street, Congress, or anything else for that matter! The credit exclusively goes to the Lord, as He blesses His Children.

(25) "WHEREFORE, SIRS, BE OF GOOD CHEER: FOR I BELIEVE GOD, THAT IT SHALL BE EVEN AS IT WAS TOLD ME."

The diagram is:

1. The phrase, *"Wherefore, sirs, be of good cheer,"* presents pretty much that which Jesus said to His Disciples after they had labored all night, attempting to make headway against an adverse wind, but to no avail (Mat. 14:27). In fact, this was the first good news the 276 people had heard. However, the storm had not abated, with the ship continuing to take terrible punishment.

2. *"For I believe God, that it shall be even as it was told me,"* insinuates that possibly some did not believe what Paul was saying. This is understandable, considering that none of these people knew the Lord, with the exception of the three. In fact, they were pagans, having no understanding of God at all! However, the outcome was not predicated on their Faith or the lack thereof, but rather on what the Angel had told Paul. So, they were safe irrespective!

3. In fact, I wonder what the reaction of

these people was as Paul began to relate to them that an Angel had visited him during the night. Quite possibly, he was only able to relate this to a part of the total number in the ship, it being very difficult to get everyone together, especially in a storm. It would seem that it would have been very dangerous to have attempted to assemble everyone on the deck, considering the storm. And yet, quite possibly this was done!

4. Knowing very little about the Lord and even less about Angels, some probably wondered what Paul was talking about. And yet, this was the only hope to which they could cling.

5. This world, even as this ship of old, is heading toward a storm called the *"Great Tribulation"* (Mat. 24:21). To be sure, it is going to be severe, even so severe that it will seem like the destruction of all of mankind. Then, as now, the only answer is Jesus Christ in that He has given us His Word that all can be saved who come to Him (I Thess. 5:9).

(26) "HOWBEIT WE MUST BE CAST UPON A CERTAIN ISLAND."

The way is:

1. As Paul revealed more of what the Angel had told him, it was probably somewhat perplexing to these mariners. Thinking they were drifting toward North Africa, they were, no doubt, surprised to hear that they would be cast upon a certain island.

2. As previously stated, the shoals and sandbars of North Africa were a graveyard for ships.

3. In their minds, they had thought that if the storm did not get them, the shoals would. So, the idea of an island encouraged them somewhat, but what island, inasmuch as the Angel did not give that information?

(27) "BUT WHEN THE FOURTEENTH NIGHT WAS COME, AS WE WERE DRIVEN UP AND DOWN IN ADRIA, ABOUT MIDNIGHT THE SHIPMEN DEEMED THAT THEY DREW NEAR TO SOME COUNTRY."

The synopsis is:

1. The phrase, *"But when the fourteenth night was come,"* pertained to the length of time after leaving Fair Havens. So the storm had lasted now for about two weeks.

2. *"As we were driven up and down in Adria,"* probably refers to the Adriatic Sea, which is a part of the Mediterranean. However, some claim it was the Sea of Adria, but irrespective, it was close to the island of Malta.

NOTES

3. *"About midnight the shipmen deemed that they drew near to some country,"* proclaims by some that they could hear waves breaking on the beach or rocks at some distance, even as some ancient manuscripts of the New Testament read.

(28) "AND SOUNDED, AND FOUND IT TWENTY FATHOMS: AND WHEN THEY HAD GONE A LITTLE FURTHER, THEY SOUNDED AGAIN, AND FOUND IT FIFTEEN FATHOMS."

The exposition is:

1. The phrase, *"And sounded, and found it twenty fathoms,"* represented a depth of about 120 feet.

2. *"And when they had gone a little further, they sounded again, and found it fifteen fathoms,"* represented a depth of about 90 feet. The fathom came to be standardized at six feet.

(29) "THEN FEARING LEST WE SHOULD HAVE FALLEN UPON ROCKS, THEY CAST FOUR ANCHORS OUT OF THE STERN, AND WISHED FOR THE DAY."

The direction is:

1. The phrase, *"Then fearing lest we should have fallen upon rocks,"* pertained to hearing the waves breaking upon the rocks, which caused them to fear for the ship, especially considering that it was only a little after midnight. Consequently, they could see little, if anything, and, therefore, decided to drop anchor.

2. *"They cast four anchors out of the stern, and wished for the day,"* represents that which was common for that time. Ancient ships did not have large anchors and, therefore, had to have several smaller ones, as here.

3. No doubt remembering what Paul had said about an island, they were very anxious for the night to be over, so they could hopefully ascertain where they were.

(30) "AND AS THE SHIPMEN WERE ABOUT TO FLEE OUT OF THE SHIP, WHEN THEY HAD LET DOWN THE BOAT INTO THE SEA, UNDER COLOUR

NOTES

AS THOUGH THEY WOULD HAVE CAST ANCHORS OUT OF THE FORESHIP."

The structure is:

1. The phrase, *"And as the shipmen were about to flee out of the ship, when they had let down the boat into the sea,"* portrays some, if not all, the ship's crew about to take the only small boat they had, attempting to escape to shore, in effect, deserting the ship.

2. *"Under colour as though they would have cast anchors out of the foreship,"* presents their deception, but Paul was watching, possibly suspecting something of this nature, or else, it was told him.

(31) "PAUL SAID TO THE CENTURION AND TO THE SOLDIERS, EXCEPT THESE ABIDE IN THE SHIP, YOU CANNOT BE SAVED."

The form is:

1. The phrase, *"Paul said to the centurion and to the soldiers,"* presents the Apostle taking this deception to the centurion.

2. Williams said, *"'Except these abide in the ship, you cannot be saved,' does not contradict the assurance given in Verse 24. The one was a Divine pledge; the other, an indispensable condition of escape. Divine agency and human instrumentality are both found within the Will of God."*

3. With most every promise given by God, there are conditions to such promises. In other words, the Believer has to play his part.

4. Of course, the Lord can do anything, but at the same time, He expects us to obey Him.

5. In fact, considering that the storm was still raging, if all of these men had gotten into this small boat and attempted to make it to shore in darkness, it is virtually certain that all of them would have drowned. If the waves did not swamp them, they most likely would have dashed on the rocks anyway.

(32) "THEN THE SOLDIERS CUT OFF THE ROPES OF THE BOAT, AND LET HER FALL OFF."

The exegesis is:

1. Evidently, the shipmen had let the boat down into the water, with the ropes still attached. They were then going to climb down and leave.

2. However, the centurion believed Paul and gave instructions for the soldiers to cut the ropes still tied to the boat, which they did, with the boat then quickly drifting away, foiling the attempt.

(33) "AND WHILE THE DAY WAS COMING ON, PAUL BESOUGHT THEM ALL TO TAKE MEAT, SAYING, THIS DAY IS THE FOURTEENTH DAY THAT YOU HAVE TARRIED AND CONTINUED FASTING, HAVING TAKEN NOTHING."

The diagram is:

1. The phrase, *"And while the day was coming on, Paul besought them all to take meat, saying,"* concerns the day that would shortly approach, and all would need strength.

2. So, despite the storm, they evidently did the best they could in attempting to prepare a meal of some sort.

3. *"This day is the fourteenth day that you have tarried and continued fasting, having taken nothing,"* does not mean, as some believe, that all 276 of these people had been fasting this length of time. As we have already stated, these pagans certainly would not have fasted, at least as Christians think of fasting.

4. The Greek word for *"nothing,"* as used here, shows that it means they had eaten no regular meals. The emphasis is not so much on the food or lack thereof, but rather on all the men. In other words, all of them suffered alike, whether by seasickness or the impossibility of trying to prepare food under these circumstances.

5. Again we emphasize that the *"fasting"* that Paul mentioned here had nothing to do with Christian fasting, but was rather a severe difficulty imposed upon all concerned because of the circumstances. In fact, they had a little something to eat, but it had been very sparse.

(34) "WHEREFORE I PRAY YOU TO TAKE SOME MEAT: FOR THIS IS FOR YOUR HEALTH: FOR THERE SHALL NOT AN HAIR FALL FROM THE HEAD OF ANY OF YOU."

The pattern is:

1. The phrase, *"Wherefore I pray you to take some meat,"* does not necessarily have

NOTES

to do with meat as we presently think of such. The word then referred to all types of food.

2. *"For this is for your health,"* refers to the fact that they should attempt to force at least some food down, irrespective of their seasickness, which, no doubt, some of them still had. As well, as one might imagine, whatever food they did have, it must have been in terrible condition considering the storm of the last two weeks. Everything in the ship, more than likely, would have been affected in some way by the storm. So, they were to attempt to eat something, irrespective as to how bad it tasted, how unappetizing it looked, etc.

3. *"For there shall not an hair fall from the head of any of you,"* once again expresses assurance, which the Lord had, no doubt, given Paul.

(35) "AND WHEN HE HAD THUS SPOKEN, HE TOOK BREAD, AND GAVE THANKS TO GOD IN PRESENCE OF THEM ALL: AND WHEN HE HAD BROKEN IT, HE BEGAN TO EAT."

The synopsis is:

1. The phrase, *"And when he had thus spoken, he took bread, and gave thanks to God in presence of them all,"* presents the Apostle taking the bread and lifting up his voice to God, thanking Him not only for the food but, as well, for His Protection. Paul did that before all of those unbelievers. Once again, Paul let everyone know that their only hope was in God.

2. *"And when he had broken it, he began to eat,"* probably represents that the bread was very hard and, therefore, evidently not wet.

(36) "THEN WERE THEY ALL OF GOOD CHEER, AND THEY ALSO TOOK SOME MEAT."

The way is:

1. The idea is that after they had taken some nourishment, they were *"all of good cheer."*

(37) "AND WE WERE IN ALL IN THE SHIP TWO HUNDRED THREESCORE AND SIXTEEN SOULS."

The rule is:

1. Of the 276 people on board, which meant that the ship was quite large, how many of these were crewmen, soldiers, or prisoners is not known.

2. If all of the crewmen were going to get into the rowboat, attempting an escape, this probably meant that they only numbered about 30 or so. Therefore, the balance of the number consisted of prisoners and soldiers. It is possible that the centurion had 100 soldiers with him, which was the normal complement for centurions, but he probably didn't have that many; consequently, the greatest number on board were evidently prisoners.

(38) "AND WHEN THEY HAD EATEN ENOUGH, THEY LIGHTENED THE SHIP, AND CAST OUT THE WHEAT INTO THE SEA."

The account is:

1. The wheat was cast into the sea in order to make the ship lighter that they might get closer to the shore the next morning. The lighter it was, the higher it rode in the water.

2. In their minds, they had now given up hope of saving the ship and, therefore, its cargo.

3. Consequently, they would do everything they could in order to save their lives.

(39) "AND WHEN IT WAS DAY, THEY KNEW NOT THE LAND: BUT THEY DISCOVERED A CERTAIN CREEK WITH A SHORE, INTO THE WHICH THEY WERE MINDED, IF IT WERE POSSIBLE, TO THRUST IN THE SHIP."

The overview is:

1. The phrase, *"And when it was day, they knew not the land,"* simply means they did not recognize anything. Actually they were several miles from the harbor of Valetta.

2. *"But they discovered a certain creek with a shore,"* is now called *"Paul's Bay,"* and fits exactly that which is recorded in this Chapter. There are places near the west side of the bay where the depth is actually 20 fathoms and then a little farther in, 15 fathoms.

3. *"Into the which they were minded, if it were possible, to thrust in the ship,"* represents the reason they threw the wheat overboard. As stated, they wanted to take the ship as close to the shore as possible.

NOTES

(40) "AND WHEN THEY HAD TAKEN UP THE ANCHORS, THEY COMMITTED THEMSELVES UNTO THE SEA, AND LOOSED THE RUDDER BANDS, AND HOISTED UP THE MAINSAIL TO THE WIND, AND MADE TOWARD SHORE."

The account is:

1. The phrase, *"And when they had taken up the anchors,"* in the Greek text, actually means that they cut the ropes holding the anchors, leaving them on the sea bottom.

2. *"They committed themselves unto the sea,"* means that the ship was not now anchored, and they would have to take measures to get it where they desired it to be.

3. *"And loosed the rudder bands,"* pertained to two or more rudders at the side, contained by all ancient ships.

4. These bands constituted some type of fastenings by which the rudders could be taken out of the water when storms became so bad that the rudders were of no use. They also could be let down into the water again when needed. When they loosened the bands, the rudders fell into the water, which helped them to steer the ship, if possible, into the creek.

5. *"And hoisted up the mainsail to the wind, and made toward shore,"* pertains to the sail that was suspended from the foremast to the bowsprit. In fact, we find about 50 nautical terms in this Chapter, which gives us an idea of the operation of ships of that particular time.

(41) "AND FALLING INTO A PLACE WHERE TWO SEAS MET, THEY RAN THE SHIP AGROUND; AND THE FOREPART STUCK FAST, AND REMAINED UNMOVABLE, BUT THE HINDER PART WAS BROKEN WITH THE VIOLENCE OF THE WAVES."

The structure is:

1. The phrase, *"And falling into a place where two seas met, they ran the ship aground,"* presents them not making it to the creek to where they had at first intended, but actually getting caught in a narrow channel that was too shallow to make it through. There is a little island called Salmoneta near the entrance to the bay. The rush of breakers on both sides of the island give the appearance of two seas meeting.

2. *"And the forepart stuck fast, and remained unmovable, but the hinder part was broken with the violence of the waves,"* proclaims that the storm was still blowing. Consequently, the ship was literally coming apart under their very feet.

(42) "AND THE SOLDIERS' COUNSEL WAS TO KILL THE PRISONERS, LEST ANY OF THEM SHOULD SWIM OUT, AND ESCAPE."

The rule is:

1. The reason for this was that Roman law condemned guards to death if prisoners escaped under their watch.

(43) "BUT THE CENTURION, WILLING TO SAVE PAUL, KEPT THEM FROM THEIR PURPOSE; AND COMMANDED THAT THEY WHICH COULD SWIM SHOULD CAST THEMSELVES FIRST INTO THE SEA, AND GET TO LAND."

The pattern is:

1. The phrase, *"But the centurion, willing to save Paul, kept them from their purpose,"* presents this man as now knowing that Paul was not just another prisoner. He had witnessed that which Paul had stated come to pass exactly as the Apostle had predicted. So, the idea of killing Paul was the last thing this centurion wanted to do.

2. The word *"save"* is very strong in the Greek text, which means that the soldiers were intent on carrying out their purpose, having possibly already gathered the prisoners together. The centurion had to use his authority, and strongly so, to stop the proposed grisly proceedings.

3. *"And commanded that they which could swim should cast themselves first into the sea, and get to land,"* presents the centurion giving instructions that the manacles or chains were to be loosed from the prisoners in order that they may be able to swim.

4. The word *"commanded,"* once again, is a strong term, implying that he did so over the objections of those under his command. Nevertheless, he prevailed.

(44) "AND THE REST, SOME ON BOARDS, AND SOME ON BROKEN PIECES OF THE SHIP. AND SO IT CAME TO PASS, THAT THEY ESCAPED ALL SAFE TO LAND."

The account is:

1. The phrase, *"And the rest, some on boards, and some on broken pieces of the ship,"* pertained to those who could not swim.

2. *"And so it came to pass, that they escaped all safe to land,"* fulfilled exactly that which the Angel had conveyed to Paul.

3. As the entirety of this episode proclaims, the Lord will always see us through, that is, if we have Faith in Him; however, this does not mean that such a course will be uneventful. As here described, the terrible hardships and discomforts of the storm were not removed, just as many storms of other varieties are not removed presently for the Child of God. However, even as the Psalmist said, *"The LORD delivers us out of them all"* (Ps. 34:19).

"Saved by the Blood of the Crucified One;
"Now ransomed from sin and a new work begun.
"Sing praise to the Father and praise to the Son,
"Saved by the Blood of the Crucified One!"

"Saved by the Blood of the Crucified One!
"All hail to the Father, all hail to the Son,
"All hail to the Spirit, the great Three in One!
"Saved by the Blood of the Crucified One!"

"Saved! Saved! My sins are all pardoned,
"My guilt is all gone!
"Glory, I'm saved! Glory, I'm saved!
"Saved! Saved! I am saved,
"By the Blood of the Crucified One!
"Glory, I'm saved! Glory, I'm saved!"

CHAPTER 28

(1) "AND WHEN THEY WERE ESCAPED, THEN THEY KNEW THAT THE ISLAND WAS CALLED MELITA."

NOTES

The way is:

1. The island of Malta now belongs to Great Britain and is situated about 50 miles south of Sicily in the Mediterranean.

2. It is small, about 20 miles long and 12 miles wide. It consists mostly of rock, actually, of white, soft freestone. There isn't much soil with which to grow crops.

(2) "AND THE BARBAROUS PEOPLE SHOWED US NO LITTLE KINDNESS: FOR THEY KINDLED A FIRE, AND RECEIVED US EVERY ONE, BECAUSE OF THE PRESENT RAIN, AND BECAUSE OF THE COLD."

The pattern is:

1. The phrase, *"And the barbarous people showed us no little kindness,"* is not meant by Luke to be an insult by the use of the word *"barbarous."* Those who were influenced by Greek culture and language referred to all people as such who did not fit that particular mold. In fact, many countries and civilizations in history, such as the Egyptians, had done the same thing.

2. Luke expressed himself readily respecting the *"kindness"* shown to all of the victims of the storm.

3. *"For they kindled a fire, and received us every one, because of the present rain, and because of the cold,"* presents the Maltese evidently seeing the people struggle ashore, and even with the storm still blowing, did the best they could to make preparations against the rain and cold.

4. The plight of the shipwrecked party must have been lamentable, with them drenched to the skin, no change of clothes, and a cold wind blowing.

(3) "AND WHEN PAUL HAD GATHERED A BUNDLE OF STICKS, AND LAID THEM ON THE FIRE, THERE CAME A VIPER OUT OF THE HEAT, AND FASTENED ON HIS HAND."

The direction is:

1. Christ is the End of the Law, which means that He has satisfied the demands of the broken Law.

2. If we look in Faith to Him, His Blood will redeem us from the wrath and judgment of God upon our sins.

PAUL

The phrase, *"And when Paul had gathered*

NOTES

a bundle of sticks, and laid them on the fire," presents the Apostle as never thinking of himself as too good to do anything that needed to be done. In other words, no task was too menial or beneath his station in life, and yet, he was one of the greatest men of God who ever lived. To be frank, the servant mentality was at least one of the reasons for his greatness.

Many in the Kingdom of God presently seem to have the very opposite opinion of themselves. Hard work or tasks of this nature are beneath them, or so they think. Actually, if the experience of Paul is any example, which it certainly is, I think the Lord would say of such people that not only are such tasks not beneath them, but rather, too good for them. Christians who are afraid of hard work, or else, prideful, are of little use to the Kingdom of God.

THE VIPER

The phrase, *"There came a viper out of the heat, and fastened on his hand,"* presents Satan as having been unsuccessful in killing Paul with the storm and now trying another tactic. This poisonous snake, evidently small, was picked up by mistake by Paul as he gathered the sticks of wood, or else, other types of combustible material, such as thorny heather, which grows in abundance on this island and is, as well, used as firewood.

Some argue that Malta does not have any snakes. While that, no doubt, is true at present, in no way does it mean that such was true nearly 2,000 years ago. The lengths to which people will go in attempting to disprove the Bible are absolutely ridiculous.

As well, this is as close as Paul or any of the other Apostles ever came to handling snakes. This was done by accident, with the viper shaken off into the fire.

The claim for this absurdity is found in Mark 16:18, *"They shall take up serpents."*

However, claiming that this refers to the handling of poisonous snakes is a complete misrepresentation of the Scripture. The Greek word for *"take up"* is *"airo"* and means *"to take up and remove, take away, put away, do away with, or kill."* In no correct way can this Greek word be twisted in order to mean the handling of poisonous vipers in order to prove one's Faith. The actual meaning is that the Believer will put away demon spirits by the use of the Name of Jesus.

DEMON SPIRITS

Jesus said, *"Behold, I give unto you power to tread on serpents and scorpions, and over all the power of the enemy: and nothing shall by any means hurt you"* (Lk. 10:19).

As is obvious, Jesus was not speaking of literal serpents and scorpions, but rather demon spirits. Actually, Satan is referred to as *"that old serpent, called the devil, and Satan"* (Rev. 12:9).

Furthermore, Jesus, continuing to speak about this very thing, said, *"Notwithstanding in this rejoice not, that the spirits are subject unto you; but rather rejoice, because your names are written in Heaven"* (Lk. 10:20).

So, He plainly referred to these *"serpents and scorpions"* as *"spirits,"* which, as stated, refers to demon spirits and not literal vipers.

For those who do not understand Mark 16:18 and, thereby, attempt to prove their Faith by handling poisonous reptiles, I do not question their motives or love for God. However, I do boldly say that the Bible does not teach such a thing, and consequently, that is the reason that down through the years, scores of these people have died from snake bites while attempting to prove their Faith. Even if successful, there is no proof of Faith in such acts, as should be glaringly obvious!

(4) "AND WHEN THE BARBARIANS SAW THE VENOMOUS BEAST HANG ON HIS HAND, THEY SAID AMONG THEMSELVES, NO DOUBT THIS MAN IS A MURDERER, WHOM, THOUGH HE HAS ESCAPED THE SEA, YET VENGEANCE SUFFERS NOT TO LIVE."

The status is:

1. The phrase, *"And when the barbarians saw the venomous beast hang on his hand,"* presents the type of serpent that literally chews its victims, all the while pumping venom into the wound. Normally, Paul's hand and arm would have immediately begun to swell, with the toxin taking its

deadly effect, and death coming in about 30 minutes, or no more than an hour. The Maltese people personally observed the bite of the serpent.

2. *"They said among themselves, No doubt this man is a murderer, whom, though he has escaped the sea, yet vengeance suffers not to live,"* presents these people jumping to conclusions as many do.

3. Paul probably did not have any manacles on his arms at present, as did none of the other prisoners, because most could not have gotten ashore with such, but would have drowned. Quite possibly there were marks on his wrists where the chains had been, which made him recognizable as a prisoner.

4. These people were superstitious, but yet, many modern Believers have the same opinion respecting difficulties that happen to fellow Believers. Many automatically jump to the conclusion that the person has sinned, and the difficulties are some type of judgment from God.

5. While such may happen occasionally, the far greater majority of the time, it is not true. Bad things do happen to good people, and it is not all the time because of sin in their lives or a lack of Faith. As well, these things are common to mankind, and God has not promised that He will never let them happen to us.

(5) "AND HE SHOOK OFF THE BEAST INTO THE FIRE, AND FELT NO HARM."

The rule is:

1. The phrase, *"And he shook off the beast into the fire,"* is the very place this snake should have been.

2. Speaking in a spiritual sense, Holy Spirit fire is the one thing Satan cannot stand. Satan and his evil spirits can bear with most of that which we think is so necessary to the Kingdom of God; however, against Holy Spirit fire, he is helpless! Consequently, he little hinders until the Holy Spirit begins to come on the scene. By that, I speak of Spirit-filled Believers, who alone can cause Satan problems (Acts 1:8).

3. *"And felt no harm,"* does not mean that he did not feel the pain of the bite, but rather did not begin to swell instantly, as was the case normally!

NOTES

(6) "HOWBEIT THEY LOOKED WHEN HE SHOULD HAVE SWOLLEN, OR FALLEN DOWN DEAD SUDDENLY: BUT AFTER THEY HAD LOOKED A GREAT WHILE, AND SAW NO HARM COME TO HIM, THEY CHANGED THEIR MINDS, AND SAID THAT HE WAS A GOD."

The order is:

1. The Incarnation was the way in which our Lord bound Himself to our woeful fortunes and carried to us the benefits that came by the Cross.

2. We must never forget His Death was for our sins.

THE MIRACLE!

The phrase, *"Howbeit they looked when he should have swollen, or fallen down dead suddenly,"* proclaims the usual reaction because they had previously seen what happened to people who were bitten. As well, they had personally seen the snake bite Paul, even it hanging on his hand. So they knew the reptile had bitten full force.

The phrase, *"But after they had looked a great while, and saw no harm come to him,"* proclaims that at first, they thought of him as being a murderer or some such criminal. As such, they fully expected his hand to begin swelling immediately, with death coming in a few minutes. However, none of this happened!

When they saw Paul continuing with his duties, suffering no ill effects whatsoever, at a point in time (whatever a great while meant), they began to have second thoughts.

The phrase, *"They changed their minds, and said that he was a god,"* probably referred to Hercules. This particular *"god"* was worshipped by the Phoenicians and was said to be a *"dispeller of evil."* Tradition said that Hercules had destroyed two serpents that attacked him in a cradle when he was a baby.

These pagans changing from one superstition to the other is understandable. Not knowing the Lord, they were greatly influenced by circumstances and happenings, whether good or bad, attempting to read omens in almost everything.

However, it is not at all understandable

NOTES

why many Christians, who ought to know better, as well, vacillate from one extreme to the other. In other words, many are little led by the Spirit of God because they little know the Word of God.

THE ACCEPTANCE OF PAUL

With all the things that happened to Paul, many of them very adverse, I wonder how he would have been accepted in modern Christian circles. In the so-called Faith community, I am concerned that he would not have been accepted at all, claiming that all of these negative things happened to him because of a lack of Faith, an improper confession, etc.

I think, as well, that his insistence on the great Gospel of grace with no attachment to the Law of Moses, or any other type of law for that matter, would have been a turn-off for most. In other words, he would have been looked at as too narrow.

Considering his emphasis on the Holy Spirit, I know that he would not have been accepted in most of the Church world, even including many Pentecostal circles. However, I think that would matter little to Paul, even as it mattered little then. His driving ambition was to please the Lord, in other words, to hear from Heaven and then do what the Lord said do. To be sure, this did not set well in many circles, but irrespective and regardless of the price, Paul never deviated from that course—and thank God he didn't!

As stated, I am afraid that in the minds of many modern Christians, the Preacher of the Gospel is either a *"criminal"* or a *"god."* If circumstances are the yardstick, such will be the attitude of most. However, if the Word of God is the yardstick, which it must be, that is, if we are to rise above the pagans, then our knowledge will be on a surer foundation.

(7) "IN THE SAME QUARTERS WERE POSSESSIONS OF THE CHIEF MAN OF THE ISLAND, WHOSE NAME WAS PUBLIUS; WHO RECEIVED US, AND LODGED US THREE DAYS COURTEOUSLY."

The diagram is:

1. The phrase, *"In the same quarters were possessions of the chief man of the island, whose name was Publius,"* proclaims this man, according to his name, as a Roman, with him probably holding his office under the governor of Sicily. As the Roman official on the island, he would have been responsible for any Roman soldiers and their prisoners who might come there.

2. Because of its central position in the Mediterranean Sea, the Romans had made this island an important naval station.

3. *"Who received us, and lodged us three days courteously,"* more than likely only pertained to Paul, Luke, and Aristarchus. Julius, the Roman centurion, was probably included, along with one or two others. The structure of the Text indicates that the entirety of the 276 people were not invited, as would be obvious.

4. Paul and his party were invited, no doubt, because of the miracle regarding the serpent. Publius would have been informed of this and, accordingly, would have treated Paul with great deference.

5. These three days of being entertained by the head Roman official of the island were a tremendous respite from the two weeks in a storm-tossed vessel. It is positive that they enjoyed these comforts exceedingly so. As well, the entirety of their stay of some three months proved to be a very enjoyable time, which the Lord had, no doubt, arranged!

(8) "AND IT CAME TO PASS, THAT THE FATHER OF PUBLIUS LAY SICK OF A FEVER AND OF A BLOODY FLUX: TO WHOM PAUL ENTERED IN, AND PRAYED, AND LAID HIS HANDS ON HIM, AND HEALED HIM."

The overview is:

1. The way to all Salvation and victory is found totally and completely in the Cross (Rom. 6:3-5).

2. With the Believer understanding that everything we receive from God comes by the means of the Cross, such must be the object of our Faith.

HEALING

The phrase, *"And it came to pass, that the father of Publius lay sick of a fever and of a bloody flux,"* presents medical terms, which Luke would have used, being a physician. The man had a recurring fever and dysentery.

"To whom Paul entered in, and prayed, and laid his hands on him, and healed him," gives us information about several things.

First of all, as stated, Publius had, no doubt, been informed of Paul suffering no ill effect from the snake bite. It is certain that he discussed these things with Paul and the others, with Paul informing him of the Lord Jesus Christ and His Power to save and to heal. So, this tells us that the Lord uses healings and miracles to whet the interest of unbelievers in Christ, especially if they have a physical need. Untold numbers have been brought to Christ as a result of physical desperation. In other words, the doctors could do no more for them, with their situation, consequently, being terminal. However, they heard of someone, whether Preacher or layperson, who believed that God could heal the sick and perform miracles, with the results being that they were miraculously healed and saved. This is not an isolated thing but has happened enumerable times. Consequently, Publius had evidently asked Paul to go pray for his father.

THE LAYING ON OF HANDS

As well, we see here the *"laying on of hands,"* as Jesus said should be respecting prayer for the sick (Mk. 16:18). However, it should be noted that any Believer, not just Preachers, can carry out this function and expect the Lord to do great things. Jesus said, *"These signs shall follow them who believe"* (Mk. 16:17).

And yet, the Lord is not limited to the *"laying on of hands,"* considering that He has healed, and does heal, in many and varied ways. For instance, the Scripture says that Peter's shadow brought healing to people (Acts 5:15), with the handkerchiefs and aprons effecting the same thing respecting Paul (Acts 19:12). As well, Jesus, at times, just spoke the Word, and the individual was healed (Lk. 7:7-10). However, the *"laying on of hands,"* as here, remains the method more often used.

In effect and ideally, the Believer becomes the Lord's Hand extended, which, as well, provides a point of contact for one's Faith.

NOTES

It is not that the Lord needs such for the healing or miracle to be brought about, but that *"laying on of hands"* is an aid to the Believer as a point of contact, as stated, for one's Faith, among other things.

Also, we do not find Luke, the physician, having anything to do with these cures. All were done by prayer and believing God. So the modern theory that Luke accompanied Paul as his personal physician to keep him well is out of harmony with truth. Not one thing is ever mentioned of this in all the history of Luke with Paul.

LUKE

The truth seems to be that Luke, who was a physician, had given up his trade in order to help Paul in whatever capacity.

And yet, doctors, nurses, hospitals, and medicine are not wrong in the Sight of God but are, in effect, God-given skills accompanied by much training. In fact, the Lord heals people in hospitals constantly and if being in a hospital or under the care of a doctor is wrong, I think such healings by the Lord would be few and far between.

When Ezekiel, the Prophet, described the coming Millennial Temple, which will be built in the coming Kingdom Age, he described the river that would flow out from under the threshold of the Temple, and how that trees will grow on both sides of this river. He then went on to say, *"And the leaf thereof* (shall be) *for medicine"* (Ezek. 47:12).

When the Bible speaks of the coming Perfect Age when the Lord will actually transfer His Headquarters from Heaven to Earth, we are given a view of the Throne of God and the river that proceeds out of it. As well, we see the Tree of Life, one on either side and one in the middle of the river. Concerning those trees, the Bible says, *"And the leaves of the Tree were for the healing of the nations"* (Rev. 22:1-2).

MEDICINE

The Holy Spirit is telling us in these accounts that these leaves will have some type of medicinal properties, which will stop all sickness and even aging. So, if it is wrong to take medicine now, or if it is a hindrance

NOTES

to one's Faith, then, of necessity, the same would be true in the coming Kingdom Age and Perfect Age to come, which we know is incorrect.

At the same time, if the Lord specifically tells a person not to take medicine, as He has with some, by all means, He should be obeyed. Otherwise, doctors, nurses, hospitals, and medicine can be and, in fact, should be, a blessing to people. However, even though I believe the Lord uses doctors and medicine at times, He is not dependent on such in any capacity, as should be obvious.

(9) "SO WHEN THIS WAS DONE, OTHERS ALSO, WHICH HAD DISEASES IN THE ISLAND, CAME, AND WERE HEALED."

The rule is:

1. The phrase, *"So when this was done,"* proclaims a spark being provided that encouraged others to come and believe as well.

2. *"Others also, which had diseases in the island, came, and were healed,"* proclaims many healings and possibly even miracles, which were obvious, but with Paul also preaching the Gospel to these people, even though it is not stated. It seems they were not Greek speaking, or Luke would not have referred to them as barbarians (Acts 28:2).

3. Paul probably used an interpreter. This being a Roman naval station, there were, no doubt, a number of people on the island who could speak Greek along with the native language. There is another truth, also, that should be brought out respecting this scenario.

4. Many times, even as here, the Lord will work mightily in healings and miracles, regarding people who have never heard the Gospel. After the initial thrust, it seems not as many healings are recorded. Even though the Lord does continue to heal, it seems to be on a more limited basis.

5. Evidently, this is done by the Holy Spirit in order to attract immediate attention, among other things. I realize that many discount what I have just said, claiming that it is all relative to Faith.

6. Of course, Faith plays an important part in anything received from the Lord. However, one cannot honestly say these people at Malta had great Faith, especially considering that they had never heard the Word of God. Even if Paul preached to them, which he no doubt did, still their Faith would have been very weak—at least for most of them—and for the obvious reasons. But yet, the implication is that all were healed.

7. So, we must conclude that even though Faith definitely played a part in this, it was probably not the greatest factor, with that being the reason I have given.

(10) "WHO ALSO HONORED US WITH MANY HONORS; AND WHEN WE DEPARTED, THEY LADED US WITH SUCH THINGS AS WERE NECESSARY."

The diagram is:

1. The phrase, *"Who also honoured us with many honours,"* evidently indicates material things, such as clothing, food, gifts of money, etc.

2. These people had experienced a Move of God seldom known, and as a result, were thankful. No doubt, many had been healed who were at the point of death, or at least had been seriously debilitated. Consequently, they were now fit and able, with life far better than it had been previously.

3. This is what the Lord does! He brings good things to all people who will dare to believe Him. Isn't this far better than the idols they had been worshiping? Isn't it much better than these fake religions that took everything and gave nothing? It is the same presently!

4. The Lord, Who is no respecter of persons, will do the same for any and all who will come to Him believing. Jesus plainly said, *"I am come that they might have life, and that they might have it more abundantly"* (Jn. 10:10).

5. James said, *"Every good gift and every perfect gift is from above, and cometh down from the Father of lights, with Whom is no variableness, neither shadow of turning"* (James 1:17).

6. That simply means that God gave good gifts then, and He continues to do so now. As well, He will never vary from that position. What a promise!

7. *"And when we departed, they laded us with such things as were necessary,"* no doubt, referred to the entirety of the 276

people who had been shipwrecked.

8. This tells us that as a result of Paul's touch with God, all of those on the ship were blessed exceedingly so, even though they did not know the Lord. In fact, all of them owed their very lives to him and, more specifically, to the Lord. How much they knew and understood this, we are not told!

(11) "AND AFTER THREE MONTHS WE DEPARTED IN A SHIP OF ALEXANDRIA, WHICH HAD WINTERED IN THE ISLE, WHOSE SIGN WAS CASTOR AND POLLUX."

The synopsis is:

1. The phrase, *"And after three months we departed in a ship of Alexandria,"* evidently portrays another grain ship from the same city where the wrecked ship had been based (Acts 27:6).

2. The *"three months"* here mentioned were probably November, December, and January.

3. *"Which had wintered in the isle,"* explains these three months as being very stormy, even as we have just seen.

4. More than likely, this ship, even as the ship on which Paul had sailed, had thought they would be able to make their destination but was caught, consequently, having to tie up for the winter. I am sure that the captains of these vessels did their very best not to be trapped in these situations, but obviously, some would try to get through at the last hour but would not be successful.

5. *"Whose sign was Castor and Pollux,"* presents these two signs as the favorite divinities of Mediterranean seamen at that time. It was the custom to have their images, whatever they were, on the head and stern of their ships.

6. Paul left this island a lot different than the way it was found. The Gospel of Jesus Christ had been preached here, with many beautiful and wonderful things taking place. This meant that this shipwreck, although hurtful to its owners, was a blessing in disguise for the people of this island. In fact, the people would never be the same again, as are all who are introduced to Christ.

(12) "AND LANDING AT SYRACUSE, WE TARRIED THERE THREE DAYS."

The overview is:

NOTES

1. Syracuse was the capital of Sicily, about 80 miles north of Malta. It was actually one of the most famous and beautiful cities of antiquity, founded and colonized in about 730 B.C. by the Greeks. The Romans made it the capital of the province.

2. As said, the ship was there three days, and it does not seem that Paul was allowed to go ashore during this time.

(13) "AND FROM THENCE WE FETCHED A COMPASS, AND CAME TO RHEGIUM: AND AFTER ONE DAY THE SOUTH WIND BLEW, AND WE CAME THE NEXT DAY TO PUTEOLI."

The construction is:

1. The phrase, *"And from thence we fetched a compass, and came to Rhegium,"* evidently means the wind was not favorable, so they were blown a little more easterly than they desired to go. Actually, they were not able to go through the Strait of Messina at that particular time but had to stop at Rhegium, now called Reggio.

2. *"And after one day the south wind blew, and we came the next day to Puteoli,"* refers to a very favorable wind, with them immediately passing through the strait and on to Puteoli, about 180 miles from Rhegium, which took only one sailing day.

3. Puteoli was the chief port on the Bay of Naples, with Rome having no good harbors at that time. An artificial harbor was later made by Emperor Claudius. (Puteoli was about 60 miles from Rome.)

4. This city, which is now called Pozzuoli, was built about 470 B.C. It was famous for its temple of Jupiter Serapis, which was not built according to the Grecian and Roman, but according to the Asiatic pattern.

5. As well, the grain ships from Alexandria usually came here. It is said that the whole population of Puteoli went out to see them sail into the harbor with their topsails at full spread, which they alone were allowed to carry, in order to hasten their arrival, so important to Italy was the wheat trade with Alexandria.

(14) "WHERE WE FOUND BRETHREN, AND WERE DESIRED TO TARRY WITH THEM SEVEN DAYS: AND SO WE WENT TOWARD ROME."

The rule is:

1. Sin is defined as *"missing the mark"* but, more particularly, missing God's mark.
2. It is a disobedience of His Word.

THE BRETHREN

The phrase, *"Where we found brethren,"* means that Paul was allowed to leave the ship, along with Luke and Aristarchus, and without any guard. It should be obvious that the centurion trusted Paul, especially after seeing all the things concerning the Apostle in the last few months.

The word *"found"* implies that Paul had to search out the Church in Puteoli City, which he did. How large it was and how the Gospel came there is not exactly known.

Some think that perhaps some of the Jews were in Jerusalem on the Day of Pentecost, consequently, bringing back word. We do know that many Jews from Rome were present at Pentecost (Acts 2:10). So, during this approximately 30 years, no doubt, many others in this area had found the Lord as well.

"And were desired to tarry with them seven days," either means the centurion allowed Paul to remain with these brethren for this length of time, or else, he had business in the city that required seven days.

ROME

However, the structure of the Greek text implies that the decision to remain there that long was that of Paul and not the centurion. If this is correct, and it probably is, it shows this Roman as attempting to be as kind to the Apostle as possible.

As well, Paul, no doubt, ministered extensively to these people, possibly every night. They needed the teaching and fellowship of the Apostle, and, as well, Paul enjoyed extensively being with them.

"And so we went toward Rome," now found them finishing this perilous journey on foot.

After all the conspiracies of the Jews who sought to take away his life, after the two years' delay at Caesarea, after the perils of that terrible shipwreck, despite the counsel of the soldiers to kill the prisoners, and despite the *"venomous beast,"* the Apostle to the Gentiles now traversed the last few

NOTES

miles to Rome, the colossal capital of the heathen world.

The Word of the Lord, *"You must bear witness also at Rome"* (Acts 23:11) had triumphed *"over all the power of the enemy"* (Lk. 10:19). Doubtless, the hearts of both Paul and Luke beat quicker when they first caught sight of the city on the seven hills.

(15) "AND FROM THENCE, WHEN THE BRETHREN HEARD OF US, THEY CAME TO MEET US AS FAR AS APPII FORUM, AND THE THREE TAVERNS: WHOM WHEN PAUL SAW, HE THANKED GOD, AND TOOK COURAGE."

The exegesis is:

1. The phrase, *"And from thence, when the brethren heard of us,"* evidently means that after it was determined that Paul would remain in Puteoli for seven days, a runner apparently went to the capital and informed the brethren that Paul was coming and approximately what time he would be at these two respective places.
2. *"They came to meet us as far as Appii Forum,"* refers to a town about 40 miles south of Rome. Paul, with his associates, the centurion, and soldiers, were on the famous Roman road, the Appian Way. There a delegation of Believers met him. They had come out to give him a royal welcome and then to escort him into Rome, which was, no doubt, greatly appreciated by the Apostle.
3. The phrase, *"And The Three Taverns,"* refers to a village, which actually meant, *"Three Shops."* It was about 30 miles from Rome. Another delegation met him there. So now there must have been quite a group!
4. *"Whom when Paul saw, he thanked God, and took courage,"* refers to the fellowship, which the Apostle greatly enjoyed, and, as well, the show of affection was, no doubt, tremendously encouraging. That these people would take the time to walk this long distance shows how much they loved Paul and, above all, how much they loved the Lord. Also, Paul, no doubt, plied them with questions concerning the Church in Rome and other things about the capital as well.

He had absolutely no idea what awaited him, but he knew the Lord wanted him there (Acts 23:11). Considering the opposition that Satan threw up against him, he

NOTES

knew the Lord would do a great thing, whatever it might be.

(16) "AND WHEN WE CAME TO ROME, THE CENTURION DELIVERED THE PRISONERS TO THE CAPTAIN OF THE GUARD: BUT PAUL WAS SUFFERED TO DWELL BY HIMSELF WITH A SOLDIER WHO KEPT HIM."

The account is:

1. Whatever the difficulty, the far greater part of the time, one can label sin as the cause.

2. The only answer for sin, and I mean the only answer, is the Cross of Christ (Heb. 10:12).

THE CAPITAL OF THE ROMAN EMPIRE

The phrase, *"And when we came to Rome,"* pertains to one journey ending but, in effect, another beginning.

It is said that the city of Rome was founded by Romulus about 753 B.C.

In New Testament times, Rome was in full flush of her growth. Multistory tenement blocks housed a population of over 1 million people, drawn from every quarter and every walk of life.

The aristocracy, becoming just as international through the domestic favors of the Caesars, lavished the profits of their business interests of three continents on beautiful suburban villas and country estates. The Caesars themselves had furnished the heart of the city with an array of public buildings perhaps never equaled in any capital. The same concentration of wealth and power provided the overcrowded masses with generous economic subsidies and entertainment.

Rome, as well, attracted literary and artistic talent from foreign parts. As the seat of the senate and of the Caesarean administration, Rome maintained diplomatic contact with every other state and province in its empire.

THE ORIGIN OF CHRISTIANITY AT ROME

So far as the New Testament goes, it is not clear how the circle of Christians was established in Rome, although the Church there probably had its beginnings with Jews from Rome who were in Jerusalem on the Day of Pentecost and others who were won to Christ in the following days.

Paul's first known link with Rome was when he met Aquila and Priscilla at Corinth (Acts 18:2). They had left the city as a result of Claudius' expulsion of the Jews. Since the Scripture is unclear whether they were already Christians or not, speculation is useless. However, we do know that they became stalwarts of the Faith after meeting Paul, but we are not able to derive much information from that source, at least as to the strength of the Church in Rome at that time.

PAUL AND THE CHURCH AT ROME

When Paul wrote his Epistle to the Romans, he stated that it was his plan to visit his friends in that city on the way to Spain (Rom. 15:24). Actually, a considerable circle of these is named (Rom., Chpt. 16), and they were well known, it seems, in Christian circles abroad (Rom. 1:8). However, it seems that many, if not most, of these people addressed by Paul were those who had contact with him previously regarding other Churches in other cities.

As well, these brethren who met Paul in these two villages, to which we have just referred, do not appear again, neither in connection with Paul's dealings with the Jewish authorities, nor, so far as the brief notice goes, during his two years' imprisonment. In fact, if his Epistle to the Philippians written from Rome is any indication, it seems that the Church at Rome, at least during crisis times, was of little support or help to Paul (Phil. 1:12-16).

Then later, during his second imprisonment in Rome, actually just before his death, in writing about his first imprisonment, he said, *"At my first answer no man stood with me, but all men forsook me: I pray God that it may not be laid to their charge."*

He then went on to say, *"Notwithstanding the Lord stood with me, and strengthened me ... And I was delivered out of the mouth of the lion,"* who some think was Nero (II Tim. 4:16-17).

So, information respecting the founding of the Church in Rome is sketchy, and yet,

NOTES

there is some evidence that its numbers came to be quite large, whatever its origin.

A HIRED HOUSE

The phrase, *"The centurion delivered the prisoners to the captain of the guard,"* pertained to the commander of Nero's Praetorian Guard. This was the general in charge of the Roman legion stationed at the Roman Praetorium to guard the Emperor Nero and, as well, the palace.

The phrase, *"But Paul was suffered to dwell by himself with a soldier that kept him,"* obviously means that Paul was treated differently than the other prisoners. He was evidently granted a special favor, probably on the good report of the courteous Julius, and was allowed to dwell in his own hired house but was fastened by a single chain to a Praetorian. These guards served in shifts, with different guards drawing the duty from time to time. Thus, it probably was the case that the entirety, or at least some, of the Praetorian Guard came to know the Gospel.

The evidence is that even though Paul was allowed this private apartment (evidently large enough for a considerable number of people to gather, as Verses 23 through 25 indicate), he was personally responsible for the rent.

(17) "AND IT CAME TO PASS, THAT AFTER THREE DAYS PAUL CALLED THE CHIEF OF THE JEWS TOGETHER: AND WHEN THEY WERE COME TOGETHER, HE SAID UNTO THEM, MEN AND BRETHREN, THOUGH I HAVE COMMITTED NOTHING AGAINST THE PEOPLE, OR CUSTOMS OF OUR FATHERS, YET WAS I DELIVERED PRISONER FROM JERUSALEM INTO THE HANDS OF THE ROMANS."

The synopsis is:

1. The phrase, *"And it came to pass, that after three days Paul called the chief of the Jews together,"* not only refers to the main Jewish leader in Rome, but all the other leaders as well. He did not waste any time, as is obvious, in doing this.

Paul always had a great love for his people but without it being very much returned. Every time he went into a city, he first went to the synagogue, at least if one existed in the area. He would minister to them, proving from the Old Testament that Jesus was indeed the Messiah, fulfilling all the predictions of the Prophets concerning this One to come. However, he was mostly met with outright hostility because their hatred of Christ had preceded the arrival of the Apostle. So now, he would call the Jewish leaders together as well!

The phrase, *"And when they were come together, he said unto them, Men and brethren,"* and the following account seem to indicate that the brethren of Verse 15 had no connection with these Jewish leaders. So, this meant that those who met Paul were probably a mixture of Jews and Gentiles from this *"sect"* in Jerusalem, as these Jewish leaders referred to Christianity (Acts 28:22).

At this time, the records show there were several Jewish synagogues in Rome. In fact, the Roman government was somewhat lenient toward the Jews, even favoring them by allowing them the privilege of governing themselves in making laws and ordinances for their own community.

"Though I have committed nothing against the people, or customs of our fathers, yet was I delivered prisoner from Jerusalem into the hands of the Romans," proclaims Paul relating the situation exactly as it had happened. In other words, he was saying that the Jewish Sanhedrin had accused him of high crimes, even though he had done nothing against them, nor had he broken the Law of Moses in any way. (The word *"people,"* as it is used here, refers to *"Jews."*)

As well, it seems these Jewish leaders little knew Paul. Strangely enough, the Sanhedrin in Jerusalem, it seems, had not sent any word concerning Paul, or even Christianity in general, although they would have had plenty of time to have done so.

(18) "WHO, WHEN THEY HAD EXAMINED ME, WOULD HAVE LET ME GO, BECAUSE THERE WAS NO CAUSE OF DEATH IN ME."

The rule is:

1. The phrase, *"Who, when they had examined me,"* pertains to the two trials, one under the Roman governor Felix and

the other under Festus of the same office

2. *"Would have let me go, because there was no cause of death in me,"* pertained to the Romans, not the Jews, as the next Verse explains.

3. Actually, Paul was examined first by the tribune, then by Lysias, then by Felix, then by Festus, and finally, by King Herod Agrippa II, all ready to acquit him.

(19) "BUT WHEN THE JEWS SPOKE AGAINST IT, I WAS CONSTRAINED TO APPEAL UNTO CAESAR; NOT THAT I HAD OUGHT TO ACCUSE MY NATION OF."

The overview is:

1. The phrase, *"But when the Jews spoke against it,"* pertained not to the Jewish people but the Sanhedrin, the Jewish leadership in Jerusalem.

2. This shows us that Festus' proposal in Acts 25:9 was made in consequence of the opposition of the Jews to the acquittal, which he was disposed to pronounce.

3. The phrase, *"I was constrained to appeal unto Caesar,"* proclaims the Apostle having done this in order to save his life.

4. *"Not that I had ought to accuse my Nation of,"* means that he in no way was there to bring charges against the Jews or to cause them problems in any manner.

5. Reading this and feeling the spirit of the Apostle, we must come to the conclusion that nothing could be more delicate, more conciliatory, or more truly patriotic than Paul's manner of addressing the Jews at this time. Himself a Hebrew of the Hebrews, devoted to his kinsmen according to the flesh, never even putting forward his own privilege as a Roman citizen till the last necessity, he showed himself the constant friend of his own people in spite of all their ill usage.

6. Undazzled by the splendor of Rome and the power of the Roman people, his heart was with his own despised Nation, *"That they might be saved."* He wished to be well with them; he wanted them to understand his position; and he spoke to them as a kinsman and a brother. His appeal to Caesar, as stated, had been of necessity—to save his life, but he was not going to accuse his brethren before the dominant race. His first desire was that they should be his friends and share with him the hope of the Gospel of Christ.

NOTES

(20) "FOR THIS CAUSE THEREFORE HAVE I CALLED FOR YOU, TO SEE YOU, AND TO SPEAK WITH YOU: BECAUSE THAT FOR THE HOPE OF ISRAEL I AM BOUND WITH THIS CHAIN."

The direction is:

1. The weakness of the Law was it commanded but had no power to have those commandments obeyed.

2. Like a discrowned king, it posted its proclamations but had no army at its back to execute them.

PAUL'S DIALOGUE WITH THE JEWS

The phrase, *"For this cause therefore have I called for you, to see you, and to speak with you,"* is meant to proclaim to these men that this situation had come about, not because of that which the Sanhedrin claimed, or even a political squabble, but rather for the cause of Christ. Behind all the accusations and demands for his life, a smoke screen, incidentally, concerning the Law of Moses and the Temple, etc., the real reason was the Lord Jesus Christ. In fact, the Jewish leaders in Jerusalem hated Jesus so much that they would little refer to Him in any manner in their accusations, rather resorting to other particulars. Irrespective, the entirety of the situation was 100 percent because of Jesus.

"Because that for the hope of Israel I am bound with this chain," refers to the Messianic hope of Israel in restoring the Kingdom of David, which, of course, is wrapped up in Jesus Christ (Acts 8:13-34; 14:22; 15:13-17; 17:3, 7, 18; 18:5, 28; 19:8; 20:25).

Hervey translates Verse 20 in this manner, *"I have asked you to come to me because this chain which binds me is not a token of a renegade Israelite who has come to Rome to accuse his Nation before the heathen master, but of a faithful Israelite, who has endured bondage rather than forsake the hope of his fathers."*

JESUS, THE FULFILLMENT

The simple matter was, Paul claimed that Jesus Christ was the fulfillment of all the prophecies and, therefore, the Messiah,

NOTES

with the Jewish Sanhedrin denying such and doing so vehemently.

The *"hope of Israel"* was a common phrase referring to the Messiah because this was the reason that God formed these people out of the loins of Abraham and the womb of Sarah. They were raised up for this particular purpose.

At this time, as is obvious, Rome ruled the world, which included Israel. Consequently, this *"hope"* was even more pronounced now than ever, in order for this yoke to be thrown off of God's chosen People. In fact, this was at least one of the reasons they did not recognize Jesus.

In fulfillment of the prophecies, Jesus came as a suffering Messiah, Who would redeem His People, as well as all of mankind, at least those who would believe, but Israel did not understand His Mission, not considering themselves in need of Redemption. In their minds, they were the seed of Abraham and, consequently, in covenant with Jehovah, hence, John the Baptist saying to them, *"And think not to say within yourselves, we have Abraham to our father: for I say unto you, that God is able of these stones to raise up children unto Abraham"* (Mat. 3:9).

They were looking for a triumphant Messiah Who would use His Power to deliver them from Rome and restore the throne of David, thereby, making them the dominant Nation in the world once again. In fact, even though it is a moot point, if such a thing had happened, Israel, in her acute self-righteousness, would have been a far worse tyrant than Rome. There is no evil like religious evil, and worse still, there is no evil like self-righteousness.

So, the *"hope of Israel"* is Jesus, Whom Paul proclaimed as the Messiah and Lord of Glory, with the Jewish leadership in Jerusalem proclaiming Him as a blasphemer and impostor.

MODERN ISRAEL

In fact, the problems of modern Israel will be found to be wrapped around this *"hope."* It doesn't matter how many peace accords between the Palestinians and the Israelis, these are accords that the Palestinians will not keep. They have no interest in a part of Israel. They want every Jew dead and the entirety of the Nation of Israel to revert to the Palestinians. They hate the Jews.

I realize that most would say, *"Well, it's because Israel will not give the Palestinians a part of their country so they can establish a country of their own."* No, that has nothing to do with it. Let me ask this question:

In World War II, leading Muslims helped the Germans in every way they could to kill more and more Jews. They were instrumental in helping to slaughter thousands of Jews. Why did they do that then? There was no land to be argued over and no Nation of Israel, but still, the leading Muslims did everything they could to slaughter Jews. So, we should understand from this that this problem is of far greater magnitude than modern diplomacy can handle. It is not a matter of boundaries, but rather between the half-brothers of Isaac and Ishmael, both sons of Abraham.

The great promise of this *"hope"* was given by God to Isaac, saying, *"In Isaac shall your seed be called"* (Gen. 21:12). Some 400 years later, the land promised to Abraham and his seed was possessed. It was called Israel after the grandson of Abraham. Approximately 500 years after that time, David became the king of Israel, being God's choice, with Saul, who was demanded by the people years before, being an aberration, i.e., *"a work of the flesh."* All told, Israel occupied the land for about 1,600 years when they were destroyed as a Nation by the Romans in A.D. 70. However, Jews remained in the land constantly throughout the following centuries, even though intruders came and went.

About 600 years after Christ, a man by the name of Muhammad wrote the Koran, claiming that Ishmael was the promised seed and not Isaac. As well, he claimed that Jesus Christ, although a Prophet, was not the Son of God, and that he, Muhammad, was God's Prophet, in other words, of greater importance than Christ. Out of this came the religion of Islam, presently claiming approximately 1 billion adherents. So, the struggle is between Isaac and Ishmael and continues unto this hour, with the

Palestinians claiming the Promised Land as well as Israel. As should be obvious, and going back to the time of Abraham, the Muslims are approximately 2,600 years late with their claims.

THE PRESENT STRUGGLE

Unfortunately, as stated, the Palestinian Accords, which, in effect, have Israel trading land for peace, will not bring peace, as it has not brought peace. In fact, more Israelis are being killed by terrorism since the Accords than before.

As a result of these problems, which will only increase, the *"hope of Israel"* will gradually come more and more to the fore. When the Antichrist makes his debut, Israel will herald to the world that this *"hope"* has finally been realized. Their Messiah has come, or so they think!

After about three and one-half years, he will show his true colors and actually attack Israel, which will begin the greatest time of suffering these people have ever known. Jeremiah called it *"the time of Jacob's trouble"* (Jer. 30:7). As stated, Jesus said it would be *"great tribulation,"* in fact, greater than Israel has ever known before or will ever know again (Mat. 24:21).

This horrible time will last for about three and one-half years, with the conclusion looking like their sure destruction. In fact, they will then cry for the Messiah as never before, that *"hope"* being their only hope!

He will not fail them; He will come! Zechariah said, *"Then shall the LORD go forth, and fight against those nations, as when He fought in the day of battle"* (Zech. 14:3). John the Beloved described Him coming back, *"KING OF KINGS, AND LORD OF LORDS"* (Rev. 19:16).

To be sure, at that time, the chain that bound Paul and, in fact, has bound so many others for the Cause of Christ, will then be eternally broken. In other words, such a chain will never touch the arms of a Child of God again!

At the Second Coming, the Jews will accept Jesus Christ, the very One they crucified, as their Saviour, their Lord, and their Messiah. Then their dark night will finally come to an end, with the sun rising and, as well, the *"Son"* arising, which will give them the life for which they had so long sought. Then, once again, David will be their king, under Jesus Christ, Who will be the President, so to speak, of the entirety of the world. Then the world will know 1,000 years of peace and prosperity as it has never known before.

NOTES

(21) "AND THEY SAID UNTO HIM, WE NEITHER RECEIVED LETTERS OUT OF JUDAEA CONCERNING YOU, NEITHER ANY OF THE BRETHREN WHO CAME SHOWED OR SPOKE ANY HARM OF YOU."

The direction is:

1. The phrase, *"And they said unto him, We neither received letters out of Judaea concerning you,"* probably pertained to the fact that Roman law punished unsuccessful prosecutors of Roman citizens. Considering this, the Jewish leaders in Jerusalem, knowing that Paul was innocent, probably thought it wisdom not to accuse him before Caesar.

2. *"Neither any of the brethren who came showed or spoke any harm of you,"* pertaining at least to those who were from Jerusalem, had maybe been warned not to say anything, and for the reasons given.

3. It is difficult to comprehend that these Jewish leaders in Rome had never heard of Paul, but from the terminology given here, this somewhat seems to be the case, or else, their knowledge of him was scant.

(22) "BUT WE DESIRE TO HEAR OF YOU WHAT YOU THINK: FOR AS CONCERNING THIS SECT, WE KNOW THAT EVERY WHERE IT IS SPOKEN AGAINST."

The diagram is:

1. Deliverance from depravity is an essential part of Biblical Salvation, in fact, the most important part in some points of view.

2. This is made possible by the Cross, and made possible by the Cross alone!

SPOKEN AGAINST ...

The phrase, *"But we desire to hear of you what you think,"* proclaims a great opportunity now presented to Paul.

This phrase does lend some small credence to the thought that maybe they had heard of Paul but had sketchy information. However, it may well have pertained only to

NOTES

their desire to learn something about Christianity, of which they seemed to know little, at least at this particular time.

"For as concerning this sect, we know that every where it is spoken against," pertained primarily to the Jews, the very ones who should have been beneficiaries of the Man and the Message, the Lord Jesus Christ. However, very shortly, Rome, even under Nero, would turn bitterly against Christians, instituting a policy by the state of extreme persecution, which actually took the lives of untold thousands in the coming years. It is that of which Jesus spoke when He said in the Olivet Discourse, *"Then shall they deliver you up to be afflicted, and shall kill you: and you shall be hated of all nations for My Name's sake"* (Mat. 24:9).

As well, at this present time, true Bible Christianity continues to be *"everywhere spoken against,"* which it has always been. To be sure, there is much which calls itself *"Christian,"* but little adheres to the Word of God and, as such, has very little, if any, opposition from anyone. Regrettably, that brand is in the far greater majority.

BIBLE CHRISTIANITY

Being on television, I have dealt with the news media for years. At first I was naive, thinking that they desired the truth and if such were freely and openly given to them, and they could prove it was the truth, they would be fair, etc. How wrong I was!

I soon found out that the greater majority of the news media had no concern whatsoever as to what the truth was concerning the Gospel, especially considering that they had long since made up their minds, which could not be changed by the truth or facts. Irrespective as to how truthful or factual something was, time and time again, I have watched them twist and turn it until they made it seem to be something sinister or crooked. I told one just the other day, *"You people would make the Sermon on the Mount seem like a plot to overthrow the government."*

Bible Christianity has never been popular, is not popular now, and never will be popular, at least in this present world's system. In fact, concerning popularity with the world, one can easily judge how close something is to God. That which is close to God is going to be treated exactly as Paul was treated—the religion of that day (Judaism) hated him, and the Roman government would soon turn on him as well.

(23) "AND WHEN THEY HAD APPOINTED HIM A DAY, THERE CAME MANY TO HIM INTO HIS LODGING; TO WHOM HE EXPOUNDED AND TESTIFIED THE KINGDOM OF GOD, PERSUADING THEM CONCERNING JESUS, BOTH OUT OF THE LAW OF MOSES, AND OUT OF THE PROPHETS, FROM MORNING TILL EVENING."

The overview is:

1. There are enemies to the Cross of Christ (Phil. 3:18).

2. They are anyone, and for all time, who attempts to substitute something else in place of the Cross.

TO HEAR PAUL TEACH

The phrase, *"And when they had appointed him a day, there came many to him into his lodging,"* proclaims an excellent opportunity for Paul to present Jesus to these people, of which he took full advantage.

As we have previously stated, even though Paul was technically a prisoner of Rome, even chained constantly to a Roman soldier except perhaps when he went to bed, he was allowed to have his own apartment, which must have had at least one large room in order to accommodate the people. No doubt, he personally had to stand the expense of these private quarters. However, the Lord provided.

THE KINGDOM OF GOD

The phrase, *"To whom he expounded and testified the Kingdom of God,"* pertained to the great subject matter of the Gospel and all its parts—grace, Righteousness, and glory, all through Jesus Christ.

He, no doubt, was attempting to get these Jewish leaders to see that the Kingdom of God was all wrapped up in Jesus Christ. This is that to which they all aspired, even from the time of Abraham, and was really their very purpose in this world. In other words, Jesus was and is the Kingdom. Even though the Kingdom of God covers every aspect of life, whether spiritual, economical, material, physical, scientific, mental, or sociological, still, it is all headed up in the Lord Jesus Christ. He is the One of Whom the Prophets testified and to Whom the Law of Moses pointed in all its many parts.

In other words, the very purpose of Israel was Jesus Christ, as the very purpose of the Church is Jesus Christ.

Both John the Baptist and Jesus came preaching, saying, *"Repent ye: for the Kingdom of Heaven is at hand"* (Mat. 3:1-2, 17).

THE KINGDOM OF HEAVEN

The message was simple: the *"Kingdom of Heaven"* (rule of Heaven) was at hand because Jesus was present. Without Him, there could be no *"kingdom"* and, therefore, when the Jews rejected Him, they rejected the kingdom as well!

In fact, they wanted the kingdom, but they wanted it on their terms. To be frank, the whole world wants the same thing. Sadly, they rejected His terms, as most of the world does, and lost it all, as there are no other terms, at least that God will recognize.

The phrase, *"Persuading them concerning Jesus, both out of the Law of Moses, and out of the Prophets, from morning till evening,"* pointed to Jesus as the Subject and the Bible as the proof.

In fact, the one infallible authority that all the Apostles appealed to as declaring that Jesus of Nazareth was the promised Messiah was the Old Testament, i.e., the Bible, and all true servants of God in all subsequent centuries have acted and do act similarly.

In effect, Paul explained that this was the kingdom proposed to be set up on Earth; that it was not to be confined to the Nation of Israel and the Hebrew people, but was to embrace the whole world and all nations, and that its King was to be Jesus of Nazareth.

There are three important terms that should be remembered:

1. *"The Kingdom of God"* (Acts 28:23).
2. *"The salvation of God"* (Acts 28:28).
3. *"The high-calling of God"* (Phil. 3:14).

The first is the subject of the Book of Acts; the second is the theme of the Epistle to the Romans; and the third is revealed in the Epistle to the Ephesians.

NOTES

Paul spent an entire day, from *"morning till evening,"* opening the Word of God to these Jews. Considering that he was speaking to men who knew the Word, at least after a fashion, there is no doubt that he made a telling argument, and that the Spirit of God helped him mightily to do so.

(24) "AND SOME BELIEVED THE THINGS WHICH WERE SPOKEN, AND SOME BELIEVED NOT."

The composition is:

1. The phrase, *"And some believed the things which were spoken,"* evidently means they embraced Jesus as their Messiah, Lord, and Saviour. They believed that He died on Calvary for their sins and rose from the dead on the third day. Thus, they became born-again believers! Paul probably recommended them to the Churches in the area.

2. Such is imperative that he did so, for to go back into false doctrine, as Judaism had become, at least in its rejection of Christ, would have spelled spiritual doom for anyone.

3. *"And some believed not,"* pretty well describes, at least most of the time, the response to Christ. Some believe, while others don't!

4. Once again, the focal point is Jesus. Consequently, this means that all of these men who sat there that day, in fact, religious leaders who studied the Bible constantly, were eternally lost despite all their religious activity. It is the same presently!

5. Millions claim Salvation and even to having accepted Christ, but sadly, there is no evident fruit of such a claimed union. For the most part, these people have only embraced a mental affirmation of Christ, with no real revelation in their hearts and, as such, have never really been saved. That is the reason a false Salvation is the worst thing there could ever be. It lulls people into believing something that they really do not have.

6. Most of this is brought about because of the Holy Spirit not being present in the proceedings. Much of the Church has rejected Him, even though they would deny such. In fact, without the Spirit of God,

NOTES

there is no way for a work of regeneration to take place (Jn. 16:7-15).

7. When Paul said that *"some believed,"* he was simply saying that they believed that Jesus was the Son of God, died on Calvary to pay the price for the sins of man, and then rose from the dead.

8. It also means that man must see himself as he really is, a sinner without God and with no hope of saving himself. He must believe that Jesus alone is the Saviour and accept what He did at Calvary and the Resurrection.

9. He must believe, as well, that none of the good things he has done, or the bad things he has not done, adds anything to his Salvation. It is all of Christ, and that he must believe. If so, he is saved (Jn. 3:16; Rom. 10:9, 10, 13; Eph. 2:8-9; Rev. 22:17).

(25) "AND WHEN THEY AGREED NOT AMONG THEMSELVES, THEY DEPARTED, AFTER THAT PAUL HAD SPOKEN ONE WORD, WELL SPOKE THE HOLY SPIRIT BY ISAIAH THE PROPHET UNTO OUR FATHERS."

The structure is:

1. The phrase, *"And when they agreed not among themselves, they departed,"* proclaims that which the truth always does—brings disagreement and a line of separation (Lk. 12:51).

2. Considering the passage of Scripture with which Paul closed this session that memorable day, which we will momentarily address, it seems that the disagreement concerning Jesus Christ was quite pronounced, even with the unbelievers becoming very strong in their denunciation. I think it must have been that way, or else, such a passage would not have been used.

3. The phrase, *"After that Paul had spoken one word, well spoke the Holy Spirit by Isaiah the Prophet unto our fathers,"* proclaims the instrument as Isaiah, but the Speaker as the Holy Spirit.

(26) "SAYING, GO UNTO THIS PEOPLE, AND SAY, HEARING YOU SHALL HEAR, AND SHALL NOT UNDERSTAND; AND SEEING YOU SHALL SEE, AND NOT PERCEIVE."

The direction is:

1. The phrase, *"Saying, Go unto this people,"* beginning this passage by Isaiah (Isa. 6:9-10), presents the sixth of seven times it is recorded by the Holy Spirit (Isa. 6:9; Mat. 13:14; Mk. 4:12; Lk. 8:10; Jn. 12:40; Acts 28:26; Rom. 11:8). This last passage predicts Israel's future Repentance and acceptance of the King and His Kingdom.

2. Primarily, this message was to Israel, but it is also applicable to any and all who reject the Word of God.

3. The message presented here by the Holy Spirit is that *"unbelief"* will stop people from hearing the truth, even though it is presented to them (Rom. 11:20).

4. *"And say, Hearing you shall hear, and shall not understand; and seeing you shall see, and not perceive,"* means that all hear the Word alike, but all do not show a like attitude of Faith in it. All saw the same thing that Paul set before them, but all did not choose to believe it.

5. The responsibility is with the people and not with God or His Word. All can believe and accept it alike if they desire to do so. Never make the mistake that God is responsible for the Faith of some and the unbelief of others. The fault is never with God, but always with the person.

6. An excellent example is the sun. It softens wax and hardens clay. The fault is not in the sun, but in the material on which it shines.

(27) "FOR THE HEART OF THIS PEOPLE IS WAXED GROSS, AND THEIR EARS ARE DULL OF HEARING, AND THEIR EYES HAVE THEY CLOSED; LEST THEY SHOULD SEE WITH THEIR EYES, AND HEAR WITH THEIR EARS, AND UNDERSTAND WITH THEIR HEART, AND SHOULD BE CONVERTED, AND I SHOULD HEAL THEM."

The way is:

1. If we are to live for God and do so successfully, we must do this thing God's Way, and that Way is the Cross.

2. If we try to live for the Lord by any other method, irrespective as to what it is, we will find the sin nature ruling us, which presents itself as a miserable situation.

HEART

The phrase, *"For the heart of this people*

NOTES

is waxed gross," presents the reason for the rejection of the Lord; it is the heart.

"Heart" in the Greek text is *"kardia"* and means *"the chief organ of physical life."* As is obvious, it occupies the most important place in the human system regarding the physical man.

However, by an easy transition, the word came to stand for man's entire mental and moral activity, both the rational and the emotional elements. In other words, the heart is used figuratively for the hidden springs of the personal life, which includes the feelings and passions of the soul and spirit of man.

The Bible describes human depravity as in the *"heart"* because sin is a principle that has its seat in the center of man's inward life, and then *"defiles"* the whole circuit of his action (Mat. 15:19-20).

On the other hand, Scripture also regards the heart as the sphere of divine influence (Acts 15:9; Rom. 2:15). The heart, as lying deep within, contains *"the hidden man,"* the real man (I Pet. 3:4). It represents the true character but, at the same time, conceals it.

THE JEWISH UNDERSTANDING OF THE HEART

The Hebrews thought in terms of subjective experience rather than objective scientific observation, which is spiritually legitimate providing it is scriptural and, thereby, avoided the modern error of over-departmentalization.

To them, the heart was essentially the whole man, with all his attributes, physical, intellectual, and spiritual, of which the Hebrew thought and spoke. Also, the heart was conceived of as the governing center of all of these. It is the heart that makes a man or a beast what he is and governs all his actions (Prov. 4:23).

Character, personality, will, and mind are modern terms that all reflect something of the meaning of *"heart"* in its Biblical usage, which, as well, speaks of the soul and the spirit, as stated.

THE BRAIN AND THE HEART

There is no suggestion in the Bible that the brain is the center of consciousness, thought, or will. It is the heart that is so regarded, and though it is used of emotions also, that usage is more frequently the lower organs (bowels), insofar as they are distinguished and are connected with the emotions.

As a broad general statement, it is true that the Bible places the spiritual focus one step lower in the anatomy than most popular modern speech, which uses *"mind"* for consciousness, thought, and will, and *"heart"* for emotions.

THE MIND

The *"mind"* is perhaps the closest modern term to the Biblical usage of *"heart,"* and many passages do lean in that direction (Prov. 16:23; Eccl. 1:17). The *"heart"* is, however, a wider term, and the Bible does not distinguish the rational or mental processes in the way that Greek philosophy does.

C. Ryder Smith suggests that: *"The First great Commandment probably means 'You shall love the Lord your God with all your heart—that is with all your soul and with all your mind and with all your strength'"* (Mk. 12:30, 33).

The heart of man does not always do that, however. It is not what it should be (Gen. 6:5; Jer. 17:9), and the Old Testament reaches the highest point in the realization that a change of heart is needed (Jer. 24:7; Ezek. 11:19), and that, of course, is fulfilled in the New Testament (Eph. 3:17).

THE HEART THAT IS RIGHT WITH GOD

There are the exceptional people whose hearts are right with God (I Ki. 15:14; Ps. 37:31; Acts 13:22), though it is obvious from what we know of David, the example referred to in the last passage, that this is not true in an absolute sense, but that Repentance, even with these, at times, is still necessary (II Ki. 23:25).

Actually, the right attitude of the heart begins with it being broken or crushed (Ps. 51:17), symbolic of humility and penitence, and synonymous with *"a broken spirit."* This is what Isaiah was saying and Paul was repeating that Israel did not have.

This brokenness is necessary because it is the hard or stony heart that will not submit to the Will of God (Ezek. 11:19).

Alternatively, it is the *"fat"* or *"uncircumcised"* heart that fails to respond to God's Will (Isa. 6:10; Ezek. 44:7).

THE LORD AND THE HEART

The Lord knows the heart of each one and is not deceived by outward appearance (I Sam. 16:7), but a worthy prayer is, nevertheless, that He should search and know the heart (Ps. 139:23) and make it clean (Ps. 51:10). A *"new heart"* must be the aim of the wicked (Ezek. 18:31), and that will mean that God's Law has to become no longer merely external but *"written on the heart,"* which will make it clean (Jer. 31:33).

Thus it is that the heart, the spring of all desires, must be guarded (Prov. 4:23), and the teacher aims to win his pupil's heart to the right way (Prov. 23:26).

It is the pure in heart who shall see God (Mat. 5:8), and it is through Christ's dwelling in the heart by Faith that the Saints can comprehend the Love of God (Eph. 3:17).

The phrase, *"And their ears are dull of hearing, and their eyes have they closed,"* simply means that the person will not *"hear,"* nor will he *"see,"* even though the truth is presented unto him. In other words, it is a willful rejection of truth, which brings about a willful judgment of the hardening of the heart.

THE PERSON IS RESPONSIBLE

This plainly tells us that it is the person responsible for the closed ears and eyes, and not God.

It is bad enough to never have an opportunity to hear the Gospel but worse still to hear it and then reject it. As such, one is never left in a static position, but rather, always falls to a far lower level morally and spiritually.

The phrase, *"Lest they should see with their eyes, and hear with their ears, and understand with their heart, and should be converted, and I should heal them,"* portrays, as stated, that the individual has willfully refused to see or hear, irrespective of the Word of God being presented, and the Holy Spirit dealing with them.

As a result, the person cannot be saved or spiritually healed.

NOTES

If one is to notice, in order to emphasize the point, the Holy Spirit says the same thing in several different ways in order that the truth not be lost, especially considering its significance.

He purposely outlines how the individual through unbelief refuses to hear or see the Gospel, and then He purposely states how such affects the individual.

It should be said, as well, that no philosophy of man has this effect on a person. Whether accepted or rejected, it only stimulates the intellectual. However, the Word of God empowered by the Holy Spirit, although heard by the intellect, is also received into the spirit of man and demands an answer. If accepted, the ears constantly hear more of the Word of God, with the eyes constantly seeing more, and with the heart growing more tender toward God. This is a process that actually never stops as long as the Word of God is received by Faith.

A GRADUAL PROCESS

The opposite effect is brought about upon rejection. It is not a sudden thing but actually a gradual process in both cases, whether accepted or rejected.

If rejected, the spiritual ears gradually become duller, with the spiritual eyes gradually becoming more closed and the heart less receptive.

After awhile, as with Israel of old, there is nothing left toward God, even though the person may continue to be very religious.

This is the reason that Israel could reject Christ, even though He performed miracles as the world had never seen before and spoke as never man spoke. They simply could not *"see"* because a blind man cannot see. They could not *"hear"* because a deaf man cannot hear. Consequently, one can *"show"* a blind man all the proof in the world, but he simply cannot see such proof. As well, one can *"speak"* all the right things to the deaf man, but he does not hear. Along with that, the *"heart"* is hardened, which means a Revelation of the Holy Spirit has no effect either.

The reader must understand that the type of spiritual blindness and deafness addressed here is not that of the unconverted who simply do not know God, but

NOTES

rather that of those who claim to know God and, in fact, are deeply religious. I remind the reader that it was not the drunks or the harlots who crucified Christ, but rather the religious leadership of Israel.

(28) "BE IT KNOWN THEREFORE UNTO YOU, THAT THE SALVATION OF GOD IS SENT UNTO THE GENTILES, AND THAT THEY WILL HEAR IT."

The diagram is:

1. The phrase, *"Be it known therefore unto you, that the Salvation of God is sent unto the Gentiles,"* presents Paul's last statement to the Jewish leadership of Rome that day. As stated, those who refused to believe must have been rabid in their denunciation of Christ, or else, Paul would not have spoken as strongly as he did.

2. First of all, he, in effect, said that the *"Salvation of God"* is found only in Jesus, which meant that Israel, who had rejected Christ, had no Salvation.

3. As well, this *"Salvation"* found only in Christ would be presented to the Gentiles, as it was already being presented to the Gentiles. In effect, this fulfilled the prophecy of Noah given some 2,400 years before when he said, *"Blessed be the LORD God of Shem."*

4. Shem was one of the sons of Noah whose lineage would bring the Messiah into the world, hence, the word *"blessed."* Abraham and all his seed were in the lineage of Shem.

5. Noah also prophesied, *"God shall enlarge Japheth, and he shall dwell in the tents of Shem"* (Gen. 9:26-27).

6. From Japheth, another of Noah's sons, the white, Caucasian Gentiles came, along with the yellow races.

7. Israel is in the lineage of Shem and, therefore, blessed by God with the privilege of bringing the Messiah into the world. Due to the Nation rejecting their Messiah, the blessings intended for Shem were instead given to *"Japheth."* Hence, *"Japheth"* will and, in fact, has dwelled in the tents of *"Shem,"* i.e., *"received the blessing of God* (Jesus) *intended for the lineage of Shem, i.e., Israel."*

Consequently, Paul spoke of the Gospel going to the Gentiles.

8. The phrase, *"And they will hear it,"* speaks of a receptive ear and obedient heart toward Jesus, which Israel did not and, in fact, would not have. As is obvious, this speaks of the Church, which now numbers approximately 1 billion people on the Earth, not counting Catholicism (only a small remnant of that great number truly know Christ).

(29) "AND WHEN HE HAD SAID THESE WORDS, THE JEWS DEPARTED, AND HAD GREAT REASONING AMONG THEMSELVES."

The structure is:

1. The phrase, *"And when he had said these words, the Jews departed,"* proclaims doing such, but with the Gospel of Jesus Christ ringing in their ears.

2. As well, they had received a stinging rebuke from Paul in the quoting of this passage from Isaiah and then the proclamation of the Gospel going to the Gentiles. All was designed by the Holy Spirit almost as a last resort, which it probably was, to reach their souls.

3. *"And had great reasoning among themselves,"* probably was related to Paul at a later time by those who had believed.

4. Maybe some of these came back at a later date and gave their hearts and lives to the Lord Jesus Christ.

5. So, Israel's action occasioned the sending of the Gospel to the Gentiles, and that enriched them partially (Rom. 11:11). However, Israel's Repentance, which definitely will come at the Second Coming, will occasion the incorporation of all the Gentile nations with the Kingdom of God, and then will be manifested the completion of the Kingdom of God on Earth. This will take place in the coming Kingdom Age (Zech. 12:10-14; 13:1-6; 14:20-21).

(30) "AND PAUL DWELT TWO WHOLE YEARS IN HIS OWN HIRED HOUSE, AND RECEIVED ALL WHO CAME IN UNTO HIM."

The exegesis is:

1. The phrase, *"And Paul dwelt two whole years in his own hired house,"* presents the Lord refreshing his beloved and precious servant with rest. At the same time, He taught him the humbling lesson that the success of the Gospel message did

NOTES

not wholly depend upon him, as it depends on no individual person.

2. During these years of imprisonment, he wrote his main Epistles and carried upon his heart the care of all the Churches. This multiple ministry was exercised in Rome, the capital of the then-known world. These facts destroy the platform on which the Vatican Church is built.

3. Some believe that Paul was released after these two years when he was called before the emperor, and the Jerusalem Jews had sent no accusation and no lawyer to represent them.

4. Others believe there was no trial, and the case was automatically dismissed at the end of the two years because no charges were presented. Roman law gave the prosecution a limited time to present its case, depending on the distance they had to come. Philemon, Verse 22, shows Paul did expect to be released.

5. Whichever it was, the appearing before Nero or the dismissal of the case, the Will of God was carried out in Paul's life and ministry. He did truly bear witness of Jesus at Rome (Acts 23:11).

6. *"And received all who came in unto him,"* no doubt, strengthened the Church mightily in Rome and, as well, saw many saved and baptized with the Holy Spirit.

(31) "PREACHING THE KINGDOM OF GOD, AND TEACHING THOSE THINGS WHICH CONCERN THE LORD JESUS CHRIST, WITH ALL CONFIDENCE, NO MAN FORBIDDING HIM."

The rule is:

1. If the blood of animals and the blood of men are precious to God, what shall we say about the Blood of God's Son, our redeeming Saviour?

2. In Acts 20:28, the Apostle Paul says that the Church was purchased by the Blood of Christ. This is an amazing and astonishing expression.

THE KINGDOM OF GOD

The phrase, *"Preaching the Kingdom of God,"* refers to the Rule of God in the human heart and life. It is that for which the Spirit strives, and that which the Preacher must proclaim. It is that for which Jesus told us to pray, *"Your Kingdom come, Your Will be done in Earth, as it is in Heaven"* (Mat. 6:10).

The phrase, *"And teaching those things which concern the Lord Jesus Christ,"* proclaims Christ as the center, the core, and the circumference of the message. As stated, Jesus Christ and His acceptance is the Kingdom of God, which will finally be brought to totality and completion when Israel at long last accepts Him, which they one day shall. Then, that which we refer to as the *"Lord's Prayer"* will be answered. The kingdom will be on Earth, even as it is now in Heaven.

"With all confidence, no man forbidding him," presents a mighty boldness on the part of Paul in the presentation of the Gospel, no doubt, given him by the Holy Spirit, which undoubtedly saw a great harvest.

It is said that even some from Caesar's household were converted (Phil. 4:22). Maybe this came about through the witness of some of the soldiers to the whole Praetorian Guard or palace (Phil. 1:13).

As well, the Lord saw to it that no man hindered Paul from this great presentation of the Gospel, not Jew or Roman!

THE BOOK OF ACTS

What followed those two years, what became of Paul, and what of his saintly biographer, we shall never know, at least this side of Glory. It has pleased God to draw a curtain over the events, which we cannot penetrate. Here our history ends because nothing more had happened when it was given to the Church.

Instead of vain regrets because it reached no further, let us devoutly thank God for all that this Book has taught us. As well, let us strive to show ourselves worthy members of that great Gentile Church, whose foundation by Peter and Paul, and whose marvelous increment, through the labors of him who once laid it waste, has been so well set before us in this Book called, *"The Acts of the Apostles."*

Actually, the Book of Acts has no formal ending, and that is the way it was designed by the Holy Spirit. In truth, it continues on unto this very hour.

As I finish my efforts regarding this Commentary, I know that within ourselves, we have little or nothing to offer, and yet, how many times in the last few months has the Spirit of God covered my heart as I attempted to dictate the notes that comprise this effort! The tears have often flowed as I stood before Peter and then Paul. What a journey it has been.

And yet, all in all, Jesus has become more and more real as I have seen Him work mightily in the lives of these great Apostles, and all by the Power, yes, the Power of the Holy Spirit.

God help me, even as it was said of Paul, that I may ever *"preach the Kingdom of God, and teach those things which concern the Lord Jesus Christ."*

If anything matters at all, that alone matters all!

"Jesus see me at Your Feet,
"With my sacrifice complete;
"I am bringing all to You,
"Yours alone I'll be."

"Oh how patient You have been,
"With my pride and inbred sin;
"Oh what mercy You have shown,
"Grace and love unknown!"

"Lord, I loathe myself and sin,
"Enter now and make me clean;
"Make my heart just like Your Own;
"Come, Lord, take Your Throne."

"Praise the Lord, the work is done;
"Praise the Lord, the victory won!
"Now the Blood is cleansing me,
"From all sin I'm free."

NOTES

BIBLIOGRAPHY

CHAPTER 1

Kenneth S. Wuest, *Wuest's Word Studies in the Greek New Testament: Mark*, Grand Rapids, Eerdmans Publishing Company, 1942.

H. D. M. Spence, *The Pulpit Commentary: Acts 1:3*, Grand Rapids, Eerdmans Publishing Company, 1978.

CHAPTER 2

George Williams, *Williams' Complete Bible Commentary*, Grand Rapids, Kregel Publications, 1994, Pg. 29.

CHAPTER 4

George Williams, *Williams' Complete Bible Commentary*, Grand Rapids, Kregel Publications, 1994, pg. 824.

CHAPTER 5

C. H. Mackintosh, *Notes on the Book of Exodus*, New York, Loizeaux Brothers, 1880, Pg. 311.

H. D. M. Spence, *The Pulpit Commentary: Acts*, Grand Rapids, Eerdmans Publishing Company, 1978.

CHAPTER 6

H. D. M. Spence, *The Pulpit Commentary: Acts*, Grand Rapids, Eerdmans Publishing Company, 1978.

H. D. M. Spence, *The Pulpit Commentary: St. Luke*, Grand Rapids, Eerdmans Publishing Company, 1978.

CHAPTER 9

H. D. M. Spence, *The Pulpit Commentary: St. Luke*, Grand Rapids, Eerdmans Publishing Company, 1978.

George Williams, *Williams' Complete Bible Commentary*, Grand Rapids, Kregel Publications, 1994, pg. 832.

CHAPTER 12

George Williams, *Williams' Complete Bible Commentary*, Grand Rapids, Kregel Publications, 1994, pg. 835.

CHAPTER 13

H. D. M. Spence, *The Pulpit Commentary: St. Luke 13:1*, Grand Rapids, Eerdmans Publishing Company, 1978.

J. C. Ryle – Sermon - http://www.biblebb.com/files/ryle/christ_crucified.htm.

CHAPTER 14

E. M. Bounds.

CHAPTER 15

Richards, Lawrence, *Expository Dictionary of Bible Words*, Grand Rapids, Zondervan Publishing House, 1985, pg. 32.

NOTES

CHAPTER 16

H. D. M. Spence, *The Pulpit Commentary: Acts 16:9*, Grand Rapids, Eerdmans Publishing Company, 1978.

H. D. M. Spence, *The Pulpit Commentary: Acts 16:25*, Grand Rapids, Eerdmans Publishing Company, 1978.

CHAPTER 20

H. D. M. Spence, *The Pulpit Commentary: Acts 20:7*, Grand Rapids, Eerdmans Publishing Company, 1978.

Orr, James, M.A., D.D. General Editor. *Entry for "HUMILITY". International Standard Bible Encyclopedia*, 1915.

D. L. Moody.

H. D. M. Spence, *The Pulpit Commentary: Acts 20:38*, Grand Rapids, Eerdmans Publishing Company, 1978.

CHAPTER 21

Edited by James Orr, *International Standard Bible Encyclopedia,* Wm. B. Eerdmans Publishing Co., 1939, http://www.internationalstandardbible.com/P/paul-the-apostle-4.html.

Ibid.

Von Harnack, *History of Dogma*, New York, Williams and Norgate, 1905, Pg. 94.

CHAPTER 23

George Williams, *Williams' Complete Bible Commentary*, Grand Rapids, Kregel Publications, 1994, Pg. 846.

H. D. M. Spence, *The Pulpit Commentary: Acts 23:6*, Grand Rapids, Eerdmans Publishing Company, 1978.

Ibid.

CHAPTER 26

H. D. M. Spence, *The Pulpit Commentary: Acts 26:29*, Grand Rapids, Eerdmans Publishing Company, 1978.

CHAPTER 27

George Williams, *Williams' Complete Bible Commentary*, Grand Rapids, Kregel Publications, 1994, Pg. 849.

CHAPTER 28

H. D. M. Spence, *The Pulpit Commentary: Acts 28:20*, Grand Rapids, Eerdmans Publishing Company, 1978.

I. Howard Marshall, A. R. Millard, J. I. Packer, Donald J. Wiseman, *New Bible Dictionary*, InterVarsity Press, 1996, Pg. 456.

REFERENCE BOOKS

Atlas Of The Bible—Rogerson

Expository Dictionary of Bible Words—L. O. Richards

Matthew Henry Commentary On The Holy Bible—Matthew Henry

New Bible Dictionary—Tyndale

Strong's Exhaustive Concordance Of The Bible

The Christology of the New Testament—W. Bousset, Kyrios Christos, O. Cullmann

The Complete Word Study Dictionary

The Essential Writings—Josephus

The Interlinear Greek—English New Testament—George Ricker Berry

The International Standard Bible Encyclopedia

The Pulpit Commentary—H. D. M. Spence

The Son of Man in Myth and History—F. H. Borsch

The Student's Commentary On The Holy Scriptures—George Williams

The Zondervan Pictorial Encyclopedia Of The Bible

Vine's Expository Dictionary Of New Testament Words

Webster's New Collegiate Dictionary

Word Studies In The Greek New Testament, Volume I—Kenneth S. Wuest

Young's Literal Translation Of The Holy Bible

INDEX

The index is listed according to subjects. The treatment may include a complete dissertation or no more than a paragraph. But hopefully it will provide some help.

As well, even though extended treatment of a subject may not be carried in this Commentary, one of the other Commentaries may well include the desired material.

A BIBLICAL EXAMPLE 239
A BOLD STAND 656
ABRAHAM 181
ABSTAIN FROM POLLUTIONS OF IDOLS 431
ACCUSERS 730
A CHILD? 556
A CHILD OF THE DEVIL 360
A CHOSEN VESSEL 256
A CORRECT CONCEPTION 305
ACUTE PERSECUTION 400
A DAY OF REST 586
A DECISION NOW 641
A DEFINITE AND DISTINCT WORK OF GRACE 221
A DEVELOPED FAITH 264
A DISAPPOINTMENT! 223
A DRAMATIC STATEMENT 611
A FELLOWSHIP OF CHURCHES 170
A GRADUAL PROCESS 792
A HELLENISTIC JEW 210
A HIRED HOUSE 784
ALEXANDRIA 531
ALL NATIONS 398
ALL, NOT JUST A PART 616
ALL THE COUNSEL OF GOD 616
ALL THINGS 615
ALL WHO BELIEVE 378
ALWAYS SOMETHING GOOD 715
A MAN OF ETHIOPIA 241
A MIST AND A DARKNESS 362
A MORAL TEST 237
A MORE CONVENIENT SEASON? 721
ANANIAS 254, 261
AND FINALLY 414
AND FROM BLOOD 431
AND FROM FORNICATION 431
AND FROM THINGS STRANGLED 431
A NEW RELIGION? 726
AN EXAMPLE 621
AN EXAMPLE WE SHOULD HEED! 653
AN IMPROPER UNDERSTANDING OF JESUS 415
AN IMPROPER UNDERSTANDING OF THE CROSS 678
AN OPEN HEART 452
ANOTHER CASE IN POINT 680
ANOTHER FAITH? 764
ANOTHER JESUS 401
ANOTHER JESUS, ANOTHER SPIRIT, AND ANOTHER GOSPEL 414
ANTIOCH 322, 529
AN UNSCRIPTURAL POSITION ALWAYS LEADS TO UNSCRIPTURAL RESULTS 619
A PERFECT WILL FOR YOUR LIFE 446
A PERMISSIVE WILL OF GOD? 446
A PERSONAL EXAMPLE 229, 250
A PERSONAL EXPERIENCE 174, 223, 356, 397, 408, 459, 706
A POINT OF CONTACT 558
A POINT TO CONSIDER! 561
APOLLOS 530
A POSSESSION 184
APOSTASY 597
APOSTLE 610
A POWERFUL TESTIMONY 572
APPOINTED 404
A PROPER RELATIONSHIP WITH CHRIST 368
AQUILA AND PRISCILLA 512
A ROMAN CITIZEN 473
A SPIRITUAL PROBLEM 593

AS THE LORD WILLS 235
AT GREAT PRICE 569
ATHENS 487
ATTENTION TO THE WORD OF GOD 452
A VISION OF JESUS 638
A WASTED EFFORT 375
A WAY OF LIFE 611
A WORK OF THE HOLY SPIRIT 352
A ZEAL FOR GOD 669
BABBLER? 491
BARNABAS 438
BARNABAS AND MARK 438
BELIEVE 714
BELIEVE ON CHRIST JESUS 541
BELIEVERS MULTIPLIED 162
BELIEVING 608
BELIEVING ON THE LORD JESUS CHRIST 320
BE OF GOOD CHEER 697
BIBLE CHRISTIANITY 390, 589, 788
BIBLE INTERPRETATION 477
BIBLE SALVATION 467
BISHOP 330, 405
BLASPHEMY 516
BOLDNESS 383
BRITISH ISRAELISM 740
BUILT UP IN THE FAITH 631
BUT WHAT ABOUT THE TEN COMMANDMENTS 412
BY THE HOLY SPIRIT 636
CAESAR 727
CAESAREA 703
CAN A BELIEVER BE DEMON POSSESSED? 457
CARE OF THE CHURCHES 580
CAUSES OF PERSECUTION 212
CERTAIN BRETHREN 354
CERTAIN DISCIPLES 534
CERTAIN MEN 407
CERTAIN PROPHETS AND TEACHERS 353
CHILDREN OF THE STOCK OF ABRAHAM 370
CHOSEN 675
CHRIST 214
CHRIST AND THE CROSS 561
CHRIST AND THE FULFILLMENT OF THE LAW 658
CHRIST AS THE PREACHER 216
CHRISTIANITY 274
CHRISTIANS 713
CHRISTIANS AND JEWS 712
CHRISTIAN SEPARATION 552
CHRIST OPENED THEIR MINDS 658
CHRIST'S BODY 164
CHURCH 628
CHURCH DENOMINATIONS 167
CHURCH DISCIPLINE 170
CHURCH GOVERNMENT 166
CHURCH MEMBERSHIP 590
CIRCUMCISION 314, 407
COME OVER INTO MACEDONIA AND HELP US 449
COMMON OR UNCLEAN 283
CONDITIONS 384
CONFESSION? 765
CONFRONTING ERROR 416
CONSTANT SEEKING OF THE LORD 595
CONTENTION 438
CONTRARY TO THE LAW 521
CONTROVERSIES 612
CORINTH 511
CORNELIUS 273
CORNELIUS THE CENTURION 289
COVENANT 198
CURIOUS ARTS 567
DAVID 368
DEACONS 173
DECEPTION 669, 679
DECEPTION AND SELF-WILL 670
DELIVERANCE 196
DEMONS IN THE EPISTLES 560
DEMON SPIRITS 454, 568, 776
DENOMINATIONALISM 169
DEPART 682
DESPISERS 380
DETRACTORS 527
DEVELOPMENT OR EXPLOITATION? 764
DID PETER GO TO ROME? 346
DISCIPLES 636
DISCIPLESHIP AT PRESENT 163
DISCIPLINE 619
DISPOSITION 712
DIVINE COMPULSION 514
DIVISION 627
DOCTRINE, DISPOSITION, AND DIRECTION 482
DOES IT MEAN SUCH A BELIEVER IS LOST? 425
DOING GOOD 300
EARNEST EXPECTATION 614
EASTER, A PAGAN FESTIVAL 336
ECCLESIASTICAL AUTHORITIES OUTSIDE THE LOCAL CHURCH 622
EIGHT WAYS GOD SPEAKS TO INDIVIDUALS: 645
EITHER CAUSED OR ALLOWED BY THE LORD 391
ELECTION ASSURES THE BELIEVER OF HIS SECURITY IN CHRIST 258
ELECTION IS A CHOICE OF INDIVIDUAL SINNERS TO BE SAVED IN AND THROUGH CHRIST 258
ELECTION IS A CHOICE PREDICATED ON GRACE (ROM. 11:5) 257
ELECTION IS A SOVEREIGN CHOICE BY GOD 257

ELECTION SHOWS THAT SALVATION IS ALL OF GOD AND NONE OF MAN 258
EMPTY NOTHINGS 396
ENTERING INTO REST 586
ENTER THE EPICUREANS AND STOICS 490
EPHESUS 525, 534, 578
EQUIPS FOR SERVICE 536
ERROR CANNOT RECEIVE ANYTHING FROM THE LORD 766
EVERYTHING GOD DOES IS GOOD 399
EVIL SPIRITS RELATIVE TO THE GOSPELS 560
EXACTLY WHAT WAS PAUL SPEAKING OF WHEN HE REFERRED TO HOPE? 714
EXHORTATION 582
EYEWITNESS ACCOUNTS OF JESUS 588
FAITH 362, 413, 469, 519, 582, 660
FAITH AS A BAROMETER 765
FAITHFUL TO THE WORD 516
FAITH IN HIM 306
FAITH IS MORE THAN MERE FACTS 246
FAITH IS RELIANCE ON GOD 470
FAITH, NOT WORKS, THE MEANS OF JUSTIFICATION 378
FAITH, THE MANNER IN WHICH GOD OPERATES 607
FAITH TOWARD OUR LORD JESUS CHRIST 606
FALLEN FROM THE TRUTH 309
FALLING FROM GRACE 425
FALSEHOOD 669
FALSE PROPHETS 508, 693
FALSE PROPHETS AND THE TRUE GOSPEL 630
FALSE WAYS OF SALVATION 467
FAMILY WORSHIP CENTER 444
FASTING 354
FASTING AND PRAYER 538
FEAR 563
FEED THE FLOCK 624
FESTUS 722
FINALLY 623
FINDING PAUL 327
FINDING THE LORD 503
FOLLOWING THE HOLY SPIRIT 308
FOLLOWING THE LEADING OF THE LORD 594
FORBIDDEN OF THE HOLY SPIRIT 444
FORGIVENESS OF SINS 748
FOR GOD WAS WITH HIM 300
FOUR COMMANDS 430
FOUR DAUGHTERS 643
FOUR HUNDRED AND FIFTY YEARS 367
FROM THE BEGINNING OF THE WORLD 429
FROM THE POWER OF SATAN UNTO GOD 747
FRUIT OF THE SPIRIT 537
FULL OF THE HOLY SPIRIT AND FAITH 324
FUTURE HAPPENINGS 544
GALILEE 299
GENESIS AND PHYSICAL SCIENCE 496
GENTILES 682
GIFTS 557
GIFTS OF THE SPIRIT 537
GIVING GOD THE GLORY 348
GLADNESS AND REJOICING 539
GOD 289
GOD? 732
GOD AND HUMILITY 599
GOD AS THE FIRST CAUSE 497
GOD GAVE THEM UP 398
GOD IS GREATER 497
GOD IS LONGSUFFERING 399
GOD KNOWS THE HEART 421
GOD'S GOVERNMENT 620
GOD'S KINGDOM 544
GOD'S PLAN 674
GOD'S WILL 524
GOD'S WORD CAN NEVER BE USED AGAINST HIMSELF 392
GOD THE CREATOR 397
GOOD NEWS 323
GOOD WORKS 507
GO TELL OTHERS 345
GRACE 248, 283
GRACE AND THE CROSS OF CHRIST 613
GRACE AS IT IS SEEN BY GOD 612
GRACE ON THE PART OF GOD 423
GREAT CLAIMS 751
GREAT OPPOSITION 386
GREEK PHILOSOPHY 489
GREEK THOUGHT CONCERNING HUMILITY 599
GRIEVOUS WOLVES 626
GROPING 503
GUIDELINES OF HONESTY 621
HANDKERCHIEFS AND APRONS 558
HARDSHIPS 601
HARMONY 478
HAVING BELIEVED 535
HEALING 778
HEALTH AND WEALTH 765
HEART 790
HEATHEN PRACTICES 568
HEAVEN AND EARTH 204
HE CLEARED UP THE MYSTERY 658
HE IS LORD OF ALL 296
HE IS LORD OF HEAVEN AND EARTH 498
HE PRESENTED JESUS AS NO OTHER HUMAN BEING 639

HERESY 767
HEROD 331
HEROD AGRIPPA 332
HEROD THE ETHNARCH 331
HEROD THE GREAT 331
HEROD THE KING 331
HEROD THE TETRARCH 331
HE WILL TELL YOU WHAT YOU OUGHT TO DO 294
HIERARCHY 597
HINDRANCES TO RECEIVING: PRIDE 229
HINDRANCES TO RECEIVING: UNBELIEF 228
HINDRANCES TO RECEIVING: YIELDING 228
HIS BRINGING UP 638
HIS DEFENSE OF HIS TEACHING 197
HIS PERSONAL DEFENSE 197
HIS WITNESS 676
HIS WORK 645
HOLY SPIRIT CONVICTION 720, 735
HOPE 714
HOPE AS USED IN THE OLD TESTAMENT 715
HOW DOES SATAN THINK HE CAN SUCCEED? 340
HOW DOES THE HOLY SPIRIT WORK? 411
HOW DO WE EXPLAIN SUCH? 577
HOW GOOD GOD IS 233
HOW IS ONE TO KNOW? 361
HOW IS THE CROSS OF CHRIST AN OFFENSE? 380
HOW IS THE CROSS OF CHRIST THE POWER OF GOD? 625
HOW RIGHT HE WAS! 692
HOW THE HOLY SPIRIT DWELLS IN MEN 646
HOW THE HOLY SPIRIT WORKS 457, 592
HUMANISTIC PSYCHOLOGY 419, 458
HUMILIATION 243
HUMILITY 598
HUMILITY AND THE CROSS OF CHRIST 600
HUMILITY IS PRAISED 598
HUMILITY, THE OPPOSITE OF SELF-EXALTATION 599
I AM CLEAN 517
I AM READY 648
I BELIEVE 245
I COMMEND YOU TO GOD 631
IDEAS THAT ARE NOT SCRIPTURAL 232
IDOLATRY AND LICENTIOUSNESS 511
IDOL GODS 495
IGNORANT WORSHIP 495
ILL GOTTEN GAINS 458
IMMUNITIES AND RIGHTS 473
IMPUTED RIGHTEOUSNESS 283
IN CONSEQUENCE OF THE SPIRIT 636
IN SUMMARY 550
INTERPRETATION PECULIAR TO THE BIBLE 478
IN THE FACE OF JESUS CHRIST 253
IN THE SPIRIT 569
IRAQ 182
IS INTERRACIAL MARRIAGE A SIN? 500
IS IT POSSIBLE THAT A LACK OF FAITH COULD PLAY A PART IN SUCH DIFFICULTIES? 461
IS IT THE WILL OF GOD? 502
ISLAM 277
ISRAEL 428, 730
ISRAEL AND THE GENTILES 260
ISRAEL FAR AHEAD OF OTHER NATIONS 408
IT IS CHRIST WHO HAS DELIVERED US 410
IT IS THE LORD'S INTENTION THAT WE TURN THESE DIFFICULTIES INTO A SACRIFICIAL OFFERING! 462
IT TAKES FAITH 229
I WILL RETURN 427
I WORK A WORK 381
JAMES 426, 650
JAMES THE JUST 346
JAPHETH AND SHEM 276
JERUSALEM 329, 680
JESUS 209, 555, 587, 628, 659
JESUS! 591
JESUS ALWAYS AS THE SON? 565
JESUS AND FAITH 607
JESUS AND FRUIT 693
JESUS AND GRACE 424
JESUS AND HIS DEATH 297, 374
JESUS AND THE KINGDOM 545
JESUS AND THE LAW 521
JESUS AND THE SECOND COMING 297
JESUS AND THE TEMPLE 726
JESUS AS THE SUPREME EXAMPLE 599
JESUS CHRIST 491, 576
JESUS CHRIST AND HIM CRUCIFIED 350
JESUS CHRIST IS THE JUDGE 303
JESUS CHRIST, THE SON OF GOD 749
JESUS EVER SUPREME 639
JESUS IS GOD 296
JESUS MAGNIFIED 563
JESUS MUST RETURN 614
JESUS SATISFIED THE LAW IN EVERY RESPECT 412
JESUS, THE FULFILLMENT 785
JESUS THE SAVIOUR 712
JEWISH CHRISTIANS 432
JEWS 483
JEWS AND GENTILES 581
JEWS FIGHTING CHRISTIANS 582
JOB 333
JUDGES 367
JUDGE THE WORLD IN RIGHTEOUSNESS 506
JUDGMENT 349

JUDGMENT IS INEVITABLE 509
JUDGMENT TO COME 720
JUSTIFICATION? 627
JUSTIFICATION BY FAITH 379, 608
JUSTIN MARTYR 587
KICKING AGAINST THE GOADS 251
KINGDOM LIFESTYLE IN THE GOSPELS 548
KING IN A DEEPER SENSE 564
KNOW 561
LACK OF FAITH? 765
LAW AND COVENANT IN ISRAEL 408
LEADERSHIP 291
LEAVEN 418
LED BY THE HOLY SPIRIT 692
LED BY THE SPIRIT 445
LETTERS 249
LIGHT 753
LINGUISTIC? 262
LOCAL CHURCH AUTHORITY 169
LOGIC 503
LOGOS 236
LORD, WHAT WILL YOU HAVE ME TO DO? 252
LOYALTY 441
LUKE 450, 779
LYDIA 451
LYDIA, THE SELLER OF PURPLE 453
MANY BELIEVED 566
MANY PEOPLE SAVED 482
MANY WHO SPEAK IN TONGUES ARE NOT, IN FACT, PENTECOSTAL! 538
MARRIAGE 501
MARY 342
MARY AND CATHOLICS 453
MEDICINE 779
MESSIAH! 564
MIDNIGHT 463
MINDS EVIL AFFECTED 388
MIRACLES TODAY? 556
MODERN ISRAEL 786
MODERN LAW! 411
MODERN LAW AND THE LAW OF MOSES 410
MONEY 235, 567
MORAL 285
MORE ABOUT WATER BAPTISM 677
MORE NOBLE 486
MORE RULES OF INTERPRETATION 478
MOSES 197
MUCH DISPUTING 420
MY COVENANT 184
NICODEMUS 590
NO CORRUPTION 375
NO DIFFERENCE 422
NO ETERNAL MATTER BEFORE CREATION 497
NO FINAL FULFILLMENT OF HIS WORK 325
NO GODS 572
NO SMALL DISSENSION 415
NO SUCH THING AS AN HONORARY GODHEAD! 297
NOT AN OPTIONAL EXPERIENCE 224
NOTHING IS IMPOSSIBLE WITH GOD 344
OBEY OR DISOBEY 286
OBJECTIVE TRUTH 669
OBVIOUS! 537
OF YOUR OWN SELVES 627
OLD TESTAMENT 654
OMNIPOTENT, OMNISCIENT, AND OMNIPRESENT 458
ONE BLOOD 499
ONE BLOOD, BUT FIVE RACES (ACTS 17:26) 500
ONE FINAL ATTEMPT 341
ONE MORE WORD ABOUT PAUL! 600
ONLY GOD CAN REMOVE SIN 305
ONLY JESUS 653
ONLY ONE REQUIREMENT 225
ONLY TALK 624
OPENING AND ALLEGING 476
OPPOSITION 259, 537, 583
OPPOSITION FROM THE JEWS 400
OPPRESSED OF THE DEVIL 300
ORIGINAL SIN 237
OUR FIRST HOLY SPIRIT SERVICE 223
OUR PARACLETE 226
OVERSEERS 618
PASTOR 596
PAUL 210, 264, 310, 326, 512, 530, 572, 602, 626, 650, 687, 690, 722, 734, 760, 775
PAUL AND FEAR 769
PAUL AND THE CHURCH AT ROME 783
PAUL AND THE JEWS 521
PAUL AND THE LAW 656
PAUL ANSWERS THAT QUESTION HIMSELF 601
PAUL LEAVING CORINTH 524
PAUL'S COMPANY 640
PAUL'S DEFENSE 668, 713
PAUL'S DIALOGUE WITH THE JEWS 785
PAUL'S DISPUTE WITH THE JUDAIZERS 469
PAUL'S GREAT EFFORTS 528
PAUL'S JOURNEY 637
PAUL'S LIFE 610
PAUL'S MESSAGE 365
PAUL'S POSITION 656
PAUL'S SECOND MISSIONARY JOURNEY 440
PAUL'S STAND FOR THE TRUTH 420
PAUL'S STATEMENT 711
PAUL'S STATEMENT ABOUT WATER BAPTISM 678
PAUL THE APOSTLE 527

PENTECOSTALS? 537
PERFECT 556
PERFECT LOVE AND FEAR 769
PERSECUTING THE LORD 745
PERSECUTION 211, 386
PERVERSION 361
PETER 313, 336, 407, 427
PETER AND PAUL 379
PETER'S FIRST ADDRESS AT PENTECOST 296
PETER THE ROCK 291
PHARISEES 691
PHARISEES AND SADDUCEES 690
PHILOSOPHY 492
PHILO, THE JEWISH PHILOSOPHER OF ALEXANDRIA 491
PLEASING THE JEWS 334
PLEASING THE LORD 716
POWER 350
PRAYER 172, 279, 288, 336, 761
PRAYER AND FASTING 405
PRAYER AND THE CROSS OF CHRIST 280
PRAYER AND THE HOLY SPIRIT 280
PRAYER IN THE NAME OF JESUS 280
PRAYER IS THE HIGHEST EXERCISE 280
PRAYERS AND ALMS 276
PRAYING AND CONFESSION 344
PREACHED THE WORD 216
PREACHERS 164
PREACHING 215
PREACHING CHRIST 217
PREACHING THE GOSPEL 303
PREACHING THE LORD JESUS 322
PRECISION 498
PRESUMPTION? 583
PRIDE 767
PRISCILLA AND AQUILA 525
PRISON 335
PROBLEMS! 171
PROCLAIMING CHRIST OPENLY 302
PROMISES KEPT 374
PROVISIONS OF THE ATONEMENT 614
PSYCHOLOGY? 624
PURCHASED WITH HIS OWN BLOOD 626
PURIFYING THEIR HEARTS BY FAITH 422
QUALITY DIFFERS 232
QUESTIONS 333, 732
RACISM 501
RACISM AND DENOMINATIONALISM 501
RAISED FROM THE DEAD 732
REASONING WITH THE JEWS 526
RECEIVING APOLLOS 532
RECEIVING THE HOLY SPIRIT 221
REJECTING LIGHT 517
RELAX IN HIM 231
RELIANCE ON JESUS 625
RELIGION 314, 454, 493
RELIGION THE GREATEST DECEIVER OF ALL 670
RELIGIOUS HIERARCHY 168
REMISSION OF SINS 306
REPENT 237
REPENTANCE 170, 505, 604, 750
RESCUE PAUL 696
RESISTING THE HOLY SPIRIT 205
RESPONSIBILITY 609
RESTORATION 741
RESURRECTION 691, 694
RHODA 343
RIGHTEOUSNESS 720
RIGHTEOUSNESS, TEMPERANCE, AND JUDGMENT TO COME 720
ROMAN CITIZENSHIP 685
ROMAN LAW 701
ROMAN LAW AND ESTABLISHED SAFEGUARDS 701
ROME 570, 782
RULES 171
SAILED TO CYPRUS 358
SAINTS AS A BLESSING 770
SALVATION 246, 385, 735
SALVATION BY THE BLOOD OF JESUS 652
SALVATION IS NOT ONLY PRESENT BUT FUTURE AS WELL! 468
SALVATION OF SOULS 539
SALVATION ORIGINATES IN THE LOVE OF GOD 305
SANCTIFIED 632, 749
SANG PRAISES UNTO GOD 463
SATAN AND THE WILL OF GOD 770
SATAN'S LIES 226
SAUL 248, 628
SCRIPTURALLY IGNORANT 363
SCRIPTURAL OFFICES IN THE CHURCH 168
SCRIPTURES OUT OF CONTEXT 765
SEARCH THE SCRIPTURES 583
SEDUCTION 629
SEEKER SENSITIVE? 514
SEEKING THE LORD 502
SELF-RIGHTEOUSNESS 371
SENT FORTH BY THE HOLY SPIRIT 357
SEPARATE LIFESTYLES 552
SEPARATE ME BARNABAS AND SAUL 356
SEPARATION BUT NOT ISOLATION 182
SEPARATION FROM FALSE DOCTRINE 553
SERVICE FOR CHRIST 343
SIGNS AND WONDERS 389, 539
SIGNS AND WONDERS IN THE LAND OF EGYPT 196

SIMON PETER 282, 420
SIMULATED HUMILITY 599
SIN! 237
SIN AND ITS FORGIVENESS 238
SIN AND THE CROSS 515
SINLESSNESS AND THE MESSIANIC CLAIM 577
SIN OFFERING 376
SIX 482
SIXTEEN HUNDRED YEARS OF LAW 415
SOCIAL IMPLICATIONS 502
SOLDIERS 704
SOME BELIEVED 481
SON OF MAN 209
SPEAKING BOLDLY IN THE LORD 389
SPEAKING WITH OTHER TONGUES! 225
SPEAKING WITH TONGUES 310
SPECIAL MIRACLES 555
SPIRIT-FILLED BELIEVERS 299
SPIRIT-FILLED PEOPLE? 592
SPIRITUAL AUTHORITY 618
SPIRITUAL SLEEP 629
SPOKEN AGAINST ... 787
SPOKEN BY THE LORD 646
STRANGE GODS? 492
STRENGTHENING THE CHURCHES 443
SUBJECTIVE TRUTH 490
SUBMISSION 620
SUBSEQUENT TO SALVATION 225
SUNDAY 587
SYMBOLISM 283
TAKE HEED 617
TARRYING 227
TARSUS 267
TEMPERANCE 720
TERRIFIED 252
TESTIFIED OF JESUS IN JERUSALEM 697
THAT CHRIST SHOULD SUFFER 752
THAT IS IN ME 749
THAT WAY 552
THAT WHICH THE LORD DID 224
THAT WORD, I SAY, YOU KNOW 298
THE ABSALOM SPIRIT 627
THE ACCEPTANCE OF PAUL 778
THE ACTION OF GALLIO 523
THE ACTIONS OF THE CHIEF CAPTAIN 686
THE ANGEL OF THE LORD 348
THE ANGEL THAT SPOKE TO CORNELIUS 294
THE ANOINTING 299
THE ANSWER 396
THE ANSWER AS GIVEN BY PAUL 725
THE ANSWER AS GIVEN BY THE LORD 284
THE APOSTASY 402
THE APOSTLE PAUL 751
THE APPEAL OF ERROR 693
THE APPEARANCE OF CHRIST TO PAUL 679, 696
THE APPEARANCE OF PAUL 734
THE ARK OF THE COVENANT 659
the AUTHORITY OF THE BELIEVER 610
THE BAPTISM OF REPENTANCE 540
THE BAPTISM WITH THE HOLY SPIRIT 591, 630
THE BASIS OF JUDGMENT 304
THE BASIS OF PAUL'S DOCTRINE OF GRACE 611
THE BEGINNING OF WISDOM 492
THE BELIEVER'S RELATIONSHIP WITH THE LORD 461
THE BIBLICAL BASIS FOR THE PRESENT KINGDOM 549
THE BIG PROBLEM WITH SOCRATES AND PLATO 490
THE BOOK OF ACTS 794
THE BOOK OF ACTS AND THE EPISTLES 166
THE BOOK OF HEBREWS 565
THE BOUNDS OF THEIR HABITATION 499
THE BRAIN AND THE HEART 791
THE BRETHREN 266, 782
THE CALLED PREACHER 215
THE CALLING 676
THE CAPITAL OF THE ROMAN EMPIRE 783
THE CATHOLIC CHURCH 213
THE CAUSE 624
THE CAUSE OF CHRIST 174
THE CAUSE OF THE FALL OF MAN 670
THE CHANGE FROM THE GOSPELS TO THE EPISTLES 515
THE CHARACTERISTICS OF TRUE BIBLICAL HUMILITY 600
THE CHIEF RULER OF THE SYNAGOGUE 523
THE CHRISTIAN CHURCH 214
THE CHRONOLOGY 420
THE CHURCH 166, 349, 555
THE CHURCH AND ISRAEL 428
THE CHURCH AT ANTIOCH 352
THE CHURCH AT CORINTH 581
THE CHURCH AT EPHESUS 526
THE COMING KINGDOM 550
THE COMING OF THE LORD 539
THE COMMAND 224
THE COMMISSION 746
THE COMMISSION GIVEN TO PAUL 747
THE CORRECT OBJECT OF FAITH 413
THE COUNCIL 691
THE COURSE 611
THE COURT OF THE WOMEN 662
THE COVENANT OF CIRCUMCISION 186
THE CREATOR 496

THE CROSS 311, 341, 375, 498, 548, 767
THE CROSS OF CHRIST 257, 325, 457, 480
THE CROSS OF CHRIST AND THE WILL OF GOD 447
THE CROSS, PROTECTION AGAINST DECEPTION 671
THE CURSE 698
THE DAVIDIC THRONE 740
THE DAYS OF UNLEAVENED BREAD 584
THE DECLARATION 345
THE DELIVERANCE OF THIS GIRL 455
THE DENIAL OF TRUTH 302
THE DIFFERENCES BETWEEN ISRAEL AND THE CHURCH 198
THE DISCIPLES 403
THE DISPENSATION OF GRACE 424
THE DISSENSION 695
THE DIVINE AGENCY 612
THE DOCTRINE OF CREATION 496
THE DOCTRINE OF THE LORD 363
THE DREAM 445
THE EARLY CHURCH 168, 260
THE EARLY CHURCH AND GENTILES 259
THE EARLY CHURCH AND THE APOSTLES 350
THE EARLY CHURCH IN ANTIOCH 322
THE EFFECTS OF SIN 237
THE EFFORTS OF SATAN 698
THE ELDERS OF THE CHURCH 596
THE EMPEROR AND THE LAW 701
THE ENDTIME 546
THE EPICUREANS AND STOICS 489
THE ESSENTIAL NATURE OF PREACHING 515
THE EVANGELIST AND HIS APPEARANCE 642
THE EXISTENCE OF EVIL SPIRITS 559
THE FAITH OF PAUL 767
THE FEAST 527
THE FIGURE OF WATER BAPTISM 541
THE FIRE OF THE CHURCH 640
THE FIRST AND THE LAST 353
THE FIRST CENTURY 298
THE FIRST DEACONS? 165
THE FIRST RESURRECTION OF LIFE 752
THE FLOCK 618
THE FORWARD LOOK TO THE KINGDOM 545
THE FUNCTION OF THE LAW 409
THE FUNDAMENTAL DOCTRINES OF PHARISAISM 692
THE GALL OF BITTERNESS 238
THE GENTILES 750
THE GENTILES AND THE HOLY SPIRIT 309
THE GIFT INSTEAD OF THE GIVER 765
THE GIFT OF GOD 236
THE GOAL OF DISCIPLING 164
THE GOAL OF THE HOLY SPIRIT 601
THE GODHEAD 504
THE GOOD NEWS OF THE KINGDOM 546
THE GOSPEL 273
THE GOSPEL AND THE HOLY SPIRIT 747
THE GOSPEL OF GRACE MUST NOT BE DILUTED 650
THE GOSPEL OF JESUS CHRIST 576
THE GOSPEL OF THE KINGDOM 544
THE GOSPEL STORY 246
THE GOVERNOR 706
THE GRACE OF GOD 423
THE GREATNESS OF THE WORK OF GOD 523
THE GREAT POWER OF THE APOSTOLIC AGE 637
THE GREAT QUESTION 311
THE GREAT SIGNIFICANCE OF THE TITLE *"LORD!"* 564
THE GREAT TRIBULATION 341
THE GREAT WHITE THRONE JUDGMENT 506
THE HAND OF THE LORD IS AGAINST YOU 361
THE HEALING 277
THE HEALING OF THE MUSLIM GIRL 277
THE HEART THAT IS RIGHT WITH GOD 791
THE HEBREW SCHOLAR OF HIS TIME 637
THE HELP OF GOD 751
THE HIGH PRIEST? 690
THE HISTORY OF THE SANHEDRIN 687
THE HOLY ONE 376
THE HOLY SPIRIT 221, 308, 317, 323, 535, 542, 562, 618, 642
THE HOLY SPIRIT AND INTERPRETATION 479
THE HOLY SPIRIT AND THE WILL OF GOD 446
THE HOLY SPIRIT BAPTISM CAN BE RECEIVED INSTANTLY 226
THE HOLY SPIRIT BAPTISM IS A GIFT 227
THE HOLY SPIRIT GUIDES INTO ALL TRUTH 553
THE HOLY SPIRIT IN THE NEW TESTAMENT 325
THE HOLY SPIRIT IN THE OLD TESTAMENT 325
THE HOLY SPIRIT IS NOT THE FATHER OR THE SON 645
THE HOLY SPIRIT SAID 355, 356
THE HOLY SPIRIT WILL NOT SPEAK FOR YOU 230
THE HOME OF MARY 342
THE HUMAN ELEMENT IN THE BIBLE 477
THE IMPORTANCE OF HUMILITY 598
THE INHERITANCE 632, 748
THE INSTRUCTIONS OF THE LORD 392
THE INTERPRETATION OF THE THOUGHTS OF ANOTHER 477
THE JEW 575
THE JEWISH UNDERSTANDING OF THE HEART 791
THE JEWS 554, 712, 726
THE JEWS AND CIVIL AUTHORITIES 524
THE JEWS AND THE APOSTLES 390
THE JUDGMENT OF GOD 179, 507

THE JUDGMENT SEAT 728
THE KINGDOM AND THE NEW BIRTH 549
THE KINGDOM IN THE NEW TESTAMENT 545
THE KINGDOM IN THE OLD TESTAMENT 544
THE KINGDOM MUST FOCUS ON THE PERSON OF JESUS 546
THE KINGDOM OF DARKNESS AND THE KINGDOM OF LIGHT 568
THE KINGDOM OF GOD 543, 550, 613, 788, 794
THE KINGDOM OF HEAVEN 335, 544, 614, 789
THE LAST ADAM 181
THE LAST JUDGMENT 303
THE LATTER RAIN OUTPOURING! 592
THE LAW 528
THE LAW AND ITS TRUE MEANING 654
THE LAW FULFILLED IN CHRIST 655
THE LAW OF MOSES 282, 379, 431, 651
THE LAW OF MOSES AND THE BELIEVER 659
THE LAW OF THE FATHERS 668
THE LAW WAS EVER MEANT TO BE TEMPORAL 409
THE LAYING ON OF HANDS 223, 235, 542, 779
THE LEADING OF THE LORD 594, 647
THE LENGTH OF THE JUDGMENT 304
THE LETTER 705
THE LIE 663
THE LIFE OF CHRIST 243
THE LIGHT OF THE GOSPEL 505
THE LIVELY ORACLES 199
THE LOCAL CHURCH 330, 404
THE LORD AND THE HEART 792
THE LORD HAS SENT ME 261
THE LORD JESUS CHRIST 506, 676, 741
THE LORD SPOKE TO PAUL 674
THE LORD'S PRAYER 549
THE MAGISTRATES 474
THE MAN AND HIS MESSAGE 617
THE MANNER OF THEIR DELIVERANCE 365
THE MEANING OF THE OLD JEWISH SABBATH 585
THE MESSAGE IS GREATER 215
THE MESSAGE OF THE EVANGELIST 641
THE MESSAGE, THE MESSENGER, AND THE MINISTRY 352
THE MESSENGER 206
THE MESSIAH 204
THE MIND 791
THE MINISTRY OF APOLLOS 532
THE MINISTRY OF PAUL 327
THE MINISTRY OF THE WORD 172
THE MINISTRY OF TIMOTHY 441
THE MIRACLE! 777
THE MIXING OF THE LAW AND THE GOSPEL 652
THE MOST HIGH 203
THE MURDER OF JAMES, THE BROTHER OF JOHN 332
THE NAME AS IT LOOKED TOWARD THE END OF THIS AGE 564
THE NAME OF JESUS 563
THE NATION OF ISRAEL 680
THE NECESSITY OF CONVERSION 306
THE NEW CHURCHES 488
THE NEW TESTAMENT AND THE JUDGMENT OF GOD 507
THE NEW TESTAMENT CHURCH HAD NO ECCLESIASTICAL HIERARCHY 622
THE OATH 190
THE OBJECT OF THIS FAITH 378
THE OFFERING OF SACRIFICE 462
THE OFFSPRING OF GOD 504
THE OLDEST AGENCY 216
THE OLD TESTAMENT AND GENTILES 259
THE ONLY ANSWER TO SIN IS REPENTANCE 238
THE OPENING 480
THE ORDAINING OF ELDERS 404
THE ORIGIN OF CHRISTIANITY AT ROME 783
THE OUTPOURING OF THE SPIRIT 539
THE PASSING AWAY OF THE LAW 659
THE PASSOVER 335
THE PERSECUTION OF THE CHURCH 212
THE PERSONALITY OF THE HOLY SPIRIT 645
THE PERSON AND MINISTRY OF THE HOLY SPIRIT 298
THE PERSON IS RESPONSIBLE 792
THE PERSON OF JESUS AND TITLES 566
THE PHARISEES 418
THE PHILOSOPHERS 489
THE PHILOSOPHY OF ARISTOTLE 490
THE PHILOSOPHY OF CHRISTIANITY 590
THE PHILOSOPHY OF SOCRATES 489
THE PLEA TO PAUL 647
THE POTENTIAL OF THE CROSS 257
THE POWER OF GOD 748
THE POWERS OF DARKNESS 483
THE PRAYER OF STEPHEN 209
THE PREACHER OF THE GOSPEL 481
THE PREACHING OF THE GOSPEL 392
THE PRESENT KINGDOM 547
THE PRESENT KINGDOM IN THE EPISTLES 547
THE PRESENT STRUGGLE 787
THE PRESERVATION OF THE LAW OF MOSES 691
THE PRESSURE OF THE HOLY SPIRIT 513
THE PRICE PAID IN ORDER THAT MEN COULD BE FORGIVEN 238
THE PRINCE OF PEACE REFUSED IS THE KINGDOM REFUSED 401

THE PRINCIPLE AND FOUNDATION OF FAITH 470
THE PRINCIPLE OF PARALLELISM 479
THE PRINCIPLES OF PLATO 490
THE PRISONER OF JESUS CHRIST 610
THE PROBLEM AND THE SOLUTION 393
THE PRODUCING OF HUMILITY 598
THE PROMISE 190, 222
THE PROPER RESPONSE 612
THE PROPHETIC KINGDOM 550
THE PSYCHOLOGIZING OF THE CHURCH 508
THE PURIFICATION PROCESS 657
THE PURPOSE OF THE CHURCH 622
THE QUEEN OF SHEBA 241
THE QUESTION 689
THE REACH OF AN EVANGELISTIC MINISTRY 641
THE REASON FOR THE INCARNATION 374
THE REASON FOR YOUR SALVATION 234
THE RECOVERY OF SPIRITUAL SIGHT TO THE BLIND 747
THE RELATIONSHIP BETWEEN THE CHURCH AND ISRAEL 198
THE RELIGIOUS HIERARCHY OF ISRAEL 181
THE RELIGIOUS WORLD 735
THE RESPONSE OF CHRIST TO THE PUBLICAN 608
THE RESULTS OF PERSECUTION 214
THE RESURRECTION 492, 506, 715
THE RESURRECTION, A CARDINAL DOCTRINE 694
THE RESURRECTION OF CHRIST 301
THE REVELATION OF GOD TO CORNELIUS 290
THE ROMAN CATHOLIC INQUISITION 213
THE ROMAN CENTURION 685
THE ROMAN PERSECUTION BEGINS 212
THE ROMANS AND THE SANHEDRIN 687
THE ROYAL FAMILY OF ENGLAND 740
THE RULE OF FAITH AND LIFE 479
THE RULE OF LAW 701
THE SAMARITANS 216
THE SAME GIFT 320
THE SANHEDRIN 743
THE SCHISM 652
THE SCRIPTURAL POSITION 620
THE SECOND COMING 428
THE SECOND TIME 284
THESE WORDS 307
THE SIGNIFICANCE OF ALL OF THIS 716
THE SIGNIFICANCE OF CHRIST'S PERSON 296
THE SIGNIFICANCE OF THE MACEDONIAN CALL 449
THE SIMILARITIES BETWEEN THE CHURCH AND ISRAEL 198
THE SINLESSNESS OF CHRIST ASSURED 576
THE SON OF GOD 565
THE SOUND OF ALARM 538
THE SPIRIT OF DARKNESS 453
THE SPIRIT WORLD OF DARKNESS 340
THE SPIRIT WORLD OF LIGHT 341
THE STORM 764
THE SUBSTITUTE AND THE SUBSTANCE 586
THE SUPREME COURT IN ATHENS 493
THE SURE MERCIES OF DAVID 376
THE SYMBOL 314
THE SYNAGOGUE 543
THE TAKING OF THE GOSPEL TO THE WORLD 352
THE TEMPLE 726
THE TENTH CHAPTER OF ACTS 273
THE TESTIMONY 604
THE TESTIMONY OF PAUL 742
THE THINKING OF JAMES 658
THE THIRD RACE 213
THE THRONE OF DAVID IN ISRAEL BEING CUT OFF 740
THE TIMES OF IGNORANCE 504
THE TITLE *"LORD"* 564
THE TOWNCLERK 577
THE TRANSPARENCY OF MESSAGE AND MOTIVE 514
THE TRIBUNE 702
THE TRUTHS ON FAITH GIVEN BY JAMES 470
THE TUMULT 662
THE TWELVE APOSTLES 163
THE TYPE OF FEAR 769
THE VIPER 776
THE VISION 275, 287, 448, 519
THE VISION OF JESUS 744
THE VOICE 250, 281
THE VOICE OF HIS MOUTH 676
THE VOW 525, 657
THE WAY 713
THE WAY OF CHRIST 249
THE WAY OF GOD MORE PERFECTLY 532
THE WAY OF THE HOLY SPIRIT 642
THE WAY OF THE LORD 603
THE WAYS OF GOD 445
THE WIDOWS 162
THE WILL OF GOD 173, 368, 438, 770
THE WILL OF GOD? 698
THE WISDOM OF GOD 497
THE WISDOM OF PAUL 527
THE WITNESS 304
THE WITNESS OF THE SPIRIT 609
THE WORD 296, 308
THE WORD *"DISCIPLE"* 163
THE WORD OF GOD 383, 486, 630, 694, 754
THE WORD OF GOD AND THE CROSS OF CHRIST 350
THE WORD OF GOD AND THE POWER OF THE HOLY SPIRIT 679

THE WORD OF GOD IN BRIEF 617
THE WORD OF GOD INCREASED 174
THE WORD OF HIS GRACE 389, 631
THE WORD OF THE LORD 557
THE WORD OF THE LORD JESUS 554
THE WORD OF THIS SALVATION 371
THE WORDS OF JESUS 605
THE WORDS OF THE LORD JESUS CHRIST 746
THE WORK OF THE HOLY SPIRIT 469
THE WORK OF THE SPIRIT 230
THE WORLD 625
THE WRATH OF GOD 180
THEY MINISTERED TO THE LORD 354
THEY TOOK HIM DOWN FROM THE CROSS 373
THEY WERE NOT FAITHLESS 344
THINGS? 766
THINGS WHICH CORNELIUS DID 275
THIS MAY BE THE SINGLE GREATEST HINDRANCE 231
THIS POWER 234
THIS SIMPLE TRUTH 653
THIS THING WAS NOT HIDDEN 755
THREE TIMES 285
THROUGH GRACE 533
THROUGH HIS NAME 305
THUS SAITH THE LORD 615
THUS SAYS THE HOLY SPIRIT 645
TIMOTHY 440
TO BELIEVE INTO 246
TO HEAR FROM GOD 616
TO HEAR PAUL TEACH 788
TO KNOW THE WILL OF GOD 676
TONGUES 536, 542
TO OPPOSE FALSE DOCTRINE 419
TORTURE 461
TO THINK DIFFERENTLY, TO CHANGE ONE'S MIND 605
TRIBULATION 403
TRUE PREACHING AND REVELATION 515
TRUSTING GOD 333
TRUST IN THE LORD 609
TRUTH 337
TRUTH AND ERROR 693
TWELVE TRIBES 739, 741
TWIN DIRECTIONS 654
TWO WAYS 514
TWO YEARS 722
UNBELIEF 551
UNBELIEVERS 483
UNBELIEVING JEWS 388
UNCIRCUMCISED IN HEART 205
UNSCRIPTURAL AUTHORITY 618
USURP AUTHORITY 644
VEERING OFF COURSE 448
VEX CERTAIN OF THE CHURCH 332
VISIONS 254
VOLUNTARY SUBMISSION 622
WAS THAT CORRECT? 619
WATER BAPTISM 311, 677
WATER BAPTIZED 452
WENT UP BY REVELATION 416
WE SHALL BE SAVED 425
WESTERN CIVILIZATION 326
WE TURN TO THE GENTILES 384
WHAT ABOUT BELIEF IN THE INTERCESSION OF CHRIST? 606
WHAT ABOUT BELIEVERS WHO DO NOT CONFESS THEIR SINS TO THE LORD? 605
WHAT ARE DEMON SPIRITS? 455
WHAT BEING A CHRISTIAN ACTUALLY MEANS 328
WHAT DECEPTION IS 669
WHAT DOCTRINE IS SCRIPTURAL? 167
WHAT DOES BIBLE SALVATION NOT INCLUDE? 468
WHAT DOES IT MEAN TO BELIEVE ON THE LORD JESUS CHRIST? 468
WHAT DOES IT MEAN TO BE SAVED? 466
WHAT DOES IT MEAN TO FALL FROM GRACE 425
WHAT DOES IT MEAN TO HAVE FAITH IN CHRIST? 606
WHAT DOES IT TAKE TO ROB THE BELIEVER OF HIS VICTORY? 463
WHAT DOES THIS MEAN? 656
WHAT DO THEY DO? 456
WHAT GOD HAS CLEANSED 284
WHAT GOD INTENDED 478
WHAT GOOD DOES THE FOLLOWING DO ANYONE? 361
WHAT HUMILITY ACTUALLY MEANS 599
WHAT IS ELECTION? 256
WHAT IS GRACE? 611
WHAT IS NEW TESTAMENT SUBMISSION? 621
WHAT IS THE GOSPEL OF THE GRACE OF GOD? 611
WHAT IS THE KINGDOM OF GOD? 613
WHAT IS THE LAW OF MOSES? 408
WHAT IS THE MINISTRY OF THE EVANGELIST? 640
WHAT IS THE PENTECOSTAL WAY? 538
WHAT IS THIS GOSPEL OF THE KINGDOM? 547
WHAT IS WICKEDNESS? 237
WHAT PAUL'S QUESTION TEACHES US 536
WHAT SHALL I DO LORD? 673
WHAT THE BIBLE SAYS ABOUT JUDGMENT 507
WHAT THE LORD SHOWED ME 232
WHAT TYPE OF CHURCH SHOULD ONE ATTEND? 167
WHAT TYPE OF FAITH? 378

WHAT WAS THE PURPOSE OF THE HOLY SPIRIT IN GIVING THESE WARNINGS? 609
WHAT WILL SEPARATION COST ME? 553
WHAT YOU MUST DO 252
WHEN THIS JUDGMENT WILL BE 303
WHERE DID THE CHURCH COME UP WITH ALL THE UNSCRIPTURAL OFFICES WHICH SEEM SO PREVALENT PRESENTLY? 623
WHERE DID THE NORTH AMERICAN INDIANS COME FROM? 500
WHERE DO DEMON SPIRITS COME FROM? 456
WHO ARE YOU, LORD? 251
WHO IS THE HOLY SPIRIT? 355
WHOSOEVER 307
WHO WILL BE THE JUDGES? 304
WHY? 334, 461, 715
WHY DID THESE JEWS HATE PAUL SO MUCH? 703
WHY DOES THE BELIEVER NEED CERTAIN DIFFICULTIES? 462
WHY DO SOME REJECT AND OTHERS ACCEPT? 551
WHY TONGUES? 233
WHY WOULD ANY BELIEVER REJECT THE LIGHT OF THE HOLY SPIRIT? 537
WHY WOULD THEY DO SUCH A THING? 396
WICKED AND UNGODLY 689
WILLFUL BLINDNESS AND IDOLATRY 203
WILL RELIGIOUS MEN ACCEPT THIS WITNESS 421
WISDOM 350
WITHSTANDING GOD 320
WITNESS 398
WOMEN PREACHERS 643
WONDER AND PERISH 381
WORKS OF GOD 536
WORKS WHICH FOLLOW TRUE REPENTANCE 750
WORSHIP 241, 536
YOU WILL SPEAK IN TONGUES 231

NOTES

NOTES

NOTES

NOTES

NOTES

NOTES

NOTES

NOTES

NOTES

NOTES

NOTES

NOTES

NOTES